115

African States and Rulers

THIRD EDITION

African States and Rulers

THIRD EDITION

John Stewart

McFarland & Company, Inc., Publishers
Jefferson, North Carolina, and London

Library of Congress Cataloguing-in-Publication Data

Stewart, John, 1952–
African states and rulers / John Stewart. — 3d ed.
p.   cm.
Includes bibliographical references and index.

ISBN 0-7864-2562-8 (illustrated case binding : 50# alkaline paper)

1. Africa — Politics and government — Dictionaries.
2.   Africa — Kings and rulers — Biography — Dictionaries.
I. Title.
DT31.S7859   2006   960.03 — dc22   2006005823

British Library cataloguing data are available

On the cover: Colossus of Rameses ©2006 Photodisc Images;
Antique map ©2006 Pictures Now

Manufactured in the United States of America

McFarland & Company, Inc., Publishers
Box 611, Jefferson, North Carolina 28640
www.mcfarlandpub.com

For my brother Pete

Table of Contents

Preface
1

An Overview of African Geopolitical History
3

The States and Rulers
5

A Chronology
245

Appendix A: The Modern Countries
with Their Historical Constituents
303

Appendix B: The Colonial Powers' Holdings
308

Appendix C: Dates of Admission into the United Nations
311

Bibliography
313

Index of Places and Persons
317

Index of Rulers
323

Preface

This is the third edition of *African States and Rulers*, first published in 1988. The second edition, published in 1999, differed from the first in format, being, in, my view, clearer. This third edition follows closely the second in that respect.

The bulk of the book, the alphabetical list of countries, was simplified during the re-formatting for the second edition, and, again in this third edition, so that now the reader need look only for the political entity desired; Sudan, for example. The story of the Sudan is now given from its beginning to the present day, so gone are the old headings of "Anglo-Egyptian Sudan," "Sudan (Self-Rule)" and "Sudan Republic." However, under the new heading "Sudan" is given only the story of the Sudan as defined geographically by us today. That is to say, other polities that have existed within the boundaries of present-day Sudan, such as Darfur, the Funj Sultanate, or Dongola, and, indeed, Southern Sudan, will be found under their own headings, because, by themselves, they are not synonymous with modern Sudan. They are separate countries.

This format consideration reaches its epitome with Egypt. In the first edition I had split up Egyptian history into eras which, although they lent themselves very well to natural segmentation — by dynasty, or by some other obvious epoch — required too much manual back and forth for the reader. Now, the story of Egypt (as defined roughly geographically today) is told under one roof.

Since the second edition, each entry has been revised and updated, and some entries have been augmented where such augmentation would make things clearer. Some entries, such as Southern Sudan, have been expanded beyond the normal size of an entry because the subject is so complex. Reduction of complexity to simplicity, while always the aim, sometimes still requires considerable space.

Obviously much has happened in Africa since 1999 — new heads of state and government, new affairs of consequence to be discussed, and even new countries, several of them.

The appendices have been updated too, where necessary, as has the chronology of Africa, which enables the reader to see at a glance what was happening all over the continent at any given time.

There are two indexes at the back of the book. The first, the "Index of Places and Persons," gathers proper nouns, as it were, that are found in the text but that are not, in themselves, rulers or entry headings. This index is formatted in a traditional way.

The second and more important index is to the rulers themselves. An index of African rulers poses presentation problems. How does one index Abu Yahya Zakariyya I? Or Jean-Baptiste Vigoureux du Plessis? With the latter, does one look under "V" for "Vigoureux" or "D" for "du Plessis" or under "P"? It can get more complicated than that, given the non–Western style of many of the rulers' names. This book has to be indexed in such a way as to provide the reader with the greatest convenience. There can be no other consideration.

What I chose to do in the second edition, and I follow that procedure closely here, is to use every element of a name as an index entry, so the reader cannot go wrong. In each of these reformatted iterations of a name, a bold initial letter to a name element indicates the alphabetical element under which the entry would have been found were this a traditional index. The index thus does away with inversion, the traditional way of indexing a name. ("Smith, John" is easy, but what does one do with "Jean-Baptiste Vigoureux du Plessis"?) This system of indexing also eliminates the *see* reference.

Many or even most book indexes would give either page numbers or entry numbers. With an index of this magnitude and complexity, what I've chosen to do, as I did with the second edition of 1999, is to give in full the names of the countries each indexed person is associated with. When an entry to which an index item refers is a long one — Egypt, say — each ruler in the index has a date in parentheses as well (the entries unfold chronologically, so the date device speeds the reader to the desired reference).

This is the best format I could come up with, and it seems to work.

John Stewart
West Jefferson, North Carolina
Fall 2005

An Overview of African Geopolitical History

The history of Africa can be somewhat conveniently divided into three distinct phases: the precolonial, the colonial, and the postcolonial periods. From a general perspective, the three phases comprise:

1. The period up to the late 19th century.
2. The period between the late 19th century and the 1960s.
3. The period since the 1960s.

This is of course very general, but it serves as a rough guide. There were European possessions in Africa as far back as the ancient days. Ethiopia has never been colonized. And South Africa was colonized by Europeans in the seventeenth century.

In the days before the Europeans arrived in force, kingdoms and empires grew up all over Africa, some lasting for centuries and achieving a fame and a magnificence equal to or greater than some of their European counterparts.

But perhaps the history of Africa should be viewed geographically rather than chronologically, especially as there are two distinct parts to the continent — North Africa and Sub-Saharan Africa. North Africa was subject to a set of historical circumstances very different from those influencing the Sub-Saharan. Being on or near the Mediterranean, North Africa has always been part of, or close to, the mainstream of European civilization, while the continent south of the Sahara spent centuries largely without contact with Europeans.

Phoenician sailors certainly seem to have voyaged through the Straits of Gibraltar and, hugging the coast, may well have traveled as far south as the Guinea coast. But it was the Portuguese in the fifteenth and sixteenth centuries, driven by the quest for slaves and gold, who first established themselves on this coast. Then other Europeans came, and after a time the Guinea coast was teeming with European-owned factories staffed by British, French, Dutch, Spanish, Portuguese, German, Scandinavian, and other functionaries. Mercenaries and adventurers abounded. European companies were chartered with the express purpose of trading between the Guinea coast, Europe, and the new American colonies.

Aside from European colonization, the greatest influence in Africa has been Islam, which, from the seventh century, swept over North Africa and then spread south across the Sahara and down the east coast of Africa.

The Dutch, in 1652, began the colony which would become South Africa, and from there they established other settlements in the hinterland. The Portuguese also came down the east coast of Africa and opened up the interior from there. But it was not until the nineteenth century that European exploration of the interior began in force. With this initial penetration of inland Africa, the desire for gold, palm oil and other indigenous commodities overtook the slave trade, which was anyway being abolished by one European country after another throughout the nineteenth century.

The nineteenth century was the real beginning of the colonial period, the "Scramble for Africa," with European states vying with one another for control of large and small chunks of the continent, a toehold here, a fingerhold there, a massive portion somewhere else. Once colonized, the countries had their boundaries arranged by cartographers and treaty-makers, until a map of Africa was in place similar to the one of today. Some of the colonial powers behaved well toward their subjects, but most did not. In the end, the human desire for freedom impelled the indigenous peoples to revolt against foreign domination and occupation. What made independence possible in such comparatively short order was, however, a growing awareness at home (i.e., among the ever-increasingly educated electorates in the colonialists' home countries) of two major factors, one sociologically based and the other economically driven. The first, which had been present and festering for decades, was an anti-empire sentiment, a feeling of embarrassment about subjugating other people against their wishes. At the same time, the colonies were becoming an intolerable expense to the taxpayers in the home countries. So, the colonies had to go. And they did — suddenly, most of them in the 1960s, too suddenly, some say, for the Africans who had had little or no experience at government. The Europeans left, voluntarily or involuntarily, taking with them their money and expertise.

As a result, the postcolonial period, or the period of independence, has been, in most cases, one of struggle to keep afloat.

Non-African powers have been ever ready to enter into the affairs of a distressed African country. The Chinese, Russians, Cubans, Americans, British, and French have all used Africa as an ideological battleground since independence, each trying to gain political influence. In short, it has been yet another scramble for Africa.

There are reasons to be optimistic about Africa's future despite its pressing problems. Uganda's determined fight against AIDS is a strong ray of hope not just for Africa but for the world. South Africa — blacks and whites — struck one of the great blows for freedom. Niger, Nigeria, Senegal and Kenya are on the way to stability, and the Arab countries of North Africa have all been pretty stable for years. Libya, with its amazing volte-face, is now an ally of the West. Once AIDS is beaten, and it will be, the rest of Africa can only go upwards.

The States and Rulers

Abbeokuta see **Abeokuta**

Abd al-Wadid Kingdom see **Tlemcen**

Abeokuta. 1829–16 Sept. 1914. *Location:* in southwestern Nigeria, just to the north of Lagos, to the southwest of Ibadan, and close to the border of Benin. *Capital:* Abeokuta. *Other names:* Abbeokuta; Egbaland; Egba Kingdom; Egba State; Egba United Government (after 1893).

History: Founded about 1830 by Sodeke, a refugee from the Egba Forest, near Ibadan. Many people from the Egba branch of the Yoruba peoples came to live here, mostly from the disintegrating Oyo (q.v.) which was then being attacked by the Fulani. In this rocky stronghold they found a refuge from the slavers of Ibadan and Dahomey, hence the name Abeokuta (meaning "refuge among rocks"). British interest in the area began in 1842 when the first missionaries arrived. The Battle of Abeokuta in 1851 was the high point of a war with the kingdom of Dahomey. The king of Abeokuta helped the British suppress the slave trade in the area, and in 1893, after the Yoruba Civil Wars (1877–1893), the king, encouraged by the governor of Lagos, signed an agreement with the British government which recognized the internal independence of the country as the Egba United Government, but which brought the country under direct British influence. It also united the rival local factions. In 1899 the railroad came to Abeokuta from Lagos, and this increased trade enormously. It also increased the desire of the British to take the country over completely. The style of government Abeokuta had adopted in 1893 was based on the British model, but only based on it, and the corruption and brutality that still existed were not acceptable to the British. In 1914 Abeokuta renounced its independence, and, along with Jebu, and other districts, was constituted into the province of Abeokuta, a fundamental part of the Nigeria Southern Provinces of the newly formed colony and protectorate of Nigeria. From that time the local king continued an administration, under the supervision of the British. In 1939 it became part of the new Nigeria Western Region, and remained as such until 1 Oct. 1960, when Nigeria became independent from Britain. It later became a province of the Western State in Nigeria.

Military Leaders: ca. 1830–1844 Sodeke. *Sabuas (Chiefs):* 1844–1854 Okukenun. *Alakes (Kings):* 8 Aug. 1854–Sept. 1862 Okukenun. *Regents:* 1862–1868 Shomoye. *Alakes (Kings):* 20 Nov. 1869–30 Dec. 1877 Ademola I; 18 Jan. 1879–18 Sept. 1881 Oyekan; 9 Feb. 1885–27 Jan. 1889 Oluwajin; 18 Sept. 1891–11 June 1898 Oshukalu; 8 Aug. 1898–28 May 1920 Gbadebo I; 27 Sept. 1920–27 Dec. 1962 Ademola II; 29 Sept. 1963–16 Oct. 1971 Gbadebo II; 5 Aug. 1972–3 Feb. 2005 Oyebade Lipede.

Abomey see **Dahomey**

Abuja. 1828–1902. *Location:* in present-day Niger State in western Nigeria. *Capital:* Abuja (since 12 Dec. 1991 this city has also been the capital of Nigeria).

History: In 1804, Makau, the ruler of Zaria, was driven out of his country by the Fulani and sought refuge at the Koro town of Zuba, his vassal state. Zuba now became his capital, from which he waged war against the Fulani. In 1828 his brother Jatau (also known as Abu Ja, or Abu the Red) founded the town and independent Hausa amirate of Abuja. Before that Abuja had been the homeland of four small Koro chiefdoms, vassals of Zaria. When Abuja began disrupting trade between Lokoja and Zaria, the British occupied it in 1902, and it became part of the protectorate of Northern Nigeria. It formed a part of North-Western State in Nigeria until 1976, when the name of that state changed to Niger State (not to be confused with the country of Niger).

Amirs: 1828–2 Aug. 1851 Abu Ja (also known as Jatau); 2 Aug. 1851–29 July 1877 Abu Kwaka (also known as Dogon Sarki); 29 July 1877–Aug. 1902 Ibrahim Ayalai (also known as Dodon Gwari); 1902–1917 Muhamman Gani; May 1917–3 March 1944 Musa Angulu; 13 March 1944–1979 Suleimanu Barau; 1979–1993 Ibrahim Dodo Musa; 1993–10 May 1994 Awal Ibrahim; 10 May 1994–Jan. 2000 Bashir Suleimanu Barau; Jan. 2000–Awal Ibrahim.

Abyssinia see **Ethiopia**

Acholi see **Nkore**

Adaiel see **Adal**

Adajel see **Adal**

Adal [i]. ca. 900–1285. *Location:* the Zeila area in the extreme north of what is today Somalia, almost on the border with Djibouti, on the Gulf of Aden. *Capital:* Zeila. *Other names:* Adel; Adaiel; Adajel; Zeila; Zaila.

History: Adal was a sultanate founded about 900, and was the center of Arab trade with the interior of what is today Somalia and Ethiopia. In 1285 it became part of Ethiopia.

Rulers: unknown.

Adal [ii]. 1415–1526. *Location:* eastern Shoa, on the border of what are today Eritrea and Djibouti. *Capital:* Harar (from ca. 1522). *Other names:* Adel; Adaiel; Adajel; Harar.

History: In 1415 the old sultanate of Ifat was conquered and made part of the Ethiopian Empire. About the same time the ruling Walashma dynasty of Ifat recreated in the same area the old sultanate of Adal, and ruled there until 1526, when it was conquered by the first amir of Harar. Harar, as a town, had, in fact, become the capital of the last sultan of Adal. Adal then became incorporated into the new amirate of Harar. Today Adal is a region composed of the Danakils, and most of it lies in Eritrea, but its southern part is in Djibouti.

Sultans: 1415–1422 Sabr ad-Din II; 1422–1425 al-Mansur II; 1425–1432 Jamal ad-Din II; 1432–1445 Badlai (also known as Shahah ad-Din); 1445–1471 Muhammad I; 1471–1472 Ibrahim I; 1472–1487 Shams ad-Din; 1487–1488 Ibrahim II; 1488–1518 Muhammad II; 1518–1519 Ali; 1519–1520 Fakhr ad-Din; 1520–1526 Abu Bakr.

Adamawa. 1806–Sept. 1901. *Location:* Cameroun/Nigeria border. *Capital:* Yola (from 1841); Jobolio (1839–1841); Ribadu (1830–1839); Gurin (1806–1830). *Other names:* Fumbina; Fombina; Yola; Southland.

History: This area had previously been called Fumbina (or Southland), and was a Fula homeland. Adama (son of Ardo Hassana, a Fula nobleman), a high-ranking Fulani officer, conquered the territory and renamed it Adamawa, and it became a Muslim amirate subject to the Fulani Empire. In fact, it was the easternmost amirate in the empire. Heinrich Barth, the German explorer, visited Yola in 1851, and during the weak rule of one of Adama's sons, Saanda, the Royal Niger Company established trading posts here. In 1901 Zubeiru tried to force the British to leave Yola, and that year the country was partitioned between Kamerun and the pro-

tectorate of Northern Nigeria, and the British part became known as Yola Province. Bobbo Ahmadu, the fourth of Adama's sons, became the new amir, but only in Yola, in the British sector. In 1914 Yola Province fell under Nigeria Northern Region, and during the first two years of World War I was a battlefield for the Germans and British. In 1916, when the Germans were defeated in Kamerun, their part of Adamawa mostly became part of British Cameroons. The name Adamawa was revived in Nigeria in 1926 when Yola and Muri provinces were merged to form Adamawa Province. The Cameroons part joined Nigeria in 1954, and thus most of what was originally Adamawa now fell under Nigeria, and became part of Northern Cameroon. In 1961 the people of Yola Province voted to become part of an independent Nigeria if they could have a new province, which they got (Sardauna), and Adamawa is now a division of that province.

Lamidos (Amirs): 1806–1848 Adama; 1848–1872 Hamman Lawal; 1872–1890 Saanda; 1890–8 Sept. 1901 Zubeiru; 8 Sept. 1901–1909 Bobbo Ahmadu; 1909–1910 Muhammadu Yerima Iya; 1910–23 Aug. 1924 Abba; 1924–1928 Muhammadu Bello (also known as Maigari); 1928–1946 Mustafa; 1946–June 1953 Ahmadu; June 1953–(?) Aliyu Mustafa.

Adam Kok's Land. 1826–26 Dec. 1861. *Location:* southern Orange Free State, between the Modder and Orange rivers. *Capital:* Philippolis (founded 1821 by Dr. John Philip, a missionary). *Other names:* Philippolis.

History: In 1820 Adam Kok II left Griquatown (see Griqualand West), which he had ruled jointly with Barend Barends since 1813, and he set up in Campbell Lands (see Cornelis Kok's Land). From 1824 to 1826 he lived as a rustler, and then he moved southeast to create a state around the town of Philippolis, eliminating the Bushmen who had lived here prior to that. Kok thus initiated the difference between the East and West Griquas (see Griqualand West). He died in 1835, and after a period of civil war, Adam Kok III came to power. In 1838 his lands were defined by treaty, and in Nov. 1843 he signed a peace treaty, placing himself under British protection. In 1848 the British recognized his independence, but in 1861 Adam Kok III, after whom the state was actually named rather than for his father, sold the area to the Orange

Free State for £4,000 and, with his people, some 3,000 in all, trekked over the Drakensberg Mountains to found Griqualand East, at the suggestion of the British.

Kaptyns (Captains): 1826–12 Sept. 1835 Adam Kok II; 12 Sept. 1835–July 1837 Abraham Kok; July 1837–Sept. 1837 Barend Lucas (acting); Sept. 1837–26 Dec. 1861 Adam Kok III.

Adel see **Adal**

Adja-Tado see **Allada**

Adjatché see **Porto-Novo**

Adrar. ca. 1800–9 Jan. 1909. *Location:* desert country in western Mauritania, close to the Spanish Sahara border, containing several oases. *Capital:* Atar.

History: Around 1800 the dynasty of Ulad Yahya ibn Uthman began to rule in Adrar (the Berber word for "uplands") and lasted until the French proclaimed a protectorate, and brought the country into the Civil Territory of Mauritania. The population is about 10,000.

Amirs: ca. 1800–(?) Uthman Ould Fadl Ould Sinan; (?)–(?) Sidi Ahmad; (?)–(?) Muhammad; (?)–1871 Ahmad II; 1871–1891 Sidi Ahmad III; 1891–ca. 1899 al-Mukhtar Ahmad; ca. 1899–1909 Sheikh Hassana; 1909–March 1932 Sidi Ahmad IV.

Afars and Issas Territory see **Djibouti**

Africa [i]. 29 B.C.–A.D. 297. *Location:* Tunisia and western Libya. *Capital:* Colonia Julia Carthago (also known as Carthage). *Other names:* Africa Roman Province.

History: In 29 B.C. Augustus Caesar united Africa Nova (see Numidia) and Africa Vetus (see Carthage) to form the large Roman province of Africa, which was placed under the control of the senate. In A.D. 297 the emperor Diocletian, in his reformation of the empire, split that province into three parts: Byzacena, Tripolitania, and a smaller province in what is now northern Tunisia, called Africa (see Africa [ii]).

Praetors: 29 B.C.–A.D. 12 [unknown]; A.D. 12–15 Lucius Nonius Asprenas; 15–16 Lucius Aelius Lamia; 16–17 Aulus Vibius Habitus; 17–18 Marcus Furius Camillus; 18–21 Lucius Apronius; 21–23 Quintus Junius Blaesus; 23–24 Publius Cornelius Dolabella; 24–26 [unknown]; 26–29 Caius Vivius Marsus; 29–35 Marcus Junius Silanus; 35–36 Caius Rubellius Blandus; 36–37 Servius Cornelius Cethegus; 37–38 [unknown]; 38–39 Lucius Calpurnius Piso; 39–40 [unknown]; 40–41 Lucius Salvius Otho; 41–43 Quintus Marcius Barea Soranus; 43–44 [unknown]; 44–46 Servius Sulpicius Galba; 46–47 Marcus Servilius Nonianus; 47–51 [unknown]; 51–52 Lucius Tampius Flavianus; 52–53 Titus Statilius Taurus; 53–56 Marcus Pompeius Silvanus Staberius Flavinus; 56–57 Quintus Sulpicius Camerinus Peticus; 57–58 Cnaeus Hosidius Geta; 58–59 Quintus Curtius Rufus; 59–60 [unknown]; 60–61 Aulus Vitellius; 61–62 Lucius Vitellius; 62–63 Servius Cornelius Scipio Salvidienus Orfitus; 63–64 Titus Flavius Vespasianus; 64–68 [unknown]; 68–68 Caius Vipstanus Apronianus; 68–121 [unknown]; 121–121 Lucius Minicius Natalis; 121–139 [unknown]; 139–140 Minicius; 140–141 Titus Prifernius Paetus Rosianus Geminus; 141–142 Sextus Julius Major; 142–143 Publius Tullius Varro; 143–(?) [unknown]; (?)–(?) Ennius Proculus; (?)–153 [unknown]; 153–ca. 154 Lucius Minicius Natalis Quadronius Verus; ca. 154–ca. 155 Marcellus; ca. 155–ca. 157 Severus; ca. 157–158 Lucius Hedius Rufus Lollianus Avitus; 158–160 Claudius Maximus; 160–161 Egrilius Plarianus; 161–162 Titus Prifernius Paetus Rosianus Geminus; 162–163 Quintus Voconius Saxa Fides; 163–164 Sextus Cocceius Severianus Honorinus; 164–164 Servius Cornelius Scipio Salvidienus Orfitus; 164–165 Marcus Antonius Zeno; 165–297 [unknown].

Africa [ii]. 297–439. *Location:* northern Tunisia. *Capital:* Colonia Julia Carthago (also known as Carthage). *Other names:* Africa Roman Province.

History: In 297 the emperor Diocletian reformed the Roman Empire, and split the old province of Africa (see Africa [i]) into three parts: Byzacena, Tripolitania (see Tripolitania Roman Province), and Africa, the last named being the subject of this entry. In 320 Tripolitania and Byzacena became component parts of the greater Roman colony of Africa Proconsularis, while Africa, as a province, continued to be independent. In 439 Africa fell to the Vandals (see Vandal North Africa), and three years later so did Africa Proconsularis, which still comprised Byzacena and Tripolitania.

Rulers: 297–439 [unknown].

Africa Nova see **Numidia**

Africa Occidental Española see **Western Sahara**

Africa Proconsularis. 320–442. *Location:* Tunisia and western Libya. *Capital:* Leptis Magna. *Other names:* Proconsular Africa.

History: In 320 the two Roman provinces of Tripolitania and Byzacena became the two component parts of the greater colony of Africa Proconsularis, thus named because it came under the administration of the Roman proconsuls. The two parts remained autonomous colonies, except that from 320 they reported to the Praetorian Prefect or the Consul of Africa Proconsularis. In 442 the whole of Roman Africa fell to the Vandals (see Vandal North Africa).

Praetorian Prefects: 320–322 Menander; 322–333 [unknown]; 333–336 Lucius Aradius Valerius Proculus Felix; 336–337 Gregorius; 337–337 Nestorius Timonianus; 337–339 [unknown]; 339–340 Euagrius; 340–341 Antonius Marcellinus; 341–342 Aconius Catullinus; 342–344 [unknown]; 344–346 Placidus; 346–347 Vulcacius Rufinus; 347–349 Ulpius Limenius; 349–350 Hermogenes; 350–352 Anicetus; 352–353 Vulcacius Rufinus; 353–354 Flavius Philippus; 354–355 Maecilius Hilarianus; 355–356 Taurus; 356–356 Lollianus Mavortius; 356–361 Taurus; 362–365 Mamertinus; 365–367 Vulcacius Rufinus; 367–375 Sextus Petronius Probus; 375–377 [unknown]; 377–378 Antonius; 378–382 Hesperius; 382–382 Severus; 382–382 Syagrius; 382–383 Hypatius; 383–384 Sextus Petronius Probus; 384–384 Atticus; 384–385 Praetextatus; 385–385 Neoterius; 385–386 Principius; 386–387 Eusignias; 387–388 Sextus Petronius Probus; 388–389 Trifolius; 390–390 Polemius; 390–393 [unknown]; 393–394 Flavianus; 395–395 Dexter; 395–396 Eusebius; 396–396 Hilarius; 397–399 Mallius Theodorus; 399–400 Valerius Messala; 400–405 Rufius Synesius Hadrianus; 406–407 Longinianus; 407–408 Curtius; 408–409 Theodorus; 409–409 Caecillianus; 409–409 Liberius; 409–410 Lampadius; 410–410 Faustinus; 410–410 Macrobius; 410–412 Melitius; 412–413 Johannes; 413–414 Synesius Hadrianus; 414–415 Seleucus; 416–421 Junius Quartus Palladius; 422–422 Johannes; 422–423 Marinianus; 423–423 Venantius; 423–426 Proculus; 426–427 Bassus; 427–428 Portogenes; 428–429 Volusianus; 430–430 Theodosius; 430–431 Decius Aciniancius Albinus; 431–432 Flavianus; 433–435 Petronius Maxi mus; 435–435 Flavius Bassus; 435–437 Petronius Maximus; 437–439 Flavius Bassus; 439–442 Petronius Maximus. *Proconsuls (where appropriate):* 358–358 Sextus Petronius Probus; 373–373 Quintus Aurelius Symmachus; 373–374 Constantius; 377–378 Nicomachus Flavianus; 378–380 Fallonius Probus Allypsius; 380–380 Alfenius Ceionius Camenius; 385–385 Pastorius; 390–390 Pacatus Drepanius; 393–394 Magnilius; 394–394 Macianus.

Africa Roman Province see **Africa [i]**

Africa Roman Province see **Africa [ii]**

Africa Vetus see **Carthage**

African Islands see **Amirante Islands**

African Republic see **Dutch African Republic**

Afrique Équatoriale Française see **French Equatorial Africa**

Afrique Occidentale Française see **French West Africa**

Agaie. 1832–24 June 1898. *Location:* in Niger State, in west central Nigeria. *Capital:* Agaie. *Other names:* Argeyes.

History: The original inhabitants of this area were the Mama peoples. They were superseded by the Dibo (also known as the Zitako, or Ganagana). This loose group was taken over by the Fulani in 1822, and in an enlarged form the area became an amirate in 1832. Mallam Baba continued to rule, but made his son, Abdullahi, amir. In 1897 Agaie aided Bida, the neighboring amirate, in its struggle against the Royal Niger Company, and as a consequence was taken over by the company in 1898 (see Northern Nigeria). In 1908 Agaie, which has always been populated mainly by Nupe peoples, became part of the newly formed Niger Province of the protectorate of Northern Nigeria. In 1975 Niger Province became Niger State (not to be confused with the country of Niger).

Governors: 1822–1832 Mallam Baba. *Regents:* 1832–1848 Mallam Baba. *Amirs:* 1832–1857 Abdullahi; 1857–1877 Muhammadu (also known as Mamman Diko); 1877–1900 Nuhu; 1900–24

July 1919 Abubakar I; 19 Aug. 1919–1926 Abubakar II; 1926–April 1935 Abdullahi; April 1935–1953 Aliyu; Oct. 1953–(?) Muhammadu Bello.

Agalega Islands. No dates. *Location:* about 600 miles north of Mauritius, in the Indian Ocean. *Capital:* Sainte Rita (on South Island).

History: The Agalegas, comprising North and South Islands, were a French possession until 3 Oct. 1810, when they were taken by the British. They then became a dependency of Mauritius, from where they were administered. On 12 March 1992 they went to form part of the newly formed Republic of Mauritius. The population has always been around 250.

Aghlabid Empire. 9 July 800–26 March 909. *Location:* Tunisia and eastern Algeria (i.e. Ifriqiyah). *Capital:* Joint capitals of Tunis and al-Qayrawan. *Other names:* Ifriqiyah; Ifriqa; Ifrikiyah; Banu al-Aghlab Dynasty.

History: In 800 the Abbasid governor of Africa (see Omayyad and Abbasid North Africa), Ibrahim ibn al-Aghlab, founded his own dynasty there, an orthodox Muslim Arab dynasty that controlled much of North Africa for a century. In 827 the Aghlabids took Sicily and eventually conquered much of southern Italy before being subdued by the Fatimids (see Fatimid North Africa). See also Tripolitania.

Sultans: 9 July 800–5 July 812 Ibrahim ibn al-Aghlab; Oct. 812–25 June 817 Abdallah I; 25 June 817–10 June 838 Ziyadat-Allah I; 10 June 838–18 Feb. 841 Abu-Iqal al-Aghlab; 18 Feb. 841–10 May 856 Muhammad I; 10 May 856–28 Dec. 863 Ahmad; 28 Dec. 863–23 Dec. 864 Ziyadat-Allah II; 23 Dec. 864–16 Feb. 875 Muhammad II; 16 Feb. 875–902 Ibrahim II; 902–28 July 903 Abdallah II; 28 July 903–26 March 909 Ziyadat-Allah III.

Agona see **Akwamu**

Aïr see **Bornu Empire**

Aiyubid Empire see **Egypt**

Ajashe see **Porto-Novo**

Ajuda see **Whydah**

Akim. ca. 1500–1899. *Location:* between Denkyira and Akwamu, in Ghana. *Capital:* Nsauoen.

History: Founded about 1500, the kingdom of Akim lasted 400 years until it was taken into the Gold Coast Northern Territories by the British. Its history was largely dominated by its struggles for control of power in the area between its two neighbors, Denkyira and Akwamu. Akim's first dynasty ended about 1733, its second about 1817, its third in 1866, and its fourth in 1912.

Kings: ca. 1500–ca. 1520 Kuntunkununku; ca. 1520–ca. 1540 Apeanin Kwaframoa Woyiawonyi; ca. 1540–ca. 1560 Damram; ca. 1560–ca. 1580 Pobi Asomaning; ca. 1580–ca. 1600 Oduro; ca. 1600–ca. 1620 Boakye I; ca. 1620–ca. 1640 Boakye II; ca. 1640–ca. 1660 Agyekum Owari I; ca. 1660–ca. 1680 Boakye III; ca. 1680–ca. 1700 Agyekum Owari II; ca. 1700–ca. 1733 Agyekum Owari III; ca. 1733–ca. 1738 Ofori Panin; ca. 1738–1742 Bakwante; 1742–ca. 1744 Pobi; ca. 1744–ca. 1750 Owusu Akyem Ohenkoko (The "Red King"); ca. 1750–ca. 1760 Twum Ampoforo Okasu; ca. 1760–1770 Obirikorane; 1770–(?) Apraku; (?)–1811 Atta Wusu Yiakosan; 1811–ca. 1815 Kofi Asante Baninyiye; ca. 1815–1817 Twum. *Queens:* 1817–1851 Dokua. *Kings:* 1851–(?) [unknown]; (?)–(?) Atta Panyin; (?)–1866 Atta Biwom; 1866–1888 Amoaka Atta I; 1888–1911 Amoaka Atta II; April 1911–1 Nov. 1912 Amoaka Atta III; 1 Nov. 1912–Aug. 1943 Nana Ofori Atta I; 13 Sept. 1943–1958 Nana Ofori Atta II; 1958–1966 Amoaka Atta IV; 1973–1 May 1976 Nana Ofori Atta III; 2 Aug. 1976–17 March 1999 Kuntunkununku II.

Aksum see **Axum**

Aku. ca. 1826–1880. *Location:* in Sierra Leone. *Capital:* Aku.

History: Founded about 1826, Aku was made a part of Sierra Leone by the British in 1880.

Kings: ca. 1826–1840 Thomas Will; 1840–5 Dec. 1867 John Macaulay (also known as Atapa); 5 Dec. 1867–1880 Isaac Benjamin Pratt.

Akwamu. 1480–1730. *Location:* in southern Ghana. *Capital:* Ayandawaase (from 1575); Aseremankese (1480–1575). *Other names:* Twifo-Heman, or Twifu-Heman (1480–1560).

History: In 1480 Agyen Kokobo founded the Akan state of Twifo-Heman. In 1560 Otumfo Asare of Twifo-Heman founded Akwamu, one of the two famous Akan (also known as Bron) states (the other being Ashanti), making his capital at Aseremenakese. Fifteen years later the capital was moved to Ayandawaase. The sale of gold made the king of Akwamu aggressive, and he expanded his territory in the late 1600s, taking the Ga and Fante towns along the coast. In 1679 Ladoku became a vassal state of Akwamu, as did Agona in 1689. In 1702 the people of Akwamu crossed the Volta River to occupy Whydah, and in 1710 conquered the Ewe people of the Ho region. Much of their time, however, was taken up in the eternal fight with their powerful neighbor, Akim, and in 1730 Akim conquered Akwamu.

Chiefs: 1480–1500 Agyen Kokobo; 1500–1520 Ofusu Kwabi; 1520–1540 Oduro; 1540–1560 Ado. *Nanas or Akwamuhenes (Kings):* 1560–1575 Otumfo Asare; 1575–1585 Akotia; 1585–1600 Ansa Saseraku I; 1600–1621 Ansa Saseraku II; 1621–1638 Ansa Saseraku III; 1638–1660 Abuako Dako; 1660–1682 Afera Kuma; 1682–1689 Ansa Saseraku IV; 1689–1702 Manukure; 1702–1726 Akwano Panyini; 1726–1730 Dako Booman.

Albania see **Griqualand West**

Aldabra Islands. No dates. *Location:* an atoll 265 miles northwest of Madagascar, in the Indian Ocean. *Capital:* None. *Notes:* The Aldabras comprise four uninhabited islands (although they have at times sustained a population up to a couple of hundred): South Island (or Grand Terre; the largest of the Aldabras, and famous for its giant tortoises); West Island (or Île Picard); Polymnie; Middle Island; and several islets in the lagoon, e.g. Île Michel. The Aldabras also include Assumption Island, to the south, and Astove Island.

History: The Aldabras were a French possession until 3 Oct. 1810, when they were captured by the British along with Réunion and the other French holdings in the Indian Ocean, and placed under the direct administration of Victoria, in the Seychelles, until 8 Nov. 1965 when, along with Farquhar and Des Roches Islands, and the Chagos Archipelago, they became part of the British colony known as the British Indian Ocean Territory. On 29 June 1976, when the BIOT effectively came to an end, the Aldabras were returned to the newly-independent Seychelles.

Alegranza see **Canary Islands** and **Gran Canaria**

Alfred see **Natal** and **Transkeian Territories**

Algeria. 5 July 1830– . *Location:* the heavily populated areas of Algeria have always been the towns along the Mediterranean coast of North Africa, between Morocco and Tunisia. The hinterland is less densely populated, extending as it does into the Sahara, and bordering Libya on the east and Mauritania on the west, and Mali and Niger in the south. *Capital:* Algiers (also known as al-Djazaiir). *Other names:* Algérie; al-Djazaiir; al-Jaza'ir; Algerian Democratic and Popular Republic (1962–); Algeria (1962–1962); French Algeria (1881–1962); French Algeria Military Province (1842–1881); French Algerian Possessions (1839–1842); French Possessions in North Africa (1830–1839).

History: By 1827 the French had a fortified trading post near Bône. In April of that year the French consul and the dey (the Turkish ruler of the Regency of Algiers) got into an argument in which the dey threatened to withdraw his concession to the French, the consul became very rude to the dey, and the dey flicked the consul with a fly-whisk. To avenge this insult Charles X, King of France, instituted a naval blockade of Algiers, but the only result of this was the loss of the trading post. A French naval and military expedition arrived in Algiers on 14 June 1830, and on 5 July the dey surrendered. The French claimed that this move helped out all countries concerned in Mediterranean trade, as it put an end to privateering. However, as everyone knew, the corsairs had not been a real threat for a long time, and the French had only taken Algiers for their own commercial purposes. In addition, the French appealed to the local Algerian majority (who were not Turkish) in that they evicted the hated Ottoman overlords. The territory of Algiers at that time extended along the coast, but not into the hinterland of what would later become Algeria. Although the name "Algeria" was not used until 1839, the idea of French Algeria began in 1830, as the French Possessions in North Africa. Oran was taken from the Turks in 1831, Bône in 1832, and Constantine on 13 Oct. 1837. With the exception of Constantine, all of these major towns and their environs had been ruled by Turkey since 1518. In 1839 the country became known as the French Algerian Possessions, and in Feb. 1842 it became a French military province called Algeria. It was still very much a coastal country. The hinterland and desert had not yet been conquered. In these early days of French rule there was trouble from Abdelkedir (see Mascara). On 23 Dec. 1847 Mascara surrendered, and from this time until 1954 there was little real resistance to French rule. In 1848 Algeria was declared a French territory. Old soldiers settled in Algeria in droves. On 26 Aug. 1881 Algeria became a civil province and the three northern départements of Algiers, Oran and Constantine were made integral parts of France. Algeria reverted to military rule on 31 Dec. 1896, and in the early 20th century France conquered most of the desert regions (using the Foreign Legion mainly) and brought the limits of Algeria close to those of today. However, there were several million Muslims living in Algeria, subjected people in their own land, living with standards considerably below those of the Europeans, and the passive status quo could not last. Independence movements began in the 1930s, and trouble began just after World War II. French repression was shockingly savage, to the Muslims as well as to the French people themselves. A certain autonomy was granted, but a lot of empty promises were made too. In 1954 a concerted uprising took place by the Front de Libération National (FLN), another in 1955, much more extensive, and in 1956 Ferhat Abbas, the prime mover for Algerian independence since the 1930s, went to Cairo, where he set up an Algerian government in exile (see Algerian Republic (Provisional Government) in 1958. This government shortly thereafter moved to Tunis. By this time the war was in full swing, with the Muslims on the one hand and the French settlers and the Army on the other. It also led to a schism in France itself, between those who favored independence and those who did not. In 1961 certain high-ranking French officers in Algeria revolted against France, but were soon crushed. On 18 March 1962 a cease fire was arranged, and the war came to an end. However, the French nationalists in Algeria, led by General Raoul Salan, had organized the O.A.S. (Organisation de l'Armée Secrète) which began a terrorist campaign to make the agreements between de Gaulle and the Algerian Muslims impossible to ratify as a reality. However, the vast majority of French settlers in Algeria had returned, or were returning, to France. On 1 July 1962 the Algerians voted for an independent Algeria in association with France, and on 3 July de Gaulle recognized their independence.

Later in 1962 (25 Sept.) the country declared itself the Democratic and Popular Republic of Algeria. In the 1960s Algeria made its opposition to Israel felt, when it broke ties with the USA, embarked on an alliance with the U.S.S.R., and declared war on Israel. The country also had to deal with the Europeans leaving and what that did to the structure of the country, a tyrannical president (ben Bellah), and a coup in 1965. The 1980s began with a devastating earthquake, and in 1986 came a bad depression when oil prices dropped. The decade ended with mass rioting. In 1992 President Boudiaf was assassinated, and, throughout the rest of the 1990s, with conditions in Algeria worsening, there was a serious Islamic Fundamentalist problem which set the country back, not only domestically, but internationally. This led to civil war, aggravated by a growing Berber nationalist movement. There was a 5.8 earthquake near Oran in 1999, and on 11 Nov. 2001, following a major storm, there was the worst flooding in 20 years. On 25 Feb. 2003 a government workers' strike paralyzed the country, and to cap it all off there was a 6.7 earthquake on 21 May, 2003, and a major locust plague in 2004. Large portions of the country were faced with starvation, poverty and enormous unemployment. On 16 Jan. 2005 the government agreed to make certain concessions to the Berbers.

Military Commanders: 5 July 1830–12 Aug. 1830 Comte Bourmont; 12 Aug. 1830–21 Feb. 1831 Comte Clausel; 21 Feb. 1831–6 Dec. 1831 Baron Berthezène; 6 Dec. 1831–29 April 1833 Duc de Rovigo; 29 April 1833–27 July 1834 Théophile Viorol (acting). *Governors-General of the French Possessions in North Africa:* 27 July 1834–8 July 1835 Comte d'Erlon; 8 July 1835–12 Feb. 1837 Comte Clausel; 12 Feb. 1837–12 Oct. 1837 Comte de Danrémont; 12 Oct. 1837–11 Nov. 1837 [unknown] (acting); 11 Nov. 1837–Dec. 1840 Comte Valée; Dec. 1840–22 Feb. 1841 [unknown] (acting); 22 Feb. 1841–Feb. 1842 Thomas Bougeaud de la Piconnerie. *Governors-General of French Algeria:* Feb. 1842–1 Sept. 1845 Thomas Bougeaud de la Piconnerie (created the Duc d'Isly in 1844); 1 Sept. 1845–6 July 1847 Christophe de Lamoricière (acting); 6 July 1847–27 Sept. 1847 Marie-Alphonse Bedeau (acting); 27 Sept. 1847–24 Feb. 1848 Duc d'Aumale; 24 Feb. 1848–29 April 1848 Eugène Cavaignac; 29 April 1848–9 Sept. 1848 Nicolas Changarnier; 9 Sept. 1848–22 Oct. 1850 Baron Charon; 22 Oct.

1850–10 May 1851 Comte d'Hautpoul; 10 May 1851–11 Dec. 1851 Aimable Pelissier; 11 Dec. 1851–31 Aug. 1858 Comte Randon. *Ministers for Algeria and the Colonies:* 24 June 1858–24 March 1859 Prince Napoléon Bonaparte; 24 March 1859–24 Nov. 1860 Comte de Chasseloup-Laubat; 24 Nov. 1860–22 May 1864 Aimable Pelissier (created the Duc de Malakoff in 1856). *Governors-General:* 22 May 1864–1 Sept. 1864 Édouard de Martimprey; 1 Sept. 1864–27 July 1870 Duc de Magenta; 27 July 1870–23 Oct. 1870 Baron Durieu (acting); 23 Oct. 1870–16 Nov. 1870 Jean Walsin-Esterhazy (acting); 24 Oct. 1870–16 Nov. 1870 Henri Didier (did not take office); 16 Nov. 1870–8 Feb. 1871 Charles du Bouzet (acting); 8 Feb. 1871–29 March 1871 Alexis Lambert (acting); 29 March 1871–10 June 1873 Comte de Gueydon; 10 June 1873–15 March 1879 Antoine Chanzy; 15 March 1879–26 Nov. 1881 Albert Grévy (acting); 26 Nov. 1881–18 April 1891 Louis Tirman; 18 April 1891–28 Sept. 1897 Jules Cambon; 28 Sept. 1897–1 Oct. 1897 Auguste Loze (declined appointment); 1 Oct. 1897–26 July 1898 Louis Lépine; 26 July 1898–3 Oct. 1900 Édouard Julien-Laferrière; 3 Oct. 1900–18 June 1901 Celestin Jonnart (acting); 18 June 1901–11 April 1903 Paul Revoil; 11 April 1903–5 May 1903 Maurice Varnier (acting); 5 May 1903–22 May 1911 Celestin Jonnart (acting); 22 May 1911–29 Jan. 1918 Charles Lutaud; 29 Jan. 1918–29 Aug. 1919 Celestin Jonnart (acting); 29 Aug. 1919–28 July 1921 Jean-Baptiste Abel; 28 July 1921–17 April 1925 Théodore Steeg; 17 April 1925–12 May 1925 Henri Dubief; 12 May 1925–20 Nov. 1927 Maurice Viollette; 20 Nov. 1927–3 Oct. 1930 Pierre Bordes; 3 Oct. 1930–21 Sept. 1935 Jules Carde; 21 Sept. 1935–19 July 1940 Georges Le Beau; 19 July 1940–16 July 1941 Jean Abrial; 16 July 1941–20 Sept. 1941 Maxime Weygand (acting); 20 Sept. 1941–20 Jan. 1943 Yves Chatel; 20 Jan. 1943–3 June 1943 Marcel Peyrouton; 3 June 1943–8 Sept. 1944 Georges Catroux; 8 Sept. 1944–11 Feb. 1948 Yves Chataigneau; 11 Feb. 1948–9 March 1951 Marcel Naegelen; 9 March 1951–11 April 1951 [unknown] (acting); 11 April 1951–26 Jan. 1955 Roger Léonard; 26 Jan. 1955–30 Jan. 1956 Jacques Soustelle; 30 Jan. 1956–6 Feb. 1956 Georges Catroux. *Residents-General:* 10 Feb. 1956–15 May 1958 Robert La Coste; 15 May 1958–28 May 1958 André Mutter. *Delegates-General:* 16 June 1958–19 Dec. 1958 Raoul Salan; 19 Dec. 1958–24 Nov. 1960 Paul Delouvrier; 24 Nov. 1960–19 March 1962 Jean Morin; 19 March 1962–3 July 1962 Christian Fouchet. *Presidents of the Provisional Executive Council:* 28 March 1962–4 Aug. 1962 Abdur Rahman Farès. *Provisional Prime Ministers:* 5 July 1962–4 Aug. 1962 Yusuf ben Khedda; 4 Aug. 1962–25 Sept. 1962 Ahmed ben Bella. *Presidents:* 25 Sept. 1962–20 Sept. 1963 [none]; 20 Sept. 1963–19 June 1965 Ah med ben Bella; 19 June 1965–27 Dec. 1978 Houari Boumedienne; 27 Dec. 1978–9 Feb. 1979 Rabah Bitat (interim); 9 Feb. 1979–11 Jan. 1992 Chadli Bendjedid; 11 Jan. 1992–16 Jan. 1992 Sid Ahmad Ghozali (acting). *Chairmen of the High State Council:* 16 Jan. 1992–29 June 1992 Muhammad Boudiaf; 2 July 1992–31 Jan. 1994 Ali Kafi. *Presidents:* 31 Jan. 1994–27 April 1999 Liamine Zéroual; 27 April 1999–Abdul Aziz Bouteflika. *Prime Ministers:* 25 Sept. 1962–26 Sept. 1962 Ahmed ben Bella (provisional); 26 Sept. 1962–20 Sept. 1963 Ahmed ben Bella; 8 March 1979–22 Jan. 1984 Muhammad Abdelghani; 22 Jan. 1984–5 Nov. 1988 Abdelhamid Brahimi; 5 Nov. 1988–9 Sept. 1989 Kasdi Merbah; 9 Sept. 1989–5 June 1991 Mouloud Hamroche; 5 June 1991–8 July 1992 Sid Ahmad Ghozali; 8 July 1992–21 Aug. 1993 Belaid Abdesalam; 21 Aug. 1993–11 April 1994 Redha Malik; 11 April 1994–31 Dec. 1995 Mokdad Sifi; 31 Dec. 1995–15 Dec. 1998 Ahmad Ouyahia; 15 Dec. 1998–23 Dec. 1999 Ismail Hamdani; 23 Dec. 1999–26 Aug. 2000 Ahmad ben Bitour; 26 Aug. 2000–5 May 2003 Ali Benflis; 5 May 2003–Ahmad Ouyahia. *Note:* du Bouzet (1870–1871) and Lambert (1871–1871) were also Prefects of Oran. *Note:* In times of no Prime Minister, the President held that office.

Algerian Republic (Provisional Government). 18 Sept. 1958–3 July 1962. *Location:* Algeria, but the provisional government worked out of Tunis. *Capital:* Tunis (but for a very short while before that, in Sept. 1958, in Cairo). *Other names:* Gouvernement Provisoire de la République Algérienne; GPRA.

History: In 1956 the Algerian freedom fighter, Ferhat Abbas, went to Cairo to join the FLN (Front de Libération National) (see Algeria for more details). In 1958 an Algerian Government in Exile was put together in Cairo, and in Sept. 1958 moved to Tunis. In 1962, when independence was won by the Muslims in Algeria, this provisional government moved back to Algiers.

Presidents: 28 March 1962–3 July 1962 Abdur

Rahman Farès. *Prime Ministers:* 18 Sept. 1958–
22 Dec. 1959 Ferhat Abbas; 22 Dec. 1959–19
Jan. 1960 Krim Belkassim; 19 Jan. 1960–27 Aug.
1961 Ferhat Abbas; 27 Aug. 1961–3 July 1962
Yusuf ben Khedda.

Algiers. 944–1830. *Location:* on the Mediterranean coast of what is now Algeria, i.e. as the
city of Algiers, with environs. *Capital:* Algiers
("al-Jaza'ir" means "the islands," which once existed in Algiers Bay). *Other names:* al-Djazaiir;
al-Jaza'ir; Alger.

History: The islands in Algiers Bay were settled to some extent by the Phoenicians, who
called the area Icosium (a name meaning "gulls'
island"). There was a Roman town where Algiers
is today (although only a small one), which was
also called Icosium. The city of Algiers, roughly
as it corresponds to today's city, was built in 944
by the Sanhaja chieftain Abu al-Futuh Buluggin,
son of Ziri ibn Manad at-Talkali (the founder of
the Zirids) (see Zirid Kingdom). In 1082 the Almoravid Empire took the city, and in turn it was
taken by the Almohad Empire in 1152. In the
13th century it was taken by the Abd al-Wadid
dynasty (see Tlemcen), of which sultanate it
formed a part. But it had a large degree of autonomy. As early as 1302 the Spanish had had a
presence in Algiers, and a considerable trade
grew up between Spain and Algiers. In 1516 the
amir of Algiers, Salim at-Teumi, invited the corsairs Aruj and Khair ad-Din, the two corsair
brothers, to expel the Spanish, who had fortified
their island base in the harbor. Instead Aruj conquered the Algiers area, and it became the Pashalik of Algiers, but in 1520 his brother, another
legendary Barbary pirate, Khair ad-Din (Barbarossa) lost it to the Kabyles. Barbarossa then
went buccaneering in the Mediterranean for five
years, but returned in 1525 and re-took Algiers,
recreating the old Pashalik. From then on Algiers and all the surrounding area were ruled by
a beylerbey (bey of beys), who delegated Algiers
to a khalifah when he was out of the country. In
1530 Khair ad-Din expelled the Spanish, and Algiers became the capital of the Barbary pirates.
In 1577 the term "pasha" started to be used for
the ruler, the khalifahs were discontinued, and
in 1587 the beylerbeys were abolished. In 1671
the Turks took Algiers, and it became Algiers
Regency, a regency of the Ottoman Empire. In
1830 the dey of Algiers lost Algiers to the French
(see Algeria).

Rulers: 944–(?) [unknown]. *Abd al-Wadid
Amirs:* (?)–1516 Salim at-Teumi. *Pashas:* 1516–
Oct. 1518 Aruj; Oct. 1518–1520 Khair ad-Din
(Barbarossa). *Kabyle rulers:* 1520–1525 [un-
known]. *Beylerbeys:* 1525–4 July 1546 Khair ad-
Din (Barbarossa) (in residence only until 15 Oct.
1535). *Khalifahs (Governors):* 15 Oct. 1535–Dec.
1543 Hassan Agha; Dec. 1543–1544 Hajji Beshir
Pasha; 1544–4 July 1546 Hassan Pasha. *Beyler-
beys:* 4 July 1546–May 1552 Hassan Pasha (in
residence only until Sept. 1551). *Khalifahs (Gov-
ernors):* Sept. 1551–May 1552 Saffah. *Beylerbeys:*
May 1552–June 1557 Salah Raïs (in residence
only until 1556). *Khalifahs (Governors):* 1556–
June 1557 Hassan Corso. *Beylerbeys:* June 1557–
1557 Tekelerli (in residence only until June
1557). *Khalifahs (Governors):* June 1557–1557
Yusuf; 1557–1557 Yahya. *Beylerbeys:* 1557–1562
Hassan Pasha (in residence only until May 1561).
Khalifahs (Governors): June 1561–Sept. 1562
Hassan Agha; Sept. 1562–1562 Ahmad. *Beylerbeys:* 1562–March 1568 Hassan Pasha (in residence only until 1567). *Khalifahs (Governors):*
1567–March 1568 Muhammad ibn Salah Raïs.
Beylerbeys: March 1568–May 1577 Eulj Ali (also
known as Lucciali) (in residence only until 10
Oct. 1571). *Khalifahs (Governors):* 10 Oct. 1571–
1574 Arab Ahmad; 1574–May 1577 Ramdan.
Pashas: May 1577–1580 Hassan Veneziano;
1580–1582 Ja'far; 1582–1588 Hassan Veneziano;
1588–1589 Deli Ahmad; 1589–1592 Hizr;
1592–1594 Hajji Shaban; 1594–1594 Mustafa;
1594–1596 Hizr; 1596–1598 Mustafa; 1598–
1599 Hassan; 1599–1603 Suleiman; 1603–1605
Hizr; 1605–1607 Köse; 1607–1610 Rizvan; 1610–
1613 Köse Mustafa; 1613–1616 Sheikh Hussein;
1616–1616 Köse Mustafa; 1616–Jan. 1617 Suleiman Katanya; Jan. 1617–1619 Sheikh Hussein;
1619–1621 Sherif Koja; 1621–1621 Hizr; 1621–
1622 Mustafa; 1622–1622 Khusrev; 1622–1623
[vacant]; 1623–1626 Murad; 1626–1627 [va-
cant]; 1627–1629 Hussein; 1629–1629 Yunus;
1629–1634 Hussein; 1634–1636 Yusuf; 1636–
1638 Abu'l Hassan Ali; 1638–Aug. 1640 Sheikh
Hussein; Aug. 1640–1642 Abu Jemal Yusuf;
1642–1645 Mehmed Brusali; 1645–1645 Ali Bijnin; 1645–1647 Mahmud Brusali; 1647–1650
Yusuf; 1650–1653 Mehmed; 1653–1655 Ahmad;
1655–1656 Ibrahim; 1656–1658 Ahmad; 1658–
1659 Ibrahim; 1659–1671 Ismail. *Aghas (Military Commanders):* 1659–1660 Halil; 1660–1661
Ramadan; 1661–1665 Shaban; 1665–1671 Hajj
Ali. *Deys:* 1671–Jan. 1682 Muhammad I; Jan.

1682–22 July 1683 Hasan I; 22 July 1683–1686 Husain I; 1686–Dec. 1688 Ibrahim; Dec. 1688–July 1695 Shaban; July 1695–Dec. 1698 Ahmad I; Dec. 1698–1699 Hasan II; 1699–Oct. 1705 Mustafa I; Oct. 1705–April 1706 Husain II Khoja; April 1706–March 1710 Muhammad II Bektash. *Pashas/Deys:* March 1710–17 June 1710 Ibrahim I; 17 June 1710–4 April 1718 Ali I; 4 April 1718–18 May 1724 Muhammad III; 18 May 1724–1731 Kurd Abdi; 1731–Nov. 1745 Ibrahim II; Nov. 1745–Feb. 1748 Kuchuk Ibrahim II; Feb. 1748–11 Dec. 1754 Muhammad IV. *Deys:* 11 Dec. 1754–Feb. 1766 Ali II; Feb. 1766–11 July 1791 Muhammad V; 11 July 1791–June 1798 Hasan III; June 1798–1 July 1805 Mustafa II; 1 July 1805–15 Nov. 1808 Ahmad II; 15 Nov. 1808–Feb. 1809 Ali III ar-Rasul; Feb. 1809–March 1815 Ali IV; March 1815–11 April 1815 Muhammad VI; 11 April 1815–2 May 1817 Umar; 2 May 1817–1 March 1818 Ali V Khoja; 1 March 1818–5 July 1830 Husain III.

Alhucemas see **Melilla** and **Morocco** and **Spanish Morocco**

Allada. ca. 1440–22 June 1894. *Location:* about 75 miles inland from the coast of what is today the Republic of Benin. *Capital:* Allada. *Other names:* Allada Protectorate (1891–1894); Allada Empire (ca. 1440–1891); Ardrah; Ardrah Empire; Empire of Ardrah; Ardra; Adja-Tado.

History: Founded about 1440 by the Adja peoples, the country of Allada grew into a small empire, and about the year 1600 three brothers went different ways. Kopon stayed to rule Allada, Do-Aklin went north to found the kingdom of Abomey (see Dahomey), while Te-Agdanlin founded the kingdom of Adjaché, or Porto-Novo, as it became known. Between 1724 and 1742 Allada was ruled by its sister state of Abomey, which was the great power in the area, and on 18 Nov. 1891 the French placed a protectorate over Allada. In 1894 it became part of the French colony of Dahomey (see Benin [ii]).

Kings: ca. 1440–ca. 1445 Aholuho Adja; ca. 1445–ca. 1450 De Nufion; ca. 1450–ca. 1458 Djidomingba; ca. 1458–ca. 1470 Dassu; ca. 1470–ca. 1475 Dassa; ca. 1475–ca. 1490 Adjakpa; ca. 1490–ca. 1495 Yessu; ca. 1495–ca. 1498 Azoton; ca. 1498–ca. 1510 Yessu; ca. 1510. 1520 Akonde; ca. 1520–ca. 1530 Amamu; ca. 1530–ca. 1540 Agagnon; ca. 1540–ca. 1550 Agbangba; ca. 1550–ca. 1560 Hueze; ca. 1560–ca.

1580 Agbande; ca. 1580–ca. 1585 Kin-Ha; ca. 1585–ca. 1587 Mindji; ca. 1587–ca. 1590 Akolu; ca. 1590–1610 Kopon (the first historic king); 1610–(?) Hunungungu; (?)–ca. 1660 Lamadje Pokonu; ca. 1660–(?) Tezifon; (?)–(?) gBagwe; (?)–March 1724 De Adjara; March 1724–1742 ruled direct from Abomey; 1742–(?) Mijo; (?)–1845 [unknown]; 1845–(?) Deka; (?)–(?) Ganhwa; (?)–1879 Gangia Sindje; 1879–4 Feb. 1894 Gi-gla No-Don Gbé-non Mau; 4 Feb. 1894–ca. 1898 Gi-gla Gunhu Hugnon; ca. 1898–15 Dec. 1923 Djihento.

Almohad Empire. 3 April 1147–1268. *Location:* Algeria, Morocco, Tunisia, and southern Spain. *Capital:* Marrakesh (from 1147); Tinmallal (1123–1147). *Other names:* Muwahhid Dynasty.

History: The Almohads began in 1121, their first ruler, a Masmuda Berber from the Atlas Mountains named Muhammad ibn Tumart, starting a long rebellion against the Almoravid Empire. Muhammad, who would be today termed an Islamic Fundamentalist, ruled his people from 1121 to 1128 and was succeeded by Abd al-Mu'min al-Kumi (1128–1163). In 1147 the Almohads finally took over the old Almoravid territory, and extended it greatly over the years, going as far as Egypt in the east and Spain in the west. By 1152 they had taken a large part of what is today Tunisia and by 1160 the Tripolitania part of Libya. By this time they had brought all the Berbers of North Africa under one rule. Between 1236 and 1247 they lost Tripoli and Tunis to the Hafsid Kingdom; between 1236 and 1239 they lost Tlemcen and other parts of Algeria to the Abd al-Wadids (see Tlemcen), and in 1268 they relinquished the rest (i.e. Morocco) to the Merinid Empire.

Amirs (or Caliphs): 3 April 1147–May 1163 Abd al-Mu'min al-Kumi; May 1163–29 June 1184 Yusuf II Abu Yakub; 10 Aug. 1184–Dec. 1198 Yakub I (also known as Abu Yusuf al-Mansur); Jan. 1199–27 Dec. 1213 Muhammad III an-Nasir; 28 Dec. 1213–6 Jan. 1224 Yusuf III (also known as Abu Yakub al-Mustansir); 7 Jan. 1224–5 Sept. 1224 Abd al-Wahid al-Makhluwi; 5 Sept. 1224–Oct. 1227 Abdallah II Abu Muhammad al-Abdil; Oct. 1227–1230 Yahya V al-Mu'tasim and Idris III al-Ma'mun (joint amirs); 1230–16 Oct. 1232 Idris III al-Ma'mun; 17 Oct. 1232–22 Dec. 1242 Rashid I (also known as Abd al-Wahid II); 23 Dec. 1242–1248 Ali IV (also known as as-Sa'id al-Mu'tadid); 1248–Oct. 1266

Umar I al-Murtada; Oct. 1266–1268 Idris IV Abu l'Ula al-Wathiq (also known as Abu Dabbus).

Almoravid Empire. 1031–3 April 1147. *Location:* Morocco, western Algeria, and southern Spain. *Capital:* Marrakesh (from 1086, when the city was founded by Yusuf ibn Tashufin); Fez (1065–1086); Ajmat (1031–1065). *Other names:* Murabitun Dynasty.

History: The al-Murabitun (Warrior Monks of the Ribat) or Almoravids were a grouping of Berber tribes (principally the Goddala, Lamtuna, and Massufa) of the Veiled Sanhajah clan of the Sahara. They conquered Morocco and western Algeria between 1063 and 1082, and ruled much of the Maghrib as successors to the old Idrisid State, as well as most of what had been Muslim Spain (with the exception of Valencia, which was held by El Cid). It was under the Almoravids that Spain and North Africa were united as a single empire. The Almoravids did not take Tunis or the Hammadid Kingdom because the rulers of both of those states were Zirids, a clan allied to the Veiled Sanhajah. They saw themselves as an orthodox amirate, and paid homage to the Abbasid caliph in Baghdad. But by 1120 the Christians had started to re-conquer Spain, and the Almohads were posing a problem in Morocco, and in 1147 the Almoravid Empire was succeeded by the Almohad Empire.

Amirs: 1031–(?) Yahya ibn Ibrahim; (?)–1056 Yahya ibn Umar; 1056–1061 Abu Bakr ibn Umar; 1061–2 Sept. 1106 Yusuf ibn Tashufin; 3 Sept. 1106–1142 Ali ibn Yusuf; 1142–22 Feb. 1145 Tashufin ibn Ali; 22 Feb. 1145–1146 Ibrahim ibn Tashufin; 1146–3 April 1147 Ishaq ibn Ali.

Aloa see **Alwah**

Alodia see **Alwah**

Alphonso Group see **Amirante Islands**

Aluyi see **Barotseland**

Alva see **Alwah**

Alwah. (?)–1504. *Location:* south of Dongola, on the Nile, roughly in the area of Merowe and the 4th Cataract, in the central Sudan. *Capital:* Soba (also known as Subah). *Other names:* Alva; Aloa; Alodia.

History: One of the major kingdoms of the Nilotic Sudan in the Dark Ages, it became Christian in 580, and in 1504 gave way to the Funj Sultanate.

Rulers: [unknown].

Amasuta see **Lesotho**

Amathembuland see **Tembuland**

Amatongaland see **Tongaland**

Ambas Bay. 1858–28 March 1887. *Location:* Ambas Bay, Cameroun. *Capital:* Victoria. *Other names:* Victoria (its name from 1858 to 1884).

History: Founded as a colony in 1858 by British Baptist missionaries, and named Victoria after the Queen. On 12 July 1884 the German flag was hoisted in the area and the Germans formed the German Crown Lands of North West Africa. This very clearly signaled the first move of the German Crown to take over all of North West Africa. The following week, on 19 July, 1884, the British government placed a protectorate over Victoria, and renamed it Ambas Bay Protectorate. Nonetheless, in 1887, it became part of the German holdings, which in 1900 became Kamerun.

Rulers: [unknown].

Amboland see **Ovamboland**

Amhara see **Ethiopia**

Amirante Islands. No dates. *Location:* a group of coral islands in the western Indian Ocean, about 200 miles southwest of the Seychelles. *Other names:* the Amirantes; the Amirante Group; the Amirante Archipelago. *Notes:* The population is always around 200. The Amirantes consist of a number of coral islets and atolls: African Islands (4 islands); Alphonso Group (3 islands); St. Joseph Group (8 islands); Poivre Islands (9 islands, and named for Pierre Poivre, intendant of the Île de France — later Mauritius).

History: On 3 Oct. 1810 the British took the group from the French, whose possession it had been until then. The islands then became a dependency of Mauritius, until 1922, when they were placed under the administration of the Seychelles. On 29 June 1976 they became part of the new Republic of the Seychelles.

Anambra State see **Biafra**

Andries-Ohrigstad see **Ohrigstad**

Andruna. ca. 1550–1852. *Location:* in the Comoros. *Capital:* [unknown].

History: This was the first Comoran sultanate after Mayotte to become part of the French Protectorate of Mayotte (see Comoros). This happened in 1852.

Sultans: ca. 1550–1835 [unknown]; 1835–1852 Tsimiharo.

Anecho see **Little Popo**

Angaziya see **Gran Comoro**

Anglo-Egyptian Condominium see **Sudan**

Anglo-Egyptian Sudan see **Sudan**

Angola. 1 Feb. 1575– . *Location:* West Africa, between Namibia and the Congo. *Capital:* Luanda (from 1975 onwards); Nova Lisboa (founded 1912 as Huambo, re-named Nova Lisboa in 1927, and re-named Huambo in 1975); Luanda (1576–1912. Until 1627 Luanda was called São Paulo de Loanda, it was named for the ancient chiefdom of Luanda). *Other names:* Republic of Angola, or Angola Republic (from 1992); People's Republic of Angola, or Angola People's Republic (1975–1992); Angola Overseas Province (1951–1975); Angola Colony (1914–1951); Portuguese West Africa (1589–1914); Angola Donataria (1575–1589); São Paulo de Loanda (1575–1589).

History: The coast of what is today Angola was discovered by the Portuguese navigator Diogo Cam in 1482. Portuguese missionaries went out, and then the Army. In 1575 Paulo Dias de Novais was given a stretch of land as a donataria by the Portuguese government. This land lay south of the Congo Estuary, and was the germ of Portuguese West Africa, which the area became after the death of Novais in 1589, when the land was returned to the Portuguese Crown. The fact that Portugal itself belonged to Spain from 1580 to 1656 made no difference to the running of this part of Africa, or the name of it. During the 17th century the territory held by the Portuguese was increased, e.g. Benguela was colonized in 1617, and the kingdoms of Ndongo, Ovimbundu, Kongo, and others were subjugated. In 1641 the Dutch captured all the Portuguese coastal possessions (including the capital, Luanda), and held them for seven years, having forced the Portuguese into the interior (see Dutch West Africa). On 14 Feb. 1885 the Berlin Conference recognized Portuguese West Africa as a colony, and granted the exclave of Cabinda (just across the mouth of the River Congo, on the border of what today are the two Congos) as part of that colony. On 15 Aug. 1914 the entire country became the colony of Angola, and on 11 June 1951 Angola became an overseas province of Portugal. As the country moved toward independence, the FNLA (Frente Nacional de Libertação de Angola) was formed, and set up a government in exile based in Léopoldville in the Congo (see Angola Revolutionary Government in Exile for more details). In 1974 a military coup ousted the Portuguese government. A transitional local government was set up on 31 Jan. 1975, but it collapsed in July of that year. The three groups that had been fighting for independence all wanted control of the new republic. The three groups were Jonas Savimbi's UNITA (backed by the U.S. and South Africa), Holden Roberto's National Front (see Angola Revolutionary Government in Exile), and the Soviet-backed MPLA, the last of which refused to countenance a coalition government. Civil war broke out between the factions. The MPLA won, having captured Luanda with the help of Cuban troops and Soviet military equipment. Antonio Agostinho Neto, a Marxist, and the head of the MPLA, was elevated to the presidency, and on 11 Nov. 1975 the country officially became totally independent of Portugal, as the Angola People's Republic, after 14 years of guerrilla fighting. (See also Angola Democratic People's Republic). The civil war, which carried on for years, killed thousands, drove the whites out of Angola, and ruined the country. When he died Neto was succeeded by his disciple, José Eduardo dos Santos. In 1985, though, after he was "elected" to a second five-year term of office, dos Santos began to remove the very Cuban troops who were supporting him. A cease-fire was arranged between Angola, Cuba and South Africa in Aug. 1988, and in Dec. 1990 a cease-fire was agreed to between the government and UNITA. In Sept. 1992 free elections were held, dos Santos was overwhelmingly re-elected in his campaign against Savimbi, and the country became known as the Republic of Angola, to distance it from the former Marxist-sounding name of Angola People's Republic. The USA formally recognized the Republic of Angola on 19 May 1993. However, UNITA was not happy with the 1992 elections and continued the civil war, causing great distress in Angola, including famine. On 20 Nov. 1994 a new peace treaty was signed. However, in 1998 civil war broke out again, Savimbi was killed on 22 Feb., 2002, and in Aug. 2002 the war ended, leaving in its wake a starving and AIDS-riddled country.

Donatarios: 1 Feb. 1575–1589 Paulo Dias de Novais. *Governors:* 1589–1591 Luis Serrão; 1591–June 1592 André Pereira; June 1592–1593 Francisco de Almeida; 1593–1594 Jerénimo de Almeida; 1594–1602 João de Mendonça; 1602–1603 João Coutinho; 1603–1606 Manuel Pereira; 1606–Sept. 1607 [unknown]; Sept. 1607–1611 Manuel Forjaz; 1611–1615 Bento Cardoso; 1615–1617 Manuel Pereira; 1617–1621 Luis de Vasconcelos; 1621–1623 João de Sousa; 1623–1623 Pedro Coelho; 1623–1624 Simão de Mascarenhas; 1624–4 Sept. 1630 Fernão de Sousa; 4 Sept. 1630–1635 Manuel Coutinho; 1635–18 Oct. 1639 Francisco da Cunha; 18 Oct. 1639–Oct. 1645 Pedro de Meneses; Oct. 1645–1646 Francisco de Souto-Maior; 1646–24 Aug. 1648 a triumvirate junta was in power; 24 Aug. 1648–1651 Salvador de Sá e Benavides; 1651–March 1652 [unknown] (acting); March 1652–1653 Rodrigo Henriques; 1653–Oct. 1654 Bartolomeu da Cunha (acting); Oct. 1654–18 April 1658 Luis Chicorro; 18 April 1658–1661 João Vieira; 1661–Sept. 1666 André de Negreiros; Sept. 1666–Feb. 1667 Tristão da Cunha; Feb. 1667–Aug. 1669 juntas were in power; Aug. 1669–1676 Francisco de Távora; 1676–1680 Pires de Sousa e Meneses; 1680–1684 João da Silva e Sousa; 1684–1688 Luis da Silva; 1688–1691 João de Lencastre; 1691–1694 Gonçalo de Meneses; 1694–1697 Henrique de Magalhães; 1697–1701 Luis de Meneses; 1701–1703 Bernardino Távares; 1703–1705 a junta was in power; 1705–1709 Lourenço de Almada; 1709–1713 Antonio Castro e Ribafria; 1713–1717 João de Noronha; 1717–1722 Henrique de Figueiredo e Alarcão; 1722–1725 Antonio de Carvalho; 1725–1726 José da Costa (acting); 1726–1732 Paulo de Albuquerque; 1732–1738 Rodrigo de Meneses; 1738–1748 João de Magalhães; 1748–1749 Fonseca Coutinho (acting); 1749–1753 Marquês de Lovradio; 1753–1758 Antonio da Cunha; 1758–1764 Antonio de Vasconcelos; 1764–1772 Francisco de Sousa Coutinho; 1772–1779 Antonio de Lencastre; 1779–1782 João da Câmara; 1782–1784 juntas were in power; 1784–1790 Barão de Moçâmedes; 1790–1797 Manuel Vasconcelos; 1797–1802 Miguel de Melo; 1802–1806 Fernando de Noronha; 1806–1807 [unknown]; 1807–1810 Antonio da Gama; 1810–1816 José Barbosa; 1816–1819 Luis da Mota Feo e Torres; 1819–1821 Manuel de Albuquerque; 1821–1822 Joaquim de Lima; 1822–1823 a junta was in power; 1823–1823 Cristóvão Dias; 1823–1829 Nicolau Branco; 1829–1834 Barão de Santa Comba Dão; 1834–1836 a junta was in power; 1836–1836 Domingos de Oliveira Daun. *Governors-General:* 1837–1839 Manuel Vidal; 1839–1839 Antonio de Noronha; 1839–1842 Manuel Malheiro (acting); 1842–1843 José Leite; 1843–1844 [unknown]; 1844–1845 Lourenço Possolo; 1845–1848 Pedro da Cunha; 1848–1851 Adrião Pinto; 1851–1853 Antonio de Sousa; 1853–1854 Visconde de Pinheiro; 1854–1860 José do Amaral; 1860–1861 Carlos Franco; 1861–1862 Sebastião de Calheiros e Meneses; 1862–1865 José Baptista de Andrade; 1865–1868 Francisco Cardoso; 1868–1869 [unknown]; 1869–1870 José do Amaral; 1870–1873 José da Ponte e Horta; 1873–1876 José Baptista de Andrade; 1876–1878 Caetano de Almeida e Albuquerque; 1878–1880 Vasco de Carvalho e Meneses; 1880–1882 Antonio Dantas; 1882–1886 Francisco Ferreira do Amaral; 1886–25 Aug. 1892 Guilherme Capelo; 25 Aug. 1892–Sept. 1893 Jaime Godins (acting); Sept. 1893–1896 Álvaro Ferreira; 1896–1897 Guilherme Capelo; 1897–1900 Antonio Curto; 1900–1903 Francisco Moncada; 1903–1904 Eduardo da Costa; 1904–1904 Custodio de Borja; 1904–1906 Antonio Curto (acting); 1906–1907 Eduardo da Costa; 1907–1909 Henrique Couceiro; 1909–1909 Álvaro Ferreira (acting); 1909–1910 José Roçadas; 1910–1911 Caetano Gonçalves (acting); 1911–1912 Manuel Coelho; 1912–1915 José Norton de Matos; 1915–1916 Antonio de Eça; 1916–1917 Pedro do Amorim; 1917–1918 Jaime de Castro Morais; 1918–1919 Filomeno Cabral; 1919–1920 Mimosa Guera (acting); 1920–1921 Visconde de Pedralva. *Governors-General/High Commissioners:* 1921–1924 José Norton de Matos; 1924–1924 João Soares; 1924–1925 Antero de Carvalho; 1925–1926 Francisco Chaves; 1926–1928 Antonio Ferreira; 1928–1929 Antonio Mora; 1929–1930 Filomeno Cabral; 1930–1931 José Sousa Faro; 1931–1934 Eduardo Viana; 1934–1935 Julio Lencastre; 1935–1939 Antonio Mateus; 1939–1941 Manuel Mano;

1941–1942 Abel Souto-Maior; 1942–1943 Álvaro Morna; 1943–1947 Vasco Alves; 1947–1947 Fernando Mena; 1947–1955 José Carvalho; 1955–1956 Manuel Gaivão (acting); 1956–15 Jan. 1960 Horacio Rebelo; 15 Jan. 1960–23 June 1961 Álvaro Távares; 23 June 1961–26 Sept. 1962 Venancio Deslandes; 26 Sept. 1962–27 Oct. 1966 Jaime Marquês; 27 Oct. 1966–Oct. 1972 Camilo de Miranda Rebocho Vaz; Oct. 1972–May 1974 Fernando Santos e Castro; May 1974–15 June 1974 Joaquim Pinheiro (acting); 15 June 1974–24 July 1974 Jaime Marquês; 24 July 1974–24 Jan. 1975 Antonio Coutinho (acting); 24 Jan. 1975–Aug. 1975 Antonio Cardoso; Aug. 1975–Aug. 1975 Ernesto de Macedo (interim); Aug. 1975–11 Nov. 1975 Leonel Cardoso. *Presidents of Military Junta:* 24 July 1974–1974 Antonio Coutinho. *Presidents of Provisional Government:* 1974–1974 Antonio Coutinho. *Presidents:* 11 Nov. 1975–10 Sept. 1979 Antonio Agostinho Neto; 21 Sept. 1979–José Eduardo dos Santos; *Prime Ministers:* 31 Jan. 1975–July 1975 Antonio Coutinho; 14 Nov. 1975–9 Dec. 1978 Lopo do Nascimento; 19 July 1991–27 Nov. 1992 Fernando Van Dunem; 2 Dec. 1992–3 June 1996 Marcolino Moco; 8 June 1996–5 Dec. 2002 Fernando Van Dunem; 5 Dec. 2002–Fernando dos Santos. *Note:* In times of no Prime Minister, the President held that office.

Angola Democratic People's Republic. 23 Nov. 1975–11 Feb. 1976. *Location:* as Angola. *Capital:* Huambo (for a history of this city, see the "capital" section under Angola). *Other names:* Democratic People's Republic of Angola.

History: After Neto and his Soviet-backed MPLA formed an Angolan government at Luanda, in 1975, the two dispossessed freedom groups, UNITA (National Union for the Total Independence of Angola), led by Dr. Jonas Savimbi, and the FNLA (National Front for the Liberation of Angola), led by Holden Roberto (see also Angola Revolutionary Government in Exile), joined forces later in November and formed their own joint government at Huambo. The Communist and Capitalist powers of the world lined up over this struggle. Cuban troops helped the MPLA win the war and take Huambo in Feb. 1976. The Organization of African Unity recognized the MPLA government as a member on 11 Feb. 1976, and from that date the rival government was finished politically, although the FNLA and UNITA continued guerrilla warfare

until 1984 when the FNLA members surrendered. Only UNITA remains a "problem." *Prime Ministers (UNITA):* 23 Nov. 1975–11 Feb. 1976 José Ndele. *Prime Ministers (FNLA):* 23 Nov. 1975–11 Feb. 1976 Johnny Pinnock.

Angola Revolutionary Government in Exile. 5 April 1962–11 Nov. 1975. *Location:* as Angola, but this government in exile was based out of Léopoldville, in the Congo (later known as Zaire). *Capital:* Léopoldville (known as Kinshasa after 1965). *Other names:* Governo Revolucionario de Angola no Exilio; GRAE.

History: In 1962 the FNLA (Frente Nacional de Libertação de Angola), the Revolutionary Front for the Liberation of Angola, set up a government in exile, based in Léopoldville, in the Congo. In 1963 it was recognized by its host country [see Congo (Zaire)], as well as by the Organization of African Unity, and in 1972 it was renamed the Supreme Council for the Liberation of Angola, under the auspices of the OAU. In 1975 Portugal granted independence to Angola, and the country became the People's Republic of Angola. The government in exile ceased to be.

Prime Ministers: 5 April 1962–11 Nov. 1975 Holden Roberto.

Anjouan. ca. 1500–1866. *Location:* one of the islands in the Comoros, in the Indian Ocean. *Capital:* Domoni (latterly); Mutsamudu (formerly). *Other names:* Ansouani; Nzwani; Anjouan Sultanate; Joanna (Red Sea pirates' slang, but became almost official in the English-speaking world).

History: Founded about 1500, the sultanate of Anjouan became part of the Mayotte Protectorate (see Comoros) in 1866. However, in 1997 an interesting independence movement began (see Nzwani).

Sultans: ca. 1500–ca. 1506 Muhammad I; ca. 1506–(?) Hassan; (?)–(?) Muhammad II; (?)–(?) Msindra. *Queens:* (?)–ca. 1590 Alimah I. *Regents:* ca. 1590–ca. 1605 Sayid Alawi. *Sultans:* ca. 1605–ca. 1610 Hussein. *Regents:* ca. 1610–ca. 1619 Sayid Idarus; ca. 1619–ca. 1632 Sayid Abu Bakr. *Queens:* ca. 1632–ca. 1676 Alimah II; ca. 1676–ca. 1711 Alimah III. *Sultans:* ca. 1711–1741 Sheikh Salim; 1741–1782 Sheikh Ahmad; 1782–1788 Abdallah I. *Queens:* 1788–1792 Halimah. *Sultans:* 1792–1796 Abdallah I; 1796–1816 Alawi; 1816–1832 Abdallah II; 1832–1833 Ali; 1833–

1836 Abdallah II; 1836–1837 Alawi II; 1837–
1852 Salim; 1852–Feb. 1891 Abdallah III; Feb.
1891–2 April 1891 Salim II; 2 April 1891–14 April
1892 Sayid Umar; 14 April 1892–July 1912 Sayid
Muhammad.

Ankole see **Nkore**

Annobón. 1 Jan. 1474–1926. *Location:* now
known as Pagalu, an island belonging to Equatorial Guinea, in the Gulf of Guinea, about 400
miles southwest of the island of Macías Nguema
Biyogo (formerly Fernando Po), and 93 miles
southwest of the island of São Tomé. *Capital:*
San Antonio de Praia (local headquarters), but
administered from Santa Isabel on Fernando Po.
Other names: Anno Bom.

History: Discovered on New Year's Day (Anno
Bom) in 1474, by Ruy de Sequeira, Annobón Island became a Portuguese possession on 7 Jan.
1494. Between 1580 and 1656 Portugal itself belonged to Spain, but this made no difference to
Annobón, as far as administration went. On 1
March 1778, along with the island of Fernando
Po, it became a Spanish possession via the Treaty
of El Parado, and in 1926 it became part of Spanish Guinea (see Equatorial Guinea). In 1960 it
became one of the two component parts of a new
province of Metropolitan Spain, called Fernando
Po and Annobón.

Rulers: 1 Jan. 1474–7 Jan. 1494 [none]; 7 Jan.
1494–1926 ruled direct from Fernando Po, except during the time of the British occupation of
Fernando Po from 1827 to 1855.

Ansouani see **Anjouan**

Antemoro see **Madagascar**

Anyidi Revolutionary Government see **Southern Sudan**

Aoukar see **Ghana Empire**

Arab Democratic Republic see **Western Sahara**

Arab North Africa. 647–649; 667–697. *Loca-
tion:* North Africa (what are today Libya,
Tunisia, and Algeria). *Capital:* al-Qayrawan.
Other names: Ifriqa; Ifriqiyah.

History: In 647 the Arabs conquered Byzantine North Africa, but in 649 the Byzantines re-

gained it by using the simple expedient of
bribery. In 667 the Arabs took it again, this time
holding it until 697, when the Byzantines took
it for the last time.

Governors: 647–649 Abdallah ibn Sa'd; 649–
667 held by the Byzantines; 667–669 Mu'awaiyah; 669–675 Uqba; 675–682 Abu'l Muhagir
Dinar; 682–683 Uqba; 683–686 during this
time the area that is today Tunisia was in Berber
hands; 686–689 Abd al-Malik; 689–697 Hassan.

Arago see **Lafia**

Ardrah see **Allada**

Argeyes see **Agaie**

Argungu. 1516–1902. *Location:* part of what is
now the Sokoto Province of Northwestern State,
in Nigeria. *Capital:* Argungu (1827–1902);
Birnin Kebbi (ca. 1700–1805); Surame (until ca.
1700). *Other names:* Kebbi (1516–1827); Kebbawa Kingdom; Birnin Lalaba Dan Badau (in
the early days of the kingdom).

History: In 1516 the Songhai captain Muhammadu Kantu made himself ruler of the Kebbawa
people who lived between the Niger River and
Zamfara. He called his state Kebbi, one of the
Banza Bakwai (see Hausa States), and its first
capital was at Surame. At the height of its power
Kebbi included the states of Yauri and Nupe,
but in 1805 the armies of the Fulani Empire
sacked the Kebbawa capital of Birnin Kebbi, and
forced the submission of the Kebbawa Kingdom
by 1813. Resistance to the Fulani continued until,
in 1827, Samaila II, the rebel king in exile, established Argungu (from the local term "a yi
gungu" meaning "let us gather in one place") as
his new capital, and that year the new country
became known as Argungu. The Fulani amirates
of Sokoto and Gwandu finally conquered Argungu in 1831, and placed governors in charge,
but the Kebbawa sarkin (king), Yakubu Nabame
(Samaila's son) continued to rule in exile until
1849, when he defeated the Fulani, expelled
them from Argungu, and returned to power. Despite the fact that Sokoto, by an 1866 treaty, recognized Argungu as an independent kingdom,
there was continued fighting between the Fulani
and the Kebbawa until the British arrived in
1902. They recognized Samaila III as amir of Argungu (not king, however), but took the amirate

as part of the protectorate of Northern Nigeria. In 1906 a considerable portion of the amirate that lay in the west was given to French West Africa.

Sarkins (Kings) of Kebbi: 1516–1561 Muhammadu Kantu; 1561–1596 Ahmadu I; 1596–1619 Dawuda; 1619–1621 Ibrahimu I; 1621–1636 Suleimanu I; 1636–1649 Muhammadu; 1649–1662 Maliki Dan Ibrahimu; 1662–1674 Umaru Ciwa; 1674–1676 Muhammadu Kaye; 1676–1684 Ibrahimu II; 1684–1686 Muhammadu na Sifawa; 1686–1696 Ahmadu Dan Amaru; 1696–1700 Tomo; 1700–1717 Muhammadu Dan Ciwa; 1717–1750 Samaila; 1750–1754 Muhammadu Dan Tagande; 1754–1775 Abdullahi Toga; 1775–1803 Suleimanu II; 1803–1803 Abubakar Ukar; 1803–1805 Muhammadu Fodi (or Hodi). *Sarkins (Kings) in exile:* 1805–1826 Muhammadu Fodi (or Hodi); 1826–1827 Samaila II (also known as Karari). *Sarkins (Kings) of Argungu:* 1827–1831 Samaila II (also known as Karari). *Sarkins (Kings) in exile:* 1831–1849 Yakubu Nabame. *Sarkins (Kings):* 1849–1854 Yakubu Nabame; 1854–1859 Yusufu Mainassara; 1859–1860 Muhammadu Ba Are; 1860–1883 Abdullahi Toga; 1883–1902 Samaila III (or Sama). *Amirs:* 1902–1915 Samaila III (or Sama); 1915–1920 Suleimana; 1920–1934 Muhammadu Sama; 1934–1942 Muhammadu Sani; 1942–1953 Samaila IV; 1953–Oct. 1959 Muhammadu Shefe; Jan. 1960–(?) Muhammadu Mera.

Aride Island see **Seychelles**

Asante see **Ashanti**

Ascension. No dates. *Location:* a small island 700 miles northwest of Saint Helena, in the southern Atlantic Ocean. *Capital:* George Town (locally called Garrison).

History: Discovered on Ascension Day, 1501, by the Portuguese navigator João da Nova Castela, and uninhabited until 6 Oct. 1815, when Napoleon arrived on Saint Helena as a captive of the British. A few British troops were based here from that time. Until 1822 Ascension was under the rule of the British Admiralty, and then it was transferred to the Colonial Office, and became a dependency of Saint Helena, being ruled from there through an administrator on Ascension. Great Britain's first satellite station was installed there in 1966.

Aseb see **Assab**

Ashanti. ca. 1570–6 March 1957. *Location:* central Ghana. *Capital:* Kumasi (from ca. 1665. Named for the "kum" tree); Asumenya Santemanso (until ca. 1665). *Other names:* Ashanti Colony (1901–1957); Ashanti Protectorate (1896–1901); Ashanti Empire (ca. 1680–1896); Ashanti Union; Asante; Asanti; Asiante; Asianti; Ashantee; Sianti; Siante.

History: About 1570 Twum founded the Twi-speaking Akan (or Bron) state of Ashanti, a people (also known as the Asantefo) bound loosely together until about 1680, when Osei Tutu founded the Ashanti Empire, and threw off his and other local tribes' subjection to the state of Denkyira. Osei Tutu's predecessor as chief of the Ashanti, Obiri, had founded the capital at Kumasi about 1665. In 1701 the Ashanti conquered Denkyira. In later years the empire grew, and with its vassal states to the north and south, the Ashanti controlled most of what is today Ghana. Slaves and gold were the main drives of the Ashanti in their inexorable expansion. However, Ashanti eventually declined, and there were two main reasons for its loss of power. One was the halting of the slave trade by the Europeans in the area, and the other was the fact that the Ashanti could not successfully control the states that they conquered. In 1824 Britain, pledged to defend the coastal tribes (of what later became Ghana) against the Ashanti, waged the First Ashanti War, and lost. In 1826 the British finally managed to defeat the Ashanti, however. In 1874 came the Second Ashanti War. It ended when Sir Garnet Wolseley marched into Kumasi. On 27 Aug. 1896 Britain placed a protectorate over Ashanti, and the legendary empire came to an end. But for some years there was alarming resistance to this move, culminating in the Third Ashanti War. The British had demanded that the Ashanti surrender their symbol of power, the Golden Stool, but the demand was refused. War began on 2 April 1900, and by the end of the year the Ashanti had been effectively subdued. On 26 Sept. 1901 Ashanti was made a British colony (effective as from 1 Jan. 1902), as part of the Gold Coast, but administered separately, the administration reporting to Accra (cf. Gold Coast Northern Territories and Gold Coast Colony Region). Thus, in 1901 the country that later became Ghana consisted of three major parts: Gold Coast (in the south), Ashanti (mid-country), and the Northern Territories. The British failed to understand the Ashantis, and times were difficult for everyone in Ashanti until the 1920s. In 1926 the long-exiled Kwaka Dua, who had been in the Seychelles, was allowed back into his country, and also allowed to resume his role of paramount chief of the Ashantis (but not as king). In 1935 the kingdom was in some way restored (under close British control, of course), and Prempeh II assumed the throne. In 1951 the Gold Coast achieved self-rule, and the mechanism was put in train to make the colony of Ashanti a region of the newly-emerging country that would soon become Ghana, and this was achieved in 1952. On 6 March 1957, at Ghana's independence (see Ghana), the colony of Ashanti became a region called Brong-Ahafo, and the Ashanti themselves little more than a memory as far as the rest of the world went.

Chiefs: ca. 1570–ca. 1590 Twum; ca. 1590–ca. 1600 Antwi; ca. 1600–ca. 1630 Kobia Amanfi; ca. 1630–ca. 1659 Oti Akenten; ca. 1659–ca. 1678 Obiri Yeboa; ca. 1678–ca. 1680 Osei Tutu. *Asantahenes (Kings):* ca. 1680–Dec. 1712 Osei Tutu; Dec. 1712–1717 [unknown]; 1717–1720 [vacant]; 1720–May 1750 Osei Opoku Ware; May 1750–1764 Kwasi Obodun; 1764–1777 Osei Kojo (also known as Kwadwo); 1777–1801 Osei Kwame; 1801–1801 Opuku Fofie; 1801–21 Jan. 1824 Osei Bonsu (also known as Osei Tutu Quamina); 21 Jan. 1824–1838 Yau Akoto; 1838–1867 Kwaka Dua I; 1867–4 Feb. 1874 Karikari; 4 Feb. 1874–1883 Mansa Bonsu; 1883–1884 Civil War contenders; 1884–June 1884 Kwaka Dua II; June 1884–23 March 1888 [vacant]; 23 March 1888–17 Jan. 1896 Prempeh I (also known as Kwaka Dua III); 17 Jan. 1896–2 Jan. 1935 [vacant]; 2 Jan. 1935–June 1970 Prempeh II; 6 July 1970–25 Feb. 1999 Opoku Ware II; 1999–Osei Tutu II. *Residents:* 27 Aug. 1896–1900 Donald Stewart; 1900–1901 Cecil Armitage (acting); 1901–1902 Donald Stewart. *Chief Commissioners:* 1902–1904 Sir Donald Stewart; 1904–1920 Francis Fuller; 1920–1923 Charles Harper; 1923–1931 John C. Maxwell; 1931–1933 Harry Newlands; 1933–1936 Francis Jackson; 1936–1941 Hubert Stevenson; 1941–1946 Edward Hawkesworth; 1946–1951 Charles Butler; 1951–1952 William Beaton. *Regional Officers:* 1952–1954 William Beaton; 1954–1955 Arthur Loveridge; 1955–6 March 1957 Arthur Russell.

Asiante see **Ashanti**

Assab. 5 July 1882–1 Jan. 1890. *Location:* a port on Assab Bay, on the southern Eritrean coast, and its surrounding hinterland. *Capital:* Assab. *Other names:* Aseb; Assab Protectorate.

History: A terminus of caravan routes across the Danakil desert from the highlands of Ethiopia, the coastal strip of Assab, and especially its port (Assab) became, after the construction of the Suez Canal, a desirable property. In 1869 it was acquired, for £1,880, from Sultan Berehan of Raheita by an Italian shipping company represented by Giuseppe Sapeto, for use as a coaling station. In March 1870, it was taken over by the Società di Navigazione Rubattino (a steamship company) which itself was acquired by the Italian government in 1882. Assab was not actually occupied until 1880. In 1882 the Italian government established a colony in Assab. This was Italy's first colonial possession in Africa, and was opposed by Egypt, Turkey and Britain. However, on 5 July 1882 it was declared an official Italian colony. Between 1883 and 1885 the Italians did the same with Massawa, and between 1883 and 1888 with the Danakil country, the Italians purchasing both from the Sultan of Aussa. In 1888 a protectorate, known as Assab Protectorate, combined all three areas as one protectorate, called Assab Protectorate. In turn, in 1890, this protectorate went to form part of the colony of Eritrea. Today Assab is a major Eritrean port.

Commandants: Dec. 1882–1885 Giulio Pestalozza; 1885–1 Jan. 1890 [unknown].

Assinie see **Ivory Coast**

Assumption Island. No dates. *Location:* south of the Aldabra Islands, in the Indian Ocean.

History: Assumption was a French possession until 3 Oct. 1810, when the British took all the French holdings in this part of the Indian Ocean. It was made a dependency of the Aldabras, which in turn was a dependency of the Seychelles, but in 1965 it became a part of the newly formed British Indian Ocean Territory. On 29 June 1976, when the Seychelles became a republic, Assumption became a part of that new country.

Astove. No dates. *Location:* south of the Cosmoledo Islands, in the Indian Ocean. *History:* This island, like Assumption Island, was politically part of the dependency of the Aldabra Islands, which belonged to the Seychelles until

1965, when it became part of the newly formed colony known as the British Indian Ocean Territory. On 29 June 1976 all the component parts of the BIOT, with the exception of the Chagos Archipelago, went to the new Republic of the Seychelles.

Aubad Island see **Somalia**

Auyo see **Hadejia**

Awfat see **Ifat**

Awlad Muhammad Dynasty see **Fezzan**

Awome see **New Calabar**

Axum. 250–ca. 950. *Location:* around the border of what are today Ethiopia and Sudan, on the Tigre Plateau. *Capital:* Nazaret (now Adama) (latterly); Axum (formerly). *Other names:* Axume; Aksum; Axumite Empire; Axumite Kingdom; Ethiopian Empire.

History: Axum's place in history is as a kingdom that bridged the gap between the old quasi-historical land of Punt, and the countries that led to today's Ethiopia. In short, it brought myth and history together. Settled by the Habashi from Abaseni in Arabia, Axum extended over much of present-day Ethiopia and Sudan. It became the great ivory market of North Africa. About 325 Axum conquered Merowe, thus ending the kingdom of Kush, and shortly after this the kings of Axum became Christians. About 950 the dynasty was overthrown by Agau chief Judith, and Axum was abandoned shortly thereafter. In 1150 the Zagwe dynasty re-established the kingdom at Roha (see Ethiopia).

Kings: 250–ca. 300 Aphilas Bisi-Dimele; ca. 300–325 [unknown kings reigned]; 325–328 Ezana (also known as Aiezanes); 328–356 Ezana (Aiezanes) and Shiazana (joint kings); 356–370 Ella Abreha and Ella Asfeha (joint kings); 370–374 Arfed; 374–379 Adhana; 379–380 Rete'a; 380–381 Asfeh; 381–386 Asbeha; 386–401 Ameda; 401–401 Abreha; 401–402 Shahel; 402–404 Gobaz; 404–408 Suhal; 408–418 Abreha; 418–424 Adhana; 424–434 Yo'ab; 434–436 Sahan; 436–446 Ameda; 446–448 Shahel; 448–451 Sabah; 451–463 Sahem; 463–466 Sahem and Gobaz (joint kings); 466–474 Gobaz; 474–475 Agabe and Lewi (joint kings); 475–486 Ella Amida; 486–489 Jacob and David (joint kings); 489–504 Armah; 504–505 Zitana; 505–514 Jacob II; 514–542 Caleb (also known as El-Eshaba); 542–550 Beta Esrael; 550–564 Gabra Masqal; 564–578 Quastantinos; 578–591 Wasan Sagad; 591–601 Feresanay; 601–623 Adreaz; 623–633 Eklewudem; 633–648 Germa Safar; 648–656 Zergaz; 656–677 Mikael; 677–696 Baher Ikela; 696–720 Hezba Seyon; 720–725 Asagum; 725–741 Latem; 741–762 Tulatem; 762–775 Adegos; 775–775 Ayzur; 775–780 Dedem Almaz; 780–790 Wedemdem; 790–820 Demawedem; 820–825 Rema Armah; 825–845 Degnajan; 845–846 Gedajan. *Queens:* 846–885 Judith. *Kings:* 885–905 Degnajan; 905–ca. 950 Del Nead.

Ayu see **Jema'a**

Ayyubid Empire see **Aiyubid Empire**

Bab Island see **British Somaliland**

Babur see **Biu**

Badagry see **Lagos**

Bade see **Bedde**

Baguirmi. 1513–21 March 1899. *Location:* the Baguirmi area of present-day Chad. *Capital:* Cekna (from 1902); Massenya (until 1902). *Other names:* Bagirmi.

History: A Barma people situated between Bornu and Wadai, they seem to have come from the east, around the area that is today the Sudan, and they formed a kingdom at their capital of Massenya, in 1513. The history of Baguirmi is one of wars with, and paying tribute to, its two large neighbors. About 1600 they converted to Islam, and expanded, conquering tribes mostly to the south, and engaging heavily in the slave trade. In 1870 the country was conquered by Wadai, and became a tributary state thereof. In 1892 the Sudanese adventurer Rabih invaded and destroyed Baguirmi, and in 1897 the sultan (or mbang) asked France for protection. In 1899 it was taken into the French sphere of influence, in 1900 becoming part of the Military Territory and Protectorate of Chad. In 1918 the mbangs became chefs-de-canton of the Massenya District of Chad, the sultanate being abolished in 1960, but re-instated in 1970. Under French administration, the area formed the Chari-Baguirmi prefecture of Chad.

Mbangs (Sultans): 1513–1528 Birni Bessé; 1528–1540 Lubatko; 1540–1561 Malo; 1561–1602 Abdallah; 1602–1620 Omar; 1620–1631 Dalai; 1631–1661 Bourkomanda I; 1661–1670 Abderrahman Woli; 1670–1676 Dalo Birni; 1676–1704 Abdel Kadir Woli; 1704–1719 Bar; 1719–1734 Wanga; 1734–1739 Bourkomanda Tad Lélé; 1739–1749 Loel; 1749–1784 Muhammad al-Amin; 1784–1806 Abderrahman Guarang I; 1806–1806 Ngarba Bira; 1806–1846 Bourkomanda II; 1846–1858 Abd al-Kedir; 1858–1882 Abou Sekin Muhammad; 1882–1885 Bourkomanda III; 1885–1918 Abderrahman Guarang II; 1918–1935 Abd al-Kedir (also known as Manga); 1935–1960 Yusuf; 14 June 1970–Muhammad Yusuf.

Bahr al-Ghazal. 29 Jan. 1869–30 April 1884. *Location:* in the southern Sudan, it borders the Central African Republic. *Capital:* Waw. *Other names:* Bahr al-Ghazal; Bahr al-Jazal.

History: In 1869 the Egyptians created the province of Bahr al-Ghazal (named after the river of the same name, meaning "Gazelle River" in Arabic), part of the Egyptian Sudan (see Sudan). In 1885 it became part of the Mahdist State (again, see Sudan). It later became a province of the Sudan, but from 1936 to 1956 it was united with the province of Equatoria.

Governors: 29 Jan. 1869–1872 Hajji Mehmed Nazir; 1872–March 1878 Zubeir Pasha; March 1878–June 1878 Idris Wad Daftar; June 1878–1879 Mehmed; 1879–Sept. 1880 Romolo Gessi Pasha; Sept. 1880–Dec. 1881 [unknown] (acting); Dec. 1881–28 April 1884 Frank Lupton; 28 April 1884–30 April 1884 Ali Musa Bey Sawqi.

Bahrite Mameluke Empire see **Mameluke Empire**

Bakélé see **Gabon**

Bakgatlaland. ca. 1470–23 March 1885. *Location:* in the southeastern part of Botswana, just north of Gaberones. *Capital:* Mochudi. *Other names:* Bakgatla Kingdom.

History: The Bakgatla (Kgatla), which was a tribe of the Tswana (also known as Batswana, Botswana, or Bechuana) group, and formed one of the major divisions of what became the Bechuanaland Protectorate in 1885.

Kings: ca. 1470–(?) Malekeleke; (?)–ca. 1500 Masilo; ca. 1500–(?) Legabo; (?)–(?) Pogopi;

(?)–ca. 1600 Botlolo; ca. 1600–(?) Mogala; (?)–(?) Matshego; (?)–(?) Kgafela: (?)–(?) Tebele; (?)–(?) Pheto I (also known as Masellane); (?)–ca. 1700 Mare; ca. 1700–(?) Modimokwana; (?)–(?) Kgwefane; (?)–ca. 1780 Molefe; ca. 1780–ca. 1790 Makgotso; ca. 1790–ca. 1805 Pheto II; ca. 1805–ca. 1810 Senwelo; ca. 1810–ca. 1817 Letsebe; ca. 1817–ca. 1817 Senwelo; ca. 1817–ca. 1823 Motlotle; ca. 1823–ca. 1833 Molefi I; ca. 1833–ca. 1836 Kgotlamaswe; ca. 1836–ca. 1836 Molefi I; ca. 1836–ca. 1848 Pilane; ca. 1848–1874 Kgamanyane; 1874–1875 Bogatsu; 1875–1924 Lentswe. *Regent:* 1924–1929 Isang; *Kings:* 1929–1936 Kgosi Molefi II; 1936–1942 Mmusi; 1942–1945 Bakgatla; 1945–1958 Kgosi Molefi II; 1958–1963 Mmusi; 1963–Lentswe II.

Bakongo see **Kongo**

Bakwenaland. ca. 1570–23 March 1885. *Location:* in the southeastern part of Botswana, north of the Kalahari Desert. *Capital:* Molepolole. *Other names:* Bakwena Kingdom; Land of the Crocodile People.

History: The Bakwena (or Kwena) were a major tribe of the Tswana (also known as Batswana, Botswana, or Bechuana) group. In turn the Bakwena subdivided into Bamangwatoland, Batwanaland, and Bangwaketseland. Their country went to form part of Bechuanaland Protectorate in 1885.

Kings: ca. 1570–(?) Masilo I; (?)–ca. 1600 Malope; ca. 1600–(?) Kwena; (?)–(?) Phokotsea; (?)–(?) Kgabo I; (?)–ca. 1700 Tebele; ca. 1700–(?) Kgabo II; (?)–(?) Masilo II; (?)–ca. 1770 Motsodhi; ca. 1770–ca. 1785 Motswasele I; ca. 1785–ca. 1795 Seitlhamo; ca. 1795–ca. 1803 Legwale; ca. 1803–ca. 1803 Malehe; ca. 1803–ca. 1807 Tshosa; ca. 1807–1821 Motswasele II; 1821–1829 Morvakgomo; 1829–1892 Setshele I; 1892–1911 Sebele I; 1911–1917 Setshele II; 1917–1931 Sebele II; 1931–1962 Kgosi Kgari Setshele III; 1963–21 Sept. 1970 Neale; Oct. 1970–1978 Bonewamang; 1979–(?) Setshele III; (?)–March 1996 Moithali; 1996–Jan. 2002 Kgosikwena; 17 Aug. 2002–Kgari II .

Bali see **Ifat**

Bamaleteland. ca. 1470–23 March 1885. *Location:* in the southeastern part of Botswana, on the South African border. *Capital:* Gaberones (see also Batlokwaland, which shared the same capital). *Other names:* Bamalete Kingdom.

History: The Bamalete (also known as Malete) Kingdom went to form part of Bechuanaland Protectorate in 1885. The Malete were a major tribe of the Tswana (also known as Batswana, Botswana, or Bechuana) group.

Kings: ca. 1470–(?) Badimo; (?)–(?) Phatle; (?)–ca. 1500 Malete; ca. 1500–(?) Lesokwana; (?)–(?) Mokgware; (?)–(?) Digope; (?)–(?) Dira; (?)–ca. 1600 Mmusi; ca. 1600–(?) Maphalaola; (?)–(?) Maoke; (?)–(?) Mongatane; (?)–(?) Maio; (?)–ca. 1700 Kgomo; ca. 1700–(?) Mokgwa; (?)–(?) Marumo; (?)–ca. 1780 Poo I; ca. 1780–ca. 1805 Mokgojwa; ca. 1805–ca. 1820 Poo II; ca. 1820–1886 Mokgosi I; 1886–1896 Ikaneng; 1896–1906 Mokgosi II; 1906–1917 Bailutle; 1917–1937 Seboko I; 1937–1945 Ketswerebothata; 1945–1966 Mokgosi III; 1966–1996 Kelemogile; 1 June 1996–21 June 2001 Seboko II; 21 June 2001–7 Jan. 2002 Tumelo. *Queen:* 7 Jan. 2002–Mosadi.

Bamangwatoland. ca. 1610–23 March 1885. *Location:* within the Motloutse Basin, in the large northeastern quadrant of Botswana, bordering Zimbabwe and South Africa. *Capital:* Serowe. *Other names:* Bamangwatoland.

History: The Bamangwato (or Ngwato) were a powerful subdivision of the Bakwena, which in turn was a main tribe of the Tswana (also known as Batswana, Botswana, or Bechuana) group. Their lands helped make up what became Bechuanaland Protectorate in 1885. The king of the Bamangwato was overlord of all Bechuanaland.

Kings: ca. 1610–(?) Ngwato; (?)–(?) Molwa; (?)–(?) Tamasiga; (?)–(?) Seogola; (?)–ca. 1710 Madirana; ca. 1710–(?) Kesitihoe; (?)–(?) Makgasama; (?)–ca. 1770 Molete; ca. 1770–ca. 1780 Mokgadi; ca. 1780–ca. 1795 Mathiba; ca. 1795–ca. 1817 Khama I; ca. 1817–ca. 1827 Kgari. *Regents:* ca. 1827–1833 Sedimo. *Kings:* 1833–1835 Khama II; 1835–1857 Sekgoma I; 1857–1858 Matsheng; 1858–1866 Sekgoma I; 1866–1872 Matsheng; 1872–1873 Khama III; 1873–1875 Sekgoma I; 1875–21 Feb. 1923 Khama III; 21 Feb. 1923–17 Nov. 1925 Sekgoma II; 17 Nov. 1925–19. Jan. 1926 Gorewang (Chairman of the Council of Regency); 10 Jan. 1926–14 Sept. 1933 Tshekedi Khama (regent); Sept. 1933–4 Oct. 1933 Seregola (acting regent); 4 Oct. 1933–23 June 1949 Tshekedi Khama (regent); 23 June 1949–8 March 1950 Seretse Khama; 13 March 1950–26 May 1952 Keaboka Khamane; 13 May 1953–May 1964 Rasebolai Khamane; May 1964–1974 Leeapeetswe; 1974–1979 Mokgatsha Mokgedi; 5 May 1979–Ian Seretse Khama.

Bambara Kingdoms see **Kaarta** and **Segu** and **Timbuktu**

Bamoun. 1394–14 July 1884. *Location:* around the Cameroun town of Foumba. *Capital:* Bamoun (also known as Mfom Ben, or Foumban). *Other names:* Bamun; Bamum; Bamoum.

History: Nchare, founder of the Bamoun (also known as Mum) dynasty, and son of a Tikar chief, set out on a conquering expedition going south, and established himself in the Bamoun area, proclaiming himself king of the Pambans, and subjugating 18 chiefs. Then he founded the town and sultanate of Bamoun. The kingdom was extended in the last half of the 18th century, and in 1884 the country came under German domination (see Kamerun), although the sultanate of Bamoun still exists. One of the late 1-9th-century mfons, Nyoja Ibrahim, invented an alphabet, and wrote a history of the Bamoun.

Mfons (Sultans): 1394–1418 Nchare Yen; 1418–1461 Ngoupou; 1461–1498 Monjou; 1498–1519 Mengap; 1519–1544 Ngouh I; 1544–1568 Fifen; 1568–1590 Ngouh II; 1590–1629 Ngapna; 1629–1672 Ngouloure; 1672–1757 Koutou; 1757–1814 Mbouombouo; 1814–1817 Ngbetnkom; 1817–1818 Mbeikuo; 1818–1865 Ngouhouo; 1865–1889 Nsangou; 1889–1931 Nyoja Ibrahim; 1931–1933 [vacant]; 1933–(?) al-Hajj (or El Hadj) Saeidou Nyimoluh Nyoju.

Banana Island. ca. 1770–1820. *Location:* outside Yauri Bay, south of Freetown, off the coast of Sierra Leone. *Capital:* [unknown].

History: Four famous native kings ruled Banana Island until it was incorporated into the Crown colony of Sierra Leone in 1820. The Caulker family then went on to rule Bumpe.

Kings: ca. 1770–1791 James Cleveland; 1791–1797 William; 1797–1810 Stephen Caulker; 1810–1820 Thomas Caulker.

Bangwaketseland. ca. 1650–23 March 1885. *Location:* south of Bakwenaland and north of the Kalahari Desert, in the southeastern portion of Botswana. *Capital:* Kanye. *Other names:* Bawanketseland; Bangwaketse Kingdom.

History: Founded about 1650, the Bangwaketse (also known as Ngwaketse) was one of the subdivisions of the Bakwena, a major tribe of the Tswana (also known as Batswana, Botswana, or Bechuana) group. The Bangwaketse lands went to help make up Bechuanaland Protectorate in 1885.

Kings: ca. 1650–(?) Ngwaketse; (?)–(?) Seepaptiso; (?)–(?) Leema; (?)–(?) Khutwe; (?)–(?) Khutwane; (?)–ca. 1770 Makaba I; ca. 1770–ca. 1795 Mongala (also known as Molete); ca. 1795–1825 Makaba II. *Regents:* 1825–1843 Sebego and Segotshane (joint regents); 1843–1845 Segotshane. *Kings:* 1845–July 1889 Gaseitswiwa; July 1889–1 July 1910 Bathoen; 1 July 1910–1916 Seepapitso II. *Regents:* 1916–1918 Kgosimotse; 1918–1919 Malope; 1919–1923 Tshosa; 1923–1925 Gagoangwe; 1925–1928 Ntebogang. *Kings:* 1928–1 July 1969 Kgosi Bathoen; 16 Jan. 1970–1973 Seepapitso III 1973–(?) Mookgami (acting); (?)–(?) Seepapitso IV; 2000–22 April 2003 Seatla Gaseitsiwe (acting); 2003–1 Sept. 2004 Kgabosetso II Mosielele (acting).

Banjol see **Gambia**

Banu al-Aghlab see **Aghlabid Empire**

Banu al-Wadid see **Tlemcen**

Banu Hafs see **Hafsid Kingdom**

Banu Hammad see **Hammadid Kingdom**

Banu Khurasan Tunis see **Tunisia**

Banu Rustum see **Rustumid Amirate**

Banu Wattas see **Wattasid Empire**

Banu Zayyan see **Tlemcen**

Banyon Point see **Fort James**

Banza Bakwai see **Hausa States**

Baol. ca. 1550–1877. *Location:* on the Senegal coast and inland, occupying the area south of Dakar. *Capital:* Lambaye.

History: A vassal state of Dyolof, Baol was conquered by Kayor about 1550, and was a vassal state of Kayor until 1686. In 1877 the French took it as part of their colony of Senegal.

Kings: ca. 1550–ca. 1560 Niokhor; ca. 1560–1593 Amari; 1593–(?) Mamalik Thioro; (?)–(?) Tié N'Della; (?)–(?) Tié Kura; (?)–(?) M'Bissan Kura; (?)–ca. 1664 Tiande; ca. 1664–ca. 1690 M'Bar; ca. 1690–1693 Tié Yaasin Demba; ca. 1693–1697 Tié Tieumbeul; 1697–1719 Lat Sukaabe; 1719–1719 Mali Kumba Dyaring; 1719–1749 Ma-Kodu Kumba; 1749–ca. 1752 Mawa; ca. 1752–ca. 1758 M'Bissan N'Della; ca. 1758–1777 Ma-Kodu Kumba; 1777–1809 [vacant]; 1809–1815 Tié-Yaasin Dieng; 1815–ca. 1822 Amadi Dyor; ca. 1822–1832 Birayma Fatma; 1832–1855 Isa Tein-Dyor; 1855–ca. 1857 Tié-Yaasin N'Gone; ca. 1857–1859 Ma-Kodu Kodu Kumba; 1859–1862 Mali Kumba N'Gone; 1862–1890 Tié-Yaasin Gallo; 1890–3 July 1894 Tanor Gogne.

Baquate see **Mauretania Tingitana**

Barbary States. A term used between the 16th and 19th centuries to denote the Maghrib, i.e. Morocco, Algeria, Tunisia and Tripolitania. The term comes from the word "Berber," who were the original inhabitants of the area. The Barbary Pirates flourished between the 16th century (most notably Khair ad-Din, or Barbarossa as he was also known) and 1830, and were a menace to ordinary shipping in the Mediterranean and off the Atlantic coast of Morocco. The pirates operated out of Algiers, Oran, Bougie, and other ports along the Mediterranean coast, as well as the Moroccan ports of Rabat–Salé and Masmouda (see also Masmouda). The most feared of these pirates were probably the Sallee Rovers out of Rabat (see Bou Regreg). The Sallee Rovers died out in the 1750s, but the Mediterranean corsairs were not finally extinguished until France took Algiers in 1830. Capture of booty was their prime aim, but they would take any human being they could. The rich could redeem themselves, but the poor faced only slavery or death.

Barca see **Cyrenaica** and **Pentapolis**

Barca Dynasty see **Carthage**

Barma see **Baguirmi**

Barnu see **Bornu**

Barolongland. ca. 1470–23 March 1885. *Location:* in the extreme southeastern corner of Botswana, on the South African border. *Capital:* Lobatsi. *Other names:* Barolong Kingdom.

History: One of the oldest South African tribes of the Tswana (also known as Batswana, Botswana, or Bechuana) group, the Barolong (or Rolong) formed a major division of what became Bechuanaland Protectorate in 1885. In 1760 the Barolong had split into the Tshidi branch (staying in Bechuanaland) and the Seleka branch (going into what became South Africa proper).

Kings: ca. 1470–(?) Morolong; (?)–ca. 1500 Noto; ca. 1500–(?) Morare; (?)–(?) Mabe; (?)–(?) Mabudi; (?)–ca. 1600 Maloto; ca. 1600–(?) Mabeo; (?)–(?) Modiboya; (?)–(?) Tshesebe; (?)–(?) Setlhare; (?)–ca. 1700 Masepha; ca. 1700–(?) Mokgopha; (?)–(?) Thibela; (?)–ca. 1760 Tau; ca. 1760–(?) Ratshidi (also known as Tsile); (?)–ca. 1805 Thutlwa; ca. 1805–(?) Leshomo; (?)–1849 Tawana; 1849–19 Oct. 1896 Montshiwa; 19 Oct. 1896–1903 Besele; 1903–1911 Badirile; 1911–1915 Lekoko; 1915–1917 Joshua; 1917–1919 Bakolopang; 1919–1954 Letla Moreng; 1954–(?) Tiego Tawana (acting); (?)–1970 Kabelepile; 1970–1977 Besele II; 1977–1982 R. Motlhatledi; 1982–17 June 2001 Besele II; 23 Feb. 2002–Letla Moreng II.

Barotseland. ca. 1550–11 June 1891. *Location:* since 1969 the old Barotseland has formed the Western Province of Zambia; and from 1964 to 1969 it was the Barotse Province of Zambia. *Capital:* Lealui. *Other names:* Lozi Empire; Lotse Empire; Kololo-Rotse Empire (1838–1864 only).

History: The Barotse (also known as the Lozi, or Lotse) peoples were originally called the Aluyi. They founded the Lozi Empire around the middle of the 16th century, and the nation was solidified around 1800 by Mulambwa. There were two vaguely defined divisions of Barotseland around this time, North Barotseland and South Barotseland, each with their own kings. In 1838 they were conquered by the Kololo, a neighboring clan (the Lozi word "Aluyi" is translated into Kololo as "Barotse," hence the more well-known name of the Barotse), but in 1864 Prime Minister Njekwa expelled the Kololo. In the 1880s the Barotse gradually became subject to Britain, and in 1891 the country became part of Zambesia (see Rhodesia), then of the Rhodesia Protectorate (again, see Rhodesia), and then of North Western Rhodesia. From 1911 Barotseland formed a large part of Northern Rhodesia (see Zambia). In the 1950s and 1960s the Barotse Native Government sought independent statehood, but this was rejected by Britain in 1961.

Litungas (Kings): ca. 1600–(?) Mboo (also known as Mwana Silundu, or Muyunda); (?)–(?) Inyambo; (?)–(?) Yeta I; (?)–(?) Ngalama; (?)–(?) Yeta II; (?)–(?) Ngombala; (?)–(?) Yubya; (?)–(?) Mwanawina I (also known as Musanawina); (?)–1780 Mwananyanda (also known a Musananyanda); 1780–1830 Mulambwa; 1830–1838 Silumelume and Mubukwanu (joint litungas); 1838–1841 Mubukwanu; 1841–1860 Ima Siku. *Regents:* 1860–1864 Sipopa (also known as Sepopa) and Njekwa (joint regents). *Litungas (Kings):* 1864–Aug. 1876 Sipopa (also known as Sepopa); Aug. 1876–Oct. 1876 Mowa Mamili (regent); Oct. 1876–May 1878 Mwanawina II; May 1878–Aug. 1878 [vacant]; Aug. 1878–Aug. 1884 Lubosi (also known as Lewanika); Sept. 1884–July 1885 Tatila Akufuna (usurper); July 1885–Nov. 1885 [vacant]; Nov. 1885–4 Feb. 1916 Lubosi (also known as Lewanika); 4 Feb. 1916–13 March 1916 Mokamba (regent); 3 March 1916–June 1945 Litia (or Yeta III); June 1945–June 1946 Shemakone Kalonga Wina (regent); June 1946–June 1948 Imwiko Lewanika; June 1948–Aug. 1948 Shemakone Kalonga Wina (regent); Aug. 1948–13 Nov. 1968 Mwanawina III; 13 Nov. 1968–15 Dec. 1968 Hastings Noyoo (regent); 15 Dec. 1968–1977 Godwin Mbikusita (or Lewanika II); 1977–7 July 2000 Ilute; Oct. 2000–Lubosi Imwiko. *Kololo Rulers:* 1838–1851 Sebitwane (King); 1851–1851 Mamosecane (Queen); 1851–1864 Sekeletu (King). *Prime Ministers:* 1864–1871 Njekwa; 1871–1878 [unknown]; 1878–1884 Silumbu; 1884–1885 Mataa; 1885–1898 Mwauluka; 1898–1919 [unknown]; 1919–(?) Mataa. *Note:* Mubukwanu was also the king of South Barotseland from about 1820 to 1830.

Barqah see **Cyrenaica**

Barra see **Fort James**

Barrakunda Falls see **Fort James**

Basa Cove see **Bassa Cove**

Bashar see **Wase**

Basia Cove see **Bassa Cove**

Basotho-QwaQwa see **QwaQwa**

Bassa Cove. Dec. 1832–1 April 1839. *Location:* on the south side of the St. John River, on the

Liberian coast, about 50 miles south of Monrovia, in what is now Grand Bassa County. Edina, which after 1837 became part of Bassa Cove Colony, lay on the north side of the river, in what is now Bong County. *Capital:* Bassa Cove (from 1835); Port Cresson (until 1835, and named for colonizer Elliott Cresson). *Other names:* Basa Cove; Basia Cove; Port Cresson (until 1835).

History: Founded in 1832 as Port Cresson, by Black Quakers of the New York and Pennsylvania Colonization Societies sometime in December 1832, Port Cresson (also known as Bassa Cove) was destroyed in June 1835 in a raid by Joe Harris, the local Bassa leader. A month later, in July 1835, the colony was reformed by the Young Men's Colonization Society of Pennsylvania, with the official name of the Colony of Bassa Cove. In 1837 the little colony gained extra ground with the inclusion of Edina, and in 1839 this enlarged colony of Bassa Cove became part of the Commonwealth of Liberia. In 1841 Bassa Cove became Buchanan.

Chief Magistrates: Dec. 1832–June 1835 Edward Hankinson.

Bastaards see **Griqualand West** and **Namibia** and **Rehoboth**

Baster Gebiet see **Rehoboth**

Basters see **Namibia**

Basutoland see **Lesotho**

Batawana see **Batwanaland**

Bathurst see **Gambia**

Batlokoa Lands see **Sekonyela's Land**

Batlokwaland. ca. 1660–23 March 1885. *Location:* in the southeastern part of Botswana, on the South African border. *Capital:* Gaberones (see also Bamaleteland, which shared the same capital). *Other names:* Batlokoaland; Batlokwa Kingdom.

History: Founded about 1660, the Batlokwa (or Tlokwa) tribe was a major division of the Tswana (also known as Batswana, Botswana, or Bechuana) group, and formed one of the major divisions of what became Bechuanaland Protectorate in 1885.

Kings: ca. 1660–ca. 1680 Tshwaana; ca. 1680–ca. 1700 Mosime; ca. 1700–ca. 1730 Mothubane; ca. 1730–ca. 1750 Mokgwa; ca. 1750–ca. 1770 Taukobong; ca. 1770–ca. 1780 Makabe; ca. 1780–ca. 1815 Bogatswe; ca. 1815–ca. 1820 Kgosi; ca. 1820–1825 Leshage; 1825–1835 Bashe; 1835–1880 Matlapeng; 1880–1931 Gaborone I; 1931–1948 Matlala; 1948–1973 Kgosi Gaborone II; 1973–(?) Kema (acting); (?)–2002 Michael Gaborone (acting); 20 Aug. 2002–Moshibidu Gaborone.

Batswanaland see **Batwanaland** and **Bechuanaland Protectorate**

Batwanaland. ca. 1795–23 March 1885. *Location:* within the Okavango Depression, the large northwestern quadrant of Botswana, bordering Namibia. *Capital:* Maun. *Other names:* Batwana Kingdom; Batawana; Tswanaland; Batswanaland; Twanaland; Tawanaland.

History: One of the major divisions of the country that became Bechuanaland Protectorate in 1885. The Batwana (also known as Twana) were a subdivision of the Bakwena, which in turn was a major tribe of the Tswana (also known as Batswana, Botswana, or Bechuana) group.

Kings: ca. 1795–ca. 1820 Tawana I; ca. 1820–ca. 1828 Moremi I; ca. 1828–ca. 1830 Sedumedi; ca. 1830–ca. 1840 Mogalakwe; ca. 1840–1874 Letsholathebe I; 1875–1876 Meno; 1876–1876 Dithapo I; 1876–4 Nov. 1890 Moremi II; 1891–1891 Dithapo II; 1891–1906 Sekgoma; 1906–1906 Sekgathole; 1906–1933 Mathiba; 1933–1934 Monaamabura; 1934–1936 Dibolayang; 1936–1937 Guetsalwe; 1937–1946 Moremi III. *Queens:* 1947–1958 Dulano Seezo (also known as Elizabeth); 1958–1981 Letsholathebe II; 1981–1995 Mathiba (acting); 1995–Tawana II.

Bauchi. 1805–Feb. 1902. *Location:* in the north-central part of what is now Nigeria, it forms a part of North-Eastern State. *Capital:* Bauchi (from 1902); Rauta (1877–1902); Bauchi (1809–1877. Also called Yakubu for many years after the death of the town's illustrious founder); Inkil (1805–1809). *Other names:* Bautschi; Inkil (its name before 1809).

History: Uthman Dan Fodio, creator of the Fulani Empire, embarked on a jihad (holy war) between 1804 and 1809, conquering most of the kingdoms in Northern Nigeria and surrounding areas. Most of these kingdoms, including Inkil, became amirates. Dan Fodio had 14 Masu-tuta (flag bearers) who led his jihad. All were Fulani, except Yakubu, the amir of Inkil, who was a Ger-awa and a long-time disciple of Dan Fodio. In 1809 Yakubu founded the town of Bauchi. In 1902, due to the flagrant disregard for British law about slave dealing, as well as the misrule of the amir Umaru, the amirate of Bauchi (the name means "land of slaves") became part of Northern Nigeria, as Bauchi Province.

Amirs: 1805–1843 Yakubu; 1843–1879 Ibrahim; 1879–1885 Usman; 1885–1902 Umaru; 1902–1903 Muhammadu; 1903–1908 Hassan; 1908–1941 Yakubu II; 1941–28 Sept. 1954 Yakubu III; May 1955–(?) Adamu Jumba; 1998– Suleiman Tiya Adamu Jumba.

Baule. ca. 1710–ca. 1840. *Location:* between the Kumbu and Bandama rivers, in Côte d'Ivoire. *Capital:* Wareba.

History: The Baule people, an Ashanti–Bron tribe, arrived at their destination from Ashanti about the middle of the 18th century under the leadership of their queen, Awura Pokou. By 1840 the kingdom had disintegrated because of quarrels between the ruling families, and became part of the French Ivory Coast.

Queens: ca. 1710–ca. 1750 Asae Pokou; ca. 1750–ca. 1760 Awura Pokou; ca. 1750–ca. 1760 Awura Danse; ca. 1760–ca. 1770 [unknown]. *Kings:* ca. 1770–ca. 1790 Akwa Bini; ca. 1790– ca. 1840 [unknown].

Baure see **Daura-Baure**

Bautschi see **Bauchi**

Bawanketseland see **Bangwaketseland**

Bechuanaland see **Botswana**

Bechuanaland North see **Botswana**

Bechuanaland Protectorate. 1884–30 Sept. 1885. *Location:* same as modern-day Botswana, plus the Bechuanaland part of northern Cape Colony. *Capital:* none.

History: In 1821 the Scottish missionary Robert Moffat established himself at Kuruman and remained there for 50 years. He had an enormous influence on Bechuanaland (i.e. the land of the Tswana peoples, or the Batswana; or as they were known in English, "Bechuana"). He was joined in 1841 by David Livingstone, and so the ties between the British Cape Colony to the south and the land of the Bechuana became very close. In 1836 the Cape claimed legal jurisdiction over the southern part of Bechuanaland, even though the Tswana tribes were regarded as independent. The principal native kingdoms were: Batlokwaland, Batwanaland, Bakwena-land, Bangwaketseland, Bamangwatoland, Baro-longland, Bakgatlaland, and Bamaleteland. After 1852 the Boers began to encroach on Bechuana-land, and by the 1870s certain local kings were asking for British protection. Although the British were unwilling to place a protectorate over Bechuanaland at this stage, they sent in Col. Charles Warren to occupy the southern part of the country, and until April 1881 a small British police force was stationed there. After they left the country fell into a state of anarchy, and the Boers began establishing republics there (see Goshen and Stellaland). Faced with this aggression, as well as German colonization going on in South West Africa, and finally as the result of the Boers proclaiming their own protectorate over Bechuanaland, the British government finally placed a protectorate of their own over what would, in Sept. 1885, become the British Crown Colony of British Bechuanaland. Cecil Rhodes wanted this territory as part of South Africa, as a launching board for forays into Zambesia. On 23 March 1885 the British extended this protectorate north over the Molopo River, and thus was created a huge protectorate, still called Bechuanaland. Later in 1885 the protectorate, too unwieldy to manage successfully, was split up, the north becoming known as Bechuanaland Protectorate (a smaller version, for which see Botswana) and the south becoming the Crown colony of British Bechuanaland.

Deputy Commissioners: April 1884–30 July 1884 John Mackenzie; 30 July 1884–Sept 1884 Cecil Rhodes. *Military Commanders:* 23 March 1885–24 Sept. 1885 Sir Charles Warren; 24 Sept. 1885–30 Sept. 1885 Lt.-Col. Frederick Carrington.

Bedde. 1825–1902. *Location:* the Bedde Division of Bornu Province, in North-Eastern State, in Nigeria. *Capital:* Gashua (latterly); Gorgo-ram (formerly). *Other names:* Bade (name comes from Birnin-Bedr, their Arabian ancestral home); Bede.

History: The Bade tribe left Kanem and the Lake Chad area in the 13th century and kept on the move until they reached Dadigar. There they seem to have split up, one group staying at Dadigar and three others going elsewhere, one of them to Tagali. The Tagali group became dominant around 1475, and the later royal family (whose list of rulers appears below) left Dadigar in the 18th century and moved to Gazai, then united with their cousins at Tagali, then on to Gayin, Gidgid, Agama Kasha, Sagmaga, Satako, and finally to Gorgoram, which they built in 1825. Rabih (see Rabih's Empire) captured Gorgoram in 1893, and in 1902 the country became the Bedde Amirate of the British protectorate of Northern Nigeria.

Mais (Kings): (?)–(?) Dugum Bugia; (?)–ca. 1820 Dugum Akuya; ca. 1820–1842 Lawan Babuje; 1842–1893 Alhaji; 1893–1897 Duna; 1897–April 1919 Saleh; Feb. 1920–1941 Sule; 1942–1945 Umara; 1945–(?) Umar Suleiman.

Beledugu see **Kaarta**

Belgian Congo see **Congo (Zaire)**

Belgian Ruanda–Urundi see **Ruanda-Urundi**

Benadir Coast Protectorate see **Italian Somaliland**

Benguela see **Angola** and **Dutch West Africa**

Beni see **Benin [i]**

Beni Saif see **Kanem**

Benin [i]. 1170–18 Feb. 1897. *Location:* in southern Nigeria. *Capital:* Usama (also known as Benin City), Great Benin.

History: Although the term "Benin" used to be applied to the Slave Coast of what is now Nigeria, as well as to the entire Niger River Delta and a small part of the country to the east of the delta, it means, in this specific entry, the state ruled from the town of Usama. This kingdom used to command a very extensive area, and gave its name to the term as used in its wider meaning (see above). The state of Benin was one of the most highly developed and organized of the West African states. However, this was also the home of the "juju" and of human sacrifice. The Portuguese discovered Great Benin (as they came

to call it over the years) about 1485, and a great slave trade developed between the Bini (or Beni, as the people are called). The British first arrived in Benin in 1553, and they also built up a great trade with the Bini, in, among other products, ivory, palm oil, and pepper. But by 1863, when Richard Burton went there to try (unsuccessfully) to put a stop to the huge number of human sacrifices, most of Benin's subject states had broken away and become independent, Benin had lost much of its coastline, and the town of Benin City was disintegrating. In 1885 the British placed a protectorate over what remained of Benin's coastline. In 1897 several British subjects were massacred by the Bini, and the British pronounced a protectorate over the kingdom, as well as allied city states along the Nigerian coastline, thus making them all part of the Niger Coast Protectorate (see Southern Nigeria). The oba was exiled to Calabar, and the chiefs were executed. Benin City was partly burned, and in 1899 the British went in again and totally subjugated the country. In 1914 the country became the Benin Province of Southern Nigeria.

Obas (Chiefs): 1170–1200 Oranmiyan; 1200–1220 Eweka I; 1220–1231 Uwakhuahen; 1231–1255 Ehenmihen; 1255–1280 Ewedo; 1280–1295 Oguola; 1295–1299 Edoni; 1299–1334 Udagbedo; 1334–1370 Ohen; 1370–1390 Egbeka; 1390–1410 Orobiru; 1410–1440 Uwaifiokun; 1440–1473 Ewuare; 1473–1477 Ezoti; 1477–1481 Olua; 1481–1504 Ozolua; 1504–1550 Esigie; 1550–1578 Orhogbua; 1578–1608 Ehengbuda; 1608–1640 Ohuan (also known as Odogbo); 1640–1661 Ahenzae; 1661–1669 Alenzae; 1669–1675 Akengboi; 1675–1684 Ahenkpaye; 1684–1689 Akenbedo; 1689–1700 Oreoghene; 1700–1712 Ewuakpe; 1712–1713 Ozuere; 1713–1735 Akenzua I; 1735–1750 Eresonyen; 1750–1804 Akengbuda; 1804–1816 Obanosa; 1816–1817 Ogbebo; 1817–1848 Osemwede; 1848–1888 Adolo; 1888–1897 Ovonramven; 1897–1914 [unrecognized]; 1914–5 April 1933 Egbeka II; 5 April 1933–(?) Akenzua II.

Benin [ii]. 22 June 1894– . *Location:* in Northwest Africa, between Togo and Nigeria. *Capital:* Porto-Novo (from 1975); Cotonou (1894–1975). *Other names:* Republic of Benin, or République Populaire du Bénin, or People's Republic of Benin (1975–); Republic of Dahomey (1960–1975); Autonomous Republic of Dahomey

(1958–1960); Overseas Territory of Dahomey (1946–1958); Dahomey Colony and Dependencies (1911–1946); Dahomey Colony (1894–1911).

History: In 1894 the French colony of Porto-Novo, along with the three French protectorates of Cotonou, Whydah, and Allada, all lying along the coast of what is today Benin, were all joined together to form the French colony of Dahomey, named for the kingdom of Dahomey that the French had made into a protectorate in 1891. In 1899 Dahomey became part of French West Africa. In 1900 the kingdom of Dahomey was officially abolished by the French, and the inland territory belonging to the kingdom was annexed by the French government. On 24 June 1911, after the French had subdued the lands further north, the country became known as Dahomey Colony and Dependencies, the hinterland becoming the dependencies. On 13 Oct. 1946 the whole country became an overseas province of the 4th republic of France, and on 4 Dec. 1958 it became a self-governing republic within the French Community. On 1 Aug. 1960 the country became completely independent of France, as the Republic of Dahomey. On 30 Nov. 1975 (effective as from 4 Dec. 1975) the country's name changed to the Republic of Benin, named after the old state of Benin (see Benin [i]). Since independence the country has been blighted by one coup after another, ethnic warfare, widespread poverty, and between 1974 and 1989 it was a Communist country. In 1991 free elections were held for the first time in 30 years, but Marxists were in and out of power in the 1990s.

Lieutenant-Governors: 22 June 1894–3 July 1899 Victor Ballot; 3 July 1899–8 Oct. 1899 Jean-Baptiste Fonsagrives (acting); 8 Oct. 1899–26 Nov. 1900 Pierre Pascal (acting); 26 Nov. 1900–30 June 1902 Victor Liotard; 30 June 1902–Oct. 1902 Charles Marchal (acting); Oct. 1902–1 Sept. 1903 Victor Liotard; 1 Sept. 1903–15 Jan. 1904 Eugène Décazes; 15 Jan. 1904–28 June 1904 Jean Penel (acting); 28 June 1904–5 May 1906 Victor Liotard; 5 May 1906–9 June 1906 Joseph Lhuerre (acting); 9 June 1906–16 July 1906 Charles Marchal (acting); 16 July 1906–8 March 1908 Charles Marchal; 8 March 1908–22 Sept. 1908 Antoine Gaudart (acting); 22 Sept. 1908–9 Oct. 1908 Charles Brunet (acting); 9 Oct. 1908–25 April 1909 Jean Peuvergne; 25 April 1909–29 June 1909 Henri Malan; 29 June 1909–10 Feb. 1910 Raphaël Antonetti (acting); 10 Feb. 1910–6 March 1911 Henri

Malan; 6 March 1911–24 June 1911 Raphaël Antonetti; 24 June 1911–9 May 1912 Émile Merwaert; 9 May 1912–11 July 1912 Charles Noufflard (acting); 11 July 1912–7 April 1917 Charles Noufflard; 7 April 1917–July 1919 Gaston Fourn (acting); July 1919–1 May 1921 Gaston Fourn; 1 May 1921–28 Feb. 1922 Pierre Chapon-Baissac (acting); 28 Feb. 1922–1 April 1924 Gaston Fourn; 1 April 1924–26 Nov. 1924 Alphonse Choteau (acting); 26 Nov. 1924–29 Aug. 1928 Gaston Fourn; 29 Aug. 1928–4 April 1929 Lucien Geay (acting); 4 April 1929–8 Feb. 1931 Dieudonné Reste; 8 Feb. 1931–7 Jan. 1932 Théophile Tellier; 7 Jan. 1932–2 Aug. 1932 Louis-Placide Blacher; 2 Aug. 1932–22 July 1933 Louis Aujas (acting); 22 July 1933–24 Aug. 1934 Jules de Coppet; 24 Aug. 1934–15 Feb. 1935 Jean de Santi (acting); 15 Feb. 1935–22 Sept. 1935 Maurice Bourgine; 22 Sept. 1935–1936 Jean de Santi (acting); 1936–12 Jan. 1937 Maurice Bourgine; 12 Jan. 1937–7 Aug. 1937 Henri Martinet (acting); 7 Aug. 1937–7 April 1938 Ernest Gayon (acting); 7 April 1938–1 June 1938 Henri Martinet (acting). *Governors:* 1 June 1938–27 Aug. 1940 Armand Annet; 27 Aug. 1940–18 Sept. 1940 Pierre Saliceti (acting); 18 Sept. 1940–26 Aug. 1943 Léon Truitard; 26 Aug. 1943–21 May 1946 Charles Assier de Pompignan; 21 May 1946–14 Jan. 1948 Robert Legendre (acting); 14 Jan. 1948–13 Jan. 1949 Jean-Georges Chambon; 13 Jan. 1949–19 Sept. 1949 Jacques-Alphonse Boissier; 19 Sept. 1949–Nov. 1951 Claude Valluy (acting); Nov. 1951–21 June 1955 Charles-Henri Bonfils; 21 June 1955–21 March 1958 Casimir Biros; 21 March 1958–15 July 1958 Bernard Hepp (acting); 15 July 1958–4 Dec. 1958 René Tirant (acting). *High Commissioners:* 4 Dec. 1958–1 Aug. 1960 René Tirant. *Heads of State:* 1 Aug. 1960–11 Dec. 1960 Hubert Maga. *Presidents:* 11 Dec. 1960–28 Oct. 1963 Hubert Maga; 28 Oct. 1963–19 Jan. 1964 Christophe Soglou (interim); 19 Jan. 1964–27 Nov. 1965 Sourou Apithy; 27 Nov. 1965–29 Nov. 1965 Justin Ahomadegbé; 29 Nov. 1965–22 Dec. 1965 Tairou Congacou; 22 Dec. 1965–17 Dec. 1967 Christophe Soglou; 17 Dec. 1967–22 Dec. 1967 Revolutionary Military Committee in power; 22 Dec. 1967–1 Aug. 1968 Alphonse Alley; 1 Aug. 1968–10 Dec. 1969 Émile Zinsou. *Presidents of the Committee:* 10 Dec. 1969–7 May 1970 Maurice Kouandété. *Presidents:* 7 May 1970–7 May 1972 Hubert Maga; 7 May 1972–26 Oct. 1972 Justin Ahomadegbé; 27 Oct. 1972–4 April 1991

Mathieu Kérékou (after 29 Sept. 1980 sometimes referred to as Ahmad Kérékou); 4 April 1991–4 April 1996 Nicéphore Soglou; 4 April 1996– Mathieu Kérékou. *Prime Ministers:* 4 Dec. 1958–22 May 1959 Sourou Apithy; 22 May 1959–1 Aug. 1960 Hubert Maga; 19 Jan. 1964–27 Nov. 1965 Justin Ahomadegbé; 22 Dec. 1967–1 Aug. 1968 Maurice Kouandété; 9 April 1996–8 May 1998 Adrien Houngbédji. *Note:* In times of no Prime Minister, the President or Head of State held that office.

Benin, Bight of see **Bight of Benin**

Benue Province see **Lafia**

Berauna see **Phazania**

Berber Tunisia see **Tunisia**

Betsimisaraka see **Madagascar**

Bexley see **Liberia**

Biafra. 30 May 1967–15 Jan. 1970. *Location:* eastern Nigeria. *Capital:* Umuahia (administrative capital from Oct. 1967); Enugu (from May to Oct. 1967. Enugu was founded in 1917. "Enu ugwu" means "at the top of the hill"). *Other names:* The Republic of Biafra (named for the Bight of Biafra).

History: In September and October 1966 there was a massacre of Ibos in the north of Nigeria. The Eastern Region of Nigeria, which was mostly populated by Ibos, had as its military governor an Ibo named Lt.-Col. Odumegwu Ojukwu. Ojukwu ordered all non–Ibos out of his region in October 1966, and took a hard line over the issue of states' rights. After unsuccessful talks with other regions of the Federal Republic of Nigeria, and equally unsuccessful demands that the power of Nigeria's central government be diminished (Ojukwu was afraid that the central power was being taken over by the Hausa, traditional enemies of the Ibo), the Eastern Region seceded in May 1967, unilaterally declaring itself a republic. In July war began with Nigeria. By October Enugu had been taken by the Nigerian forces and by late 1968 Biafra had been reduced to one tenth its original size, and did not have a real capital city. Most of its towns had been captured and its people bombed and starved into submission. But by now there

was considerable international sympathy for the Biafrans. Tanzania, Zambia, Ivory Coast, and Gabon all recognized Biafra as an independent republic by 1968, and France was on the point of doing so. The Pope and other powers organized relief to be flown in, and mercenaries abounded. In April 1969 federal forces captured the "capital" of Umuahia, and soon afterwards the Biafrans re-captured Owerri and made it their headquarters. On 10 Jan. 1970 this town was re-taken by the federal forces, and basically it was all over. Ojukwu fled to the Ivory Coast, leaving Maj.-Gen. Phillip Effiong to see to the details of surrender. In 1970 Biafra rejoined Nigeria, and the Federal powers were quick to rehabilitate the Biafrans, and the expected revenge did not take place. Biafra now occupies the four states of Cross River, Anambra, Imo, and Rivers.

Presidents: 30 May 1967–8 Jan. 1970 Odumegwu Ojukwu; 8 Jan. 1970–15 Jan. 1970 Phillip Effiong (acting).

Biafra, Bight of see **Bight of Biafra**

Biafra and Benin, Bights of see **Bights of Biafra and Benin**

Bight of Benin. 1 Feb. 1852–6 Aug. 1861. *Location:* Lagos, Nigeria, and the area surrounding it. *Capital:* Lagos.

History: In 1852 another British sphere of influence came into being — the Bight of Benin (cf. the Bight of Biafra), with headquarters at Lagos. In 1861 the kingdom of Lagos came to an end, and the city of Lagos became a British possession. At that point the Bight of Benin administratively fell under Lagos. In 1867 the Bight of Biafra assumed responsibility for the Bight of Benin (which was now minus Lagos), and the two became the Bights of Biafra and Benin. *Consuls:* May 1852–1853 Louis Fraser; 1853– April 1859 Benjamin Campbell; April 1859– 1860 George Brand; 1860–Jan. 1861 Henry Hand; Jan. 1861–May 1861 Henry Foote; May 1861–6 Aug. 1861 William McCoskry (acting).

Bight of Biafra. 30 June 1849–1867. *Location:* eastern Nigeria coast. *Capital:* Fernando Po; Bonny (local headquarters).

History: By the 1840s the slave trade was moribund in this area, and palm oil had taken its place. The British and the local kingdoms traded on a great scale, and in 1849 a British consul was appointed at Bonny to safeguard British interests. For the first few years he was also the governor of Fernando Po. John Bee croft, the consul, negotiated unsuccessfully with King Kosoko of Lagos to stop the slave trade out of Lagos, and in 1851 the British took the town. Kosoko fled, his uncle was placed on the throne and signed a treaty banning slavery and human sacrifice. In 1861 Lagos became a British possession, and in 1867 the Bight of Biafra and the Bight of Benin were united as the Bights of Biafra and Benin, a British sphere of influence.

Consuls: 30 June 1849–10 June 1854 John Beecroft; 10 June 1854–1855 James Lynslager (acting); 1855–1861 Thomas Hutchinson; 1861–Dec. 1864 Richard Francis Burton; Dec. 1864–1867 Charles Livingstone.

Bights of Biafra and Benin. 1867–5 June 1885. *Location:* basically southern Nigeria, excluding Lagos. *Capital:* Fernando Po; Bonny (local headquarters).

History: In 1867 the Bight of Biafra and the Bight of Benin were joined by the British as one administrative unit. This was still only a "sphere of influence," not a colony or protectorate, but in 1884 the British began declaring protectorates over the local kingdoms (see Niger Coast Protectorate for details). By 1885 they were calling the area the Oil Rivers, and in 1885 the British declared a protectorate over the whole coast, including Lagos.

Consuls: 1867–1873 Charles Livingstone; 1873–1878 George Hartley; 1878–13 Sept. 1879 David Hopkins; 13 Sept. 1879–5 June 1885 Edward Hyde Hewett.

Bini see **Benin [i]**

Bintang see **Fort James**

Biram. ca. 1100–1805. *Location:* in northern Nigeria, in the extreme east of what is now Kano Province. *Capital:* Biram.

History: Founded by Garin Gabas as an early native state of the Hausa persuasion, it had a long and mostly unrecorded history until taken over by the Fulani Empire in 1805, as part of Hadejia.

Kings: ca. 1100–(?) Biram; (?)–(?) Bomi; (?)–(?) Tumku; (?)–(?) Maji; (?)–(?) Kurada; (?)–ca. 1210 Yarima; ca. 1210–(?) Kumari; (?)–(?) Dan

kwafan; (?)–(?) Jatau; (?)–(?) Amale; (?)–ca. 1300 Mamadu; ca. 1300–(?) Dango; (?)–(?) Yahaya; (?)–(?) Dan Asan; (?)–(?) Abore; (?)–(?) Sakaina; (?)–ca. 1405 Musa I; ca. 1405–(?) Kujera; (?)–(?) Adam; (?)–(?) Ali; (?)–(?) Tagwai; (?)–ca. 1500 Jimami; ca. 1500–(?) Barikurgu; (?)–(?) Gamajiya Dayau; (?)–(?) Bako; (?)–(?) Burwai; (?)–(?) Gwarma; (?)–ca. 1600 Buri; ca. 1600–(?) Usuman; (?)–(?) Gadbo; (?)–(?) Abdu; (?)–(?) Tukur; (?)–ca. 1700 Buba; ca. 1700–(?) Kankarau; (?)–(?) Asawa; (?)–(?) Muhamman Bako; (?)–(?) Kawu; (?)–(?) Barwa; (?)–1805 al-Hajj Abu Bakar; 1805–1805 Musa II.

Bird Island see **Seychelles**

Bissau. 1687–1707; 1753–1879. *Location:* an island off the coast of southern Guinea-Bissau. *Capital:* São José de Bissau. *Other names:* Bissao.

History: In 1687 the second Portuguese settlement in what is today Guinea-Bissau was founded (see also Cacheu). In 1696 Bissau became a captaincy, placed under the rule of a Captain-Major. It was a major port for the slave trade to South America, and was maintained from Cacheu. In 1707 Bissau was abandoned, but revived in 1753 by the Grão-Pará Company belonging to the Marquês de Ponbal. By the early 1800s Bissau was more important to the Portuguese than the original settlement of Cacheu, and in 1879 Bissau, the Cacheu area and all the other Portuguese settlements in what is now Guinea-Bissau became Portuguese Guinea. *Rulers:* 1687–1696 ruled from Cacheu.

Capitães-Mores (Captains-Major: 1696–1699 José da Câmara; 1699–1707 Rodrigo da Fonseca; 1753–(?) Nicolau Pino de Araújo; (?)–ca. 1757 [unknown]; ca. 1757–1759 Manuel Pires; 1759–(?) Duarte Róis; (?)–ca. 1763 [unknown]; ca. 1763–(?) Filipe de Souto-Maior; (?)–ca. 1770 [unknown]; ca. 1770–ca. 1775 Sebastião da Cunha Souto-Maior; ca. 1775–ca. 1777 [unknown]; ca. 1777–(?) Inacio Baião; (?)–1793 [unknown]; 1793–ca. 1796 José Antonio Pinto; ca. 1796–1799 [unknown]; 1799–(?) João de Neves Leão; (?)–1803 [unknown]; 1803–(?) Antonio Faria; (?)–1805 [unknown]; 1805–1811 Manuel de Gouveia; 1811–(?) Antonio Figueiredo; (?)–ca. 1820 [unknown]; ca. 1820–ca. 1821 João Semedo; ca. 1821–1822 [unknown]; 1822–(?) Joaquim de Matos; (?)–1825 Domingos de Abreu Picaluga; 1825–1827 Joaquim de Matos; 1827–(?) Francisco Muacho; (?)–ca. 1829 [unknown]; ca. 1829–1830 Caetano Nozolini; 1830–(?) Joaquim de Matos; (?)–1834 Caetano Nozolini; 1834–(?) Joaquim de Matos; (?)–1836 [unknown]; 1836–1836 José Vieira; 1836–1839 Honorio Barreto; 1839–1840 José Barbosa; 1840–1841 Honorio Barreto; 1841–1842 José Machado; 1842–1842 Antonio Santos; 1842–1843 Antonio Torres; 1843–1844 José Coelho; 1844–1845 Alois Dziezaski; 1845–1847 Joaquim Alpoim; 1847–1848 Carlos de Sousa; 1848–1850 Caetano Nozolini; 1850–1851 [unknown]; 1851–(?) Alois Dziezaski; (?)–1852 [unknown]; 1852–1852 Libanio dos Santos; 1852–1853 José da Ávila; 1853–1854 José da Silva; 1854–1854 Pedro Ferreira; 1854–1855 [unknown]; 1855–1858 Honorio Barreto; 1858–1858 Antonio de Albuquerque Cota Falcão; 1858–1859 Honorio Barreto; 1859–1860 [unknown]; 1860–1862 Antonio Zagalo; 1862–1863 [unknown]; 1863–(?) Joaquim Marquês; (?)–1867 [unknown]; 1867–1868 Bernardo Moreira; 1868–1869 Manuel Meira; 1869–1871 Álvaro Caldeira; 1871–1871 José do Crato; 1871–(?) Joaquim Marquês; (?)–ca. 1877 [unknown]; ca. 1877–1879 Antonio Vieira.

Biu. ca. 1535–1 Jan. 1900. *Location:* in Bornu State, in northeastern Nigeria. *Capital:* Biu (from 1878, and permanently from 1904); Kogu (ca. 1763–1878); Limbur (until ca. 1763). *Other names:* Babur.

History: Founded by Bornu emigré Yamta the Great, this Bura (adjective meaning "of Biu") kingdom resisted the Fulani Empire and was taken into the brand new British protectorate of Northern Nigeria in 1899 (effective as from 1 Jan. 1900). In 1918 the area was made a division of Nigeria and in 1920 was made into an amirate.

Mais (Kings): ca. 1535–1580 Yamtara Wala (Yamta the Great, and also known as Yamta Abdullahi Ula); 1580–(?) Mari Vira Hyel; (?)–(?) Dira Wala; (?)–(?) Yamta Amba; (?)–ca. 1670 Yamta Kupaya Wadi; ca. 1670–(?) Mari Watila Tampta; (?)–(?) Yamtara Bangwe; (?)–(?) Mari Luku; (?)–(?) Jakwa Birtitik; (?)–(?) Thlama Bahara; (?)–(?) Tayar Warinki; (?)–ca. 1740 Dakwai; ca. 1740–ca. 1750 Mari Kopchi (also known as Kwabchi); ca. 1750–ca. 1760 Di Forma; ca. 1760–ca. 1770 Garga Moda; ca. 1770–ca. 1780 Dawi Moda; ca. 1780–ca. 1783 Di Biya; ca. 1783–1783 Di Rawa; 1783–1793 Garga Kopchi (also known as Kwabchi); 1793–1838 Mari Watirwa; 1838–1873 Ari Paskur; 1873–1891 Mari Biya; 1891–1908 Garga Kwomting; 1908–1935

Ari I (also known as Dogo); 1935–1951 Ari II (also known as Gurgur); 1951–1959 Muhammadu Aliyu (also known as Maidalla Madu); 1959–(?) Maidalla Mustafa Aliyu.

Boa Vista see **Cape Verde**

Bobo see **Burkina Faso**

Bobo Dioulasso see **Burkina Faso**

Boina see **Madagascar**

Bolewa see **Daniski** and **Fika**

Bomvanaland see **Cape Colony** and **Transkeian Territories**

Bonaparte see **Réunion**

Bône see **Algeria**

Bong County see **Bassa Cove**

Bonny. ca. 1450–5 June 1885. *Location:* in Degema Province, Rivers State, on the Nigerian coast. *Capital:* Bonny. *Other names:* Grand Bonny; Ibani; Ubani; Okoloba.

History: Originally a chiefdom, Bonny became a kingdom dealing in slaves. In the 1830s, with the abolition of the slave market, the country became a leading trader in palm oil. On 30 June 1849 a British consul was installed at Bonny to safeguard British interests in the area. Bonny became one of the Oil River States (see Niger Coast Protectorate), and it became part of the protectorate in 1885.

Chiefs: ca. 1450–(?) Alagbariye; (?)–(?) Okapara Ndole; (?)–(?) Opu Amakubu; (?)–(?) Okpara Asimini. *Kings:* (?)–(?) Asimini; (?)–(?) Edimini; (?)–(?) Kamba; (?)–(?) Kamalu; (?)–(?) Dappa; (?)–(?) Amakiri; (?)–ca. 1705 Appinya (also known as Apia); ca. 1705–(?) Warri. *Joint Kings:* (?)–(?) Awusa (also known as King Holiday); (?)–(?) Egbani (also known as Igbani); (?)–(?) Bupuor; (?)–ca. 1750 Ipuor. *Kings:* ca. 1750–1792 Perekule (also known as Captain Pepple); 1792–1792 Fubra (also known as Agbaa). *Joint Kings:* 1792–(?) Fubra II; 1792–1829 Opobo. *Kings:* 1829–1830 Bereibibo. *Regents:* 1830–1835 Madu. *Kings:* 1835–23 Jan. 1853 Dappa (also known as William, or Bill Pepple); 23 Jan. 1853–13 Aug. 1855 Agba Fubra (also known as Dappo). *Regents:* 13 Aug. 1855–1861 a series of regents. *Kings:* 1861–1863 Dappa (also known as William, or Bill Pepple); 1863–1885 Jaja (also known as George); 1885–25 Aug. 1891 Oko Jumbo.

Bono. ca. 1420–1723. *Location:* in Takyiman State, in Ghana. *Capital:* Bono-Mansu.

History: An Akan state of Ghana, formed about 1420 by the Fante tribe from the Sudan, it was a great gold mining and distributing center. Bono was finally subjugated by the Ashanti in 1723.

Namas (Kings): ca. 1420–ca. 1430 Asaman. *Regents:* ca. 1430–c. 1440 Ameyaw Kese. *Nanas (Kings):* ca. 1440–ca. 1450 Akumfi I; ca. 1450–ca. 1480 Obunumankona; ca. 1480–ca. 1500 Takyi Akwamo; ca. 1500–ca. 1520 Gyako I; ca. 1520–ca. 1550 Dwambera; ca. 1550–ca. 1560 Afena Yaw; ca. 1560–1577 Berempon Katakyira; 1577–1591 Yebowa Ananta; 1591–1600 Ati Kwame; 1600–1615 Ameyaw Kurompe; 1615–1621 Afena Diamono; 1621–1631 Owusu Aduam; 1631–1641 Akumfi II; 1641–1646 Kofu; 1646–1651 Owusu Akyempo; 1651–1666 Gyamfi; 1666–1674 Boakyi; 1674–1694 Kyereme; 1694–1723 Ameyaw Kwaakye.

Bophuthatswana. 1 June 1972–27 April 1994. *Location:* within, and surrounded by, South Africa. *Capital:* Mmabatho. *Other names:* Republic of Bophuthatswana; Repaboliki ya Bophuthatswana.

History: On 1 June 1972 Bophuthatswana became self-governing. This was the bantustan (or native homeland) of the Tswana peoples, and comprised six scattered exclaves throughout the Transvaal and Orange Free State provinces. On 6 Dec. 1977 it became the second bantustan (Transkei being the first) to gain independence from South Africa, but like the other bantustans (Transkei, Ciskei, Venda, QwaQwa, GazaNkulu, KwaZulu, KwaNdebele, KaNgwane, and Lebowa) it was recognized only by South Africa and the other bantustans. In 1994 South Africa became a black state, and there was no further need for bantustans. Bophuthatswana had already been terminated as a bantustan, due to Mangope's intransigence.

Chief Ministers: 1 June 1972–6 Dec. 1977 Lucas Mangope. *Presidents:* 6 Dec. 1977–10 Feb. 1988 Lucas Mangope; 10 Feb. 1988–10 Feb. 1988 Rocky Ismael Peter Malabane-Metsing; 10 Feb. 1988–13 March 1994 Lucas Mangope.

Borkou–Ennedi–Tibesti see **Chad**

Borku see **Chad**

Bornu. ca. 850–ca. 1260. *Location:* northeastern Nigeria, west of Lake Chad, in the Northern Region of Nigeria. *Capital:* [unknown]. *Other names:* Bornu State; Barnu; Bornou.

History: One of several small states founded on the dissolution of the old Zaghawa Kingdom (see also Kanem) around 850, this one by the Sao peoples. On the southwest of Lake Chad, it lived in the shadow of its neighbor, Kanem across the water, until about 1200 when the Kanuri from Kanem began expanding into Bornu, taking it over totally about 1260. It then became part of the growing state of Kanem-Bornu (see Bornu Empire).

Rulers: [unknown].

Bornu Empire. ca. 1256–1902. *Location:* around Lake Chad, on the Nigeria-Niger border. *Capital:* Yerwa (from 1907); Kukawa (1814–1907); Birni Ngazargamu (founded as the new capital in 1475); Yamia (also known as Muniyo) (until 1475); Birni Kimi (before that); Wudi (before that); Njimi (the first capital). *Other names:* Bornu; Bornou; Barnu; Regnum Organa; Kanem-Bornu; Kanem-Bornu Empire; Canem-Bornu.

History: Kanem reached its peak in the 13th century, and as the old state of Bornu collapsed about this time, Kanem took it over and Kanem-Bornu was born. Dunama Dibbelemi, king of Kanem, was the first undisputed ruler of the new Kanem-Bornu Empire. Kashim Biri succeeded his successor, by which time Kano, Wadai, Adamawa, and all of Bornu were under the control of the new empire. The Sefawa Mais (Kings) continued to rule, as they had done in Kanem. However, Old Kanem had relapsed into a rebellious state under the Bulala, a tribe who had been there for centuries. They captured Njimi and plagued the new Kanem-Bornu Empire for a long time thereafter. This necessitated a shift of power from Old Kanem to Old Bornu, and by 1400 the empire became simply the Bornu Empire. In the early 1500s Kanem was reconquered from the Bulala and the land of Aïr was also taken. The empire reached its peak under Idris Alooma, but the latter half of the 17th century saw the beginning of the collapse of the Bornu Empire, with Tuaregs invading, as well as famine, and by 1700 it was in a state of decadence. After the Fulani invasions of the early 19th century (see Fulani Empire), Bornu became split into several amirates, and by March 1808 had effectively ceased to exist. However, by 1824 the Fulani had been expelled by the fakir al-Kanemi, and the Bornu Empire was re-activated, and regained strength. In 1846 the Sefawa dynasty of Mais (Kings) ended and a series of Shehus (Sheikhs) ruled until 1893, when the empire ended, being conquered by Rabih (see Rabih's Empire). In 1902 part of Bornu went into the British protectorate of Northern Nigeria; another part had already (1900) gone to the French Military Territory and Protectorate of Chad. In 1907 the capital moved to Yerwa (also, erroneously, known as Maiduguri).

Emperors: ca. 1256–1259 Dunama Dibbelemi; 1259–1260 Kade; 1260–1288 Kashim Biri (also known as Abd al-Kadim); 1288–1307 Biri II Ibrahim; 1307–1326 Ibrahim I; 1326–1346 Abdallah II; 1346–1350 Selma; 1350–1351 Kure Ghana as-Saghir; 1351–1352 Kure Kura al-Kabir; 1352–1353 Muhammad I; 1353–1377 Idris I Nigalemi; 1377–1386 Daud Nigalemi; 1386–1391 Uthman I; 1391–1392 Uthman II; 1392–1394 Abu Bakr Liyatu; 1394–1398 Umar ibn Idris; 1398–1399 Sa'id; 1399–1400 Kade Afunu. *Mais (Kings):* 1400–1432 Biri III; 1432–1433 Uthman III Kaliwama; 1433–1435 Dunama III; 1435–1442 Abdallah III Dakumuni; 1442–1450 Ibrahim II; 1450–1451 Kadai; 1451–1455 Ahmad Dunama IV; 1455–1456 Muhammad II; 1456–1456 Amr; 1456–1456 Muhammad III; 1456–1461 Ghaji; 1461–1466 Uthman IV; 1466–1467 Umar II; 1467–1472 Muhammad IV; 1472–1504 Ali Ghajideni; 1504–1526 Idris Katarkamabi; 1526–1545 Muhammad V Aminami; 1545–1546 Ali II Zainami; 1546–1563 Dunama V Ngumaramma; 1563–1570 Dala (also known as Abdallah); 1570–1580 Aissa Kili; 1580–1603 Idris Alooma (also known as Alawma); 1603–1617 Muhammad Bukalmarami; 1617–1625 Ibrahim III; 1625–1645 Umar III; 1645–1685 Ali III; 1685–1704 Idris IV; 1704–1723 Dunama VI; 1723–1737 Hamdan; 1737–1752 Muhammad VII Erghamma; 1752–1755 Dunama VII Ghana; 1755–1793 Ali IV ibn Haj Hamdun; 1793–March 1808 Ahmad ibn Ali; March 1808–1810 Dunama Lafiami; 1810–1814 Muhammad VIII; 1814–1817 Dunama Lafiami; 1817–1846 Ibrahim; 1846–1846 Ali Delatumi. *Protectors of Bornu:*

1817–1824 Muhammad al-Amin al-Kanemi (also known as Laminu); 1824–1846 Umar. *Shehus (Sheikhs):* 1846–1853 Umar; 1853–1854 Abdarrahman; 1854–1881 Umar; 1881–1884 Bukar Kura; 1884–1885 Ibrahim; 1885–1893 Hashim; 1893–1893 Kiyari Muhammad al-Amin. *Conqueror and Ruler:* 1893–22 April 1900 Rabih az-Zubayr ibn Fadl-Allah. *Rulers:* 22 April 1900–23 Aug. 1901 Fadl-Allah (son of Rabih). *Shehus (Sheikhs):* 1902–Feb. 1922 Bukar Garbai; 1922–1937 Umar Sanda Kura; 1937–1969 Umar Sanda Kiyarimi; 1969–(?) Umar Baba Ya Mairami.

Borozwi see **Rozwi**

Botswana. 30 Sept. 1885– . *Location:* southern Africa, north of the Republic of South Africa, and east of Namibia. *Capital:* Gaborone (formerly known as Gaberones. The town was founded about 1892, and named for Chief Gaberone Matlapin. It was the capital since 1965); Mafeking (in South Africa. This was the external capital from 1885 to 1965). *Other names:* Republic of Botswana (from 1966); Bechuanaland (until 1966).

History: In September 1885 the British divided the huge Bechuanaland Protectorate into two more manageable segments. The southern one was the Crown colony of British Bechuanaland, which ultimately became part of Cape Colony in South Africa. The northern one remained a protectorate and the British continued to call it Bechuanaland Protectorate (this would eventually become Botswana). This was the area occupied by most of the Tswana tribes, and the chief of the Bamangwato was the native overlord of all Bechuanaland, while the same British administrator essentially ran both the new protectorate and the new crown colony, as if they had still been one. On 9 May 1891 the protectorate became Bechuanaland High Commission Territory, with the British resident commissioner reporting to the High Commissioner in Mafeking. In 1892 this protectorate was considerably enlarged with the acquisition of much native land, and the country did, as Rhodes had wanted (see Bechuanaland Protectorate) become the springboard for the colonization of the Rhodesias. In 1895 Rhodes's plans to acquire the protectorate for his company were thwarted by chiefs Khama III, Sebele and Bathoen traveling to London with missionary support, and pleading with the British government to remain under

British protection. In 1948 Seretse Khama married an Englishwoman named Ruth Williams, and this disturbed the British government so much that they exiled him from Bechuanaland. This led to problems in Bechuanaland. On 1 Aug. 1964 the High Commission Territories of Bechuanaland, Swaziland and Basutoland ceased to exist in preparation for independence, and Bechuanaland became self-governing on 3 March 1965. On 30 Sept. 1966 Botswana came into being, as an independent republic within the British Commonwealth. The country's main problems are AIDS and unemployment, AIDS having devastated Botswana.

Chief Native Administrators: 1952–3 March 1965 Rasebolai Khamane. *Prime Ministers:* 3 March 1865–30 Sept. 1966 Sir Seretse Khama. *British Resident Administrators:* 30 Sept. 1885–19 Nov. 1895 Sidney Shippard (knighted 1887); 19 Nov. 1895–21 Dec. 1897 Francis Newton: 21 Dec. 1897–Jan. 1901 Hamilton Goold-Adams; Jan. 1901–1906 Ralph Williams; 1906–1816 Francis Panzera; 1916–1917 Edward Garraway; 1917–1920 James MacGregor; 1920–1920 Jules Ellenberger (acting); 1920–1923 James MacGregor; 1923–1926 Jules Ellenberger; 1926–1926 Rowland Daniel (acting); 1926–1927 Jules Ellenberger; 1927–1930 Rowland Daniel; 1930–1937 Charles Rey (knighted 1932); 1937–1942 Arden Clarke (from 1951 he would be Sir Charles Arden-Clarke); 1942–1946 Aubrey Forsyth-Thompson; 1946–1950 Anthony Sillery; 1950–1953 Edward Beetham; 1953–1955 William Mackenzie; 1955–1959 Martin Wray; 1959–1 Aug. 1964 Peter Fawcus. *Commissioners:* 1 Aug. 1964–1965 Peter Fawcus (knighted 1965); 1965–30 Sept. 1966 Hugh Norman-Walker. *Presidents:* 30 Sept. 1966–13 July 1980 Sir Seretse Khama; 13 July 1980–18 July 1980 Quett Masire (also known as Ketumile Masire) (acting); 18 July 1980–31 March 1998 Quett Masire (also known as Sir Ketumile Masire); 1 April 1998–Festus Mogae. *Note:* for list of High Commissioners see South Africa.

Bou Regreg. 1627–1641. *Location:* Salé–Rabat, Morocco. *Capital:* Salé. *Other names:* Bu Regreg; Bu Ragrag; Bou Ragrag; Republic of Bou Regreg; Morisco Republic; Salé Republic.

History: In 1608 expatriate Moriscos (Spanish Muslims) were expelled from Spain, settled in Rabat, in Morocco, and strongly fortified it. More Moriscos settled across the Bou Regreg River in Salé. Thus two cities were set up by these Hornacheros (Moriscos from Hornacho in Spain)—Sla al-Qadim (Old Salé) and Sla al-Jadid (New Salé, or Rabat). From this base the Hornachero pirates, especially the dreaded Sallee Rovers (the most notorious of all the Barbary Pirates) raided shipping in the Atlantic with the protection of the Moroccan sultan. The two cities combined to form the pirate republic of Bou Regreg. Incorporated into Morocco in 1641, the pirates continued to raid unimpeded from Rabat-Salé until the 1750s.

Presidents: 1627–1641 Abu Abdallah Muhammad ibn Ahmad az-Ziyani. *Governors of Rabat:* 1629–1630 Muhammad ibn Abdel Kadir; 1630–1637 Ahmad ibn Ali; 1637–1647 Abdallah ibn Ali al-Kasri.

Boujdour see **Western Sahara**

Bourbon see **Réunion**

Boussouma see **Mossi States**

Brakna. ca. 1650–18 Oct. 1904. *Location:* in Mauritania. *Capital:* Shamama (from 1780).

History: Around 1650 the dynasty of Ulad Nurmash began ruling in Brakna, and by 1780 the dynasty of Ulad Abd Allah (also known as Ulad Saiyyid) had taken over. In 1904 the French took it over as part of the Civil Territory of Mauritania. As part of Mauritania, it formed the cercle of Brakna.

Amirs: ca. 1650–(?) Nurmash; (?)–1728 Muhammad al-Hiba; 1728–1762 Ahmad al-Hiba; 1762–1780 Ali; 1780–1780 Ahmayada; 1780–1800 Muhammad; 1800–1817 Sidi Ali I; Jan. 1818–1841 Ahmaddu I; 1841–1842 Moukhtar Sidi; 1842–1851 Muhammad ar-Rajal; 1851–Dec. 1858 Muhammad Sidi; Dec. 1858–1893 Sidi Ali II; 1893–Dec. 1903 Ahmaddu II; Dec. 1903–18 Oct. 1904 Sidi Muhammad. *Rebel Leaders:* Dec. 1903–28 Oct. 1910 Sheikh Mahl Aynin; 28 Oct. 1910–6 May 1912 Hamid al-Hiba. *Sultans:* 6 May 1912–1919 Hamid al-Hiba; 1919–1919 Talib Hiyar; 1919–7 April 1934 Maribbi Rabbu.

Brandenburger Gold Coast Settlements see **Hollandia**

Brass. ca. 1450–5 June 1885. *Location:* right on the delta of the Niger River, and at the mouth of the Brass River, in Nigeria. *Capital:* Brass town (named for the "Barasin," which means "let go," it was also called Brass, and formerly Nembe. It was called Nembe when the country was called Nembe, and the capital lay 35 miles inland. Until the end of the 19th century this town was called Brass by the Europeans. Then, out of trade expediency, the capital was shifted to the mouth of the Brass River, to Tuwon (also known as Twon), which the Europeans erroneously read as "Town." Hence Brass Town, or Brasstown). *Other names:* Nembe; Nimby; Itebu; Debe.

History: The origins of the Nembe area are obscure, but it is likely that people from Benin (see Benin [i]) came to the delta under the leadership of Kala-Ekule. One of the early kings was named Nembe, and from him came the name of the country. Like Bonny, Brass became a major slave-dealing city-state, then, on the abolition of the slave trade, made an agreement with Britain in 1856, and went into the palm-oil business. In 1885 it became part of the Oil Rivers Protectorate (see Southern Nigeria). The incursions of other Europeans traders in the palm-oil trade, and the prohibitive regulations of the Royal Niger Company, threatened Brass with extinction, and on 29 Jan. 1895 the Brass men attacked and destroyed the Royal Niger Company's station at Akassa. 43 of the prisoners taken back to Nembe were eaten. This was unacceptable to the British, and in March 1896 they sacked Nembe, and King Koko was deposed in 1898. Brass is now the seat of Yanagoa Province, in Rivers State, southern Nigeria.

Amanyanabos (Kings): ca. 1450–ca. 1500 Kala-Ekule; ca. 1500–(?) Ogbodo; (?)–(?) Nembe; (?)–(?) Owagi; (?)–(?) Ogio; (?)–(?) Peresuo; (?)–ca. 1700 Obia; ca. 1700–(?) Basuo; (?)–ca. 1780 Mingi I; ca. 1780–(?) Ikata (also known as Mingi II); (?)–1800 Gboro (also known as Mingi III); 1800–1830 Kulo (also known as King Forday, or Mingi IV); 1830–1846 Amain (also known as King Boy, or Mingi V); 1846–1863 Kien (also known as Mingi VI); 1863–1879 Ockiya VII (also known as Mingi VII); 1879–1889 interregnum; 1889–1898 Koko (also known as Mingi VIII); 1898–1926 ruled directly by the British; 1926–1936 Anthony Ockiya (also known as Mingi IX); 1936–(?) Allagoa (also known as Mingi X); (?)–Mingi IX.

Brava see **Cape Verde**

Brazzaville see Congo and **French Equatorial Africa**

British Bechuanaland. 30 Sept. 1885–16 Nov. 1895. *Location:* in the northern part of Cape Province (formerly Cape Colony), South Africa. *Capital:* Vrijburg (also known as Vryburg).

History: In Sept. 1885 Bechuanaland Protectorate was split into two parts. The northern section remained a protectorate, and carried on the name Bechuanaland Protectorate (it would eventually become Botswana). The southern part became a Crown colony called British Bechuanaland. This Crown colony included the United States of Stellaland, and in 1895 became part of the Cape.

Military Commanders: 30 Sept. 1885–23 Oct. 1885 Lt.-Col. Frederick Carrington. *Administrators:* 23 Oct. 1885–16 Nov. 1885 Sidney Shippard (he would be knighted in 1887).

British Central Africa Protectorate see **Malawi**

British East Africa see **Kenya**

British Indian Ocean Territory. 8 Nov. 1965– . *Location:* Indian Ocean. *Capital:* London, England (from 1976); Victoria, Seychelles (1965–1976). *Other names:* BIOT.

History: The BIOT was a British colony formed in 1965 from certain islands which were formerly dependencies of Mauritius or the Seychelles, viz. the Chagos Archipelago (which is outside the province of this book), the Aldabras, and the Farquhar and Des Roches Islands. The reason for the creation of this colony was so that the UK and the USA could have defense and communications installations in the Indian Ocean. Because of that, over a thousand migrant copra workers were expelled to Mauritius. On June 29, 1976, all except the Chagos Archipelago were transferred to the Seychelles, which became a republic that year. Only the Chagos were left to form the much depleted BIOT. No civilian population now resides in the colony. *Rulers:* The high commissioners of BIOT were the same men as the governors of the Seychelles, at least until 1976. From that time BIOT was administered from the Foreign and Commonwealth Office in London, by non-resident commissioners and administrators.

British Kaffraria. 10 May 1835–17 April 1866. *Location:* the present-day Ciskei, i.e. the area of South Africa between the Keiskamma and Kei rivers. *Capital:* King William's Town (1847–1866); Grahamstown (1835–1847); King William's Town (1835–1835). *Other names:* Queen Adelaide Land, or Eastern Province (1835–1847); Queen Adelaide Province (1835–1835).

History: In 1835 Sir Benjamin D'Urban (Governor of Cape Colony) and Colonel Harry Smith annexed the area as a natural extension of the Cape Colony's eastern boundary, forcing out the Xhosa natives, and naming it Queen Adelaide Province, in honor of the wife of King William IV of the United Kingdom. King William's Town was founded by D'Urban that year and named for the king. On 5 Dec. 1835 D'Urban and Smith disannexed the province and re-admitted the Xhosa. Five days after the disannexation the province became a separately administered district of the Cape, was re-named Queen Adelaide Land, or Eastern Cape Province, and for the next twelve years was administered by the lieutenant-governors of the Eastern Districts of Cape Colony, through a local man in Grahamstown, which replaced King William's Town as the local capital. On 17 Dec. 1847 the area was annexed by Harry Smith and became the colony of British Kaffraria. Smith had rebuilt King William's Town in 1847, and that became the new capital. On 7 March 1860 the country's dependence on the Cape was removed and it became the Crown colony of British Kaffraria. In 1866, however, it merged into Cape Colony, becoming the two districts of King William's Town and East London. Later on this region became the Ciskei.

Administrators: 10 May 1835–5 Dec. 1835 Col. Harry Smith. *Lieutenant-Governors:* 10 Dec. 1835–13 Sept. 1836 Col. Harry Smith (acting); 13 Sept. 1836–9 Aug. 1838 Sir Andries Stockenstroom; 9 Aug. 1838–31 Aug. 1839 John Hare (acting); 31 Aug. 1839–Sept. 1846 John Hare; Sept. 1846–9 April 1847 Direct rule from Cape Colony; 9 April 1847–4 Nov. 1847 Sir Henry Young; 4 Nov. 1847–17 Dec. 1847 Direct rule from Cape Colony. *Chief Commissioners:* 23 Dec. 1847–Oct. 1852 George Mackinnon; Oct. 1852–7 March 1860 John Maclean. *Lieutenant-Governors:* 7 March 1860–24 Dec. 1864 John Maclean. *Governor's Deputies:* 24 Dec. 1864–17 April 1866 Robert Graham. *Kings:* 1760–1785 Rarabe. *Regents:* 1785–1797 Ndlambe; *Kings:* 1797–13 Nov. 1829 Ngqika (also known as Gaika); 13 Nov. 1829–1 June 1878 Sandile. *Note:* The Xhosa rulers of the area were the Rarabe offshoot of the main Xhosa line. For Xhosa rulers before Rarabe, see the entry Transkeian Territories.

British Pondoland. 25 Sept. 1894–30 May 1910. *Location:* in Kaffraria, South Africa, immediately southwest of Natal. *Capital:* none. *Other names:* Pondoland; Mpondoland.

History: In 1894 Pondoland East and Pondoland West were annexed to Cape Colony and governed from there, as part of the Transkeian Territories. The area was called British Pondoland until 1910, when the Union of South Africa came into existence, and then it simply disappeared into history as part of the Cape.

Rulers: 25 Sept. 1894–30 May 1910 direct Cape rule.

British Somaliland. 7 Sept. 1877–1 July 1960. *Location:* northeast Africa, to the east of Ethiopia, on the Gulf of Aden. *Capital:* Hargeysa (from 1941); Berbera (until 1941. Berbera was founded about 300 B.C. by Ptolemy Philadelphus, and the name means "land of the Barbarians"). *Other names:* Somaliland; Somalia, or Somalia State (1960–1960); Somali Protectorate (1887–1960); Egyptian Somaliland (1877–1884);

History: This country was taken by the Egyptians as a step in their conquest of Africa (an ambition that was not limited to the extent of the East African lakes, as they claimed). The Egyptian flag was hoisted in Berbera in 1870, and at first Britain objected to these moves. However, by 1877 they had come to regard the Egyptian presence as a safe bulwark against possible encroachment from less friendly powers. Internal problems in Egypt placed a strain on the new empire, and in 1884 the Egyptians were forced to pull out of Somaliland in order to concentrate on the Mahdi threat (see Sudan). At that point the British moved into the area, occupying Berbera and other coastal towns, and the country became British Somaliland. The British East India Company had had a considerable influence on the area since 1840, when they concluded treaties with the local rulers and established suitable harbors for their ships. On 20 July 1887 the British placed a protectorate over the country, and in 1888 took in the three small British protectorates of Mussa Island, Bab Island, and Aubad Island. Also in 1888 the boundaries between British and French territory were defined, and those between British and Italian territory in 1894 and between British and Ethiopian in 1897. At first the country was regarded as a dependency of Aden (therefore falling under the administration of India); the protectorate was transferred to the Foreign Office in 1898. In 1905 it passed to the Colonial Office. Between 1899 and 1921 the main threat to stability in the area was a Somali fanatic/hero named Muhammad ibn Abdallah Hassan (nicknamed "The Mad Mullah" by the British) who, with his army of dervishes, created havoc in the protectorate. The Italians occupied British Somaliland briefly during World War II. The British ruled the protectorate until 26 June 1960, when it became an independent country known as the State of Somalia. This new state lasted a mere five days before it united with Italian Somaliland to form the country of Somalia as we know it today.

Governors: 7 Sept. 1877–1878 Rauf Pasha; 1878–1884 [unknown]. *Residents/Political Agents:* 1884–1888 Frederick Hunter; 1888–1893 Edward Stace; 1893–1896 Charles Sealy; 1896–1897 William Ferris; 1897–1898 James Sadler. *Consuls-General:* 1898–1901 James Sadler; 1901–1903 Eric Swayne; 1903–1904 Harry Cordeaux (acting); 1904–1905 Eric Swayne. *Administrators:* 1905–1907 Harry Cordeaux; 1907–1907 Sir William Manning (acting); 1907–Jan. 1910 Harry Cordeaux; Jan. 1910–Jan. 1910 Horace Byatt (acting); Jan. 1910–July 1911 Sir William Manning; July 1911–1912 Horace Byatt; 1912–1913 Geoffrey Archer (acting); 1913–May 1914 Horace Byatt. *Commissioners:* May 1914–Oct. 1919 Geoffrey Archer. *Governors:* Oct. 1919–1920 Geoffrey Archer (knighted 1920); 1920–1921 Arthur Lawrance (acting); 1921–17 Aug. 1922 Sir Geoffrey Archer; 17 Aug. 1922–1925 Gerald Summers (knighted 1925); 26 Jan. 1926–18 June 1932 Harold Kittermaster (knighted 1928). *Commissioners:* 18 June 1932–1935 Arthur Lawrance (knighted 1934). *Governors:* 1935–2 March 1939 Sir Arthur Lawrance; 2 March 1939–18 Aug. 1940 Vincent Glenday; 18 Aug. 1940–29 March 1941 Italian occupation. *Military Governors:* 29 March 1941–3 March 1943 Arthur Chater; 3 March 1943–1948 Gerald Fisher. *Governors:* 1948–1954 Gerald Reece (knighted 1950); 1954–1959 Theodore Pike (knighted 1956); 1959–26 June 1960 Sir Douglas Hall. *Prime*

Ministers: 19 May 1956–26 June 1960 Abdallah Issa; 26 June 1960–1 July 1960 Muhammad Ibrahim Egal.

British Togoland. 27 Dec. 1916–13 Dec. 1956. *Location:* in the Volta Region, southeastern Ghana. It has no port. *Capital:* Ho (founded in the early 18th century). *Other names:* Togo; Togoland; West Togo; Togoland British Trust Territory (1946–1956); Togoland British Mandate (1920–1923).

History: In 1916 the French–British Condominium (see Togoland) came to an end in Togoland, and the country was divided into West Togo (British) and East Togo (French). The French were not satisfied with this division, as it gave the main port of Lomé to the British. On 30 Sept. 1920 France and Britain both received League of Nations mandates for their areas, and the French gained Lomé in exchange for some country inland. On 11 Oct. 1923 the British mandate was handed over to the Gold Coast, to be ruled from there as a territory of that colony, or rather, the northern section was ruled as if it were a part of Gold Coast Northern Territories, and the southern section as if it were a part of the Gold Coast proper. The southern section, the more advanced of the two, was known as the Ho District. On 13 Dec. 1946 British Togoland became a United Nations Trust Territory, still administered by Britain from Accra in the Gold Coast. From 1951 the southern section elected three members to the legislative assembly of the colony of the Gold Coast, but this system was not implemented in the northern section. In 1956, by virtue of UN resolution No. 425, it became politically part of the Gold Coast as that country prepared for independence as the Dominion of Ghana. The French part of Togo followed a very similar course (see Togo).

Rulers: 27 Dec. 1916–30 Sept. 1920 ruled direct from the Gold Coast. *Administrators:* 30 Sept. 1920–11 Oct. 1923 Francis Jackson; 11 Oct. 1923–13 Dec. 1956 ruled direct from Accra in the Gold Coast.

British West Africa. 17 Oct. 1821–13 Jan. 1850; 19 Feb. 1866–28 Nov. 1888. *Location:* Gambia, Sierra Leone, Gold Coast, Lagos, in northwest Africa.

Capital: Freetown (in Sierra Leone). *Other names:* British West African Settlements, or British West Africa Settlements, or West Africa

Settlements, or West African Settlements, or W.A.S. (1866–1888); West African Territories, or W.A.T. (1821–1850).

History: In 1821 all British forts and settlements in Northwest Africa were placed under the administration of a Governor-in-Chief, based in Freetown, Sierra Leone. The three constituent parts of the new organization all became territories, therefore, and were as follows:

1. Gambia, which, in 1829, became Bathurst Settlement and Dependencies in the Gambia, and then in 1843 separated from the WAT and became a separate colony called Gambia; 2. Gold Coast, which detached from the W.A.T. in 1828 to be run by a Committee of Merchants (although the links between that government and that of Sierra Leone remained strong). In 1843 the Gold Coast became the property of the Crown once more; 3. Sierra Leone, the only territory that remained as such until the dissolution of the West African Territories in 1850. The W.A.T. was the precursor of the West African Settlements, which were formed in 1866, and ruled by the Governor of Sierra Leone, from Freetown again. This time the constituent parts were four in number—1. Gold Coast; 2. Lagos; 3. Sierra Leone; and 4. Gambia. On 24 July 1874 the Gold Coast and Lagos broke away to form their own colony, Gold Coast Colony (with Lagos) (see Ghana). This left Sierra Leone and the Gambia as the only two components of the W.A.S., which was re-constituted on 17 Dec. 1874. In Oct. 1888 Sierra Leone and the Gambia left, and on 28 Nov. 1888 the West African Settlements (and British West Africa) came to an end as a separate entity.

Rulers: 17 Oct. 1821–13 Jan. 1850 same as those for Sierra Leone. *Rulers:* same as those for Sierra Leone.

Bron States see **Akwamu** and **Baule**

Brong-Ahafo see **Ashanti**

Bu Regreg see **Bou Regreg**

Bubi see **Fernando Po**

Buchanan see **Bassa Cove** and **Liberia** and **Petit Dieppe**

Buduu see **Nkore**

Buganda. 1395–26 Dec. 1890. *Location:* in Uganda. *Capital:* Nabulagala (1882–1890); Lubaga (1880–1882); Kikandwa (1879–1880); Lubaga (1875–1879); Kabodha (1872–1875); Nabulagala (1870–1872); Nnakawa (1865–1870); Bbanda (1862–1865); Nakatema (1860–1862); Nabulagala (1856–1860); Mulago (1850–1856); Mengo (until 1850). *Other names:* Kingdom of Uganda.

History: For centuries Buganda was a native kingdom dominated by Bunyoro, but in the 16th and 17th centuries it gradually broke free. In 1862 John Hanning Speke was the first white man into Buganda. It had been only 12 years since King Mutesa I had even heard such a race. In 1874 General Gordon, then the governor of Equatoria Province in the Egyptian Sudan, attempted to bring Buganda and Bunyoro into his political realm, but the British government prevented this. In the 1870s Buganda became a battleground between the Anglicans and Muslims from Zanzibar, both of whom were trying to save Mutesa's soul. And, in 1879 the Catholics joined the battle. Under Mutesa's tyrannical son, Mwanga, not only were all these religions terribly persecuted, but they all fought among themselves. With this obsession about religion dominating the thoughts and actions of the people of Buganda, and with Karl Peters and his German adventurers threatening the country with annexation, the British moved in. In 1890 Buganda was taken over by Britain, as a fundamental part of Uganda, although the kings of Buganda continued to have influence on local chiefs and in the administration of the colony, until the monarchy was abolished in 1967. In 1993 the Ugandan government restored the kingdom, but only as a ceremonial institution.

Kabakas (Kings): 1395–1408 Kintu; 1408–1420 Cwa I Nabaka; 1420–1447 Kimera; 1447–1474 Tembo; 1474–1501 Kiggala; 1501–1528 Kiyimbo; 1528–1555 Kayima; 1555–1582 Nakibinge; 1582–1609 Mulundo and Jemba and Suna I (all jointly); 1609–1636 Sekamanya and Kimbugwe (jointly); 1636–1663 Katerrega; 1663–1690 Mutebi and Kayemba (jointly); 1690–1717 Tebandeke and Ndawula (jointly); 1717–1744 Kagulu and Mawanda and Kikulwe (all jointly); 1744–1771 Kagulu and Namagula and Kyabaggu (all jointly); 1771–1798 Junju and Semakookiru (jointly); 1798–1825 Kamanya; 1825–1852 Suna II; 1852–10 Oct. 1884 Mutesa I Walugembe Makaobya; 10 Oct. 1884–1888 Danieri Mwanga;

1888–Oct. 1888 Mutebi II Kiwena; Oct. 1888–Oct. 1889 Kalema; Oct. 1889–July 1897 Danieri Mwanga; July 1897–Nov. 1897 no king ruled; Nov. 1897–20 Nov. 1939 Daudi Cwa II; 20 Nov. 1929–30 Nov. 1953 Mutesa II; 30 Nov. 1953–17 Oct. 1955 tribe unrecognized; 17 Oct. 1955–24 May 1966 Mutesa II; 8 May 1966–8 Sept. 1967 [vacant].

Bugio see **Madeira**

Bugisu see **Nkore**

Bukedi see **Nkore**

Bulala see **Bornu Empire** and **Kanem**

Bumpe. 1820–1888. *Location:* in Sierra Leone. *Capital:* Bumpe.

History: The Caulker family had ruled Banana Island until it fell under British rule in Sierra Leone. The Caulkers moved to Bumpe, which they ruled until 1888, when it also became part of Sierra Leone.

Kings: 1820–1832 Thomas Caulker; 1832–1842 Charles Caulker; 1842–1857 Canreba; 1857–1864 Thomas Theophilus Caulker; 1864–1888 Richard Canreba Caulker; 1888–1895 [vacant]; 1895–1898 Richard Canreba Caulker; 1898–1901 [vacant]; 1901–(?) James Canreba Caulker.

Bunce Island see **Sierra Leone**

Bunyoro. ca. 1400–30 July 1896. *Location:* between Lake Victoria and Lake Albert, in Uganda. *Capital:* Mparo. *Other names:* Unyoro Kingdom.

History: Founded by northern invaders the kingdom became pre-eminent in the area. Finally, by the 18th century, it lost sway to Buganda. In 1896 it became absorbed into the British protectorate of Uganda, by having "protection" thrust upon it. It became part of the Western Province of Uganda. As with Buganda, the monarchy was abolished in 1967. In 1993 the Ugandan government restored the monarchy, but only as a ceremonial institution.

Omukamas (Kings): ca. 1400–(?) Isingoma Mpuga Rukidi; (?)–(?) Ochaki Rwangira; (?)–(?) Oyo Nyimba; (?)–(?) Winyi I Rubembeka; (?)–(?) Olimi I Kalimbi; (?)–ca. 1550 Nyabongo I Rulemu; ca. 1550–ca. 1580 Winyi II Ruban-giramasega; ca. 1580–(?) Olimi II Ruhundwangeye; (?)–(?) Nyarwa Omuzarra Kyaro; (?)–(?) Cwa I Mali Rumoma Mahanga. *Queens:* (?)–(?) Mashamba. *Okumakas (Kings):* (?)–(?) Kyebambe I Omuzikiya; (?)–ca. 1710 Winyi III Ruguruka; ca. 1710–(?) Nyaika and Kyebambe II Bikaju (jointly); (?)–1731 Olimi III Isansa; 1731–1782 Duhaga I Cwa Mujwiga; 1782–1786 Olimi IV Kasoma; 1786–1835 Kyebambe III Nyamutukura; 1835–1848 Nyabongo II Mugenyi; 1848–1852 Olimi V Rwakabale; 1852–1869 Kyebambe IV (also known as Kamurasi); 1869–1870 Kabigumere; 1870–1898 Cwa II Kabarega; 1898–1902 Kitahimbwa Karukare; 1902–1924 Duhaga II Bisereko; 1924–8 Sept. 1967 Winyi IV Gafabusa.

Burkina Faso. 20 Feb. 1895– . *Location:* in North west Africa, essentially north of Ghana and south of Mali. *Capital:* Ouagadougou (also known as `Wagadugu, and founded as a town about 1050). *Other names:* Burkina; the Republic of Burkina Faso; Haute-Volta, or Upper Volta (1895–1984).

History: In 1895 the French placed a protectorate over Yatenga, and Gwiriko in the Volta region of Northwest Africa, and called the new territory the protectorate of Haute Volta (also known as Upper Volta). On 13 Sept. 1896 the French occupied Wagadugu and brought it into the protectorate in 1897, as was Gurma, who had asked for French protection, and the lands of the Bobo and of the Lobi. The Lobi, however, were not so willing, and with their poisoned arrows wreaked havoc among the French troops until they were finally subdued in 1903. An Anglo-French convention fixed the boundaries between the new protectorate and the British Northern Territories of the Gold Coast. The new protectorate was ruled by the military, and they employed their usual administrative decisions called "cercles," while keeping the chiefs in power locally. On 18 Oct. 1904 Haute Volta became part of the new French colony of Upper Senegal and Niger (which would eventually become Mali). On 1 March 1919 a large piece of Upper Senegal and Niger was carved out to form the new colony of Haute Volta. This new colony consisted of the areas of Bobo Dioulasso, Ouagadougou, Gurma (also known as Fada N'Gourma), Say, Dedougou, Gaoua, and Dori. Later in 1919 a governor was appointed to administer this colony, but on 5 Sept. 1932 (effective as from 1 Jan.

1933) Haute Volta was dismembered by the French, being split up between the French Sudan (the old Upper Senegal and Niger and the future Mali), which got Ouahigouya and parts of Dori and Dedougou; the colony of Niger, which got Fada (formerly called Gurma, or Fada N'Gourma) and the other part of Dori; and the protectorate of the Ivory Coast, which got the rest in a lump called Haute Côte d'Ivoire (also known as Upper Ivory Coast). On 4 Sept. 1947 the old colony of Haute Volta was re-established as the Overseas Territory of Haute Volta, with its own territorial assembly. On 11 Dec. 1958 it became an autonomous republic, called the Voltaic Republic, or La République de Haute Volta (Upper Volta), on the way to independence. In 1959 Haute Volta, Dahomey, the Ivory Coast and Niger formed a loose political and economic union called the Sahel-Bénin Union. Independence finally arrived on 5 Aug. 1960. A pro–French government was elected, and in Sept. 1962 Haute Volta became a member of the United Nations. In 1980 the military took over the country. On 5 Aug. 1984 the Republic of Upper Volta changed its name to Burkina Faso, a name meaning "country of honest men." In 1986 Thomas Sankara, the president, declared it a "jamahiriyya" (i.e. a Muslim republic), and in 1987 another coup, in which Sankara was killed, placed Campaoré in power. The country has been beset by ethnic wars, widespread poverty, one coup after another, droughts, and strained relations with its neighbors. It went to war with Mali in 1974 and again in 1985.

Commandants: 20 Feb. 1895–June 1898 Georges Destenave; June 1898–18 Oct. 1904 Col. Crane. [ruled between 18 Oct. 1904 and 9 Nov. 1919 by the lieutenant-governors of the colony of Upper Senegal and Niger]. *Lieutenant-Governors:* 9 Nov. 1919–6 Aug. 1921 Édouard Hesling (appointed 16 May 1919); 6 Aug. 1921–26 May 1922 Louis Fousset (acting); 26 May 1922–9 May 1924 Édouard Hesling; 9 May 1924–10 Dec. 1924 Louis Fousset (acting); 10 Dec. 1924–May 1926 Édouard Hesling; May 1926–Nov. 1926 Louis Fousset (acting); Nov. 1926–7 Aug. 1927 Édouard Hesling; 7 Aug. 1927–13 Jan. 1928 Robert Arnaud (acting); 13 Jan. 1928–10 Jan. 1929 Albéric Fournier; 10 Jan. 1929–1 Dec. 1929 Louis Fousset (acting); 1 Dec. 1929–20 Jan. 1930 Henri Chessé (acting); 20 Jan. 1930–1 Aug. 1930 Albéric Fournier; 1 Aug. 1930–20 Jan. 1931 François Bernard (acting); 20

Jan. 1931–22 Dec. 1932 Albéric Fournier; 22 Dec. 1932–31 Dec. 1932 Gabriel Descemet. *Administrators:* 31 Dec. 1932–1 Jan. 1933 Henri Chessé (acting). [ruled between 1 Jan. 1933 and 4 Sept. 1947 as described above]. *Administrators:* 4 Sept. 1947–29 April 1948 Gaston Mourgues (acting). *Governors:* 29 April 1948–22 March 1950 Albert Mouragues; 22 March 1950–Oct. 1950 Lucien Geay (acting); Oct. 1950–25 April 1952 Albert Mouragues; 25 April 1952–Oct. 1952 Roland Pré (acting); Oct. 1952–23 Feb. 1953 Albert Mouragues; 23 Feb. 1953–3 Nov. 1956 Salvador-Jean Etcheber; 3 Nov. 1956–15 July 1958 Yvon Bourges; 15 July 1958–11 Dec. 1958 Max Berthet (acting). *High Commissioners:* 11 Dec. 1958–Feb. 1959 Max Berthet; Feb. 1959–5 Aug. 1960 Paul Masson. *Presidents:* 11 Dec. 1959–5 Aug. 1960 Maurice Yaméogo; 5 Aug. 1960–8 Dec. 1960 [country run by Maurice Yaméogo, now styled Prime Minister]; 8 Dec. 1960–3 Jan. 1966 Maurice Yaméogo. *Chiefs of State:* 3 Jan. 1966–13 Feb. 1971 Sangoulé Lamizana. *Presidents:* 13 Feb. 1971–25 Nov. 1980 Sangoulé Lamizana. *Heads of the Military Committee of Recovery:* 25 Nov. 1980–7 Nov. 1982 Saye Zerbo. *Chairmen of the Provisional Committee of Popular Salvation:* 7 Nov. 1982–4 Aug. 1983 Jean-Baptiste Ouedraogo. *Chairmen of the National Revolutionary Council:* 4 Aug. 1983–4 Aug. 1984 Thomas Sankara. *Heads of State:* 4 Aug. 1984–15 Oct. 1987 Thomas Sankara; 15 Oct. 1987–Blaise Campaoré. *Prime Ministers:* 27 April 1958–8 Dec. 1960 Maurice Yaméogo; 16 July 1978–25 Nov. 1980 Joseph Conombo; 10 Jan. 1983–17 May 1983 Thomas Sankara; 16 June 1992–20 March 1994 Youssouf Ouedraogo; 20 March 1994–6 Feb. 1996 Marc-Christian Kaboré; 6 Feb. 1996–6 Nov. 2000 Kadré Desiré Ouedraogo; 7 Nov. 2000–Paramanga Yonli. *Note:* In times of no Prime Minister, the President or Head of State held that office, except in the peculiar reversal of this situation with Yaméogo in 1960 (see above).

Burundi [i]. ca. 1675–6 April 1903. *Location:* as the Burundi of today. *Capital:* Usumbura (today's Bujumbura).

History: Originally, and possibly before the 14th century, the Tutsi from Ethiopia invaded the area that is now Burundi, and conquered the Hutu. About 1675 the Tutsi king Ntare I built a kingdom there, and during his reign conquered the areas of Nkoma, Bututsi, Kilimiro, and

Buyenzi. Conquest and internecine struggles marked the history of Burundi until it became part of the protectorate of German East Africa in 1903, even though the Germans never really ruled the area (cf. Ruanda). After World War I Burundi's fate was inexorably bound up with that of Ruanda (see Ruanda–Urundi).

Bami (Kings; Bami is the plural of Mwami): ca. 1675–ca. 1705 Ntare I Rushatse; ca. 1705–ca. 1725 Mwezi I; ca. 1725–ca. 1760 Ntare II Kivimira; ca. 1760–ca. 1768 Mwezi II; ca. 1768–ca. 1795 Mwambutsa I; ca. 1795–1810 Mutaga I Seenyamwiiza; 1810–1852 Ntare II Rugaamba; 1852–21 Aug. 1908 Mwezi II Kisabo; 21 Aug. 1908–10 Nov. 1915 Mutaga II; 16 Dec. 1915–8 July 1966 Mwambutsa II; 8 July 1966–28 Nov. 1966 Ntare III Ndiziye (also known as Charles Ndiziye).

Burundi [ii]. 1959– . *Location:* east central Africa. *Capital:* Bujumbura. *Other names:* République du Burundi, or Republic of Burundi (1966–); Kingdom of Burundi (1961–1966); Urundi (alternative name, 1961–1962).

History: In 1959 the Belgian Trust Territory of Ruanda–Urundi was officially divided into two component parts — Rwanda and Burundi. On 26 Jan. 1961 Burundi formed a local government, and on 29 Sept. 1961 was given limited self-rule as the Kingdom of Burundi, being ruled by the Tutsi minority who had, as in Ruanda, ruled nominally throughout foreign occupation. On 1 July 1962, on the breaking up of the Trust Territory, the Kingdom of Burundi became fully independent of Belgium (see also Rwanda). On 28 Nov. 1966 Burundi became a republic, and the monarchy was abolished. There was a Hutu rebellion (i.e. the majority Hutu rebelling against the minority Tutsi government) in 1972–1973, which decimated 10,000 Tutsi and 15,000 Hutu (conservative count). Over 100,000 Hutu are reported to have fled the country for Tanzania and Zaire. In the 1980s the government decided to allow free elections, and as a quite natural consequence, a Hutu (Melchior Ndadaye) was elected president. He was killed in an attempted coup, however, on 21 Oct. 1993. There was much inter-tribal violence in the wake of this assassination, and over 150,000 Burundians died. While the bloodbath was going on, the president of Burundi, Cyprien Ntaryamira, and the president of Rwanda, were killed in a mysterious plane crash on 6 April 1994. This led to a fantastic scene of massacres and outrageous violence in Rwanda. This left the Burundian carnage looking pale in comparison, but the Burundians tried to catch up with the Rwandans in this regard in 1995. There was a military coup in Burundi on 25 July 1996, and for the next several years neighbors imposed sanctions on Burundi. There were two failed coups in 2001. With poverty and AIDS as only two of the major pressing problems, the situation remained explosive. *Mwamis (Kings):* (see preceding entry, Burundi [i] for king list).

Governors of Ruanda-Urundi: 29 Sept. 1961–1 July 1962 Jean-Paul Harroy. *Presidents:* 28 Nov. 1966–1 Nov. 1976 Michel Micombero. *Heads of the Supreme Council of the Revolution:* 9 Nov. 1976–Jan. 1980 Jean-Baptiste Bagaza. *Presidents:* Jan. 1980–3 Sept. 1987 Jean-Baptiste Bagaza. *Leaders of the Military Committee for National Salvation:* 3 Sept. 1987–9 Sept. 1987 Pierre Buyoya. *Presidents:* 9 Sept. 1987–10 July 1993 Pierre Buyoya; 10 July 1993–21 Oct. 1993 Melchior Ndadaye; 21 Oct. 1993–27 Oct. 1993 François Ngeze; 27 Oct. 1993–5 Feb. 1994 Sylvio Kinigi (acting); 5 Feb. 1994–6 April 1994 Cyprien Ntaryamina; 8 April 1994–1 Oct. 1994 Sylvestre Ntibantunganya (acting); 1 Oct. 1994–25 July 1996 Sylvestre Ntibantunganya; 25 July 1996–11 June 1998 Pierre Buyoya (interim); 11 June 1998–30 April 2003 Pierre Buyoya; 30 April 2003–19 Aug. 2005 Domitien Ndayizeye; 19 Aug. 2005–Pierre Nkurunziza. *Prime Ministers:* 26 Jan. 1961–28 Sept. 1961 Joseph Cimpaye; 29 Sept. 1961–13 Oct. 1961 Prince Louis Rwagasore; 20 Oct. 1961–10 June 1963 Chief André Muhirwa; 17 June 1963–1 April 1964 Pierre Ngendamdumwe; 1 April 1964–7 Jan. 1965 Albin Nyamoya; 7 Jan. 1965–15 Jan. 1965 Pierre Ngendamdumwe; 15 Jan. 1965–25 Jan. 1965 Pie Masumboko (acting); 25 Jan. 1965–30 Sept. 1965 Joseph Bamina; 1 Oct. 1965–9 July 1966 Léopold Biha; 13 July 1966–28 Nov. 1966 Michel Micombero; 14 July 1972–6 June 1973 Albin Nyamoya; 13 Nov. 1976–Jan. 1980 Édouard Nzambimana; 19 Oct. 1988–10 July 1993 Adrien Sibomana; 10 July 1993–7 Feb. 1994 Sylvio Kinigi; 7 Feb. 1994–22 Feb. 1995 Anatole Kanyenkiko; 22 Feb. 1995–31 July 1996 Antoine Nduwayo; 31 July 1996–12 June 1998 Pascal Firmin Ndimira. *Note:* in times of no Prime Minister, the President or Head of State held that office.

Bushmen see **Cape Colony** and **Namibia**

Busoga see Uganda

Bututsi see Burundi [i]

Buyenzi see Burundi [i]

Byzacena. 297–442. *Location:* southern Tunisia. *Capital:* Hadrumatum. *Other names:* Byzacium.

History: in 297 Diocletian reformed the Roman Empire, and out of the Province of Africa (see Africa [i]) were created three new provinces: Africa (see Africa [ii]), Tripolitania, and Byzacena. From about 395 Byzacena came under the Prefecture of Italy (Subdivision: Diocese of Africa), and in 442 it all went to the Vandals (see Vandal North Africa).

Rulers: 297–442 [unknown].

Byzantine North Africa. April 534–647; 649–667; 697–703. *Location:* North Africa (i.e. Libya, Tunisia, and Algeria). *Capital:* Carthage.

History: In 533 the Byzantine general, Belisarius, acting for the emperor Justinian, invaded Vandal North Africa, and a year later had taken all former Vandal territory there. An administration was set up under a prefect, and it took 12 years to pacify the country. Over the years Constantinople lost interest in North Africa, due to pressing problems closer to home, and also because of the gross corruption that was rampant throughout the North African administration. In 647 the Arabs invaded and captured the Byzantine territory (see Arab North Africa). They were bought off, however, and Byzantine rule returned in 649. The whole country alternated between Arabs and Byzantines until 703, when North Africa became, finally, an Arab land.

Prefects: April 534–May 534 Archelaus. *Military Commanders:* May 534–Sept. 534 Belisarius; Sept. 534–535 Salomon. *Prefects:* 535–Dec. 536 Salomon; Dec. 536–Dec. 536 Symmachus. *Military Commanders:* Dec. 536–539 Germanus. *Prefects:* 539–543 Salomon; 544–Dec. 545 Areobindus; Dec. 545–May 546 Athanasius. *Military Commanders:* May 546–546 Artabanus; 546–Sept. 552 Johannes Troglita. *Prefects:* Sept. 552–555 Paulus; 555–Oct. 558 Boethius; Oct. 558–Dec. 562 Johannes Troglita. *Military Commanders:* Dec. 562–June 563 Johannes Rogathinos. *Prefects:* June 563–563 Areobindus. *Military Commanders:* 563–565 Marcianus. *Prefects:* 565–565 Thomas; 565–569 Lucius Mappius. *Military Commanders:* 569–

May 570 Theodorus; May 570–571 Theoctistus; 571–574 Amabilis; 574–578 [unknown]. *Prefects:* 578–578 Thomas. *Military Commanders:* 578–578 Gennadius; 578–Aug. 582 Vitalius. *Prefects:* Aug. 582–590 Theodorus; 590–July 591 Johannes; July 591–594 Gennadius. *Exarchs:* 594–Oct. 598 Pantaleon; Oct. 598–July 600 Gennadius. *Prefects:* July 600–602 Innocentius. *Exarchs:* 602–611 Heraclius; 611–614 [unknown]; 614–617 Caesarius; 617–619 [unknown]; 619–June 627 Nicetas. *Prefects:* June 627–633 Gregorius. *Exarchs:* 633–641 Petrus. *Prefects:* 641–July 645 Gregorius. *Exarchs:* July 645–647 Gregorius. [Arab rule, 647–649]. *Byzantine Rulers:* 649–667 [unknown]. [Arab rule, 667–697]. *Byzantine Governors:* 697–703 Johannes.

Cabinda see Angola

Cabo Verde see Cape Verde

Cacheu. 1614–1879. *Location:* in the northern part of Guinea-Bissau, at the mouth of the Cacheu River. *Capital:* Cacheu.

History: Nuno Tristão, the Portuguese discoverer, was probably the first to visit the area which is today Guinea-Bissau, in 1446. By 1588 it had been settled from the Cape Verde Islands, and in 1614 an administration was begun, subject to the Cape Verde government. In 1640 it became a captaincy, answerable to Lisbon. In 1676 the short-lived Cacheu Company was granted a trade monopoly in the area by the Portuguese government. In 1687 Bissau was founded to the south, and in 1696 became a captaincy of its own, but maintained by a second Cacheu Company. In 1703 the Cacheu Company's contract was canceled, and Bissau was abandoned temporarily. By 1850 Cacheu had lost its importance as a captaincy, and in 1879 the area, along with Bissau and others, merged into Portuguese Guinea, and Cacheu became a municipality within the new country.

Administrators: 1614–ca. 1615 João de Sousa; ca. 1615–ca. 1616 Baltasar de Castelo Branco; ca. 1616–ca. 1622 [unknown]; ca. 1622–(?) Francisco de Távora; (?)–ca. 1625 [unknown]; ca. 1625–(?) Francisco Sodré Pereira; (?)–ca. 1633 [unknown]; (?)–1634 Francisco Nunes de Andrade; 1634–(?) Paulo da Silva; (?)–ca. 1640 Manuel da Silva Botelho. *Capitães-Mores (Captains-Major):* ca. 1640–1641 Luis de Magalhães; 1641–1644 [unknown]; 1644–1649 Gonçalo de

Gamboa Ayala; 1649–1650 Gaspar Vogado; 1650–1654 João Fidalgo; 1654–1655 [unknown]; 1655–(?) Francisco da Cunha; (?)–1658 [unknown]; 1658–1662 Manuel Contrim; 1662–1664 Antonio Ornelas; 1664–(?) João Moutinho; (?)–(?) Manuel de Almeida; (?)–(?) Ambrosio Gomes; (?)–ca. 1674 [unknown]; ca. 1674–(?) Sebastião da Rosa; (?)–1676 [unknown]; 1676–1682 Antonio Bezerra; 1682–1685 Gaspar Pacheco; 1685–1686 João de Oliveira; 1686–1687 [unknown]; 1687–1688 Antonio Bezerra; 1688–1689 Rodrigo da Fonseca; 1689–1690 José da Câmara; 1690–1691 Domingos de Carvalho; 1691–1707 Santos Castanho; 1707–(?) Paulo de Abreu e Lima; (?)–1715 [unknown]; 1715–1718 Antonio Bezerra, Jr.; 1718–(?) Inacio Ferreira; (?)–ca. 1721 [unknown]; ca. 1721–(?) Antonio Bezerra, Jr.; (?)–ca. 1723 [unknown]; ca. 1723–(?) Pedro de Barros; (?)–ca. 1726 [unknown]; ca. 1726–(?) Manuel Lobo; (?)–ca. 1729 [unknown]; ca. 1729–1731 João Perestrelo; 1731–(?) Antonio Bezerra, Jr.; (?)–1733 [unknown]; 1733–ca. 1734 João de Carvalho; ca. 1734–ca. 1737 [unknown]; ca. 1737–(?) Damião de Bastos; (?)–ca. 1741 [unknown]; ca. 1741–(?) Nicolau Pino de Araújo; (?)–1748 [unknown]; 1748–1751 João de Távora; 1751–ca. 1755 Francisco Souto-Maior; ca. 1755–ca. 1765 [unknown]; ca. 1765–1770 Sebastião Souto-Maior; 1770–1775 [unknown]; 1775–(?) Antonio Vaz de Araújo; (?)–1785 Antonio de Meneses; 1785–1786 João Barreto; 1786–(?) Luis de Araújo e Silva; (?)–1798 [unknown]; 1798–(?) Lopo Henriques; (?)–1800 [unknown]; 1800–(?) Manuel de Gouveia; (?)–ca. 1802 [unknown]; ca. 1802–1803 José Torvão; 1803–(?) João Pinto; (?)–1811 [unknown]; 1811–1814 Joaquim de Figueiredo e Góis; 1814–1815 [unknown]; 1815–(?) João Goodolfim; (?)–1819 João de Meneses Drumont; 1819–1820 [unknown]; 1820–ca. 1820 [unknown]; ca. 1820–1821 José Correia de Barros; 1821–(?) João de Araújo Gomes; (?)–1823 [unknown]; 1823–ca. 1825 João Goodolfim; ca. 1825–ca. 1826 [unknown]; ca. 1826–(?) Antonio Santos; (?)–ca. 1835 [unknown]; ca. 1835–(?) José Ferreira; (?)–1838 [unknown]; 1838–(?) Delfim dos Santos; (?)–1842 [unknown]; 1842–1844 Antonio Chaves; 1844–1846 José do Crato; 1846–1847 Honorio Barreto; 1847–ca. 1849 José do Crato; ca. 1849–1879 [unknown].

Calabar see **New Calabar**

Calbaria see **New Calabar**

Caldwell see **Liberia**

Cameroons. 4 March 1916–1 Oct. 1954. *Location:* in eastern Nigeria, on the border with Cameroun. *Capital:* Lagos (in Nigeria); Buea (local headquarters). *Other names:* British Cameroons; West Cameroon; West Cameroons; Western Cameroon; British Cameroon (the name Cameroun comes from "Rio de Camarões" meaning "River of Prawns," the name given by the early Portuguese explorers to the Wouri River Estuary).

History: In 1916 the French-British Condominium of Cameroun (also known as Cameroon, or Cameroons) (see Kamerun) was divided up between the French and the British. The British got the western part, one-fifth of the whole, and bordering Nigeria, and it was attached to the Eastern Provinces of Nigeria, and divided into three districts. The French got the eastern four-fifths. The French part became known as Cameroun, and the British as Cameroons. On 28 June 1919, at the Treaty of Versailles, France and Britain were granted League of Nations mandates over their respective territories in Cameroun/Cameroons (cf. Togo). This became effective on 22 July 1920. On 13 Dec. 1946 both French Cameroun and the British Cameroons became United Nations Trust Territories, and from this point the fortunes of the two countries differ more than they had in the past. While French Cameroun went through the de-colonialization process to become the republic it is today, the British Cameroons was joined to Nigeria on 1 Oct. 1954, where it became one of the autonomous regions of that country. It was then divided into Northern Cameroons and Southern Cameroons. In February 1961 Southern Cameroons voted to become part of the French-speaking Republic of Cameroun, and on 1 Oct. 1961 did so, while the Northern Cameroons had voted to become an integral part of Nigeria, which happened on 1 June 1961. British Cameroons then followed the destiny of Nigeria.

Rulers: 4 March 1916–1949 Ruled from Lagos, Nigeria. *Special Residents:* 1949–1 Oct. 1954 Edward Gibbons.

Cameroun. 4 March 1916– . *Location:* northwest Africa, between Nigeria and Gabon. *Capital:* Yaoundé (founded in 1888, it was the capital from 1946); Douala (1940–1946); Yaoundé

(1922–1940); Douala (1916–1922). *Other names:* East Cameroon; East Cameroons; French Cameroon; French Cameroons; Cameroun Français (1916–1954); République du Cameroun, or Republic of Cameroun (from 1984); United Republic of Cameroun (1972–1984); Federal Republic of Cameroun (1961–1972); Republic of Cameroun (1960–1961); Autonomous Republic of Cameroun (1959–1960); Cameroun Trust Territory (1946–1959); Cameroun Mandate (1921–1946); Cameroun Territory (1916–1921).

History: In 1916 the French-British Condominium of Cameroun was divided up into the French part and the British. The French got the majority of it (see Cameroons for more details of this division). On 22 July 1920 the area became a League of Nations Mandate, and on 23 March 1921 French Cameroun was given a degree of autonomy. On 13 Dec. 1946 it became a United Nations Trust Territory. On 1 Jan. 1959 Cameroun became an autonomous republic within the French Community, and on 1 Jan. 1960 it became fully independent as the Republic of Cameroun. In February 1961 the autonomous region of Southern Cameroons in Nigeria voted to become part of the new Republic of Cameroun, and the country became known as the Federal Republic of Cameroun on 1 Oct. 1961. This created a federal government which consisted of two parts, East and West Cameroun, the East being French-speaking and the West being English-speaking. The President was to be French- and the Vice-President English-speaking. On 2 June 1972 the country became the United Republic of Cameroun, but on 21 Jan. 1984 President Paul Biya discarded this name and the country reverted to the name Republic of Cameroun. There was a coup attempt that year, and a national strike in 1990. There has been strained relations with Nigeria over oil, corruption, rigged elections, and there are problematic separatist movements, but AIDS and poverty remain the major problems.

Governors: 4 March 1916–8 Oct. 1916 Joseph Aymerich; 8 Oct. 1916–6 March 1919 Lucien Fourneau; 6 March 1919–7 Dec. 1919 Jules Carde (acting); 7 Dec. 1919–Oct. 1920 Jules Carde; Oct. 1920–23 March 1921 Auguste Bonnecarrère (acting). *Commissioners:* 23 March 1921–24 April 1921 Auguste Bonnecarrère (acting); 24 April 1921–March 1923 Jules Carde; March 1923–29 April 1923 Albéric Fournier (acting); 29 April 1923–27 Dec. 1924 Théodore Marchand; 27 Dec. 1924–11 May 1925 Ernest Bleu (acting); 11 May 1925–2 March 1926 Théodore Marchand; 2 March 1926–31 Oct. 1926 Ernest Bleu (acting); 31 Oct. 1926–26 April 1929 Théodore Marchand; 26 April 1929–26 Oct. 1929 Ernest Bleu (acting); 26 Oct. 1929–19 June 1931 Théodore Marchand; 19 June 1931–6 Feb. 1932 Ernest Bleu (acting); 6 Feb. 1932–31 Aug. 1932 Théodore Marchand; 31 Aug. 1932–22 Sept. 1932 Auguste Bonnecarrère (acting); 22 Sept. 1932–7 July 1934 Auguste Bonnecarrère; 7 July 1934–1936 Jules Repiquet; 1936–Jan. 1937 Gaston Guibet (acting); Jan. 1937–7 Oct. 1937 Pierre-François Boissons; 7 Oct. 1937–9 March 1938 Pierre Aubert (acting); 9 March 1938–16 Nov. 1938 Pierre-François Boissons; 16 Nov. 1938–29 Aug. 1940 Richard Brunot. *Governors:* 29 Aug. 1940–12 Nov. 1940 Philippe Leclerc de Hauteclocque; 12 Nov. 1940–20 July 1943 Pierre Cournarie; 20 July 1943–15 Nov. 1944 Hubert Carras; 15 Nov. 1944–16 Jan. 1946 Henri Nicolas; 16 Jan. 1946–16 March 1946 Alexis Leger (acting). *High Commissioners:* 16 March 1946–25 March 1947 Robert Delavignette; 25 March 1947–April 1947 Robert Casimir (acting); April 1947–7 July 1949 René Hoffherr; 7 July 1949–10 Jan. 1950 Robert Casimir (acting); 10 Jan. 1950–2 Dec. 1954 Jean-Louis Soucadaux; 2 Dec. 1954–17 April 1956 Roland Pré; 17 April 1956–29 Jan. 1958 Pierre Messmer; 29 Jan. 1958–19 Feb. 1958 Jean-Paul Ramadier; 19 Feb. 1958–1 Jan. 1960 Xavier Torré. *Presidents:* 5 May 1960–6 Nov. 1982 Ahmadou Ahidjo; 6 Nov. 1982–Paul Biya. *Prime Ministers:* 15 May 1957–18 Feb. 1958 André-Marie Mbida; 18 Feb. 1958–5 May 1960 Ahmadou Ahidjo; 14 May 1960–1 Oct. 1961 Charles Assalé. *Prime Ministers of East Cameroun:* 1 Oct. 1961–June 1965 Charles Assalé; June 1965–20 Nov. 1965 Vincent de Paul Ahanda; 20 Nov. 1965–2 June 1972 Simon Tchoungi. *Prime Ministers of West Cameroun:* 1 Oct. 1961–11 Jan. 1968 John Foncha; 11 Jan. 1968–2 June 1972 Solomon Tandeng. *Prime Ministers:* 30 June 1975–6 Nov. 1982 Paul Biya; 6 Nov. 1982–22 Aug. 1983 Bello Bouba Maigari; 22 Aug. 1983–21 Jan. 1984 Luc Ayang; 26 April 1991–9 April 1992 Sadou Hayatou; 9 April 1992–19 Sept. 1996 Simon Achidi Achu; 19 Sept. 1996–8 Dec. 2004 Peter Mafani Musonge; 8 Dec. 2004–Ephraim Inoni. *Note:* In times of no Prime Minister, the President held that office.

Campbell Lands see **Cornelis Kok's Land**

Canary Islands. No dates. *Location:* seven main islands and six islets off the Atlantic coast of Morocco. The islands are: Gran Canaria, Tenerife, Lanzarote, Hierro, Fuerteventura, La Palma, and Gomera. Three of the islets are inhabited — Alegranza, Graciosa, and Lobos. *Capital:* Las Palmas (founded in 1478, and named for the palms in the area. The capital from 1480); Acatife (1405–1480). *Other names:* Islas Canarias (named for the large number of big dogs on the islands in the ancient days, the Roman word "canis" meaning "dog"); The Canaries; Fortunate Islands (pre–1405 name).

History: The Romans knew of the Canary Islands, but during the Dark Ages they became legendary in Europe, even though the Arabs were trading there from the end of the 10th century. Many Europeans visited there in the 13th and 14th centuries, and found that the Guanches and Canarios were the local people of the Fortunate Islands (as they were then called by the Europeans). These peoples, of Berber stock, were exterminated by the Spanish from the time of Juan de Béthencourt's systematic conquest of the islands in 1404 and 1405. De Béthencourt established a regal dynasty in the Canaries (as they were renamed) on the orders of Henry III of Castile, returning to Spain in Dec. 1406 leaving his nephew Maciot in charge. Maciot, however, was such a bad ruler that Queen Catherine of Castile forced him to sell his royal office to the Queen's envoy, Pedro Barba de Campos. However, Maciot went to Lisbon, where he sold it again, this time to Prince Henry of Portugal. A few years later he sold it yet again, this time to Enrique de Guzmán, Count of Niebla. When he died in 1422, Juan de Béthencourt, the original proprietor, left the islands (although he had no right to do so) to his brother Reynaud. As for de Guzmán, he later sold the kingdom to Guillén Peraza, a Spanish nobleman, whose heirs were persuaded to sell to Ferdinand and Isabella of Spain in 1476. Prince Henry and Portugal claimed the islands on and off until 1479, having bought the kingdom, and having pacified the island of Gomera between 1420 and 1479. But, in 1479, they recognized Spain's claim to the Canaries. In 1480 Gran Canaria, the only island of the group really "civilized" by that year, became a Spanish colony in its own right, and in 1483 a few straggling Guanche survivors surrendered to the Spanish. La Palma was conquered in 1491, and in 1495 Spain brought Tenerife

under control, and it became the second most important of the Canary Islands. For the history of Gran Canaria between 1480 and 1821 see that entry. For the history of Tenerife between 1495 and 1821 see that entry. In 1589 the Canary Islands as a group became a Spanish captaincy-general, but only for six years, and then in 1595 Gran Canaria and Tenerife again became their own colonies. In 1625, however, the captaincy-general was re-instituted. In 1821 the Canaries became a province of Spain, and in 1912 a protectorate. A movement for autonomy in 1902 had been crushed by the Spanish. In 1927 the islands were split into two separate Spanish provinces — Santa Cruz de Tenerife and Las Palmas de Gran Canaria (and for these see the entries for Gran Canaria and Tenerife respectively). On 16 Aug. 1982 the island group became autonomous.

Rulers: ca. 1350–ca. 1402 Gumidafe (ruled in Gran Canaria); ca. 1402–ca. 1405 Artemi (ruled in Gran Canaria); ca. 1400–ca. 1405 Guarafia (ruled in Lanzarote). *Kings:* 15 Dec. 1405–1415 Maciot de Béthencourt; 1415–1418 Pedro Barba de Campos; 1418–(?) Enrique de Guzmán, Count of Niebla; (?)–(?) Guillén Peraza I; (?)–1444 Guillén Peraza II; 1444–1476 Diego de Herrera; 1476–6 March 1480 [unknown]. *Captains-General:* 1589–1591 Marqués de Bedmar; 1591–1595 [unknown]; 1625–1626 Francisco de Andía Irarrazábal y Zárate; 1626–1629 [unknown]; 1629–1634 Juan de Rivera y Zambrana; 1634–1638 Iñigo de Brizuela y Urbina; 1638–1644 Luis de Córdoba y Arce; 1644–1650 Pedro de Guzmán; 1650–1659 Alfonso Dávila y Guzmán; 1659–1661 Sebastián de Corcuera y Gaviría; 1661–1665 Jerónimo de Quiñones; 1665–1666 Juan de Toledo; 1666–1671 Conde de Puertolano; 1671–1676 Juan Mogrobejo; 1676–1677 [unknown]; 1677–1681 Jerónimo de Velasco; 1681–1685 Conde de Guaro; 1685–1689 Francisco Barahona; 1689–1697 Marqués de Fuensagrada; 1697–1701 Conde del Palmar; 1701–1705 Miguel de Otazo; 1705–1709 Agustín Laurenzana; 1709–1713 Francisco Medina y Salazar; 1713–1718 Ventura de Landaeta y Horna; 1718–1719 José de Chavez y Osorio; 1719–1722 Juan de Mur Aguirre y Argaiz; 1722–1723 [unknown]; 1723–1735 Marqués de Valhermoso; 1735–1741 Francisco Emparan; 1741–1744 Andrés Pignately; 1744–1745 José de Lima; 1745–1746 Luis Salazar; 1746–1747 [unknown]; 1747–1764 Juan de Urbina; 1764–1764 Pedro Moreno y Pérez de Oteyro; 1764–1768 Domingo

Gómez; 1768–1775 Miguel de Heredia; 1775–1779 Marqués de los Tabalosos; 1779–1784 Marqués de la Cáñada Ibáñez; 1784–1789 Marqués de Branciforte; 1789–1791 José de Avellaneda; 1791–1799 Antonio de Otero y Santallana; 1799–1803 José de Perlasca; 1803–1809 Marqués de Casa Cagigal; 1809–1810 Carlos Luján; 1810–1810 Duque del Parque; 1810–1811 Ramón Carvajal; 1811–1820 Pedro de la Buría; 1820–1821 [unknown]. *Administrators:* 1821–1927 [unknown]. *Presidents of the Government:* 8 May 1983–30 July 1987 Jerónimo Saavedra Acevedo; 30 July 1987–28 Dec. 1988 Fernando Fernández Martín; 28 Dec. 1988–11 July 1991 Lorenzo Cullén; 11 July 1991–2 April 1993 Jerónimo Saavedra Acevedo; 2 April 1993–16 July 1999 Manuel Rojas; 16 July 1999–8 July 2003 Román Rodríguez; 8 July 2003–Adán Martín Menis.

Canem see **Kanem**

Cape Colony. 6 April 1652–30 May 1910. *Location:* the southern portion of South Africa. *Capital:* Cape Town (founded by Jan Van Riebeeck on 6 April 1652 as De Kaapsche Vlek, meaning the Cape Hamlet, it had become known as Kaapstad by about 1690. It was referred to as Cape Town by the British by 1773, and this is the name that stuck). *Other names:* Hottentot Hollandia (an early name); Table Bay (an early name); Colony of Cape of Good Hope (1652–1795); The Cape; Cape of Good Hope Province (since 1910).

History: The original inhabitants of the Cape were the San, or Bushmen, and they were pushed out by the Khoikhoi, or Hottentots. In 1487 the Portuguese explorer Dias discovered what he called the Cabo da Boa Esperança (Cape of Good Hope). It was the Hottentots whom the first Europeans encountered when they landed. Over the next 150 years or so there were several landings made by Europeans, and a few settlements were considered, but nothing came of them until the Dutch East India established a settlement at Cape Town in 1652 to serve as a refreshment station for ships en route to the East Indies. This settlement became a colony, and gradually the Cape Colony area widened, taking in the local Bantu chiefdoms. However, by as late as 1691 there were still only 1,000 Europeans at the Cape, mostly Dutch, but also several French Huguenots, some Scandinavians, and a sprinkling of other nationalities, including Asians and some African slaves. The Dutch East India Company ruled the Cape until the British, by the Capitulation of Rustenburg, seized it on 16 Sept. 1795. Technically they held it for the Prince of Orange, and at the end of Britain's war with the Dutch, under the terms of the Treaty of Amiens, they handed it back to the Batavian Government of Holland on 20 Feb. 1803. On 10 Jan. 1806, at the Capitulation of Papendorp, Britain again took the Cape, and on 13 Aug. 1814, it became legally a British colony. It was a reluctant acquisition, being effected only to stop Britain's rivals and enemies from blockading the British path to India. Until 1835 the Cape basically equaled South Africa, in that there were no settlements outside of it. But shortly thereafter came the founding of the Transvaal, Natal, and the Orange River states. It was in the 19th century that Cape Colony did most of its expanding. In 1879 it acquired Fingoland; in 1880 Griqualand West and the diamond fields therein; on 26 Aug. 1885 it annexed Tembuland, in Kaffraria, and in 1886 Bomvanaland. It was the diamond industry that changed Cape Colony, making it immeasurably richer than it had ever been before. On 1 Dec. 1872 the colony achieved a degree of self-rule, and a prime minister was elected. On 30 May 1910 the Cape, Transvaal, Natal and Orange River all joined to form the Union of South Africa. The Cape became a province thereof.

Dutch Commanders: 7 April 1652–6 May 1662 Jan Van Riebeeck; 6 May 1662–27 Sept. 1666 Zacharias Wagenaar; 27 Sept. 1666–18 June 1668 Cornelis Van Quaelbergen; 18 June 1668–25 March 1670 Jacob Borghorst; 25 March 1670–30 Nov. 1671 Pieter Hackius; 30 Nov. 1671–25 March 1672 Coenrad Van Breitenbach (Leader of the Council of Policy); 25 March 1672–2 Oct. 1672 Albert Van Breughel (acting); 2 Oct. 1672–14 March 1676 Isbrand Goske; 14 March 1676–29 June 1678 Johann Bax; 29 June 1678–12 Oct. 1679 Hendrik Crudop (acting); 12 Oct. 1679–1 June 1691 Symon Van Der Stel. *Dutch Governors:* 1 June 1691–11 Feb. 1699 Symon Van Der Stel; 11 Feb. 1699–3 June 1707 Willem Van Der Stel; 3 June 1707–1 Feb. 1708 Johan D'Ableing (acting); 1 Feb. 1708–27 Dec. 1711 Louis Van Assenburgh; 27 Dec. 1711–28 March 1714 Willem Helot (acting); 28 March 1714–Sept. 1724 Pasques de Chavonne; 8 Sept. 1724–25 Feb. 1727 Jan de la Fontaine (acting); 25 Feb. 1727–23 April 1729 Pieter Noodt; 23 April

1729–8 March 1730 Jan de la Fontaine (acting); 8 March 1730–31 Aug. 1737 Jan de la Fontaine; 31 Aug. 1737–19 Sept. 1737 Adriaan Van Kervel; 20 Sept. 1737–14 April 1739 Daniel Van Den Henghel (acting); 14 April 1739–27 Feb. 1751 Hendrik Swellengrebel; 27 Feb. 1751–11 Aug. 1771 Ryk Tulbagh; 12 Aug. 1771–18 May 1774 Joachim Van Plettenberg (acting); 4 Sept. 1772–23 Jan. 1773 Pietre Van Oudtshoorn (died on voyage out); 18 May 1774–14 Feb. 1785 Joachim Van Plettenberg; 14 Feb. 1785–24 June 1791 Cornelis Van De Graaff; 24 June 1791–3 July 1792 Johan Rhenius (acting). *Dutch Commissioners-General:* 3 July 1792–2 Sept. 1793 Sebastian Nederburgh; 3 July 1792–2 Sept. 1793 Simon Frijkenius; 2 Sept. 1793–16 Sept. 1795 Abraham Sluysken. *British Military Commanders:* 16 Sept. 1795–15 Nov. 1795 Admiral Sir George Elphinstone, General Alured Clarke, and General James Craig (jointly). *British Commandants:* 15 Nov. 1795–5 May 1797 General James Craig (knighted 1797). *British Governors:* 5 May 1797–20 Nov. 1798 George, Earl Macartney; 21 Nov. 1798–9 Dec. 1799 Francis Dundas (acting); 10 Dec. 1799–20 April 1801 Sir George Yonge; 20 April 1801–20 Feb. 1803 Lord Glenbervie (did not leave Britain); 20 April 1801–20 Feb. 1803 Francis Dundas (acting). *Batavian Commissioners-General:* 21 Feb. 1803–25 Sept. 1804 Jacob de Mist. *Batavian Governors:* 1 March 1803–10 Jan. 1806 Jan Janssens. *British Governors:* 10 Jan. 1806–17 Jan. 1807 David Baird (acting); 17 Jan. 1807–21 May 1807 Henry Grey (acting); 22 May 1807–4 July 1811 Alexander, Earl of Caledon; 4 July 1811–5 Sept. 1811 Henry Grey (acting); 6 Sept. 1811–18 Oct. 1813 Sir Francis Cradock; 18 Oct. 1813–Jan. 1814 Robert Meade (acting); 7 Jan. 1814–6 April 1814 Sir Francis Cradock; 6 April 1814–12 Jan. 1820 Lord Charles Somerset; 13 Jan. 1820–30 Nov. 1821 Sir Rufane Donkin (acting); 30 Nov. 1821–5 March 1826 Lord Charles Somerset; 5 March 1826–9 Sept. 1828 Richard Bourke (acting); 9 Sept. 1828–10 Aug. 1833 Sir Lowry Cole; 10 Aug. 1833–16 Jan. 1834 Thomas Wade (acting); 16 Jan. 1834–20 Jan. 1835 Sir Benjamin D'Urban; 20 Jan. 1835–30 Dec. 1835 John Bell (acting); 30 Dec. 1835–22 Jan. 1838 Sir Benjamin D'Urban; 22 Jan. 1838–18 March 1844 Sir George Napier; 18 March 1844–10 Oct. 1846 Sir Peregrine Maitland. *High Commissioners/Governors:* 10 Oct. 1846–27 Jan. 1847 Sir Peregrine Maitland; 27 Jan. 1847–1 Dec. 1847 Sir Henry Pottinger; 1

Dec. 1847–31 March 1852 Sir Harry Smith; 31 March 1852–26 May 1854 Sir George Cathcart; 26 May 1854–5 Dec. 1854 Charles Darling (acting); 5 Dec. 1854–20 Aug. 1859 Sir George Grey; 20 Aug. 1859–4 July 1860 Robert Wynyard (acting); 4 July 1860–15 Aug. 1861 Sir George Grey; 15 Aug. 1861–15 Jan. 1862 Robert Wynyard (acting); 15 Jan. 1862–20 May 1870 Sir Philip Wodehouse; 20 May 1870–31 Dec. 1870 Charles Hay (acting); 31 Dec. 1870–31 March 1877 Sir Henry Barkley; 31 March 1877–15 Sept. 1880 Sir Bartle Frere; 15 Sept. 1880–27 Sept. 1880 Henry Clifford (Officer Administering); 27 Sept. 1880–22 Jan. 1881 Sir George Strahan (Officer Administering); 22 Jan. 1881–30 April 1881 Sir Hercules Robinson; 30 April 1881–Aug. 1881 Sir Leicester Smythe (Officer Administering); Aug. 1881–25 April 1883 Sir Hercules Robinson; 25 April 1883–26 March 1884 Sir Leicester Smythe (Officer Administering); 26 March 1884–7 April 1886 Sir Hercules Robinson; 7 April 1886–7 July 1886 Sir Henry Torrens (Officer Administering); 7 July 1886–1 May 1889 Sir Hercules Robinson; 1 May 1889–13 Dec. 1889 Henry Smyth (Officer Administering); 13 Dec. 1889–14 Jan. 1891 Sir Henry Loch; 14 Jan. 1891–1 Dec. 1892 Sir William Cameron (Officer Administering); 1 Dec. 1892–May 1894 Sir Henry Loch; May 1894–July 1894 Sir William Cameron (Officer Administering); July 1894–30 May 1895 Sir Henry Loch; 30 May 1895–21 April 1897 Sir Hercules Robinson (created Baron Rosmead in 1896); 21 April 1897–5 May 1897 Sir William Goodenough (Officer Administering); 5 May 1897–2 Nov. 1898 Sir Alfred Milner; 2 Nov. 1898–14 Feb. 1899 Sir William Butler (Officer Administering); 14 Feb. 1899–6 March 1901 Sir Alfred Milner. *High Commissioners:* 6 March 1901–1 April 1905 Sir Alfred Milner (created Baron Milner in 1901 and Viscount Milner in 1902); 2 April 1905–17 June 1909 William Palmer, 2nd Earl of Selborne; 17 June 1909–21 Sept. 1909 Sir Walter Hely-Hutchinson (acting); 21 Sept. 1909–30 May 1910 Sir Henry Scobell (acting). *Governors:* 6 March 1901–30 May 1910 Sir Walter Hely-Hutchinson. *Prime Ministers:* 29 April 1872–5 Feb. 1878 Sir John Molteno; 6 Feb. 1878–8 May 1881 Gordon Sprigg; 9 May 1881–12 May 1884 Sir Thomas Scanlen; 13 May 1884–24 Nov. 1886 Sir Thomas Upington; 25 Nov. 1886–16 July 1890 Sir Gordon Sprigg; 17 July 1890–12 Jan. 1896 Cecil Rhodes; 13 Jan. 1896–13 Oct. 1898 Sir Gordon Sprigg; 14 Oct.

1898–17 June 1900 William Schreiner; 18 June 1900–21 Feb. 1904 Sir Gordon Sprigg; 22 Feb. 1904–2 Feb. 1908 Sir Starr Jameson (formerly Dr. Leander Starr Jameson); 3 Feb. 1908–30 May 1910 John Merriman.

Cape Mesurado see **Liberia**

Cape of Good Hope see **Cape Colony**

Cape Town see **Cape Colony**

Cape Verde. 1462– . *Location:* about 365 miles off the coast of northwest Africa. *Capital:* Praia (before 1974 this city, which is on the island of São Tiago, was known as Villa de Praia, and has been the capital since 1769); Cidade de Ribeira Grande (founded in 1462, this was the capital from 1495 to 1769). *Other names:* Islas do Cabo Verde; Cape Verde Islands; Cabo Verde; Arquipélago de Cabo Verde; Cap Vert; República de Cabo Verde (1975–); Ribeira Grande (1495–1587).

History: The Portuguese have the first substantial claim to discovery of the Cape Verde Islands when in 1460 Diogo Gomes and Antonio da Nola sighted and named the islands, although the Venetian captain Alvise Cadamosto, working for Prince Henry the Navigator, may have visited there in 1456. The name comes from the nearest cape on the mainland of Africa, which was called the Green Cape. The island of São Tiago was settled in 1462, and the town of Ribeira Grande (the oldest European town in the tropics) was built on Santo Antão soon afterwards. The islands were granted by King Afonso V of Portugal to his brother, Prince Ferdinand, and in 1466 the settlers on Cape Verde were given exclusive slave trading rights in the Guinea area. On Ferdinand's death in 1470 the islands reverted to the Crown, to be given at once by the new king, João II to Prince Manuel. However, all this time the islands were in the hands of Portuguese nobles until 1495, when Prince Manuel came to the throne, and the Cape Verde Islands were taken over by the Crown, and given as donatarias (gifts, or donations, made by the Portuguese government to private individuals with enough money to run them). Ribeira Grande itself was the main donataria, and the others — the islands of Santo Antão, São Vicente, São Tiago, São Nicolao, Maio, Boa Vista, Sal, Fogo, and Brava — were all grouped together as the Dominion of Cape Verde. A capitão-mor (captain-major) or corregedor (magistrate) administered each one. Slaves were brought in from the earliest times, and the people of Cape Verde descend from them and from the Portuguese and other European settlers on the islands. Cape Verde grew rich on slaves and gold, and Sir Francis Drake twice attacked Ribeira Grande, in 1585 and 1592. By 1587, Portugal was being ruled by Spain (Portugal was a part of Spain from 1580 to 1656), and Madrid wished to centralize the different Cape Verde/Ribeira Grande donatarias, and bring them under one governor, and thus they were grouped together as the Colony of Cape Verde. In 1712 the French sacked the town of Ribeira Grande, and it was subsequently abandoned, in 1770. In 1854 the Portuguese government freed the public slaves in Cape Verde, and in 1857 began moves to do the same for privately owned slaves, this latter move being finally accomplished by 1876. The last century of Portuguese rule was noted for ever-increasingly bad conditions, famine and mismanagement, corruption and poverty. On 11 June 1951 Cape Verde became an overseas province of Portugal, and on 19 Dec. 1974 the Portuguese government signed an agreement with the African Party for the Independence of Guinea-Bissau and the Cape Verde Islands, and Cape Verde achieved self-rule as an autonomous republic, effective 31 Dec. 1974. On 5 July 1975 Cape Verde finally became a full-fledged republic, and allied itself with Guinea-Bissau. In fact there were plans to unify with Guinea-Bissau in 1980, but a coup in Guinea-Bissau in November of that year ended such hopes. A prolonged drought in the 1990s caused massive emigration.

Rulers: 1462–1495 [unknown]. *Capitães-Mores/Corregedores of the Islands forming the Dominion of Cape Verde:* 1495–1587 [unknown]. *Capitães-Mores/Corregedores of Ribeira Grande:* 1495–1550 [unknown]; 1550–1555 Jorge Pimentel; 1555–1558 Manuel de Andrade; 1558–1562 Luis de Evangelho; 1562–1565 Bernardo de Alpoim; 1565–1569 Manuel de Andrade; 1569–1578 Antonio Tinoco; 1578–1583 Gaspar de Andrade; 1583–1587 Diogo Magro. *Governors of Cape Verde:* 1587–1591 Duarte da Gama; 1591–1595 Brás de Melo; 1595–1596 Amador Raposo; 1596–1603 Francisco da Gama; 1603–1606 Fernão de Brito; 1606–1611 Francisco da Silva; 1611–1614 Francisco de Sequeira; 1614–1618 Nicolao de Castilho; 1618–1622 Francisco de

Moura; 1622–1622 Francisco Roulim; 1622–1624 Manuel de Guerra (acting); 1624–1628 Francisco da Cunha; 1628–1632 João Corte-Real; 1632–1636 Cristóvão de Cabral; 1636–1639 Jorge de Castilho; 1639–1640 Jerónimo de Cavalcanti e Albuquerque; 1640–1645 João da Cunha; 1645–1646 Lourenço Garro; 1646–1648 Jorge de Araújo; 1648–1648 Roque de Barros do Rego; 1648–1650 Council of Government; 1650–1650 Gonçalo de Gamboa Ayala; 1650–1651 Pedro Cardoso; 1651–1653 Jorge Castelo Branco; 1653–1658 Pedro Barreto; 1658–1663 Francisco de Figueroa; 1663–1667 Antonio Galvão; 1667–1671 Manuel da Costa Pessoa; 1671–1676 Manuel de Melo; 1676–1676 João Pássaro; 1676–1678 Council of Government; 1678–1683 Manuel da Costa Pessoa; 1683–1687 Inacio Barbosa; 1687–1688 Veríssimo da Costa; 1688–1690 Vitoriano da Costa; 1690–1691 Diogo Esquivel; 1691–1692 Council of Government; 1692–1696 Manuel da Câmara; 1696–1696 Antonio Mena; 1696–1698 Council of Government; 1698–1702 Antonio Salgado; 1702–1707 Gonçalo de Lemos Mascarenhas; 1707–1711 Rodrigo da Fonseca; 1711–1715 José da Câmara; 1715–1716 Council of Government; 1716–1720 Serafim de Sá; 1720–1725 Antonio Vieira; 1725–1726 Council of Government; 1726–1728 Francisco de Nóbrega Vasconcelos; 1728–1733 Francisco Grans; 1733–1737 Bento Coelho; 1737–1738 José Barbosa; 1738–1741 ruled by a Chamber Senate; 1741–1752 João de Santa Maria; 1752–1752 Antonio de Faria; 1752–1757 Luis Antonio da Cunha d'Eça; 1757–1761 Manuel de Sousa e Meneses; 1761–1761 Marcelino de Ávila; 1761–1764 Antonio Bezerra; 1764–1766 Bartolomeu de Sousa Tigre; 1766–1767 João Henriques; 1767–1768 Council of Government; 1768–1777 Joaquim Lobo; 1777–1781 Antonio de Sousa e Meneses; 1781–1782 Duarte de Almeida; 1782–1783 Francisco de São Simão (acting); 1783–1785 Council of Government; 1785–1790 Antonio de Faria e Maia; 1790–1795 Francisco Carneiro; 1795–1796 José d'Eça; 1796–1802 Marcelino Bastos; 1802–1803 Council of Government; 1803–1818 Antonio de Lencastre; 1818–1822 Antonio Pussich; 1822–1826 João de Mata Chapuzet; 1826–1830 Caetano de Vasconcelos; 1830–1831 Duarte Macedo; 1831–1833 José de Lencastre; 1833–1835 Manuel Martins; 1835–1836 Joaquim Marinho; 1836–1837 Domingos Arouca; 1837–1839 Joaquim Marinho; 1839–1842 João de Melo;

1842–1845 Francisco Paula; 1845–1847 José de Noronha; 1847–1848 Council of Government; 1848–1851 João de Melo; 1851–1854 Fortunato Barreiros; 1854–1858 Antonio Arrobas; 1858–1860 Sebastião Meneses; 1860–1861 Januário de Almeida; 1861–1864 Carlos Franco; 1864–1869 José de Carvalho e Meneses; 1869–1876 Caetano de Almeida e Albuquerque; 1876–1878 Lopes de Macedo; 1878–1879 Vasco de Carvalho e Meneses; 1879–1881 Antonio de Sampaio; 1881–1886 João de Vasconcelos; 1886–1889 João de Lacerda; 1889–1890 Augusto de Carvalho; 1890–1893 José de Melo; 1893–1894 Fernão de Magalhães e Meneses; 1894–1898 Alexandre Serpa Pinto; 1898–1900 João de Lacerda; 1900–1902 Arnaldo de Rebelo; 1902–1903 Francisco de Paula Cid; 1903–1904 Antonio de Freitas; 1904–1907 Amancio Cabral; 1907–1909 Bernardo de Macedo; 1909–1910 Martinho Montenegro; 1910–1911 Antonio Ortigão; 1911–1911 Artur de Campos; 1911–1915 Joaquim Biker; 1915–1918 Abel da Costa; 1918–1919 Teófilo Duarte; 1919–1921 Manuel da Maia Magalhães; 1921–1922 Filipe de Carvalho; 1922–1924 Council of Government; 1924–1926 Julio de Abreu; 1926–1927 João de Almeida; 1927–1931 Antonio Guedes Vaz; 1931–1941 Antonio de Figueiredo; 1941–1943 José Martins; 1943–1949 João de Figueiredo; 1949–1953 Carlos Roçadas; 1953–1957 Manuel Amaral; 1957–1958 Antonio Correia (acting); 1958–1963 Silvinio Marquês; 1963–Dec. 1970 Leão Monteiro; Jan. 1971–19 Dec. 1974 Antonio dos Santos. *High Commissioners:* 19 Dec. 1974–31 Dec. 1974 Antonio dos Santos; 31 Dec. 1974–5 July 1975 Almeida d'Eça. *Ruling Council:* 30 Dec. 1974–5 July 1975 Carlos Reis, Amaro da Luz, and Manuel Faustino. *Presidents:* 8 July 1975–22 March 1991 Aristides Pereira; 22 March 1991–22 March 2001 Antonio Mascarenhas Monteiro; 22 March 2001–Pedro Pires. *Prime Ministers:* 15 July 1975–28 Jan. 1991 Pedro Pires; 28 Jan. 1991–29 July 2000 Carlos Veiga; 29 July 2000–19 Jan. 2001 Gualberto de Rosario; 1 Feb. 2001–José María Neves.

Caprivi Strip see **Namibia**

Cardagos Carajos Shoals see **Saint Brandon Islands**

Carthage. ca. 814 B.C.–29 B.C. *Location:* in Tunisia. *Capital:* Utica (capital of Africa Vetus);

Carthage (the name means "new town," and today it is a suburb of Tunis. It was the capital of Carthage). *Other names:* Africa Vetus (146 B.C.–29 B.C.); Carthago, Karchedon, or Kart-Hadshat, or Kart-Hadasht (all alternative names for Carthage).

History: The coast of Tunis was first visited by Phoenicians about two millennia B.C. In the 16th century B.C. merchants from Sidon established a post at Cambe, near the later town of Bordj-Jedid. Carthage was traditionally founded by Phoenicians about 814 B.C.; legend says by Dido (right name Elissa), the Tyrian princess, fleeing from her brother Pygmalion. However, this event is probably confused in Carthaginian history with the founding of a town in Cyprus about that time. In truth the Phoenicians first arrived in Carthage about 720 B.C. The state of Carthage (not the city) dates from about 550 B.C., the beginning of Carthage's supremacy in the Mediterranean. By this time the Carthaginian empire was divided into three provinces: Zeugitana, Byzacena, and the Emporia. The inhabitants were called Poeni by the Romans, and the country was run as a republic, based on wealth rather than birth. About 550 B.C. Malchus, the sufet (principal senator) conquered Sicily, but failed in Sardinia, for which crime he was expelled by the Senate. But he returned, conquered Carthage, and was finally executed by his own party. His successor was Mago, the son of Hanno of a ruling house known as the Barca, and Mago conquered Sardinia and the Balearic Islands. In 509 B.C. the first Carthaginian–Roman treaty was made, allotting Italy to the Romans and Africa to the Carthaginians. Carthage naturally produced great sailors, the pre-eminent one in this period being Hanno, son of Hamilcar, who sailed through the Straits of Gibraltar and established settlements along the West African coast, possibly even as far south as the Guinea Coast, and including the islands of Madeira and the Canaries. Wars with the Greeks and especially for the control of Sicily occupied decades of Carthaginian time. The first Punic War, between Carthage and Rome, lasted from 268 to 241 B.C., and was fought over Sicily and control of the Tyrhennian Sea. Between 237 and 228 B.C. Hamilcar embarked on the conquest of Spain, and the second Punic War with Rome lasted from 218 B.C. to 201 B.C., the Carthaginian leader being the famous Hannibal. Elephants were used in war by the Carthagini-

ans from the 3rd century B.C., as they had been used in Egypt and Syria before that, and Hannibal made good use of them in his war. The Third Punic War lasted three years, and culminated in the fall of the city and state of Carthage in 146 B.C. The Romans destroyed it, cursed the city of Carthage and forbade any future settlement there. They replaced the Carthaginian empire with their own province of Africa Vetus, and established a new capital at Utica. However, in 122 B.C. the curse was lifted, and a new Roman city went up on the old site of the city of Carthage. This was Colonia Iunonia, but it did not last. In 29 B.C. the Emperor Augustus united Africa Vetus with another province, Africa Nova, to form the Roman province of Africa (see Africa [i]). As for the subsequent history of Carthage the city, another Roman headquarters was established here in 13 B.C., called Colonia Julia Carthago. Carthage remained an important town for the Romans and the African Christians. It was a Vandal stronghold, and when the Byzantines conquered it in A.D. 553, it received the new name of Colonia Justiniana Carthago. In the late 7th century the Arabs captured it, and it was finally destroyed in 698.

Sufets (Judges): ca. 550 B.C.–ca. 535 B.C. Malchus; ca. 535 B.C.–ca. 500 B.C. Mago; ca. 500 B.C.–ca. 485 B.C. Hasdrubal; ca. 485 B.C.– ca. 465 B.C. Hamilcar; ca. 400 B.C. Himilco; ca. 240 B.C. Hamilcar; ca. 235 B.C. Hanno; ca. 220 B.C. Hasdrubal; ca. 210 B.C. Mago II; ca. 196 B.C. Hannibal; ca. 149 B.C. Hasdrubal II. *Only known Roman Praetor:* ca. 88 B.C. Publius Sextilius.

Cayor see **Kayor**

Cazembe see **Kazembe**

Central African Council see **Federation of Rhodesia and Nyasaland**

Central African Empire see **Central African Republic**

Central African Republic. 1893– . *Location:* north central Africa. *Capital:* Bangui (from 1906); Abiras (1894–1906). *Other names:* République Centrafricaine; C.A.R.; Central African Empire (1976–1979); Ubangi-Shari, or Oubangui-Chari (1894–1958); Ubangi-Bomu, or Oubangui-Bomou (1893–1894).

History: The first territory carved out by the French in what would later become the Central African Republic was Ubangi-Bomu, in 1893. In 1894 the French expanded out from Gabon and the Congo into the forks of the two rivers, the Ubangi and the Shari, and on 13 July 1894 Ubangi-Bomu began to be administered, and the name was changed to the colony of Ubangi-Shari. On 11 Feb. 1906 Ubangi-Shari and Chad were combined to form the greater colony of Ubangi-Shari–Chad, with each of the components becoming territories, and with the capital being at Bangui, the Ubangi-Shari capital. On 12 April 1916 Ubangi-Shari–Chad came to an end, and the colony of Ubangi-Shari came back into existence, the lieutenant-governor of which continued to rule Chad through a military commandant there. On 30 June 1934 Ubangi-Shari became a region of the colony of French Equatorial Africa. On 31 Dec. 1937 it became an overseas territory of France, while continuing to form part of the A.E.F. (Afrique Équatoriale Française). On 1 Dec. 1958 it gained self-rule as the autonomous Central African Republic, within the French Community. On 13 Aug. 1960 it became fully independent as the Central African Republic. All freedom in politics was done away with, and the country became a Chinese puppet. A coup led by Army leader Jean-Bédel Bokassa at the end of 1965 removed the ineffectual David Dacko (Bokassa's cousin), and cut ties with China. Dacko was arrested and remained so until 1976, when he became an adviser to Bokassa. Things went from bad to worse as Bokassa proved himself an insane tyrant. In 1971 Bokassa, who, when he was a young man had wanted to be a Catholic priest but instead had served for years with distinction in the French Army, now made himself a general, and in 1972 president for life. He survived several assassination attempts; he made a woman prime minister, the first time this had happened in Africa; and he received a visit from Muammar Qadaffi of Libya, whereupon Bokassa promptly adopted Islam and changed his name (for a short while anyway) to Salah ad-Din Ahmad (or Saladin). When Qadaffi failed to come through with the financial aid he had promised, Bokassa coincidentally lost all desire to be a Muslim, and became Jean-Bédel Bokassa again, Catholic. By 1976 he was suffering from a Napoleon complex, and had himself crowned emperor and changed the name of the country, on 4 Dec. 1976, to the Central African Empire. The coronation cost the country approximately $20 million. Bokassa ordered schoolchildren to wear new uniforms made in a factory owned by him. The children objected and demonstrated against this edict on 20 and 21 Jan. 1979. On 18 April 1979 Bokassa personally, with the aid of his Imperial Guard, executed over 100 of these children. After the country could no longer contain the excesses of Bokassa's reign, a bloodless coup, aided by the French, got rid of him, while he was visiting his friend Qadaffi in Libya, and the country became the Central African Republic again, on 21 Sept. 1979, again under the presidency of David Dacko. Bokassa went into exile in the Ivory Coast, and subsequently to France. However, Dacko had not learned from his long period of incarceration, and slipped back into his old ways of repressions and corruption. In 1981 General André Kolingba came to power in another bloodless coup, and offered freedom of elections, that is until he was found to be losing in the Oct. 1992 elections, when he promptly canceled that freedom and the elections at the same time. However, since that time a certain freedom has been achieved, along with a degree of stability for the inhabitants. A postscript on the awful Bokassa: For some mysterious reason in Oct. 1986 he returned to the C.A.R., where he had, in Dec. 1980, been sentenced to death in absentia, and stood trial on charges of cannibalism, murder, embezzlement, illegal detentions, and a host of other charges. He was sentenced to death, but this was commuted to life imprisonment at hard labor in Feb. 1988, by the gracious consent of President André Kolingba. In 1996 there were three Army mutinies, and a civil war in 1997; the French had to intervene. In the early 2000s there were many attempted coups, and a successful one in 2003. AIDS is rampant, as is poverty and ethnic warfare.

Rulers: 1893–13 July 1894 [unknown, if any]. *Commissioners:* 13 July 1894–20 Oct. 1894 Col. Eugène Décazes; 20 Oct. 1894–1897 Victor Liotard. *Lieutenant-Governors:* 1897–1899 Victor Liotard. *Commissioners:* 1900–May 1904 Adolphe Cureau. *Governors-Delegate:* May 1904–22 Aug. 1905 Alphonse Iaeck (acting); 22 Aug. 1905–16 Feb. 1906 Victor Emmanuel Merlet (acting); 16 Feb. 1906–4 April 1906 Louis Lamy. *Lieutenant-Governors:* 4 April 1906–28 Feb. 1909 Émile Merwaert; 28 Feb. 1909–5 Aug. 1910 Lucien Fourneau (acting); 5 Aug. 1910–10 June 1911 Paul

Adam (acting); 10 June 1911–24 Nov. 1913 Frédéric Estèbe; 24 Nov. 1913–12 Oct. 1916 Pierre Adam; 12 Oct. 1916–17 July 1917 Victor Emmanuel Merlet; 17 July 1917–16 May 1919 Auguste Lamblin (acting); 16 May 1919–31 Aug. 1920 Auguste Lamblin; 31 Aug. 1920–Dec. 1921 Henri Dirat (acting); Dec. 1921–17 Aug. 1923 Auguste Lamblin; 17 Aug. 1923–Nov. 1924 Pierre François (acting); Nov. 1924–1 July 1926 Auguste Lamblin; 1 July 1926–July 1928 Georges-David Prouteaux (acting); July 1929–22 Oct. 1929 Auguste Lamblin; 22 Oct. 1929–30 Oct. 1930 Georges-David Prouteaux (acting); 30 Oct. 1930–8 March 1933 Adolphe Deitte; 8 March 1933–Jan. 1934 Pierre Bonnefont (acting); Jan. 1934–17 Aug. 1934 Adolphe Deitte. *Governors-Delegate:* 17 Aug. 1934–21 May 1935 Adolphe Deitte; 21 May 1935–30 May 1935 Richard Brunot; 30 May 1935–Dec. 1935 Pierre Bonnefont (acting); Dec. 1935–24 Oct. 1936 Richard Brunot. *Governors:* 24 Oct. 1936–28 March 1939 Charles-Max Masson de Saint-Félix; 28 March 1939–15 July 1941 Pierre de Saint-Mart (acting); 15 July 1941–30 May 1942 Pierre de Saint-Mart; 30 May 1942–30 July 1942 André Latrille; 30 July 1942–3 April 1946 Henri Sautot; 3 April 1946–24 May 1946 Jean Chalvet; 24 May 1946–13 Oct. 1946 Henri LaCour (acting); 13 Oct. 1946–5 April 1948 Jean Chalvet; 5 April 1948–30 Nov. 1948 Jean Mauberna (acting); 1 Dec. 1948–27 Jan. 1949 Auguste Éven (acting); 27 Jan. 1949–4 Jan. 1950 Pierre Delteil; 4 Jan. 1950–10 March 1950 Auguste Éven (acting); 10 March 1950–9 July 1951 Ignace Colombani; 9 July 1951–19 Oct. 1951 Pierre Raynier (acting); 19 Oct. 1951–16 Feb. 1954 Louis Grimald; 16 Feb. 1954–29 Jan. 1958 Louis Sanmarco; 29 Jan. 1958–1 Dec. 1958 Paul Bordier. *High Commissioners:* 1 Dec. 1958–13 Aug. 1960 Paul Bordier. *Presidents:* 13 Aug. 1960–17 Nov. 1960 David Dacko (interim); 17 Nov. 1960–31 Dec. 1965 David Dacko; 1 Jan. 1966–22 Feb. 1972 Jean-Bédel Bokassa. *Presidents for Life:* 22 Feb. 1972–7 April 1976 Jean-Bédel Bokassa. *Marshals of the Republic:* 7 April 1976–4 Dec. 1976 Jean-Bédel Bokassa. *Emperors:* 4 Dec. 1976–21 Sept. 1979 Bokassa I. *Presidents:* 21 Sept. 1979–1 Sept. 1981 David Dacko. *Chairmen of the Committee of National Recovery:* 1 Sept. 1981–21 Sept. 1985 André Kolingba. *Presidents:* 21 Sept. 1985–19 Sept. 1993 André Kolingba; 22 Oct. 1993–15 March 2003 Ange-Félix Patassé; 15 March 2003–François Bozizé. *Prime Ministers:* 8 Dec. 1958–29 March 1959 Barthélémy Boganda; 30 March 1959–5 May 1959 Abel Goumba (acting); 5 May 1959–13 Aug. 1960 David Dacko; 2 Jan. 1975–7 April 1976 Élisabeth Domitienne; 5 Sept. 1976–4 Dec. 1976 Ange-Félix Patassé; 8 Dec. 1976–14 July 1978 Ange-Félix Patassé; 14 July 1978–21 Sept. 1979 Henri Maidou; 26 Sept. 1979–22 Aug. 1980 Bernard Ayandho; 12 Nov. 1980–4 April 1981 Jean-Pierre Lebouder; 4 April 1981–1 Sept. 1981 Simon Bozanga; 15 March 1991–4 Dec. 1992 Édouard Franck; 4 Dec. 1992–26 Feb. 1993 Timothée Malendoma; 26 Feb. 1993–25 Oct. 1993 Énoch Dérant Lakoué; 25 Oct. 1993–12 April 1995 Jean-Luc Mandaba; 12 April 1995–6 June 1996 Gabriel Koyambounou; 6 June 1996–30 Jan. 1997 Jean-Paul Ngoupande; 30 Jan. 1997–18 Feb. 1997 Michel Gbzera-Brio (acting); 18 Feb. 1997–15 Jan. 1999 Michel Gbzera-Brio; 15 Jan. 1999–1 April 2001 Anicet Georges Dologuélé; 1 April 2001–15 March 2003 Martin Ziguélé; 23 March 2003–11 Dec. 2003 Abel Goumba; 11 Dec. 2003–13 June 2005 Celestin Gaombalet; 13 June 2005–Elie Doté. *Note:* In times of no Prime Minister, the President held that office.

Cerf Island see **Seychelles**

Ceuta. No dates. *Location:* Ceuta, Morocco, across the Straits of Gibraltar from Spain. *Capital:* Ceuta. *Other names:* Sebta or Cibta (the Arabic name); Septon (Byzantine name); Ad Septem Fratres (Roman name).

History: Originally Ceuta was the site of a Carthaginian colony, and then it passed through the stages shared by most of North Africa in general, i.e. Roman, Vandal, and Byzantine. The emperor Justinian restored its walls in 535. In 618 it was captured by the Visigoths, and remained the last major city to hold out against the Arab invasion of North Africa. That was in 711, when the last governor, Julian, surrendered the city. Over the next several centuries it changed ownership many times between one Berber or Arab faction or another, and in 1415 the Portuguese captured this key Mediterranean port from the Merinids (see Merinid Empire). This was Europe's first modern colony. From 1580 to 1640, although Spain ruled Portugal, Portugal maintained her overseas possessions. In 1640 Ceuta went to Spain, however. From 1694 to 1720 Mulay Ismail as-Samin, the Moorish leader, besieged Ceuta, and this was but one of many sieges suffered by the city, which had become an important trading center. The British occupied it briefly, with the consent of Spain, between 1810 and 1814, during the Napoleonic Wars, and in 1847, with the establishment of the Spanish Captaincy-General of North Africa (see Spanish Morocco), Ceuta, like Melilla, became a district of that organization. As a result of the 1860 war with Morocco, Spain was able to increase its area around the city. On 27 Nov. 1912, with the establishment of Spanish Morocco, Ceuta became a comandáncia (as did Melilla), attached to the province of Cádiz. In 1918 Ceuta and Melilla gained some territory when the third comandáncia, Larache, became extinct. On 7 April 1956 Ceuta became a presidio (or plaza), a part of Metropolitan Spain. The Mayor of Ceuta represents this African exclave in the Spanish cortes. In Sept. 1994 Ceuta gained a certain amount of autonomy, and on 14 March 1995 it became the autonomous city of Ceuta.

Captains-General: 1415–1430 Pedro, Conde de Viana; 1430–1434 Duarte, Conde de Viana; 1434–1437 Pedro, Conde de Viana; 1437–1438 Duarte, Conde de Viana; 1438–1445 Fernão, Conde de Vila Real; 1445–1447 Antonio Pacheco; 1447–1450 Duque de Bragança; 1450–1460 Conde de Odemira; 1460–1461 [unknown]; 1461–1464 Pedro, Conde de Vila Real; 1464–1479 João Rodrigues de Vasconcelos Ribeiro; 1479–1481 Rui Mendes de Vasconcelos Ribeiro; 1481–1487 João de Noronha; 1487–1491 Conde de Linhares; 1491–1509 Fernão, Conde de Alcoutim; 1509–1512 Pedro Alardo; 1512–1517 Pedro, Conde de Alcoutim; 1517–1518 [unknown]; 1518–1519 Conde de Portalegre; 1519–1521 Gomes da Silva de Vasconcelos; 1521–1522 [unknown]; 1522–1524 João de Noronha; 1524–1525 Pedro, Conde de Alcoutim; 1525–1529 Gomes da Silva de Vasconcelos; 1529–1539 Nunho de Noronha; 1539–1540 [unknown]; 1540–1549 Afonso de Noronha; 1549–1549 Antão de Noronha; 1549–1550 Martim da Silva; 1550–1553 Pedro de Meneses; 1553–1553 Pedro da Cunha; 1553–1553 João Rodrigues Pereira; 1553–1555 Martim da Silva; 1555–1557 Jorge Vieira; 1557–1562 Fernão de Meneses; 1562–1563 Conde de Vila Real; 1563–1564 Fernão de Meneses; 1564–1565 Pedro da Cunha; 1565–1566 [unknown]; 1566–1567 Francisco Pereira; 1567–1574 Duque de Vila Real; 1574–1577 Diogo Lopes de França; 1577–1578 Duque de Vila Real; 1578–1580 Dionisio Pereira; 1580–1586 Jorge Pessanha; 1586–1591 Gil da Costa; 1591–1592 Francisco de Andrade; 1592–1594 Duque de Caminha; 1594–1597 Mendo de Ledesma; 1597–1601 Duque de Caminha; 1601–1602 [unknown]; 1602–1605 Afonso de Noronha; 1605–1616 Duque de Caminha; 1616–1622 Conde de Vila Real; 1622–1623 [unknown]; 1623–1623 Duque de Caminha; 1623–1624 Antonio Albuquerque; 1624–1625 Conde da Tôrre; 1625–1625 Gonçalo Alcoforado; 1625–1626 Duque de Caminha; 1626–1627 [unknown]; 1627–1627 Dinís de Mascarenhas de Lencastre; 1627–1634 Jorge de Mendonça Pessanha; 1634–1636 Brás Teles de Meneses; 1636–1637 [unknown]; 1637–1637 Fernão Teles de Meneses; 1637–1640 Francisco de Almeida. *Governors:* 1640–1641 Francisco de Almeida (interim); 1641–1644 Marqués de Miranda de Auta; 1644–1645 [unknown]; 1645–1646 Marqués de Malagón; 1646–1653 Marqués de Torcifal; 1653–1661 Marqués de Tenorio; 1661–1662 [unknown]; 1662–1665 Marqués de Castelo Mendo; 1665–1672 Marqués de Sentar; 1672–1677 Conde de Torres Vedras; 1677–1677 Antonio Chacón y Ponce de León; 1677–1678 Diego de Portugal; 1678–1679 Antonio Chacón y Ponce de León; 1679–1681 Conde de Puñonrostro; 1681–1689 Francisco de Velasco y Tovar; 1689–1692 Francisco Varona; 1692–1695 Marqués de Valparaíso; 1695–1698 Marqués de Valdecañas; 1698–1702 Marqués de Villadarias; 1702–1704 Marqués de Gironella; 1704–1705 [unknown]; 1705–1709 Juan Francisco de Araña; 1709–1715 Gonzalo Chacón y Arellano Sandoval y Rojas; 1715–1719 Francisco Fernández y Rivadeo; 1719–1719 Francisco Pérez Mancheño; 1719–1720 Príncipe de Campo Flórido; 1720–1720 Juan Francisco de Araña; 1720–1725 Francisco Fernández y Rivadeo; 1725–1731 Comte de Charny; 1731–1738 Marqués de Santa Cruz; 1738–1739 Antonio Manso Maldonaldo; 1739–1745 Marqués de Campofuerte; 1745–1745 Juan Antonio Tineo y Fuertes; 1745–1746 Juan de Palafox y Centurión; 1746–1751 José Horcasitas y Oleaga; 1751–1751 Marqués de la Matilla; 1751–1755 Marqués de Croix; 1755–1760 Miguel Carreño; 1760–1763 Marqués de Warmarch; 1763–1776 Diego Osorio; 1776–1783 Marqués de Casa Tremañes; 1783–1784 Domingo de Salcedo; 1784–1791 Miguel Porcel y Manrique de Araña Menchaca y Zaldívar; 1791–1792 José de Sotomayor; 1792–1794 José de Urrutia y las Casas;

1794–1795 Conde de Santa Clara; 1795–1795 Diego de la Peña; 1795–1798 José Vassallo; 1798–1801 José Bautisto de Castro; 1801–1805 Antonio Terrero; 1805–1807 Francisco de Horta; 1807–1808 Ramón de Carvajal; 1808–1809 Carlos Luján; 1809–1810 Carlos Gand; 1810–1813 José María Alós; 1813–1813 José María Lastres; 1813–1813 Pedro Grimarest; 1813–1814 Fernando Gómez de Buitrón; 1814–1815 Pedro Grimarest; 1815–1816 Luis Antonio Flores; 1816–1818 Juan de Pontons y Mujica; 1818–1820 José de Miranda; 1820–1820 Vincente Rorique; 1820–1822 Fernando Gómez de Buitrón; 1822–1823 Álvaro Chacón; 1823–1823 Manuel Fernández; 1823–1823 Antonio Quiroga; 1823–1824 Juan María Muñoz; 1824–1826 José de Miranda; 1826–1826 Joaquín Bureau; 1826–1826 Julio O'Neill; 1826–1830 Juan María Muñoz; 1830–1833 Carlos Ullmann; 1833–1835 Mateo Ramírez; 1835–1835 Carlos Espinosa; 1835–1836 Joaquín Gómez Ansa; 1836–1837 Francisco Sanjuanena; 1837–1837 Bernardo Tacón; 1837–1844 José María Rodríguez Vera; 1844–1847 Antonio Ordóñez; 1847–27 Nov. 1912 administered by the captains-general of Spanish North Africa; 27 Nov. 1912–7 April 1956 administered by the governors-general of Spanish Morocco, through an administrator in Ceuta. *Presidents:* 19 June 1995–24 July 1996 Basilio López; 24 July 1996–26 Aug. 1999 Jesús Ramos; 26 Aug. 1999–7 Feb. 2001 Antonio Casarramona; 7 Feb. 2001–Juan Lara.

Chad. 5 Sept. 1900– . *Location:* central North Africa. *Capital:* N'Djamena (until 6 Sept. 1973 this town was called Fort Lamy, and was founded 13 April 1900, being named for Major Lamy of the French Army, who was killed nearby). *Other names:* Tchad; République du Tchad, or the Republic of Chad (from 1958); Autonomous Republic of Chad (1958–1960).

History: Before 1900 much of what is today Chad belonged to Rabih's Empire. In 1900 Borku, one of the areas thus controlled, was declared a French protectorate, and that day the southern part of what is today Chad was formed into a military territory and protectorate by the French. On 5 July 1902 it became the Protectorate of Chad, and on 11 Feb. 1906 it became a territorial part of the colony of Ubangi-Shari–Chad, being administered by military commandants responsible to Bangui (the capital of the greater colony). On 3 June 1909 Wadai became a part of Chad, and on 12 April 1916, on the breakup of the colony of Ubangi-Shari–Chad, Chad became an independent unit again, but still answerable to Bangui. It achieved colonial status on 17 March 1920. On 30 June 1934 Chad became a region of the colony of French Equatorial Africa, and on 31 Dec. 1937 it became an overseas territory of France, but still part of the A.E.F. (Afrique Équatoriale Française). On 28 Nov. 1958 it became an autonomous republic within the French Community, being primed for independence from France, which it finally achieved on 11 Aug. 1960, as the republic of Chad. The French continued to administer Borkou–Ennedi–Tibesti (B.E.T.) until 23 Jan. 1965, when they pulled out and this prefecture was incorporated into the Republic of Chad. Since that time there has been a continual problem with the Chad National Liberation Front (FROLINAT), i.e. the Northern rebels (Muslims), who have been attempting to overthrow the Southern (Christian) government. French troops have been into Chad, on and off, for years, assisting the government. In Oct. 1971 Hissène Habré, who had been sent to the North by Tombalbaye to negotiate with FROLINAT, defected and joined Goukouni Oueddi's faction of FROLINAT, leading the Armed Forces of the North (FAN). In 1973 Tombalbaye began to Africanize Chad, in other words to remove French influence. He re-named himself N'garta Tombalbaye. In 1975 General Odingar, chief of staff, led a military coup that toppled and killed President Tombalbaye. Odingar released General Félix Malloum, who had earlier been jailed by Tombalbaye for plotting his overthrow, and Malloum became the new head of state. FROLINAT objected to this too, and continued to rebel. Goukouni Oueddi became the new leader of FROLINAT, supported by Libya. In Aug. 1978 Malloum and Habré (still with FROLINAT) formed a coalition government, but they could not agree, and, after an unsuccessful coup attempt by Habré, the fight continued until rebel forces took over the government under Goukouni Oueddi in 1979. Habré became Minister of Defense, but he rebelled against Oueddi, and was thrown out of the government. Libyan troops were in Chad at the request of the Oueddi government, between Dec. 1980 and Nov. 1981. Libya had every intention (and still does) of making Chad a province of Libya. Rebel forces, under Hissène Habré, captured the capital in

June 1982 and forced the president, Oueddi, to flee the country. In 1983 France sent 3,000 troops to Chad to support the government in their fight against Libyan-backed Oueddi supporters, and in Sept. 1984 an agreement was reached whereby France and Libya would both evacuate at the same time. Libya reneged on the deal, and it was not until March 1987 when government forces finally pushed them out. In Dec. 1990 Habré was toppled by the Patriotic Salvation Movement, led by Idriss Déby, and supported by Libya. A Habré invasion of the country in Dec. 1991 was repulsed. Déby has survived several coup attempts, from the time he took power. Free elections were supposedly held in 1996, but there was constant fighting in Chad until the early 2000s. Chad has never recovered from a long drought in the 1960s and 1970s, from the ethnic wars within its own boundaries, the wars with its neighbors, the constant coups, corruption, general poverty, and now AIDS. In addition, thousands of refugees from the Sudan swarm into Chad.

Military Commandants: 5 Sept. 1900–1901 Georges Destenave; 1901–5 July 1902 Col. Julien; 5 July 1902–1904 Étienne Largeau; 1904–11 Feb. 1906 Henri Gouraud; 11 Feb. 1906–1908 Étienne Largeau; 1908–1909 Constant Millot; 1909–9 Nov. 1910 Alexandre Moll; 9 Nov. 1910–1911 Joseph Maillard; 1911–1912 Étienne Largeau; 1912–1912 James-Édouard Hirtzman; 1912–1913 Gabriel Briand; 1913–1915 Étienne Largeau; 1915–12 April 1916 Gabriel Briand; 12 April 1916–1918 Clément Martelly; 1918–10 Aug. 1920 Albert du Carré. *Lieutenant-Governors:* 10 Aug. 1920–30 Jan. 1923 Fernand Lavit; 30 Jan. 1923–1925 Dieudonné Reste; 1925–9 April 1925 Antoine Touzet; 9 April 1925–25 Jan. 1926 Dieudonné Reste; 25 Jan. 1926–13 Jan. 1928 Jules de Coppet (acting); 13 Jan. 1928–21 April 1929 Adolphe Deitte; 21 April 1929–22 Nov. 1929 Émile Buhot-Launay; 22 Nov. 1929–14 May 1932 Jules de Coppet; 14 May 1932–26 Jan. 1933 Georges-David Prouteaux (acting); 26 Jan. 1933–30 June 1934 Richard Brunot. *Governors-Delegate:* 30 June 1934–17 Aug. 1934 Richard Brunot; 17 Aug. 1934–21 May 1935 Adolphe Deitte; 21 May 1935–30 May 1935 Richard Brunot; 30 May 1935–23 Oct. 1936 Pierre Bonnefont (acting); 23 Oct. 1936–24 Oct. 1936 Émile Buhot-Launay (acting); 24 Oct. 1936–31 Dec. 1937 Max de Masson de Saint-Félix. *Chefs du Térritoire:* 31 Dec. 1937–28 March 1938

Charles-Max Masson de Saint-Félix; 28 March 1938–19 Nov. 1938 Émile Buhot-Launay; 19 Nov. 1938–14 Dec. 1938 Félix Éboué; 14 Dec. 1938–1939 Charles Dagain (acting); 1939–12 Nov. 1940 Félix Éboué; 12 Nov. 1940–30 July 1941 Pierre Lapie; 30 July 1941–5 Nov. 1943 André Latrille; 5 Nov. 1943–10 Aug. 1945 Jacques Rogué; 10 Aug. 1945–13 Oct. 1946 Auguste Éven (acting. *Governors:* 13 Oct. 1946–24 Nov. 1948 Jacques Rogué; 24 Nov. 1948–1949 Paul Le Layec; 1949–1950 Henri de Mauduit; 1950–27 Jan. 1951 M. Casamata (acting); 27 Jan. 1951–29 Oct. 1951 Charles Hanin (acting); 29 Oct. 1951–3 Nov. 1956 Ignace Colombani; 3 Nov. 1956–28 Nov. 1958 Jean Troadec. *High Commissioners:* 28 Nov. 1958–16 Dec. 1958 [vacant]; 16 Dec. 1958–11 Feb. 1959 Daniel Doustin; 11 Feb. 1959–12 March 1959 M. Sahoulba (acting); 12 March 1959–23 March 1959 Ahmand Koulamallah; 12 March 1959–12 Aug. 1960 [vacant]. *Presidents of Government Council:* 13 May 1957–16 Dec. 1958 Daniel Doustin. *Heads of State:* 12 Aug. 1960–23 April 1962 François Tombalbaye. *Presidents:* 23 April 1962–13 April 1975 François Tombalbaye (from 1973 known as N'garta Tombalbaye); 13 April 1975–15 April 1975 General Noël Odingar (acting). *Presidents of the Supreme Military Council:* 15 April 1975–23 March 1979 Félix Malloum. *Chairmen of the Provisional Government:* 23 March 1979–29 April 1979 Goukouni Oueddi; 29 April 1979–22 Aug. 1979 Lol Muhammad Shawa. *Presidents of the Provisional State Council:* 22 Aug. 1979–7 June 1982 Goukouni Oueddi. *Leaders of the Revolutionary Council:* 7 June 1982–19 June 1982 Hissène Habré. *Heads of State:* 19 June 1982–21 Oct. 1982 Hissène Habré. *Presidents:* 21 Oct. 1982–2 Dec. 1990 Hissène Habré; 4 Dec. 1990–Idriss Déby. *Prime Ministers:* 24 March 1959–12 Aug. 1960 François Tombalbaye; 29 Aug. 1978–23 March 1979 Hissène Habré; 19 May 1982–7 June 1982 Djidingar Done Ngardoum (acting); 4 March 1991–20 May 1992 Jean Alingué Bawoyea; 20 May 1992–7 April 1993 Joseph Yodoyman; 7 April 1993–6 Nov. 1993 Fidèle Moungar; 6 Nov. 1993–8 April 1995 Delwa Kassire Koumakoye; 8 April 1995–16 May 1997 Koibla Djimasta; 17 May 1997–13 Dec. 1999 Nassour Guelengdoussia Ouaido; 13 Dec. 1999–11 June 2002 Nagoum Yamassoum; 12 June 2002–24 June 2003 Haroun Kabedi; 24 June 2003–3 Feb. 2005 Moussa Faki; 3 Feb. 2005–Pascal Yoadimnaji.

Note: In times of no Prime Minister, the President or other Head of State held that office.

Chafarinas see **Morocco** and **Spanish Morocco**

Chagos Archipelago see **British Indian Ocean Territory**

Changamire see **Rozwi**

Chão see **Madeira**

Christopolis see **Liberia**

Circassian Mameluke Empire see **Egypt**

Cirenaica see **Cyrenaica**

Ciskei. 4 Dec. 1981–27 April 1994. *Location:* eastern Cape Province, South Africa. *Capital:* Bisho. *Other names:* Republic of Ciskei; Iriphabliki Yeciskei.

History: On 1 Aug. 1972 the South African Bantustan of Ciskei (also known as the Native Homeland of the Xhosa peoples) achieved self-government. In 1981 the country became the fourth Bantustan to achieve independence from South Africa, and the first to opt for independence using the referendum system. Like Transkei, Bophuthatswana and Venda it was not recognized internationally. In 1994, with the white government in South Africa coming to an end, the Bantustans were no longer necessary, and Ciskei became part of South Africa.

South African Commissioner-General: 1 Sept. 1976–4 Dec. 1981 J.J. Engelbrecht. *Chief Ministers:* 1 Aug. 1972–21 May 1973 J.T. Mabandla; 21 May 1973–1975 Lennox Sebe; 1975–1975 Charles Sebe (acting); 1975–4 Dec. 1981 Lennox Sebe. *Presidents:* 4 Dec. 1981–4 March 1990 Lennox Sebe. *Chairmen of the Military Committee and Council of State:* 4 March 1990–22 March 1994 Joshua Oupa Gqozo. Administrators: 23 March 1994–26 April 1994 Pieter Goosen and Bongani Finca.

Coetivy. No dates. *Location:* an island, north of the Agalegas, in the Indian Ocean.

History: Taken by the British from the French on 3 Oct. 1810, Coetivy, a dependency, was transferred from Mauritius to Seychelles in 1908, and was administered from there, as it had been from Mauritius. On 30 June 1976 it became part of the Republic of the Seychelles.

Comoros. 25 March 1841– . *Location:* a republic composed of a group of islands in the Indian Ocean, halfway between the northern tip of Madagascar and the northern half of Mozambique. The name Comoro comes from "kamar," an Arab word meaning "moon." The three principal islands are Ngazidja (formerly known as Gran Comoro, or Grande Comore), Nzwani (also known as Ndzouani, and formerly known as Anjouan), and Moili (formerly known as Mohéli). There is another island, Mayotte, which, although it was part of the Comoros for six months in 1975–1976, did not go the way the rest of the Comoros went. It remains a French overseas department, and is treated separately in this work (see Mayotte Department). *Capital:* Moroni (on the island of Ngazidja. This was the capital from 1962); Dzaoudzi (1887–1962); Chingoni (1841–1887). *Other names:* Les Comores; Comoro Archipelago; République des Comores, or Republic of the Comoros (1975–1978); Jumhuriyat al-Qumur al-Itthadiya al-Islamiyah, or the Federal Islamic Republic of the Comoros (from 1978); Province de Mayotte et Dependences (alternative French name, 1914–1946); Mayotte (this name was used interchangeably with that of Comoros from 1887 to 1946).

History: These were basically Muslim islands when the French came. In 1841 Andriantsuli, the local king of Mayotte, ceded that island to the French, who occupied it in 1843. The neighboring island kingdoms in the archipelago gradually became part of the new French protectorate of Mayotte, as it now became known. Andruna joined in 1852; Anjouan in 1866; Mohéli in 1886; and Moroni in 1893. By the time Moroni was included, Mayotte Protectorate had become known as the Comoros Protectorate (on 5 Sept. 1887). On 9 April 1908 the Comoros became a dependent territory of Madagascar, another French possession. On 23 Feb. 1914 the Comoros became a colony, but remained a dependent province of Madagascar, and administered from Tananarive, Madagascar, through a local man at Dzaoudzi, in the Comoros. In 1925 the Comoros were given their own local administration, and on 13 Oct. 1946 they became an overseas territory of the Fourth Republic of France, and lost their dependence on Madagascar. In 1958 the country voted to remain part of France, rather than become an autonomous republic within the French Community. However, on 22 Dec. 1961 it became an autonomous state. In 1968 it won the right to form political parties and hold elections, and on 22 Dec. 1974 the islands voted on independence from France. All but the basically Christian island of Mayotte chose independence, and on 6 July 1975 the Republic of the Comoros was unilaterally declared by Ahmad Abdallah. Although Mayotte remained a part of the new republic, another vote made it an overseas department of France on 9 Feb. 1976. However, the Comoros claims Mayotte as a fundamental part of the republic. The Comoros have been bedeviled by coups and assassinations since independence, the most famous being the 1978 invasion by French mercenaries led by Col. Bob Denard. In 1995 the official French army had to go in and depose the latest coup leaders. In the late 1990s the islands of Nzwani and Mwali broke away. Coups abounded in the 1990s and early 2000s, and in 2001 the Comoros Union came into being, granting autonomy to the three major islands, including Nzwani and Moili that had seceded (Grande Comore is the other one).

Commandants: 25 March 1841–29 Aug. 1843 no French administration; 29 Aug. 1843–16 June 1844 Paul Rang; 16 June 1844–22 Oct. 1844 Capt. A. Thiebault (acting); 22 Oct. 1844–5 Jan. 1846 Auguste Lebrun; 5 Jan. 1846–11 Dec. 1849 Pierre Passot. *Commissioners:* 11 Dec. 1849–13 June 1851 Stanislas Livet; 13 June 1851–18 Oct. 1853 Philibert Bonfils; 18 Oct. 1853–12 Dec. 1855 André Brisset; 12 Dec. 1855–12 Dec. 1857 André-César Vérand; 12 Dec. 1857–14 Aug. 1860 Charles Morel; 14 Aug. 1860–10 Dec. 1864 Charles Gabrié; 10 Dec. 1864–8 July 1868 Joseph Colomb; 8 July 1868–15 April 1869 Joseph Hayes (acting); 15 April 1869–21 May 1869 L.G. Leguay (acting); 21 May 1869–4 March 1871 Joseph Colomb; 4 March 1871–19 Dec. 1871 Jules Ventre de la Touloubre (acting); 19 Dec. 1871–1 March 1875 Jules Ventre de la Touloubre; 1 March 1875–16 Sept. 1875 Claude Fontaine (acting); 16 Sept. 1875–26 Dec. 1875 François Perriez; 26 Dec. 1875–2 Jan. 1878 Jules Ventre de la Touloubre; 2 Jan. 1878–15 Jan. 1879 M.J. Roblin (acting); 15 Jan. 1879–7 Sept. 1879 Charles-Henri Vassal; 7 Sept. 1879–16 Dec. 1879 Charles Rayet (acting); 16 Dec. 1879–17 April 1880 Numa Sasias (acting); 17 April 1880–4 June 1882 François Perriez; 4 June 1882–21 Feb. 1883 Édouard Marie (acting); 21 Feb.

1883–3 March 1885 François Perriez; 3 March 1885–19 Aug. 1887 Philotée Gerville-Réache; 19 Aug. 1887–5 Sept. 1887 Paul Celeron de Blainville. *Administrators:* 5 Sept. 1887–4 May 1888 Paul Celeron de Blainville; 4 May 1888–1893 Clovis Papinaud; 1893–30 March 1896 Étienne Lacascade; 30 March 1896–5 Aug. 1897 Gentian Péréton; 5 Aug. 1897–7 March 1899 Louis Micon; 7 March 1899–18 Sept. 1900 Clovis Papinaud. *Governors:* 18 Sept. 1900–15 Oct. 1902 Pierre Pascal; 15 Oct. 1902–28 Feb. 1905 Albert Martineau; 28 Feb. 1905–3 March 1906 Jean Joliet; 3 March 1906–9 April 1908 Fernand Foureau. *Administrators:* 9 April 1908–8 Sept. 1908 Fernand Foureau; 8 Sept. 1908–1 May 1911 Charles Vergnes. *Governors:* 1 May 1911–28 Sept. 1911 Frédéric Estèbe; 28 Sept. 1911–21 Feb. 1913 Gabriel Garnier-Mouton; 21 Feb. 1913–23 Feb. 1914 Honoré Catron; 23 Feb. 1914–13 Oct. 1946 ruled direct from Madagascar. *Administrators-Superior:* 13 Oct. 1946–31 Dec. 1948 Eugène Alaniou; 31 Dec. 1948–Dec. 1950 Roger Rémy (acting); Dec. 1950–21 April 1956 Pierre Coudert; 21 April 1956–11 Feb. 1958 Georges Arnaud (acting); 11 Feb. 1958–30 June 1959 Georges Arnaud; 30 June 1959–14 Dec. 1960 Gabriel Savignac (acting); 14 Dec. 1960–27 Feb. 1962 Louis Saget. *High Commissioners:* 27 Feb. 1962–22 May 1962 Louis Saget; 22 May 1962–15 Feb. 1963 Yves de Daruvar; 15 Feb. 1963–26 July 1966 Henri Bernard; 26 July 1966–1969 Antoine Columbani; 1969–6 July 1975 Jacques Mouradian. *Presidents:* 7 July 1975–3 Aug. 1975 Ahmad Abdallah. *Provisional Heads of State:* 3 Aug. 1975–5 Aug. 1975 Ali Soilih. *Presidents of National Executive Council:* 5 Aug. 1975–3 Jan. 1976 Prince Sa'id Muhammad Jaffar. *Presidents:* 3 Jan. 1976–13 May 1978 Ali Soilih; 13 May 1978–21 May 1978 Sa'id Attourmani; 21 May 1978–3 Oct. 1978 Ahmad Abdallah and Muhammad Ahmad (jointly); 3 Oct. 1978–22 Oct. 1978 [vacant]; 22 Oct. 1978–26 Nov. 1989 Ahmad Abdallah; 26 Nov. 1989–20 March 1990 Sa'id Muhammad Djohar (acting); 1990–29 Sept. 1995 Sa'id Muhammad Djohar. *Heads of Transitional Military Committee:* 29 Sept. 1995–2 Oct. 1995 Combo Ayuba. *Presidents:* 2 Oct. 1995–5 Oct. 1995 Muhammad Taki Abdulkarim and Sa'id Ali Kamal (jointly); 5 Oct. 1995–26 Jan. 1996 Caabi al-Yachurtu (acting); 26 Jan. 1996–25 March 1996 Sa'id Muhammad Djofar; 25 March 1996–6 Nov. 1998 Muhammad Taki Abdulkarim; 6 Nov. 1998–30 April 1999 Tajjidine ben Sa'id Massonde (interim). *Chief of Staff of National Development:* 30 April 1999–6 May 1999 Azali Assoumani; *Heads of State:* 6 May 1999–21 Jan. 2002 Azali Assoumani; 21 Jan. 2002–26 May 2002 Hamada Bolero (acting); 26 May 2002–Azali Assoumani *Prime Ministers:* 22 Dec. 1961–16 March 1970 Sa'id Muhammad Sheikh; 16 March 1970–16 July 1972 Sa'id Ibrahim ibn Ali; 16 July 1972–Oct. 1972 Sa'id Muhammad Jaffar al-Angadi; 26 Dec. 1972–6 July 1975 Ahmad Abdallah; 6 Jan. 1976–22 Dec. 1978 Abdullahi Muhammad; 22 Dec. 1978–25 Jan. 1982 Salim ben Ali; 8 Feb. 1982–31 Dec. 1984 Ali Mroudjae; 10 May 1992–10 July 1992 Muhammad Taki Abdulkarim (provisional); 1 Jan. 1993–26 May 1993 Ibrahim Abderrahman Halidi; 26 May 1993–19 June 1993 Sa'id Ali Muhammad; 20 June 1993–2 Jan. 1994 Ahmad ben Sheikh Attoumane; 2 Jan. 1994–14 Oct. 1994 Muhammad Abdou Mahdi; 14 Oct. 1994–29 April 1995 Khalifa Houmadi; 29 April 1995–27 March 1996 Caabi al-Yachurtu; 27 March 1996–27 Dec. 1996 Tajiddine ben Sa'id Massonde; 27 Dec. 1996–2 Jan. 1997 Ahmad Abdou (acting); 2 Jan. 1997–9 Sept. 1997 Ahmad Abdou; 7 Dec. 1997–30 May 1998 Nourdine Bourhane; 22 Nov. 1998–30 April 1999 Abbas Djoussouf; 7 Dec. 1999–29 Nov. 2000 Bianrifi Tarmidi; 29 Nov. 2000–15 April 2002 Hamadi Madi HamHamadi . *Note:* In times of no Prime Minister, the President or Head of State held that office.

Congo. 5 Feb. 1883– . *Location:* west central Africa. *Capital:* Brazzaville (founded in 1883, built on the site of Nntamo, and named for the French explorer and administrator Pierre Savorgnan de Brazza). *Other names:* République du Congo, or Republic of Congo (from 1991); République Populaire du Congo, or People's Republic of Congo (1970–1991); Moyen-Congo, Middle Congo or Lower Congo (1883–1958); Congo Français, or French Congo (1883–1960).

History: In 1883 the French protectorate of Moyen-Congo was established to protect French interests in the area. The name Congo came from the river of the same name, which in turn comes from the old kingdom of Kongo. On 27 April 1886 Moyen-Congo became part of the new protectorate of French Equatorial Africa, the capital of this new protectorate being at Brazzaville (see also Portuguese Congo for another attempt at colonization in the Congo). On

29 June 1886 Moyen-Congo became a colony, and on 11 Dec. 1888 it went to form, along with Gabon, the greater territory of Moyen-Congo–Gabon (see Lower Congo–Gabon), which on 5 July 1902 became a colony. The administrators of Moyen-Congo also handled Gabon. On 29 Dec. 1903 the two territories were separated, and Moyen-Congo became a colony again. A large part of the colony was in German hands between 1911 and 1916, as part of Kamerun. On 30 June 1934 Moyen-Congo became a region of the colony of French Equatorial Africa, and on 31 Dec. 1937, still part of the A.E.F. (Afrique Équatoriale Française), Moyen-Congo became an overseas territory of France. On 28 Nov. 1958 it achieved self-rule as an autonomous republic within the French Community, and was bound for independence as the Republic of the Congo. On 15 Aug. 1960 it became independent of France. Just before this the Belgian Congo, its neighbor, had become free, and was known as the Congo also. To avoid confusion between the two, the old French colony became known as Congo (Brazzaville), while the old Belgian colony became known as Congo (Léopoldville). In 1964 Congo (Brazzaville) became a Marxist state, and Congo (Léopoldville) became known as the Democratic Republic of the Congo, but the confusion of names remained, so in 1965 it changed to Congo (Kinshasa). This did little good until 1971 when the old Belgian colony changed its name to Zaire. Then there was only one country called the Congo. By that time (on 1 Jan. 1970) the old French colony had changed its name to the People's Republic of Congo. In Feb. 1991 the name changed back to the Republic of Congo. In 1997 the old Belgian colony changed its name from Zaire to the Democratic Republic of Congo. So now there are two Congos again, and this time the confusion is even greater. Coups (1968, 1979 and 1997) and attempted coups, gross corruption, severe economic depression (1988–1989), poverty, assassinations (1977), ethnic wars, and civil wars (1993–1994 and 1997–1999) have plagued Congo. In between all that there was a supposedly "first democratic election" in 1992. And now there is AIDS as well.

Commissioners: 5 Feb. 1883–27 April 1886 Pierre Savorgnan de Brazza; 27 April 1886–12 Aug. 1889 direct rule by the Commissioner-General of French Equatorial Africa at Brazzaville. *Lieutenant-Governors:* 12 Aug. 1889–27

April 1894 Fortuné de Chavannes; 27 April 1894–1 May 1899 Albert Dolisie; 1 May 1899–11 July 1902 Jean-Baptiste Lemaire; 11 July 1902–5 April 1906 Émile Gentil; 5 April 1906–16 Jan. 1908 Adolphe Cureau; 16 Jan. 1908–17 Nov. 1908 Édouard Dubosc-Taret (acting); 17 Nov. 1908–27 June 1910 Adolphe Cureau; 27 June 1910–28 July 1911 Édouard Dubosc-Taret (acting); 28 July 1911–16 April 1916 Lucien Fourneau; 16 April 1916–17 July 1917 Jules Carde; 17 July 1917–2 April 1919 Jules Le Prince (acting); 2 July 1919–16 May 1919 Edmond Cadier; 16 May 1919–21 Aug. 1919 Jean Marchand (acting); 21 Aug. 1919–17 Aug. 1922 Matteo Alfassa; 17 Aug. 1922–24 April 1923 Georges Thomann (acting); 24 April 1923–21 July 1925 Jean Marchand (acting); 21 July 1925–1 Dec. 1929 ruled direct by Governor-General of French Equatorial Africa; 1 Dec. 1929–4 Dec. 1930 Marcel Marchessou (acting); 4 Dec. 1930–May 1931 Pierre Bonnefont (acting); May 1931–1932 Charles-Max Masson de Saint-Félix; 1932–21 Nov. 1932 Émile Buhot-Launay; 21 Nov. 1932–10 Feb. 1941 ruled direct by Governor-General of French Equatorial Africa. *Lieutenant-Governors:* 10 Feb. 1941–21 Feb. 1942 Gabriel Fortune; 21 Feb. 1942–19 July 1942 Jean Capagorry (acting); 19 July 1942–20 Aug. 1945 Gabriel Fortune; 20 Aug. 1945–30 April 1946 direct rule by Governor-General of French Equatorial Africa; 30 April 1946–16 May 1946 Christian Laigret (acting); 16 May 1946–6 Nov. 1946 direct rule by Governor-General of French Equatorial Africa; 6 Nov. 1946–31 Dec. 1947 Numa-François Sadoul; 31 Dec. 1947–1 March 1950 Jacques-Georges Fourneau; 1 March 1950–25 April 1952 Paul Le Layec; 25 April 1952–15 July 1953 Jean-Georges Chambon; 15 July 1953–19 Feb. 1954 Ernest-Eugène Rouys (acting); 19 Feb. 1954–2 Nov. 1956 Ernest-Eugène Rouys; 2 Nov. 1956–29 Jan. 1958 Jean-Michel Soupault; 29 Jan. 1958–28 Nov. 1958 Charles Dériaud (acting). *High Commissioners:* 28 Nov. 1958–7 Jan. 1959 Charles Dériaud (acting); 7 Jan. 1959–15 Aug. 1960 Gui-Noël Georgy. *Presidents:* 15 Aug. 1960–15 Aug. 1963 Fulbert Youlou; 16 Aug. 1963–19 Dec. 1963 Alphonse Massemba-Débat (acting); 19 Dec. 1963–2 Aug. 1968 Alphonse Massemba-Débat. *Heads of National Revolutionary Council:* 2 Aug. 1968–4 Aug. 1968 Marien Ngouabi. *Presidents:* 4 Aug. 1968–4 Sept. 1968 Alphonse Massemba-Débat; 4 Sept. 1968–1 Jan. 1969 Alfred Raoul; 1 Jan. 1969–5 Jan. 1970

Marien Ngouabi. *Presidents of State Council:* 5 Jan. 1970–25 Aug. 1973 Marien Ngouabi. *Presidents:* 25 Aug. 1973–18 March 1977 Marien Ngouabi. *Chairmen of the Military Committee:* 18 March 1977–5 Feb. 1979 Joachim Yhombi-Opango. *Presidents:* 8 Feb. 1979–31 March 1979 Denis Sassou-Nguesso (interim); 31 March 1979–20 Aug. 1992 Denis Sassou-Nguesso; 20 Aug. 1992–25 Oct. 1997 Pascal Lissouba; 25 Oct. 1997–Denis Sassou-Nguesso. *Prime Ministers:* 26 July 1958–8 Dec. 1958 Jacques Opangoult; 8 Dec. 1958–15 Aug. 1960 Fulbert Youlou; 24 Dec. 1963–15 April 1966 Pascal Lissouba; 6 May 1966–12 Jan. 1968 Ambroise Noumazalay; 25 Aug. 1973–11 Dec. 1975 Henri Lopes; 13 Dec. 1975–7 Aug. 1984 Louis-Sylvain Ngoma (also known as Louis-Sylvain Goba); 11 Aug. 1984–7 Aug. 1989 Ange-Édouard Poungui; 7 Aug. 1989–3 Dec. 1990 Alphonse Poaty-Souchalaty; 3 Dec. 1990–8 Jan. 1991 Pierre Moussa (interim); 8 Jan. 1991–8 June 1991 Louis-Sylvain Ngoma (also known as Louis-Sylvain Goba); 8 June 1991–2 Sept. 1992 André Milongo; 2 Sept. 1992–6 Dec. 1992 Stéphane-Maurice Bongho-Nouarra; 6 Dec. 1992–23 June 1993 Antoine Dacosta; 23 June 1993–23 April 1996 Jacques Yhombi-Opango; 27 Aug. 1996–8 Sept. 1997 Charles-David Ganao; 8 Sept. 1997–15 Oct. 1997 Bernard Kolelas; 7 Jan. 2005–Isidore Mvouba. *Note:* In times of no Prime Minister, the President or Head of State held that office.

Congo (Brazzaville) see **Congo**

Congo Free State see **Congo (Zaire)**

Congo (Kinshasa) see **Congo (Zaire)**

Congo (Léopoldville) see **Congo (Zaire)**

Congo (Zaire). 22 April 1884– . *Location:* central Africa. *Capital:* Kinshasa (its name from 1 July 1965. Named for a village once on the site of this city); Léopoldville (its name until 1 July 1965. This city, later called Kinshasa, was founded in 1881 by Henry M. Stanley, the explorer and agent for King Léopold of the Belgians, for whom Stanley named the town); Boma (1886–1923). *Other names:* Democratic Republic of the Congo (from 1997); Zaire, or République du Zaïre, or Republic of Zaire (1971–1997); Congo (Kinshasa), or Congolese Republic, or République Congolaise, or Republic of the

Congo (all alternative names from 1965 to 1971); Democratic Republic of the Congo, or Independent Republic of the Congo (alternative names from 1960 to 1971); Congo (Léopoldville) (alternative name from 1960 to 1965); Belgian Congo, or Congo Belge (1908–1960); Belgian State of Congo (1908–1908); Congo Free State, or État Indépendant du Congo, or State of Congo, or Kongo Free State (all alternative names between 1885 and 1908); International Association of the Congo (1884–1885).

History: The Portuguese were the first Europeans here, in the late 15th century. At that time the kingdom of Kongo held sway. During the scramble for Africa, by the European powers in the second half of the 19th century, Léopold II, king of the Belgians, formed an international cartel of businessmen to exploit the Congo. This was in 1876, and he sent the famous explorer Henry M. Stanley in to discover new land for the cartel. Later the king sent Stanley back into the Congo to make acquisitions from the local chiefs. At the Conference of Berlin, in 1884 the International Association of the Congo was recognized internationally as the private African estate of King Léopold, and also as a state, covering a good deal of what later became the Belgian Congo. On 5 Feb. 1885 (effective 1 July 1885) it became known as Congo Free State. Because of Léopold's excesses with the natives, especially his brutal treatment of them on the rubber plantations, the Belgian government, on 20 Aug. 1908, took it over as the Belgian State of Congo, a move that was confirmed by an act of the Belgian parliament on 18 Oct. 1908. On 15 Nov. 1908 the country became known as the Belgian Congo. In 1933 Katanga was made a part of the Belgian Congo, as its richest province. Nationalist activities led to Belgium agreeing to independence on 27 June 1960, and three days later, on 30 June 1960 the country did, indeed, become independent, as Congo (Léopoldville), so named in order to distinguish it from its neighbor across the River Congo, i.e. Congo (Brazzaville), the former French colony. These early years of the new state were extremely troublous and indicative and typical of the way events would unfold in the Congo for the next half century. It is the all-too-typical African story: the Belgians created an artificial country — a very big one — containing too many disparate tribes who for centuries had hated each other and who only refrained from wiping each other out because the

Belgians were there with their big guns. Once the Belgians left the trouble began immediately. A new Congo, totally unable to run itself, even if it had the will to do so, plunged headlong into disaster which has bedeviled it for half a century. There were two main parties, the right wing, led by Joseph Kasavubu, and the left wing, led by Patrice Lumumba. Neither party could gain pre-eminence, so a coalition government was formed, with Kasavubu as president and Lumumba as prime minister. In the first few weeks the extreme violence let loose by independence (tribal violence and the mutiny in the Belgian-officered army) caused about 15,000 of the European population to flee the country, with their expertise and money, and United Nations troops moved in. The army was brought back into line by strongman Col. Joseph Desiré Mobutu. The Belgian mining corporations financed and inspired Luanda leader Moise Tshombe to secede Katanga from the Congo, and he did, on 11 July 1960, declaring a new Katanga Republic, in the southeast of the country, with its capital at Elisabethville, and Tshombe as president. On 8 Aug. 1960 Albert Kalonji also broke away in south central Congo, to form his own South Kasai Republic, at Bakwanga. Later in August 1960 Kalonji and Tshombe formed a federation of their two states, but on 27 Aug., when the Kasai state was a mere 19 days old, it was captured by government forces. In Sept. 1960 Kasavubu dismissed Lumumba at Léopoldville, but Lumumba's supporters objected strongly to this move. The dispute was settled by a 14 Sept. 1960 coup led by Col. Mobutu, who allowed Kasavubu to remain as president, arrested Lumumba, and expelled the Communist advisers. On 13 Dec. 1960 Antoine Gizenga, former deputy prime minister under Lumumba, and now claiming to be the official ruler of the Congo, formed his own Stanleyville Republic, which did not last long, however. Lumumba was murdered by Tshombe's followers in Feb. 1961. Tshombe's Republic of Katanga repulsed government forces and it was only due to UN pressure on him that he agreed to re-unify with the Congo, in Jan. 1963. The United Nations finally left on 30 June 1964 and Moise Tshombe, at Kasavubu's invitation, became prime minister shortly thereafter. On 1 Aug. 1964 the country became the Democratic Republic of the Congo. On 7 Sept. 1964 left-wing rebels set up their own Stanleyville People's Republic, also known as the Congolese

People's Republic. This was with the intention of overthrowing Tshombe's legitimate government. This republic did not last long either, because Tshombe brought in mercenaries and rebuilt his army along more professional lines. On 1 July 1965 the country became known as Congo (Kinshasa) (after the new name of the capital), or the Congolese Republic. In Oct. 1965, after a period of being unable to work with him, Kasavubu dismissed Tshombe. This led to renewed violence in the Congo, and Mobutu led another coup, on 25 Nov. 1965, which removed Kasavubu and installed Mobutu. On 21 Oct. 1971 the country changed its name to Zaire, after the newly renamed River Congo (now the Zaire River. The name "zaire" means "great river," specifically the Congo River). Whereas the name of the country caught on immediately (it was so welcome because it ended the confusion between the two Congos), the new name of the river was used only in the country of Zaire. The rest of the world continued to call it the River Congo (or the Congo River). The Congolese National Liberation Front invaded Shaba Province (the old Katanga) in March 1977. The 1980s and 1990s especially were notorious in Zaire for gross corruption, government repression, and poverty, and in 1997 Mobutu was finally toppled. The day after that, on May 17, 1997, the name of the country was changed to the Democratic Republic of the Congo, and the river became the Congo again. There was another Army mutiny in 1998 (the second one of the decade) and then ethnic wars began in earnest. President Kabila was assassinated in 2001, and in 2004 there were two attempted coups and an uprising in East Congo, following which Rwanda and Uganda invaded parts of the country. The old specter haunting the Congo is poverty, and the new specter is AIDS.

Kings/Governors: 22 April 1884–1 July 1885 Léopold, King of the Belgians. *Kings:* 1 July 1885–18 Oct. 1908 Léopold, king of the Belgians. *Administrators-General:* 22 April 1884–26 March 1887 Francis de Winton. *Administrators:* 22 April 1884–June 1884 Sir Frederic Goldsmid. *Governors-General:* 26 March 1887–1 March 1888 Camille Janssen; 1 March 1888–1889 Hermann Ledeganck (acting); 1889–17 April 1891 Camille Janssen. *Governors:* 17 April 1891–8 May 1891 Henri-Ernest Gondry; 8 May 1891–26 Aug. 1892 Camille-Aimé Coquilhat; 26 Aug. 1892–4 Sept. 1896 Joseph Wahis; 4 Sept. 1896–21 Dec.

1900 Francis Dhanis; 21 Dec. 1900–Dec. 1900 Col. Bartels (acting); Dec. 1900–20 May 1912 Joseph Wahis; 20 May 1912–20 Aug. 1916 Félix Fuchs; 20 Aug. 1916–Jan. 1921 Joseph Henry; Jan. 1921–1923 Maurice Lippens; 1923–27 Dec. 1927 Joseph Rutten; 27 Dec. 1927–14 Sept. 1934 Auguste Tilkens; 14 Sept. 1934–31 Dec. 1946 Pierre Ryckmans; 1 Jan. 1947–Jan. 1951 Eugène Jungers; Jan. 1951–5 July 1958 Léon Pétillon; 5 July 1958–30 June 1960 Henri Cornelis. *Presidents:* 24 June 1960–25 Nov. 1965 Joseph Kasavubu; 25 Nov. 1965–1 Dec. 1965 Joseph Desiré Mobutu (provisional); 1 Dec. 1965–16 May 1997 Joseph Desiré Mobutu (also known as Mobutu Sese Seko). *Head of State:* 17 May 1997–29 May 1997 Laurent Kabila. *Presidents:* 29 May 1997–16 Jan. 2001 Laurent Kabila; 16 Jan. 2001–26 Jan. 2001 Joseph Kabila (interim); 26 Jan. 2001–Joseph Kabila. *Prime Ministers-Designate:* 17 June 1960–19 June 1960 Joseph Kasavubu. *Prime Ministers:* 19 June 1960–21 June 1960 Joseph Kasavubu; 21 June 1960–5 Sept. 1960 Patrice Lumumba; 5 Sept. 1960–9 Feb. 1961 Joseph Ileo (prime minister elect); 9 Feb. 1961–1 Aug. 1961 Joseph Ileo; 1 Aug. 1961–10 July 1964 Cyrille Adoulla; 10 July 1964–13 Oct. 1965 Moise Tshombe; 13 Oct. 1965–25 Nov. 1965 Léonard Mulamba. *First State Commissioners:* 6 July 1977–6 March 1979 Mpinga Kasenda; 6 March 1979–27 Aug. 1980 Bo-Boliko Lokonga; 27 Aug. 1980–23 April 1981 Nguza Karl-I-Bond; 23 April 1981–5 Nov. 1982 N'Singa Udjuu; 5 Nov. 1982–31 Oct. 1986 Kengo wa Dondo; 22 Jan. 1987–7 March 1988 Mabi Mulumba; 7 March 1988–26 Nov. 1988 Sambwa Pida Nbagui; 26 Nov. 1988–4 May 1990 Kengo wa Dondo; 4 May 1990–1 April 1991 Lunda Bululu; 1 April 1991–22 July 1991 Mulumba Lukeji; 22 July 1991–24 July 1991 Étienne Tshisekedi wa Mulumba (refused to serve); 24 July 1991–29 Sept. 1991 Mulumba Lukeji; 29 Sept. 1991–20 Oct. 1991 Étienne Tshisekedi wa Mulumba; 1 Nov. 1991–25 Nov. 1991 Bernardin Mungul Diaka; 25 Nov. 1991–14 Aug. 1992 Nguza Karl-I-Bond; 15 Aug. 1992–18 March 1993 Étienne Tshisekedi wa Mulumba; 18 March 1993–14 Jan. 1994 Faustin Birindwa; 6 July 1994–24 March 1997 Léon Kengo wa Dondo; 2 April 1997–9 April 1997 Étienne Tshisekedi wa Mulumba; 9 April 1997–16 May 1997 Likulia Bolongo. *Note:* First State Commissioner is equivalent to Prime Minister. *Note:* In times of no First State Commissioner, the President held that office.

Constantine. 1637–13 Oct. 1837. *Location:* in northern Algeria. *Capital:* Qusantina (also known as Constantine). *Other names:* Qusantina.

History: This is the ancient city of Cirta, a major port in Numidia. It was devastated during the war between Rome and Numidia, and rebuilt by the emperor Constantine, for whom it is named. It did not fall victim to the Vandal conquest of North Africa, but did become an Arab city in the 7th century. Despite mismanagement by the Arabs, and despite continual conquest and reconquest by the Turks and other local powers, it continued to flourish as a Mediterranean seaport, finally becoming the Turkish beylik of Qusantina in 1637, subject to the beylerbey of Algiers. In 1826 the local Kabyle population declared independence from Algiers, and elected Hajji Ahmad as bey. The French tried unsuccessfully to storm the town in 1836, and in 1837 the city state was taken by the French, and it became part of the French Possessions in North Africa (see Algeria), becoming a department of Algeria.

Beys: 1637–(?) Ferhad Bey; (?)–ca. 1700 [unknown]; ca. 1700–1713 Ali Kojja Bey; 1713–1736 Kalyan Hassan; 1736–1754 Hassan; 1754–1756 [vacant]; 1756–1771 Ahmad al-Kollo; 1771–1792 Salah; 1792–1826 during this period a total of 17 beys ruled, including Mustafa Inglis; 1826–1837 Hajji Ahmad.

Corisco see **Equatorial Guinea**

Cornelis Kok's Land. 1813–1857. *Location:* in Orange Free State. *Capital:* Campbell. *Other names:* Campbell Lands (1813–1824).

History: In 1813 the Rev. John Campbell of the London Missionary Society established a Griqua state with its capital at Campbell. It was Campbell who gave the Griquas their name (they were a mixture of races) and the area was loosely ruled until 1819 when Adam Kok left Griquatown (see Griqualand West) and established his rule (as kaptyn, or captain) in Campbell. In 1824 Cornelis Kok II, Adam's younger brother, succeeded to the captaincy and the area became known as Cornelis Kok's Land (see also Adam Kok's Land). During Cornelis's lifetime his boundaries were restructured by all the neighboring white powers and in 1857 Kok and his lands became part of the Orange Free State.

Residents: 1813–1819 Rev. John Campbell.

Kaptyns (Captains): 1819–May 1824 Adam Kok II; May 1824–1857 Cornelis Kok II.

Cosmoledo Islands. No dates. *Location:* 12 islands in the Indian Ocean, 70 miles east of the Aldabras. On 3 Oct. 1810 the British took them from the French. They formed a dependency of the Seychelles until 29 June 1976, when they became part of the new Republic of the Seychelles.

Côte d'Ivoire. 1843– . *Location:* on the Gulf of Guinea, in Northwest Africa. *Capital:* Yamoussoukro (official capital); Abidjan (the de facto capital, and the real capital from 1934); Bingerville (from 1900 to 1934, this town was named after Louis-Gustave Binger, the lieutenant-governor); Grand Bassam (1893–1900); Assinie (1889–1893); Grand Bassam (1843–1889). *Other names:* Ivory Coast (the official name until Sept. 1985, when it was changed to Côte d'Ivoire (which has always been the French name); République de Côte d'Ivoire, or Republic of the Ivory Coast (from 1958); French Gold Coast (alternative name from 1843 to 1893); Assinie (alternative name from 1889 to 1893); Grand Bassam (alternative name from 1843 to 1883).

History: French trading posts were established at Assinie and Grand Bassam, and then forts built at these two places. After acquisitions were made from local chiefs, in 1843 French protectorates of a sort were established at Grand Bassam and Assinie. A little later, at Gabon, a similar thing happened (see Gabon). On 4 Aug. 1860 the Ivory Coast (named for the ivory trade of the early Portuguese dealers in the area) became a territory of the colony of Ivory Coast–Gabon. On 22 Nov. 1878 the French government handed control of the Ivory Coast over to the firm called A. Verdier & Co., who made their headquarters at the already established capital of Grand Bassam. On 16 Dec. 1883 the colony of Ivory Coast–Gabon came to an end, and Verdier continued to run the Ivory Coast as a company possession until 10 Jan. 1889, when all the areas along the coast were brought together under a French protectorate, and administered from Assinie. Expansion began in the hinterland, and on 10 March 1893 Ivory Coast became a colony. That year, 1893, it gained the French protectorate of Kong. On 5 Sept. 1932 (effective 1 Jan. 1933) the French colony of Upper Volta was dismembered, and parts of it went to the French Sudan, Niger and (the largest part) to the Ivory

Coast. This part that went to the Ivory Coast was called Upper Ivory Coast, or Haute Côte d'Ivoire. However, on 1 Jan. 1938 Upper Ivory Coast was constituted a single administrative district. Ivory Coast was under the Vichy government until 1942, when it joined the Free French cause. On 13 Oct. 1946 the Ivory Coast became an overseas province of France, and in 1947, at the request of the inhabitants, the Upper Ivory Coast went to the newly reformed Upper Volta. In Sept. 1958 a referendum was held in the Ivory Coast on the issue of the country becoming an autonomous republic within the French Community. It was affirmative, and the autonomous republic came into being on 4 Dec. 1958. On 7 Aug. 1960 it gained full independence as the Republic of the Ivory Coast. In Sept. 1985 the country's name changed to Côte d'Ivoire by public proclamation. The president, Félix Houphouët-Boigny, was in power from the time Côte d'Ivoire became a republic until 1993. The country was held up as a shining example of what could go right with a sub-Saharan African state (it was the only one), but when Houphouët-Boigny died the country fell apart, rapidly. There is a lot of truth to the theory that he held it all together, but the truth is that toward the end of his regime he was losing his grip. There was an attempted coup in 1980, great poverty, high unemployment, and AIDS. The Côte d'Ivoire suffered its first successful coup in 1999, then ethnic wars, then the French had to step in. There was another attempted coup in 2001 and an Army mutiny in 2002. After a civil war the U.N. went in in April 2004, then there was another civil war from Nov. 2004 until 2005. By this time the Europeans had left (always a bad blow for an African country), and the U.N. were imposing sanctions. Côte d'Ivoire was no longer the shining example of Africa.

Commandants: 1843–1843 Charles de Kerhallet; 1843–1844 Thomas Besson; 1844–1845 Joseph Pellegrin; 1845–1847 M. Conjard; 1847–1848 Adolphe Pigeon; 1848–1850 Jean-Jules Boulay; 1851–1853 Charles Martin des Pallières; 1853–1854 François Chirat; 1854–1855 Pierre Mailhetard; 1856–1856 Noël Bruyas; 1857–1857 Charles Brossard de Corbigny; 1858–1859 Pierre Mailhetard; 1859–4 Aug. 1860 [unknown]; 4 Aug. 1860–1862 Charles Liébault; 1862–1863 Joseph Alem; 1863–1863 Jean Noyer; 1863–1864 Jacques Desnouy; 1864–1866 Jean Martin; 1866–1867 Léon Noël; 1867–1869 Alfred Pou-

zols; 1869–1871 Jean-Louis Vernet. *Residents:* 1871–1886 Arthur Verdier; 1886–9 March 1890 Marcel Treich-Laplène; 9 March 1890–14 June 1890 Octave Péan (acting); 14 June 1890–1892 Jean Desailles; 1892–1892 Eloi Bricard (acting); 1892–12 Nov. 1892 Julien Voisin (acting); 12 Nov. 1892–10 March 1893 Paul Heckman. *Governors:* 10 March 1893–1895 Louis-Gustave Binger; 1895–1895 Paul Cousturier (acting); 1895–1896 Joseph Lemaire (acting); 1896–25 Feb. 1896 Pierre Pascal (acting); 25 Feb. 1896–13 May 1896 Eugène Bertin (acting); 13 May 1896–14 May 1896 Jean-Baptiste Castaing (acting); 14 May 1896–19 March 1897 Louis Mouttet (acting); 19 March 1897–1898 Louis Mouttet; 1898–1898 Pierre Bonhomme (acting); 1898–1898 Jean Penel (acting); 1898–1898 Pierre Capest (acting); 1898–11 Sept. 1898 M. Ribes (acting); 11 Sept. 1898–5 Nov. 1902 Henri Roberdeau; 5 Nov. 1902–25 Nov. 1902 Albert Nébout (acting); 25 Nov. 1902–4 May 1903 Joseph Clozel (acting); 4 May 1903–17 July 1904 Joseph Clozel; 17 July 1904–6 Jan. 1905 Émile Merwaert (acting); 6 Jan. 1905–19 Nov. 1905 Joseph Clozel; 19 Nov. 1905–27 Oct. 1906 Albert Nebout (acting); 27 Oct. 1906–25 Aug. 1907 Joseph Clozel; 25 Aug. 1907–25 April 1908 Albert Nebout (acting); 25 April 1908–28 April 1909 Gabriel Angoulvant; 28 April 1909–Aug. 1909 Pierre Brun (acting); Aug. 1909–12 May 1911 Gabriel Angoulvant; 12 May 1911–9 March 1912 Casimir Guyon (acting); 9 March 1912–22 May 1913 Gabriel Angoulvant; 22 May 1913–29 Oct. 1913 Casimir Guyon (acting); 29 Oct. 1913–4 Sept. 1914 Gustave Julien (acting); 4 Sept. 1914–16 June 1916 Gabriel Angoulvant; 16 June 1916–1 Dec. 1916 Maurice Lapalud (acting); 1 Dec. 1916–27 Dec. 1916 Gabriel Angoulvant; 27 Dec. 1916–Jan. 1918 Maurice Lapalud (acting); Jan. 1918–June 1919 Raphaël Antonetti; June 1919–22 Sept. 1919 Maurice Beurnier (acting); 22 Sept. 1919–24 Jan. 1922 Raphaël Antonetti; 24 Jan. 1922–28 Sept. 1922 Pierre Chapon-Baissac (acting); 28 Sept. 1922–2 April 1924 Raphaël Antonetti; 2 April 1924–2 July 1925 Richard Brunot (acting); 2 July 1925–20 May 1927 Maurice Lapalud; 20 May 1927–March 1928 Maurice Bourgine (acting); March 1928–25 Aug. 1930 Maurice Lapalud; 25 Aug. 1930–28 Oct. 1930 Jules Brévié; 28 Oct. 1930–16 Jan. 1931 Jean-Paul Boutonnet (acting); 16 Jan. 1931–3 March 1931 Dieudonné Reste; 3 March 1931–28 Dec. 1932 Raoul Bourgine (acting); 28 Dec. 1932–7 May 1935 Dieudonné Reste; 7 May 1935–28 June 1935 Alphonse de Pouzois (acting); 28 June 1935–7 March 1936 Adolphe Deitte; 7 March 1936–28 Nov. 1936 Julien Lamy (acting); 28 Nov. 1936–16 July 1938 Gaston Mondon; 16 July 1938–27 Jan. 1939 Louis Bressalles (acting). *Governors:* 27 Jan. 1939–5 March 1940 Horace Crocicchia (acting); 5 March 1940–1 Jan. 1941 Horace Crocicchia; 1 Jan. 1941–29 Sept. 1942 Hubert Deschamps; 29 Sept. 1942–3 Aug. 1943 Georges Rey; 3 Aug. 1943–26 Aug. 1943 Jean-François Toby; 26 Aug. 1943–16 Aug. 1945 André Latrille; 16 Aug. 1945–April 1946 Henri de Mauduit; April 1946–20 Feb. 1947 André Latrille; 20 Feb. 1947–20 May 1947 Oswald Durand (acting); 20 May 1947–29 Jan. 1948 Oswald Durand; 29 Jan. 1948–10 Nov. 1948 Georges Orselli; 10 Nov. 1948–25 April 1952 Laurent Péchoux; 25 April 1952–10 July 1952 Pierre-François Pelieu; 10 July 1952–19 Feb. 1954 Victor Bailly; 19 Feb. 1954–18 Feb. 1956 Pierre Messmer; 18 Feb. 1956–28 May 1956 Pierre Lami (acting); 28 May 1956–23 Feb. 1957 Pierre Lami; 23 Feb. 1957–4 Dec. 1958 Ernest de Nattes. *High Commissioners:* 4 Dec. 1958–1960 Ernest de Nattes; 1960–7 Aug. 1960 Yves Guéna. *Presidents:* 7 Aug. 1960–27 Nov. 1960 Félix Houphouët-Boigny (interim); 27 Nov. 1960–7 Dec. 1993 Félix Houphouët-Boigny; 7 Dec. 1993–24 Dec. 1999 Henri Konan Bédié; 24 Dec. 1999–25 Oct. 2000 Robert Guéi; 25 Oct. 2000–Laurent Gbagbo. *Prime Ministers:* 4 Dec. 1958–31 April 1959 Auguste Denis (provisional); 2 May 1959–7 Aug. 1960 Félix Houphouët-Boigny; 7 Nov. 1990–7 Dec. 1993 Alassane Ouattara; 117 Dec. 1993–24 Dec. 1999 Daniel Kablan Duncan; 18 May 2000–23 Oct. 2000 Seydou Diarra; 27 Oct. 2000–25 Jan. 2003 Affi N'Guessan; 25 Jan. 2003–Seydou Diarra. *Note:* In times of no Prime Minister, the President held that office.

Cotonou. 19 May 1868–22 June 1894. *Location:* Kotonou, Benin. *Capital:* Cotonou. *Other names:* Kotonu.

History: In 1868 the French established a protectorate over the coastal kingdom of Kotonu. An administration does not seem to have been set up until 1878, in the form of a French consul. In 1883 the power at Cotonou became vested in the resident of the French protectorate of Porto-Novo. In 1894 Cotonou became part of the French colony of Dahomey (see Benin).

Consuls: 1878–1881 Albert Ardin d'Elteil; 1881–1883 Victor Bareste; 1883–22 June 1894 ruled from Porto-Novo.

Crocodile People see **Bakwenaland**

Cross River State see **Biafra**

Curieuse Island see **Seychelles**

Cush see **Kush**

Cyrenaica. 15 Oct. 1912–24 Dec. 1951. *Location:* eastern Libya. *Capital:* Benghazi (from 1943); al-Marj (also known as Barce) (1942–1943); Bengasi (the Italian spelling) (until 1942). *Other names:* Cirenaica (the Italian name); Barca; Barqah.

History: Cyrenaica was of great importance in the Mediterranean in ancient days. Originally a Greek, and then a Ptolemaic colony, it became a Roman province in 96 B.C. In the 640s it became an Arab territory, and by the 19th century was an Ottoman province. By 1912 the Italians had conquered the three principal areas of what we now know as Libya, viz. Tripolitania, Cyrenaica (15 Oct. 1912), and the Fezzan. The Italians divided the country into two protectorates, Cirenaica and Tripolitania. On 17 May 1919 Cirenaica became a colony, but on 24 Jan. 1929 the Italians re-united Cirenaica and Tripolitania to form Libya, although Cirenaica continued to be administered separately. In 1942 this was the first part of Libya to be taken by the Allies in World War II. In 1943 the Tripolitania area and the Fezzan were captured and the Italians changed sides. The French and British split up Libya between them, the French getting the Fezzan, and the British getting Cyrenaica (their spelling) and Tripolitania. On 1 June 1949 the amir, Idris, proclaimed the independence of Cyrenaica, calling it the Kingdom of Libya. The British did not quite agree, but did give autonomy to the area in preparation for the real independence which was to come for all of Libya in 1951.

Governors: 15 Oct. 1912–Oct. 1913 Ottavio Briccolo; Oct. 1913–5 Aug. 1918 Giovan-Battista Ameglio; 5 Aug. 1918–5 Aug. 1919 Vincenzo Garioni; 5 Aug. 1919–23 Nov. 1921 Nobile Giacomo Di Martino; 23 Nov. 1921–1 Oct. 1922 Luigi Pintor; 1 Oct. 1922–1 Dec. 1922 Eduardo Baccari; 1 Dec. 1922–7 Jan. 1923 Oreste

De Gasperi; 7 Jan. 1923–24 May 1924 Luigi Bongiovanni; 24 May 1924–22 Nov. 1926 Ernesto Mombelli; 2 Dec. 1926–18 Dec. 1928 Attilio Teruzzi; 21 Jan. 1929–24 Jan. 1929 Domenico Siciliani. *Vice-Governors:* 24 Jan. 1929–13 March 1930 Domenico Siciliani; 13 March 1930–30 May 1934 Rodolfo Graziani; 1 June 1934–23 April 1935 Guglielmo Nasi; 23 April 1935–21 Dec. 1942 administered direct from Tripoli. *British Military Administrators:* 21 Dec. 1942–10 March 1943 Duncan Cumming. *Chief Administrators:* 10 March 1943–30 Oct. 1945 Duncan Cumming; 30 Oct. 1945–1946 Peter Acland; 1946–1948 James Haugh; 1948–17 Sept. 1949 Eric Vully de Candole. *Residents:* 17 Sept. 1949–24 Dec. 1951 Eric Vully de Candole. *Amirs:* 21 Dec. 1942–24 Dec. 1951 Idris al-Mahdi as-Sanusi. *Prime Ministers-Designate:* 5 July 1949–7 Nov. 1949 Fathi al-Kikhya (never took office). *Prime Ministers:* 9 Nov. 1949–18 March 1950 Umar Mansur al-Kikhya; 18 March 1950–24 Dec. 1951 Muhammad as-Saqizli. *United Nations High Commissioners:* 17 March 1950–24 Dec. 1951 Adrian Pelt.

Cyrene see **Pentapolis**

Dadigar see **Bedde**

Dagbon see **Dagomba**

Dagomba. ca. 1440–1896. *Location:* mid–Ghana. *Capital:* Yendi. *Other names:* Dagbon.
   History: Legend has it that the kingdom of Dagomba was founded in the 14th century. Actually, 1440 is more correct. About 1680 Dagomba was subjugated by the Ashanti Empire, and remained so until 1874 when the Ashanti were defeated by the British. In 1896 Dagomba became part of the British protectorate of Ashanti.
   Kings: ca. 1440–ca. 1475 Nyagse; ca. 1475–ca. 1500 Zulande; ca. 1500–ca. 1520 Nagalogu; ca. 1520–ca. 1525 Datorli; ca. 1525–ca. 1530 Buruguyomda; ca. 1530–ca. 1560 Zoligu; ca. 1560–ca. 1600 Zonman; ca. 1600–ca. 1630 Ninmitoni; ca. 1630–ca. 1640 Dimani; ca. 1640–ca. 1645 Yanzo; ca. 1645–ca. 1660 Darizegu; ca. 1660–ca. 1680 Luro; ca. 1680–ca. 1690 Tutugri; ca. 1690–ca. 1695 Zagale; ca. 1695–ca. 1700 Zokuli; ca. 1700–ca. 1710 Gungobili; ca. 1710–ca. 1720 Zangina; ca. 1720–ca. 1730 Andani Sigili; ca. 1730–ca. 1745 Ziblim Bunbiogo; ca. 1745–

ca. 1760 Gariba; ca. 1760–ca. 1780 Ziblim Na Saa; ca. 1780–ca. 1785 Ziblim Bandamda; ca. 1785–ca. 1815 Andani I; ca. 1815–ca. 1820 Mahama I; ca. 1820–ca. 1830 Ziblim Kulunku; ca. 1830–ca. 1845 Sumani Zoli; ca. 1845–ca. 1863 Yakubu I; ca. 1863–ca. 1882 Abdullai I; ca. 1882–1899 Andani II; 1899–1900 Darimani; 1900–1920 al-Hassan; 1920–1938 Abdullai II; 1938–1948 Mahama II; 1948–1953 Mahama III; 1953–1968 Abdullai III; 1968–1969 Andani III; 1969–1974 Muhammad Abdullai IV; 1974–27 March 2002 Yakubu II.

Dahomey. ca. 1600–22 June 1894. *Location:* Benin. *Capital:* Abomey. *Other names:* Danhomé; Allada (from 1730); Abomey (1600–1730).
   History: About 1590 Akolu, the ruler of Allada died, leaving three sons. One stayed at Allada, another founded the kingdom of Porto-Novo, while the third, Do-Aklin, with his son Dakodonu, after a series of adventures founded the kingdom of Abomey (although Agasu, the Leopard, is the mythical founder of the Abomey dynasty). Do-Aklim and his people intermarried with the indigenous Gedevi tribe. Thus the Fon ethnic group was formed. Wegbaja was the great king of this dynasty. Abomey captured Allada in 1724 and the kingdom of Whydah in 1729. In 1730 the name of the kingdom changed to Dahomey. Long before the reign of Gezo, the Amazons were formed as the first reliably documented female army (although Gezo claimed them as his idea). In 1851 Gezo entered into a commercial agreement with France, in which he undertook to protect their fort at Whydah. Gezo, an enlightened monarch, died in 1858, and was succeeded by his son Gelele, not so enlightened. He raided neighbors, persecuted Christians, and encouraged the slave trade. The British annexed Lagos in 1861 in order to have a station from which to engage him in warfare if necessary. On 3 Dec. 1891 the French established a military protectorate over the country. In 1892 there was war between the French and Dahomey, and French troops entered Abomey on 17 Nov. 1892. gBehanzin, Gelele's equally nasty son, fled and finally surrendered to the French on 25 Jan. 1894. That year the French colony of Dahomey officially came into being, and the kingdom came to a close, although kings continued to rule nominally for a while.
   Kings: ca. 1600–ca. 1625 Do-Aklim; ca.

1625–1645 Dakodonu; 1645–1645 Ganye Hesu; 1645–1685 Wegbaja; 1685–1708 Akaba (also known as Wibega). *Queens:* 1685–1708 Hangbe (ruled jointly with Akaba). *Kings:* 1708–April 1732 Aguja (also known as Tossu); April 1732–17 May 1774 Tegbesu (also known as Avissu); 17 May 1774–1789 Kpengla (also known as gNansunu); 1789–17 May 1790 [vacant]; 17 April 1790–1797 Agonglo (also known as Sindozan). *Regents:* 1797–1804 Adanzan. *Kings:* 1804–1818 Adanzan; 1818–1858 Gezo (also known as Gangkpe); 1858–29 Dec. 1889 Gelele (also known as Glele); 30 Dec. 1889–15 Jan. 1894 gBehanzin; 15 Jan. 1894–1898 Agbo Agoli.

Dahomey Portuguese Protectorate. 5 Aug. 1885–22 Dec. 1887. *Location:* Benin. *Capital:* none. *Other names:* Portuguese Dahomey.

History: The Portuguese claimed a protectorate over the Dahomey coastline, but in reality their only possession in the area was the old fort at Whydah. By 1887 they had relinquished all claims in favor of France (see Porto-Novo).

Rulers: 5 Aug. 1885–22 Dec. 1887 none.

Dala Hill see **Kano**

Damagaram. 1731–30 July 1899. *Location:* the Zinder area of southern Niger. *Capital:* Zinder (1822–1899); Kianza (1802–1822); Gueza (1731–1802). *Other names:* Zinder (alternative name from 1822).

History: Founded in 1731 as a vassal state of the Bornu Empire, Damagaram became independent about 1800, and in 1899 was taken by the French as part of French West Africa, becoming, in 1900, the base for the Autonomous Military Territory of Zinder (see Niger).

Kings: 1731–1746 Mallam ibn Maina; 1746–1757 Babami; 1757–1775 Tanimun; 1775–1782 Assafa; 1782–1787 Abaza; 1787–1790 Mallam Babu Saba; 1790–1799 Dauda; 1799–1812 Ahmadu I; 1812–1822 Suleiman I; 1822–1841 Ibrahim I; 1841–1843 Tanimun II; 1843–1850 Ibrahim I; 1850–1851 Muhammad Kace; 1851–1884 Tanimun II; 1884–1884 Ibrahim II; 1884–1893 Suleiman II; 1893–30 July 1899 Ahmadu II; 30 July 1899–1906 Ahmadu III; 1906–1922 Bellama; 27 Feb. 1923–3 Sept. 1950 Barma Mustafa; 1950–1978 Umaru Sanda; 1978–9 July 2001 Abubakar; 26 July 2001–Mamadu Mustafa.

Damaraland see **Namibia**

Danakil Territory see **Massawa**

Danhomé see **Dahomey**

Danish Gold Coast. 1658–30 March 1850. *Location:* the eastern coast of what is now Ghana. *Capital:* Fort Christiansborg (from 1685); Fort Frederiksborg (until 1685). *Other names:* Danish Guinea.

History: In 1653 the Danes arrived on the Gold Coast to compete in trade with the other powers (see Gold Coast, Dutch Gold Coast, and Portuguese Gold Coast). In 1658 they captured Fort Frederiksborg, the old Swedish capital there (see Swedish Gold Coast), expelling the remaining Swedes from the Gold Coast. Until 1750 the Danish forts were run by the West India and Guinea Company, but after that year the Danish Crown managed affairs in the colony. In 1850 the forts and ports of Christiansborg (later the nucleus of Accra), Keta, Kongosteen, Fort Frederiksborg, and Fort Augustenborg, were sold to the British, who incorporated them into the Gold Coast (q.v.). That year the Danes left the Gold Coast.

Opperhoveds (Chief Heads): 1658–16 April 1659 Samuel Smidt; 16 April 1659–Oct. 1659 no Danish rule; Oct. 1659–6 June 1662 Joost Cramer; 6 June 1662–10 Sept. 1664 Henning Albrecht (acting); 10 Sept. 1664–1669 Henning Albrecht; 1669–1674 Bartolomaus von Grone stein; 1674–1680 Conrad Crul (acting); 1680–1680 Peter With (acting); 1680–2 Feb. 1681 Peter Valck (acting); 2 Feb. 1681–1 July 1681 Magnus Prang; 1 July 1681–11 July 1684 [unknown]; 11 July 1684–1687 Hans Lykke; 1687–5 Jan. 1691 Nikolaj Fensman; 5 Jan. 1691–1692 Jørgen Meyer; 1692–1694 Harding Petersen; 1694–6 Dec. 1696 Thomas Jacobsen; 6 Dec. 1696–23 Dec. 1698 Erik Lygaard (acting); 23 Dec. 1698–31 Aug. 1703 Johan Trawne; 11 Sept. 1703–23 April 1704 Hartvig Meyer. *Vice-Opperhoveds:* 23 April 1704–5 May 1705 Peter Sverdrup; 5 May 1705–25 May 1705 Peter Petersen. *Opperhoveds:* 25 May 1705–17 Aug. 1711 Erik Lygaard; 17 Aug. 1711–26 Nov. 1717 Bfantz Boye; 26 Nov. 1717–6 Aug. 1720 Knud Røst; 6 Aug. 1720–24 Jan. 1722 Peter Østrup; 25 Jan. 1722–22 Jan. 1723 David Hernn; 22 Jan. 1723–30 Oct. 1723 Niels Østrup; 7 Nov. 1723–27 April 1724 Christian Syndermann; 27 April 1724–1 March 1727 Hendrik von Suhm; 4 March 1727–18 Sept. 1727 Fred Pahl; 18 Sept. 1727–24 Dec. 1728 Andreas

Willennsen; 24 Dec. 1728–12 Aug. 1735 Anders Waerøe; 12 Aug. 1735–14 June 1736 Severin Schilderup; 14 June 1736–20 June 1740 Enewald Borris; 20 June 1740–26 May 1743 Peter Jørgensen; 26 May 1743–3 Feb. 1744 Christian Dorph; 3 Feb. 1744–11 March 1745 Jørgen Billsen; 11 March 1745–23 March 1745 Thomas Brock; 23 March 1745–23 April 1745 Johan Wilder; 23 April 1745–21 June 1746 August Hackenborg; 21 June 1746–6 March 1751 Joost Platfusz; 6 March 1751–8 March 1751 Magnus Lützow; 8 March 1751–21 July 1752 Magnus Hacksen (acting); 21 July 1752–11 March 1757 Carl Engmann; 11 March 1757–14 Feb. 1762 Christian Jessen; 14 Feb. 1762–20 Oct. 1766 Carl Resch. *Governors of Guinea:* 20 Oct. 1766–11 Jan. 1768 Christian Tychsen; 11 Jan. 1768–2 July 1769 Frantz Kyhberg (acting); 2 July 1769–11 June 1770 Gerhard Wrisberg; 11 June 1770–13 June 1770 Joachim Otto (acting); 13 June 1770–15 June 1772 Johan Frohlich (acting); 15 June 1772–24 June 1777 Niels Aarestrup (acting); 24 June 1777–2 Dec. 1780 Conrad von Hemsen; 2 Dec. 1780–21 April 1788 Jens Kiøge (acting); 21 April 1788–23 Oct. 1789 Johan Kipnasse (acting); 23 Oct. 1789–July 1792 Andreas Biørn; July 1792–25 Jan. 1793 Andreas Hammer (acting); 25 Jan. 1793–30 June 1793 Andreas Hammer; 30 June 1793–3 Aug. 1793 Bendt Olrich; 3 Aug. 1793–17 Aug. 1795 Frantz von Hager (acting); 17 Aug. 1795–Oct. 1795 [unknown] (acting); Oct. 1795–31 Dec. 1799 Johan Wrisberg; 31 Dec. 1799–3 Oct. 1802 Johan Ahnholm (acting); 3 Oct. 1802–15 April 1807 Johan Wrisberg; 15 April 1807–1 March 1817 Christian Schiønning (acting); 3 March 1817–5 Oct. 1817 Johan Richter; 5 Oct. 1817–6 May 1819 Jens Reiersen (acting); 6 May 1819–25 Nov. 1819 Philip Wrisberg (never took office); 6 May 1819–1 Jan. 1821 Christian Svanekjaer (acting); 1 Jan. 1821–5 Sept. 1821 Peter Steffens; 5 Sept. 1821–23 Dec. 1823 Matthias Thønning (acting); 23 Dec. 1823–7 May 1825 Johan von Richelieu; 7 May 1825–30 Sept. 1827 Niels Brøch (acting); 30 Sept. 1827–1 Aug. 1828 Jens Flindt; 1 Aug. 1828–20 Jan. 1831 Heinrich Lind (acting); 29 Jan. 1831–21 Oct. 1831 Ludwig von Hein; 21 Oct. 1831–4 Dec. 1831 Helmut von Ahrenstorff; 4 Dec. 1831–1 March 1833 Niels Brøch; 1 March 1833–21 July 1834 Heinrich Lind; 21 July 1834–26 Dec. 1834 Edvard von Gandil (acting); 26 Dec. 1834–19 Aug. 1837 Frederik Mørch (acting); 19 Aug. 1837–18 March 1839 Frederik Mørch; 19 March 1839–18 Aug. 1839 Hans Giede (acting); 18 Aug. 1839–24 May 1842 Lucas Dall (acting); 24 May 1842–26 Aug. 1842 Bernhardt Wilkens (acting); 26 Aug. 1842–15 March 1844 Edvard Carstensen (acting); 15 March 1844–5 July 1844 Edvard Ericksen (acting); 5 July 1844–9 Oct. 1844 Georg Lutterodt (acting); 9 Oct. 1844–10 April 1847 Edvard Carstensen (appointed 30 July 1844); 10 April 1847–20 Feb. 1850 Rasmus Schmidt (acting); 20 Feb. 1850–30 March 1850 Edvard Carstensen. *Nominal Governors:* April 1850–17 Aug. 1850 Edvard Carstensen.

Daniski. 1447–1806. *Location:* northern Nigeria. *Capital:* Daniski Hill.

History: The Bolewa people came from the Lake Chad area to northern Nigeria in 1447, and settled in the Daniski Hills, establishing their capital at Daniski Hill, and displacing the Ngamo tribe. In 1806 their moi (king) founded Fika and left Daniski.

Sarkis: 1447–1454 Idriso; 1454–1463 Atman. *Mois (Kings):* 1463–1471 Moi Albo; 1471–1488 Mele Manso; 1488–1498 Anbanga; 1498–1554 Bunowo; 1554–1596 Barma Dan Moi Bunowo; 1596–1611 Gandowo; 1611–1621 Langawa Daka; 1621–1639 Halbo; 1639–1674 Mama Kayi; 1674–1684 Bawa Kayi; 1684–1709 Mele Fusan; 1709–1710 Buraima Wamu; 1710–1721 Mama Mulu; 1721–1728 Adam Bakam; 1728–1745 Mama Korya; 1745–1749 Mama Gimsi; 1749–1752 Sule Ladi; 1752–1770 Aji Daka; 1770–1787 Langawa; 1787–1796 Uthman Gana; 1796–1804 Mammadi Gizze; 1804–1805 Mele Filata; 1805–1806 Moi Buraima.

Darfur. 1603–6 Nov. 1916. *Location:* eastern Sudan. *Capital:* al-Fasher (this was the first permanent capital, established as such about 1790). *Other names:* Dar Fur; Fur.

History: In 1603 the Keira dynasty was founded in Darfur, thus beginning the recorded history of that state. In the first few years of his reign, Suleiman Solong conquered Kordofan. After about 1670 the sultans established their "fasher" (capital) at a different place, until about 1790, when it was fixed at al-Fasher. On 24 Oct. 1874 it was taken by Egypt, and became the Darfur Province of the Egyptian Sudan. In Dec. 1883 it was overrun by the forces of the Mahdi, and it became a fundamental part of his state, and after the fall of the Mahdi, on 21 March

1899, Darfur was re-established as a sultanate. In 1915 the sultan of Darfur revolted against Anglo-Egyptian rule in the Sudan, and was killed in 1916, whereupon Darfur became a province of the Anglo-Egyptian Sudan (see Sudan). For the recent troubles in Darfur see Sudan.

Sultans: 1603–1637 Suleiman Solong; 1637–1682 Musa ibn Suleiman; 1682–1722 Ahmad Bakr ibn Musa; 1722–1732 Muhammad I Dawra; 1732–1739 Umar Lele; 1739–1756 Abu'l Qasim; 1756–1787 Muhammad II Tairab; 1787–1801 Abdarrahman ar-Rashid; 1801–1839 Muhammad III al-Fadhl; 1839–1873 Muhammad IV Hussain; 1873–24 Oct. 1874 Ibrahim. *Governors:* 24 Oct. 1874–1881 Hassan Bey Hilmi; 1881–Dec. 1883 Rudolf Karl Slatin. *Sultans:* 21 March 1899–6 Nov. 1916 Ali Dinar ibn Zakariyya.

Daura. ca. 700–1903. *Location:* on the Niger-Nigeria border. *Capital:* Daura (the latter capital. The name means "blacksmith" in ancient Tuareg); Tsofon Birni (the original capital).

History: The senior of all the Hausa States, it was taken over about the year 1000 by Kazuru. He arrived in the area and married the 17th queen of Daura. In 1805 the Fulani amir Mallam Ishaku conquered the Habe kingdom of Daura, and made it a Muslim amirate (see Fulani Empire). The deposed king, Gwari Abdu, escaped first to Kwargdom, then to Tsirkau, and on to Murya, and then to Nguru. Then he returned to Murya, where he stayed. He waged war on the Fulani, but was unable to recapture it from the Fulani. Gwari Abdu died about 1809, and his brother Lukudi became de jure Sarkin Daura (King of Daura) of the Habe dynasty. He forced the Fulani out of a sector of the old kingdom, a sector called Zango, and about 1825 set up a rival kingdom in the town of Zango (see Daura-Zango). Another branch of the Habe from Daura, under Danshuhunni, had already set up a second rival dynasty at the town of Dan Mairam. When Danshuhunni was killed, his son Tsofo moved on to found, about 1825, the rival kingdom of Daura-Baure, with its capital at Baure. In 1903 the Fulani amirate of Daura was split up between the French and the British, and a reformed amirate known as Daura was formed in the British protectorate of Northern Nigeria.

Magajiyas (Queens): ca. 700–(?) Kufuru (also known as Kofano); (?)–(?) Gino (also known as Gufano); (?)–(?) Yakumo (also known as Yak-wano); (?)–(?) Yakunya (also known as Yakaniya); (?)–(?) Walzamu (also known as Waizam); (?)–(?) Yanbamu; (?)–(?) Gizirgizit (also known as Gadar Gadar); (?)–(?) Innagari (also known as Anagiri); (?)–(?) Daura; (?)–(?) Gamata; (?)–(?) Shata; (?)–(?) Batatume; (?)–(?) Sandamata; (?)–(?) Jamata; (?)–(?) Hamata; (?)–(?) Zama; (?)–ca. 1000 Shawata. *Sarkins (Kings):* ca. 1000–ca. 1030 Abayajidda (also known as Kazuru); ca. 1030–ca. 1070 Bawo; ca. 1070–ca. 1100 Gazaura; ca. 1100–(?) Gakuna; (?)–(?) Jaaku; (?)–(?) Jaketake; (?)–ca. 1200 Yakama; ca. 1200–(?) Jaka; (?)–(?) Ada Hamta; (?)–(?) Ada Jabu; (?)–(?) Dagamu; (?)–(?) Ada Yaki; (?)–(?) Hamdogu; (?)–ca. 1300 Yabau; ca. 1300–(?) Naji; (?)–(?) Gani; (?)–(?) Wake; (?)–(?) Kamutu; (?)–(?) Rigo; (?)–(?) Gaga; (?)–ca. 1400 Jabu; ca. 1400–(?) Zamnau; (?)–(?) Shashimi; (?)–(?) Ada Inda; (?)–(?) Doguma; (?)–ca. 1500 Ada Gamu; ca. 1500–(?) Ada Sunguma; (?)–(?) Shafau; (?)–(?) Ada Sabau; (?)–(?) Ada Doki; (?)–(?) Nagama; (?)–(?) Ada Kube; (?)–ca. 1600 Hamama; ca. 1600–(?) Dagajirau; (?)–(?) Kamu; (?)–(?) Ada Guguwa; (?)–(?) Hamida; (?)–(?) Abdu Kawo; (?)–(?) Nagama; (?)–ca. 1700 Hanatari; ca. 1700–(?) Rifau; (?)–(?) Hazo; (?)–(?) Dango; (?)–(?) Bawan Allah; (?)–(?) Kalifah; (?)–(?) Tsofo; (?)–(?) Jiro; (?)–1805 Gwari Abdu. *Amirs:* 1805–(?) Mallam Ishaku; (?)–(?) Yusufu; (?)–(?) Muhamman; (?)–(?) Zubeiru; (?)–(?) Bello; (?)–(?) Altine; (?)–(?) Maigardo; (?)–(?) Sogiji; (?)–1906 Murnai.

Daura-Baure. ca. 1825–1903. *Location:* 36 miles southeast of Daura, in southern Niger. *Capital:* Baure. *Other names:* Baure.

History: In 1805 the kingdom of Daura was conquered by the Fulani amir Mallam Ishaku, and two sets of noble families fled Daura and eventually established rival kingdoms not far from their original home. One of these groups was led by the deposed Habe king, Gwari Abdu, whose brother Lukudi would, around 1825, form the kingdom of Daura-Zango. Another branch was led by Danshuhunni. At first they resided at the town of Dan Mairam, but when Danshuhunni was killed, his son Tsofo founded the town of Baure, around which the kingdom of Daura-Baure grew up as a rival not only to the amirate under the Fulani conquerors, but also to Daura-Zango. Daura-Baure spent most of its history as a vassal state of Damagaram (which had its capital at Zinder). In 1903 Daura-Baure became part of the autonomous French military territory of Zinder (see Niger).

Sarkins (Kings): ca. 1825–(?) Tsofo; (?)–(?) Habu; (?)–(?) Jibo; (?)–(?) Zakari; (?)–(?) Abdu; (?)–1903 Hallaru.

Daura-Zango. ca. 1825–1903. *Location:* 12 miles east of Daura, in southern Niger. *Capital:* Zango. *Other names:* Zango.

History: In 1805 the kingdom of Daura was conquered by the Fulani amir Mallam Ishaku. The deposed king, Gwari Abdu, fled, dying at Murya about 1809, and eventually his brother, Lukudi founded the town of Zango. Around this town Lukudi established the rival kingdom of Daura-Zango about 1825. Zango spent most of its time as a vassal state of Damagaram (which had its capital at Zinder). In 1903 Zango became free of Damagaram, but only because the French and British divided the area up between them. Damagaram, and a portion of the amirate of Daura, and a portion of Daura-Zango all joined the autonomous French military territory of Zinder (see Niger), while the ruling portion of Daura-Zango, as well as most of the amirate of Daura, became part of the British protectorate of Northern Nigeria.

Sarkins Daura (Kings of Daura-Zango): ca. 1825–1828 Lukudi; 1828–1843 Nuhu; 1843–1856 Muhamman Sha; 1856–1862 Haruna; 1862–1868 Dan Aro; 1868–1888 Tafida; 1888–1890 Suleimanu; 1890–1895 Yusufu; 1895–1904 Tafida; 1904–1911 Mallam Musa; 1911–1912 interregnum; 1912–1963 Abdurrahman; 1963–(?) al-Hajj Muhammadu Bashar.

Dawa see **Hadejia**

Dawaro see **Ifat**

Dedougou see **Burkina Faso**

Dei see **Liberia**

Dembe see **Brass**

Denis Island see **Seychelles**

Denkyira. 1550–1701. *Location:* Ghana–Côte d'Ivoire. *Capital:* Abankeseso. *Other names:* Denkyera.

History: In 1550 the Denkyira people founded their community, the state of Denkyira itself being formed in 1620. In 1701 the Ashanti conquered it.

Chiefs: 1550–1560 Ayekeraa; 1560–1570 Yao Awirri; 1570–1590 Anim Kokobo Boadee; 1590–1601 Ahaha; 1601–1609 Ahihi; 1609–1649 Warempe Ampem (also known as Mumuromfi); 1649–1671 Boadu Akafo Berempon (also known as Adafo Biaka); 1671–1690 Boa Amponsem (also known as Boa Siante); 1690–1710 Ntim Gyakari.

Denyanke Dynasty see **Futa Toro**

Des Roches Islands see **Farquhar and Des Roches Islands**

Deserta Grande see **Madeira**

Desertas Group see **Madeira**

Dia Ogo Dynasty see **Futa Toro**

Diallon see **Futa Jallon**

Dibo see **Agaie**

Diego Ruy's Island see **Rodrigues**

Diego Suarez. 1886–6 Aug. 1896. *Location:* the present-day town of Antsirana, and its environs, in northern Madagascar. *Capital:* Diego Suarez.

History: Diego Suarez was the name given to a bay in northern Madagascar, discovered in 1500 by Portuguese navigator Diogo Dias. It is generally reckoned that it was here that the pirate republic of Libertalia was set up. At the end of the French war with the local Hova peoples, the French built a naval station here, and in 1886 the local king ceded Diego Suarez to France as a colony. In 1896 it became a part of the overall French colony of Madagascar, as the District of Diego Suarez.

Commandants: 1886–1887 Henri Caillet; 1887–6 Aug. 1896 Ernest-Emmanuel Froger.

Diggers' Republic see **Klipdrift Republic**

Digue Island see **Seychelles**

Dire Dawa see **Ethiopia**

Diva Morgabin see **Réunion**

Djallon see **Futa Jallon**

Djibouti. 11 March 1862– . *Location:* northeast Africa, at the southern entrance to the Red Sea. *Capital:* Djibouti (the capital from 1892. This town was built around 1880); Obock (1884–1892). *Other names:* Jibuti; Djibuti; Jamhariyya Djibouti, or République du Djibouti, or Republic of Djibouti (1977–); Térritoire Français des Afars et des Issas, or French Territory of the Afars and Issas, or Territory of the Afars and Issas (1967–1977); French Somaliland (1896–1967); Obock, or Obok (alternative names from 1862 to 1896); French Coast of the Somalis, or Côte Française des Somalis (1862–1884, although this name lingered on in France until 1967).

History: In the 1830s and 1840s the French explored this area of the Red Sea, signing treaties with the local Afar and Issas leaders in 1859. In 1862 they bought the seaport of Obock, and in 1884 a commandant was appointed at Obock, and the place was finally occupied by the French, when it was renamed the colony of Obock on 24 June 1884. Around the colony of Obock the whole coastline was gradually brought under a French protectorate (e.g. Tadjouna) until 1896, when the area was renamed French Somaliland. In 1896 the country became the protectorate of French Somaliland. The interior was developed in the 1920s and 1930s. During World War II the British occupied it, but the French administration continued. Internal autonomy was granted in 1956, and in 1958, by a choice of the local people, it became the French Somaliland Overseas Territory. The Afars and Europeans said "oui," and the Issas said "non." The Afars are Danakils, and the Issas are Somalis, and both belong to the Hamitic group. On March 19, 1967, another local vote (held as a referendum on March 19, 1967, and effective as from 6 July 1967) led to the country remaining associated with France, and the name of the country became the French Territory of the Afars and Issas. The leader of the African People's League for Independence, Hassan Gouled Aptidon (an Issa) pressed for independence, and another referendum in May 1977 (this time with the Issas registering to vote, which had not necessarily happened before) led to independence on 27 June 1977. The country became the Republic of Djibouti. Both Ethiopia and Somalia have laid claims to it, but they have now renounced such claims, although each accuses the other of trying to claim it. Ethnic wars broke out immediately (1977–1980), then there were wars with Ethiopia and Somalia. The first years of the 1990s were dominated by an Afar rebellion. This was ended by a peace treaty in Dec. 1994. Then there were more rebellions until 2001. AIDS, poverty, high unemployment, and corruption are just some of the problems that constantly bedevil Djibouti. *Rulers:* 11 March 1862–24 June 1884 none.

Commandants: 24 June 1884–7 Sept. 1887 Léonce Lagarde. *Governors:* 7 Sept. 1887–7 March 1899 Léonce Lagarde; 7 March 1899–23 March 1899 Louis Mizon (acting); 28 March 1899–13 April 1900 Alfred Martineau; 13 April 1900–6 Dec. 1900 Gabriel Angoulvant (acting); 6 Dec. 1900–7 Sept. 1901 Adrien Bonhoure; 7 Sept. 1901–June 1902 Louis Ormières (acting); June 1902–23 May 1903 Adrien Bonhoure; 23 May 1903–Dec. 1903 Albert Dubarry (acting); Dec. 1903–2 April 1904 Adrien Bonhoure; 2 April 1904–5 Aug. 1904 Albert Dubarry (acting); 5 Aug. 1904–9 Sept. 1905 Pierre Pascal; 9 Sept. 1905–13 Oct. 1905 Raphaël Antonetti (acting); 13 Oct. 1905–19 May 1906 Louis Ormières (acting); 19 May 1906–19 June 1906 M. Patte (acting); 19 June 1906–July 1908 Pierre Pascal: July 1908–5 Jan. 1909 Jean-Baptiste Castaing (acting); 5 Jan. 1909–June 1911 Pierre Pascal; June 1911–Dec. 1911 Jean-Baptiste Castaing (acting); Dec. 1911–1915 Pierre Pascal; 1915–1916 Paul Simoni; 1916–1918 Victor Fillon; 1918–1924 Jules Lauret; 1924–1932 Pierre Chapon-Baissac; 1932–7 May 1934 Louis-Placide Blacher; 7 May 1934–18 July 1935 Jules de Coppet; 18 July 1935–20 Dec. 1935 Achille Silvestre; 20 Dec. 1935–1 May 1937 Armand Annet; 1 May 1937–27 April 1938 François Pierre-Alype (acting); 27 April 1938–2 May 1939 Hubert Des champs (acting); 2 May 1939–1940 Hubert Deschamps; 1940–7 Aug. 1940 Gaëtan Germain; 7 Aug. 1940–4 Dec. 1942 Pierre Nouailhetas; 4 Dec. 1942–30 Dec. 1942 Christian Dupont; 30 Dec. 1942–22 June 1943 Charles Bayardelle; 22 June 1943–7 Jan. 1944 Michel Saller (acting); 7 Jan. 1944–1 May 1944 Michel Saller; 1 May 1944–14 May 1945 Jean Chalvet; 14 May 1945–Dec. 1945 Jean-Louis Beyriès (acting); Dec. 1945–30 April 1946 Jean Chalvet; 30 April 1946–1 March 1950 Paul Sirieix; 1 March 1950–6 April 1954 Numa-François Sadoul; 6 April 1954–13 Aug. 1954 Roland Pré; 13 Aug. 1954–7 Aug. 1957 Jean Petitbon; 7 Aug. 1957–1958 Maurice Meker; 1958–16 Nov. 1962 Jacques Compain; 16 Nov. 1962–15 Sept. 1966 René Tirant; 15 Sept.

1966–6 June 1967 Louis Saget. *High Commissioners:* 6 July 1967–5 Feb. 1969 Louis Saget; 5 Feb. 1969–21 Aug. 1971 Dominique Ponchardier; 21 Aug. 1971–Dec. 1974 Georges Thiercy; Dec. 1974–9 Feb. 1976 Christian Dablanc; 9 Feb. 1976–27 June 1977 Camille d'Ornano. *Presidents of the Council of Government:* June 1974–May 1977 Ali Aref Bourhan. *Presidents:* 24 June 1977–8 May 1999 Hassan Gouled Aptidon; 8 May 1999–Ismael Guelleh. *Prime Ministers:* 6 July 1967–June 1974 Ali Aref Bourhan; 12 July 1977–17 Dec. 1977 Ahmad Dini; 5 Feb. 1978–21 Sept. 1978 Abdallah Kamil; 30 Sept. 1978–6 Feb. 2001 Barket Gourad Hamadou; 4 March 2001–Dileita Muhammad Dileita. *Note:* In time of no Prime Minister, the President held that office.

Djolof see Dyolof

Doma. 1232–1901. *Location:* Northern Nigeria. *Capital:* Doma. *Other names:* Gara.

History: In 1232 the kingdom of Doma was founded by Andoma. In 1901 it was taken by the British and became part of their protectorate of Northern Nigeria.

Kings: 1232–(?) Andoma; (?)–(?) Aseil; (?)–ca. 1300 Akau; ca. 1300–(?) Akwei; (?)–(?) Adago; (?)–ca. 1390 Oka; ca. 1390–(?) Okabu; (?)–ca. 1480 Okaku; ca. 1480–ca. 1500 Aboshe; ca. 1500–(?) Oga I; (?)–(?) Atta I; (?)–ca. 1600 Anao; ca. 1600–(?) Akwe I; (?)–(?) Aboshi; (?)–ca. 1700 Adra; ca. 1700–(?) Asabo; (?)–ca. 1800 Anawo; ca. 1800–(?) Oga II; (?)–(?) Ogu; (?)–(?) Atta II; (?)–ca. 1855 Ari; ca. 1855–(?) Akwe II; (?)–(?) Amaku; (?)–(?) Atta III; (?)–(?) Ausu; (?)–(?) Agabi; (?)–(?) Agulu; (?)–1901 Agabo; 1901–1930 Atta IV.

Dongo see Ndongo

Dongola. ca. 675–1323. *Location:* northern Sudan. *Capital:* Dunqulah. *Other names:* Dunqulah.

History: About 675 Mukurra and the land of the Nobatae (see Nubia) united to form the kingdom of Dongola. The country was occupied by the Aiyubids from Egypt between 1174 and 1210. It was a Christian state until 1323, when it became Muslim under the Mamelukes (see Mameluke Empire).

Kings: ca. 675–ca. 710 Merkurios; ca. 710–ca. 722 [unknown]; ca. 722–ca. 738 Kyriakos; ca. 738–ca. 744 Zacharias I; ca. 744–ca. 768 Simon; ca. 768–ca. 780 Markos; ca. 780–ca. 790 Abraham; ca. 790–ca. 810 Michael; ca. 810–ca. 822 Joannes; ca. 822–ca. 831 Zacharias III; ca. 831–ca. 831 Qanun (pretender); ca. 831–ca. 854 Zacharias III; ca. 854–ca. 860 Ali Baba; ca. 860–ca. 870 Israel; ca. 870–892 Georgios I; 892–ca. 912 Asabysos; ca. 912–ca. 943 Istabanos; ca. 943–ca. 958 Kubri ibn Surun; ca. 958–ca. 969 Zacharias IV; ca. 969–ca. 980 Georgios II; ca. 980–ca. 999 Simeon; ca. 999–ca. 1030 Rafael; ca. 1030–ca. 1080 Georgios III; ca. 1080–ca. 1089 Salomo; ca. 1089–ca. 1130 Basileios; ca. 1130–ca. 1158 Georgios IV; ca. 1158–ca. 1174 Moise; ca. 1174–ca. 1210 Aiyubid occupation; ca. 1210–ca. 1268 Yahya; ca. 1268–ca. 1274 David; ca. 1274–April 1276 David II; April 1276–ca. 1277 Shekanda; ca. 1277–1279 Mashqadat; 1279–1286 Barah; 1286–1293 Shamamun; 1293–1304 Mameluke occupation; 1304–1305 Amai; 1305–1312 Kudanbes; 1312–1323 Mameluke occupation.

Dori see Burkina Faso

Dorobe Dynasty see Kayor

Dunqulah see Dongola

Dutch African Republic. Nov. 1838–16 Dec. 1856. *Location:* western Transvaal, South Africa. *Capital:* Potchefstroom (founded in 1838, the oldest town in the Transvaal). *Other names:* African Republic (alternative name from 1852 to 1856); Republic of Potchefstroom (1838–1852).

History: Formerly Matabele country under Mzilikazi, the Matabele were driven out of the area in 1838 by Boers led by Hendrik Potgieter, who had felt frustrated in Winburg. The new republic was named for Potgieter, Scherl, and Stockenstroom, the three Boer leaders, and was the first Boer republic north of the Vaal River. On 17 Jan. 1852 it became recognized as independent, as the Dutch African Republic. The town of Pretoria was founded in 1855. In 1856 it became known as the South African Republic (see Transvaal for details about the development of the country from that point).

Head Commandants: Nov. 1838–1845 Hendrik Potgieter; 1845–Jan. 1851 Andries Pretorius. *Commandants-General:* Jan. 1851–23 July 1853 Andries Pretorius; 23 July 1853–16 Dec. 1856 Marthinus Pretorius. *Commandants:* 1847–17 Jan. 1852 Gert Kruger.

Dutch Gold Coast. 1598–21 Feb. 1871. *Location:* Ghana coast. *Capital:* Elmina (from 1637); Moree (until 1637).

History: In 1598 the Dutch arrived at the Gold Coast. In 1637 they captured the Portuguese fort of Elmina, and in 1642 they expelled the Portuguese entirely from the Gold Coast (see Portuguese Gold Coast). In the 1860s they began selling their posts to the British (see Gold Coast), and by 1871 had moved out of the Gold Coast. Their major posts were Elmina, Axim, Kormantin, Accra, and Takoradi.

Administrators: 1598–1624 [unknown]. *Directors-General:* 1624–1 Oct. 1638 Adriaan Jacobs; 1 Oct. 1638–18 July 1639 Nikolaas Van Ypren; 18 July 1639–6 Jan. 1641 Arend Montfort; 6 Jan. 1641–18 Dec. 1645 Jacob Ruyghaver; 18 Dec. 1645–9 April 1650 Jacob Van Der Well; 9 April 1650–11 June 1650 Hendrik Doedens. *Governors:* 11 June 1650–15 March 1651 Arent Cocq. *Directors-General:* 15 March 1651–24 Jan. 1656 Jacob Ruyghaver; 24 Jan. 1656–27 April 1659 Jean Valkenburg; 27 April 1659–7 April 1662 Jasper Van Houssen; 7 April 1662–23 Dec. 1662 Dirk Wilré; 23 Dec. 1662–2 June 1667 Jean Valkenburg. *Governors:* 2 June 1667–12 Dec. 1668 Huybert Van Ongerdonk. *Directors-General:* 12 Dec. 1668–12 June 1675 Dirk Wilré; 12 June 1675–13 Sept. 1676 Johan Root; 13 Sept. 1676–26 March 1680 Abraham Meermans; 26 March 1680–1 Aug. 1683 Daniel Verhoutert; 1 Aug. 1683–15 July 1685 Thomas Ernsthuis; 15 July 1685–29 Jan. 1690 Nikolaas Sweerts; 29 Jan. 1690–25 March 1694 Joel Smits; 25 March 1694–9 June 1696 Jan Staphorst; 9 June 1696–2 June 1702 Jan Van Sevenhuysen; 2 June 1702–5 Nov. 1705 Willem de la Palma; 5 Nov. 1705–10 Oct. 1708 Pieter Nuyts. *Governors:* 10 Oct. 1708–14 Aug. 1709 Henrikus Van Wiessel. *Directors-General:* 14 Aug. 1709–16 April 1711 Adriaan Schoonheidt; 16 April 1711–11 June 1716 Hieronimus Haring; 11 June 1716–9 April 1718 Abraham Robberts; 9 April 1718–14 Oct. 1722 Willem Bullier; 14 Oct. 1722–28 May 1723 Abraham Houtman. *Governors:* 28 May 1723–14 Dec. 1723 Mattheus De Krane. *Directors-General:* 14 Dec. 1723–11 March 1727 Pieter Valkenier; 11 March 1727–6 March 1730 Robert Norri; 6 March 1730–13 March 1734 Jan Pranger; 13 March 1734–21 Feb. 1736 Antonius Van Overbeek; 21 Feb. 1736–15 Oct. 1736 [unknown]; 15 Oct. 1736–16 March 1740 Francis De Bordes. *Governors:* 17 March 1740–7 March

1741 Francis Barbrius. *Directors-General:* 8 March 1741–11 April 1747 Baron Jacob De Petersen; 11 April 1747–14 July 1754 Jan Van Voorst; 14 July 1754–24 Oct. 1755 Nikolaas Van Der Nood De Gieterre. *Governors:* 25 Oct. 1755–16 Jan. 1758 Roelof Ulsen. *Directors-General:* 16 Jan. 1758–12 March 1759 Lambert Van Tets; 13 March 1759–2 March 1760 Jan Huydecooper; 2 March 1760–10 July 1763 David Erasmi. *Governors:* 11 July 1763–31 Aug. 1764 Hendrik Walmbeek. *Directors-General:* 31 Aug. 1764–11 Sept. 1764 [unknown]; 11 Sept. 1764–8 June 1767 Jan Huydecooper. *Governors-General:* 8 June 1767–10 June 1769 Jan Huydecooper. *Directors-General:* 10 June 1769–11 April 1780 Pieter Woortman; 11 April 1780–10 May 1780 [unknown]. *Governors:* 10 May 1780–30 Dec. 1780 Jacobus Van Der Puye. *Directors-General:* 30 Dec. 1780–12 March 1784 Pieter Volkmar. *Governors-General:* 15 March 1784–14 Feb. 1785 Servaas Gallé. *Directors-General:* 14 Feb. 1785–26 May 1786 Adolph Thierens. *Governors-General:* 2 June 1786–24 Aug. 1787 Servaas Gallé. *Presidents:* 8 Sept. 1787–19 March 1790 Lieven Van Burgen Van Der Grijp. *Directors-General:* 19 March 1790–23 March 1794 Jacobus De Veer; 23 March 1794–26 May 1794 [unknown]. *Presidents:* 26 May 1794–10 Jan. 1795 Lieven Van Burgen Van Der Grijp. *Governors:* 10 Jan. 1795–3 June 1796 Otto Duim. *Directors-General:* 3 June 1796–10 Aug. 1796 [unknown]; 10 Aug. 1796–1 May 1798 Gerhardus Van Hamel. *Governors-General:* 8 May 1798–28 April 1804 Cornelis Bartels. *Presidents:* 29 April 1804–15 June 1805 Izaak De Roever. *Governors-General:* 16 June 1805–21 July 1807 Pieter Linthorst. *Presidents:* 22 July 1807–11 Aug. 1808 Johannes Hoogenboom. *Directors-General:* 12 Aug. 1808–23 Feb. 1810 Jan Koning. *Commandants-General:* 23 Feb. 1810–1 March 1816 Abraham De Veer. *Governors-General:* 1 March 1816–22 April 1818 Herman Daendels. *Presidents:* 22 April 1818–10 Jan. 1820 Frantz Christian Oldenborg. *Commanders/Presidents:* 10 Jan. 1820–27 July 1821 Johannes Oosthout. *Commanders:* 27 July 1821–11 Jan. 1823 Frederick Last (acting); 11 Jan. 1823–6 May 1823 Librecht Timmink (acting); 6 May 1823–14 May 1824 Willem Poolman; 14 May 1824–25 Dec. 1824 Hendrik Mouwe (acting); 25 Dec. 1824–2 Jan. 1825 Johan Pagenstecher (acting); 2 Jan. 1825–12 Nov. 1826 Frederick Last (acting); 12 Nov. 1826–4 Oct. 1828 Jacobus Van Der Breggen Paauw (acting); 4 Oct. 1828–17 April 1833 Frederick Last; 17 April 1833–17 May 1833 Jan Cremer (acting); 17 May 1833–2 Feb. 1834 Eduard Van Ingen (acting); 2 Feb. 1834–16 March 1834 Marthinus Swarte (acting); 16 March 1834–2 Dec. 1836 Christiaan Lans; 2 Dec. 1836–28 Oct. 1837 Hendrikus Tonneboeijer (acting); 29 Oct. 1837–5 Aug. 1838 Anthony Van Der Eb (acting). *Governors:* 5 Aug. 1838–7 March 1840 Hendrik Bosch; 7 March 1840–1846 Anthony Van Der Eb; 1846–1847 W.G.F. Derx; 1847–1852 Anthony Van Der Eb; 1852–1856 Hero Schomerus; 1856–1856 P.J. Runckel; 1856–1857 W.G.F. Derx; 1857–1857 Jules Van Der Bossche; 1857–1862 Cornelis Nagtglas; 1862–1865 Col. Henry Elias; 1865–1866 A. Magnin; 1866–1867 Willem Van Idzinga; 1867–1869 Col. Georg Boers; 1869–1871 Cornelis Nagtglas; 1871–1871 Jan Hugenholz; 1871–21 Feb. 1871 Jan Fergusson (acting).

Dutch West Africa. 1641–1648. *Location:* the coastal areas of Angola. *Capital:* Luanda. *Other names:* Luanda.

History: In 1641 the Dutch, in their war against the Portuguese, captured the coastal areas of Portuguese West Africa, including Benguela and the capital Luanda. In 1648 the Portuguese, who had been pushed into the interior, recovered their possessions.

Directors: 1641–1642 Pieter Moorthamer; 1642–1648 Cornelis Ouman.

Dyolof. ca. 1350–July 1889. *Location:* in Senegal. *Capital:* Linger (also known as Linguère). *Other names:* Wolof; Djolof; Ouolof.

History: Founded about 1350, Dyolof lasted 500 years, and was the main power in what is now the interior of Senegal. In the 14th century Kayor became a satellite state of the Djolof. In the 15th century Djolof and its vassal states became an empire, known as the Wolof Empire, and traded profitably with the Portuguese — mostly in slaves. In 1549 Kayor threw off Wolof dominance and became an independent nation, thus cutting off the empire's access to the sea. Thus began the deterioration of the empire, and in 1889 the empire, or what remained of it, became a part of the French colony of Senegal.

Burbas (Kings): ca. 1350–ca. 1370 N'Dyadya N'Dyaye; ca. 1370–ca. 1390 Sare N'Dyaye; ca. 1390–ca. 1420 N'Diklam Sare; ca. 1420–ca. 1440 Tyukuli N'Diklam; ca. 1440–ca. 1450 Leeyti Tyukuli; ca. 1450–ca. 1465 N'Dyelen Mbey Leeyti; ca. 1465–ca. 1481 Birayma N'Dyeme Eter; ca. 1481–ca. 1488 Tase Daagulen; ca. 1488–ca. 1492 Birayma Kuran Kan; ca. 1492–ca. 1527 Bukaar Biye-Sungule; ca. 1527–ca. 1543 Birayma Dyeme-Kumba; ca. 1543–ca. 1549 Leele Fuli Fak; ca. 1549–ca. 1566 al-Buri Penda; ca. 1566–ca. 1597 Lat-Samba; ca. 1597–ca. 1605 Gireun Buri Dyelen; ca. 1605–ca. 1649 Birayma Penda; ca. 1649–ca. 1670 Birayma Mba; ca. 1670–ca. 1711 Bakar Penda; ca. 1711–ca. 1721 Bakan-Tam Gan; ca. 1721–ca. 1740 al-Buri Dyakher; ca. 1740–ca. 1748 Birayamb; ca. 1748–ca. 1750 Birawa Keme; ca. 1750–ca. 1755 Lat-Kodu; ca. 1755–ca. 1763 Bakaa-Tam Buri-Nyabu; ca. 1763–ca. 1800 Mba Kompaas; ca. 1800–ca. 1818 Mba Buri-Nyabu; ca. 1818–ca. 1838 Birayamb Kumba-Gey; ca. 1838–1845 al-Buri Tam; 1845–1847 Baka Kodu; 1847–1849 Birayamb Aram; 1849–1849 Birayma-Penda; 1849–1849 Mbanyi Paate; 1849–1849 Lat-Koddu; 1849–1850 interregnum; 1850–1855 Birayamb Ma-Dyigen; 1855–1856 al-Buri Peya; 1856–1858 Bakan-Tam Yaago; 1858–1863 Taanor; 1863–1871 Bakan-Tam Khaari; 1871–1875 Amadou Seeku; 1875–May 1890 Ali Buri N'Dyaye; 3 June 1890–3 Nov. 1895 Samba; 3 Nov. 1895–1900 Buuna.

Dyula see **Kenedugu** and **Kong**

East Caprivi see **Namibia**

East London District see **British Kaffraria**

East Mauretania see **Mauretania East**

East Nupe. 1796–1805. *Location:* in Niger State, west-central Nigeria. *Capital:* Gbara. *Other names:* Nupe East.

History: In 1796 the kingdom of Nupe temporarily split into two, East Nupe and West Nupe, due to civil war between the two inheriting brothers. East Nupe retained the capital of Gbara, while West Nupe was founded with its capital at Raba. In 1805 the two rival states were re-united as Nupe.

Sarkins Gbara (Kings at Gbara): 1796–1805 Jimada.

East Pondoland see **Pondoland East**

East Sister Island see **Seychelles**

Eastern Cape Province see **British Kaffraria**

Eastern Nigeria see **Nigeria Eastern Region**

Eastern Province see **Uganda**

Edina. 1832–1837. *Location:* in today's Bong County, Liberia, on the opposite bank of the St. John's River from Bassa Cove. *Capital:* Edina.

History: In 1832 Edina was formed as a colony, or settlement, by the New York and Pennsylvania Colonization Societies. In 1837 it became part of Bassa Cove.

Rulers: [unknown].

Efik see **New Calabar**

Egba United Government see **Abeokuta**

Egbaland see **Abeokuta**

Egwanga see **Opobo**

Egypt. ca. 3100 B.C.– . *Location:* the extreme northeastern portion of Africa. *Capital:* Cairo (named al-Mansuriyah from 969, when it was founded, until 974). Name al-Qahir means "the planet Mars," under whose sign the city was founded; al-Fustat (905–969); al-Qata'i (870–905); al-Askar (750–870); al-Fustat (642–750); Alexandria (332 B.C.–A.D. 642); Sebennytus (335 B.C.–332 B.C.); Memphis (338 B.C.–335 B.C.); Sebennytus (31st and 30th Dynasties, 380 B.C.–338 B.C.); Mendes (29th Dynasty, 399 B.C.–380 B.C.); Sais (28th Dynasty, 404 B.C.–399 B.C.); Memphis (27th Dynasty, 525 B.C.–404 B.C.); Sais (26th Dynasty, 656 B.C.–525 B.C.); Thebes (25th Dynasty, ca. 715 B.C.–656 B.C.); Sais (24th Dynasty, ca. 730 B.C.–ca. 715 B.C.); Thebes (rival 23rd Dynasty, ca. 817 B.C.–ca. 715 B.C.); Bubastis (rival 22nd Dynasty, ca. 945 B.C.–ca. 715 B.C.); Tanis (21st Dynasty, ca. 1085 B.C.–ca. 945 B.C.); Pi-Ramesse (20th Dynasty, ca. 1200 B.C.–ca. 1085 B.C.); Pi-Ramesse (19th Dynasty, ca. 1280 B.C.–ca. 1200 B.C.); Thebes (19th Dynasty, ca. 1320 B.C.–ca. 1280 B.C.); Thebes (18th Dynasty, ca. 1359 B.C.–ca. 1320 B.C.); Tell al-Amarna (also known as Akhenaton) (18th Dynasty, ca. 1374 B.C.–ca. 1359 B.C.); Memphis (18th Dynasty, ca. 1465 B.C.–ca. 1374 B.C.); Thebes (18th Dynasty, ca. 1567 B.C.–ca. 1465 B.C.); Idj-Towy (17th Dynasty, ca. 1650 B.C.–ca. 1567 B.C.); unknown city in eastern Delta (16th Dynasty, ca. ca. 1674 B.C.–ca. 1567 B.C.); Avaris (15th Dynasty, ca. 1674 B.C.–ca. 1567 B.C.); Xois in the western Delta (14th Dynasty, ca. 1786 B.C.–ca. 1602 B.C.); Idj-Towy (12th and 13th Dynasties, ca. 1991 B.C.–ca. 1674 B.C. Near al-Fayyum, and now called al-Lisht); Nowe (11th Dynasty, ca. 2040 B.C.–ca. 1991 B.C. Also known as Nuwe, or, as the Greeks called it, Thebes); Neni-Nesu (9th and 10th Dynasties, ca. 2160 B.C.–ca. 2040 B.C. The Greeks called it Heracleopolis); Thinis (may have been capital of the 1st and 2nd Dynasties); Memphis (3100 B.C.–ca. 2160 B.C. Memphis was formerly called "White Wall." It may have been the capital of the 1st and 2nd Dynasties, and from the time of the 3rd Dynasty was definitely the capital until the time of the 9th Dynasty). *Other names:* Masr (local name); Arab Republic of Egypt, or Egyptian Arab Republic (from 1971); United Arab Republic, or UAR (1958–1971); Republic of Egypt (1953–1958); Kingdom of Egypt (1922–1953); Protectorate of Egypt (1914–1922); Mameluke Empire (1250–1517); Aiyubid Empire (1171–1250); Fatimid Egypt (969–1171); Lagid Egypt (Lagus was the father of Ptolemy, and this was a name given to Egypt during the Ptolemaic dynasty); Keme, Kmt (the earliest local names for Egypt, both meaning "the black land" because of the black alluvial soil on the banks of the Nile). The name "Egypt" is from the Greek "Aigyptos."

History: About 3100 B.C. Menes is believed to have united Upper Egypt and Lower Egypt. The dates, of course, are very uncertain and highly speculative as far as accuracy is concerned, but must have been in that general time period. Menes's identity, and even his existence, is doubted by many scholars, but someone united the two kingdoms, and almost overnight Egypt became a country of great sophistication during the 1st Dynasty. The reasons for the dynastic change are not clear; possibly a south–north struggle, which led to a reunification under the first king of the 2nd Dynasty. By ca. 2686 B.C. the 2nd Dynasty had come to an end, and so had the pre-historical Egypt. The period called the Old Kingdom was about to begin, with the 3rd Dynasty. During this dynasty Zoser built the Step Pyramid at Saqqarah, the first monument of any great size to be built completely of stone (Imhotep was the architect). Other pyramids were built during this dynasty. It was Zoser who fixed Egypt's southern boundary at the First

Cataract. The 4th Dynasty (ca. 2613 B.C.–ca. 2496 B.C.) was the great dynasty, the Golden Age of pyramid building at Giza (pyramids proper, as opposed to step pyramids). This was the dynasty that included such great kings (pharaohs) as Snefru and Cheops. The geographical boundaries of Egypt expanded under this dynasty, a strong centralized government was created, peace and prosperity reigned in Egypt, and many innovations and huge technological advances were made. The 5th Dynasty was the one that emphasized the cult of Ra (also known as Re), the Sun-God, at Heliopolis, and which built its tombs south of Giza, at Abu-Sir. The government was decentralized during the 6th Dynasty (ca. 2345 B.C.–ca. 2181 B.C.), and provincial governorates (or nomes) came into being, with the nomarchs answerable to the King. These nomarchs gradually assumed more and more power. Trade with Nubia to the south was increased, and the nomarch of Elephantine (the southern boundary of Egypt at that time) was made governor of all Upper Egypt. Pepi II is said to have reigned 94 years. It is not known how long the 7th Dynasty lasted, or indeed what the dynasty consisted of. The country was certainly in much confusion during this period, and all direction was gone. It seems likely that the 7th Dynasty was merely a succession of kings or princes of Memphis, who each survived only short terms at the helm of a nominal government. The 8th Dynasty is also a mystery, and it may not have actually existed. If it did, it lasted from ca. 2174 B.C. to ca. 2160 B.C., and was probably based at Memphis. It seems likely that it controlled a certain amount of Upper and Lower Egypt, but really the country was still in the hands of the nomarchs. The 9th Dynasty began with Akhtoy, the nomarch of Heracleopolis in Upper Egypt who, about 2160 B.C. declared himself King of Egypt, and began to weld the neighboring nomes together. He took most of Egypt, established his capital at Neni-Nesu (called Heracleopolis in Greek) but his successors did not have the same energy, and twilight falls over the rest of the dynasty, which marks the beginning of what is called the First Intermediate Period. The 10th Dynasty, an extension of the previous dynasty, saw a certain stability come to the country, but it failed to reunite Egypt as one nation. The rise of Thebes in the south occurred during this period, when Mentuhotep I became not only the founder of the 11th Dynasty, but also ruler of Upper Egypt. Mentuhotep founded a dynasty in the Nome of Thebes about 2133 B.C., and about 2040 B.C. his successor Mentuhotep II conquered the Delta and reunified Egypt. This marks the beginning of what is called the Middle Kingdom. About 1991 B.C. the vizier of Egypt, Amenemhet, who was also Governor of Upper Egypt, seized the throne and established his own dynasty, the 12th, a great dynasty, and moved his family to Idj-Towy. It was during this dynasty that contact with Asia and the Aegean flourished in a big way for the first time. At home the nomes were abolished, and the country split into three regions, all responsible to the vizier. During this period the southern boundary of Egypt reached the Second Cataract. The arts flourished as never before and peace and prosperity reigned, and the cult of Osiris reached its peak. The end of the dynasty (in ca. 1786 B.C.) marks the beginning of what is called the Second Intermediate Period. During the 13th Dynasty central governmental control was gradually lost, and the 14th Dynasty co-existed with the 13th, and even continued to exist until ca. 1602 B.C. This 14th Dynasty was based in Xois, in the western Delta region. Apparently it lasted 184 years and had 76 kings, but, as it corresponded for a large part of its existence with a proper, viable dynasty (the 13th), then the 14th Dynasty could really only have been of local importance, if it existed at all. If it did, it would have continued well into the Hyksos period. The main threat during this period was from Asiatics who had been encouraged into Egypt during the 12th Dynasty. Grouped around the eastern Delta region, the Hyksos occupied the town of Avaris in the eastern Delta about 1720 B.C., and formed the Seth cult. As central power in the last years of the 13th Dynasty weakened, so grew the power of the Hyksos, and they took Memphis around 1674 B.C., and thus began 15th Dynasty, known as the Dynasty of the Great Hyksos (as opposed to the Minor Hyksos of the 16th Dynasty). However, the name "Hyksos" was not used until much later to describe these Asiatics. The name means "Shepherd Kings," and came probably from the Egyptian "heqa-khase" meaning "ruler of a foreign principality." The Hyksos introduced the horse and chariot into Egypt, and were Semitic peoples. It is doubtful whether they ruled all of Egypt — probably only Lower Egypt. About 1674 B.C. another dynasty came into being, the 16th, contemporaneous for a few years with the 15th Dynasty. This 16th Dynasty was another branch of Asiatics, referred to as the Minor Hyksos. About 1650 B.C. yet another dynasty came into being, the 17th, and these kings were probably descended from those of the 13th Dynasty. They ruled Southern, or Upper Egypt as rivals (or colleagues) of the Hyksos in the North. About 1567 B.C. this dynasty had succeeded in taking all of Egypt, and the two Hyksos dynasties crumbled. The 18th Dynasty, a direct continuation of the 17th, succeeded to a unified Egypt. This was the beginning of the period known as the New Kingdom, with its capital at Thebes. This was the dynasty with the famous pharaohs ("per'o" in Ancient Egyptian, and basically the same word as "Farouk") or kings—Thutmose III, the Amenhoteps (including Akhenaton), and best remembered of all, Tutankhamen. Wars increased territory (most of the Levant and the Middle East) and revenue, and the pyramids gave way to rock-cut tombs as burial places for the pharaohs. The southern boundary of Egypt was extended to the Fourth Cataract during this dynasty. In ca. 1320 B.C., when Horemheb, the last of the kings of this dynasty, died without male issue, he nominated his vizier Rameses to follow him on the throne. This was the 19th Dynasty. Wars with the Libyans and Hittites featured early in the dynasty. This was the time of the Biblical "Exodus," the relevant pharaoh probably being Merneptah. At the end of the dynasty myriad internal factions caused havoc, and about 1200 B.C. Senakht founded the 20th Dynasty and restored order. His son, Rameses II, was the last great pharaoh, and spent much of his reign repelling invasions. The rest of the dynasty saw the diminishing of the empire, and the rise of the high priests in Egypt. On the death of Rameses XI the Governor of Tanis, Smendes, became pharaoh, and founder of the 21st Dynasty, about 1085 B.C. During this dynasty Egypt lost control of Nubia and its Asiatic empire. Pharaoh Siamon married his daughter to King Solomon of Israel. At Thebes a hereditary dynasty of high priests developed late in the 20th Dynasty, and are often referred to as Dynasty 20b. In 945 B.C. Sheshonk, the leader of the Meshwesh Libyan captive race in Egypt, took the throne and established the 22nd Dynasty. He politically intermarried his people with the high priest families of Thebes, thus trying to cement the whole kingdom. About 931 B.C. She-

shonk sacked Jerusalem. About 817 B.C. a rival dynasty sprang up in Thebes, the 23rd Dynasty, and about 730 B.C. yet another, the 25th Dynasty, with its capital at Sais. This last was the dynasty of the Libyan nobleman Tefnakhte who tried to conquer Egypt from Sais, in the western Delta. He captured Memphis and proceeded south, to the annoyance of the Kushites in what is today the Sudan (see Kush). Piankh (also known as Piy) the Kushite king, took Thebes in 730 and beat the Northerners, and retired back to Kush. Tefnakhte then rebelled again and in 720 B.C. his son succeeded to the dynastic throne. This king was buried alive by Shabaka, the founder of the 25th Dynasty, in ca. 715 B.C. That year brought the 23rd Dynasty to an end as well as the 22nd, as the Kushites (or Ethiopians, as they were also called) swept all before them as they conquered all of Egypt as the 25th Dynasty. Wars with Assyria were the main problems during this dynasty, and about 656 B.C. the Assyrians finally expelled the Kushites, returned to Assyria, and Psamtik I (son of Necho) of the Delta region formed the 26th Dynasty, with its capital at Sais. Psamtik took all of Egypt. There was a great Greek immigration during this period, as well as trading. In 525 B.C. the Persian Cambyses invaded Egypt and conquered the whole country, which then became a Persian province, also known as the 27th Dynasty. Together with the Libyan oases and Cyrenaica, it formed the 6th Persian Satrapy. Until 486 B.C. the Persians governed it well, and with great tolerance, but that year Xerxes put down a rebellion in the Delta and from then on treated Egypt as a conquered province in fact as well as on paper. Xerxes was the first major Achaemenid ruler of Persia who never visited Egypt and he was assassinated in 645 B.C. This sparked off an Athenian-backed revolt in the Delta, led by the Libyan Inaros who, after eleven years of warfare was caught and crucified. Around 450 B.C. Herodotus made a celebrated trip to Egypt. In 404 B.C., with the Persians occupied elsewhere, Amyrtaeus, a Libyan nobleman, revolted in the Delta after the death of Darius II in Persia. Amyrtaeus's rule was recognized all over Egypt, as the 28th Dynasty. In 399 B.C. a new dynasty, the 29th, appeared out of the town of Mendes, in the eastern Delta. Under Achoris this dynasty forged close political and military links with Greece, in order to repel the Persians. In 380 B.C. General Nectanebo usurped the throne and established his own dynasty, the 30th. Much building took place during this dynasty, as well as three Persian invasions — the third, in 343 B.C. succeeding, and Nectarebe, the last king of the 30th Dynasty, fled to Nubia. The Persian 31st Dynasty lasted a mere five years before Artaxerxes III, the Persian Emperor, died, and a Nubian prince named Khababasha (or Hababasha) gained control of Egypt. By 335 B.C., however, Persia had regained control, but in 332 B.C. Alexander the Great walked into Egypt without a battle. He ruled through a governor until his death in 323 B.C. He founded the town of Alexandria, and one of his successors, Ptolemy, ruled Egypt as the satrap and, from 305 B.C., as the king. The Ptolemaic Dynasty ruled Egypt until 30 B.C., when it became a Roman province with the death of Cleopatra VII. The country became Octavian's own personal property, administered as a province of Rome, by a prefect. In A.D. 330 Constantine organized his empire into Christian dioceses, and Egypt was one of them. In 395 control of Egypt passed to Byzantium, who ruled it until 616, when the Persians gained control for 12 years, ruling through a traitorous patriarch until they were expelled by a combination of Roman Emperor Heraclius and the Arabs. The Muslims could not be stopped, however, and in 639 they marched into Byzantine Egypt, and, under Amr ibn al-As, took town after town until, in 642 the Byzantines left. In 645 the Byzantines attempted to re-conquer Alexandria (their former capital), but they were quickly put down by the Arabs. The Muslims changed little of Byzantine provincial rule, but they moved the capital to al-Fustat. In July 658 the first of the Omayyad governors assumed office, and for the next 92 years the Omayyad caliphate in Damascus ruled Egypt through the Egyptian governor. Arabic replaced Greek as the national language in 706. On 9 Aug. 750 the caliphate became Abbasid. On 15 Sept. 868 the Tulunids began a 37-year rule in Egypt which lasted until 10 Jan. 905, when the Abbasid general Muhammad ibn Suleiman regained power there for his caliph. On 2 Sept. 935 the governor of Egypt, Muhammad al-Ikhshid, made himself the independent sovereign of Egypt and Syria. The Abbasids were virtually finished by this time anyway, and in Egypt the Ikhshids ruled until 5 Aug. 969 from al-Fustat, their capital, when the Fatimid general Gohar conquered Egypt and made Cairo his new capital. The Fatimid Empire had been founded in 909 and named for Fatima, the daughter of the Prophet. Ruled by Caliphs from Tunisia, the empire spread over North Africa and Arabia. In 1073 Badr, Commander of the Armies, seized power. These commanders, also known as viziers (or wazirs) actually ruled, and on 10 Sept. 1171 Saladin (Salah ad-Din), the Vizier, brought an end to the Fatimid Empire. Saladin's empire, the Aiyubid Empire, comprised Egypt (with its local capital at Cairo) as well as parts of Libya, the Levant and the Red Sea coasts, and had its imperial capital at Damascus, until 2 May 1250 when the Sultan's bodyguards, the Bahrite Mamelukes, revolted, creating their own dynasty. They expanded the frontiers of the empire, and on 26 Nov. 1382 the Circassian Mamelukes took over. In its later years this dynasty fell more and more under the power of the amirs until, on 22 Jan. 1517, Egypt was conquered by the Sultan of Turkey, and a pasha was installed to supervise the Mameluke beys who effectively continued to rule the country as administrators. On 25 July 1798 Egypt (most of the northern and administrative part, anyway) was conquered by Napoleon, and the following year he left General Kléber in charge. In 1801 the French were defeated by the British and Turks at Alexandria; Cairo was surrendered in June, and in September the Napoleonic troops left Alexandria, and on 27 June 1801 Egypt became an Ottoman pashalik again. In 1811 the Viceroy, Muhammad Ali (also known as Mahomet Ali, or Mehmet Ali) created an autonomous state in Egypt, virtually independent of Constantinople, with himself as Vali (or viceroy). On 3 May 1833 Turkey recognized Egypt's independence of action, and on 13 Feb. 1841 Muhammad Ali gained Egypt as an hereditary possession, and this became an hereditary vice-royalty in 1866, a move which gave Egypt almost total independence from the Porte (the Sultan's capital). The Vali became a khedive. On 17 Nov. 1869 the Suez Canal was opened, and on 15 Sept. 1882 Egypt became a British sphere of influence, because the khedive refused to pay his dues to the Sultan of Turkey, and Britain helped out. The British moved in, although in theory Egypt was an Ottoman state until 18 Dec. 1914, when the British protectorate of Egypt came into being. The khedive of Egypt was the nominal ruler throughout the British occupation. However, after 1914 a British High Commissioner ruled, with a

British-placed sultan in nominal office. In 1922 Britain granted independence to Egypt, and the sultan became king shortly thereafter. A British High Commissioner remained until 1936. On 23 July 1952 the Egyptian Army seized power, ousted King Farouk, and colonels Naguib and Nasser assumed control (Sadat also took part in the coup). On 18 June 1953 a republic was declared. The Suez Crisis began in 1956 when Nasser nationalized the Canal and closed it to international traffic. On 1 Feb. 1958 Egypt and Syria joined together to form the United Arab Republic (UAR). At the same time Egypt and Yemen formed the United Arab States (dissolved in 1961). In 1961 Syria withdrew from the UAR, but Egypt kept the name until 2 Sept. 1971 when Sadat changed it to the Arab Republic of Egypt. In 1967, during the Six-Day War with Israel, Egypt lost Sinai, not to regain it until 1979, when Begin of Israel and Sadat of Egypt made peace after 31 years of enmity and war between the two countries. Sadat was assassinated on 6 Oct. 1981, and succeeded by Hosni Mubarrak, who continued friendly relations with Israel. Egypt has been suffering from Fundamentalist extremisms in the 1990s and early 200s, as well as a rising poverty.

1st Dynasty Kings: ca. 3100 B.C.–(?) Menes (also known as Narmer, Min, or Meni); (?)–(?) Aha; (?)–(?) Djer; (?)–(?) Djet; (?)–(?) Den; (?)–(?) Anedjib; (?)–(?) Semerkhet; (?)–ca. 2890 B.C. Qa'a. *2nd Dynasty Kings:* ca. 2890 B.C.–(?) Hetepsekhemwy; (?)–(?) Re'neb; (?)–(?) Ninetjer; (?)–(?) Weneg; (?)–(?) Sened; (?)–(?) Peribsen; (?)–(?) Khasekhem; (?)–ca. 2686 B.C. Khasekhemwy (may be confounded with Khasekhem). *3rd Dynasty Kings:* ca. 2686 B.C.–ca. 2680 B.C. Sanakht; ca. 2680 B.C.–ca. 2661 B.C. Zoser (also known as Djoser); ca. 2661 B.C.–(?) Sekhemkhet; (?)–(?) Kha'ba; (?)–ca. 2613 B.C. Huni. *4th Dynasty Kings:* ca. 2613 B.C.–ca. 2589 B.C. Snefru (also known as Snofru); ca. 2589 B.C.–ca. 2558 B.C. Cheops (also known as Khufu); ca. 2558 B.C.–ca. 2549 B.C. Ra'djedef; ca. 2549 B.C.–ca. 2530 B.C. Chephren (also known as Khafre); ca. 2530 B.C.–ca. 2512 B.C. Menkaure (also known as Mycerinus); ca. 2512 B.C.–ca. 2496 B.C. Shepsekaf. *5th Dynasty Kings:* ca. 2496 B.C.–(?) Userkaf; (?)–(?) Sahure; (?)–(?) Neferirkare; (?)–(?) Shepseskare; (?)–(?) Neferefre; (?)–(?) Niuserre; (?)–(?) Menkauhor; (?)–(?) Djedkare Izezi; (?)–ca. 2345 B.C. Unas (also known as Unis). *6th Dynasty Kings:* ca. 2345

B.C.–ca. 2340 B.C. Teti; ca. 2340 B.C.–2335 B.C. Userkare; ca. 2335 B.C.–ca. 2286 B.C. Pepi I Meryre; ca. 2286 B.C.–ca. 2281 B.C. Antyemsaf I Merenre; ca. 2281 B.C.–ca. 2187 B.C. Pepi II Neferkare; ca. 2187 B.C.–ca. 2184 B.C. Antyemsaf II Merenre; ca. 2184 B.C.–ca. 2182 B.C. Menkare. *7th Dynasty Kings:* ca. 2182 B.C.–ca. 2174 B.C. [unknown]. *8th Dynasty Kings:* ca. 2174 B.C.–ca. 2160 B.C. [unknown]. *9th Dynasty Kings:* ca. 2160 B.C.–(?) Akhtoy (also known as Achthoes); (?)–ca. 2130 B.C. [unknown names of an indeterminate number of kings]. *10th Dynasty Kings:* ca. 2130 B.C.–(?) [indeterminate number of unknown names of kings]; (?)–(?) Merikare; (?)–ca. 2040 B.C. [unknown]. *Kings of Upper Egypt:* [The Theban Dynasty which ruled in Upper Egypt from ca. 2133 B.C. until the re-unification of Egypt in ca. 2040 B.C. was as follows] ca. 2133 B.C.–ca. 2117 B.C. Mentuhotep I and Sehertowy Intef (joint kings); ca. 2117 B.C.–ca. 2068 B.C. Intef II; ca. 2068 B.C.–2060 B.C. Intef III; ca. 2060 B.C.–ca. 2040 B.C. Mentuhotep II Nebhepetre. *11th Dynasty Kings:* ca. 2040 B.C.–ca. 2009 B.C. Mentuhotep II Nebhepetre; ca. 2009 B.C.–ca. 1997 B.C. Mentuhotep III Sankhkare; ca. 1997 B.C.–ca. 1991 B.C. Mentuhotep IV Nebto were. *12th Dynasty Kings:* ca. 1991 B.C.–ca. 1962 B.C. Amenemhet I Shetepibre; ca. 1972 B.C.–ca. 1928 B.C. Sesostris (also known as Senwosre) I Kheperkare; ca. 1929 B.C.–ca. 1895 B.C. Amenemhet II Nubkaure; ca. 1897 B.C.–ca. 1878 B.C. Sesostris (also known as Senwosre) II Khakheperre; ca. 1878 B.C.–ca. 1842 B.C. Sesostris (also known as Senwosre) III Khakaure; ca. 1842 B.C.–ca. 1797 B.C. Amenemhet III Nemare; ca. 1798 B.C.–ca. 1789 B.C. Amenemhet IV Makherure. *12th Dynasty Queens:* ca. 1789 B.C.–ca. 1786 B.C. Sebekhnofru Sebbekhare. *13th Dynasty Kings:* ca. 1786 B.C.–(?) Sebekhotep I; (?)–(?) Amenemhet V Sekhemkare; (?)–(?) Amenemhet VI Sehetepibre; (?)–(?) Sankhibre; (?)–(?) Hetepibre; (?)–(?) Sebekhotep II; (?)–(?) Renseneb; (?)–(?) Awibre Hor; (?)–(?) Sedjefakare; (?)–(?) Khutowere; (?)–(?) Sesostris (also known as Senwosre) IV Seneferibre; (?)–(?) Userkare Khendjer; (?)–(?) Semenkhkare; (?)–(?) Sebekemsaf I Sekhemre Wadjkhau; (?)–(?) Sebekhotep III Sekhemre Sewadjtowy; (?)–(?) Neferhotep I Khasekhemre; (?)–(?) Sebekhotep V Khaankre; (?)–(?) Neferhotep II Mersekhemre; (?)–(?) Sebekhotep VI Khahotepre; (?)–(?) Neferhotep III Sekhemre Sankhtowy; (?)–(?) Wahibre Iayeb; (?)–(?) Merneferre Iy; (?)–(?) Merhetepre Ini; (?)–ca. 1674 B.C. Djedneferre Dudimose. *14th Dynasty Kings:* [unknown 76 kings, which may have been only local rulers]. *15th Dynasty Kings:* ca. 1674 B.C.–(?) Mayebre Sheshni (also known as Salitis); (?)–(?) Meruserre Yakhuber; (?)–(?) Sewesewenre Khayan; (?)–(?) Auserre Apopi I; (?)–(?) Ahenenre Apopi II; (?)–ca. 1567 B.C. Asehere Khamudy. *16th Dynasty Kings:* [unknown]. *17th Dynasty Kings of Upper Egypt:* ca. 1650 B.C.–(?) Sekhemre Wahkha Rahotep; (?)–(?) Sekhemre Wepmae Intef; (?)–(?) Sekhemre Herhimae Intef; (?)–(?) Sekhemre Shedtowe Sebekemsaf; (?)–(?) Sekhemre Smentowe Djehuty; (?)–(?) Sankhenre Mentuhotep; (?)–(?) Swadjenre Nebirierau; (?)–(?) Neferkare Nebirierau; (?)–(?) Semenmedjatre; (?)–(?) Seuserenre; (?)–(?) Sekhemre Shedwast; (?)–(?) Nubkheperre Intef; (?)–(?) Senakhtenre; (?)–(?) Sekenenre Tao I; (?)–(?) Sekenenre Tao II; (?)–ca. 1570 B.C. Wadjkheperre Kamose; ca. 1570 B.C.–ca. 1567 B.C. Ahmose Nebpehtire. *18th Dynasty Kings:* ca. 1567 B.C.–ca. 1546 B.C. Ahmose Nebpehtire; ca. 1546 B.C.–ca. 1526 B.C. Amenhotep I Djeserkare; ca. 1526 B.C.–ca. 1512 B.C. Thutmose I Akheperkare; ca. 1512 B.C.–ca. 1504 B.C. Thutmose II Akheperenre; ca. 1504 B.C.–ca. 1450 B.C. Thutmose III Mankheperre (did not become effective until ca. 1482 B.C.). *18th Dynasty Queens Regent:* ca. 1504 B.C.–ca. 1482 B.C. Hatshepsut Makare (from ca. 1502 B.C. until ca. 1482 B.C. she ruled as effective king [sic]. *18th Dynasty Pharaohs (Kings):* ca. 1452 B.C.–ca. 1425 B.C. Amenhotep II Akheprure (ruled jointly until ca. 1450 B.C.); ca. 1425 B.C.–ca. 1417 B.C. Thutmose IV Menkheprure; ca. 1417 B.C.–ca. 1379 B.C. Amenhotep III Nebmare; ca. 1379 B.C.–ca. 1374 B.C. Amenhotep IV Neferkheprure Waenre; ca. 1374 B.C.–ca. 1362 B.C. Akhenaton (formerly Amenhotep IV); ca. 1364 B.C.–ca. 1361 B.C. Smenkhare Ankheprure (ruled jointly until ca. 1362 B.C.); ca. 1361 B.C.–ca. 1352 B.C. Tutankhaton (from ca. 1359 B.C. known as Tutankhamen Nebkheprure); ca. 1352 B.C.–ca. 1348 B.C. Ay Kheperkheprure Itnute; ca. 1348 B.C.–ca. 1320 B.C. Horemheb Djeserkheprure. *19th Dynasty Pharaohs (Kings):* ca. 1320 B.C.–ca. 1318 B.C. Rameses I Menpehtire; ca. 1318 B.C.–ca. 1304 B.C. Seti Menmare Merneptah; ca. 1304 B.C.–ca. 1237 B.C. Rameses II the Great Usermare Miamun; ca. 1237 B.C.–ca. 1223 B.C. Merneptah Binere Meryamun Hotphimae; ca. 1223 B.C.–ca. 1217 B.C. Amenmesse Menmire; ca. 1217 B.C.–ca. 1210 B.C. Seti II Usikheperure Merneptah; ca.

1210 B.C.–ca. 1203 B.C. Siptah Akhenre Merneptah; ca. 1203 B.C.–ca. 1200 B.C. Tausert (also known as Tewosre) Sitre Meryamun (may have been the widow of Siptah, which is most likely; or she may have been a king, or he may have been a king). *20th Dynasty Pharaohs (Kings):* ca. 1200 B.C.–ca. 1198 B.C. Senakht Userkhaure; ca. 1198 B.C.–ca. 1166 B.C. Rameses III Usermare Meryamun; ca. 1166 B.C.–ca. 1160 B.C. Rameses IV Hekamare Setpenamun; ca. 1160 B.C.–ca. 1156 B.C. Rameses V Usermare Sekhepereure; ca. 1156 B.C.–ca. 1148 B.C. Rameses VI Nebmare Meryamun; ca. 1148 B.C.–ca. 1145 B.C. Rameses VII Usermare Meryamun; ca. 1145 B.C.–ca. 1140 B.C. Rameses VIII Usermare Akhenamun; ca. 1140 B.C.–ca. 1121 B.C. Rameses IX Neferkare Setpenre; ca. 1121 B.C.–ca. 1113 B.C. Rameses X Khepermare Setpenre; ca. 1113 B.C.–ca. 1085 B.C. Rameses XI Menmare Setneptah. *21st Dynasty Pharaohs (Kings):* ca. 1085 B.C.–ca. 1059 B.C. Nesbanebded (also known as Smendes) Hedjkheperre; ca. 1059 B.C.–ca. 1054 B.C. Amenemnisu Hekawise Neferkare; ca. 1954 B.C.–ca. 1001 B.C. Psusennes I (also known as Psibkhaemne) Akheperre; ca. 1001 B.C.–ca. 983 B.C. Amenemope Usermare; ca. 983 B.C.–ca. 960 B.C. Siamon Nutekheperre; ca. 960 B.C.–945 B.C. Psusennes II (also known as Psibkhaemne) Titkheprure. *21st Dynasty High Priests:* ca. 1094 B.C.–ca. 1087 B.C. Herihor; ca. 1987 B.C.–ca. 1074 B.C. Piankh; ca. 1074 B.C.–ca. 1050 B.C. Pinudjem I; ca. 1050 B.C.–(?) Menkheperre; (?)–(?) Nesbanebded; (?)–ca. 945 B.C. Pinudjem II. *22nd Dynasty Kings:* ca. 945 B.C.–ca. 924 B.C. Sheshonk I Hedjkheperre (also known as Shishak); ca. 924 B.C.–ca. 890 B.C. Osorkhon I Sekhemkheperre; ca. 890 B.C.–ca. 889 B.C. Sheshonk II Hekenkheperre; ca. 889 B.C.–ca. 874 B.C. Takelot I Usermare; ca. 874 B.C.–ca. 850 B.C. Osorkhon II Usermare; ca. 850 B.C.–ca. 825 B.C. Takelot II Hedjkheperre; ca. 825 B.C.–ca. 773 B.C. Sheshonk III Usermare; ca. 773 B.C.–ca. 767 B.C. Pimay Usermare (also known as Pami); ca. 767 B.C.–ca. 730 B.C. Sheshonk V Akheperre; ca. 730 B.C.–ca. 715 B.C. Osorkhon IV Akheperre. *23rd Dynasty Kings:* ca. 817 B.C.–ca. 793 B.C. Redebast Usermare (ruled jointly after ca. 804 B.C.); ca. 804 B.C.–ca. 783 B.C. Iuput I (ruled jointly until ca. 793 B.C.); ca. 783 B.C.–ca. 777 B.C. Sheshonk IV; ca. 777 B.C.–ca. 749 B.C. Osorkhon III (ruled jointly after ca. 754 B.C.); ca. 754 B.C.–ca. 734 B.C. Takelot III (ruled jointly until ca. 749 B.C.); ca.

734 B.C.–ca. 731 B.C. Rudamen; ca. 731 B.C.–ca. 720 B.C. Iuput II; ca. 720 B.C.–ca. 715 B.C. Sheshonk VI. *24th Dynasty Kings:* ca. 730 B.C.–ca. 720 B.C. Tefnakhte Shepsesre; ca. 720 B.C.–ca. 715 B.C. Bekenrinef (also known as Bocchoris) Wahkare. *25th Dynasty Kings:* ca. 715 B.C.–ca. 702 B.C. Shabaka; ca. 702 B.C.–690 B.C. Shebitku; 690 B.C.–664 B.C. Taharqa; 664 B.C.–656 B.C. Tanuatamon. *26th Dynasty Kings:* 664 B.C.–610 B.C. Psamtik I Wahibre; 610 B.C.–595 B.C. Necho II Wehembre; 595 B.C.–589 B.C. Psamtik II Neferibre; 589 B.C.–570 B.C. Apries (also known as Hophra, or Haaibre) Wahimbre; 570 B.C.–526 B.C. Ahmose Khnemibre; 526 B.C.–525 B.C. Psamtik III Ankhkaenre. *27th Dynasty Emperors of Persia:* 525 B.C.–1 July 522 B.C. Cambyses (also known as Kambujiyah II); 1 July 522 B.C.–522 B.C. Smerdis (also known as Bardiya-Gaumata); 522 B.C.–Nov. 486 B.C. Darius the Great (also known as Darayavahush I); Nov. 486 B.C.–Dec. 465 B.C. Xerxes I (also known as Khshayarsa I); Dec. 465 B.C.–424 B.C. Artaxerxes I (also known as Artakhshayarsa I); 424 B.C.–423 B.C. Xerxes II (also known as Khshayarsa II); 423 B.C.–July 423 B.C. Sogdianos; July 423 B.C.–March 404 B.C. Darius II (also known as Darayavahush II); March 404 B.C.–404 B.C. Artaxerxes II (also known as Artakhshayarsa II). *27th Dynasty Governors of Egypt:* 1 July 522 B.C.–517 B.C. Aryandes; 517 B.C.–485 B.C. Pherendates I; 485 B.C.–484 B.C. [unknown]; 484 B.C.–460 B.C. Achaimenes; 460 B.C.–404 B.C. [unknown]. *28th Dynasty Kings:* 404 B.C.–399 B.C. Amyrtaeus (also known as Amonirdisu). *29th Dynasty Kings:* 399 B.C.–393 B.C. Nefaurud (also known as Nepherites I); 393 B.C.–393 B.C. Setneptah Usire Pshenmut; 393 B.C.–380 B.C. Achoris (also known as Hakor) Khnemmaere; 380 B.C.–380 B.C. Nefaurud (also known as Nepherites II). *30th Dynasty Kings:* 380 B.C.–362 B.C. Nectanebo (also known as Nekhtnebef Kheperkhare); 362 B.C.–360 B.C. Setpenanhur Irmaenre Djeho (also known as Takhos); 360 B.C.–343 B.C. Nectarebe (also known as Nekhtharehbe Snedjembre). *31st Dynasty Emperors of Persia:* 343 B.C.–Sept. 338 B.C. Artaxerxes III (also known as Artakhshayarsa III); Sept. 338 B.C.–338 B.C. Arsha. *31st Dynasty Governors of Egypt:* 343 B.C.–338 B.C. Pherendates II. *Kings:* 338 B.C.–335 B.C. Khababasha. *Emperors of Persia:* 335 B.C.–332 B.C. Darius III (also known as Darayavahush III). *Persian Governors of Egypt:* 335 B.C.–333 B.C. Sabakes; 333

B.C.–332 B.C. Mazakes. *Emperors:* 332 B.C.–13 June 323 B.C. Alexander the Great. *Alexandrian Military Governors of Egypt:* 332 B.C.–13 June 323 B.C. Kleomenes of Naucratis. *Satraps:* 13 June 323 B.C.–7 Nov. 305 B.C. Ptolemy (from 304 B.C. he would be called Ptolemy Soter). *Kings and Queens:* 7 Nov. 305 B.C.–ca. Jan. 282 B.C. King Ptolemy I Soter I (called Soter only after 304 B.C.); 290 B.C.–ca. Jan. 282 B.C. Queen Berenice I; 26 June 285 B.C.–24 Oct. 247 B.C. King Ptolemy II Philadelphus; ca. 277 B.C.–July 270 B.C. Queen Arsinoe II; 24 Oct. 247 B.C.–18 Oct. 221 B.C. King Ptolemy III Euergetes I; 245 B.C.–18 Oct. 221 B.C. Queen Berenice II; 18 Oct. 221 B.C.–28 Nov. 205 B.C. King Ptolemy IV Philopator; 217 B.C.–204 B.C. Queen Arsinoe III; *Prime Ministers:* 18 Oct. 221 B.C.–202 B.C. Sosibius (the real power behind the throne). *Kings and Queens:* 28 Nov. 205 B.C.–ca. May 180 B.C. King Ptolemy V Epiphanes; ca. Feb. 193 B.C.–176 B.C. Queen Cleopatra I; ca. May 180 B.C.–Oct. 164 B.C. King Ptolemy VI Philometor; 173 B.C.–Oct. 164 B.C. Queen Cleopatra II; 170 B.C.–163 B.C. King Ptolemy VIII Euergetes (also known as Physcon); 163 B.C. ca. July 145 B.C. King Ptolemy VI Philometor; 163 B.C.–115 B.C. Queen Cleopatra II (from 136 B.C. to 28 June 116 B.C. as Rival Queen, and from 28 June 116 B.C. to 115 B.C. as Queen Regent); 147 B.C.–Aug. 145 B.C. King Ptolemy VII Neos Philopator; Aug. 145 B.C.–28 June 116 B.C. King Ptolemy VIII Euergetes (also known as Physcon); ca. 136 B.C.–28 June 116 B.C. Queen Cleopatra III; 28 June 116 B.C.–Oct. 110 B.C. King Ptolemy IX Soter II (also known as Lathyrus); 28 June 116 B.C.–115 B.C. Queen Cleopatra IV; 115 B.C.–Oct. 110 B.C. Queen Cleopatra V Selene; 115 B.C.–101 B.C. Queen Cleopatra III (Queen Regent); Oct. 110 B.C.–ca. Feb. 109 B.C. King Ptolemy X Alexander I; ca. Feb. 109 B.C.–March 107 B.C. King Ptolemy IX Soter II (also known as Lathyrus); ca. Feb. 109 B.C.–March 107 B.C. Queen Cleopatra V Selene; March 107 B.C.–88 B.C. King Ptolemy X Alexander I; 101 B.C.–80 B.C. Queen Berenice III; 88 B.C.–80 B.C. King Ptolemy IX Soter II (also called Lathyrus); 80 B.C.–80 B.C. Ptolemy XI Alexander II; 80 B.C.–58 B.C. King Ptolemy XII Auletes; 80 B.C.–58 B.C. Queen Cleopatra VI Traephaeana; 58 B.C.–55 B.C. Queen Berenice IV; 55 B.C.–51 B.C. King Ptolemy XII Auletes; 52 B.C.–47 B.C. King Ptolemy XIII Theos Philopator; 52 B.C.–12 Aug. 30 B.C. Queen Cleopatra VII (the most famous queen of that name); 47 B.C.–July 44 B.C. Ptolemy XIV Theos Philopator II; July 44 B.C.–12 Aug. 30 B.C. Ptolemy XV Caesar (also known as Caesarion). *Roman Prefects:* 30 B.C.–26 B.C. Cornelius Gallus; 26 B.C.–25 B.C. Petronius; 25 B.C.–24 B.C. Aelius Gallus; 24 B.C.–13 B.C. Petronius; 13 B.C.–7 B.C. Rubrius Barbarus; 7 B.C.–23 Sept. A.D. 1 Turranius; 23 Sept. A.D. 1–(?) Maximus; (?)–17 Aquila; 17–21 Vitrasius Pollio; 21–ca. 31 Galerius; ca. 31–ca. 32 Vitrasius Pollio; ca. 32–32 Julius Severus; 32–37 Avillius Flaccus; 37–37 Aemilius Rectus; 37–38 Seius Strabo; 38–28 April 39 Naevius Sertorius Macro; 28 April 39–42 Vitrasius Pollio; 42–ca. 47 Aemilius Rectus; ca. 47–48 Julius Postumus; 48–5 April 54 Vergilius Capito; 5 April 54–55 Lusius; 55–56 Metius Modestus; 56–60 Claudius Balbillus; 60–67 Julius Vestinus; 67–28 Sept. 68 Caecina Tuscus; 28 Sept. 68–71 Julius Alexander; 71–(?) Julius Lupus; (?)–2 Feb. 82 Paulinus; 2 Feb. 82–86 Stettius Africanus; 86–10 April 90 Septimus Vegetus; 10 April 90–14 March 95 Metius Rufus; 14 March 95–98 Petronius Secundus; 98–29 Aug. 103 Pompeius Planta; 29 Aug. 103–105 Vibius Maximus; 105–109 Minicius Italus; 109–116 Sulpicius Simius; 116–117 Rutilius Lupus; 117–23 April 118 Marcius Turbo; 23 April 118–18 Feb. 121 Rhammius Martialis; 18 Feb. 121–20 March 126 Haterius Nepos; 20 March 126–25 Feb. 134 Flavius Titianus; 25 Feb. 134–(?) Petronius Mamertinus; (?)–30 March 139 Valerius Eudaemon; 30 March 139–12 Jan. 148 Avidius Heliodorus; 12 Jan. 148–150 Petronius Honoratus; 150–29 Aug. 154 Munatius Felix; 29 Aug. 154–ca. 159 Sempronius Liberalis; ca. 159–ca. 160 Volusius Maecianus; ca. 160–163 Valerius Proculus; 163–6 Jan. 165 Annius Syriacus; 6 Jan. 165–10 May 166 Domitius Honoratus; 10 May 166–ca. 167 Flavius Titianus; ca. 167–26 Oct. 175 Bassaeus Rufus; 26 Oct. 175–177 Calvisius Statianus; 177–180 Pactumeius Magnus; 180–181 Maenius Flavianus; 181–(?) Flavius Priscus; (?)–6 March 193 Marcus Aurelius Papirius Dionysius; 6 March 193–195 Mantennius Sabinus; 195–11 July 197 Ulpius Primianus; 11 July 197–202 Aemilius Saturninus; 202–202 Maecius Laetus; 202–16 March 215 Subatianus Aquila; 16 March 215–5 June 216 Septimius Heracleitus; 5 June 216–218 Valerius Datus; 218–13 Aug. 219 Basilianus; 13 Aug. 219–June 232 Geminius Chrestus; June 232–(?) Maevius Honorianus; (?)–(?) Julianus; (?)–17 July 250 Epagathus; 17 July 250–(?) Appius Sabinus; (?)–(?) Aemilianus; (?)–(?) Firmus; (?)–(?) Celerinus; (?)–(?) [unknown]; (?)–(?) [unknown]; (?)–ca. 302 [unknown]; ca. 302–28 Feb. 303 Pompeius; 28 Feb. 303–307 Culcianus; 307–17 Aug. 323 Satrius Arrianus; 17 Aug. 323–28 March 338 Sabinianus; 28 March 338–26 Feb. 354 Flavius Antonius Theodorus; 26 Feb. 354–ca. 357 Longinianus; ca. 357–2 July 357 Parnasius; 2 July 357–360 Pomponius Metrodorus; 360–2 Dec. 362 Artemius; 2 Dec. 362–ca. 367 Ecdicius; ca. 367–370 Tatianus; 370–ca. 372 Publius; ca. 372–374 Tatianus; 374–375 Aelius Palladius; 375–377 Tatianus; 377–17 March 380 Hadrianus; 17 March 380–380 Julianus; 380–381 Paulinus; 381–14 May 382 Bassianus; 14 May 382–8 May 383 Palladius; 8 May 383–384 Hypatius; 384–18 Dec. 384 Antoninus; 18 Dec. 384–25 July 385 Florentius; 25 July 385–17 Feb. 386 Paulinus; 17 Feb. 386–30 April 388 Florentius; 30 April 388–18 Feb. 390 Erythrius; 18 Feb. 390–16 June 391 Alexander; 16 June 391–5 March 392 Euagrius; 5 March 392–9 April 392 Potamius; 9 April 392–22 June 392 Hypatius; 22 June 392–Aug. 392 Potamius; Aug. 392–392 Claudius Septimus Eutropius; 392–395 Potamius; 395–5 Feb. 396 Charmosynus; 5 Feb. 396–30 March 396 Gennadius (also known as Torquatus); 30 March 396–17 June 397 Remigius; 17 June 397–(?) Archelaus; (?)–403 [unknown]; 403–404 Pentadius; 404–(?) Euthalius; (?)–415 [unknown]; 415–(?) Orestes; (?)–422 [unknown]; 422–(?) Callistus; (?)–435 [unknown]; 435–(?) Cleopater; (?)–442 [unknown]; 442–(?) Charmosinus; (?)–451 [unknown]; 451–(?) Theodorus; (?)–453 [unknown]; 453–(?) Florus; (?)–468 [unknown]; 468–(?) Alexander; (?)–476 [unknown]; 476–477 Boethus; 477–478 Anthemius; 478–479 Theoctistus; 479–(?) Theognostus; (?)–482 [unknown]; 482–(?) Pergamius; (?)–485 [unknown]; 485–(?) Eutrechius; (?)–487 [unknown]; 487–487 Theodorus; 487–(?) Arsenius; (?)–501 [unknown]; 501–(?) Eustathius; (?)–ca. 510 [unknown]; ca. 510–(?) Theodosius; (?)–520 [unknown]; 520–(?) Licinius; (?)–527 [unknown]; 527–(?) Hephaestus; (?)–535 [unknown]; 535–(?) Dioscorus; (?)–537 [unknown]; 537–(?) Rhodon; (?)–539 [unknown]. *Roman Duci (Dukes):* 539–542 Petrus Marcellinus Felix Liberius; 542–(?) Ioannes Laxarion; (?)–ca. 560 [unknown]; ca. 560–(?) Favorinus; (?)–566 [unknown]; 566–(?) Iustinus; (?)–582 [unknown]; 582–(?) Ioannes;

(?)–ca. 585 [unknown]; ca. 585–(?) Paulus; (?)–ca. 588 [unknown]; ca. 588–(?) Ioannes; (?)–ca. 592 [unknown]; ca. 592–(?) Constantinus; (?)–ca. 595 [unknown]; ca. 595–(?) Menas; (?)–600 [unknown]; 600–603 Petrus (also known as Iustinus); 603–ca. 606 [unknown]; ca. 606–(?) Ioannes; (?)–614 [unknown]; 614–(?) Niketas; (?)–616 [unknown]. *Persian Patriarch-Prefects:* 616–628 Benjamin. *Roman Military Prefects:* 628–629 [unknown]; 629–641 Anastasius; 641–17 Sept. 642 Theodorus. *Arab Governors:* 17 Sept. 642–644 Amr ibn al-As (also known as al-Asi); 644–654 Abdallah ibn Sa'd; 654–655 Keys ibn Sa'd; 655–656 Abdallah ibn Sa'd; 656–July 658 Muhammad ibn Abu Bakr. *Omayyad Governors:* July 658–Jan. 664 Amr ibn al-As (also known as al-Asi); Jan. 664–Feb. 664 Abdallah ibn Amr; Feb. 664–665 Otba ibn Abi Sufyan; 665–20 May 667 Okbar ibn Amr; 20 May 667–9 April 682 Maslama ibn Mukhallad; 9 April 682–14 May 682 Muhammad ibn Maslama; 14 May 682–April 684 Sa'id ibn Yezid; April 684–11 Feb. 685 Abd ar-Rahman ibn Ghadam; 11 Feb. 685–1 July 703 Abd al-Aziz ibn Marwan; 1 July 703–30 Jan. 709 Abdallah ibn Abd al-Malik; 30 Jan. 709–14 Nov. 714 Kurra ibn Sharik; 14 Nov. 714–Nov. 717 Abd al-Malik ibn Rifa'a; Nov. 717–1 April 720 Ayyub ibn Shurahbil; 1 April 720–May 721 Bishr ibn Safwan; May 721–724 Handhala ibn Safwan; 724–2 May 724 Muhammad ibn Abd al-Malik; 2 May 724–27 April 727 al-Hurr ibn Yusuf; 27 April 727–16 May 727 Hafs ibn al-Walid; 16 May 727–30 May 727 Abd al-Malik ibn Rifa'a; 30 May 727–July 735 al-Walid ibn Rifa'a; July 735–12 Jan. 737 Abd ar-Rahman ibn Khalid; 12 Jan. 737–2 July 742 Handhala ibn Safwan; 2 July 742–21 March 745 Hafs ibn al-Walid; 21 March 745–7 April 745 Hassan ibn Atahiya; 7 April 745–4 Oct. 745 Hafs ibn al-Walid; 4 Oct. 745–19 March 748 al-Hawthara ibn Suheyl; 19 March 748–March 750 al-Mughira ibn Obeydallah; March 750–9 Aug. 750 Abd al-Malik ibn Marwar. *Abbasid Governors:* 9 Aug. 750–2 April 751 Salih ibn Ali; 2 April 751–27 Oct. 753 Abu Awn; 27 Oct. 753–21 Feb. 755 Salih ibn Ali; 21 Feb. 755–26 Aug. 758 Abu Awn; 26 Aug. 758–28 April 759 Musa ibn Ka'ab; 28 April 759–18 Dec. 760 Muhammad ibn al-Ashath; 18 Dec. 760–14 Feb. 762 Humeyd ibn Kahtaba; 14 Feb. 762–30 April 769 Yezid ibn Hatim; 30 April 769–Feb. 772 Abdallah ibn Abderrahman; Feb. 772–18 Sept. 772 Muhammad ibn Abderrahman; 18 Sept. 772–14 Sept. 778 Musa ibn Olayy; 14 Sept. 778–18 March 779 Isa ibn Lukman; 18 March 779–1 June 779 Wadih; 1 June 779–Aug. 779 Mansur ibn Yezid; Aug. 779–15 Sept. 780 Abu Salih Yahya; 15 Sept. 780–6 Sept. 781 Salim ibn Sawada; 6 Sept. 781–1 July 784 Ibrahim ibn Salih; 1 July 784–10 July 785 Musa ibn Musab; 10 July 785–11 Aug. 785 As Ama ibn Amr; 11 Aug. 785–April 786 al-Fadl ibn Salih; April 786–15 Sept. 787 Ali ibn Suleiman; 15 Sept. 787–15 Feb. 789 Musa ibn Isa; 15 Feb. 789–28 Dec. 789 Maslama ibn Yahya; 28 Dec. 789–2 June 790 Muhammad ibn Zuheyr; 2 June 790–15 June 791 Dawud ibn Yezid; 15 June 791–June 792 Musa ibn Isa; June 792–1 Jan. 793 Ibrahim ibn Salih; 1 Jan. 793–12 Oct. 793 Abdallah ibn al-Mussayab; 12 Oct. 793–1 Nov. 794 Ishaq ibn Suleiman; 1 Nov. 794–9 Jan. 795 Harthama ibn Ayan; 9 Jan. 795–27 March 796 Abd al-Malik ibn Salih; 27 March 796–2 Nov. 796 Obeydallah ibn al-Mahdi; 2 Nov. 796–17 Aug. 797 Musa ibn Isa; 17 Aug. 797–2 Nov. 797 Obeydallah ibn al-Mahdi; 2 Nov. 797–4 Aug. 798 Ismail ibn Salih; 4 Aug. 798–10 Dec. 798 Ismail ibn Isa; 10 Dec. 798–21 June 803 al-Leyth ibn al-Fadl; 21 June 803–15 Sept. 805 Ahmad ibn Ismail; 15 Sept. 805–30 July 806 Obeydallah al-Abbasi; 30 July 806–24 Feb. 808 al-Hussein ibn Gemil; 24 Feb. 808–25 Dec. 808 Malik ibn Delhem; 25 Dec. 808–11 July 810 al-Hassan ibn at-Takhtah; 11 July 810–25 March 811 Hatim ibn Harthama; 25 March 811–25 March 812 Gabir ibn al-Ashath; 25 March 812–13 Nov. 813 Abbad al-Balkhi; 13 Nov. 813–21 June 814 al-Muttalib; 21 June 814–4 Sept. 814 al-Abbas ibn Musa; 4 Sept. 814–3 April 815 al-Muttalib; 3 April 815–30 Sept. 816 as-Sari ibn al-Hakam; 30 Sept. 816–28 Feb. 817 Suleiman ibn Ghalib (pretender); 28 Feb. 817–10 Dec. 820 as-Sari ibn al-Hakam; 10 Dec. 820–7 Jan. 822 Muhammad ibn as-Sari; 7 Jan. 822–17 April 826 Obeydallah ibn as-Sari; 17 April 826–Dec. 828 Abdallah ibn Tahir; Dec. 828–21 Jan. 829 [unknown] (acting); 21 Jan. 829–27 Jan. 829 Isa ibn Yezid; 27 Jan. 829–28 April 829 Omeyr ibn al-Wahid; April 829–June 829 [unknown] (acting); June 829–830 Isa ibn Yezid; 830–28 Feb. 830 al-Motasim; 28 Feb. 830–18 Feb. 831 Abdaweyh ibn Gaabela; 18 Feb. 831–832 Isa ibn Mansur; 832–March 832 al-Mamun (also the caliph); March 832–June 834 Nasr ibn Abdallah (also known as Keydar); June 834–9 Sept. 834 al-Muzaffar ibn Keydar; 9 Sept. 834–12

Feb. 839 Musa al-Hanafi; 12 Feb. 839–5 Feb.
841 Malik ibn Keydar; 5 Feb. 841–6 Oct. 843 Ali
ibn Yahya; 6 Oct. 843–Dec. 847 Isa ibn Mansur; Dec. 847–15 Feb. 848 [unknown] (acting);
15 Feb. 848–3 April 849 Harthama ibn an-
Nadr; 3 April 849–3 May 849 Hatim ibn Harthama; 3 May 849–27 May 850 Ali ibn Yahya;
27 May 850–27 May 851 Ushaq ibn Yahya (also
known as Khut); 27 May 851–24 Sept. 852 Abd
al-Wahid ibn Yahya; 24 Sept. 852–22 Nov. 856
Anbasa ibn Ishaq; 22 Nov. 856–13 March 867
Yezid ibn Abdallah; 13 March 867–7 April 868
Muzahim ibn Khakan; 7 April 868–June 868
Ahmad ibn Muzahim; June 868–15 Sept. 868
Arguz Tarkhan. *Tulunid Sultans:* 15 Sept.
868–20 May 884 Ahmad ibn Tulun; 20 May
884–Jan. 896 Khumarawayh; Jan. 896–26 July
896 Jaysh; 26 July 896–30 Dec. 904 Harun; 30
Dec. 904–10 Jan. 905 Shayban. *Abbasid Military
Commanders:* 10 Jan. 905–Aug. 905 Muhammad
ibn Suleiman. *Abbasid Military Governors:* Aug.
905–Aug. 905 Muhammad ibn Suleiman. *Ab-
basid Governors:* Aug. 905–Sept. 905 Isa; Sept.
905–May 906 Muhammad al-Khalangi (usurper);
May 906–9 May 910 Isa; 9 May 910–13 June 910
[unknown] (acting); 13 June 910–23 June 910
Abu'l Abbas; 23 June 910–27 Aug. 915 Tekin al-
Khassa al-Gezeri; 27 Aug. 915–8 Aug. 919
Dhuka ar-Rumi; 8 Aug. 919–22 July 921 Tekin
al-Khassa al-Gezeri; 22 July 921–25 July 921
Mahmun ibn Hamal; 25 July 921–14 Aug. 921
Tekin al-Khassa al-Gezeri; 14 Aug. 921–17 Aug.
923 Hilal ibn Bedr; 17 Aug. 923–12 Feb. 924
Ahmad ibn Keyghalagh; 12 Feb. 924–16 March
933 Tekin al-Khassa al-Gezeri; 16 March
933–30 Sept. 933 Muhammad ibn Tekin; 933–
933 Muhammad ibn Tugh ("The Ikhshid") (did
not take office); 30 Sept. 933–934 Ahmad ibn
Keyghalagh; 934–2 Sept. 935 Muhammad ibn
Tekin. *Ikhshid Kings:* 2 Sept. 935–24 July 946
Muhammad al-Ikhshid; 24 July 946–29 Dec.
960 Unujur; 1 Jan. 961–7 Feb. 965 Ali; 8 Feb.
965–23 April 968 Abu al-Misq Kafur; 23 April
968–5 Aug. 969 Ahmad. *Ikhshid Viziers:* 946–8
Feb. 965 Abu al-Misq Kafur. *Fatimid Military
Administrators:* 5 Aug. 969–June 973 Gohar. *Fatimid Caliphs:* June 973–10 Dec. 975 al-Mu'izz;
10 Dec. 975–14 Oct. 996 al-Aziz; 14 Oct.
996–13 Feb. 1021 al-Hakim; 13 Feb. 1021–13
June 1036 az-Zahir; 13 June 1036–29 Dec. 1094
al-Mustansir; 31 Dec. 1094–8 Dec. 1101 al-
Musta'li; 8 Dec. 1101–17 Oct. 1130 al-Amir;
1131–Oct. 1149 al-Hafiz; Oct. 1149–16 April 1154

az-Zafir; 16 April 1154–23 July 1160 al-Fa'iz; 23
July 1160–10 Sept. 1171 al-Adid. *Fatimid Maliks
(or Viziers, or Military Commanders):* June 973–
23 Feb. 991 ibn Kallis; 23 Feb. 991–June 1050
[vacant]; June 1050–March 1058 al-Yazuri;
March 1058–27 Jan. 1074 [vacant]; 27 Jan.
1074–April 1094 Badr al-Jamali; April 1094–
Dec. 1121 al-Afdal Shahanshah; Dec. 1121–4 Oct.
1125 ibn al-Batai'hi (also known as al-Mamun);
4 Oct. 1125–21 Sept. 1130 [vacant]; 21 Sept.
1130–8 Dec. 1131 Abu Ali; 8 Dec. 1131–Aug. 1132
Yanis; Aug. 1132–29 March 1134 [vacant]; 29
March 1134–15 Feb. 1137 Bahram; 15 Feb. 1137–
14 June 1139 Rudwan; 14 June 1139–1143 [un-
known]; 1143–ca. 1152 Salih ibn Ruzzik; ca.
1152–April 1153 ibn as-Salar; April 1153–1154
Abbas; 1154–1161 Salih ibn Ruzzik; 1161–1163 al-
Adil Ruzzik; 1163–30 Aug. 1163 Shawar; 31 Aug.
1163–May 1164 Dirgham; May 1164–18 Jan. 1169
Shawar; 18 Jan. 1169–23 March 1169 Shirkuh;
23 March 1169–10 Sept. 1171 Saladin (also known
as Salah ad-Din). *Aiyubid Sultans:* 10 Sept.
1171–4 March 1193 Saladin (also known as Yusuf
ibn Aiyub, or Salah ad-Din); 4 March 1193–29
Nov. 1198 al-Aziz Uthman; 29 Nov. 1198–1200
Nasir ad-Din Muhammad; Feb. 1200–31 Aug.
1218 al-Adil Abu Bakr I (also known as Sa-
phadin); 2 Sept. 1218–8 March 1238 Malik al-
Kamil; 8 March 1238–31 May 1240 al-Adil Abu
Bakr II; 1 June 1240–21 Nov. 1249 as-Salih
Aiyub. *Aiyubid Queens-Regent:* 21 Nov. 1249–27
Feb. 1250 Sheger ad-Durr. *Aiyubid Sultans:* 27
Feb. 1250–2 May 1250 Turanshah. *Bahrite
Mameluke Queens:* 2 May 1250–31 July 1250
Sheger ad-Durr. *Bahrite Mameluke Sultans:* 31
July 1250–10 April 1257 Aibak; 15 April 1257–
Nov. 1259 Nur ad-Din; Nov. 1259–24 Oct. 1260
al-Mudhaffar Kuts; 24 Oct. 1260–1 July 1277
Baibars I; 3 July 1277–Aug. 1279 Sa'id Barakh
Khan; Aug. 1279–Nov. 1279 al-Adil Salamish;
Nov. 1279–10 Nov. 1290 al-Mansur Qala'un; 12
Nov. 1290–12 Dec. 1293 al-Ashraf Khalil; 14
Dec. 1293–Dec. 1294 Muhammad an-Nasir;
Dec. 1294–7 Dec. 1296 al-Adil ad-Din Ket-
bugha; 7 Dec. 1296–16 Jan. 1299 al-Mansur
Lagin; 16 Jan. 1299–March 1309 Muhammad
an-Nasir; April 1309–5 March 1310 Baibars II;
5 March 1310–6 June 1341 Muhammad an-
Nasir; 8 June 1341–1341 Abu Bakr; 1341–1342
Al'a ad-Din Kujuk; 1342–1343 Ahmad; 1343–
1344 Ismail; 1344–1345 Shaabaan I; 1345–Dec.
1347 Hajji I; Dec. 1347–1351 Hassan; 1351–1354
Salih; 1354–1361 Hassan; 1361–1363 al-Mansur

ad-Din Muhammad; 1363–1368 Shaabaan II; 1368–1380 al-Mansur Al'a ad-Din; 1380–26 Nov. 1382 as-Salih Hajji. *Circassian Mameluke Sultans:* 26 Nov. 1382–1 June 1389 Barquq; 1 June 1389–1 Feb. 1390 as-Salih Hajji (temporary Bahrite sultan); 1 Feb. 1390–20 June 1399 Barquq; 20 June 1399–20 Sept. 1405 Faraq; 20 Sept. 1405–20 Nov. 1405 Abdul Aziz; 20 Nov. 1405–28 May 1412 Faraq; 28 May 1412–6 Nov. 1412 al-Adil al-Musta'in; 6 Nov. 1412–13 Jan. 1421 Sheikh al-Mu'aiyad; 13 Jan. 1421–29 Aug. 1421 al-Muzaffar Ahmad; 29 Aug. 1421–30 Nov. 1421 ad-Dahir Tatar; 30 Nov. 1421–1 April 1422 as-Salih Muhammad; 1 April 1422–7 June 1438 al-Ashraf Barsabay; 7 June 1438–9 Sept. 1438 al-Aziz Yusuf; 9 Sept. 1438–1 Feb. 1453 Abu Sa'id Jaqmaq; 1 Feb. 1453–19 March 1453 Abu s-Sadat Uthman; 19 March 1453–26 Feb. 1461 Ainal; 26 Feb. 1461–28 June 1461 Ahmad; 28 June 1461–9 Oct. 1467 Khoshkhakham; 9 Oct. 1467–3 Dec. 1467 Bilbay; 3 Dec. 1467–31 Jan. 1468 Temerbeg; 31 Jan. 1468–7 Aug. 1496 Qait Bey; 7 Aug. 1496–31 Oct. 1498 Muhammad; 31 Oct. 1498–21 Nov. 1498 [unknown] (acting); 21 Nov. 1498–28 June 1500 Khansoo; 30 June 1500–25 Jan. 1501 Janbalat; 27 Jan. 1501–20 April 1501 Tooman Bey; 22 April 1501–15 Oct. 1516 al-Ghuri; 17 Oct. 1516–25 Aug. 1517 Tooman Bey I. *Ottoman Pashas:* 25 Aug. 1517–29 Sept. 1522 Kha'ir Bey; 1 Oct. 1522–27 May 1523 Mustafa; 28 May 1523–June 1523 Qasim; June 1523–19 Aug. 1523 [unknown] (acting); 19 Aug. 1523–Feb. 1524 Ahmad; Feb. 1524–24 March 1525 Qasim; 24 March 1525–April 1525 [unknown] (acting); April 1525–14 June 1525 Ibrahim; 15 June 1525–22 Jan. 1535 Suleiman (also known as Khadim); 23 Jan. 1535–10 Dec. 1536 Khusru; 11 Dec. 1536–8 June 1538 Suleiman; 9 June 1538–11 April 1549 Daud; 12 April 1549–Dec. 1553 Ali Semiz; Dec. 1553–31 May 1556 Muhammad (also known as Dukagin); 1 June 1556–8 May 1559 Iskander; 9 May 1559–25 Aug. 1560 Ali Khadim; 26 Aug. 1560–26 Jan. 1564 Lala Shahin; 1 Feb. 1564–20 April 1566 Ali Sufu; 21 April 1566–26 Dec. 1567 Mahmud; 27 Dec. 1567–13 Dec. 1568 Sinan; 14 Dec. 1568–24 June 1571 Tsherkes Iskander; 25 June 1571–2 May 1573 Sinan; 3 May 1573–13 Jan. 1575 Hussein; 14 Jan. 1575–28 June 1580 Masih (also known as Khadim); 29 June 1580–16 June 1583 Hassan (also known as Khadim); 17 June 1583–7 Oct. 1585 Ibrahim; 8 Oct. 1585–30 May 1587 Sinan (also known as Defter); 31 May 1587–30 April 1591 Uways; 2 May 1591–10 May 1595 Hafiz Ahmad; 11 May 1595–30 March 1596 Kurd; 1 April 1596–16 July 1598 Sayyid Muhammad; 17 July 1598–30 July 1601 Khidr; 31 July 1601–14 Sept. 1603 Yawuz Ali; 15 Sept. 1603–24 Sept. 1604 Ibrahim al-Hajj; 25 Sept. 1604–16 July 1605 Muhammad (also known as Gurji); 17 July 1605–27 May 1607 Hassan ibn Hussein; 29 May 1607–July 1611 Muhammad (also known as Oghuz); July 1611–29 April 1615 Muhammad (also known as Sufi); 30 April 1615–8 Feb. 1618 Ahmad; 9 Feb. 1618–1 Nov. 1618 Mustafa Lefkeli; 2 Nov. 1618–6 Aug. 1619 Ja'far; 6 Aug. 1619–16 Aug. 1620 Mustafa; 17 Aug. 1620–5 March 1622 Hussein (also known as Miri); 7 March 1622–16 July 1622 Muhammad (also known as Babar); 17 July 1622–5 July 1623 Ibrahim; 6 July 1623–12 Oct. 1623 Mustafa (also known as Qara); 13 Oct. 1623–12 Feb. 1624 Ali (also known as Tshetshedji); 13 Feb. 1624–16 May 1626 Mustafa (also known as Qara); 17 May 1626–8 Sept. 1628 Bairam; 8 Sept. 1628–15 Oct. 1630 Muhammad (also known as Tabany-Yasy); 16 Oct. 1630–11 July 1631 Musa; 12 July 1631–13 March 1633 Khalil; 14 March 1633–17 Oct. 1635 Ahmad (also known as Baqirdji); 21 Oct. 1635–5 Oct. 1637 Hussein (also known as Deli); 6 Oct. 1637–29 Aug. 1640 Muhammad (also known as Juwan Qapiji Sultanzade); 30 Aug. 1640–3 Oct. 1642 Mustafa (also known as Naqqash); 4 Oct. 1642–22 April 1644 Maqsud; 22 April 1644–15 April 1646 Ayyub; 16 April 1646–2 Dec. 1647 Muhammad (also known as Haydar Agha Zade); 2 Dec. 1647–20 Dec. 1647 Mustafa (also known as Mustari); 20 Dec. 1647–28 Feb. 1649 Muhammad (also known as Sharaf); 1 March 1649–Feb. 1651 Ahmad (also known as Tarkhunji); Feb. 1651–9 Sept. 1652 Abd ar-Rahman (also known as Khadim); 10 Sept. 1652–28 May 1656 Muhammad (also known as Khasseki); 29 May 1656–20 June 1657 Mustafa (also known as Khaliji-Zade-Damad); 21 June 1657–30 June 1660 Muhammad (also known as Shahsuwar-Zade-Ghazi); 1 July 1660–22 May 1661 Mustafa (also known as Gurji); 23 May 1661–1 April 1664 Ibrahim (also known as Defterdar); 2 April 1664–20 Feb. 1667 Umar (also known as Silahdar); 21 Feb. 1667–14 Nov. 1668 Ibrahim (also known as Sufi); 14 Nov. 1668–29 Dec. 1669 Ali (also known as Qaraqash); 30 Dec. 1669–9 June 1673 Ibrahim; 10 June 1673–28 July 1675 Hussein (also known as Jambalat-Zade); 29 July 1675–11 May 1676 Ahmad (also known as Defterdar); 12 May 1676–18 June 1680 Abd ar-Rahman; 19 June 1680–29 April 1683 Uthman; 1 May 1683–31 March 1687 Hamza; 1 April 1687–14 Nov. 1687 Hassan; 15 Nov. 1687–15 Oct. 1689 Hassan (also known as Damad); 16 Oct. 1689–12 April 1691 Ahmad (also known as Mufattish Kiaya); 12 April 1691–30 July 1695 Ali (also known as Khaznadar); 1 Aug. 1695–30 Sept. 1697 Ismail; 1 Oct. 1697–9 Oct. 1699 Hussein (also known as Firari); 9 Oct. 1699–6 May 1704 Muhammad (also known as Qara); 7 May 1704–7 Oct. 1704 Suleiman; 7 Oct. 1704–31 Aug. 1706 Muhammad (also known as Rami); 1 Sept. 1706–Sept. 1707 Ali; Sept. 1707–28 Oct. 1709 Hassan (also known as Damad); 28 Oct. 1709–Aug. 1710 Ibrahim; Aug. 1710–30 July 1711 Khalil (also known as Khosej); 1 Aug. 1711–30 Aug. 1714 Wali; 1 Sept. 1714–29 June 1717 Abdi; 1 July 1717–9 Sept. 1720 Ali (also known as Kiaya); 10 Sept. 1720–30 April 1721 Rajab; 1 May 1721–30 Sept. 1725 Muhammad (also known as Nishanji); 1 Oct. 1725–Feb. 1726 Ali Muraly; Feb. 1726–29 Sept. 1727 Muhammad (also known as Nishanji); 30 Sept. 1727–Oct 1727 Abdi; Oct. 1727–10 July 1729 Abu Bakr; 11 July 1729–30 June 1733 Abdallah (also known as Heupruluzade); 1 July 1733–1734 Muhammad (also known as Silahdar); 1734–1734 Uthman; 1734–Dec. 1734 Abu Bakr; Dec. 1734–1741 Ali (also known as Hakimzade); 1741–3 July 1743 Yahya; 3 July 1743–28 Feb. 1744 Muhammad Sa'id; 1 March 1744–31 Aug. 1748 Muhammad (also known as Raghib); 1 Sept. 1748–Jan. 1752 Ahmad (also known as al-Hajj); Jan. 1752–Dec. 1752 Muhammad Melek; Dec. 1752–Oct. 1755 Hassan ash-Sharawi; Oct. 1755–Dec. 1756 Ali (also known as Hakimzade); Dec. 1756–29 April 1757 Sa'id ad-Din; 30 April 1757–1760 Muhammad Sa'id; 1760–Dec. 1762 Mustafa (also known as Bahir Keuse); Dec. 1762–Jan. 1765 Ahmad; Jan. 1765–1766 Bakr; 1766–April 1767 Hamza (also known as Silahdar Mahir); April 1767–April 1767 Muhammad Melek; April 1767–1768 Muhammad (also known as Ruqim); 1768–1768 Muhammad (also known as Diwitdar). *Ottoman Governors:* 1768–13 April 1773 Ali Bey al-Kabir; 13 April 1773–10 June 1775 Abu'dh Dhahab (also known as Mehmed Bey); 26 June 1775–Aug. 1777 Murad Bey; Aug. 1777–Feb. 1778 Ismail Bey; Feb. 1778–1786 Murad Bey; 1786–1790 Ismail Bey; 1790–25 July 1798 Murad Bey and Ibrahim Bey (joint governors). *French Military Commanders:* 25 July 1798–22 Aug. 1799 Napo-

léon Bonaparte; 22 Aug. 1799–14 June 1800 Jean-Baptiste Kléber; 14 June 1800–27 June 1801 Jacques de Menou. *Ottoman Governors:* 27 June 1801–10 Aug. 1801 Nasih Pasha; 10 Aug. 1801 Jan. 1802 Kuchuk Hussein Pasha; Jan. 1802–3 May 1803 Khusrau Pasha; 3 May 1803–June 1803 Taher Pasha; June 1803–July 1803 Khurshid Pasha; July 1803–31 Jan. 1804 Ali Pasha Jazairli; 31 Jan. 1804–March 1804 [unknown] (acting). *Ottoman Valis:* March 1804–2 Nov. 1805 Khurshid Pasha; 2 Nov. 1805–1 Sept. 1848 Muhammad Ali; 1 Sept. 1848–10 Nov. 1848 Ibrahim. *Ottoman Diwan Presidents:* 10 Nov. 1848–30 Nov. 1848 Sa'ib Pasha. *Ottoman Valis:* 30 Nov. 1848–13 July 1854 Abbas I; 14 July 1854–18 Jan. 1863 Muhammad Sa'id; 18 Jan. 1863–1866 Ismail. *Ottoman Khedives:* 1866–25 June 1879 Ismail; 25 June 1879–7 Jan. 1892 Tewfiq; 7 Jan. 1892–19 Dec. 1914 Abbas II Hilmi. *Sultans:* 19 Dec. 1914–9 Oct. 1917 Hussein Khamil; 9 Oct. 1917–15 March 1922 Fuad (also known as Ahmad Fuad I). *Kings:* 15 March 1922–28 April 1936 Fuad I; 28 April 1936–22 July 1952 Farouk; 26 July 1952–18 June 1953 Fuad II. *Presidents:* 18 June 1953–14 Nov. 1954 Muhammad Naguib; 17 Nov. 1954–28 Sept. 1970 Gamal Abdel Nasser; 29 Sept. 1970–15 Oct. 1970 Muhammad Anwar as-Sadat (interim); 15 Oct. 1970–6 Oct. 1981 Muhammad Anwar as-Sadat; 10 Oct. 1981–13 Oct. 1981 Sufi Abu Talib (acting); 13 Oct. 1981–Muhammad Hosni Mubarrak. *British Agents/Consuls-General:* 11 Sept. 1882–15 Sept. 1882 Sir Evelyn Baring; 15 Sept. 1882–11 Sept. 1883 Sir Edwin Malet; 15 Sept. 1883–1891 Sir Evelyn Baring; 1891–1892 Arthur Hardinge (acting); 1892–24 April 1907 Sir Evelyn Baring (created Baron Cromer in 1892, Viscount Cromer in 1899, and Earl Cromer in 1901); 7 May 1907–12 July 1911 Sir Eldon Gorst; 16 July 1911–18 Dec. 1914 Horatio, Lord Kitchener. *British High Commissioners:* 18 Dec. 1914–9 Jan. 1915 Sir Milne Chatham (acting); 9 Jan. 1915–1 Jan. 1917 Sir Arthur MacMahon; 1 Jan. 1917–17 Oct. 1919 Sir Reginald Wingate; 17 Oct. 1919–26 Feb. 1925 Edmund, Lord Allenby; 26 Feb. 1925–21 Oct. 1925 [unknown] (acting); 21 Oct. 1925–8 Aug. 1929 Sir George Lloyd; 8 Aug. 1929–16 Dec. 1933 Sir Percy Loraine; 8 Jan. 1934–1936 Sir Miles Wedderburn Lampson. *Prime Ministers:* 15 Aug. 1878–18 Feb. 1879 Nubar Pasha; 2 Feb. 1882–25 May 1882 Mahmud Sami. *War Ministers:* 25 May 1882–17 June 1882 Ahmad Arabi. *Prime Ministers:* 17 June 1882–28 Aug. 1882

Ragib Pasha; 28 Aug. 1882–15 Sept. 1882 Sherif Pasha; 15 Sept. 1882–8 Dec. 1882 Riaz Pasha; 8 Dec. 1882–30 Oct. 1883 Nubar Pasha; 30 Oct. 1883–7 Jan. 1884 Sherif Pasha; 7 Jan. 1884–8 June 1888 Nubar Pasha; 8 June 1888–12 May 1891 Riaz Pasha; 13 May 1891–15 Jan. 1893 Mustafa Fehmy Pasha; 18 Jan 1893–16 April 1894 Riaz Pasha; 16 April 1894–11 Nov. 1895 Nubar Pasha; 12 Nov. 1895–12 Nov. 1908 Mustafa Fehmy Pasha; 12 Nov. 1908–20 Feb. 1910 Butros Ghali; 22 Feb. 1910–3 April 1914 Muhammad Sa'id Bey; 5 April 1914–21 April 1919 Hussein Rushdi Pasha; 21 April 1919–28 Nov. 1919 Muhammad Sa'id Pasha; 28 Nov. 1919–19 May 1920 Yusef Wahba Pasha; 19 May 1920–15 March 1921 Tewfiq Nesim Pasha; 15 March 1921–1 March 1922 Adli Yegen Pasha; 1 March 1922–30 Nov. 1922 Abdul Khalik Pasha Sarwat; 30 Nov. 1922–5 Feb. 1923 Tewfiq Pasha; 5 Feb. 1923–15 March 1923 [vacant]; 15 March 1923–17 Jan. 1924 Yehia Ibrahim Pasha; 28 Jan. 1924–24 Nov. 1924 Sa'd Zaghlul Pasha; 25 Nov. 1924–6 June 1926 Ahmad Pasha Ziwar; 6 June 1926–18 April 1927 Adli Yegen Pasha; 18 April 1927–16 March 1928 Abdul Khalik Pasha Sarwat; 16 March 1928–25 June 1928 Nahhas Pasha; 25 June 1928–2 Oct. 1929 Muhammad Mahmud Pasha; 2 Oct. 1929–30 Dec. 1929 Adli Yegen Pasha; 31 Dec. 1929–21 June 1930 Nahhas Pasha; 21 June 1930–21 March 1933 Ismail Sidqi Pasha; 24 March 1933–6 Nov. 1934 Yehia Ibrahim Pasha; 15 Nov. 1934–22 Jan. 1936 Muhammad Tewfiq Nesim; 30 Jan. 1936–10 May 1936 Ali Maher Pasha; 10 May 1936–30 Dec. 1937 Nahhas Pasha; 30 Dec. 1937–18 Aug. 1939 Muhammad Mahmud Pasha; 18 Aug. 1939–22 June 1940 Ali Maher Pasha; 28 June 1940–14 Nov. 1940 Hassan Sabry; 14 Nov. 1940–8 Feb. 1942 Hussein Sirry Pasha; 8 Feb. 1942–8 Oct. 1944 Nahhas Pasha; 9 Oct. 1944–24 Feb. 1945 Ahmad Pasha; 24 Feb. 1945–8 Feb. 1946 Nokrashy Pasha; 8 Feb. 1946–8 Dec. 1946 Ismail Sidqi Pasha; 9 Dec. 1946–28 Dec. 1948 Nokrashy Pasha; 28 Dec. 1948–26 July 1949 Abdul Hidi Pasha; 26 July 1949–12 Jan. 1950 Hussein Sirry Pasha; 12 Jan. 1950–27 Jan. 1952 Nahhas Pasha; 27 Jan. 1952–1 March 1952 Ali Maher Pasha; 1 March 1952–29 June 1952 Naguib al-Hilaili Pasha; 2 July 1952–20 July 1952 Hussein Sirry Pasha; 24 July 1952–7 Sept. 1952 Ali Maher Pasha; 7 Sept. 1952–18 June 1953 Muhammad Naguib; 25 Feb. 1954–27 Feb. 1954 Gamal Abdel Nasser; 27 Feb. 1954–18 April 1954 [va-cant]; 18 April 1954–17 Nov. 1954 Gamal Abdel Nasser; 24 Sept. 1962–29 Sept. 1965 Ali Sabry; 29 Sept. 1965–10 Sept. 1966 Zahariah Mohieddin; 10 Sept. 1966–19 June 1967 Sidqi Suleiman; 20 June 1970–17 Jan. 1972 Mahmoud Fawzi; 17 Jan. 1972–27 March 1973 Aziz Sidqi; 25 Sept. 1974–13 April 1975 Abdul Aziz Hegazy; 13 April 1975–2 Oct. 1978 Mamdouh Salem; 2 Oct. 1978–12 May 1980 Mustafa Khalil; 7 Oct. 1981–13 Oct. 1981 Muhammad Hosni Mubarrak; 2 Jan. 1982–5 June 1984 Ahmad Fuad Mohieddin; 5 June 1984–17 July 1984 Kamal Hassan Ali (acting); 17 July 1984–4 Sept. 1985 Kamal Hassan Ali; 4 Sept. 1985–12 Nov. 1986 Ali Lutfi; 12 Nov. 1986–2 Jan. 1996 Atif Sidqi; 4 Jan. 1996–19 Oct. 1999 Kamal al-Ganzouri; 19 Oct. 1999–9 July 2004 Atef Ebeid; 9 July 2004–Ahmad Nazif. *Note:* In times of no Prime Minister [except where it says the position was vacant], the Khedive or President fulfilled that function.

Ekwanga see **Opobo**

Ekwu see **Kom**

Elliotdale see **Kreli's Country**

Elobey see **Equatorial Guinea**

Emporia see **Carthage**

EPLF see **Eritrea**

EPRDF see **Eritrea**

Equatoria Province. 26 May 1871–April 1889. *Location:* southern Sudan. *Capital:* Gondokoro. *Other names:* Mongalla; al-Istiwa'iyah.

History: It was the plan of Ismail, the Khedive of Egypt, to conquer Africa. Samuel Baker, a British explorer working for Ismail, set out to annex all the land between the southern Sudanese town of Gondokoro and the Great Lakes. He reached Gondokoro in 1870, and renamed it Ismailia. Baker was made governor of this territory, which was named Equatoria and made into a province of the Egyptian Sudan (see Sudan). In 1874 Baker was succeeded by Col. (later Maj.-Gen.) Gordon (also known as "Chinese" Gordon, and later as "Gordon of Khartoum"). The efforts of these two governors to crush the slave trade in the area were largely unsuccessful, but they did succeed in conquering a lot of territory, as far south as Uganda. In 1889 it fell to the Mahdi (also see Sudan). It later became known officially as Mongalla (until 1936, after which it reverted to the name Equatoria), and between 1936 and 1956 included Bahr al-Ghazal (q.v.).

Governors: 26 May 1871–Aug. 1873 Samuel Baker Pasha; Aug. 1873–March 1874 Mehmed Reuf Pasha; March 1874–Oct. 1876 Charles Gordon Pasha; Oct. 1876–1877 Henry Prout Bey; 1877–Aug. 1877 Alexander Mason Bey; Aug. 1877–1878 Ibrahim Pasha Fawzi; 1878–April 1889 Mehmed Emin Pasha (also known as Eduard Schnitzer).

Equatorial Guinea. 1926– . *Location:* the mainland part, Río Muni, lies on the west central African coast, between Gabon and Cameroun. Bioko (formerly Fernando Po) is an island about 20 miles off the coast of Cameroun, in the Bight of Biafra. Pagalu (formerly Annobón) is another island, 400 miles to the southwest of Bioko. *Capital:* Malabo (formerly called Santa Isabel), which is the capital of the entire country, and was between 1959 and 1963 the capital of the island province (see below); Bata (between 1959 and 1963 it was the capital of the province of Río Muni). *Other names:* República de Guinea Ecuatorial, or Republic of Equatorial Guinea (from 1963); Overseas Provinces of Spanish Guinea (1959–1963); Spanish Territories of the Gulf of Guinea (1938–1959); Spanish Guinea (1926–1938).

History: In 1926 the Spanish possessions of Río Muni, Fernando Po, and Annobón were united as Spanish Guinea. In 1938 the area became known as the Spanish Territories of the Gulf of Guinea. On 30 July 1959 (effective as from 1 Jan. 1960) the country became two overseas provinces of Spain, each under a civil governor—Río Muni as one of them, which also included the estuary islets of Corisco, Elobey Chico and Elobey Grande; the two islands of Fernando Po and Annobón formed the other province; both provinces together were termed Spanish Guinea Overseas Provinces. On 15 Dec. 1963 it became the partially self-governing country of Equatorial Guinea. In 1964 Fernando Po was given autonomy status, and on 12 Oct. 1968 the whole country became independent as the Republic of Equatorial Guinea. Fernando Po became Macías Nguema Biyogo (later just Bioko), and Annobón became Pagalu. There has been a clash between the more advanced island and the

more backward Río Muni of the mainland, and from 1972 the whole country was hampered by the brutal regime of dictator Macías Nguema Biyogo. The Europeans left under his administration, and the country went bankrupt. Biyogo was ousted in a military coup in Aug. 1979 and executed. The first free elections were held in 1993, and another in 1996, but they were hopelessly fixed by the party in power. In 1997 oil was discovered, which would have raised the standard of living of the population, but most of the revenue went into the president's personal coffers. In March 2004 the government foiled a coup led by South African mercenaries. Equatorial Guinea is the only independent Spanish-speaking state in Africa, but like the rest of sub-Saharan Africa it is plagued by poverty and AIDS.

Governors: 1926–1931 Miguel de Prado; 1931–1932 Gustavo de Sostoa y Sthamer; 1032–1933 [unknown]; 1933–1934 Estanislao García; 1934–1935 Ángel Feltrer; 1935–1936 Luis Saéz; 1936–1937 [unknown]; 1937–1937 Manuel de Mendívil y Elío; 1937–1941 Juan Fontán y Lobé; 1941–1943 Mariano Alonso; 1943–1949 Juan Rubío; 1949–1962 Faustino González; 1962–15 Dec. 1963 Francisco Rodríguez. *High Commissioners:* 15 Dec. 1963–1964 Francisco Rodriguez; 1964–1966 Pedro Alcubierre; 1966–12 Oct. 1968 Victor Díaz del Río. *Presidents of the Government Council:* 15 Dec. 1963–12 Oct. 1968 Bonifácio Ondo Edu. *Presidents:* 12 Oct. 1968–14 July 1972 Francisco Macías Nguema Biyogo. *Presidents for Life:* 14 July 1972–3 Aug. 1979 Francisco Macías Nguema Biyogo. *Presidents:* 3 Aug. 1979–10 Oct. 1979 Teodoro Obiang Nguema Mbasogo (interim); 10 Oct. 1979–Teodoro Obiang Nguema Mbasogo. *Prime Ministers:* 15 Aug. 1982–23 Jan. 1992 Cristino Seriche Bioko; 23 Jan. 1992–1 April 1996 Silvestre Siale Bileka; 1 April 1996–4 March 2001 Ángel Serafín Seriche Dougan; 4 March 2001–Cándido Rivas. *Note:* In times of no Prime Minister, the President held that office. *Note:* On 26 Sept. 1975 Macías dropped the Francisco part of his name, and in 1976 he changed Macías to Macie.

Eritrea. 1 Jan. 1890– . *Location:* on the Red Sea coast of northeast Africa, to the north of Ethiopia and to the south and east of the Sudan. *Capital:* Asmara (from 1935); Massawa (1890–1935). *Other names:* Eritrean Autonomous State (1952–1962); British Eritrea (1941–1952).

History: In 1890 the Italian colony of Eritrea was born. The Italians named it after the Mare Erythraeum, the Roman name for the Red Sea. It was created by the Italians as an extension of prior protectorates in the area, e.g. Assab and Massawa. In 1896 it ceased being a military administration, and became civil. On 15 May 1902 the territory of the Kanama people was acquired by Eritrea, and on 16 May 1908 the boundary between Eritrea and Ethiopia was fixed. In 1935 Eritrea became the launching pad for the Italian conquest of Ethiopia (or Abissinia, as they called it). In this the Italians were aided, as they always had been, by the native army known as the Askari. On 9 May 1936 Eritrea became a province of Italian East Africa. On 5 May 1941, after Britain had captured the Italian possessions in East Africa, Eritrea became a British prize of war, and in the peace treaty of 1947 Italy renounced all claims in Africa. On 11 Sept. 1952 it became the Autonomous State of Eritrea, independent except that it was ruled by Ethiopia, the two countries being called an Ethiopian–Eritrean Federation. On 14 Nov. 1962 Eritrea became the 14th Province of Ethiopia, and that year the Eritrean Liberation Front was formed, and later the Eritrean People's Liberation Front (EPLF) was also formed. These groups at one time had captured most of Eritrea and set up a rudimentary government. The reason for the conflict was that Eritrea wanted independence, and Ethiopia, by granting such an independence, would lose not only its only seaports, but also its only petroleum refinery. In 1978 the Ethiopian Army crushed (but did not stamp out) the rebels, who subsequently returned to guerrilla warfare. On 18 Sept. 1987 the new Ethiopian government granted autonomy again to Eritrea. On 29 May 1991 Isaias Afwerki, secretary-general of the People's Front for Democracy and Justice (PFDJ), which then served, and still does, as Eritrea's legislative body, announced the formation of a provisional government in Eritrea (the PGE), in preparation for the referendum on independence for Eritrea, to be held on 23–25 April 1993. The result was a landslide for independence, which, after a 31-year struggle, was declared on 24 May 1993. A five-year war with Yemen began immediately, over islands in the Red Sea. That was followed by a war (1998–2000) with Ethiopia over disputed border territory. Ethiopia won and Eritrea lost territory. In the early 2000s the new country was faced with drought, famine, starvation, and AIDS, as well as political repression and the persecution of religious minorities.

Italian Commandants: 1 Jan. 1890–30 June 1890 Baldassare Orero; 30 June 1890–28 Feb. 1892 Giacomo Gandolfi; 28 Feb. 1892–22 Feb. 1896 Oreste Baratieri; 22 Feb. 1896–17 Dec. 1897 Antonio Baldissera. *Italian Governors:* 16 Dec. 1897–25 March 1907 Ferdinando Martini; 25 March 1907–17 Aug. 1915 Giuseppe Salvago-Raggi; 17 Aug. 1915–16 Sept. 1916 Giovanni Cerrina-Ferroni (acting); 16 Sept. 1916–20 July 1919 Nobile Giacomo Di Martino; 20 July 1919–20 Nov. 1920 Camillo De Camillis; 20 Nov. 1920–14 April 1921 Ludovico Pollera; 14 April 1921–1 June 1923 Giovanni Cerrina-Ferroni; 1 June 1923–1 June 1928 Jacopo Gasparini; 1 June 1928–16 July 1930 Corrado Zoli; 16 July 1930–15 Jan. 1935 Riccardo Astuto; 15 Jan. 1935–18 Jan. 1935 Ottone Gabelli. *Italian High Commissioners:* 18 Jan. 1935–27 Nov. 1935 Emilio De Bono; 28 Nov. 1935–31 May 1936 Pietro Badoglio (also Viceroy of Ethiopia); 31 May 1936–June 1936 Alfredo Guzzoni; June 1936–9 April 1937 Emilio De Bono; 9 April 1937–15 Dec. 1937 Vincenzo De Feo; 15 Dec. 1937–2 June 1940 Giuseppe Daodice; 2 June 1940–5 May 1941 Luigi Frusci. *British Chief Administrators:* 5 May 1941–4 May 1942 William Platt; 4 May 1942–9 Sept. 1944 Stephen Longrigg; 9 Sept. 1944–14 Aug. 1945 C.D. McCarthy; 14 Aug. 1945–1 Nov. 1946 John Benoy; 1 Nov. 1946–19 Feb. 1951 Francis Drew; 19 Feb. 1951–11 Sept. 1952 Duncan Cumming. *U.N. Commissioners:* 19 Feb. 1951–11 Sept. 1952 Edoardo Matienzo. *Ethiopian Governors:* 11 Sept. 1952–Aug. 1955 Ato Tedla Bairu; Aug. 1955–Dec. 1959 Betwoded Asfaha Wolde Mikael; Dec. 1959–1964 Abiye Abebe; 1964–Dec. 1970 Ras Asrata-Medhin Kassa; Dec. 1970–Aug. 1974 Debbe Haile Maryan; Aug. 1974–19 Feb. 1975 Immanuel Amde Michael; 19 Feb. 1975–(?) General Getachew Nadu. *Heads of State:* 24 May 1993–Isaias Afwerki.

Essmara see **Western Sahara**

Ethiopia. 1117– . *Location:* northeast Africa. *Capital:* Addis Ababa (from 1889. The city was founded in 1887, and named by the Empress Taitu, wife of Menelik II. The name means "new flower"); Entoto (1880–1889); Magdala (1855–1880); Gonder (1632–1855); Danqaz (the second capital of the Amhara Empire, until 1632);

Tegulat (the first capital of the Amhara Empire, from 1270); *Other names:* Abyssinia, or Abissinia (as the Italians called it); Ethiopia Federal Democratic Republic (from 1991); People's Democratic republic of Ethiopia (1987–1991); Gonder Ethiopia (1632–1855); Amhara Empire (1270–1632); Zagwe Ethiopia, or Roha Empire (1117–1268).

History: Like Egypt, Ethiopia is an ancient country. Its origins as a nation are obscure, and clouded in myth, but it seems certain that a nation of sorts existed here several centuries B.C. This may have been the land of Punt, or part of it, and some of the Ancient Egyptian texts refer to the people as Habashat, which name became Abyssinia in more recent times. There is a confusion between the word "Ethiopian," meaning from the country as we know it today, and the general ancients' term "Ethiopian," meaning "negro." So, Sudan and Nubia were often called Ethiopia in the days of antiquity. There are indications that the Sabaeans from Saba'a in Arabia settled here, and this led the later Ethiopians to interpret this as Sheba (hence their claim to have been ruled by the Queen of Sheba, and for their royal line to b descended from the union of Solomon and Sheba). From A.D. 250 to about 950 the country was part of the Axumite Empire (see Axum), which was also called the Ethiopian Empire, and some time in the 330s Christianity was adopted as the religion by the King Ezana. About 340 the first Christian Bishop of Ethiopia, Frumentius, was consecrated, and the Ethiopian Church became a part of the Egyptian Church, which later became the Coptic Church. Around 950 Axum was destroyed by Queen Judith, a local rival who had been converted to Judaism. The Ethiopians in time produced a new dynasty called the Zagwe, and, added to by a large influx of Copts escaping from Muslim Egypt, this dynasty established a new empire in 1117 at Roha. This new empire was called the Ethiopian Empire, or the Roha Empire. It is at this point that the modern state of Ethiopia may be said to have its origins. In 1270 the Zagwe dynasty came to an end, to be replaced by the Amhara, the legitimate heirs of the old Axumite Empire. They moved the capital to Tegulat, in Shewa (also known as Shoa) (the capital later shifted to Danqaz). They ruled, as a very Christian empire, with the assistance of the Coptic Church, and successfully combated the encroachment of Islam from all sides. Sub-

sequent to the Portuguese discovery of Ethiopia in 1520, the legend of Prester John, a fabulously rich Christian king of Ethiopia, grew up in Europe, but it had as much basis in fact as the previous Prester John of Asia a few centuries before. In the 16th and 17th centuries Catholic missionaries entered Ethiopia in droves. On 14 June 1632, after much civil strife, this dynasty came to an end, to be replaced in turn by that of the new emperor, Fasiladas, at his capital at Gonder. This period, between 1632 and 1855 is often referred to as Gonder Ethiopia, or the Gonderian Age. This was a new era for Ethiopia. The missionaries were expelled, and the town of Gonder became the second largest city in Africa, after Cairo. By the 19th century lack of unity was bringing an end to the Gonderian dynasty. On 11 Feb. 1855 Tewodoros II (also known as Theodore, or Lij Kasa), became Emperor of Ethiopia. Theodore took Magdala as his capital (this was shifted to Entoto in 1880, and then to Addis Ababa in 1889) and in time he unified Ethiopia. Gojjam and Tigre were brought in in 1855, and Shoa in 1856. Theodore took the last Shoan king's son Menelik as a captive, and then embarked on a repressive campaign of subjugation. Menelik escaped from captivity and proclaimed himself king of Shoa. Finally, Theodore went mad, and imprisoned the British envoy and some other Europeans based on the groundless accusation that they were planning an Egyptian coup to overthrow him. Gen. Sir Charles Napier advanced on Magdala to free the captives, and Theodore shot himself. Three claimants then fought for power in Ethiopia, and in 1872 Kasa, the chief of the Tigre, won the day, and had himself installed as Emperor John IV. In 1887 Harar became part of the Empire, and on 2 May 1889, via the Treaty of Uccialli, a treaty of friendship between Menelik and the Italians, Italy saw fit to declare a protectorate over the Ethiopian Empire, and called it Abyssinia. On 6 Nov. 1889 Menelik II became Emperor of Ethiopia. This marked the start of the modern era in Ethiopia. Gradually the Italian Abyssinian Protectorate was becoming recognized by more and more countries, although not by the Ethiopians, and Menelik denounced it on 9 Feb. 1891. In Nov. 1895 war broke out between Ethiopia and Italy, and on 1 March 1896 the Italians were soundly defeated by Menelik's forces at the Battle of Adowa. The "protectorate" was terminated a few months later, on 26 Oct. 1896, by the Treaty of

Addis Ababa. In 1897 the kingdom of Kaffa was conquered by Menelik, and various treaties with France, Britain and Italy over the next 11 years fixed the boundaries of Ethiopia. On 9 May 1936 the Italians invaded, and Ethiopia became the central component of Italian East Africa. Ethiopia was divided into four provinces — Amhara, Galla and Sidama, Harar, and Shoa. The King of Italy, Vittorio Emanuele, ruled through his viceroys. On 5 May 1941 Haile Selassie, the Emperor of Ethiopia, regained control of his country with British assistance (notably in the form of Orde Wingate). In 1962 Eritrea officially became a part of the Empire, and on 12 Sept. 1974 Haile Selassie, the "Lion of Judah," was deposed by a revolutionary council, and Ethiopia became a military state, ruled by the Dergue, a 120-member socialist government. The monarchy was abolished in March 1975, and on 10 Sept. 1984 the country became communist when it established the Workers' Party of Ethiopia as the only legal political party. Ethiopia's problems were vast and seemingly unsolvable — famine, poverty, illiteracy and the threats from neighbors. On 10 Sept. 1987 the government handed over power to the people, and the country became known as the People's Democratic Republic of Ethiopia. Mengistu Haile Mariam was elected by the people. On 18 Sept. 1987 autonomous status was granted to five regions: Eritrea, Tigrai, Assab, Dire Dawa, and Ogaden. On 21 May 1991 the Ethiopian People's Revolutionary Democratic Front (EPRDF) toppled Mariam from power, and he fled the country. The EPRDF set up a provisional government, and in 1993 Eritrea won its independence. Free elections were held in Ethiopia in 1995. The previous year a new constitution had been drawn up, dividing the country into ethnic regions, each with a right to secede. Constant drought, famine and poverty, ethnic wars, and the war with Eritrea in 1998–2000 have all made things worse in Ethiopia. *Rulers:* 250–ca. 950 see Axum.

Zagwe Emperors: 1117–1133 Marari; 1133–1172 Yemrehana Krestos; 1172–1212 Gabra Maskal Lalibela; 1212–1260 Na'akueto La'ab; 1260–1268 Yetbarak. *Amhara Emperors:* 1270–1285 Yekuno Amlak (also known as Tasfa Iyasus); 1285–1294 Salomon I (also known as Yagbe'a Seyon); 1294–1295 Bahr Asqad (also known as Senfa Ar'ed); 1295–1296 Hezba Asqad; 1296–1297 Kedma Asqad; 1297–1298 Djin; 1298–1299 Saba Asqad; 1299–1314 Wedem Ar'ed; 1314–1344 Amda

Seyon (also known as Gabra Maskal); 1344–1372 Newaya Krestos (also known as Safya Ar'ed); 1372–1382 Newaya Maryam; 1382–1411 Dawit I (also known as David I); 1411–1414 Tewodoros I (also known as Theodore I); 1414–Sept. 1429 Yeshaq I (also known as Isaac I); Sept. 1429–March 1430 Endreyas; March 1430–June 1433 Takla Maryam (also known as Hezba Nan); June 1433–Nov. 1433 Sarwe Iyasus (also known as Mehreka Nan); Nov. 1433–June 1434 Amda Iyasus; June 1434–6 Sept. 1468 Zara Yaqob (also known as Constantine I); 6 Sept. 1468–19 Nov. 1478 Ba'eda Maryam I; 19 Nov. 1478–May 1494 Eskender; May 1494–Dec. 1494 Amda Seyon II; Dec. 1494–31 July 1508 Na'od (also known as Anbasa Bazar); 22 Aug. 1508–2 Sept. 1540 Lebna Dengel Dawit II (also known as David II); 13 Sept. 1540–23 March 1559 Galawdewos (also known as Caludius); 3 April 1559–23 Jan. 1563 Admas Sagad (also known as Minas); 31 Jan. 1563–2 Aug. 1597 Sarsa Dengel (also known as Malak Sagad); 2 Aug. 1597–1603 Yaqob I; Sept. 1603–24 Oct. 1604 Za Dengel (also known as Asnaf Sagad); 24 Oct. 1604–10 March 1607 Yaqob I; 10 March 1607–14 June 1632 Susneyos (also known as Seltan Sagad). *Gonder Emperors:* 14 June 1632–18 Oct. 1667 Fasiladas (also known as Alam Sagad); 18 Oct. 1667–19 July 1682 John I (also known as Yohannes I, or A'alaf Sagad); 19 July 1682–March 1706 Iyasu I (also known as Adyam Sagad); March 1706–30 June 1708 Takla Haymanot I; 14 July 1708–14 Oct. 1711 Tewoflos (also known as Asrar Sagad); 14 Oct. 1711–19 Feb. 1716 Yostos (also known as Dsahai Sagad); 19 Feb. 1716–18 May 1721 Dauti III (also known as Dawit III, or David III, or Adbar Sagad); 18 May 1721–19 Sept. 1730 Bakaffa (also known as Asma Giyorgis); 19 Sept. 1730–26 June 1755 Iyasu II. *Gonder Regents:* 19 Sept. 1730–26 June 1755 Menetewab. *Gonder Emperors:* 26 June 1755–7 May 1769 Iyoas I (also known as Adyam Sagad); 7 May 1769–17 Oct. 1769 Yohannes II (also known as John II); 17 Oct. 1769–15 Sept. 1777 Takla Haymanot II; 15 Sept. 1777–20 July 1779 Salomon; 20 July 1779–8 Feb. 1784 Takla Giyorgis (also known as Fehr Sagad); 8 Feb. 1784–24 April 1788 Iyasu III (also known as Ba'ala Segab); 24 April 1788–26 July 1789 Takla Giyorgis (also known as Fehr Sagad); 26 July 1789–Jan. 1794 Hezekiyas; Jan. 1794–15 April 1795 Takla Giyorgis (also known as Fehr Sagad); 15 April 1795–Dec. 1795 Ba'eda Maryam II; Dec. 1795–May 1796 Takla Giyorgis (also known as Fehr

Sagad); 21 June 1796–15 July 1797 Walda Salomon; Aug. 1797–4 Jan. 1798 Yonas; 4 Jan. 1798–20 May 1799 Takla Giyorgis (also known as Fehr Sagad); 20 May 1799–1799 Walda Salomon; 1799–24 March 1800 Demetros; 24 March 1800–June 1800 Takla Giyorgis (also known as Fehr Sagad); June 1800–June 1801 Demetros; June 1801–3 June 1818 Egwala Seyon; 3 June 1818–3 June 1821 Iyoas II; 3 June 1821–April 1826 Gigar; April 1826–April 1826 Ba'eda Maryam III; April 1826–18 June 1830 Gigar; 18 June 1830–18 March 1832 Iyasu IV; 18 March 1832–8 June 1832 Gabra Krestos; 8 June 1832–Oct. 1832 interregnum; Oct. 1832–Aug. 1840 Sahla Dengel; Sept. 1840–Oct. 1841 Yohannes III (also known as John III); Oct. 1841–1850 Sahla Dengel; 1850–1851 Yohannes III (also known as John III); 1851–11 Feb. 1855 Sahla Dengel. *Modern Emperors:* 11 Feb. 1855–13 April 1866 Lij Kasa (also known as Tewodoros II, or Theodore II); 14 April 1868–12 Jan. 1872 Takla Giyorgis II; 12 Jan. 1872–10 March 1889 Yohannes IV (also known as John IV); 12 March 1889–3 Nov. 1889 disputed succession; 3 Nov. 1889–15 May 1911 Sahle Mariam (also known as Menelik II); 15 May 1911–27 Sept. 1916 Lij Iyasu. *Empresses:* 30 Sept. 1916–2 April 1930 Zauditu. *Emperors:* 30 Sept. 1916–12 Sept 1974 Ras Dejazmatch Tafari (also known as Haile Selassie). *Nominal Kings:* 12 Sept. 1974–21 March 1975 Asfa Wossen. *Italian Governors-General:* 5 May 1941–19 May 1941 Duca D'Aosta (acting); 19 May 1941–6 July 1941 Pietro Gazzera (acting); 6 July 1941–22 Nov. 1941 Guglielmo Nasi (acting). *Heads of Provisional Military Government:* 12 Sept. 1974–28 Nov. 1974 Aman Andom; 28 Nov. 1974–3 Feb. 1977 Teferi Benti (acting). *Chairmen of Military Council:* 11 Feb. 1977–10 Sept. 1984 Mengistu Haile Mariam. *Secretaries-General:* 10 Sept. 1984–10 Sept. 1987 Mengistu Haile Mariam. *Presidents:* 10 Sept. 1987–21 May 1991 Mengistu Haile Mariam; 21 May 1991–27 May 1991 Tesfaye Gebre Kidan (acting); 27 May 1991–21 July 1991 Meles Zenawi (provisional); 21 July 1991–22 Aug. 1995 Meles Zenawi; 22 Aug. 1995–8 Oct. 2001 Negasso Gidada; 8 Oct. 2001–Girma Wolde-Giorgis Lucha. *Prime Ministers:* 5 May 1941–3 April 1958 Makonnen Endalkatchon; 3 April 1958–Dec. 1960 Abede Aragai; 17 April 1961–28 Feb. 1974 Tshafe Tezaz Aklilu Habte-Wold; 28 Feb. 1974–22 July 1974 Makonnen Endalkatchon; 22 July 1974–12 Sept. 1974 Mikael Imru; 10 Sept. 1987–8 Nov. 1989

Fikre Selassie Wogderess; 8 Nov. 1989–26 April 1991 Hailu Yemenu (acting); 26 April 1991–27 May 1991 Tesfaye Dinka (acting); 6 June 1991–29 July 1991 Tamirat Laynie (acting); 29 July 1991–22 Aug. 1995 Tamirat Laynie; 23 Aug. 1995–Meles Zenawi. *Note:* In times of no Prime Minister, the Emperor, President or other head of state, held that office.

Ethiopia see **Kush**

Europa Island. No dates. *Location:* an uninhabited French possession and wildlife sanctuary, lying between Madagascar and Mozambique, it occupies 28 sq km, and is claimed by Madagascar. *Other names:* Île Europa.
Rulers: Administered by a French commissioner in Réunion.

Fada N'Gourma see **Gurma**

Fagi see **Hadejia**

FAN see **Chad**

Fang see **Río Muni**

Fante see **Bono**

Farquhar and Des Roches Islands. No dates. *Location:* two groups of islands, closely related, and always linked politically, lying between the Aldabras and the Agalegas, in the Indian Ocean.
History: On 3 Oct. 1810 the British took these islands from the French, and they became a dependency of the Seychelles. In 1965 they were transferred to the British Indian Ocean Territory (BIOT), and on 29 June 1976 transferred back to the Seychelles. They now form part of the Republic of the Seychelles.

Fatajar see **Ifat**

Fatimid North Africa. 6 Jan. 910–973. *Location:* Tunisia–eastern Algeria. *Capital:* al-Mansuriyya (from 947; this was a town outside al-Qayrawan); al-Mahdiya (established as a town in 912, it was the capital from 921 to 947); Raqqada (near al-Qayrawan, was the capital until 921).
History: The Fatimids, named after Fatima (the daughter of the Prophet), from whom they claimed descent, emerged as a principal part of the Isma'ili movement in the 9th century. Their

aim was to overthrow the Abbasids. Very little is known of their early days because the organization was naturally secret. In 909 the leader of the Isma'ilis in North Africa, Abu Abdallah ash-Shi'i conquered the entire province of Ifriqiya (today's Tunisia and eastern Algeria) from the Aghlabids (who were vassals of the Abbasids). He then rescued his colleague Ubaydallah from captivity in Sijilmassa, and Ubaydallah became the first Fatimid caliph, as Mahdi Ubaydallah. He conquered al-Qayrawan, the major Aghlabid Empire capital, and set up his first headquarters on the coast at al-Mahdiya. He also murdered Abu Abdallah ash-Shi'i. His main aim, however, was to establish a Fatimid caliphate, and with this in mind he tried conquering Egypt in 913–914, and again in 919–920, but failed both times. Under al-Mu'izz the empire extended out to include Morocco, all of Algeria, and Sicily. In 969 the Fatimids conquered Egypt. This was the end of the first phase of the Fatimid Empire. The second phase was from 972 when the caliph al-Mu'izz transferred his capital to Cairo (see Egypt), leaving behind his general, Yusuf ibn Ziri, who thus began the Zirid dynasty (see Zirid Kingdom). In 973 the Zirids took power in the part of North Africa previously under Fatimid control, although strictly speaking the Zirids remained vassals of the Fatimids until 1045.

Caliphs: 6 Jan. 910–4 March 934 al-Mahdi Ubaydallah; 4 March 934–18 May 946 al-Qa'im; 18 May 946–18 March 953 al-Mansur; April 953–973 al-Mu'izz. *Viceroys:* Aug. 972–973 General Yusuf ibn Ziri.

Fazzan see **Fezzan**

Federation of Rhodesia and Nyasaland. 23 Oct. 1953–31 Dec. 1963. *Location:* present-day Zimbabwe, Zambia, and Malawi. *Capital:* Salisbury, Southern Rhodesia. *Other names:* Central African Federation.

History: A British-controlled federation brought comprising three states — Nyasaland (see Malawi), Northern Rhodesia (see Zambia), and Southern Rhodesia (see Zimbabwe). Such a federation had been discussed by the European residents of the three countries even before 1938, when a Royal Commission looked into the matter. An inter-territorial advisory body was recommended, and due to the War, it finally came into operation in 1945, as the Central African Council. By the 1950s it had become more or less

a dead issue, until the spark for federation was rekindled in March 1951 primarily by its old boosters Sir Godfrey Huggins (in Southern Rhodesia) and Roy Welensky (in Northern Rhodesia). British Central Africa was approved, against the wishes of the Africans in Northern Rhodesia and Nyasaland, and was brought about by Order in Council No. 1199 of 1 Aug. 1953 (effective 23 Oct.). Although it was a well-meaning effort, differences between the three caused the breakup of the federation. The northern blacks feared that the strongest of the three, Southern Rhodesia, which also had the largest white population, would take over and that Northern Rhodesia and Nyasaland would never achieve their independence. Great economic strides were made under federation, and a considerable liberalization of policy toward the black Africans. This, plus the growing number of African countries achieving independence, made a British federation a difficult concept to believe in, and it was just a matter of time before the federation came to an end, which it did on the last day of 1963.

Governors-General: 23 Oct. 1953–24 Jan. 1957 John, Baron Lewellin; 24 Jan. 1957–31 Dec. 1963 Simon Ramsay, 16th Earl of Dalhousie. *Prime Ministers:* 18 Dec. 1953–31 Oct. 1956 Sir Godfrey Huggins (created 1st Viscount Malvern in 1955); 1 Nov. 1956–31 Dec. 1963 Sir Roy Welensky. *Deputy Prime Ministers:* 18 Dec. 1953–31 Oct. 1956 Sir Roy Welensky.

Félicité Island see **Seychelles**

Fernando Po. 1472–1926. *Location:* in the Bight of Biafra, about 60 miles south of Nigeria, this is the island now known as Bioko, belonging to Equatorial Guinea. *Capital:* Santa Isabel (its name at all times other than 1827–1855, when it was called Port Clarence). *Other names:* Fernando Póo; Bioko (its current name); Macías Nguema Biyogo (its name for a long time during the rule of the man with the same name); Formosa (its original name, until 1494); Puerto de Isabel (an alternative Spanish name during the period 1855–1926).

History: The island was discovered in 1472 by Fernão do Pó, a Portuguese navigator, and named Formosa (meaning "beautiful"). The original inhabitants were the Bubi. On 7 June 1494 it was renamed Fernando Póo (the word Póo being the Portuguese spelling, while Po is the Spanish), and became a Portuguese possession. Between 1580 and 1656 Spain ruled Portugal, but this made no difference to the administration of Fernando Po. On 1 March 1778, along with the island of Annobón, it became a Spanish possession, but in 1781 the Spanish abandoned it, considering it unsuitable due to yellow fever problems. However, it remained a Spanish property, and in 1827 they leased part of the island to the British. The British also considered it an unfit place to settle, but put a naval base there, in order to help with the suppression of the slave trade. Administering this base was a British superintendent, who also received a Spanish commission as the governor of the island. The British named their headquarters Port Clarence. Between 1839 and 1841 the Spanish repeatedly refused to sell Fernando Po to the British, and in 1843 the British gave up their naval base, transferring it to Freetown in Sierra Leone, and selling their Port Clarence facilities to a Baptist mission. In 1844 the Spanish actively reclaimed the island, but continued the appointment of John Bee croft as governor. On 30 June 1849 Beecroft also became the British consul for the Bight of Biafra. In 1855 the Spanish decided to try colonization again, and Spanish adventurers went in to pacify Río Muni, the area in mainland Africa. A Spanish governor was sent out to Fernando Po, and the Baptist missionaries were duly ejected in 1858. The British consulate remained on Fernando Po until 1885, although not as governor any longer. For a list of the British Consuls of the Bight of Biafra, see that entry. During the British administration many freed slaves settled on the island. From 1879 the Spanish basically used Fernando Po as a penal colony for captured Cuban rebels. In 1885 a Spanish protectorate was placed over Río Muni, and in 1900 it became a Spanish colony. In 1926 the three Spanish possessions in this area — Fernando Po, Río Muni, and Annobón were grouped together to form Spanish Guinea.

Rulers: 1472–7 June 1494 none; 7 June 1494–1781 [unknown]; 1781–1827 none. *British Superintendents/Governors:* 1827–1829 William Owens; 1829–1830 Edward Nicolls; 1830–1832 John Beecroft (acting); 1832–1833 Edward Nicolls; 1833–10 June 1854 John Bee croft; 10 June 1854–1855 James Lynslager (acting). *Spanish Governors:* 1855–1858 Domingo Mustrich; 1858–1858 Carlos Chacón y Michelena; 1858–1862 José de la Gándara y Navarro; 1862–1865 Pantaleón Ayllón; 1865–1868 José Barrera; 1868–1869 Joaquín Gallardo; 1869–1869 Antonio Maymó; 1869–1870 Zoilo Acaña; 1870–1871 [unknown]; 1871–1871 Frederico Anrich; 1871–1872 [unknown]; 1872–1874 Ignacio Tudela; 1874–1875 [unknown]; 1875–1877 Diego Chamorro; 1877–1879 Alejandro Salgado; 1879–1880 Enrique Santaló; 1880–1883 José de Oca; 1883–1885 Antonio Cano; 1885–1887 José de Oca; 1887–1888 Luis Navarro; 1888–1889 Antonio Guerra; 1889–1890 José de la Ibarra; 1890–1892 José de Barrasa; 1892–1892 Antonio Martínez; 1892–1893 Eulogio Merchán; 1893–1895 José de la Puente Basseve; 1895–1897 Adolfo de España y Gómez de Humarán; 1897–1898 Manuel Rico; 1898–1900 José Vera; 1900–1901 Francisco Dueñas; 1901–1905 José de la Ibarra; 1905–1906 José de la Cerna; 1906–1906 Diego Saavedra y Magdalena; 1906–1907 Ángel Barrera y Luyando; 1907–1908 Luis Ramos Izquierdo; 1908–1909 José Anchorena; 1909–1910 [unknown]; 1910–1924 Ángel Barrera y Luyando; 1924–1926 Carlos Tovar de Revilla.

Fez see **Morocco**

Fezzan. ca. 1566–15 Oct. 1912; 29 Jan. 1943–24 Dec. 1951. *Location:* southwest Libya. *Capital:* Murzuq (ca. 1566–1912); Sabha (1943–1951). *Other names:* Fazzan; French Fezzan (1943–1951); Fezzan Pashalik (1842–1912); Kingdom of Fazzan, or Awlad Muhammad Dynasty (ca. 1566–1842).

History: This was basically the old country of Phazania, and from this name comes the name Fezzan. After the eclipse of Phazania in 666, the country followed the destiny of the Arabs who conquered it from time to time. In the 13th century it was part of the Bornu Empire. About 1566 al-Mustansir ibn Muhammad set up a kingdom in the Fezzan. During its lifetime, the kingdom was constantly invaded by armies from Tripoli, and quite often occupied (these periods of occupation are reflected in the ruler list, below). In 1804 the last of the Awlad Muhammad Dynasty was killed by the Tripolitanian general, Yusuf al-Mukni, who in turn set himself up as sultan of the Fezzan. He as deposed by Abd al-Jalil, an Arab chieftain, who reigned for almost eleven troublesome years before being killed in battle by the Osmanli Turks in 1842. The Fezzan, by then an area disputed by the Turks and various local sects, was conquered by the Turks, and it became a sanjaq, or province (or pashalik). On 15 Oct. 1912 the Italians captured it and dismembered it, and finally occupied it in 1914. It thus became part of the Italian possessions in North Africa that would soon become Libya. On 29 Jan. 1943, after the allied victory over Italy in North Africa, the British and the French split Libya up into three parts — Tripolitania and Cyrenaica (both of which went to the British), and Fezzan, which went to the French. In 1951 all three divisions were merged and became the Kingdom of Libya. Fezzan became a vilayat (province) of the Kingdom, and remained that way until 1963, when Libya became a unitary state.

Sultans: ca. 1566–1580 al-Mustansir ibn Muhammad; 1580–1599 an-Nasir; 1599–1612 al-Mansur. *Tripolitanian Governors:* 1612–1614 [unknown]. *Sultans:* 1614–1623 Tahir I. *Tripolitanian Governors:* 1623–1626 [unknown]. *Sultans:* 1626–1658 Muhammad I; 1658–1682 Nagib; 1682–1689 Muhammad II Nasir. *Tripolitanian Governors:* 1689–1689 Muhammad al-Mukni. *Sultans:* 1689–1689 Temmam; 1689–1690 Muhammad III. *Tripolitanian Governors:* 1690–1690 Ali al-Mukni. *Sultans:* 1690–1718 Muhammad II Nasir; 1718–1767 Ahmad I; 1767–1775 Tahir II; 1775–1789 Ahmad II; 1789–1804 Muhammad IV al-Hakim; 1804–1804 Muhammad V al-Mustansir; 1804–1831 Yusuf al-Mukni; 1831–1842 Abd al-Jalil. *Pashas:* 1842–1846 Bekir; 1846–1855 Hassan al-Balazi; 1855–1859 [unknown]; 1859–1865 Halim; 1865–1865 Hamid Bey (acting); 1865–1870 Halim; 1870–(?) [unknown]; (?)–ca. 1882 Mustafa Faik; ca. 1882–(?) [unknown]; (?)–ca. 1900 [unknown]; ca. 1900–ca. 1906 Mahmud Bey; ca. 1906–1909 Samih Bey. *Sanusi Governors:* 1909–15 Oct. 1912 Sayid Muhammad al-Abid. *French-placed Administrators:* 29 Jan. 1943–1945 no fixed administration; 1945–12 Feb. 1950 Ahmad Saif an-Nasir. *French Military Governors:* 1947–1950 Maurice Sarazac. *French Residents:* 1950–24 Dec. 1951 Maurice Sarazac. *Chiefs of Fezzan:* 12 Feb. 1950–24 Dec. 1951 Ahmad Saif an-Nasir.

Figuig see **French Morocco**

Fika. 1806–27 Dec. 1899. *Location:* Bornu Province, northeastern Nigeria. *Capital:* Fika (built about 1805 and called Lafiya Moi until about 1807).

History: Founded as an amirate about 1806 by King Buraima of the Bolewa tribe who had moved his kingdom from Daniski. It was never taken by the Fulani Empire or by the Sudanese adventurer Rabih (see Rabih's Empire) in the 1890s. In 1899 it became part of the soon-to-be-announced British protectorate of Northern Nigeria. In 1924 the capital of the amirate was moved to Potiskum. Fika is known for its dates.

Amirs: 1806–1822 Buraima; 1822–1844 Adam; 1844–1857 Disa Siri; 1857–1867 Mammadi Gaganga; 1867–1871 Ismaila; 1871–1882 Mammadi Buye; 1882–1882 Aji; 1882–1885 Mama (also known as Muhammad); 1885–1902 Sule (also known as Suleiman); 1902–1922 Disa (also known as Idrissa); 1922–1976 Muhammadu ibn Idrissa; 1976–(?) Mania Alsali; (?)–Muhammad Abali.

Filali Morocco see **Morocco**

Filane Empire see **Fulani Empire**

Fingoland. 1835–1879. *Location:* in the Transkei area of South Africa. *Capital:* Nqamakwe.

History: The Fingos (also known as the Mfengu. The name comes from a Bantu word "amaFengu," meaning "the wanderers") were refugees displaced as a result of the Mfecane (the Zulu movements of the 1820s), and later they were granted lands by the British for fighting on the British side during the Xhosa War of 1835. Over the years, and through successive Xhosa wars, they increased their land at the expense of the Xhosa. In 1879 they were incorporated into the British Cape Colony, as part of the Transkei District of the Transkeian Territories.

Rulers: 1835–1879 [unknown].

Five Towns see **Pentapolis**

FLN see **Algeria** and **Algerian Republic (Provisional Government)**

FNLA see **Angola** and **Angola Democratic People's Republic** and **Angola Revolutionary Government in Exile**

Fogo see **Cape Verde**

Fombina see **Adamawa**

Fon see **Dahomey**

Formosa see **Fernando Po**

Fort-Dauphin. 24 Sept. 1642–27 Aug. 1674. *Location:* the extreme southeastern point of Madagascar. *Capital:* Fort-Dauphin. *Other names:* Fort Dauphin.

History: In 1642 the French founded Fort-Dauphin as an East India trading base, but it was never used for this purpose. From 1667 to 1671 it was the headquarters of the Compagnie des Indes Orientales, but was abandoned in 1674 after the French had been partially massacred there. Fort-Dauphin's importance in history is that it was the first French toe-hold on the island of Madagascar, and was the basis for their continual claim on Madagascar from then on. In fact, in the late 18th century a fresh French attempt at settlement at Fort-Dauphin was made, by the Comte de Modave, but it failed.

Governors: 24 Sept. 1642–4 Dec. 1648 Jacques Pronis; 4 Dec. 1648–12 Feb. 1655 Étienne de Flacourt; 12 Feb. 1655–23 May 1655 Jacques Pronis (acting); 23 May 1655–1655 Jean des Perriers; 1655–1656 Martin Gueston (acting); 1656–29 May 1657 Luc de Champmargou (acting); 29 May 1657–9 May 1661 Pierre de Rivau; 9 May 1661–8 July 1665 Luc de Champmargou; 8 July 1665–14 Dec. 1665 Pierre de Beausse; 14 Dec. 1665–Sept. 1666 Gilles Montauban; Sept. 1666–10 March 1667 Luc de Champmargou (acting); 10 March 1667–4 Dec. 1670 Marquis de Montdevergue; 4 Dec. 1670–26 June 1671 Jacob Blanquet de la Haye; 26 June 1671–6 Dec. 1672 Luc de Champmargou; 6 Dec. 1672–27 Aug. 1674 Jean de la Bretesche.

Fort James. 1455–25 May 1765. *Location:* the mouth of the Gambia River. *Capital:* Fort James (1661–1765); St. Andrew's Island (1651–1661). *Other names:* James Fort; James Island; Gambia; Dutch Gambia (1659–1661); Courlander (or Kurlander) Gambia Settlements (1651–1659).

History: The Portuguese were the first Europeans here, in 1455 and were already trading by the beginning of the 16th century, looking for slaves and gold. Certain Portuguese living in England brought the country to the attention of Queen Elizabeth, who, in 1588, granted trade rights to a Company of Devon and London Merchants. Because of this grant it is often claimed that this was Britain's first African colony, but although these merchants went out to the Gambia, and traded, there was no settlement. In 1618 James I granted the rights to the Company of Adventurers of London. Again they were in search of gold, which they believed came from Timbuktu. The Company's first agent, George Thompson, was murdered by Portuguese and natives, but successive agents built a fort near the mouth of the Gambia River. In 1651 James, Duke of Courland (a small Baltic state) saw in the Gambia a chance to improve the fortunes of his country. His agents bought what they renamed St. Andrew's Island, in the Gambia River, from the King of Barra, and the island of Banjol from the King of Kombo. Due to war at home, the colonists were stranded, and the Courlander settlements were doomed. In 1659 the Dutch West India Company made an arrangement with the Duke of Courland's agent in Holland whereby the Company would take over the Courlander settlements in the Gambia. The Courlander commandant was expelled, and the colony was without any form of government until he was allowed to return in 1660. The British took over the fort on St. Andrew's Island on 19 March 1661, renaming it Fort James, in honor of the Duke of York. It was a fort rebuilt to keep the Dutch out. King Charles II of England had that year formed the Royal Adventurers Trading in Africa, and this company was designed to make Britain enter the slave trade at a roaring pace. On 18 Nov. 1668 the Company, not finding the trade too profitable, sublet its operations to the Gambia Adventurers. This move became effective on 1 Aug. 1669. In 1684, after twelve years of legal wrangles between the two companies, they both relinquished their claims on the Gambia in favor of the Royal African Company, which had taken over effective control of the place as far back as 1678. Under the Royal African Company other establishments were created up the river and along the coast — Macarthy Island, Barrakunda Falls, Bintang, Banyon Point, and Juffure. On 27 July 1695 the French captured Fort James, and the place became known as the French Gambia, although it lay unoccupied for four years. In April 1699, at the conclusion of the war between England and France, the Royal African Company resumed its position in the Gambia. The island was abandoned between 1709 and 1713. On 13 June 1750, with the effective demise of the Royal African Company, the Gambia (or Fort James as it was still officially called) fell into the hands of the Company of Merchants Trading to Africa.

On 25 May 1765 the British posts in Senegal and the Gambia were merged to form the first British colony in Africa, that of Senegambia (see Senegambia Colony). Gambia passed to the Crown effectively in April 1766. The British did nothing of significance in the Gambia until 1816, when they occupied the island of Banjol and renamed it St. Mary. The rest of this history of the area is told under Gambia.

Agents: 1618–1619 George Thompson; 1619–(?) Richard Jobson; (?0–(?) [unknown]. *Commandants:* 1651–1654 Heinrich Fock; 1654–1659 Otto Stiel; 1659–1660 no fixed rule; 1660–19 March 1661 Otto Stiel. *Agents:* 19 March 1661–1661 Francis Kerby; 1661–1662 Morgan Facey; 1662–26 Jan. 1664 Stephen Ustick; 26 Jan. 1664–1666 John Ladd; 1666–1672 [unknown]; 1672–1674 Rice Wright; 1674–1677 [unknown]; 1677–1680 Thomas Thurloe; 1680–1681 Thomas Forde; 1681–1684 John Kastell; 1684–1688 Alexander Cleeve; 1688–8 June 1693 John Booker; 8 June 1693–1695 William Heath; 1695–27 July 1695 John Hanbury; 27 July 1695–April 1699 French rule, but the island was deserted; April 1699–1700 Thomas Corker; 1700–1700 Paul Pindar; 1700–1701 Thomas Gresham; 1701–Nov. 1702 Henry Bradshaw; Nov. 1702–7 Dec. 1703 Humphrey Chishull; 7 Dec. 1703–4 Sept. 1704 Thomas Weaver; 4 Sept. 1704–22 June 1706 John Chidley; 22 June 1706–Aug. 1706 Joseph Dakins (acting); Aug. 1706–2 Dec. 1706 John Tozer; 2 Dec. 1706–20 May 1709 John Snow; 20 May 1709–13 Nov. 1713 island abandoned; 13 Nov. 1713–Dec. 1714 William Cooke; Dec. 1714–9 Oct. 1717 David Francis; 9 Oct. 1717–4 Feb. 1721 Charles Orfeur. *Governors:* 4 Feb. 1721–6 Oct. 1721 Thomas Whitney; 6 Oct. 1721–13 April 1723 Henry Glynne; 13 April 1723–28 Oct. 1723 Joseph Willey; 28 Oct. 1723–2 Nov. 1725 Robert Plunkett; 2 Nov. 1725–1728 Anthony Rogers; 1728–1728 Richard Hull; 1728–1729 Charles Cornewall; 1729–29 Nov. 1729 Daniel Pepper (acting); 29 Nov. 1729–7 Feb. 1733 Anthony Rogers; 7 Feb. 1733–16 Jan. 1737 Richard Hull; 16 Jan. 1737–1745 Charles Orfeur; 1745–13 June 1750 John Gootheridge; 13 June 1750–1752 James Alison (acting); 1752–1754 James Skinner; 1754–1755 Robert Lawrie; 1755–1758 Tobias Lisle; 1758–25 May 1765 Joseph Debat. *Rulers:* For the administrators of the British possessions in the Gambia after 1765 see Senegambia Colony.

Fort Victoria see **Port Natal**

Fortunate Islands see **Canary Islands**

Foumbina see **Adamawa**

Fourth Shore see **Libya**

Fouta Djalon see **Futa Jallon**

Fouta Toro see **Futa Toro**

Free Province of New Holland in South East Africa see **Natal**

Freedom Province see **Sierra Leone**

Freetown see **Sierra Leone**

FRELIMO see **Mozambique**

French Coast of the Somalis see **Djibouti**

French Congo see **Congo**

French Equatorial Africa. 27 April 1886–28 Nov. 1958. *Location:* this was a federation that took in the countries that today are Chad, Gabon, Congo, and the Central African Republic. In the early days, though, French Equatorial Africa was confined to the coastal areas, because, for the most part, inland exploration had not yet taken place. *Capital:* Brazzaville (1910–1958); Libreville (1886–1910). *Other names:* Afrique Équatoriale Française; A.E.F.; Federation of French Equatorial Africa; Congo Français et Dependances, or French Congo (its name between 1891 and 1910).

History: In 1886 a central administration was placed over all French possessions in the west central African area, and called the protectorate of French Equatorial Africa. This included the two possessions of Moyen-Congo (see Congo) and Gabon. On 30 April 1891 the federation's named changed to the French Congo and Dependencies, the capital of the Federation remaining in Libreville, which was in Gabon. In 1893 Ubangi-Bomu (see Central African Republic) was added to the federation, and on 13 July 1894 this territory became known as Ubangi-Shari. Chad did not become the fourth component until 17 March 1920, when it had finally achieved colonial status. On 15 Jan. 1910 the federation changed its name back to French Equatorial Africa, and on 30 June 1934 it became a giant colony, with its four component parts of Ubangi-Shari, Chad, Moyen-Congo, and Gabon. All these parts now became regions of the new colony, and in 1937 they became overseas territories of France. During World War II the A.E.F. was Free French, with Brazzaville as the center of Free French activity in Africa. In 1958 the A.E.F. broke up, and autonomy was granted to all the parts thereof.

Commissioners-General: 27 April 1886–28 Sept. 1897 Pierre Savorgnan de Brazza; 28 Sept. 1897–2 Dec. 1898 Henri de la Mothe; 2 Dec. 1898–April 1899 Martial Merlin (acting); April 1899–28 April 1900 Henri de la Mothe; 28 April 1900–Dec. 1900 Jean-Baptiste Lemaire (acting); Dec. 1900–2 March 1903 Louis Grodet; 2 March 1903–Oct. 1903 Émile Gentil (acting); Oct. 1903–21 Jan. 1904 Louis Grodet; 21 Jan. 1904–28 June 1908 Émile Gentil. *Governors-General:* 28 June 1908–24 Sept. 1909 Martial Merlin; 24 Sept. 1909–3 May 1910 Charles Rognon (acting); 3 May 1910–18 July 1910 Adolphe Cureau (acting); 18 July 1910–17 Nov. 1910 Martial Merlin; 17 Nov. 1910–7 March 1911 Charles Rognon (acting); 7 March 1911–16 May 1911 Charles Vergnes (acting); 16 May 1911–1912 Martial Merlin; 1912–23 March 1913 Charles Vergnes (acting); 23 March 1913–17 Nov. 1913 Georges Poulet (acting); 17 Nov. 1913–14 Sept. 1914 Frédéric Estèbe (acting); 14 Sept. 1914–15 May 1917 Martial Merlin; 15 May 1917–17 June 1919 Gabriel Angoulvant; 17 June 1919–July 1919 Frédéric Estèbe (acting); July 1919–16 May 1920 Gabriel Angoulvant; 16 May 1920–5 Sept. 1920 Maurice Lapalud (acting); 5 Sept. 1920–9 Oct. 1921 Jean Augagneur; 9 Oct. 1921–19 July 1922 Matteo Alfassa (acting); 19 July 1922–21 Aug. 1923 Jean Augagneur; 21 Aug. 1923–8 July 1924 Robert de Guise (acting); 8 July 1924–16 Oct. 1924 Matteo Alfassa (acting); 16 Oct. 1924–15 May 1925 Raphaël Antonetti; 15 May 1925–14 Dec. 1925 Matteo Alfassa (acting); 14 Dec. 1925–15 Nov. 1929 Raphaël Antonetti; 15 Nov. 1929–30 Aug. 1930 Matteo Alfassa (acting); 30 Aug. 1930–9 April 1931 Raphaël Antonetti; 9 April 1931–5 Nov. 1931 Matteo Alfassa (acting); 5 Nov. 1931–4 Dec. 1932 Raphaël Antonetti; 4 Dec. 1932–11 Dec. 1933 Matteo Alfassa (acting); 11 Dec. 1933–14 Oct. 1934 Raphaël Antonetti; 14 Oct. 1934–20 March 1935 Georges Renard; 20 March 1935–5 April 1936 Marcel Marchessou

(acting); 5 April 1936–25 Nov. 1938 Dieudonné Reste; 25 Nov. 1938–9 Feb. 1939 Léon Solomiac (acting); 9 Feb. 1939–21 April 1939 Dieudonné Reste; 21 April 1939–3 Sept. 1939 Léon Solomiac (acting); 3 Sept. 1939–17 July 1940 Pierre-François Boissons; 17 July 1940–28 Aug. 1940 Louis Husson; 28 Aug. 1940–11 Aug. 1941 René de Larminat; 11 Aug. 1941–15 Feb. 1944 Félix Éboué; 15 Feb. 1944–2 Oct. 1944 Charles Bayardelle (acting); 2 Oct. 1944–8 March 1945 Charles Bayardelle; 8 March 1945–June 1945 Henri Sautot (acting); June 1945–3 Aug. 1946 Charles Bayardelle; 3 Aug. 1946–5 June 1947 Jean-Louis Soucadaux (acting); 5 June 1947–Aug. 1947 Laurent Péchoux (acting); Aug. 1947–17 Sept. 1947 Charles Luizet; 17 Sept. 1947–15 Nov. 1947 Jean-Louis Soucadaux (acting); 15 Nov. 1947–26 March 1948 Jean-Louis Soucadaux; 26 March 1948–21 Sept. 1951 Bernard Cornut-Gentille; 21 Sept. 1951–20 Jan. 1958 Paul Chauvet. *High Commissioners:* 20 Jan. 1958–15 July 1958 Pierre Messmer; 15 July 1958–28 Nov. 1958 Yvon Bourges.

French Gambia. 11 Feb. 1779–3 Sept. 1783. *Location:* the Gambia River. *Capital:* Saint Louis, in Senegal.

History: In 1778 the French captured their former possessions in Senegal from the British (see Senegambia Colony), and in 1779 took the British settlements on the Gambia River, thus effectively ending the British colony of Senegambia. From 1779 to 1783 (i.e. until the Treaty of Paris in 1783) Gambia was in French hands. In 1783 these settlements were returned to Britain, although they were not to be re-occupied until 1816 (see Gambia).

Administrators: 11 Feb. 1779–3 Sept. 1783 direct rule from Saint Louis, in Senegal.

French Gold Coast see **Ivory Coast,** and **Petit Dieppe**

French Guinea see **Guinea**

French Morocco. 4 Aug. 1907–2 March 1956. *Location:* Morocco as we know it today, minus the Spanish sections in the extreme south of the country, as well as Ceuta and Melilla. *Capital:* Rabat. *Other names:* Morocco; Maroc; Maroc Français; French Protectorate of Morocco (1912–1956); French-Occupied Morocco (1907–1912).

History: France's involvement with Morocco

dates back to 1830 when France seized Algiers, and it increased from then on. The rebel Abdelkader (see Mascara) caused a strain on this relationship in the 1830s and 1840s and France took portions of Morocco and added them to Algeria. Basically France wanted to control North Africa, at least the eastern part, and by 1904 Morocco had become a French sphere of influence, although Moroccan independence was affirmed by all the world powers (see Morocco). In fact, as early as 20 July 1901 Morocco had granted France control of the Frontier Police. In 1902 France and Spain secretly agreed to carve up Morocco between them, but the actual details of the division that was discussed never took place. In the same year the French and Italians agreed to the Italians taking Libya and the French taking Morocco, and that each one should respect the territories of the other. In 1904 Britain agreed to France taking Morocco, and Spain and France agreed to a new division of the country, with France getting the lion's share. So, by the end of 1904 France had the green light from all the other involved powers to go ahead and conquer Morocco. In 1904 France occupied the Figuig area south of Oujda. In 1907 Oujda itself was occupied, and gradually the rest of the country too. The sultan was deposed by his successor late in 1907. By 1911 Fez and Meknes were also occupied. In 1911 the Germans made a protest against this takeover when they anchored their gunboat "Panther" off Agadir, but they were bought off with a piece of French territory which they could add to Togo. On 30 March 1912 the French declared a protectorate over their occupied territory. Tangier was a special case, becoming an international zone in 1923. The 1920s also saw a real threat in the uprising of Abdel Krim (see Rif Republic). The contributions made by the Spanish, and particularly the French, in Morocco, were vast, and brought Morocco out of the old world into the new, but in 1956 both French and Spanish Morocco came to an end, Tangier was given back to the sultan, and Morocco became its own master again (see Morocco).

Residents-General: 24 May 1912–13 Dec. 1916 Hubert Lyautey; 13 Dec. 1916–7 April 1917 Henri Gouraud (acting); 7 April 1917–24 Sept. 1925 Hubert Lyautey; 24 Sept. 1925–4 Oct. 1925 [unknown] (acting); 4 Oct. 1925–1 Jan. 1929 Théodore Steeg; 1 Jan. 1929–July 1933 Lucien Saint; Aug. 1933–22 March 1936 Henri

Ponsot; 22 March 1936–17 Sept. 1936 Marcel Peyrouton; 17 Sept. 1936–14 Nov. 1942 Augustin Noguès; 14 Nov. 1942–5 June 1943 [unknown]; 5 June 1943–3 March 1946 Gabriel Puaux; 3 March 1946–14 May 1947 Eirik Labonne; 14 May 1947–28 Aug. 1951 Alphonse Juin; 28 Aug. 1951–20 May 1954 Augustin Guillaume; 20 May 1954–20 June 1955 François La Coste; 20 June 1955–29 Aug. 1955 Gilbert Grandval; 29 Aug. 1955–9 Nov. 1955 Comte Boyer de la Tour du Moulin; 9 Nov. 1955–2 March 1956 André Dubois. *Note:* For list of Sultans see Morocco. *Note:* For list of Prime Ministers, see Morocco.

French Possessions in North Africa see **Algeria**

French Somaliland see **Djibouti**

French Sudan see **Mali**

French Territory of the Afars and Issas see **Djibouti**

French West Africa. 16 June 1895–6 April 1959. *Location:* North West Africa — comprising the countries that would later become Guinea, Mali, Côte d'Ivoire, Senegal, Benin, Mauritania, Niger, and Burkina Faso. *Capital:* Dakar (from 1904); Gorée (1902–1904); Saint Louis (1895–1902). *Other names:* Afrique Occidentale Française; A.O.F.

History: In 1895 the Federation of French West Africa was born, taking in the following components (as they were then known): French Guinea, French Sudan, Ivory Coast, and Senegal. In 1899 Dahomey joined, in 1919 Upper Volta, in 1921 Mauritania, and in 1922 Niger. From the inception of French West Africa to 11 Nov. 1902 the Governor-General of French West Africa was also the Governor of Senegal, both polities being ruled from Saint Louis. The same thing happened briefly in 1907–1908. During World War II Pierre-François Boissons, the High Commissioner in A.O.F. remained under orders to the Vichy French until Nov. 1942, when he transferred the allegiance of French West Africa to the Free French. The A.O.F. became defunct by the end of 1958, although on paper it continued until 1959. There was no administration after Jan. 1959, and the A.O.F. officially came to an end in April.

Governors-General: 16 June 1895–28 Sept.

1895 Jean-Baptiste Barthélemy Chaudié (acting); 28 Sept. 1895–1 Nov. 1900 Jean-Baptiste Barthélemy Chaudié; 1 Nov. 1900–26 Jan. 1902 Noël Ballay; 26 Jan. 1902–15 March 1902 Pierre Capest (acting); 15 March 1902–15 Dec. 1907 Ernest Roume; 15 Dec. 1907–9 March 1908 Martial Merlin (acting); 9 March 1908–14 April 1915 Amédée Merlaud-Ponty; 14 April 1915–3 June 1917 Joseph Clozel; 3 June 1917–22 Jan. 1918 Joost Van Vollenhouven; 22 Jan. 1918–28 Feb. 1919 Gabriel Angoulvant; 28 Feb. 1919–16 Sept. 1919 Charles Brunet (acting); 19 Sept. 1919–27 May 1922 Martial Merlin; 27 May 1922–1 Dec. 1922 Marcel Olivier (acting); 1 Dec. 1922–18 March 1923 Martial Merlin; 18 March 1923–15 Oct. 1930 Jules Carde; 15 Oct. 1930–27 Sept. 1936 Jules Brévié; 27 Sept. 1936–14 July 1938 Jules de Coppet; 14 July 1938–28 Oct. 1938 Léon Geismar (acting); 28 Oct. 1938–18 April 1939 Pierre-François Boissons; 18 April 1939–25 June 1940 Léon Cayla. *High Commissioners:* 25 June 1940–1 July 1943 Pierre-François Boissons; 1 July 1943–May 1946 Pierre Cournarie; May 1946–27 Jan. 1948 René Barthes; 27 Jan. 1948–24 May 1951 Paul Béchard; 24 May 1951–21 Sept. 1952 Paul Chauvet (acting); 21 Sept. 1952–5 July 1956 Bernard Cornut-Gentille; 5 July 1956–July 1958 Gaston Cusin. *High Commissioners-General:* July 1958–21 Jan. 1959 Pierre Messmer; 21 Jan. 1959–6 April 1959 no administration.

Frigate Island see **Seychelles**

FROLINAT see **Chad**

Fuerteventura see **Canary Islands** and **Gran Canaria**

Fulani Empire. 21 Feb. 1804–15 March 1903. *Location:* Northern Nigeria, southern Niger, and parts of Cameroun. *Capital:* Sokoto and Gwandu (jointly from 1809); Sifawa (1807–1809); Gwandu (July 1805–1807); Sabon Gari (March 1805–July 1805). *Other names:* Sokoto Caliphate (alternative name for the Sokoto division of this empire from 1809); Filane Empire.

History: The Fulani (also known as the Fulbe, or Fula) peoples established many states in West Africa over the centuries, e.g. Futa Jallon, Yatenga, Masina, Futa Toro, Baguirmi, and Gobir. The Fulani subsequently became fanatical Muslims, and between 1804 and 1812 Uthman Dan Fodio, the Muslim warrior and fundamentalist mystic, at the head of his Fulani Army, conquered the states of Katsina, Kano, Zaria, Daura, Gombe, Misau, Kazaure, Katagum, Bauchi, Adamawa, Ilorin, and Nupe, establishing an amirate over each, and himself as the caliph over the whole lot. In 1809 Dan Fodio split his empire into two parts, one based at Sokoto, in the east (which he gave to his son Muhammad Bello), and the other at Gwandu, in the west, which he gave to his other son Abdullahi Dan Fodio. Sokoto as a town had existed since 1200, within the old state of Gobir, and in 1809 Uthman Dan Fodio made it his capital. In 1903 most of the Fulani Empire went to form part of the British protectorate of Northern Nigeria, while some went to Zinder (see Niger). The sultans continued to rule in Sokoto, and the amirs in Gwandu, answerable, of course, to the British authorities in Nigeria.

Sarkins (Military Commanders): 21 Feb. 1804–21 April 1817 Uthman Dan Fodio (also known as Usman Dan Fodio). *Sultans:* 21 April 1817–26 Oct. 1837 Muhammad Bello; 26 Oct. 1837–Nov. 1842 Abubakr Atiku I; Nov. 1842–21 Oct. 1859 Aliyu; 21 Oct. 1859–2 Nov. 1866 Ahmadu Atiku; 2 Nov. 1866–20 Oct. 1867 Aliyu Karami; Oct. 1867–March 1873 Ahmadu Rufai; March 1873–March 1877 Abubakr Atiku II; March 1877–Sept. 1881 Mu'azu; Sept. 1881–25 March 1891 Umaru; 25 March 1891–10 Oct. 1902 Abdarrahman; 13 Oct. 1902–15 March 1903 Atahiru Ahmadu (also known as Muhammad Atahiru I); March 1903–June 1915 Muhammad Atahiru II; 1915–1924 Muhammad Maiturare; 1924–Jan.1931 Muhammad Tambari; 1931–1938 Hassan Shahu; 17 June 1938–1 Nov. 1988 Sidiq Abubakr; 6 Nov. 1988–20 April 1996 Ibrahim Dasuki; 21 April 1996–Ibrahim Muhammad Maccido.

Fumbina see **Adamawa**

Funchal. 1418–1580. *Location:* Madeira. *Capital:* Funchal (founded 1421 by João Gonçalves Zarco).

History: In 1418 the Madeira Islands were discovered by João Gonçalves Zarco, a Portuguese navigator. In 1420 settlement began of Porto Santo, Funchal, and Machico. The big island of Madeira was split up into two donatarias (lands granted to a noble family by the Crown): Funchal and Machico, while the small island of

Porto Santo was its own donataria. In 1580, when Spain took over Portugal, the donatarias were canceled, and the island group was made into a colony (see Madeira). Wine and sugar were the main thrusts of the economy.

Rulers: 1418–1580 [unknown].

Fung see **Funj Sultanate**

Funj Sultanate. 1504–12 June 1821. *Location:* central Sudan. *Capital:* Sennar (from 1515). *Other names:* Fung Kingdom; Sennar; Sennaar; Senaar.

History: In 1504 Amara Dunkas founded the sultanate around the town of Sennar. A peak in power was reached in the late 17th century, then it declined until 1762, when the Hamaj clan began ruling through puppet sultans. The Turkish-Egyptian Army conquered the area in 1821, and Funj became incorporated, along with Nubia and Kordofan into the newly formed state of Sudan.

Sultans: 1504–1534 Amara Dunkas; 1534–1551 Nayil ibn Amara; 1551–1558 Abd al-Kadir I; 1558–1569 Amara II Abu Sakaykin; 1569–1586 Dakin al-Adil; 1586–1587 Dawra ibn Dakin; 1587–1591 Tabl; 1591–1592 interregnum; 1592–1604 Unsa I; 1604–1606 Abd al-Kadir II; Nov. 1606–1611 Adlan I; 1611–1617 Badi I Sid al-Qum; 1617–1645 Rubat I; 1645–28 Dec. 1680 Badi II Abu Daqan; 28 Dec. 1860–6 June 1692 Unsa II; 6 June 1692–13 April 1716 Badi III al-Ahmar; 13 April 1716–8 June 1720 Unsa III; 8 June 1720–8 July 1724 Nul; 8 July 1724–25 March 1762 Badi IV Abu Shulukh; 25 March 1762–1769 Nasir ibn Badi; 1769–1776 Ismail ibn Badi; 1776–1789 Adlan II; 1789–1789 Tabl II; 1789–1790 Badi V; 1790–1790 Hassab Rabihi; 1790–1791 Nawwar; 1791–1796 Badi VI; 1796–1803 Ranfi; 1803–12 June 1821 Badi VI.

Fur see **Darfur**

Futa Jallon. ca. 1700–14 July 1881. *Location:* west-central Guinea. *Capital:* Timbo. *Other names:* Diallon; Djallon; Jalon; Futa Jalon; Futa Dyallo; Fouta Jalon.

History: Formed about 1700, the kingdom of Futa Jallon was composed of Diallon peoples, and was the major political unit of what became the French territory of Rivières du Sud (see Guinea), into which it merged in 1881.

Amirs: ca. 1700–1715 Muhammad Sa'idi; 1715–1720 Musa Ba Kikala; 1720–1720 Sam-bigu; 1720–1720 Nuhu Ba Kikala; 1720–1727 Malik Si; 1727–1776 Ibrahim Musa; 1776–1791 Ibrahima Sori I; 1791–1796 Sa'adu; 1796–1797 Ali Bilma; 1797–1799 Salihu; 1799–1799 Abdullahi Ba Demba; 1799–1810 Abdelkader; 1810–1814 Abdullahi Ba Demba; 1814–1822 Abdelkader; 1822–1822 Bu Bakar; 1822–1822 Yahya; 1822–1823 Amadu; 1823–1839 Bu Bakar; 1839–1840 Yahya; 1840–1843 Umaru Sori; 1843–1845 Bakari; 1845–1848 Ibrahima Sori II; 1848–1850 Umaru Sori; 1850–1852 Ibrahima Sori II; 1852–1854 Umaru Sori; 1854–1856 Ibrahima Sori II; 1856–1858 Umaru Sori; 1858–1860 Ibrahima Sori II; 1860–1862 Umaru Sori; 1862–1864 Ibrahima Sori II; 1864–1866 Umaru Sori; 1866–1868 Ibrahima Sori II; 1868–1870 Umaru Sori; 1870–1871 Ibrahima Sori II; 1871–1872 Umaru Sori; 1872–1873 Ibrahima Sori III; 1873–1875 Ahmadu Dara Alfaya; 1875–1877 Umaru Ba Demba; 1877–1879 Ahmadu Dara Alfaya; 1879–1881 Ibrahima Sori III; 1881–1883 Ahmadu Dara Alfaya; 1883–1885 Ibrahima Sori III; 1885–1887 Ahmadu Dara Alfaya; 1888–1890 Ibrahima Sori III; 1890–1892 Bu Bakar III; 1892–June 1894 Ahmadu Dara Alfaya; June 1894–Jan. 1896 Bu Bakar III; Jan. 1896–Feb. 1896 Modi Abdulaye; Feb. 1896–18 Nov. 1896 Bu Bakar III; 18 Nov. 1896–1 Dec. 1896 Umaru Ba Demba; 1 Dec. 1896–30 Oct. 1897 Alfa Ibrahima Sori; 26 Nov. 1897–1906 Baba Alimu; 1906–1912 Bu Bakar IV.

Futa Toro. 1513–24 Oct. 1877. *Location:* northeast of Dakar, Senegal. *Capital:* Podor. *Other names:* Fouta Toro.

History: Founded by the Dia Ogo dynasty about 850, then ruled by various peoples until 1513, when the Denyanke dynasty came into being. In 1877 it became part of Senegal.

Kings: 1513–1535 Dengella Koli I; 1533–1538 Dengella Koli II; 1538–ca. 1765 a series of 15 kings whose names have not come down in history; ca. 1765–1776 Sule-Budu; 1776–1804 Abdelkedir; 1804–ca. 1859 [unknown]; ca. 1859–ca. 1868 Mustafa; ca. 1868–1875 Ahmadu Sego; 1875–Feb. 1891 Abdul Bu Bakar.

Gabon. 9 Feb. 1839– . *Location:* west central Africa, on the Atlantic coast. *Capital:* Libreville (from 1849); Fort d'Aumale (1843–49). *Other names:* République Gabonaise, or Republic of Gabon (1958–); Gabun; Gaboon; Gabon and Gulf of Guinea Settlements (1883–86); Gulf of Guinea Settlements (1843–49).

History: In 1839 the French began settlements along the coast of Gabon, and called them the Gulf of Guinea Settlements. The name Gabon comes from a Portuguese word "gabão," meaning "hooded cloak," which the Gabon Estuary looked like to the early explorers. On 11 June 1843 Fort d'Aumale was founded, as a naval post on the Gabon coast, and effectively as the capital, and the area became a French protectorate known as the Gabon Settlements. A commandant-particulier was installed to rule over the territories acquired along the coast. On 28 March 1844 the chiefdom of Glass became French; on 4 Nov. 1846 the area of George's Creek became part of the settlements, as did the Como and Remboue Rivers region (formerly part of the Séké and Bakélé chiefdoms) on 2 Dec. 1846; on 14 Feb. 1848 the Mondah (also formerly part of the Séké) also came under French control. In 1847 Libreville was founded as a town for freed slaves (the name meaning "Free Town" in French), and in Aug. 1849 replaced Fort d'Aumale as the capital. Cape Esterias fell to the French on 18 Sept. 1852. In 1854 the island of Gorée was detached from the French colony of Senegal, and made into a separate colony, which also included the Gabon Settlements. Thus Gabon became a territory of Gorée, with a Commandant-Supérieur ruling the whole colony, and a commandant-particulier running Gabon. This lasted until 4 Aug. 1860, when the French decided to link the Ivory Coast and Gabon as one political unit called Ivory Coast-Gabon, and the Gabon Settlements became a territory of this unit, with its local capital still at Libreville. On 16 Dec. 1883 the French split the two up and both Ivory Coast and Gabon became French colonies. However, on 27 April 1886 the French created an umbrella protectorate covering all their possessions in the area, and called it Afrique Équatoriale Française (French Equatorial Africa, or A.E.F.), and Gabon became one of its territories, with Libreville also the capital of the new A.E.F. The A.E.F. system was new, and the French were struggling for the best way to rule the vast area under their control in this part of Africa, so, on 29 June, 1886, after only a few months, Gabon became an autonomous French colony, ruled by a lieutenant-governor. Two years later it was considered more effective to combine the two colonies of Moyen-Congo and Gabon, and so the large territory of Moyen-Congo-Gabon was formed on 11 Dec. 1888, with the capital at Brazzaville, and the local Gabonese administrative headquarters at Libreville. On 5 July 1902 this political unit became the colony of Moyen-Congo–Gabon (or Lower Congo–Gabon), and Gabon remained a territory within this large colony, which in turn was ruled by the governor of French Congo (as French Equatorial Africa was known between 1891 and 1910). On 29 Dec. 1903 the colony of Moyen-Congo-Gabon was dissolved, and the two units went back to being colonies, Moyen-Congo and Gabon respectively. For the first three weeks Gabon fell under the administrative control of the governor-general of French West Africa, based in Saint Louis, Senegal, but after that time the lieutenant-governor of Gabon was answerable to the Commissioner-General (or Governor-General as he was known after 1908) of the French Congo (or French Equatorial Africa, as it became known as again, after 1910). On 30 June 1934 French Equatorial Africa, until then a federation of French colonies with a Governor-General ruling from Brazzaville, became a colony itself, with four component "regions"— Chad, Moyen-Congo, Gabon, and Ubangi-Shari. On 31 Dec. 1937 Gabon became an overseas territory of France, still with its local administrative capital at Libreville, and still answerable to the Governor-General of French Equatorial Africa. It kept this status under the Fourth Republic of France, and on 28 Nov. 1958 became an autonomous republic, paving the way for independence, which happened on 17 Aug. 1960. There was a coup in 1964, but M'Ba, who had been ousted, was restored soon afterwards by the French. Political repression and election-rigging led to riots in 1989. Along with the rest of sub–Saharan Africa Gabon faces the two major threats of poverty and AIDS.

Commanders: 9 Feb. 1839–11 June 1843 Capt. Louis Bouët-Willaumez. *Commandants-Particulier:* 11 June 1843–1844 Antoine Devoisins; 1844–1844 Joseph-Marie Millet; 1844–1846 André Brisset; 1846–1847 Jean Carilès; 1847–1847 André Brisset; 1847–25 March 1848 Victor-Joseph Roger; 25 March 1848–3 Aug. 1848 Alphonse Sordeaux; 3 Aug. 1848–Dec. 1848 Eugène Desperles; Dec. 1848–10 Aug. 1849 Étienne Deschanel; 10 Aug. 1849–15 Dec. 1850 Jean Martin; 15 Dec. 1850–1853 Alexis Vignon; 1853–1857 Théophile Guillet; 1857–1859 Alexis Vignon; 1859–4 Aug. 1860 Pierre Mailhetard; 4 Aug. 1860–1861 César Pradier; 1861–

1863 Paul Bruë; 1863–1866 Charles Baur; 1866–1867 Joseph Brunet-Millet; 1867–1868 Laurent Aube; 1868–1869 Frédéric Bourgarel; 1869–1871 Hippolyte Bourgoin; 1871–1873 Gustave Garraud; 1873–1875 Charles Panon de Hazier; 1875–1876 Félix Clément; 1876–1878 Jules Boitard; 1878–1879 Paul Caudière; 1879–1880 Augustin Dumont; 1880–1882 Jules Hanet-Cléry; 1882–16 Dec. 1883 Émile Masson; 16 Dec. 1883–1885 Jean Cornut-Gentille; 1885–27 April 1886 Georges Pradier. *Governors of the French Equatorial African Protectorate:* 27 April 1886–29 June 1886 Pierre Savorgnan de Brazza. *Lieutenant-Governors:* 29 June 1886–27 Aug. 1887 Noël Ballay; 27 Aug. 1887–25 Dec. 1887 Capt. Gourgas (acting); 25 Dec. 1887–12 March 1889 Noël Ballay; 12 March 1889–1 June 1894 Fortuné de Chavannes; 1 June 1894–1 May 1899 Albert Dolisie; 1 May 1899–5 July 1902 Émile Gentil. *Commissioners-General of the French Congo:* 5 July 1902–2 March 1903 Louis Grodet; 2 March 1903–Oct. 1903 Émile Gentil (acting); Oct. 1903–29 Dec. 1903 Louis Grodet. *Governors-General of French West Africa:* 29 Dec. 1903–21 Jan. 1904 Ernest Roume. *Lieutenant-Governors:* 21 Jan. 1904–19 April 1905 Louis Ormières; 19 April 1905–5 Aug. 1905 Paul Cousturier (acting); 5 Aug. 1905–27 April 1906 Alfred Fourneau; 27 April 1906–23 April 1907 Charles Noufflard (acting); 23 April 1907–26 April 1907 Alfred Martineau; 26 April 1907–Dec. 1908 Édouard Telle (acting); 20 Jan. 1909–10 Feb. 1909 Frédéric Weber (acting); 10 Feb. 1909–9 Nov. 1909 Charles Rognon (acting); 9 Nov. 1909–June 1911 Léon Richaud (acting); June 1911–21 Feb. 1912 Georges Poulet; 21 Feb. 1912–18 April 1914 Paul Adam (acting); 18 April 1914–1 June 1917 Casimir Guyon; 1 June 1917–12 June 1918 Georges Thomann (acting); 12 June 1918–30 June 1919 Maurice Lapalud; 30 June 1919–13 April 1920 Jean Marchand (acting); 13 April 1920–12 March 1921 Jean Marchand; 12 March 1921–Aug. 1921 Georges Thomann (acting); Aug. 1921–29 May 1922 Jean Marchand; 29 May 1922–15 June 1923 Edmond Cadier (acting); 15 June 1923–29 July 1924 Louis Cercus (acting); 29 July 1924–26 Sept. 1926 Joseph Bernard; 26 Sept. 1926–Aug. 1927 Adolphe Deitte (acting); Aug. 1927–13 April 1928 Joseph Bernard; 13 April 1928–Sept. 1929 Adolphe Deitte (acting); Sept. 1929–19 June 1931 Joseph Bernard; 19 June 1931–Sept. 1931 Louis Vingarassamy (acting); Sept. 1931–26 Sept. 1934 Louis Bonvin. *Superior-Administrators:* 26 Sept. 1934–1935 Louis Bonvin; 1935–24 Oct. 1936 Charles Assier de Pompignan (acting). *Delegate-Governors:* 24 Oct. 1936–11 Sept. 1937 Louis Bonvin; 11 Sept. 1937–29 Aug. 1938 Georges Parisot; 29 Aug. 1938–2 Nov. 1939 Georges Masson (acting); 2 Nov. 1939–14 Nov. 1940 Georges Masson; 14 Nov. 1940–26 March 1941 Lt.-Col. Parent (acting). *Governors:* 26 March 1941–30 May 1942 Victor Valentin-Smith; 30 May 1942–26 Aug. 1943 Charles Assier de Pompignan; 26 Aug. 1943–5 Nov. 1943 Paul Vuillaume; 5 Nov. 1943–Dec. 1943 André Servel (acting); Dec. 1943–19 Nov. 1944 Paul Vuillaume; 19 Nov. 1944–28 March 1946 Numa-François Sadoul; 28 March 1946–31 Dec. 1947 Roland Pré; 31 Dec. 1947–6 April 1949 Numa-François Sadoul; 6 April 1949–19 Oct. 1951 Pierre-François Pelieu; 19 Oct. 1951–25 April 1952 Charles Hanin (acting); 25 April 1952–29 Jan. 1958 Yves Digo; 29 Jan. 1958–28 Nov. 1958 Louis Sanmarco. *High Commissioners:* 28 Nov. 1958–July 1959 Louis Sanmarco; July 1959–17 Aug. 1960 Jean Risterucci. *Presidents:* 17 Aug. 1960–17 Feb. 1964 Léon M'Ba; 17 Feb. 1964–19 Feb. 1964 Jean-Hilaire Aubame (Usurper Head of State with title Provisional Prime Minister); 20 Feb. 1964–27 Nov. 1967 Léon M'Ba; 28 Nov. 1967–Omar Bongo (until 1973 known as Albert-Bernard Bongo). *Chief Ministers:* 28 Nov. 1958–27 Feb. 1959 Léon M'Ba. *Prime Ministers:* 27 Feb. 1959–17 Aug. 1960 Léon M'Ba; 16 April 1975–3 May 1990 Léon Mébiame; 3 May 1990–7 June 1991 Casimir Oyé-M'Ba; 15 June 1991–2 Nov. 1994 Casimir Oyé M'Ba; 9 Dec. 1994–23 Jan. 1999 Paulin Obame-Nguema; 23 Jan. 1999–Jean-François Ntoutoumane. *Note:* in times of no Prime Minister, the President held that office.

Gaiya see **Kano**

Galekaland see **Kreli's Country**

Galla and Sidama see **Ethiopia**

Gambaga see **Mossi States**

Gambia. 23 Aug. 1816– . *Location:* North West Africa. *Capital:* Banjul (named Bathurst until 1973, this town was founded in 1816, and named for Henry Bathurst, British Colonial Secretary). *Other names:* The Gambia; Republic of The

Gambia (1970–); Gambia Colony and Protectorate (1901–1963); Bathurst Colony (1816–1821); St. Mary (1816); Banjol (1816).

History: The story of the first settlements in the area of the Gambia is told in more detail in the entry Fort James. The list of rulers of the British possessions in the Gambia between 1765 and 1779 are given under the entry Senegambia. In 1816 certain British traders from Senegal, forced to leave that country when it reverted to France after the Napoleonic Wars, arrived at the Gambia River and occupied the island of Banjol, renaming it St. Mary. Power fell into the hands of the Royal African Corps. The town, which had also had the name Banjol, was renamed Bathurst that same year, but very soon the name of the colony became Bathurst. The colony prospered, and began to expand along the coast and into the interior. On 17 Oct. 1821 all forts and settlements in Northwest Africa were placed under the rule of the West African Territories (or W.A.T.) (see British West Africa), with headquarters at Freetown, in Sierra Leone. On 12 Dec. 1829 the name of the Gambian territory became Bathurst Settlements and Dependencies in the Gambia. On 11 April 1843 Gambia (as it became known now) broke away from the W.A.T. and became a separate colony. On 19 Feb. 1866 it became a component of the West African Settlements (W.A.S.) (again, see British West Africa), again ruled from Freetown. On 24 July 1874 the W.A.S. lost two of its component parts, the Gold Coast and Lagos. This left only two, Sierra Leone and Gambia. Gambia became a colony again on 28 Nov. 1888, with the inevitable demise of the West African Settlements. In 1894 the hinterland of Gambia was opened up as a protectorate, which formed an addition to the colonial settlement of the coastal and riverine areas of the Gambia River, and on 11 Jan. 1901 the country became Gambia Colony and Protectorate. On 3 Oct. 1963 the Gambia achieved self-rule, and on 18 Feb. 1965 it became a dominion of the British Commonwealth. On 23 April 1970 Gambia finally achieved republic status. Drought and severe famine rocked the country in the 1970s and 1980s. On 1 Feb. 1982 Senegal and Gambia united in the Senegambia Confederation, although each country, of course, continued to be its own entity. The Senegambia idea came to an amicable end in Sept. 1989. In 1994 Dawda Jawara was ousted in a bloodless coup. AIDS is no more a problem in

Gambia than it is in the USA, but the country does have to face huge unemployment.

Administrators: 23 Aug. 1816–1 Aug. 1826 Alexander Grant; 1 Aug. 1826–12 Dec. 1829 Lt.-Col. Alexander Findlay. *Lieutenant-Governors:* 12 Dec. 1829–23 Feb. 1830 Lt.-Col. Alexander Findlay; 23 Feb. 1830–22 Sept. 1837 George Rendall; 22 Sept. 1837–Oct. 1838 Thomas Ingram (acting); Oct. 1838–May 1839 William Mackie; May 1839–Jan. 1840 Thomas Ingram (acting); Jan. 1840–Oct. 1841 Sir Henry Huntley; Oct. 1841–11 April 1843 Thomas Ingram (acting). *Governors:* 11 April 1843–Oct. 1843 Capt. Henry Frowd Seagram; Oct. 1843–1844 Edmund Norcott; 1844–1847 Commander Charles Fitzgerald; 1847–1852 Sir Richard Macdonnell; 1852–1852 Arthur Kennedy (never arrived); 1852–Sept. 1859 Col. Luke O'Connor; Sept. 1859–19 Feb. 1866 Col. George D'Arcy. *Administrators:* 19 Feb. 1866–1869 Admiral Charles Patey. *Officers Administering:* 1869–1871 Alexander Bravo. *Administrators:* 1871–1873 Thomas Callaghan; 1873–1875 Sir Cornelius Kortright; 1875–1877 Dr. Samuel Rowe; 1877–1884 Dr. Valesius Gouldsbury; 1884–1886 Alfred Moloney; 1886–1886 James Hay (acting); 1886–1888 Gilbert Carter (acting); 1888–1891 Gilbert Carter (knighted 1890); 1891–1900 Robert Llewellyn (knighted 1898); 1900–11 Jan. 1901 Sir George Denton. *Governors:* 11 Jan. 1901–21 Dec. 1911 Sir George Denton; 21 Dec. 1911–11 April 1914 Sir Henry Galway (until 1911 known as Gallwey); 11 April 1914–1918 Edward Cameron (knighted 1916); 1918–1919 Herbert Henniker (acting); 1919–1920 Sir Edward Cameron; 1920–3 Jan. 1921 Herbert Henniker (acting); 3 Jan. 1921–10 March 1927 Cecil Armitage (knighted 1926); 10 March 1927–29 Nov. 1928 Sir John Middleton; 29 Nov. 1928–11 Sept. 1930 Sir Edward Denham; 11 Sept. 1930–12 April 1934 Richmond Palmer (knighted 1934); 12 April 1934–22 Oct. 1936 Arthur Richards (knighted 1935); 22 Oct. 1936–23 March 1942 Sir Thomas Southorn; 23 March 1942–29 March 1947 Hilary Blood (knighted 1944); 29 March 1947–1 Dec. 1949 Andrew Wright (knighted 1948); 1 Dec. 1949–19 June 1958 Percy Wyn-Harris (knighted 1952); 19 June 1958–29 March 1962 Sir Edward Windley; 29 March 1962–18 Feb. 1965 Sir John Paul. *Governors-General:* 18 Feb. 1965–9 Feb. 1966 Sir John Paul; 9 Feb. 1966–23 April 1970 al-Hajji Sir Farimang Singhateh. *Presidents:* 24 April 1970–22 July

1994 Sir Dawda Jawara. *Chairmen of the Armed Forces Provisional Ruling Council:* 23 July 1994–27 Sept. 1996 Capt. Yahya Jammeh. *Presidents:* 27 Sept. 1996–18 Oct. 1996 Capt. Yahya Jammeh (interim); 18 Oct. 1996–Capt. Yahya Jammeh. *Chief Ministers:* March 1961–May 1962 Pierre N'Jie. *Prime Ministers:* May 1962–24 April 1970 Dawda Jawara (knighted 1966). *Note:* In times of no Prime Minister, the President or Head of State held that office.

Ganagana see **Agaie**

Gando, Gandu see **Gwandu**

Gao see **Songhai**

Gaoua see **Burkina Faso**

Garamantes see **Phazania**

Garun Gabbas see **Hadejia**

Gatarwa see **Hadejia**

Gazaland. 1824–28 Dec. 1895. *Location:* on the border between southern Mozambique and Zimbabwe, between Delagoa Bay and the Pungwe River. *Capital:* Xai Xai (also known as Chai Chai). *Other names:* Gaza; Shangana; Vatua; Landeen; Gaza Empire.

History: The Gaza Empire (named after Gaza, a Bantu chief) was built in the early 1820s by Nguni leader Soshangane (son of Gaza), from various tribes who were being oppressed by the Zulu king Dingaan. Soshangane had great success in territorial expansion, conquering land as far north as the Zambesi, and massacring Portuguese inhabitants at Delagoa Bay, Inhambane, Sofala, and Sena. Although the Portuguese retook these forts, they had great difficulty holding them against the Matshangana (as Soshangane's people were called). About 1850 a Goanese named Gouveia arrived in the area and set himself up as king. He was not finally disposed of until the 1800s, when the British South African Company threw him out. In 1891 the British made an offer to king Gungunyane to accept a British protectorate, but this was refused. In 1895 the Portuguese conquered it as part of Mozambique.

Kings: 1824–11 Oct. 1858 Soshangane (also known as Manikusa); 11 Oct. 1858–1862 Ma-

wewe; 1862–Aug. 1884 Mzila; Aug. 1884–28 Dec. 1895 Gungunyane.

GazaNkulu. 1 Feb. 1973–27 April 1994. *Location:* on the Transvaal–Venda border, in South Africa. *Capital:* Giyani. *Other names:* Gaza Nkulu National State. GazaNkulu was the Bantustan (National Homeland) for the Shangaan (also known as Thonga) peoples. In 1973 it achieved a status of self-government, but still remained part of South Africa. In 1994 the homelands, now no longer needed, were abolished. *Chief Ministers:* 1 Feb. 1973–25 March 1993 Prof. Hudson Ntsanwisi; 25 March 1993–April 1993 Edward Mkinga (acting); April 1993–26 April 1994 Samuel Nxumalo.

Gcalekaland see **Kreli's Country**

Gedevi see **Dahomey**

Geedy Dynasty see **Kayor**

Gelwar Dynasty see **Kayor**

George's Creek see **Gabon**

German East Africa. 27 May 1885–14 Nov. 1918. *Location:* Tanganyika and (after 1895) Urundi, and (after 1899) Ruanda. *Capital:* Dar es-Salaam (founded in 1862 by the Sultan of Zanzibar on the site of the village of Mzizima, it was the capital of German East Africa from 1891); Bagamoyo (until 1891). *Other names:* German East African Protectorate.

History: In 1885 Karl Peters, a German adventurer in East Africa, made several treaties with the local rulers (e.g. Karagwe), and wound up with a large stretch of land ruled over by his company, the German East African Company. The beginning of the protectorate of Witu would seem to mark the inception of what can be called German East Africa, and other protectorate treaties followed in short order, e.g. Usagora, on 14 Aug. 1885. Incidentally, the British proclaimed a protectorate of their own over Witu on 18 June 1890. By 1890 the German East African Company was in trouble, being unable to handle uprisings, and the German government established its own rule from 28 Oct. 1890 (effective as from 1 Jan. 1891), as an official German protectorate. During World War I the British and Belgians occupied the area, dividing it up between them. The Germans put up resistance until 14 Nov. 1914, by which time the War was over. At the Treaty of Versailles in 1919, the Germans' territory was divided up between the British and the Belgians as Tanganyika and Ruanda-Urundi (Portugal was awarded the Kionga triangle in the south, which went to Mozambique), and this became effective on 10 Jan. 1920.

Administrators: 27 May 1885–28 April 1888 Karl Peters. *Reichskommissars:* 28 April 1888–1 Jan. 1891 Herrmann von Wissmann. *Military Commanders:* 1 Jan. 1891–21 Feb. 1891 Herrmann von Wissmann. *Governors:* 21 Feb. 1891–1891 Julius von Soden; 1891–1891 Capt. Ruediger (acting); 1891–15 Sept. 1893 Julius von Soden; 15 Sept. 1893–1 May 1895 Friedrich von Schiele; 1 May 1895–3 Dec. 1896 Herrmann von Wissmann; 3 Dec. 1896–12 Feb. 1901 Eduard von Liebert; 12 Feb. 1891–22 April 1906 Graf Adolf von Götzen; 22 April 1906–July 1912 Baron Albrecht von Rechenburg; July 1912–14 Nov. 1918 Heinrich Schnee.

Ghana. 1621– . *Location:* North West Africa. *Capital:* Accra (from 1877. The name comes from the Akan word "akran," meaning "black ants," which abound here. Accra was formerly a native village); Osu (1874–1877); Cape Coast Castle (1664–1874); Kormantin (1621–1664). *Other names:* Republic of Ghana (1960–); Dominion of Ghana (1957–1960); Gold Coast (1621–1957).

History: The English started arriving along the Gold Coast in 1618, and an administration of company factors was inaugurated in 1621. In 1632 the Company of Merchants Trading to Guinea established a central government over the English Gold Coast Settlements, but they lost it in 1651 to the Company of London Merchants, who, in turn, lost it in 1658 to the East India Company. On 10 Jan. 1662 the Company of Royal Adventurers took it over. In 1664, with Holland and England at war over the Gold Coast, the Dutch Admiral De Ruyter bombarded and destroyed all the English forts except the newly-built capital at Cape Coast Castle. On 27 Sept. 1672 the Royal African Company took over the Gold Coast settlements (or rather the English settlements on the coast — there were still Danish Gold Coast Settlements and Dutch Gold Coast Settlements at that stage, and there had been Portuguese Gold Coast Set-

tlements and Swedish Gold Coast Settlements, as well as some French Gold Coast settlements at Petit Dieppe. The Prussians would come later, for which see Hollandia). The English were not the only nation on the Gold Coast, by any means, and they were all heavily involved in the slave and gold trade. The Royal African Company built several new forts, and repaired Cape Coast Castle. On 1 May 1707 England and Scotland were joined, and the term British Gold Coast Settlements now began to be applied to the area. On 23 June 1751 the Company of Merchants Trading to Africa took over the British settlements from the dying Royal African Company, and with this change came a more central and stable government. However, with the British abolition of the slave trade in 1807, the Company faded, and on 7 May 1821 Britain assumed the Gold Coast as a Crown colony. On 17 Oct. 1821 Britain made their new acquisition a territory of the West African Territories (W.A.T.) (see British West Africa), and it was made subordinate to Sierra Leone. On 25 June 1828 the Gold Coast broke away from this federation, and a Committee of Merchants assumed temporary control from the Crown, although the links with Sierra Leone remained strong. In 1843 the British Crown resumed control of its Gold Coast territories, making the Gold Coast a Crown colony again, but re-linking it with Sierra Leone. On 13 Jan. 1850 the country became the individual and separate Crown colony of the Gold Coast. On 30 March 1850 Britain acquired the Danish Gold Coast Settlements, and on 19 Feb. 1866 the West African Settlements (W.A.S.) (see British West Africa) were created by the British government, to be ruled by the Governor of Sierra Leone. The four component parts of the W.A.S. were Gold Coast, Gambia, Sierra Leone, and Lagos. On 24 July 1874 Gold Coast and Lagos broke away, and together formed a new entity, Gold Coast Colony (with Lagos). On 13 Jan. 1886 the two component parts of this colony separated, and the individual colony of the Gold Coast came back into existence. In the long period that followed, great changes took place. The original colony of the Gold Coast had always been in the south (of what would eventually become Ghana), by the ocean, and in 1896 the British protectorate of Ashanti was created out of the conquered empire of that name. In 1901 this became the colony of Ashanti. The Ashanti areas lay mid-country, and in the north were the Gold Coast Northern Territories. In 1945 an experiment was tried when the Gold Coast Colony Region was created within the main country, to the south of Ashanti, and answerable to Accra. It was created as a separate region, but still belonged to the overall British possession of the Gold Coast. A similar position existed with Ashanti and the Northern Territories. This was when the British were splitting the Gold Coast into regions, and when Nationalism was beginning to cause problems to the British administration. On 8 Feb. 1951 the Gold Coast was granted internal autonomy, with powers over Ashanti and the Northern Territories as well. The "region" idea was dropped in 1953, although Ashanti and Northern Territories continued to exist until independence. On 13 Dec. 1956 the Gold Coast was enlarged by the addition of British Togoland, and on 6 March 1957 the Gold Coast became the first black African country to achieve dominion status within the British Commonwealth. At this point it changed its name to Ghana, named for the old empire in what is now Mali. The country finally became a republic on 1 July 1960. Kwame Nkrumah (right name: Francis Kofi) was the first giant Ghanaian figure, but he had two sides to him, one that made enormous domestic improvements to the country, and the other that ran the country into debt, and eliminated opposition to his dictatorship, a socialist dictatorship that was officially granted him by the people in a 1964 referendum. Nkrumah was ousted in a police-Army coup in 1966. Since that time Ghana's history has been one largely of coups and violence. The strong man in Ghana for over 20 years from 1979 was Flight-Lieutenant Jerry Rawlings. There was ethnic warfare in 1994, and AIDS looms large as the major health threat

Governors: 1621–1623 Sir William St. John; 1623–1660 [unknown]; 1660–(?) William Greenhill; (?)–1685 [unknown]; 1685–(?) Henry Nurse; (?)–1691 [unknown]; 1691–(?) John Bloome; (?)–1697 [unknown]; 1697–1701 Governor Baggs; 1701–1708 Thomas Dalby; 1708–23 June 1751 [unknown]; 23 June 1751–23 Jan. 1756 Thomas Melvill; 23 Jan. 1756–17 Feb. 1756 William Tymewell; 17 Feb. 1756–15 Oct. 1757 Charles Bell (acting); 15 Oct. 1757–10 May 1761 Nassau Senior (acting); 10 May 1761–15 Aug. 1763 Charles Bell; 15 Aug. 1763–1 March 1766 William Mutter; 1 March 1766–11 Aug. 1766 John Hippisley; 11 Aug. 1766–21 April 1769 Gilbert Petrie; 21 April 1769–11 Aug. 1770 John Grossle; 11 Aug. 1770–20 Jan. 1777 David Mill; 20 Jan. 1777–25 March 1780 Richard Miles; 25 March 1780–20 May 1781 John Roberts; 20 May 1781–29 April 1782 John Weuves (acting); 29 April 1782–29 Jan. 1784 Richard Miles; 29 Jan. 1784–24 Jan. 1787 James Mourgan; 24 Jan. 1787–27 April 1787 Thomas Price; 27 April 1787–20 June 1789 Thomas Norris; 20 June 1789–15 Nov. 1791 William Fielde; 15 Nov. 1791–31 March 1792 John Gordon; 31 March 1792–16 Dec. 1798 Archibald Dalzel; 16 Dec. 1798–4 Jan. 1799 Jacob Mould; 4 Jan. 1799–28 April 1800 John Gordon; 28 April 1800–30 Sept. 1802 Archibald Dalzel; 30 Sept. 1802–8 Feb. 1805 Jacob Mould; 8 Feb. 1805–4 Dec. 1807 George Torrane; 4 Dec. 1807–21 April 1816 Edward White; 21 April 1816–19 Jan. 1817 Joseph Dawson; 19 Jan. 1817–27 March 1822 John Hope Smith; 27 March 1822–17 May 1822 Sir Charles Macarthy; 17 May 1822–Dec. 1822 Maj. James Chisholm (acting); Dec. 1822–21 Jan. 1824 Sir Charles Macarthy; 21 Jan. 1824–17 Oct. 1824 Maj. James Chisholm (acting); 17 Oct. 1824–22 March 1825 Maj. Edward Purdon (acting); 22 March 1825–March 1826 Charles Turner; March 1826–18 May 1826 [unknown] (acting); 18 May 1826–15 Nov. 1826 Sir Neil Campbell; 15 Nov. 1826–11 Oct. 1827 Henry Ricketts; 11 Oct. 1827–10 March 1828 Col. Hugh Lumley (acting); 10 March 1828–5 June 1828 Capt. George Hingston (acting); 5 June 1828–25 June 1828 Henry Ricketts; 25 June 1828–19 Feb. 1830 John Jackson (acting); 19 Feb. 1830–26 June 1836 George Maclean; 26 June 1836–15 Aug. 1838 William Topp (acting); 15 Aug. 1838–1843 George Maclean; 1843–8 March 1845 Worsley Hill; 8 March 1845–15 April 1846 James Lilley (acting); 15 April 1846–31 Jan. 1849 William Winniett; 31 Jan. 1849–13 Jan. 1850 James Fitzpatrick (acting); 13 Jan. 1850–4 Dec. 1850 Sir William Winniett; 4 Dec. 1850–14 Oct. 1851 James Bannerman (acting); 14 Oct. 1851–June 1853 Stephen Hill; June 1853–Aug. 1853 James Fitzpatrick (acting); Aug. 1853–Feb. 1854 Brodie Cruickshank (acting); Feb. 1854–Dec. 1854 Stephen Hill; Dec. 1854–March 1857 Henry Connor (acting); March 1857–14 April 1858 Sir Benjamin Pine; 14 April 1858–20 April 1860 Henry Bird (acting); 20 April 1860–14 April 1862 Edward Andrews; 14 April 1862–20 Sept. 1862 William Ross (acting); 20 Sept. 1862–1864 Richard Pine. *Lieutenant-*

Governors: 1864–1864 William Hackett. *Governors:* 1864–1865 Richard Pine; 1865–1865 Rokeby Jones (acting); 1865–April 1865 W.E. Mockler. *Lieutenant-Governors:* April 1865–19 Feb. 1866 Edward Conran. *Governors:* 19 Feb. 1866–Feb. 1867 Edward Conran; Feb. 1867–Aug. 1868 Herbert Ussher; Aug. 1868–Nov. 1869 W.H. Simpson (acting); Nov. 1869–July 1871 Herbert Ussher; July 1871–1872 Charles Salmon (acting); 1872–April 1872 Herbert Ussher. *Governors-in-Chief:* April 1872–1872 John Pope-Hennessey. *Administrators:* 1872–Nov. 1872 Charles Salmon (acting); Nov. 1872–7 March 1873 Robert Harley. *Governors-in-Chief:* 7 March 1873–17 March 1873 Robert Keate; 17 March 1873–2 Oct. 1873 Robert Harley and Alexander Bravo (acting, jointly); 2 Oct. 1873–4 March 1874 Sir Garnet Wolseley. *Administrators:* 4 March 1874–30 March 1874 Col. Maxwell (acting); 30 March 1874–June 1874 William Johnston (acting); June 1874–24 July 1874 George Strahan. *Governors:* 24 July 1874–7 April 1876 George Strahan. *Lieutenant-Governors:* 7 April 1876–Dec. 1876 Charles Lees; Dec. 1876–5 June 1877 Sanford Freeling. *Governors:* 5 June 1877–13 May 1878 Sanford Freeling. *Lieutenant-Governors:* 13 May 1878–June 1879 Charles Lees. *Governors:* June 1879–1 Dec. 1880 Herbert Ussher. *Lieutenant-Governors:* 1 Dec. 1880–4 March 1881 William Griffith. *Governors:* 4 March 1881–13 May 1882 Sir Samuel Rowe; 13 May 1882–4 Oct. 1882 Alfred Moloney (acting). *Lieutenant-Governors:* 4 Oct. 1882–24 Dec. 1882 William Griffith. *Governors:* 24 Dec. 1882–29 April 1884 Sir Samuel Rowe; 29 April 1884–24 April 1885 William Young; 24 April 1885–11 April 1887 William Griffith; 11 April 1887–26 Nov. 1887 F.B.P. White (acting); 26 Nov. 1887–30 June 1889 Sir William Griffith; 30 June 1889–18 Feb. 1890 Frederic Hodgson (acting); 18 Feb. 1890–12 June 1891 Sir William Griffith; 12 June 1891–24 Nov. 1891 Frederic Hodgson (acting); 24 Nov. 1891–12 Aug. 1893 Sir William Griffith; 12 Aug. 1893–7 March 1894 Frederic Hodgson (acting); 7 March 1894–7 April 1895 Sir William Griffith; 7 April 1895–19 April 1896 William Maxwell; 19 April 1896–23 Oct. 1896 Frederic Hodgson (acting); 23 Oct. 1896–6 Dec. 1897 Sir William Maxwell; 6 Dec. 1897–29 May 1898 Frederic Hodgson (acting); 29 May 1898–27 Dec. 1898 Frederic Hodgson; 27 Dec. 1898–13 July 1899 William Low (acting); 13 July 1899–28 June 1900 Sir Frederic Hodgson; 28 June 1900–11 July 1900 William Low (acting); 11 July 1900–29 Aug. 1900 Sir Frederic Hodgson; 29 Aug. 1900–17 Dec. 1900 William Low (acting); 17 Dec. 1900–30 July 1902 Mathew Nathan; 30 July 1902–20 Dec. 1902 Leonard Arthur (acting); 20 Dec. 1902–9 Feb. 1904 Sir Mathew Nathan; 9 Feb. 1904–3 March 1904 Herbert Bryan (acting); 3 March 1904–10 May 1905 Sir John Rodger; 10 May 1905–12 Nov. 1905 Herbert Bryan (acting); 12 Nov. 1905–2 April 1906 Sir John Rodger; 2 April 1906–2 Sept. 1906 Herbert Bryan (acting); 2 Sept. 1906–9 Oct. 1907 Sir John Rodger; 9 Oct. 1907–28 March 1908 Herbert Bryan (acting); 28 March 1908–30 March 1909 Sir John Rodger; 30 March 1909–29 Aug. 1909 Herbert Bryan (acting); 29 Aug. 1909–1 Sept. 1910 Sir John Rodger; 1 Sept. 1910–21 Nov. 1910 Herbert Bryan (acting); 21 Nov. 1910–5 Feb. 1911 James Thorburn; 5 Feb. 1911–16 June 1911 Herbert Bryan (acting); 16 June 1911–29 June 1912 James Thorburn; 29 June 1912–26 Dec. 1912 Herbert Bryan (acting); 26 Dec. 1912–1 May 1914 Sir Hugh Clifford; 1 May 1914–27 Aug. 1914 Sir William Robertson (acting); 27 Aug. 1914–5 May 1915 Sir Hugh Clifford; 5 May 1915–16 Nov. 1915 Ransford Slater (acting); 16 Nov. 1915–18 Nov. 1916 Sir Hugh Clifford; 18 Nov. 1916–23 April 1917 Ransford Slater (acting); 23 Nov. 1917–1 April 1919 Sir Hugh Clifford; 1 April 1919–8 Oct. 1919 Ransford Slater (acting); 9 Oct. 1919–2 June 1920 Gordon Guggisberg; 2 June 1920–6 Oct. 1920 Ransford Slater (acting); 6 Oct. 1920–11 July 1921 Gordon Guggisberg; 11 July 1921–12 Dec. 1921 Richard W.H. Wilkinson (acting); 12 Dec. 1921–2 April 1923 Gordon Guggisberg (knighted 1922); 2 April 1923–17 Aug. 1923 John C. Maxwell (acting); 18 Aug. 1923–1 Oct. 1923 Arthur J. Philbrick (acting); 1 Oct. 1923–31 March 1924 Sir Gordon Guggisberg; 31 March 1924–1 Sept. 1924 John C. Maxwell (acting); 1 Sept. 1924–6 July 1925 Sir Gordon Guggisberg; 6 July 1925–10 Nov. 1925 John C. Maxwell (acting); 10 Nov. 1925–11 April 1926 Sir Gordon Guggisberg; 11 April 1926–27 Sept. 1926 John C. Maxwell (acting); 27 Sept. 1926–24 April 1927 Sir Gordon Guggisberg; 24 April 1927–19 July 1927 John C. Maxwell (acting); 19 July 1927–18 April 1930 Sir Ransford Slater; 18 April 1930–22 Sept. 1930 G.C. du Boulay (acting); 22 Sept. 1930–30 Jan. 1931 Sir Ransford Slater; 30 Jan. 1931–20 April 1931 Geoffrey Northcote (acting); 20 April 1931–8

Dec. 1931 Sir Ransford Slater; 8 Dec. 1931–14 Dec. 1931 G.C. du Boulay (acting); 14 Dec. 1931–5 April 1932 Sir Ransford Slater; 5 April 1932–29 Nov. 1932 Geoffrey Northcote (acting); 30 Nov. 1932–13 May 1934 Sir Shenton Thomas; 13 May 1934–23 Oct. 1934 Geoffrey Northcote (acting); 24 Oct. 1934–24 Oct. 1941 Sir Arnold Hodson; 24 Oct. 1941–29 June 1942 George London (acting); 29 June 1942–2 Aug. 1947 Sir Alan Burns; 2 Aug. 1947–12 Jan. 1948 George London (acting); 12 Jan. 1948–15 Feb. 1949 Sir Gerald Creasy; 15 Feb. 1949–28 March 1949 Sir Robert Scott (acting); 28 March 1949–11 June 1949 Thorleif Mangin (acting); 11 June 1949–11 Aug. 1949 Sir Robert Scott (acting); 11 Aug. 1949–6 March 1957 Sir Arden Clarke (after 1951 known as Sir Charles Arden-Clarke). *Governors-General:* 6 March 1957–14 May 1957 Sir Charles Arden-Clarke; 14 May 1957–13 Nov. 1957 Kobrina Arku Korsah (acting); 13 Nov. 1957–1 July 1960 William Hare, Earl of Listowel (appointed in June 1957). *Presidents:* 1 July 1960–24 Feb. 1966 Kwame Nkrumah. *Chairmen of the National Liberation Council:* 24 Feb. 1966–3 April 1969 Joseph Ankrah; 3 April 1969–7 Aug. 1970 Akwasi Afrifa; 7 Aug. 1970–31 Aug. 1970 Nii Amaa Ollennu (acting). *Presidents:* 31 Aug. 1970–13 Jan. 1972 Edward Akufo-Addo. *Chairmen of the National Redemption Council:* 13 Jan. 1972–5 July 1978 Ignatius Acheampong; 5 July 1978–4 June 1979 Frederick Akuffo. *Chairmen of the Armed Forces Revolutionary Council:* 5 June 1979–24 Sept. 1979 Jerry Rawlings. *Presidents:* 24 Sept. 1979–31 Dec. 1981 Hilal Limann. *Military Leaders:* 31 Dec. 1981–11 Jan. 1982 Jerry Rawlings (interim). *Chairmen of the Provisional National defense Council:* 11 Jan. 1982–3 Nov. 1992 Jerry Rawlings. *Presidents:* 3 Nov. 1992–7 Jan. 2001 Jerry Rawlings; 7 Jan. 2001–John Kufuor. *Prime Ministers:* 5 March 1952–1 July 1960 Kwame Nkrumah; 29 Aug. 1969–13 Jan. 1972 Kofi Busia. *Note:* In times of no Prime Minister, the President or Head of State held that office.

Ghana Empire. ca. 350–1240. *Location:* mostly in what is today Mali, but also partly in what is today Mauritania. *Capital:* Kumbi (this was the 11th century capital). *Other names:* Wagadu; Land of Gold; the Kingdom of Ghana; Aoukar; Ancient Ghana.

History: Ghana was the first great trading empire of Medieval West Africa. The original inhabitants may have been Berbers, but by the 8th century its people were black Mande-speaking Soninke tribes and the empire was an enormous trading post and carrier of goods from one part of Africa to another. By the year 800 Ghana was very powerful, its actual name being Wagadu. The "ghana" was the king himself. There were many capitals, and the empire absorbed vassal state after vassal state, but by the 11th century the great empire began to decline. The Almoravids in the north were the main cause of Ghana's disintegration. Kumbi was taken in 1076, and the slow death of the empire followed, with the area shrinking as vassal states dropped away. By 1240 it was all over and what was left of the Ghana Empire became part of the greater still Mali Empire. This ancient empire gave its name to the modern state of Ghana.

Kings: ca. 350–ca. 350 Kaya Maja; ca. 350–ca. 622 there were 21 kings, whose names have not come down to us; ca. 622–ca. 750 there were 21 kings, whose names have not come down to us; ca. 750–ca. 750 Majan Dyabe Sisse; ca. 750–ca. 1040 [unknown number of kings whose names are also unknown]; ca. 1040–1062 Bassi; 1062–1068 Tunka Menin; 1068–1076 [unknown]; 1076–ca. 1090 Kambine Diaresso; ca. 1090–ca. 1100 Suleiman; ca. 1100–ca. 1120 Banna Bubu; ca. 1120–ca. 1130 Majan Wagadu; ca. 1130–ca. 1140 Gane; ca. 1140–ca. 1160 Musa; ca. 1160–ca. 1180 Birama; ca. 1180–ca. 1200 Diara Kante; ca. 1200–1234 Sumanguru; 1234–1240 [unknown].

Giubaland see **Jubaland**

Giza see **Egypt**

Glass see **Gabon**

Glorioso Islands. No dates. *Location:* a group of French islands northwest of Madagascar, and claimed by Madagascar. They occupy 5 sq. km., and include various islands and rocks, notably Île Glorieuse. *Capital:* none. *Other names:* Îles Glorieuses. *Rulers:* Administered by a French commissioner resident in Réunion.

Gobir. ca. 1100–1900. *Location:* on the Niger-Nigeria border. *Capital:* Alkalawa (from 1734); Birnin Lalle (ca. 1720–1734); Goran Rami (unknown dates); Maigali (unknown dates).

History: Gobir took its name from its ancestral home in Yemen, Arabia. Legend has it that it was one of the seven Hausa States founded by one of the sons of Bawo, son of Abdullahi, King of Bagdad. Gobir, the northernmost outpost of Hausaland (another way of saying the Hausa States), was a state as early as about 1100. Seemingly apart from major events in the area until 1731, it then engaged in a war with the kingdom of Kano until 1743. By 1799 the Gobirawa (people from Gobir) were the most powerful in Hausaland. But soon the Habe dynasty was to be defeated by the Fulanis under Uthman Dan Fodio (see Fulani Empire), and after Sept. 1808 the rulers of Gobir were Fulani amirs. The Gobirawa fled north, building the town of Tsibiri, from which they harassed the Fulani. In 1900 the country became part of two colonial subdivisions — one French and the other British. The northern part of Gobir became part of Zinder (see Niger), and the southern part became one of the northern sections of the British protectorate of Northern Nigeria.

Sultans: (?)–(?) Duma; (?)–(?) Banaturumi; (?)–(?) Sanakafo; (?)–(?) Majigu; (?)–(?) Batutua; (?)–(?) Bawa; (?)–(?) Birtakiskis; (?)–(?) Sirtengi; (?)–(?) Barankimi; (?)–(?) Madaura; (?)–(?) Dangoma; (?)–(?) Zerama; (?)–(?) Biamusu; (?)–(?) Umi; (?)–(?) Shiruma; (?)–(?) Majanjara; (?)–(?) Kasu; (?)–(?) Chida; (?)–(?) Goji; (?)–(?) Jilabataji; (?)–(?) Ginsarana; (?)–(?) Bawa Nesso; (?)–(?) Badadella; (?)–(?) Chiroma; (?)–(?) Muzakha I; (?)–(?) Muzakha II; (?)–(?) Barankimi; (?)–(?) Ishifi; (?)–(?) Alezzi Kalajuma; (?)–(?) Bachiri; (?)–(?) Muhammadu; (?)–(?) Dalla Gungumi; (?)–(?) Dalla Dawaki; (?)–(?) Chiroma; (?)–(?) Muhammadu; (?)–(?) Maji; (?)–(?) Babba; (?)–(?) Chiroma; (?)–(?) Akal; (?)–(?) Gumsara; (?)–(?) Chiroma; (?)–(?) Maji; (?)–(?) Babba; (?)–ca. 1715 Chiroma; ca. 1715–(?) Muhammadu Dan Chiroma; (?)–(?) Barbandoma (also known as Chuba Dan Muhammadu); (?)–(?) Bachiri (also known as Akili Dan Chuba); (?)–(?) Yako (also known as Uban Doro); (?)–(?) Soba Dan Doro; (?)–(?) Nyakum; (?)–(?) ibn Ashe; (?)–1742 Akal; 1742–1770 Babari Dan ibn Ashe; 1770–1777 Dan Gudi Dan Babari; 1777–1795 Bawa Jan Gwarzo; 1795–1801 Yakuba Dan Babari; 1801–1803 Nafata Dan Babari (also known as Muhamman); 1803–1804 Yunfa Dan Nafata; 1804–Sept. 1808 Salihu; Sept. 1808–1814 Modibbo Dan Fodio; 1814–1817 Gwamki; 1817–1835 Ali; 1835–1858 Mayaki; 1858–1858 Baciri VII; 1858–1883 Bawa Dan Gwamki; 1883–1886

Ibrahim; 1886–1889 Mainassara Maji; 1889–1890 Almu; 1890–1890 Ibrahim; 1890–1894 Mainassara Maji; 1894–1897 Almu; 1897–April 1898 Ibrahimu Na Mai Fura; April 1898–Jan. 1899 Bakon Dare; Jan. 1899–1907 Umaru Dacili; 1907–14 Nov. 1912 Baturi; 1912–(?) Dan Buddi; (?)–(?) Dan Magaji; (?)–(?) Tumbulki; (?)–ca. 1936 Gulbi; ca. 1936–1937 Salau; 1937–1939 Kunto; 1939–1963 Labo Salau; 1963–1975 Agada Nagogo; 1975–Muhammadu Bawa. *Note:* While this is the most complete list one can compile from available data (mostly oral tradition), its accuracy cannot be substantiated. The early sultans date from the time that the Gobirawa were in the Yemen, or en route to Africa, and written records are virtually non-existent.

Goddala see **Almoravid Empire**

Gojjam. ca. 1620–1855. *Location:* now a northwestern province of Ethiopia, south of Lake Tana. *Capital:* Debra Markos. *Other names:* Gojam.

History: A powerful kingdom of Ethiopia which, in 1855, went to make up the Ethiopian Empire (see Ethiopia).

Kings: ca. 1620–(?) Sarsa Krestos; (?)–ca. 1740 unknown kings; ca. 1740–ca. 1777 Ras Goskol; ca. 1777–1793 Ras Abeto Haylu; 1793–1798 Ras Mar'ed; 1798–1805 Dejaz Saude; 1805–1806 Dejaz Mar'ed Gwalo; 1806–1813 Dejaz Saude; 1813–ca. 1820 Dejaz Walad Rafael; ca. 1820–1828 Dori; 1828–1828 Matantu; 1828–1842 Ras Gosho II; 1842–March 1844 Ras Beru Gugsa; March 1844–Dec. 1844 Merso; Dec. 1844–1852 Ras Gosho II; 1852–1853 Ras Kasa; 1853–1854 Ras Ali II; 1854–1855 Tedla Haylu.

Gold Coast see **Ghana**

Gold Coast Colony Region. 1945–1953. *Location:* south Ghana, south of the Ashanti Region. *Capital:* Accra. *Other names:* Gold Coast Colony.

History: In 1945 this area was created as a separate region by the Gold Coast government. It still belonged to the overall British possession of the Gold Coast. A similar position existed with Ashanti and the Gold Coast Northern Territories (qq.v.). This idea of regions was dropped in 1953, although Ashanti and Northern Territories continued to exist until 1957, when Ghana became a dominion within the British Commonwealth.

Chief Commissioners: 1945–1950 Thorleif Mangin; 1950–1953 Arthur Loveridge.

Gold Coast Northern Territories. 1899–6 March 1957. *Location:* the northern segment of Ghana. *Capital:* Tamale. *Other names:* Northern Territories; Northern Territories Civil Protectorate (1907–1957); Northern Territories Military Protectorate (1899–1907).

History: In 1899 the British occupied the northernmost part of what later became Ghana. By 1906, when the entire Gold Coast was delimited as a colony, the Northern Territories were fully organized as a military territory. On 1 Jan. 1907 the Northern Territories became a civil territory. In 1957, when the new dominion of Ghana came into being, the Northern Territories ceased to exist, and they became the basis for the Northern Region of Ghana.

Chief Commissioners: 1899–1904 Arthur Morris; 1904–1910 Alan Watherston; 1910–1920 Cecil Armitage; 1920–1924 Arthur J. Philbrick; 1924–1930 Arthur Walker-Leigh; 1930–1933 Francis Jackson; 1933–1942 William Jones; 1942–1946 George Gibbs; 1946–1948 William Ingrams; 1948–1950 Edward Jones; 1950–1953 Geoffrey Burden. *Regional Officers:* 1953–1954 Arthur Loveridge; 1954–1957 Sydney Mac-Donald-Smith.

Goldesia see **Nigeria**

Gombe. 1804–Feb. 1902. *Location:* northeastern Nigeria. *Capital:* Gombe (this has been the name of the capital since 1919); Doma (the name of the capital from 1913 to 1919, when it was renamed Gombe); Gombe (this was another town, and was the capital from 1824 to 1913. It was renamed Gombe Aba, or Old Gombe, in 1843).

History: Founded as an amirate in 1804 by Buba Yero, a Fulani chief of the Sokoto Caliphate (see Fulani Empire). In 1902 it became a part of the British protectorate of Northern Nigeria.

Chiefs: 1804–1841 Buba Yero; 1841–1844 Suli; 1844–1881 Koiranga; 1881–1888 Zailani; 1888–1895 Hassan; 1895–1898 Tukur; 1898–1922 Umaru; 1922–1935 Haruna; Jan. 1936–(?) Abubakr; (?)–Usuman.

Gomera see **Canary Islands**

Gonçalo Álvarez see **Gough Island**

Gonder see **Ethiopia**

Gondokoro see **Equatoria Province** and **Uganda**

Gonja. ca. 1495–ca. 1713. *Location:* Ghana-Côte d'Ivoire. *Capital:* Pembi.

History: Founded about 1495, Gonja was conquered about 1713 by Dagomba.

Kings: ca. 1495–ca. 1554 Sumayla Ndewura Dyakpa; ca. 1554–1583 Wadih (also known as Naba); 1583–1623 Ma'ura; 1623–1666 Dyakpa Lanta (also known as Lata); 1666–1688 Thaara (also known as Suleiman); 1688–1709 [unknown]; 1709–ca. 1713 [unknown].

Goosen see **Goshen**

Gorée. 10 Feb. 1763–30 Jan. 1779. *Location:* an island off the coast of Senegal. *Capital:* Saint Louis (in Senegal).

History: The Portuguese navigator Diniz Diaz landed here in 1444, and the Portuguese occupied the island. In 1617 the Dutch, who had long used it as a port of call, bought it from the local chief, and called it Gorée, for the Dutch island of the same name. In 1663 Commodore Robert Holmes took Gorée from the Dutch, but the following year Admiral De Ruyter took it back. The French took it in 1677 and made it an integral part of Senegal. In 1758 the British took it, but in 1763 returned it to the French. Britain kept its other Senegalese possessions until 1779, when France re-took everything, and Gorée merged into Senegal again. When the French abolished slavery in their colonies, Gorée's importance faded away.

Commandants: 12 Sept. 1763–Nov. 1764 Pierre Poncet de la Rivière; Nov. 1764–March 1765 [unknown] (acting); March 1765–July 1767 Jean-Georges le Baillif des Mesnager; July 1767–March 1768 Claude Le Lardoux de la Gastière; March 1768–4 Oct. 1768 M. Maizière (acting); 4 Oct. 1768–10 Dec. 1772 Pierre de Rastel de Rocheblaye; 10 Dec. 1772–10 Dec. 1772 Antoine Louis Desmarets de Montchaton (acting); 10 Dec. 1772–Nov. 1774 Charles Boniface; Nov. 1774–Dec. 1777 Joseph Le Brasseur; Dec. 1777–Aug. 1778 Alexandre Ar…mé…ny de Paradis; Aug. 1778–30 Jan. 1779 Charles Boucher (acting).

Gorée and Dependencies. 1854–1859. *Location:* off the coast of Senegal. *Capital:* Gorée. *Other names:* Gorée.

History: In 1854 the islet of Gorée was detached from the French colony of Senegal, and made into a separate colony, which also included the Gabon Settlements. A commandant-supérieur had overall control of the colony, and the island of Gorée was administered by a commandant-particulier under him. In 1859 Gorée was re-attached to the colony of Senegal, and in the following year the Gabon Settlements became the territory of Gabon.

Commandants-Supérieurs: 1854–1856 Jérôme Monléon; 1856–1859 Auguste Prôtet. *Commandants-Particuliers of Gorée:* 1854–1856 Timoléon Ropert; 1856–1859 Jean d'Alteyrac; 1859–1859 Georges de Cools. *Note:* For commandants-particuliers of Gabon Settlements, see Gabon.

Goshen. 24 Oct. 1882–7 Aug. 1883. *Location:* eastern British Bechuanaland, part of Korannaland. *Capital:* Rooigrond. *Other names:* Het Land Goosen; Goosen; Land Goosen (named Goshen from the Bible).

History: A Boer republic, founded on the Rooigrond, and set up on land ceded to the Boers by Bechuana chief Moshete. It merged with Stellaland to form the United States of Stellaland in 1883.

Administrators: 24 Oct. 1882–7 Aug. 1883 Gey Van Pettius.

Gough Island. No dates. *Location:* an island, about 225 miles south southeast of Tristan da Cunha in the South Atlantic, about halfway between Africa and South America. *Capital:* none. *Other names:* Gonçalo Álvarez.

History: Discovered about 1505 by Portuguese sailors, and named Gonçalo Álvarez. It was rediscovered in 1731 by Capt. Gough. In 1938, along with Tristan da Cunha, Gough became a dependency of Saint Helena.

Gouiriko see **Gwiriko**

Graaff-Reinet. 6 Feb. 1795–22 Aug. 1796. *Location:* on the Sunday River, in the Cape of Good Hope Colony, South Africa. *Capital:* Graaff-Reinet (founded in 1786 and named for Governor Van De Graaff and his wife, whose name was Reinet).

History: Formed in 1785 as an administrative district of the Cape (see Cape Colony), and ruled by a landdrost (magistrate) and a secretary from the chief town of Graaff-Reinet. In 1795 the

Boers of the area rebelled against the liberal, anti-racist laws of the then landdrost Honoratus Maynier, and expelled him, declaring themselves an independent colony, answerable only to Holland (see also Swellendam). Not an independent republic as such, it submitted to the British in 1796, and became a Cape district again.

Presidents of the War Council: 6 Feb. 1795–22 Aug. 1796 Adriaan Van Jaarsveld. *National Landdrosts:* 6 Feb. 1795–22 Aug. 1796 Carl Gerotz.

Graciosa see **Canary Islands** and **Gran Canaria**

GRAE see **Angola Revolutionary Government in Exile**

Grain Coast see **Liberia**

Gran Comoro. ca. 1515–1893. *Location:* Comoros. *Capital:* Moroni. *Other names:* Moroni; Angaziya; Grande Comore; Ngaridza.

History: Founded about 1515 as the Sultanate of Ngaridza, the island of Gran Comoro fell under French protection in 1893 as part of Mayotte.

Sultans: ca. 1515–ca. 1600 seven sultans including Tibi; ca. 1600–ca. 1843 [unknown]; ca. 1843–ca. 1850 Sayid Hamza; ca. 1850–1875 Sayid Ahmad; 1875–1909 Sayid Ali.

Gran Canaria. 6 March 1480– . *Location:* the largest of the Canary Islands. *Capital:* Las Palmas (founded 1478 and named for the palms nearby). *Other names:* Grand Canary.

History: Gran Canaria was occupied by the Spanish in 1480. In 1589 the colony of Gran Canaria, as with the colony of Tenerife, became a territory of the Captaincy-General of the Canary Islands. The captain-general, based on Gran Canaria, also served as governor of Gran Canaria. In 1595 Tenerife and Gran Canaria again became individual colonies. This lasted until 1625, when a captaincy-general situation again came into being. In 1821 Gran Canaria became part of the Spanish province of the Canary Islands, and remained that way until 1927, when the island was grouped together with the islands of Fuerteventura, Lanzarote, Alegranza, Graciosa, and Lobos, to form the Spanish province of Las Palmas de Gran Canaria. On 8 May 1983 the two provinces of Las Palmas de Gran Canaria and Santa Cruz de Tenerife (see Tenerife) were joined to form the self-governing province of the Canary Islands.

Governors: 6 March 1480–1491 Pedro de Vera; 1491–1494 Francisco de Maldonaldo; 1494–1495 [unknown]; 1495–1497 Alfonso Fajardo; 1497–1498 [unknown]; 1498–1502 Lope de Valenzuela; 1502–1502 Antonio de Torres; 1502–1503 [unknown]; 1503–1505 Alonso Esudero; 1505–1517 Lope de Sosa y Mesa; 1517–1518 Pedro de Castilla; 1518–1520 Fernán de Guzmán; 1520–1521 Bernardino de Anaya; 1521–1523 Pedro de Castilla; 1523–1526 Diego de Herro; 1526–1529 Martín Cerón; 1529–1531 Bernardo del Nero; 1531–1532 [unknown]; 1532–1535 Martín Cerón; 1535–1536 Agustín de Zurbarán; 1536–1538 Bernardino de Ledesma; 1538–1540 Juan de Legarte; 1540–1543 Agustín de Zurbarán; 1543–1546 Alonso del Corral; 1546–1549 Juan de Miranda; 1549–1553 Rodrigo de Acuña; 1553–1555 Luis de Vigil; 1555–1557 Rodrigo de Acuña; 1557–1558 Francisco Marquez y Pedrosa; 1558–1559 [unknown]; 1559–1562 Juan Pacheco de Benavides; 1562–1565 Diego de Águila y Toledo; 1565–1568 [unknown]; 1568–1571 Pedro de Herrera; 1571–1575 Juan Alonso de Benavides; 1575–1578 Diego de Melgarejo; 1578–1579 [unknown]; 1579–1584 Martín de Benavides; 1584–1586 Tomás de Cangas; 1586–1589 Álvaro de Acosta. *Governors-General:* Marqués de Bedmar; 1591–1595 [unknown]. *Governors:* 1595–1599 Alonso de Alvorado y Ulloa; 1599–1601 Antonio Pamachamoso; 1601–1607 Jerónimo de Valderrama y Tovar; 1607–1612 Luis de Mendoza; 1612–1615 Francisco de la Rúa; 1615–1621 Fernando Osorio; 1621–1624 Pedro de Barrionuevo y Melgoza; 1624–1625 Gabriel de Lara. *Rulers:* 1625–1821 ruled by the Captain-General of the Canary Islands; 1821–8 May 1983 [unknown].

Grand Bassa see **Bassa Cove**

Grand Bassam see **Ivory Coast**

Grand Bonny see **Bonny**

Grand Canary see **Gran Canaria**

Grand Dieppe see **Petit Dieppe**

Grand Sesters see **Liberia**

Grand Terre see **Aldabra Islands**

Grande Comore see **Comoros**

Granville Town see **Sierra Leone**

Great Namaqualand see **Namibia**

Great Zimbabwe see **Mwene Mutapa Empire**

Greenville see **Liberia** and **Mississippi-in-Africa**

Griqualand East. 26 Dec. 1861–Oct. 1874. *Location:* eastern South Africa, south of Natal. *Capital:* Kokstad (founded in 1862, and named for Adam Kok III). *Other names:* New Griqualand (it is now called Emboland).

History: In 1861 two thousand Griquas left Adam Kok's Land under their leader Adam Kok III, and trekked over the Drakensberg Mountains to No Man's Land. They renamed their new home Griqualand East (cf. Griqualand West). In 1874 it became part of Cape Colony.

Kaptyns (Captains): 26 Dec. 1861–Oct. 1874 Adam Kok III. *Residents:* 1873–Oct. 1874 Joseph Orpen.

Griqualand West. 1813–15 Oct. 1880. *Location:* Bechuanaland–South Africa border. *Capital:* Kimberley (founded 1871, and named for the Earl of Kimberley, it was the capital from 1871); Griquatown (until 1871, this town was founded in 1802 as Klaarwater [Clear Water], and named thus by the Rev. Kramer and the Rev. Anderson, on account of the spring there. Originally a London Mission Society station, it was renamed Griquatown in 1813 by the Rev. John Campbell). *Other names:* Waterboer's Land (1820–1871); Griquatown (1813–1820).

History: In the late 18th century Adam Kok, a Bastaard, and named after his profession (cook), was compelled to leave the Stellenbosch area of the Cape, and headed north, gathering half-breed Bastaards and Griqua Hottentots en route. He died in 1795, and his son Cornelis Kok I, settled on the Orange River, and Cornelis's two sons, Adam Kok II and Cornelis Kok II both settled in the village of Klaarwater, which John Campbell renamed in 1813 (see also Cornelis Kok's Land). Adam Kok II and Barend Barends ruled between them until 1819, when Andries Waterboer took over. Barends went north to become involved with the Matabele, and Adam Kok II went on to form Adam Kok's Land (which he named after his son, Adam Kok III). Cornelis Kok II went north to Campbell Lands, which later became Cornelis Kok's Land. Griquatown became known as Waterboer's Land, and in 1838 Waterboer extended his country's boundaries by treaty. In 1855 the territory of Albania came within his rule, and in 1860 Nicolaas Waterboer gained all of Cornelis Kok's Land, which Cornelis Kok had given to Adam Kok III in 1857. In 1867 diamonds were discovered in Waterboer's Land. The British in Cape Colony, and the Boers in the South African Republic (see Transvaal) both wanted the area for themselves, naturally, but from 1867 to 1870 Waterboer was the claimant to whom the Keate Award gave the diamond lands. On 27 Oct. 1871, having asked for British protection, Waterboer accepted a British protectorate, and his land, now called Griqualand West (a name that had been in use for about eight years as an alternative to Waterboer's Land), was attached to the Cape. On 17 July 1873 it became the Crown Colony of Griqualand West (see also Klipdrift Republic). In 1877 it was re-attached to the Cape, this move not becoming effective until 1880.

Kaptyns (Captains): 1813–1819 Adam Kok II and Barend Barends (jointly); 1819–13 Dec. 1852 Andries Waterboer; 23 Dec. 1852–27 Oct. 1871 Nicolaas Waterboer. *Civil Commissioners:* 27 Oct. 1871–10 Jan. 1873 Joseph Orpen. *Administrators:* 10 Jan. 1873–17 July 1873 Richard Southey. *Lieutenant-Governors:* 17 July 1873–3 Aug. 1875 Richard Southey; 4 Aug 1875–March 1879 Owen Lanyon; March 1879–15 Oct. 1880 James Rose-Innes, Jr.

Griqualand West Republic see **Klipdrift Republic**

Gross-Friedrichsburg see **Hollandia**

Guanche see **Canary Islands**

Guinea. 5 Aug. 1849– . *Location:* North West Africa. *Capital:* Conakry (founded 1884 as the local headquarters, and named for a village nearby, Conakry was the capital from 1891); Saint Louis (in Senegal. This was the capital until 1891). *Other names:* Guinée; République du Guinée, or Republic of Guinea, or People's Revolutionary Republic of Guinea (from 1958);

French Guinea (1893–1958); Rivières du Sud, or South Rivers (1849–1893).

History: Beginning in 1838 Louis Bouët-Willaumez and some other French naval officers surveyed this part of the Guinea coast (the Guinea coast then being the internationally accepted term for the entire coast of Africa from what is now Equatorial Guinea to Morocco, and the name "guinea" coming from the Berber word "aguinaw" meaning "black man"). They established a settlement on the Río Nuñez which, in 1849 the French government made into a protectorate, calling it Rivières du Sud. This new protectorate was answerable to the French African capital of Saint Louis, in Senegal. In 1880 the French took Tomba Island, and in 1881 Futa Jallon. Various settlements were made along the coast and in the interior, and on 12 Oct. 1882 Rivières du Sud officially became a territory of France and a dependency of Senegal, with a lieutenant-governor answerable still to Saint Louis. On 1 Aug. 1889 (effective 1 Jan. 1890) the country became a partially autonomous colony, and on 17 Dec. 1891 a fully autonomous colony. On 10 March 1893 it became the colony of French Guinea, and on 16 June 1895 the colony became a part of French West Africa, remaining so until the break up of that federation in 1958. The colony was enlarged in the 1890s by the addition of hinterland acquired from Sierra Leone and from Liberia, and in 1904 the British ceded the Los Islands to French Guinea. On 13 Oct. 1946 French Guinea became an overseas territory of France (its inhabitants becoming French citizens), and in 1958, when the French began giving away their African colonies, Guinea became the only one that elected not to go through the decompression stage of being an autonomous republic, and not to become part of the French Community. Instead, on 2 Oct. 1958, it became the Republic of Guinea, the first of the French northwest African colonies to go. Thus, without French backing, Guinea turned to the communist countries for assistance. Sékou Touré was the great Guinean patriot, and became the first president. In 1960 the French attempted to overthrow him, and this became Touré's excuse to embark on a reign of terror and suppression of political opponents. Touré survived several assassination attempts and an invasion in Nov. 1970 of Guinean exiles and mercenaries. Touré died in a Cleveland, Ohio, hospital in 1984. Army coups and attempted coups, and gross corruption, have been the order of the day in Guinea since independence. In 1996 there was an unsuccessful Army revolt, and in the late 1990s there was an influx of over 400,000 refugees from Liberia and Sierra Leone. In 2000–2001 there were border wars with Liberia and Sierra Leone, and new ethnic warfare in 2004, and another attempted coup, as well as an attempted assassination of President Conté. AIDS and poverty pose the big health problems.

Rulers: 5 Aug. 1849–12 Oct. 1882 administered direct by the governors of Senegal, at Saint Louis. *Lieutenant-Governors:* 12 Oct. 1882–1890 Jean-Marie Bayol; 1890–22 July 1892 Noël Ballay; 22 July 1892–June 1893 Paul Cousturier (acting); June 1893–23 April 1895 Noël Ballay; 23 April 1895–28 May 1896 Paul Cousturier (acting); 28 May 1896–21 June 1898 Noël Ballay; 21 June 1898–12 April 1900 Paul Cousturier (acting); 12 April 1900–2 Nov. 1900 Noël Ballay; 2 Nov. 1900–28 Sept. 1904 Paul Cousturier; 28 Sept. 1904–15 Oct. 1904 Antoine Frezouls (acting); 15 Oct. 1904–27 Feb. 1906 Antoine Frezouls; 27 Feb. 1906–16 May 1907 Jules Richard (acting); 16 May 1907–25 July 1907 Joost Van Vollenhoven (acting); 25 July 1907–18 Feb. 1908 Georges Poulet (acting); 18 Feb. 1908–24 Sept. 1909 Victor Liotard; 24 Sept. 1909–Jan. 1910 Georges Veillat (acting); Jan. 1910–4 July 1910 Victor Liotard; 4 July 1910–Nov. 1910 Georges Poulet (acting); Nov. 1910–9 May 1912 Camille Guy; 9 May 1912–7 March 1913 Jean-Louis Poiret (acting); 7 March 1913–6 March 1914 Jean Peuvergne; 6 March 1914–13 June 1914 Jean-Louis Poiret (acting); 13 June 1914–23 Oct. 1915 Jean Peuvergne; 23 Oct. 1915–12 Oct. 1916 Jean-Louis Poiret (acting); 12 Oct. 1916–9 April 1919 Jean-Louis Poiret; 9 April 1919–20 Jan. 1920 Fernand Lavit (acting); 20 Jan. 1920–15 Feb. 1922 Jean-Louis Poiret; 15 Feb. 1922–13 Nov. 1922 Jules Vidal (acting); 13 Nov. 1922–26 March 1925 Jean-Louis Poiret; 26 March 1925–Dec. 1925 Robert Simon (acting); Dec. 1925–7 April 1927 Jean-Louis Poiret; 7 April 1927–13 April 1928 Antoine Paladi (acting); 13 April 1928–21 Oct. 1928 Jean-Claude Tissier (acting); 21 Oct. 1928–21 July 1929 Jean-Louis Poiret; 21 July 1929–28 Feb. 1931 Louis Antonin (acting); 28 Feb. 1931–1 Jan. 1932 Robert de Guise; 1 Jan. 1932–13 June 1933 Joseph Vadier; 13 June 1933–6 Dec. 1933 Antoine Paladi (acting); 6 Dec. 1933–8 July 1935 Joseph Vadier; 8 July 1935–24 Nov. 1935 Louis-Placide Blacher (acting); 24 Nov. 1935–7 March 1936 Joseph Vadier. *Governors:* 7 March 1936–21 Nov. 1936 Louis-Placide Blacher (acting); 21 Nov. 1936–4 Sept. 1937 Louis-Placide Blacher; 4 Sept. 1937–26 Jan. 1938 Pierre Tap (acting); 26 Jan. 1938–10 June 1939 Louis-Placide Blacher; 10 June 1939–1 Oct. 1939 Félix Martiné (acting); 1 Oct. 1939–12 Feb. 1940 Louis-Placide Blacher; 12 Feb. 1940–Aug. 1942 Félix Giacobbi; Aug. 1942–25 March 1944 Horace Crocicchia; 25 March 1944–30 April 1946 Jacques-Georges Fourneau (acting); 30 April 1946–13 Oct. 1946 Éduard Terrac; 13 Oct. 1946–Jan. 1948 Éduard Terrac (acting); Jan. 1948–9 Feb. 1951 Roland Pré; 9 Feb. 1951–April 1953 Paul Sirieix; April 1953–23 June 1955 Jean-Paul Parisot; 23 June 1955–3 June 1956 Charles-Henri Bonfils; 3 June 1956–29 Jan. 1958 Jean-Paul Ramadier; 29 Jan. 1958–2 Oct. 1958 Jean Mauberna. *Heads of State:* 2 Oct. 1958–12 Nov. 1958 Ahmed Sékou Touré (interim); 12 Nov. 1958–15 Jan. 1961 Ahmed Sékou Touré. *Presidents:* 15 Jan. 1961–26 March 1984 Ahmed Sékou Touré; 27 March 1984–3 April 1984 Louis Lansana Béavogui (interim). *Heads of Military Committee for National Redress:* 3 April 1984–5 April 1984 Lansana Conté. *Presidents:* 5 April 1984–Lansana Conté. *Prime Ministers:* 26 April 1972–26 March 1984 Louis Lansana Béavogui; 5 April 1984–18 Dec. 1984 Diara Traoré; 9 July 1996–12 March 1999 Sidia Touré; 12 March 1999–3 Feb. 2004 Ladime Sidimé; 23 Feb. 2004–30 April 2004 François Fall; 9 Dec. 2004–Cellou Diallo. *Note:* In times of no Prime Minister, the President of other Head of State held that office.

Guinea-Bissau. 1879– . *Location:* West Africa, between Cape Roxo and the Cajet River. *Capital:* Bissau (established in 1687 as a fortified Portuguese post, it was the capital from 1941); Bolama (until 1941). *Other names:* Republic of Guinea-Bissau (from 1973); Portuguese Guinea (until 1973).

History: In 1879 Bissau and the erstwhile Cacheu, as well as neighboring areas in what is today Guinea-Bissau, were released from their dependence on Cape Verde, and transformed into the colony of Portuguese Guinea. On 11 June 1951 Portuguese Guinea became an overseas province of Portugal. From the 1960s a guerrilla war started, its intention being to throw off Portuguese rule. This war lasted more than ten years, during which time a rebel government was formed in the interior of the country that gradually gained more and more support. On 24 Sept. 1973, the country gained its independence as the Republic of Guinea-Bissau. The independence of Guinea-Bissau was fully recognized by the Portuguese on 10 Sept. 1974. There were plans afoot in 1980 to unite with the Cape Verde Islands, but these fell through in November of that year because of a coup in Guinea-Bissau. In 1998 civil war broke out, and a coup in 1999 ousted Vieira. In Nov. 2000 there was an Army rebellion, and President Yala was ousted in Sept. 2003 by another Army coup. AIDS is rampant, as is poverty.

Governors: 1879–1881 Agostinho Coelho; 1881–1884 Pedro de Gouveia; 1884–1885 [unknown]; 1885–1886 Francisco Barbosa; 1886–1887 José de Brito; 1887–30 May 1887 Eusébio Castella do Vale; 30 May 1887–4 Sept. 1888 Francisco da Silva; 4 Sept. 1888–1890 Joaquim da Graça Correia e Lança; 1890–30 April 1891 Augusto dos Santos; 30 April 1891–1895 Luis de Vasconcelos e Sá; 1895–26 May 1895 Eduardo Oliveira; 26 May 1895–1897 Pedro de Gouveia; 1897–1898 Álvaro da Cunha (acting); 1898–1899 Albano Ramalho; 1899–1900 Álvaro da Cunha (acting); 1900–1903 Joaquim Biker; 1903–1904 Alfredo Martins; 1904–1904 João Valente; 1904–1906 Carlos Pessanha; 1906–1909 João Muzanty; 1909–23 Oct. 1910 Francelino Pimentel; 23 Oct. 1910–Aug. 1913 Carlos Pereira; Aug. 1913–1914 José Sequeira; 1914–1915 José Duque; 1915–1917 José Sequeira; 1917–1918 Carlos Ferreira; 1918–1919 José Duque; 1919–1919 José Marinho; 1919–1920 Henrique Guerra; 1920–1921 [unknown]; 1921–1926 José Caroço; 1926–1927 [unknown]; 1927–1931 Antonio de Magalhães; 1931–1932 João Zilhão; 1932–1940 Luis Antonio Viegas; 1940–1941 [unknown]; 1941–25 April 1945 Ricardo Vaz Monteiro; 25 April 1945–1950 Manuel Rodrigues; 1950–1951 [unknown]; 1951–1953 Raimundo Serrão; 1953–1956 Diogo de Melo e Alvim; 1956–1958 Álvaro Távares; 1958–1962 Antonio Correia; 1962–1965 Vasco Rodrigues; 1965–24 May 1968 Arnaldo Schultz; 24 May 1968–July 1973 Antonio de Spínola; July 1973–30 Aug. 1973 [unknown] (acting); 30 Aug. 1973–April 1974 José Rodrigues; 2 May 1974–1974 Lt.-Col. San Gouveia; 1974–10 Sept. 1974 Carlos Fabião. *Presidents:* 26 Sept. 1973–14 Nov. 1980 Luis de Almeida Cabral. *Presidents of the Council of the Revolution:* 14 Nov. 1980–14 May 1984 João Bernardo "Nino" Vieira. *Chairmen of*

the Council of State: 16 May 1984–7 May 1999 João Bernardo "Nino" Vieira; 11 May 1999–17 Feb. 2000 Malam Sanhá; 17 Feb. 2000–14 Sept. 2003 Kumba Ialá; 14 Sept. 2003–28 Sept. 2003 Verissimo Seabra (interim); 28 Sept. 2003–24 July 2005 Henrique Rosa (interim); 24 July 2005–João Bernardo "Nino" Vieira. *Principal Commissioners:* 26 Sept. 1973–7 July 1978 Francisco Mendes; 7 July 1978–28 Sept. 1978 Constantino Teixeira (acting); 28 Sept. 1978–14 Nov. 1980 João Bernardo "Nino" Vieira; 14 May 1982–8 March 1984 Victor Saúde María; 27 Dec. 1991–5 Nov. 1994 Carlos Correia; 5 Nov. 1994–26 May 1997 Manuel Saturnino da Costa; 6 June 1997–3 Dec. 1998 Carlos Correia; 3 Dec. 1998–19 Feb. 2000 Francisco Fadul; 19 Feb. 2000–19 March 2001 Caetano N'Tchoma; 21 March 2001–9 Dec. 2001 Faustino Imbali; 9 Dec. 2001–16 Nov. 2002 Alamara Nhassa; 16 Nov. 2002–14 Sept. 2003 Mário Pires; 28 Sept. 2003–10 May 2004 Artur Sanhá; 10 May 2004–Carlos Gomes Júnior. *Note:* Principal Commissioner is the same as Prime Minister. *Note:* In times of no Principal Commissioner, the President or Chairman held that office.

Gumel. 1749–1903. *Location:* Kano Province, Northern Nigeria. *Capital:* Gumel (from 1845); Tumbi (until 1845). *Other names:* Gummel; Laute; Lautaye.

History: The name Gumel comes from "Gubele"—Fulani for a "short-horned cow." Founded as an amirate in 1749 by a Kano native named Dan Juma, with his Mangawa followers. About 1755 it became a tributary state of the Bornu Empire, but was never part of the Fulani Empire. Gumelawa history has been one of wars with Hadejia, Kano, and Damagaram, and in 1903 it became part of the British protectorate of Northern Nigeria.

Amirs: 1749–1754 Dan Juma I (also known as Danyuma); 1754–1760 Adamu Karro; 1760–1777 Dan Juma I (also known as Danyuma); 1777–1804 Maikota (also known as Danmaigatiny Uata, or Tanoma); 1804–1811 Kalgo (also known as Damgalke); 1811–1828 Dan Auwa (also known as Danyawa); 1828–1843 Muhammad (also known as Dan Tanoma); 1843–1850 Cheri; 1850–1852 Muhammar Atu; 1852–1861 Cheri; 1861–1872 Abdullahi; 1872–1896 Abubakr; 1896–1915 Ahmadu; 1915–1944 Mamman na Kota; May 1944–1981 Maina Mamman (also known as Muhammadu); 1981–Ahmad Muhammad Sani.

Gunagwa see **Yauri**

Gurma. 1204–20 Jan. 1895. *Location:* southeast Burkina Faso. *Capital:* Fada N'Gurma (also known as Fada N'Gourma, or Fa'N'Gurma). *Other names:* Fada N'Gourma; Gourma.

History: This was one of the Mossi States, and composed of Gurmanche peoples. Founded in 1204 it was made part of the French protectorate of Upper Volta (see Burkina Faso).

Kings: 1204–1248 Diaba Lompo; 1248–1292 Tidarpo; 1292–1336 Untani; 1336–1380 Banydoba; 1380–1395 Labi Diebo; 1395–ca. 1425 Tenin; ca. 1425–ca. 1470 Tokurma; ca. 1470–ca. 1520 Gima; ca. 1520–ca. 1553 Gori; ca. 1553–1571 Bogora; 1571–1615 Kampadiboaghi; 1615–ca. 1659 Kampadi; ca. 1659–1684 Tantiari; 1684–1709 Lissoangui; 1709–1736 Yendabri; 1736–1761 Yembirima; 1761–1791 Baghama; 1791–1820 Yanghama; 1820–1849 Yenkirma; 1849–1853 Yentiabri; 1853–1856 Yempabu; 1856–1883 Yempadigu; 1883–1892 Yentuguri; 1892–1911 Batchande; 1911–1952 Kambambori; 1952–1 Jan. 1954 [vacant]; 1 Jan. 1954–26 Nov. 1961 Hamtiuri; 26 Nov. 1961–1973 [vacant]; 1973–1975 Tenmiama; 30 May 1975–Yentangu.

Gurmanche see **Gurma**

Gwandara see **Jema'a**

Gwandu. 1808–March 1903. *Location:* in Sokoto Province, in northwestern Nigeria, Gwandu formerly occupied both banks of the Niger River, but now lies only west of the river. *Capital:* Gwandu (named for the Royal farmlands, or "gandu" nearby). *Other names:* Gandu; Gando.

History: In 1808 Uthman Dan Fodio split his Fulani Empire into two amirates, Sokoto and Gwandu. Sokoto was the main Fulani power throughout the 19th century, with Gwandu distinctly the weaker sister. In 1903 Gwandu went the way of the Empire (otherwise known as the Sokoto Caliphate), most of it becoming incorporated into the British protectorate of Northern Nigeria, and other parts being taken by the French. See Fulani Empire for more details.

Amirs: 1808–1828 Abdullahi Dan Fodio; 1828–1833 Muhammar (also known as Muhammad I); 1833–1858 Halilu (also known as Khalil); 1858–1860 Haliru I; 1860–1864 Aliyu; 1864–1868 Abdulkadir; 1868–1868 Almustafa; 1875–1876 Hanuf; 1876–1888 Malik; 1888–

1897 Umaru Bakatara; 1897–1898 Abdullahi Bayero; 1898–May 1903 Bayero Aliyu; May 1903–March 1906 Auhammmadu (also known as Muhammad II); March 1906–March 1915 Haliru II; March 1915–Jan. 1918 Muhammadu Bashiru; Jan. 1918–1938 Usman; 1938–12 Jan. 1954 Yahya; 13 Jan. 1954–(?) Harun; (?)–Mustafa Haruna Jokolo.

Gwari see **Hausa States** and **Lapai**

Gwiriko. 1714–1890. *Location:* in the bend of the Black Volta River, in the Bobo Lands of Burkina Faso. *Capital:* [unknown]. *Other names:* Gouiriko.

History: This Dyula state was an extension of the Watara Empire of Kong, and was founded by Famagan Watara, brother of the founder of Kong. It was taken by the French in 1890, eventually forming part of the protectorate of Upper Volta (see Burkina Faso).

Kings: 1714–1729 Famagan Watara; 1729–1742 Famagan denn Tieba; 1742–1749 Kere Massa; 1749–1809 Magan Oule Watara; 1809–1809 Dramani; 1809–1839 Diori Watara; 1839–1851 Bako Moru Watara; 1851–1854 Laganfiela Moru; 1854–1878 Ali Dian; 1878–1885 Kokoroko Dia; 1885–1892 Sabana; 1892–1897 Tieba Niandane Watara; 1897–1909 Pintieba Watara; 1909–1915 Karamoko.

Habashi see **Axum** and **Ethiopia**

Habe Dynasty see **Daura** and **Gobir** and **Hadejia**

Hadeija see **Hadejia**

Hadejia. ca. 1460–7 April 1906. *Location:* in Kano Province, North-Eastern State, in the north central portion of Nigeria. *Capital:* Hadejia. *Other names:* Hadeija.

History: A small kingdom of uncertain origin, it is said to have been founded by Hadiya, a Kanuri hunter from Manchinna, who heads a list of 32 Habe kings. Only the last three are known by name. For a long time this kingdom was a tributary of Bornu. In 1805, Umaru, the sarkin (king), pledged allegiance to Uthman Dan Fodio, the leader of the Fulani Empire, and in 1808 Umaru's brother, Sambo, joined his country with the petty chiefdoms of Auyo, Garun Gabbas, Gatarwa, Kazura, Fagi, and Dawa to form the amirate of Hadejia. In 1851 the amir Bohari rebelled against the Fulani Empire, and went on a conquering rampage, enlarging his territory considerably. After his death, Hadejia again became part of the Fulani Empire. In 1903 the amirate submitted (nominally, at least) to the British, but in 1906 the amir became openly hostile to the British. In April 1906 the British marched into the capital and took it after five hours of fighting. They installed Haruna as amir, and Hadejia became a part of Kano Province, in the protectorate of Northern Nigeria.

Sarkins (Kings): ca. 1460–(?) [29 unknown sarkins]; (?)–(?) Baude; (?)–(?) Musa; (?)–1805 Abubakr; 1805–1808 Umaru; 1808–1808 Moman Kankia. *Amirs:* 1808–1845 Sambo; 1845–1847 Garko; 1847–1848 Abdulkadiri; 1848–1850 Bohari; 1850–1851 Amadu; 1851–1863 Bohari; 1863–1865 Umaru; 1865–1885 Haru; 1885–1906 Muhammadu; 1906–1909 Haruna; 1909–1925 Abdulkadiri; 1925–1950 Usman; June 1950–1984 Haruna; 1984–11 Sept. 2002 Abubakr Maje Haruna; 14 Sept. 2002–Hamadu Abubakr Maje.

Hadiya see **Hadejia**

Hadrumatum see **Byzacena**

Hafsid Kingdom. 1236–18 Aug. 1534. *Location:* Tunisia, plus the present-day area of Constantine in Algeria, plus Tripolitania in Libya. *Capital:* Tunis. *Other names:* Banu Hafs Dynasty.

History: Named for the founder of the house, Abu Hafs Umar, a Berber chieftain, the kingdom was established in 1236 by his grandson Abu Zakariyya, the Almohad governor of Tunis, who declared himself independent. Its history is one of continual division, reunification, and fighting with the Abd al-Adid Kingdom (see Tlemcen), the Merinid Kingdom and the European powers, and it reached its zenith under al-Mustansir, who made a remarkable peace treaty with the Crusaders, and was left untouched. In 1534 the Corsairs under Barbarossa (Khair ad-Din) took Tunis, and, although the Hafsids continued to rule nominally, their real power was finished from 1534. In 1574 Tunis became a Turkish pashalik.

Sultans: 1236–Oct. 1249 Abu Zakariyya Yahya I; Oct. 1249–17 May 1277 Abu Abdallah Muhammad I al-Mustansir; 17 May 1277–Aug. 1279 Abu Zakariyya Yahya II al-Wathiq; Aug. 1279–28 Jan. 1283 Abu Ishaq Ibrahim I; 28 Jan.

1283–June 1283 Abu Faris (pretender); June 1283–12 July 1284 interregnum; 12 July 1284–4 Nov. 1295 Abu Hafs Umar I; 5 Nov. 1295–18 Aug. 1309 Abu Abdallah Muhammad II Abu Asida; 18 Aug. 1309–4 Sept. 1309 Abu Yahya Abu Bakr ash-Shahid; 4 Sept. 1309–14 Nov. 1311 Abu al-Baqa Khalid I; 14 Nov. 1311–Oct. 1317 Abu Yahya Zakariyya I; Oct. 1317–8 June 1318 Abu Darba; 8 June 1318–19 Oct. 1346 Abu Yahya Abu Bakr; 19 Oct. 1346–15 Sept. 1347 Abu Hafs Umar II; 15 Sept. 1347–10 April 1348 occupied by the Merinids; 10 April 1348–1350 Abu al-Abbas Ahmad al-Fadl; 1350–1357 Abu Ishaq Ibrahim; 1357–1357 occupied by the Merinids; 1357–1369 Abu Ishaq Ibrahim; 1369–9 Nov. 1370 Abu al-Baqa Khalid II; 9 Nov. 1370–4 June 1394 Abu al-Abbas Ahmad; 4 June 1394–18 July 1434 Abu Faris Abd al-Aziz; 18 July 1434–16 Aug. 1434 interregnum; 16 Aug. 1434–16 Sept. 1435 Abu Abdallah Muhammad IV al-Muntasir; 16 Sept. 1435–1488 Abu Amr Uthman; 1488–1489 Abu Zakariyya Yahya II; 1489–13 Oct. 1490 Abd al-Mu'min; 13 Oct. 1490–15 May 1494 Abu Zakariyya Yahya II; 15 May 1494–1526 Abu Abdallah Muhammad V; 1526–1542 Mulay al-Hassan; 1542–Dec. 1569 Ahmad (also known as Hamida); Dec. 1569–1573 interregnum; 1573–13 Sept. 1574 Mulay Muhammad.

Hajji Omar's Empire see **Tukolor Empire**

Halphoolaren see **Tukolor Empire**

Hamaj see **Funj Sultanate**

Hammadid Kingdom. 1014–1152. *Location:* Algeria. *Capital:* al-Qalat (built in 1007, the word means "the fortress"). *Other names:* Banu Hammad Dynasty.

History: In 1014 Hammad ibn Buluggin, a Zirid (see Zirid Kingdom), declared his independence. Reaching a peak of importance at the end of the 11th century, it fell to the Almohad Empire in 1152.

Kings: 1014–1028 Hammad ibn Buluggin; 1028–1055 al-Qa'id; 1055–1055 Muhsin; 1055–1056 interregnum; 1056–1062 Buluggin ibn Muhammad; 1062–1088 an-Nasir ibn Alannas; 1088–1104 al-Mansur ibn an-Nasir; 1104–1104 Badis ibn al-Mansur; 1104–1105 interregnum; 1105–1122 al-Aziz ibn al-Mansur; 1122–1152 Yahya ibn al-Aziz.

Harar. 1526–Jan. 1887. *Location:* east central Ethiopia. *Capital:* Harar (founded in the 7th century, it was the capital from 1526 to 1577, and again from 1647 to 1875). *Other names:* Harer; Hararghe; Harrar.

History: In 1526 Ahmad Gran, the first amir of the Muslim state of Harar, conquered Adal, and took its capital Harar as his own, and named his new state after the town. Sir Richard Burton was the first European visitor (in the 1850s), and another famous visitor was Rimbaud, the French poet. From 1875 to 1885 the city of Harar was occupied by the Turks, and in 1887 the country was conquered by Menelik II of Ethiopia, and Harar became Harar Province, ruled first by Haile Selassie's father, Ras Makonnen, as governor, and then, in the same position, by the future Lion of Judah himself, from 1910.

Sultans: 1526–1543 Ahmad Gran ibn Ibrahim; 1543–1567 Nur ibn Mujahid; 1567–1569 Uthman al-Habashi; 1569–1571 Talha ibn al-Abbas; 1571–1573 Nasir ibn Uthman; 1573–1576 Muhammad ibn Nasir; 1576–1576 Mansur ibn Muhammad; 1576–1583 Muhammad ibn Ibrahim; 1583–1647 unknown rulers in the desert; 1647–1653 Ali ibn Daud; 1653–1671 Hashim; 1671–1700 Abdallah; 1700–1721 Talha; 1721–1732 Abu Bakr; 1732–1733 Khalaf; 1733–1747 Hamid; 1747–1756 Yusuf; 1756–1783 Ahmad ibn Abu Bakr; 1783–1783 Muhammad; 1783–1794 Abd ash-Shakur ibn Yusuf; 1794–1821 Ahmad ibn Muhammad; 1821–1826 Abd ar-Rahman ibn Muhammad; 1826–1834 Abd al-Karim ibn Muhammad; 1834–1852 Abu Bakr ibn Abd al-Mannan; 1852–1856 Ahmad ibn Abu Bakr; 1856–1875 Muhammad ibn Ali; 1875–Jan. 1887 Abdallah ibn Muhammad.

Harper see **Maryland**

Hausa States. Also Hausaland. Terms used interchangeably with, but far more often than, Habe Land, Habash Land, and Hau-Sha Land. The Hausa peoples are, and were, to be found in northern Nigeria and southern Niger. The largest ethnic group in the area, the Hausa formed seven major and seven minor states called, respectively, the Hausa Bakwai and the Banza Bakwai (i.e. the seven true Hausa states, and the seven bastards). The Hausa Bakwai were: Daura, Kano, Zaria, Gobir, Katsina, Rano, and Biram. The Banza Bakwai were: Zamfara, Kebbi, Nupe, Gwari, Yauri, Bauchi, and Kwararafa. The legend has it that Bayajida came from Bagdad to Daura, in what is now Northern Nigeria. His son, Bawo, was the father of six sons who founded the seven original Hausa states. Seven other states were formed out of the lands of non-Hausa peoples. The Hausa states began as pagans, then be-came Muslims. They were virtually all taken over by Uthman Dan Fodio and his Fulani Empire.

Haut-Senegal–Niger see **Mali**

Haute Volta see **Burkina Faso**

Heidelberg see **Transvaal**

Heliopolis see **Egypt**

Hereroland. ca. 1730–21 Oct. 1885. *Location:* in Namibia. *Capital:* no central government. *Other names:* Herreroland.

History: Founded about 1730, the land of the Hereros was made part of German South West Africa (see Namibia) in 1885. There was a major Herero rebellion in 1904, in which the Germans decimated the Hereros.

Chiefs: ca. 1730–(?) [unknown]; (?)–1861 Tjamuaha. *Paramount Chiefs:* 1861–1890 Maherero; 1890–1917 Samuel Maherero; 1917–1970 Hosea Kutako.

Hierro see **Canary Islands**

Himba see **Namibia**

Hogbonu see **Benin**

Hollandia. May 1682–1720. *Location:* Gold Coast. *Capital:* Gross-Friedrichsburg (founded 1683). *Other names:* Gross-Friedrichsburg; Prussian Gold Coast Settlements (1701–1720); Brandenburger Gold Coast Settlements (1682–1701).

History: In 1682 the Brandenburg Electorate (later Prussia) founded settlements along the coast of what is today the Republic of Ghana. In 1701, when Brandenburg became the nucleus of the Kingdom of Prussia, these settlements officially became Prussian settlements. Fort Dorothea (Accada) was their secondary fort. After 1716 these settlements were effectively abandoned, and in 1720 sold to the Dutch (see Dutch Gold Coast Settlements).

Governors: May 1682–1683 Philip Bloncq;

1683–1684 Nathaniel Dillinger; 1684–1686 Karl von Schnitter; 1686–1691 Johann Niemann; 1691–1693 Johann Tenhoof; 1693–1695 Jakob Tenhoof; 1695–1697 Gijsbrecht Van Hoogveldt; 1697–1699 Jan Van Laar; 1699–1701 Jan de Visser; 1701–1704 Adriaan Grobbe; 1704–1706 Johann Münz; 1706–1709 Heinrich Lamy; 1709–1710 Frans de Lange; 1710–1716 Nicolas Dubois; 1716–1716 Anton Van Der Meden; 1716–1720 the settlements were abandoned by the Prussians.

Hottentots see **Cape Colony** and **Namibia**

Hottentot Hollandia see **Cape Colony**

Houeda see **Whydah**

Hova see **Diego Suarez** and **Madagascar**

Huti see **Burundi [i]** and **Burundi [ii]** and **Ruanda** and **Rwanda**

Hyksos see **Egypt**

Ibadan. ca. 1750–1893. *Location:* Western State, Nigeria, just over 100 miles northeast of Lagos. *Capital:* Ibadan (the name "Eba Odan" means "near the savannah," and the town was originally the war capital of the Yoruba peoples).

History: Founded about 1750 by Yoruba refugees from all over what is now western Nigeria, Ibadan in 1829 became the leading city of the area. There was never a hereditary ruler of Ibadan — it was ruled by a rule-of-the-fittest system. In 1893 it became part of the Niger River Delta Protectorate (see Northern Nigeria). It was one of the largest cities in Africa.

Chiefs: ca. 1750–(?) Maye; (?)–(?) Laborinde; (?)–(?) Lakanle I; (?)–(?) Olyedun; (?)–(?) Lakanle II; (?)–(?) Ohuyole; (?)–1855 Opeagbe; 1855–ca. 1866 Olugboda; ca. 1866–ca. 1870 Ogunmola; ca. 1870–ca. 1872 Oruwusi; ca. 1872–(?) Latosisa; (?)–ca. 1892 [vacant]; ca. 1892–1893 Fijabi.

Ibani see **Bonny**

Ibea see **Kenya**

Icosium see **Algiers**

Idah see **Igala**

Iddo Island see **Lagos**

Idrisid State. 6 Feb. 789–974. *Location:* northern Morocco and northwest Algeria. *Capital:* Hajar an-Nasr (937–974); Fez (this town was founded between 790 and 808, and was the Idrisid capital from 807 to 927); Walila (until 807).

History: Founded by Idris, a descendant of Ali, as a state free from the persecution of the Abbasids. It became a group of principalities after 828, all of these principalities answerable to the King. In 920 the Idrisid capital, Fez, was taken by the Fatimids, to be won back by the Idrisids in 925. Just over a year later the king was defeated by rival Berber tribes, and was killed. The Fatimids ruled Fez again, and then in 937 the Idrisids came to power for the third time, this time with a new capital. By 974 the Abbasids were ruling there.

Kings: 6 Feb. 789–June 791 Idris I ibn Abdallah; June 791–Sept. 828 Idris II (also known as Mulay Idris II); Sept. 828–April 836 Muhammad al-Mustansir; April 836–Feb. 849 Ali I; Feb. 849–863 Yahya I; 863–866 Yahya II; 866–880 Ali II ibn Umar; 880–905 Ali III al-Miqdam; 905–920 Yahya IV; 920–925 Fatimid rule; 925–927 Hassan al-Hajjam; 927–937 Fatimid rule; 937–948 al-Qasim Gannum; 948–954 Abu'l Aish Ahmad; 954–974 Hassan II.

Idu Aysh see **Tagant**

Idutywa. Aug. 1858–Dec. 1864. *Location:* British Kaffraria, Southern Africa. *Capital:* Idutywa. *Other names:* Idutywa Reserve.

History: Formed as a dependency of the Crown Colony of British Kaffraria, it was composed of Bantu fragments of Umhala's clan. In 1864 it merged into British Kaffraria, and later became part of the Transkei District of the Transkeian Territories. The bulk of the inhabitants are Fingo (see Fingoland).

Special Magistrates: Aug. 1858–Sept. 1858 John Gawler; Sept. 1858–May 1860 George Colley; May 1860–Sept. 1861 W.G.B. Shepstone; Sept. 1861–Dec. 1864 William B. Chalmers.

Ifat. 1285–1415. *Location:* eastern Shoa, on the Ethiopia–Somalia border. *Capital:* Goncho. *Other names:* Awfat.

History: In 1285 the first Walashma sultan created the state of Ifat by conquering the states of Fatajar, Dawaro, and Bali, as well as Adal. A Muslim state, it continually revolted against Ethiopia until, in 1415, it became part of Ethiopia, as Adal.

Sultans: 1285–ca. 1304 Umar ibn Dunyahuz; ca. 1304–ca. 1321 Jaziwi; ca. 1321–ca. 1328 Haqq ad-Din I; ca. 1328–ca. 1330 Hussein; ca. 1330–ca. 1331 Nasir; ca. 1331–ca. 1335 al-Mansur I; ca. 1335–ca. 1337 Jamal ad-Din I; ca. 1337–ca. 1343 Abut; ca. 1343–ca. 1344 Zubair. *Queens:* ca. 1344–ca. 1352 Ma'at Laila. *Sultans:* ca. 1352–ca. 1354 Sabr ad-Din I; ca. 1354–ca. 1360 Qat-Ali; ca. 1360–ca. 1366 Harbi Ar'ed; ca. 1366–ca. 1373 Haqq ad-Din II; ca. 1373–1415 Sa'd ad-Din Ahmad.

Ife. ca. 1000–1900. *Location:* 50 miles east of Ibadan, in Oyo Province, Western State, in southwestern Nigeria. *Capital:* Ife (formerly called Ile-Ife, it is one of the oldest Yoruba towns). *Other names:* Ile-Ife.

History: Traditionally founded by one of the sons of the Yoruba god Oduduwa, and said to be where mankind began, Ife is one of the oldest Yoruba towns (cf. Ijebu). It is held by them to be a sacred city, in fact their chief religious center. Ife did not become subject to the Fulani Empire, but the slave trade wars of the 1820s and 1830s weakened it. In 1900 it became part of the Niger River Delta Protectorate (see Northern Nigeria).

Only known Onis (Kings): ca. 1300 Adimu; (?)–1930 Adesoji; 25 Sept. 1930–7 July 1980 Aderemi Adesoji; Nov. 1980–Okunade Adele Sijuwade Olubuse.

Ifni. 1860–4 Jan. 1969. *Location:* a Spanish enclave on the coast of southern Morocco. It had a coastline of 50 miles and extended only 15 miles inland. *Capital:* Sidi Ifni (from 1912. The name "Ifni" means "rocky desert").

History: The Spanish had once occupied Santa Cruz de la Mar Pequeña on the Moroccan coast, and using this as their precedent persuaded the Sultan of Morocco to give them Ifni. They did not occupy it, however, and on 27 Nov. 1912 they made Ifni a Spanish protectorate. In 1934 Spanish troops finally occupied it, and in 1952 it became a territory of Spanish West Africa (see Western Sahara). On 14 Jan. 1958 it became a separate Spanish province, and on 4 Jan. 1969 was given back to Morocco.

Rulers: 1860–1934 no central administration. *Administrators:* 1934–1952 [unknown, if any]. *Rulers:* 1952–1956 ruled direct by Governor-General of Spanish Morocco. *Administrators:* 1956–14 Jan. 1958 [unknown]. *Governors:* 14 Jan. 1958–1959 Mariano Quirce; 1959–1961 Pedro Alcubierre; 1961–1963 Joaquín Coronado; 1963–1965 Adolfo Campos; 1965–1967 Marino Larrasquito; 1967–4 Jan. 1969 José Rodríguez.

Ifrikiyah see **Aghlabid Empire**, **Arab North Africa**, and **Omayyad and Abbasid North Africa**

Igala. ca. 1525–1901. *Location:* in Kabba Province, in north central Nigeria. *Capital:* Idah. *Other names:* Idah.

History: The Igala (or Igara) people grew up around the present-day town of Idah, which they founded as their capital at the beginning of the 16th century. In 1901 the country became part of the British protectorate of Northern Nigeria.

Kings: ca. 1525–(?) Abutu Eje; (?)–(?) Ebelejonu; (?)–ca. 1600 Agenapoje; ca. 1600–(?) Idoko; (?)–(?) Ayagba; (?)–(?) Akogu; (?)–ca. 1700 Ocholi; ca. 1700–(?) Agada; (?)–(?) Amacho; (?)–(?) Itodo; (?)–ca. 1800 Ogalla; ca. 1800–(?) Idoko Adegbe; (?)–(?) Onuche; (?)–1835 Ekalaga; 1835–1856 Amocheje; 1856–1870 Aku Odiba; 1870–1876 Okoliko; 1876–1900 Amaga; 1900–1903 Ocheje Onokpa; 1903–1905 [vacant]; 1905–1911 Oboni; 1911–1919 Oguche Akpa; 1919–1926 Atabor; 1926–1945 Obaje Ocheje; 1945–23 June 1956 Ame; 20 Oct. 1956–Alii.

Ijebu. (?)–20 May 1892. *Location:* western Nigeria. *Capital:* Ijebu-Ode. *Other names:* Jebu.

History: Traditionally founded by one of the sons of Oduduwa, a Yoruba god, Ijebu was the main go-between for centuries for the Lagos area and its trade with the Yoruba country. The Ijebu are a division of the Yoruba. In 1892 Ijebu became part of the Niger River Delta Protectorate (see Northern Nigeria).

Only known Kings: ca. 1892–(?) Gbelegbura I; (?)–(?) Ogbagba I; Sept. 1933–1959 Daniel Adesanya Gbelegbura II; 1959–Sikiru Adetona Ogbagba II.

Ikhshid Egypt see **Egypt**

Ikum Island see **Yauri**

.

Île Bonaparte see **Réunion**

Île de Bourbon see **Réunion**

Île de France see **Mauritius**

Île de Labourdonnais see **Seychelles**

Ile-Ife see **Ife**

Ilha do Cerne see **Mauritius**

Ilorin. ca. 1780–5 March 1897. *Location:* Northern Nigeria. *Capital:* Ilorin (founded about 1785, the name probably means "town of the elephant"). *Other names:* Illorin; Yoruba.

History: Ilorin, founded by Yoruba peoples toward the end of the 18th century, was a Yoruba vassal state of Oyo. In 1810 the Fulani Empire conquered Ilorin, and placed a kakanfo (military commander) named Afonja in power there. In 1817 Afonja proclaimed the independence of Ilorin, and in this he was assisted by a Fulani from Sokoto named Mallam Alimi. In 1829 Alimi's son, Abd as-Salami, became the first amir of Ilorin. In 1897 the amirate of Ilorin became part of the Niger River Delta Protectorate (see Northern Nigeria), and in 1900 became the only part of Yorubaland to fall under the British protectorate of Northern Nigeria.

Kings: ca. 1780–1810 [unknown]. *Kakanfos (Fulani Military Commanders):* 1810–1817 Afonja. *Independent rulers:* 1817–1818 Afonja; 1818–1829 Mallam Alimi ibn Zubeiru. *Amirs:* 1829–1842 Abd as-Salami; 1842–1860 Shi'ta; 1860–1868 Zubeiru; 1868–1891 Shi'ta Aliyu; 1891–1895 Moma; 1895–14 Jan. 1915 Suleimanu; 1915–Nov. 1919 Shu'aibu (also known as Bawa); 17 Feb. 1920–June 1959 Abd al-Kadiri; 30 June 1959–1991 Zulkarnayni Gambari.; 1992–Aug. 1994 Malam; 1995–Ibrahim Sulu Gambari.

Imerina see **Madagascar**

Imo State see **Biafra**

Inaccessible Island see **Tristan da Cunha**

Ingwavuma see **Tongaland**

Inkil see **Bauchi**

International Association of the Congo see **Congo (Zaire)**

Issas see **Djibouti**

Italian East Africa. 9 May 1936–5 May 1941. *Location:* Ethiopia, Italian Somaliland and Eritrea. *Capital:* Addis Ababa.

History: Early in 1935 a dispute had arisen between the Italians in Somaliland (see Italian Somaliland) and the Ethiopians over a trifling incident concerning ownership of wells at Walwal, on the border of Italian Somaliland and Ethiopia. This was merely an excuse for Italian expansion, and on 3 Oct. 1935 Italy invaded Ethiopia (or Abissinia, as they called it), and by 1936 had conquered the entire Ethiopian Empire. Haile Selassie, the Ethiopian emperor, escaped to Switzerland via Djibouti and Jerusalem. Together with their existing Italian Crown Colony of Southern Somaliland (also known as Italian Somaliland) and their colony of Eritrea, the invaders created Italian East Africa. Ethiopia was divided into four provinces—Amhara, Galla and Sidama, Harar, and Shoa. Vittorio Emanuele, the Italian king, ruled through his viceroys. Haile Selassie, in exile and pleading for League of Nations support, was astonished to find that that league supported Italy. Haile Selassie then moved to England. The Italians built roads and undertook other major improvements, but armed resistance began in Ethiopia against them. Ras Imru was the first major resistance leader, and a failed attempt to assassinate Italian viceroy Marshal Graziani in Feb. 1937 was followed by heavy reprisals against the patriots. It was not until Italy declared war on the Allies during World War II that things changed for Haile Selassie, who now moved to Khartoum to muster anti-Italian forces. On 26 Sept. 1941 the British took Italian Somaliland, and placed a governor in charge. This marked the real end of Italian rule in East Africa. In May 1941, with British assistance (notably in the form of an officer named Orde Wingate), Haile Selassie regained control of his country, which now became the Ethiopian Empire again, and Eritrea fell to the British. In Feb. 1947 Italy formally renounced any claim on Ethiopia.

Emperors: 9 May 1936–5 May 1941 Vittorio Emanuele II of Italy. *High Commissioners:* 3 Oct. 1935–27 Nov. 1935 Emilio De Bono; 27 Nov. 1935–22 May 1936 Pietro Badoglio. *Governors-General:* 22 May 1936–21 May 1937 Rodolfo Graziani; 21 Dec. 1937–5 May 1941 Duca D'Aosta.

Italian Somaliland. 3 Aug. 1889–1 July 1960. *Location:* northeast Africa. *Capital:* Mogadiscio (also known as Mogadishu). *Other names:* Somaliland Italian Trusteeship (1949–1960); Southern Somaliland (1905–1941); Benadir Coast Protectorate, or Italian Benadir (1889–1905).

History: In 1889 Italy acquired this stretch of the coast of what is today Somalia, and they called it the Benadir Coast Protectorate, but it was not administered by them until 15 May 1893, when the Filonardi Company took it over. In 1896 the Italian government took it over again, and it was run by a Royal Commission until 25 May 1898, when the Milanese Commercial Society took it over. This society also was known as the Benadir Company, and had been founded by Antonio Cecchi (killed in 1896). On 16 March 1905 the Benadir Coast Protectorate became an Italian colony known as Italian Somaliland or Southern Somaliland, and in July 1910 it became a crown colony. In 1926 Jubaland became part of this colony, and in 1935 the country itself became part of Italian East Africa. When that conglomerate fell apart at the hands of the British on 26 Feb. 1941 the British placed a governor in charge. This marked the end of real Italian rule in East Africa. On 21 Nov. 1949 (effective 1 April 1950) the British gave the country back to Italy on a U.N. trusteeship basis, and the country became known as Somalia. Because the land was so bleak of prospect, this was looked on as a punishment. Thus, Italy regained control of its former colony, but only because no one else wanted it. On 1 July 1960 this United Nations trust territory became independent and joined the neighboring newly founded state of Somalia (formerly British Somaliland), to form Somalia as we know it today.

Rulers: 3 Aug. 1889–15 May 1893 none. *Governors:* 15 May 1893–1896 Vincenzo Filonardi. *Royal Commissioners:* 1896–1897 Vincenzo Filonardi; 1897–1897 Ernesto Dulio; 1897–25 May 1898 Giorgio Sorrentino. *Governors:* 25 May 1898–16 March 1905 Ernesto Dulio. *Royal Commissioners-General:* 16 March 1905–1906 Luigi Mercatelli. *Vice Commissioners-General:* 1906–1906 Alessandro Sapelli (acting). *Governors:* 1906–1907 Giovanni Cerrina-Ferroni (acting). *Royal Civil Commissioners:* 1907–1908 Tommaso Carletti. *Governors:* 1908–1908 Tommaso Carletti; 1908–July 1910 Gino Macchioro (acting); July 1910–1916 Giacomo Di Martino;

1916–21 June 1920 Giovanni Cerrina-Ferroni; 21 June 1920–8 Dec. 1923 Carlo Ricci; 8 Dec. 1923–1 June 1928 Cesare De Val Cismon; 1 June 1928–1 July 1931 Guido Corni; 1 July 1931–7 March 1935 Maurizio Rava; 7 March 1935–22 May 1936 Rodolfo Graziani; 22 May 1936–24 May 1936 Angelo De Rubeis (acting); 24 May 1936–15 Dec. 1937 Ruggero Santi; 15 Dec. 1937–11 June 1940 Francesco Saverio Caroselli; 11 June 1940–31 Dec. 1940 Gustavo Pesenti; 31 Dec. 1940–9 March 1941 Carlo De Simone. *British Military Administration Governors:* 26 Feb. 1941–1941 Reginald H. Smith; 1941–1943 William E.H. Scupham; 1943–1948 Dennis Wickham; 1948–1948 Eric Vully de Candole; 1948–21 Nov. 1949 Geoffrey Gamble. *Administrators:* 21 Nov. 1949–1953 Giovanni Fornari; 1953–1955 Enrico Martino; 1955–1958 Enrico Anzilotti; 1958–1 July 1960 Mario Di Stefani. *Prime Ministers:* 29 Feb. 1956–1 July 1960 Abdullahi Issa Muhammad.

Itebu see **Brass**

Itsekiri see **Warri**

Ivory Coast see **Côte d'Ivoire**

Ivory Coast–Gabon see **Ivory Coast**, and **Gabon**

Jama'are see **Jemaari**

James Fort see **Fort James**

James Island see **Senegambia Colony**

Jebu see **Ijebu**

Jema'a. 1810–1902. *Location:* Zaria Province, North-Central State, in central Nigeria. *Capital:* Kafanchan (from 1933) Jema'an Sarari (1926–1933); Jema'an Darroro (the capital from 1810 to 1926. The name means "disciples of a holy man of Darroro").

History: In 1810 Mallam Uthman, a Fulani priest who had gathered together a mass of his people exiled from Kajuru, established Jema'a as a vassal state of Zaria. Uthman and his son Musa enlarged the amirate by conquering the Gwandara, Kagoro, Kaje, Kagoma, Mora, and Ayu peoples, but continued to pay tribute to Zaria until 1902, when it became part of Nasarawa

Province of the British protectorate of Northern Nigeria.

Amirs: 1810–1833 Mallam Uthman; 1833–1837 Abdullahi; 1837–1846 Musa. *Regents:* 1846–1849 Abdarrahman (also known as Atona). *Amirs:* 1849–1850 Musa; 1850–1869 Adamu; 1869–1881 Muhammadu Adda; 1881–1911 Abdullahi (also known as Machu); 1911–1915 Muhammadu; 1915–Nov. 1926 Abdullahi; March 1927–1960 Muhammadu ibn Muhammadu; 1960–1961 [ruled by regents]; 1961–Nov. 1998 Isa dan Muhammadu; May 1999–Muhammadu dan Isa.

Jemaari. 1811–Oct. 1903. *Location:* in Bauchi Province, North-Eastern State, in the north-central portion of Nigeria. *Capital:* Jemaari (founded 1811). *Other names:* Jama'are; Jamaari.

History: Jemaari was founded in 1811 by Hama Wabi, a Fulani flag-bearer (one of the leaders of the Fulani jihad, or holy war). In 1903 it became part of the British protectorate of Northern Nigeria. It was, and is, Nigeria's smallest amirate, and was at first (1903) made part of the Katagum Division of Kano Province, but was transferred to Bauchi Province in 1926.

Amirs: 1811–1824 Hama Wabi I (also known as Muhammadu Wabi I); 1824–1854 Sambolei; 1854–1861 Muhammadu Maudo; 1861–1885 Sambo Gabaima; 1885–11 Jan. 1918 Mohama Wabi II; 4 March 1918–1928 Muhammadu Goji Yerima; 1928–1975 Muhammadu Wabi III; 1975–Muhammadu Wabi IV.

Jibuti see **Djibouti**

Joanna see **Anjouan**

Jolof see **Dyolof**

Juan de Nova Island. *Location:* a French island, occupying 4 sq km, between Madagascar and Mozambique. A wildlife sanctuary, no people live there, and it is claimed by Madagascar. *Other names:* Île Juan de Nova.

Rulers: Administered by a French commissioner resident in Réunion.

Jubaland (i). 15 July 1924–1 July 1926. *Location:* Lower Juba Province, at the extreme south of Somalia, on the border with Kenya. *Capital:* Kismayu (known by the Italians as Chisimaio). *Other names:* Giuba Land; Giuba; Juba; Oltre Giuba.

History: This small area of land, south of the Juba River (Somalia's principal river), was held by the Imperial British East Africa Company until 1 July 1895, when it became part of the British East Africa Protectorate (see Kenya). In 1924 most of Jubaland (with its key port of Kismayu) was ceded by Kenya Colony and Protectorate to Italy. In 1926 it became part of the Italian Crown Colony of Southern Somaliland (see Italian Somaliland).

High Commissioners/Governors: 15 July 1924–1 July 1926 Corrado Zoli.

Jubaland (ii). 3 Sept. 1998–18 June 2001 . *Location:* Somalia. *Capital:* Kismayo. *History:* This is one of the four self-proclaimed states to break away from the troubled Somali government. It was set up by the Somali Patriotic Movement and the Dogil and Rahanwein clans. In 1999 the leader was ousted by the Allied Somali Forces, and in 2001 the Juba Valley Alliance (formerly the Allied Somali Forces) set up a new administration supporting the central Somali government. This effectively put an end to the fledgling state. *Rulers:* 3 Sept. 1998–11 June 1999 Muhammad Siyad Hersi Morgan.

Juda see **Whydah**

Juffure see **Fort James**

Jukun see **Kororofa** and **Muri**

Kaarta. ca. 1610–1870. *Location:* in Mauritania. *Capital:* Kaarta. *Other names:* Bambara Kingdom of Kaarta; Beledugu.

History: For the founding of Kaarta in about 1610, see Segu. In 1870 Kaarta was taken over by the Tukolor Empire.

Kings: ca. 1610–1640 Nya Ngolo; 1640–1670 Sounsan (also known as Sunsa); 1670–1690 Massa; 1690–1700 Sekolo (also known as Bemfa); 1700–1709 Foro-Kolo (also known as Fulakoro); 1709–1760 Seba-Mana (also known as Sebe); 1760–1780 Deni ba Bo (also known as Denibabo); 1780–1789 Sira Bo (also known as Sirabo); 1789–1802 Desse-Koro (also known as Dase); 1802–1811 Nntin Koro (also known as Tegenkoro); 1811–1815 Sara-ba (also known as Sekuba); 1815–1818 Moussa Koura Bo (also known as Musa Kurabo); 1818–1833 Bodyan Mori Ba (also known as Bodian Moriba); 1833–1835 period of anarchy; 1835–1844 Nyaralen

Gran (also known as Garan); 1844–1854 Ma-marikan-dyan (also known as Kandia Mamadi); 1854–1870 Diringa Mori; 1870–1870 Bussei.

Kabyle Algiers see **Algiers** and **Constantine**

Kacinna see **Katsina**

Kaffa see **Ethiopia**

Kaffraria Proper see **Transkeian Territories**

Kagoma see **Jema'a**

Kagoro see **Jema'a**

Kaje see **Jema'a**

Kajuru see **Jema'a**

Kalabari see **New Calabar**

Kalahari see **Namibia**

Kalundwe see **Luba Empire**

Kamerun. 12 July 1884–4 March 1916. *Location:* as the present-day Republic of Cameroun, but with some boundary differences, for example, after 1912 it included a large piece of Moyen-Congo. *Capital:* Douala (1914–1916); Buea (1884–1914). *Other names:* Cameroun French-British Condominium (1914–1916); German Cameroons Protectorate, or Cameroun German Protectorate (alternative names from 1900 to 1916); German Crown Land of North West Africa, or Crown Land of North West Africa (1884–1900).

History: In 1884 the German flag was hoisted in what is now Cameroun. Various protectorates (e.g. Ambas Bay, on 19 July 1884) followed until the German lands covered a vast area. On 1 Jan. 1900 the name of the German Crown Lands of North West Africa changed to Kamerun. On 26 Sept. 1914 the British and French captured most of this huge country and ruled it jointly as a military condominium, even though technically the Germans did not formally surrender their protectorate until 18 Feb. 1916. On 4 March 1916 this country was split into two — French Cameroun Territory (see Cameroun) and British Cameroons Territory (see Cameroons).

Reichskommissars: 12 July 1884–19 July 1884

Gustav Nachtigal; 19 July 1884–1 April 1885 Max Buchner (acting); 1 April 1885–3 July 1885 Eduard von Knorr (acting). *Governors:* 3 July 1885–13 May 1887 Julius von Soden; 13 May 1887–4 Oct. 1887 Jesko von Puttkamer (acting); 4 Oct. 1887–17 Jan. 1888 Eugen von Zimmerer; 17 Jan. 1888–26 Dec. 1889 Julius von Soden; 26 Dec. 1889–17 April 1890 Eugen von Zimmerer (acting); 17 April 1890–3 Aug. 1890 Markus Graf Pfeil; 3 Aug. 1890–14 Aug. 1890 Herr Kurz (acting); 14 Aug. 1890–2 Dec. 1890 Jesko von Puttkamer (acting); 2 Dec. 1890–7 Aug. 1891 Herr Leist (acting); 7 Aug. 1891–5 Jan. 1892 Bruno von Schuckmann (acting); 5 Jan. 1892–27 June 1893 Eugen von Zimmerer (acting); 27 June 1893–24 Feb. 1894 Herr Leist (acting); 24 Feb. 1894–31 Dec. 1894 Eugen von Zimmerer (acting); 1 Jan. 1895–28 March 1895 Jesko von Puttkamer (acting); 27 March 1895–4 May 1895 Herr von Lücke (acting); 5 May 1895–26 Oct. 1895 Jesko von Puttkamer (acting); 27 Oct. 1895–Sept. 1896 Theodor Seitz (acting); Sept. 1896–15 Aug. 1897 Jesko von Puttkamer (acting); 15 Aug. 1897–10 Sept. 1897 Theodor Seitz (acting); 11 Sept. 1897–12 Jan. 1898 Jesko von Puttkamer (acting); 12 Jan. 1898–13 Oct. 1898 Theodor Seitz (acting); 14 Oct. 1898–17 Jan. 1900 Jesko von Puttkamer (acting); 17 Jan. 1900–31 July 1900 August Köhler (acting); 1 Aug. 1900–6 Sept. 1900 Herr Diehl (acting); 6 Sept. 1900–15 Nov. 1900 Herr von Kamptz (acting); 16 Nov. 1900–3 Feb. 1902 Jesko von Puttkamer (acting); 3 Feb. 1902–5 Oct. 1902 Herr Plehn (acting); 9 Oct. 1902–9 May 1904 Jesko von Puttkamer (acting); 9 May 1904–8 Nov. 1904 Karl Ebermaier (acting); 9 Nov. 1904–31 Jan. 1905 Otto Gleim (acting); 31 Jan. 1905–6 Jan. 1906 Jesko von Puttkamer (acting); 6 Jan. 1906–Nov. 1906 Herr Oberst Müller (acting); Nov. 1906–1 July 1907 Otto Gleim (acting); 1 July 1907–10 Feb. 1909 Theodor Seitz; 10 Feb. 1909–Oct. 1909 Herr Hansen (acting); Oct. 1909–27 Aug. 1910 Theodor Seitz; 27 Aug. 1910–Sept. 1910 Herr Steinhausen (acting); Sept. 1910–25 Oct. 1910 Herr Hansen (acting); 25 Oct. 1910–Oct. 1911 Otto Gleim; Oct. 1911–29 March 1912 Herr Hansen (acting); 29 March 1912–9 Oct. 1913 Karl Ebermaier; 9 Oct. 1913–1914 Herr Full (acting); 1914–18 Feb. 1916 Karl Ebermaier. *French/British Military Commanders:* 26 Sept. 1914–7 April 1915 Joseph Aymerich. *French/British Administrators:* 7 April 1915–4 March 1916 Joseph Aymerich.

Kanama see **Eritrea**

Kanem. 784–ca. 1260. *Location:* north and east of Lake Chad, in Chad. *Capital:* Njimi; Kawar (the first capital). *Other names:* Canem.

History: Originally the Zaghawa Kingdom prevailed around the area of Lake Chad. One tribal division, the Beni Saif (or Sefawa), under their leader Dugu (son of Ibrahim, son of Sebu, son of Aisa), founded Kanem on the east side of the lake, about 784. Humé became a Muslim in 1086. With a key position in Sahara trade, Kanem flourished and expanded. By the turn of the 13th century it was becoming universally known, and the Kanuri people of Kanem were expanding into Bornu. Kanem reached its peak at this time, when it really became known as Kanem–Bornu (see Bornu). Old Kanem relapsed into a rebellious state under the Bulala, a tribe who had been there for centuries. They captured the capital, Njimi, and plagued the new Kanem-Bornu Empire for a long time thereafter. *Mais (Kings):* 784–835 Dugu; 835–893 Fune; 893–942 Arju (also known as Aritse); 942–961 Katuri; 961–1019 Boyoma (also known as Adyoma); 1019–1035 Bulu; 1035–1077 Argi; 1077–1081 Shuwa; 1081–1085 Jil; 1085–1097 Humé ibn Abd al-Jalil; 1097–1150 Dunama I ibn Humé; 1150–1176 Biri I; 1176–1194 Bikorom (also known as Dala, or Abdallah I); 1194–1221 Abd al-Jalil (also known as Jilim); 1221–1259 Dunama Dibbelemi; 1259–1260 Kade.

Kanem-Bornu see **Bornu Empire**

Kangaba. ca. 1050–ca. 1237. *Location:* on the Niger River, in present-day Mali. *Capital:* Kangaba (1200–1237); Dodu (1090–1200); Kiki (1050–1090). *Other names:* Kingdom of Mali.

History: Reckoned to have been founded around 1050 by Mandingo tribesmen, as the successor to an older Kangaba country in the same area. It was a vassal state of the Ghana Empire. In 1237 its king, Sundiata Keita, revolted against Ghana, and by 1240 had brought to extinction the Ghana Empire. About this time marks the end of the Ghana Empire, and of the kingdom of Kangaba, and the beginning of the successor to both of them — the Mali Empire.

Kings: ca. 1050–ca. 1090 Taraore; ca. 1090–ca. 1150 Baraonendana; ca. 1150–ca. 1190 Hamama; ca. 1190–ca. 1200 Di Jigi Bilali; ca. 1200–ca. 1218 Keita Nari fa Majan; ca. 1218–1228 Danagaram Tumo; 1228–1230 Soninke rule; 1230–ca. 1237 Mari Jata I (also known as Sundiata Keita).

KaNgwane. April 1981–27 April 1994. *Location:* on the Transvaal–Swaziland border, in Southern Africa. *Capital:* Nyamasane. *Other names:* Swazi; Swazi Territory.

History: The National State of KaNgwane was a Bantustan (or native homeland) allowed for the Swazis by the South African government (the Ngwani were the race from which the Swazi came). The dominant political figure, Enos Mabuza, was made chief councillor on 8 Oct. 1977, and the country was given a legislative assembly in 1978, and self-government in 1981. The country was threatened with a merger with the kingdom of Swaziland in June 1982, but the Supreme Court overruled South Africa's decision to effect this. In 1994, with the coming of black power to South Africa, the need for bantustans disappeared.

Chief Executive Councillor: April 1981–18 June 1982 Enos Mabuza. *Administrator:* 18 June 1982–9 Dec. 1982 N.J. Badenhorst. *Chief Executive Councillor:* 9 Dec. 1982–Aug. 1984 Enos Mabuza. *Chief Ministers:* Aug. 1984–1 April 1991 Enos Mabuza; 15 April 1991–26 April 1994 Manqisi Zitha.

Kaniok see **Luba Empire**

Kano. (?)–3 Feb. 1903. *Location:* around the present-day town of Kano, midway between the Niger River and Lake Chad, in Northern Nigeria. *Capital:* Kano (from about 1100); Sheme (from about 998 to ca. 1100) Dala Hill (until ca. 998. It is now a section of Kano City, it was founded by a chief named Dala, who came here from origins unknown).

History: The original settlement of Kano belonged to an early, semi-mythical race of people based around Dala Hill. Kano was named for an early inhabitant, a Gaiya smith named Kano. In Dec. 998 the country was conquered by the Habe people from the East, who formed the kingdom of Kano. Bagauda was their first king. He was one of the grandsons of Bayajidda, the legendary ancestor of the Hausa peoples, and Bagauda formed Kano as one of the seven true Hausa states (see Hausa States). Islam was introduced in the 1340s. The history of the kingdom is one of constant warfare with Katsina, its prin-

cipal rival, and of subjugation to the other kingdoms or empires of the day, most notably Bornu,
Zazzau and the Songhai Empire. In March 1807
the Fulani Empire conquered the kingdom of
Kano, and an amirate was set up. In 1903 Col.
Morland, at the head of a British force, captured
the town of Kano, and installed a new amir. The
amirate became Kano Province within the protectorate of Northern Nigeria. In 1968 this province became Kano State, within the country of
Nigeria (a case similar to, say, California vis a vis
the USA).

Chiefs: (?)–(?) Dala; (?)–(?) Garageje; (?)–(?)
[unknown]; (?)–(?) Buzame; (?)–(?) Barbushe;
(?)–(?) [unknown]; (?)–Dec. 998 Jankare. *Sarkis
Kano (Kings of Kano):* Dec. 998–Jan. 1063
Bagauda (also known as Yakano); Jan. 1063–Jan.
1095 Warisis; Jan. 1095–Nov. 1133 Gajemasu;
Nov. 1133–Oct. 1135 Nawata and Gawata
(jointly); Oct. 1135–Dec. 1193 Yusa (also known
as Tsaraki); Dec. 1193–May 1247 Naguji; May
1247–Jan. 1290 Gujjua; Jan. 1290–July 1306
Shekkarau; July 1306–June 1342 Tsamia (also
known as Barandamasu); June 1342–March 1349
Osumanu (also known as Zamnagawa); March
1349–Feb. 1385 Yaji I; Feb. 1385–Dec. 1389
Bugaya; Dec. 1389–May 1409 Kanajeji; May
1409–Jan. 1421 Umaru; Jan. 1421–Jan. 1437
Dauda; Jan. 1437–Jan. 1452 Abdullahi Burja;
Jan. 1452–Jan. 1452 Dakauta (one night); Jan.
1452–Feb. 1452 Atuma; Feb. 1452–Sept. 1462
Yakubu; Sept. 1462–Aug. 1498 Muhamman
Rumfa; Aug. 1498–May 1508 Abdullahi; May
1508–Aug. 1564 Muhamman Kisoki; Aug.
1564–Jan. 1565 Yakufu; Jan. 1565–March 1565
Dauda Abasama I; March 1565–May 1572
Abubakr Kado; May 1572–Jan. 1582 Muham-
man Shashere; Jan. 1582–Dec. 1617 Muhamman
Zaki; Dec. 1617–Nov. 1622 Muhamma Nazaki;
Nov. 1622–Jan. 1648 Kutumbi; Jan. 1648–Jan.
1649 al-Hajj; Jan. 1649–Dec. 1650 Shekkarau;
Dec. 1650–Dec. 1651 Muhamman Kukuna;
Dec. 1651–Dec. 1651 Soyaki; Dec. 1651–Sept.
1659 Muhamman Kukuna; Sept. 1659–1670
Bawa; 1670–May 1702 Dadi; May 1702–July
1730 Muhamma Sharefa; July 1730–Feb. 1743
Kumbari; Feb. 1743–May 1752 al-Hajji Kabe;
May 1752–May 1768 Yaji II; May 1768–Feb.
1776 Baba Zaki; Feb. 1776–Dec. 1780 Dauda
Abasama II; Dec. 1780–March 1807 Muhamma
Alwali. *Sarkins Kano (Amirs of Kano):* March
1807–22 Aug. 1819 Sulimanu; 21 Sept. 1819–
Dec. 1845 Ibrahim Dabo; 9 Feb. 1846–26 Aug.

1855 Osumanu (also known as Uthman I); 16
Sept. 1855–Nov. 1882 Abdullahi; Nov. 1882–
July 1892 Muhammad Bello; July 1892–16
March 1895 Tukur; 16 March 1895–3 Feb. 1903
Aliyu Babba (also known as Abu); 3 April 1903–1
May 1919 Muhammadu Abbas; 1 May 1919–
Sept. 1919 [vacant]; Sept. 1919–1926 Osumanu
II (also known as Uthman II, or Usuman Dan
Abdullahi); 1926–25 Dec. 1953 Abdullahi Chi-
roma Bayero; 1 Jan. 1954–1963 Muhammadu
Sanusi; 1963–8 Oct. 1963 Muhammadu Inuwa
Abbas; 12 Oct. 1963–(?) Ado Bayero.

Kanuri see **Bornu** and **Hadejia**

Kaokoland see **Namibia**

Kaokoveld see **Namibia**

Karagwe. ca. 1450–1885. *Location:* in Tanzania.
Capital: Bukoba. *Other names:* Karague.

History: About 1450 the Bahinda dynasty
came to the fore in Karagwe (see also Nkore). In
1885 it had a German protectorate placed over
it (see German East Africa).

Mugabes (Kings): ca. 1450–ca. 1490 Ruhinda
Kizarabagabe; ca. 1490–ca. 1520 Ntare I; ca.
1520–ca. 1550 Ruhinda II; ca. 1550–ca. 1575
Ntare II; ca. 1575–ca. 1595 Ruhinda III; ca.
1595–ca. 1620 Ntare III; ca. 1620–ca. 1645
Ruhinda IV; ca. 1645–ca. 1675 Ntare IV; ca.
1675–ca. 1700 Ruhinda V; ca. 1700–ca. 1725
Rusatira; ca. 1725–ca. 1750 Mehiga; ca. 1750–
ca. 1774 Kalemera Bwirangenda; ca. 1774–ca.
1794 Ntare V Kiitabanyoro; ca. 1794–ca. 1819
Ruhinda VI Orushongo; ca. 1819–1853 Ndagara
I; 1853–1883 Rumanyika; 1883–1886 Kayenje
Kalemera II; 1886–1893 Nyamukuba Ndagara
II; 1893–1916 Kanyorozi Ntare VI; 1916–1939
Rumanyika II; 1939–1963 Ruhinda VII.

Karamanli Tripoli see **Tripolitania**

Karanga see **Rozwi**

Karchedon see **Carthage**

Karekare see **Potiskum**

Kart-Hadasht see **Carthage**

Kasai see **South Kasai Republic**

Katagum. 1807–Oct. 1903. *Location:* now in Bauchi Province, North-Eastern State, in the north central portion of Nigeria. *Capital:* Azare (from 1916); Katagum (from 1814 to 1916. Built in 1814); Tashena (until 1814).

History: Founded as a Muslim amirate in 1807 by Fulani warrior Mallam Zaki (see Fulani Empire). In 1826 it was conquered by the Bornu Empire, but in the same year it was won back. Wars with Hadejia in the 1850s weakened it and in 1903 it surrendered to the British and became part of the protectorate of Northern Nigeria. It became a sub-province of the province of Kano, and in 1926 was divided again, this time between Kano and Bauchi provinces.

Sarkins (Amirs): 1807–1814 Mallam Zaki (also known as Ibrahim Zakiyul Kalbi); 1814–1816 Suleimanu; 1816–1846 Dankawa; 1846–1851 Abdurahman; 1851–1868 Kadri (also known as Abdulkadiri); 1868–1896 Moma Haji; 1896–May 1905 Abdulkadiri II; 1905–1909 Muhammadu; 1909–1947 Abdulkadiri III; 1947–(?) Umaru Faruku; (?)–Muhammadu Kabir Umar.

Katanga see **Oyo**

Katanga Republic. 11 July 1960–15 Jan. 1963. *Location:* southeastern Congo (Zaire). *Capital:* Elisabethville (established in 1910, and after 1966 called Lubumbashi). *Other names:* Shaba.

History: The province of Katanga was brought into the Congo Free State in 1892, despite Cecil Rhodes's plans to make it a part of the British territory that would become Northern Rhodesia (see Zambia). The Union Minière du Haut-Katanga virtually ruled Katanga from 1906 (when it was granted the concession by the Congo Free State government) until the independence of the Congo. In 1960 the Belgian mining corporations financed and inspired Luanda leader Moise Tshombe (also then the premier of Katanga) to secede Katanga from Congo (Léopoldville), and independence was declared, with Tshombe as president. In early 1961 Tshombe's followers murdered Patrice Lumumba, the leftist former premier of Congo (Léopoldville). The Congolese army failed to win back Katanga, until then its richest province, but the United Nations put pressure on Tshombe to re-unify. Katanga was then divided into two provinces — North Katanga (came into effect in July 1962) and Lualaba and East Katanga (June 1963). Katanga is important to

world powers because only the riches in Katanga can pay back the loans to the country that became Zaire. Katanga is now officially called the Shaba Province of the Democratic Republic of the Congo.

Presidents: 11 July 1960–15 Jan. 1963 Moise Tshombe.

Katsina. ca. 1015–April 1903. *Location:* in the Zaria Province of Northern Nigeria, on the border with Niger. *Capital:* Katsina (fourth capital); Durbita Kusheyi (third capital); Ambuttai (second capital); Durombsi (first capital). *Other names:* Katsena; Kacinna (named for a local princess); Kecinna; Ketsina.

History: Around 1015 the kingdom of Katsina was founded by Kumayo, as one of the Hausa Bakwai (see Hausa States), or True Hausa States. Islam came to Katsina about 1450, and in the early 1700s the state reached its peak of power. Katsina, the city, was the largest town in the Hausa States in the 17th and 18th centuries. In 1806 Katsina became a Fulani amirate when Umaru Dallaji, a Fulani warrior (see Fulani Empire) captured Katsina City, after a long and heroic defense. Many of the nobility and ordinary people of Katsina fled north to what is now Niger, and formed a separate Katsina chiefdom which periodically raided the amirate. In March 1903 the amirate was visited by Sir Frederick Lugard, and the following month became a part of the British protectorate of Northern Nigeria without any ado. However, the following year the amir showed his true colors when he revolted. He was deposed by the British, and a new amir was installed. In 1931 Katsina Province was formed from Zaria and Kano Provinces.

Kings: ca. 1015–ca. 1100 Kumayo; ca. 1100–ca. 1180 Ramba-Ramba; ca. 1180–ca. 1250 Bata tare; ca. 1250–ca. 1300 Jarnanata; ca. 1300–ca. 1350 Sanau; ca. 1350–ca. 1410 Korau; ca. 1410–1452 Ibrahim Yanka Dari; 1452–1492 Yidda Yaki; 1492–1541 Muhammadu Korau; 1541–1543 Ibrahim Sura; 1543–1568 Ali Mura bus; 1568–1572 Muhammadu Toya Rero; 1572–1585 Aliyu Karya Giwa; 1585–1589 Usman Tsagarana; 1589–1595 Aliyu Jan Hazo I; 1595–1612 Muhammadu Mai-sa-Maza-Gudu; 1612–1614 Aliyu Jan Hazo II; 1614–1631 Maje Ibrahim; 1631–1634 Abd al-Karim; 1634–1635 Ashafa; 1635–1644 Ibrahim Gamda; 1644–1655 Muhammadu Wari; 1655–1667 Suleiman; 1667–1684 Usman No Yi Nawa; 1684–1701 Muhammadu Toya Rero II;

1701–1704 Muhammadu Wari II; 1704–1706 Uban Yari (also known as Muhammadu Dan Wari); 1706–1715 Karya Giwa II; 1715–1728 Jan Hazo III; 1728–1740 Tsagarana Hassan; 1740–1750 Muhammadu Kabiya (also known as Mai-Kere); 1750–1751 Tsagarana Yahya; 1751–1758 Karya Giwa III; 1758–1767 Muhammadu Wari III; 1767–1784 Karya Giwa IV; 1784–1801 Agwaragi; 1801–1802 Tsagarana Gwozo; 1802–1804 Bawa Dan Gima; 1804–1805 Mare Mawa Mahmudu; 1805–1806 Magajin Halidu. *Amirs:* 1806–1835 Umaru Dallaji; 1835–1844 Sidiku; 1844–1869 Muhamman Bello; 1869–1870 Ahmadu Rufai; 1870–1882 Ibrahim; 1882–1887 Musa; 1887–1904 Abubakr; 2 Jan. 1905–Nov. 1906 Yero; Nov. 1906–29 Jan. 1944 Muhammadu Dikko; 5 Aug. 1944–19 March 1981 Usman Nagogo; April 1981–Kabir dan Uthman Nagogo.

Kavangoland see **Namibia**

Kayor. 1549–1885. *Location:* now a province of Senegal. *Capital:* Mbul. *Other names:* Cayor.

History: The Wolof nation originated in Walo, north of Kayor, about the year 1100. They were a mixture of tribes. The first two Wolof states were Walo and Dyolof. Kayor became a vassal state of Dyolof, but in 1549 became independent. A matrilineal society, the first dynasty, the Geedy, produced eleven kings (or "damels"). Then came the Muyoy dynasty, then the Dorobe, the Sonyo, the Gelwar, and finally the Wagadu. In 1885 Kayor was annexed by the French to the colony of Senegal.

Damels (Kings): 1549–1549 Detye Fu-N'Diogu; 1549–1593 Amari; 1593–1600 Samba; 1600–1610 Khuredya; 1610–1640 Biram Manga; 1640–1647 Dauda Demba; 1647–1664 Dyor; 1664–1681 Birayma Yaasin-Bubu; 1681–1683 Detye Maram N'Galgu; 1683–1684 Faly; 1684–1691 Khuredya Kumba Dyodyo; 1691–1693 Birayma Mbenda-Tyilor; 1693–1693 Dyakhere; 1693–1697 Dethialaw; 1697–1719 Lat Sukaabe; 1719–1748 Isa-Tende; 1748–1749 Isa Bige N'Gone; 1749–1757 M'Bathio Samb; 1757–1758 Birayma Kodu; 1758–1759 Isa Bige N'Gone; 1759–1760 Birayma Yamb; 1760–1763 Isa Bige N'Gone; 1763–1766 Dyor Yaasin Isa; 1766–1777 Kodu Kumba; 1777–1790 Birayma Faatim-Penda; 1790–1809 Amari; 1809–1832 Birayma Fatma; 1832–1855 Isa Tein-Dyor; 1855–1859 Birayma-Fal; 1859–May 1861 Ma-Kodu; May 1861–Dec. 1861 Ma-Dyodyo; 1862–

1863 Lat-Dyor; Jan. 1864–1868 Ma-Dyodyo; 1868–Dec. 1882 Lat-Dyor; Jan. 1883–Aug. 1883 Amari; 1883–1886 Samba.

Kazaure. 1807–1906. *Location:* Northern Nigeria. *Capital:* Kazaure (after 1824); Damberta (until 1824).

History: Kazaure was born as an amirate in 1807 and named for a local hunter by Dan Tunku, the Fulani founder of the amirate. In the year of his death, Dan Tunku achieved independence for Kazaure, and the same year, 1824, his son moved the capital from Damberta. In 1906 the capital was taken by the British, and the amirate became a part of the protectorate of Northern Nigeria.

Amirs: 1807–1824 Dan Tunku; 1824–1857 Dambo; 1857–1886 Muhamman Zangi; 1886–1914 Muhamman Mayaki; 1914–1922 Muhammadu Tura; 1922–1941 Umaru Na'uka; 1941–1969 Adamu ibn Abdulmumini; 19 Dec. 1969–1974 al-Hajj Ibrahim Adamu; 1974–(?) Muhammadu dan Adamu; (?)–Najib Husaini Adamu.

Kazembe. ca. 1710–1899. *Location:* this kingdom straddled the border of what are now Zambia and Congo (Zaire), extending as far north as south-central Katanga. *Capital:* Kazembe. *Other names:* Cazembe.

History: About 1710 Lunda settlers with Portuguese weapons established a kingdom in the Luapula Valley, which became the strongest and most extensive of the Lunda–Luba kingdoms (see Luba and Lunda). By 1899 it had been colonized by the British (see Zambesia) and the Belgians (see Belgian Congo).

Kazembes (Kings): ca. 1710–ca. 1740 Nganda Bilonda; ca. 1740–ca. 1760 Kaniembo; ca. 1760–ca. 1805 Ilunga; ca. 1805–ca. 1850 Kibangu Keleka; ca. 1850–1854 Mwongo Mfwama; 1854–1862 Cinyanta Munona; 1862–1870 Mwonga Nsemba; 1870–1872 Cinkonkole Kafuti; 1872–1885 Lukwesa Mpanga; 1885–1899 Kaniembo Ntemena.

Kazura see **Hadejia**

Keana. ca. 1700–1900. *Location:* Northern Nigeria. *Capital:* [unknown].

History: Founded around 1700 by Keana, it was taken as part of the British protectorate of Northern Nigeria in 1900.

Kings: ca. 1700–(?) Keana; (?)–(?) Madafu; (?)–(?) Egwa; (?)–(?) Oshu; (?)–ca. 1789 Azagia I; ca. 1789–ca. 1791 Asiki; ca. 1791–ca. 1795 Alago; ca. 1795–1815 Agadi; 1815–1818 Otaki; 1818–1830 Onyatiko; 1830–1852 Adasho; 1852–1862 Aladoga; 1862–1899 Azagia II; 1899–1900 Ago.

Kebbi see **Argungu**

Keccina see **Katsina**

Keffi. ca. 1750–1902. *Location:* Northern Nigeria. *Capital:* Keffi (name means "stockade").

History: The Kano-allied kingdom of Keffi is of unknown origin. In 1802 it became a Fulani state (see Fulani Empire), and in 1902 it was taken by the British as part of their protectorate of Northern Nigeria.

Kings: ca. 1750–1802 Kareshi; 1802–1820 Abdu Zanga; 1820–1835 Maizabo; 1835–1859 Jibrilu; 1859–1862 Muhamman; 1862–1877 Ahmadu I; 1877–1894 Sidi Umaru; 1894–1902 Ibrahim; 1902–1921 Abdullahi; 1921–1923 Abubakar; 1923–1928 Abdullahi; 1928–1933 Muhammadu Mayaki; 1933–1948 Abubakar; 7 March 1948–(?) Ahmadu Maikwato; (?)–Yamusa II.

Keme see **Egypt**

Kenedugu. ca. 1650–1 May 1898. *Location:* on the border of Mali and Burkina Faso. *Capital:* Sikasso; Bougoula (their first capital, in the very early days). *Other names:* Sikasso; Kénédougou.

History: Nanka Traore and his people, the Dyula, founded the small kingdom of Kenedugu in the middle of the 17th century around the town of Bougoula. By 1750 his descendant, Daoula Ba Traore, had established an organized state. Much of the 19th century was taken up by war with the Walata family of Kong, and with Gwiriko. The French took it over as part of their colony of the French Sudan (see Mali) in 1898.

Faamas (Kings): ca. 1650–(?) Nanka Traore; (?)–ca. 1750 series of kings whose names have not come down; ca. 1750–(?) Daoula Ba Traore; (?)–ca. 1800 [unknown]; ca. 1800–ca. 1820 Tapri Traore; ca. 1820–ca. 1825 Moussa Toroma; ca. 1825–1835 Famorhoba; 1835–1845 Nyanamagha; 1845–1845 Tyemonkonko; 1845–1877 Daoula Ba Traore II; 1877–28 Jan. 1893 Tieba Traore; 28 Jan. 1893–1 May 1898 Babemba Traore.

Kenya. 3 Sept. 1888– . *Location:* East Africa, between Tanzania in the south and Ethiopia in the north. Uganda is to the west and the Indian Ocean to the east. Until 1920 the country also included the Zanzibar coast. *Capital:* Nairobi (from 1905. This town began in 1897 as a colonial railway settlement, and the name comes from a stream nearby, Enkare Nairobi, meaning "cold water"); Mombasa (until 1905. This town was founded by Arabs in the 11th century and most likely named for Mombasa in Oman). *Other names:* Djumhuriya Kenya, or the Republic of Kenya (from 1964); British East Africa, or East Africa (1888–1920); Ibea (its general name from 1888 to 1895, the name coming from the initials of the Imperial British East Africa Company).

History: The British had a presence in Mombasa in the 1820s. In 1877 the Sultan of Zanzibar offered a considerable portion of what is now Kenya to the British, but the British refused, not yet aware of what Africa had to offer. In the mid 1880s the scramble for East Africa between Germany and Great Britain resulted in the Imperial British East Africa Company taking possession in 1888 of what is now Kenya, as a means of access to Uganda. The Germans, led by the adventurer Karl Peters, proved a major thorn in the side of the BEAC, and on 18 June 1890 the British took over the German protectorate of Witu (also known as Vitu), making it a protectorate of their own. Witu was a coastal sultanate lying between the mouth of the Ozi River and the northern limit of Manda Bay. The Uganda venture ruined the Company (too much effort expended on building a railroad from the coast), and on 1 July 1895 the British Foreign Office took over the colony as the autonomous British East Africa Protectorate. Between 1896 and 1903 the railway project was finally carried through by the British government, and built by Indian laborers (which accounts for the large Indian population in Kenya) at a cost to the British tax payers of over £5 million. The railroad led from Mombasa to the Victoria Nyanza, and it was discovered, much to the surprise of the British, that the climate of the high plateaux made them an excellent place for Europeans to live. This and the presence of a completed railway to the coast produced settlers and land grants. In 1905 the British refused the Zionist request to make part of the territory the new Jewish homeland, and also that year the administration of East Africa was transferred to the Colonial Office. On 23 July 1920 British East Africa became Kenya Colony and Protectorate, the colony being inland, and the protectorate a strip of coastland 10 miles deep, over which the sultan of Zanzibar had nominal authority. The country was renamed Kenya for the mountain (the Kikuyu word "kerenyaga" means "white mountain"). Jubaland, until 1924, was a part of Kenya, and was transferred to Italy. The British government was hotly in favor of rights for the native Kenyan population, whereas the white settlers, under Lord Delamere (the head of the white community since 1903), were definitely not, and this caused friction. Added to this the Indians were pressing for representation, something they had been deliberately denied by the British government and settlers alike. In 1944 Kenya became the first East African possession to include a black African in its legislative council, a man appointed by the Governor. More and more black Africans became legislators over the next few years. The Mau Mau was formed in 1948 as a Kikuyu movement for independence and the expulsion of whites, and its inordinate violence caused Britain to declare a state of emergency in Kenya in 1952. Jomo Kenyatta, the leading Kenyan nationalist, was arrested and jailed, even though it was never proved that he was associated with the dreaded Mau Mau. By the mid-50s the British had crushed the Mau Mau menace, but the state of emergency ended only in 1960. In Aug. 1961 Kenyatta was finally released by the British authorities. In June 1963 Kenya became partially self-governing, and on 12 Dec. 1963 it became dominion, within the British Commonwealth. On 12 Dec. 1964 the country became a republic, and changed the pronunciation of its name to "kennya," as opposed to the British "keenya." Kenyatta did not allow an opposition party in Kenya until 1967. In 1969 Tom Mboya, a cabinet minister, and the man most likely to succeed Kenyatta, was assassinated. The death of Mboya, a leading member of the Luo tribe, sparked tribal violence and unrest, and Kenyatta blamed the opposition party for the assassination, and clamped down hard, banning the party and arresting its leaders. This established a trend for Kenyatta, a trend of wiping out the opposition. In all of this, he found a worthy successor in Daniel arap Moi. Aside from corruption and repression under the Kenyatta and Moi governments, things went relatively well in Kenya until the 1990s, when tribal violence flared in the western provinces, wiping out thousands of people and homes. Daniel arap Moi was forced to resign in 2002 by the rules of the constitution.

Commissioners: 3 Sept. 1888–May 1890 George Mackenzie; May 1890–Feb. 1891 Sir Francis de Winton; Feb. 1891–1891 George Mackenzie; 1891–1892 Ernest Berkeley; 1892–Jan. 1895 John Pigott; Jan. 1895–20 June 1904 same as the Consuls-General of Zanzibar; 20 June 1904–Oct. 1905 Sir Donald Stewart; Oct. 1905–12 Dec. 1905 [unknown] (acting); 12 Dec. 1905–31 Dec. 1905 James Sadler. *Governors:* 31 Dec. 1905–16 Sept. 1909 James Sadler (knighted 1907); 16 Sept. 1909–July 1912 Sir Percy Girouard; July 1912–3 Oct. 1912 Charles Bowring (acting); 3 Oct. 1912–22 July 1919 Henry Belfield (knighted 1914); 22 July 1919–15 Aug. 1922 Sir Edward Northey; 15 Aug. 1922–2 Oct. 1925 Sir Robert Coryndon; 2 Oct. 1925–1930 Sir Edward Grigg; 1930–1930 Henry Moore (acting); 1930–13 Feb. 1931 Sir Edward Grigg; 13 Feb. 1931–1936 Sir Joseph Byrne; 1936–6 April 1937 [unknown] (acting); 6 April 1937–9 Jan. 1940 Sir Robert Brooke-Popham; 9 Jan. 1940–1942 Sir Henry Moore; 1942–1942 Gilbert Rennie (acting); 1942–11 Dec. 1944 Sir Henry Moore; 11 Dec. 1944–30 Sept. 1952 Sir Philip Mitchell; 30 Sept. 1952–1957 Sir Evelyn Baring; 1957–1958 Richard Turnbull (acting); 1958–23 Oct. 1959 Sir Evelyn Baring; 23 Oct. 1959–1962 Sir Patrick Renison; 1962–4 Jan. 1963 [unknown] (acting); 4 Jan. 1963–12 Dec. 1963 Sir Malcolm MacDonald. *Governors-General:* 12 Dec. 1963–12 Dec. 1964 Sir Malcolm MacDonald. *Presidents:* 12 Dec. 1964–22 Aug. 1978 Jomo Kenyatta; 22 Aug. 1978–10 Oct. 1978 Daniel arap Moi (acting); 10 Oct. 1978–30 Dec. 2002 Daniel arap Moi; 30 Dec. 2002–Mwai Kibaki. *Prime Ministers:* April 1962–12 Dec. 1964 Jomo Kenyatta. *Note:* In times of no Prime Minister, the President held that office.

Ketsina see **Katsina**

Kgatlaland see **Bakgatlaland**

Khoikhoi see **Cape Colony**

Khumalo see **Matabeleland**

Khurasan see **Tunis**

Kikonja see **Luba Empire**

Kilwa see **Zeng Empire**

King William's Town District see **British Kaffraria**

Kinyarwanda see **Rwanda**

Kionga Triangle see **German East Africa**

Kitara see **Nkore**

Klein Vrijstaat see **Little Free State**

Klipdrift Republic. 1870–13 Dec. 1870. *Location:* the Klipdrift diamond fields, 20 miles northwest of Kimberley, Cape Province, South Africa. *Capital:* Klipdrift (founded in 1870, and renamed in 1873 as Barkly West, for Sir Henry Barkly, governor of the Cape). *Other names:* The Diggers' Republic; the Republic of Griqualand West.

History: In 1870, three years after the first diamond was discovered in the area, the diggers (who had signed a treaty with local Griqua chief Jan Bloem at Nooigedacht) proclaimed a free republic because Pretorius of the South African Republic (see Transvaal) was threatening to annex the area. This forced the British, later in 1870, to march in and take over the Diggers' Republic. This marked the end of the rule of Stafford Parker, a former British able-bodied seaman. A year later, on 27 Oct. 1871, the Klipdrift fields merged into Cape Colony, as part of Griqualand West.

Presidents: 1870–13 Dec. 1870 Stafford Parker.

Kmt see **Egypt**

Knights of Malta see **Tripolitania**

Kololo-Rotse Empire see **Barotseland**

Kom. ca. 1720–14 July 1884. *Location:* west Cameroun. *Capital:* Laikom.

History: The Ekwu clan traveled extensively before Jina settled in Laikom and founded the Kom dynasty. Jina was the son of Bo, and the rule has passed through the family to the present day. In 1884 Kom became part of the German Crown Land in North West Africa (see Kamerun).

Chiefs: ca. 1720–ca. 1740 Jina; ca. 1740–(?) Kumanbong; (?)–(?) Kwo; (?)–1830 Nkwain; 1830–1855 Tufoyn; 1855–1865 Kumong; 1865–1912 Yu; 1912–1926 Nggam; 1926–1954 Ndi; 1954–1966 Lo'o; 1966–(?) Nsom.

Kombo see **Fort James**

Kong. ca. 1710–20 Feb. 1888. *Location:* Côte d'Ivoire. *Capital:* Kong.

History: The Dyula state of Kong was founded in the early 18th century by Shehu Umar Watara, brother of the founder of Gwiriko. In 1888 it was visited by Louis Binger, and he persuaded the sheikh to place Kong under a French protectorate. In 1893 this protectorate became part of the colony of the Ivory Coast (see Côte d'Ivoire), as the administrative district known as the Cercle du Kong. Samory (see Samory's Empire) captured much of Kong in the 1890s.

Sheikhs: ca. 1710–(?) Shehu Umar Watara; (?)–(?) [unknown]; (?)–(?) [unknown]; (?)–(?) [unknown]; (?)–(?) [unknown]; (?)–ca. 1815 [unknown]; ca. 1815–(?) Bakary Watara; (?)–ca. 1850 [unknown]; ca. 1850–(?) Kurakara; (?)–ca. 1899 Dabila; ca. 1899–1895 Karamoko; 1895–1962 gBon Culibaly.

Kongo. ca. 1350–ca. 1850. *Location:* northern Angola and parts of Congo (Zaire) and Congo. *Capital:* Mbanza (also called São Salvador). *Other names:* Bakongo; Congo.

History: Named for the Bakongo people, this large kingdom was very powerful by 1400. Aside from that nothing is known of this kingdom until Diogo Cão (Cam) discovered it in 1483. A good relationship developed between Kongo and Portugal, with the Bakongo becoming Christianized and somewhat Europeanized. In the late 1660s the Portuguese abandoned the area (see Angola), long after it had been recognized by the Vatican as a Christian kingdom and had fallen into ruin. It later (at an uncertain date) became part of Portuguese West Africa (see Angola) and part of Moyen-Congo (see Congo) and Congo Free State [see Congo (Zaire)]. A man calling himself Pedro VII of Kongo died in 1955.

Manis (Kings): ca. 1350–1483 [unknown]; 1483–1508 João I (also known as Nzinga); 1508–1543 Afonso I (also known as Nzinga Mbemba); 1543–1545 Pedro I (also known as Nkang Mbemba); 1545–1561 Diogo I; 1561–1562 Afonso II; 1562–1563 Bernardo I; 1563–1582 Enriques I; 1582–1587 Álvaro I; 1587–1609 Jaga Álvaro II; 1609–1615 Bernardo II; 1615–1621 Álvaro III; 1621–1624 Pedro II; 1624–1626 García I; 1626–1631 Ambrosio; 1631–1635 Álvaro IV; 1635–1636 Álvaro V; 1636–1641 Álvaro VI; 1641–1661 García II Afonso; 1661–1665 Antonio I; 1665–1666 Álvaro VII; 1666–1666 Álvaro VIII; 1666–1667 Afonso III; 1667–1669 Pedro III; 1669–1674 Álvaro IX and Pedro III and Rafael (jointly); 1674–1678 Daniel and Pedro III (jointly); 1678–1683 Pedro III; 1683–1709 João II; 1709–1717 João II and Pedro IV (jointly); 1717–(?) Pedro V; (?)–ca. 1850 series of kings whose names have not come down.

Konkiok see **Wase**

Kontagora. 1864–Jan. 1901. *Location:* part of Niger Province, western Nigeria, it lies on the east bank of the Niger River, to the north of Nupe. *Capital:* Kontagora (founded in 1864, the name means "lay down your gourds").

History: Created out of Kamberi country in the late 1850s by Fulani chieftain Umaru Nagwamatse, and established as an amirate in 1864, it was brought into the British protectorate of Northern Nigeria in 1901, as Kontagora Province. It is now a division of Niger Province.

Sarkins Sudan (Kings): 1864–1876 Umaru Nagwamatse; 1876–1880 Abubakar Modibbo; 1880–1901 Ibrahim Nagwamatse; 1901–April 1903 kingdom not recognized; April 1903–26 Oct. 1929 Ibrahim Nagwamatse; 26 Oct. 1929–Feb. 1961 Umaru Maidubu; Feb. 1961–Jan. 1974 Mu'azu; 21 Jan. 1974–al-Hajji Saidu Naemaska.

Korannaland see **Stellaland**

Kordofan. (?)–Dec. 1883. *Location:* in the Sudan. *Capital:* al-Ubaid (also known as El Obeid). *Other names:* Kurdufan.

History: The country of Kordofan (the Nubian word "kurta" means "men") was never actually an independent state. By about 1500 Funj settlers began moving there, and over the next century and a half did so in ever increasing numbers. In the early 17th century the country was occupied by Suleiman Solong, the sultan of Darfur. Kordofan became a province of the Funj Sultanate in 1748. In 1772 this rule was temporarily thrown off, but re-established in 1784. In 1821 the Egyptians conquered all of the Sudan, and on 16 Aug. 1821 Kordofan became a muridia (province) of the Egyptian Sudan (see Sudan). At the end of 1883 the Mahdi swallowed it up (again, see Sudan).

Sultans: ca. 1600–ca. 1650 Muhammad I; ca. 1650–ca. 1700 Muhammad II; ca. 1700–(?) Isawi; (?)–1748 Hashim. *Funj Governors:* 1748–1772 Sheikh Muhammad Abu'l Kaylak. *Sultans:* 1772–1784 Hashim. *Funj Governors:* 1784–16 Aug. 1821 Maqdum Musallam. *Governors:* 16 Aug. 1821–1822 Mehmed Bey; 1822–1825 Halim Bey; 1825–1827 Suleiman Bey Harputli; 1827–1833 Rustum Bey; 1833–1843 [unknown]; 1843–1848 Mustafa Kiridli; 1848–1850 [vacant]; 1850–1850 Musa Pasha Hamdi; 1850–1857 [vacant]; 1857–1859 Hassan Ali Pasha Arnavut; 1859–1862 [unknown]; 1862–1865 Hassan Ali Pasha Arnavut; 1865–1873 [unknown]; 1873–1874 Mehmed Sa'id Pasha Wahbi; 1874–1879 [unknown]; 1879–Dec. 1883 Mehmed Sa'id Pasha Wahbi.

Kororofa. ca. 1600–1901. *Location:* on the border of Northern Nigeria and Niger. *Capital:* Kororofa. *Other names:* Kwararafa; Jukun.

History: A Hausa state of the Jukun peoples, formed around the turn of the 17th century and based on descent from a semi-mythical kingdom of the late Middle Ages. In 1901 it was divided up between French West Africa and the British protectorate of Northern Nigeria.

Kings: ca. 1600–ca. 1630 Agbu Kendja; ca. 1630–ca. 1671 Katapka; ca. 1671–(?) Agwabi; (?)–(?) Dawi; (?)–(?) Agigbi; (?)–(?) Nani To; (?)–(?) Dadju; (?)–ca. 1750 Zike; ca. 1750–ca. 1775 Kuwya; ca. 1775–ca. 1800 Matsweu Adi; ca. 1800–1815 Ashu Manu I; 1815–1848 Zikeenya; 1848–1866 Agbu Manu I; 1866–1871 Ashu Manu II; 1871–1902 Agudu Manu; 1903–1915 Agbu Manu II; 1915–1927 Ashu Manu III.

Kosi Bay see **Tongaland**

Kotonu see **Benin**

Koya-Temne. ca. 1505–31 Aug. 1896. *Location:* in Sierra Leone. *Capital:* Robanna (after 1720); Port Lokko (1680–1720); Lokko (1560–1680). *Other names:* Temne; Koya; Quiah.

History: Founded about 1505, Koya-Temne was one of the major political divisions of Sierra Leone before the British took over the country.

Kings: ca. 1505–ca. 1550 Farima I; ca. 1550–ca. 1560 Farima II; ca. 1560–1605 Farima III; 1605–1610 Sangrafare (also known as Pedro); 1610–1630 Borea I; 1630–1664 Borea II; 1664–1680 Felipe II; 1680–1720 Naimbanna I; 1720–1793 Naimbanna II; 1793–1807 Farima IV; 1807–1817 Bai Foki; 1817–1825 Moriba; 1825–1826 Kunia Banna (also known as Jack Coby); 1826–1840 Fatima; 1840–1859 Moribu Kindo; 1859–1872 Bai Kanta (also known as Alexander). *Regents:* 1872–1890 Alimani Lahai Bundu. *Kings:* 1890–1898 Bai Kompa (also known as William Rowe); 1898–1898 Fula Mansa Gbanka. *Sub-Kings of Ko-Fransa:* 1770–1788 Tom I; 1788–1796 Jimmy; 1796–1807 Tom II.

Kreli's Country. 1750– . *Location:* in Kaffraria, South Africa. *Capital:* Kentani. *Other names:* Gcalekaland; Galakaland; Sarili's Country (alternative name from 1835 to 1893).

History: Gcaleka, after whom Galekaland was named, was left in control of his (the northern) branch of the Xhosa when his father Phalo emigrated to the south with his other son Rarabe (see British Kaffraria for rulers of the Rarabe branch of the Xhosa). Galekaland began effectively at this time. From 1835 to 1886 it was known as Kreli's Country. On 28 June 1881 Kreli surrendered to the British and was given land in Elliotdale, and in 1886 Kreli's Country was annexed to Cape Colony, as part of the Transkei District of the Transkeian Territories.

Chiefs: 1750–1792 Gcaleka; 1792–1804 Khawuta. *Regents:* 1804–1820 Nqoko. *Chiefs:* 1820–12 May 1835 Hintsa; 12 May 1835–19 May 1835 interregnum; 19 May 1835–Feb. 1893 Kreli (also known as Sarili); Feb. 1893–1902 Sigcawu; 1902–1921 Gwebinkumbi. *Regents:* 1921–1923 Daliza; 1923–1933 Ngangomhlaba; 1933–(?) Zwelidumile.

Kurdufan see **Kordofan**

Kush. ca. 860 b.c.–ca. a.d. 325 *Location:* in the Sudan. *Capital:* Meroë (from ca. 590 b.c.–ca. a.d. 325); Napata (until ca. 590 b.c.). *Other names:* Cush; Nubia; Ethiopia.

History: The area that today is the Sudan was formerly an Egyptian-occupied country called Old Nubia (as opposed to Nubia). The northern division of this country was called Wawat (with headquarters at Aswan) and the southern division was called Kush (with headquarters at Napata). This was the state of affairs for almost five centuries until, by the 11th century b.c., with the decline of Egypt, Kush assumed more and more autonomy until, by about 860 b.c., it became an independent kingdom. The Greeks called it Ethiopia; the Ancient Egyptians called it Kush; and its own particular Nubian-Egyptian culture was maintained throughout its history. Under its king Kashta it turned the tables on its northern neighbor by conquering Upper Egypt, and under Kashta's son Piankhi (see Egypt) all of Egypt became Kushite in the 25th Dynasty. In 671 b.c. this situation ended with the Assyrian invasion of Egypt and the Kushites retired to their home. Kush remained the dominant kingdom in the Sudan until about a.d. 325 when their capital, Meroë was destroyed by the king of Axum.

Kings: ca. 860 b.c.–(?) Kashta; (?)–(?) Alara; (?)–(?) Piankhi I; (?)–(?) Kashta II; (?)–(?) Neferkare Shabaha II; (?)–(?) Jadkaure Shebitku; (?)–ca. 671 b.c. Hunefertemre; ca. 671 b.c.–(?) Urdamen; (?)–(?) Bakare Tanuatamun; (?)–(?) Piankhi II; (?)–(?) Neferankh Asrumeri Amen; (?)–ca. 653 b.c. Piankhi III; ca. 653 b.c.–ca. 643 b.c. Hukare Atlanersa; ca. 643 b.c.–ca. 623 b.c. Sekherpereure Senkamanishen; ca. 623 b.c.–ca. 593 b.c. Ankhikare Anlamani; ca. 593 b.c.–ca. 568 b.c. Merkare Aspelta; ca. 568 b.c.–ca. 555 b.c. Wajkare Amtalqa; ca. 555 b.c.–ca. 542 b.c. Sekhemkare Malenaqen; ca. 542 b.c.–ca. 538 b.c. Neferkare Analmaaye; ca. 538 b.c.–ca. 519 b.c. Amaninatakilebte; ca. 519 b.c.–ca. 510 b.c. Karkamani; ca. 510 b.c.–ca. 487 b.c. Setepkare Astabarqamen; ca. 487 b.c.–ca. 468 b.c. Sejertawi Asasunaq; ca. 468 b.c.–ca. 463 b.c. Nasakhma; ca. 463 b.c.–ca. 435 b.c. Heperkare Maluiane; ca. 435 b.c.–ca. 431 b.c. Talakhamane; ca. 431 b.c.–ca. 405 b.c. Neferabre Herinutarekamen; ca. 405 b.c.–ca. 404 b.c. Baskakaren; ca. 404 b.c.–ca. 369 b.c. Sameramne Herusaatef; ca. 369 b.c.–ca. 350 b.c. [unknown]; ca. 350 b.c.–ca. 335 b.c. Ahratan; ca. 335 b.c.–ca. 310 b.c. Ankhkare Nastasen; ca. 310 b.c.–ca. 295 b.c. Amanibakhi; ca. 295 b.c.–ca. 275 b.c. Khnemabre Arkaqamani; ca. 275 b.c.–ca. 260 b.c. Amanislo. *Queens:* ca. 260 b.c.–ca. 250 b.c. Bartare. *Kings:* ca. 250 b.c.–ca. 235 b.c. Amanitekha; ca. 235 b.c.–ca. 218 b.c. Arnekhamani; ca. 218 b.c.–ca. 200 b.c. Arqamani; ca. 200 b.c.–ca. 185 b.c. Tabirqa; ca. 185 b.c.–ca. 170 b.c. [unknown]; ca. 170 b.c.–ca. 160 b.c. Shanakdakhete; ca. 160 b.c.–ca. 145 b.c. [unknown]; ca. 145 b.c.–ca. 120 b.c. Naqrisan; ca. 120 b.c.–ca. 100 b.c. Tanyidamani; ca. 100 b.c.–ca. 80 b.c. [unknown]; ca. 80 b.c.–ca. 65 b.c. [unknown]; ca. 65 b.c.–ca. 33 b.c. Nawidemak; ca. 33 b.c.–ca. 24 b.c. Teriteqas; ca. 24 b.c.–ca. 15 b.c. Akinidad; ca. 15 b.c.–ca. a.d. 12 Natakamani; ca. a.d. 12–ca. 17 Serkarer; ca. 17–ca. 35 Pisakar; ca. 35–ca. 45 Amanitaraqide; ca. 45–ca. 62 Amanitenmemide. *Queens:* ca. 62–ca. 85 Amanikhatashan. *Kings:* ca. 85–ca. 103 Tarekeniwal; ca. 103–ca. 108 Amanikhalika; ca. 108–ca. 132 Aritenyesbekhe; ca. 132–ca. 137 Aqrakamani; ca. 137–ca. 146 Adeqetali; ca. 146–ca. 165 Takideamani; ca. 165–ca. 184 [unknown]; ca. 184–ca. 194 [unknown]; ca. 194–ca. 209 Teritedakhetey; ca. 209–ca. 228 Aryesbekhe; ca. 228–ca. 246 Teridnide; ca. 246–ca. 266 Teqerideamani; ca. 266–ca. 283 Tamelerdeamani; ca. 283–ca. ca. 300 Yesbekheamani; ca. 300–ca. 308 Lakhideamani; ca. 308–ca. 320 Maleqerabar; ca. 320–ca. 325 Akhedakhetiwal.

Kutama see **Rustumid Amirate**

KwaNdebele. Oct. 1977–27 April 1994. *Location:* north central Transvaal, South Africa. *Capital:* Siyabuswa. *Other names:* South Ndebele.

History: In 1977 the National State of KwaNdebele, the homeland (or bantustan) of the Southern Matabele (also known as the Ndebele), achieved self-rule. It never achieved independence, as did Bophuthatswana, and some other homelands. In 1994, with the establishment of black rule in South Africa, the bantustans ceased to be necessary.

Chief Executive Councillor: Oct. 1977–April 1981 Simon Sikosana. *Chief Ministers:* April 1981–17 Nov. 1986 Simon Sikosana; 17 Nov. 1986–27 Nov. 1986 Klaas Mtshiweni (acting); 27 Nov. 1986–3 Feb. 1989 George Mahlangu; 3 Feb. 1989–30 April 1990 Jonas Mabena; 30 April 1990–26 April 1994 Prince James Mahlangu.

Kwara State see **Lafiagi**

Kwararafa see **Kororofa**

KwaZulu. 1 April 1972–27 April 1994. *Location:* northern Natal, South Africa. *Capital:* Ulundi; Nongoma (the first capital).

History: Formerly the Zulu territorial Authority, the National State of KwaZulu was a bantustan (or native homeland) formed for the Zulus by the South African government. It was composed of more than 30 discontinuous exclaves throughout Natal. Gatsha Buthelezi, who had been until then the chief executive councillor, was named chief minister. The country became self-governing in 1977. In 1994, with the establishment of black rule in South Africa, the bantustans ceased to be necessary.

Chief Ministers: 1 April 1972–26 April 1994 Gatsha Buthelezi.

Kwenaland see **Bakwenaland**

Kyrene see **Pentapolis**

La Digue Island see **Seychelles**

La Laguna see **Tenerife**

La Palma see **Canary Islands**

Laayoune see **Western Sahara**

Ladoku see **Akwamu**

Lafia. 1780–1900. *Location:* central Nigeria. *Capital:* Lafia (from 1804. Formerly called Lafian Beri-Beri, the name "Lafia" means "comfortably settled"); Anane (until 1804).

History: Originally this was the home of the Arago people. It was captured and established as a political entity in 1780 by expatriate traders from Bornu led by Dunama, who, in 1804, proclaimed himself sarkin (or chief) of Lafia. Dunama's successor expanded the frontiers of Lafia by conquest. In 1873 Lafia was captured by troops from Sokoto, and Abdullahi Dalla Bahagu, grandson of the original Dunama, was placed in power. Lafia never became a Fulani amirate, but maintained its independence until 1900, when it became an amirate of the British protectorate of Northern Nigeria. It formed part of Benue Province, in the state of Benue-Plateau, until 1976, when it became part of Plateau State.

Sarkins (Chiefs): 1780–1809 Dunama. *Amirs:* 1809–1814 Musa Dan Jaji; 1814–1819 Umar I; 1819–1844 Laminu; 1844–1849 Musa Gana; 1849–1866 Abdullahi Dalla; 1866–1868 Ari; 1868–1873 Umar II; 1873–1881 Abdullahi Dalla

Bahagu; 1881–1903 Muhamman Agwe I. *Amirs:* 1903–1918 Musa; 1918–1926 Abdullahi; 1926–1933 Muhammadu Angulu; 1933–1949 Muhamman Agwe II; 1949–Dec. 1952 Makwangiji Na'ali (acting); Dec. 1952–1978 Yusufu Musa; 1978–Isa Mustafa Agwe.

Lafiagi. 1824–1900. *Location:* west central Nigeria, on the south bank of the Niger River. *Capital:* Lafiagi (built in 1810).

History: The name means "a small hill" in Nupe, and it was founded as a town by two Fulani chiefs from Gwandu, Mallam Maliki and Manzuma. In 1824 the amirate was founded. In 1900 it became part of the British protectorate of Northern Nigeria, being placed in Ilorin Province, later part of Kwara State.

Chiefs: 1810–1824 Mallam Maliki. *Amirs:* 1824–1833 Manzuma; 1833–1834 Aliyu; 1834–1845 Abdulkadiri; 1845–1853 Aliyu; 1853–1868 Abdulkadiri; 1868–1882 Ibrahim Halilu; 1882–1891 Aliyu; 1891–1892 Abdurrahim; 1892–1915 Ahmadu; 1915–1945 Muhamman Bello; 1945–1949 Abubakr Kawu. *Chiefs:* 1949–1951 Maliki; 1951–1961 Abubakr Ceceko; 11 Oct. 1961–(?) Umaru Oke-Ode; (?)–Sa'du Kawu Khaliru.

Lago de Curama see **Lagos**

Lagos. ca. 1700–1906. *Location:* Lagos Island and surrounding areas, in Southern Nigeria. *Capital:* Lagos (named by the Portuguese initially as Lago de Curamo, then renamed by them as Onin, and finally as Lagos, partly for the lagoons nearby, and partly for a harbor in Portugal. The city of Lagos is now the capital of Nigeria). *Other names:* Eko (before 1861. This name means "war camp" in Yoruba).

History: The Yoruba settled the island of Lagos (or Eko as they called it then), but it was a vassal state of Benin (see Benin [i]), under which Lagos acted as a western province. By the early 1800s it was a major slave-trading center, and independent from Benin, but on 6 Aug. 1861 it was taken over by the British. The administrator took over the consulship of the Bight of Benin as well. This British possession included not only the island of Lagos but also Iddo Island, Badagry, Palma, and Leckie. The headquarters remained at Lagos Town. On 22 Aug. 1862 the area became known as the Lagos Settlement, and on 19 Feb. 1866 the country became one of the four territories of the West African Settlements

(see British West Africa). On 24 July 1874, together with the Gold Coast, it broke away from the W.A.S. and a new colony was formed — Gold Coast Colony (with Lagos). Thus Lagos remained a territory, but of this new colony (of which the Gold Coast was decidedly the senior partner), until 13 Jan. 1886, when Lagos became its own colony. On 18 Oct. 1887 a protectorate was established in the hinterland of Lagos, and the colony and the protectorate were ruled side by side until 27 Dec. 1899 (effective as from 1 Jan. 1900), when the protectorate (but not the colony) went to form part of the new Southern Nigeria Protectorate (see Southern Nigeria). The colony of Lagos continued as such until 16 Feb. 1906, when it went to form part of the new Southern Nigeria Colony and Protectorate (again, see Southern Nigeria).

Obas (Kings): ca. 1700–(?) Ashikpa; (?)–(?) Ado; (?)–(?) Gabaro; (?)–ca. 1805 Akinshemoyin; ca. 1805–ca. 1808 Kekere; ca. 1808–1811 Olugun Kutere; 1811–1821 Adele I; 1821–ca. 1832 Oshinlokun; ca. 1832–1833 Idewu Ogulari; 1833–1834 Adele I; 1834–1841 Oluwole; 1841–July 1845 Akitoye I; July 1845–Feb. 1852 Kosoko; Feb. 1852–1853 Akitoye I; 1853–1885 Docemo (also known as Dosumu); 1885–1900 Oyekan I; 1900–1920 Eshugbayi Eleko; 1920–1931 Samusi Olusi; 1931–1932 Eshugbayi Eleko; 1932–1 Oct. 1949 Falolu; 1 Oct. 1949–12 July 1964 Alaiyeluwa Oba Adeniji Adele II; 12 July 1964–11 March 1965 S.A. Agoro (regent); 11 March 1965–7 March 2003 Adeyinka Oyekan II; 7 March 2003–24 May 2003 Teslim Binadu-Eko (acting); 24 May 2003–Okolu I. *Governors:* 6 Aug. 1861–22 Jan. 1862 William McCoskry (acting); 22 Jan. 1862–1863 Henry Freeman; 1863–1864 W.R. Mullinar (acting); 1864–April 1865 John Glover (acting); April 1865–19 Feb. 1866 John Glover. *Administrators:* 19 Feb. 1866–Feb. 1866 Charles Patey; Feb. 1866–1870 John Glover; 1870–1870 Miles Cooper (acting); 1870–1870 John Glover; 1870–1871 W.H. Simpson (acting); 1871–1872 J. Gerrard (acting); 1872–1872 Henry Fowley (acting); 1872–1873 George Berkeley; 1873–1873 Charles Lees (acting); 1873–1874 George Strahan; 1874–24 July 1874 John Shaw (acting); 24 July 1874–1875 Charles Lees; 1875–1878 John Dumaresq (acting); 1878–1878 F. Simpson (acting); 1878–1878 Malcolm Brown (acting); 1878–1880 Alfred Moloney (acting). *Lieutenant-Governors:* 1880–1880 Brandford Griffith. *Administrators:*

1880–1883 C.D. Turton. *Deputy-Governors:* 1883–1883 Alfred Moloney; 1883–1883 Fred Evans; 1883–1884 Brandford Griffith; 1884–1884 Murray Rumsey; 1884–1885 Knapp Burrow; 1885–13 Jan. 1886 C. Pike. *Governors:* 13 Jan. 1886–1889 Alfred Moloney; 1889–1890 George Denton (acting); 1890–1891 Sir Alfred Moloney; 1891–1897 Gilbert Carter (knighted 1893); 1897–1899 Henry McCallum (knighted 1898); 1899–1902 Sir William MacGregor; 1902–1903 Henry Reeve (acting); 1903–Aug. 1904 Henry Reeve; Aug. 1904–16 Feb. 1906 Walter Egerton (knighted 1905).

Lamtuna see **Almoravid Empire**

Land Goosen see **Goshen**

Land of Gold see **Ghana Empire**

Land of Punt see **Punt**

Landeen see **Gazaland**

Lanzarote see **Canary Islands** and **Gran Canaria**

Lapai. 1825–24 June 1898. *Location:* Niger State, west central Nigeria. *Capital:* Lapai (after 1936 the capital became Badeggi-Lapai).

History: This was originally the land of the Gbari people (also known as the Gwari), who lived under the domination of the kingdom of Zazzau (later known as Zaria). In 1825 Lapai was created a separate amirate of the Fulani Empire, in the place of the Gwari people who had lived there in the kingdom of Payi (hence the name Lapai). In 1897 the neighboring state of Bida was at war with the British Royal Niger Company, and Lapai took Bida's side, which was a mistake. The Company came into Lapai and burned the capital. In 1898 Lapai became part of the Niger River Delta Protectorate (see Northern Nigeria), and in 1900 it became part of British protectorate of Northern Nigeria. In 1908 it became part of Niger Province, in Nigeria.

Amirs: 1825–1832 Dauda Maza; 1832–1835 Yamusa; 1835–1838 Baji; 1838–1874 Jantabu; 1874–1875 Atiku; 1875–1893 Bawa; 1893–1907 Abdulkadiri; 1907–1923 Ibrahim; 1923–April 1937 Aliyu Gana; 1937–Nov. 1954 Umaru; 1954–13 June 2002 Muhammadu Kobo; 10 Aug. 2002–Umaru Bago.

Larache see **Ceuta**

Las Palmas de Gran Canaria see **Gran Canaria**

Lautaye see **Gumel**

Laute see **Gumel**

Lebowa. 2 Oct. 1972–27 April 1994. *Location:* northern Transvaal, South Africa. *Capital:* Lebowakgomo.

History: The National State of Lebowa was the bantustan (or native homeland) for the Northern Sotho peoples ("lebowa" means "north"), and included the Pedi. It consisted of three main exclaves (parcels of land not connected to each other), as well as several small extraneous tracts of land. It achieved self-government in 1972, but continued to remain part of South Africa. In 1994 the homelands were abolished, and Lebowa became part of South Africa.

Chief Ministers: 2 Oct. 1972–8 May 1973 Maurice Matlala; 8 May 1973–7 Oct. 1987 Cedric Phatudi; 7 Oct. 1987–21 Oct. 1987 Z.T. Seleki (acting); 21 Oct. 1987–1989 Mogoboya Radomike. *Prime Ministers:* 1989–26 April 1994 Mogoboya Radomike. .

Leckie see **Lagos**

Léopoldville see **Congo (Zaire)**

Leptis Magna see **Tripolitania**

Lesotho. 1822– . *Location:* Lesotho is a tiny independent state entirely surrounded by South Africa. *Capital:* Maseru (from 11 March 1869. Founded as the administrative capital by James Bowker. The name means "place of red sandstone"); Thaba Bosiu (from July 1824 until 1869. The name means "hill of night"); Butha-Buthe (until 1824). *Other names:* Basutoland (until 1966); Amasuta (an early name).

History: In 1822 Moshoeshoe I, leader of the Basotho, arrived in the area that would eventually become the core of Lesotho, and built a kingdom. After warding off other tribes, Moshoeshoe faced losing his country to the Boers, who were settling on his land in increasing numbers. He thus worked for British protection, and on 13 Dec. 1843 Britain recognized the kingdom, and it became a British protectorate. In 1849 the British reduced the borders of Basutoland, and the little kingdom was basically cast adrift by the British to fend for itself against its neighbors, mostly the Boers again, who were about to take over the whole country when, on 12 March 1868 Basutoland became a Crown protectorate, i.e. a British agent was sent to advise the king. This stopped the Boers, and assured Basutoland its own integrity. On 11 Aug. 1871 the country was annexed to Cape Colony, as an autonomous territory. This was a very unpopular move in Basutoland, with the British unable or unwilling to understand their Basuto charges. Revolts took place, and culminated in the Gun War of 1880, when the British tried to disarm the people. Peace was not restored until 1883. The Cape was tired of its responsibility toward Basutoland, and on 2 Feb. 1884 (effective as from 18 March 1884) the country became Basutoland High Commission Territory (cf. Swaziland and Bechuanaland). A high commissioner ruled through resident commissioners, and much internal self-government was awarded to the Basutos. The Basutos remained loyal to the British at best, and neutral at worst, over the next several years, and this was largely due to their fear for their future, regarding the ever present threat of South African control. In 1909, when the unification of South Africa was imminent, the leaders of the proposed Union wanted possession of Basutoland, but it did not happen. This problem surfaced again in 1933, and has done, in one form or another, occasionally since then. On 1 Aug. 1964 the country was granted self-rule, and on 4 Oct. 1966 it became the independent kingdom of Lesotho. A huge number of Lesotho citizens worked in South Africa, and sent money home. This revenue formed the greatest portion of the Gross National Product. South Africa acted with great circumspection over its Lesotho problems, one of which was the influx of Lesotho citizens streaming into South Africa to work, and yet not spending in their adopted country, and at the same time not only refusing to accept South African control, but actively aiding rebels fighting the South African government. This came to a head in Jan. 1986 when South Africa imposed a blockade on Lesotho, and this was followed by a military coup in Lesotho, and the new government became more co-operative with South Africa. There was another coup in 1991, Moshoeshoe went into exile in London, returned

in 1992, but did not resume the throne. The first free elections in 23 years took place in 1993. In Sept. 1998 riots took place over election frauds, and South Africa and Botswana had to send troops in to restore order. Lesotho was bedeviled in the early 2000s by droughts, scandals, political corruption, rebel factions, AIDS, poverty and starvation.

Motlotlehis (Kings): 1822–11 March 1870 Moshoeshoe I; 11 March 1870–20 Nov. 1891 Letsie I; 20 Nov. 1891–19 Aug. 1905 Lerotholi; 19 Aug. 1905–19 Sept. 1905 Letsie II (king designate); 19 Sept. 1905–28 Jan. 1913 Letsie II; Feb. 1913–11 April 1913 Griffith (king designate); 11 April 1913–July 1939 Griffith; Aug. 1939–Dec. 1940 Seeiso. *Queens Regent:* Dec. 1940–12 March 1960 MaNtsebo. *Paramount Chiefs:* 12 March 1960–1 Aug. 1964 Moshoeshoe II (also known as Constantine Sereng Seeiso). *Motlotlehis (Kings):* 1 Aug. 1964–2 Feb. 1970 Moshoeshoe II (also known as Constantine Sereng Seeiso). *Queens Regent:* 2 Feb. 1970–4 Dec. 1970 Mamaohato. *Motlotlehis (Kings):* 4 Dec. 1970–12 Nov. 1990 Moshoeshoe II (also known as Constantine Sereng Seeiso); 12 Nov. 1990–14 Sept. 1994 Letsie III (also known as Letsie David Seeiso). *Queens Regent:* 14 Sept. 1994–25 Jan. 1995 Mamaohato. *Motlotlehis (Kings):* 25 Jan. 1995–15 Jan. 1996 Moshoeshoe II (also known as Constantine Sereng Seeiso). *Queens Regent:* 15 Jan. 1996–7 Feb. 1996 Mamaohato. *Motlotlehis (Kings):* 7 Feb. 1996–Letsie III (also known as Letsie David Seeiso). *High Commissioner's Agents:* 14 March 1868–April 1868 Walter Currie; April 1868–11 March 1869 James Bowker (acting); 11 March 1869–May 1870 James Bowker; May 1870–Aug. 1871 William Surmon; Aug. 1871–11 Aug. 1871 Charles Griffith. *Governor's Agents:* 11 Aug. 1871–1877 Charles Griffith; 1877–9 Dec. 1877 Emile Rolland (acting); 9 Dec. 1877–1878 Charles Griffith; 1878–10 Oct. 1878 Emile Rolland (acting); 10 Oct. 1878–25 Aug. 1881 Charles Griffith; 25 Aug. 1881–16 March 1883 Joseph Orpen (acting); 17 March 1883–18 March 1884 Matthew Blyth (acting). *Resident Commissioners:* 18 March 1884–18 Sept 1894 Marshall Clarke (knighted 1886); 18 Sept. 1894–1895 Godfrey Lagden; 1895–1895 Herbert Sloley (acting); 1895–1901 Godfrey Lagden (knighted 1897); 1901–1913 Herbert Sloley (knighted 1911); 1913–1913 James MacGregor (acting); 1913–1915 Sir Herbert Sloley; 1915–1917 Robert Coryndon; 1917–April 1926 Edward Garraway (knighted

1926); April 1926–March 1935 John Sturrock (knighted 1934); March 1935–Aug. 1942 Edmund Richards (knighted 1941); Aug. 1942–Nov. 1946 Arden Clarke (from 1951 he would be known as Sir Charles Arden-Clarke); Nov. 1946–24 Oct. 1951 Aubrey Forsyth-Thompson; 24 Oct. 1951–Sept. 1956 Edwin Arrowsmith; Sept. 1956–1961 Alan Chaplin; 1961–April 1965 Alexander Giles (knighted 1965). *British Government Representatives:* April 1965–4 Oct. 1966 Sir Alexander Giles. *High Commissioners for Basutoland, Bechuanaland, and Swaziland:* 1 Aug. 1964–4 Oct. 1966 Sir Hugh Stephenson. *Tona Kholas (Prime Ministers):* 6 June 1965–7 July 1965 Chief Sekhonyana Maseribane; 7 July 1965–20 Jan. 1986 Chief Leabua Jonathan. *Chairmen of Military Council:* 24 Jan. 1986–2 May 1991 Justin Lekhanya; 2 May 1991–2 April 1993 Elias Tutsoane Ramaema. *Tona Kholas (Prime Ministers:* 2 April 1993–17 Aug. 1994 Ntsu Mokhehle; 17 Aug. 1994–19 Sept. 1994 Hae Phoofolo; 19 Sept. 1994–29 May 1998 Ntsu Mokhehle; 29 May 1998–Pakalitha Mosisili. *Note:* See South Africa for list of High Commissioners, who, after 1931 were no longer responsible for South Africa, only for the High Commission Territories of Basutoland, Bechuanaland, and Swaziland.

Liberia. 15 Dec. 1821– . *Location:* on the southwest coast of West Africa. Sierra Leone borders it on the west, Guinea on the north, and Côte d'Ivoire on the east. The Atlantic forms its southern boundary. *Capital:* Monrovia (from 1824. This town was built on the site of the original Cape Mesurado Colony, and named Monrovia in 1824 for President James Monroe of the USA, by either local resident Robert Goodloe Harper, or the Rev. Ralph Randolph Gurley); Thompson Town (until 1824). *Other names:* the Republic of Liberia (1847–); the Commonwealth of Liberia (1839–1847); the Colony of Liberia (1824–1839); Cape Mesurado Colony (the official name of the colony from 1821 to 1824); Christopolis (an early name given to the colony by its founder Jehudi Ashmun).

History: In the 14th century Norman merchants from Dieppe established two settlements that they called Grand Dieppe and Petit Dieppe (see Petit Dieppe for details), or (collectively) the French Gold Coast, in what are now the Buchanan and Greenville areas, respectively, of Liberia. This area of the Grain Coast (so called

from the roaring trade in "grains of paradise," otherwise known as Amomum or Melegueta pepper) was named Cape Montserrado in 1461 by the Portuguese navigator Pedro de Sintra. Between 1663 and 1664 two forts built by the English Royal Company of Adventurers existed on this coast, at Mesurado and Grand Sesters, but they were destroyed by the Dutch. From the late 18th century onwards, this area was considered for the repatriation of former American slaves, but Sierra Leone, with its better harbor, was used instead. The American Colonization Society (ACS) was formed on 1 Jan. 1817 by a few white North American philanthropists and clergymen, with the intention of sending a few blacks to Africa to found a state, to convert the continent to Christianity, to begin the expansion of American trade, and to rid the USA of the free negroes — or rather, "those considered undesirables." In 1821 Eli Ayres of the ACS bought the coastal lands of what would become Liberia from local Dei chieftains, and made it the site of the first Liberian colony. Among the early settlers were Lott Carey, who arrived in 1821, and representatives of US firms, but the real founder of Liberia was a white American named Jehudi Ashmun who went out in 1822. Under his leadership, the infant colony took off. But it was an unpopular, hard-won country. Liberia would be settled by 19,000 blacks from the USA between 1822 and 1867. Malaria and African hostiles would kill many, and the Liberian motto was (and still is) "The Love of Liberty Brought Us Here." On 15 Aug. 1824 the colony of Cape Mesurado expanded and became the Colony of Liberia (a name coined by either the Rev. Ralph Gurley, another white American, and a colleague of Ashmun's, or local citizen Robert Goodloe Harper, the same man who named Monrovia, and who in turn had a town — Harper — named after him; the name "liber" meaning "free" in Latin). Other, separate, colonies began to spring up in the area: New Georgia, in 1824; and Port Cresson (see Bassa Cove), and Edina, both in 1832. In 1834 Maryland was founded, and in 1835 the colonies of Bassa Cove (successor to Port Cresson) and Mississippi-in-Africa were created, while in 1837 Edina became part of Bassa Cove. On 1 April 1839, having expanded some way into the interior, the Colony of Liberia took in Bassa Cove and New Georgia, and the new, enlarged state became the Commonwealth of Liberia, the first governor being Thomas

Buchanan, cousin of James Buchanan, who would later become president of the USA. Buchanan was the last white administrator of Liberia, although his successor, Joseph Jenkins Roberts, from Virginia, was what used to be called an octoroon. The Commonwealth consisted of the counties of Grand Bassa and Montserrado, which in turn consisted of the settlements of Monrovia, New Georgia, Caldwell, Millsburg, Bexley, Marshall, Bassa Cove, and Edina. In 1842 Mississippi-in-Africa was admitted into the Commonwealth, as Sinoe County. On 26 July 1847 the country became independent of the ACS, as the Republic of Liberia, but with a constitution based on that of the USA. International recognition was quick in coming, and by the following year most countries had accepted the new republic. The USA would not do so until 1862. During Roberts' administration, the British Navy finally ended the slave trade operating out of Liberian ports. In 1857 Maryland, by now a republic, became part of Liberia, and in 1880 the chiefdom of Medina was incorporated. In 1910 the French took, by agreement, a large portion of the Liberian hinterland which Monrovia, for decades, had been unable to control. About this time the USA stepped in to save Liberia from economic ruin and total governmental failure. In effect, the USA became the caretakers of Liberia. In 1926 Firestone, the American company, was granted a million acres in Liberia, for the development of rubber, which had always been one of the major local commodities. Firestone became the dominant presence in Liberia, building roads, harbors and railroads. There was a scandal involving forced labor and slavery which, in 1930 brought down the government of Charles King. William Tubman, who utterly dominated Liberian politics for over a quarter of a century, was either the most popular man in the country by a long way, or the elections were rigged. Liberia achieved stability and prosperity under Tubman. However, after Tubman poverty became a raging issue in Liberia, and the Second Republic of Liberia came into effect in 1980 when after a very violent coup President Tolbert (Tubman's successor) was toppled, and killed, and Master Sergeant Samuel Doe succeeded him. Doe survived a coup in 1985, but civil war began in 1989. Rebel troops from the northeast, the National Patriotic Forces of Liberia, led by Charles Taylor, fast approached the capital, and killed Doe in 1990.

Years of tribal violence followed, and international peace-keeping forces were unsuccessful in their efforts to restore order. Half of the population of Liberia became refugees as a result. In 1996 Ruth Perry became the first woman head of state in modern African history, and the civil war ended in 1997. There was civil war again in 2001–2003. In 2003 President Taylor, surrounded by scandal and corruption, went into exile. AIDS is rampant.

Colonial Agents: 15 Dec. 1821–25 April 1822 Dr. Eli Ayres; 25 April 1822–4 June 1822 Frederick James (acting); 4 June 1822–8 Aug. 1822 Elijah Johnson (acting); 8 Aug. 1822–2 April 1823 Jehudi Ashmun; 2 April 1823–14 Aug. 1823 Elijah Johnson (acting); 14 Aug. 1823–22 Aug. 1824 Jehudi Ashmun (acting); 22 Aug. 1824–26 March 1828 Jehudi Ashmun; 26 March 1828–8 Nov. 1828 Lott Carey (acting); 8 Nov. 1828–22 Dec. 1828 Colston Waring (acting); 22 Dec. 1828–19 April 1829 Richard Randall; 19 April 1829–14 Sept. 1829 Joseph Mechlin, Jr. (acting); 14 Sept. 1829–27 Feb. 1830 Joseph Mechlin, Jr.; 27 Feb. 1830–12 April 1830 John Anderson (acting); 12 April 1830–4 Dec. 1830 Anthony Williams (acting); 4 Dec. 1830–24 Sept. 1833 Joseph Mechlin, Jr.; 24 Sept. 1833–1 Jan. 1834 George McGill (acting); 1 Jan. 1834–10 May 1835 John Pinney; 10 May 1835–12 Aug. 1835 Nathaniel Brander (acting); 12 Aug. 1835–25 Sept. 1836 Ezekiel Skinner; 25 Sept. 1836–1 April 1839 Anthony Williams (acting). *Governors:* 1 April 1839–3 Sept. 1841 Thomas Buchanan; 3 Sept. 1841–20 Jan. 1842 Joseph Roberts (acting); 20 Jan. 1842–26 July 1847 Joseph Roberts. *Presidents of the Convention:* 26 July 1847–Oct. 1847 Samuel Benedict. *Presidents-Elect/Governors:* Oct. 1847–3 Jan. 1848 Joseph Roberts. *Presidents:* 3 Jan. 1848–2 Jan. 1856 Joseph Roberts; 2 Jan. 1856–4 Jan. 1864 Stephen Benson; 4 Jan. 1864–6 Jan. 1868 Daniel Warner; 6 Jan. 1868–4 Jan. 1870 James Payne; 4 Jan. 1870–26 Oct. 1871 Edward Roye; 26 Oct. 1871–1 Jan. 1872 James Smith; 1 Jan. 1872–24 Feb. 1876 Joseph Roberts; 24 Feb. 1876–1 Jan. 1878 James Payne; 1 Jan. 1878–20 Jan. 1883 Anthony Gardner; 20 Jan. 1883–4 April 1884 Alfred Russell; 4 April 1884–4 Jan. 1892 Hilary Johnson; 4 Jan. 1892–12 Nov. 1896 Joseph Cheeseman; 12 Nov. 1896–10 Dec. 1900 William Coleman; 10 Dec. 1900–4 Jan. 1904 Garretson Gibson; 4 Jan. 1904–1 Jan. 1912 Arthur Barclay; 1 Jan. 1912–5 Jan. 1920 Daniel Howard; 5 Jan.

1920–3 Dec. 1930 Charles King; 3 Dec. 1930–1 Jan. 1944 Edwin Barclay; 1 Jan. 1944–23 July 1971 William Tubman; 23 July 1971–12 April 1980 William Tolbert. *Chairmen of the People's Redemption Council:* 12 April 1980–26 July 1984 Samuel Doe. *Presidents of the Interim National Assembly:* 26 July 1984–6 Jan. 1986 Samuel Doe. *Presidents:* 6 Jan. 1986–9 Sept. 1990 Samuel Doe; 9 Sept. 1990–22 Nov. 1990 interregnum; 22 Nov. 1990–7 March 1994 Amos Sawyer. *Heads of Transitional Council of State:* 7 March 1994–1 Sept. 1995 David Kpormakor; 1 Sept. 1995–3 Sept. 1996 Wilton Sankawulo; 3 Sept. 1996–2 Aug. 1997 Ruth Perry. *Presidents:* 2 Aug. 1997–11 Aug. 2003 Charles Taylor; 11 Aug. 2003–14 Oct. 2003 Moses Blah; 14 Oct. 2003–Gyude Bryant.

Libertalia. ca. 1680–ca. 1691. *Location:* northern Madagascar (although see below for various alternatives). *Capital:* [unknown]. *Other names:* Libertatia; International Republic of Libertalia.

History: The following account is somewhat vague, and lacks accurate dates. Indeed, the whole history of the Pirate Republic of Libertalia (or Libertatia — even the name is uncertain) is shrouded not so much in mystery as in legend. Historians never wrote about this republic, only story tellers did so. Even the location of the pirates' stronghold is debated — some say it was on the southeastern coast of Madagascar, some say on the northwest, and yet others say on the island of Anjouan in the Comoros. It is most likely, however, that it was where Diego Suarez was later established. Most important is the name of the place — Libertalia or Libertatia. Around 1672 a French seaman named Capt. Misson and an ex-Vatican priest named Lieutenant Caraccioli, formed a pirate crew on board a captured ship, the *Victoire.* With their oyster the whole world, they plied their trade from the Caribbean to Africa, and wound up in Madagascar and the Comoros. They holed up in Anjouan for a while, fighting in local wars. Caraccioli was now captain of his own ship, and he and Misson founded a republic in Madagascar, naming it Libertalia. Soon they were joined by Capt. Thomas Tew, another pirate. Soon their colony, and the Red Sea pirate trade, increased. A government was set up, but after a raid by local natives during which Caraccioli was killed, and after the loss of Tew's ship, Misson and Tew left for the Americas, Misson drowning en route. Tew was to die several years later.

Lords Conservator: Capt. Misson. *Admirals:* Capt. Thomas Tew. *Secretaries of State:* Capt. Caraccioli.

Libia. 24 Jan. 1929–29 Jan. 1943. *Location:* as modern-day Libya, although not as extensive in the southern region. *Capital:* Tripoli. *Other names:* Italian Libya; Libya; The Fourth Shore.

History: The ancients used the name Libya to mean all of North Africa. The name comes from a Cyrenaican tribe reckoned to have existed about 2,000 b.c. However, the modern Libya was not created until 1929, when the Italians brought together their colonies of Tripolitania and Cirenaica (see Cyrenaica) under one administrative Italian roof. The new entity was called Libia (Libya in English), although Cirenaica continued to be administered separately by a vice-governor. On 1 Jan. 1934 Libia became a colony. On 25 Oct. 1938 it was declared a part of Italy (effective as from 9 Jan. 1939), and over 30,000 Italians were settled here. In 1943 the Cirenaica area (i.e. the eastern area) was lost to the Allies during World War II, and in 1943 so were Tripolitania and the Fezzan (i.e. the southern area). The result was British Cyrenaica (see Cyrenaica), British Tripolitania (see Tripolitania), and French Fezzan (see Fezzan).

Governors-General: 24 Jan. 1929–31 Dec. 1933 Pietro Badoglio; 1 Jan. 1934–28 June 1940 Italo Balbo; 28 June 1940–30 June 1940 Giuseppe Bruni; 30 June 1940–11 Feb. 1941 Rodolfo Graziani; 11 Feb. 1941–19 July 1941 Italo Garibaldi; 19 July 1941–29 Jan. 1943 Ettore Bastico.

Libode District see **Pondoland West**

Libya. 24 Dec. 1951– . *Location:* North Africa, between Tunisia and Algeria on the west, and Egypt on the east. The Mediterranean forms the northern boundary. *Capital:* Tripoli. *Other names:* Libi; Libyan Arab Jamahiriyya, or People's Socialist Libyan Arab Jamahiriyya (from 1977); Libyan Arab People's Republic (1976–1977); Libyan Republic, or Libyan Arab Republic (1969–1976); Kingdom of Libya (1951–1969); United Kingdom of Libya (1963–1969); Federal Kingdom of Libya (1951–1963).

History: In 1949 British Cyrenaica (see Cyrenaica) became an autonomous state, headed by the Sanusi leader, Idris. The locals called the place the Kingdom of Libya, even then, and referred to the amir as the King. Idris formed a

Libyan government, however, on 29 March 1951, in readiness for the moment later in the year, when foreign forces left Libya altogether, that is as occupying forces. The kingdom actually came into effect on Jan. 2, 1952. The three components which made up this new kingdom were: Cyrenaica, Tripolitania and the Fezzan. From 1951 to 1963 the three provinces of Cyrenaica, Tripolitania, and Fezzan were granted autonomy under a federal kingdom, but the provinces were abolished on 27 April 1963 and the country became a unitary state. Idris gained much foreign aid from the UK and the USA for allowing those countries to build air bases in Libya. In 1959 oil was discovered in Libya in a big way, and made the country rich. On 1 Sept. 1969 Colonel Muammar al-Qadaffi, at the head of a military junta, usurped King Idris, and seized power, creating the Libyan Republic. He closed down the foreign air bases, seized the oil and banking businesses, and succeeded in alienating the Western powers. On 5 Jan. 1976 the country became known as the Libyan Arab People's Republic, and on 2 March 1977 the name changed again, to the Libyan Arab Jamahiriyya ("jamahiriyya" means "republic"). This was a socialist centralized republic. Libya engaged in a war with Egypt in July 1977, and also occupied the northern regions of Chad that year, hoping to acquire uranium. These Libyan forces were eventually expelled, in March 1987, by the Chadian army, leaving over a billion dollars' worth of equipment behind. Col. Qadaffi became known for, among other things, his aid to terrorists throughout the world, and for harboring (although not sincerely, it seems) deposed African tyrants. In 1986 there was a virtual war with the USA. Beginning in the late 1990s Qadaffi did a volte face and became the good scout of the Middle East, aligning strenuously with the West, admitting to his past evil deeds (some of them, anyway), seeming to rectify them, and expelling terrorists.

Kings: 24 Dec. 1951–1 Sept. 1969 Idris al-Mahdi as-Sanusi (also known as Idris I). *Military Revolutionary Leaders:* 1 Sept. 1969–13 Sept. 1969 Muammar al-Qadaffi. *Chairmen of the Revolutionary Command Council:* 13 Sept. 1969–5 Jan. 1976 Muammar al-Qadaffi. *Secretaries-General:* 5 Jan. 1976–1 March 1979 Muammar al-Qadaffi; 1 March 1979–7 Jan. 1981 Abd al-Ali al-Obeidi; 7 Jan. 1981–16 Feb. 1984 Muhammad az-Zaruq Rajab; 16 Feb. 1984–1 March 1987 Miftah al-Istah; 1 March 1987–7 Oct. 1990 Umar Mustafa al-Muntasir; 7 Oct. 1990–29 Jan. 1994 Abu Za'id Umar Durda; 29 Jan. 1994–29 Dec. 1997 Abd al-Majid al-Qa'ud; 29 Dec. 1997–1 March 2000 Muhammad Ahmad al-Mangush; 1 March 2000–Mubarrak ash-Shamikh. *National Leaders:* 1 March 1979–Muammar al-Qadaffi. *Prime Ministers:* 24 Dec. 1951–15 Feb. 1954 Mahmud Bey Muntasir; 19 Feb. 1954–11 April 1954 Muhammad as-Saqizli; 12 April 1954–23 May 1957 Mustafa ben Halim; 26 May 1957–16 Oct. 1960 Abd al-Majid Kubar; 16 Oct. 1960–21 March 1963 Muhammad ben Uthman; 21 March 1963–24 Jan. 1964 Muhiaddin Fekini; 24 Jan. 1964–21 March 1965 Mahmud Bey Muntasir; 21 March 1965–28 June 1967 Hussein Maziq; 29 June 1967–25 Oct. 1967 Abd al-Qadir Badri; 25 Oct. 1967–4 Sept. 1968 Abd al-Hamid al-Bakkush; 4 Sept. 1968–1 Sept. 1969 Wanis al-Qadaffi (also known as Wanis al-Gadaffi); 8 Sept. 1969–16 Jan. 1970 Suleiman al-Maghrebi; 16 July 1972–2 March 1977 Abdal-Salem Jallud. *Note:* In times of no Prime Minister, Col. Qadaffi held that post.

Lijdenburg see **Lydenburg**

Lijdenrust see **Lydenrust**

Little Free State. 10 March 1886–2 May 1891. *Location:* southwest of Swaziland, in eastern Transvaal. *Capital:* This republic was too small to have a capital, as such. *Other names:* Klein Vrijstaat.

History: In 1886 Umbandine of Swaziland ceded a very small area in the southwest of his kingdom to F.I. Maritz and J.F. Ferreira, two Transvaal officials. The Republic of Klein Vrijstaat (population 72) was proclaimed, intended by the Boers as a first foothold in Swaziland. In 1891 it became Ward 1 of the District of Piet Retief in the South Africa Republic (see Transvaal).

Rulers: 10 March 1886–22 May 1891 ruled by a triumvirate.

Little Popo. ca. 1750–19 July 1883. *Location:* 30 miles east of Lomé, in Togo, on the Bight of Benin. *Capital:* Little Popo. *Other names:* Petit Popo; Anecho.

History: Founded about 1750, the kingdom of Little Popo became a French protectorate on 19 July 1883. In 1885 it became part of the German protectorate of Togoland.

Kings: ca. 1750–ca. 1775 Quam Dessu; ca. 1775–ca. 1800 Foli Arlonko; ca. 1800–1820 Aholin; 1820–1859 Akuete Zankli Lawson I. *Regents:* 1859–1868 Late Adjromitan. *Kings:* 1869–19 July 1883 Alexandre Boevi Lawson II; 19 July 1883–1906 Georges Betnui Lawson III; 1906–1918 Jackson Kpavuvu Lawson IV; 1918–1922 [vacant]; 1922–1948 Frederick Boevi Lawson V; 1948–1955 Glin Lawson VI.

Lobi see **Burkina Faso**

Lobos see **Canary Islands** and **Gran Canaria**

Lokoja see **Abuja**

Los Islands see **Guinea**

Lotse see **Barotseland**

Louisbourg. 11 Feb. 1774–27 May 1786. *Location:* the Bay of Antongil, in northeast Madagascar. *Capital:* Louisbourg (named for King Louis XV of France).

History: In 1774 Maritius Beynowski, a Pole recently escaped from Siberia, was commissioned by France to found a settlement here. France refused him a protectorate, however, and in 1777 he received monies from the new government of the United States of America and proclaimed himself king of the whole northeast coast of Madagascar. He was killed by the French in 1786.

Kings: 11 Feb. 1774–27 May 1786 Maritius Beynowski.

Lounda see **Lunda**

Lower Congo–Gabon. 11 Dec. 1888–29 Dec. 1903. *Location:* Congo and Gabon combined. *Capital:* Brazzaville. *Other names:* Moyen-Congo–Gabon.

History: In French Equatorial Africa in the late 19th century it was difficult to establish satisfactory administrative systems due to the constantly shifting and expanding boundaries of the French territories, as more and more land opened up through exploration, and conquest. Thus, in 1888 it was found by the French to be expedient to combine their two colonies of Moyen-Congo (see Congo) and Gabon, with headquarters at Brazzaville. On 5 July 1902 this "super-territory" became a colony. It did not last long, however,

as Moyen-Congo and Gabon went back to being their own colonies.

Rulers: see both Congo and Gabon for exact dates.

Lower Egypt. ca. 5000 b.c.–ca. 3100 b.c. *Location:* the part of present-day Egypt north of Cairo, i.e. the Nile Delta area. *Capital:* Buto (latterly); Behdet (formerly). *Other names:* Northern Egypt.

History: Lower Egypt and Upper Egypt were the two kingdoms that developed in pre-dynastic times in Egypt. Horus, the falcon, was the chief god of Lower Egypt, which was the country of the Red Crown (Upper Egypt having the White Crown). Around 3100 b.c. Menes of Upper Egypt conquered the Northern Kingdom and united the two into the 1st Dynasty of Egypt.

Kings: (?) Tiu; (?)–(?) Thes; (?)–(?) Askiu; (?)–(?) Waznar.

Lozi Empire see **Barotseland**

Lualaba see **Katanga Republic**

Luanda see **Angola** and **Dutch West Africa**

Luba Empire. ca. 1585–ca. 1885. *Location:* southern Congo (Zaire). *Capital:* Munza (ca. 1620–ca. 1885); Mwibele (ca. 1585–ca. 1620). *Other names:* Luba Kingdom.

History: About 1560 a powerful warrior, Kongolo, invaded the area and subjugated the several local chiefdoms, thus creating the first Luba Empire. He was joined by Ilunga Mbili, a hunter, who later returned to his homeland. A son, Ilunga Kalala, was born to Ilunga Mbili's wife (she was Kongolo's half-sister), and when he came of age he developed into a great warrior and extended Kongolo's kingdom. Kongolo, jealous of the young man's success, and afraid of his power, attempted to have him killed. Kalala defeated Kongolo in war and established the second Luba Empire about 1620. Several other Luba kingdoms (vassals of Ilunga Kalala) were established in the area around this time (e.g. Kalundwe, Kikonja, Kaniok). Also out of Luba came Lunda (which far outstripped its parent in the northeast) and Kazembe (which arose in what is now northern Zambia around 1710). About 1885 the Luba Empire was incorporated into the Congo Free State [see Congo (Zaire)].

Emperors: ca. 1585–ca. 1620 Kongolo; ca. 1620–ca. 1640 Ilunga Kalala; ca. 1640–ca. 1650 Kasongo Mwine Kibanza; ca. 1650–ca. 1670 Ngoi Sanza; ca. 1670–ca. 1685 Kasongo Kabundulu; ca. 1685–ca. 1700 Kumwimba; ca. 1700–ca. 1715 Kasongo Bonswe; ca. 1715–ca. 1740 Mwine Kombe Dai; ca. 1740–ca. 1742 Kadilo; ca. 1742–ca. 1749 Kekenya; ca. 1749–ca. 1769 Kaumbo; ca. 1769–ca. 1780 Miketo; ca. 1780–ca. 1810 Ilunga Sunga; ca. 1810–ca. 1840 Kumwimba Ngombe; ca. 1840–ca. 1840 Ndai Mujinga; ca. 1840–ca. 1870 Ilunga Kaabala; ca. 1870–ca. 1880 Muloba; ca. 1880–ca. 1882 Kitamba; ca. 1882–1885 Kasongo Kalombo. *Kings:* 1885–1891 Dai Mande; 1891–Oct. 1917 Kasongo Nyembo.

Lunda. ca. 1500–25 May 1891. *Location:* southern Congo (Zaire). *Capital:* Musumba. *Other names:* Lounda; Lunda Kingdom; Mwata Yamvo Empire.

History: Of unknown extraction, the Lunda Kingdom was introduced to Luba culture (see Luba Empire) by Cibinda Ilunga, a Luba nobleman who, about 1620, came to Lunda and married a Lundan princess. Lunda became the biggest of the Luba states. By 1680 the Lunda Empire (as it had now become) had expanded enormously, and the Mwata Yamvo (as the ruler had long been known) developed a reputation that spread over most of Africa. In 1891 the Lunda Empire became part of the Congo Free State [see Congo (Zaire)].

Kings: ca. 1500–ca. 1516 Mwaaka. *Mwata Yamvos (Great Rulers):* ca. 1516–ca. 1550 Yala Maaku; ca. 1550–ca. 1590 Kunde; ca. 1590–ca. 1600 Luedji; ca. 1600–ca. 1620 Nkonda Matit; ca. 1620–ca. 1630 Cibinda Ilunga; ca. 1630–ca. 1660 Yavu Ilunga; ca. 1660–ca. 1687 Yavu a Nawej; ca. 1687–ca. 1719 Mbal Iyavu; ca. 1719–ca. 1720 Mukas Munying Kabalond; ca. 1720–ca. 1748 Muteba Kat Kateng; ca. 1748–ca. 1766 Mukas Waranankong; ca. 1766–ca. 1773 Nawej Mufa Muchimbunj; ca. 1773–ca. 1802 Chikombi Iyavu; ca. 1802–1852 Nawej Ditend; 1852–1857 Mulaji Nam Wan; 1857–1873 Muteba Chikombu; 1873–1874 Mbala Kmong Isot; 1874–1883 Mbumb Muteba Kat; 1883–1884 Chimbindu Kasang; 1884–1884 Kangapu Nawej; 1884–1886 Mudib; 1886–1887 Mutand Mukaz; 1887–Nov. 1887 Mbala Kalong; Nov. 1887–1903 Mushidi; 1903–1920 Muteba III; 1920–1951 Kamba; 1951–June 1963 Ditend Yavu;

1963–1965 Musidi; Dec. 1965–27 Nov. 1973 Muteba IV; 27 Nov. 1973–1984 Mbumba; 1984–27 Jan. 2005 Kawel; Jan. 2005–Kaumb.

Luo see **Kenya**

Lydenburg. 1846–4 April 1860. *Location:* east central Transvaal, in South Africa. *Capital:* Lydenburg (founded in 1849 and named for the "lijden" or "sufferings" of the pioneers). *Other names:* Republiek Lijdenburg.

History: In 1846 the Republic of Ohrigstad was abandoned due to plague and tsetse fly. The survivors left for the south to form a new territory around the town that would eventually become Lydenburg. The country expanded by taking in the old area of Ohrigstad, and Lydenburg was officially declared a republic on 17 Dec. 1856. In May 1858 it expanded even more by taking in the Republic of Utrecht. In 1860 Lydenburg merged into the South African Republic (see Transvaal). This move made the Transvaal a unified Boer state.

Commandants-General: 1846–1850 Andries Pretorius (acting); Jan. 1851–1859 Willem Joubert; 1859–4 April 1860 Joseph Van Dyck.

Lydenrust. 20 Oct. 1885–1887. *Location:* southwest Africa. *Capital:* Grootfontein. *Other names:* Lijdenrust; Upingtonia (its name between 1885 and 1886).

History: A Boer republic founded in 1885 by 46 Thirstland trekkers and named Upingtonia for Sir Thomas Upington, the Prime Minister of Cape Colony, in the hope that the Cape would support the fledgling republic. It did not, so in 1886 Upingtonia accepted Bismarck's offer of German protection and was renamed Lydenrust (or Lijdenrust). German protection did not amount to much and the hostiles became too much for the young republic, which ceased to exist in 1887.

Presidents: 20 Oct. 1885–1887 G.D.P. Prinsloo.

Maba see **Wadai**

Macarthy Island see **Fort James**

Machico. 1418–1580. *Location:* Madeira Island, Madeira. *Capital:* Machico.

History: This was a Portuguese donataria (see Port Santo for details of its history), named for a legendary character, Robert Machim, who arrived here with a girl he eloped with from England. In 1580, when Spain took over Portugal, Machico became part of the colony of Madeira. *Rulers:* 1418–1580 [unknown].

Macías Nguema Biyogo Island see **Fernando Po** and **Equatorial Guinea**

Macina see **Masina**

Madagascar. ca. 1300– . *Location:* in the Indian Ocean, off the east coast of Africa. *Capital:* Antananarivo (called Tananarive by the French, this was the capital from 1630); Ambohidrabiby (ca. 1575–1630); Alasora (ca. 1540–ca. 1575); Imerinanjaka (ca. 1500–ca. 1540). *Other names:* République Malgache, or Malagasy Republic (1958–1975); Hova Kingdom, or Imerina Kingdom (ca. 1300–1810).

History: About 2,000 years the big red island of Madagascar was settled by peoples from Malaya and Indonesia. Africans and Arabs were added over the centuries. The Hova peoples founded their civilization in the Ikopa Valley in the center of Madagascar about 1250. The kingdom of Imerina was founded about 1300. The first European to see Madagascar was Diogo Dias, the Portuguese navigator, on 10 Aug. 1500, and he named it the Isle of St. Lawrence, it being the feast day of that saint when Dias discovered it. During the first 20 years of the 17th century Portuguese missionaries were unsuccessful in their attempts to find converts on the coastal parts of the island, and in the second quarter of that century English settlements on the southwest coast, and at Nossi-Bé also failed. In 1642 Fort-Dauphin was established by the French as an East India trading post, and this was the first European foothold on the island. It lasted until 1674, and France, from that time, maintained a claim on the whole island. About 1680 pirates founded the International Republic of Libertalia in Madagascar, but by 1691 that had gone too. From 1710 to 1794 the kingdom of Imerina was split into four, with sub-kings ruling at the four capitals of Ambohidratimo, Ambohimanga, Antananarivo, and Ambohidrabiby. In the 18th century the kingdom of Betsimisaraka was created by Ratsimilaho, the son of an English pirate and a local woman. In 1794 King Andrianampoinimerina re-united the whole country, with its capital, again, at Antananarivo. In 1803

a French agency was established at Antananarivo, by Sylvain Roux, but this was taken by the English in 1811, and for several years thereafter a British resident, James Hastie, lived at Antananarivo. In 1810 the kingdom of Imerina became known as Madagascar, and the enlightened king, Radama I, came to he throne. By 1828 Radama had conquered most of the other chiefdoms on the island, taking in Antemoro, Sakalava, Betsimisaraka, Zafi-Raminia, Menaba, and Boina, and aided in this endeavor by the British in their attempt to keep the French from gaining the island. At that time the French maintained only the island bases of Sainte-Marie and Nossi-Bé, In 1828 Radama died, aged 36, and was succeeded by the xenophobic queen Ranavalona I. In 1835 she banned Christianity, which had made great headway under Radama, and which had advanced the country considerably. Under Queen Ranavalona Madagascar plunged into the dark ages, and all foreign contact was lost. A farcical attempt in 1845 by the French and British navies to take the port of Tamatave, failed. In 1861, though, the queen died, and Radama II, her son, opened up the kingdom again. He and the three queens who succeeded him allowed the French to gain great control of the island. The real power in Madagascar at this time was the prime minister, Rainilaiarivony, who had married three queens in a row. By 17 Dec. 1885, the French had succeeded in gaining such control over the whole island that a French administration was established. The treaty they signed provided for French control over Malagasy foreign relations. In 1886, as another result of this treaty, the French established another colony in the northern part of the island, Diego Suarez. On 5 Aug. 1890 the French placed a protectorate over most of Madagascar. On 6 Aug. 1896 this protectorate became a colony, and took in the three other French possessions on or around the island: Diego Suarez, Nossi-Bé, and Sainte-Marie. At the same time the kingdom of Madagascar came to an end, with the monarch remaining as a figurehead until she was exiled to Réunion. Madagascar declared in favor of Vichy France in 1940, and in order to prevent the Japanese taking over the island, the British took temporary control of Madagascar on 25 Sept. 1942, with the French governor-general continuing to administer the island. On 13 Oct. 1946 the island was given back to France, when it became an overseas territory. Nationalist sentiment in

Madagascar, which had first come to light during World War I, now came to the fore. On 14 Oct. 1958, as the result of a vote, Madagascar became a semi- autonomous republic within the French Community, and changed its name to the Malagasy Republic. On 26 June 1960 the Malagasy Republic became fully independent. In 1972 a coup, motivated by distrust of the government's reliance of France, and to increasing poverty on the island, resulted in the Sovietization of Madagascar and the island becoming effectively closed to the Western World. A state of emergency was declared. Tyranny set in as a natural consequence of this action. On 21 Dec. 1975 the country changed its name to the Democratic Republic of Madagascar. By 1979 the country was in economic ruins, and had to rely on Western aid for survival. By 1991 the autocratic Ratsiraka had lost control of the government and Albert Zafy set up a "second government" that was recognized by several countries. Ratsiraka was forced to yield many of his powers, but he lost the 1993 election to Zafy and a "democracy" came into being. However, Zafy soon became power-mad too and he was impeached in 1996. Ratsiraka won the 1997 election. He decentralized government by creating autonomous provinces, but the governors of the provinces remained his puppets. Marc Ravalomanana, the new savior of Madagascar, won the 2002 election, but Ratsiraka rigged the results and refused to step down. Ravalomanana declared himself president on 22 Feb. 2002. Four days later he named Jacques Sylla as his prime minister, and so there were now two governments. This almost led to civil war. In April and May 2002 several provinces declared themselves independent and established a joint capital for themselves. Ratsiraka moved his "government" there, while Ravalomanana stayed in the capital. Finally Ravalomanana was installed as the new president on 6 May 2002, and on 15 June 2002 Ratsiraka fled to France.

Kings: ca. 1300–ca. 1320 Andrianerimerina; ca. 1320–ca. 1500 ten kings whose names have not come down. *Queens:* ca. 1500–ca. 1520 Rafohy; ca. 1520–ca. 1540 Rangita. *Kings:* ca. 1540–ca. 1575 Andramanelo; ca. 1575–ca. 1610 Ralambo; ca. 1610–ca. 1630 Andrianjaka; ca. 1630–ca. 1650 Andriantsitakatrandriana; ca. 1650–ca. 1670 Andriantsimitoviaminanandran-dehibe; ca. 1670–ca. 1675 Razakatsitakatrandriana; ca. 1675–1710 Andrianamasinavalma;

1710–1794 four kings (see above); 1794–1810 Andrianampoinimerina; 1810–27 July 1828 Radama I. *Queens:* 28 July 1828–16 Aug. 1861 Ranavalona I. *Kings:* 23 Aug. 1861–12 May 1863 Radama II. *Queens:* 12 May 1863–30 March 1868 Rasoaherina; 1 April 1868–13 July 1883 Ranavalona II; 13 July 1883–28 Feb. 1897 Ranavalona III. *Residents-General:* 28 April 1886–March 1888 Charles Le Myre de Villiers; March 1888–12 Dec. 1889 Arthur Larrouy; 12 Dec. 1889–11 Oct. 1891 Maurice Bompard; 11 Oct. 1891–Oct. 1892 M. Lacoste (acting); Oct. 1892–1894 Arthur Larrouy; 1894–1 Dec. 1895 Charles Le Myre de Villiers; 1 Dec. 1895–28 Sept. 1896 Hippolyte Laroche. *Governors-General:* 28 Sept. 1896–21 April 1899 Gen. Joseph Galliéni; 21 April 1899–3 July 1900 Gen. Pennequin (acting); 3 July 1900–11 May 1905 Gen. Joseph Galliéni; 11 May 1905–23 Dec. 1905 Charles Louis Lepreux (acting); 23 Dec. 1905–13 Dec. 1909 Jean Augagneur; 13 Dec. 1909–16 Jan. 1910 Hubert Garbit (acting); 16 Jan. 1910–31 Oct. 1910 Henri Core (acting); 31 Oct. 1910–5 Aug. 1914 Albert Picquié; 5 Aug. 1914–13 Oct. 1914 Hubert Garbit (acting); 13 Oct. 1914–24 July 1917 Hubert Garbit; 24 July 1917–1 Aug. 1918 Martial Merlin; 1 Aug. 1918–12 July 1919 Abraham Schrameck; 12 July 1919–22 June 1920 Casimir Guyon (acting); 22 June 1920–13 March 1923 Hubert Garbit; 13 March 1923–20 Feb. 1924 Charles Brunet (acting); 20 Feb. 1924–24 Jan. 1926 Marcel Olivier; 24 Jan. 1926–18 March 1927 Hugues Berthier (acting); 18 March 1927–30 Jan. 1929 Marcel Olivier; 30 Jan. 1929–1 May 1930 Hugues Berthier (acting); 1 May 1930–19 June 1931 Léon Cayla; 19 June 1931–29 Jan. 1932 Louis Bonvin (acting); 29 Jan. 1932–12 Oct. 1933 Léon Cayla; 12 Oct. 1933–29 Oct. 1934 Joseph Bernard (acting); 29 Oct. 1934–31 March 1936 Léon Cayla; 31 March 1936–17 April 1937 Léonce Jore (acting); 17 April 1937–22 April 1939 Léon Cayla; 22 April 1939–10 June 1939 Léon Réallon (acting); 10 June 1939–30 July 1940 Jules de Coppet; 30 July 1940–11 April 1941 Léon Cayla; 11 April 1941–25 Sept. 1942 Armand Annet. *British Occupied Territories Administrators:* 25 Sept. 1942–1943 Anthony Sillery. *Governors-General:* 25 Sept. 1942–7 Jan. 1943 M. Bech (acting); 7 Jan. 1943–3 May 1943 Paul de Gentilhomme; 3 May 1943–1944 Pierre de Saint-Mart; 1944–27 March 1946 Paul de Saint-Mart; 27 March 1946–19 May 1946 Robert Boudry (acting); 19 May 1946–13 Oct. 1946 Jules de Coppet. *High*

Commissioners: 13 Oct. 1946–Dec. 1947 Jules de Coppet; Dec. 1947–Feb. 1948 [unknown] (acting); Feb. 1948–3 Feb. 1950 Pierre de Chevigné; 3 Feb. 1950–1953 Isaac Bargues; 1953–26 June 1960 Jean-Louis Soucadaux. *Presidents:* 27 April 1959–18 May 1972 Philibert Tsiranana. *Titular Heads of State:* 18 May 1972–8 Oct. 1972 Philibert Tsiranana. *Heads of the National Army:* 18 May 1972–8 Oct. 1972 Gabriel Ramanantsoa. *Presidents:* 8 Oct. 1972–5 Feb. 1975 Gabriel Ramanantsoa; 5 Feb. 1975–11 Feb. 1975 Richard Ratsimandrava. *Heads of the National Military Directorate:* 11 Feb. 1975–15 June 1975 Gilles Andriamahazo. *Presidents of the Supreme Revolutionary Council:* 15 June 1975–21 Dec. 1975 Didier Ratsiraka. *Presidents:* 21 Dec. 1975–9 March 1993 Didier Ratsiraka; 9 March 1993–5 Sept. 1996 Albert Zafy; 5 Sept. 1996–9 Feb. 1997 Norbert Ratsirahonana (acting); 9 Feb. 1997–5 July 2002 Didier Ratsiraka; 5 July 2002–Marc Ravalomanana. *Prime Ministers:* 14 July 1864–6 Aug. 1896 Rainilaiarivony; 21 Dec. 1975–30 July 1976 Joel Rakotomalala; 12 Aug. 1976–14 Aug. 1977 Justin Rakotoniaina; 14 Aug. 1977–Dec. 1987 Desiré Rakotoarijaona; Dec. 1987–Feb. 1988 Victor Ramahatra (acting); Feb. 1988–8 Aug. 1991 Victor Ramahatra; 8 Aug. 1991–9 Aug. 1993 Guy Razanamasy; 9 Aug. 1993–30 Oct. 1995 Francisque Ravony; 30 Oct. 1995–28 May 1996 Emmanuel Rakotovahiny; 28 May 1996–5 Sept. 1996 Norbert Ratsirahonana; 5 Sept. 1996–21 Feb. 1997 Emmanuel Rakotovahiny; 21 Feb. 1997–23 July 1998 Pascal Rakotomavo; 23 July 1998–31 May 2002 Tantely Andrianarivo; 31 May 2002–5 July 2002 Jean-Jacques Rasolondraiba; 5 July 2002 Jacques Sylla. *Note:* In times of no Prime Minister, the monarch, the president, or other head of state held that office.

Madeira. 1580– . *Location:* an archipelago of several islands, two of them inhabited (Madeira and Porto Santo), 360 miles off the coast of Northwest Africa, in the Atlantic Ocean. The uninhabited islands are divided into two groups—the Desertas and the Selvagens. The Desertas comprise three islets 11 miles southeast of Madeira: Chão, Bugio, and Deserta Grande, as well as a rock, Sail Rock. The Selvagens (or Salvage Islands) comprise three rocks located 156 miles south of Madeira. *Capital:* Funchal. *Other names:* Ilhas de Madeira; Funchal Islands; Funchal District (alternative name from 1834).

History: In 1580, with the Spanish takeover of Portugal, the three donatarias, Funchal, Machico (these two on the island of Madeira), and Porto Santo (its own island), were united as the colony of Madeira (still run by the Portuguese. Spain ruled Portugal until 1656). In 1775 slavery was abolished. Between 1801 and 1802, and again between 1807 and 1814, Britain occupied the islands, with, however, nominal Portuguese rule continuing for those periods. In 1834 Madeira became a metropolitan district (overseas province) of Portugal. *Governors-General:* 1580–1581 [unknown]; 1581–1585 João Leitão; 1585–1591 Tristão da Veiga; 1591–1595 Antonio de Barreido; 1595–1600 Diogo de Azambuja e Melo; 1600–1603 Cristóvão de Sousa; 1603–1609 João d'Eça; 1609–1614 Manuel Coutinho; 1614–1618 Jorge da Câmara; 1618–1622 Pedro da Silva; 1622–1624 Francisco Henriques; 1624–1625 [unknown]; 1625–1626 Fernão de Saldanha; 1626–1628 Jerónimo Fernando; 1628–1634 Francisco de Sousa; 1634–1636 João de Meneses; 1636–1640 Luis Pinto; 1640–1642 [unknown]; 1642–1645 Nunho Freire; 1645–1648 Manuel Mascarenhas; 1648–1651 Manuel da Silva; 1651–1655 Bartolomeu de Vasconcelos; 1655–1660 Pedro da Silva da Cunha; 1660–1665 Diogo Furtado; 1665–1668 Francisco de Mascarenhas; 1668–1669 [unknown]; 1669–1672 Pires de Sousa e Meneses; 1672–1676 João de Saldanha e Albuquerque; 1676–1680 Alexandre de Moura e Albuquerque; 1680–1684 João de Brito; 1684–1688 Pedro Brandão; 1688–1690 Lourenço de Almada; 1690–1694 Rodrigo da Costa; 1694–1698 Pantaleão de Sá e Melo; 1698–1701 Antonio de Melo; 1701–1704 João de Ataíde e Azevedo; 1704–1712 Duarte Pereira; 1712–1715 Pedro Álvares da Cunha; 1715–1718 João da Gama; 1718–1724 Jorge de Sousa e Meneses; 1724–1727 Francisco Freire; 1727–1734 Filipe Mascarenhas; 1734–1737 João Branco; 1737–1747 Francisco Gurjão; 1747–1751 João do Nascimento; 1751–1754 Álvaro de Távora; 1754–1757 Manuel de Saldanha e Albuquerque; 1757–1759 Gaspar Brandão; 1759–1767 José de Sá; 1767–1777 João Pereira; 1777–1781 João Coutinho; 1781–1798 Diogo Coutinho; 1798–1800 [unknown]; 1800–1803 José da Câmara; 1803–1807 Ascenso Freire; 1807–1813 Pedro de Antas e Meneses; 1813–1814 Luis de Gouveia e Almeida; 1814–1815 [unknown]; 1815–1819 Florencio de Melo; 1819–1821 Sebastião Botelho; 1821–1822 Rodrigo de Melo;

1822–1823 Antonio de Noronha; 1823–1827 Manuel de Portugal e Castro; 1827–1828 José Valdês; 1828–1830 José Monteiro; 1830–1834 Álvaro de Sousa e Macedo. *Administrators:* 1834–[unknown].

Mafwe see **Namibia**

Maghrib see **Algeria** and **Barbary States** and **Morocco** and **Tunisia**

Mahdist State see **Sudan**

Mahé see **Seychelles**

Mahoré see **Mayotte**

Maio see **Cape Verde**

Makdishu see **Mogadishu**

Makuria see **Mukurra**

Malagasy Republic see **Madagascar**

Malawi. 21 Sept. 1889– . *Location:* the extreme north of Southern Africa. *Capital:* Lilongwe (established as a town in 1947, it was chosen as the new capital in 1964, effective as from 1 Jan. 1975); Zomba (built in 1885, and named for Mount Zomba, on whose slope the town is situated, it was the capital until 1 Jan. 1975). *Other names:* Nyasaland (the generally used name between 1891 and 1964); British Central Africa (alternative name from 1891 to 1907); Shiré River Protectorate, or Shiré Heights Protectorate (1889–1891).

History: In 1889 a protectorate was proclaimed by Britain over the Shiré River, then the local area most populated with British. On 1 Feb. 1891 (effective as from 14 May 1891) it expanded to become Nyasaland, and on 22 Feb. 1893 the name of the country changed to the British Central Africa Protectorate. On 6 July 1907 (effective as of 30 Sept. 1907) the country became the British protectorate of Nyasaland. Between 1953 and 1963, along with Southern Rhodesia and Northern Rhodesia, Nyasaland went to form the Federation of Rhodesia and Nyasaland. There was agitation for independence, led by Dr. Hastings Banda, who was jailed by the British from 1959 to 1960. A state of emergency was declared in Nyasaland in 1959. On 1 Feb. 1963 Nyasa-

land gained self-rule (effective 9 May 1963), and on 6 July 1964 it gained independence as the dominion of Malawi (the name means "land of flames"), remaining within the British Commonwealth. On 6 July 1966 it declared itself a republic. Hastings Banda was the strongman (read "dictator") in Malawi for almost 30 years, and he allowed no political parties other than his own. There was an awesome drought in 1992, uprisings against Banda, and Western aid was suspended. In 1994 free elections were held for the first time, and Banda was defeated. Malawi, crippled by AIDS, also faces mass starvation.

Commissioners: 21 Sept. 1889–14 May 1891 Harry Johnston. *Commissioners/Consuls-General:* 14 May 1891–1894 Harry Johnston; 1894–1894 John S. Brabant (acting); 1894–1894 Alfred Sharpe (acting); 1894–16 April 1896 Harry Johnston (knighted 1896); 16 April 1896–14 July 1897 Alfred Sharpe (acting); 14 July 1897–1903 Alfred Sharpe; 1903–1903 Francis Pearce (acting); 1903–31 March 1907 Sir Alfred Sharpe; 1 April 1907–6 July 1907 Francis Pearce (acting). *Governors:* 6 July 1907–30 Sept. 1907 Francis Pearce (acting); 1 Oct. 1907–1 May 1908 Sir William Manning (acting); 1 May 1908–1 April 1910 Sir Alfred Sharpe; 1 April 1910–3 July 1910 Francis Pearce (acting); 4 July 1910–6 Feb. 1911 Henry Wallis (acting); 6 Feb. 1911–23 Sept. 1913 Sir William Manning; 23 Sept. 1913–1921 George Smith (knighted 1914); 1921–1921 Richard Rankine (acting); 1921–12 April 1923 Sir George Smith; 12 April 1923–27 March 1924 Richard Rankine (acting); 27 March 1924–30 May 1929 Sir Charles Bowring; 30 May 1929–7 Nov. 1929 Wilfred Davidson-Houston (acting); 7 Nov. 1929–22 Nov. 1932 Shenton Thomas (knighted 1931); 22 Nov. 1932–9 April 1934 Sir Hubert Young; 9 April 1934–21 Sept. 1934 Kenneth Hall (acting); 21 Sept. 1934–14 Jan. 1939 Sir Harold Kittermaster; 14 Jan. 1939–20 March 1939 [unknown] (acting); 20 March 1939–8 Aug. 1942 Sir Donald Mackenzie-Kennedy; 8 Aug. 1942–27 March 1947 Sir Edmund Richards; 27 March 1947–30 March 1948 ruled by acting governors; 30 March 1948–31 May 1951 Geoffrey Colby (knighted 1949); 31 May 1951–11 Nov. 1954 ruled by acting governors; 11 Nov. 1954–10 April 1956 Sir Geoffrey Colby; 10 April 1956–10 April 1961 Sir Robert Armitage; 10 April 1961–6 July 1964 Sir Glyn Jones. *Governors-General:* 6 July 1964–6 July 1966 Sir Glyn Jones. *Presidents:* 6 July 1966–6 July 1971 Hastings Banda. *Presidents for*

Life: 6 July 1971–17 May 1994 Hastings Banda. *Presidents:* 21 May 1994–Bakili Muluzi. *Prime Ministers:* 1 Feb. 1963–6 July 1966 Hastings Banda.

Maleteland see Bamaleteland

Mali. 6 Sept. 1880– . *Location:* North West Africa. *Capital:* Bamako (the capital from 1908, this town was originally a local settlement, and occupied by the French in 1880); Kayès (until 1908). *Other names:* République du Mali, or Republic of Mali (from 1960); République Soudainaise, or Republic of the Sudan (1958–1960); Soudain Français, or French Sudan (1920–1958); Haut-Sénégal–Niger, or Upper Senegal and Niger (1904–1920); Sénégambie–Niger, or Senegambie–Niger, or Senegambia and Niger (1902–1904); Haut-Sénégal–Niger, or Upper Senegal–Middle Niger, or Upper Senegal and Niger (1899–1902); Soudain Français, or French Sudan (1890–1899); Haut-Sénégal, or Upper Senegal, or Upper River (1880–1890).

History: In earlier history this land formed a fundamental part of the territory of the Ghana Empire, and then the Mali Empire, and subsequently the Songhai Empire and Timbuktu. As far as the Europeans were concerned, the area that is today Mali was opened up by Louis Faidherbe, the great French administrator of Senegal from the 1850s. In 1880 a commandant-supérieur was appointed by the French government to look after French interests what became known as the Territory of Upper Senegal. On 21 March 1881 the French placed a protectorate over the country, and named it Upper Senegal. On 18 Aug. 1890 it became known as the Territory of the French Sudan. On 27 Aug. 1892 it became a military territory, and on 21 Nov. 1893 a civil territory. On 16 June 1895 it became the colony of the French Sudan, and on 17 Oct. 1899 it became subject to Senegal, and became known as Upper Senegal and Niger Territory. Trading posts were set up in Gao, and at other points on the Niger River, and the territory was divided into "cercles," or civil administrative districts. On 1 Oct. 1902 it was renamed Senegambia and Niger Territories, still subject to Senegal. On 18 Oct. 1904 it became the colony of Upper Senegal and Niger. On 4 Dec. 1920 it became the French Sudan again, and on 13 Oct. 1946 became an overseas territory of France. On 24 Nov. 1958 it gained autonomy within the French Community, as the Sudanese Republic. On 17 Jan. 1959 (effective as from 4 April 1959) it joined with the similarly autonomous Republic of Senegal to form the Mali Federation, both countries retaining their republican status however. On 20 June 1960 the Federation as a body was granted full independence by France. On 20 Aug. 1960 the Mali Federation came to an end. The Sudanese Republic changed its name on 22 Sept. 1960 to the Republic of Mali (named after the old Mali Empire). A devastating famine in 1973–74 killed an enormous number of people, and in the 1980s drought plagued Mali. There was a war with Burkina Faso in 1985. In 1991 a coup ended the long regime of Moussa Traoré, and the main problem since then has been from Tuareg rebel groups. Other problems are corruption, AIDS, repression, poverty, coups and attempted coups.

Commandants-Supérieurs: 6 Sept. 1880–3 Sept. 1883 Gustave Borgnis-Desbordes; 3 Sept. 1883–18 June 1884 Charles Boilève; 18 June 1884–4 Sept. 1884 Antoine Combes (acting); 4 Sept. 1884–Sept. 1885 Antoine Combes; Sept. 1885–Aug. 1886 Henri Frey; Aug. 1886–28 Oct. 1888 Joseph Galliéni; 28 Oct. 1888–9 Oct. 1891 Louis Archinard; 9 Oct. 1891–27 Aug. 1892 Pierre Humbert. *Lieutenant-Governors:* 27 Aug. 1892–Sept. 1892 Pierre Humbert (acting); 3 Oct. 1892–2 Aug. 1893 Louis Archinard; 2 Aug. 1893–Dec. 1893 François Bonnier (acting); Dec. 1893–12 July 1895 Louis Grodet; 12 July 1895–1898 Louis de Trentinian; 1898–1899 René Audéoud; 1899–17 Oct. 1899 Louis de Trentinian. *Delegates:* 17 Oct. 1899–18 Oct. 1904 Amédée Merlaud-Ponty. *Lieutenant-Governors:* 18 Oct. 1904–1 Sept. 1906 Amédée Merlaud-Ponty; 1 Sept. 1906–1 Jan. 1907 Jean Peuvergne (acting); 1 Jan. 1907–28 Aug. 1907 Amédée Merlaud-Ponty; 28 Aug. 1907–1908 Jean Peuvergne; 1908–May 1909 [unknown] (acting); May 1909–17 Dec. 1909 Joseph Clozel; 17 Dec. 1909–14 Aug. 1910 Henri Lejeune (acting); 14 Aug. 1910–13 Jan. 1912 Joseph Clozel; 13 Jan. 1912–Aug. 1912 Philippe Henry (acting); Aug. 1912–12 Dec. 1912 Joseph Clozel; 12 Dec. 1912–Aug. 1913 Philippe Henry (acting); Aug. 1913–16 June 1915 Joseph Clozel; 16 June 1915–1 July 1915 Philippe Henry (acting); 1 July 1915–28 July 1916 Louis Thiébaud (acting); 28 July 1916–20 April 1917 Raphaël Antonetti; 20 April 1917–21 May 1917 Albert Nébout (acting); 21 May 1917–20 Feb. 1918 Louis Periquet (acting); 20 Feb.

1918–20 Aug. 1919 Auguste Brunet; 20 Aug. 1919–March 1920 Marcel Olivier; March 1920–10 Aug. 1920 Jean Terasson de Fougères (acting); 10 Aug. 1920–Jan. 1921 Théodore Maillet (acting); Jan. 1921–21 Aug. 1921 Marcel Olivier; 21 Aug. 1921–26 Feb. 1924 Jean Terasson de Fougères (acting); 26 Feb. 1924–23 April 1924 Jean Terasson de Fougères; 23 April 1924–6 May 1924 Jean Joseph Carreau (acting); 6 May 1924–Feb. 1925 Albéric Fournier (acting); Feb. 1925–30 April 1926 Jean Terasson de Fougères; 30 April 1926–Nov. 1926 Gabriel Descemet (acting); Nov. 1926–2 April 1928 Jean Terasson de Fougères; 2 April 1928–28 Jan. 1929 Gabriel Descemet (acting); 28 Jan. 1929–31 Dec. 1930 Jean Terasson de Fougères; 31 Dec. 1930–4 April 1931 Joseph Court (acting); 4 April 1931–11 June 1931 Gabriel Descemet (acting); 11 June 1931–31 March 1933 Louis Fousset; 31 March 1933–22 May 1933 René Desjardins (acting); 22 May 1933–30 Nov. 1933 Léon Solomiac (acting); 30 Nov. 1933–19 Feb. 1935 Louis Fousset; 19 Feb. 1935–22 Nov. 1935 Félix Éboué (acting); 22 Nov. 1935–9 Nov. 1936 Matteo Alfasa; 9 Nov. 1936–4 Dec. 1936 Ferdinand Rougier (acting); 4 Dec. 1936–1937 Ferdinand Rougier. *Governors:* 1937–1937–28 March 1938 Ferdinand Rougier; 28 March 1938–15 Nov. 1940 Jean Desanti (acting); 15 Nov. 1940–17 April 1942 Jean Rapenne (acting); 17 April 1942–29 Dec. 1942 Auguste Calvel (acting); 29 Dec. 1942–15 May 1946 Auguste Calvel; 15 May 1946–25 Feb. 1949 Edmond Louveau; 25 Feb. 1949–3 Feb. 1950 Lucien Geay (acting); 3 Feb. 1950–April 1952 Edmond Louveau; April 1952–10 July 1952 Victor Bailly; 10 July 1952–23 Feb. 1953 Salvador-Jean Etcheber; 23 Feb. 1953–2 Dec. 1953 Albert Mouragues; 2 Dec. 1953–10 Feb. 1954 Lucien Geay (acting); 10 Feb. 1954–3 Nov. 1956 Lucien Geay. *High Commissioners:* 3 Nov. 1956–24 Nov. 1958 Henri Gipoulon; 24 Nov. 1958–20 June 1960 Jean-Charles Sicurani. *Presidents:* March 1959–4 April 1959 Modibo Keita; 4 April 1959–20 Aug. 1960 [vacant during the lifetime of the Mali Federation, but Keita was the president in all but name]; 20 Aug. 1960–19 Nov. 1968 Modibo Keita. *Military Leaders:* 19 Nov. 1968–6 Dec. 1968 Yoro Diakité and Moussa Traoré. *Chairmen of the Military Committee of National Liberation:* 6 Dec. 1968–19 Sept. 1969 Moussa Traoré. *Presidents:* 19 Sept. 1969–26 March 1991 Moussa Traoré; 26 March 1991–6 June 1992 Amadou Toumani Touré; 8 June 1992–8 June 2002 Alpha Oumar Konaré; 8 June 2002–Amadou Toumani Touré. *Prime Ministers:* April 1957–4 April 1959 Jean-Marie Koné; 16 April 1959–20 June 1960 Modibo Keita; 6 Dec. 1968–19 Sept. 1969 Yoro Diakité; 6 June 1986–6 June 1988 Mamadou Dembelé; 2 March 1991–8 June 1992 Soumana Sacko; 8 June 1992–12 April 1993 Younoussi Touré; 12 April 1993–4 Feb. 1994 Abdulaye Sékou Sow; 4 Feb. 1994–15 Feb. 2000 Ibrahim Boubakar Keita; 15 Feb. 2000–18 March 2000 Mande Sidibe; 18 March 2000–9 June 2002 Modibo Keita II; 9 June 2002–30 April 2004 Ahmad Ag Hamani; 30 April 2004–Ousman Maïga. *Note:* In times of no Prime Minister, the President or other Head of State held that office.

Mali Empire. ca. 1237–1464. *Location:* West Africa, from the coast of Senegal to the Niger River. *Capital:* Djeriba (also known as Niani). *Other names:* Malinke Empire; Mandingo Empire.

History: About 1237 Sundiata Keita, the king of Kangaba, conquered the Ghana Empire, thus establishing the new Mandingo empire of Mali (the name "Mali" means "where the king lives"). A Mandingo himself, Sundiata Keita ruled until 1255, when his successor adopted the title of Mansa (Emperor). Under Mansa Musa the empire reached its peak. By the beginning of the 15th century revolts and invasions began to take their toll and the empire started on the long, crumbling road to extinction. It was replaced as the major power in this part of Africa by the Songhai Empire, although nominal mansas continued to rule until the end of the 17th century.

Military Commanders: ca. 1237–1255 Mari Jata I (also known as Sundiata Keita). *Mansas (Emperors):* 1255–1270 Ali; 1270–1274 Wati; 1274–1274 Khalifa; 1274–1285 Abu Bakr I; 1285–1300 Sakura (usurper); 1300–1305 Qu; 1305–1310 Muhammad; 1310–1312 Abu Bakr II; 1312–1337 Musa I (also known as Kankan Musa); 1337–1341 Magha I; 1341–1360 Suleiman; 1360–1360 Qasa; 1360–1374 Mari Jata II; 1374–1387 Musa II; 1387–1388 Magha II; 1388–1390 Sandaki (usurper); 1390–ca. 1420 Magha III; ca. 1420–1460 Musa III; ca. 1460–ca. 1480 Mule; ca. 1480–1496 Muhammad II; 1497–1536 Muhammad III; 1536–1590 [unknown]; 1590–ca. 1610 Nyani Mansa Muhammad; ca. 1610–ca. 1670 [unknown]; ca. 1670–(?) Mama Magha.

Mali Federation. 4 April 1959–20 Aug. 1960. *Location:* Mali and Senegal. *Capital:* Dakar (originally a coastal village, the name comes from the Wolof word "dakhar," meaning "the tamarind tree"). *Other names:* Sudan Federation.

History: On 17 Jan. 1959 (effective as from 4 April 1959) the autonomous French republics of Senegal and the Sudanese Republic (which would later become Mali) joined together politically to form the Mali Federation, an autonomous body within the French Community, composed, therefore, of two component territories, Senegal and the Sudanese Republic. Two other countries were to have joined the Mali Federation — Upper Volta and Dahomey — but they backed out at the last moment. On 20 June 1960 the whole federation became independent from France, as a federation and as two separate countries within that federation. In August 1960 Senegal seceded from the union, and the two countries of the Republic of Senegal and the Sudanese Republic went their separate ways.

Presidents: 4 April 1959–20 Aug. 1960 Modibo Keita. *Vice Presidents:* 4 April 1959–20 Aug. 1960 Mamadou Dia. *Heads of the Federal Assembly:* 4 April 1959–20 Aug. 1960 Léopold Senghor.

Mali Kingdom see **Kangaba**

Malinke Empire see **Mali Empire**

Malta, Knights of see **Tripolitania**

Mama see **Agaie**

Mameluke Empire see **Egypt**

Mamprusi see **Mossi States**

Manchinna see **Hadejia**

Mandara. ca. 1500–1902. *Location:* in Cameroun. *Capital:* Mora (from 1894); Dulo (ca. 1580–1894). *Other names:* Wandala.

History: The kingdom of Mandara was founded around 1500 and in 1902 was taken over by the Germans as part of Kamerun.

Kings: ca. 1500–(?) Sukda; (?)–(?) [unknown]; (?)–ca. 1600 Ti-Maya; ca. 1600–ca. 1619 Sankré; ca. 1619–(?) Aldawa Nanda; (?)–(?) [unknown]; (?)–ca. 1715 Naldawa Nazariza. *Sultans:* ca. 1715–ca. 1737 Mai Bukar Aji; ca. 1737–1757 Mahmadi Makia; 1757–1773 Ti-Kse Bldi; 1773–1828 Bukar D'Gjiama; 1828–1842 Hiassae; 1842–1894 Bukar Narbanha; 1895–1911 Umar Adjara; 1911–1915 Bukar Afade; 1915–1922 Umar Adjara; 1922–May 1924 Amada; May 1924–March 1926 Kola Adama; March 1926–18 March 1942 Bukar Afade; 18 March 1942–(?) Hamidu Umar.

Mandingo Empire see **Mali Empire**

Mandinka Empire see **Samory's Empire**

Mangawa see **Gumel**

Mantateesi see **Sekonyela's Land**

Maqdishu see **Mogadishu**

Maqurrah see **Mukurra**

Marinid Empire see **Morocco**

Marshall see **Liberia**

Maryland. 12 Feb. 1834–19 Feb. 1857. *Location:* present-day Maryland County, Liberia (i.e. on Cape Palmas). *Capital:* Harper (founded in 1834, and formerly called Cape Palmas, it was renamed for Robert Goodloe Harper, a local citizen and supporter). *Other names:* Maryland-in-Africa; Maryland-in-Liberia; Republic of Maryland-in-Liberia (1854–1857).

History: Founded in 1834 by James Hall of the Maryland State Colonization Society, the "independent African state of Maryland became the independent republic of Maryland-in-Liberia on 8 June 1854. In 1857 it became part of Liberia, as Maryland County.

Governors: 12 Feb. 1834–Feb. 1836 Dr. James Hall; Feb. 1836–1 July 1836 Oliver Holmes, Jr.; 1 July 1836–28 Sept. 1836 ruled by a three-man committee; 28 Sept. 1836–1848 John Russwurm; 1848–1848 Dr. Samuel F. McGill (acting); 1848–9 June 1851 John Russwurm; 9 June 1851–8 June 1854 Samuel F. McGill (acting); 8 June 1854–Dec. 1855 William A. Prout; Dec. 1855–June 1856 Boston Drayton (acting); June 1856–19 Feb. 1857 Boston Drayton.

Mascara. 22 Nov. 1832–23 Dec. 1847. *Location:* northern Algeria. *Capital:* No capital from 1843 to 1847; Tiaret (1835–1843. Also known as

Tahart, the name means "the lioness." The town is now called Tagdemt); Mascara (until 1835. The name "Mascara" means "mother of soldiers," and was founded as a Turkish military garrison in 1701). *Other names:* Mascara Amirate.

History: In 1832 Abd al-Qadir (or Abdelkedir, as the French called him), the legendary Algerian leader, formed his own state, a real political state, in the armpit of the French (see Algeria). He harassed the French to such an extent that in 1837 France signed the Treaty of Tafna with him, which gave Abdelkedir control of the entire interior of the provinces of Oran and the Titteri. The town of Mascara had been laid to ruins by the French in 1835 and Abdelkedir had moved his capital to the fortress of Tiaret. In 1840 the French moved against him in force, and took Tiaret in 1843. From that time Abdelkedir was mostly in Morocco. In 1847 he was obliged to surrender, and the Amirate of Mascara (the first modern state in what is now Algeria) became part of the French Military Province of Algeria.

Amirs: 22 Nov. 1832–23 Dec. 1847 Abd al-Qadir (also known as Abdelkedir).

Mashonaland see **Rhodesia**

Masina. ca. 1400–1862. *Location:* in Mali. *Capital:* Hamdallahi (from 1819). *Other names:* Macina.

History: Founded about 1400 by the Fulani, Masina was conquered by the Tukolor Empire in 1862.

Kings: ca. 1400–1404 Majan Dyallo; 1404–1424 Birahim I; 1424–1433 Ali I; 1433–1466 Kanta; 1466–1480 Ali II; 1480–1510 Nguia; 1510–1539 Sawadi; 1539–1540 Ilo; 1540–1543 Amadi Sire; 1543–1544 Hammadi I; 1544–1551 Bubu I; 1551–1559 Ibrahim; 1559–1583 Bubu II; 1583–ca. 1595 Hammadi II; ca. 1595–1599 Moroccan rule; 1599–1603 Hammadi II; 1603–1613 Bubu III; 1613–1625 Birahim II; 1625–1627 Silamaran; 1627–1663 Hammadi III; 1663–1663 Hammadi IV; 1663–1673 Ali III; 1673–1675 Gallo; 1675–1696 Gurori I; 1696–1706 Gueladio; 1706–1761 Guidado; 1761–1780 Hammadi V; 1780–1801 Ya Gallo; 1801–1810 Gurori II; 1810–1814 [unknown]. *Sheikhs:* 1814–1844 Hamadu I; 1844–1852 Hamadu II; 1852–1862 Hamadu III; 1862–1863 under Tukolor military government. *Tukolor Regents:* 1863–1864 Sidi al-Bakka; 1864–1864 Sheikh Abidin al-Bakha'i. *Sheikhs:* 1864–1871 Badi Tali; 1871–1872 Badi Sidi; 1872–1873 Ahmadu. *Tukolor Regents:* 1873–1874 Sheikh Abidin al-Bakha'i.

Masmouda. ca. 1602–1614. *Location:* on the Moroccan coast. *Capital:* Masmouda. *Other names:* Masmuda; Masmouda Pirates Republic.

History: Founded by buccaneer Captain Henry Mainwaring, this republic took its name from the Berber tribe, the Masmudah. In 1614 it was incorporated into the Sa'did state of Morocco.

Rulers: ca. 1602–1614 [unknown].

Massaesyli see **Mauretania**

Massawa. 6 Feb. 1885–1 Jan. 1890. *Location:* a port on the Red Sea, on the central Eritrean coast, and including a little hinterland. *Capital:* Massawa (the largest Ethiopian port at one time, it stands on the two connected islands of Massawa and Taulud). *Other names:* Mitsiwa; Massaua.

History: The Turks occupied Massawa from 1557 until they gave it to Egypt in 1865. In 1885 Massawa was taken by the Italians. That and Assab were combined in 1890 with the Danakil area to form the Italian colony of Eritrea, the capital of which, until 1900, was Massawa.

Commandants: 6 Feb. 1885–15 Dec. 1885 Tancredi Saletta; 15 Dec. 1885–18 March 1887 Carlo Gene; 18 March 1887–Oct. 1887 Tancredi Saletta; Nov. 1887–1888 Alessandro Di San Marzano; 1888–20 Dec. 1889 Antonio Baldissera; 20 Dec. 1889–1 Jan. 1890 Baldassare Orero.

Massufa see **Almoravid Empire**

Masubia see **Namibia**

Matabeleland. Nov. 1837–Jan. 1894. *Location:* in Zimbabwe. *Capital:* Bulawayo (from 1881. Founded in 1838); Inyati (1837–1870). *Other names:* Ndebeleland; Moselekatze's Land; Mzilikazi's Land; Matabele Empire.

History: Mzilikazi (also known as Moselekatze), was the leader of the northern Khumalo branch of the Zulu under the supreme Zulu commander, Chaka. He betrayed Chaka and was condemned to death. In 1817 he fled Zululand, taking his substantial army with him, and settled north of the Vaal River, near what is now Pretoria. By 1836 they were a major force in Southern Africa, the name "Matabele" meaning

"Men of the long shields." In 1836–1837 Mzilikazi and his cross-sectional band of warriors
were defeated by the Boers and forced across the
Limpopo into what is now Zimbabwe. Here they
formed the Matabele Empire which covered all
of what is today Zimbabwe. Mzilikazi died in
1868 and after two years of successional disputes
his son Lobengula came to the throne. On 11
Feb. 1888 Matabeleland came under British
domination as Zambesia (see Rhodesia) was
roughly hewn, and the Matabele fell under a
British protectorate until 1894 when the tribe
was finally conquered. It was added to the protectorate of Mashonaland to form South Zambesia (see Rhodesia).

Chiefs of the northern Khumalo: (?)–(?) Zazalita; (?)–(?) Langa; (?)–(?) Mangete; (?)–1818
Mashobane; 1818–Nov. 1837 Mzilikazi (also
known as Moselekatze). *Matabele Kings:* Nov.
1837–9 Sept. 1868 Mzilikazi (also known as
Moselekatze). *Regents:* 9 Sept. 1868–24 Jan. 1870
Nombate. *Matabele Kings:* 24 Jan. 1870–Jan.
1894 Lobengula.

Matshangana see Gazaland

Mauretania. (?)–ca. 100 B.C.; 38 B.C.–A.D. 42
Location: north of the Atlas Mountains, in
northern Morocco and northern Algeria. *Capital:* Iol (until 25 B.C.); Caesarea (after 25 B.C.).

History: Of ancient origin, Mauretania was
inhabited for centuries by tribes known to the
Romans as Massaesyli, or Mauri. Around 100
B.C. the country was divided into two parts—
Mauretania East and Mauretania West. In 38
B.C. Bocchus III united these two divisions, as
Mauretania. Five years later, in 33 B.C., he gave
his united kingdom to the Romans as a gift. The
Romans allowed the Mauretanians to continue
to rule, but in A.D. 42 the Romans occupied it
and divided it again, this time into Mauretania
Caesariensis (the old Mauretania East) and Mau-
retania Tingitana (the old Mauretania West).

Kings: ca. 206 B.C. Baqa; ca. 206–38 B.C. series of kings whose names have not come down;
38 B.C.–25 B.C. Bocchus III; 25 B.C.–A.D. 23
Caius Julius Juba II; A.D. 23–A.D. 40 Ptolemaeus; A.D. 40–A.D. 42 Aedemon.

Mauretania Caesariensis. A.D. 42–ca. 395. *Location:* northern Algeria. *Capital:* Caesarea Mauretaniae (from about 300); Caesarea (later named
Cherchel, this was the capital until about 300).

History: In A.D. 42 Mauretania was divided
into two sections—Mauretania Caesariensis
(meaning "of Caesar") and Mauretania Tingitana (meaning "of Tingis"). In A.D. 297, out of
a part of Caesariensis, was formed Mauretania
Sitifensis. About 395 the rest of Caesariensis
came under the Roman Prefecture of Italy (Subdivision: Diocese of Africa).

Rulers: 42–ca. 395 [unknown].

Mauretania East. ca. 100 B.C.–38 B.C. *Location:*
northern Algeria. *Capital:* Iol. *Other names:* East
Mauretania.

History: About 100 B.C. Mauretania was divided into Mauretania East and Mauretania
West. In 38 B.C. it was re-united by Bocchus III
into Mauretania.

Kings: ca. 100 B.C.–85 B.C. Bocchus I; 85
B.C.–82 B.C. Volux; 82 B.C.–ca. 51 B.C. Bogud;
ca. 51 B.C.–38 B.C. Bocchus III. *Note:* for Bocchus II see Mauretania West.

Mauretania Sitifensis. 297–435. *Location:* eastern Algeria. *Capital:* Sitifis (later known as
Sétif).

History: Formed out of the eastern part of
Mauretania Caesariensis by Diocletian in A.D.
297, Sitifensis went to the Vandals by agreement
in 435 (see Vandal North Africa).

Rulers: 297–435 [unknown].

Mauretania Tingitana. A.D. 42–ca. 395. *Location:* northern Morocco. *Capital:* Tingis (now
Tangier).

History: In A.D. 42 Mauretania was formally
annexed by the Romans and divided into Mauretania Tingitana in the west and Mauretania
Caesariensis in the east. Because the Mauretanians were good warriors, they were heavily used
by the Romans in their legions, and the Romans
recognized the tribal chiefs. About the year 300
the Romans gave up a lot of Tingitana to the
Baquate tribe, and around 395 the rest came
under the Roman Prefecture of Gaul (Subdivision: The Diocese of Spain).

Rulers: A.D. 42–ca. 395 [unknown].

Mauretania West. ca. 100 B.C.–38 B.C. *Location:* northern Morocco. *Capital:* Tingis (now
Tangier). *Other names:* West Mauretania.

History: About 100 B.C. Mauretania was divided up into Mauretania West and Mauretania
East. In 38 B.C. Bocchus III re-united the two
to re-form Mauretania.

Kings: ca. 100 B.C.–ca. 85 B.C. Iphthas; ca. 85 B.C.–ca. 70 B.C. Askalis; ca. 70 B.C.–ca. 56 B.C. Bocchus II; ca. 56 B.C.–ca. 51 B.C. Sosus; ca. 51 B.C.–38 B.C. Bogud II. *Note:* For Bocchus I and II see Mauretania East.

Mauri see Mauretania

Mauritania. 12 May 1903– . *Location:* North West Africa. *Capital:* Nouakchott (developed as a city and as the capital after independence in 1960); Saint Louis (in Senegal, this was the capital until 1960). *Other names:* Mauritanie; Islamic Republic of Mauritania, or Republic of Mauritania (from 1958).

History: In 1903 a protectorate was established over most of what is today the Republic of Mauritania, by the French commandant Coppolani. It was really an extension of the protectorate of Trarza which the French had created the year before. By 1903–1904 most of the other kingdoms and amirates in the area had been brought into the new protectorate of Mauritania (the name means "land of the Moors"). On 18 Oct. 1904 it became the Civil Territory of Mauritania. In 1905 Coppolani was assassinated. In 1907 Tagant was occupied by the French, and Adrar in 1909. In 1920 (effective as from 1 Jan. 1921) the country became a French colony. On 7 Aug. 1949 the country became an overseas territory of France, and on 28 Nov. 1958 it became the Autonomous Republic of Mauritania, within the French Community, en route to independence from France, which took place on 28 Nov. 1960. Mauritania held southern Spanish Sahara (see Western Sahara) from 28 Feb. 1976 until 1980. Mauritania has been plagued with constant coups, droughts, poverty, starvation, chronic racial tension between the Moors and the blacks, rioting, conflict with Senegal in the 1990s, several attempted coups in the early 2000s, and a horrendous locust plague in 2004. On 3 Aug. 2005, while President Taya was out of the country, the Army effected a coup.

Commandants: 12 May 1903–12 May 1905 Xavier Coppolani; 12 May 1905–27 May 1905 Capt. Frerejean (acting); 27 May 1905–Sept. 1907 Bernard Capdebosq; Sept. 1907–1909 Col. Henri Gouraud; 1909–1909 Col. Claudel (acting); 1909–1 Jan. 1910 Col. Aubert (acting); 1 Jan. 1910–1 March 1912 Col. Henri Patey; 1 March 1912–April 1914 Col. Charles Mouret; April 1914–17 Nov. 1916 Louis Obissier; 17 Nov.

1916–11 Dec. 1920 Henri Gaden. *Lieutenant-Governors:* 11 Dec. 1920–Dec. 1927 Henri Gaden; 13 Jan. 1928–27 Jan. 1928 Alphonse Choteau; 27 Jan. 1928–Oct. 1928 René Chazal (acting); Oct. 1928–21 Nov. 1929 Alphonse Choteau; 21 Nov. 1929–19 June 1931 René Chazal; 19 June 1931–22 June 1933 Gabriel Descemet; 22 June 1933–7 April 1934 Louis Antonin (acting); 7 April 1934–5 July 1934 Gabriel Descemet; 5 July 1934–Aug. 1934 Adolphe Deitte; Aug. 1934–1 Sept. 1934 Jean-Baptiste Chazelas (acting); 1 Sept. 1934–15 April 1935 Richard Brunot; 15 April 1935–10 Sept. 1935 Jean-Baptiste Chazelas (acting); 10 Sept. 1935–1 Sept. 1936 Jules de Coppet; 1 Sept. 1936–24 Oct. 1936 Jean-Louis Beyriès (acting); 24 Oct. 1936–7 Aug. 1938 Oswald Durand (acting); 7 Aug. 1938–Nov. 1938 Charles Dumas (acting); Nov. 1938–28 Aug. 1941 Jean-Louis Beyriès (acting); 28 Aug. 1941–4 May 1944 Jean-Louis Beyriès; 4 May 1944–31 July 1945 Christian Laigret; 31 July 1945–30 April 1946 René Babin (acting); 30 April 1946–19 July 1947 Georges Poirier (acting); 19 July 1947–31 Dec. 1947 Lucien Geay; 1 Jan. 1948–7 Aug. 1949 Henri de Mauduit; 7 Aug. 1949–21 Sept. 1950 Édouard Terrac (acting). *Governors:* 21 Sept. 1950–25 April 1952 Jacques Rogué; 25 April 1952–6 April 1954 Pierre Messmer; 6 April 1954–23 June 1955 Albert Mouragues; 23 June 1955–14 May 1956 Jean-Paul Parisot; 14 May 1956–5 Oct. 1958 Albert Mouragues. *High Commissioners:* 5 Oct. 1958–Feb. 1959 Henri Bernard; Feb. 1959–28 Nov. 1960 Pierre Anthonioz. *Presidents:* 20 Aug. 1961–10 July 1978 Mohktar Ould Daddah. *Leaders of Military Committee for National Salvation:* 10 July 1978–3 June 1979 Mustafa Ould Saleck. *Presidents:* 3 June 1979–4 Jan. 1980 Muhammad Mahmud Ould Ahmad Louly; 4 Jan. 1980–12 Dec. 1984 Muhammad Ould Haidalla; 12 Dec. 1984–3 Aug. 2005 Maaouya Ould Sidi Ahmad Taya. *Chairman of the Military Council:* 4 Aug. 2005–Ely Ould Muhammad Vall. *Chairmen of the Executive Council:* 21 May 1957–23 June 1959 Mokhtar Ould Daddah. *Prime Ministers:* 23 June 1959–20 Aug. 1961 Mokhtar Ould Daddah; 6 April 1979–27 May 1979 Ahmad Ould Bouceif; 27 May 1979–31 May 1979 Ahmad Salem Ould Sidi (interim); 31 May 1979–4 Jan. 1980 Muhammad Ould Haidalla; 12 Dec. 1980–25 April 1981 Sidi Ahmad Ould Bneijara; 26 April 1981–8 March 1984 Maaouya Ould Sidi Ahmad Taya; 20 April 1992–2 Jan. 1996 Sidi

Muhammad Ould Boubaker; 2 Jan. 1996–6 July 2003 Sheikh al-Afia Ould Muhammad Khouna; 6 July 2003–Sghair Ould M'Bareck. *Note:* In times of no Prime Minister, the President held that office.

Mauritius. 1507– . *Location:* east of Madagascar, in the Indian Ocean. The administrative and political unit of Mauritius includes Rodrigues. *Capital:* Port Louis (from 1736, when it was built); no capital before 1736. *Other names:* Île Maurice; Île de France (1722–1810); Ilha do Cerne (1507–1598).

History: The island of Mauritius was discovered in 1507 by the Portuguese and named Ilha do Cerne ("Island of the Tree-Heart"). It remained unclaimed until 1598, when the Dutch took possession and renamed it Mauritius, after Maurits von Nassau, Stadholder of Holland. It remained uninhabited (except by dodoes) until 31 July 1638, when it became a Dutch colony and a way station en route to the East Indies. However, in 1658 the Dutch abandoned it in favor of the Cape of Good Hope (see Cape Colony). In 1664 the Dutch partially re-settled the island, but abandoned it forever in 1710. The island lay neglected until 1715, when the Compagnie des Indes (French East India Company) claimed it. In April 1722 Guillaume d'Arse renamed it Île de France, and the Compagnie began to populate it with people from the island of Bourbon (see Réunion). Port Louis was built in 1736, as the first capital. After 1727 the governor of Île de France was the governor-general of all the French possessions in the Indian Ocean. In July 1767 the French government took it over as a colony. On 3 Oct. 1810 it was captured (as were all the French holdings in the Indian Ocean during the Napoleonic Wars except Rodrigues, which Col. Keating had taken on 4 Aug. 1809) by the British, and they occupied Île de France until 30 May 1814, when it was ceded to Britain and became Mauritius again, a British colony. The Seychelles were ruled from Mauritius until 1903. In 1908 Mauritius lost Coetivy to the Seychelles, and in 1922 the Farquhar and Des Roches Islands, as well as others in the area. On 12 March 1968 the country became independent from Britain, as a dominion of the British Commonwealth, and on 12 March 1992 it became a republic. This republic includes not only the island of Mauritius and surrounding islets, but also Rodrigues (with Diego Garcia),

the Saint Brandon Islands, and the Agalega Islands (which are about 600 miles to the north), and it also claims the British possession of the Chagos Archipelago, and the French island of Tromelin. Rodrigues declared its autonomy.

Commanders: 1664–1664 Jacobus Nieuwland; 1664–1665 [unknown]; 1665–1667 Georg Wreede; 1667–1668 Jan Van Laar; 1668–1669 Dirk Smient; 1669–1672 Georg Wreede; 1672–1673 Pieter Col; 1673–1677 Hubert Hugo; 1677–1692 Isaäc Lamotius; 1692–1703 Roelof Dieodati; 1703–1710 Abraham Van De Velde. *Governors:* 1715–1718 none; 1718–April 1722 Joseph Beauvollier de Courchant; April 1722–1723 Denis de Nyon; 1723–Dec. 1725 Antoine Desforges-Boucher; Dec. 1725–Aug. 1727 Denis de Brousse (acting); Aug. 1727–Aug. 1729 Pierre-Bênoit Dumas; Aug. 1729–June 1735 Nicolas de Maupin. *Governors-General:* June 1735–Feb. 1740 Bertrand-François Mahé, Comte de la Bourdonnais; Feb. 1740–Aug. 1740 Didier de Saint Martin (acting); Aug. 1740–March 1746 Bertrand-François Mahé, Comte de la Bourdonnais; March 1746–Feb. 1747 Didier de Saint Martin (acting); Feb. 1747–14 March 1750 Pierre David; 14 March 1750–Jan. 1756 Jean-Baptiste Bouvet de Lozier; Jan. 1756–Nov. 1759 René de la Villebague; Nov. 1759–July 1767 Antoine Marc Desforges-Boucher; July 1767–Nov. 1768 Jean Dumas; Nov. 1768–June 1769 Jean Stenauer (acting); June 1769–Aug. 1772 François Desroches; Aug. 1772–Dec. 1776 Charles de Ternay; Dec. 1776–3 May 1779 Antoine de la Brillane; 3 May 1779–30 Jan. 1780 François de Souillac (acting); 30 Jan. 1780–5 April 1785 François de Souillac; 5 April 1785–28 June 1785 Charles de Fresne (acting); 28 June 1785–Nov. 1785 Chevalier de Fleury (acting). *Governors-General of the Îles de France et de Bourbon:* Nov. 1785–16 Feb. 1787 François de Souillac; 16 Feb. 1787–Nov. 1789 Joseph d'Entrecasteaux. *Governors-General of the French Establishments to the East of the Cape of Good Hope:* Nov. 1789–Aug. 1790 Thomas de Conway; Aug. 1790–17 June 1792 David Charpentier de Cossigny; 17 June 1792–28 July 1800 Joseph de Malartic; 29 July 1800–Sept. 1803 François de la Morlière; Sept. 1803–3 Oct. 1810 Charles Décaen. *Governors:* 3 Oct. 1810–1811 Sir Robert Farquhar; 1811–1811 Henry Warde (acting); 1811–1817 Sir Robert Farquhar; 1817–1818 Gage Hall; 1818–1819 John Dalrymple (acting); 1819–1820 Ralph Darling (acting); 1820–1823

Sir Lowry Cole; 1823–1833 Sir Charles Colville; 1833–1840 Sir William Nicolay; 1840–1842 Sir Lionel Smith; 1842–1849 Sir William Gomm; 1849–1850 Sir George Anderson; 1851–1857 Sir James Higginson; 1857–1863 Sir William Stevenson; 1863–Dec. 1870 Sir Henry Barkly; 1871–1874 Sir Arthur Hamilton-Gordon; 1874–1879 Sir Arthur Phayre; 1879–1880 Sir George Bowen; 1880–1882 Sir Frederick Broome; 1883–1887 Sir John Pope-Hennessey; 1887–1888 Francis Fleming (acting); 1888–1889 Sir John Pope-Hennessey; 1889–1892 Sir Charles Lees; 1892–1894 Sir Hubert Jerningham; 1894–1894 Charles King-Harman (acting); 1894–1897 Sir Hubert Jerningham; 1897–1903 Sir Charles Bruce; 1903–20 Aug. 1904 [unknown] (acting); 20 Aug. 1904–1911 Cavendish Boyle; 1911–13 Nov. 1911 George Smith (acting); 13 Nov. 1911–1914 John Chancellor (knighted 1913); 1914–1914 John Middleton (acting); 1914–18 May 1916 Sir John Chancellor; 18 May 1916–1921 Sir Hesketh Bell; 1921–1921 Edward Denham (acting); 1921–19 Feb. 1925 Sir Hesketh Bell; 19 Feb. 1925–30 Aug. 1930 Herbert Read; 30 Aug. 1930–21 Oct. 1937 Wilfred Jackson (knighted 1931); 21 Oct. 1937–5 July 1942 Sir Bede Clifford; 5 July 1942–May 1949 Sir Donald Mackenzie-Kennedy; May 1949–26 Sept. 1949 [unknown] (acting); 26 Sept. 1949–30 July 1953 Sir Hilary Blood; 30 July 1953–22 April 1954 [unknown] (acting); 22 April 1954–25 Oct. 1959 Sir Robert Scott; 30 Oct. 1959–17 Sept. 1962 Sir Colville Deverell; 17 Sept. 1962–12 March 1968 Sir John Rennie. *Governors-General:* 12 March 1968–3 Sept. 1968 Sir John Rennie; 3 Sept. 1968–Aug. 1970 Sir Len Williams; Aug. 1970–Oct. 1970 Sir Abdul Raman Osman (acting); Oct. 1970–Dec. 1971 Sir Len Williams; Dec. 1971–Feb. 1972 Sir Abdul Raman Osman (acting); Feb. 1972–27 Dec. 1972 Sir Len Williams; 27 Dec. 1972–31 Oct. 1977 Sir Abdul Raman Osman; 31 Oct. 1977–24 March 1978 Henry Garrioch (acting); 24 March 1978–26 April 1979 Sir Abdul Raman Osman; 26 April 1979–17 Jan. 1986 Dayendranath Burrenchobay; 17 Jan. 1986–12 March 1992 Sir Veerasamy Ringadoo. *Presidents:* 12 March 1992–30 June 1992 Sir Veerasamy Ringadoo (acting); 1 July 1992–15 Feb. 2002 Cassam Uteem; 15 Feb. 2002–18 Feb. 2002 Angidi Chettiar (acting); 18 Feb. 20002–25 Feb. 2002 Ariranga Pillay; 25 Feb. 2002–1 Oct. 2003 Karl Offmann; 1 Oct. 2003–Raouf Bundhun (acting). *Chief Ministers:* 26 Sept. 1961–12 March

1964 Seewoosagur Ramgoolam. *Prime Ministers:* 12 March 1964–11 June 1982 Seewoosagur Ramgoolam (knighted 1965); 11 June 1982–27 Dec. 1995 Aneerood Jugnauth; 27 Dec. 1995–17 Sept. 2000 Navin Ramgoolam; 17 Sept. 2000–30 Sept. 2003 Aneerood Jugnauth; 30 Sept. 2003–Paul Berenger.

Mayotte. ca. 1515–25 March 1841. *Location:* one of the Comoros Islands, in the Indian Ocean. *Capital:* Chingoni (latterly); Msamboro (formerly). *Other names:* Mayuta; Mahoré.

History: The sultanate of Mayotte, founded about 1515, had several encounters with French pirates, as did all of the islands in the Comoros. In 1835 the neighboring island of Anjouan conquered Mayotte, and Anjouani qadis (governors) ruled for six years until 1841, when the French took Mayotte over as a protectorate. This stopped the pirate problem.

Sultans: ca. 1515–ca. 1530 Hassan I; ca. 1530–ca. 1550 Muhammad; ca. 1550–ca. 1590 Isa. *Queens-Regent:* ca. 1590–ca. 1596 Amina. *Regents:* ca. 1595–ca. 1620 Bwana Fuma ibn Ali. *Sultans:* ca. 1620–ca. 1640 Ali I; ca. 1640–ca. 1680 Umar; ca. 1680–ca. 1700 Ali II. *Queens-Regent:* ca. 1700–ca. 1714 Aisa; ca. 1714–ca. 1720 Monavo Fani. *Sultans:* ca. 1720–1727 Abu Bakr; 1727–1752 Salim I; 1752–1790 Bwana Kombo I; 1790–1807 Salim II; 1807–1817 Salih; 1817–1829 Ahmad; 1829–1832 Bwana Kombo II; 1832–19 Nov. 1835 Andrianametaka. *Anjouan Qadis (Governors):* 19 Nov. 1835–ca. 1838 Umar; ca. 1838–25 March 1841 Adriantsuli.

Mayotte Department. 9 Feb. 1976– . *Location:* in the Comoros. *Capital:* Mamoutzou (latterly); Dzaoudzi (formerly). *Other names:* Territorial Collectivity of Mayotte; Mahoré.

History: The Comoros became independent of France in 1975. On 22 Dec. 1974 and again on 9 Feb. 1976 one of the Comoros Islands, Mayotte, voted to remain a French territory, an overseas dependency of France. However, the Republic of the Comoros claims the island as part of their country.

Commissioners of the Republic (or Prefects): 9 Feb. 1976–30 April 1978 Jean-Marie Cousirou; 30 April 1978–15 April 1980 Jean Rigotard; 15 April 1980–24 Jan. 1981 Philip Kessler; 24 Feb. 1981–6 Jan. 1982 Pierre Sevellec; 25 Jan. 1982–25 Nov. 1982 Yves Bonnet; 5 Jan. 1983–1984 Christian Pellerin; 1984–1986 Francois Bonelle;

1986–1986 Guy Dupuis; 1986–23 Nov. 1988 Akli Khider; 23 Nov. 1988–17 Oct. 1990 Daniel Limodin; 17 Oct. 1990–24 Feb. 1993 Jean-Paul Coste; 9 March 1993–17 Jan. 1994 Jean-Jacques Debacq; 17 Jan. 1994–20 Feb. 1996 Alain Weil; 20 Feb. 1996–15 July 1998 Philippe Boisadam; 31 Aug. 1998–8 Oct. 2001 Pierre Bayle; 8 Oct. 2001–4 July 2002 Philippe de Mester; 4 July 2002–17 Jan. 2005 Jean-Jacques Brot; 17 Jan. 2005–Jean-Paul Kihl. *Presidents of the General Council:* Jan. 1983–(?) Younoussa Bamana; 2 April 2004–Said Omar Oili.

Mayotte Protectorate see **Comoros**

Mbire Empire see **Mwene Mutapa Empire**

Medina see **Liberia**

Melilla. 1497– . *Location:* northern Morocco. *Capital:* Melilla.

History: Melilla was a Berber town of antiquity (named Rusaddir) when it fell to the Spanish in 1497. It became the property of the family of the Duke of Medina Sidonia and remained thus until 1556 when the Spanish Crown took it over. In 1508 Velez de la Gomera was brought under Spanish rule and placed in the administration of Melilla. In 1673 Alhucemas was also brought under Spanish rule and placed under the administration of Melilla. In 1847 the Spanish Captaincy-General of North Africa (see Spanish Morocco) was created, and Melilla became a territory of that body, and was known as the District of Melilla. Like the District of Ceuta, Melilla had its own governor, as before, except that now the governor of Ceuta became the governor-general of the captaincy. On 27 Nov. 1912, upon the establishment of Spanish Morocco, Melilla became a comandáncia, and to all intents and purposes remained autonomous, ruled by a commander, answerable to the governor-general of Spanish Morocco. On 7 April 1956, with the departure of the Spanish (and the French) from Morocco, Spain maintained Melilla as a presidio (or plaza) of Metropolitan Spain. It is represented in the Spanish cortes by the Mayor of Melilla. In Sept. 1994 a limited measure of self-rule was granted by Spain, and on 14 March 2005 it became the autonomous city of Melilla.

Rulers: 1497–1556 [unknown]. *Governors:* 1556–1559 Alonso de Urrea; 1559–1561 [unknown]; 1561–1568 Pedro de Córdoba; 1568–1571 Francisco de Córdoba; 1571–1595 Antonio de Tejada; 1595–1596 Jerónimo de los Barrios; 1596–1601 Martín Dávalos y Padilla; 1601–1603 [unknown]; 1603–1611 Pedro de Herredia; 1611–1612 [unknown]; 1612–1617 Domingo de Dieguez; 1617–1618 Gaspar de Mondragón; 1618–1619 Domingo de Ochoa; 1619–1620 Diego de Leyva; 1620–1622 Francisco Rodríguez de Sanabria; 1622–1624 Francisco Ruíz; 1624–1625 [unknown]; 1625–1632 Luis de Sotomayor; 1632–1633 Pedro Moreo; 1633–1635 Tomás Mejía de Escobedo; 1635–1637 [unknown]; 1637–1648 Gabriel de Penalosa y Estrada; 1648–1649 [unknown]; 1649–1649 Luis de Sotomayor; 1649–1650 Jordán Jerez; 1650–1651 [unknown]; 1651–1655 Pedro Palacio y Guevara; 1655–1656 Diego de Arce; 1656–1669 Luis de Velázquez y Angulo; 1669–1672 Francisco Osorio y Astorga; 1672–1674 Diego de Arce; 1674–1675 [unknown]; 1675–1680 José Frias; 1680–1683 Diego Toscano y Brito; 1683–1684 [unknown]; 1684–1686 Diego Pacheco y Arce; 1686–1687 [unknown]; 1687–1687 Francisco López Moreno; 1687–1688 Antonio Domínguez de Durán; 1688–1691 Bernabé Ramos y Miranda; 1691–1692 [unknown]; 1692–1697 Antonio de Zúñiga y la Cerda; 1697–1703 Domingo Canal y Soldevila; 1703–1704 [unknown]; 1704–1707 Blas de Trincheria; 1707–1711 Diego de Flores; 1711–1714 Juan Jerónimo Ungo de Velasco; 1714–1715 Patricio Gómez de la Hoz; 1715–1716 Conde de Desallois; 1716–1719 Pedro Borrás; 1719–1719 Francisco Ibáñez y Rubalcava; 1719–1730 Alonso de Guevara y Vasconcelos; 1730–1732 Juan Andrés del Thoso; 1732–1757 Antonio Villalba y Angulo; 1757–1758 Francisco de Alba; 1758–1767 Narciso Vázquez y Nicuesa; 1767–1772 Miguel Fernández de Saavedra; 1772–1777 José Carrión y Andrade; 1777–1779 Bernardo Tortosa; 1779–1780 [unknown]; 1780–1782 Antonio Manso; 1782–1786 José Granados; 1786–1788 José Naranjo; 1788–1798 José Rivera; 1798–1800 Fernando Moyano; 1800–1814 Ramón Conti; 1814–1821 Jacinto Díaz Capilla; 1821–1823 Antonio Mateos y Malpartida; 1823–1824 Juan Pérez del Hacho y Oliván; 1824–1826 Luis Cappa y Rioseco; 1826–1829 Manuel García; 1829–1830 Juan Serrano y Reyna; 1830–1835 Luis Cappa y Rioseco; 1835–1838 Rafael Delgado y Moreno; 1838–1839 [unknown]; 1839–1847 Demetrio María de Benito y Hernández; 1847–1848 Manuel Arcaya; 1848–1850

Ignacio Chacón; 1850–1854 José de Castro y Méndez; 1854–1856 Manuel del Villar; 1856–1858 José Morcillo Ezquerra; 1858–1860 Manuel del Villar; 1860–1861 Luis de la Breche; 1861–1862 Felipe del Espinar; 1862–1863 Manuel Álvarez Maldonado; 1863–1864 Tomás O'Ryan y Vázquez; 1864–1866 Bartolomé Benavides y Campuzano; 1866–1868 José Salcedo y González; 1868–1871 Pedro Beaumont y Peralta; 1871–1873 Bernardo Alemañy y Perote; 1873–1879 Andrés Cuadra y Bourman; 1879–1880 Manuel Macías y Casado; 1880–1880 Ángel Navascués; 1880–1881 Evaristo García y Reyna; 1881–1886 Manuel Macías y Casado; 1886–1887 Teodoro Camino y Alcobendas; 1887–1888 Mariano de la Iglesia y Guillén; 1888–1888 Juan Villalonga y Soler; 1888–1889 Rafael Assin y Bazán; 1889–1891 José Mirelis y González; 1891–1893 Juan García y Margallo; 1893–1894 Manuel Macías y Casado; 1894–1894 Juan Arolas y Esplugues; 1894–1895 Rafael Cerero; 1895–1898 José Alcántara Pérez; 1898–1899 Fernando Alameda y Liancourt; 1899–1904 Venancio Hernández y Fernández; 1904–1905 Manuel Serrano y Ruíz; 1905–1905 Enrique Segura y Campoy; 1905–1910 José Marina y Vega; 1910–27 Nov. 1912 José García Aldave. *Rulers:* 27 Nov. 1912–7 April 1956 ruled by the governor-general of Spanish Morocco through a commander in Melilla; 7 April 1956–1991 ruled direct from Spain, through the mayor of Melilla. *Presidents:* 1991–3 March 1998 Ignacio Rivera; 3 March 1998–5 July 1999 Enrique Hernández; 5 July 1999–19 July 2000 Mustafa Aberchán; 19 July 2000–Juan Ortiz.

Memphusi see **Mossi States**

Menaba see **Madagascar**

Merina see **Madagascar**

Merinid Empire see **Morocco**

Meroë see **Kush** and **Nubia**

Merowe see **Kush** and **Nubia**

Meshwesh see **Egypt**

Messau see **Misau**

Mesurado see **Liberia**

Michel, Île see **Aldabra Islands**

Middle Island see **Aldabra Islands**

Middle Islet see **Tristan da Cunha**

Millsburg see **Liberia**

Mining Republic see **South Kasai Republic**

Mirambo. ca. 1858–1895. *Location:* in Tanzania. *Capital:* Umyanyembe. *Other names:* Myamwezi; Unyamwezi.

History: An East African sultanate, it became part of the protectorate of German East Africa in 1895.

Sultans: ca. 1858–ca. 1860 Fundakira; ca. 1860–ca. 1865 Msavila; ca. 1865–1876 Kiyungi; 1876–1893 Isike. *Queens:* 1893–1893 Mugalula. *Sultans:* 1894–1898 Kutagamoto; 1898–1898 Koswika.

Misau. 1831–1903. *Location:* Northern Nigeria. *Capital:* Misau. *Other names:* Mesau; Messau; Missau.

History: Founded in 1831 by Mamman Manga, son of a Fulani warrior, and enlarged in the 1870s, this amirate was taken over by the British and made part of the protectorate of Northern Nigeria.

Amirs: 1831–1833 Mamman Manga (also known as Moma Manga); 1833–1850 Amadu; 1850–1861 Usman; 1861–1886 Mamman Sali (also known as Moma Sali); 1886–1900 Hama Manga; 1900–1903 Amadu; 1903–Oct. 1926 Mamman al-Hajji (also known as Moma Alhaji); Oct. 1926–(?) Ahmadu Waziri; (?)–Mamman Manga III. *Premiers:* 14 Feb. 1918–Oct. 1926 Ahmadu Waziri.

Mississippi-in-Africa. 1835–1842. *Location:* on the Sinoe River, Liberia. *Capital:* Greenville (called Sinoe until 1838, and renamed for James Green, a colonization advocate). *Other names:* Mississippi; Greenville; Sinoe.

History: In 1835 the Mississippi and Louisiana State Colonization Societies founded this colony in what is now Liberia, for freed slaves from the American state of Mississippi only. In 1842 it was admitted to the Commonwealth of Liberia, as Sinoe County.

Governors: 1835–June 1837 [vacant]; June 1837–10 Sept. 1838 Josiah Finley; 10 Sept. 1838–1842 [vacant].

Mitsiwah see **Massawa**

MLSTP see **São Tomé and Príncipe**

Moçambique see **Mozambique**

Mogadishu. ca. 1238–ca. 1400. *Location:* Mogadishu, Somalia. *Capital:* Mogadishu. *Other names:* Maqdishu; Mogadiscio; Aristocratic Republic of Mogadishu; Makdishu; Republic of Mogadishu.

History: An early Arab settlement on the east coast of Africa, Mogadishu became a republic for a brief while in the 13th century, after which it reverted to being a sultanate.

Heads of the Republic: ca. 1238–(?) Sheikh Muhammad; (?)–ca. 1300 [unknown]; ca. 1300–ca. 1331 Sheikh Abubakr; ca. 1331–(?) Tewfik; (?)–(?) Rahman; (?)–ca. 1390 Yusuf; ca. 1390–ca. 1400 Fahr ad-Din.

Mohéli. (?)–1886. *Location:* one of the Comoros Islands. *Capital:* Fomboni. *Other names:* Moili; Mwali; Mohilla.

History: Of uncertain origin, the sultanate of Mohéli became a part of the French protectorate of Mayotte in 1886. For its history as a separate state in the 1990s see Mwali.

Sultans: 1828–1842 Andriamanetaha. *Queens:* 1842–1868 Jumbe Fatimah. *Sultans:* 1868–1871 Muhammad; 1871–1888 Marjani; 1888–1912 Salima Masimba.

Mombasa. 1593–1 July 1895. *Location:* the great port of Mombasa, in Coast Province, Kenya, and also its surrounds. *Capital:* Mombasa. *Other names:* Mvita (the Swahili name meaning "war").

History: Mombasa (which takes its name from Mombasa in Arabia) was a thriving Arab port from the 11th century on. After sacking the town several times from 1505 onwards, the Portuguese captured Mombasa in 1593. On 12 Dec. 1698 they lost it when the Omani imam Sa'if ibn Sultan stormed the port. The Portuguese were subsequently expelled, and the area of Mombasa much extended by the Omanis. On 12 March 1728 Portuguese from Goa re-captured it, but on 21 Sept. 1729 the Omanis took it again. This time the Portuguese left that particular coast forever. The Omani governors resumed their rule until 1746 when the governor was murdered and his brother, Ali ibn Uthman al-Mazrui, assumed the title of sultan and declared his independence from Oman. Thus came into power the Mazrui dynasty of Mombasa. In December 1823 Admiral William Owen of the British Navy established a protectorate over Mombasa, the area then being disputed by the Sultan of Muscat and the Sultan of Mombasa. However, this protectorate was never ratified by the British government, and in 1826 the al-Bu Sa'id dynasty of Oman (who had extended their territories to include most of East Africa north of Lourenço Marques and south of the Horn of Africa, and who were later to rule in Zanzibar) attacked Mombasa, took it over, and ushered the British governor out of the country. The Busaidi installed their own governor, and in 1837 Mombasa came under the administration of Zanzibar. The Mombasans revolted against Zanzibari rule in 1875, but the rebellion was put down with British aid. In 1887 the Sultan of Zanzibar allowed the British to take it over, and on 1 July 1895 Mombasa became part of the colony of British East Africa (later Kenya). Until 1963, when Kenya became independent, Mombasa was part of the sultanate of Zanzibar, and administratively formed part of Kenya Protectorate as opposed to Kenya Colony.

Portuguese Capitães-Mores (plural of Capitão-Mor, or Captain-Major): 1593–1596 Mateus de Vasconcelos; 1596–1598 Antonio de Andrade; 1598–1606 Rui Soares de Melo; 1606–1609 Gaspar Pereira; 1609–1610 Pedro de Abreu; 1610–1614 Manuel Pereira; 1614–1620 Simão Pereira; 1620–1625 Francisco Pereira; 1625–1626 João Semedo; 1626–1629 Marçal de Macedo; 1629–15 Aug. 1631 Pedro de Gambôa; 15 Aug. 1631–1635 Pedro Botelho; 1635–1639 Francisco de Seixas e Cabreira; 1639–1642 Martim Manuel; 1642–1643 [unknown]; 1643–1646 Manuel Coutinho; 1646–1648 Diogo da Silva; 1648–1651 Antonio de Meneses; 1651–1653 Francisco de Seixas e Cabreira; 1653–158 [unknown]; 1658–1663 José da Silva; 1663–1667 Manuel de Campos; 1667–1670 João Cota; 1670–1671 [vacant]; 1671–1673 José da Costa; 1673–1676 Manuel de Campos; 1676–1679 Francisco de Faria; 1679–(?) Manuel Franco; (?)–1682 Pedro Henriques; 1682–1686 Leonardo da Costa; 1686–1688 João Portugal; 1688–1693 Duarte de Melo; 1693–1694 Pascual Sarmento; 1694–1696 João Leão; 1696–1697 Antonio de Melo; 1697–1698 Príncipe de Faza; 1698–12 Dec. 1698 Leonardo Souto-Maior. *Omani Military Commanders:* 12 Dec. 1698–Dec. 1698 Imam Sa'if ibn Sultan; Dec. 1698–12

March 1728 Nasr ibn Abdallah al-Mazrui. *Portuguese Capitães-Mores:* 12 March 1728–21 Sept. 1729 Álvaro de Melo e Castro. *Omani Governors:* 21 Sept. 1729–1735 [unknown]; 1735–1739 Sa'id al-Hadermi; 1739–1746 Muhammad ibn Uthman al-Mazrui; 1746–1746 Ali ibn Uthman al-Mazrui. *Mazrui Sultans:* 1746–1755 Ali ibn Uthman al-Mazrui; 1755–1773 Masud ibn Nasir; 1773–1782 Abdallah ibn Muhammad; 1782–1811 Ahmad ibn Muhammad; 1811–1825 Abdallah ibn Muhammad; 1825–1826 Suleiman ibn Ali. *British Governors:* Dec. 1823–13 Feb. 1824 Adm. William Owen; 13 Feb. 1824–29 May 1824 J.J. Reitz; 29 May 1824–Sept. 1824 [vacant]; Sept. 1824–1826 Lt. Emery. *Busaidi Governors:* 1826–March 1835 Salem ibn Ahmad (also known as Muhammad Asmani al-Mazrui); March 1835–1836 Nasr ibn Ahmad; 1836–1837 Rashid ibn Salem; 1837–1837 Khamis ibn Rashid; 1837–1860 Abdallah ibn Hamish; 1860–1873 Mubarrak ibn Rashid; 1873–1 July 1895 Rashid ibn Hamish.

Mondah see **Gabon**

Monomatapa see **Mwene Mutapa Empire**

Monrovia see **Bassa Cove** and **Liberia**

Mora see **Jema'a**

Morisco Republic see **Bou Regreg**

Morocco. 1268– . *Location:* the extreme northwest of Africa. *Capital:* Rabat (founded in the 12th century as a ribat, or military post, it was the capital of French Morocco between 1907 and 1956, and of Morocco itself from 1956); between 1666 and 1907 the capital was mostly either at Rabat or Fez, but occasionally at Meknès or Marrakesh; Tafilalt (1631–1666); Marrakesh (1524–1631); Fez (1472–1524); Asila (1465–1472). *Other names:* Maghrib; Maroc; Marruecos; al-Mamlakah al-Maghribiyyah, or Kingdom of Morocco (from 1957); Sultanate of Morocco (1956–1957); French Morocco (the name given to most of the country between 1907 and 1956); Spanish Morocco (the name given to the Spanish possessions between 1847 and 1956).

History: There are various points in Maghribi history at which one might say the state of Morocco took form, as a cohesive unit, with roughly the parameters it has today. Probably the most opportune is 1268, when the Merinids (also known as the Marinids, or Banu Marin) took over from the Almohads as the third Berber dynasty to rule all of Morocco. However, the preceding Almohad Empire had constituted a much larger territory than just Morocco, as had their predecessor, the Almoravid Empire. The Banu Marin were a tribe of the Zanatah group, and had been in existence since about 1150, in eastern Morocco. In 1248 they captured Fez, making it their capital instead of their old headquarters at Taza. They made several attempts to recapture Spanish possessions in Spain, and toward the end of its lifetime the empire fell into anarchy. Around 1428 the viziers became virtual rulers of Morocco under the Merinids and in 1459 they set up their own dynasty — the Wattasids (also known as the Banu Wattas) which, by 23 May 1465, had replaced the Merinids as the official ruling power in the Western Maghrib. A weak dynasty, however, the Banu Wattas controlled only Northern Morocco, and throughout the lifetime of the dynasty the Portuguese settled various towns on the coast of Morocco. These were: Alcazarseguer in 1458; Anfa in 1469; Arzila in 1471; Tangier in 1471 (see Tangier); Massa in 1488; Agadir in 1505; Safi in 1508; Azammour in 1513; Mazagan in 1514; Mehdia in 1515; and Agouz in 1519. The legitimacy of the Banu Wattas was never fully recognized and by 1511 the Sa'did Dynasty was already beginning to take over. By that stage Mulay Ahmad, the sheikh of the Sharifian Sa'di tribe, with his capital at Sous, was declared leader of a jihad to expel the Portuguese who had settled under the weak Wattasid Empire. In 1524 the Sa'dids captured Marrakesh and made it their capital, setting up a rival government to the Banu Wattas. In 1548 they also seized Fez. By 28 Jan. 1549 the Sa'dids were the masters of Morocco, but they had little support as the new rulers. By the early 17th century the dynasty was in decline and being ruled by different factions from Fez and Marrakesh. In 1659 the country was taken over by the Alawids. The Alawids had come from Arabia in the times of the Merinid Empire and based themselves in the oases of Tafilalt. By 1631 they had risen to enormous power in Morocco. In 1666 Mulay Rashid was officially proclaimed sultan of Morocco, and his dynasty has ruled Morocco ever since, with a little help from the French and the Spanish, as well as from the Portuguese and British at times. Spain had long had control over what today is Southern Morocco (see Western Sahara and Ifni), as well as possession of Ceuta and Melilla, two enclaves in the north, but it was the French who took over the bulk of Morocco in 1907 (see French Morocco). In 1912 the Spanish occupied a large part of Northern Morocco known as the Rif. The sultan, Muhammad V, very pro–French (more as a matter of expediency, though, than as a true sentiment), attached himself to Vichy France during World War II, although when the Allies landed at Casablanca he expediently changed to the correct side. The nationalist party, Istiqlal, was founded in 1944, and Muhammad, tired of expediency, became a nationalist after the War, and was deposed and exiled by the French in 1953, being replaced on the throne by his uncle, Muhammad VI. Istiqlal objected strenuously to this move, and the new sultan survived several assassination attempts. In 1955 Muhammad V came back to still the troubled waters. In 1956 France returned its part of Morocco to the Moroccans, and the Spanish returned the Rif, and the independent sultanate of Morocco came into being. Tangier was a unique case. In 1923, until then a French Moroccan town, it had became the International Zone of Tangier (see Tangier), but in 1956 the town also reverted to the new sultanate. Spain kept Ifni and Río de Oro (which became Spanish Sahara in 1958), as well as Ceuta and Melilla and the northern Moroccan islands of Alhucemas, Chafarinas, and Velez de la Gomera. On 11 Aug. 1957 the sultanate of Morocco became the Kingdom of Morocco that we know today, and in 1961, Hassan, son of Muhammad V, became king. From 1963 to 1970 Morocco was at war with Algeria, and a state of emergency was declared in 1965. In 1969 Spain gave Ifni to Morocco, and in 1976 they evacuated Spanish Sahara, leaving that country to its fate (see Western Sahara for details). Hassan was captured in a coup attempt in 1971, survived two assassination attempts that year, and as a result purged the Army. The war with POLISARIO raged in the 1970s and 1980s because the main internal problem in Morocco has been the Western Sahara question. Should Morocco have possession, or should it become a free state? This is a matter for a referendum in Western Sahara.

Merinid Kings: 1196–1218 Abu Muhammad Abd al-Haqq I; 1218–1240 Uthman I; 1240–12 Nov. 1244 Muhammad I; 12 Nov. 1244–30 July 1258 Abu Yahya Abu-Bakr; 30 July 1258–20 March 1286 Abu Yusuf Yakub; 20 March 1286–10 May 1307 Abu Yakub Yusuf; 10 May 1307–23 July 1308 Abu Thabit Amir; 23 July 1308–Nov. 1310 Abu'l Rabi Suleiman; Nov. 1310–Sept. 1331 Abu Sa'id Uthman II; Sept. 1331–Sept. 1348 Abu'l Hassan Ali I; Sept. 1348–3 Dec. 1358 Abu Inan Faris; 3 Dec. 1358–July 1359 Muhammad II as-Sa'id; Aug. 1359–1 Oct. 1361 Abu Salim Ali II; 1 Oct. 1361–Nov. 1361 Abu Umar Tashufin; Nov. 1361–29 Dec. 1361 Abd al-Halim; 29 Dec. 1361–30 Aug. 1366 Abu Zayyan Muhammad III; 30 Aug. 1366–23 Oct. 1372 Abu'l Faris Abd al-Aziz I; 23 Oct. 1372–18 June 1374 Abu Zayyan Muhammad IV; 18 June 1374–1384 Abu'l Abbas Ahmad; 1384–28 Sept. 1386 Musa; 28 Sept. 1386–9 Nov. 1386 Abu Zayyan Muhammad V; 20 Nov. 1386–1393 Abu'l Abbas Ahmad; 1393–1396 Abu'l Faris Abd al-Aziz I; 1396–1398 Abdallah; 1398–1420 Abu Sa'id Uthman III; 1420–1428 interregnum; 1428–May 1465 Abu Muhammad Abd al-Haqq II. *Wattasid Sultans:* 23 May 1465–1505 Muhammad ash-Sheikh; 1505–1524 Muhammad II al-Bartuqali; 1524–1545 Ahmad al-Wattasi; 1545–1547 Muhammad III al-Qasri; 1547–28 Jan. 1549 Ahmad al-Wattasi. *Sa'did Sheiks:* 1511–1517 Muhammad al-Qa'im; 1517–1525 Ahmad I al-Araj; 1525–28 Jan. 1549 Muhammad II al-Mahdi. *Sa'did Sultans:* 28 Jan. 1549–23 Oct. 1557 Muhammad II al-Mahdi; 23 Oct. 1557–21 Jan. 1574 Abdallah al-Ghalib; 31 March 1574–1576 Muhammad III al-Mutawakkil; 1576–4 Aug. 1578 Abd al-Malik al-Ghazi; 15 Aug. 1578–19 Aug. 1603 Ahmad II al-Mansur; 19 Aug. 1603–1610 Zaydan an-Nasir; 1610–1613 Muhammad IV al-Ma'mun (ruled from Fez); 1610–1626 Zaydan an-Nasir (ruled from Marrakesh); 1613–1624 Abdallah II (ruled from Fez); 1624–1626 Abd al-Malik III (ruled from Fez); 1626–1628 Zaydan an-Nasir; 1628–10 March 1631 Abd al-Malik II; 10 March 1631–21 Feb. 1636 al-Walid; 21 Feb. 1636–1655 Muhammad V al-Asgher; 1655–1659 Ahmad II al-Abbas. *Alawid Sheikhs:* 1631–1635 Muhammad I ash-Sharif; 1635–3 Aug. 1664 Muhammad II; 3 Aug. 1664–1666 Mulay Rashid. *Alawid Sultans:* 1666–27 March 1672 Mulay Rashid; 27 March 1672–21 March 1727 Mulay Ismail as-Samin; 21 March 1727–April 1728 Ahmad adh-Dhahabi; April 1728–June 1728 Abd al-Malik; June 1728–5 March 1729 Ahmad adh-Dhahabi; 5 March 1729–29 Sept. 1734 Abdallah; 29 Sept. 1734–12 May 1736 Ali al-Araj; 12 May 1736–1736 Abdallah; 1736–1738 Muhammad III;

1738–1740 al-Mustadi ibn Ismail; 1740–1745 Abdallah; 1745–1745 Zayin al-Abidin; 1745–1748 Abdallah; 1748–1748 Muhammad III; 1748–1757 Abdallah; 1757–11 April 1790 Muhammad III; 11 April 1790–15 Feb. 1792 Yazid; 15 Feb. 1792–1793 Hisham; 1793–19 Nov. 1822 Suleiman; 19 Nov. 1822–28 Aug. 1859 Abd ar-Rahman; 28 Aug. 1859–12 Sept. 1873 Muhammad IV; 25 Sept. 1873–7 June 1894 Hassan I; 7 June 1894–4 Jan. 1908 Abd al-Aziz; 4 Jan. 1908–11 Aug. 1912 Abd al-Hafiz; 11 Aug. 1912–17 Nov. 1927 Yusuf; 17 Nov. 1927–14 Aug. 1953 Muhammad V (also known as Sidi Muhammad ben Yusuf); 14 Aug. 1953–16 Aug. 1953 Muhammad VI (also known as Sidi Muhammad ben Mulay Arafa); 16 Aug. 1953–21 Aug. 1953 [vacant]; 21 Aug. 1953–30 Oct. 1955 Muhammad VI (also known as Sidi Muhammad ben Mulay Arafa); 1 Nov. 1955–11 Aug. 1957 Muhammad V (also known as Sidi Muhammad ben Yusuf). *Kings:* 11 Aug. 1957–26 Feb. 1961 Muhammad V (also known as Sidi Muhammad ben Yusuf); 26 Feb. 1961–23 July 1999 Hassan II (also known as Mulay Hassan); 23 July 1999–Muhammad VI. *Grand Viziers:* 1908–1909 Muhammad al-Muqri; 1911–1913 Muhammad al-Muqri; 1917–Oct. 1955 Muhammad al-Muqri. *Prime Ministers:* 7 Dec. 1955–15 April 1958 M'barek ben Mustafa al-Bakai; 12 May 1958–3 Dec. 1958 Ahmad Balafrej; 16 Dec. 1958–20 May 1960 Abdallah Ibrahim; 3 May 1961–13 Nov. 1963 Ahmad Reda Guedira; 13 Nov. 1963–7 June 1965 Ahmad Bahmini; 7 July 1967–6 Oct. 1969 Muhammad Benhima; 6 Oct. 1969–6 Aug. 1971 Ahmad Laraki; 6 Aug. 1971–2 Nov. 1972 Muhammad Karim Lamrani; 2 Nov. 1972–22 March 1979 Ahmad Osman; 22 March 1979–19 Nov. 1983 Maati Bouabid; 30 Nov. 1983–30 Sept. 1986 Muhammad Karim Lamrani; 30 Sept. 1986–11 Aug. 1992 Azzedine Laraki; 11 Aug. 1992–25 May 1994 Muhammad Karim Lamrani (acting); 25 May 1994–4 Feb. 1998 Abdellatif Filali; 14 March 1998–9 Oct. 2002 Abd ar-Rahman al-Youssoufi; 9 Oct. 2002–Driss Jettou. *Note:* For list of French residents-general, see French Morocco. *Note:* For list of Spanish high commissioners see Spanish Morocco. *Note:* In times of no Prime Minister, the King held that office.

Moroni see **Comoros** and **Gran Comoro**

Moselekatse's Land see **Matabeleland**

Mossi States. The Southern Mossi chiefdoms were: Mamprusi (also known as Memphusi), Dagomba, and Nanumba — all in today's Ghana. The Northern Mossi chiefdoms were: Tenkodogo, Zandoma, Gurma, Wagadugu, and Yatenga — all in today's Burkina Faso. About the year 1100 a Dagomba king called Nedega, who ruled at Gambaga, appeared in the Volta area. His daughter Yenenga married a Man dingo hunter named Riala. Ouidriaogo, their son, founded the Mossi Empire at Tenkodogo. Rawa, his son, founded the kingdom of Zandana which, later, under his grandson Yadega, became the state of Yatenga. In the east, Rawa's brother, Diaba, founded Gurma, while Oubri (flourished probably around 1350), one of their nephews, founded Wagadugu. Separately these states existed as kingdoms (or chiefdoms) within the family-related Mossi Empire. By 1900, after three years of French colonial rule, the Mossi Empire had been reduced to three major states — Gurma, Wagadugu, and Yatenga. Small kingdoms within Wagadugu were Rotenga, Zitenga, and Riziam. There were 34 rulers (emperors) of the Mossi Empire.

Moyen-Congo see **Congo**

Moyen-Congo–Gabon see **Lower Congo-Gabon**

Mozambique. 1501– . *Location:* a country on the southeast coast of Africa, it is bordered on the north by Tanzania, Malawi, and Zambia; on the west by Zimbabwe and the Transvaal province of South Africa; and on the south by the Tongaland District of Natal province of South Africa; on the east it is bounded by the Indian Ocean. *Capital:* Maputo (until 3 Feb. 1976 called Lourenço Marques, which was named for a Portuguese trader and explorer in 1544. The town developed around a fortress built in 1787, and became a city in 1887. It was the capital from 1897); Mozambique (1554–1897); Sofala (1512–1554); Kilwa (1501–1512. This town is located in what is today Kenya); Sofala (local headquarters from 1501 to 1507). *Other names:* Moçambique; República de Moçambique, or Republic of Mozambique (from 1990); República Popular de Moçambique, or People's Republic of Mozambique (1975–1990); Portuguese East Africa (alternative name from 1501 to 1975); Provincia de Moçambique, or Overseas Province of Mozambique (1951–1975); Colony of Mozambique (1836–1951); Colony of Mozambique, the Zambesi and Sofala (1752–1836); Colony of Mozambique, Sofala, Ríos de Cuama and Monomatapa (1609–1752); Captaincy-General of Mozambique (1569–1609); Captaincy of Sofala and Mozambique (1507–1569); Captaincy of Sofala (1501–1507).

History: In 1497 Vasco da Gama landed on the coast of what is today Mozambique. On 1 March 1498 he landed at what is now the city of Mozambique. Driven almost exclusively by wild tales of the fantastically rich gold and silver mines of a semi-legendary ruler in the interior named the "monomatapa" (see Mwene Mutapa Empire), the Portuguese early determined to take control of the country as far as they could. In 1501 a Portuguese administration was commenced at Sofala, subject to Goa in India, and a fort was built there, and a settlement established, by 1505. On 8 Sept. 1507, with the opening up of the coast, the country became known as the Captaincy of Sofala and Mozambique, still subject to Goa. Posts began to be built up the Zambesi River, such as Tete and Sena in the early 1530s. Still obsessed with the Monomatapa's mines, the Portuguese finally reached him and found the truth. There were no mines. In 1569 the country, by now growing in importance and development, became the Captaincy-General of Mozambique. Spain ruled Portugal between 1580 and 1656, but the Portuguese continued to administer Mozambique. In 1609 it became the Colony of Mozambique, Sofala, Ríos de Cuama and Monomatapa, but was popularly known as Mozambique or Portuguese East Africa. In 1752 it was freed of its dependence on Goa and became an individual autonomous colony of Portugal, with the official name of Mozambique, the Zambesi and Sofala. In March 1836 it became simply the Colony of Mozambique. In 1878 slavery was abolished in Mozambique. In 1919, at the Treaty of Versailles (effective 10 Jan. 1920), Mozambique gained the Kionga triangle in the north, a stretch of land that had been part of German East Africa. On 11 June 1951 it became an overseas province of Portugal. From 1962 onwards the Mozambique Liberation Front (FRELIMO) waged a guerrilla war for independence. In 1969, Samora Machel, who had worked his way up through the FRELIMO ranks, succeeded Eduardo Mondlane as leader of the organization. In 1974 Portugal peacefully handed over power to FRELIMO, who began a local administration on 20 Sept. 1974. However, this move was not made so peacefully, large sectors of the country objecting to the Communist-oriented FRELIMO. On 25 June 1975 the country became the People's Republic of Mozambique, a Communist country, and most of the white people left. Dependent economically on South Africa, and beleaguered by famines and civil wars (notably the continuous rebellion of RENAMO, the Mozambique National Resistance), the government formally abandoned Communism in 1989 (effective 30 Nov. 1990), and the country became the Republic of Mozambique. Free elections were held, and on 7 Aug. 1992 a truce was signed between the government and RENAMO. There was a bad drought in 1992 which led to famine and starvation, and then civil war. More than a million refugees fled the country. In 2000 Mozambique was just recovering from the civil war when a major cyclone hit the country and the worst flooding in years. Gross corruption by extraordinarily incompetent rulers has, along with the massive AIDS problem, brought Mozambique to its knees.

Capitães-Mores (plural of Capitão-Mor, or Captain-Major): 1501–4 May 1505 Sancho de Tovar; 4 May 1505–March 1506 Pedro de Nhuya; March 1506–Dec. 1506 Manuel Fernandes; Dec. 1506–8 Sept. 1507 Nunho Vaz Pereira; 8 Sept. 1507–Feb. 1508 Vasco de Abreu; Feb. 1508–1509 Rui Patalim (acting); 1509–24 June 1512 Antonio de Saldanha; 24 June 1512–June 1515 Simão de Azevedo; June 1515–July 1515 Sancho de Tovar (acting); July 1515–June 1518 Cristóvão de Távora; June 1518–July 1521 Sancho de Tovar; July 1521–1525 Diogo de Sepúlveda; 1525–1528 Lopo de Almeida; 1528–1531 Antonio de Meneses; 1531–1538 Vicente Pegado; 1538–1541 Aleixo Chicorro; 1541–1548 João de Sepúlveda; 1548–1551 Fernão de Távora; 1551–1553 Diogo de Mesquita; 1553–1557 Diogo de Sousa; 1557–1560 Sebastião de Sá; 1560–1564 Pantaleão de Sá; 1564–1567 Jerónimo Barreto; 1567–1569 Pedro Rolim. *Captains-General:* 1569–June 1573 Francisco Barreto; June 1573–1577 Vasco Homem (acting); 1577–1577 Fernando Monroi (acting); 1577–1577 Simão de Silveira (acting); 1577–1582 Pedro de Castro; 1582–1586 Nunho Pereira; 1586–1589 Jorge de Meneses; 1589–1590 Lourenço de Brito; 1590–1595 Pedro de Sousa; 1595–1598 Nunho da Cunha e Ataíde; 1598–1601 Álvaro Abranches; 1601–1604 Vasco de Mascarenhas; 1604–1607 Sebastião de Macedo; 1607–1609 Estévão de Ataíde. *Governors:* 1609–1611 Nunho Pereira; 1611–1612 Estévão de Ataíde; 1612–1612 Diogo de Madeira (acting); 1612–1614 João de Azevedo; 1614–1618 Rui Sampaio; 1618–1623 Nunho Pereira; 1623–1624 Lopo de Almeida; 1624–1627 Diogo de Meneses; 1627–1631 Nunho Pereira; 1631–1632 Cristóvão de Brito e Vasconcelos (acting); 1632–1633 Diogo de Meneses; 1633–1634 Filipe de Mascarenhas; 1634–1639 Lourenço de Souto-Maior; 1639–1640 Diogo de Vasconcelos; 1640–1641 Antonio de Brito Pacheco; 1641–1642 Francisco da Silveira; 1642–1646 Júlio Moniz da Silva; 1646–1648 Fernão Baião; 1648–1651 Álvaro de Távora; 1651–1652 Francisco de Mascarenhas; 1652–1657 Francisco de Lima; 1657–1661 Manuel de Sampaio; 1661–1664 Manuel de Mascarenhas; 1664–1667 Antonio de Melo e Castro; 1667–1670 Inacio de Carvalho; 1670–1673 João Freire; 1673–1674 Simão da Silva; 1674–1674 André da Fonseca; 1674–1676 Manuel da Silva (acting); 1676–1682 João Freire; 1682–1686 Caetano de Melo e Castro; 1686–1689 Miguel de Almeida; 1689–1692 Manuel Pinto; 1692–1693 Tomé Correia; 1693–1694 Francisco de Mesquita (acting); 1694–1695 Estévão da Costa; 1695–1696 Francisco da Costa; 1696–1699 Luis Sampaio; 1699–1703 Jácome Sarmento; 1703–1706 João de Almeida; 1706–1707 Luis de Brito Freire; 1707–1712 Luis da Câmara; 1712–1714 João de Almeida; 1714–1715 Francisco de Mascarenhas; 1715–1719 Francisco de Souto-Maior; 1719–1721 Francisco de Alarcão e Souto-Maior; 1721–1723 Álvaro de Melo e Castro; 1723–1726 Antonio Sequeira e Faria; 1726–1730 Antonio Fróis; 1730–1733 Antonio de Melo; 1733–1736 José Leal; 1736–1739 Nicolau de Almeida; 1739–1743 Lourenço de Noronha; 1743–1746 Pedro da Gama e Castro; 1746–1750 Caetano de Sá; 1750–March 1758 Francisco de Melo e Castro; March 1758–April 1758 João de Melo; April 1758–28 May 1759 David Marquês Pereira; 28 May 1759–1763 Pedro de Saldanha e Albuquerque; 1763–1765 João Barba; 1765–June 1779 Baltasar do Lago; June 1779–1780 provisional administration; 1780–1781 José de Vasconcelos e Almeida; 1781–4 Jan. 1782 Vicente de Maia e Vasconcelos (acting); 4 Jan. 1782–21 Aug. 1782 Pedro de Saldanha e Albuquerque; 21 Aug. 1782–1786 a junta was in power; 1786–

1793 Antonio de Melo e Castro; 1793–1797 Diogo Coutinho; 1797–Sept. 1801 Francisco Meneses da Costa; Sept. 1801–Aug. 1805 Isidro de Almeida Sousa e Sá; Aug. 1805–Dec. 1807 Francisco do Amaral Cardoso; Dec. 1807–14 Aug. 1809 a junta was in power; 14 Aug. 1809–Aug. 1812 Antonio de Melo e Castro de Mendonça; Aug. 1812–Feb. 1817 Marcos de Abreu e Meneses; Feb. 1817–Sept. 1818 João de Albuquerque; Sept. 1818–Nov. 1819 a junta was in power; Nov. 1819–June 1821 João Brito-Sanches; June 1821–June 1824 two juntas were in power; June 1824–Jan. 1825 João da Silva; Jan. 1825–Aug. 1829 Xavier Botelho; Aug. 1829–Jan. 1832 Paulo de Brito; Jan. 1832–March 1834 a junta was in power; March 1834–March 1836 José Pegado. *Governors-General:* March 1836–March 1837 provisional rule; March 1837–Oct. 1837 Antonio de Melo; Oct. 1837–March 1838 Marquês de Aracaty; March 1838–25 March 1840 Council of Government; 25 March 1840–May 1841 Joaquim Marinho; May 1841–15 Feb. 1843 João Xavier; 15 Feb. 1843–May 1847 Rodrigo de Abreu e Lima; May 1847–Oct. 1851 Domingos do Vale; Oct. 1851–April 1854 Joaquim de Magalhães; April 1854–Sept. 1857 Vasco de Carvalho e Meneses; Sept. 1857–Feb. 1864 João de Almeida; Feb. 1864–April 1864 Council of Government; April 1864–Oct. 1867 Antonio de Canto e Castro; Oct. 1867–Sept. 1868 Antonio de Lacerda; Sept. 1868–Feb. 1869 Council of Government; Feb. 1869–April 1869 Antonio de Almeida; April 1869–Dec. 1869 Fernão Leal; Dec. 1869–June 1870 Council of Government; June 1870–Aug. 1870 Inacio Alves (acting); Aug. 1870–Dec. 1873 José do Amaral; Dec. 1873–Aug. 1874 Council of Government; Aug. 1874–Dec. 1877 José de Carvalho e Meneses; Dec. 1877–Jan. 1880 Francisco da Cunha; Jan. 1880–Aug. 1881 Augusto Sarmento; Aug. 1881–Feb. 1882 Carlos de Arcos; Feb. 1882–April 1882 João d'Ávila (acting); April 1882–April 1885 Agostinho Coelho; April 1885–July 1885 Council of Government; July 1885–March 1889 Augusto de Castilho Barreto e Noronha; March 1889–July 1889 José d'Almeida (acting); July 1889–July 1890 José Ferreira; July 1890–2 July 1891 Joaquim Machado; 2 July 1891–May 1893 Rafael de Andrade; May 1893–13 Jan. 1894 Francisco da Silva; 13 Jan. 1894–July 1894 João Correia e Lança (acting); July 1894–Jan. 1895 Fernão de Magalhães e Meneses; Jan. 1895–Dec. 1895 Antonio Enes; Jan. 1896–March 1896 João Correia e Lança (acting); March 1896–Nov. 1897 Joaquim de Albuquerque; Nov. 1897–Aug. 1898 Baltasar Cabral; Aug. 1898–Dec. 1898 Carlos Alberto Schultz Xavier; Dec. 1898–March 1900 Álvaro Ferreira; March 1900–May 1900 Júlio da Costa; May 1900–Oct. 1900 Joaquim Machado; Oct. 1900–Dec. 1902 Manuel Gorjão; Dec. 1902–Feb. 1905 Tomás Rosado; Feb. 1905–Oct. 1906 João de Sequeira; Oct. 1906–Nov. 1910 Alfredo de Andrade; Nov. 1910–May 1911 José Ribeiro; May 1911–Feb. 1912 José de Azevedo e Silva; Feb. 1912–March 1913 José de Magalhães; March 1913–April 1914 Augusto dos Santos; April 1914–May 1915 Joaquim Machado; May 1915–Oct. 1915 Alfredo Coelho; Oct. 1915–April 1918 Álvaro de Castro; April 1918–April 1919 Pedro do Amorim; April 1919–March 1921 Manuel da Fonseca. *High Commissioners/Governors-General:* March 1921–Sept. 1923 Manuel Camacho; Sept. 1923–Sept. 1924 Manuel da Fonseca (acting). *Governors-General/High Commissioners:* Sept. 1924–May 1926 Victor Hugo de Azevedo Coutinho; May 1926–Nov. 1926 Ivens Ferraz (acting). *High Commissioners/Governors-General:* Nov. 1926–April 1938 José Cabral. *Governors-General/High Commissioners:* April 1938–1940 José de Oliveira; 1941–1946 José de Bettencourt; 1946–May 1947 [unknown] (acting); May 1947–Dec. 1948 Luis de Sousa e Vasconcelos e Funchal; Dec. 1948–1958 Gabriel Teixeira; 1958–1961 Pedro de Barros; 1961–1964 Manuel Rodrigues; 1964–1969 José da Costa Almeida; 1969–Oct. 1971 Eduardo Arantes e Oliveira; Oct. 1971–1973 Manuel dos Santos; 1973–17 Aug. 1974 Henriques de Melo; 17 Aug. 1974–12 Sept. 1974 Ferro Ribeiro (acting); 12 Sept. 1974–25 June 1975 Victor Crespo. *Presidents:* 25 June 1975–19 Oct. 1986 Samora Machel; 19 Oct. 1986–2 Feb. 2005 Joaquim Chissanó; 2 Feb. 2005–Armando Guebuza. *Prime Ministers:* 20 Sept. 1974–25 June 1975 Joaquim Chissanó; 17 July 1986–16 Dec. 1994 Mario Machungo; 21 Dec. 1994–17 Feb. 2004 Pascoal Mocumbi; 17 Feb. 2004–Luisa Diogo.

MPLA see **Angola** and **Angola People's Democratic Republic**

Mpondoland see **Pondoland**

Mtetwa Empire see **Zululand**

Mukurra. ca. 340–ca. 675. *Location:* in the Sudan. *Capital:* Old Dunqulah. *Other names:* Maqurrah; Makuria.

History: One of the major kingdoms of the Nilotic Sudan during the Dark Ages, Mukurra was converted to Christianity about 550. About 675 the state swallowed up Nubia (the land of the Nobatae) and the new, enlarged kingdom became known as Dongola.
Rulers: ca. 340–ca. 675 [unknown].

Mum see **Bamoun**

Murabitun Dynasty see **Almoravid Empire**

Muri. 1833–Sept. 1901. *Location:* Northern Nigeria. *Capital:* Jalingo (from 1917); Mutum Biyu (1910–1917); Lau (1901–1910); Jalingo (1893–1901); Muri (until 1893). *Other names:* Hammuruwa Kingdom; Muri Protectorate (1892–1893).

History: By 1817 the Fulani Empire had taken most of the Muriwa (people of Muri) territory and Hamman Ruwa, the Fulani captain, was made governor of the area. In 1833 he gained independence for Muri as an amirate of the empire. In 1892 the perennial enemy, the Jukun (see Kororofa) attacked again, and the amir of Muri enlisted the aid of a French adventurer, Louis Mizon who, due to his rather vague connection with the French Army, succeeded in placing a perfectly legal French protectorate over the amirate, in 1892, with himself as governor. In 1893, however, Mizon was expelled, and the Muriwa moved to a new capital, Jalingo. In 1901 the amirate became part of the British protectorate of Northern Nigeria, as the Lau Division of Muri Province.

Governors: 1817–1833 Hamman Ruwa. *Amirs:* 1833–1836 Ibrahim; 1836–1836 Hamman; 1836–1848 Ibrahim; 1848–1861 Hamman; 1861–1869 Hamadu; 1869–1873 Burba; 1873–1874 Abubakar; 1874–June 1896 Muhammadu Nya; 1897–1903 Hassan; 1903–1953 Muhammadu Mafindi; 1953–1966 Muhammadu Tukur; 1966–12 Aug. 1986 Umaru; 1986–Tafida. *Governors:* 1892–1893 Capt. Louis Mizon.

Mussa Island see **British Somaliland**

Muwahhid Dynasty see **Almohad Empire**

Muyoy Dynasty see **Kayor**

Mvita see **Mombasa**

Mwali. 11 Aug. 1997–1998. *Location:* as Mohéli, in the Comoros. *Capital:* Fomboni. *Other names:* Moili, Mohéli.

History: In 1997 the Comoran island of Mohéli declared itself the autonomous state of Mwali, but recognition did not follow. In 1998 it slipped quietly back into the Comoran fold, so quietly that there is no actual date for its readmission. In 2002 it accepted the compromise of being an autonomous province within the new Union of the Comoros, with a president from 19 May 2002 — Soidri Ahmad. See also Nzwani.

Presidents: 11 Aug. 1997–1998 Said Muhammad Soefou. *Prime Ministers:* 11 Aug. 1997–1998 Muhammad Said Fazul.

Mwata Yamvo Empire see **Mwene Mutapa Empire**

Mwene Mutapa Empire. ca. 1330–ca. 1888. *Location:* it occupied a great deal of what are today Zimbabwe and Mozambique. *Capital:* Mount Fura (from about 1445); Zimbabwe (until about 1445). *Other names:* Mbire Empire; Mwata Yamvo Empire; Monomatapa; Monomotapa; Mwenemutapa.

History: About 1330 a kingdom grew up, probably in succession to one in the ancient city of Zimbabwe (also known as Great Zimbabwe), between the Zambesi and Limpopo Rivers, and founded by Mbire. His great-great grandson, Nyatsimba, acquired the title "Mwene Mutapa" (meaning "ravager of the lands"), and was the first great conqueror and expander of the state into an empire. From the 1530s the Portuguese influence grew stronger and stronger, and legends about the incredibly rich mineral mines of the monomatapa grew wilder and wilder (they are still legion today, and for more information see Mozambique). In 1629 the Mwene Mutapa of the day attempted to expel the Portuguese, but they deposed him and installed a successor. Colonial rule was beginning, and the power of the Mwene Mutapa sagged until by the end of the 17th century it was virtually eclipsed by the crescent power of Rozwi. Technically, though, the state continued to exist as a small chiefdom in the north of what is now Zimbabwe, until it became incorporated into Zambesia (see Rhodesia).

Kings: ca. 1330–(?) Mbire; (?)–(?) [unknown]; (?)–(?) [unknown]; (?)–ca. 1430 [unknown].

Mwene Mutapas: ca. 1430–ca. 1450 Nyatsimba Mutota; ca. 1450–1480 Matope Nyanhehwe Nebedza; 1480–1480 Mabura Maobwe; 1480–1490 Nyahuma Mukombero; 1490–1494 Changamire; 1494–1530 Chikuyo Chisamarengu; 1530–1550 Neshangwe Munembire; 1550–1560 Chivere Nyasoro; 1560–1589 Negomo Chisamhuru; 1589–1623 Gatsi Rusere; 1623–1629 Nyambu Kapararidze; 1629–1652 Mavura Mhande Felipe; 1652–1663 Siti Kazurukamusapa; 1663–1692 Kamharapasu Mukombwe; 1692–1694 Nyakambira; 1694–1707 Nyamaende Mhande; 1707–1711 Nyenyedzi; 1711–1719 Boroma Dangwarangwa; 1719–1735 Samatambira Nyamhandu I; 1735–1740 Nyatsutsu; 1740–1759 Dehwe Mapunzagutu; 1759–1785 Changara; 1785–1790 Nyamhandu II; 1790–1810 Chiwayo; 1810–1835 Nyasoro; 1835–1868 Kataruza; 1868–1870 Kandeya; 1870–1887 Dzuda; 1887–1917 Chioko.

Mzilikazi's Land see **Matabeleland**

Namaland see **Namibia** and **Rehoboth**

Namaqualand see **Namibia**

Namib see **Namibia**

Namibia. 24 April 1884– . *Location:* southwest Africa. *Capital:* Windhoek (the capital since 1891, this town was founded in 1870, the name meaning "place of smoke"); Otjimbigwe (1884–1891). *Other names:* South West Africa (1915–1968); German South West Africa (1884–1915).

History: Germany's first colonial move, this area of South West Africa was subdued in the early 1880s, the first settlements being made on 24 April 1883. The town of Lüderitz was taken in the same year, and the rest of the country in 1884. Prior to this the area was split into three basic regions: Ovamboland in the north; Damaraland in the center; and Great Namaqualand in the south. Windhoek became the central town (although not the capital until 1891). The coastline contained the isolated British colony of Walvis Bay; the rest of the country was in the hands of the German South-West Africa Colonial Company. In 1889 the German government relieved the company of the area owing to the company's financial difficulties. Heinrich Goering (Herman's father) continued to rule in the protectorate, however. On 14 Sep. 1902 the country became a German colony. Effective control of the Hottentots and Hereros was not complete until 1906. In 1915 the Germans lost the country to South African troops, and on 15 July 1915 it became the protectorate of South West Africa, under a South African military governor. On 1 Jan. 1921 South West Africa became a South African League of Nations Class C mandate. Class C authorized the occupying power to exercise full control over the territory as an integral part of its own state. On 11 Dec. 1946, at the time that United Nations trusteeships were being awarded to former mandates, South Africa refused one for South West Africa. South Africa continued to rule their territory as before, except that their mandate was now recognized by the U.N. South Africa wanted to annex the area, but the United Nations refused permission for this. On 27 Oct. 1966 the U.N. took away the mandate by virtue of U.N. General Assembly Resolution No. 2145, claiming that South Africa had not fulfilled its obligations in South West Africa, and so it became a United Nations Supervised Territory. On 19 May 1967 the U.N. established an 11-member U.N. Council for South West Africa, to administer the territory until independence (at that stage independence was scheduled for June 1968), but the South Africans would not allow the Council entry into South West Africa. South Africa simply refused to accept the termination of the old mandate. On 12 June 1968 the U.N. changed the name of the country to Namibia (the name comes from the Namib Desert—a name meaning "area where nothing lives"), and this represented the final stage of the country's history before independence. S.W.A.P.O. (the South West Africa People's Organization of Namibia), formerly the Ovambo People's Organization, and consisting mainly of Ovambos (the largest ethnic group in the country) came to the fore in demanding self-determination. Led by Sam Nujoma and Hendrik Witbooi, S.W.A.P.O. (founded as early as 1958) engaged in political discussion and guerrilla warfare to achieve their aims, but South Africa refused to deal with them. In 1977 Walvis Bay was incorporated into South Africa, and this port (lying in the center of the Namibian coastline) added another obstacle to settlement of the independence question. In 1977 an administrator-general was sent by South Africa to Namibia. The occupation of Namibia by South Africa was a fact, and continued to be looked upon as illegal by most of the world, including the United Nations. Keen to alleviate world hostility, on 22 Dec. 1988 South Africa did, with Angola and Cuba, sign a U.S.–mediated agreement to end South African administration of South West Africa, to provide for a cease-fire, to afford the Namibians a transition to independence, and to recognize Namibia's independence within the following year or two. Another question was that of the bantustans (or native homelands) in Namibia. On 2 Oct. 1968 South Africa created a model homeland for the Ovambos, and called it Ovamboland, giving it some degree of self-rule. However, the "model" turned out to be inaccessible to the rest of the world. On 1 May 1973 Ovamboland achieved self-government, but the inaccessibility remained. In 1980 South Africa terminated the "model" bantustan of Ovamboland, and government fell completely back into the hands of South Africa. There were nine other bantustans created in Namibia: Kavangoland, created 10 Oct. 1972, in Northeastern Namibia, with its capital at Rundu, was a homeland for the Kavango peoples (or Okavango). It was a strip of land about three miles wide, along the Okavango River. East Caprivi was a bantustan for the Mafwe and the Masubia peoples, and was on the Caprivi Strip in Northeastern Namibia. It was created in March 1972 and its capital was Ngwese. Kaokoland was in the Kaokoveld in Northwestern Namibia, and its capital was Ohopoho. It was the homeland for the Himba and Tjimba-Herero peoples. Damaraland was in the Namib Desert, and was the homeland for the Damaras. Its capital was Weltwitschia. Hereroland was in the Kalahari desert and was the bantustan for the Hereros. Namaland was in the south, and had as its capital Gibeon. It was the homeland for the Namas (the former Namaquas). Bushmanland was also in the Kalahari, and was the homeland for the Bushmen (also known as the San). Tswanaland was a fabricated homeland for a fabricated group of tribes—the "Tswanas." Essentially it was a convenient dumping ground for a lot of "inconvenient" natives. Finally, Rehoboth Gebiet, in Central Namibia, had its capital at Rehoboth. This was the bantustan for the Basters (Bastaards), and was the traditional home of these people (see also Rehoboth), their old homeland from 1870 to 1885). On 21 March 1990 Namibia finally became an independent republic. The enclave of Walvis Bay remained a South African port until 1 March 1994, when the new South African regime gave it back to Namibia. AIDS is so prevalent that it is hard to imagine how the country is going to survive it.

Reichskommissars: 24 April 1884–30 Dec. 1886 no fixed rule; 30 Dec. 1886–1890 Heinrich Goering; 1890–March 1891 [unknown] (acting); March 1891–14 Sept. 1892 Kurt von François. *Landeshauptmänner:* 14 Sept. 1892–15 March 1895 Kurt von François; 15 March 1895–1899 Theodor Leutwein. *Governors:* 1899–19 Aug. 1905 Theodor Leutwein; 19 Aug. 1905–Nov. 1905 [unknown] (acting); Nov. 1905–26 Aug. 1907 Friedrich von Lindequist; 26 Aug. 1907–20 June 1910 Bruno von Schuckmann; 17 Nov. 1910–15 July 1915 Theodor Seitz. *Military Commanders:* June 1904–19 Nov. 1905 Lothar von Trotha; 19 Nov. 1905–1906 Col. Dame; 1906–26 Aug. 1907 Col. Berthold von Deimling. *Military Governors:* 15 July 1915–30 Oct. 1915 Gen. P.S. Beves. *Administrators:* 31 Oct. 1915–1 Oct. 1920 Sir Howard Gorges; 1 Oct. 1920–31 March 1926 Gysbert Hofmeyer; 1 April 1926–1 April 1933 Albertus Werth; 1 April 1933–1 April 1943 David Conradie; 1 April 1943–6 Dec. 1951 Petrus Hoogenhout; 6 Dec. 1951–1 Dec. 1953 Albertus Van Rhijn; 1 Dec. 1953–1 Dec. 1963 Daniel Viljoen; 1 Dec. 1963–1 Nov. 1968 Wenzel du Plessis; 1 Nov. 1968–1 Nov. 1971 Johannes Van De Wath; 1 Nov. 1971–1 Sept. 1977 Barend Van Der Walt. *Administrators-General:* 1 Sept. 1977–2 Aug. 1979 Marthinus Steyn; 2 Aug. 1979–4 Sept. 1980 Gerrit Van Niekerk Viljoen; 4 Sept. 1980–1 Feb. 1983 Danie Hough; 1 Feb. 1983–1 July 1985 Willie Van Niekerk; 1 July 1985–21 March 1990 Louis Pienaar. *Commissioners-General:* 1 May 1970–21 March 1990 Jannie De Wet. *United Nations Commissioners:* 13 June 1967–(?) Constantine Stavropoulos (acting); 18 Dec. 1973–1 Jan. 1977 Sean MacBride; 1 Jan. 1977–1 April 1982 Martti Ahtissari; 1 April 1982–31 June 1987 Brajesh Chandra Mishra; 31 June 1987–21 Dec. 1988 Bernt Carlsson. *Local Government:* 17 June 1985–21 March 1990 provisional, with rapidly alternating ministers. *Presidents:* 21 March 1990–21 March 2005 Sam Nujoma; 21 March 2005–Hifekepunye Pohamba. *Prime Ministers:* 21 March 1990–28 Aug. 2002 Hage Geingob; 28 Aug. 2002–21 March 2005 Theo-Ben Gurirab; 21 March 2005–Nahas Angula. *Chiefs of the Hereros:* 27 Oct. 1966–26 July 1970 Hosea Kutako; 26 July 1970–21 March 1990 Clemens Kapuuo.

Nanumba see **Mossi States**

Nasarawa Province see **Jema'a**

Natal. 2 Dec. 1836–30 May 1910. *Location:* the eastern part of South Africa, today's Natal province. *Capital:* Pietermaritzburg (founded in 1839 and named for Piet Retief and Gerrit Maritz); no fixed capital before 1839. *Other names:* Natalia (alternative name, 1838–1843); De Vrije Provincie van Nieuwe Holland in Zuid Oost Afrika, or the Free Province of New Holland in South East Africa (1836–1838).

History: Boer emigrants from Cape Colony under Gerrit Maritz, Jacobus Uys, Hendrik Potgieter, and Piet Retief, founded this polity in 1836. On 20 Oct. 1838 it became Natalia, or the Republic of Natal. Later that year it acquired the British settlement of Port Natal, and in 1839 Southern Zululand and the land of the Mpondos (see Pondoland). On 12 May 1843 it was taken over by the British as a colony, and officially named Natal. On 31 May 1844 it was annexed by Cape Colony as the District of Natal. Some Boers accepted British rule, and others left for the Transvaal. Southern Zululand and Pondoland were restored to their original owners, and on 12 July 1856 the District of Natal became a British Crown colony. On 1 Jan. 1866 it extended its borders to include the District of Alfred, and on 10 May 1893 Natal became self-governing. In 1897 it extended its boundaries again by including Zululand. In 1902 it added parts of southern Transvaal, and in 1910 was one of the four self-ruling colonies to form the Union of South Africa (see South Africa). It then became the Province of Natal.

Commandants-General: 2 Dec. 1836–6 June 1837 Gerrit Maritz. *Governors/Commandants-General:* 6 June 1837–6 Feb. 1838 Piet Retief; 6 Feb. 1838–23 Sept. 1838 Gerrit Maritz; 23 Sept. 1838–20 Oct. 1838 Andries Pretorius. *Military Leaders:* 20 Oct. 1838–23 Nov. 1838 Andries Pretorius. *Commandants-General:* 23 Nov. 1838–9 Aug. 1842 Andries Pretorius; 9 Aug. 1842–12 May 1843 Gerrit Rudolf. *Special Commissioners:* 12 May 1843–31 May 1844 Henry Cloete. *Rulers:* 31 May 1844–4 Dec. 1845 direct Cape rule. *Lieutenant-Governors:* 4 Dec. 1845–1 Aug. 1849 Martin West; 2 Aug. 1849–19 April 1850 Edmond Boys; 19 April 1850–12 Oct. 1852 Benjamin Pine; 12 Oct. 1852–31 Jan. 1853 Edmond Boys; 1 Feb. 1853–22 March 1853 Maj.

W.R. Preston (acting); 22 March 1853–3 March 1855 Benjamin Pine; 3 March 1855–5 Nov. 1856 Henry Cooper; 5 Nov. 1856–31 Dec. 1864 John Scott. *Acting Administrators:* 31 Dec. 1864–26 July 1865 John Thomas; 26 July 1865–24 May 1867 John Bissett. *Lieutenant-Governors:* 24 May 1867–19 July 1872 Robert Keate; 19 July 1872–30 April 1873 Anthony Musgrave. *Officers Administering:* 30 April 1873–22 July 1873 Thomas Milles. *Lieutenant-Governors:* 22 July 1873–1 April 1875 Sir Benjamin Pine. *Officers Administering:* 1 April 1875–3 Sept. 1875 Sir Garnet Wolseley. *Lieutenant-Governors:* 3 Sept. 1875–20 April 1880 Sir Henry Bulwer. *Lieutenant-Governors:* 20 April 1880–5 May 1880 William Bellairs; 5 May 1880–2 July 1880 Henry Clifford. *Governors:* 2 July 1880–17 Aug. 1880 Sir George Colley. *Officers Administering:* 17 Aug. 1880–14 Sept. 1880 Henry Alexander. *Governors:* 14 Sept. 1880–27 Feb. 1881 Sir George Colley. *Officers Administering:* 28 Feb. 1881–3 April 1881 Sir Evelyn Wood; 3 April 1881–9 Aug. 1881 Redvers Buller; 9 Aug. 1881–22 Dec. 1881 Sir Evelyn Wood; 22 Dec. 1881–6 March 1882 Charles Mitchell. *Governors:* 6 March 1882–23 Oct. 1885 Sir Henry Bulwer. *Officers Administering:* 23 Oct. 1885–18 Feb. 1886 [unknown]. *Governors:* 18 Feb. 1886–5 June 1889 Sir Arthur Havelock. *Officers Administering:* 5 June 1889–1 Dec. 1889 [unknown]. *Governors:* 1 Dec. 1889–13 July 1893 Sir Charles Mitchell. *Officers Administering:* 13 July 1893–27 Sept. 1893 Seymour Haden. *Governors:* 28 Sept. 1893–6 March 1901 Sir Walter Hely-Hutchinson. *Officers Administering:* 6 March 1901–13 May 1901 [unknown]. *Governors:* 13 May 1901–7 June 1907 Sir Henry McCallum. *Officers Administering:* 7 June 1907–2 Sept. 1907 [unknown]. *Governors:* 2 Sept. 1907–23 Dec. 1909 Sir Mathew Nathan. *Officers Administering:* 23 Dec. 1909–17 Jan. 1910 [unknown]. *Governors:* 17 Jan. 1910–30 May 1910 Paul, 3rd Baron Methuen. *Chief Ministers:* 4 July 1893–14 Feb. 1897 Sir John Robinson; 15 Feb. 1897–4 Oct. 1897 Harry Escombe; 5 Oct. 1897–8 June 1899 Henry Binns (knighted 1898); 9 June 1899–17 Aug. 1903 Sir Albert Hime; 18 Aug. 1903–16 May 1905 George Sutton; 16 May 1905–22 Nov. 1906 Charles Smythe; 28 Nov. 1906–30 May 1910 Frederick Moor.

Natalia see **Natal**

Ndebeleland see **Matabeleland**

Ndongo. ca. 1358–ca. 1675. *Location:* southern Angola. *Capital:* Mbanza Kabassa. *Other names:* Dongo.

History: In the 14th century the Ngola peoples came from Central Africa and settled in southern Angola. The latter part of the history of Ndongo is one of war with the Portuguese, and in the late 17th century it became part of the Portuguese Imperial system (see Angola).

The only known rulers of Ndongo are: *Chiefs:* ca. 1358 Ngola-a-Nzinga. *Kings:* ca. 1619–1624 Ngola Nzinga Mbandi. *Queens:* 1624–1663 Jinga (also known as Anna de Souza Nzina).

Negretia see **Nigeria**

Nembe see **Brass**

New Africa see **Numidia**

New Calabar. ca. 1550–5 June 1885. *Location:* Niger Delta, Nigeria. *Capital:* Elem Kalabari. *Other names:* Calabar; Kalabari; Calbaria; Awome.

History: There were two Calabars — New Calabar and Old Calabar (the latter so called after the 17th century to avoid confusion with New Calabar). Originally there were two states on this part of the Nigerian coast: Efik, at the mouth of the Cross River, and Kalabari, 150 miles to the west, on the Niger Delta. Legend says that Kalabari was named for the founder of the tribe, Kalabari (at an unknown date), but it is not known how the name Calabar came to be applied to the state of Efik. However, by about 1650 Old Calabar was the name being given to the Cross River state and New Calabar to the Niger Delta state. Over the years New Calabar (Kalabari) became the main slave trading state on the Niger Coast and then, like Bonny and Brass, it became a dealer in palm oil when the slave trade was abolished. In 1885 it became part of the Oil Rivers Protectorate (see Southern Nigeria).

Kings: ca. 1550–ca. 1575 Kalabari; ca. 1575–ca. 1590 Owoma; ca. 1590–ca. 1600 Opukoroye; ca. 1600–ca. 1620 Owerri Daba; ca. 1620–ca. 1655 Igbessa; ca. 1655–ca. 1680 Kamalo (also known as King Robert); ca. 1680–ca. 1720 Mangi Suku; ca. 1720–ca. 1726 Igonibaw; ca. 1726–ca. 1733 Ngbesa; ca. 1733–ca. 1740 Omuye; ca. 1740–ca. 1745 Bokoye; ca. 1745–ca. 1750 Daba; ca. 1750–ca. 1770 Kalagba; ca.

1770–ca. 1790 Amakiri; ca. 1790–ca. 1835 Amakuru (also known as Amakiri II); ca. 1835–April 1863 Karibo (also known as Amakiri III); April 1863–ca. 1900 Abe (also known as Amakiri IV, or Prince Will).

New Georgia. 1824–1 April 1839. *Location:* on Stockton Creek, Liberia. *Capital:* [unknown].

History: In 1824 the US government settled New Georgia with Congo recaptives (slaves rescued by the Americans in mid-ocean). In 1839, with the Colony of Liberia, it went to form the Commonwealth of Liberia.

Rulers: 1824–1 April 1839 [unknown].

New Griqualand see **Griqualand East**

New Oyo see **Oyo**

New Republic. 16 Aug. 1884–11 Sept. 1887. *Location:* northwest Zululand (in northern Natal), South Africa. *Capital:* Vrijheid (also known as Vryheid, the name means "freedom"). *Other names:* Nieuwe Republiek; Republiek Vrijheid.

History: In 1884, in return for helping to place Dinuzulu on the Zulu throne, Transvaal Boers (including Louis Botha) took half of Zululand and, incorporating the districts of Vrijheid, Utrecht, and Wakkerstrom, created the New Republic. By 1885 they were claiming three quarters of Zululand, and on 22 Oct. 1886 Britain recognized the New Republic, but with considerably withdrawn boundaries. In 1887 it became incorporated into Natal, as the District of Vrijheid.

Presidents: 16 Aug. 1884–11 Sept. 1887 Lukas Meyer.

Ngamo see **Daniski**

Ngaridza see **Gran Comoro**

Ngola see **Ndongo**

Nguni see **Gazaland** and **Swaziland** and **Tembuland**

Ngwaketseland see **Bangwaketseland**

Ngwani see **KaNgwane** and **Swaziland**

Ngwatoland see **Bamangwatoland**

Nieuwe Republiek see **New Republic**

Niger. 23 July 1900– . *Location:* North West Africa. *Capital:* Niamey (the origin of the name is uncertain and there are several legends concerning it. It was the capital from 1926); Zinder (1911–1926); Niamey (1903–1910); Sorbo Haoussa (1900–1903). *Other names:* Zinder (1900–1910).

History: In 1900 the French expanded their Upper Senegal and Niger Territory (see Mali) and created the Térritoire Militaire Autonome de Zinder (Autonomous Military Territory of Zinder) out of states such as Damagaram and others in the area. On 22 June 1910 this territory became a separate colonial unit, the Térritoire Militaire du Niger (the Military Territory of Niger), named after the River Niger (from "gher n-gheren" which means "river among rivers" in Tamashak). It was still attached to what Upper Senegal and Niger had now become, viz. the French Sudan, but on 4 Dec. 1920 the country became detached as the Térritoire Civil du Niger (Civil Territory of Niger). On 13 Oct. 1922 it became the colony of Niger. On 13 Oct. 1946 it became an overseas territory of France. On 19 Dec. 1958 it became an autonomous republic within the French Community in preparation for independence, which took place on 3 Aug. 1960, when the country went into its final stage as the Republic of Niger. There were no free elections until 1993, and in the 1960s the government's stability was continually threatened by coup attempts, and in the 1970s by famine in the wake of the drought of 1968–1975. Gross corruption within the administration was another major problem. In 1974 Hamani Diori, longtime strongman of Niger, was ousted in a coup, and under his successor, Seyni Kountché, the economy of Niger improved somewhat. Coups, restiveness, and violence, dominated the Niger scene in the 1990s, although in 1995 peace was made between the government and the Tuareg rebels, who had been fighting since 1990. In 1996 a coup took place that placed the Army back in control of Niger. Maïnassara was assassinated in April 1999, and the country has been relatively stable since then.

Commandants: 23 July 1900–23 Sept. 1900 no fixed central administration; 23 Sept. 1900–1901 Lt.-Col. Péroz; 1901–Oct. 1904 Henri Gouraud; Oct. 1904–(?) Col. Noël; (?)–(?) Joseph Aymerich; (?)–(?) Col. Lamolle; (?)–22

June 1910 Col. Cristofari; 22 June 1910–27 Sept. 1911 Paul Venel; 27 Sept. 1911–1912 Col. Hocquart; 1912–24 Feb. 1913 Charles de Maugras (acting). *Commissioners:* 24 Feb. 1913–4 Dec. 1913 Charles de Maugras (acting); 4 Dec. 1913–15 Nov. 1915 Paul Venel; 15 Nov. 1915–24 Jan. 1918 Charles Mourin; 24 Jan. 1918–Aug. 1919 Félix Méchet; Aug. 1919–1920 Claude Lefebvre; 1920–5 July 1920 Maurice Renauld (acting); 5 July 1920–1921 Lucien Rueff; 1921–13 Oct. 1922 Jules Brévié. *Lieutenant-Governors:* 13 Oct. 1922–1923 Jules Brévié; 1923–1925 Léonce Jore (acting); 1925–9 Oct. 1929 Jules Brévié; 9 Oct. 1929–21 Nov. 1929 Jean-Baptiste Fayout (acting); 21 Nov. 1929–30 Oct. 1930 Alphonse Choteau; 30 Oct. 1930–9 Sept. 1931 Louis-Placide Blacher; 9 Sept. 1931–25 May 1933 Théophile Tellier; 25 May 1933–May 1934 Maurice Bourgine; May 1934–16 March 1935 Léon Pêtre; 16 March 1935–Aug. 1936 Joseph Court; Aug. 1936–Dec. 1936 Auguste Calvel (acting). *Governors:* Dec. 1936–29 April 1938 Joseph Court; 29 April 1938–18 Feb. 1939 Jean-Baptiste Chazelas (acting); 18 Feb. 1939–7 Nov. 1940 Jean Rapenne; 7 Nov. 1940–8 Dec. 1940 Léon Solomiac (acting); 8 Dec. 1940–4 March 1942 Maurice Falvy; 4 March 1942–30 April 1946 Jean-François Toby; 30 April 1946–13 Oct. 1946 Jacques Gosselin (acting); 13 Oct. 1946–20 Nov. 1946 Jean-François Toby (acting); 20 Nov. 1946–24 Nov. 1948 Jean-François Toby; 24 Nov. 1948–25 Feb. 1949 Lucien Geay (acting); 25 Feb. 1949–29 March 1950 Ignace Colombani (acting); 29 March 1950–11 Feb. 1952 Jean-François Toby; 11 Feb. 1952–23 Feb. 1953 Fernand Casimir (acting); 23 Feb. 1953–21 Dec. 1954 Jean-François Toby; 21 Dec. 1954–3 Nov. 1956 Jean-Paul Ramadier; 3 Nov. 1956–29 Jan. 1958 Paul Bordier; 29 Jan. 1958–25 Aug. 1958 Louis Rollet (acting). *High Commissioners:* 25 Aug. 1958–3 Aug. 1960 Don-Jean Colombani. *Chairmen of Government Council:* 19 Dec. 1958–3 Aug. 1960 Hamani Diori. *Presidents:* 3 Aug. 1960–9 Nov. 1960 Hamani Diori (interim); 9 Nov. 1960–15 April 1974 Hamani Diori; 17 April 1974–10 Nov. 1987 Seyni Kountché; 10 Nov. 1987–16 April 1993 Ali Seibou; 16 April 1993–27 Jan. 1996 Mahamane Ousmane; 27 Jan. 1996–9 April 1999 Ibrahim Baré Maïnassara; 9 April 1999–22 Dec. 19999 Daouda Wanké; 22 Dec. 1999–Tandja Mamadou. *Prime Ministers:* 1957–14 Dec. 1958 Djibo Bakari; 14 Dec. 1958–19 Dec. 1958 Hamani Diori; 24 Jan. 1983–14 Nov.

1983 Oumarou Mamane; 14 Nov. 1983–15 July 1988 Hamid Algabid; 15 July 1988–10 Dec. 1989 Oumarou Mamane; 2 March 1990–1 Nov. 1991 Aliou Mahamidou; 1 Nov. 1991–27 March 1992 Amadou Cheiffou (transitional); 27 March 1992–17 April 1993 Amadou Cheiffou; 17 April 1993–28 Sept. 1994 Mahammadou Issoufou; 28 Sept. 1994–8 Feb. 1995 Souley Abdulaye; 8 Feb. 1995–21 Feb. 1995 Amadou Cissé; 21 Feb. 1995–27 Jan. 1996 Amadou Hama; 27 Jan. 1996–21 Dec. 1996 Boukari Adji; 21 Dec. 1996–24 Nov. 1997 Amadou Cissé; 27 Nov. 1997–1 Dec. 1997 Ibrahim Hassabe Mayaki (acting); 1 Dec. 1997–Ibrahim Hassabe Mayaki. *Note:* In times of no Prime Minister, the President or other Head of State held that office.

Niger Coast Protectorate see **Southern Nigeria**

Niger Districts Protectorate see **Northern Nigeria**

Niger Province see **Lapai**

Niger Sudan see **Nigeria**

Niger River Delta Protectorate see **Northern Nigeria**

Nigeria. 1 Jan. 1914– . *Location:* North West Africa. *Capital:* Abuja (from 12 Dec. 1991); Lagos (originally called "Eko," meaning "war camp," the Portuguese called it "Lago de Curama," then "Onin," then "Lagos" for a harbor in Portugal. This was the capital of Nigeria until 12 Dec. 1991).

History: Following the instructions of the British government, Sir Frederick Lugard, in one of the classic examples of colonial building, united the British colony and protectorate of Southern Nigeria and the protectorate of Northern Nigeria, to form Nigeria Colony and Protectorate, a move that became effective on 1 Jan. 1914. The name Nigeria was chosen for the new colony at that time on the suggestion of Lady Lugard (she was Flora Shaw at the time), rather than the proposed names Niger Sudan, Negretia, and Goldesia. The colony part of Nigeria corresponded to the old colony of Lagos, while the protectorate part, comprising the southern and northern regions, continued to be administered separately (see Nigeria Southern Provinces and Nigeria Northern Region), both answerable to Lagos. In 1939, in order to make the demarcated lines more compatible with ethnic groupings, Southern Provinces was divided into two — Nigeria Eastern Region and Nigeria Western Region, both administered separately. On 1 Oct. 1954 a measure of self-rule came to the whole country when it merged with the British Trust Territory of the Cameroons to form the partially autonomous Federation of Nigeria. On 1 Oct. 1960 the whole country became a dominion of the British Commonwealth, and on 1 Oct. 1963 a federal republic within the Commonwealth. In 1966 Abubaka Tafawa Balewa was ousted in a coup and murdered. From 1967 to 1970 Biafra broke away to form its own country. Nigeria's history has been plagued by coups, violent riots, repression, drought, high unemployment, and gross government corruption, which has led to a disastrous economy at times. On 12 Dec. 1991 the capital officially moved from Lagos to Abuja, but it was some time before all the government machinery made the move. By the 2000s a major attempt was being made to control corruption. A major drought continued into the 200s, and in 2004 there was a locust plague.

Governors-General: 1 Jan. 1914–July 1919 Sir Frederick Lugard. *Governors:* 8 Aug. 1919–1921 Sir Hugh Clifford; 1921–1921 Donald Cameron (acting); 1921–May 1925 Sir Hugh Clifford; May 1925–13 Nov. 1925 [unknown] (acting); 13 Nov. 1925–1930 Sir Graeme Thompson; 1930–17 June 1931 [unknown] (acting); 17 June 1931–1935 Sir Donald Cameron; 1935–1 Nov. 1935 John Maybin (acting); 1 Nov. 1935–1 July 1940 Sir Bernard Bourdillon; 1 July 1940–1 July 1940 Sir John Shuckburgh (never took office); 1 July 1940–1942 Sir Bernard Bourdillon; 1942–1942 Sir Alan Burns (acting); 1942–18 Dec. 1943 Sir Bernard Bourdillon; 18 Dec. 1943–1947 Sir Arthur Richards; 1947–5 Feb. 1948 [unknown] (acting); 5 Feb. 1948–1952 Sir John MacPherson; 1952–1952 Arthur Benson (acting); 1952–1 Oct. 1954 Sir John MacPherson. *Governors-General:* 1 Oct. 1954–15 June 1955 Sir John MacPherson; 15 June 1955–16 Nov. 1960 Sir James Robertson; 16 Nov. 1960–1 Oct. 1963 Nnamdi Azikiwe. *Presidents:* 12 Dec. 1959–1 Oct. 1960 Nnamdi Azikiwe; 1 Oct. 1960–1 Oct. 1963 [vacant]; 1 Oct. 1963–15 Jan. 1966 Nnamdi Azikiwe. *Heads of Military Council:* 15 Jan. 1966–29 July 1966 Johnson Aguiyi-Ironsi; 29 July 1966–29 July 1975 Yokubu Gowon. *Heads*

of State: 29 July 1975–13 Feb. 1976 Murtala Ramat Muhammad. *Heads of Military Government:* 13 Feb. 1976–1 Oct. 1979 Olusegun Obasanjo. *Presidents:* 1 Oct. 1979–31 Dec. 1983 Alhajji Shehu Shagari. *Chairmen of Supreme Military Council:* 3 Jan. 1984–27 Aug. 1985 Muhammad Buhari. *Presidents:* 30 Aug. 1985–26 Aug. 1993 Ibrahim Babangida; 26 Aug. 1993–17 Nov. 1993 Ernest Shonekan (interim). *Chairmen of Provisional Ruling Council:* 17 Nov. 1993–8 June 1998 Gen. Sani Abacha; 9 June 1998–29 May 1999 Gen. Abdusalam Abubakar; 29 May 1999–Olusegun Obasanjo. *Chief Ministers:* May 1952–1 Oct. 1954 Nnamdi Azikiwe. *Premiers:* 2 Sept. 1957–15 Jan. 1966 Sir Abubaka Tafawa Balewa. *Prime Ministers:* 15 Jan. 1966–17 Jan. 1966 Mallam Dipchairina (acting); 15 Feb. 1976–31 Dec. 1983 Shehu Musa Yar Adua. *Note:* In times of no Prime Minister, the President or other Head of State held that office.

Nigeria Eastern Region. 1939–1 Oct. 1960. *Location:* southeastern Nigeria. *Capital:* Enugu. *Other names:* Eastern Nigeria.

History: In 1939 Nigeria Southern Provinces was divided into two — Nigeria North Eastern Region and Nigeria North Western Region, in order to make the demarcated lines more compatible with ethnic groupings. Both of these regions were administratively answerable to the Nigerian capital in Lagos. In 1960, with independence for Nigeria, these regions ceased to exist as colonial divisions.

Chief Commissioners: 1939–1943 George Shute; 1943–1948 Frederick Carr; 1948–1951 James Pyke-Nott. *Lieutenant-Governors:* 1951–1952 James Pyke-Nott; 1952–1954 Clement Pleass (knighted 1953). *Governors:* 1954–1956 Sir Clement Pleass; 1956–1 Oct. 1960 Sir Robert Stapledon. *Premiers:* 1 Oct. 1954–1959 Nnamdi Azikiwe; Jan. 1960–1 Oct. 1960 Michael Okpara.

Nigeria Northern Region. 1 Jan. 1914–1962. *Location:* Northern Nigeria. *Capital:* Kaduna (this was the capital from 1917 to 1962. The name means "crocodile" in Hausa and the town was built in 1913); Zungeru (1914–1917). *Other names:* Northern Region.

History: In 1914, upon amalgamation (see Nigeria Southern Provinces for details), the Northern Region of Nigeria continued to be ruled separately, subject to Lagos. This was the only division of Nigeria which continued to exist after independence in 1960.

Lieutenant-Governors: 1 Jan. 1914–1917 Charles Temple; 1917–1921 Herbert Goldsmith; 1921–1925 William Gowers; 1925–1930 Richmond Palmer; 1930–1932 Cyril Alexander. *Chief Commissioners:* 1932–1937 George Browne; 1937–1943 Theodore Adams; 1943–1947 John Patterson; 1947–1951 Eric Thompstone. *Lieutenant-Governors:* 1951–1952 Eric Thompstone; 1952–1954 Bryan Sharwood-Smith (knighted 1953). *Governors:* 1954–2 Dec. 1957 Sir Bryan Sharwood-Smith; 2 Dec. 1957–1962 Sir Gawain Bell. *Premiers:* 1 Oct. 1954–1962 Alhaji Ahmadu Bello.

Nigeria Southern Provinces. 1 Jan. 1914–1939. *Location:* Southern Nigeria. *Capital:* Enugu (from 1928); Calabar (until 1928). *Other names:* Southern Region.

History: In 1914, with the amalgamation of all colonies and protectorates in the area into Nigeria Colony and Protectorate, the new country was divided into the Colony (corresponding to the old colony of Lagos), and the Protectorate, which now comprised the Southern Provinces and Nigeria Northern Region, and both parts of the protectorate continued to be administered separately, albeit both answerable to Lagos. In 1939 the Southern Provinces split into two — Nigeria Western Region and Nigeria Eastern Region.

Lieutenant-Governors: 1 Jan. 1914–1920 Alexander Boyle; 1921–1925 Harry Moorhouse; 1925–1929 Upton Ruxton; 1929–1930 Cyril Alexander; 1930–1935 Walter Buchanan-Smith. *Chief-Commissioners:* 1935–1939 William Hunt.

Nigeria Western Region. 1939–1 Oct. 1960. *Location:* southwestern Nigeria. *Capital:* Ibadan. *Other names:* Western Nigeria.

History: In 1939 Southern Nigeria Provinces was divided into two regions (see Nigeria Eastern Region for details). In 1960 they ceased to exist when the dominion of Nigeria came into being.

Chief Commissioners: 1939–1946 Gerald Whiteley; 1946–1951 Theodore Hoskins-Abrahall. *Lieutenant-Governors:* 1951–1951 Theodore Hoskins-Abrahall; 1951–1954 Hugo Marshall. *Governors:* 1954–1 Oct. 1960 Sir John Rankine. *Premiers:* 1 Oct. 1954–Dec. 1959 Obafemi Awolowo; Dec. 1959–1 Oct. 1960 Samuel Akintola.

Nightingale Island see **Tristan da Cunha**

Nile Provisional Government see **Southern Sudan**

Nimby see **Brass**

Nimule see **Uganda**

Ninisi see **Wagadugu**

Nkole see **Nkore**

Nkoma see **Burundi [i]**

Nkore. ca. 1430–1896. *Location:* southwest Uganda. *Capital:* Mbarara. *Other names:* Nkole; Ankole; Ankhole.

History: About 1430 the Bahinda dynasty from Karagwe began to rule in Nkore, one of the old Ugandan chiefdoms (others were Buganda, Bunyoro, the many tribes forming Busoga, as well as Bukedi, Toro, Kitara, Buduu, Acholi, and Bugisu). The Nkole people consist of nine parts Iru and one part Hima. In 1896 Nkore was placed under the ever-growing British protectorate of Uganda. In 1967 the kingdom was abolished (it was restored in 1993.

Mugabes (Kings): ca. 1430–ca. 1446 Ruhinda; ca. 1446–ca. 1475 Nkuba; ca. 1475–ca. 1503 Nyaika; ca. 1503–ca. 1531 Nyabugaro Ntare I; ca. 1531–ca. 1559 Rushango; ca. 1559–ca. 1587 Ntare II Kagwejegyerera; ca. 1587–ca. 1615 Ntare III Rugaamba; ca. 1615–ca. 1643 Kasasira; ca. 1643–ca. 1671 Kitera and Kumongye (jointly); ca. 1671–ca. 1699 Mirindi; ca. 1699–ca. 1727 Ntare IV Kitabanyoro; ca. 1727–ca. 1755 Macwa; ca. 1755–ca. 1783 Rwabirere and Karara I and Karaiga (all jointly); ca. 1783–ca. 1811 Kahaya I and Nyakashaija and Bwarenga and Rwebishengye (all jointly); ca. 1811–ca. 1839 Rwebishengye and Kayunga and Gasiyonga I (all jointly); ca. 1839–ca. 1867 Mutambuka; ca. 1867–1895 Ntare V; 1895–1944 Kahaya II; 1944–8 Sept. 1967 Gasiyonga II; 8 Sept. 1967–1993 monarchy abolished; 1993–Gasiyonga II.

No Man's Land see **Griqualand East**

Nobatae see **Nubia**

North Bechuanaland see **Bechuanaland**

North Eastern Rhodesia. 29 Jan. 1900–17 Aug. 1911. *Location:* Zambia. *Capital:* Fort Jameson (now known as Chipata, it was established in 1899, and named for Dr. Leander Starr Jameson, later Sir Starr Jameson).

History: North Eastern Rhodesia had been administered separately since 1895, although still part of the British South Africa Company (BSAC) protectorate of Rhodesia (see Rhodesia), and in 1900 the protectorate was divided up officially into three parts — North Eastern Rhodesia, North Western Rhodesia, and Southern Rhodesia (see Zimbabwe). In 1911 North Eastern Rhodesia and North Western Rhodesia were merged to form Northern Rhodesia (see Zambia).

Deputy Administrators: 29 Jan. 1900–31 May 1900 Robert Codrington. *Administrators:* 31 May 1900–24 April 1907 Robert Codrington; 24 April 1907–Jan. 1909 Lawrence Wallace (acting); Jan. 1909–16 May 1911 Leicester Beaufort; 16 May 1911–17 Aug. 1911 Hugh Marshall (acting).

North Island see **Agalega Islands**

North Island see **Seychelles**

North West Madagascar see **Nossi-Bé**

North Western Rhodesia. 29 Jan. 1900–17 Aug. 1911. *Location:* Zambia. *Capital:* Lealui.

History: In 1900 the British South Africa Company (BSAC) protectorate of Rhodesia was divided into three parts. The largest part, all the land south of the Zambesi, was called Southern Rhodesia (see Zimbabwe), while the territory north of the river was halved between North Western Rhodesia and North Eastern Rhodesia. In 1911 North Eastern Rhodesia and North Western Rhodesia merged to form Northern Rhodesia (see Zambia), still under BSAC control.

Residents in Barotseland: 29 Jan. 1900–18 Sept. 1900 Robert Coryndon. *Administrators:* 18 Sept. 1900–8 April 1907 Robert Coryndon; 8 April 1907–20 Oct. 1907 Hugh Hole (acting); 20 Oct. 1907–Feb. 1908 John Carden (acting); Feb. 1908–16 Dec. 1908 Robert Codrington; Jan. 1909–17 Aug. 1911 Lawrence Wallace (acting).

North Zambesia see **Rhodesia**

Northern Egypt see **Lower Egypt**

Northern Nigeria. 5 June 1885–1 Jan. 1914. *Location:* Northern Nigeria. *Capital:* Lokoja (founded in 1860 by William Balfour Baikie). *Other names:* Niger River Delta Protectorate, or Royal Niger Company (1886–1899); Niger Districts Protectorate (1885–1886).

History: Sir George Goldie arrived in North West Africa in 1877, and in 1879 he combined all the British commercial interests on the Niger River into the United African Company. In 1885 he created a large protectorate over a good deal of what is today Northern Nigeria. On 10 July 1886 his company was chartered as the Royal Niger Company, and the name of the area under his control became the Niger River Delta Protectorate. Goldie's company made treaties, fought battles, and was generally responsible for bringing British rule to Northern Nigeria. In 1899 the British government revoked Goldie's charter and took over the area for itself, as the protectorate of Northern Nigeria. This became effective on 1 Jan. 1900. By 15 March 1903 conquest of Northern Nigeria was complete. In 1914 the protectorate and Southern Nigeria Colony and Protectorate united to form Nigeria.

Northern Rhodesia see **Zambia**

Nossi-Bé. 14 July 1840–6 Aug. 1896. *Location:* off the northwest coast of Madagascar. *Capital:* Hellville (named by Governor Pierre Passot for Admiral de Hell, French commander in the Indian Ocean). *Other names:* Nosy-Bé (the name means "great island"); Nossi-Vey; North West Madagascar Territory (alternative name, 1840–1843).

History: In 1840 the Sakalava ruler of the northwest portion of Madagascar ceded the island of Nossi-Bé to France. It was used as a naval station, and was placed under the administration of Bourbon (see Réunion). On 25 March 1843 it was transferred to Mayotte in the Comoros, as a dependent colony. In 1878 it became a separate colony of France, and in 1896, when the whole of Madagascar became a French colony, Nossi-Bé became part of it.

Governors: 3 Feb. 1841–1842 François Gouhot; 1842–1842 Capt. Pierre Passot; 1842–1845 Charles Morel; 1845–1848 Henri-Martin Lamy; 1848–1851 Jean-Ernest Marchaisse; 1851–1851 Alexandre Berg; 1851–1852 Jean Lapeyre-Bellair; 1852–1853 Thomas Dupuis; 1853–1854 André Brisset; 1854–1855 Louis Arnoux; 1855–1856 Joseph Septans; 1856–1858 Thomas Dupuis; 1858–1860 Paul-Gustave Sachet; 1860–1861 Justin Dupérier; 1861–1865 Vincent Derussat; 1865–1866 Pierre Lucas; 1866–1868 Joseph Hayes; 1868–1869 Louis Chériner; 1869–1870 Aimé Champy; 1870–1871 Jules Ventre de la Touloubre; 1871–1872 Jean-Baptiste Barnier; 1872–1873 Marie-Alexandre Leclos; 1873–1874 Honoré Léchelle; 1874–1875 Claude Fontaine; 1875–1876 Joseph Carle; 1876–1876 Arthur-Paul Feutray; 1876–1878 François Ferriez; 1878–1883 Alphonse Seignac-Lesseps; 1883–1886 Alexandre Le Maître; 1886–1888 Léon Clément-Thomas; 1888–1889 Furcy Augustin Armanet; 1889–6 Aug. 1896 Joseph François.

Nosy Boraha see **Sainte Marie de Madagascar**

Nubia. ca. 325–ca. 675. *Location:* northern Sudan. *Capital:* Pachoras (also known as Bukharas, it is the town that today is called Faras). *Other names:* Nobatae; Nobatia.

History: The country referred to by the ancients as Nubia (or Old Nubia) was actually Kush (q.v.). The Nobatae, or X-Group, a Nilotic Sudanese group, ruled Nubia from about 325 after Meroë was destroyed (see Kush). The Nobatae were converted to Christianity about 540. Engulfed by Mukurra about 675, the two states became known as Dongola. The name Nubia continued until as late as 1821 when the Egyptians conquered the area (see Sudan).

Rulers: [unknown].

Numidia. 201 B.C.–29 B.C. *Location:* Algeria. *Capital:* Cirta (or Kirtha — from the Phoenician meaning "a city." It was renamed Constantine in A.D. 313). *Other names:* Africa Nova, or New Africa (the name of the Roman province that Numidia became in 46 B.C.).

History: Numidia was the Roman name for the country that is now Algeria. From the 6th century B.C. it was inhabited by a variety of semi-nomadic tribes. In 206 B.C. Masinissa, a local leader and until then an ally of Carthage, went over to the Roman side, and by 201 B.C. had united the country and was ruling as the king of the Roman client state of Numidia. On his death, the Romans split his kingdom between his three sons, and this division stayed in force

until 112 B.C. when Jugurtha re-unified the kingdom for seven years before the Romans won back control. Numidian territory was heavily reduced. In 49 B.C. Juba attempted to throw off Roman rule, but was defeated in 46 B.C. by Julius Caesar, who formed the province of Africa Nova from Numidia. In 29 B.C. Augustus Caesar united Africa Nova with Africa Vetus (see Carthage) to form the new Roman province of Africa (see Africa [I]).

Kings: 201 B.C.–148 B.C. Masinissa; 148 B.C.–118 B.C. Micipsa and Gulussa and Mastanabal (joint kings); 118 B.C.–117 B.C. Adherbal and Hiempsal I and Jugurtha (joint kings); 117 B.C.–112 B.C. Adherbal and Jugurtha (joint kings); 112 B.C.–105 B.C. Jugurtha; 105 B.C.–ca. 88 B.C. Gauda; ca. 88 B.C.–ca. 62 B.C. Hiempsal II; ca. 62 B.C.–46 B.C. Juba I. *Praetors:* 46 B.C.–44 B.C. Publius Sitius; 44 B.C.–29 B.C. Arabion.

Nupe. 1531–1796; 1805–1901. *Location:* Niger Province, Nigeria. *Capital:* Bida (from 1857); Raba (1835–1857); Zugurma (1830–1835); Adama Lulu (1810–1830); Raba (1805–1810); Bedeghi (1776–1796); Biaghi (1766–1776); Bedeghi (1760–1766); Biaghi (1741–1760); Labuji (1717–1741); Jebba (ca. 1660–1717); Pategi (ca. 1580–ca. 1660); Gbara (now called Jimunli, was the capital from about 1550 to about 1580); Bida-Nupiko (1531–ca. 1550).

History: Tsoede, the illegitimate son of Attah of Idah, founded the kingdom of Nupe in 1531. In 1796 the kingdom temporarily split up into two parts — West Nupe and East Nupe. In 1805 the two separate countries were re-united. In 1835 Nupe became part of the Fulani Empire, as an amirate, and in 1901 it was incorporated into the British protectorate of Northern Nigeria, as the amirate of Bida, within Niger Province.

Etsus (Kings): 1531–1591 Tsoede (also known as Edegi, or Choede); 1591–1600 Shaba (also known as Tsoacha); 1600–1625 Zaulla (also known as Zavunla, or Zagulla); 1625–1670 Jiga (also known as Jia, or Jigba); 1670–1679 Mamman Wari; 1679–1700 Abdu Waliyi; 1700–1710 Aliyu; 1710–1713 Ganamace (also known as Sachi Gana Machi); 1713–1717 Ibrahima; 1717–1721 Idrisu I (also known as Ederisu); 1721–1742 Tsado (also known as Chado, or Abdullahi); 1742–1746 Abu Bakr Kolo; 1746–1759 Jibrin (also known as Jibrilu); 1759–1767 Ma'azu; 1767–1777 Majiya I (also known as Zubeiru); 1777–1778 Iliyasu; 1778–1795 Ma'azu; 1795–

1795 Alikolo Tankari; 1795–1796 Mamma; 1796–1805 there were two separate states (see above); 1805–1810 Majiya II; 1810–1830 Idrisu II; 1830–1834 Majiya II; 1834–1835 Tsado. *Amirs:* 1835–1841 Uthman Zaki; 1841–1847 Masaba; 1847–1856 Umar Bahaushe; 1856–1859 Uthman Zaki; 1859–1873 Masaba; 1873–1884 Umar Majigi; 1884–1895 Malik; 1895–17 Feb. 1901 Abu-Bakr; Feb.1901–26 Feb. Feb. 1916 Muhammad; 6 March 1916–1926 Bello; 1926–Feb. 1935 Sa'id; 28 Feb. 1935–29 Oct. 1962 Muhammad Ndayako; 29 Oct. 1962–(?) Uthman Sarki; (?)–10 Jan. 1975 Musa Bello; Jan. 1975–Umaru Sanda Ndayako.

Nupe East see **East Nupe**

Nupe West see **West Nupe**

Nyamwezi see **Mirambo**

Nyasaland see **Malawi**

Nzwani. 4 Aug. 1997–10 March 2002. *Location:* the island of Anjouan, in the Comoros. *Capital:* Mutsamudu. *Other names:* Ndzouani; Anjouan; L'État d'Anjouan.

History: In 1997, after a referendum in which the populace of the island of Anjouan voted overwhelmingly in favor of the proposition, the island declared independence and became the unrecognized Republic of Nzwani. This was a unilateral declaration. On 10 March 2002 it became the autonomous province of Anjouan within the newly-formed Union of the Comoros. Mr Bacar became the new president on 14 April 2002. See also Mwali.

Presidents: 4 Aug. 1997–1 Aug. 1999 Abdallah Ibrahim. Head of State: 1 Aug. 1999–9 Aug. 2001 Said Abeid Abderemane. 10 Aug. 2001–25 Aug. 2001 [ruled by presidium]. Head of State: 25 Aug. 2001–10 March 2002 Muhammad Bacar. *Prime Ministers:* 8 March 1998–7 July 1998 Chamassi Sa'id Umar; 19 July 1998–1998 Abdou Mhindi. *Note:* In times of no Prime Minister, the President held that office.

Nzwani see also **Anjouan**

Obock see **Djibouti**

Ogaden see **Ethiopia**

Ohrigstad. 11 Aug. 1845–1846. *Location:* eastern Transvaal. *Capital:* Andries-Ohrigstad (founded in 1845). *Other names:* Andries-Ohrigstad.

History: Hendrik Potgieter left Potchefstroom (see Dutch African Republic) in 1845 after Britain took over Natal, and he headed northwest, buying a new area of land from the Pedi tribe, and building a new republic around the town of Andries-Ohrigstad, named after the head of a Dutch trading company. In 1846 Potgieter left to found Zoutpansberg, and shortly thereafter the small republic of Ohrigstad came to an end, plagued by fever and tsetse fly. The inhabitants repaired south to found the territory of Lydenburg.

Head Commandants: 1 Aug. 1845–1846 Hendrik Potgieter; 1846–1846 [unknown].

Oil Rivers Protectorate see **Southern Nigeria**

Okoloba see **Bonny**

Old Africa see **Carthage**

Old Calabar see **New Calabar** and **Nigeria**

Old Oyo see **Oyo**

Oltre Giuba see **Jubaland**

Omar al-Hajj's Empire see **Tukolor Empire**

Omayyad and Abbasid North Africa. 703–9 July 800. *Location:* Algeria, Tunisia, and Libya. *Capital:* al-Qayrawan. *Other names:* Ifriqiyah; Ifrikiya; Ifriqa; Abbasid North Africa (from 750).

History: In 703 the Omayyad (also known as the Umayyad) Caliphate conquered Byzantine North Africa. A total of about 100,000 Arab soldiers manned the country, and mostly in what is now Tunisia and eastern Algeria. However, their reign was despotic, and their outrages led to a revolt in 740, and by 742 the rebels had taken most of Omayyad territory. On 9 Aug. 750 the caliphate in Bagdad became Abbasid, and the Abbasids reconquered most of North Africa. In 800 North Africa fell to the Aghlabid Empire.

Governors: 703–715 Abd ar-Rahman Musa; 715–718 Muhammad ibn Yazid; 718–720 Ismail; 720–721 Yazid; 721–721 Muhammad ibn Aus al-Ansari; 721–729 Bisr; 729–734 Ubayda; 734–741 Ubayd Allah; 741–742 Kultum; 742–747

Hanzala; 747–755 Abd ar-Rahman; 755–758 Habib; 758–July 758 Asim Warfaguma; July 758–Aug. 761 Abd ar-Rahman; Aug. 761–765 Muhammad; 765–765 Isa; 765–765 Ali; 765–766 al-Aghlab; 766–767 al-Hassan; 768–772 Abu Ja'far Hazarmard Umar; 772–24 March 787 Abu Halid Yazid; 24 March 787–788 Daud; 788–2 Feb. 791 Abu Hatim Rawh; 2 Feb. 791–794 Nasr; 794–795 al-Fadl; 795–796 Hartama; 796–800 Muhammad ibn Muqatil; 800–800 Tammam; 800–9 July 800 Muhammad ibn Muqatil.

Oorlam Territory. 1838–1886. *Location:* Namibia. *Capital:* Windhoek.

History: The Oorlam Khoikhoi were one branch of the Oorlam peoples who controlled a section of what is today Namibia prior to the German takeover in 1884. Jager Afrikaner's son, Junker, arrived in the area that would later become Windhoek in 1838, and his family became the predominant one in the country. In 1885 Jan Jonker ceded territory to the Germans and in 1886 accepted a protectorate (see Namibia).

Rulers: 1800–1823 Jager Afrikaner; 1823–1861 Junker Afrikaner; 1861–1863 Christiaan Afrikaner; 1863–1889 Jan Jonker Afrikaner.

Opobo. 1870–19 Dec. 1884. *Location:* Uyo province of Southern Nigeria. *Capital:* Opobo (named by Jaja for Opobo, a great ruler of Bonny). *Other names:* Opubo; Ekwanga; Egwanga.

History: In 1870 Jubo Jubogha, a nobleman from Bonny, came to the slave-trading village of Egwanga and set up the kingdom of Opobo. Known as Jaja (or Chief Jaja) by the Europeans, Jubo destroyed the economic power of Bonny and turned Opobo into the chief oil-trading state along the Niger Delta. In 1884 Opobo was taken over by the British (see Bights of Biafra and Benin). Jubo was deposed in 1887.

Kings: 1870–19 Dec. 1884 Jubo Jubogha (also known as Chief Jaja).

Oran. 1509–1831. *Location:* the area around, and including, the city of Oran, on the coast of Algeria. *Capital:* Oran. *Other names:* Wahran (Arab name); Orán (Spanish name).

History: In 1509 the Spanish occupied the town of Oran. In 1708 the Turks took it, but in 1732 the Spanish re-took it. In 1790 the town was devastated by an earthquake, and in 1792 the

Spanish returned it to the Turks, who settled a Jewish community there. In 1831 Oran was taken by the French and it became part of the French Possessions in North Africa (see Algeria).

Spanish Governors: 1509–1509 Conde de Oliveto; 1509–1510 Rui Díaz de Rojas; 1510–1512 Diego de Córdoba; 1512–1517 Martín de Argote; 1517–1522 Diego, Marqués de Comares; 1522–1523 Luis, Marqués de Comares; 1523–1525 Luis de Cárdenas; 1525–1531 Luis, Marqués de Comares; 1531–1534 Pedro de Godoy; 1534–1558 Martín, Conde de Alcandete; 1558–1564 Alonso, Conde de Alcandete; 1564–1565 Andrés Ponce de León; 1565–1567 Hernán de Guzmán; 1567–1571 Marqués de Navarrés; 1571–1573 Felipe de Borja; 1573–1574 Diego, Conde de Comares; 1574–1575 Luis de Bocanegra; 1575–1585 Marqués de Cortes; 1585–1589 Pedro de Padilla; 1589–1594 Diego, Conde de Comares; 1594–1596 Gabriel de Zúñiga; 1596–1604 Francisco, Conde de Alcandete; 1604–1607 Conde de Teba; 1607–1608 Diego de Toledo y Guzmán; 1608–1616 Conde de Aguilar de Inestrillas; 1616–1625 Duque de Maqueda; 1625–1628 Marqués de Velada; 1628–1632 Visconde de Santa Clara de Avellido; 1632–1639 Marqués de Flores Dávila; 1639–1643 Marqués del Viso; 1643–1647 Marqués de Viana; 1647–1652 Marqués de Flores Dávila; 1652–1660 Marqués de San Román; 1660–1666 Duque de San Lúcar; 1666–1672 Marqués de los Vélez; 1672–1675 Diego de Portugal; 1675–1678 Íñigo de Toledo y Osorio; 1678–1681 Marqués de Algava; 1681–1682 Conde de la Monclova; 1682–1683 Conde de Cifuentes; 1683–1685 Marqués de Osera; 1685–1687 Marqués de Santa Cruz de Paniagua; 1687–1687 Conde de Bracamonte; 1687–1691 Conde de Guaro; 1691–1692 Comte de Charny; 1692–1697 Duque de Cansano; 1697–1701 Marqués de Casasola; 1701–1704 Juan Francisco de Araña; 1704–1707 Carlos Carafa; 1707–1708 Marqués de Valdecañas. *Turkish Governors:* 1708–1717 Saban Bey; 1717–1732 [unknown]. *Spanish Governors:* 1732–1733 Marqués de Santa Cruz de Mercenado; 1733–1733 Marqués de Villadarias; 1733–1739 José Vallejo; 1738–1742 José de Aramburu; 1742–1748 Alexandre de la Mothe; 1748–1752 Marqués de la Real Corona; 1752–1758 Juan Antonio de Escoiquiz; 1758–1765 Juan Zermeño; 1765–1767 Cristóbal de Córdoba; 1767–1770 Conde de Bolognino; 1770–1774 Eugenio de Alvorado y Perales Hurtado y Colomo; 1774–1778 Pedro Zermeño; 1778–1779

Luis de Carvajal; 1779–1785 Pedro Guelfi; 1785–1789 Luis de las Casas y Aragorri; 1789–1790 Marqués de Campo Santo; 1790–1791 Conde de Cumbre Hermosa; 1791–1792 Juan de Courten. *Turkish Governors:* 1792–(?) Mehmed Bey al-Kabir; (?)–ca. 1800 Osman Bey; ca. 1800–(?) Mustafa Bey al-Manzalah; (?)–ca. 1804 Mehmed Bey Makkalas; ca. 1804–(?) [unknown]; (?)–1831 Hassan Bey.

Orange Free State. 3 Feb. 1848–30 May 1910. *Location:* Orange Free State Province of South Africa. *Capital:* Bloemfontein. *Other names:* Oranje Vrij Staat; Orange River Free State; Orange River; Orange River Colony (1900–1910); Orange River Republic (alternative name from 1854 to 1900); Orange River Sovereignty, or Orange River Territory (1848–1854).

History: In 1848 Sir Harry Smith finally annexed to Britain all land between the Orange and Vaal Rivers, leaving it in the hands of the British resident of Transorangia, who had been there for some years. This area included Transorangia (the major component) and the Boer republic of Winburg (which Smith had also annexed), and Smith called it the Orange River Sovereignty. On 23 Feb. 1854 the country achieved independence as the Boer state of Orange River. On 10 April 1854 it changed its name to the Orange Free State, a name that has stuck, regardless of the status or official name the country has had since. It expanded its boundaries in 1861, 1866 and 1871. On 21 May 1900, during the South African War, Britain took it over again, as the Orange River Colony. Marthinus Steyn, the president of the Free State, continued to rule until 1902 (although in absentia from 1900 — he spent 1900 to 1906 in Europe), returning to the colony to head the National Political Party of the colony. Self-rule was granted on 6 Dec. 1906, and the country began more and more to be called the Orange Free State again. At the stroke of midnight on 30–31 May 1910 the four colonies of Orange River (or Orange Free State), Natal, the Cape (see Cape Colony) and the Transvaal all joined together to form the Union of South Africa.

Residents: 3 Feb. 1848–23 July 1852 Henry Warden; 23 July 1852–23 Feb. 1854 Henry Green. *Special Commissioners:* 6 April 1853–23 Feb. 1854 Sir George Clerk. *Leaders of the Provisional Government of Seven:* 23 Feb. 1854–15 May 1854 Josias Hoffman. *Presidents:* 15 May 1854–10 Feb. 1855 Josias Hoffman. *Chairmen of the Provisional Government of Four:* 10 Feb. 1855–27 Aug. 1855 Jacobus Venter. *Presidents:* 27 Aug. 1855–25 June 1859 Jacobus Boshof; 25 June 1859–15 Dec. 1859 Elias Snyman (acting); 15 Dec. 1859–8 Feb. 1860 Jacobus Venter; 8 Feb. 1860–15 April 1863 Marthinus Pretorius; 15 April 1863–20 June 1863 Joseph Allison (acting); 20 June 1863–5 Nov. 1863 Jacobus Venter (acting); 5 Nov. 1863–31 Aug. 1872 Jan Brand; 31 Aug. 1872–4 Oct. 1872 Friedrich Höhne (acting); 4 Oct. 1872–16 June 1873 Committee comprising William Collins, Fried rich Schnehage, and Gerhardus du Toit; 16 June 1873–16 July 1888 Jan Brand (knighted 1882); 16 July 1888–10 Jan. 1889 Pieter Blignaut (acting); 11 Jan. 1889–17 Nov. 1895 Francis Reitz; 17 Nov. 1895–21 Feb. 1896 Pieter Blignaut (acting); 21 Feb. 1896–30 May 1902 Marthinus Steyn; 30 May 1902–31 May 1902 Christiaan De Wet (acting). *Governors:* Jan. 1901–21 June 1902 Sir Hamilton Goold-Adams (acting); 21 June 1902–1 April 1905 Alfred, Baron Milner (created Viscount Milner in 1902); 2 April 1905–7 June 1907 William Palmer, 2nd Earl of Selborne; 7 June 1907–30 May 1910 Sir Hamilton Goold-Adams. *Party Presidents:* 6 Dec. 1906–30 May 1910 Marthinus Steyn. *Prime Ministers:* 6 Dec. 1906–30 May 1910 Abraham Fischer.

Orange River see **Orange Free State**

Ouadaï see **Wadai**

Ouagadougou see **Wagadugu**

Ouahigouya see **Burkina Faso** and **Yatenga**

Oualo see **Walo**

Oubangui-Chari see **Central African Republic**

Oued Eddahab see **Western Sahara**

Ouidah see **Whydah**

Ouolof see **Dyolof**

Ouere see **Warri**

Ovamboland. 2 Oct. 1968–July 1980. *Location:* northern Namibia. *Capital:* Oshakati. *Other names:* Owambo; Amboland.

History: Established as the first bantustan (native homeland) in Namibia by the South African government, the Ovamboland Homeland was not recognized internationally as a self-governing state. It was meant to be the homeland for the Ovambo (also known as the Ambo) peoples, and was the subject of considerable press put out by the South African government extolling its success as a "model" bantustan. The problem was, however, foreigners could not get in to see it. Set up in 1968, it achieved self-government on 1 May 1973, but in July 1980 the South African government decided to end the experiment.

Chief Ministers: 2 Oct. 1968–14 Jan. 1972 Uushona Shiimi; 14 Jan. 1972–16 Aug. 1975 Chief Filemon Elifas; 16 Aug. 1975–July 1980 Cornelius Njoba.

Ovimbundu see Angola

Oyo. ca. 1400–1900. *Location:* Oyo State, Nigeria. *Capital:* New Oyo (from about 1840); Old Oyo (from about 1550 to about 1840); unknown capital before ca. 1550. *Other names:* Katanga [sic]; New Oyo (from ca. 1840); Old Oyo (the name used retrospectively for the older state).

History: Oyo was founded by a farming section of the Yoruba tribe. The people became cavalrymen, and their Alafins (Kings) began to expand the area into an empire. In the 1550s Orompotu established the old city of Oyo, which by the 1830s had broken up. At this stage Atiba became the founder of both a new dynasty and the new town of Oyo. In 1900 Oyo was incorporated into the British protectorate of Northern Nigeria.

Alafins (Kings): ca. 1400–(?) Oranyan (son of Oduduwa); (?)–(?) Ajaka; (?)–(?) Sango; (?)–(?) Ajika; (?)–(?) Aganju; (?)–(?) Kori; (?)–ca. 1520 Oluaso; ca. 1520–(?) Onigbogi; (?)–(?) Ofinran; (?)–ca. 1555 Egunoju; ca. 1555–ca. 1580 Orompotu; ca. 1580–ca. 1590 Ajiboyede; ca. 1590–1614 Abipa; 1614–ca. 1640 Abalokun; ca. 1640–ca. 1652 Oluodo; ca. 1652–ca. 1690 Ajagbo; ca. 1690–ca. 1692 Odarawu; ca. 1692–(?) Kanran; (?)–(?) Jayin; (?)–(?) inter regnum; (?)–ca. 1724 Ayibi; ca. 1724–ca. 1725 Osiyago; ca. 1725–ca. 1735 Ojigi; ca. 1735–ca. 1740 Gberu; ca. 1740–1746 Amuniwaiye; 1746–1754 Onisile; 1754–1754 Agboluje; 1754–1770 Majeogbe; 1770–April 1789 Abiodun; May 1789–1796 Aole; 1976–1796 Awonbioju; 1796–1796 Adebo; 1796–1797 Maku; 1797–1802 interregnum; 1802–1830 Majotu; 1830–1833 Amodo; 1833–1835 Oluewu; ca. 1836–1859 Atiba; 1859–1875 Adelu; 1875–1905 Adeyemi I; 1905–1911 Lawani; 1911–1943 Ladigbolu I; 1943–1946 Adeniran; 1946–1956 [vacant]; 1956–1970 Ladigbolu II; 1970–19 Nov. 1970 interregnum; 19 Nov. 1970–(?) Lamidi Adeyemi II.

Pagalu see Annobón

Palma see Lagos

Pamban see Bamoun

Pedi see Lebowa and Ohrigstad

Pemba see Zanzibar

Pentapolis. 631 B.C.–75 B.C. *Location:* eastern Libya. *Capital:* Cyrene (also known as Kyrene). *Other names:* Kyrene; Cyrene.

History: In 631 B.C. the people of Thera (present day Santorini), an island in the Aegean, were told by the Delphic Oracle to found this new land. After opposition from the natives, they established themselves at the Five Towns (or Pentapolis) of Cyrene, Barca, Apollonia, Berenice, and Arsinoë. In 331 B.C. the country was incorporated into Egypt, as the territory of Pentapolis (or Kyrene). In 96 B.C. it became a Roman territory, and in 75 B.C. it became part of the Roman province of Cyrenaica.

Kings: 631 B.C.–(?) Battus I; ca. 599 B.C.–ca. 580 B.C. Arsecilaus I; ca. 580 B.C.–ca. 554 B.C. Battus II; ca. 554 B.C.–ca. 550 B.C. Arsecilaus II; ca. 550 B.C.–ca. 550 B.C. Learchus (usurper); ca. 550 B.C.–ca. 525 B.C. Battus III; ca. 525 B.C.–ca. 515 B.C. Arsecilaus III; ca. 515 B.C.–ca. 465 B.C. Battus IV; ca. 465 B.C.–ca. 460 B.C. Arsecilaus IV; ca. 460 B.C.–331 B.C. Democratic rule. *Emperors:* 331 B.C.–13 June 323 B.C. Alexander the Great. *Governors:* 323 B.C.–322 B.C. Thibron of Sparta. *Satraps:* 322 B.C.–313 B.C. Ptolemy (later called Ptolemy Soter). *Strategoi:* 313 B.C.–308 B.C. Ophellas. *Kings:* 308 B.C.–258 B.C. Magas; 258 B.C.–257 B.C. Demetrios. *Queens:* 258 B.C.–246 B.C. Berenice. *Kings:* 246 B.C.–240 B.C. Ptolemy III Euergetes of Egypt; 240 B.C.–240 B.C. Ekdelos and Demophanes (joint usurpers); 240 B.C.–222 B.C. Ptolemy III Euergetes of Egypt; 222 B.C.–205 B.C. Ptolemy IV Philopator of Egypt; 205 B.C.–204 B.C. Philemon; 204 B.C.–200 B.C. [unknown]; 200 B.C.–149 B.C. under rule from Numidia; 149 B.C.–116 B.C. Ptolemy VIII Euergetes (also known as Physcon) of Egypt; 116 B.C.–110 B.C. Ptolemaios Aspion. *Tyrants:* 110 B.C.–110 B.C. Nikostratos; 110 B.C.–110 B.C. *Kings:* 110 B.C.–96 B.C. Ptolemaios Aspion; 96 B.C.–75 B.C. under Roman rule. *Note:* Strategoi is plural of Strategos (General).

Petit Dieppe. 1364–1413. *Location:* the Greenville area of Liberia. *Capital:* [unknown]. *Other names:* French Gold Coast (this was the collective name given by the Normans to their two settlements here of Grand Dieppe and Petit Dieppe).

History: In 1364 Norman adventurers established two settlements on the coast of what is now Liberia. One, in the area we now call Buchanan, was called Grand Dieppe, and the other (in what is now the Greenville area) was called Petit Dieppe. Very little is known of this whole episode, and some historians doubt the authenticity of it all.

Rulers: [unknown].

Pewenet see **Punt**

PFDJ see **Eritrea**

PGE see **Eritrea**

Phazania. ca. 430–666. *Location:* Libya. *Capital:* Murzuq (name means "sea of sand"). *Other names:* Fezzan; Fazan.

History: Part of the territory of the Garamantes, Phazania was thus part of the land conquered by the Romans in 19 B.C. and named Phazania. About A.D. 430, after the Vandals had taken most of North Africa (see Vandal North Africa), Phazania gained its independence under a Berauna dynasty. In 666 the Arabs conquered it and it became part of the Arab world (see Arab North Africa). It formed the basis of the later Fezzan.

Rulers: ca. 430–666 [unknown].

Philippolis see **Adam Kok's Land**

Picard, Île see **Aldabra Islands**

Piet Retief District see **Little Free State**

Plantation Island see **Shenge**

Plateau State see **Lafia**

Poivre Islands see **Amirante Islands**

POLISARIO see **Western Sahara**

Polymnie see **Aldabra Islands**

Pondoland. 7 Oct. 1844–29 Oct. 1867. *Location:* in Kaffraria, Southern Africa, immediately southwest of Natal. *Capital:* Port St Johns. *Other names:* Mpondoland.

History: In 1844 Faku was recognized by the British as ruler of the land of the Mpondos (Pondoland). In 1867, on his death, Pondoland was split into two parts — Pondoland East and Pondoland West.

Chiefs: ca. 1552–(?) Kondwana; (?)–(?) Ncindise; (?)–(?) Cabe; (?)–(?) Cilwayo; (?)–(?) Dayeni; (?)–(?) Tahle; (?)–(?) Nyawuza; (?)–1824 Ncqungushe; 1824–29 Oct. 1867 Faku.

Pondoland East. 29 Oct. 1867–25 Sept. 1894. *Location:* Pondoland. *Capital:* Qakeni (about 8 miles from Lusikisiki). *Other names:* East Pondoland.

History: See Pondoland West for details.

Chiefs: 29 Oct. 1867–28 Oct. 1887 Mqikela; 28 Oct. 1887–15 Feb. 1888 [vacant]; 15 Feb. 1888–25 Sept. 1894 Sigcau.

Pondoland West. 29 Oct. 1867–25 Sept. 1894. *Location:* Pondoland. *Capital:* Nyandeni (in the Libode District). *Other names:* West Pondoland.

History: In 1867, on the death of Faku, Pondoland was divided into two parts — East and West Pondoland (see also Pondoland East). In 1894 the two separate countries were re-united as British Pondoland, and annexed to Cape Colony.

Chiefs: 29 Oct. 1867–29 Aug. 1876 Ndamase; 29 Aug. 1876–25 Sept. 1894 Nqiliso.

Port Cresson see **Bassa Cove**

Port Natal. 7 Aug. 1824–24 Dec. 1839. *Location:* the coastline around Durban, Natal province, South Africa. *Capital:* Durban (this city was built on the old town of Port Natal, and was laid out on 23 June 1835, and named for Sir Benjamin D'Urban, the governor of Cape Colony. Durban was the capital of the state of Port Natal from 1835 to 1838); Port Natal (1824–1828). *Other names:* Fort Victoria, or Victoria (alternative name from 1838 to 1839).

History: Vasco da Gama discovered and named the coast of Natal on Christmas Day 1497 (the name Natal meaning Christmas). From 1686 to 1725 the Dutch expressed some interest in the area but, in the early 19th century, Chaka, the Zulu king, conquered all of what is today Natal. In 1824 he ceded an area around port Natal, 100 miles by 30, to Lt. Francis Farewell, who claimed the area for Britain. Farewell and his companions colonized the area, but on 30 April 1828 the settlement broke up due to the instability of the country following the assassination of Chaka. A few European settlers remained, and then on 6 May 1835 Allan Gardiner, a sailor turned missionary, settled a new population in Port Natal, renaming the town Durban. Dingaan, the Zulu king, ceded all of Southern Natal to Gardiner who intended it to be a district of Cape Colony. This new territory swallowed up the area that had once been administered by Lt. Francis Farewell. However, Gardiner's settlement came to an end on 4 Feb. 1838, and Gardiner left the colony. Again, only a few farmers remained. In November 1838 Maj. Samuel Charters, military secretary to Sir George Napier (governor of the Cape) arrived to take possession of Durban and the colony of Port Natal for the Cape. He built a stockade, Fort Victoria, and in January 1839 he left for the Cape. The British pulled out on 24 Dec. 1839 and the land became part of Natalia (see Natal).

Commanders: 7 Aug. 1824–30 April 1828 Lt. Francis Farewell; 30 April 1828–6 May 1835 no formal British rule. *Administrators:* 6 May 1835–4 Feb. 1838 Allan Gardiner; 4 Feb. 1838–Nov. 1838 no formal British rule. *Military Administrators:* Nov. 1838–Jan. 1839 Maj. Samuel Charters; Jan. 1839–24 Dec. 1839 Henry Jervis.

Porto-Novo. 1688–22 June 1894. *Location:* around Porto-Novo, in the present-day Republic of Benin. *Capital:* Porto-Novo (now the capital of the Republic of Benin). *Other names for the kingdom:* Hogbonu; Ajashe; Adjatshe; Adjatché.

History: From the same stock as Abomey (see Dahomey), the kingdom of Porto-Novo was created in 1688, and was then called Hogbonu (later Ajashe). It became a leading slave-trading state,

and on 25 Feb. 1863 the French placed a protectorate over it, much to the consternation of the British. On 2 Jan. 1865 this protectorate came to an end and the kingdom was re-established as the sole monarchy in the area. However, on 14 April 1882 the French re-instituted their protectorate, and on 22 June 1893 Porto-Novo became a French colony. On 22 June 1894, exactly a year later, the colony was merged into the French colony of Dahomey.

Kings: 1688–1729 Té-Agbanlin I; 1729–1739 Hiakpon; 1739–1746 Lokpon. *Queens:* 1746–1752 Hude. *Kings:* 1752–1757 Messe; 1757–1761 Huyi; 1761–1765 Gbeyon; 1765–1775 interregnum; 1775–1783 Ayikpe; 1783–1794 Ayaton; 1794–1807 Huffon; 1807–1816 Ajohan; 1816–1818 Toyi; 1818–1828 Hueze; 1828–1836 Toyon; 1836–1848 Meyi; 1848–1864 Sodji; 1864–1872 Mikpon; 1872–1874 Messi; 1874–7 Feb. 1908 Tofa; 7 Feb. 1908–1913 Gbedissin; 1913–1929 Hudji; 1929–1930 Toli; 1930–1940 Gbehinto; 1941–(?) Gbesso Toyi. *Agents:* 25 Feb. 1863–2 Jan. 1865 Marius Daumas; June 1882–1883 Bonaventure Colonna de Lecca; 1883–1883 Henri Guilman; 1883–1884 Daniel Germa; 1884–July 1884 Léopold Maignot; July 1884–1886 Charles Disnematin-Dorat; 1886–1886 Émmanuel Roget; 1886–1887 Jean-Marie Bayol; 1887–16 June 1887 Gentian Péréton; 16 June 1887–11 July 1888 Victor Ballot. *Administrators:* 11 July 1888–1889 Paul de Beeckmann. *Residents:* 1889–19 Oct. 1889 Louis Tautain; 19 Oct. 1889–22 Dec. 1891 Victor Ballot. *Lieutenant-Governors:* 22 Dec. 1891–22 June 1894 Victor Ballot. *Note:* From 1883 these administrators were also the administrators of Cotonou. *Note:* Disnematin-Dorat was also Military Commandant of Cotonou. *Note:* Roget was also Commandant of Cotonou.

Porto Santo. 1418–1580. *Location:* Porto Santo Island, Madeira. *Capital:* Vila de Porto Santo ("Vila," for short).

History: In 1418 the Madeiras were discovered by Juan Gonçalves Zarco, a Portuguese navigator. In 1420 settlement began of Porto Santo, as well as Machico and Funchal. Wine and sugar were the main thrusts of the economy. The big island of Madeira was split up into two donatarias (parcels of land given to prominent Portuguese families by the Crown)—Funchal and Machico, while the small island of Porto Santo was made a separate donataria. In 1580 the Portuguese Crown canceled the donatarias and made the entire Madeira Island group a colony of Portugal (see Madeira).

Rulers: 1418–1580 [unknown].

Portuguese Congo. 26 Feb. 1884–26 June 1884. *Location:* Congo (at the mouth of the River Congo). *Capital:* none. *Other names:* Congo Portugues.

History: In 1884 the Portuguese overstepped their bounds and set up an area of interest within the French sphere of influence in the Congo. A few months later they were persuaded to move out.

Rulers: unknown, if any.

Portuguese Dahomey see **Dahomey Portuguese Protectorate**

Portuguese Gold Coast. 19 Jan. 1482–9 Jan. 1642. *Location:* the coast of what is today Ghana. *Capital:* São Jorge da Mina (also known as El Mina) (this was the capital until 1637). *Other names:* São Jorge da Mina.

History: In 1482 the Portuguese came to the Gold Coast, with their base at São Jorge da Mina (Saint George of Mina). In 1637 their headquarters were taken by the Dutch (see Dutch Gold Coast) and by 1642 all Portuguese territory in the area had been ceded to the Dutch.

Capitães-Mores (plural of Capitão-Mor, or Captain Major): 19 Jan. 1482–1484 Diogo de Azambuja; ca. 1486 Álvaro Vaz Pestano; ca. 1487 João Fogaça; ca. 1493 Lopo Soares de Albergaria; ca. 1502–ca. 1504 Nuno Vaz de Castelo Branco; ca. 1504–1504 Antonio de Miranda de Azevedo; 1504–1505 Diogo Lopes de Sequeira; 1505–(?) Martinho da Silva; (?)–ca. 1508 [unknown]; ca. 1508–1509 Capitão Bobadilha; 1509–ca. 1510 Manuel de Gois; ca. 1510–1513 Afonso Caldeira; 1513–ca. 1517 [unknown]; ca. 1517–1519 Fernão Lopes Correia; 1519–1522 Duarte Pacheco Pereira; 1522–1524 Afonso de Albuquerque; 1524–1525 João de Barros; 1525–1529 [unknown]; 1529–(?) Estévão da Gama; 1536–1539 Manuel de Albuquerque; 1539–1541 Antonio de Miranda; 1541–(?) Lopo de Sousa Coutinho; (?)–1545 [unknown]; 1545–(?) Diogo Soares de Albergaria; 1548–1550 Lopo de Sousa Coutinho; 1550–1552 Diogo Soares de Albergaria; 1552–ca. 1555 Rui de Melo; ca. 1555–ca. 1557 [unknown]; ca. 1557–(?) Afonso Gonçalves Botofago; (?)–1562 Rui Gomes de Azevedo; 1562–(?) Manuel de Mesquita Perestrelo; (?)–1564 [unknown]; 1564–(?) Martím Afonso; (?)–1570 [unknown]; 1570–(?) Antonio de Sá; (?)–ca. 1574 [unknown]; ca. 1574–(?) Mendio da Mota; (?)–ca. 1579 [unknown]; ca. 1579–(?) Vasco Fernandes Pimentel; (?)–1584 João Rodrigues Peçanha; 1584–(?) Bernardinho Ribeiro Pacheco; (?)–1586 [unknown]; 1586–ca. 1595 João Róis Coutinho; ca. 1595–ca. 1596 Duarte Lobo da Gama; ca. 1596–1608 Cristóvão da Gama; 1608–1613 Duarte de Lima; 1613–1613 João do Castro; 1613–ca. 1615 Pedro da Silva; ca. 1615–1616 [unknown]; 1616–1624 Manuel da Cunha e Teive; 1624–ca. 1625 Francisco de Souto-Maior; ca. 1625–(?) [unknown]; (?)–(?) Luis Tomé de Castro; (?)–1629 João da Sera de Morais; 1629–ca. 1632 [unknown]; ca. 1632–1634 Pedro de Mascarenhas; 1634–9 Jan. 1642 Antonio da Rocha Magalhães.

Portuguese Guinea see **Guinea-Bissau**

Portuguese West Africa see **Angola**

Potchefstroom see **Dutch African Republic**

Potiskum. ca. 1809–1901. *Location:* Northern Nigeria. *Capital:* Potiskum.

History: About 1809, in the middle of the troubles created by the Fulani Empire, a chief of the Ngizim tribe founded the town of Potiskum, extending the area under his control and ruling his own people and the local Karekare tribe. In 1901 Potiskum became part of the British protectorate of Northern Nigeria, and in 1909 the town of Potiskum became the center for the newly-formed Fika Province.

Mois (Kings): ca. 1809–(?) Bauya; (?)–(?) Awani; (?)–(?) Dungari; (?)–(?) Dowi; (?)–1836 Muzgai; 1836–1839 Jaji; 1839–1859 Nego; 1859–1886 Numainda; 1886–1895 Gubbo; 1895–1901 Bundi; 1901–1915 Agudum.

Praslin Island see **Seychelles**

Príncipe (i). 1470–1753. *Location:* the smaller island that goes to make up São Tomé and Príncipe. It is 90 miles northeast of the island of São Tomé. *Capital:* Santo Antonio (from 1500). *Other names:* Prince Island.

History: Discovered by the Portuguese in 1470, the island of Príncipe was made a donataria in 1500. A donataria was a parcel of land given to a Portuguese family of high rank and standing by the Portuguese Crown. In 1753 it became a part of the Portuguese possessions of São Tomé and Príncipe. The major problem here was the tsetse fly.

Rulers: 1470–1500 none; 1500–1753 [unknown].

Príncipe (ii). 28 April 1995– . *Location:* as Príncipe (i). *Capital:* Santo Antonio.

History: In 1995 the island province of Príncipe declared itself an autonomous region from São Tomé.

Presidents of Regional Government: 28 April 1995–12 April 2002 Damião Vaz d'Almeida; 12 April 2002–Zeferino dos Prazeres.

Proconsular Africa see **Africa Proconsularis**

Providence Group. No dates. *Location:* three islands 170 miles east of Madagascar. They were formed by the piling up of sand on a crescent-shaped surface reef.

History: Taken by the British from the French on 3 Oct. 1810, the Providence Group continued to be administered from Mauritius (as they had been under the French) until 1922, when they became a dependency of the Seychelles. On 30 June 1976 they became part of the new Republic of the Seychelles.

Prussian Gold Coast see **Hollandia**

Puerto de Isabel see **Fernando Po**

Punt. ca. 3500 B.C.–(?) B.C. *Location:* probably somewhere in the area of Somalia, Eritrea and/or Djibouti, but certainly by the Red Sea. *Capital:* [unknown]. *Other names:* Pwnt; Pwani; Punue; Pewenet; Puanet; Land of Punt.

History: A semi-mythical land visited by certain Egyptian pharaohs in the ancient days (Punt was the Egyptian name for the country). When the country began as a state and when it ended is unknown. Indeed, the whole country may not have existed.

Rulers: [unknown].

Puntland. 23 July 1998– . *Location:* Northeastern Somalia. *Capital:* Garowe. *Other names:* Puntland State; State of Puntland.

History: Created by the Harti and Darog clans, its leaders declared an autonomous republic in 1998, naming it for Punt (qv). It did not

try for international recognition. Abdullahi's main rival, Jama Ali Jam, began a civil war, but Abdullahi eventually won. The country was severely damaged during the 2004 tsunami.

Presidents: 23 July 1998–30 June 2001 Abdullahi Yusuf; 1 July 2001–14 Nov. 2001 Haji Nur (acting); 14 Nov. 2001–8 May 2002 Jama Ali Jama; 8 May 2002–10 Oct. 2004 Abdullahi Yusuf; 10 Oct. 2004–8 Jan. 2005 Muhammad Abdi Hasha; 8 Jan. 2005–Gen. Muhammad Muse Hersi Adde

Queen Adelaide Land see **British Kaffraria**

Queen Adelaide Province see **British Kaffraria**

Quiah see **Koya-Temne**

Qusantina see **Constantine**

QwaQwa. 1 Nov. 1974–27 April 1994. *Location:* In Orange Free State, on the border with Lesotho, in Southern Africa. *Capital:* Phuthaditjhaba. *Other names:* Qwa Qwa; Basotho-Qwa-Qwa.

History: QwaQwa National State was the bantustan (or national homeland) created for the Southern Sotho tribes of the Kwena and Tlokwa. Formerly it was called Witzieshoek, which means "Wetsie's corner" then Basotho Ba Borwa (from April 1969 when the tribes combined into a single territory), then Basotho QwaQwa (from 1 April 1972), QwaQwa being a translation of Witzieshoek. Wessels Mota was chief councillor. On 1 Nov. 1974 the new homeland achieved self-government within the Republic of South Africa. In 1994 the homelands were abolished as they were no longer necessary, South Africa being transferred to the black South Africans.

Chief Executive Councillor: 1 Nov. 1974–Feb. 1975 Wessels Mota. Chief Ministers: Feb. 1975–19 May 1975 Wessels Mota; 19 May 1975–26 April 1994 Tsiame Kenneth Mopale.

Rabih's Empire. 1893–23 Aug. 1901. *Location:* Nigeria, east of Lake Chad. *Capital:* Dikwa (from 1893); Logone (this was Rabih's capital, or rather his base of operations, from 1892 to 1893). *Other names:* Rabeh's Empire.

History: A Sudanese general, Rabih az-Zubayr ibn Fadl Allah, arrived in the area of Lake Chad about 1879 with 400 followers, on the run from the Egyptians. By raiding towns he grew in power until he had several thousand troops. In 1893 he occupied the Bornu Empire and his own empire dates properly from that time. He established his capital in the town of Dikwa and took over much of the Fulani Empire. In 1900 he and his forces met the French at Kusseri and Rabih was killed. For a short while he was succeeded by his son Fadl Allah, but his vast holdings became part of either French West Africa or the British protectorate of Northern Nigeria.

Emperors: 1893–22 April 1900 Rabih az-Zubayr ibn Fadl-Allah; 22 April 1900–23 Aug. 1901 Fadl-Allah.

Rano see **Hausa States**

Regnum Organa see **Bornu Empire**

Rehoboth. 1870–15 Sept. 1885. *Location:* Great Namaqualand in central Namibia. *Capital:* Rehoboth. *Other names:* Baster Gebiet; Rehoboth Republic; Land of the Bastaards.

History: In 1870 the Bastaards (or Basters) settled in their own land. A people of mixed races, usually of Afrikaaners who had "married" Nama women, they came from Cape Colony and settled in Rehoboth. In 1885 the country became part of German South West Africa.

Kaptyns (Captains): 1870–15 Sept. 1885 Hermanus Van Wyk.

Rehoboth Gebiet see **Namibia**

RENAMO see **Mozambique**

Réunion. 1502– . *Location:* an island 425 miles southeast of Madagascar, and 130 miles southwest of Mauritius, in the Indian Ocean. *Capital:* Saint Denis (from about 1736); Saint Paul (from 1649 to about 1736); no capital before 1649. *Other names:* Département d'Outremer Réunion (official name from 1946); Réunion Colony (1848–1946); Bourbon, or Île de Bourbon (1810–1848); Bonaparte, or Île Bonaparte (1801–1810); Réunion des Patriotes (alternative name from 1793 to 1801); Bourbon, or Île de Bourbon (1649–1793); Santa Apollonia, or Mascarenhas (1513–1649); Diva Morgabin (1502–1513).

History: This island was discovered by the Portuguese in 1502 and named Diva Morgabin. On 9 Feb. 1513 it was discovered again, by Pedro Mascarenhas, and re-named Santa Apollonia, because it was first seen by Mascarenhas on Saint Apollonia's Day. Santa Apollonia was uninhabited in 1638 when Capt. Goubert, of Dieppe, landed there, and another Frenchman in his party, François Cauche, hoisted the French flag. In 1642 it was officially claimed for France by Jacques Pronis. Pronis deported a dozen French mutineers to the island from Fort-Dauphin, the French colony in Madagascar. These convicts became the first settlers on what was to become Réunion. In 1645 these convicts were returned to France, and in 1649 France officially annexed the island, renaming it Île de Bourbon (which became simply Bourbon). The first colonist came out from France in 1662. From 1674 to 1763 Bourbon was ruled by the Compagnie des Indes Orientales (French East India Company). In the early 1730s refugee French pirates from Madagascar arrived. On 5 Nov. 1763 the island became a French Crown Colony. Mocha coffee, and later sugar, were the crops that made the island prosperous. In 1793, with the fall of the House of Bourbon, its name was not unexpectedly changed (given events in the mother country at that time), to Réunion. In 1801 its name was changed again, this time to Île Bonaparte (which soon became simply Bonaparte), in honor of Napoleon Bonaparte, the new ruler of France. On 8 July 1810 the island was taken by the British, and renamed Bourbon. After being occupied by the British for almost five years Bourbon was handed back to France in April 1815, with the stipulation (readily accepted by the French) that the island continue to be named Bourbon. In 1848 the island changed its name again, this time to Réunion, and it became a colony of France. At the same time slavery was abolished, and the island's 60,000 slaves became "French citizens." On 19 March 1946 Réunion became an overseas department of Metropolitan France. Since the 1980s it has been seeking more autonomy.

Rulers: 1502–1642 none; 1642–1649 [unknown]. *Commandants:* 1649–5 Aug. 1665 no central administration; 5 Aug. 1665–8 May 1671 Étienne Régnault; 9 May 1671–Nov. 1674 Jacques de Lahure; Nov. 1674–17 June 1678 Henri Esse d'Orgeret; 18 June 1678–Jan. 1680 Germain de Fleuricourt; 16 Jan. 1680–1 Dec. 1686 Bernardin de Quimper; 2 Dec. 1686–9 Dec. 1689 Jean-Baptiste Drouillard; 11 Dec. 1689–26 Nov. 1690 Henri Habet de Vauboulon; 26 Nov. 1690–11 Aug. 1693 Michel Firélin; 11

Aug. 1693–1693 M. Pradès and M. Lemayeur; 1693–2 July 1696 Athanase Touchard (President of the Directory of St Paul); 1 Aug. 1696–6 June 1698 Joseph Bastide; 21 Oct. 1699–13 May 1701 Jacques de la Cour de la Saulais; 12 June 1701–5 March 1709 Jean-Baptiste de Villers; 7 March 1709–24 March 1710 François Desbordes de Charanville; 22 April 1710–14 Nov. 1715 Pierre Parat de Chaillenest; 4 Dec. 1715–14 Feb. 1718 Henri Justamont; 6 Sept. 1718–22 Aug. 1723 Joseph Beauvollier de Courchant; 23 Aug. 1723–1 Dec. 1725 Antoine Desforges-Boucher; 2 Dec. 1725–28 May 1727 Hélie Dioré; 21 July 1727–11 July 1735 Pierre-Benoît Dumas; 12 July 1735–1 Oct. 1735 Bernard François Mahé, Comte de la Bourdonnais; 2 Oct. 1735–30 Sept. 1739 Alfred Lémery-Dupont; 11 Nov. 1739–12 Dec. 1743 Pierre d'Héguerty; 13 Dec. 1743–8 May 1745 Didier de Saint-Martin; 15 May 1745–31 Oct. 1745 Jean-Baptiste Azéma; 1 Nov. 1745–18 Dec. 1745 Didier de Saint-Martin. *Governors:* 29 Dec. 1745–28 March 1747 Gaspard de Ballade; 14 April 1747–11 Nov. 1748 Didier de Saint-Martin; 22 Nov. 1748–17 March 1749 Gaspard de Ballade; 24 May 1749–23 Aug. 1749 Antoine Marc Desforges-Boucher; 6 Sept. 1749–16 Oct. 1750 Joseph Brénier; 16 Oct. 1750–14 Dec. 1752 Jean-Baptiste Bouvet de Lozier; 14 Dec. 1752–14 Jan. 1756 Joseph Brénier; 12 July 1757–15 Oct. 1757 Antoine Marc Desforges-Boucher; 19 Oct. 1757–6 Sept. 1763 Jean-Baptiste Bouvet de Lozier; 7 Sept. 1763–14 Oct. 1763 Jean Sentuary. *Commandants:* 5 Nov. 1763–30 March 1767 François Bertin d'Avesnes; 31 March 1767–4 Nov. 1767 Martin-Adrien Bellier. *Governors:* 4 Nov. 1767–4 Oct. 1773 Guillaume de Bellecombe; 15 Dec. 1773–15 Oct. 1776 Jean Steinauer; 26 Oct. 1776–30 April 1779 François de Souillac; 25 May 1779–22 Aug. 1781 Joseph Murinay de Saint-Maurice; 25 Aug. 1781–21 April 1785 André Chalvet de Souville; 2 May 1785–15 Feb. 1788 Hélie Dioré; 21 Feb. 1788–15 Aug. 1790 David Charpentier de Cossigny; 8 Sept. 1790–18 Oct. 1792 Dominique de Chermont; 19 Oct. 1792–11 April 1794 Jean-Baptiste Vigoureux du Plessis; 12 April 1794–1 Nov. 1795 Pierre-Alexandre Roubaud; 2 Nov. 1795–7 Oct. 1803 Philippe Jacob de Cordemoy; 10 Nov. 1803–31 Dec. 1805 François Magallon de Lamorlière; 9 Jan. 1806–25 Sept. 1809 Nicolas de Regnac des Brulys; 9 Oct. 1809–8 July 1810 Jean Brunteau de Sainte-Suzanne. *British Governors:* 8 July 1810–20 Dec. 1810 Robert Farquhar; 1811–

1811 Henry Warde; 1811–26 April 1811 Henry Keating; 26 April 1811–10 July 1811 Robert Farquhar; 10 July 1811–5 April 1815 Henry Keating. *Governors:* 6 April 1815–30 June 1817 Athanase Bouvet de Lozier; 1 July 1817–9 Sept. 1818 Hilaire Lafitte de Courteil; 13 Sept. 1818–14 Feb. 1821 Pierre-Bernard de Milius; 15 Feb. 1821–14 Oct. 1826 Louis Desaulses de Freycinet; 20 Oct. 1826–4 July 1830 Achille de Penfentenio de Cheffontaines; 5 July 1830–7 Nov. 1832 Étienne Mengin Duval d'Ailly; 8 Nov. 1832–4 May 1838 Jacques Cuvillier; 5 May 1838–14 Oct. 1841 Adm. Louis de Hell; 15 Oct. 1841–4 June 1846 Charles Bazoche; 5 June 1846–13 Oct. 1848 Joseph Graëb; 13 Oct. 1848–7 March 1850 Joseph-Napoléon Sarda-Garriga; 9 March 1850–14 Feb. 1851 De Barolet de Puligny (acting); 15 Feb. 1851–8 Aug. 1852 Louis Doret; 8 Aug. 1852–8 Jan. 1858 Louis Hubert-Delisle; 11 Jan. 1858–27 March 1858 M. Leferre (acting); 28 March 1858–19 Sept. 1864 Rodolphe Darricau; 4 Jan. 1865–23 Sept. 1869 Marc Dupré; 27 Sept. 1869–18 Sept. 1875 Louis de Lormel; 19 Nov. 1875–29 April 1879 Pierre Faron; 6 May 1879–23 March 1886 Pierre Cuinier; 23 March 1886–11 Oct. 1886 Jean-Baptiste Lougnon (acting); 11 Oct. 1886–16 Dec.1887 Étienne Richaud; 16 Dec. 1887–21 Aug. 1888 Jean-Baptiste Lougnon (acting); 22 Aug. 1888–10 July 1893 Louis Manès; 11 July 1893–21 June 1895 Henri Danel; 22 June 1895–12 Aug. 1895 Henri Roberdeau (acting); 13 Aug. 1895–19 May 1896 Benedict de Cordemoy (acting); 19 May 1896–30 Oct. 1900 Laurent Beauchamp; 30 Oct. 1900–19 Feb. 1901 Charles Madre (acting); 19 Feb. 1901–29 July 1905 Paul Samary; 29 July 1905–30 Aug. 1896 Fernand Theron (acting); 30 Aug. 1906–7 Nov. 1906 Marius Herignon (acting); 8 Nov. 1906–27 Dec. 1907 Adrien Bonhoure; 1 Jan. 1908–19 March 1908 Henri Core (acting); 19 March 1908–18 Jan. 1910 Lucien Guy; 18 Jan. 1910–17 Sept. 1910 Philippe Jullien; 18 Sept. 1910–28 July 1912 François Rodier; 30 Aug. 1912–22 Nov. 1913 Hubert Garbit (acting); 23 Nov. 1913–1 June 1919 Pierre Duprat; 2 June 1919–26 July 1920 Victor Brochard (acting); 27 July 1920–5 Sept. 1922 Frédéric Estèbe; 6 Sept. 1922–21 Aug. 1923 Henri Cleret de Langavant; 22 Aug. 1923–2 Oct. 1924 Maurice Lapalud; 31 March 1925–28 Nov. 1932 Jules Repiquet; 29 Nov. 1932–13 June 1934 Louis Fabre (acting); 14 June 1934–29 May 1936 Alphonse Choteau; 17 Aug. 1936–27 Oct. 1938 Léon Truitard; 28 Oct. 1938–29 Dec.

1939 Joseph Court; 30 Dec. 1939–1 Dec. 1942 Pierre Aubert; 1 Dec. 1942–19 March 1946 André Capagorry. *Prefects:* 19 March 1946–17 July 1947 André Capagorry; 16 Aug. 1947–1 June 1950 Paul Demange; 1 June 1950–4 July 1952 Roland Béchoff; 4 July 1952–14 May 1956 Pierre Philip; 12 June 1956–1 March 1963 Jean-François Perreau-Pradier; 1 March 1963–1 Sept. 1966 Alfred Diefenbacher; 11 Sept. 1966–22 Oct. 1969 Jean Vaudeville; 29 Oct. 1969–21 Aug. 1972 Paul Cousserau; 28 Aug. 1972–14 April 1975 Claude Vieillescazes; 14 April 1975–12 May 1977 Robert Lamy; 16 May 1977–22 May 1980 Bernard Landouzy; 29 May 1980–1 Aug. 1981 Jacques Seval (acting); 1 Aug. 1981–Nov. 1982 Michel Levallois. *Government Commissioners:* Nov. 1982–15 March 1984 Michel Levallois; 26 March 1984–9 April 1986 Michel Blangy; 25 April 1986–11 Sept. 1989 Jean Anciaux; 11 Sept. 1989–18 July 1991 Daniel Constantin; 18 July 1991–1 Dec. 1992 Jacques Dewatre; 2 Dec. 1992–2 Jan. 1995 Hubert Fournier; 9 Jan. 1995–29 Nov. 1995 Pierre Steinmetz; 29 Nov. 1995–15 July 1998 Robert Pommies; 5 Aug. 1998–2 July 2001 Jean Daubigny; 31 July 2001–13 Aug. 2004 Gonthier Friederici; 16 Aug. 2004–4 June 2005 Dominique Vian; 16 July 2005–Laurent Cayrel.

Rhodesia. 30 Oct. 1888–29 Jan. 1900. *Location:* as Zambia. *Capital:* Salisbury (founded 12 Sept. 1890 as Fort Salisbury, and named for Lord Salisbury, the British Prime Minister).

History: In 1888, when Cecil Rhodes and his company (which in 1889 would become the British South Africa Company, or BSAC) began infiltrating the huge expanse of land that now comprises Zambia and Zimbabwe, there were no European possessions there at all. Barotseland was the principal state north of the Zambesi, while south of the river two great kingdoms predominated — Mashonaland and Matabeleland. The Matabele had long passed their peak of power and the British placed a protectorate over them on 11 Feb. 1888. However, the Matabele refused to accept this, and it was not until Jan. 1894 that they were finally conquered and brought into Zambesia. In 1888 the British began calling the entire country (both sides of the Zambesi) "Zambesia," after the river, and on 30 Oct. 1888 the country was officially named Zambesia. What was left of the Mwene Mutapa Empire (which was not much by then) was incorporated into Zambesia. On 29 Oct.

1889 Mashonaland was made a British protectorate, and on 11 June 1891 the Barotse, who had become more and more subject to the British, became part of Zambesia. On 23 Jan. 1894, with Matabeleland now merged into Mashonaland Protectorate, Zambesia was divided into North Zambesia and South Zambesia, with the Zambesi River as the boundary. On 3 May 1895 the two Zambesias merged to form Rhodesia Protectorate. This was the first time the name Rhodesia was used, named of course for Cecil Rhodes, the only man after whom two countries (Northern Rhodesia and Southern Rhodesia) have been named. It was decided, for no apparent reason, to pronounce the name Rhodesia (as we know it today) with the stress on the second syllable rather than the first, i.e *Rhodes*-ia. On 29 Jan. 1900 the British protectorate of Rhodesia split into three parts — Southern Rhodesia (see Zimbabwe), North Western Rhodesia, and North Eastern Rhodesia.

Resident Commissioners of Mashonaland Protectorate: 29 June 1890–17 Sept. 1891 Archibald Colquhoun (acting). *Chief Magistrates of Mashonaland Protectorate:* 18 Sept. 1891–8 Oct. 1893 Dr. Leander Starr Jameson; 8 Oct. 1893–May 1894 Andrew Duncan (acting); May 1894–9 Sept. 1894 Dr. Leander Starr Jameson. *Administrators:* 9 Sept. 1894–28 Oct. 1894 Dr. Leander Starr Jameson; 28 Oct. 1894–1 April 1895 Francis Rhodes (acting); 1 April 1895–June 1895 Dr. Leander Starr Jameson; June 1895–2 May 1896 Joseph Vintcent (acting); 2 May 1896–23 July 1897 Earl Grey; 24 July 1897–5 Dec. 1898 William Milton (acting); 5 Dec. 1898–29 Jan. 1900 William Milton. *Administrators of Mashonaland:* 5 Dec. 1898–Jan. 1899 Sir Thomas Scanlen (acting); Jan. 1899–22 June 1899 position filled by William Milton, also the administrator of Rhodesia; 22 June 1899–5 Dec. 1899 Capt. Arthur Lawley; 5 Dec. 1899–29 Jan. 1900 position again filled by Milton. *Administrators of Matabeleland:* Nov. 1896–Feb. 1897 Capt. Arthur Lawley (acting); Feb. 1897–4 Dec. 1898 Capt. Arthur Lawley. *Deputy Administrators of Matabeleland:* 5 Dec. 1898–29 Jan. 1900 Capt. Arthur Lawley. *Residents in Barotseland:* 8 April 1897–29 Jan. 1900 Robert Coryndon. *Administrators of North Eastern Rhodesia:* 1 July 1895–June 1897 Patrick Forbes; June 1897–10 July 1898 Henry Daly (acting). *Deputy Administrators of North Eastern Rhodesia:* 11 July 1898–29 Jan. 1900 Robert Coryndon.

Rhodesia see **Zambia** and **Zimbabwe**

Ribeira Grande see **Cape Verde**

Rif see **Spanish Morocco**

Rif Republic. Feb. 1923–27 May 1926. *Location:* in the area called the Rif, in northern Morocco. *Capital:* Ajdir. *Other names:* Jumhuriyya Rifiya, or Republic of the Rif.

History: In 1923 Berber warlord and bandit chief Abd al-Karim (called Abdel Krim by the French, his name is also seen as Abd al-Qrim) formed a republic within Spanish Morocco, and succeeded in maintaining this "republic" for five years until halted by a massive French–Spanish combined operation. By this time Abdel Krim had awakened much sympathy throughout the world for his cause, which was to expel the foreigners from his country. On 27 May, 1926 he was forced to surrender, and was exiled to Réunion, in the Indian Ocean. This was the end of the Rif Republic.

Presidents/Princes of the Rif: Feb. 1923–27 May 1926 Abd al-Karim (also known as Abd al-Qrim, or Abdel Krim). *Prime Ministers:* Feb. 1923–27 May 1926 ben Hajj Hatmi.

Río de Oro see **Western Sahara**

Río Muni. 9 Jan. 1885–1926. *Location:* the mainland part of Equatorial Guinea. *Capital:* Ruled from Santa Isabel, on Fernando Po.

History: The main local people in this territory were (are) the Fang. In 1885 the Spanish infiltrated the mainland of what would later become Equatorial Guinea, and called it Río Muni, after the estuary into which the larger rivers of the area flow. On 27 June 1900 Río Muni was delimited as a colony. In 1926 Río Muni and the islands of Fernando Po and Annobón were all united to form the colony known as Spanish Guinea (later Equatorial Guinea).

Rulers: 9 Jan. 1885–27 June 1900 none; 27 June 1900–1926 ruled direct from Fernando Po.

Rivers State see **Biafra**

Rivières du Sud see **Guinea**

Riziam see **Mossi States**

Rodrigues (i). 1507–3 March 1992. *Location:* an island in the Indian Ocean, 350 miles east of Mauritius. *Capital:* Port Mathurin (from 1638). *Other names:* Rodriguez; Diego Ruy's Island (1507–1638).

History: Discovered as an uninhabited island by the Portuguese in 1507, it was colonized by the French in 1638, and renamed Rodrigues (two syllables, as per the French pronunciation). In 1809 the British seized it from the French, and on 30 May 1814 the colony was awarded to the British, and it kept the name Rodrigues, but became a dependency of Mauritius. The British abolished slavery there, and this proved the undoing of the country's economy. In 1992, when Mauritius became a republic, Rodrigues continued to be a part of it.

Rulers: 1507–1638 none; 1638–30 May 1814 [unknown]; 30 May 1814–1992 ruled from Port Louis, Mauritius, through a locally-placed magistrate and council of 17 islanders.

Rodrigues (ii). 12 Oct. 2002– . *Location:* as Rodrigues (i). *Capital:* Port Mathurin.

History: In 2002 Rodrigues declared itself autonomous from Mauritius (qv).

Chief Commissioners: 12 Oct. 2002–4 Feb. 2003 Jean Spéville; 4 Feb. 2003–Serge Clair. *Chief Executives:* 24 Oct. 2002–23 Oct. 2004 Claude Wong Su; 24 Oct. 2004–Jean-Claude Pierre-Louis.

Roha Empire see **Ethiopia**

Rolongland see **Barolongland**

Rostemid Kingdom see **Rustumid Amirate**

Rotenga see **Mossi States**

Royal Niger Company see **Northern Nigeria**

Rozwi. ca. 1480–1838. *Location:* Zimbabwe and parts of Botswana. *Capital:* Dhlo Dhlo. *Other names:* Borozwi; Rozvi; Varozvi; Changamire.

History: A Karanga empire established about 1480 by Changamire I (son of Matope of the Mwene Mutapa Empire. A later Changamire (Dunbo) overthrew the Portuguese in his area of the Zambesi, and his name became the title of the ruler of Rozwi (i.e. the "Changamire," meaning "the King"). The mfecane (the turmoil created in Southeast Africa by the Zulu migrations) caused the demise of the Rozwi Empire, and it was swallowed up by Matabeleland in 1838.

Kings: ca. 1480–1494 Changamire I; 1494–1530 Changamire II; 1530–ca. 1660 [unknown]; ca. 1660–ca. 1695 Changamire Dunbo; ca. 1695–ca. 1700 [unknown]; ca. 1700–1710 Changamire Negamo; 1710–(?) [unknown]; (?)–(?) Chirisamaru; (?)–ca. 1825 [unknown]; ca. 1825–ca. 1828 Changamire Baswi; ca. 1828–1831 Changamire Chirisamaru II; 1831–1866 Changamire Tohwechipi.

Ruanda. ca. 1350–1890. *Location:* Rwanda. *Capital:* Kigali. *Other names:* Rwanda.

History: The Tutsi (also known as the Watusi), skilled warriors, came to the Ruanda-Urundi area in the mid–14th century, and peacefully assumed dominance over the Hutu population. They ruled until 1890 when the Germans placed a protectorate over them (see German East Africa), as they had already done over Burundi (see Burundi [i]). The Tutsi continued to rule, even more than nominally, because the Germans never really gained control of the country. During World War I the Belgians captured this area, as well as Burundi, and in 1920 they united the two countries as Ruanda-Urundi.

Mwamis (Kings): ca. 1350–ca. 1386 Ndahiro Ruyange; ca. 1386–ca. 1410 Ndoba; ca. 1410–ca. 1434 Samembe; ca. 1434–ca. 1458 Nsoro Samukondo; ca. 1458–ca. 1482 Ruganza Bwimba; ca. 1482–ca. 1506 Cyilima Rugwe; ca. 1506–ca. 1528 Kigeri I Mukobanya; ca. 1528–ca. 1552 Mibambwe I Mutabaazi; ca. 1552–ca. 1576 Yuhi I Gahima; ca. 1576–ca. 1600 Ndahiro II Cyaamatare; ca. 1600–ca. 1624 Ruganza II Ndoori; ca. 1624–ca. 1648 Mutara I Seemugeshi; ca. 1648–ca. 1672 Kigeri II Nyamuheshera; ca. 1672–ca. 1696 Mibambwe II Gisanura; ca. 1696–ca. 1720 Yuhi II Mazimpaka; ca. 1720–ca. 1744 Keremeera Rwaaka; ca. 1744–ca. 1768 Cyilima II Rujugira; ca. 1768–ca. 1792 Kigeri III Ndabarasa; ca. 1792–ca. 1797 Mibambwe III Seentaabyo; ca. 1797–ca. 1830 Yuhi III Gahandiro; ca. 1830–1853 Mutara II Rwoogera; 1853–1895 Kigeri IV Rwabugiri; 1895–Nov. 1896 Mibambwe IV Rutulindwa; Nov. 1896–1931 Yuhi IV Musinga; 16 Nov. 1931–25 July 1959 Mutara III Rudahigwa; 1959–28 Jan. 1961 Kigeri V Ndahundirwa.

Ruanda-Urundi. 21 May 1916–1 July 1962. *Location:* Rwanda and Burundi combined, in East Africa. *Capital:* Bujumbura (also known as Usumbura, this was the capital from 1924 to 1962, although it was the local headquarters from 1916); Léopoldville (in the Belgian Congo, this was the administrative capital from 1923 to 1924); Boma (in the Belgian Congo, this was the administrative capital from 1916 to 1923).

History: In 1916 the Belgians the British captured German East Africa and split it up between them. The British got the larger part, which four years later they would call Tanganyika. The Belgian part became Ruanda-Urundi, and the Belgians administered it from Boma in the Belgian Congo through local headquarters in Bujumbura. On 30 May 1919 the country was officially awarded to the Belgians by the League of Nations. It was still governed through the Belgian Congo. On 23 Aug. 1923 (effective as from 20 Oct. 1924) Ruanda-Urundi became a League of Nations mandate. On 21 Aug. 1925 it became a mandated territory (a subtly different constitution), and was split administratively into Ruanda and Urundi. On 3 Dec. 1946 it became a United Nations Trust Territory, still dependent on the Belgian Congo. However, nationalism was growing in Ruanda-Urundi, so in 1959 two individual component parts were created within the Trust Territory, viz. Rwanda and Burundi. On 28 Jan. 1961 the Rwanda Provisional Government proclaimed Rwanda a republic (see Rwanda for details of this country after this date). On 29 Sept. 1961 Burundi was given a certain degree of autonomy as the Kingdom of Burundi (see Burundi [ii] for details of this country after this time). On 1 July 1962 Belgium gave up the Trust Territory of Ruanda-Urundi, and the two halves went their own way.

Governors: 21 May 1916–1920 Justin Malfeyt. *Residents-General:* 1920–1922 Alfred Marcorati; 1922–1928 Pierre Ryckmans. *Vice Governors-General:* 1928–30 June 1932 Charles Voisin; 30 June 1932–3 Dec. 1946 Pierre Jungers; 11 Dec. 1946–1952 Léon Pétillon; 1952–1955 Alfred Claeys-Boúúaert; 1955–1959 Jean-Paul Harroy. *Residents-General:* 1959–1 July 1962 Jean-Paul Harroy. *Note:* For the kings of Ruanda and Burundi, see Ruanda and Burundi [i] respectively. *Note:* For prime ministers of Rwanda and Burundi during this period, see Rwanda and Burundi [ii] respectively.

Rudolph Province see **Uganda**

Rusaddir see **Melilla**

Rustumid Amirate. 776–31 July 911. *Location:* Tahert, Algeria (near present-day Tiaret). *Capital:* Wargla (from 909); Tahert (until 909). *Other names:* Tahert; Tahart; Rostemid Kingdom; Banu Rustum.

History: A city-state in Northwestern Algeria, Tahert was the center of the heterodox Kharijite doctrine for over a hundred years, and was ruled by Abd ar-Rahman ibn Rustum and his descendants, as the Banu Rustum dynasty, or the Rustumids. With the Aghlabid Empire in the east and the Idrisid State in the west, it was finally destroyed by the Kutama mountain tribes led by Abu Abdallah ash-Shi'i.

Amirs: 776–784 Abd ar-Rahman ibn Rustum; 784–823 Abd al-Wahhab; 823–871 Abu Sa'id al-Aflah; 871–871 Abu Bakr; 871–894 Abu al-Yaqzan Muhammad; 894–907 Abu Hatim Yusuf; 907–909 Yaqub ibn al-Aflah; 909–909 Abu Suleiman; 909–31 July 911 Yaqub ibn al-Aflah.

Rwanda. 1959– . *Location:* east central Africa. *Capital:* Kigali. *Other names:* Ruanda.

History: The Tutsi minority in Rwanda had reigned nominally since European occupation, and in 1959 the Hutu majority revolted and overthrew the monarchy. The Belgian Trust Territory of Ruanda–Urundi was officially divided up into two parts — Rwanda and Burundi (see Burundi [ii]), but the whole lot was still ruled by Belgium. On 10 Oct. 1960 Rwanda formed its own local government, and on 28 Jan. 1961 the Rwanda Provisional Government proclaimed a republic, and abolished the monarchy. At the same time Burundi formed its own government. The United Nations did not recognize the new self-declared republic of Rwanda, but under their aegis elections were held later in 1961. On 1 July 1962, with the dismemberment of the Trust Territory, the Democratic and Sovereign Republic of Rwanda came into being. With the Hutu in power, the Tutsis rebelled in 1963 and the bloodshed was horrendous. Thousands of Tutsis went into exile. Burundi invaded in 1964. There was a coup in 1973, and more Tutsi rebellions led to a coup in which Juvénal Habyarimana toppled President Kayibanda. Habyarimana survived a coup in 1980, and a civil war in 1990, and by 1991 had begun to democratize the country again. Habyarimana and the president

of Burundi were both killed in a plane crash under possibly mysterious circumstances, on 6 April 1994, and this led to astonishing violence in Rwanda in the mid–1990s between the Tutsis and the Hutu. There was civil war again by 1997. In 2000 Bizimungu resigned, and Kagale became the first Tutsi president of Rwanda. Rwanda, like all the southern African countries, is faced with an overwhelming AIDS problem, and on top of that poverty, a huge refugee problem, disease, and corruption.

Presidents: 28 Jan. 1961–26 Oct. 1961 Dominique Mbonyumutwa; 26 Oct. 1961–5 July 1973 Grégoire Kayibanda; 5 July 1973–6 April 1994 Juvenal Habyarimana; 6 April 1994–19 July 1994 Théodore Sindikubwayo; 19 July 1994–23 March 2000 Pasteur Bizimungu; 23 March 2000–Paul Kagame. *Prime Ministers:* 10 Oct. 1960–28 Jan. 1961 Joseph Gitera; 12 Oct. 1991–2 April 1992 Sylvestre Nsanzimana; 2 April 1992–18 July 1993 Dismas Nsengiyaremye; 18 July 1993–7 April 1994 Agathe Uwilingiyumana; 9 April 1994–19 July 1994 Jean Kambanda; 19 July 1994–31 Aug. 1995 Faustin Twagiramungu; 31 Aug. 1995–8 March 2000 Pierre-Celestin Rwigema; 8 March 2000–Bernard Makuza.

Saharan Arab Democratic Republic see **Western Sahara**

Sahel-Bénin Union see **Burkina Faso**

Sail Rock see **Madeira**

St. Andrew's Island see **Fort James**

St. Anne Island see **Seychelles**

Saint Brandon Islands. (?)–12 March 1992. *Location:* a group of uninhabited islets northeast of Mauritius, in the Indian Ocean. *Other names:* St. Brandon Islands; Cardagos Carajos Shoals.

History: On 3 Oct. 1810 the British took these islands from the French, and they became a dependency of Mauritius. In 1992, when Mauritius became a republic, the Saint Brandons went with it.

Saint Helena. 1651– . *Location:* an island in the southern Atlantic Ocean, 1200 miles west of Africa. It has two dependencies: Ascension (from 1922) and Tristan da Cunha with its associated island, Gough Island (since 1938). *Capital:*

Jamestown (built in 1658, and named for the Duke of York, afterwards James II). *Other names:* St. Helena.

History: Discovered as an uninhabited island on 21 May 1502 by the Portuguese navigator João da Nova Castela, Saint Helena was named by him for the mother of the Roman emperor Constantine. The Portuguese established a station here, with a chapel, but not a permanent settlement. Fernão López was the first settler. A traitor from India, he was mutilated and marooned on the island with four slaves, and died there in 1546. Two Japanese ambassadors from Rome landed there in 1584, and Thomas Cavendish, the English navigator, landed here in June 1588 during his circumnavigation of the globe. A few other sailors, of various nationalities, visited Saint Helena over the next several decades, and in 1645 the Dutch attempted a settlement, but it proved fruitless after a six-year try. It was left to the English East India Company to make the first real permanent settlement here. They occupied the island as soon as the Dutch had left, and settlement began in 1658. On 1 Jan. 1673 the Dutch captured the island, and occupied it for a few months until they were expelled by an English force led by Capt. Richard Munden on 5 May 1673. On 16 Dec. 1673 Charles II granted the island to the East India Company. Due to its position, it became a very prosperous island with all the ships stopping off their and refitting for considerable periods of time. Saint Helena was a shockingly bad place for slaves, of which there were many working the plantations, until 1792, when more humane laws were passed regarding their treatment (the slaves were all freed between 1826 and 1836). On 6 Oct. 1815 Napoleon was exiled here after Waterloo, and the island became a Crown Colony. The British Crown assumed direct responsibility for the colony as long as their notorious prisoner was staying at Longwood, 2½ miles southwest of Jamestown, for six years, until he died on 5 May 1821, whereupon the East India Company immediately resumed control of the island's affairs. In 1833 an Act was passed in the British Parliament, and on 22 April 1834 Saint Helena evolved into its final state, a permanent colony of the United Kingdom. The Suez Canal, which enabled ships to get to India by a different (shorter) route, was the main reason for the decline of Saint Helena, after 1870. The garrison was removed in 1906 (although there were British troops there during World War I). From the time of Napoleon, Saint Helena was used as a place of exile for defeated or deposed African leaders, as well as a jail for more ordinary criminals. In 1922 Ascension Island was made a dependency of Saint Helena, and in 1938 a similar thing happened to Tristan da Cunha and its associate satellite Gough Island.

Governors: 1659–1661 John Dutton; 1661–1671 Robert Stringer; 1671–1672 Richard Coney; 1672–1673 Anthony Beale; 1673–1673 Richard Munden; 1673–1674 Richard Kedgwin; 1674–1678 Gregory Field; 1678–1690 John Blackmore; 1690–April 1693 Capt. Joshua Johnson; April 1693–1697 Richard Kelinge; 1697–1707 Capt. Stephen Poirier; 1707–1708 Thomas Goodwin; 1708–1711 John Roberts; 1711–1714 Benjamin Boucher; 1714–1719 Isaac Pyke; 1719–1723 Edward Johnson; 1723–1727 John Smith; 1727–1731 Edward Byfield; 1731–1738 Isaac Pyke; 1738–1739 John Goodwin; 1739–1741 Robert Jenkins; 1741–1741 Thomas Lambert; 1741–1743 George Powell; 1743–1747 David Dunbar; 1747–1764 Charles Hutchison; 1764–1782 John Skottowe; 1782–1788 Daniel Corneille; 1788–1800 Robert Brooke; 1800–1801 Francis Robson; 1801–1808 Robert Patton; 1808–1813 Alexander Beatson; 1813–1816 Mark Wilks; 1816–1823 Sir Hudson Lowe; 1823–1828 Alexander Walker; 1828–1836 Charles Dallas; 1836–1842 George Middlemore; 1842–1846 Hamelin Trelawny; 1846–1851 Patrick Ross; 1851–1856 Thomas Browne; 1856–1863 Edward Drummond-Hay; 1863–1870 Charles Elliot; 1870–1873 Charles Patey; 1873–1884 Hudson Janisch; 1884–1887 Grant Blunt; 1887–1897 William Grey-Wilson; 1897–1903 Robert Sterndale; 1903–1911 Henry Gallwey (knighted 1910, and after 1911 known as Sir Henry Galway); 1911–1917 Harry Cordeaux; 1917–1919 Lt.-Col. William Dixon (acting); 1919–1920 Harry Cordeaux; 1920–1925 Robert Peel; 1925–1932 Charles Harper; 1932–1938 Steuart Davis; 1938–18 March 1941 Guy Pilling; 18 March 1941–31 May 1947 William Gray; 31 May 1947–11 Jan. 1954 George Joy; 11 Jan. 1954–12 Feb. 1958 James Harford; 12 Feb. 1958–27 Feb. 1962 Robert Alford; 27 Feb. 1962–1968 Sir John Field; 1968–1972 Sir Dermot Murphy; 1972–1977 Sir Thomas Oates; 1977–1981 G.C. Guy; 1981–3 Aug. 1984 John Massingham; 3 Aug. 1984–1988 Francis Baker; 1988–1991 Robert Frederick Stimson; 1991–1995 Alan Hoole; 1995–1999 David Smallman; 24 June 1999–29 Sept. 2004 David Hollamby; 29 Sept. 2004–15

Oct. 2004 John Styles (acting); 15 Oct. 2004–Michael Clancy.

Saint Joseph Group see **Amirante Islands**

St. Lawrence Island see **Madagascar**

Saint Mary see **Gambia**

Sainte Marie de Madagascar. 30 July 1750–6 Aug. 1896. *Location:* a little island off the northeastern coast of Madagascar, now known as Nossi Boraha. *Capital:* Saint Denis (on the island of Réunion, from where Sainte Marie was administered from 1819 to 1843, and again from 1878 to 1896); Chingoni (on the island of Mayotte, in the Comoros, from where Sainte Marie was administered from 1843 to 1853); Ambodifototra (local headquarters from 1819). *Other names:* Sainte-Marie.

History: In 1750 this island was ceded to France by the local ruler, but remained virtually unoccupied until it became a French colony on 15 Oct. 1818. In 1819 the French administration began, and the territory of Sainte Marie was placed under the island of Réunion. On 25 March 1843 it became a dependent colony of Mayotte, in the Comoros. In 1853 it became a separate colony, but in 1878 it reverted to being a territory of Réunion. In 1896 it was taken in by France (along with the other French possessions on Madagascar, Diego Suarez and Nossi-Bé) to form part of the new French colony of Madagascar.

Administrators: 30 July 1750–July 1754 M. Gosse; July 1754–1819 no fixed central administration; 1819–15 April 1821 Jean-Louis Carayon; 15 April 1821–2 April 1823 Jean-Baptiste Roux; 2 April 1823–29 April 1823 François Albrand; 29 April 1823–Oct. 1826 Hercule Blévec; Oct. 1826–May 1827 Capt. Giraud (acting); May 1827–1829 Hercule Blévec; 1829–1830 Jean-Louis Carayon; 1830–1841 direct administration from the island of Bourbon (now known as Réunion); 1841–25 March 1843 Raimond Vergès. *Commandants:* 25 March 1843–1849 Raimond Vergès; 1849–1850 Pierre-Balthasar Mermier; 1850–1851 André Brisset; 1851–1853 Pierre-Balthasar Mermier; 1853–1853 Félix Grébert; 1853–1855 Jean-Pierre Durand; 1855–1858 Jean-Baptiste Raffenel; 1858–1868 Jean-Paul de la Grange; 1868–1874 Louis Blandinières; 1874–1878 Charles-Henri Vassal; 1878–6 Aug. 1896 administered direct from Réunion.

Sakalava see **Madagascar**

Sal see **Cape Verde**

Salé–Rabat see **Bou Regreg**

Samory's Empire. 1879–29 Sept. 1898. *Location:* Guinea. *Capital:* Bissandugu. *Other names:* Mandinka Empire.

History: In 1847 the 17-year-old Samory Touré from Sanankoro in present-day Guinea, became a trader, later serving in the army of a Mandinka war-leader. In 1879 he formed his empire (otherwise called the Mandinka Empire) by conquest. From 1882 until his capture in 1898 Samory resisted the French, and died in exile in Gabon in 1900. His empire became part of French West Africa.

Emperors: 1879–29 Sept. 1898 Samory Touré.

San see **Namibia**

Sanhajah see **Almoravid Empire** and **Zirid Kingdom**

Santa Apollonia see **Réunion**

Santa Cruz de la Mar Pequeña. 1476–1524. *Location:* somewhere on the coast of Morocco opposite the Canary Islands, probably in the area of Ifni. *Capital:* Unknown exactly, but probably Santa Cruz. *Other names:* Santa Cruz; Santa Cruz de Mar Pequeña.

History: In 1476 the Spanish established a fort and post here to aid in the colonization of the Canary Islands. For almost fifty years they used it as a slave-dealing entrepôt. It was destroyed by the Moors in 1524, and the concept was abandoned.

Rulers: [unknown].

Santa Cruz de Tenerife see **Tenerife**

Santo Antão see **Cape Verde**

SANU see **Southern Sudan**

Sao see **Bornu**

São Antão see **Cape Verde**

São Jorge de Mina see **Portuguese Gold Coast**

São Nicolau see **Cape Verde**

São Paolo de Loanda see **Angola**

São Tiago see **Cape Verde**

São Tomé. 1470–1753. *Location:* the major of the two islands that form São Tomé and Príncipe, on the Equator, off the coast of West Africa, in the Bight of Biafra. *Capital:* São Tomé (from 1485). *Other names:* Saint Thomas.

History: In 1470 the island of São Tomé was discovered by the Portuguese (cf. Príncipe). In 1485 it became a donataria (i.e. a parcel of land given by the Portuguese Crown to a family of standing). In 1522, however, the Crown took possession of the island. Between 1580 and 1656 Spain ruled Portugal, but the administration in São Tomé (as in Príncipe) remained unchanged. From 1641 to 1644 the Dutch occupied São Tomé (but not Príncipe), but the Portuguese administration continued. In 1753 São Tomé joined with Príncipe to form the Portuguese Possessions of São Tomé and Príncipe.

Rulers: 1470–1485 none. *Capitães-Mores (plural of Capitão-Mor, or Captain-Major):* 1485–1490 João de Paiva; 1490–1493 João Pereira; 1493–1499 Álvaro Souto-Maior; 1499–ca. 1510 Fernão de Melo; ca. 1510–(?) [unknown]; (?)–ca. 1516 [unknown]; ca. 1516–ca. 1517 Diogo de Alcáçova; ca. 1517–1522 João de Melo; 1522–(?) Vasco Estevens; (?)–1531 [unknown]; 1531–ca. 1535 Henrique Pereira; ca. 1535–1541 [unknown]; 1541–1545 Diogo Pereira; 1545–1546 [unknown; 1546–ca. 1554 Francisco de Paiva; ca. 1554–ca. 1558 [unknown]; ca. 1558–(?) Pedro Botelho; (?)–1560 [unknown]; 1560–1564 Cristóvão de Sousa; 1564–1569 Francisco de Gouveia; 1569–1571 Francisco Teles; 1571–1575 Diogo Salema; 1575–ca. 1582 Antonio Maciel; ca. 1582–ca. 1584 [unknown]; ca. 1584–1586 Francisco de Figueiredo. *Governors:* 1586–1587 Francisco de Figueiredo; 1587–1591 Miguel de Moura; 1591–1592 Duarte da Silva; 1592–1593 Francisco de Vila Nova (acting); 1593–1597 Fernando de Meneses; 1597–ca. 1598 Vasco de Carvalho; ca. 1598–1601 João da Cunha (acting); 1601–1604 Antonio Monteiro (acting); 1604–(?) Pedro de Andrade; (?)–1609 João da Cunha (acting); 1609–1609 Fernando de Noronha; 1609–1609 João da Cunha (acting); 1609–1611 Constantino Távares; 1611–1611 João da Cunha (acting); 1611–1611 Francisco Teles de Meneses;

1611–1613 Luis de Abreu; 1613–1614 Feliciano Carvalho; 1614–1616 Luis de Abreu; 1616–1620 Miguel Baharem; 1620–1621 Pedro da Cunha; 1621–1623 Félix Pereira; 1623–1627 Jerónimo de Melo Fernando; 1627–1628 André Maracote; 1628–1632 Lourenço de Távora (acting); 1632–1632 Francisco Barreto de Meneses; 1632–1636 Lourenço de Távora (acting); 1636–1636 Antonio de Carvalho; 1636–1640 Lourenço de Távora (acting); 1640–1640 Manuel Carneiro; 1640–1641 Miguel de Melo e Albuquerque (acting); 1641–1642 Paulo da Ponte (acting); 1642–ca. 1650 Lourenço de Távora; ca. 1650–1656 [unknown]; 1656–ca. 1657 Cristóvão do Rego; ca. 1657–ca. 1661 [unknown]; ca. 1661–(?) Pedro da Silva; (?)–1669 [unknown]; 1669–1671 Paulo de Noronha; 1671–1673 ruled by a Chamber Senate; 1673–1677 Julião de Campos Barreto; 1677–1680 Bernardim Freire de Andrade; 1680–1683 Jacinto de Figueiredo e Abreu; 1683–1686 João da Cunha (acting); 1686–1686 Antonio Lemos; 1686–1689 Bento de Sousa Lima; 1689–1693 Antonio Lacerda; 1693–1694 Antonio de Barredo; 1694–1695 [unknown]; 1695–1696 José Sodré; 1696–1697 João Matos; 1697–1702 Manuel da Câmara; 1702–1709 José do Castro; 1709–1710 Vicente Pinheiro; 1710–1715 ruled by a junta; 1715–1716 Bartolomeu Ponte; 1716–1717 ruled by a Chamber Senate; 1717–1720 Antonio Mendonça; 1720–1722 ruled by a junta; 1722–1727 José da Câmara; 1727–1734 Serafim Sarmento; 1734–1736 Lopo Coutinho; 1736–1741 José Souto-Maior; 1741–1741 Antonio de Castelo Branco; 1741–1744 ruled by a Chamber Senate; 1744–1744 Francisco de Conceição; 1744–1745 Francisco de Alva Brandão (acting); 1745–1747 ruled by a Chamber Senate; 1747–1748 Francisco das Chagas; 1748–1751 ruled by a Chamber Senate; 1751–1751 Antonio Neves; 1751–1753 ruled by a Chamber Senate.

São Tomé and Príncipe. 1753– . *Location:* two principal islands, São Tomé and Príncipe, in the Bight of Biafra, off the coast of West Africa. *Capital:* São Tomé (capital of the whole country, and also of the island of São Tomé; the capital city of the island of Príncipe is Santo Antonio). *Other names:* República Democrática de São Tomé e Príncipe, or the Democratic Republic of São Tomé and Príncipe (from 1975).

History: In 1753 the Portuguese Crown possession of São Tomé and the Portuguese donataria of Príncipe merged into one government, the Portuguese Possessions of São Tomé and Príncipe. On 11 June 1951 the country became an overseas province of Portugal. In 1973, largely as the result of agitation by the MLSTP (Movement for the Liberation of São Tomé and Príncipe) led by Dr. Manuel Pinto da Costa (who had founded it the year before), a local government was set up, recognized by the Organization of African Unity. A certain amount of autonomy was then granted to the country by Portugal. On 21 Dec. 1974, following a coup in Portugal itself, São Tomé and Príncipe achieved real autonomy, and a transitional government was set up. On 12 July 1975 the country achieved full independence as the Democratic Republic of São Tomé and Príncipe. Miguel Trovoada, the prime minister, was arrested and imprisoned in 1979, and in 1981 exiled to Lisbon. Da Costa survived numerous coup and assassination attempts, but in the first multi-party elections, in 1991, Trovoada, who had recently returned to São Tomé from exile, at the head of the new Party of Democratic Convergence, became the new president (da Costa refused to be a candidate in a race in which he might be beaten). In 1995 Príncipe declared itself to be an autonomous region, but ten years later the country is still known as São Tomé and Príncipe

Governors: 1753–1755 ruled by a Chamber Senate; 1755–1755 Lopo Coutinho; 1755–1758 ruled by a Chamber Senate; 1758–1761 Luis da Mota e Melo; 1761–1767 ruled by a Chamber Senate; 1767–1768 Lourenço Palha; 1768–1770 ruled by a Chamber Senate; 1770–1778 Vicente Ferreira; 1778–1782 João de Azambuja; 1782–1788 Cristóvão de Sá; 1788–1797 João Leote; 1797–1797 Inacio Coutinho; 1797–1797 Manuel de Carvalho; 1797–1798 Varela Borca; 1798–1799 Manuel da Mota; 1799–1799 Francisco de Vide; 1799–1802 João Baptista da Silva; 1802–1805 Gabriel do Castro; 1805–1817 Luis Lisboa; 1817–1824 Felipe de Freitas; 1824–1830 João de Brito; 1830–1834 Joaquim da Fonseca; 1834–1836 Provisional Government in power; 1836–1837 Fernando de Noronha (acting); 1837–1838 Leandro da Costa; 1838–1839 José de Urbanski; 1839–1843 José da Costa; 1843–2 March 1843 Leandro da Costa; 2 March 1843–1 May 1846 José Marquês; 1 May 1846–30 Sept. 1847 ruled by a Chamber Senate; 30 Sept. 1847–20 Nov. 1847 Carlos de Morais e Almeida; 20 Nov. 1847–20 July 1848 ruled by a Chamber Senate; 20 July 1848–12 Dec. 1849 José Pessôa; 12 Dec. 1849–9

March 1851 Leandro da Costa; 9 March 1851–20 March 1853 José Marquês; 20 March 1853–28 July 1855 Francisco da Pina Rolo; 28 July 1855–March 1857 Adrião Passálaqua; March 1857–15 Jan. 1858 ruled by a Chamber Senate; 15 Jan. 1858–May 1858 Francisco Correia; May 1858–1859 ruled by a Chamber Senate; 1859–21 Nov. 1860 Luis Pereira e Horta; 21 Nov. 1860–8 July 1862 José de Melo; 8 July 1862–17 Nov. 1862 ruled by a Chamber Senate; 17 Nov. 1862–30 March 1863 José da Costa Moura; 30 March 1863–8 Jan. 1864 João Baptista Brunachy; 8 Jan. 1864–2 Aug. 1865 Estanislau de Assunção e Almeida; 2 Aug. 1865–30 July 1867 João Baptista Brunachy; 30 July 1867–30 Sept. 1867 Antonio da Fonseca; 30 Sept. 1867–30 May 1869 Estanislau de Assunção e Almeida; 30 May 1869–7 Oct. 1872 Pedro Lopes; 7 Oct. 1872–28 Oct. 1873 João de Carvalho; 28 Oct. 1873–1 Nov. 1876 Gregorio Ribeiro; 1 Nov. 1876–28 Sept. 1879 Manuel de Assunção e Almeida; 28 Sept. 1879–28 Nov. 1879 Francisco Ferreira do Amaral; 28 Nov. 1879–3 Jan. 1880 Custódio de Borja (acting); 3 Jan. 1880–30 Dec. 1881 Vicente de Melo e Almada; 30 Dec. 1881–26 Jan. 1882 Augusto Leão (acting); 26 Jan. 1882–24 May 1884 Francisco da Silva; 24 May 1884–8 Aug. 1885 Custódio de Borja; 8 Aug. 1885–19 Sept. 1885 Augusto Cabral (acting); 19 Sept. 1885–25 Sept. 1885 Custódio de Borja; 25 Sept. 1885–25 Feb. 1886 Augusto Cabral (acting); 25 Feb. 1886–25 Aug. 1886 Custódio de Borja; 25 Aug. 1886–9 March 1890 Augusto Sarmento; 9 March 1890–26 June 1891 Firmeno da Costa; 26 June 1891–8 Dec. 1894 Francisco de Miranda; 8 Dec. 1894–8 April 1895 Jaime Godins (acting); 8 April 1895–5 April 1897 Cipriano Jardim; 5 April 1897–5 April 1899 Joaquim da Graça Correia e Lança; 5 April 1899–3 Jan. 1901 Amancio Cabral; 3 Jan. 1901–8 May 1901 Francisco Vieira (acting); 8 May 1901–8 Oct. 1902 Joaquim de Brito; 8 Oct. 1902–7 June 1903 João Guimarães; 7 June 1903–14 Dec. 1903 João Ferreira; 14 Dec. 1903–13 April 1907 Francisco de Paula Cid; 13 April 1907–24 June 1907 Vitor Lemos e Melo (acting); 24 June 1907–24 Oct. 1908 Pedro Berquó; 24 Oct. 1908–13 March 1909 Vitor Lemos e Melo (acting); 13 March 1909–13 June 1910 José da Fonseca; 13 June 1910–21 July 1910 Jaime do Rego; 21 July 1910–7 Aug. 1910 Henrique de Oliveira (acting); 7 Aug. 1910–11 Nov. 1910 Fernando de Carvalho; 12 Nov. 1910–28 Nov. 1910 Carlos Pimentel e Melo (acting); 28

Nov. 1910–14 June 1911 Antonio Guedes; 14 June 1911–24 Dec. 1911 Jaime do Rego; 24 Dec. 1911–13 May 1913 Mariano Martins; 13 May 1913–31 May 1915 Pedro Machado. 31 May 1915–6 June 1915 José de Sousa e Faroo; 6 June 1915–28 July 1918 Rafael Oliveira (acting); 28 July 1918–11 June 1919 João Ferreira; 11 June 1919–25 Sept. 1920 Avelino Leite; 25 Sept. 1920–22 Oct. 1920 José Velez (acting); 22 Oct. 1920–2 July 1921 Eduardo de Lemos (acting); 2 July 1921–23 Jan. 1924 Antonio Pereira; 23 Jan. 1924–8 July 1926 Eugénio Branco; 8 July 1926–31 Aug. 1928 José Rato; 31 Aug. 1928–30 Jan. 1929 Sebastião Barbosa (acting); 30 Jan. 1929–31 Oct. 1929 Francisco Penteado; 31 Oct. 1929–17 Dec. 1933 Luis Fernandes; 17 Dec. 1933–8 May 1941 Ricardo Vaz Monteiro; 8 May 1941–5 April 1945 Amadeu de Figueiredo; 5 April 1945–July 1948 Carlos Gorgulho; July 1948–8 Oct. 1950 Afonso de Sousa; 8 Oct. 1950–28 June 1952 Mario Castro (acting); 28 June 1952–18 April 1953 Guilherme Pinto; 18 April 1953–19 May 1953 Fernando Rodrigues (acting); 19 May 1953–July 1953 Afonso de Sousa (acting); July 1953–Aug. 1954 Francisco Barata; Aug. 1954–15 June 1955 Luis Faria; 15 June 1955–5 Dec. 1956 José Machado (acting); 5 Dec. 1956–13 Oct. 1957 Octavio Gonçalves; 13 Oct. 1957–Aug. 1963 Manuel Amaral; Aug. 1963–30 Oct. 1963 Alberto Campos (acting); 30 Oct. 1963–1972 Antonio Sebastião. *High Commissioners:* 1973–21 Dec. 1974 João Gonçalves; 21 Dec. 1974–12 July 1975 Pires Veloso. *Presidents:* 12 July 1975–3 April 1991 Manuel Pinto da Costa; 3 April 1991–3 Sept. 2001 Miguel Trovoada; 3 Sept. 2001–Fradique de Menesez. *Leaders of MLSTP:* 1973–21 Dec. 1974 Manuel Pinto da Costa. *Prime Ministers:* 21 Dec. 1974–12 July 1975 Leonel d'Alva; 12 July 1975–Oct. 1979 Miguel Trovoada; 8 Jan. 1988–8 Feb. 1991 Celestino Rocha da Costa; 8 Feb. 1991–16 May 1992 Daniel Lima dos Santos Daio; 16 May 1992–2 July 1994 Norberto José d'Alva Costa Alegre; 7 July 1994–25 Oct. 1994 Evaristo Carvalho; 25 Oct. 1994–29 Dec. 1995 Carlos de Graça; 29 Dec. 1995–19 Nov. 1996 Armindo Vaz de Almeida; 19 Nov. 1996–5 Jan. 1999 Raul Bragança; 5 Jan. 1999–26 March 2002 Guilhermo Posser da Costa; 26 March 2002–3 Oct. 2002 Gabriel Costa; 3 Oct. 2002–15 Sept. 2004 María das Neves; 15 Sept. 2004–8 June 2005 Damião Vaz d'Almeida; 8 June 2005–María do Carmo Silveira. *Note:* In times of no Prime Minister, the President held that office.

São Vicente see **Cape Verde**

Sarili's Country see **Kreli's Country**

Say see **Burkina Faso**

Séchelles see **Seychelles**

Sefawa see **Kanem**

Segu. ca. 1600–10 March 1861. *Location:* in Mali. *Capital:* Segu-koro (from 1750); Ngoi (1736–1750); Segu-koro (ca. 1600–1736). *Other names:* Ségou.

History: Segu and Kaarta were the two Bambara states founded in the early 17th century by two brothers — Barama-Ngolo and Nya Ngolo (the latter founding Kaarta). Segu expanded, and in 1861 was swallowed up in the Tukolor Empire. From 1861 to 1890 the dynasty continued to rule in exile, and in 1890 Mari, the last ruler, was killed by the French.

Kings: ca. 1600–1620 Barama-Ngolo; 1620–1640 Soma; 1640–1660 Fa Sine; 1660–1710 Mamari Biton; 1710–1711 Bakari; 1711–1736 De-Koro; 1736–1740 Tonmassa Dembele (also known as Tonmansa); 1740–1744 Kanouba-Nyouma Bari; 1744–1748 Kafadyougou; 1748–1750 a period of anarchy; 1750–1787 Ngolo Dyara; 1787–1808 Man-nsor; 1808–1827 Da Kaba; 1827–1839 Tye-Folo; 1839–1840 Nyene-Mba I; 1840–1843 a period of anarchy; 1843–1849 Ben; 1849–1851 Kon-Maran; 1851–1854 Demba; 1854–1856 Touro-Koro Mari; 1856–10 March 1861 Ali; 13 April 1861–1870 Kege Mari; 1878 Nyene-Mba II; 1878–1878 Mamuru; 1878–1883 Massatana; 1883–1887 Karanoko; 1887–29 May 1890 Mari Dyara.

Seguia El-Hamra see **Western Sahara**

Séké see **Gabon**

Sekonyela's Land. 1822–Sept. 1853. *Location:* the Caledon River Valley, South Africa. *Capital:* Joalaboholo. *Other names:* Sikonyela's Land; Batlokoa Lands.

History: As a result of Zulu king Chaka's movements in the early 1820s all the tribes in the area were pushed out and forced to move on. This caused havoc in South Africa and was called the "mfecane" or "hammering." The kingdom of Basutoland was formed as a result of this mfecane, as was the area of land ruled by Sekonyela, son of King Mokotjo of the Batlokoa ("the people of the Wild Cat") and his Mantateesi. Deadly rival to Moshoeshoe of Basutoland, Sekonyela was driven out by Moshoeshoe and finally granted land in the Herschel District of Cape Colony by Sir George Clerk of the British government. In 1853 this land was swallowed up into the administration of the Cape.

Kings: 1822–July 1856 Sekonyela; July 1856–1881 Lelingoanna and Lehana (jointly).

Seleka see **Barolongland**

Selvagens see **Madeira**

Senaar see **Funj Sultanate**

Senegal. 1626– . *Location:* North West Africa. *Capital:* Dakar (from 1904); Saint Louis (1817–1904); Freetown (in Sierra Leone. This was the British capital which administered Senegal from 1809 to 1817); Saint Louis (1693–1809); no capital (1693–1693); Saint Louis (1659–1693); no fixed central administrative capital before 1659). *Other names:* République Sénégalaise, or République du Sénégal (from 1958).

History: The first explorers to the area of the mouth of the Senegal River were the Portuguese, but the French established settlements here in 1626, under the command of the Compagnie Normande. These settlements were not permanent, neither were those under its successor company, the Compagnie du Cap Vert et du Sénégal, which took over the area in 1658. On 28 May 1664 the ownership changed hands once again, to Colbert's Compagnie des Indes Occidentales. On 9 April 1672 the Compagnie du Sénégal took it over, and the settlements changed hands again in 1682, this time to the Compagnie d'Afrique. On 12 Sept. 1684 the Compagnie du Guinée took it over. In January 1693 the British took the area for the first time, but kept it only until July that year, when the French took it back and the Compagnie du Guinée resumed control. In March 1696 the Royal Company of Senegal took it over, and it became a colony. On 15 Dec. 1718 the Compagnie des Indes Orientales took it over and continued to run it as a colony. On 30 April 1758 the British took over all the French possessions in the Senegal area, including the island of Gorée, an integral part of Senegal. On 10 Feb. 1763 the British returned Gorée (and only Gorée) to the

French, but continued to run Senegal under the administration of the Royal African Company. On 25 May 1765 the coastal and mainland areas of Senegal under British control merged with the British posts on the Gambia River to form the first British Crown colony in Africa — Senegambia. Senegal thus became a territory of this Crown colony. Saint Louis was the capital of Senegambia. On 30 Jan. 1779 the French took back their Senegalese possessions from the British (and the Gambia Settlements as well on 11 Feb. 1779) and, incorporating Gorée into the Senegalese settlements, created the Térritoire du Sénégal. The British colony of Senegambia officially came to an end at the Treaty of Paris in 1783, by which Britain regained the Gambia Settlements, and France legally secured her Senegalese possessions. On 13 July 1809 the French again lost all their Senegalese possessions to the British. On 25 Jan. 1817 the French got them back, and this brought an end to the incessant power struggle between France and Britain in this area. Senegal now became a French colony. The French expanded into the hinterland especially during and after the administration of Governor Faidherbe. From 1854 to 1859 Gorée was detached and made a separate colony called Gorée and Dependencies, the dependencies including the Gabon settlements. In 1895 Senegal became the administrative base for French West Africa and until 1902 was ruled by the Governor-General of that Federation. On 13 Feb. 1904, due to the large amount of hinterland that it had taken as a protectorate, the country became known as Senegal Colony and Protectorate, and the capital was moved from Saint Louis to Dakar. From 1907 to 1908 Senegal was again ruled direct by French West Africa. On 13 Oct. 1946 Senegal became an overseas territory of France. On 25 Nov. 1958 it became the autonomous republic of Senegal, in the French Community, on the way to independence. On 17 Jan. 1959 (effective as from 4 April 1959) Senegal and its neighbor, the autonomous republic of the Sudanese Republic, joined to form the Mali Federation, an autonomous body still within the French Community, with Dakar as its capital. The Senegalese leaders, Léopold Senghor and Mamadou Dia, were head of the Federal Assembly and vice-president respectively of the Mali Federation. On 20 June 1960 the Mali Federation as a unit became independent of France, and the two individual components also became independent. On 20 Aug. 1960 Senegal seceded from the Union, and the two countries went their separate ways, one as the Sudanese Republic (later to become Mali), and the other as la République du Sénégal. The Republic of Senegal was formally proclaimed on 5 Sept. 1960. The leader of Senegal for many years was the famous poet and scholar Léopold Senghor who was, rather surprisingly, a repressive dictator. The country suffered from a long drought in the late 1960s and early 1970s. On 1 Feb. 1982 Senegal and Gambia joined politically to form the Senegambia Confederation, although each country, of course, retained its own identity. The Senegambia idea came to an amicable end in Sept. 1989. In the 1990s and early 2000s the region of Casamance, almost separated geographically from the rest of Senegal by Gambia, has been trying to secede.

Compagnie Normande Governors: 1626–1631 Thomas Lambert; 1631–1641 Jacques Fuméchon; 1641–1648 Jean Caullier; 1649–1650 M. de Soussy; 1651–1658 M. Mésineau. *Compagnie du Cap Vert et du Sénégal Governors:* 1658–1661 M. Raguenet; 1661–28 May 1664 M. de Boulay. *Colbert's West India Company Governors:* 28 May 1664–1668 M. Jacquet; 1668–9 April 1672 M. de Richemont. *Compagnie du Sénégal Governors:* 1672–1673 M. de Richemont (acting). *Compagnie du Sénégal Directors:* 1674–1682 Jacques Fuméchon. *Compagnie d'Afrique Directors:* 1682–12 Sept. 1684 Denis Basset. *Compagnie du Guinée Directors:* 12 Sept. 1684–1689 Louis Moreau de Chambonneau; 1689–1690 Michel Jajolet de la Courbe; 1690–Jan. 1693 Louis Moreau de Chambonneau. *British Governors:* Jan. 1693–July 1693 none. *Compagnie du Guinée Directors:* July 1693–March 1696 Jean Bourguignon. *Royal Company of Senegal Directors:* March 1696–4 April 1697 Jean Bourguignon (acting); 4 April 1697–1702 André Bruë; 1702–1706 Joseph LeMaître; 1706–1710 Michel Jajolet de la Courbe; 1710–1711 Guillaume de Mustellier; 1711–2 May 1713 Pierre de Richebourg; 2 May 1713–20 April 1714 [unknown]; 20 April 1714–15 Dec. 1718 André Bruë. *Compagnie des Indes Directors:* 15 Dec. 1718–May 1720 André Bruë; May 1720–April 1723 Nicolas Després de Saint-Robert; April 1723–1725 Julien Dubellay; 1725–1726 Nicolas Després de Saint-Robert; 1726–1726 Arnaud Plumet; 1726–1733 Jean Levens de la Roquette; 1733–7 March 1733 M. Lejuge; 7 March 1733–1736 Sebastien De-

vaulx (acting); 1736–1738 Sebastien Devaulx; 1738–1746 Pierre David; 1746–30 April 1758 Jean-Baptiste Estoupan de la Bruë. *British Governors:* 30 April 1758–10 Feb. 1763 Richard Worge. *British Royal African Company Governors:* 10 Feb. 1763–25 May 1765 John Barnes. *Governors of Senegambia Colony:* 25 May 1765–30 Jan. 1779 these men ruled Senegal direct. See that entry for list of governors. *French Commandants:* 30 Jan. 1779–31 Jan. 1779 Charles Boucher (acting); 31 Jan. 1779–March 1779 Duc de Lauzun; March 1779–7 March 1781 Jacques-Joseph Eyriès; 7 March 1781–July 1782 J.B. Bertrand (acting); July 1782–Feb. 1784 Anne-Guilin Dumontêt; Feb. 1784–Feb. 1786 Louis Le Gardeur de Repentigny; Feb. 1786–June 1786 Stanislas de Boufflers; June 1786–Feb. 1787 François Blanchot de Verly (acting); Feb. 1787–Dec. 1787 Stanislas de Boufflers; Dec. 1787–1790 François Blanchot de Verly; 1790–May 1792 Charles Boucher (acting); May 1792–Jan. 1801 François Blanchot de Verly; Jan. 1801–2 July 1801 M. de Charbonnes (acting); 2 July 1801–27 Oct. 1802 Louis Laserre; 27 Oct. 1802–Sept. 1807 François Blanchot de Verly; Sept. 1807–13 July 1809 Pierre Levasseur. *British Governors:* 13 July 1809–1811 Charles Maxwell; 1811–1814 Charles Macarthy; 1814–19 April 1816 Thomas Brereton; 19 April 1816–25 Jan. 1817 [unknown] (acting). *French Commandants:* 25 Jan. 1817–17 June 1817 [unknown] (acting); 17 June 1817–Dec. 1817 Julien Schmaltz; Dec. 1817–13 March 1819 Capt. Fleuriau (acting); 13 March 1819–14 Aug. 1820 Julien Schmaltz; 14 Aug. 1820–1 March 1821 Louis Lecoupé de Montereau; 1 March 1821–18 May 1827 Jacques-François Roger; 18 May 1827–7 Jan. 1828 M. Gerbidon (acting). *French Governors:* 7 Jan. 1828–11 May 1829 Jean Guillaume Jubelin; 11 May 1829–24 May 1831 Pierre Brou; 24 May 1831–18 Oct. 1833 Thomas Renault de Saint-Germain; 18 Oct. 1833–13 Nov. 1833 M. Cadest (acting); 13 Nov. 1833–10 May 1834 Germain Quernel; 10 May 1834–1 July 1836 Louis Pujol; 1 July 1836–Dec. 1836 Louis Malavois; Dec. 1836–13 Sept. 1837 Louis Guillet (acting); 13 Sept. 1837–12 April 1839 Julien Soret; 12 April 1839–19 May 1841 Guillaume Charmasson de Puy-Laval; 19 May 1841–7 May 1842 Jean-Baptiste Montagniès de la Roque; 7 May 1842–5 Feb. 1843 Édouard Pageot des Noutières; 5 Feb. 1843–8 Dec. 1843 Louis Bouët-Willaumez; 8 Dec. 1843–July 1844 M. Laborel (acting); July 1844–11 Dec. 1845 Pierre

Thomas (acting); 11 Dec. 1845–20 March 1846 François Ollivier; 20 March 1846–30 Aug. 1846 M. Hoube (acting); 30 Aug. 1846–24 Aug. 1847 Ernest Bourdon de Grammont; 24 Aug. 1847–7 Sept. 1847 M. Caille (acting); 7 Sept. 1847–Nov. 1847 Léandre Berlin-Duchâteau (acting); Nov. 1847–1848 Auguste Baudin; 1848–1848 Léandre Berlin-Duchâteau (acting); 1848–11 Oct. 1850 Auguste Baudin; 11 Oct. 1850–April 1853 Auguste Prôtet; April 1853–31 Jan. 1854 André-César Vérand (acting); 31 Jan. 1854–16 Dec. 1854 Auguste Prôtet; 16 Dec. 1854–4 Sept. 1858 Louis Faidherbe; 4 Sept. 1858–12 Feb. 1859 A. Robin (acting); 12 Feb. 1859–1 June 1861 Louis Faidherbe; 1 June 1861–1 Dec. 1861 Léopold Stéphan (acting); 1 Dec. 1861–13 May 1863 Jean-Bernard Jauréguiberry; 13 May 1863–14 July 1863 Jean Pinet-Laprade (acting); 14 July 1863–1 May 1865 Louis Faidherbe; 1 May 1865–12 Dec. 1865 Jean Pinet-Laprade (acting); 12 Dec. 1865–18 Aug. 1869 Jean Pinet-Laprade; 18 Aug. 1869–17 Oct. 1869 Ferdinand Tredos (acting); 17 Oct. 1869–18 June 1876 François Victorien Valière; 18 June 1876–April 1880 Col. Louis Brière de l'Isle; April 1880–4 Aug. 1881 Louis de Lanneau; 4 Aug. 1881–Oct. 1881 Marie-Auguste Deville de Perrière (acting); Oct. 1881–28 June 1882 Henri Canard; 28 June 1882–15 Nov. 1882 Aristide-Marie Villon; 15 Nov. 1882–28 June 1883 René Servatius; 28 June 1883–25 July 1883 Adolphe Le Boucher (acting); 25 July 1883–15 April 1884 Henry Bordiaux (acting); 15 April 1884–14 April 1886 Alphonse Seignac-Lesseps; 14 April 1886–29 April 1888 Jules Genouille; 29 April 1888–22 Sept. 1890 Léon Clément-Thomas; 22 Sept. 1890–19 May 1895 Henri de la Mothe; 19 May 1895–28 June 1895 Louis Mouttet (acting); 28 June 1895–28 Sept. 1895 Jean-Baptiste Barthélemy Chaudié; 28 Sept. 1895–15 March 1902 the governor of Senegal was also the governor-general of French West Africa (see that entry for list of governor-generals); 15 March 1902–11 Nov. 1902 Ernest Roume (governor-general of French West Africa and acting governor of Senegal). *Lieutenant-Governors:* 11 Nov. 1902–26 Aug. 1907 Lucien Guy; 26 Aug. 1907–15 Dec. 1907 Joost Van Vollenhouven (acting); 15 Dec. 1907–17 Dec. 1908 again Senegal was ruled direct by French West Africa, and the governor-general of French West Africa also filled the role of acting lieutenant-governor of Senegal (see French West Africa for list of governors-general throughout this period); 17 Dec. 1908–23 Feb. 1909 Maurice Gourbeil; 23 Feb. 1909–2 May 1909 Antoine Gaudart (acting); 2 May 1909–7 July 1909 Jean Peuvergne; 7 July 1909–13 Nov. 1909 Antoine Gaudart (acting); 13 Nov. 1909–5 Feb. 1911 Jean Peuvergne; 5 Feb. 1911–13 May 1914 Henri Core; 13 May 1914–Dec. 1916 Raphaël Antonetti; Dec. 1916–20 March 1917 [unknown] (acting); 20 March 1917–23 Sept. 1920 Fernand Lévecque; 23 Sept. 1920–17 Sept. 1921 Théophile Pascal (acting); 17 Sept. 1921–24 July 1925 Pierre Didelot; 24 July 1925–23 May 1926 Théodore Maillet (acting); 23 May 1926–23 Oct. 1926 Joseph Cadier (acting); 23 Oct. 1926–12 March 1929 Léonce Jore; 12 March 1929–4 July 1930 Maurice Beurnier; 4 July 1930–15 Aug. 1931 Théodore Maillet; 15 Aug. 1931–14 Oct 1931 Benoît-Louis Rebonne; 14 Oct. 1931–22 May 1933 Maurice Beurnier; 22 May 1933–24 Dec. 1933 Léon Solomiac (acting); 24 Dec. 1933–Dec. 1936 Maurice Beurnier. *French Governors:* Dec. 1936–25 Oct. 1938 Louis Lefebvre; 25 Oct. 1938–30 Dec. 1940 Georges Parisot; 1 Jan. 1941–22 Dec. 1942 Georges Rey; 22 Dec. 1942–2 Dec. 1943 Hubert Deschamps; 2 Dec. 1943–June 1945 Charles Dagain; June 1945–April 1946 Pierre Maestracci; April 1946–May 1947 Oswald Durand; 20 May 1947–19 Oct. 1950 Laurent Wiltord; 19 Oct. 1950–25 April 1952 Victor Bailly; 25 April 1952–1954 Lucien Geay; 1954–19 Feb. 1954 Daniel Goujon; 19 Feb. 1954–31 Oct. 1955 Maxime Jourdan; 31 Oct. 1955–10 Feb. 1957 Don-Jean Colombani; 10 Feb. 1957–25 Nov. 1958 Pierre Lami. *French High Commissioners:* 25 Nov. 1958–20 June 1960 Pierre Lami. *Presidents of Council:* 25 Nov. 1958–4 April 1959 Mamadou Dia. *Rulers:* 4 April 1959–20 Aug. 1960 Mamadou Dia. *Presidents:* 20 Aug. 1960–6 Sept. 1960 Léopold Senghor (interim); 6 Sept. 1960–31 Dec. 1980 Léopold Senghor; 1 Jan. 1981–1 April 2000 Abdou Diouf; 1 April 2000–Abdulaye Wade. *Prime Ministers:* 20 Aug. 1960–17 Dec. 1962 Mamadou Dia; 28 Feb. 1970–31 Dec. 1980 Abdou Diouf; 1 Jan. 1981–3 April 1983 Habib Thiam; 3 April 1983–29 April 1983 Moustapha Niasse (interim); 8 April 1991–3 July 1998 Habib Thiam; 3 July 1998–2 April 2000 Mamadou Lamine Loum; 2 April 2000–3 March 2001 Moustapha Niasse; 3 March 2001–4 Nov. 2002 Madior Boye; 4 Nov. 2002–21 April 2004 Idrissa Seck; 21 April 2004–Macky Sall. *Note:* In times of no Prime Minister, the President held that office.

Senegambia and Niger see **Mali**

Senegambia Colony. 25 May 1765–11 Feb. 1779. *Location:* Senegal minus Gorée, along with the British posts in the Gambia. *Capital:* Saint Louis (overall headquarters, as well as the local headquarters for Senegal); James Island (local Gambia headquarters). *Other names:* Senegambia Province.

History: In 1765 the Royal African Company posts in Senegal were merged with those on the Gambia River (see Fort James), and all these areas were reconstituted as the Province of Senegambia, the first British Crown colony in Africa (Gambia passing to the Crown effectively in April 1766). On 30 Jan. 1779 the French retook their former Senegalese possessions and on 11 Feb. 1779 took the Gambia posts which, soon after this action were abandoned. This marked the end of Senegambia as a British colony, although on paper the colony lasted until the Treaty of Paris on 3 Sept. 1783, when the Gambia possessions were returned to Britain (although Britain did not occupy them until 1816. See Gambia). As far as the Senegalese part of Senegambia went, it was ruled as a military territory by the French until 13 July 1809, when the French lost everything in Senegal to the British again (see Senegal).

Governors: 25 May 1765–Nov. 1775 Charles O'Hara; Nov. 1775–8 April 1777 Matthias MacNamara; 8 April 1777–18 Aug. 1778 John Clarke; 18 Aug. 1778–11 Feb. 1779 William Lacy (never assumed office); 18 Aug. 1778–11 Feb. 1779 George Fall (acting). *Gambia Superintendents of Trade:* 25 May 1765–April 1766 Joseph Debat. *Lieutenant-Governors of Gambia:* April 1766–24 Jan. 1774 Joseph Debat; 24 Jan. 1774–Aug. 1774 William Myres; Aug. 1774–Nov. 1775 Matthias MacNamara; Nov. 1775–Dec. 1775 Thomas Sharpless (acting); Dec. 1775–8 Aug. 1776 Joseph Wall; 8 Aug. 1776–1776 George Fall (acting); 1776–18 Aug. 1778 William Lacy (acting); 18 Aug. 1778–11 Feb. 1779 George Fall (acting).

Senegambia Confederation. 1 Feb. 1982–30 Sept. 1989. *Location:* Senegal and Gambia combined. *Capital:* Dakar. *Other names:* La Confédération du Sénégambie; Federation of Senegambia; Senegambia; Sénégambie.

History: On 14 Nov. and 17 Dec. 1981 the Republic of Senegal and the Republic of the Gambia signed long-planned agreements which came into effect on 1 Feb. 1982, forming the two countries into a political confederation, adopting joint defense and monetary policies, but retaining individual sovereignty. Although the two countries speak a different language, the peoples are closely related. In 1989 the confederation dissolved amicably.

Presidents: 1 Feb. 1982–Sept. 1989 Abdou Diouf. *Vice-Presidents:* 1 Feb. 1982–30 Sept. 1989 Sir Dawda Jawara.

Sennaar see **Funj Sultanate**

Serra Leão see **Sierra Leone**

Seychelles. 1744– . *Location:* an archipelago of 115 islands, northeast of Madagascar, in the Indian Ocean. Mahé is the largest island, and the others include: Praslin, Silhouette, Frigate, Bird, Denis, La Digue, Félicité, East Sister, West Sister, Curieuse, Aride, North Island, St. Anne, and Cerf. The Republic of the Seychelles as we know it today also includes, as a fundamental part of the state, the following detached island groups: the Farquhar and Des Roches Islands, the Amirante Islands, the Aldabra Islands, the Cosmoledo Islands, Assumption Island, Coetivy, and Astove. *Capital:* Victoria (from 1814. This city is on Mahé Island, and was named for Queen Victoria); Mahé (1770–1814); no capital before 1770. *Other names:* Séchelles, or Îles de Séchelles; Île de Labourdonnais, or Îles de Labourdonnais (1744–1756).

History: These islands were on a Dutch map of 1502, but the first recorded landings took place here in 1609, by the English East India Company. In 1742 and 1744 Bertrand-François Mahé, Comte de la Bourdonnais, then French governor of Île de France (see Mauritius) sent Capt. Lazare Picault to explore these islands. Until then they had been a favorite hiding place for pirates in the area (for example, see Libertalia). Picault finally landed on Mahé Island (which he named), and he named the group after his superior. In 1756 the French staked a serious claim to the islands and named them the Séchelles. In 1770 the group became a French colony. In 1794 the British captured the colony and occupied it, but the French administration remained in place, under the British flag, until 1810, when the British finally annexed it and it became a British colony called the Seychelles, dependant on Mauritius, and ruled from Mauritius through a local man in the Seychelles. On 30 May 1814 it was officially ceded to Britain, who administered it and Mauritius as a single colony until 1872, when they were divided. In Aug. 1903 the Seychelles became a separate British Crown Colony. In 1908 Coetivy was transferred from Mauritius, and in 1922 so were the Farquhar Islands. In 1965 the governor of the Seychelles also became the High Commissioner for the British Indian Ocean Territory (BIOT), a group of islands farther east in the Indian Ocean, to which Seychelles lost some islands. In 1967 and 1970 certain measures of self-rule were granted to the Seychelles, and on 1 Oct. 1975 the country became self-governing. On 29 June 1976 it won independence and became the Republic of the Seychelles, still within the British Commonwealth. At that point the Seychelles also got back all of the islands they had lost to the BIOT in 1965. In 1977 a coup brought France-Albert René to power. Another attempted coup, in 1981, led by Mike Hoare out of South Africa, failed.

Rulers: 1744–1770 none. *Commandants:* 1770–1772 M. de Launay; 1772–1775 M. Anselme; 1775–1778 M. Le Roux de Kermeseven; 1778–1781 M. Saint-Amant de Romainville; 1781–1783 M. Berthelot de la Coste; 1783–1786 Capt. François de Souillac; 1786–1789 M. Motais de Narbonne; 1789–1792 Louis de Malavois; 1792–1794 Charles Esnouf; 1794–1810 Jean-Baptiste Quéau de Quincy. *Civil Agents/Commissioners:* 1810–1811 Jean-Baptiste Quéau de Quincy (acting); 1811–1812 Bartholomew Sullivan; 1812–1815 Bibye Lasage; 1815–1822 Edward Madge. *Civil Agents:* 1822–1837 George Harrison; 1837–1839 Arthur Wilson. *Civil Commissioners:* 1839–1850 Charles Mylius; 1850–1852 Robert Keate; 1852–1862 George Wade; 1862–1868 Swinburne Ward. *Chief Civil Commissioners:* 1868–1874 William Franklyn; 1874–1879 Charles Salmon; 1879–1880 Arthur Havelock; 1880–1882 Francis Blunt; 1882–1888 Arthur Barkly. *Administrators:* 1888–1895 Thomas Griffith; 1895–1899 Henry Stewart; 1899–Aug. 1903 Ernest Sweet-Escott. *Governors:* Aug. 1903–1904 Sir Ernest Sweet-Escott; 1904–1912 Sir Walter Davidson; 1912–1918 Sir Charles O'Brien; 1918–1921 Sir Eustace Twistleton-Wykeham-Fiennes; 1921–1927 Sir Joseph Byrne; 1927–1928 Sir Malcolm Stevenson; 1928–1934 Montagu Honey (knighted 1932); 1934–1936 Sir Gordon Lethem; 1936–5 Jan. 1942 Sir Arthur Grimble; 5 Jan. 1942–July 1947 Sir William Logan; July 1947–14 May 1951 Sir Percy Selwyn-Clarke; 14 May 1951–18 Oct. 1953 Frederick Crawford; 18 Oct. 1953–1958 Sir William Addis; 1958–7 Nov. 1961 Sir John Thorp; 7 Nov. 1961–1967 Earl of Oxford and Asquith; 1967–1969 Sir Hugh Norman-Walker; 1969–1973 Sir Hugh Greatbatch; 1973–1 Oct. 1975 Sir Colin Allen. *High Commissioners:* 1 Oct. 1975–29 June 1976 Sir Colin Allen. *Presidents:* 29 June 1976–5 June 1977 James Mancham; 5 June 1977–14 April 2004 France-Albert René; 14 April 2004– James Michel. *Chief Ministers:* 1970–1 Oct. 1975 James Mancham. *Prime Ministers:* 1 Oct. 1975–29 June 1976 James Mancham; 29 June 1976–5 June 1977 France-Albert René. *Note:* In times of no Prime Minister, the President held that office.

Shaba see **Katanga Republic**

Shangaan see **GazaNkulu**

Shangana see **Gazaland**

Sharifian Sa'di see **Morocco**

Shenge. 1810–1888. *Location:* off the coast of Sierra Leone. *Capital:* Shenge. *Other names:* Plantation Island.

History: Founded in 1810 by the Caulker family, Shenge lasted as a political unit until 1888 when it became part of Sierra Leone.

Kings: 1810–1831 George Stephen Caulker I; 1831–1842 Thomas Stephen Caulker; 1842–1849 [vacant]; 1849–15 Aug. 1871 Thomas Stephen Caulker; 15 Aug. 1871–1881 George Stephen Caulker II. *Regents:* 1881–1888 Thomas Neale Caulker.

Shewa see **Shoa**

Shiré River see **Malawi**

Shoa. ca. 1470–3 Nov. 1889. *Location:* central Ethiopia. *Capital:* Ankober (from 1813); Qundi (1808–1813); Doqait (1745–1808); unknown capital before 1745. *Other names:* Shewa.

History: Shoa was a kingdom in Central Ethiopia which in 1856 was made a part of the Ethiopian Empire (see Ethiopia). Indeed, it became the central part of the empire. In 1886 Menelik II, who had been captured by the

Ethiopian emperor Theodore, won back the kingdom of Shoa, and in 1889 he became the emperor of Ethiopia himself.

Neguses (Kings): ca. 1470–1510 Malak Sagad; 1510–(?) [vacant]; (?)–1580 Negasse I; 1580–1625 Gabriel; 1625–1703 Negasse II; 1703–1718 Asfa Wossen; 1718–1745 Abbiye; 1745–1775 Amme-hayes; 1775–1808 Asfa Wossen II; 1808–1813 Ras Wossen Seged; 1813–1847 Ras Sahle Selassie; 1847–1855 Hayla Melekot; 1855–1886 ruled as part of Ethiopia; 1886–3 Nov. 1889 Menelik II.

Siante see **Ashanti**

Sierra Leone. 14 May 1787– . *Location:* North West Africa. *Capital:* Freetown; Granville Town (1791–1792; 1787–1789). *Other names:* Freetown (alternative name from 1792 to 1799); Freedom Province (1787–1789).

History: Originally there were several local chiefdoms here. Portuguese sailors named the peninsula at the mouth of the Rokel River Serra Leão, after the lion shape of the mountains thereon. From the time of the late 15th century ships from many Europeans countries sailed into the harbor that lies close to where Freetown is today. The English built trading posts on Bunce Island and York Island in the 16th century, and traders settled there under the protection of the local chiefs, but there was no attempt at a European administration of the region. In 1787 freed slaves from England were settled on the coastal lands, sponsored by Henry Smeathman and Granville Sharp, the English abolitionist, who saw this move as a step against slavery in North West Africa. They were awarded a section of land by a local Temne chief, King Tom, and they named it Freedom Province, and their chief town Granville Town. In 1789 Granville Town was burned to the ground by King Jimmy, Tom's successor. In 1791 the Sierra Leone Company was formed in London, with the same ideals that Granville Sharp had had, and, using the settlers who remained from Freedom Province, the Company, in Jan. 1791, formed a new settlement on the ashes of the old one. Granville Town was somewhat revived, and in 1792 the tiny and lonely population was boosted by the arrival of Nova Scotian blacks from Canada, who had won their freedom as British soldiers in the American Revolutionary War. Also, in 1792 Freetown, the new capital, was built. On 5 July 1799 the slowly growing settlement of Freetown became the colony of Sierra Leone, still run by the Company. In 1800 the country was added to by the impor-

tation of a group of Maroons, Jamaican trouble-makers who had been expelled to Nova Scotia. In 1807 Britain ruled the slave trade illegal, and that year (effective as from 1 Jan. 1808) the colony of Sierra Leone (or Freetown as it was also known) became a British Crown Colony, and a naval base for anti-slavery activities. From the very beginning, Britain's policy in Sierra Leone was enlightened and progressive. On 17 Oct. 1821 it was one of the three colonies (Gold Coast and Gambia being the other two) that went to make up the West African Territories (see British West Africa). It was the dominant territory of the W.A.T., the capital of the federation being at Freetown. In 1828 the Gold Coast broke away, and in 1843 the Gambia did too, leaving Sierra Leone as the only component of the W.A.T. By On 13 Jan. 1850, with the dissolution of the W.A.T., Sierra Leone went back to being a colony. On 19 Feb. 1866 the British tried the federation idea again, with the West African Settlements (W.A.S.) (again see British West Africa). This time there were four components: Sierra Leone, Gambia, Gold Coast, and Lagos. Again, Sierra Leone was the dominant member, with the capital of the federation being at Freetown. In 1874 Gold Coast and Lagos broke away to form their own, joint, colony, and in Oct. 1888 Sierra Leone and Gambia went their own ways. On 28 Nov. 1888, when the W.A.S. officially broke up, Sierra Leone became a colony again. It was only the threat of French incursion that made the British think about expansion of the colony. Therefore the hinterland was explored, conquered and developed, and was finally made a protectorate. On 24 Aug. 1895 the polity of Sierra Leone Colony and Protectorate came into being, the colony being the coastal areas around Freetown, and the protectorate being the hinterland. Some of the northern chiefs, who had not been consulted about the protectorate, waged a small war with the British in 1898, but, aside from that, British rule remained peaceful for its entire existence. With the 20th century came the beginnings of nationalism. With Britain's post–World War II policy of eventual independence for the African colonies, Sierra Leone's nationalists were groomed for self-government. On 27 April 1961 the whole country became a dominion of Great Britain, and Sir Henry Lightfoot-Boston became the first native-born governor-general, in 1962. On 17 March 1967 Siaka P. Stevens won the election as prime minister, but

David Lansana, head of the Army, seized power in a coup on 21 March. Lansana, who declared martial law, and removed Sir Henry Lightfoot-Boston from office as governor-general, served a prime minister for two days before being arrested and jailed by other officers. A National Reform Council was set up, with Lt.-Col. Ambrose Genda at its head. However, four days later, on 27 March, Genda was removed by another lieutenant-colonel, Andrew Juxon-Smith. On 19 April 1968 another coup, led by Patrick Conteh, expelled the military and on 22 April restored civilian government to Sierra Leone. On 19 April 1971 it became fully independent as the Republic of Sierra Leone, but still within the British Commonwealth. A one-party political system was introduced in 1978, following a referendum, and for a few years the country was stable, but became increasingly poverty-stricken and the government more and more corrupt. The 1990s and early 2000s were plagued by coups and civil wars.

Administrators: 14 May 1787–Sept. 1787 Capt. B. Thompson. *Governors:* 1788–(?) John Taylor. *Agents:* Jan. 1791–June 1791 Mr Falconbridge; June 1791–March 1792 [unknown]. *Superintendents:* March 1792–July 1792 John Clarkson. *Governors:* July 1792–31 Dec. 1792 John Clarkson; 31 Dec. 1792–March 1794 William Dawes; March 1794–6 May 1795 Zachary Macaulay; 6 May 1795–March 1796 William Dawes; March 1796–April 1799 Zachary Macaulay; April 1799–May 1799 John Gray; May 1799–1800 Thomas Ludlum; 1800–Jan. 1801 John Gray; Jan. 1801–Feb. 1803 William Dawes; Feb. 1803–1803 William Day; 1803–1805 Thomas Ludlum; 1805–4 Nov. 1805 William Day; 4 Nov. 1805–1806 [unknown]; 1806–1 Jan. 1808 Thomas Ludlum; 1 Jan. 1808–21 July 1808 Thomas Ludlum (acting); 21 July 1808–12 Feb. 1810 Thomas Thompson; 12 Feb. 1810–May 1811 Edward Columbine; May 1811–1 July 1811 Robert Bones (acting); 1 July 1811–July 1814 Charles Maxwell; July 1814–Dec. 1814 Charles Macarthy (acting); Dec. 1814–Jan. 1815 J. Mailing (acting); Jan. 1815–March 1815 R. Purdie (acting); March 1815–June 1815 William Appleton (acting); June 1815–July 1815 Capt. H.B. Hyde (acting); July 1815–1 Jan. 1816 Charles Macarthy (acting); 1 Jan. 1816–July 1820 Charles Macarthy (knighted 1820); July 1820–1821 Alexander Grant (acting); 1821–17 Oct. 1821 Lt.-Col. Burke (acting); 17 Oct. 1821–Nov. 1821

Alexander Grant (acting); Nov. 1821–21 Jan. 1824 Sir Charles Macarthy; 21 Jan. 1824–5 Feb. 1825 Daniel Hamilton (acting); 5 Feb. 1825–7 March 1826 Sir Charles Turner; 8 March 1826–1826 Kenneth Macaulay (acting); 1826–Aug. 1826 Samuel Smart (acting); Aug. 1826–Dec. 1827 Sir Neil Campbell. *Lieutenant-Governors:* Dec. 1827–May 1828 Hugh Lumley; May 1828–9 June 1828 Dixon Denham; 9 June 1828–1828 Hugh Lumley; 1828–Nov. 1828 Samuel Smart (acting); Nov. 1828–1829 Henry Ricketts (acting); 1829–1830 Augustine Evans; 1830–1830 Alexander Fraser (acting); 1830–July 1833 Alexander Findlay; July 1833–Dec. 1833 Michael Melville (acting); Dec. 1833–1834 Octavius Temple; 1834–Feb. 1835 Thomas Cole (acting); Feb. 1835–1837 Henry Campbell (acting); 1837–1837 Thomas Cole (acting). *Governors:* 1837–1840 Richard Doherty; 1840–April 1841 John Jeremie; April 1841–Sept. 1841 J. Carr (acting); Sept. 1841–Jan. 1842 William Fergusson (acting); Jan. 1842–July 1844 George MacDonald; July 1844–1845 William Fergusson; 1845–1852 Norman MacDonald; 1852–1854 Arthur Kennedy; 1854–1854 Robert Dougan (acting); 1854–1855 Stephen Hill; 1855–1855 Robert Dougan (acting); 1855–1859 Stephen Hill; 1859–1860 Alexander Fitzjames (acting); 1860–1861 Stephen Hill; 1861–1862 William Hill and Lt.-Col. Smith (acting, jointly); 1862–1865 Samuel Blackall; 1865–19 Feb. 1866 Col. Chamberlayne (acting). *Governors-in-Chief:* 19 Feb. 1866–1867 Samuel Blackall; 1867–1867 Gustavus Yonge (acting); 1867–1868 Samuel Blackall; 1868–1869 Sir Arthur Kennedy; 1869–1869 John Kendall (acting); 1869–1871 Sir Arthur Kennedy; 1871–1871 John Kendall (acting); 1871–1871 Capt. Sheppard (acting); 1871–Jan. 1872 Sir Arthur Kennedy; Jan. 1872–Feb. 1872 John Kendall (acting); Feb. 1872–7 March 1873 John Pope-Hennessey; 7 March 1873–17 March 1873 Robert Keate; 17 March 1873–2 Oct. 1873 Robert Harley and Alexander Bravo (acting jointly); 2 Oct. 1873–4 March 1874 Sir Garnet Wolseley; 4 March 1874–17 Dec. 1874 George Berkeley; 17 Dec. 1874–1875 George French (acting); 1875–1875 Cornelius Kortright; 1875–1876 Dr. Samuel Rowe; 1876–1877 Cornelius Kortright; 1877–1877 Horatio Huggins (acting); 1877–1880 Dr. Samuel Rowe (knighted 1880); 1880–1881 William Streeten; 1881–1881 Sir Samuel Rowe; 1881–1881 Franas Pinkett (acting); 1881–1883 Arthur Havelock; 1883–1883 Franas

Pinkett (acting); 1883–1884 Arthur Havelock; 1884–1884 Arthur Tarleton (acting); 1884–1885 Franas Pinkett (acting); 1885–1886 Sir Samuel Rowe; 1886–1887 James Hay (acting); 1887–1888 Sir Samuel Rowe; 1888–1888 J.M. Maltby (acting); 1888–28 Nov. 1888 James Hay (acting); 28 Nov. 1888–1889 James Hay (knighted 1889); 1889–1889 Lt.-Col. Patchett and Maj. Foster (acting, jointly); 1889–1890 J.M. Maltby (acting); 1890–1891 Sir James Hay; 1891–1892 J.J. Crooks (acting); 1892–1892 W.H.Q. Jones (acting); 1892–1893 Sir Francis Fleming; 1893–1893 W.H.Q. Jones (acting); 1893–1894 Sir Francis Fleming; 1894–1894 W.H.Q. Jones (acting); 1894–1895 Frederic Cardew; 1895–24 Aug. 1895 Lt.-Col. Caulfeild (acting); 24 Aug. 1895–1897 Frederic Cardew (knighted 1897); 1897–1897 J.C. Gore (acting); 1897–1897 Lt.-Col. Caulfeild (acting); 1897–1899 Sir Frederic Cardew; 1899–1899 Mathew Nathan (acting); 1899–1900 Sir Frederic Car dew; 1900–11 Dec. 1900 Lt.-Col. Caulfeild (acting); 11 Dec. 1900–3 Oct. 1904 Sir Charles King-Harman; 3 Oct. 1904–1910 Leslie Probyn (knighted 1909); 1910–1913 Sir Edward Merewether; 1913–1913 Claud Hollis (acting); 1913–1915 Sir Edward Merewether; 1915–9 March 1916 [unknown]; 9 March 1916–1921 Richard W.H. Wilkinson; 1921–1921 James Maxwell (acting); 1921–4 May 1922 Richard W.H. Wilkinson; 4 May 1922–24 Sept. 1927 Ransford Slater (knighted 1924); 24 Sept. 1927–1929 Sir Joseph Byrne; 1929–1930 Mark Young (acting); 1930–23 May 1931 Sir Joseph Byrne; 23 May 1931–17 July 1934 Arnold Hodson (knighted 1932); 17 July 1934–21 May 1937 Henry Moore (knighted 1935); 21 May 1937–5 July 1941 Douglas Jardine (knighted 1938); 5 July 1941–4 Sept. 1947 Sir Hubert Stevenson; 4 Sept. 1947–Dec. 1952 Sir George Beresford-Stooke; Dec. 1952–1 Sept. 1956 Sir Robert Hall; 1 Sept. 1956–27 April 1961 Maurice Dorman (knighted 1957). *Governors-General:* 27 April 1961–7 July 1962 Sir Maurice Dorman; 7 July 1962–1962 Sir Henry Lightfoot-Boston (acting); 1962–21 March 1967 Sir Henry Lightfoot-Boston; 27 March 1967–19 April 1968 Andrew Juxon-Smith (also Chairman of the National Reformation Council); 22 April 1968–31 March 1971 Banja Tejan-Sie (acting); 31 March 1971–19 April 1971 Christopher Okoro Cole (acting). *Presidents:* 19 April 1971–21 April 1971 Christopher Okoro Cole (acting); 21 April 1971–28 Nov. 1985 Siaka P. Stevens; 28 Nov. 1985–29 April 1992 Joseph

Saidu Momoh. *Chairmen of the Provisional Ruling Council:* 29 April 1992–1 May 1992 Valentine Strasser (acting); 1 May 1992–16 Jan. 1996 Valentine Strasser; 17 Jan. 1996–29 March 1996 Julius Maada Bio (acting). *Presidents:* 29 March 1996–25 May 1997 Ahmad Tejan Kabbah. *Heads of the Armed Forces Revolutionary Council:* 25 May 1997–12 Feb. 1998 Johnny Paul Koroma. *Presidents:* 12 Feb. 1998–Ahmad Tejan Kabbah. *Chief Ministers:* 1954–14 Aug. 1958 Milton Margai. *Prime Ministers:* 14 Aug. 1958–28 April 1964 Milton Margai; 29 April 1964–17 March 1967 Milton Margai (knighted 1965); 17 March 1967–21 March 1967 Siaka P. Stevens (never served); 21 March 1967–23 March 1967 David Lansana; 23 March 1967–27 March 1967 Ambrose Genda (Chairman of the National Reformation Council — never served); 20 April 1968–26 April 1968 Anti-Corruption Revolutionary Movement in power, led by Patrick Conteh; 26 April 1968–Sept. 1970 Siaka P. Stevens; Sept. 1970–Sept. 1970 Sheku Bochari Kawusu Conteh (acting); Sept. 1970–19 April 1971 Siaka P. Stevens. *Note:* In times of no Prime Minister, the Governor-General, President or other Head of State held that office.

Sikasso see **Kenedugu**

Sikonyela's Land see **Sekonyela's Land**

Silhouette Island see **Seychelles**

Sinoe see **Liberia** and **Mississippi-in-Africa**

Slave Coast see **Benin [i]**

Sofala see **Gazaland** and **Mozambique**

Sokoto see **Fulani Empire**

Somalia. 1 July 1960– . *Location:* northeast Africa. *Capital:* Mogadishu (also known as Maqdishu, Mogadisho, and Mogasiscio, this town was founded about 950 by Arabs). *Other names:* Jamhuuriyada Demuqraadiga Soomaaliyeed, or Democratic Republic of Somalia (from 1969).

History: On 1 July 1960 Italian Somaliland and the state of Somalia (see British Somaliland), which had been independent of the British for a mere five days, united to form Somalia as we know it today. The 1960s were terrible for the country economically, and there was a war with Ethiopia from 1964 to 1967. On 21 Oct. 1969, following a coup in which the president was assassinated, the country became the Democratic Republic of Somalia. Somalis used to dream of a "Greater Somalia" taking in not only Somalia but also the Ogaden region of Ethiopia, the southern part of Djibouti, and the eastern strip of Kenya; in short all the Somali-populated areas. Now, they dream about food. Repression, lack of cohesion, grinding poverty and starvation made it easy for the Communists to take the country over in the 1970s. There was another war with Ethiopia in 1977–1978, and civil war raged in the 1980s and 1990s. After a 1991 coup, President Barre fled the country, and in July 1992 the United Nations declared Somalia a country without a government. In the 1990s the civil war between rival rebel groups led to famine and abortive U.S. and U.N. involvement. Barre died in exile in Lagos on 2 Jan. 1995, and the U.N. pulled out on 3 March 1995. The country was devastated by floods in 1997, and by the tsunami in 2004. In 2000 a concerted effort was made to re-form a centralized government, but this has been generally unsuccessful. A fresh wave of fighting between warlords began in 2005. Several entities within Somalia have broken away to form their own republics: see Somaliland Republic, Jubaland, Southwestern Somaliland, and Puntland.

Presidents: 1 July 1960–6 July 1961 Aden Abdallah Osman Daar (acting); 6 July 1961–10 June 1967 Aden Abdallah Osman Daar; 10 June 1967–15 Oct. 1969 Abdi Rashid Shermarke; 15 Oct. 1969–21 Oct. 1969 Sheikh Mokhtar Muhammad Hussein (acting). *Presidents of the Supreme Revolutionary Council:* 21 Oct. 1969–1 July 1976 Muhammad Siyad Barre. *Secretaries-General:* 1 July 1976–26 Jan. 1991 Muhammad Siyad Barre; 29 Jan. 1991–21 July 1991 Ali Mahdi Mahmud (interim); 21 July 1991–Nov. 1991 Ali Mahdi Mahumd. Nov. 1991–8 Oct. 2000 [no recognized government]. *Head of National Salvation Council:* 3 July 1997–(?) Ali Mahdi Mahmud. *Presidents:* 22 Aug. 2000–27 Aug. 2000 Abdallah Derow Isaq (acting); 27 Aug. 2000–24 Oct. 2004 Abdiqasim Salad Hassan (in exile in Djibouti until 13 Oct. 2000, then his rule was limited only to the Mogadishu area); 14 Oct. 2004–Abdullahi Yusuf Ahmad (in exile in Nairobi until 13 June 2005, then from 26 July 2005 in Jowhar). *Other presidential claimants:* 15 June

1996–1 Aug. 1996 Muhammad Farah Aydid; 4 Aug. 1996–20 March 1998 Hussein Aydid; July 2003–Abdinur Ahmad Darman (controlled part of Mogadishu and Southern Somalia). Chairmen of the Somali Reconciliation Council: 26 March 2001–(?) rotated monthly. *Prime Ministers:* 1 July 1960–12 July 1960 Muhammad Ibrahim Egal; 12 July 1960–14 June 1964 Abdi Rashid Shermarke; 14 June 1964–27 Sept. 1964 Abdi Rizak Hajji Hussein (acting); 27 Sept. 1964–10 June 1967 Abdi Rizak Hajji Hussein; 10 June 1967–21 Oct. 1969 Muhammad Ibrahim Egal; 30 Jan. 1987–3 Sept. 1990 Muhammad Ali Samatar; 3 Sept. 1990–24 Jan. 1991 Muhammad Hawadle Madar; 24 Jan. 1991–Nov. 1991Umar Arteh Ghalib. Nov. 1991–8 Oct. 2000 [no recognized government]. 8 Oct. 2000–28 Oct. 2001 Ali Khalif Galaid; 28 Oct. 2001–12 Nov. 2001 Osman Jama Ali (acting); 12 Nov. 2001–8 Dec. 2003 Hassan Abshir Farah; 8 Dec. 2003–3 Nov. 2004 Muhammad Abdi Yusuf; 3 Nov. 2001–Ali Muhammad Ghedi (in exile in Nairobi until 18 June 2005, then in Jowhar).

Somaliland see **Italian Somaliland**

Somaliland Republic. 28 May 1991–. *Location:* Northwestern corner of Somalia. *Capital:* Hargeysa. *Other names:* Republic of Somaliland.

History: On 24 May 1991 the Somali National Movement, which was headed by Muhammad Egal and some other old leaders from the British Somaliland days, declared an independent Somaliland Republic, a Muslim state, the same size as the British country was in those old days. Four days later it came into existence. Being an idealistic, rather than a tangible, country, it is naturally not recognized internationally. They have a flag (adopted on 14 Oct. 1996), but no law and order.

Presidents: 28 May 1991–16 May 1993 Abd ar-Rahman Ahmad Ali Tur; 16 May 1993–3 May 2002 Muhammad Ibrahim Egal; 3 May 2002–Dahir Riyale Kahir (acting).

Songhai. ca. 500–1640. *Location:* Mali, and later, as an empire, most of the western Sahara, centered on Mali. *Capital:* Dendi (from 1591); Gao (1010–1591); Kukya (until 1010). *Other names:* Songhai Empire (from 1464); Kingdom of Songhai, or Sonrhai (until 1464).

History: About the year 500 the Songhai people, who had come from the middle Niger region established their kingdom, with a line of kings called "dias." At the turn of the 7th century they came to Gao, their capital remaining at Kukya. In 1010 the 15th dia, Kossoi, was converted to Islam, and moved his capital to Gao. The town of Gao, then the state of Gao, went to form the nucleus of what became the Songhai Empire. In 1325 Gao became part of the Mali Empire. In 1335 the last of the dias died, and a new era of "sunnis" or "shihs" (sheikhs) began. In 1375 the second sunni, Suleiman-Mar, won back independence from the Mali Empire. In 1464 Sunni Ali became king of Gao and Songhai lands, entering into a phase of expansion which began the Songhai Empire (as opposed to just the Songhai Kingdom). The empire reached its height under the first of the ten Askia kings, Askia the Great. In 1582 Morocco invaded with firearms, and in 1591 the key cities of Gao and Timbuktu were taken. The Songhai Empire was virtually finished, and the emperor fled to Dendi, where he and his successors continued to rule in exile. Only guerrilla raids by groups of Songhais kept the name of the empire alive. The Moroccans left in 1618, but by about 1640 Songhai had been reduced to a group of small, weak states in the southeastern section of the former empire.

Dias (Kings): ca. 500–ca. 837 unknown series of kings; ca. 837–ca. 849 Alayaman; ca. 849–861 Za Koi; 861–873 Takoi; 873–885 Akoi; 885–897 Ku; 897–909 Ali Fai; 909–921 Biyai Komai; 921–933 Biyai Bei; 933–945 Karai; 945–957 Yama Karaonia; 957–969 Yama Dombo; 969–981 Yama Danka Kibao; 981–993 Kukorai; 993–1005 Kenken; 1005–1025 Za Kosoi; 1025–1044 Kosai Dariya; 1044–1063 Hen Kon Wanko Dam; 1063–1082 Biyai Koi Kimi; 1082–1101 Nintasanai; 1101–1120 Biyai Kaina Kimba; 1120–1139 Kaina Shinyunbo; 1139–1158 Tib; 1158–1177 Yama Dao; 1177–1196 Fadazu; 1196–1215 Ali Koro; 1215–1235 Bir Foloko; 1235–1255 Yosiboi; 1255–1275 Duro; 1275–1295 Zenko Baro; 1295–1325 Bisi Baro; 1325–1332 Bada. *Sunnis (Sheikhs):* 1332–1340 Ali Konon; 1340–1347 Salman Nari; 1347–1354 Ibrahim Kabay; 1354–1362 Uthman Kanafa; 1362–1370 Bar Kaina Ankabi; 1370–1378 Musa; 1378–1386 Bukar Zonko; 1386–1394 Bukar Dalla Boyonbo; 1394–1402 Mar Kirai; 1402–1410 Muhammad Dao; 1410–1418 Muhammad Konkiya; 1418–1426 Muhammad Fari; 1426–1434 Karbifo; 1434–1442 Mar Fai Kolli-Djimbo; 1442–1449 Mar Arkena; 1449–1456 Mar Aran-dan; 1456–1464 Suleiman Daman. *Emperors:* 1464–6 Nov. 1492 Sunni Ali (also known as Sonni Ali); 6 Nov. 1492–1493 Baru; 3 March 1493–26 Aug. 1528 Askia the Great (formerly Muhammad Touray); 26 Aug. 1528–12 April 1531 Musa; 12 April 1531–22 April 1537 Muhammad Bunkan; 22 April 1537–2 March 1538 Askia the Great; 2 March 1538–1539 Ismail; 1539–25 March 1549 Ishaq I; 25 March 1549–Aug. 1582 Dawud; Aug. 1582–15 Dec. 1586 Muhammad II (also known as al-Hajj); 15 Dec. 1586–9 April 1588 Muhammad Bani; 9 April 1588–14 April 1591 Ishaq II; 14 April 1591–1591 Muhammad Gao; 1591–1599 Nuh; 1599–1612 Harun; 1612–1618 al-Amin; 1618–1635 Dawud II; 1635–1640 Ismail.

Soninke see **Ghana Empire**

Sonyo Dynasty see **Kayor**

Soudan Français see **Mali**

South Africa. 31 May 1910– . *Location:* the southernmost portion of Africa. *Capital:* Pretoria (administrative capital); Cape Town (legislative capital); Bloemfontein (judicial capital, from 1961). *Other names:* Azania (African name); Republiek Van Zuid-Afrika, or the Republic of South Africa (from 1961); Union of South Africa (1910–1961).

History: On the stroke of midnight, 30–31 May 1961 the four British colonies of Cape Colony, Transvaal, Natal, and Orange River Colony were united to form the Union of South Africa, ruled over by a British-appointed governor-general and a South African prime minister and government. On 1 July 1910 South Africa became a dominion of the British Empire, and set about establishing race laws to keep the vast black majority (roughly 70 per cent) in a condition of subjugation. South Africa sided with Britain during World War I. In 1922 Jan Smuts, the strongman of South Africa in those days, almost succeeded in getting Southern Rhodesia to become a part of South Africa, and this plan was only thwarted at a referendum held that year by Southern Rhodesians. On 11 Dec. 1931 South Africa became a fully self-governing dominion, with the Monarch of the United Kingdom continuing as head of state of the Union of South Africa, and the British governor-general and high commissioner remaining. During the 1930s the blacks began to express discontent about the racial policies of South Africa. When World War II broke out, South Africa voted on whether to remain neutral or to support Britain. Jan Smuts narrowly won over J.B.M. Hertzog and the country went with Britain. On 30 May 1961 all this changed and the Union of South Africa became a republic, leaving the Commonwealth at the same time. South Africa was known to the outside world primarily a restrictive and oppressive state, with the vast black majority excluded from any form of franchise in a form of racial separation known as apartheid. This brought the world down on white South Africa, and finally, in the mid–1980s things began to change. On Feb. 11, 1990 President deKlerk freed black activist Nelson Mandela after 27 years imprisonment. In 1994 the vote was given to all adults, regardless of color, and the bantustans (or homelands), now no longer necessary, were incorporated back into South Africa. In 1994 Nelson Mandela was elected president, and white rule was over in South Africa, after 332 years. The provinces were re-structured into nine: Eastern Province, Free State, Gauteng, KwaZulu/Natal, Mpumalanga (formerly Eastern Transvaal), Northern Province (formerly Northern Transvaal), Northern Cape, North-West, and Western Cape. The 2000s offer high unemployment but the most grisly specter hanging over the future of South Africa is AIDS.

Governors-General/High Commissioners: 31 May 1910–17 July 1912 Herbert John, 1st Viscount Gladstone; 17 July 1912–11 Nov. 1912 John, Baron de Villiers (acting GG) and Sir Reginald Harte (acting HC); 11 Nov. 1912–11 July 1914 Herbert John, 1st Viscount Gladstone; 11 July 1914–8 Sept. 1914 John, Baron de Villiers (acting GG) and Sir James Murray (acting HC); 8 Sept. 1914–17 July 1920 Viscount Buxton; 17 July 1920–3 Sept. 1920 Sir James Rose-Innes (acting GG); 3 Sept. 1920–20 Nov. 1920 Sir James Rose-Innes (acting GG) and Beresford Carter (acting HC); 20 Nov. 1920–5 Dec. 1923 Prince Arthur of Connaught; 5 Dec. 1923–10 Dec. 1923 Sir James Rose-Innes (acting GG); 10 Dec. 1923–21 Jan. 1924 Sir James Rose-Innes (acting GG) and Sir Rudolf Bentinck (acting HC); 21 Jan. 1924–21 Dec. 1930 Earl of Athlone. *Governors-General:* 21 Dec. 1930–26 Jan. 1931 Jacob de Villiers (acting); 26 Jan. 1931–17 March 1937 George Villiers, Earl of Clarendon; 17 March 1937–5 April 1937 John Curlewis (acting); 5 April 1937–17 July 1943 Sir Patrick Duncan; 17 July 1943–31 Dec. 1945 Nicolaas De Wet (acting); 31 Dec. 1945–20 Sept. 1950 Brand Van Zyl; 28 Sept. 1950–1 Jan. 1951 [unknown] (acting); 1 Jan. 1951–25 Nov. 1959 Ernest Jansen; 25 Nov. 1959–12 Jan. 1960 [unknown] (acting); 12 Jan. 1960–18 May 1961 Charles Swart. *Officers Administering:* 18 May 1961–30 May 1961 L.C. Steyn. *High Commissioners:* 21 Dec. 1930–6 April 1931 [vacant]; 6 April 1931–1 Aug. 1933 Sir Herbert Stanley; 1 Aug. 1933–1 Dec. 1933 Edward Evans (acting); 1 Dec. 1933–6 Jan. 1935 Sir Herbert Stanley; 7 Jan. 1935–3 Jan. 1940 Sir William Clark; 3 Jan. 1940–24 May 1941 Sir Walter Huggard (acting); 24 May 1941–13 May 1944 William Ormsby-Gore, Baron Harlech; 13 May 1944–23 June 1944 Harold Priestman (acting); 23 June 1944–27 Oct. 1944 Sir Walter Huggard; 27 Oct. 1944–1 Oct. 1951 Sir Evelyn Baring; 2 Oct. 1951–2 Feb. 1955 Sir John Le Rougelet; 2 Feb. 1955–4 March 1955 [unknown] (acting); 4 March 1955–Dec. 1958 Percivale Liesching; Dec. 1958–15 Jan. 1959 [unknown] (acting); 15 Jan. 1959–30 May 1961 Sir John Maud. *Presidents:* 18 May 1961–30 May 1961 Charles Swart. *State Presidents:* 31 May 1961–1 June 1967 Charles Swart; 1 June 1967–6 Dec. 1967 Theophilus Dönges (never inaugurated); 1 June 1967–10 April 1968 Tom Naude (acting); 10 April 1968–21 Feb. 1975 Jim Fouché; 21 Feb. 1975–19 April 1975 [vacant]; 19 April 1975–21 Aug. 1978 Nicolaas Diederichs; 21 Aug. 1978–29 Sept. 1978 [vacant]; 29 Sept. 1978–4 June 1979 John Vorster; 4 June 1979–19 June 1979 Marais Viljoen (interim); 19 June 1979–14 Sept. 1984 Marais Viljoen. *Executive State Presidents:* 14 Sept. 1984–18 Jan. 1989 Pieter W. Botha; 19 Jan. 1989–15 March 1989 J. Christian Heunis (acting); 15 March 1989–14 Aug. 1989 Pieter W. Botha; 15 Aug. 1989–10 May 1994 F.W. deKlerk; 10 May 1994–16 June 1999 Nelson Mandela; 16 June 1999–Thabo Mbeki. *Prime Ministers:* 15 Sept. 1910–1918 Louis Botha; 1918–1919 François Malan; 1919–27 Aug. 1919 Louis Botha; 27 Aug. 1919–3 Sept. 1919 [vacant]; 3 Sept. 1919–23 June 1924 Jan Smuts; 30 June 1924–3 Sept. 1939 James (J.B.M.) Hertzog; 5 Sept. 1939–26 May 1948 Jan Smuts; 26 May 1948–3 June 1948 [vacant]; 3 June 1948–29 Oct. 1954 Daniel Malan; 29 Oct. 1954–30 Nov. 1954 Nicolaas C. Havenga (acting); 2 Dec. 1954–24 Aug. 1958 Johannes Strijdom; 24 Aug. 1958–3 Sept. 1958 Charles Swart (acting); 3 Sept.

1958–6 Sept. 1966 Hendrik Verwoerd; 6 Sept. 1966–13 Sept. 1966 Theophilus Dönges (acting); 13 Sept. 1966–28 Sept. 1978 John Vorster; 28 Sept. 1978–14 Sept. 1984 Pieter W. Botha. *Note:* In 1984 P.W. Botha combined the offices of State President and Prime Minister to make the new office of Executive State President.

South Africa Republic see **Transvaal**

South African Republic see **Transvaal**

South Island see **Agalega Islands**

South Island see **Aldabra Islands**

South Kasai Republic. 8 Aug. 1960–1962. *Location:* south central Congo (Zaire). *Capital:* Bakwanga (founded in 1909, it was renamed Mbuji Mayi in 1966). *Other names:* État Autonome du Sud Kasaï; Mining State; Mining Republic; Kasai Republic.

History: In 1960, immediately after the independence of the Belgian Congo, Albert Kalonji broke away to form a separate government in Kasai (Kasai was named for the river, and ultimately for the Kasai tribe). Later in August he and Moise Tshombe of the Katanga Republic joined in a federation. Bakwanga was captured by Congolese troops on 27 Aug. 1960, which brought an effective end to the Mining Republic, although it maintained an identity until 1962.

Presidents: 8 Aug. 1960–23 Aug. 1960 Albert Kalonji (provisional); 23 Aug. 1960–8 Sept. 1960 Albert Kalonji. *Chefs Suprêmes:* 8 Sept. 1960–30 March 1961 Albert Kalonji. *Emperors:* 30 March 1961–1962 Albert I (also known as Albert Kalonji).

South Ndebele see **KwaNdebele**

South Rivers see **Guinea**

South West Africa see **Namibia**

South Zambesia see **Rhodesia**

Southern Egypt see **Upper Egypt**

Southern Nigeria. 5 June 1885–16 Feb. 1906. *Location:* Southern Nigeria, excluding the colony of Lagos. *Capital:* Old Calabar (after 1904 this town was called Calabar). *Other names:* Southern Nigeria Protectorate (alternative name from 1900 to 1906); Niger Coast Protectorate (1893–1900); Oil Rivers Protectorate (1885–1893).

History: Between 1884 and 1897 Britain announced a string of protectorates along the Bights of Biafra and Benin, over the Niger Delta states of Bonny, Brass, Opobo, Aboh, Old Calabar, and Benin. By 1885 the British were calling the whole area the Oil River States, because of the palm oil trade there. On 13 May 1893 this coast became known as the Niger Coast Protectorate. On 27 Dec. 1899 (effective as from 1 Jan. 1900) it became the bulk of the protectorate of Southern Nigeria. In 1906 the colony of Lagos joined the protectorate to form Southern Nigeria Colony and Protectorate.

Consuls-General: 5 Jan. 1885–1 Jan. 1891 Edward Hyde Hewett. *Vice-Consuls:* 1 Jan. 1891–3 Aug. 1891 Capt. Synge. *Commissioners/Consuls-General:* 3 Aug. 1891–1893 Claude MacDonald (knighted 1892); 1893–1893 Ralph Moor (acting); 1893–1896 Sir Claude MacDonald; 1896–Nov. 1896 Ralph Moor; Nov. 1896–4 Jan. 1897 Mr Phillips (acting); 4 Jan. 1897–Feb. 1897 [unknown] (acting); Feb. 1897–1 Jan. 1900 Ralph Moor (knighted 1897). *High Commissioners:* 1 Jan. 1900–1900 Sir Ralph Moor; 1900–1900 Henry Gallwey (after 1911 he would be known as Galway) (acting); 1900–Aug. 1904 Sir Ralph Moor; Aug. 1904–16 Feb. 1906 Walter Egerton (knighted 1905).

Southern Nigeria Colony and Protectorate. 16 Feb. 1906–1 Jan. 1914. *Location:* Southern Nigeria. *Capital:* Lagos.

History: In 1906 the British protectorate of Southern Nigeria and the colony of Lagos were united to form the British colony and protectorate of Southern Nigeria. In 1914 this unit combined with the British protectorate of Northern Nigeria to for the colony and protectorate of Nigeria.

Governors: 16 Feb. 1906–1907 Sir Walter Egerton; 1907–1907 James Thorburn (acting); 1907–1912 Sir Walter Egerton; 1912–1 Jan. 1914 Sir Frederick Lugard.

Southern Rhodesia see **Zimbabwe**

Southern Somaliland see **Italian Somaliland**

Southern Sudan. 1962– . *Location:* the provinces of Equatoria, Upper Nile, and Bahr al-

Ghazal, in Southern Sudan. *Capital:* Juba. *Other names:* NPG (alternative name, 1969–1970); Southern Sudan Provisional Government, or SSPG (1967–1969); Azania Liberation Front, or ALF (1965–1967).

History: The Southern Sudan is comprised of three of the nine Sudanese provinces, and its citizens are predominantly black Christians and those of tribal religions, as opposed to the Northern Sudan, which is largely Muslim. The problem in the Sudan reflects the basic problem throughout most of Africa (and throughout most of the world), which is the desire for ethnic unity at the expense of national unity. The Sudan developed its own cancerous example of this in its three southernmost provinces. Azanian (Black African) non-Muslims wanted to be free of Islam and the central government at Khartoum. An independence movement, or rather several independence movements, were formed from 1956 on, but the first one of any major consequence came in 1962, when William Deng, Joseph Oduho, Aggrey Jaden, and Father Lohure Saturnino created the Sudan African Closed Districts National Union, which in 1963 changed its name to the Sudan African National Union (SANU). In 1963 an army was formed, called the Anya Nya, a ragged, poverty-stricken, beaten-up army headed by Joseph Lagu, which for years struggled to achieve independence for the Southern Sudan. In 1965 SANU split over the issue of compromise with the national Sudanese government in Khartoum. The two branches of SANU that thus emerged were SANU-Inside (headed by William Deng) and SANU-in-Exile (headed by Joseph Oduho and Father Lohure Saturnino). SANU-Inside continued, within the geographic boundaries of the Sudan, until the murder of Deng in 1968, while SANU-in-Exile re-grouped and formed the Azania Liberation Front in 1965 (Azania means "Black Africa"). In 1965 Aggrey Jaden formed the Sudan African Liberation Front, and later that year this group merged with the Azania Liberation Front. In 1967 the Sudan African Liberation Front–Azania Liberation Front combine was renamed the Southern Sudan Provisional Government, with Aggrey Jaden as president. This in turn was replaced in March 1969 by the Nile Provisional Government (formed in Uganda), with Gordon Mayen as president and Maro Morgan as vice-president. The Anyidi Revolutionary Government was another major movement, founded in 1969 by Emidio Tafeng, an Anya Nya commander, as a partner to the Nile Provisional Government in the Southern Sudan, and as a likely successor to that organization, but it was soon (1970) swallowed up by Joseph Lagu's Southern Sudan Liberation Front, the political organ of the Anya Nya army. Lagu it was who succeeded, by 1971, in bringing together most of the southern political factions under the Southern Sudan Liberation Movement banner, and on 28 Feb. 1972 the SSLM was the main southern spokesman at the Addis Ababa Conference between Khartoum and the South. As a result a certain degree of autonomy was granted to the Southern Provinces, and a Southern Region High Executive Committee was set up. Some elements continued the fight for complete independence for the South. In 1978 oil was discovered in the South, and this naturally determined Khartoum to keep the South. In 1983 President Numayri introduced Islamic law to the Sudan. To the Christians and animists of the South, as well as to the non-Muslims in the North, this was a major setback. In 1983 the Southern People's Liberation Movement was formed, headed by John Garang, and rebellion broke out on a major scale, costing well over a million lives in famine and war. Khartoum stepped up its war with the South, and by the mid–1990s about three million people had become homeless in the south. Finally, in 2005 an agreement was signed whereby the South would be granted autonomy and a six-year reflective period in which to examine their hopes for independence. John Garang, the Southern leader, became the first vice president of the Sudan itself. By 2111 there would be a referendum in the South to decide on independence. John Garang died in a helicopter crash on 30 July 2005, possibly the victim of an assassination. He was irreplaceable, and riots began in Khartoum immediately after his death, leading to many killings on the streets.

Presidents of the Southern Sudan Provisional Government: 1967–March 1969 Aggrey Jaden. *Presidents of the Nile Provisional Government:* March 1969–1970 Gordon Mayen. *Presidents of the Anyidi Revolutionary Government:* 15 July 1969–1970 Emidio Tafeng Lodongi. *Leaders of the Southern Sudan Liberation Movement:* 1969–1972 Joseph Lagu. *Chairmen of the High Executive Council:* 6 April 1972–Feb. 1978 Abel Alier; Feb. 1978–30 May 1980 Joseph Lagu; 30 May

1980–5 Oct. 1981 Abel Alier; 5 Oct. 1981–23 June 1982 Gismalla Rassas (interim); 23 June 1982–5 June 1983 Joseph Tombura; 5 June 1983–25 May 1985 [unknown]; 25 May 1985–May 1986 James Loro. Chairmen of the Council for the South: 31 Jan. 1987–Jan. 1988 Matthew Abor; Jan. 1988–June 1989 Angelo Beda. *Chairmen of the Southern Sudan Co-ordination Council:* 7 Aug. 1997–31 Jan. 2000 Riek Machar; Feb. 2000–9 Dec. 2002 Gatluak Deng; 9 Dec. 2002–Riek Gai. *Chairmen of the Sudan People's Liberation Movement (SPLM):* June 1983–9 July 2005 John Garang. *Presidents of the Government of Southern Sudan:* 9 July 2005–30 July 2005 John Garang; 4 Aug. 2005–Salva Kiir.

Southwestern Somalia. 1 April 2002– . *Location:* Southwestern Somalia. *Capital:* Baidoa.

History: The Rahanwein Resistance Army declared the independence of this breakaway Somali state in 2002. Shatigadud lost the capital on 3 Oct. 2002, and since then it has been controlled by Sheikh Aden Madobe and Muhammad Ibrahim Habsade. The continued existence of this state is highly doubtful.

Presidents: 1 April 2002–? Hassan Muhammad Nur Shatigadud.

Soutpansberg see **Zoutpansberg**

Spanish Captaincy-General of North Africa see **Spanish Morocco**

Spanish Guinea see **Equatorial Guinea**

Spanish Morocco. 1847–7 April 1956. *Location:* northern Morocco and the southern — Tarfaya — region. *Capital:* Tetuán (after 1912); Ceuta (until 1912). *Other names:* Marruecos Español; Rif; Er-Rif; Spanish Captaincy-General of North Africa (1847–1912).

History: In 1847 the Captaincy-General of North Africa was created in order to bring all the Spanish enclaves along the North African coast under one administration. These enclaves were: Ceuta, Melilla, Velez de la Gomera, Alhucemas, and Chafarinas. The governor of Ceuta became the Captain-General of the whole lot. The Algeciras Act of 8 April 1906 gave France and Spain control in Morocco, and a certain territory was granted to Spain as a protectorate in 1912, basically an extension in land of the territory of the captaincy-general, but also including the far south of Morocco, the region known as Tarfaya. On 27 Nov. 1912 the captaincy-general officially became known as Spanish Morocco, a name that had long been in use anyway. Subsequent agreements decreased the size of this area to the advantage of French Morocco. After 1934 the Spanish high commissioner had jurisdiction for some years over Spanish West Africa (see Western Sahara), which was also known as the Southern Protectorate of Morocco, and which had previously been called Río de Oro (again, see Western Sahara). During World War II, on 14 June 1940, Spain took over Tangier (then an international zone), and in November 1940 incorporated it into Spanish Morocco. In Oct. 1945 Tangier went back to being an international zone. In 1956 Spain, following on the heels of France, gave her protectorate lands back to Morocco (which had become independent of France in March). Spain still holds enclaves in Morocco — Alhucemas, Chafarinas, Velez de la Gomera, Ceuta, and Melilla. Until 1969 Spain also held Ifni, but it gave it to Morocco that year. The last Spanish troops left Morocco proper on 31 Aug. 1961.

Captains-General: 1847–1851 Antonio Ros de Olano; 1851–1854 Salvador de la Puente Pita; 1854–1857 Mariano Rebigliato; 1857–1858 Carlos Tobía; 1858–1858 Manuel Gasset Mercader; 1858–1864 Ramón Gómez Pulido; 1864–1865 Manuel Álvarez Maldonaldo; 1865–1866 Ramón Gómez Pulido; 1866–1866 Antonio Peláez Campomanes; 1866–1868 José Oribe Sans; 1868–1868 Antonio del Rey y Caballero; 1868–1870 Joaquín Cristón y Gasatín; 1870–1872 Enrique Serrano Dolz; 1872–1873 Carlos Sáenz Delcourt; 1873–1873 Manuel Keller y García; 1873–1875 Fulgencio Gávila y Solá; 1875–1876 Pedro Sartorius y Tapia; 1876–1877 Fernando del Piño Villamil; 1877–1877 Juan García Torres; 1877–1878 Victoriano López Pinto; 1878–1879 José María Velasco Postigo; 1879–1881 José Aizpuru y Lorriez Fontecha; 1881–1883 José Merello y Calvo; 1883–1883 José Pascual de Bonanza; 1883–1889 Juan López Pinto y Marín Reyna; 1889–1891 Narciso de Fuentes y Sánchez; 1891–1894 Miguel Correia y García; 1894–1898 Rafael Correia y García; 1898–1901 Jacinto de León y Barreda; 1901–1903 Manuel de Aguilar y Diosdado; 1903–1907 Francisco Fernández Bernal; 1907–1908 Fernando Álvarez de Sotomayor y Flórez; 1908–1910 José García Aldave; 1910–3 April 1913 Felipe Alfau y Mendoza. *High*

Commissioners: 3 April 1913–15 Aug. 1913 Felipe Alfau y Mendoza; 17 Aug. 1913–9 July 1915 José Marina y Vega; 9 July 1915–18 Nov. 1918 Francisco Gómez y Jordana; 18 Nov. 1918–27 Jan. 1919 [unknown] (acting); 27 Jan. 1919–13 July 1922 Dámaso Berenguer y Fuste; 15 July 1922–22 Jan. 1923 Ricardo Burguete y Lana; 22 Jan. 1923–16 Feb. 1923 Miguel Villanueva (never took office); 16 Feb. 1923–14 Sept. 1923 Luis Silvela y Casado; 14 Sept. 1923–25 Sept. 1923 [unknown] (acting); 25 Sept. 1923–2 Oct. 1924 Luis Aizpuru; 2 Oct. 1924–16 Oct. 1924 [unknown] (acting); 16 Oct. 1924–2 Nov. 1925 Miguel Primo de Rivera y Orbaneja; 2 Nov. 1925–1928 José Sanjurjo, Marqués de Malmusi; 1928–19 April 1931 Francisco Gómez Jordana y Sousa; 19 April 1931–20 June 1931 José Sanjurjo, Marqués de Malmusi; 20 June 1931–May 1933 Luciano Ferrer; May 1933–23 Jan. 1934 Juan Moles; 23 Jan. 1934–March 1936 Manuel Avello; March 1936–July 1936 Juan Moles; July 1936–1936 Álvarez Buylla; 1936–1936 Sáenz de Buruaga; 1936–1936 Francisco Franco Bahamonde; 1936–Aug. 1937 Luis Orgaz y Yoldi; Aug. 1937–1939 Juan Beigbeder y Atienza; 1939–Feb. 1940 [unknown] (acting); Feb. 1940–12 May 1941 Carlos Asensio; 12 May 1941–4 March 1945 Luis Orgaz y Yoldi; 4 March 1945–March 1951 José Iglesias; March 1951–7 April 1956 Rafael Valiño y Marcen. *Khalifas (Sultan's Representatives):* 19 April 1913–9 Nov. 1923 Mulay al-Mahdi; 9 Nov. 1923–8 Nov. 1925 [vacant]; 8 Nov. 1925–7 April 1956 Mulay Hassan ben al-Mahdi. *Note:* For list of French residents-general of French Morocco, see that entry. *Note:* For list of Sultans of Morocco, see that entry. *Note:* For list of Prime Ministers of Morocco, see that entry.

Spanish Sahara see **Western Sahara**

Spanish Territories of the Gulf of Guinea see **Equatorial Guinea**

Spanish West Africa see **Western Sahara**

SSLM see **Southern Sudan**

Stanleyville People's Republic. 7 Sept. 1964–1 July 1965. *Location:* Kisangani, in Congo (Zaire). *Capital:* Stanleyville (established 1883 and first known as Falls Station, it was renamed for Henry Morton Stanley, pioneer of the Belgian Congo,

and in 1966 it was renamed again, as Kisangani). *Other names:* République Populaire du Congo, or Congolese People's Republic.

History: In 1964 rebels took over Stanleyville with the intention of overthrowing Moise Tshombe's government in the Democratic Republic of the Congo [see Congo (Zaire)]. Less than a year later the rebel government died out.

Presidents: 7 Sept. 1964–1 July 1965 Christophe Gbenye.

Stanleyville Republic. 13 Dec. 1960–5 Aug. 1961. *Location:* around Kisangani, in Congo (Zaire). *Capital:* Stanleyville (see Stanleyville People's Republic for a brief history of this city).

History: In 1960 Antoine Gizenga, the former premier of the Congo [see Congo (Zaire)] broke away and formed his own government at Stanleyville. It lasted almost a year before being taken back into the Congo.

Prime Ministers: 13 Dec. 1960–5 Aug. 1961 Antoine Gizenga.

Stellaland. 26 July 1882–7 Aug. 1883. *Location:* eastern British Bechuanaland, part of Korannaland. *Capital:* Vrijburg. *Other names:* Republic of Stellaland (named for a comet seen at the time — "stella" is Latin for "star").

History: In 1882 the Boers technically invaded British territory, and set up the Republic of Stellaland, to be followed soon after by Goshen. In 1883 the two republics merged, as the United States of Stellaland.

Administrators: 26 July 1882–7 Aug. 1883 Gerrit Van Niekerk.

Stellenbosch see **Griqualand West**

Stoltenhoff Island see **Tristan da Cunha**

Sudan. 12 June 1821– . *Location:* the largest country in Africa, it lies south of Egypt. *Capital:* Khartoum (from 1898); Omdurman (1885–1898); Khartoum (1823–1885. Khartoum was founded in 1821 as a Turkish camp, and the name means "elephant's tusk." By 1823 it was a city). *Other names:* is-Sudan (local name); The Sudan; Jumhuriyat is-Sudan, or the Republic of the Sudan (from 1985); Jumhuriyat is-Sudan ad-Dimuqratiyah, or Democratic Republic of the Sudan (1956–1985); Anglo-Egyptian Sudan, or Anglo-Egyptian Condominium (1899–1952); al-Mahdiyah, or the Mahdist State (1884–1898); Egyptian Sudan (1821–1884).

History: In 1818 the Turkish–Egyptian Army conquered the Red Sea coast of what is now the Sudan, including the strategic port of Suakin. Massawa, in Eritrea, was also included in the new territory of conquest the same year. Nubia was conquered from 1820 to 1822, and the Funj Sultanate and Kordofan in 1821 and 1822 respectively. Khartoum was founded in 1823, and in 1871 Equatoria was included within the country, and Darfur joined in 1874. Harar also became an Egyptian province in 1874, later becoming British Somaliland. In 1881 Muhammad Ahmad proclaimed himself the Mahdi (the awaited redeemer of Islam) and set about a holy war (jihad) against foreign rule, with the aim of re-establishing basic Islamic principles in the Sudan. He soon began to conquer the area, and by 6 Jan. 1884 had taken over all of the former Egyptian Sudan, although the Egyptian Sudan did not officially come to an end until General Gordon was killed at Khartoum on 26 Jan. 1885. The Mahdi died soon afterwards, and his ideals became lost in the power struggles of the new political state. By 2 Sept. 1898 the British and Egyptian forces, led by Lord Kitchener, had conquered the Sudan, and occupied it, and on 19 Jan. 1899 the country officially became the Anglo-Egyptian Condominium (the idea of a condominium being Lord Cromer's). Although both Britain and Egypt ruled the country technically, in fact only Britain did. The governors-general were nominated by the khedive of Egypt and approved by Britain. Sudanese nationalism first appeared in the early 1920s, and on 19 Nov. 1924, the governor-general of the Sudan, Sir Lee Stack, was assassinated in Cairo. On 22 Oct. 1952 the Sudan won self-rule, and on 1 Jan. 1956 it became fully independent as the Democratic Republic of the Sudan. On 17 Nov. 1958 General Ibrahim Abboud came to power after a bloodless coup, and over the next few years there were occasional attempts to overthrow the new military government. Beginning in the late 50s, and gathering momentum ever since until it looks like drawing to a successful conclusion, has been the movement (or movements) for the independence of Southern Sudan. This is of enormous consequence to both the people in the Southern Sudan and the central government in Khartoum, so much so that over the decades it has killed millions of people and ruined the country. For more on this issue, see Southern Sudan. Following a disastrous economic decade

there was another coup in 1969. President Numayri was repressive, and survived several coup attempts, but on 6 April 1985 one succeeded, and a transitional military council was set up three days later. On 15 Dec. 1985 the country became the Republic of the Sudan, with disastrous consequences, political, economic, and libertarian, to the man in the street. There was another coup in 1989, and Sudan made the mistake of supporting Iraq in the Gulf War. In 2003 a rebellion began in Darfur, in the west of the Sudan, with disastrous consequences to the nation as a whole. The Sudan has been beset by ethnic cleansing, slavery, forced labor, harboring terrorists, poverty, starvation, AIDS, and, of course, the decades of civil war with the South. However, by 2005 things were looking brighter as far as the South goes. John Garang, the southern leader, was sworn in as the first vice president of the Sudan, and as president of the newly-formed government of the Southern Sudan.

Egyptian Rulers: 12 June 1821–1825 no fixed central administration. *Governors-General:* 1825–1826 Uthman Bey; 1826–March 1826 Mahhu Bey; March 1826–June 1838 Khurshid Pasha; June 1838–6 Oct. 1843 Ahmad Pasha Abu Wadan; 6 Oct. 1843–1844 [unknown]. *Military Commanders:* 1844–1845 Ahmad Pasha al-Manikli. *Governors-General:* 1845–1846 [unknown]; 1846–1849 Khalid Pasha; 1849–1850 [unknown]; 1850–Jan. 1851 Abd al-Latif Pasha; Jan. 1851–May 1852 Rustum Pasha; May 1852–1853 Ismail Pasha Abu Jabal; 1853–1854 Salim Pasha; July 1854–Nov. 1854 Ali Pasha Sirri; Nov. 1854–1855 [unknown]; 1855–1857 Ali Pasha Jarkis; 1857–1859 Arakil Bey al-Armani (acting). *Governors:* 1859–1861 Hasan Bey Salamah; 1861–1862 Muhammad Bey Rasileh; 1862–1865 Musa Pasha Hamdi; 1865–Nov. 1865 Umar Bey Fahri (acting). *Governors-General:* Nov. 1865–1866 Ja'far Pasha Sadiq; 1866–5 Feb. 1871 Ja'far Pasha Mazhar; 5 Feb. 1871–Oct. 1872 Mumtaz Pasha; Oct. 1872–1872 Edhem Pasha (acting). *Governors:* 1872–May 1877 Ismail Pasha; May 1877–Dec. 1879 Gordon Pasha (Charles Gordon); Dec. 1879–Feb. 1882 Rauf Pasha; Feb. 1882–May 1882 Geigler Pasha (acting); May 1882–March 1883 Abd al-Qadir Pasha Hilmi; March 1883–5 Nov. 1883 Ala ad-Din Pasha Siddiq; 5 Nov. 1883–18 Feb. 1884 [unknown]; 18 Feb. 1884–26 Jan. 1885 Gordon Pasha (Charles Gordon). *Mahdis:* 29 June 1881–21 June 1885 Muhammad Ahmad ("The

Mahdi"); 21 June 1885–2 Sept. 1898 Abdallah ibn Muhammad at-Taashi ("The Khalifah"). *Military Governors:* 2 Sept. 1898–19 Jan. 1899 Horatio, Lord Kitchener. *Governors-General:* 21 Jan. 1899–23 Dec. 1899 Horatio, Lord Kitchener; 23 Dec. 1899–31 Dec. 1916 Sir Reginald Wingate; 1 Jan. 1917–19 Nov. 1924 Sir Lee Stack; 20 Nov. 1924–5 Jan. 1925 Wasey Sterry (acting); 5 Jan. 1925–17 July 1926 Sir Geoffrey Archer; 17 July 1926–31 Oct. 1926 [unknown] (acting); 31 Oct. 1926–10 Jan. 1934 Sir John Maffey; 10 Jan. 1934–19 Oct. 1940 Sir Stewart Symes; 19 Oct. 1940–19 Oct. 1940 Sir Bernard Bourdillon (never took office); 19 Oct. 1940–8 April 1947 Sir Hubert Huddleston; 8 April 1947–Dec. 1954 Sir Robert Howe; Dec. 1954–11 March 1955 [unknown] (acting); 11 March 1955–12 Dec. 1955 Sir Knox Helm. *Presidents:* 1 Jan. 1956–17 Nov. 1958 [vacant]. *President of the Supreme Council for the Armed Forces:* 17 Nov. 1958–15 Nov. 1964 Ibrahim Abboud. *Presidents:* 15 Nov. 1964–10 June 1965 [vacant]; 10 June 1965–25 May 1969 Ismail al-Azhari. *Chairmen of the Revolutionary Council:* 25 May 1969–19 July 1971 Ja'far an-Numayri. *Communist Presidents:* 19 July 1971–22 July 1971 Babakr an-Nur (never took office). *Presidents:* 22 July 1971–6 April 1985 Ja'far an-Numayri. *Chairmen of Transitional Military Council:* 9 April 1985–15 Dec. 1985 Abd ar-Rahman Siwar ad-Dahab. *Presidents:* 15 Dec. 1985–6 May 1986 Abd ar-Rahman Siwar ad-Dahab. *Chairmen of the Supreme Council:* 6 May 1986–30 June 1989 Ahmad al-Mirghani. *Chairmen of the National Salvation Revolution Command Council:* 30 June 1989–Umar al-Bashir. *Chief Ministers:* 22 Oct. 1952–Nov. 1953 Sayid Abd ar-Rahman ibn al-Mahdi; Nov. 1953–9 Jan. 1954 [unknown] (acting); 9 Jan. 1954–1 Jan. 1956 Ismail al-Azhari. *Prime Ministers:* 1 Jan. 1956–5 July 1956 Ismail al-Azhari; 5 July 1956–17 Nov. 1958 Abdallah Khalil; 1 Nov. 1964–14 June 1965 Sirr al-Khatim al-Khalifah; 14 June 1965–27 July 1966 Muhammad Mahjub; 27 July 1966–16 May 1967 Sadiq al-Mahdi; 16 May 1967–25 May 1969 Muhammad Mahjub; 25 May 1969–28 Oct. 1969 Abu Bakr Awadullah; 9 Aug. 1976–10 Sept. 1977 Rashid Bakr; 22 April 1985–15 Dec. 1985 al-Gizouli Dafalla; 6 May 1986–30 June 1989 Sadiq al-Mahdi. *Note:* In times of no Prime Minister, the President or Head of State held that office.

Sudan Federation see **Mali Federation**

SWAPO see **Namibia**

Swazi Territory see **KaNgwane**

Swaziland. 1818– . *Location:* in Southern Africa, it is a small country, surrounded on three sides by South Africa, and on one side by Mozambique, which blocks Swaziland's route to the Indian Ocean. *Capital:* Mbabane (from 1906); Bremersdorf (from 1893 to 1906, this town was founded in 1890 by a trader named Bremer); Elangeni (1818–1893).

History: A Nguni clan originally from southern Tongaland and called Ngwani, related to the Zulus, the Swazi were pursued to what is now Swaziland from the Pongolo River by the Zulus between 1818 and 1820. The Ngwani chieftaincy had been in existence for over 200 years, and the first king of Swaziland, Somhlolo (also known as Sobhuza I), represented the continual chain of monarchy. He tried to live in peace, but his son, Mswati (also known as Mswazi), after whom the country is named, was a more aggressive king, and cultivated friendship with the Boers. On the death of Mswati the Boers took an active interest in Swaziland, supporting Mbandzeni in his claim to the Paramount Chieftaincy. By 1878 there were numerous Europeans there, driven by the quest for gold and game hunting. In 1893 the Queen Regent applied to Britain for protection, which happened on 13 Nov. 1893 under Transvaal direction (i.e. Swaziland was protected from the Transvaal, rather than from Cape Town, and there was no resident in Swaziland itself). On 1 Dec. 1906 Swaziland became one of the three High Commission Territories in Southern Africa (cf. Basutoland and Bechuanaland, for which see Lesotho and Botswana respectively), directly dependant on the High Commissioner for South Africa (see South Africa for those High Commissioners after 1910, and Cape Colony for those between 1906 and 1910), and administered locally through a resident commissioner. On 1 Aug. 1964 the High Commission Territories came to an end, and Swaziland was granted limited self-rule on the way to independence. On 25 April 1967 the country became fully self-governing, and the kingdom (recognized as a kingdom by the British in 1961) was empowered to rule. On 6 Sept. 1968 Swaziland became fully independent as the Kingdom of Swaziland. The 1980s and especially the 1990s saw the king's absolute power threatened by ever increasingly violent student strikes. In 1992 there was a severe drought and famine. The 2000s have seen more pressure being applied to lessen the King's powers. AIDS is the biggest single problem in Swaziland.

Paramount Chiefs: 1818–1836 Somhlolo (also known as Sobhuza I); 1836–1868 Mswati (also known as Mswazi); 1868–1874 Ludvonga; 1874–6 Oct. 1889 Mbandzeni (also known as Umbandzeni); 23 Oct. 1889–1899 Ubanu (also known as Bunu, Boon, and Ngwane). *Ngwenyamas (Kings):* 1899–1899 Isitoso. *Paramount Chiefs:* 1899–4 Sept. 1921 Sobhuza II. *Ngwenyamas (Kings):* 4 Sept. 1921–21 Aug. 1982 Sobhuza II. *Queens-Regent:* 21 Aug. 1982–10 Aug. 1983 Dzeliwe Shongwe; 10 Aug. 1983–25 April 1986 Ntombi Thwala. *Ngwenyamas (Kings):* 25 April 1986–Mswati III. *Administrators:* 19 Feb. 1895–1902 T. Krogh; 1902–1907 Enraght Mooney. *Resident Commissioners:* 1907–1916 Robert Coryndon; 1916–Oct. 1928 Montagu Honey; Oct. 1928–1 April 1935 Thomas A. Dickson; 1 April 1935–Oct. 1935 [unknown] (acting); Oct. 1935–Nov. 1937 Allan Marwick; Nov. 1937–30 Sept. 1942 Charles Bruton; 30 Sept. 1942–25 Aug. 1946 Eric Featherstone; 25 Aug. 1946–1950 Edward Beetham; 1950–1956 David Morgan; 1956–1963 Brian Marwick. *Commissioners:* 1963–1964 Sir Brian Marwick; 1964–6 Sept. 1968 Francis Loyd (knighted 1965). *Prime Ministers:* 25 April 1967–17 March 1976 Makhosini Dhlamini; 17 March 1976–25 Oct. 1979 Maphevu Dhlamini; 25 Oct. 1979–23 Nov. 1979 Ben Nsibandze (acting); 23 Nov. 1979–23 March 1983 Mandabala Fred Dhlamini; 23 March 1983–6 Oct. 1985 Bhekimpi Dhlamini; 6 Oct. 1985–13 July 1989 Sotsha Ernest Dhlamini; 13 July 1989–25 Oct. 1993 Obed Dhlamini; 25 Oct. 1993–4 Nov. 1993 Andreas Fakudze (acting); 4 Nov. 1993–8 May 1996 Prince Jameson Mbilini Dhlamini; 8 May 1996–26 July 1996 Sishayi Nxumalo; 26 July 1996–29 Sept. 2003 Barnabas Sibusiso Dhlamini; 29 Sept. 2003–14 Nov. 2003 Paul Shabangu; 14 Nov. 2003–Themba Dhlamini.

Swedish Gold Coast. 22 April 1650–20 April 1663. *Location:* the coast of present-day Ghana. *Capital:* Fort Frederiksborg.

History: In 1640 the Swedes arrived on the Gold Coast, and by 1650 had started a colony with bases at Butri and Carlsborg (later called Cape Coast Castle). Later on Anamabo, Osu, Takoradi, Apollonia, and Fort Frederiksborg (later called Christiansborg) came under their control, but by 1663 the Swedish posts had all fallen to the Danes (see Danish Gold Coast).

Directors: 22 April 1650–1656 Hendrik Carlof. *Governors:* 1656–Feb. 1658 J. Philippus von Krusenstierna. *Commanders:* (?)–20 April 1663 Tonnies Voss.

Swellendam. 18 June 1795–Nov. 1795. *Location:* in the Breede River Valley, Cape Colony, South Africa. *Capital:* Swellendam (founded in 1743 and named for the Cape governor Hendrik Swellengrebel and his wife, née Damme, it is the third oldest settlement in the Cape).

History: In 1795, following the lead of Graaff-Reinet, the Cape Town–ruled administrative district of Swellendam revolted against the rule of the local landdrost (magistrate) and declared an independent colony, answerable to the Dutch government in Europe. Often referred to by historians as an independent republic, it submitted to the British when they took over the Cape in 1795, and was re-incorporated into Cape Colony.

National Commandants: 18 June 1795–Nov. 1795 Petrus Jacobus Delport. *Presidents of the National Assembly:* 18 June 1795–Nov. 1795 Hermanus Steyn.

Table Bay see **Cape Colony**

Tadjouna see **Djibouti**

Tagali see **Bedde**

Tagant. ca. 1580–1905. *Location:* in Mauritania. *Capital:* Tagant.

History: Founded in the late 16th century, the Muslim dynasty of Idu Aysh, descendants of the Almoravids, created the amirate of Tagant, which in 1905 was incorporated by the French into their civil territory of Mauritania.

Amirs: ca. 1580–ca. 1595 Ould Rizg; ca. 1595–ca. 1730 [unknown]; ca. 1730–ca. 1785 Sheikh Muhammad Shayin; ca. 1785–ca. 1820 Muhammad al-Bakr; ca. 1820–ca. 1831 Su'aidi Ahmad; ca. 1831–1836 Muhammad Sayin; 1836–1 April 1905 Bakar; 1 April 1905–1905 Uthman; 1905–Aug. 1918 not recognized as an amirate; Aug. 1918–(?) Abd ar-Rahman.

Tahart see **Rustumid Amirate**

Tahert see **Rustumid Amirate**

Tambookieland see **Tembuland**

Tanga see **Tangier**

Tanganyika. 9 Oct. 1916–26 April 1964. *Location:* the same as German East Africa, minus Ruanda–Urundi, or, put another way, the mainland of what is today Tanzania. On the north it was bordered by Kenya and Uganda; on the west by Ruanda–Urundi and the Belgian Congo; and on the south by Northern Rhodesia, Nyasaland, and Mozambique; on the east it was bounded by the Indian Ocean. *Capital:* Dar es-Salaam (the name means "haven of peace" in Arabic). *Other names:* Tanganyika Territory (1946–1961); British-Occupied German East Africa (1916–1920).

History: In 1916, during World War I, Britain and Belgium occupied the German East African Protectorate (see German East Africa). The Belgians got the Ruanda–Urundi part, and the British got the rest, the bigger part. At the Treaty of Versailles in 1919 (effective on 10 Jan. 1920) the League of Nations awarded the country to Britain as a mandate, and Sir Cosmo Parkinson dreamed up the name Tanganyika for the new land. From the beginning the British embarked on a policy that was very pro-native, securing the Africans' land rights and training them for government. In the 1930s two specters hung over Tanganyika: the first was the Great Depression, and the second was the fear that Tanganyika would be handed back to Germany, as a British appeasement to a colony-hungry Hitler, but this latter fear never materialized as a reality. to On 11 Dec. 1946 it became a United Nations Trust Territory, and was known as Tanganyika Territory. On 1 May 1961 it won self-rule, and on 9 Dec. 1961 became independent as a dominion of Great Britain. On 9 Dec. 1962 the Republic of Tanganyika came into being. In January 1964 President Nyerere asked the British to come in to put down an Army mutiny. Later in 1964 Tanganyika joined with Zanzibar to form the United Republic of Tanganyika and Zanzibar (see Tanzania). *Administrators:* 9 Oct. 1916–22 July 1920 Horace Byatt (knighted 1919). *Governors:* 22 July 1920–1924 Sir Horace Byatt; 1924–5 March 1925 John Scott (acting); 5 March 1925–1929 Sir Donald Cameron; 1929–1929 Douglas Jardine (acting); 1929–Jan. 1931 Sir Donald Cameron; Jan. 1931–1933 Sir Stewart Symes; 1933–19 Feb. 1934 [unknown] (acting); 19 Feb. 1934–8 July 1938 Sir Harold MacMichael; 8 July 1938–19 June 1941 Sir Mark Young; 19 June 1941–28 April 1945 Sir Wilfred Jackson; 28 April 1945–18 June 1949 Sir William Battershill; 18 June 1949–15 July 1958 Sir Edward Twining; 15 July 1958–1 May 1961 Sir Richard Turnbull. *Governors-General:* 1 May 1961–9 Dec. 1962 Sir Richard Turnbull. *Presidents:* 2 Nov. 1962–26 April 1964 Julius Nyerere. *Chief Ministers:* 2 Sept. 1960–1 May 1961 Julius Nyerere. *Prime Ministers:* 1 May 1961–22 Jan. 1962 Julius Nyerere; 22 Jan. 1962–9 Dec. 1962 Rashidi Kawawa. *Note:* In times of no Prime Minister, the President held that office.

Tanganyika and Zanzibar see **Tanzania**

Tangier. 1421–29 Oct. 1956. *Location:* one of the chief ports in northern Morocco, just across the Straits of Gibraltar from Spain. *Capital:* Tangier. *Other names:* Tanga; Tanja.

History: Tangier seems to have been named for Tingis, an ancient, pre–Roman city, which stood very close to today's Tangier, and which Augustus Caesar made a free city of the Roman Empire. It became the capital city of the old Roman Province of Mauretania Tingitana between 42 and A.D. 395 In 395 it came under the Diocese of Spain, in the Roman Prefecture of Gaul, and for the next several centuries Tangier followed the destiny of most of North Africa (see Vandal North Africa, Byzantine North Africa, and Arab North Africa). By 789 the Idrisids were in control here (see Idrisid State), and they were succeeded by the Almoravids (see Almoravid Empire), and then by the Almohads (see Almohad Empire). Then the Merinid Empire took over, and in 1421 the Merinid governor of Tangier (see Morocco) became an independent amir. On 28 Aug. 1471 the Portuguese took Tangier. Between 1580 and 1656 Portugal belonged to Spain, and therefore so did all of the Portuguese possessions, even though Portuguese governors continued to run Tangier, until 29 Jan. 1662, when, as a result of Charles II of England marrying Catherine de Braganza of Portugal, Tangier came with her (as did Bombay, in India). This was the first English possession in Africa that was not company-owned. A long siege by the Mulay Ismail as-Samin, sultan of Morocco, caused the English to abandon the town and the fortress on 6 Feb. 1684, and the town became part of Morocco, as the sultan's ambassadorial city, i.e. the town in which he received foreign visitors so that the capital Fez (or other cities that were the Moroccan capital over the years), would be left untouched by European influence. As a result of the Algeciras Act of 1906 Tangier was recognized as an international town. This was due to its being so close to the British port of Gibraltar, and having such a strategic location which might affect all European sea traffic in the Mediterranean. In 1913 negotiations between Britain, France and Spain began to make Tangier an international zone, with an international administration. However, World War I stopped the negotiations, and during the course of the War Spain hoped that it might get Tangier for itself. In 1923, as a result of the Statute of Tangier, the city and surrounding areas did, in fact, become an international zone, administered by internationally elected officials representing Britain, France (both of whom signed in 1923), Spain (signed in 1924), Portugal, the Netherlands, Belgium, and (later) the USA, Sweden, and Italy (1928). This was a neutral territory, and Spanish and French troops having to go through it on the way to or from Europe had to apply to do so from the Tangier authorities first. Tangier had its own police force of 250 Moroccans under a Belgian chief with French and Spanish lieutenants. The sultan of Morocco had the final say regarding native administration and institutions in Tangier. The Tangier legislative assembly consisted of 26 members, 17 of whom were Europeans, and rest of whom were Moroccan subjects of the Sultan. The Europeans comprised four French, four Spanish, three British, two Italian, one American, one Belgian, one Dutch, and one Portuguese, all nominated by their respective consuls. The Moroccans comprised six Muslims and three Jews. The Sultan's representative presided over the assembly. The French were the main power, though, in the International Zone, with Spain coming second. Spain expressed frustration at the working of the Zone, and Italy wanted to come in, so in 1928 the terms of the Statute of Tangier were revised. However, Spain still wanted Tangier for itself, and during World War II Spain did, in fact, take control of Tangier on 14, June 1940, and in November 1940 they made it a part of Spanish Morocco. In October 1945 the international zone

was resumed, with modifications favoring the United States, and with the USSR now involved. Italy was re-admitted in 1948. On 29 Oct. 1956, after some violent nationalist riots in 1952, Tangier reverted to a now independent Morocco. The sultan of Morocco appointed his own governor of Tangier from that time. The internationality of Tangier was formally and finally abolished on April 18, 1960, when it was re-integrated financially with Morocco.

Amirs: 1421–1437 Salih ibn Salih; 1437–28 Aug. 1471 Abu'l Hassan Ali al-Mandari. *Portuguese Governors:* 28 Aug. 1471–148? Ruis de Melo; 148?–1486 Conde de Oliveira; 1486–1489 Conde de Tarouca; 1489–1501 [unknown]; 1501–1508 Conde de Tarouca; 1508–151? [unknown]; 151?–1522 Conde de Monsanto; 1522–1531 Duarte de Meneses; 1531–1552 João de Meneses; 1552–1553 Luis de Loureiro; 1553–1562 Bernardim de Carvalho; 1562–1564 [unknown]; 1564–1566 Lourenço de Távora; 1566–1572 [unknown]; 1572–1573 Ruis de Carvalho; 1573–1574 [unknown]; 1574–1578 Duarte de Meneses; 1578–15?? Pedro da Silva; 15??–1605 [unknown]; 1605–1610 Nuño de Mendonça; 1610–1614 Afonso de Noronha; 1614–1 July 1617 Conde de Tarouca; 1 July 1617–1621 Pedro Manuel; 1621–1624 Marquês de Montalvão; 1624–1628 Conde de Linhares; 1628–1637 Conde de la Torre; 1637–1643 Conde de Sarzedas; 1643–1653 [unknown]; 1653–1656 Rodrigo de Lencastre; 1656–1661 Conde de Ericeira; 1661–29 Jan. 1662 Luis de Almeida. *English Governors:* 29 Jan. 1662–1663 Earl of Peterborough; 1663–3 May 1664 Earl of Teviot; 3 May 1664–1664 Sir Tobias Bridges (acting); 1664–April 1665 John Fitzgerald; April 1665–1666 Baron Belasyse; 1666–1669 Sir Henry Norwood; 1669–1670 Earl of Middleton; 1670–1672 Sir Hugh Cholmondeley (acting); 1672–1674 Earl of Middleton; 1674–1675 Budgett Meakin (acting); 1675–1680 Earl of Inchiquin; 1680–1681 Sir Edward Sackville; 1681–1683 Sir Piercy Kirke; 1683–6 Feb. 1684 Baron Dartmouth. *International Administrators:* 1923–1926 [unknown]; 1926–1929 Paul Alberge; 1929–14 June 1940 Joseph Le Fur; 14 June 1940–3 Nov. 1940 [unknown]. *Spanish Military Commanders:* 3 Nov. 1940–1941 Col. José Yuste; 1941–18 Nov. 1942 Col. Uriarte; 18 Nov. 1942–Oct. 1945 Col. Pothous. *International Administrators:* Oct. 1945–18 March 1948 Luis Correia; 18 March 1948–Aug. 1948 [unknown]; Aug. 1948–1951

H.L.F.C. Van Vredenbusch; 1951–Dec. 1954 José Archer; 4 Jan. 1955–29 Oct. 1956 Robert d'Hallebast. *Sultan's Representatives:* 1923–1941 al-Hajj Muhammad at-Tazi Bu Ashran; 1941–1945 [vacant]; 1945–1954 al-Hajj Muhammad at-Tazi Bu Ashran; 1954–8 July 1956 Si Ahmad at-Tazi.

Tanja see **Tangier**

Tanzania. 26 April 1964– . *Location:* Tanganyika and Zanzibar, on the east coast of Africa. *Capital:* Dar es-Salaam (executive); Dodoma (legislative). *Other names:* United Republic of Tanganyika and Zanzibar (1964–1964).

History: In 1964 the two neighboring republics of Tanganyika and Zanzibar united to form the United Republic of Tanganyika and Zanzibar. Internal self-government was maintained for Zanzibar as part of the deal. On 29 Oct. 1964 the name of the new country changed to Tanzania. There were border clashes with Uganda in the 1970s, and a war in 1978. Julius Nyerere totally dominated Tanzania from the time it became a united country until he resigned as president in 1985. He allowed no political parties other than his own, but in 1992 this changed as multi-party elections were held for the first time. Nyerere also opened Tanzania up to guerrilla movements, such as those from Angola and Mozambique, for them to use as their base in their wars for independence against the Portuguese. The problems besetting Tanzania are poverty, disease, floods, drought, corruption, and, above all, AIDS.

Presidents: 27 April 1964–5 Nov. 1985 Julius Nyerere; 5 Nov. 1985–23 Nov. 1995 Ali Hassan Mwinyi; 23 Nov. 1995–Benjamin William Mkapa. *Prime Ministers:* 17 Feb. 1972–13 Feb. 1977 Rashidi Kawawa; 13 Feb. 1977–5 Nov. 1980 Edward M. Sokoine; 7 Nov. 1980–24 Feb. 1983 Cleopa David Msuya; 24 Feb. 1983–12 April 1984 Edward M. Sokoine; 24 April 1984–6 Nov. 1985 Salim Ahmad Salim; 6 Nov. 1985–9 Nov. 1990 Joseph Warioba; 9 Nov. 1990–7 Dec. 1994 John Malecela; 7 Dec. 1994–28 Nov. 1995 Cleopa David Msuya; 28 Nov. 1995–Frederick Sumaye. *Note:* In times of no Prime Minister, the President held that office.

Tarabalus see **Tripolitania**

Tarfaya see **Spanish Morocco**

Taulud see **Massawa**

Tawanaland see **Batwanaland**

Tchad see **Chad**

Teda see **Zaghawa Kingdom**

Tekoror see **Tukolor Empire**

Tembuland. 1750–14 July 1885. *Location:* Transkei, South Africa. *Capital:* Umtata. *Other names:* Tambookieland; Thembuland; Amathembuland.

History: A branch of the Southern Nguni, the Tembu formed a kingdom in 1750, named for an early king, Tembu, brother of Xhosa. In 1885 it went to Britain as part of the Cape Colony.

Kings: ca. 1750–1800 Ndaba; 1800–10 Aug. 1830 Ngubencuka. *Regent:* 1830–1845 Fadana. *Kings:* 1845–1849 Mthikrakra. *Regents:* 1849–1863 Joyi. *Kings:* 1863–31 Dec. 1884 Nyangelizwe; 1885–22 April 1920 Dalindyebo. *Regents:* 1 Oct. 1920–1 Oct. 1924 Silimela. *Kings:* 1 Oct. 1924–6 July 1928 Jangilizwe (also known as Sampu). *Regent:* 7 July 1928–19 Aug. 1942 Jongintaba. *Kings:* 8 Jan. 1943–30 June 1954 Dabulamanzi; 30 June 1954–1980 Sabata; 1980–1987 Bambilanga; June 1988–May 1989 Zondwa; May 1989–(?) Bayelekhaya. *Queen:* 2000–Noluntu (acting).

Temne see **Koya-Temne** and **Sierra Leone**

Tenerife. 1495– . *Location:* the second largest of the Canary Islands. *Capital:* Santa Cruz de Tenerife (from 1625); La Laguna (founded in 1496 and named for the old [extinct] lagoon, this was the capital until 1625). *Other names:* Teneriffe (the origin of the name is uncertain: possibly "Tener" and "Yfe" meaning "Snow Mountain").

History: In 1495 Tenerife was conquered by Spain, and became one of the two most important of the Canary Islands (see also Gran Canaria). In 1496 the Governor of Tenerife became, for a few years, the Governor-General of all the Canaries, but as each island continued to function under its own governor, this system neither lasted long nor worked dramatically well. However, in 1589, a Captain-General was appointed to rule over all the Canaries, each island becoming a territory of the captaincy-general. In 1595 the captaincy-general was dissolved, and Tenerife resumed its status as an individual colony. In 1625, though, the captaincy-general was brought back, this time to stay, and Tenerife became a territory once more. In 1821 the captaincy-general was finally dissolved, and Tenerife, and all the other islands in the Canaries group, became part of the Spanish province of the Canary Islands. In 1912 the Canaries became a Spanish protectorate, and in 1927 this protectorate was split up into two provinces of Metropolitan Spain: Santa Cruz de Tenerife and Las Palmas de Gran Canaria (see Gran Canaria). This was due to the rivalry between the ports of Las Palmas and Tenerife. The island of Tenerife was the main constituent part of the province of Santa Cruz de Tenerife. In 1983 the Canaries, as a whole, became an autonomous province of Spain.

Governors: 1495–1525 Alonso de Lugo; 1525–1538 Pedro de Lugo; 1538–1540 Alfonso Dávila; 1540–1543 Juan Verdugo; 1543–1546 Jerónimo de Sotomayor; 1546–1548 Diego de Figueroa; 1548–1550 Juan Bautista de Ayora; 1550–1551 Duque de Estrada; 1551–1554 Juan de Miranda; 1554–1557 Juan de Cepeda; 1557–1558 [unknown]; 1558–1559 Hernando de Cañizares; 1559–1561 [unknown, but possibly a man with the last name of Plaza); 1561–1562 Alfonso de Llarena; 1562–1565 Armenteros de Paz; 1565–1567 Juan de Guevara; 1567–1570 Eugenio de Salazar; 1570–1573 Juan del Campo; 1573–1577 Juan de Fonseca; 1577–1579 Juan de Leiva; 1579–1582 Juan de Fonseca; 1582–1584 Lázaro de León; 1584–1589 Juan de la Fuente; 1589–1597 Tomás de Cangas; 1597–1601 Pedro de la Vega; 1601–1603 Luis Gudiel y Ortiz; 1603–1608 Francisco de Benavides; 1608–1615 Juan de Espinosa; 1615–1618 Melchor de Pereda; 1618–1621 Diego Bazán; 1621–1624 Rodrigo de Bohorques; 1624–1625 Diego Bracamonte. *Rulers:* 1625–1821 ruled direct by the captain-general of the Canary Islands; 1821–[unknown].

Tenkodogo see **Mossi States**

Territory of the Afars and Issas see **Djibouti**

Thembuland see **Tembuland**

Thongaland see **GazaNkulu** and **Tongaland**

Tikar see **Bamoun**

Timbuktu. 30 May 1591–1780. *Location:* in Mali. *Capital:* Timbuktu. *Other names:* Tombouctou (the French name); Timbuctu; Timbuctoo.

History: Tin Buktu ("place of Buktu — an old woman), the most mysterious town in Africa. Founded by Tuaregs as a camp about 1100, it became the terminus of one of the major Trans-Saharan caravan routes, and between the 15th and 17th centuries also a center for Islam in Africa. It became part of the Ghana Empire, the Mali Empire, and in the 1300s for a while a part of Yatenga. Then the Tuaregs ruled it until 29 Nov. 1468, when the Songhai Empire took it over. Timbuktu had always been more than just a town. It was a small state, with the city as the capital. Its fame spread to the rest of the world relatively quickly (and not just because id the euphony of its name). By 1375 it was to be found on a Spanish map. Under the Songhais Timbuktu reached its height, but in 1591 it was taken by the Moroccans, as was a lot of what is today Mali. Timbuktu became the capital of these marauding Moroccans, and was ruled by a Moroccan pasha who, more and more as the years went by, became independent from his masters in Marrakesh. The decline of Timbuktu was evident by 1780 when the Bambara tribes made a second and more permanent conquest of the city. In 1800 the Tuaregs took it over; 1813–1814 saw it in the hands of Masina; 1814–1826 in the hands of the Tuaregs once more; then from 1826 to 1844 in the hands of Masina again. From 1844 to 1862 the Tuaregs regained control of Timbuktu, and the Tukolor Empire took it from them. In July 1893 it became part of the Military Territory of the French Sudan (see Mali).

Pashas: 17 Aug. 1591–1594 Mahmud I; 1594–1597 al-Mansur I; 1597–1599 Mahmud Taba II; 1599–1600 Ammar I; 1600–1604 Suleiman; 1604–11 Oct. 1612 Mahmud Longo III; 11 Oct. 1612–13 March 1617 Ali I; 13 March 1617–June 1618 Ahmad I; June 1618–Jan. 1619 Haddu; Jan. 1619–4 Nov. 1621 Muhammad I; 4 Nov. 1621–1622 Hammu I; 1622–1627 Yusuf I; 1627–1628 Ibrahim I; 1628–July 1632 Ali II; July 1632–17 Oct. 1632 Ali III; 17 Oct. 1632–1634 Sa'ud I; 1634–1635 Abd ar-Rahman I; 1635–1637 Sa'id I; 1637–1642 Masud; 1642–1646 Muhammad II; 1646–1647 Ahmad II; 1647–1647 Hamid; 1647–1651 Yahya I; 1651–1654 Hammadi I; 1654–1654 Muhammad III; 1655–1657 Muhammad IV; 1657–1659 Muhammad

V; 1659–1659 Allal; 1659–1660 al-Hajj al-Mukhtar; 1660–1661 Hammu II; 1661–1662 Ali IV; 1662–1662 Ali V; 1662–1665 Ammar II; 1665–1665 Muhammad VI; 1666–1666 Nasir I; 1666–1667 Abd ar-Rahman II; 1667–1670 Nasir II; 1670–1670 Muhammad VII; 1671–1671 Muhammad VIII; 1672–1675 Ali VI; 1675–1678 Sa'id; 1678–1678 Abdallah I; 1679–1679 Dun-Nun I; 1680–1680 Muhammad IX; 1681–1681 Dun-Nun I; 1682–1682 Muhammad VIII; 1683–1683 Ba-Haddu Salim; 1683–1683 al-Fah Benkano; 1683–1683 Zenka; 1684–1684 Muhammad IX; 1684–1684 Ali VII; 1685–1685 al-Mubarrak I; 1686–1686 Sa'ud II; 1686–1686 al-Hassan; 1687–1687 Abdallah II; 1688–1688 al-Abbas; 1688–1688 al-Mansur II; 1689–1689 Ahmad III; 1690–1690 Sa'ud II; 1691–1691 Sanibar I; 1691–1693 Ibrahim II; 1693–1693 Baba Saiyid I; 1693–1693 al-Mubarrak I; 1693–1694 Ibrahim II; 1694–1694 Dun-Nun I; 1694–1694 Ahmad IV; 1694–1695 Sanibar I; 1695–1696 Abdallah III; 1696–1696 Hammadi II; 1696–1697 al-Mubarrak II; 1697–1697 Muhammad X; 1697–1697 Ali VIII; 1697–1697 Yahya II; 1697–1698 Abdallah IV; 1698–1699 al-Mansur II; 1699–1700 Hammadi II; 1700–1700 Abdallah IV; 1700–1701 Yusuf II; 1701–1701 Muhammad XI; 1701–1702 Ahmad V; 1702–1703 Ali IX; 1703–1703 Santa'a; 1703–1703 Mami I; 1703–1704 Muhammad XI; 1704–1704 Muhammad X; 1704–1705 Abdallah IV; 1705–1705 Sa'id III; 1705–1706 Mami I; 1706–1706 al-Mubarrak III; 1706–1707 Nasir II; 1707–1707 Abdallah IV; 1707–1708 Ali X; 1708–1708 Muhammad XII; 1708–1709 Hammadi III; 1709–1709 Yahya III; 1709–1710 Yahya IV; 1710–1711 Babakar I; 1711–1711 Yusuf II; 1711–1712 Abd al-Qadir; 1712–1712 Abdallah IV; 1712–1712 Ali IX; 1712–1713 al-Mansur III; 1713–1713 Mami I; 1713–1713 Ali X; 1713–1714 Abdallah V; 1714–1714 Ammar III; 1714–1714 Ba-Haddu II; 1714–1715 Abdallah V; 1715–1715 Ba-Haddu II; 1715–1716 Muhammad XII; 1716–1716 Ali XI; 1716–1716 Abdallah V; 1716–1719 al-Mansur II; 1719–1721 Ba-Haddu II; 1721–1722 Abd al-Ja'far I; 1722–1725 Abdallah V; 1725–1726 Mahmud IV; 1726–1726 Abd ar-Rahman III; 1726–1727 Abdallah V; 1727–1729 Ba-Haddu II; 1729–1729 Yusuf II; 1729–1731 Abdallah V; 1731–1732 Muhammad XIII; 1732–1733 al-Hassan II; 1733–1734 Muhammad XII; 1734–1735 Sa'id IV; 1735–1736 Hammadi IV; 1736–1737 Sa'id IV; 1737–1737 Hammadi IV;

1737–1738 Muhammad XII; 1738–1738 al-Fah Ibrahim III; 1738–1738 Hammadi V; 1738–1738 al-Fah Ibrahim IV; 1738–1739 Sa'id V; 1739–1740 Yahya V; 1740–1741 Baba Saiyid II; 1741–1741 al-Hassan III; 1741–1742 Sa'id V; 1742–1743 Sa'id VI; 1743–1745 Sa'id V; 1745–1746 Baba Saiyid II; 1746–1748 al-Fah Mahmud; 1748–1748 Abd al-Ja'far II; 1748–ca. 1749 Babakar II; ca. 1749–ca. 1750 Sa'id VI; ca. 1750–(?) Ali XII; (?)–(?) Ba-Haddu III; (?)–1780 Baba Ali.

Tiris El-Gharbia see **Western Sahara**

Titteri see **Mascara**

Tjimba-Herero see **Namibia**

Tlemcen. 1236–1550. *Location:* northern Algeria. *Capital:* Tlemcen (the name comes from "Tilmisan," the Moorish word for "springs"). *Other names:* Tlemsen; Abd al-Wadid Kingdom; Banu Zayyan Dynasty; Bau Abd al-Wad.

History: Related to the Merinids (see Merinid Empire), the Banu Abd al-Wad were loyal subjects of the Almohad Empire until, with the absolute decline of that empire, the Abd al-Wadid chieftain Abu Yahya Yaghmurasan ibn Zayyan, then governor of the town of Tagrart, declared his independence, and he united the towns of Tagrart and Agadir (the Algerian Agadir — not the Moroccan one) to form his country of Tlemcen, with the capital at the town of Tlemcen. Most of the time this kingdom was at war with the Merinids or the Hafsids (see Hafsid Kingdom), and several times, often for long periods of time, the Abd al-Wadids were forced out of their capital. The dynasty came to an end in 1550, and the town of Tlemcen was captured by Algerian Turks in 1559.

Kings: 1236–March 1283 Abu Yahya Yaghmurasan ibn Zayyan; March 1283–6 June 1304 Abu Sa'id Uthman I; 6 June 1304–14 April 1308 Abu Zayyan I Muhammad; 14 April 1308–22 July 1318 Abu Hammu I Musa; 22 July 1318–May 1336 Abu Tashufin I Abd ar-Rahman; May 1336–1348 occupied by the Merinids; 1348–1352 Abu Sa'id Uthman II Abd ar-Rahman and Abu Thabit (jointly); 1352–9 Feb. 1359 occupied by the Merinids; 9 Feb. 1359–20 May 1360 Abu Hammu II ibn Abi Yaqub; 20 May 1360–1360 Abu Zayyan Muhammad; 1360–1370 Abu Hammu II ibn Abi Yaqub; 1370–1372

Muhammad II; 1372–1383 Abu Hammu II ibn Abi Yaqub; 1383–1384 Muhammad II; 1384–1387 Abu Hammu II ibn Abi Yaqub; 1387–1387 Muhammad II; 1387–1389 Abu Hammu II ibn Abi Yaqub; 1389–29 May 1393 Abu Tashufin II Abd ar-Rahman; 29 May 1393–8 July 1393 Abu Thabit II Yusuf; 8 July 1393–Nov. 1393 Abu Hajjaj Yusuf; Nov. 1393–1397 Abu Zayyan II Muhammad; 1397–1400 Abu Muhammad Abdallah I; 1400–1411 Abu Abdallah Muhammad I; 1411–1411 Abd ar-Rahman ibn Musa; 1411–Nov. 1412 Abu Sa'id ibn Musa; Nov. 1412–May 1424 Abu Malik Abd al-Wahid; May 1424–1427 Abu Abdallah Muhammad II; 1427–1429 interregnum; 1429–1430 Abu Malik Abd al-Wahid; 1430–1430 Abu Abdallah Muhammad II; 1430–Jan. 1462 Abu al-Abbas Ahmad; Feb. 1462–1468 Abu Abdallah Muhammad III; 1468–1468 Abu Tashufin III; 1468–1504 Abu Abdallah Muhammad IV; 1504–1517 Abu Abdallah Muhammad V; 1517–1527 Abu Hammu III Musa; 1527–Jan. 1541 Abu Muhammad Abdallah II; Jan. 1541–7 March 1543 Abu Zayyan Ahmad; 7 March 1543–June 1543 Abu Abdallah Muhammad VI; June 1543–1550 Abu Zayyan Ahmad; 1550–1550 al-Hasan ibn Abdallah.

Tlokwaland see **Batlokwaland**

Tocolor Empire see **Tukolor Empire**

Togo. 27 Dec. 1916– . *Location:* North West Africa. *Capital:* Lomé. *Other names:* République Togolaise, or Togolese Republic, or Republic of Togo (from 1956); Associated Territory of Togo (1946–1956); French Togoland (alternative name from 1916 to 1956).

History: During World War I the French and British conquered the German colony of Togoland, and split it up between them as a jointly-administered condominium. In 1916 they partitioned it between themselves, with the French getting the bigger part, French Togo land. The British part was known as British Togoland. Both parts became League of Nations mandates, on 30 Sept. 1920. French Togo land became a United Nations trusteeship on 13 Dec. 1946, and France called it the Associated Territory of Togo. On 30 Aug. 1956 the country became a partially autonomous republic, and on 27 April 1960 it became fully independent as the Republic of Togo (the name means "water's edge" in Ewe). The early 1960s saw much violence, most of it directed toward the head of state, Sylvanus Olimpio, who was finally, after three assassination attempts, gunned down outside the U.S. Embassy on 13 Jan. 1963. His successor, Grunitzky, survived a coup attempt in 1966, but was ousted in one that took place in 1967. In the 1980s there was a huge influx of refugees into Togo from other countries, and in 1986 there was another coup attempt. Economic sanctions were imposed on Togo by Europe in 1993. Éyadéma was dictator for almost 40 years, and when he died in 2005 his son became the new president, but stepped down due to international pressure. Togo faces the AIDS specter, and also poverty and corruption.

Governors: 27 Dec. 1916–27 April 1917 Gaston Fourn; 27 April 1917–25 Jan. 1920 Alfred-Louis Woelfel; 25 Jan. 1920–30 Sept. 1920 Numa Sasias (acting); 30 Sept. 1920–1921 Alfred-Louis Woelfel. *Commissioners:* 1921–2 Jan. 1922 Alfred-Louis Woelfel; 2 Jan. 1922–22 Dec. 1922 Auguste Bonnecarrère (acting); 22 Dec. 1922–24 April 1923 Auguste Bonnecarrère; 24 April 1923–9 Oct. 1923 Léon Bauche (acting); 9 Oct. 1923–25 Feb. 1925 Auguste Bonnecarrère; 25 Feb. 1925–21 Nov. 1925 Léon Bauche (acting); 21 Nov. 1925–18 Sept. 1927 Auguste Bonnecarrère; 18 Sept. 1927–13 Jan. 1928 Bernard Sladous (acting); 13 Jan. 1928–Feb. 1929 Léon Pêtre (acting); Feb. 1929–28 May 1930 Auguste Bonnecarrère; 28 May 1930–Dec. 1930 Maurice Bourgine (acting); Dec. 1930–27 Dec. 1931 Auguste Bonnecarrère; 27 Dec. 1931–18 Oct. 1933 Robert de Guise; 18 Oct. 1933–7 May 1934 Léon Pêtre (acting); 7 May 1934–31 Dec. 1934 Maurice Bourgine. *Administrators:* 1 Jan. 1935–25 Sept. 1936 Léon Geismar; 25 Sept. 1936–1937 Michel Montagné. *Commissioners:* 1937–21 Sept. 1938 Michel Montagné (acting); 21 Sept. 1938–April 1939 Marc Antoine Gradassi (acting); April 1939–1 Jan. 1941 Michel Montagné; 1 Jan. 1941–28 Aug. 1941 Léonce Delpech (acting); 28 Aug. 1941–19 Nov. 1941 Léonce Delpech; 19 Nov. 1941–12 April 1942 Jean-François de Saint-Alary (acting); 12 April 1942–31 Aug. 1943 Pierre Saliceti; 31 Aug. 1943–10 Jan. 1944 Albert Mercadier (acting); 10 Jan. 1944–4 Nov. 1944 Jean Noutary (acting); 4 Nov. 1944–31 March 1945 Jean Noutary; 31 March 1945–July 1945 Henri-François Gaudillot (acting); July 1945–8 March 1948 Jean Noutary; 8 March 1948–20 Sept. 1951 Jean Cédile; 20 Sept. 1951–25 April 1952 Yves Digo;

25 April 1952–3 Feb. 1955 Laurent Péchoux; 3 Feb. 1955–6 Aug. 1955 Jean-Louis Bérard (acting); 6 Aug. 1955–23 March 1957 Jean-Louis Bérard; 23 March 1957–June 1957 Joseph Rigal (acting). *High Commissioners:* June 1957–27 April 1960 Georges-Léon Spénale. *Heads of State:* 27 April 1960–12 April 1961 Sylvanus Olimpio. *Presidents:* 12 April 1961–13 Jan. 1963 Sylvanus Olimpio. *Chairmen:* 13 Jan. 1963–5 May 1963 Émanuel Bodjolle. *Presidents:* 16 Jan. 1963–5 May 1963 Nicolas Grunitzky (acting); 5 May 1963–13 Jan. 1967 Nicolas Grunitzky; 13 Jan. 1967–14 April 1967 Kléber Dadjo. *Chairmen of the National Reconciliation Committee:* 14 April 1967–18 April 1967 Étienne Éyadéma. *Presidents:* 18 April 1967–5 Feb. 2005 Étienne Éyadéma (after May 1974 also known as Gnassingbé Éyadéma); 5 Feb. 2005–26 Feb. 2005 Faure Gnassingbé; 26 Feb. 2005–4 May 2005 Abbas Bonfali (interim); 4 May 2005–Faure Gnassingbé. *Chief Ministers:* 12 Sept. 1956–27 April 1958 Nicolas Grunitzky. *Prime Ministers:* 27 April 1958–16 May 1958 Nicolas Grunitzky; 16 May 1958–27 April 1960 Sylvanus Olimpio; 27 Aug. 1991–23 April 1994 Edem Kodjo; 20 April 1996–Kwassi Klutse. *Note:* In times of no Prime Minister, the President or Head of State held that office.

Togoland. 5 July 1884–27 Dec. 1916. *Location:* as the present-day Togo, plus the Volta region of the Republic of Ghana. *Capital:* Lomé (from 1897); Sebe (1887–1897); Bagida (1884–1887). *Other names:* German Togoland; Togo; Togo land French–British Condominium (1914–1916).

History: The Germans arrived at the Togo coast in 1880, following the German missionaries who had been there for forty years. In 1884, after a period of negotiations between the German representative Gustav Nachtigal and the local chiefs, the Imperial flag went up to signify the protectorate of Togoland. Before the Germans it had been little used by either the Ashanti to the west or the people of Dahomey to the east, because it did not have a decent port, and therefore the slave trade could not operate out of there. The Berlin Conference of 1885 recognized Germany's possession of Togoland, and shortly thereafter the new country's borders with the Gold Coast and Dahomey were fixed. Pacification of the interior was an easy job, and the hinterland's boundaries were negotiated and fixed in deals with France in 1897 and with Britain in

1904. Lomé was chosen to be the capital, and the Germans established a plantation economy in Togoland. The Togolese were treated badly by the Germans, forced labor being one of the factors involved. On 1 Jan. 1905 this country became a German colony. On 31 Aug. 1914, Germany surrendered Togoland to the British and French, who then occupied it as a condominium (two powers sharing the administration). At the end of 1916 Britain and France partitioned the country, France getting the larger part, which became French Togoland (see Togo), and Britain getting British Togoland.

Reichskommissars: 5 July 1884–6 July 1884 Gustav Nachtigal. *Provincial Consuls:* 6 July 1884–26 June 1885 Heinrich Randad. *Reichskommissars:* 26 June 1885–May 1887 Ernst Falkenthal; July 1887–17 Oct. 1888 Jesko von Puttkamer (acting); 17 Oct. 1888–14 June 1891 Eugen von Zimmerer; 14 June 1891–4 June 1892 [vacant]; 4 June 1892–1893 Jesko von Puttkamer. *Landeshauptmänner:* 1893–18 Nov. 1895 Jesko von Puttkamer; 18 Nov. 1895–1898 August Köhler. *Governors:* 1898–19 Jan. 1902 August Köhler; 20 Jan. 1902–1 Dec. 1902 [vacant]; 1 Dec. 1902–11 May 1905 Waldemar Horn; 11 May 1905–7 Nov. 1910 Julius Zech; 7 Nov. 1910–31 March 1911 [vacant]; 31 March 1911–19 June 1912 Edmund Brückner; 19 June 1912–31 Aug. 1914 Adolf Frederick, the Herzog of Mecklenburg. *Military Administrators:* 31 Aug. 1914–27 Dec. 1916 Gaston Fourn.

Tomba Island see **Guinea**

Tombouctou see **Timbuktu**

Tongaland. May 1895–1897. *Location:* on the east coast of South Africa, north of Zululand. *Capital:* Kosi Bay. *Other names:* Amatongaland; Thongaland.

History: In May 1895 Britain acquired Tongaland, with its admirable port of Kosi Bay. This was a move designed to block the Boers' route to the sea, and also to stop the Boers from claiming it, which they intended to do. In 1897 Tongaland became a district of **Natal**, and was renamed Ingwavuma.

Rulers: [unknown].

Toro see **Nkore**

Toucouleur Empire see **Tukolor Empire**

Transkei. 26 May 1959–27 April 1994. *Location:* three separate pieces of land in the southeastern portion of South Africa. *Capital:* Umtata (founded in the 1870s and named for the Umtata River). *Other names:* Iriphabliki Yetranskei; Republic of Transkei.

History: This was the bantustan (or native homeland) for the Xhosa peoples of South Africa, and was somewhat the same entity as the District of Transkei in the Transkeian Territories. It was created on 26 May 1959, and in May 1963 achieved self-rule. On 26 Oct. 1976 Transkei became the first of the bantustans in South Africa to gain its independence, a false independence, of course, as it was, like all the other bantustans, totally at the mercy of the whims of the South African government. Moreover, it was an independence not recognized by anyone outside of South Africa. In 1994 the bantustans effectively ceased to exist, as a new regime came to South Africa in which native homelands were no longer needed.

South African Commissioners-General: May 1963–26 Oct. 1976 D. Potgieter. *Presidents:* 26 Oct. 1976–1 Dec. 1978 Botha Sigcau; 20 Feb. 1978–20 Feb. 1986 Chief Kaiser Matanzima; 20 Feb. 1986–9 May 1994 Nyangelizwe Ndamase. *Chief Ministers:* 11 Dec. 1963–26 Oct. 1976 Chief Kaiser Matanzima. *Prime Ministers:* 26 Oct. 1976–20 Feb. 1979 Chief Kaiser Matanzima; 20 Feb. 1979–24 Sept. 1987 George Matanzima; 24 Sept. 1987–5 Oct. 1987 Maj.-Gen. Bantu Holomisa (military usurper); 5 Oct. 1987–30 Dec. 1987 Stella Sigcau. *Heads of Military Council:* 30 Dec. 1987–9 May 1994 Maj.-Gen. Bantu Holomisa.

Transkeian Territories. Dec. 1836–May 1963. *Location:* longitudinally between Natal and Great Kei River, Cape Province, South Africa, and latitudinally between the Drakensberg Mountains and the coast. *Capital:* Kokstad (1879–); Fort Peddie (until 1879, this was the main town, rather than the capital, of Kaffraria Proper). *Other names:* Kaffraria; Kaffraria Proper; Caffraria; Kaffirland; The Native Territories.

History: Kaffraria, or Kaffirland, was a British and Dutch term signifying all the land along the eastern coast of South Africa, between the Umzinkulu and Keiskamma Rivers, i.e those lands inhabited by Xhosas, Pondos, and Tembus, between Natal and the Cape. On 17 Dec. 1847

Queen Adelaide Land, a British possession in what is now the Ciskei (between the Keiskamma and the Kei Rivers) changed its name to British Kaffraria, so the rest of Kaffraria became known as Kaffraria Proper. On 1 Jan. 1866 Alfred (a part of Kaffraria Proper) went to Natal, and in April of that year British Kaffraria was swallowed up by the Cape. Between 1879 and 1894 various portions of Kaffraria Proper were annexed by the Cape, and the native reservation called Transkeian Territories (the word Transkei means "beyond the Kei River") was developed. Fingoland (annexed to the Cape in 1879) and Griqualand East (which had been annexed to the Cape in 1874), became the first component of the new Transkeian Territories in 1879. Next came Tembuland, on 26 Aug. 1885. Bomvanaland and Kreli's Country became parts of the new reserve in 1886, and finally, on 25 Sept. 1894 so did Pondoland. The rest of the Transkei had been added piecemeal over the years. The Territories were divided into four administrative districts — Transkei, Pondoland, Tembuland, and Griqualand East. There were some areas within the Territories that were white settlements, and the reserve was ruled by a magistrate. The Transkei District became a self-governing bantustan in 1963 (see Transkei).

British Residents: Dec. 1836–Feb. 1839 John Bowker; Feb. 1839–Nov. 1845 Theophilus Shepstone; Nov. 1845–Nov. 1846 John Mac lean. *Xhosa Paramount Chiefs:* (?)–(?) Mnguni; (?)–(?) Xhosa; (?)–(?) Malangana; (?)–(?) Nkosiyamntu; (?)–ca. 1550 Tshawe; ca. 1550–ca. 1580 Ngcwangu; ca. 1580–ca. 1610 Sikhomo (also known as Sikomo); ca. 1610–1640 Togu; 1640–1670 Ngconde; 1670–1702 Tshiwo; 1702–1750 Phalo. *Note:* Phalo's base was Galekaland (see under Kreli's Country). Phalo had two sons, Galeka and Rarabe. For their respective dynasties see Kreli's Country and British Kaffraria.

Transorangia. 1824–3 Feb. 1848. *Location:* between the Orange and Vet Rivers, in the southern part of today's Orange Free State province of South Africa. *Capital:* Bloemfontein.

History: In 1824 independent Boer trekkers from Cape Colony began crossing the Orange River to settle here. In 1836 Great Trek Boers arrived and in 1845 Harry Smith established the first white rule, at Bloemfontein, in the form of a British resident. In 1848 Smith, then Sir Harry Smith, finally annexed Transorangia, along with

Winburg, as the Orange River Sovereignty (see Orange Free State).

Residents: 8 March 1845–3 Feb. 1848 Henry Warden.

Transvaal. 16 Dec. 1856–30 May 1910. *Location:* as modern day Transvaal province of South Africa. *Capital:* Pretoria (from 30 Dec. 1880); Heidelberg (this was the capital between 16 Dec. 1880 and 30 Dec. 1880, and was a town founded in 1866 and named for the Heidelberg Catechism used by the Dutch Reformed Church); Pretoria (founded in 1855 and named for Andries Pretorius by his son, and originally called Pretoria Philadelphia, this city was the capital from 3 April 1860 to 16 Dec. 1880); Potchefstroom (until 3 April 1860). *Other names:* Zuid-Afrikaansche Republiek, or South African Republic, or South Africa Republic, or Z.A.R., or S.A.R. (these were all alternative names of the country between 1856 and 1877, again between 1880 and 1881, and then again from 1884 to 1900); Heidelberg Republic (the official name, but not the generally used one, for the last two weeks of 1880).

History: In 1856 the Dutch African Republic became the South African Republic. In Jan. 1858 Zoutpansberg joined the S.A.R., as did the Republic of Lydenburg on 4 April 1860, and this enlarged republic became the major Boer state across the Vaal River from Cape Colony. On 12 April 1877 Britain annexed the S.A.R., calling it the Colony of Transvaal. On 16 Dec. 1880 the Boers received permission for independence, and for two weeks the country was known as the Heidelberg Republic, although the inhabitants never had time to get used to the name. The capital was shifted to the town of Heidelberg, but on 30 Dec. 1880 the name of the country reverted to the South African Republic. On 5 April 1881 it became the state of Transvaal, but on 2 Feb. 1884 it was placed under British suzerainty again, and changed its name yet again to the South Africa Republic (not the South African Republic, as before, although everyone still called it the South African Republic, or Transvaal). On 1 Sept. 1900 it began its final metamorphosis, when it was re-annexed by Britain as the colony of Transvaal. It was officially awarded to Britain on 31 May 1902, after the South African War. On 6 Dec. 1906 the Transvaal achieved self-rule, and on 30 May 1910, at the stroke of midnight at the end of that

day, Transvaal became one of the four provinces of the Union of South Africa (see South Africa).

Presidents: 16 Dec. 1856–1 Jan. 1857 Marthinus Pretorius (acting); 1 Jan. 1857–6 Feb. 1860 Marthinus Pretorius; 6 Feb. 1860–9 Oct. 1860 Johannes Grobelaar (acting); 9 Oct. 1860–2 April 1862 Stephanus Schoeman (acting); 2 April 1862–20 Jan. 1863 Stephanus Schoeman and Willem Van Rensburg (jointly acting); 20 Jan. 1863–24 Oct. 1863 Willem Van Rensburg (acting); 24 Oct. 1863–10 May 1864 Willem Van Rensburg; 10 May 1864–16 Nov. 1871 Marthinus Pretorius; 16 Nov. 1871–1 July 1872 Daniel Erasmus (acting); 1 July 1872. 1875 Thomas Burgers; Feb. 1875–April 1876 Piet Joubert (acting); April 1876–12 April 1877 Thomas Burgers. *Administrators:* 12 April 1877–4 March 1879 Sir Theophilus Shepstone; 4 March 1879–16 Dec. 1880 Owen Lanyon (knighted 1880). *High Commissioners of South-East Africa:* 28 June 1879–29 Sept. 1879 Sir Garnet Wolseley. *Governors/High Commissioners of South-East Africa:* 29 Sept. 1879–16 Dec. 1880 Sir Garnet Wolseley. *Rulers:* 16 Dec. 1880–16 April 1883 Triumvirate of Paul Kruger, Piet Joubert, and Marthinus Pretorius. *Presidents Elect:* 16 April 1883–8 May 1883 Paul Kruger. *Presidents:* 8 May 1883–Sept. 1883 Paul Kruger; Sept. 1883–July 1884 Piet Joubert (acting); July 1884–Aug. 1900 Paul Kruger; Aug. 1900–31 May 1902 Schalk Burger (acting). *Governors:* 21 June 1902–29 Sept. 1902 Alfred, Baron Milner (created Viscount Milner in 1902); 29 Sept. 1902–3 Dec. 1905 Sir Arthur Lawley (acting); 4 Dec. 1905–2 Oct. 1906 Sir Richard Solomon (acting); 2 Oct. 1906–30 May 1910 William Palmer, 2nd Earl of Selborne. *Prime Ministers:* 4 Feb. 1907–30 May 1910 Louis Botha.

Trarza. ca. 1640–12 May 1903. *Location:* in Mauritania. *Capital:* Saint Louis, in Senegal (1902–1903); Trarza (this town was the capital until 1902, when it became merely the local headquarters answerable to the French African capital at Saint Louis).

History: The dynasty of Ulad Ahmad ibn Daman ruled the state of Trarza until it was taken over by the French commandant Coppolani on 15 Dec. 1902 as a protectorate. In 1903 Trarza became part of the new French protectorate of Mauritania.

Sultans: ca. 1640–ca. 1660 Ahmad ibn Daman; ca. 1660–1703 Addi I; 1703–1727 Ali Sandura; 1727–ca. 1758 Umar I; ca. 1758–(?)

Mukhtar Ould Amar; (?)–(?) Muhammad Babana; (?)–(?) Addi II; (?)–(?) Mukhtar II; (?)–(?) Muhammad II; (?)–ca. 1800 Ali Kuri; ca. 1800–(?) Aleit; (?)–(?) Umar Kumba II; (?)–(?) Muhammad III; (?)–(?) Mukhtar III; (?)–1833 Umar III; 1833–1860 Muhammad IV al-Habib; 1860–July 1871 Sidi Mbairika; July 1871–1873 Ahmad Salum; 1873–Oct. 1886 Sidi Ali Diombot; Oct. 1886–Dec. 1886 Sheikh Muhammad Fadl; Dec. 1886–1891 Umar Salum; 1891–1903 Ould Sidi Ahmad Salum; 1903–1903 Muhammad Salum Ould Brahim; 1903–1917 Sheikh Sa'd Bu (also known as Sidi Ould Deid); 1917–1932 Sheikh al-Khalifa (also known as Sidi Buya). *Viziers:* 1873–1898 Hayarum. *Note:* although there were other viziers, Hayarum is the only noteworthy one. *Commandants:* 15 Dec. 1902–12 May 1903 Xavier Coppolani.

Tripoli see **Tripolitania**

Tripolitania. 297–24 Dec. 1951. *Location:* northwestern Libya. *Capital:* Tripoli (from 800); Leptis Magna (297–442). *Other names:* Tripoli (800–1911); Tarabulus (the Turkish name).

History: In A.D. 297 the Roman emperor Diocletian, in his geographical reformation of the Empire, divided the large province of Africa (see Africa [i]) into three parts — Tripolitania, Byzacena, and another (smaller) province called Africa (see Africa [ii]). In 442 Tripolitania, like all of North Africa had done or was about to do, went to the Vandals (see Vandal North Africa). In April 534 the Byzantines conquered the Vandals in North Africa, and Tripolitania formed part of the Byzantine Province of Africa (see Byzantine North Africa). North Africa alternated between Byzantine rule and a loosely confederated Arab rule over the next few centuries (see Arab North Africa) until the year 703, when the Omayyads took it over (see Omayyad and Abbasid North Africa). On 9 July 800 the Aghlabid Empire conquered Tripoli as they did all of North Africa, from the Abbasids. On 26 March 909 the Fatimids took it over (see Fatimid North Africa). In 977 the Zirids replaced the Fatimids (see Zirid Kingdom). In 1148 Roger II of Sicily, a Norman adventurer, conquered Tripoli, and ruled the city and surrounding areas, as well as the eastern coast of what is now Tunisia. During the period 1158 to 1160 the Normans lost it to the newly-arriving Almohad Empire. The fall of the city of Tripoli marked the end of Norman rule in North Africa (with possibly the exception of Grand Dieppe and Petit Dieppe in Liberia, for which see Petit Dieppe). The Almohads installed the last Zirid governor to hold the office before the Normans took over (the Zirids were out of power in Africa by now, but still survived). Rule vacillated for the next 80 years or so between the Almohads and the Aiyubids (see Egypt), but the governor of Tripoli remained, for the most part, an Almohad. In the 1220s the Hafsids rose to prominence, and in 1236 proclaimed their kingdom (see Hafsid Kingdom). About 1247 they supplanted the Almohads in Tripoli. In 1327 the Hafsids voluntarily turned the town over to the Banu Ammar dynasty, but in 1401 it reverted to the Hafsids. In 1412 the Hafsids lost it to the Egyptian Mamelukes (see Egypt). In 1482 the Hafsids regained Tripoli for the last time, holding it until 26 June 1510, when the Spanish from Sicily took it. In 1530 the Spanish handed Tripoli over to the Grand Master of the Knights of Malta. Tripolitania was governed for 21 years by one of the Grand Master's representatives, and on 14 Aug. 1551 the Turks took it and it became a province of the Ottoman Empire. On 29 July 1711 the Turks awarded Tripoli to the Karamanli Dynasty. Between 1801 and 1805 Tripoli was at war with the United States of America. The USA, since 1796, had paid protection money ($83,000 a year) to the sultan, in order that American commerce in the area remain free from pirate raids. The sultan, however, now wanted more money, and the USA refused. Peace was made on 3 June 1805. In 1815 trouble flared up again, and another US squadron was sent to Tripoli, this time with more immediate effect. The Karamanlid Sultans ruled until 26 May 1835, when Tripoli again became an Ottoman province. By the late 1890s Italy had already decided to take Tripolitania and Cyrenaica, but were slow in effecting this occupation. In 1911 Germany threatened to make a move in the direction of Tripoli, so Italy declared war on Turkey and on 5 Nov. 1911 Tripolitania became an Italian protectorate. Over the period 1911–1912 the Italians conquered most of what is today Libya (including the Fezzan). During World War I the Italians pulled out of Libya, leaving garrisons only in Tripoli and Homs, and (from 1916) Zuwara. On 17 May 1919 Tripolitania became an Italian colony, and on 24 Jan. 1929 the Italians united this colony with their neighboring colony of Cirenaica (see Cyrenaica) to make Libya. On

15 Dec. 1942 the British captured Tripolitania from the Italians during World War II. In 1951 Tripolitania, Cyrenaica and the Fezzan were all united to form the modern day state of Libya.

Roman Governors: 297–442 [unknown]. *Vandal Governors:* 442–April 534 [unknown]. *Byzantine Governors:* April 534–647 [unknown]. *Arab Governors:* 647–649 [unknown]. *Byzantine Governors:* 649–667 [unknown]. *Arab Governors:* 667–697 [unknown]. *Byzantine Governors:* 697–703 [unknown]. *Omayyad Governors:* 703–9 Aug. 750 [unknown]; *Abbasid Governors:* 9 Aug. 750–9 July 800 [unknown]. *Aghlabid Governors:* there is only one recorded Aghlabid governor of Tripoli, and that is Muhammad ibn Qurhub, ca. 869. *Fatimid Governors:* there is only one recorded Fatimid governor of Tripoli, and that is Abdallah ibn Yalluf, ca. 973. *Zirid Governors:* 977–1000 Tamsulat; 1000–1001 Abu'l Hassan Yanis; 1001–1007 Yahya; 1007–1009 Fulful; 1009–1014 Warru; 1014–1022 Abu Abdallah Muhammad; 1022–1028 Khalifa; 1028–1037 Sa'id; 1037–1038 Abu'l Hassan Ali; 1038–(?) Khazrun; (?)–1053 Muhammad; 1053–(?) Abu Muhammad Abdallah; (?)–1068 al-Muntasir; 1068–1078 [unknown]; 1078–(?) Muqallab; ca. 1095 Shah Malik; (?)–1146 [unknown]; 1146–1148 Sheikh Abu Yahya. *Norman Kings:* 1148–26 Feb. 1154 Roger II of Sicily; 26 Feb. 1154–22 Jan. 1160 William I of Sicily. *Zirid Governors for the Almohads:* 1160–23 Aug. 1172 Sheikh Abu Yahya. *Aiyubid Governors:* 23 Aug. 1172–1190 Qaraqush. *Almohad Governors:* 1190–(?) [unknown]. *Aiyubid Governors:* (?)–1202 Qaraqush. *Almohad Governors:* 1202–1204 [unknown]; 1204–1207 Yahya al-Miruki; 1207–25 Feb. 1221 Abu Muhammad Abd al-Wahid; March 1221–June 1221 Abu Sa'id Abd ar-Rahman; 1221–1221 Sa'id Abu'l Ala Idris; 1221–1222 Ibrahim ibn Ismail al-Hafs (acting); 1222–1223 Sa'id Abu'l Ala Idris; 1223–1223 Abu Yahya Amran; 1224–1224 Abu Zaiyid; 1224–Aug. 1226 Abu Amran Musa; Aug. 1226–1228 [unknown]; 1228–1236 Yahya; 1236–ca. 1247 Abd ar-Rahman Yaqub. *Hafsid Governors:* ca. 1247–1279 [unknown]; 1279–1282 Murjim; 1283–(?) Muhammad ibn Isa; (?)–1318 [unknown]; 1318–1327 Muhammad ibn Abu Bakr. *Banu Ammar Sultans:* 1327–1327 Thabit I ibn Ammar; 1327–1348 Muhammad; 1348–1355 Thabit II; 1355–1371 [unknown]; 1371–1392 Abu Bakr; 1392–1397 Ali ibn Ammar; 1397–1401 Yahya and Abd al-Wahid (jointly). *Hafsid Governors:* 1401–1412 [un-

known]. *Egyptian Governors:* 1412–1421 al-Ashraf Barsabay; 1421–ca. 1480 [unknown]; ca. 1480–1482 Sheikh Abd as-Salaam al-Asman. *Hafsid Governors:* 1482–1489 Abu Bakr; 1489–1494 Sheikh Ahmad az-Zarraq; 1494–26 June 1510 [unknown]. *Spanish Governors:* 26 June 1510–1510 Pedro de Navarra; 1510–1511 Jayme de Requesens; 1511–1520 Guillem de Moncada; 1520–1530 [unknown]. *Knights of Malta Governors:* 1530–ca. 1533 Gaspard de Sanguesse; ca. 1533–ca. 1538 Georg Schilling; ca. 1538–1542 Fernand de Brancamont; 1542–1551 Christopher de Solefertan; 1551–14 Aug. 1551 Fray Gaspar de Valier. *Ottoman Aghas:* 14 Aug. 1551–1553 Murad. *Ottoman Pashas:* 1553–1565 Dragut; 1565–1568 Eulj Ali (also known as Lucciali); 1569–1580 Ja'far; 1580–1581 Murad; 1581–1584 Qa'id Ramadan; 1584–1588 Mustafa; 1588–1595 Hussein; 1595–1600 Ibrahim; 1600–1606 Iskender; 1606–1607 Selim; 1607–1609 Ali; 1609–1609 Ahmad. *Ottoman Deys:* 1610–1620 Suleiman; 1620–1631 Mustafa Sherif. *Ottoman Pashas:* 1631–1631 Kasim. *Ottoman Deys:* 1631–1631 Ramadan Agha; 1631–7 Nov. 1649 Mehmed Saqizli; 7 Nov. 1649–1672 Osman Saqizli; 1672–28 Nov. 1672 Osman Reis as-Suhali; 28 Nov. 1672–26 April 1673 Bali Javush. *Ottoman Pashas:* 26 April 1673–1675 Arnavut Halil. *Ottoman Deys:* 1675–May 1675 Mustafa Pehlevan; May 1675–3 April 1676 Ibrahim Misirli-Oglu; 5 April 1676–7 April 1676 Ibrahim Jelebi; 7 April 1676–4 April 1677 Mustafa Kapudan; 4 April 1677–27 April 1678 Baba Osman. *Ottoman Beys:* 27 April 1678–9 Sept. 1679 Ak Mehmed. *Ottoman Deys:* 9 Sept. 1679–11 June 1683 Hassan Abaza; 11 June 1683–13 June 1683 Yulk Mahmud; 13 June 1683–18 June 1684 Ali Jezairli; 18 June 1684–8 Feb. 1687 Hajji Abdallah Izmirli; 8 Feb. 1687–May 1687 [unknown]; May 1687–Nov. 1687 Ibrahim Terzi; Nov. 1687–19 May 1701 Mehmed Imam Kerdeki; 19 May 1701–11 Aug. 1701 Osman; 11 Aug. 1701–29 July 1702 Mustafa Galibuli; 29 July 1702–Oct. 1706 Mehmed Imam. *Ottoman Pashas:* Oct. 1706–Nov. 1709 Halil. *Ottoman Deys:* Nov. 1709–23 Nov. 1710 Ibrahim Alayali; 23 Nov. 1710–20 Jan. 1711 Ismail Hoja; 20 Jan. 1711–20 Jan. 1711 Hajji Rejeb; 20 Jan. 1711–4 July 1711 Mehmed Hussein Javush Bey; 4 July 1711–29 July 1711 Abu Umays Mahmud. *Karamanlid Sultans:* 29 July 1711–4 Nov. 1745 Ahmad I; 4 Nov. 1745–24 July 1754 Muhammad; 24 July 1754–30 July 1793 Ali I; 30 July 1793–20 Jan. 1795 Ali II Burghul; 20 Jan.

1795–11 June 1795 Ahmad II; 11 June 1795–20 Aug. 1832 Yusuf; 20 Aug. 1832–26 May 1835 Ali III. *Ottoman Pashas:* 27 June 1835–7 Sept. 1835 Mustafa Negib; 7 Sept. 1835–April 1837 Mehmed Reis; April 1837–1838 Tahir; 1838–3 Aug. 1838 Hassan; 3 Aug. 1838–July 1842 Ali Asker; July 1842–April 1847 Mehmed Emin; April 1847–Oct. 1848 Ragib; Oct. 1848–1849 Hajji Ahmed Izzet; 1849–Oct. 1852 Mustafa Asim; Oct. 1852–1855 Mustafa Nuri; 1855–1858 Osman Nazhar; 1858–Aug. 1860 Ahmed Izzet; Aug. 1860–April 1867 Mahmud Nedim Bey; April 1867–July 1867 Hassan (acting); July 1867–May 1870 Ali Reza; May 1870–June 1870 Mustafa (acting); June 1870–Sept. 1871 Mehmed Halid; Sept. 1871–1872 Mehmed Rashid; 1872–6 June 1873 Ali Reza; 6 June 1873–1874 Samih; 1874–1875 Mustafa Asim; 1875–1876 Mustafa; 1876–1878 Mehmed Jelaleddin; 1878–1878 Savfet; 1878–July 1879 Sabri; July 1879–May 1880 Ahmed Izzet; May 1880–Oct. 1881 Mehmed Nazif; Oct. 1881–June 1896 Ahmed Rasim; June 1896–March 1899 Nemik Bey; March 1899–July 1900 Hashim Bey; July 1900–Dec. 1903 Hafiz Mehmed; Dec. 1903–May 1904 Hassan Husni (also known as Hussein Effendi); May 1904–Aug. 1904 Abderrahman Bey (acting); Aug. 1904–1908 Rejeb; 1908–Aug. 1909 Ahmed Fawzi; Aug. 1909–Aug. 1910 Hassan Husni (also known as Hussein Effendi); Aug. 1910–5 Nov. 1911 Ibrahim. *Italian Governors:* 5 Nov. 1911–11 Oct. 1911 Raffaele Borea Ricci D'Olmo; 11 Oct. 1911–1912 Carlo Caneva; 1912–2 June 1913 Ottavio Ragni; 2 June 1913–1914 Vincenzo Garioni; 1914–1915 Luigi Druetti; 1915–1915 Giulio Cesare Tassoni; 1915–5 Aug. 1918 Giovan-Battista Ameglio; 5 Aug. 1918–17 May 1919 Vincenzo Garioni; 17 May 1919–1 Aug. 1919 [unknown] (acting); 1 Aug. 1919–6 July 1920 Vittorio Menzinger; 6 July 1920–16 July 1921 Luigi Mercatelli; 16 July 1921–3 July 1925 Giuseppe Volpi Di Misurata; 3 July 1925–1927 Emilio De Bono; 1927–1927 Ernesto Queirolo (acting); 1927–18 Dec. 1928 Emilio De Bono; 18 Dec. 1928–24 Jan. 1929 [unknown] (acting). *Ottoman Pashas Residing:* 5 Nov. 1911–1912 Bekir Samih Bey. *Ottoman Governors-General:* 1915–1917 Suleiman al-Baruni; 1917–1918 Nuri Bey; 1918–1918 Ishak Bey; 1918–1918 Osman Fuad Pasha. *Italian Governors-General:* 24 Jan. 1929–15 Dec. 1942 for the list see **Libia**). *British Deputy Chief Civil Affairs Officers:* 15 Dec. 1942–23 Jan. 1943 Maurice Lush; 23 Jan. 1943–1944 Travers Blackley.

British Chief Administrators: 1944–April 1949 Travers Blackley. *British Residents:* April 1949–24 Dec. 1951 Travers Blackley. *Tripolitanian Amirs:* July 1922–24 Dec. 1951 Idris al-Mahdi as-Sanusi.

Tripolitanian Republic. 16 Nov. 1918–1923. *Location:* Tripolitania, Libya. *Capital:* Aziziyah. *Other names:* Jumhuriyya at-Tarabulusiyah.

History: In 1918 local Libyans formed their own short-lived republic in Tripolitania. During 1923 it merged into the newly-formed Italian colony of Tripolitania.

Chairmen: 16 Nov. 1918–Nov. 1920 Suleiman al-Baruni; Nov. 1920–1923 Ahmad al-Muraiyid.

Tristan da Cunha. 1506– . *Location:* three small volcanic islands (Tristan, Nightingale, and Inaccessible), and two islets (Stoltenhoff and Middle), as well as several rocks, in the southern Atlantic Ocean, halfway between South Africa and South America. Gough Island, about 225 miles south southeast of Tristan, is associated with the group. *Capital:* Edinburgh (from 1816).

History: Tristão da Cunha, the Portuguese navigator, discovered this country in 1506. The islands were claimed by Portugal, and there were three unsuccessful attempts at colonization, one in 1656 by the Dutch, one in the 1680s by the English East India Company, and one in 1810, by an American, Jonathan Lambert (from Salem, Mass.), who settled here with two companions, but was drowned. All this time the Portuguese claim remained vague. On 14 Aug. 1816 the Tristan da Cunha Islands became a British possession when Britain placed a garrison at Edinburgh, the town on the main island of Tristan, in order to prevent any attempt to rescue Napoleon from Saint Helena (where he was in exile). The garrison was removed in May 1817, but one settler (Corp. William Glass, a Scotsman) and his family remained. By 1886 there were 97 inhabitants. In 1938 the three islands, and their associated island, Gough Island, were made dependencies of the colony of Saint Helena. In 1950 the Colonial Office appointed an administrator for Tristan, which until then had managed its own affairs. On 9 Oct. 1961 a volcano erupted on Tristan, and the inhabitants were evacuated to Britain. They returned in Nov. 1963. This disaster, however, did put Tristan da Cunha on the map.

Commandants: Nov. 1816–May 1817 Capt.

Abraham Cloete. *Administrators:* May 1817–1950 local council; 1950–managed from Saint Helena through a local administrator.

Tshidi see **Barolongland**

Tswanaland see **Botswana** and **Namibia**

Tukolor Empire. 1854–1 Jan. 1891. *Location:* Mali. *Capital:* Bandiagara (from 1884); Timbuctu (until 1884). *Other names:* Toucouleur; Tucolor; Tekoror; Halphoolaren; Empire of al-Hajj Umar, or Umar al-Hajj's Empire, or al-Hajji Umar Empire; Omar al-Hajj's Empire, or Hajji Omar's Empire.

History: In 1854 Umar al-Hajj began his jihad (holy war), conquering the Bambara state of Segu, and an empire was formed. In 1870 the state of Kaarta fell to them. The Tukolor were (and are) a tribe of Fulbe-speaking Islamic peoples from the Senegal region, and this empire passed from father to son. In 1891 the French put the son to flight, captured the empire, and incorporated it into what would become French West Africa, or to be more specific it became a section of the Military Territory of the French Sudan (see Mali).

Emperors: 1854–1864 Umar al-Hajj; 1864–1870 Mustafa; 1870–1872 Ahmadu; 1872–1873 Alamami (acting); 1873–1874 Muntaga; 1874–1 Jan. 1891 Ahmadu.

Tunis. (?)–12 May 1881. *Location:* North Africa, between Algeria and Libya. *Capital:* Tunis (from 1236); al-Mahdiya (1159–1236); Tunis (1059–1169).

History: Tunis, as a town, was founded about 1000 B.C., and the origin of its name is uncertain. The town, and the land around it was part of Carthage. Then, in 146 B.C. the Romans wiped out Carthage and took over their empire, and it became the province of Africa Vetus (again, see Carthage). In 29 B.C. Africa Vetus went to form part of the province of the Roman province of Africa (see Africa [i]). In A.D. 297 the country we now know as Tunisia was split into two Roman provinces — Byzacena in the south and Africa (see Africa [ii]) in the north. In 320 Byzacena joined with the Roman province of Tripolitania (in today's Libya) to form the Roman colony of Africa Proconsularis. In 439 Africa fell to the Vandals, and in 442 so did Byzacena. These conquered territories, along with all the other land taken by the Vandals, went to form Vandal North Africa. Over the next few centuries Tunisia was owned by the Byzantines and the Arabs (see Byzantine North Africa and Arab North Africa). In 703 the Omayyads took it over (see Omayyad and Abbasid North Africa), and on 9 July 800 the Aghlabids took it over (see Aghlabid Empire). The general Arab name for the region was Ifriqiyah. On 26 March 909 the Berbers took control of the city of Tunis, and that year the Fatimids (see Fatimid North Africa) started to overrun not only Tunisia but eastern Algeria too. On 6 Jan. 910 they expelled the Berbers from Tunis. In 973 Tunisia became a Zirid state (see Zirid Kingdom). In 1059 the house of Khurasan began to rule Tunis as representatives of the Zirids. In July 1159, with the collapse of the Zirids, Tunis became an Almohad city (see Almohad Empire). In 1236 Tunisia became the property of the Hafsid Kingdom, a kingdom founded by Abu Zakariyya Yahya, the Almohad governor of Tunis (grandson of Abu Hafs Umar, for whom he named the new kingdom). On 18 Aug. 1534 Khair ad-Din, the Turkish corsair also known as Barbarossa or Red Beard, conquered Tunis and deposed the Hafsid dynasty. Khair ad-Din took over most of what is today the Republic of Tunisia, and ruled Tunis as the beylerbeg (bey of beys). The new ruler of Tunis worried the rest of Europe with his incessant piracy, so the Spanish took Tunis on 20 July 1535. The Hafsid sultans continued to rule under Spanish or Turkish protection until 1574. In 1539 the Turks recaptured Tunis, and in 1573 Don John of Austria and his Spanish fleet, fresh from their two-year-old triumph at Lepanto, captured Tunis from the Turks, but on 13 Sept. 1574 Don John lost it to the Turks, and Tunis became a pashalik. The pasha was the head of the government, but in 1590 the deys took power as the representatives of the janissaries (in effect this was an army coup). In 1640 the beys, who had been gathering power under Murad, took over from the deys. The Muradids were the real rulers during the 17th century, but in 1702 the agha of the spahis, Ibrahim, became bey and in 1704 he became dey and pasha. On 9 July 1705 Husain ibn Ali became bey, and began the Husainid dynasty in Tunis which was to last for 250 years. Although it was still a dominion of the Ottoman Empire, Tunis was now styled a regency. In 1819 the bey abolished slavery and piracy in Tunis. In 1869, due to several decades of bad financial administration in Tunis, the government faced ruin, and Britain, France, and Italy became the guarantors of the country. In 1881, with Italy looking as if it might create a protectorate in Tunisia, France decided to invade Tunisia, and occupy it. The bey, threatened with a war if he did not surrender, surrendered, and on 11 May signed the Treaty of Kasar Sa'id. On 12 May 1881 France took the country over as the protectorate of Tunisia.

Rulers: Before 439 see Africa Proconsularis and Africa [i]; 439–April 534 ruled by the Vandals; April 534–647 ruled by the Byzantines; 647–549 ruled by the Arabs; 649–667 ruled by the Byzantines; 667–697 ruled by the Arabs; 697–703 ruled by the Byzantines; 703–Aug. 750 ruled by the Omayyads; 9 Aug. 750–9 July 800 ruled by the Abbasids; 9 July 800–26 March 909 ruled by the Aghlabids. *Kings:* 26 March 909–6 Jan. 910 Abu Abdallah as-Si'i al-Muhtasab. *Rulers:* 6 Jan. 910–973 ruled by the Fatimids; 973–July 1159 ruled by the Zirids. *Almohad governors of Tunis:* July 1159–(?) Abu Ishaq Ibrahim; (?)–1168 Abu Yahya al-Hassan; 1168–1195 [unknown]; 1195–1200 Abd al-Karim ar-Ragrag; 1200–May 1207 [unknown]; May 1207–Feb. 1221 Abu Muhammad Abd al-Wahid; Feb. 1221–May 1221 Abu Sa'id Abd ar-Rahman; May 1221–Nov. 1221 Abu Ishaq Ibrahim; Nov. 1221–1223 Sa'id Abu'l Ala Idris; 1223–Nov. 1226 Abu Sa'id Abd ar-Rahman; Nov. 1226–June 1228 Abu Muhammad Abdallah Abu; June 1228–1236 Abu Zakariyya Yahya. *Rulers:* 1236–18 Aug. 1534 ruled by the Hafsids. *Turkish Beylerbegs of Tunis:* 18 Aug. 1534–20 July 1535 Khair ad-Din (also known as Barbarossa). *Rulers:* 20 July 1535–Dec. 1569 ruled by the Hafsid sultans under Spanish or Turkish protection (see Hafsid Kingdom for list of sultans during this period); Dec. 1569–1573 Direct Ottoman rule; 1573–13 Sept. 1574 ruled by Don John of Austria as military overlord, in conjunction with the Hafsid sultan Mulay Muhammad. *Pashas:* 13 Sept. 1574–1576 Sinan; 1576–1587 Kilik Ali. *Deys:* 1587–1590 Ibrahim Ruzili; 1590–1 Oct. 1610 Uthman; 1 Oct. 1610–Dec. 1637 Yusuf. *Beys:* 1612–1631 Murad; 1631–1659 Hammuda Pasha; 1659–19 Aug. 1675 Murad II; 19 Aug. 1675–1696 Muhammad; 1696–1699 Ramdan; 1699–1702 Murad III; 1702–1704 Ibrahim ash-Sharif. *Deys:* 1704–9 July 1705 Ibrahim; 9 July 1705–4 Sept. 1735 Husain I; 4 Sept. 1735–1756 Ali I; 1756–March 1759 Muhammad I; March

1759–26 May 1782 Ali II; 26 May 1782–15 Sept. 1814 Hammuda; 15 Sept. 1814–19 Dec. 1814 Uthman; 20 Dec. 1814–23 March 1824 Mahmud; 23 March 1824–1835 Husain II; 1835–10 Oct. 1837 Mustafa; 10 Oct. 1837–29 May 1855 Ahmad I; 29 May 1855–23 Sept. 1859 Muhammad II; 23 Sept. 1859–12 May 1881 Muhammad III as-Sadiq.

Tunisia. 12 May 1881– . *Location:* as Tunis, but a larger area, more hinterland. *Capital:* Tunis. *Other names:* al-Jumhiriyyah at-Tunisiyah, or Republic of Tunisia (from 1957).

History: In 1881 Tunis was occupied, as per the Treaty of Kasar Sa'id. In effect, the country became a protectorate, although this was somewhat unofficial. The French put down a rising in the south, and took the port of Sfax on 11 July 1881. al-Qayrawan, another center of the rising, was captured on 26 Oct. 1881. Gafsa was taken on 19 Nov. 1881, and finally Gabès on 30 Nov. 1881. In 1883 the protectorate came into being on paper as well as in reality, at the Convention of La Marsa. The bey continued to be the official ruler, although totally under the control of the French. The Young Tunisian party was formed in 1907 with the aim of self-government for the Tunisians. In 1920 the Destour party was created, under the leadership of Abd ar-Rahman at-Thaalibi, with nothing short of independence as its platform. In 1922 the bey, a nationalist himself, threatened to abdicate, and the French put down the prevailing discontent with force. However, they did allow certain reforms to pacify the Tunisians. Habib Bourguiba broke away from the Destour and founded the Neo-Destour in 1934, and was the leading Tunisian political figure for over 50 years. The French banned the Neo-Destour in 1934 and over the next 20 years led a most adventurous life, most of the time being either in French jails, in German custody, or in exile. But he remained the spokesman for Tunisian independence, and he refused to go over to the Axis, who had occupied Tunisia during World War II. Mussolini's plans for an Italian Tunisia were rejected out of hand by the bey of Tunis in 1943. In 1950 the French promised autonomy for Tunisia, and on 31 July 1954 agreed to independence. Bourguiba returned to France in June 1955. On 20 March 1956 Tunisia became independent. On 25 July 1957 Tunisia was proclaimed a republic and the position of bey was discontinued. In 1961 there was war with France over the French air force base at Bizerte, and in 1963 the French left. There were border disputes with Algeria from 1962 to 1970. Bourguiba (or possibly his followers) were not above disposing of political opponents, as witness the assassination of Bourguiba's old Neo-Destour colleague Salah ben Yusuf in Aug. 1961, and the removal from political life of many others. Bourguiba became too unwell to run the country, and stepped down in 1987. He was then arrested by his successor. The popular Islamic Fundamentalist movement that was sweeping the Arab world in the 1980s and 1990s threatened to cause havoc in Tunisia, a very western-facing country, with a huge tourist trade from Europe. Bourguiba and Zine ben Ali both resisted this with great determination.

French Residents-General: 13 May 1881–18 Feb. 1882 Théodore Rouston; 18 Feb. 1882–Nov. 1886 Paul Cambon; Nov. 1886–Nov. 1892 Justin Massicault; Nov. 1892–14 Nov. 1894 Maurice Rouvier; 14 Nov. 1894–Nov. 1900 René Millet; Nov. 1900–27 Dec. 1901 Benoît de Merkel (acting); 27 Dec. 1901–29 Dec. 1906 Eugène Pichon; 7 Feb. 1907–26 Oct. 1918 Gabriel Alapetite; 26 Oct. 1918–23 Nov. 1920 Pierre Flandin; 23 Nov. 1920–Jan. 1921 [unknown] (acting); Jan. 1921–18 Feb. 1929 Lucien Saint; 18 Feb. 1929–29 July 1933 François Manceron; 29 July 1933–21 March 1936 Marcel Peyrouton; 21 March 1936–17 April 1936 [unknown] (acting); 17 April 1936–18 Oct. 1938 Armand Guillon; 18 Oct. 1938–22 Nov. 1938 [unknown] (acting); 22 Nov. 1938–3 June 1940 Eirik Labonne; 3 June 1940–22 July 1940 Marcel Peyrouton; 22 July 1940–26 July 1940 [unknown] (acting); 26 July 1940–10 May 1943 Jean-Pierre Estéva; 10 May 1943–22 Feb. 1947 Charles Mast; 22 Feb. 1947–13 June 1950 Jean Mons; 13 June 1950–Dec. 1951 Louis Périllier; Dec. 1951–13 Jan. 1952 [unknown] (acting); 13 Jan. 1952–2 Sept. 1953 Jean de Hauteclocque; 2 Sept. 1953–5 Nov. 1954 Pierre Voizard; 5 Nov. 1954–13 Sept. 1955 Comte Boyer de la Tour du Moulin; 13 Sept. 1955–20 March 1956 Roger Seydoux Fornier de Clausonne. *Beys:* 12 May 1881–28 Oct. 1882 Muhammad III as-Sadiq; 28 Oct. 1882–11 June 1902 Ali Muddat; 11 June 1902–11 May 1906 Muhammad IV al-Hadi; 11 May 1906–10 July 1922 Muhammad V an-Nasir; 10 July 1922–11 Feb. 1929 Muhammad VI al-Habib; 11 Feb. 1929–19 July 1942 Ahmad II; 19 July 1942–14 May 1943 Muhammad VII al-Muncif; 15 May

1943–25 July 1957 Muhammad VIII al-Amin. *Presidents:* 25 July 1957–18 March 1975 Habib Bourguiba. *Presidents for Life:* 18 March 1975–7 Nov. 1987 Habib Bourguiba. *Presidents:* 7 Nov. 1987–Zine ben Ali. *Prime Ministers:* 1922–26 Oct. 1926 Si Mustafa Dingizli; 26 Oct. 1926–2 March 1932 Si Halil Bu Hajib ben Salim; 2 March 1932–Dec. 1942 Sidi Muhammad al-Hadi al-Ahwa; Jan. 1943–20 Aug. 1947 Salah Eddine ben Muhammad Baccouche; 20 Aug. 1947–17 March 1950 Mustafa Kaak; 17 March 1950–28 March 1952 Muhammad Chenik; 28 March 1952–2 March 1954 Salah Eddine ben Muhammad Baccouche; 2 March 1954–16 June 1954 Muhammad as-Salih; 16 June 1954–6 July 1954 [vacant]; 6 July 1954–2 Aug. 1954 Georges Dupoizat (acting); 2 Aug. 1954–10 April 1956 Tahar ben Ammar; 10 April 1956–25 July 1957 Habib Bourguiba; 6 Nov. 1969–2 Nov. 1970 Bahi Ladgham; 2 Nov. 1970–26 Feb. 1980 Hedi Nouira; 1 March 1980–23 April 1980 Muhammad Mzali (acting); 23 April 1980–8 July 1986 Muhammad Mzali; 8 July 1986–2 Oct. 1987 Rachid Sfar; 2 Oct. 1987–7 Nov. 1987 Zine ben Ali; 7 Nov. 1987–27 Sept. 1989 Hedi Baccouche; 27 Sept. 1989–17 Nov. 1999 Hamed Karoui; 17 Nov. 1999–Muhammad Ghannouchi. *Note:* In times of no Prime Minister, the President held that office.

Tunjur see **Wadai**

Tutsi see **Burundi** [i] and **Burundi** [ii] and **Ruanda** and **Rwanda**

Twanaland see **Batwanaland** and **Bechuanaland Protectorate** and **Bophuthatswana** and **Botswana**

Twifo-Heman see **Akwamu**

Ubangi-Bomu see **Central African Republic**

Ubangi-Shari see **Central African Republic**

Ubangi-Shari-Chad. 11 Feb. 1906–12 April 1916. *Location:* present-day southern Chad and all of the Central African Republic. *Capital:* Bangui. *Other names:* Oubangui-Chari-Tchad; Ubangi-Shari and Chad Colony.

History: In 1906 the colony of Ubangi-Shari (see Central African Republic) and the protectorate of Chad joined to produce the greater colony of Ubangi-Shari-Chad, and the two components became territories of the larger colony. In 1916 Ubangi-Shari-Chad came to an end, although the lieutenant-governor of the new colony of Ubangi-Shari continued to be responsible (through a military commander) for Chad.

Lieutenant-Governors: 11 Feb. 1906–12 April 1916 same as the lieutenant-governors for Ubangi-Shari (see Central African Republic list of lieutenant-governors for this period).

Ubani see **Bonny**

Uganda. 1 July 1890– . *Location:* central East Africa, to the immediate south of the Sudan. *Capital:* Kampala (from 1958); Entebbe (founded in 1893, this was the capital from 1905 to 1958); Kampala (the name means "hill of the impala," and was selected as the capital by Capt. Frederick Lugard, in 1890, and remained the capital until 1905). *Other names:* Buganda (1890–1894).

History: On 1 July 1890 the Anglo-German agreement declared Buganda to be a British sphere of influence. The main kingdoms then (in the area that would later become Uganda) were Buganda (by far the biggest and most powerful), Bunyoro, and Nkore. On 18 Dec. 1890 Capt. Frederick Lugard occupied Buganda for the British East Africa Company, and the following week, on 26 Dec. 1890, a treaty was signed whereby the British promised to keep order in Buganda. Done by international agreement, this marked the start of Britain's long involvement with Uganda. On 1 April 1893 Buganda was declared a provisional protectorate, and on 11 April 1894 (effective 18 June) the British took it over as a full-fledged protectorate. On 30 June 1896 the kingdom of Bunyoro was taken into the protectorate and over the next five or six years the other, smaller, kingdoms were also brought in, such as Busoga on 3 July 1896. By now the new country was called Uganda. On 1 April 1902 the Eastern Province of Uganda was given to the British East Africa Colony (see Kenya), to provide it with a hinterland, and on 1 April 1905 responsibility for Uganda was transferred from the Foreign Office to the Colonial Office. In 1914 the districts of Gondokoro and Nimule were handed over to the Sudan, and in 1926 Rudolph Province was given to Kenya. The independence movement began immediately after World War II, and the British began the inevitable process of decolonization. On 1 March 1962 Uganda became self-governing, and on 9 Oct. 1962 it became a dominion of the British Commonwealth. On 9 Oct. 1963 the Common wealth of Uganda came into being and the British governor-general left the country. This marked the end of British ownership of Uganda, although the association with the British Commonwealth remained, even after Uganda became a republic. This took place on 15 April 1966, although civil unrest prevented the ratification of the republic until 8 Sept. 1967. At that time the traditional kingdoms (e.g. Buganda, Bunyoro and Nkore) were abolished. (They would be restored in 1993 by the Ugandan government, but only as ceremonial institutions). In 1971 Idi Amin, commander of the Army, overthrew the previous strongman, Milton Obote, and ruled the country as a tyrant until 11 April 1979, when Tanzanian forces, backed by Ugandan exiles, forced Amin from power. There was a coup in 1979, and another one ousted Obote in 1985. There was civil war in the 1980s. President Museveni has been popular, and the country has been fairly stable. Uganda has been a much celebrated and closely studied showcase for its systematic reduction of AIDS.

Military Administrators: 26 Dec. 1890–17 March 1893 Capt. Frederick Lugard. *Commissioners:* 17 March 1893–30 May 1893 Sir Gerald Portal; 30 May 1893–4 Nov. 1893 Capt. MacDonald (acting); 4 Nov. 1893–10 May 1894 Henry Colville; 10 May 1894–24 Aug. 1894 Frederick Jackson (acting); 24 Aug. 1894–1897 Ernest Berkeley; 1897–1897 Frederick Jackson (acting); 1897–July 1899 Ernest Berkeley; July 1899–Nov. 1901 Sir Harry Johnston; Nov. 1901–1905 James Sadler; 1905–18 Oct. 1907 Hesketh Bell. *Governors:* 18 Oct. 1907–31 Jan. 1910 Hesketh Bell (knighted 1908); 1 Feb. 1910–3 April 1911 Harry Cordeaux (never took office); 1 Feb. 1910–3 April 1911 [unknown] (acting); 3 April 1911–10 Feb. 1918 Frederick Jackson (knighted 1913); 10 Feb. 1918–15 Aug. 1922 Robert Coryndon (knighted 1919); 15 Aug. 1922–1924 Sir Geoffrey Archer; 1924–1924 John Sturrock (acting); 1924–18 May 1925 Sir Geoffrey Archer; 18 May 1925–23 Nov. 1932 William Gowers (knighted 1926); 23 Nov. 1932–17 Oct. 1935 Sir Bernard Bourdillon; 17 Oct. 1935–7 July 1940 Philip Mitchell (knighted 1937); 7 July 1940–31 Dec. 1944 Sir Charles Dundas; 1 Jan. 1945–17 Jan. 1952 Sir John Hall; 17 Jan. 1952–26 Feb.

1957 Sir Andrew Cohen; 26 Feb. 1957–19 Oct. 1961 Sir Frederick Crawford; 19 Oct. 1961–1 March 1962 Sir Walter Coutts. *Governors-General:* 1 March 1962–9 Oct. 1963 Sir Walter Coutts. *Presidents:* 9 Oct. 1963–2 March 1966 Sir Edward Mutesa II, King of Buganda; 2 March 1966–15 April 1966 Milton Obote (acting); 15 April 1966–25 Jan. 1971 Milton Obote. *Leaders of Revolutionary Council:* 25 Jan. 1971–20 Feb. 1971 Idi Amin. *Presidents:* 20 Feb. 1971–25 June 1976 Idi Amin. *Presidents for Life:* 25 June 1976–11 April 1979 Idi Amin. *Presidents:* 13 April 1979–20 June 1979 Yusufu Lule; 20 June 1979–12 May 1980 Godfrey Binaisa. *Chairmen of Military Commission:* 18 May 1980–17 Sept. 1980 Paulo Muwanga. *Presidents:* 17 Sept. 1980–27 July 1985 Milton Obote. *Chairmen of Military Council:* 29 July 1985–27 Jan. 1986 Tito Okello. *Heads of State and Chairmen of National Resistance Council:* 29 Jan. 1986–Yoweri Museveni. *Chief Ministers:* 2 July 1961–25 April 1962 Benedicte Kiwanuka. *Prime Ministers:* 25 April 1962–2 March 1966 Milton Obote; 13 Dec. 1980–27 July 1985 Erifasi Otema Allimadi; 1 Aug. 1985–25 Aug. 1985 Paulo Muwanga; 25 Aug. 1985–30 Jan. 1986 Abraham Waligo; 30 Jan. 1986–22 Jan. 1991 Samson Kisekka; 22 Jan. 1991–18 Nov. 1994 George Cosmas Adyebo; 18 Nov. 1994–7 April 1999 Kintu Mosoke; 7 April 1999–Apolo Nsimbambi. *Note:* In times of no Prime Minister, the President or other Head of State held that office.

Umar al-Hajj's Empire see **Tukolor Empire**

Umayyad North Africa see **Omayyad and Abbasid North Africa**

Union of South Africa see **South Africa**

United Arab Republic see **Egypt**

United States of Stellaland. 7 Aug. 1883–30 Sept. 1885. *Location:* Stellaland and Goshen combined. *Capital:* Vrijburg. *Other names:* Het Land Goosen; Stellaland; Bechuanaland Republic; Republic of Bechuanaland.

History: The combination into the United States of Stellaland of the two Boer republics, Stellaland and Goshen, both in Korannaland (which straddled the "Missionary Road" to the interior of Africa) led to both the Boer state of Transvaal (after 1884 called the South Africa Re-

public) and the British Cape Colony claiming them. The London Convention split the United States of Stellaland down the middle, Britain winning control of the road. The western part of the United States of Stellaland now fell under the British Bechuanaland Protectorate, while the now-renamed South Africa Republic got the rest. This was all finalized by September 1885, when it all merged into other areas (notably British Bechuanaland). This was a typically rapid political movement of land in that time and place.

Administrators: 7 Aug. 1883–30 Sept. 1885 Gerrit Van Niekerk.

Unyamwezi see **Mirambo**

Unyoro see **Bunyoro**

Upingtonia see **Lydenrust**

Upper Egypt. ca. 5000 B.C.–ca. 3100 B.C. *Location:* the part of present-day Egypt south of Cairo, but not as far south as Lake Aswan. *Capital:* Nekheb (this was the capital from about 3400 B.C. to about 3100 B.C., and was later called Hierakonpolis); Naqadah (ca. 5000 B.C.–ca. 3400 B.C.). *Other names:* Southern Egypt.

History: This kingdom, of which little is known politically, was symbolized by the White Crown worn by the kings (as opposed to the Red Crown of Lower Egypt). The chief god was Seth. Around 3100 B.C. King Menes of Upper Egypt united his country with Lower Egypt to form the 1st Dynasty of Ancient Egypt.

Only Known Kings: ca. 4500 B.C. Merimde; ca. 4000 B.C. Badari; ca. 3700 B.C. Amra; ca. 3200 B.C. Girza; ca. 3150 B.C.–ca. 3100 B.C. Menes (also known as Narmer, Meni, or Min).

Upper Ivory Coast. 1 Jan. 1938–4 Sept. 1947. *Location:* southern Burkina Faso. *Capital:* Wagadugu (known by the French as Ouagadougou). *Other names:* Haute Côte d'Ivoire.

History: On 5 Sept. 1932 the French colony of Upper Volta (see Burkina Faso) was dismembered. Parts of it went to the French Sudan (see Mali) but the bulk of it went to the Ivory Coast (see Côte d'Ivoire) and became known as Haute Côte d'Ivoire (Upper Ivory Coast). In 1938 the Upper Ivory Coast was constituted a single administrative district. In 1947 it was dismantled and, at the request of the inhabitants, placed back into the newly reconstituted overseas territory of Upper Volta.

Résidents-Supérieurs: 1 Jan. 1938–29 July 1940 Edmond Louveau; 29 July 1940–4 Sept. 1947 administered direct by the Ivory Coast.

Upper River see **Mali**

Upper Senegal see **Mali**

Upper Senegal and Niger see **Mali**

Upper Ubangi see **Central African Republic**

Upper Volta see **Burkina Faso**

Urundi see **Burundi**

Usagora see **German East Africa**

Utrecht. 1852–May 1858. *Location:* along the Buffalo River, in northern Natal. *Capital:* Utrecht (formed in 1852 and named after the Dutch town).

History: In 1852 a Boer settlement was founded and named Utrecht. In Feb. 1856 it became a republic. In May 1858 it became part of the Republic of Lydenburg.

Landdrosts (Magistrates): 1852–1855 A.T. Spies; 1855–May 1858 J.C. Steyn. *Commandants:* 1852–May 1858 J.C. Klopper.

Valvisch Bay see **Walvis Bay**

Vandal North Africa. 430–April 534. *Location:* Tunisia, Algeria, Libya. *Capital:* Carthage (from 439).

History: The Vandal conquest of North Africa should have taken place earlier than it did, but the death of their great king Alaric delayed the inevitable until 429, when Geiserich, with his 80,000 Vandals crossed from Europe. In 435 Geiserich made a deal with the Romans whereby he occupied only Numidia and Mauretania Sitifensis, but by 439 he began taking over Africa Proconsularis from the Romans. By 442 he had conquered all of Roman North Africa. In 468 a Byzantine invasion of North Africa was unsuccessful, but in 533 the Byzantine general Belisarius invaded with only 16,000 men, and a year later had conquered the Vandal empire of North Africa. By 535 the Vandals had gone (see Byzantine North Africa).

Emperors: 430–25 Jan. 477 Geiserich; 25 Jan. 477–23 Dec. 484 Hunerich; 23 Dec. 484–3 Sept. 496 Gundamund; 3 Sept. 496–6 May 523 Thrasamund; 6 May 523–19 May 530 Hilderich; 19 May 530–15 May 534 Gelimer.

Varozvi see **Rozwi**

Vatua see **Gazaland**

Velez de la Gomera see **Melilla** and **Morocco** and **Spanish Morocco**

Venda. 1 Feb. 1973–27 April 1994. *Location:* in South Africa. *Capital:* Thohoyandou. *Other names:* Vhavenda; Republiek Van Venda, or Riphabubliki ya Venda.

History: Venda (the name means "world" or "land") was the Bantustan, or homeland, of the Vhavenda tribe. It was split into two entirely separate units. On 1 June 1971 the dominant politician Patrick Mphephu became chief councillor, and on 1 Feb. 1973 the country achieved self-government. On 13 Sept. 1979 it became the third homeland to achieve independence from South Africa (see also Transkei, Bophuthatswana, and Ciskei), but this independence was not recognized internationally. In 1994, with the transfer of power in South Africa to a black regime, the bantustans were no longer needed, and Venda was re-incorporated into South Africa.

Chief Ministers: 1 Feb. 1973–1973 Patrick Mphephu; 1973–1973 Baldwin Mudau; 1973–13 Sept. 1979 Patrick Mphephu. *Presidents:* 13 Sept. 1979–17 April 1988 Patrick Mphephu; 18 April 1988–5 April 1990 Chief Frank N. Ravele. *Heads of State:* 5 April 1990–25 Jan. 1994 Gabriel Ramushwana; 25 Jan. 1994–26 April 1994 T.G. Ramabulana. *Note:* In times of no Prime Minister, the President held office.

Vhavenda see **Venda**

Victoria see **Port Natal**

Victoria Colony see **Ambas Bay**

Volta Region see **British Togoland**

Voltaic Republic see **Burkina Faso**

Vrijheid Republiek see **New Republic**

Wadai. ca. 1500–3 June 1909. *Location:* the Ouaddaï Prefecture of eastern Chad. *Capital:* Abéché. *Other names:* Ouaddaï; Ouadaï; Waday.

History: There have been three states of Wadai. The first was pre–1500. In the 14th century Wadai became a quasi independent state of Maba peoples, subject to Darfur. Nothing else is known of this state, but it was apparently destroyed toward the end of the 15th century. The second Wadai grew out of this, and in the 16th century the Tunjur tribe conquered it. In 1611 Abd al-Krim, a Maba, expelled the Tunjur, and in 1635 he became the first Muslim kolak (king). This marks the beginning of the third incarnation of Wadai. Civil wars, conquests and slave-trading form the basis of Wadai's history after 1635, and in 1909 France invaded, annexing the country to the territory of Chad. Direct French military rule did not cease until 1935, when a new kolak was installed but with very limited powers over the prefecture of Ouaddaï. The state was suppressed by Chad between 1960 and 1970.

Maliks (Kings): before 1500 [unknown]; ca. 1500–(?) Karama; (?)–(?) Gamal ad-Din; (?)–(?) Durdur; (?)–(?) al-Kamin. *Sultans:* (?)–(?) Muhammad Tunjur; (?)–(?) Yakub al-Mwakir; (?)–(?) Hamid; (?)–1635 Daud. *Kolaks (Kings):* 1635–1655 Abd al-Krim; 1655–1678 Sharuf (also known as Kharut al-Khabir); 1678–1681 Sharif (also known as Kharif); 1681–1707 Yakob Arous; 1707–1747 Kharut as-Sarhir; 1747–1795 Muhammad Jawda (also known as Joda); 1795–1803 Salih Deret; 1803–1813 Abd al-Karim (also known as Sabun); 1813–1829 Yusuf Kharifain; 1829–1834 Abd al-Aziz; 1834–1843 Adam; 1843–1858 Muhammad Sharif; 1858–1874 Ali; 1874–1898 Yusuf II; 1898–1901 Ibrahim; 1901–Dec. 1901 Abu Ghazali; 1902–3 June 1909 Muhammad Doud Mourrah; 1909–5 June 1912 Acyl (also known as Asil); 5 June 1912–1935 Direct French rule; 1935–1945 Muhammad Urada; 1945–1960 Ali Silek; 1960–1970 [vacant]; 1970–1977 Ali Silek; 1977–Ibrahim ibn Muhammadu Urada.

Wagadu see Ghana Empire and Kayor

Wagadugu. ca. 1495–13 Sept. 1896. *Location:* in Burkina Faso. *Capital:* Dazuli (from 1620); Lumbila (1590–1620); La (1520–1590); Lugusi (1517–1520); Guilongou (ca. 1495–1517). *Other names:* Ouagadougou.

History: A Mossi kingdom (see Mossi States), which grew out of Oubritenga, and founded by Oubri about 1495. Oubri was the son of Naba Zoungourana and a Ninisi woman called Poughtoenga, and was the first of a long line of moro nabas of Wagadugu. In 1896 the country was occupied by France, and in 1897 became part of the French protectorate of Upper Volta (see Burkina Faso).

Moro Nabas: ca. 1495–ca. 1517 Oubri (also known as Wubri); ca. 1517–ca. 1520 Soarba; ca. 1520–ca. 1525 Naskyemde; ca. 1525–ca. 1535 Nasbire; ca. 1535–ca. 1550 Nyingnyemdo; ca. 1550–ca. 1570 Koudoumie; ca. 1570–ca. 1590 Kouda; ca. 1590–ca. 1599 Dawema; ca. 1599–(?) Zwetembusma; (?)–(?) Nyadfo; (?)–(?) Nattia; (?)–(?) Namega; (?)–(?) Kida; (?)–(?) Kemba; (?)–ca. 1690 Kolera; ca. 1690–(?) Zana; (?)–(?) Giliga; (?)–1729 Ubra; 1729–1737 Muatiba; 1737–1744 Warga; 1744–1784 Zombre; 1784–(?) Kom I; (?)–1795 Sagha I; 1795–1825 Doulougou; 1825–1842 Sawadogho; 1842–(?) Karfo; (?)–ca. 1854 Baogo I; ca. 1854–1871 Koutou; 1871–1889 Sanem; 1889–21 Jan. 1897 Wobgho (also known as Boukhary Kou Tou); 28 Jan. 1897–16 Feb. 1905 Sigiri; 27 Feb. 1905–12 Feb. 1942 Kom II; 23 March 1942–12 Nov. 1957 Sagha II; 28 Nov. 1957–8 Dec. 1982 Kougri.; Dec. 1982–Baogo II.

Wahiguya see Yatenga

Wahran see Oran

Wakkerstrom see New Republic

Walashma Dynasty see Adal [ii]

Walata see Kenedugu

Walfisch Bay see Walvis Bay

Walo. 1186–1855. *Location:* in Senegal. *Capital:* [unknown]. *Other names:* Oualo.

History: Founded in 1186 the Wolof kingdom of Walo lasted 700 years before being annexed by Louis Faidherbe, governor of the French colony of Senegal, of which Walo then became a part.

Kings: 1186–1202 N'Dya-N'Dya; 1202–1211 Mbang Waad; 1211–1225 Barka Mbody; 1225–1242 Tyaaka Mbar; 1242–1251 [unknown]; 1251–1271 Amadu Faaduma; 1271–1278 Yerim Mbanyik; 1278–1287 Tyukli; 1287–1304

Naatago Tany; 1304–1316 Fara Yerim; 1316–1331 Mbay Yerim; 1331–1336 Dembaane Yerim; 1336–1343 N'dyak Kumba Sam Dyakekh; 1343–1348 Fara Khet; 1348–1355 N'dyak Kumba-gi tyi Ngelogan; 1355–1367 N'dyak Kumba-Nan Sango; 1367–1380 N'dyak Ko N'Dyay Mbanyik; 1380–1381 Mbany Naatago; 1381–1398 Meumbody N'dyak; 1398–1415 Yerim Mbanyik Konegil; 1415–1485 Yerim Kode; 1485–1488 Fara Toko; 1488–1496 Fara Penda Teg Rel; 1496–1503 Tyaaka Daro Khot; 1503–1508 Naatago Fara N'dyak; 1508–1519 Naatago Yerim; 1519–1531 Fara Penda Dyeng; 1531–1542 Tani Fara N'dyak; 1542–1549 Fara Koy Dyon; 1549–1552 Fara Koy Dyop; 1552–1556 Fara Penda Langan Dyam; 1556–1563 Fara Ko Ndaama; 1563–1565 Fara Aysa Naalem; 1565–1576 Naatago Kbaari Daaro; 1576–1640 Beur Tyaaka Loggar; 1640–1674 Yerim Mbanyik Aram Bakar; 1674–1708 Naatago Aram Bakar; 1708–1733 N'dyak Aram Bakar Teedyek; 1733–1734 Yerim N'date Bubu; 1734–1735 Meu Mbody Kumba Khedy; 1735–1735 Yerim Mbanyik Anta Dyop; 1735–1736 Yerim Khode Fara Mbuno; 1736–1780 N'dyak Khuri Dyop; 1780–1792 Fara Penda Teg Rel; 1792–1801 N'dyak Kumba Khuri Yay; 1801–1806 Saayodo Yaasin Mbody; 1806–1812 Kruli Mbaaba; 1812–1821 Amar Faatim Borso; 1821–1823 Yerim Mbanyik Teg; 1823–1837 Fara Penda Adam Sal; 1837–1840 Kherfi Khari Daano; 1840–1855 Mbeu Mbody Maalik.

Walvis Bay. 12 March 1878–7 Aug. 1885. *Location:* midway down the coast of Namibia. *Capital:* Walvis Bay. *Other names:* Valvisch Bay; Whale Bay; Walfisch Bay; Walvisbaai.

History: In 1878 Britain established a protectorate over Walvis Bay, the largest port in what is today Namibia, as well as the immediate coastal strip of 434 square miles, right in the heart of German territory. In 1885 this lonely enclave became part of the Cape Colony. In 1910 it went with the Cape as part of South Africa, and in 1922 was assigned to the South African Mandate of South West Africa (see Namibia) for administrative purposes. In Aug. 1977 it was re-incorporated into South Africa, but on 1 March 1994 South Africa gave it back to Namibia.

Residents: June 1878–Nov. 1880 Maj. D. Erskine; Nov. 1880–7 Aug. 1885 Maj. Benjamin Musgrave.

Wandala see **Mandara**

Warri. ca. 1475–1884. *Location:* Benue Province, in Southern Nigeria. *Capital:* Warri. *Other names:* Itsekiri; Ouwerre; Ouwere.

History: Founded by Prince Ginuwa from Benin (see Benin [i]), 60 miles to the north, the town of Warri became the capital of this Itsekiri kingdom. After a certain success in the slave trade, then in the palm-oil business, Warri fell apart and was taken over by the British in 1884 (see Bights of Biafra and Benin).

Obas (Kings): ca. 1475–ca. 1500 Ginuwa I; ca. 1500–ca. 1580 [unknown]; ca. 1580–ca. 1600 Dom Domingo; ca. 1600–ca. 1644 [unknown]; ca. 1644–(?) Antonio de Mingo; (?)–ca. 1780 [unknown]; ca. 1780–ca. 1792 Manuel Otobia (also known as Aitogbuwa); ca. 1792–ca. 1805 Sebastian Otobia (also known as Erejuwa); ca. 1805–1848 João (also known as Akengbuwa). *Queens-Regent:* 1848–1853 Dola. *Regents:* 1853–ca. 1858 Eri. *Governors of the River:* ca. 1858–Feb. 1870 Diare; Feb. 1870–1879 Chanomi; 1879–1883 Olomu; 1884–1894 Nana Olomu (also known as Eriomulu); 1894–7 Feb. 1936 [vacant]; 7 Feb. 1936–(?) Ginuwa II.; (?)–Atuwatse.

Wase. ca. 1790–1898. *Location:* Wase, Northern Nigeria. *Capital:* Wase (the town in its present incarnation was built in 1820, on the site of the old capital). *Other names:* Bashar (ca. 1790–1820).

History: From Konkiok in Bornu came the Basharawa to settle on a small hill near the present day town of Gaduk. Later they moved to the site of the present day Wase Town. The Jukun tribe took them over about this time, but shortly thereafter the Fulani attacked and conquered them and built the town of Wase. From then on Wase was a vassal state of Bauchi. The Basharawa from Wase were relocated by the Fulani to the west, to Wase Tofa, which was their capital from 1820 to 1824, and then, about 1824, to Ganua. About 1835 they were moved again, this time to Gworam, near Bashar. In 1839 they were moved to Bashar, and in 1898, along with the main chiefdom of Wase (still a Fulani country with its capital at Wase Town), the Basharawa became part of the Niger River Delta Protectorate (see Northern Nigeria). In 1902 the Fulani chiefdom at Wase officially became an amirate under the British.

Chiefs: ca. 1790–ca. 1805 Tokta; ca. 1805–

1820 Yamusa. *Fulani Madakins at Wase:* 1820–1828 Hassan. *Fulani Sarkins at Wase:* 1828–1848 Abdullahi I; 1848–1866 Hamman I; 1866–1869 Hamman II; 1869–1874 Suleimanu; 1874–1877 Muhammadu I; 1877–1898 Muhammadu II; 1898–1909 Muhammadu III (also known as Yaki); 1909–1919 Abdullahi II; 1919–1928 Muhammadu IV; 1929–1947 Abubakr; 1948– Abdullahi Maikano III. *Basharawa Chiefs:* ca. 1820–ca. 1824 Karu; ca. 1824–1835 Yamusa; 1835–1838 Karu; 1838–ca. 1880 Abubakr; ca. 1880–1892 interregnum; 1892–1892 Usmanu (never took office); 1892–1898 Abubakar.

Waterboer's Land see **Griqualand West**

Wattasid Empire see **Morocco**

Watusi see **Ruanda**

Wawat see **Kush**

Wenburg see **Winburg**

West Africa Settlements see **British West Africa**

West African Settlements see **British West Africa**

West African Territories see **British West Africa**

West Island see **Aldabra Islands**

West Mauretania see **Mauretania West**

West Nupe. 1796–1805. *Location:* around the town of Jima, in Niger Province, Nigeria. *Capital:* Raba. *Other names:* Nupe West.

History: In 1796 Jimada and Majiya, the two grandsons of Iliyasu, the king of Nupe, began a civil war which created two states out of the old kingdom of Nupe — West Nupe and East Nupe. With the death of Jimada, the country was reunited under Majiya (see Nupe).

Kings: 1796–1805 Majiya (Majiya II of Nupe).

West Pondoland see **Pondoland West**

West Sister Island see **Seychelles**

Western Nigeria see **Nigeria Western Region**

Western Sahara. 1860– . *Location:* in North West Africa, between Morocco and Mauritania, with Algeria bordering it on the east. *Capital:* Based at Tindouf, Algeria (from 1976); El-Aaiún (1958–1976); Villa Cisneros (1887–1958); no capital until 1887. *Other names:* Sahrawi Arab Democratic Republic, or Saharan Arab Democratic Republic, or SADR, or Arab Democratic Republic (from 1976); Sahara Español, or Spanish Sahara (1958–1976); Africa Occidental Española (its name from 1912 to 1958, although it had been called that before 1912); Southern Protectorate of Morocco (an alternative name from 1912 to 1958); Río de Oro (1860–1912).

History: In 1860 the Spanish acquired rights to Ifni and the stretch of coast that became Río de Oro — these courtesy of Morocco. On 9 Jan. 1885 Spain declared a protectorate over the Río de Oro settlements. On 6 April 1887, Río de Oro became a dependant protectorate of the Canary Islands, and was ruled direct from there. It was not until 1903 that Río de Oro was effectively settled, and on 27 Nov. 1912 it became Spanish West Africa. On that same day in 1912 Ifni became a protectorate of Spain, and in 1952 it became a part of Spanish West Africa. On 10 Jan. 1958 the Río de Oro part of Spanish West Africa was combined with Seguia El-Hamra to form a separate province of Metropolitan Spain, called Sahara Español (Spanish Sahara), while four days later, on 14 Jan. 1958 Ifni also became a province of Spain. On 10 April 1958 Spanish West Africa as a concept was declared dead. In 1969 Ifni was given back to Morocco. In 1973 the world's largest phosphate deposit was discovered in Spanish Sahara. Morocco had long laid claims to the area, based on the historical fact that 11th century tribes there had given their allegiance to Morocco, but they had really forfeited this claim when they handed over the land to the Spanish in 1860. Now, however, they wanted Spanish Sahara back. On 6 Nov. 1975 350,000 unarmed Moroccans entered Spanish Sahara in the "Green March." On 14 Nov. 1975 the area became jointly controlled by Spain, Morocco and Mauritania, but the Spanish were now determined to evacuate the Province of Spanish Sahara, which they finally did, on 28 Feb. 1976, leaving it to be fought over between Morocco and Mauritania. On the day the Spanish left, POLISARIO (the Popular Front for the Liberation of Seguia El-

Hamra and Río de Oro) declared a provisional government in exile of the Saharan Arab Democratic Republic, with headquarters in Algeria (they had formerly been in Mauritania). The name of the country became a problem. It was no longer Spanish, and the names that were being put forth by different groups were not mutually acceptable, so the name Western Sahara was born to satisfy all (and none) of the parties concerned. On 14 April 1976 Morocco and Mauritania divided the country up between them, Morocco gaining the upper two thirds (i.e. all of Seguia El-Hamra and half of Río de Oro) and the phosphates, while Mauritania gained the southern portion of Río de Oro (Tiris El-Gharbia). POLISARIO (founded in 1973 in order to gain independence from Spain) proved such an able guerrilla organization that both Mauritania's and Morocco's economies were shattered by the conflict. More and more nations began to recognize the Saharan Arab Democratic Republic. On 5 Aug. 1979 Mauritania withdrew from Western Sahara, and the Moroccans promptly stepped in to Tiris El-Gharbia and renamed it Oued Eddahab (the Arabic form of Río de Oro), thereby annexing all of Western Sahara as a territory of Morocco. It was split into four provinces — Boujdour, Essmara, Laayoune, and Oued Eddahab. Inevitably the SADR will become a recognized country.

Administrators of Río de Oro: 1860–1903 no local administration; 1903–27 Nov. 1912 Francisco Bens Argandoña. *Governors-General of Spanish West Africa:* 27 Nov. 1912–1925 Francisco Bens Argandoña; 1925–1932 Guillermo de la Peña Cusi; 1932–1933 Eduardo Navarro; 1933–1934 José Gonzales Deleito; 1934–1939 Antonio de Oro Pulido; 1939–1949 José López; 1949–1952 Francisco Rosalen y Burguet; 1952–1954 Venancio Gil; 1954–1957 Ramón de Santallana; 1957–10 April 1958 Enrique Quirce. *Governors-General of Spanish Sahara Province:* 10 Jan. 1958–1958 José Vázquez; 1958–1961 Mariano Alonso; 1961–1964 Pedro Alcubierre; 1964–1965 Joaquín Coronado; 1965–1967 Ángel Larrando; 1967–4 March 1971 José Tejero; 4 March 1971 1975 Fernando de Santiago y Díaz de Mendívil; 1975–28 Feb. 1976 Federico de Salazar y Nieto. *Chairmen of Revolutionary Council:* 29 Feb. 1976–9 June 1976 al-Wali Mustafa as-Sayyid; 10 June 1976–30 Aug. 1976 Mahfud Ali Beiba; 30 Aug. 1976–16 Oct. 1982 Muhammad Abdelazziz. *Heads of State of the*

SADR: 16 Oct. 1982–Muhammad Abdelazziz. *Prime Ministers of the SADR:* 5 March 1976–4 Nov. 1982 Muhammad Lamine Ould Ahmad; 4 Nov. 1982–18 Dec. 1985 Mahfud Ali Beiba; 18 Dec. 1985–16 Aug. 1988 Muhammad Lamine Ould Ahmad; 16 Aug. 1988–18 Sept. 1993 Mahfud Ali Beiba; 19 Sept. 1993–8 Sept. 1995 Buchraya Hamoudi; 8 Sept. 1995–10 Feb. 1999 Mahfud Ali Beiba; 10 Feb. 1999–29 Oct. 2003 Buchraya Hamoudi; 29 Oct. 2003–Abdelkader Taleb Oumar.

Whale Bay see **Walvis Bay**

Whydah. ca. 1580–22 June 1894. *Location:* in Benin. *Capital:* Savi. *Other names:* Ajuda; Houeda; Juda; Ouida; Ouidah.

History: The kingdom of Whydah was founded about 1580 by refugees from Allada, and grew into a slave-trading kingdom, as did all of those kingdoms in what is today the Republic of Benin. From 1727 Whydah was subjugated by the kingdom of Abomey (see Dahomey) and ruled through an Abomey governor in collaboration with the Whydah king. On 30 Nov. 1891 the French placed a protectorate over Whydah, effective as from 3 Dec. 1892. In 1894 the country became part of the French colony of Dahomey.

Kings: ca. 1580–ca. 1620 Haholo; ca. 1620–ca. 1640 Kpassé; ca. 1640–(?) [unknown]; (?)–ca. 1669 [unknown]; ca. 1669–ca. 1690 Ayohuan; ca. 1690–1703 Agbangia; 1703–1708 Amah; 1708–Feb. 1727 Huffon. *Nominal Kings:* Feb. 1727–1741 Huffon; 1741–(?) [unknown]; (?)–Dec. 1774 [unknown]; Dec. 1774–1775 Agbamy. *Abomey Governors:* Feb. 1727–1744 Dassu; 1744–ca. 1765 Dedele; ca. 1765–(?) Sekplon; (?)–(?) Bassoh; (?)–ca. 1868 [unknown]. *Kings:* ca. 1868–1879 Adjossogbé; 1879–ca. 1882 Zinhummé; ca. 1882–ca. 1884 Seklocka; ca. 1884–ca. 1887 Aguessi Dagba; ca. 1887–ca. 1890 Jagba; ca. 1890–1898 Nugbododhone.

Winburg. 17 Jan. 1837–3 Feb. 1848. *Location:* 90 miles northeast of Bloemfontein, in the Orange Free State. *Capital:* Winburg (founded 1841). *Other names:* Wenburg.

History: In early January 1837 the Boers established their first major settlement here, in a section of land they called the Sotho. They then founded the Republic of Winburg later that month, the name Winburg being chosen by

Hendrik Potgieter to commemorate a Boer victory over the Matabele king Mzilikazi. In 1848 it became part of Orange River Sovereignty (see Orange Free State).

Commandants-General: 17 Jan. 1837–1 Sept. 1838 Hendrik Potgieter; 1 Sept. 1838–3 Feb. 1848 Andries Pretorius.

Witbooi Territory. ca. 1838–12 April 1893. *Location:* in Namibia. *Capital:* Gibeon.

History: Another branch of the Oorlams (see Oorlam Territory), the Witbooi family was allied to the Afrikaner family, but ruled in a different territory. In 1893 they signed a treaty of protection with the Germans (see Namibia).

Rulers: 1798–1875 Kido Witbooi; 1875–1888 Moses Witbooi; 1888–1889 Paul Visser; 1889–1905 Hendrick Witbooi.

Witu see **German East Africa** and **Kenya**

Witzieshoek see **QwaQwa**

Wolof Empire see **Djolof**

X-Group see **Nubia**

Xhosa see **British Kaffraria** and **Ciskei** and **Fingoland** and **Kreli's Country** and **Transkei** and **Transkeian Territories**

Yako see **Mossi States**

Yanagoa Province see **Brass**

Yatenga. 1540–1895. *Location:* in Burkina Faso. *Capital:* Ouahigouya (after 1757); Gourcy (before 1757). *Other names:* Ouahigouya; Wahiguya.

History: Founded by Yadega (from Wagadugu), this Northern Mossi kingdom (see also Mossi States) was established on territory which was once part of Zandoma. In 1895 it became a French protectorate, as part of French West Africa, or more specifically of the colony of the French Sudan (see Mali).

Nabas: ca. 1540–(?) Yadega; (?)–(?) Yaulumfao; (?)–(?) Kurita; (?)–(?) Geda; (?)–(?) Tonugum; (?)–(?) Possinga; (?)–(?) Nassege; (?)–(?) Vante; (?)–(?) Bonga; (?)–(?) Sugunum; (?)–(?) Kissun; (?)–(?) Zangayella; (?)–(?) Lanlassé; (?)–ca. 1650 Nassodoba; ca. 1650–(?) Lambwegha; (?)–(?) Niago; (?)–(?) Parima; (?)–(?) Kumpaugum; (?)–(?) Nabassere; (?)–(?) Tusuru; (?)–(?) Sini; (?)–1754 Piga I; 1754–1754 Kango; 1754–1757 Wabgho; 1757–1787 Kango; 1787–1803 Sagha; 1803–1806 Kaogho; 1806–1822 Tougouri; 1822–1825 Kom; 1825–1831 Ragongo; 1831–1831 Ridimba; 1831–1834 Diogore; 1834–1850 Totebalobo; 1850–1851 interregnum; 1851–1877 Yemde; 1877–1879 Sanem; 1879–1884 Noboga; 1884–1885 Piga II; 1885–May 1894 Baogho; June 1894–27 Jan. 1899 Boulli; 4 Feb. 1899–12 Feb. 1902 Ligidi; 28 Feb. 1902–2 Sept. 1914 Kobgha; 1914–1954 Tougouri II; 1954–4 May 1960 Sigiri; May 1960–1975 Kom II; 1975–1978 Gigma; 1978–Kom III.

Yauri. ca. 1400–1901. *Location:* Sokoto Province, Northern Nigeria. *Capital:* Yelwa (from 1888); Ikum Island (1850–1888); Bin Yauri (also known as Ireshe, or Ireshe Bino, this was the capital until 1850).

History: The date of the founding of the kingdom of Yauri is very speculative and lost in the mists of time. 1400 seems a reasonable date, and a lot more accurate than 950, which was the date traditionally given. It is one of the Banza Bakwai (see Hausa States), i.e. the seven illegitimate Hausa States, as opposed to the Hausa Bakwai. It may have been founded by Katsina hunters, or by Songhai warriors, but the Gunagwa tribe seem to have been the progenitors. Long a tributary state of Kebbi (see Argungu), it pledged allegiance to the amir of Gwandu, one of the main overlords of the Fulani Empire, and the king of Yauri became an amir himself, thus continuing the dynasty rather than the unpleasant alternative. In 1850 there was a civil war, and in 1901 Yauri became part of the British protectorate of Northern Nigeria.

Kings: ca. 1400–(?) Tafarilu; (?)–(?) Kamuwa; (?)–(?) Buyanga; (?)–(?) Sakazu; (?)–(?) Yauri; (?)–(?) Kisagare; (?)–ca. 1575 Jerabana I; ca. 1575–(?) Gimba; (?)–(?) Gimba II; (?)–ca. 1615 Kasafogi; ca. 1615–(?) Jerabana II; (?)–(?) Gimba III; (?)–ca. 1650 Kasagurbi; ca. 1650–(?) Kana; (?)–(?) Jan Rina; (?)–(?) Dutsi; (?)–(?) Lafiya I; (?)–(?) Kada; (?)–(?) Gamdi; (?)–(?) Dan Ibrahimu; (?)–(?) Muhammadu; (?)–(?) Lafiya II; (?)–(?) Yanazu; (?)–(?) Umaru Gamdi; (?)–(?) Suleimanu Jerabana; (?)–(?) Aliyu Lafiya; (?)–(?) Ahmadu Jerabana; (?)–ca. 1790 Shu'aibu Madara; ca. 1790–1799 Mustafa Gazari; March 1799–ca. 1810 Albishir (also known as Dan Ayi).

Amirs: ca. 1810–Nov. 1829 Albishir (also known

as Dan Ayi); Nov. 1829–June 1835 Ibrahimu (also known as Dogon Sharki); June 1835–March 1844 Jibrilu (also known as Gajere); March 1844–Sept. 1848 Abubakar Jatau; Sept. 1848–Sept. 1850 Jibrilu (also known as Gajere); Sept. 1850–Jan. 1869 Jibrilu (also known as Gajere), Yakuba (also known as Dan Gajere), and Suleimanu Dan Addo (all three ruled jointly); Jan. 1869–Jan. 1871 Yakuba (also known as Dan Gajere); Jan. 1871–Jan. 1888 Abdullahi Gallo; Jan. 1888–Feb. 1904 Abdullahi Abarshi; Feb. 1904–1915 Jibrilu; 1915–March 1923 Aliyu; March 1923–1955 Abdullahi; 1955–(?) Muhammad Tukur; (?)–(?) S.Y. Abashi; (?)–Muhammadu Zayanu.

Yola see **Adamawa**

York Island see **Sierra Leone**

Yorubaland see **Ilorin**

Zafi-Raminia see **Madagascar**

Zaghawa Kingdom. (?)–ca. 1350. *Location:* northern Chad and part of Darfur (in the Sudan). *Capital:* Njimi.

History: A group of Arab clans in northern Chad and part of Darfur (i.e. present day Sudan) founded this kingdom. Of nomadic Berber origins they controlled much of the Trans-Saharan trade in the Middle Ages. They helped found the kingdom of Kanem, as well as Gobir. They expanded seriously in the 11th century, and reached their height in the 13th century. Their language was (is) close to that of the Teda, and about 250,000 Zaghawa exist today.

Rulers: [unknown].

Zagwe Kingdom see **Ethiopia**

Zaire see **Congo (Zaire)**

Zakzak see **Zaria**

Zambesia see **Rhodesia**

Zambia. 17 Aug. 1911– . *Location:* north of the Zambesi River, in Southern Africa. *Capital:* Lusaka (founded in 1905, and named for Lusaakas, the head man of a nearby village, this was the capital from 1935); Livingstone (named for Dr. David Livingstone, the explorer, this town is now called Maramba, and was the capital from 1911 to 1935). *Other names:* Northern Rhodesia (1911–1964).

History: In 1911 the two districts of North Western Rhodesia and North Eastern Rhodesia became one — Northern Rhodesia, still ruled by the British South Africa Company (BSAC). On 1 April 1924 the country became a British protectorate. Agitation for independence began in the late 1940s, led by Kenneth Kaunda who, over the years, spent a considerable amount of time in British prisons. On 11 Sept. 1962 (effective 22 Jan. 1964) the country gained self-rule, as Zambia (named after the Zambesi River), and on 24 Oct. 1964 it achieved independence, together with Barotseland, as the Republic of Zambia, a free nation within the British Commonwealth. In 1972 Kaunda banned all political parties aside from his own, a situation that was to last until 1991, when he was defeated in the elections. A few failed coups in the 1990s led to a state of emergency in 1993 and another in 1997. The country remains in a terrible state of poverty and disease, and by 2000 the standard of living had dropped to half of what it was in the 1960s. AIDS is the big killer. Politically, however, the 2001 elections indicated that Zambia might be emerging into democracy.

Administrators: 17 Aug. 1911–17 March 1921 Lawrence Wallace (knighted 1918); 17 March 1921–20 Sept. 1923 Sir Drummond Chaplin; 20 Sept. 1923–1 April 1924 Richard Goode (acting). *Governors:* 1 April 1924–25 July 1927 Sir Herbert Stanley; 25 July 1927–31 Aug. 1927 Richard Goode (acting); 31 Aug. 1927–1931 Sir James Maxwell; 1931–1931 Donald Mackenzie-Kennedy (acting); 1931–30 Nov. 1932 Sir James Maxwell; 1 Dec. 1932–20 March 1934 Sir Ronald Storrs; 20 March 1934–31 Aug. 1938 Sir Hubert Young; 1 Sept. 1938–9 April 1941 Sir John Maybin; 9 April 1941–15 Oct. 1941 William Logan (acting); 16 Oct. 1941–15 Oct. 1947 Sir John Waddington; 16 Oct. 1947–18 Feb. 1948 Richard Stanley (acting); 19 Feb. 1948–8 March 1954 Sir Gilbert Rennie; 8 March 1954–24 May 1954 Alexander Williams (acting); 25 May 1954–22 April 1959 Sir Arthur Benson; 22 April 1959–24 Oct. 1964 Sir Evelyn Hone. *Presidents:* 24 Oct. 1964–2 Nov. 1991 Kenneth Kaunda; 2 Nov. 1991–2 Jan. 2002 Frederick Chiluba; 23 Jan. 2002 Levy Mwanawasa. *Prime Ministers:* 22 Jan. 1964–24 Oct. 1964 Kenneth Kaunda; 28 Aug. 1973–27 May 1975 Mainza Chona; 27 May

1975–20 July 1977 Elijah Mudenda; 20 July 1977–16 June 1978 Mainza Chona; 16 June 1978–18 Feb. 1981 Daniel Lisulo; 18 Feb. 1981–24 April 1985 Nalumino Mundia; 24 April 1985–15 March 1989 Kebby Musokotwane; 15 March 1989–31 Aug. 1991 Malimba Masheke. *Note:* In times of no Prime Minister, the President held that office.

Zamfara. ca. 1200–1902. *Location:* on the border of Northern Nigeria and southern Niger. *Capital:* Anka (from about 1820); Ruwan Gora (ca. 1810–ca. 1820); Sabon Gari (ca. 1805–ca. 1810); Kiawa (ca. 1756–ca. 1805); Birnin Zamfara (ca. 1300–ca. 1756); Dutsi (until about 1300).

History: Named for a princess called Fara, the Zamfarawa (men of Fara) settled in Dutsi about 1200. About 1756 they were driven out by the Gobirawa (see Gobir), and for the next fifty years regularly changed capitals, finally settling at Anka as vassals of the Fulani Empire. In 1902 their kingdom was divided between the French Military Territory of Zinder (see Niger) and the British protectorate of Northern Nigeria.

Sarkins (Kings): ca. 1200–(?) Dakka I; (?)–(?) Jatau; (?)–(?) Jimir Dakka; (?)–(?) Kokai Kokai; (?)–(?) Dudufani I. *Queens:* (?)–ca. 1300 Algoje. *Sarkins (Kings):* ca. 1300–(?) Bakurukuru; (?)–(?) Bakawa; (?)–(?) Gimshikki; (?)–(?) Karafau; (?)–(?) Gatamma; (?)–(?) Kudandam; (?)–(?) Bardau; (?)–(?) Gubarau; (?)–(?) Tasgarin Burum; (?)–(?) Durkusa; (?)–(?) Mowashi; (?)–(?) Kigaya; (?)–(?) Tabarau; (?)–ca. 1550 Dudufani; ca. 1550–(?) Burum I and Burum II (ruled jointly as twin sarkins); (?)–(?) Taritu; (?)–ca. 1625 Fati I and Fati II (ruled jointly as twin sarkins); ca. 1625–(?) Zartai; (?)–(?) Dakka II; (?)–(?) Tasau; (?)–(?) Zaude; (?)–(?) Aliyu; (?)–(?) Hamidu Karima; (?)–(?) Abdu na Makaki; (?)–(?) Suleimana; (?)–(?) Abdu na Tamane; (?)–ca. 1715 Maliki (also known as Malu); ca. 1715–(?) Babba I; (?)–(?) Yakubu I; (?)–(?) Jimirra (also known as Jirau); (?)–ca. 1734 Falkari (also known as Fashane); ca. 1734–(?) Babba II; (?)–ca. 1756 Yakubu II; ca. 1756–ca. 1805 Maroki; ca. 1805–(?) Abarshi; (?)–(?) Fari; (?)–(?) Dan Bako; (?)–ca. 1825 Dan Gado; ca. 1825–(?) Tukudu; (?)–1829 Abdu Fari; 1829–1853 Abubakar; 1853–1877 Muhammadu Dan Gigala; 1877–1896 Hassan; 1896–1899 Muhammadu Farin Gani; 1899–1904 Abdullahi Gade; 1904–1916 Abdu Kakkadi; 1916–1928 Muhammadu Katar; 1928–1946 Muhammadu Fari; 16 Sept. 1946–(?) Ahmadu Barmo.

Zanatah see **Morocco**

Zandoma see **Mossi States** and **Yatenga**

Zang Empire see **Zeng Empire**

Zango see **Daura** and **Daura-Zango**

Zanquebar see **Zanzibar**

Zanzibar. 1698–26 April 1964. *Location:* the country of Zanzibar consisted of the island of Zanzibar, 20 miles off the coast of Tanzania, as well as the island of Pemba to the north, and other islets nearby. *Capital:* Zanzibar (originally Zanquebar, meaning probably "Land of the Zanj," or "Zeng," as in the Zeng Empire, for which see that name). *Other names:* The Isle of Cloves; Zanzibar and Pemba (from 1890); People's Republic of Zanzibar (1964); Zanzibar Sultanate (1698–1964); Zanzibar Protectorate (alternative name between 1890 and 1964).

History: Originally part of the Zeng Empire, the islands of Zanzibar and Pemba, as well as the mainland coast opposite these islands, were conquered by the Portuguese between 1503 and 1508. In 1698 the Omanis from Muscat in Arabia took control of the island of Zanzibar, and in 1832 made the town of Zanzibar the capital. On 10 March 1862 the country became a sultanate under Sayid Madjid, independent of Muscat, and a British sphere of influence. A quantity of mainland territory was acquired, but Sultan Barghash saw all of that go to Germany, Italy and Britain (see German East Africa, Italian Somaliland and Kenya). On 4 Nov. 1890, as part of a deal whereby Britain gave up Heligoland to Germany and all claims to Madagascar in favor of France, the British proclaimed a protectorate over Zanzibar itself (including the island of Pemba, to the immediate north), while the remaining portions of what had once been Zanzibar (parts of Kenya, Somalia, and Tanzania) were gobbled up by the Imperial process. There was some British naval action in Zanzibar in 1896 when the sultan died and his cousin, Khalid, seized the palace. The British, not in favor of this move, bombarded the palace, and Khalid placed himself in the care of the Germans. In 1897 slavery was abolished, and the former owners (mostly Arabs) were compensated by the British government. On 1 July 1913 Zanzibar and Pemba became part of the British East Africa Protectorate (see Kenya), and administration was transferred to the British Colonial Office. The Zanzibari administrator was now answerable to the governor of British East Africa, in Nairobi. From 1925 the Zanzibari resident was directly responsible to the Colonial Office. All this time, however, the sultan was much more than a mere puppet of the British, with whom he was a close ally. Independence movements began in the 1950s. On 24 June 1963 self-rule was granted to Zanzibar, and on 10 Dec. 1963 it gained full independence as the Sultanate of Zanzibar. On 12 Jan. 1964 the sultan was deposed in a violent revolution led by Cuban-trained Ugandan "Field Marshal" John Okello, and the Republic of Zanzibar was declared. On 26 April 1964 Zanzibar and Tanganyika joined to become the United Republic of Tanganyika and Zanzibar (see Tanzania), although Karume continued to rule Zanzibar as autonomously and as despotically as he could without risking international interference, until he was assassinated in 1972.

Omani Governors: 1698–ca. 1710 [unknown]; ca. 1710–(?) Sa'id; (?)–1746 [unknown]; 1746–(?) Abdallah ibn Gad; (?)–ca. 1804 [unknown]; ca. 1804–ca. 1822 Yaqut; ca. 1822–ca. 1823 Muhammad ibn Nasir; ca. 1823–ca. 1832 Sayid Muhammad al-Ahabagi; ca. 1832–Nov. 1833 Hamad; Nov. 1833–1836 Tuwayni; 1836–June 1840 [unknown]; June 1840–7 Nov. 1854 Khalid; 7 Nov. 1854–10 March 1862 Sayid Madjid. *Sultans:* 10 March 1862–7 Oct. 1870 Sayid Madjid; 7 Oct. 1870–26 March 1888 Sayid Barghash; 27 March 1888–17 Feb. 1890 Sayid Khalifa I; 17 Feb. 1890–5 March 1893 Seyid Ali; 5 March 1893–25 Aug. 1896 Sayid Hamed; 25 Aug. 1896–27 Aug. 1896 Sayid Khalid; 27 Aug. 1896–18 July 1902 Sayid Hamud; 20 July 1902–9 Dec. 1911 Sayid Ali; 9 Dec. 1911–9 Oct. 1960 Sayid Khalifa ibn Harub (knighted 1914); 17 Oct. 1960–24 June 1963 Sayid ibn Abdallah; 24 June 1963–30 June 1963 Sayid Abdallah ibn Khalifa; 30 June 1963–12 Jan. 1964 Sayid Jamshid ibn Abdallah. *Consuls:* 1840–1857 Atkins Hamerton; 1857–1860 Christopher Rigby; 1861–10 March 1862 Lewis Pelly; 10 March 1862–1865 Robert Playfair; 1865–1870 Henry Churchill; 1870–1873 John Kirk. *Consuls-General:* 1873–1886 John Kirk (knighted 1881); 1887–1888 Claude MacDonald (acting); 1888–5 March 1891 Sir Charles Euan-Smith; 6 March 1891–12 Dec. 1892 Sir Gerald Portal; 12 Dec. 1892–Feb. 1894 Rennell Rodd; Feb. 1894–1900 Arthur Hardinge (knighted 1897); 1900–20 June 1904 Sir Charles Elliot; 20 June 1904–1908 Basil Cave; 1908–1909 [unknown] (acting); 1909–1 July 1913 Edward Clarke. *Viziers (Wazirs, or First Ministers):* 1890–11 Oct. 1901 Sir Lloyd Matthews; 11 Oct. 1901–3 Nov. 1901 [vacant]; 3 Nov. 1901–1906 A.S. Rogers; 1906–1908 Arthur Raikes; 1908–1 July 1913 Francis Barton. *Residents:* 1 July 1913–1922 Francis Pearce; 1922–Dec. 1923 John Sinclair; Jan. 1924–Dec. 1929 Claud Hollis (knighted 1927); Dec. 1929–Oct. 1937 Richard Rankine (knighted 1932); Oct. 1937–1940 John Hall; 1940–1941 [unknown] (acting); 1941–1946 Sir Guy Pilling; 1946–1951 Sir Vincent Glenday; 1951–1952 [unknown] (acting); 1952–2 Nov. 1954 John Rankine; 2 Nov. 1954–1959 Henry Potter (knighted 1956); 1959–1960 [unknown] (acting); 1960–10 Dec. 1963 Sir George Mooring. *Presidents:* 12 Jan. 1964–7 April 1972 Abeid Amani Karume; 11 April 1972–30 June 1984 Mwingi Aboud Jumbe; 30 June 1984–19 April 1984 Ali Hassan Mwinyi (acting); 19 April 1984–17 Oct. 1985 Ali Hassan Mwinyi; 24 Oct. 1985–25 Oct. 1999 Idris Abdul Wakil; 25 Oct. 1999–8 Nov. 2000 Salmin Amour; 8 Nov. 2000–Amani Abeid Karume. *Chief Ministers:* Feb. 1961–June 1961 G.C. Lawrence; June 1961–24 June 1963 Muhammad Shamte Hamadi. *Prime Ministers:* 24 June 1963–12 Jan. 1964 Muhammad Shamte Hamadi; 14 Jan. 1964–26 April 1964 Abdallah Kassim Hanga; 21 Feb. 1983–6 Feb. 1984 Ramadani Baki; 6 Feb. 1984–22 Jan. 1988 Seif Hamad; 25 Jan. 1988–Oct. 1995 Umar Ali Juma; Oct. 1995–15 Nov. 2000 Muhammad Gharib Bilal; 15 Nov. 2000–Shamsi Nahodha. *Note:* In times of no Prime Minister, the President held that office.

Zaria. ca. 1010–March 1902. *Location:* the southernmost of the Hausa States, in Northern Nigeria. *Capital:* Zaria (the capital from about 1578, this town was founded about 1536, and named for Chief Bakwa's daughter, Zaria); Turunku; Wuciciri; Rikoci; Kawar (the first capital). *Other names:* Zazzau (its name from about 1010 to about 1578); Zegzeg; Zakzak; Zozo.

History: Around the beginning of the 11th century the Hausa state of Zazzau was founded by King Gunguma, grandson of Bayajidda (see

Kano). The name "zazzau" means "sword." In 1536 the kingdom was moved and the town of Zaria built. At the end of the 16th century the name of the kingdom was changed to Zaria, as that town became the capital. Zaria became a conquering country, then a subjugated nation, and so on, as with most of the kingdoms in the area at that time, until 1804, when the Fulani Empire took it over. The Hausa rulers went into exile in Zuba and founded Abuja. In 1808 a Fulani became ruler of Zaria, and in 1835 it became an amirate. In 1902 it was taken by the British, but the amirate continued under the ruling authority of the British protectorate of Northern Nigeria.

Sarkis (Chiefs): ca. 1010–(?) Gunguma; (?)–(?) Matani (also known as Matazo); (?)–(?) Tumso (also known as Tumsah); (?)–(?) Tamusa; (?)–(?) Sulimano; (?)–(?) Nasabo (also known as Maswaza); (?)–(?) Danzaki (also known as Dinzaki); (?)–(?) Saiwago (also known as Nayoga); (?)–(?) Kwasari (also known as Kauchi); (?)–(?) Nwaiku (also known as Nawainchi); (?)–(?) Besekal (also known as Machikai); (?)–(?) Kuna (also known as Kewo); (?)–(?) Bashikarr; (?)–(?) Maji Dadi (also known as Majidada); (?)–(?) Kirari (also known as Dihirahi); (?)–(?) Jenhako (also known as Jinjiku); (?)–ca. 1505 Sukana; ca. 1505–1530 Rabon Bawa (also known as Monan Abu); 1530–1532 Gudumua Muska (also known as Gidan Dan Masukanan); 1532–1535 Tukuariki (also known as Nohir); 1535–1536 Uwan (also known as Kawanissa). *Queens:* 1536–1539 Bakwa Turunku. *Sarkis (Chiefs):* 1539–1566 Ibrihimu; 1566–1576 Karama; 1576–1578 Kafow; 1578–1584 Ali; 1584–1597 Bako Majirua; 1597–1608 Bako Su Aliyu; 1608–1608 Bako Musa; 1608–1611 Bako Mahama Gabi (also known as Gadi); 1611–1611 Bako Hamza (king for a day); 1611–1618 Bako Abdu Ashkuku (also known as Abdaku); 1618–1621 Bako Brima (also known as Burema); 1621–1646 Bako Ali; 1646–1647 Bako Makam Rubu; 1647–1660 Bako Brima; 1660–1670 Bako Shukunu; 1670–1678 Bako Aliyu; 1678–1682 Bako Brima Hasko; 1682–1710 Bako Mahama Rubo; 1710–1718 Bako; 1718–1727 Bako Aliyu; 1727–1736 Bako Dan Musa; 1736–1738 Bako Ishihako (also known as Ishaq); 1738–1750 Bako Makam Danguma; 1750–1757 Bako Ruhawa; 1757–1758 Bako Makam Gaba; 1758–1760 Bako Mair ari Ashaka Okao; 1760–1762 Kao; 1762–1764 Bako Bawa; 1764–1770 Yonusa; 1770–1788 Baba (also known as Ya-kuba); 1788–1793 Aliyu; 1793–1795 Chikkoku; 1795–1796 Maihaman Maigano; 1796–1802 Ishihako Jatai (also known as Ishaq Jatao); 1802–1804 Makkam (also known as Muhamman Makau); 1804–1821 Mallam Musa; 1821–1834 Yan Musa; 1834–1835 Abd al-Karim. *Sarkins in Exile:* 1804–1825 Muhamman Makau; 1825–1828 Abu Ja. *Amirs:* 1835–1846 Abd al-Karim; 1846–1846 Hamada; 1846–1853 Mahoma Sani; 1853–1854 Sidi Abd al-Kadiri; 1854–1857 Abd as-Salami; 1857–1871 Abdullahi; 1871–1874 Abubakr (also known as Bawa); 1874–1879 Abdullahi; 1879–1888 Sambo; 1888–1897 Yero; 1897–1902 Kwasso; 1902–1903 Nufu Aliyu; 1903–1903 Wambai Zozo; 1903–1920 Aliyu; 1920–1924 Dallatu; 1924–1937 Ibrahim; 1937–Aug. 1959 Ja'afaru; Sept. 1959–4 Feb. 1975 Muham Madu Aminu; 11 April 1975–Idris.

Zayyanid Kingdom see **Tlemcen**

Zazzau see **Zaria**

Zegzeg see **Zaria**

Zeng Empire. 980–1515. *Location:* Somali, Kenya, Tanzania, Mozambique. *Capital:* Kilwa (on the coast of what is today Tanzania). *Other names:* Zing; Zang; Kilwa.

History: In 975 Prince Ali ibn Hasan, a Shirazi nobleman from Arabia, arrived on the east coast of Africa, founded Mombasa that year and Kilwa in 976, and after much conquest made Kilwa the capital of his new Zeng Empire. This empire brought Swahili as the language of the area. In 1513 Kilwa, the capital, became part of the Portuguese captaincy of Sofala and Mozambique (see Mozambique). By this time, however, the limits of the empire had shrunk to between Sofala and Tanga (in today's Tanzania).

Sultans: 980–1022 Ali ibn Hasan; 1022–1027 Ali ibn Baskhat; 1027–1032 Daud ibn Ali; 1032–1035 Khalid ibn Bekr; 1035–1064 Hasan ibn Suleiman; 1064–1090 Ali ibn Daud I; 1090–1100 Ali ibn Daud II; 1100–1115 Hasan ibn Daud; 1115–1117 Suleiman the Tyrant; 1117–1158 Daud ibn Suleiman; 1158–1177 Suleiman al-Hasan the Great; 1177–1180 Daud ibn Suleiman; 1180–1181 Talut ibn Suleiman; 1181–1200 Hasan ibn Suleiman; 1200–1206 Khalid; 1206–1217 Ali ibn Suleiman the Lucky; 1217–1259 Abu Suleiman; 1259–1274 Ali ibn Daud; 1274–1293 Hasan ibn Talut; 1293–1308 Suleiman ibn

Hasan; 1308–1334 Hasan Abu'l Mawahib. *Regents:* 1334–1336 Daud ibn Suleiman. *Sultans:* 1336–1357 Daud ibn Suleiman; 1357–1358 Suleiman ibn Daud; 1358–1364 Hussein ibn Suleiman; 1364–1366 Talut ibn Hussein; 1366–1368 Suleiman ibn Hussein; 1368–1392 Suleiman ibn Suleiman; 1392–1416 Hussein ibn Suleiman; 1416–1425 Muhammad al-Adil; 1425–1447 Suleiman ibn Muhammad; 1447–1460 Ismail ibn Hussein. *Regents:* 1460–1461 Muhammad Yarik. *Sultans:* 1461–1462 Ahmad ibn Suleiman; 1462–1472 Hasan ibn Ismail; 1472–1482 Sa'id ibn Hasan. *Regents:* 1482–1483 Suleiman ibn Muhammad. *Sultans:* 1483–1484 Abdallah ibn Hasan; 1484–1486 Ali ibn Hasan; 1486–1487 Sabhat ibn Muhammad; 1487–1488 Hasan ibn Suleiman. *Regents:* 1488–1491 Hasan ibn Suleiman. *Sultans:* 1488–1491 Hasan ibn Suleiman (usurper); 1491–1496 Ibrahim ibn Muhammad. *Regents:* 1496–1496 Muhammad Kiwab. *Sultans:* 1496–1500 al-Fudail. *Regents:* 1500–1504 Ibrahim ibn Suleiman; 1504–1505 Muhammad Ankony; 1505–1506 Hajji Hasan; 1506–1507 Muhammad Mikat. *Sultans:* 1507–1507 Muhammad Mikat; 1507–1508 Ibrahim ibn Suleiman. *Regents:* 1508–1510 Sa'id ibn Suleiman. *Sultans:* 1510–1515 Muhammad ibn Hussein.

Zeugitana see **Carthage**

Zimbabwe. 29 Jan. 1900– . *Location:* to the north of South Africa. *Capital:* Harare (until 1981 this city was called Salisbury). *Other names:* Zimbabwe–Rhodesia (alternative name from 1979 to 1980); Rhodesia (1964–1979); Southern Rhodesia (this was the name of the country from 1900 to 1964, and even up to 1980 it was still being called Southern Rhodesia, even though Northern Rhodesia had become Zambia in 1964).

History: In 1900 the British protectorate of Rhodesia was divided up into three separate units — Southern Rhodesia, North Eastern Rhodesia, and North Western Rhodesia. On 17 Aug. 1911 Southern Rhodesia became a British protectorate, although it was still ruled by the British South Africa Company (BSAC). On 21 Sept. 1923 it became a colony. Between 1953 and 1963 Southern Rhodesia, Northern Rhodesia and Nyasaland all joined to form the Federation of Rhodesia and Nyasaland. On 24 Oct. 1964, with the independence of Northern Rho-

desia as Zambia, the term Rhodesia now applied only to the southern colony, and so the name of Southern Rhodesia was changed (officially anyway) to Rhodesia. On 11 Nov. 1965 prime minister Ian Smith placed his country in an interesting position when he made an illegal unilateral declaration of independence (UDI). Interesting in that it started the ball rolling for the eventual takeover of the country by the black population, and illegal from Britain's point of view, in that Rhodesia was then a British possession. The British governor-general left the country (remaining in spirit only), and on 20 June 1969 the Republic of Rhodesia came into being (effective as from 2 March 1970). That Britain did not send in the gunboats was an indication that the world was changing. More subtle, long-term planning was the order of the day, and meanwhile Ian Smith ran his country as a white country until he could no longer do so in the face of the huge black majority in the country, guerilla warfare from the blacks, and in the face of world opinion. There was still the question of who really owned Rhodesia — the British or the white minority rulers in the country itself. It was decided to hand over rule to the black majority. On 21 April 1979 a new name was chosen for the country, Zimbabwe-Rhodesia. The whites continued in power for a month after this, and then power was handed over. On 11 Dec. 1979, in order to make this black independence fully legal, the new (black) government officially terminated the UDI of Ian Smith, and handed over control of the country to the British on a temporary lease and release basis, so that Britain could oversee the transfer of power. A day later, 12 Dec. 1979, the British governor-general arrived to assume responsibility for the impending transfer of the country to an independent black regime. On 18 April 1980 the deal took place, and the country became Zimbabwe, with strongman Robert Mugabe in power ever since, in the early days as a Communist tool. Over 25,000 people had been killed in the struggle for independence. Canaan Banana was the head of state in the 1980s. As an example of Mr Banana's lack of self-confidence, it became a crime, punishable by a five-year jail sentence, to make fun of his name. In the 1990s Mugabe began seizing white-owned farms with no compensation, and in 2002 he proclaimed a state of national disaster. Since independence the main problem holding Zimbabwe back has been Mugabe, but there is also AIDS, which is scandalously rampant. Drought, poverty, and huge unemployment also bedevil the country. By 2003 inflation had reached 600 percent.

Administrators of Matabeleland: 29 Jan. 1900–March 1901 Capt. Arthur Lawley. *Administrators of Southern Rhodesia:* 29 Jan. 1900–31 Oct. 1914 William Milton; 2 Nov. 1914–24 Dec. 1914 Sir Francis Newton (acting); 24 Dec. 1914–15 Oct. 1919 Drummond Chaplin (knighted 1917); 15 Oct. 1919–14 Dec. 1919 Clarkson Tredgold (acting); 14 Dec. 1919–10 Sept. 1920 Sir Drummond Chaplin; 10 Sept. 1920–10 Dec. 1920 Ernest Montagu (acting); 10 Dec. 1920–15 Nov. 1922 Sir Drummond Chaplin; 15 Nov. 1922–10 May 1923 Ernest Montagu (acting); 10 May 1923–21 Sept. 1923 Sir Drummond Chaplin. *Governors:* 21 Sept. 1923–23 Sept. 1923 Percy Flynn (acting); 23 Sept. 1923–1 Oct. 1923 [vacant]; 1 Oct. 1923–Feb. 1926 Sir John Chancellor; Feb. 1926–Sept. 1926 Murray Bissett (acting); Sept. 1926–30 May 1928 Sir John Chancellor; 30 May 1928–15 June 1928 [vacant][15 June 1928–24 Nov. 1928 Murray Bissett (acting); 24 Nov. 1928–30 June 1934 Sir Cecil Rodwell; 1 July 1934–8 Jan. 1935 Alexander Russell (acting); 8 Jan. 1935–6 Jan. 1942 Sir Herbert Stanley; 8 Jan. 1942–10 Dec. 1942 Sir Alexander Russell (acting); 10 Dec. 1942–26 Oct. 1944 Sir Evelyn Baring; 26 Oct. 1944–20 Feb. 1945 Sir Robert Hudson (acting); 20 Feb. 1945–2 Feb. 1946 Sir Campbell Tait; 2 Feb. 1946–19 July 1946 Sir Alexander Russell (acting); 19 July 1946–14 Jan. 1947 Sir Robert Hudson (acting); 14 Jan. 1947–17 Oct. 1950 Sir John Kennedy; 17 Oct. 1950–13 Nov. 1950 Walter Thomas (acting); 13 Nov. 1950–21 Nov. 1953 Sir John Kennedy; 21 Nov. 1953–26 Nov. 1954 Sir Robert Tredgold (acting); 26 Nov. 1954–28 Dec. 1959 Sir Peveril William-Powlett; 28 Dec. 1959–11 Nov. 1965 Humphrey Gibbs (knighted 1960). *Nominal Governors:* 11 Nov. 1965–24 June 1969 Sir Humphrey Gibbs. *Officers Administering:* 17 Nov. 1965–24 June 1969 Clifford Dupont. *Presidents:* 24 June 1969–16 April 1970 Clifford Dupont (acting); 16 April 1970–14 Jan. 1976 Clifford Dupont; 14 Jan. 1976–21 March 1978 John Wrathall. *Presidents of the Council of State:* 21 March 1978–1 Aug. 1978 John Wrathall; 1 Aug. 1978–2 Nov. 1978 Henry Everard (acting); 2 Nov. 1978–21 April 1979 Jack Pithey (acting). *Presidents:* 21 April 1979–23 May 1979 Jack Pithey (acting); 23 May 1979–11 Dec. 1979 Jo-

siah Gumede. *Governors-General:* 12 Dec. 1979–18 April 1980 Lord Soames. *Presidents:* 4 March 1980–31 Dec. 1987 Canaan Banana. *Executive Presidents:* 31 Dec. 1987–Robert Mugabe. *Prime Ministers:* 5 July 1933–6 Sept. 1933 George Mitchell; 12 Sept. 1933–7 Sept. 1953 Godfrey Huggins (knighted 1941); 7 Sept. 1953–8 Feb. 1958 Garfield Todd; 8 Feb. 1958–15 Dec. 1962 Sir Edgar Whitehead; 16 Dec. 1962–13 April 1964 Winston Field; 13 April 1964–23 May 1979 Ian Smith; 29 May 1979–11 Dec. 1979 Abel Muzorewa; 4 March 1980–31 Dec. 1987 Robert Mugabe. *Note:* In times of no Prime Minister, the President held that office.

Zinder see **Damagaram**, and **Niger**

Zing Empire see **Zeng Empire**

Zirid Kingdom. 973–July 1159. *Location:* northern Algeria, Tunisia, and Libya. *Capital:* Sabra al-Mansuriyah (this was the last capital); Raqqada (985–[?]); al-Qayrawan (973–985).

History: Founded by the Sanhaja chieftain Ziri ibn Manad at-Talkali from his base at Ashir, 80 miles southeast of Algiers. In 972 the Zirids moved their power base from Ashir to al-Qayrawan, and in 973 declared a kingdom under their leader Abu al-Futuh Buluggin (also known as Yusuf), the son of the founder of the Zirids. The kingdom declined in the 12th century, and in 1159 became part of the Almohad Empire. See also Tunis.

Kings: 973–984 Abu al-Futuh Buluggin (also known as Yusuf); 984–995 al-Mansur; 995–1016 Badis; 1016–1062 al-Mu'izz; 1062–1108 Tamim; 1108–1116 Yahya; 1116–1121 Ali; 1121–1167 al-Hasan.

Zitako see **Agaie**

Zitenga see **Mossi States**

Zoutpansberg. 1849–Jan. 1858. *Location:* northern Transvaal, South Africa. *Capital:* Schoemansdal (founded in 1849 and named for Stefanus Schoeman). *Other names:* Soutpansberg.

History: In 1849 Hendrik Potgieter left Ohrigstad to found yet another republic, this time at Zoutpansberg, around the town of Schoemansdal. In 1858 it became part of the South African Republic (see Transvaal).

Head Commandants: 1849–1851 Hendrik Potgieter. *Commandants-General:* 1851–Dec. 1852 Hendrik Potgieter; Dec. 1852–Nov. 1854 Pieter Potgieter; Nov. 1854–Jan. 1858 Stefanus Schoeman.

Zozo see **Zaria**

Zuba see **Abuja**

Zuid-Afrikaansche Republiek see **Transvaal**

Zululand. 1817–1 Dec. 1897. *Location:* the original Zulu kingdom comprised Natal and points north, but it shrank considerably after 1838, to northern Natal, in South Africa. *Capital:* Eshowe. *Other names:* British Zululand (1887–1897); Zulu Native Reserve (1879–1887).

History: The founding of Zululand may be attributed to Chaka (or Shaka) in 1817, when he broke away from the Mtetwa Empire that year. The Zulu were a Bantu clan of the Transkei area, and they moved north under Chaka. The land of the Zulus expanded greatly and quickly. However, in 1838 King Dingaan signed away all of Natal to Piet Retief, the Trekboer, and moved north into what became the final basic stage of Zululand. In 1879, following the Zulu War (which the British won), King Cetewayo was captured and sent to Cape Town, and Sir Garnet Wolseley split Zululand into 13 chiefdoms in order to prevent a central Zulu power base. Thus, on 1 Sept. 1879 Zululand Province came into being. A British resident was installed to advise and to be the means of communication between the chiefs and the British government. By 1883 the situation in Zululand had become very difficult, with warring factions, and with the Boers becoming involved. In 1884 Dinuzulu, the paramount chief, and Cetewayo's successor, signed away half of his land to the Boers' New Republic in return for their help in establishing himself over his rivals. On 21 June 1887 Britain annexed the country as British Zululand (or Zululand British Protectorate), with a resident commissioner responsible to the governor of Natal. In 1888 Dinuzulu rebelled, lost to the British, and was exiled to Saint Helena. On 1 Dec. 1897 Zululand, which had incorporated Tongaland, came under the direct rule of Natal, as Zululand Province. Solomon Dinuzulu would be universally recognized as paramount chief in 1925. Basically Zululand followed the destiny of Natal, until 1961, and then of the Republic of South Africa (see also KwaZulu).

Kings (Paramount Chiefs): (?)–ca. 1700 Mandalela (also known as Malandela); ca. 1700–ca. 1710 Zulu; ca. 1710–ca. 1727 Phunga (also known as Punga); ca. 1727–ca. 1745 Mageba; ca. 1745–ca. 1763 Ndaba; ca. 1763–ca. 1781 Jama; ca. 1781–1816 Senzangakhona; 1816–22 Sept. 1828 Shaka (also known as Chaka); 23 Sept. 1828–Nov. 1828 Umthlangana; Nov. 1828–29 Jan. 1840 Dingaan (also known as Dingana); 10 Feb. 1840–18 Oct. 1872 Mpande (also known as Panda); 18 Oct. 1872–28 Aug. 1879 Cetewayo (also known as Cetshwayo); 28 Aug. 1879–29 Jan. 1883 [ruled by 13 chiefs]; 29 Jan. 1883–8 Feb. 1884 Cetewayo; 21 May 1884–18 Oct. 1913 Dinuzulu; 1 Nov. 1913–4 March 1933 Solomon Dinuzulu; 2 April 1933–27 Aug. 1948 Arthur Mshiyeni (acting); 27 Aug. 1948–17 Sept. 1968 Cyprian Bhekuzulu. *Regents:* Nov. 1968–3 Dec. 1971 Gatsha Buthelezi; 3 Dec. 1971–Zwelithini Goodwill Ka Bhekuzulu. *Residents:* 8 Sept. 1879–Jan. 1880 William Wheelwright; Jan. 1880–March 1883 Sir Melmoth Osborn. *Resident Commissioners:* 22 Dec. 1882–March 1883 John W. Shepstone; March 1883–1893 Sir Melmoth Osborn; 1893–1 Dec. 1897 Marshall Clarke.

A Chronology

ca. B.C. 5000
Lower and Upper Egypt created
ca. B.C. 3500
Punt founded
ca. B.C. 3400
Nekheb replaced Naqadah as capital of Upper Egypt
ca. B.C. 3150
Menes became king of Upper Egypt
ca. B.C. 3100
Menes united Upper and Lower Egypt
ca. B.C. 3100
Memphis became the capital of Egypt
ca. B.C. 2890
2nd Dynasty began in Egypt
ca. B.C. 2686
The Old Kingdom of Egypt began with 3rd Dynasty
ca. B.C. 2680
Zoser became king of Egypt
ca. B.C. 2613
4th Dynasty began in Egypt
ca. B.C. 2589
Cheops became king of Egypt
ca. B.C. 2549
Chephren became king of Egypt
ca. B.C. 2496
5th Dynasty began in Egypt
ca. B.C. 2345
6th Dynasty began in Egypt
ca. B.C. 2182
7th Dynasty began in Egypt
ca. B.C. 2174
8th Dynasty began (perhaps) in Egypt
ca. B.C. 2160
9th Dynasty began in Egypt
ca. B.C. 2160
Heracleopolis became the capital of Egypt
ca. B.C. 2133

The Theban Dynasty began ruling in Upper Egypt
ca. B.C. 2130
10th Dynasty began in Egypt
ca. B.C. 2040
Egypt re-unified
ca. B.C. 2040
Middle Kingdom began in Egypt with the 11th Dynasty
ca. B.C. 2040
Thebes became the capital of Egypt
ca. B.C. 2000
Coast of Tunis visited by Phoenicians
ca. B.C. 1991
12th Dynasty began in Egypt
ca. B.C. 1991
Idj-Towy became the capital of Egypt
ca. B.C. 1786
13th Dynasty began in Egypt
ca. B.C. 1674
15th Dynasty began in Egypt (the Hyksos)
ca. B.C. 1650
17th Dynasty began ruling in Upper Egypt
ca. B.C. 1567
18th Dynasty began in Egypt
B.C. 16th cent.
Merchants from Sidon establish base at Cambe
ca. B.C. 1361
Tutankhamen became pharaoh of Egypt
ca. B.C. 1320
19th Dynasty began in Egypt
ca. B.C. 1304
Rameses the Great became king of Egypt
ca. B.C. 1200
20th Dynasty began in Egypt
ca. B.C. 1085
21st Dynasty began in Egypt

ca. B.C. 1000
Tunis founded as a town
ca. B.C. 945
22nd Dynasty began in Egypt
ca. B.C. 860
Kush became an independent kingdom
ca. B.C. 817
23rd Dynasty began in Egypt
ca. B.C. 814
Traditional but erroneous founding date of Carthage
ca. B.C. 730
24th Dynasty began in Egypt
ca. B.C. 730
Sais became the capital of Egypt
ca. B.C. 720
Carthage founded by Phoenicians
ca. B.C. 715
25th Dynasty began in Egypt
ca. B.C. 715
Thebes became the capital of Egypt
B.C. 671
The Assyrians invaded Egypt
B.C. 664
26th Dynasty began in Egypt
B.C. 656
Sais became the capital of Egypt again
B.C. 631
Pentapolis founded
ca. B.C. 550
State of Carthage founded
B.C. 525
27th Dynasty began in Egypt (Persian)
B.C. 525
Memphis became the capital of Egypt
B.C. 509
The first Carthaginian-Roman treaty was made
ca. B.C. 450

Herodotus made a trip to Egypt
B.C. 404

28th Dynasty began in Egypt
B.C. 404

Sais became the capital of Egypt again
B.C. 399

29th Dynasty began in Egypt
B.C. 399

Mendes became the capital of Egypt
B.C. 380

30th Dynasty began in Egypt
B.C. 380

Sebennytus became the capital of Egypt
B.C. 343

31st Dynasty began in Egypt
B.C. 338

Memphis became the capital of Egypt again
B.C. 335

Sebennytus became the capital of Egypt again
B.C. 332

Alexander the Great conquered Egypt
B.C. 332

Alexandria became the capital of Egypt
B.C. 323, June

Ptolemy became satrap of Egypt
B.C. 305, Nov.

Ptolemy became king of Egypt
B.C. 268

Beginning of First Punic War
B.C. 241

End of First Punic War
B.C. 218

Beginning of Second Punic War
B.C. 201

End of Second Punic War
B.C. 201

Numidia created
ca. B.C. 196

Hannibal became leader of Carthage
B.C. 149

Beginning of Third Punic War
B.C. 148

Numidia split into three by the Romans
B.C. 146

End of Third Punic War
B.C. 146

Carthage became Africa Vetus
B.C. 122

Colonia Iunonia built on site of city of Carthage
B.C. 112

Numidia reunified by new king Jugurtha
ca. B.C. 100

Mauretania divided into East and West
B.C. 96

Cyrenaica became a Roman province
B.C. 75

Pentapolis became part of Cyrenaica
B.C. 62

Juba I became king of Numidia
B.C. 52

Cleopatra became queen of Egypt
ca. B.C. 51

Bocchus III became king of Mauretania East
B.C. 49

Numidian rebellion under Juba
B.C. 46

Numidia defeated by Julius Caesar
B.C. 46

Numidia made into Africa Nova Province by Caesar
B.C. 38

Mauretania united under Bocchus III
B.C. 33

Bocchus III gave Mauretania to the Romans
B.C. 30

Egypt became a Roman province
B.C. 29

Africa Vetus and Africa Nova united to form Africa
B.C. 25

Caesarea became capital of Mauretania
B.C. 19

Phazania conquered and named by the Romans
B.C. 13

Colonia Julia Carthago founded on site of Carthage
A.D. 42

Mauretania annexed by the Romans and divided in two
297

Emperor Diocletian reformed the Empire
297

Old province of Africa dismembered by Romans
297

Byzacena came into being
297

Tripolitania came into being
297

Mauretania Sitifensis formed by Diocletian
297

Roman Province of Africa came into being
300

Much of Mauretania Tingitana given to the Baquate
313

Cirta renamed Constantine
320

Africa Proconsularis formed
ca. 325

Axum conquered Merowe
330

Egypt became a Christian diocese of Rome
ca. 340

Mukurra founded
ca. 350

Empire of Ghana created
395

Egypt became a part of Byzantium
395

Mauretania Tingitana came under Gaul Prefecture
395

Mauretania Caesariensis came under Italy Prefecture
ca. 395

Byzacena came under Prefecture of Italy
429

The Vandals invaded North Africa
430

Phazania became an independent kingdom
435

Mauretania Sitifensis and Numidia went to Vandals
439

Roman province of Africa fell to the Vandals
442

Byzacena fell to the Vandals
442

Africa Proconsularis fell to the Vandals
442

Vandal conquest of North Africa complete
468

Unsuccessful Byzantine invasion of North Africa
ca. 500

Songhai kingdom founded
533

Belisarius invaded Vandal North Africa

534, April
Byzantine administration of North Africa began
535
The last of the Vandal troops left North Africa
540
Nubia converted to Christianity
546
All of North Africa pacified by the Romans
ca. 550
Mukurra converted to Christianity
553
The Byzantines conquered Carthage
553
Carthage became Colonia Justiniana Carthago
580
The state of Alwah became Christian
ca. 600
The Songhai came to Gao
616
The Persians conquered Egypt
618
Ceuta captured by the Visigoths
628
The Romans expelled the Persians from Egypt
639
The Arabs began their conquest of Egypt
642
Egypt was now Arab-owned
642
al-Fustat became the capital of Egypt
645
Unsuccessful Roman attempt to take Alexandria
647
The Arabs conquered Byzantine North Africa
649
The Arabs bought off by Byzantium
658, July
Egypt became Omayyad-owned
666
Phazania conquered by the Arabs
667
The Arabs conquered Byzantine North Africa again
ca. 675
Mukurra and Nubia united to form Dongola
697

The Byzantines conquered Arab North Africa
697
Carthage conquered by the Arabs
698
Carthage destroyed by the Arabs
ca. 700
Daura founded
703
Byzantines expelled from North Africa by Omayyads
706
Arabic replaced Greek as the language in Egypt
711
Ceuta surrendered to the Arabs
750, Aug. 9
The Abbasids took over Egypt
750
al-Askar became the capital of Egypt
750, Aug. 9
Omayyad Caliphate replaced by Abbasid Caliphate
776
The Rustumid Amirate founded
784
Kanem founded
789, Feb. 6
Idrisid State founded
800, July 9
Aghlabid Empire founded
807
Fez became capital of the Idrisid State
ca. 850
The state of Bornu founded
868, Sept. 15
The Tulunids took over Egypt
870
al-Qata'i became the capital of Egypt
ca. 900
Adal founded
905, Jan. 10
The Abbasids regained control of Egypt
905
al-Fustat became capital of Egypt again
909, March 26
Aghlabid Empire conquered by the Fatimids
909
The Fatimids conquered Ifriqiya
910, Jan. 6
North Africa became Fatimid-owned
911, July 31

The Rustumid Amirate was destroyed
912
al-Mahdiya established as a town in North Africa
913
Unsuccessful Fatimid attempt to conquer Egypt
919
Unsuccessful Fatimid attempt to conquer Egypt
920
Fez taken by the Fatimids
921
al-Mahdiya became capital of Fatimid North Africa
925
Fez re-taken by the Idrisids
935, Sept. 2
The Ikhshids took over Egypt
937
Hajar an-Nasr became capital of the Idrisid State
947
al-Mansuriyya capital of Fatimid North Africa
ca. 950
Axum came to an end
969
Fatimid leader Gohar began conquest of Egypt
969, Aug. 5
The Fatimids took over Egypt
969, Aug. 5
al-Mansuriyah became the capital of Egypt
973
The Zirids took over Fatimid North Africa
974
al-Mansuriyah became Cairo
974
End of the Idrisid State
975
Mombasa founded
976
Kilwa founded
980
Zeng Empire created
985
Raqqada replaced al-Qayrawan as the Zirid capital
ca. 998
Sheme became the capital of Kano
998, Dec.
Kano conquered by the Habe people
ca. 1000
Ife founded

1007
The town of al-Qalat built
1010
Gao replaced Kukya as the Songhai capital
ca. 1010
Zazzau founded
1014
The Hammadid Kingdom established
ca. 1015
Katsina founded
1031
Ajmat became capital of Almoravid Empire
ca. 1050
The town of Wagadugu founded
ca. 1050
Kangaba founded
1059
Tunis became a Zirid-run town
1059
Tunis became the capital of Tunis
1065
Fez became capital of the Almoravid Empire
1073
The wazirs seized power in Egypt
1076
Kumbi taken by the Almoravids
1086
Marrakesh founded
1086
King Humé of Kanem became a Muslim
1090
Dodu became the capital of Kangaba
ca. 1100
Biram founded
ca. 1100
Timbuktu founded by Tuaregs
ca. 1100
Kano became the capital of Kano
ca. 1100
The Wolof nation originated in Walo
ca. 1100
Gobir founded
1117
Ethiopian Empire created
1147, April 3
The Almoravid Empire conquered by the Almohads
1148
The Norman Roger II of Sicily conquered Tripoli
1152

Hammadid Kingdom fell to the Almoravids
1158
The Almohad conquest of Tripoli began
1159
al-Mahdiya became the capital of Tunis
1159, July
The town of Tunis captured by the Almohads
1159, July
The Zirid Kingdom became part of the Almohad Empire
1160
The Almohad conquest of Tripoli complete
1170
Benin founded
1171, Sept. 10
Saladin took over Egypt
1174
The Aiyubids occupied Dongola
1186
Walo founded
ca. 1200
Zamfara founded
1204
Gurma founded
1210
The Aiyubids left Dongola
1232
Doma founded
1236
The Hafsid Kingdom established
1236
Tlemcen founded as a state
1236
The Hafsids took Tunis
1236
Tunis became the capital of Tunis
ca. 1237
Ghana and Kangaba supplanted by the Mali Empire
ca. 1238
Mogadishu became a republic
1247
The Hafsids supplanted the Almohads in Tripoli
1248
The Merinids captured Fez
1250, May 2
Bahrite Mamelukes revolted and took over Egypt
ca. 1250
The Hova founded a civilization in Madagascar
ca. 1256
The Bornu Empire created

1260
Kanem became Kanem-Bornu
1268
Almohad Empire taken over by the Merinids
1270
Tegulat became capital of Ethiopia
1285
Ifat founded
1300
Imerina founded
1300
Birnin Zamfara became the capital of Zamfara
1312
Kankan Musa became Mali emperor
1323
Dongola became part of the Mameluke Empire
1325
Gao became part of the Mali Empire
1327
The Banu Ammar dynasty gained Tripoli
ca. 1330
Mwene Mutapa Empire founded
ca. 1345
Islam introduced to Kano
ca. 1350
Ruanda founded
ca. 1350
Dyolof founded
ca. 1350
The state of Oubri flourished
ca. 1350
Kongo founded
ca. 1350
Zaghawa Kingdom came to an end
ca. 1358
Ndongo founded
1364
Petit Dieppe established
1375
The Songhai broke free of the Mali Empire
1382, Nov. 26
Circassian Mamelukes took over Egypt
1394
Bamoun founded
1395
Buganda founded
ca. 1400
Bunyoro founded
ca. 1400
Masina founded by the Fulani

ca. 1400
Mogadishu Republic became a sultanate again

ca. 1400
Oyo founded

ca. 1400
Yauri founded

1401
Tripoli reverted to the Hafsids

1404
Conquest of the Fortunate (Canary) Islands began

1405
Fortunate Islands became Canary Islands

1405
Acatife became capital of the Canary Islands

1412
The Egyptian Mamelukes took over Tripoli

1413
Petit Dieppe came to an end

1415
Adal re-created as a state from the former Ifat

1415
Ceuta taken from the Merinids by the Portuguese

1418
Madeira discovered

ca. 1420
Bono founded

1420
Settlement began of Madeira

1421
Funchal founded

1421
Tangier became an independent Merinid amirate

ca. 1428
The wazirs (later Wattasids) took over in Morocco

ca. 1430
Nkore founded

ca. 1440
Allada founded

ca. 1440
Dagomba founded

ca. 1445
Mount Fura became capital of Mwene Mutapa Empire

1446
Nuno Tristão visited what became Guinea-Bissau

1447
Daniski founded

ca. 1450
Bonny founded

ca. 1450
The Bahinda Dynasty came to the fore in Karagwe

ca. 1450
Islam came to Katsina

ca. 1450
Brass founded

1455
The Portuguese began trading in the Gambia

1458
Alcazarseguer settled by the Portuguese

1459
The Wattasids set up their dynasty

1460
Cape Verde discovered and named by the Portuguese

ca. 1460
Hadejia founded

1461
Cape Montserrado (later Mesurado) named

1462
São Tiago, Cape Verde, settled

1464
Songhai became an empire

1464
Sonni Ali became first Songhai emperor

ca. 1464
Mali Empire taken over by the Songhai Empire

1465, May 23
The Wattasids replaced the Merinids in Morocco

1465
Asila became the capital of Morocco

1468, Nov. 29
Songhai Empire took over Timbuktu

1469
Anfa settled by the Portuguese

1470
São Tomé and Príncipe discovered

ca. 1470
Shoa founded

ca. 1470
Bakgatlaland founded

ca. 1470
Bamaleteland founded

ca. 1470
Barolongland founded

1471
Arzila settled by the Portuguese

1471, Aug. 28
Tangier taken by the Portuguese

1472
Formosa (Fernando Po) discovered

1472
Fez became the capital of Morocco

1474, Jan. 1
Annobón discovered

ca. 1475
Warri founded

1476
Canary Islands became Spanish

1476
Santa Cruz de la Mar Pequeña founded

1478
Las Palmas founded in the Canary Islands

1480, March 6
Gran Canaria occupied by the Spanish

1480
Twifo-Heman founded

ca. 1480
Rozwi Empire established

1480
Las Palmas became capital of the Canary Islands

1480
Gran Canaria became a Spanish colony

1482, Jan. 19
The Portuguese came to the Gold Coast

1482
Angola discovered

1482
The Hafsids regained Tripoli for the last time

1483
The Portuguese discovered Kongo

1485
Benin discovered by the Portuguese

1485
São Tomé became a donataria

1485
São Tomé became the capital of São Tomé

1488
Massa settled by the Portuguese

1491
La Palma, in the Canary Islands, was conquered

1494, Jan. 7
Annobón became a Portuguese possession

1494
Formosa became Fernando Po

1495
Spain conquered Tenerife

ca. 1495
Gonja founded
ca. 1495
Wagadugu founded
1495
Portuguese crown took over
Cape Verde
1496
La Laguna founded as the capital of Tenerife
1497
Bartolomeu Dias discovered the Cape of Good Hope
1497
Melilla fell to the Spanish
1497
Vasco da Gama landed on the coast of Mozambique
1497, Dec. 25
Vasco da Gama discovered Natal
1498, March 1
da Gama landed at what became town of Mozambique
ca. 1500
Funj settlers began moving into Kordofan
1500
Diego Suarez discovered by the Portuguese
1500
Príncipe was made a donataria
1500
Santo Antonio became the capital of Príncipe
ca. 1500
Akim founded
ca. 1500
The second state of Wadai founded
ca. 1500
Lunda founded
ca. 1500
Anjouan founded
ca. 1500
Mandara founded
ca. 1500
Imerinanjaka became the capital of Imerina
1500, Aug. 10
Diogo Dias discovered Madagascar
1501
Ascension discovered, on Ascension Day
1501
The Captaincy of Sofala created in Mozambique
1502, May 21
Saint Helena discovered and named by Portuguese

1502
Diva Morgabin (later Réunion) discovered
1503
Portuguese conquest of Zanzibar began
1504
The Funj Sultanate created
1504
Alwah swallowed up by Funj Sultanate
1505
The first of several Portuguese sackings of Mombasa
1505
Sofala settled by the Portuguese
1505
Gough Island discovered by the Portuguese
1505
Agadir settled by the Portuguese
ca. 1505
Koya-Temne founded
1506
Tristan da Cunha discovered by the Portuguese
1507
Ilha do Cerne (Mauritius) discovered
1507
Rodrigues discovered
1507, Sept. 8
Sofala became Sofala & Mozambique
1508
Velez de la Gomera became Spanish
1508
Safi settled by the Portuguese
1508
Portuguese conquest of Zanzibar complete
1509
Oran occupied by the Spanish
1510, June 26
Tripoli taken by the Spanish from Sicily
1512
Sofala became the capital of Mozambique
1513, Feb. 9
Diva Morgabin renamed Santa Apollonia
1513
Baguirmi founded
1513
Kilwa taken by the Portuguese
1513
The Denyanke Dynasty began in Futa Toro

1513
Azammour settled by the Portuguese
1514
Mazagan settled by the Portuguese
1515
Mehdia settled by the Portuguese
1515
The end of the Zeng Empire
ca. 1515
Ngaridza (Gran Comoro) founded
ca. 1515
Mayotte founded as a sultanate
1516
The Corsairs conquered Algiers
1516
Kebbi founded
1517, Jan. 22
Egypt conquered by the Turks
1517
Lugusi became the capital of Wagadugu
1519
Agouz settled by the Portuguese
1520
The Portuguese discovered Ethiopia
1520
The Kabyles conquered Algiers
1520
La became the capital of Wagadugu
1522
Portuguese crown took São Tomé
1524
The Sa'dids captured Marrakesh
1524
Marrakesh became the capital of Morocco
1524
Santa Cruz de la Mar Pequeña destroyed by Moors
1525
The Corsairs re-conquered Algiers
ca. 1525
Igala founded
1526
Harar conquered Adal
1530
Algiers became capital of Barbary Pirates
1530
Tripoli given by the Spanish to Knights of Malta
1531
Nupe founded

1534, Aug. 18
Khair ad-Din's corsairs took Tunis
ca. 1535
Biu founded
1535, July 20
The Spanish took Tunis
ca. 1536
The town of Zaria founded
1539
Tunis re-captured by the Turks
ca. 1540
Alasora became the capital of Imerina
1540
Yatenga founded
1544
Lourenço Marques named for a Portuguese trader
1546
Fernão López, first Saint Helena settler, died
1548
The Sa'dids captured Fez
1549, Jan. 28
Morocco became a Sa'did state
1549
Kayor. Independence from Wolof
ca. 1550
Andruna founded
ca. 1550
The Denkyira people founded their community
ca. 1550
Baol conquered by Kayor
1550
The state of Tlemcen came to an end
ca. 1550
Lozi Empire founded
ca. 1550
Calabar founded
ca. 1550
Gbara replaced Bida-Nupiko as the capital of Nupe
ca. 1550
Oyo became the capital of Oyo
1551, Aug. 14
Tripoli became an Ottoman province
ca. 1552
Kondwana first chief of the Mpondos
1553
The first English arrived in Benin
1554
Mozambique replaced Sofala as capital of Mozambique

1556
The Spanish crown took over Melilla
1557
The Turks occupied Massawa
1559
The town of Tlemcen captured by Algerian Turks
1560
Akwamu founded
ca. 1560
Lokko became capital of Koya-Temne
ca. 1566
The Kingdom of Fezzan created
1569
Portuguese captaincy-general of Mozambique created
ca. 1570
The state of Ashanti founded
ca. 1570
Bakwenaland founded
1573
Don John of Austria and Spanish fleet took Tunis
1574, Sept. 13
Tunis became a Turkish pashalik
1575, Feb. 1
Paulo Dias de Novais given Angola as donataria
1575
Ayandawaase became capital of Akwamu
ca. 1575
Ambohidrabiby became the capital of Imerina
1576
São Paulo de Loanda became capital of Angola
1578
Zazzau renamed Zaria, after its new capital
1580
Madeira became a Portuguese colony
ca. 1580
Whydah founded
ca. 1580
Dulo became the capital of Mandara
ca. 1580
Pategi became the capital of Nupe
ca. 1580
Tagant founded
1582
Morocco invaded the Songhai Empire
1584
Two Japanese ambassadors landed on Saint Helena

ca. 1585
The first Luba Empire created
1587
Beylerbeys abolished in Algiers
1587
Sir Francis Drake attacked Ribeira Grande
1588
Cacheu settled
1588, June
Thomas Cavendish landed on Saint Helena
1588
An English company began trading in the Gambia
1589
Captaincy-general in Canary Islands instituted
1589
Angola returned to the Portuguese Crown
1589
Angola became Portuguese West Africa
1590
The deys took power in Tunis
1590
Lumbila became the capital of Wagadugu
1591
Dendi became the capital of the Songhai Empire
1591, May 30
Timbuktu and Gao taken by the Moroccans
1592
Sir Francis Drake attacked Ribeira Grande again
1593
Mombasa taken by the Portuguese
1595
Captaincy-general ended in Canary Islands
1598
The Dutch arrived on the Gold Coast
1598
Ilha do Cerne claimed by the Dutch as Mauritius
ca. 1600
Baguirmi converted to Islam
ca. 1600
Kororofa founded
ca. 1600
Muhammad I the first recorded sultan of Kordofan
ca. 1600
Abomey founded
ca. 1600
Segu founded

1602
Masmouda founded as a pirate republic
1603
Darfur's recorded history began
1608
Expelled Moriscos settled in Rabat
1609
Seychelles (then unnamed) visited by the English
ca. 1610
Bamangwatoland founded
ca. 1610
Kaarta founded
1611
Abd al-Krim expelled the Tunjur from Wadai
1614
Portuguese administration began in Cacheu
1614
Masmouda incorporated into Morocco
1617
Benguela colonized
1617
The Dutch bought Gorée from local chiefs
1618
Gold Coast began to receive English visitors
1618
Rights to Gambia granted to Co. of Adventurers
1620
The state of Denkyira founded
1620
Dazuli became the capital of Wagadugu
ca. 1620
Gojjam founded
ca. 1620
The second Luba Empire created
ca. 1620
Munza became capital of the Luba Empire
1621
Gold Coast began first English administration
1621
Gold Coast capital became Kormantin
1625
Captaincy-general re-established in Canary Islands
1625
Santa Cruz became capital of Tenerife
1626

Senegal settled by the Compagnie Normande
1627
Bou Regreg founded as a pirate republic
1629
The Mwene Mutapa emperor deposed by the Portuguese
1630
Antananarivo became the capital of Imerina
1631
Tafilalt became the capital of Morocco
1632
Gold Coast taken over by Company of Merchants
1632, June 14
Gonder became capital of Ethiopia
1635
Abd al-Krim became the first Muslim king of Wadai
1637
Constantine became Turkish beylik of Qusantina
1637
The Dutch captured Elmina on the Gold Coast
1637
Elmina became the capital of the Dutch Gold Coast
1637
El Mina (Portuguese Gold Coast) taken by the Dutch
1638
Diego Ruy's Island renamed Rodrigues
1638
Port Mathurin became the capital of Rodrigues
1638
The French flag hoisted on Santa Apollonia
1638, July 31
Mauritius became a Dutch colony
1640
Cacheu became a Portuguese captaincy
1640
The Swedes arrived on the Gold Coast
1640
The Songhai Empire ended
ca. 1640
Trarza founded
1640
The beys took over from the deys in Tunis

1641
Bou Regreg incorporated into Morocco
1641
Dutch captured Portuguese West African possessions
1642, Jan. 9
Portuguese Gold Coast ceded to the Dutch
1642
Santa Apollonia officially claimed for France
1642
Dutch expelled the Portuguese from the Gold Coast
1642, Sept. 24
Fort-Dauphin founded
1643
Convicts were first settlers on Bourbon
1644
The Dutch left São Tomé
1645
Bourbon convict settlers returned to France
1647
Harar became capital of Harar again
1648
Portuguese regained their West African possessions
1649
France annexed Santa Apollonia, renaming it Bourbon
1649
Saint Paul became the first capital of Bourbon
1650, April 22
Swedish Gold Coast Colony created
ca. 1650
Bangwaketseland founded
ca. 1650
The Ulad Nurmash dynasty began ruling in Brakna
ca. 1650
Kenedugu founded
1651
The Duke of Courland bought Gambia
1651
Saint Helena occupied by the British
1651
Gold Coast taken over by Co. of London Merchants
1652, April 6
Cape Colony founded as De Kaapsche Vlek
1653

The Danes arrived on the Gold Coast
1656
Portugal became independent from Spain
1656
Failed Dutch colonizing attempt at Tristan da Cunha
1658
Saint Helena began to be settled
1658
The Dutch abandoned Mauritius
1658
Compagnie du Cap Vert et du Sénégal took Senegal
1658, Feb.
The Danes expelled the last Swede from Gold Coast
1658
English Gold Coast now run by East India Company
1659
Saint Helena. East India Co. administration began
1659
The Dutch took over the Gambia
1659
Saint Louis became the capital of Senegal
1659
Morocco taken over by the Alawids
ca. 1660
Batlokwaland founded
ca. 1660
Jebba became the capital of Nupe
1661, March 19
The British took over Gambia
1661, March 19
Gambia settlements renamed Fort James
1661
The Royal Adventurers took over Fort James
1662, Jan. 10
Royal Adventurers took over Gold Coast
1662, Jan. 29
Tangier became a British possession
1662
The first proper colonists came to Bourbon
1663, April 20
Swedish Gold Coast officially taken by the Danes
1663

Gorée taken from the Dutch by the British
1663
The British built two forts on the Liberian coast
1664, May 28
Colbert's Compagnie des Indes took over Senegal
1664
The Dutch bombarded the English Gold Coast
1664
Cape Coast Castle became capital of Gold Coast
1664
The Dutch partially settled Mauritius
ca. 1665
Kumasi became capital of Ashanti
1666
Mulay Rashid proclaimed sultan of Morocco
1667
Fort-Dauphin became HQ of French East India Co.
1668, Nov. 18
The Gambia Adventurers took over Gambia
1669, Aug. 1
The Gambia Adventurers moved into Fort James
1671
Turks took Algiers
1672, April 9
Compagnie du Sénégal took over Senegal
1672, Sept. 27
Royal African Company took over Gold Coast
1673, Jan. 1
The Dutch captured Saint Helena
1673, May 5
The British expelled the Dutch from Saint Helena
1673
Alhucemas became Spanish
1673, Dec. 16
Charles II granted Saint Helena to East India Co.
1674
Bourbon taken over by the Compagnie des Indes
1674, Aug. 27
Fort-Dauphin abandoned
ca. 1675
Burundi founded
ca. 1675
Ndongo taken by the Portuguese

1676
Cacheu Company granted a monopoly in West Africa
1677
The French took Gorée from the British
1678
Royal African Company in control at Fort James
1679
Ladoku became vassal state of Akwamu
ca. 1680
Ashanti Empire founded
ca. 1680
Dagomba subjugated by Ashanti
ca. 1680
Libertalia formed
1680
Lokko became Port Lokko (in Koya-Temne)
1682, May
Hollandia founded
1682
Compagnie d'Afrique took over Senegal
1683
Gross-Friedrichsburg became capital of Hollandia
ca. 1683
Failed English colony attempt of Tristan da Cunha
1684, Feb. 6
Tangier abandoned by the British to Morocco
1684
Royal African Co. officially took over Fort James
1684, Sept. 12
Compagnie du Guinée took over Senegal
1686
Baol broke free of Kayor
1687
Bissau founded
1688
Hogbonu (Porto-Novo) founded as a kingdom
1689
Agona became vassal state of Akwamu
ca. 1691
Libertalia came to an end
1693, Jan
The British took over Senegal
1693
Saint Louis became the capital of Senegal again
1695, July 27
The French captured Fort James

1696, March
Senegal became a British colony
1696
Bissau became a Portuguese captaincy
1698
Zanzibar taken by the Omanis
1698, Dec. 12
Mombasa taken by the Omanis
1699, April
The British returned to Fort James
ca. 1700
Birnin Kebbi became capital of Argungu
ca. 1700
Futa Jallon founded
ca. 1700
Lagos founded
ca. 1700
Keana founded
1701
The Ashanti conquered Denkyira
1701
Mascara founded as a Turkish garrison
1702
Phalo became Xhosa paramount chief
1702
Ibrahim, agha of the spahis, became bey of Tunis
1703
Cacheu abandoned
1705, July 9
The Hussainid dynasty began in Tunis
1707
Bissau abandoned
1708
Oran taken by the Turks
1709, May 20
Fort James abandoned
ca. 1710
Baule founded as a state
ca. 1710
Kazembe founded
ca. 1710
Kong founded
1710
Imerina split into four parts
1710
The Dutch abandoned Mauritius
1711, July 29
Tripoli awarded by the Turks to Karamanli Dynasty
1712
The French sacked Ribeira Grande

1713, Nov. 13
Fort James re-occupied
ca. 1713
Gonja conquered by Dagomba
1714
Gwiriko founded
1715
The French East India Company claimed Mauritius
1716
Hollandia abandoned
1717
Labuji became the capital of Nupe
1718, Dec. 15
Senegal taken over by Compagnie des Indes
ca. 1720
Kom founded
1720
Robanna became the capital of Koya-Temne
1720
Hollandia sold to the Dutch
ca. 1720
Birnin Lalle became the capital of Gobir
1722, April
Mauritius renamed Île de France
1723
Bono subjugated by the Ashanti
1724
Abomey conquered Allada
1727
Abomey subjugated Whydah
1728, March 12
Portuguese re-captured Mombasa
1729
Abomey conquered Whydah
1729, Sept. 21
Mombasa re-captured by the Omanis
1730
Akwamu conquered by Akim
1730
Abomey became Dahomey
ca. 1730
Hereroland founded
1731
Damagaram founded
1731
Kano-Gobir War began
1731
Capt. Gough re-discovered Gough Island
1732
Oran re-taken by the Spanish
1734
Alkalawa became the capital of Gobir

1736
Port Louis the first capital of Île de France
1736
Ngoi became the capital of Segu
ca. 1736
Saint Denis replaced Saint Paul as Bourbon capital
1741
Biaghi became the capital of Nupe
1743
End of Kano-Gobir War
1743
Swellendam founded
1744
Île de Labourdonnais named by the French
1745
Doqait became the capital of Shoa
1746
Mombasa became independent from Oman
1748
Kordofan became a province of the Funj Sultanate
1749
Gumel founded as an amirate
1750
Danish government took over Danish Gold Coast
ca. 1750
Little Popo founded
1750, June 13
Fort James taken over by Company of Merchants
ca. 1750
Ibadan founded
1750
Galekaland founded
ca. 1750
Keffi founded
1750
Tembuland founded
1750
Segu-koro became the capital of Segu again
ca. 1750
Kiawa became the capital of Zamfara
ca. 1750
Kenedugu became an organized state
1750, July 30
Sainte Marie de Madagascar ceded to France
1751, June 23
Gold Coast taken over by Company of Merchants

1752
Mozambique, the Zambesi and Sofala became a colony
1753
Bissau revived by the Portuguese
1753
São Tomé and Príncipe united
ca. 1755
Gumel became a tributary state of the Bornu Empire
1756
Île de Labourdonnais taken by France as Séchelles
1757
Ouahigouya became the capital of Yatenga
1758, April 30
The British took all the French Senegal possessions
1760
The Barolong split into the Tshidi and the Seleka
1760
Bedeghi became the capital of Nupe
1763, Feb. 10
Britain returned Gorée to the French
ca. 1763. ca
Kogu replaced Limbur as the capital of Biu
1764
Bourbon became a French crown colony
1765, May 25
Senegambia Colony created
1766
Biaghi became the capital of Nupe
1766, April
Gambia passed effectively to British crown
1767, July
Île de France became a French colony
1769
Villa de Praia became capital of Cape Verde
ca. 1770
Banana Island created as a state
1770
The Seychelles became a French colony
1770
Mahé became the capital of the Seychelles
1770
Ribeira Grande abandoned
1772
Kordofan broke free from the Funj Sultanate

1773
Kaapstad became Cape Town
1774, Feb. 11
Louisbourg founded
1775
Slavery abolished in Madeira
1776
Bedeghi became the capital of Nupe again
1777
Beynowski proclaimed himself king of Madagascar
1778, March 1
Annobón and Fernando Po became Spanish possessions
1779, Jan. 30
France re-took Senegalese possessions from Britain
1779, Feb. 11
French captured British Gambia settlements
1780
Shamama became capital of Brakna
1780
Lafia founded
1780
Timbuktu taken by the Bambara tribes
ca. 1780
Ilorin founded as a state
1781
Fernando Po abandoned by the Spanish
1781
Senzangakhona became king of the Zulus
1783, Sept. 3
Treaty of Paris
1783, Sept. 3
French returned the Gambia to Britain
1784
Kordofan again conquered by the Funj Sultanate
1785
Graaff-Reinet formed as a Cape district
ca. 1785
The town of Ilorin founded
1786, May 27
Louisbourg came to an end with Beynowski's death
1786
Town of Graaff-Reinet founded
1787, May 14
Freedom Province founded
1787
Fortress built by Portuguese at Lourenço Marques

1789
Granville Town burned to the ground by King Jimmy
ca. 1790
al-Fasher became permanent capital of Darfur
1790
Oran devastated by an earthquake
1791, Jan
Granville Town revived by the Sierra Leone Company
1792
Oran handed back to the Turks by the Spanish
1792
Freetown built
1792
Nova Scotian blacks arrived at Freetown
1793
Bourbon was renamed Réunion
1794
Imerina (Madagascar) united
1794
The British captured and occupied the Seychelles
1795, Feb. 6
Graaff-Reinet declared itself an independent colony
ca. 1795
Batwanaland founded
1795
Adam Kok I died
1795, June 18
Swellendam declared as an independent colony
1795, Sept. 16
British seized Cape Colony from Dutch East India Co.
1795, Nov.
Swellendam became part of the Cape again
1796
Nupe split into East and West Nupe
1796
The USA began paying tribute to Tripoli pirates
1796, Aug. 22
Graaff-Reinet re-attached to the Cape
1799, July 5
The colony of Freetown renamed Sierra Leone
1798, July 25
Egypt conquered by Napoleon
1799, Aug. 22
Jean-Baptiste Kléber became governor of Egypt

ca. 1800
Damagaram broke free from the Bornu Empire
1800, June 14
Jacques de Menou became governor of Egypt
1800
Jager Afrikaner became ruler of Oorlam Khoikhoi
1800
Timbuktu taken by the Tuaregs
1800
Nova Scotian maroons arrived in Sierra Leone
1801
The French defeated at Alexandria
1801
US war with Tripoli began
1801
The British occupied Madeira
1801
Réunion renamed Île Bonaparte
1801, June
The French surrendered Cairo to the British
1801, June 27
Egypt became an Ottoman pashalik again
1801, Sept.
Napoleonic troops left Egypt
1802
Kianza became capital of Damagaram
1802
Keffi became a Fulani state
1802
The British left Madeira
1802
The town of Klaarwater founded
1803, Feb. 20
Britain handed Cape Colony back to Holland
1804, Feb. 21
The Fulani Empire created
1803
A French agency established at Antananarivo
1804
Gombe founded as an amirate
1804
Zaria became part of the Fulani Empire
1804
Mallam Musa became ruler of Zaria
1804
Lafia became the capital of Lafia
1805, March
Sabon Gari became capital of the Fulani Empire

1805
Bauchi created as a state
1805
US war with Tripoli ended
1805
Biram became part of Hadejia
1805
The Fulani conquered Daura
1805
The town of Lafiya Moi built
1805
East and West Nupe united as Nupe
1805
Hadejia pledged allegiance to the Fulani Empire
1805
East and West Nupe united
1805
Raba became the capital of Nupe
1805, July
Gwandu became capital of the Fulani Empire
1805, Nov. 2
Mehmet Ali became vali of Egypt
1806, Jan. 10
Cape Colony became British again
1806
Fika founded as an amirate
1806
Adamawa founded
1806
Katsina became a Fulani amirate
1806
Daniski came to an end
1807, March
Kano conquered by the Fulani Empire
1807
Katagum founded as an amirate
1807
The British occupied Madeira
1807
The town of Lafiya Moi became Fika
1807
The British abolished the slave trade
1807
Kazaure founded
1807
Sifawa became capital of the Fulani Empire
1808, Jan. 1
Sierra Leone became a British crown colony
1808
Fulani Empire split into Sokoto and Gwandu

1808
Hadejia became part of the Fulani Empire
1808
Qundi became the capital of Shoa
1808, Sept.
The rulers of Gobir became Fulani amirs
1809
Bauchi founded and became capital of Bauchi
1809
The British seized Rodrigues from the French
1809
The Fulani Empire split into two
ca. 1809
Potiskum founded
1809, July 13
France lost Senegalese possessions to the British
1809, Aug. 4
Col. Keating took Rodrigues for the British
1810
Britain occupied Ceuta with Spanish consent
1810
Adama Lulu became the capital of Nupe
1810
Ilorin conquered by the Fulani
1810
Jonathan Lambert tried Tristan da Cunha settlement
1810
Britain annexed Séchelles, as Seychelles
1810
Shenge founded
1810
Jema'a created as a state
1810
The town of Lafiagi built
ca. 1810
Ruwan Gora became the capital of Zamfara
1810
Imerina became Madagascar
1810, July 8
Île Bonaparte taken by British and renamed Bourbon
1810, Oct. 3
Most of the Indian Ocean islands became British
1811
Egypt made an autonomous state by Mehmet Ali
1811

British took over French residency at Antananarivo
1811
Jemaari founded
1813
John Campbell created Campbell Lands
1813
Klaarwater became Griquatown
1813
Ankober became the capital of Shoa
1813
Timbuktu fell to Masina
1814, May 30
Mauritius and Rodrigues ceded to Britain
1814, May 30
Seychelles ceded to Britain
1814
Timbuktu fell to the Tuaregs
1814
Kukawa became capital of Bornu
1814
Katagum replaced Tashena as capital of Katagum
1814
British troops left Ceuta
1814
British troops left Madeira
1814
Victoria became the capital of the Seychelles
1814, Aug. 13
Cape Colony became legally British
1815, April
Bourbon handed back to France by Britain
1815
US naval squadron sent to Tripoli
1815, Oct. 6
Napoleon arrived on Saint Helena
1816
The British occupied Banjol
1816
Edinburgh became the capital of Tristan da Cunha
1816
Banjol became St. Mary
1816
Chaka became king of the Zulus
1816, Aug. 14
Tristan da Cunha became a British possession
1816, Aug. 23
Bathurst Colony created
1817, Jan. 1

American Colonization Society formed
1817, Jan. 25
French got back Senegalese possessions from Britain
1817, May
Tristan da Cunha garrison removed
1817
Ilorin declared independence from the Fulani
1817
Zululand formed
1817
Hamman Ruwa became governor of Muri
1817
Mzilikazi fled Zululand
1817
Saint Louis became capital of Senegal
1818
Mzilikazi became chief of the Northern Khumalo
1818
Turkish-Egyptian Army conquered Red Sea coast
1818
Swaziland created, with Sobhuza I as chief
1818, Oct. 15
Sainte Marie de Madagascar became a colony
1819
Adam Kok II began ruling Campbell Lands
1819
French rule began on Sainte Marie de Madagascar
1819
Hamdallahi became capital of Masina
1819
The bey of Tunis abolished slavery and piracy
1820
Banana Island became part of Sierra Leone
1820
Anka became the capital of Zamfara
1820
Adam Kok II left Griquatown for Campbell Lands
1820
Bashar became known as Wase
1820
The town of Wase was built
1820
Egyptian conquest of Nubia began
1820

Griquatown became known as Waterboer's Land
1820
Bumpe created as a state
1821, May 5
Napoleon died on Saint Helena
1821, May 7
Gold Coast became a crown colony
1821, June 12
Funj Sultanate incorporated into the Sudan
1821
Philippolis founded
1821
Khartoum founded as a Turkish camp
1821
Canary Islands became a province of Spain
1821, Aug. 16
Kordofan became a province of the Sudan
1821, Oct. 17
West African Territories created
1821, Dec. 15
Cape Mesurado founded as a colony
1822
Ascension transferred to Colonial Office
1822
Basutoland founded by Moshoeshoe I
1822
Sekonyela's Land created
1822
Nubia fully conquered by the Egyptians
1822
Zinder became capital of Damagaram
1822, Aug. 8
Jehudi Ashmun arrived in Cape Mesurado
1823
Khartoum became the capital of the Sudan
1823, Dec.
Adm. Owen established a protectorate over Mombasa
1824
First Ashanti War
1824
Gombe became capital of Gombe
1824
Lafiagi founded as an amirate
1824

Campbell Lands became Cornelis Kok's Land
1824
Gazaland created by King Soshangane
1824
Monrovia became the capital of Liberia
1824
Kazaure became the capital of Kazaure
1824, July
Thaba Bosiu became the capital of Basutoland
1824, Aug. 7
Port Natal claimed for Britain
1824, Aug. 15
Cape Mesurado renamed Liberia
1824
New Georgia founded
1824
Boers first settled in Transorangia
1825
The town of Gorgoram built in Bedde
1825
Egyptian administration of the Sudan began
1825
Lapai founded as an amirate
ca. 1825
Daura-Zango and Daura-Baure founded as states
1826
Adam Kok's Land created at Philippolis
ca. 1826
Aku founded
1826
The al-Bu Sa'id Dynasty took over Zanzibar
1826
Katagum conquered by the Bornu Empire
1826
Timbuktu fell to Masina
1826
Constantine declared independence from Algiers
1827
The French built a fort at Bône, Algeria
1827
Spanish leased part of Fernando Po to the British
1827
Santa Isabel (Fernando Po) became Port Clarence
1827
British occupied Fernando Po

1827
Argungu founded
1828, April 30
Port Natal settlement broke up
1828
Abuja founded
1828, June 25
Gold Coast broke away from West African Territories
1828, July 27
King Radama I of Madagascar died
1828, Sept. 22
Umthlangana became the king of the Zulus
1829
Ibadan became leading city in what became Nigeria
1829
Abd as-Salami became first amir of Ilorin
1829, Dec. 12
Bathurst Settlement and Dependencies created
1830
Ribadu became capital of Adamawa
ca. 1830
Abeokuta founded as a state by Sodeke
1830
Zugurma became the capital of Nupe
1830, July 5
Algiers became French
1831
Oran taken by the French
1831
Misau founded
1831
The Fulani conquered Argungu
1832
Agaie became an amirate
1832
Bône taken by the French
1832
Zanzibar became the capital of Zanzibar
1832
Edina founded
1832, Nov. 22
Mascara founded by Abdelkedir
1832, Dec.
Port Cresson founded
1833, May 3
Turkey recognized Egypt's independence of action
1833
Muri became an independent Fulani amirate

1834, Feb. 12
Maryland-in-Liberia founded as Cape Palmas
1834, April 22
Saint Helena became a British colony
1834
Madeira became an overseas province of Portugal
1835
Adam Kok II died
1835
Tiaret became the capital of Mascara
1835
Zaria became an amirate
1835
Queen Ranavalona of Madagascar banned Christianity
1835, May 6
Port Natal re-settled by Allan Gardiner
1835, May 10
Queen Adelaide Province annexed by British
1835, May 19
Kreli began reign in Galekaland
1835, May 26
Tripoli became an Ottoman province again
1835, June
Port Cresson destroyed by the Bassa
1835, June 23
The town of Durban laid out in Port Natal
1835
Fingoland came into being
1835
Anjouan conquered Mayotte
1835
Nupe became an amirate within the Fulani Empire
1835
Raba became the capital of Nupe again
1835
The town of Mascara destroyed by the French
1835
Mississippi-in-Africa founded
1835, July
Bassa Cove founded on ashes of Port Cresson
1835, Dec. 10
Queen Adelaide Province became Queen Adelaide Land
1836, March
The colony of Mozambique created

1836
Mswati became paramount chief of Swaziland
1836
Great Trek Boers arrived in Transorangia
1836, Dec. 2
Free Province of New Holland founded
1836, Dec.
British administration began in Kaffraria
1837, Jan
Winburg founded
1837, Jan. 17
Winburg became a republic
1837
Edina became part of Bassa Cove
1837
Treaty of Tafna signed between France and Mascara
1837
The Matabele defeated by the Boers
1837
The Matabele crossed the Limpopo
1837
Mombasa came under Zanzibari administration
1837, Oct. 13
Constantine taken by the French
1837, Nov.
Matabeleland created
1838, Feb. 4
Port Natal came to an end
1838
The Kololo conquered Barotseland
1838
The French surveyed the Guinea coast
1838
The town of Sinoe in Liberia renamed Greenville
1838
Zulu king Dingaan signed away Natal to Piet Retief
1838
Rozwi became part of Matabeleland
1838
Oorlam Territory created in South West Africa
ca. 1838
Witbooi Territory created
1838, Sept. 1
Andries Pretorius became commandant of Winburg
1838, Oct. 20

Free Province of New Holland renamed Natal
1838, Nov.
Potchefstroom founded
1838, Nov.
The Cape acquired Port Natal
1839, Feb. 9
French began Gulf of Guinea Settlements
1839, April 1
Commonwealth of Liberia came into being
1839, April 1
Thomas Buchanan became first governor of Liberia
1839
Jobolio became capital of Adamawa
1839
Natalia acquired southern Zululand and Pondoland
1839
Pietermaritzburg founded
1839
The term "Algeria" used for the first time
1839, Dec. 24
Port Natal became part of Natalia
1840, Feb. 10
Mpande became king of the Zulus
1840
The French moved against Mascara in force
1840
New Oyo became the capital of Oyo
ca. 1840
Baule became part of French Ivory Coast
1840, July 14
Nossi-Bé ceded to the French
1841, Feb. 13
Mehmet Ali gained Egypt as an hereditary possession
1841, March 25
Mayotte ceded to the French as a protectorate
1841
Chingoni became capital of Mayotte
1841
Yola became capital of Adamawa
1841
Winburg founded
1841
Bassa Cove became Buchanan
1841, Sept. 3
Joseph Roberts became acting governor of Liberia

1842, Jan. 20
Joseph Roberts became governor of Liberia
1842
First missionaries arrived in Abeokuta
1842
Fezzan conquered by the Turks
1842
Mississippi-in-Africa became part of Liberia
1842, Feb.
Algeria became a French military province
1843, March 25
Nossi-Bé transferred to Mayotte
1843, March 25
Sainte Marie de Madagascar transferred to Mayotte
1843, April 11
Gambia became a separate colony
1843, May 12
Natalia became the British colony of Natal
1843
The British gave up their naval base in Fernando Po
1843
The French occupied Mayotte
1843
The French took Tiaret, the Mascara capital
1843
The town of Gombe renamed Old Gombe
1843, June 11
Gulf of Guinea Settlements now French protectorate
1843
French protectorates of Grand Bassam and Assinie
1843
Gold Coast became a crown colony
1843, Aug. 29
First French administration of Mayotte
1843, Nov.
Adam Kok III placed lands under British protection
1843, Dec. 13
Kingdom of Basutoland recognized by Britain
1844, March 20
Glass became part of Gulf of Guinea Settlements
1844, May 31
Natal became a district of the Cape

1844
The Spanish reclaimed Fernando Po
1844
The Tuaregs regained control of Timbuktu
1844, Oct. 7
Pondoland recognized by the British
1845, March 8
First white administration north of the Vaal
1845
Gumel replaced Tumbi as capital of Gumel
1845
French and British failed to take Tamatave
1845, Aug. 11
Ohrigstad founded
1846
Hendrik Potgieter left Ohrigstad
1846
Ohrigstad abandoned
1846
Lydenburg formed
1846, Nov. 4
George's Creek became part of Gulf of Guinea
1846, Dec. 2
Como and Remboue rivers part of Gulf of Guinea
1847
King William's Town capital of British Kaffraria
1847
Libreville founded as a town
1847
Spanish captaincy-general of North Africa created
1847, July 26
Liberia became a republic
1847, Dec. 17
Queen Adelaide Land became British Kaffraria
1847, Dec. 23
Mascara surrendered to the French
1848, Jan. 3
Joseph Roberts inaugurated first Liberian president
1848, Feb. 3
Orange River Territory annexed by Harry Smith
1848, Feb. 3
Winburg became part of Orange River Sovereignty
1848, Feb. 14
The Mondah taken in by Gulf of Guinea Settlements

1848
Algeria declared a French territory
1848
Bourbon renamed Réunion
1848, Nov. 30
Abbas I became vali of Egypt
1849
Britain reduced the borders of Basutoland
1849
The town of Lydenburg built
1849
Zoutpansberg formed
1849, Aug. 5
Rivières du Sud created as a French protectorate
1849, Aug.
Libreville replaced Fort d'Aumale as Gabon capital
1849, June 30
Bight of Biafra came into being
1850, Jan. 13
West African Territories came to an end
1850, Jan. 13
Gold Coast became a crown colony
1850, March 30
Danish Gold Coast sold to the British
1850
Mulago replaced Mengo as capital of Buganda
1850
Ikum Island became the capital of Yauri
1850
Civil war in Yauri
1850
Gouveia became "king" of Gazaland
1850
Kongo came to an end
1851
France and Dahomey made commercial agreement
1851
Hadejia rebelled against the Fulani Empire
1852, Jan. 17
Potchefstroom became Dutch African Republic
1852, Feb. 1
Bight of Benin came into being
1852
Andruna became part of Mayotte
1852
Utrecht founded

1852, Sept. 18
Cape Esterias (off Gabon) fell to the French
1853
Sainte Marie de Madagascar became separate colony
1853, Sept.
Sekonyela's Land became part of the Cape
1854, Feb. 23
Orange River Republic achieved independence
1854, April 10
Orange River Republic renamed Orange Free State
1854
Public (not private) slaves freed in Cape Verde
1854
Gorée became a separate colony
1854
Tukolor Empire created under Umar al-Hajj
1854, June 8
Maryland-in-Liberia became a republic
1854, Nov. 7
Sayid Madjid became the Omani governor of Zanzibar
1855, Feb. 11
Theodore became Emperor of Ethiopia
1855
The Spanish tried again to colonize Fernando Po
1855
Pretoria founded
1855
Spanish adventurers entered Río Muni
1855
Port Clarence (Fernando Po) became Santa Isabel
1855
Gojjam and Tigre became part of Ethiopia
1855
British left Fernando Po
1855
The town of Pretoria founded
1855
Magdala became capital of Ethiopia
1855
Walo became part of Senegal
1855
Territory of Albania came within Waterboer's Land
1856, Jan. 2

Stephen Benson became president of Liberia

1856, Feb.
Utrecht became a republic

1856
Nabulagala became capital of Buganda

1856
Shoa became part of Ethiopia

1856, July 12
Natal became a British crown colony

1856, Dec. 16
Dutch African Republic now South African Republic

1856, Dec. 17
Lydenburg declared a republic

1857, Jan. 1
Marthinus Pretorius became president of SAR

1857, Feb. 19
Maryland-in-Liberia became part of Liberia

1857
Cornelis Kok's Land taken by Orange Free State

1857
Bida became the capital of Nupe

1858, Jan
Zoutpansberg joined the South African Republic

1858, May
Utrecht became part of Lydenburg

1858
Victoria founded as a colony in Ambas Bay

1858
Baptist missionaries expelled from Fernando Po

ca. 1858
Mirambo created

1858, Aug.
Idutywa formed

1859
France signed treaties with Afars and Issas leaders

1859
Gorée re-attached to Senegal

1860, March 7
British Kaffraria became a crown colony

1860, April 3
Pretoria became capital of South African Republic

1860, April 4
Lydenburg merged into the South African Republic

1860
Nakatema became capital of Buganda

1860
Spain at war with Morocco

1860
Lokoja founded as a town in what became Nigeria

1860
Spain acquired Ifni and Río de Oro

1860, Aug. 4
Ivory Coast and Gabon united

1861, March 10
Segu taken over by the Tukolor Empire

1861
The British annexed Lagos

1861
Richard Burton became British consul in Fernando Po

1861, Aug. 6
Lagos taken by the British

1861, Aug. 16
Queen Ranavalona I of Madagascar died

1861, Dec. 26
Adam Kok II sold his lands to Orange Free State

1862, March 10
Zanzibar became a sultanate

1862, March 11
The French bought Obock

1862
The name French Coast of the Somalis first used

1862
Masina conquered by the Tukolor Empire

1862
Liberia recognized by the USA

1862
The town of Dar es-Salaam founded

1862
Bbanda became capital of Buganda

1862
John Hanning Speke first white man into Buganda

1862
Timbuktu taken by the Tukolor Empire

1862, Aug. 22
Lagos became the Lagos Settlement

1863, Jan. 18
Ismail became vali of Egypt

1863, Feb. 25
Porto-Novo became a French protectorate

1863
Richard Burton in Benin

1864, Jan. 4
Daniel Warner became president of Liberia

1864, May 10
Marthinus Pretorius became president of SAR

1864
The Kololo expelled from Barotseland

1864
Mustafa became new emperor of Tukolor Empire

1864
Kontagora founded as an amirate

1864, July 14
Rainilaiarivony became PM of Madagascar

1864, Dec.
Idutywa merged into British Kaffraria

1865, Jan. 2
Porto-Novo French protectorate came to an end

1865
Nnakawa became capital of Buganda

1865
The Turks gave Massawa to the Egyptians

1866, Jan. 1
The district of Alfred became part of Natal

1866, Feb. 19
West African Settlements formed

1866
Anjouan became part of Mayotte

1866
Anjouan became part of Mayotte

1866
The town of Heidelberg founded

1866
Egypt became an hereditary viceroyalty

1866
Ismail became khedive of Egypt

1866, April 17
British Kaffraria became part of Cape Colony

1867
The Bights of Biafra and Benin united

1867
Diamonds discovered in Waterboer's Land

1867, Oct. 29
Pondoland split into East and West

1868, Jan. 6
James Payne became president of Liberia

1868, March 12
Basutoland became a crown protectorate

1868, April 1
Queen Ranavalona II of Madagascar came to throne

1868, May 19
French established a protectorate over Cotonou

1868
Ludvonga became paramount chief of Swaziland

1868, Sept. 9
Mzilikazi of Matabeleland died

1869, Jan. 29
Bahr al-Ghazal created as a province

1869, March 11
Maseru became the capital of Basutoland

1869
Assab acquired by Italian shipping company

1869
Britain, France & Italy became guarantors of Tunis

1869, Nov. 17
Suez Canal opened

1870, Jan. 4
Edward Roye became president of Liberia

1870, Jan. 24
Lobengula became king of the Matabele

1870, March 11
Moshoeshoe I of Basutoland died

1870, March 11
Letsie I became king of Basutoland

1870
Egyptian flag hoisted in Berbera

1870
Opobo founded

1870
Rehoboth founded

1870
Klipdrift Republic founded

1870
Windhoek founded as a town

1870
John Kirk became consul in Zanzibar

1870
Kaarta taken over by the Tukolor Empire

1870
Nabulagala again became capital of Buganda

1870
Baguirmi conquered by Wadai

1870, Oct. 7
Sayid Barghash became sultan of Zanzibar

1870, Dec. 13
Klipdrift Republic came to an end

1871, Feb. 21
The last of the Dutch moved out of the Gold Coast

1871, May 26
Equatoria became a province of the Sudan

1871, Aug. 11
Basutoland annexed to the Cape

1871, Oct. 26
James Smith became president of Liberia

1871, Oct. 27
Waterboer's Land became Griqualand West

1871
The town of Kimberley founded

1871, Oct. 27
Klipdrift diamond fields taken by the Cape

1872, Jan. 1
Joseph Roberts became president of Liberia again

1872, April 29
John Molteno became PM of Cape Colony

1872
Kabodha became capital of Buganda

1872
Cetewayo became king of the Zulus

1872
Mauritius and Seychelles separated administratively

1872, July 1
Thomas Burgers president of South African Republic

1872, Dec. 1
Cape Colony achieved a certain self-rule

1873
Lafia captured by Sokoto

1873, July 17
Griqualand West became a crown colony

1874, March
Charles Gordon became governor of Equatoria

1874
Second Ashanti War

1874
Osu became the capital of the Gold Coast

1874
Harar became an Egyptian province

1874
Mbandzeni became paramount chief of Swaziland

1874, July 24
Gold Coast Colony (with Lagos) formed

1874, Oct.
Griqualand East became part of Cape Colony

1874, Oct. 24
Darfur became a province of the Sudan

1874, Dec. 17
West African Settlements reconstituted

1875
Lubaga became capital of Buganda

1875
Mombasa revolted unsuccessfully against Zanzibar

1875
The town of Harar occupied by the Turks

1876, Feb. 24
James Payne became president of Liberia again

1876
Final end of slavery in Cape Verde

1877, April 12
Britain annexed South African Republic as Transvaal

1877, May
General Gordon became governor of the Sudan

1877
Rauta became capital of Bauchi

1877
Yoruba Civil Wars begin in Nigeria

1877
Baol, became part of Senegal

1877
George Goldie arrived in North West Africa

1877
British refused East African offer from Zanzibar

1877
Accra became capital of the Gold Coast

1877, Sept. 7
Somaliland became Egyptian

1877, Oct. 24
Futa Toro became part of Senegal

1878, Jan. 1

Anthony Gardner became president of Liberia

1878, Feb. 6
Gordon Sprigg became PM of Cape Colony

1878, March 12
Walvis Bay became a British protectorate

1878
Biu became temporary capital of Biu

1878
Slavery abolished in Mozambique

1878
Nossi-Bé became a separate French colony

1878
Sainte Marie de Madagascar transferred to Réunion

1878
First French consul arrived in Cotonou

1878, Aug. 15
Nubar Pasha became first Egyptian PM

1878, Nov. 22
French gave Ivory Coast to Verdier & Cie.

1879
Portuguese Guinea created

1879
Kikandwa became capital of Buganda

1879
Samory's Empire created

1879
Cape Colony annexed Fingoland

1879
Rabih arrived in the Lake Chad area

1879
United African Company created by George Goldie

1879
Fernando Po became a Spanish penal colony

1879
Zulu War

1879
Fingoland incorporated into Cape Colony

1879
Kokstad became capital of Transkeian Territories

1879, Sept. 1
Zululand Province came into being

1879, June 25
Tewfiq became khedive of Egypt

1879, Dec.
Rauf Pasha became the governor of the Sudan

1880
Aku became part of Sierra Leone

1880
Entoto became capital of Ethiopia

ca. 1880
Djibouti built as a town

1880
Assab first occupied by Italians

1880
The Germans arrived on the Togo coast

1880
The Gun War in Basutoland

1880
Medina incorporated into Liberia

1880
Tomba Island became part of Rivières du Sud

1880
Lubaga again became capital of Buganda

1880, Sept. 6
Upper Senegal became a French territory

1880, Oct. 15
Griqualand West merged into the Cape

1880, Dec. 16
Transvaal renamed Heidelberg

1880, Dec. 16
Capital of Heidelberg became Heidelberg

1880, Dec. 30
Heidelberg renamed South African Republic

1880, Dec. 30
Pretoria became capital of South African Republic

1881, Jan. 22
Hercules Robinson became governor of Cape Colony

1881, March 21
Upper Senegal became a French protectorate

1881, April 5
South African Republic renamed Transvaal

1881, May 9
Thomas Scanlen became PM of Cape Colony

1881, May 11
Treaty of Kasar Sa'id between France and Tunisia

1881, May 12
Tunisia became a French protectorate

1881, June 28
Kreli surrendered to the British

1881, June 29
Muhammad Ahmad proclaimed himself the Mahdi

1881
Léopoldville founded by Henry Stanley

1881
Bulawayo became the capital of Matabeleland

1881, July 11
The French took Sfax in Tunisia

1881, July 14
Futa Jallon became part of Rivières du Sud

1881, Aug. 26
Algeria became a French civil province

1881, Oct. 26
al-Qayrawan taken by the French in Tunisia

1881, Nov. 19
Gafsa taken by the French in Tunisia

1881, Nov. 30
Gabès taken by the French in Tunisia

1882, Feb. 2
Mahmud Sami became PM of Egypt

1882, April 14
Porto-Novo became a French protectorate again

1882, May 25
Ahmad Arabi became War Minister (PM) of Egypt

1882
Nabulagala again became capital of Buganda

1882, June 17
Ragib Pasha became PM of Egypt

1882, July 5
Assab became an Italian colony

1882, July 26
Stellaland founded

1882, Aug. 28
Sherif Pasha became PM of Egypt

1882, Sept. 11
Evelyn Baring became British consul in Egypt

1882, Sept. 15
Egypt became a British sphere of influence

1882, Sept. 15
Riaz Pasha became PM of Egypt

1882, Oct. 12
Rivières du Sud became a territory of France

1882, Oct. 24
Goshen formed
1882, Dec. 8
Nubar Pasha became PM of Egypt
1883, Jan. 20
Alfred Russell became president of Liberia
1883, Feb. 5
Moyen-Congo created by the French
1883, April 16
Paul Kruger elected president of Transvaal
1883, April 24
First German settlements in South West Africa
1883, May 8
Paul Kruger became president of Transvaal
1883
Lüderitz taken by the German in South West Africa
1883
Brazzaville founded
1883
French protectorate of Tunisia recognized
1883
Stanleyville founded, as Falls Station
1883, July 19
Little Popo became a French protectorate
1883, Aug. 7
Goshen merged with Stellaland
1883
Peace restored in Basutoland after the Gun War
1883, Oct. 30
Sherif Pasha became PM of Egypt
1883, Dec. 16
Ivory Coast–Gabon split into two
1883, Dec.
Darfur became part of the Mahdist State
1883, Dec.
Kordofan became part of the Mahdist State
1884, Jan. 6
The Mahdi had control of all of the Sudan
1884, Jan. 7
Nubar Pasha became PM of Egypt
1884, Feb. 2
Transvaal renamed South Africa Republic

1884, Feb. 8
Dinuzulu became king of the Zulus
1884, Feb. 18
General Gordon became governor of the Sudan
1884, Feb. 26
The Portuguese claimed part of French Congo
1884, March 18
Basutoland became a High Commission Territory
1884, April 4
Hilary Johnson became president of Liberia
1884, April 24
German South West Africa established
1884, May 13
Thomas Upington became PM of Cape Colony
1884, June 24
Obock became a French colony
1884, June 26
The Portuguese relinquished their Congo claim
1884, July 5
Togoland became a German protectorate
1884, July 14
Bamoun came under German domination
1884
Bechuanaland became a protectorate
1884
Bandiagara became the capital of Tukolor Empire
1884
The town of Conakry founded
1884
Bagida became the capital of Togoland
1884
Warri taken over by the British
1884, April 22
Congo recognized as King Léopold's private estate
1884
The Egyptians pulled out of Somaliland
1884, July 12
German Crown Land of North West Africa formed
1884, July 14
Kom became part of German Crown Land in NW Africa
1884, July 19
Victoria Colony became Ambas Bay Protectorate

1884, Aug. 16
New Republic created
1884, Dec. 19
Opobo taken over by the British
1885, Jan. 9
Río Muni came into being
1885, Jan. 9
Río de Oro became a Spanish protectorate
1885, Jan. 26
General Gordon killed at Khartoum
1885, Feb. 6
Massawa taken by the Italians
1885, Feb. 14
Berlin Conference
1885, Feb. 14
Togoland recognized as German
1885, March 23
Bechuanaland took in several native kingdoms
1885, March 23
Charles Warren military commander of Bechuanaland
1885, May 27
Germany declared a protectorate over Witu
1885
Mafeking became capital of Bechuanaland
1885
Omdurman became the capital of the Sudan
1885
Karagwe became a German protectorate
1885
Kayor became a part of Senegal
1885
Jan Jonker Afrikaner ceded territory to the Germans
ca. 1885
Luba Empire became part of Congo Free State
1885
Little Popo became part of German Togoland
1885, June 5
Oil Rivers Protectorate created
1885, June 5
Bonny became part of Oil Rivers Protectorate
1885, June 5
New Calabar became part of Oil Rivers Protectorate
1885, June 21
The Mahdi died, to be replaced by the Khalifah
1885, July 1

Léopold's estate in Africa became Congo Free State
1885, July 14
Tembuland became part of the Cape
1885
Bahr al-Ghazal became part of Mahdist State
1885
Spanish protectorate placed over Río Muni
1885
The town of Zomba built
1885, Aug. 5
Portugal claimed protectorate over Dahomey coast
1885, Aug. 7
Walvis Bay became part of Cape Colony
1885, Aug. 14
Usagora declared a German protectorate
1885, Aug. 26
Cape Colony annexed Tembuland
1885, Sept. 15
Rehoboth became part of German South West Africa
1885, Sept. 30
Bechuanaland Protectorate split up
1885, Oct. 20
Upingtonia founded
1885, Oct. 25
Hereroland became part of German South West Africa
1885, Dec. 17
French administration formed in Madagascar
1886, Jan. 13
Gold Coast and Lagos split up
1886, March 10
Little Free State created
1886, April 27
French Equatorial Africa created
1886
Upingtonia renamed Lydenrust
1886, June 29
Moyen-Congo became a colony
1886, June 29
Gabon became a colony
1886
Cape Colony annexed Bomvanaland
1886
Oorlam Territory part of German South West Africa
1886
Diego Suarez ceded to France
1886

Boma became capital of Congo (Belgian)
1886
Mohéli became part of Mayotte
1886
Bomvanaland became part of Transkeian Territories
1886
Kreli's Country annexed to Cape Colony
1886
Menelik II won back the kingdom of Shoa
1886, July 10
Royal Niger Company chartered
1886, Oct. 22
New Republic recognized by Britain
1886, Nov. 25
Gordon Sprigg became PM of Cape Colony again
1886, Dec. 30
Heinrich Goering new reichskommissar of SW Africa
1887, Jan
Harar conquered by Ethiopia
1887, March 28
Ambas Bay taken by the Germans
1887, April 6
Río de Oro became a dependency of the Canaries
1887, June 21
Zululand annexed by Britain
1887
Dzaoudzi became capital of Mayotte
1887
Mombasa taken over by the British
1887
Villa Cisneros became capital of Río de Oro
1887
Lourenço Marques became a city
1887
Sebe became the capital of Togoland
1887
Addis Ababa founded
1887
Chief Jaja deposed in Opobo
1887
Lydenrust ceased to exist
1887, July 20
British Somaliland Protectorate created
1887, Sept. 5
Mayotte became Comoros Protectorate

1887, Sept. 11
New Republic incorporated into Natal
1887, Oct. 18
Lagos Protectorate established in the hinterland
1887, Dec. 22
Portugal gave up Dahomey claim
1888, Feb. 11
Zambesia created
ca. 1888
Mwene Mutapa Empire became part of Zambesia
1888, Feb. 20
Kong became a French protectorate
1888, June 8
Riaz Pasha became PM of Egypt
1888
Assab Protectorate created by the Italians
1888
Yelwa became the capital of Yauri
1888
Bumpe became part of Sierra Leone
1888
British Somaliland took Mussa, Bab, and Aubad
1888
Zulu rebellion
1888
Yaoundé founded as a town
1888
Shenge became part of Sierra Leone
1888, Sept. 3
British East Africa came into being
1888, Oct. 30
Zambesia created
1888, Nov. 28
West African Settlements came to an end
1888, Nov. 28
Gambia became a colony again
1888, Dec. 11
Moyen-Congo and Gabon united
1889, Jan. 10
Ivory Coast became a French protectorate
1889, April
Equatoria fell to the Mahdi
1889, May 2
Treaty of Uccialli between Ethiopia and Italy
1889, May 2
Italy declared Ethiopia protectorate of Abissinia
1889

Assinie became capital of Ivory
Coast
1889
Cecil Rhodes's company became
the BSAC
1889
Addis Ababa became capital of
Ethiopia
1889
German government took over
South West Africa
1889
Solomon Dinuzulu became king
of the Zulus
1889, July
Dyolof became part of Senegal
1889, Aug. 3
Italy acquired the Benadir Coast
of Somalia
1889, Sept. 21
Shiré River Protectorate created
1889, Oct. 23
Ubanu became paramount chief
of Swaziland
1889, Oct. 29
Mashonaland became a British
protectorate
1889, Nov. 3
Menelik II became Emperor of
Ethiopia
1889, Nov. 3
Shoa became part of Ethiopia
1890, Jan. 1
Eritrea created
1890, Jan. 1
Rivières du Sud became partially
autonomous colony
1890, May 29
Mari, the last king of Segu,
killed by the French
1890, June 18
Witu was declared a British protectorate
1890
Gwiriko taken by the French
1890
Lloyd Matthews became wazir of
Zanzibar
1890
Ruanda became a German protectorate
1890
The town of Bremersdorf
founded in Swaziland
1890, July 1
Buganda became a British sphere
of influence
1890, July 17

Cecil Rhodes became PM of
Cape Colony
1890, Aug. 5
French protectorate of Madagascar created
1890, Aug. 18
Upper Senegal renamed French
Sudan
1890, Sept. 12
Fort Salisbury founded
1890, Nov. 4
Zanzibar became a British pro-
tectorate
1890, Dec. 18
Buganda taken over by the Brit-
ish
1890, Dec. 26
British treaty signed with Bu-
ganda
1890, Dec.
Kampala became the capital of
Buganda
1891, Jan. 1
German government took over
German East Africa
1891, Jan. 1
Tukolor Empire became part of
French Sudan
1891, Feb. 1
Shiré River Protectorate re-
named Nyasaland
1891, Feb. 9
Menelik of Ethiopia denounced
the Italians
1891, April 30
French Equatorial Africa became
French Congo
1891, May 2
Little Free State part of South
Africa Republic
1891, May 9
Bechuanaland became a High
Commission Territory
1891, May 13
Mustafa Fehmy Pasha became
PM of Egypt
1891, May 14
Nyasaland came into effect
1891, May 25
Lunda became part of Congo
Free State
1891, June 11
Barotseland became part of
Zambesia
1891
Gazaland refused British protec-
torate
1891
Windhoek became capital of
German South West Africa

1891
Conakry became capital of Rivières du Sud
1891
Dar es-Salaam became capital of
German East Africa
1891, Sept. 18
Starr Jameson became Mashonaland chief magistrate
1891, Nov. 18
Allada became a French protectorate
1891, Nov. 20
Lerotholi became king of Basutoland
1891, Nov. 30
Whydah became a French protectorate
1891, Dec. 3
Dahomey became a French protectorate
1891, Dec. 17
Rivières du Sud became an autonomous colony
1892, Jan. 4
Joseph Cheeseman became president of Liberia
1892, Jan. 7
Abbas Hilmi became khedive of
Egypt
1892, May 20
Ijebu taken by Niger River Delta
Protectorate
1892
Rabih destroyed Baguirmi
1892
Djibouti new capital of French
Coast of the Somalis
1892
War between France and Dahomey
1892
Louis Mizon placed a protectorate over Muri
1892
Cecil Rhodes failed to acquire
Katanga
1892
Logone became Rabih's base of
operations
1892
Katanga became part of Congo
Free State
ca. 1892
The town of Gaberones (later
Gaborone) founded
1892, Aug. 27
French Sudan became a military
territory
1892, Nov. 17

The French entered Abomey to end Dahomey War
1892, Dec. 3
Whyda protectorate became effective
1893, Jan. 18
Riaz Pasha became PM of Egypt
1893, Feb. 22
Nyasaland became British Central Africa
1893, March 10
Ivory Coast became a French colony
1893, March 10
Rivières du Sud became French Guinea
1893, April 1
Buganda declared provisional British protectorate
1893, April 12
Witbooi Territory part of German South West Africa
1893, May 10
Natal became self-governing
1893, May 13
Oil Rivers renamed Niger Coast Protectorate
1893, May 15
Filonari Company took over Benadir Coast
1893, June 22
Porto-Novo became a French colony
1893
Kong became part of the Ivory Coast
1893
Gran Comoro became part of Mayotte
1893
Entebbe founded as a town
1893
Rabih captured Bedde capital of Gorgoram
1893
Rabih conquered Bornu Empire
1893
Kong became part of Ivory Coast
1893
Ubangi-Bomu created by the French
1893
Louis Mizon expelled from Muri
1893
Jalingo became capital of Muri
1893
Ibadan taken by Niger River Delta Protectorate
1893

Grand Bassam became capital of Ivory Coast
1893
Yoruba Wars end in Nigeria
1893
Bremersdorf became the capital of Swaziland
1893
Abeokuta became Egba United Government
1893
Rabih's Empire founded
1893
Dikwa became the capital of Rabih's Empire
1893
Moroni became part of Mayotte
1893, July
Timbuktu became part of French Sudan
1893, Nov. 13
Swaziland became a British protectorate
1893, Nov. 21
French Sudan became a civil territory
1894, Jan
Matabeleland became a British protectorate
1894, Jan. 23
Zambesia was divided into North and South
1894, April 11
Buganda taken over as a protectorate
1894, April 16
Nubar Pasha became PM of Egypt
1894, June 18
Buganda Protectorate renamed Uganda
1894, June 22
Dahomey created as a French colony
1894, June 22
Whydah became part of Dahomey
1894, June 22
Porto-Novo became part of Dahomey
1894, July 13
Ubangi-Bomu became Ubangi-Shari
1894
Cotonou became capital of Dahomey
1894
Hinterland of Gambia opened up as a protectorate
1894

Mora became the capital of Mandara
1894, Sept. 25
Pondoland East and Pondoland West went to the Cape
1895, Jan. 20
Gurma became part of Upper Volta
1895, Jan. 29
Brass outrage on Akassa
1895, Feb. 20
Upper Volta created by the French
1895, May 3
Rhodesia Protectorate formed
1895, May
Britain acquired Tongaland
1895, June 16
French West Africa created
1895
Cecil Rhodes tried and failed to buy Bechuanaland
1895
Senegal administrative base for French West Africa
1895
Mirambo became part of German East Africa
1895
Yatenga became part of French Sudan
1895, June 16
French Sudan became a colony
1895, July 1
British government took over British East Africa
1895, July 1
Mombasa became part of British East Africa
1895, July 1
Jubaland became part of British East Africa
1895, Aug. 24
Sierra Leone Colony and Protectorate created
1895, Nov.
War began between Italy and Ethiopia
1895, Nov. 12
Mustafa Fehmy Pasha became PM of Egypt
1895, Nov. 16
British Bechuanaland became part of the Cape
1895, Dec. 28
Gazaland became part of Mozambique
1896, Jan. 13
Gordon Sprigg became PM of Cape Colony again

1896, March 1
Menelik of Ethiopia beat the Italians at Adowa

1896, March
The British sacked Nembe, the Brass capital

1896
French Coast of the Somalis now French Somaliland

1896
Eritrea became a civil administration

1896
Nkore became part of Uganda

1896
British government took over Uganda Railway venture

1896, June 30
Bunyoro became part of Uganda

1896, July 3
Busoga became part of Uganda

1896, Aug. 6
Madagascar became a French colony

1896, Aug. 6
Nossi-Bé became part of Madagascar Colony

1896, Aug. 6
Diego Suarez became part of Madagascar Colony

1896, Aug. 27
Ashanti became a British protectorate

1896, Aug. 31
Koya-Temne became part of Sierra Leone

1896
Dagomba became part of Ashanti Protectorate

1896
Italian government took over Benadir Coast

1896, Sept. 13
Wagadugu conquered by the French

1896, Oct. 26
Abissinia Protectorate ended

1896, Nov. 12
William Coleman became president of Liberia

1896, Dec. 31
Algeria became a French military province again

1897, Feb. 18
Benin became part of Niger Coast Protectorate

1897, March 5
Ilorin taken by Niger River Delta Protectorate

1897, May 5

Alfred Milner became governor of Cape Colony

1897
Wagadugu became part of Upper Volta

1897
Kingdom of Kaffa conquered by Ethiopia

1897
Slavery abolished in Zanzibar

1897
Gurma became part of Upper Volta

1897
Tongaland became a district of Natal

1897
Zululand became part of Natal

1897
Lourenço Marques became capital of Mozambique

1897
Nairobi founded as a town

1897
The mbang of Baguirmi asked France for protection

1897
Lomé became the capital of Togoland

1897, Dec. 1
Zululand became a province of Natal

1898, May 1
Kenedugu became part of French Sudan

1898, May 25
Milanese Commercial Society took over Benadir Coast

1898, June 24
Lapai became part of Niger River Delta Protectorate

1898
The British deposed King Koko of Brass

1898
British Somaliland transferred to Foreign Office

1898
Khartoum became the capital of the Sudan

1898
Wase became part of Niger River Delta Protectorate

1898, June 24
Agaie taken over by the Royal Niger Company

1898, Sept. 2
British occupied all of the Sudan

1898, Sept. 2

Lord Kitchener became governor of the Sudan

1898, Sept. 29
Samory's Empire became part of French West Africa

1898, Oct. 14
William Schreiner became PM of Cape Colony

1899, Jan. 19
Anglo-Egyptian Sudan came into being

1899, Jan. 21
Lord Kitchener became governor-general of the Sudan

1899, March 21
Baguirmi became French sphere of influence

1899, March 21
Darfur re-established as a sultanate

1899
Akim became part of the Gold Coast

1899
British pacified Benin

1899
Fort Jameson established as a town

1899
Kazembe split between the British and Belgians

1899
Gold Coast Northern Territories created

1899
Britain revoked George Goldie's Nigeria charter

1899
Sobhuza II became paramount chief of Swaziland

1899, July 30
Damagaram became part of French West Africa

1899, Oct. 17
French Sudan became Upper Senegal & Niger Territory

1899, Dec. 23
Rex Wingate became governor-general of the Sudan

1899, Dec. 27
Fika became part of Northern Nigeria

1900, Jan. 1
Northern Nigeria Protectorate created

1900, Jan. 1
Southern Nigeria Protectorate created

1900, Jan. 1
Biu became part of Northern Nigeria

1900, Jan. 1
German Crown Lands in NW Africa became Kamerun

1900, Jan. 29
Rhodesia Protectorate split into three parts

1900, Jan. 29
Southern Rhodesia came into being

1900, April 2
The Third Ashanti War began

1900, April 13
Fort Lamy founded as a town

1900, April 22
Rabih met the French at Kusseri and was killed

1900, May 21
Orange River Colony created

1900
Baguirmi became part of Chad

1900
Oyo became part of Northern Nigeria

1900
Gobir split between French and British

1900
Lafia became part of Northern Nigeria

1900
Lafiagi became part of Northern Nigeria

1900
Río Muni became a Spanish colony

1900
Keana became part of Northern Nigeria

1900
Samory died in exile in Gabon

1900
Lapai became part of Northern Nigeria

1900
Ife became part of Northern Nigeria

1900
Part of Bornu became part of Chad

1900
Kingdom of Dahomey abolished by the French

1900
Bingerville became capital of Ivory Coast

1900, June 18
Gordon Sprigg became PM of Cape Colony again

1900, June 27
Río Muni delimited as a colony

1900, July 23
Zinder created as a French territory

1900, Sept. 1
South Africa Republic/Transvaal annexed by Britain

1900, Sept. 5
Borku became a French protectorate

1900, Sept. 5
Chad came into being as a military territory

1900, Dec. 10
Garretson Gibson became president of Liberia

1901, Jan. 11
Gambia Colony and Protectorate created

1901, Jan
Kontagora became part of Northern Nigeria

1901
Doma became part of Northern Nigeria

1901
Yauri became part of Northern Nigeria

1901
Nupe became part of Northern Nigeria

1901
Kororofa split between British and French

1901
Potiskum became part of Northern Nigeria

1901
Igala became part of Northern Nigeria

1901, July 20
Morocco granted France control of Frontier Police

1901, Aug. 23
Rabih's Empire split between French and British

1901, Sept.
Adamawa dismembered

1901, Sept.
Muri became part of Northern Nigeria

1901
Lau became the capital of Muri

1902, Jan. 1
Ashanti became a British colony

1902, Feb.
Bauchi became a province of Northern Nigeria

1902, Feb.
Gombe became part of Northern Nigeria

1902, March
Zaria taken by the British

1902, April 1
Eastern Province of Uganda to British East Africa

1902, May 15
Kanama territory became part of Eritrea

1902, May 31
Transvaal awarded to Britain

1902
France and Spain agreed to divide Morocco

1902
Abuja became part of Northern Nigeria

1902
Wase became an amirate

1902
Canary Islands independence movement crushed

1902
Keffi became part of Northern Nigeria

1902
Part of Bornu became part of Northern Nigeria

1902
Argungu became part of Northern Nigeria

1902
Bedde became part of Northern Nigeria

1902
Cekna became capital of Baguirmi

1902
Jema'a became part of Northern Nigeria

1902
Bauchi replaced Rauta as capital of Bauchi

1902
Zamfara divided between the French and British

1902
Natal took in pieces of southern Transvaal

1902
Gorée became capital of French West Africa

1902
Mandara became part of Kamerun

1902, June 21
Lord Milner became governor of Transvaal

1902, July 5
Chad became a French protectorate

1902, July 5
Moyen-Congo–Gabon became a French colony

1902, Sept. 14
South West Africa became a German colony

1902, Oct. 1
Upper Senegal & Niger renamed Senegambia & Niger

1902, Dec. 15
Trarza became a French protectorate

1903, Feb. 3
Kano became part of Northern Nigeria

1903, March 15
Fulani Empire ended

1903, March 15
British conquest of Northern Nigeria complete

1903, March
Gwandu became part of Northern Nigeria

1903, May 12
Mauritania became a French protectorate

1903, May 12
Trarza became part of Mauritania

1903, April 6
Burundi became part of German East Africa

1903, April
Katsina became part of Northern Nigeria

1903
Niamey became capital of Zinder

1903
The French subdued the Lobi in Upper Volta

1903
Río de Oro effectively settled

1903
Daura split between the French and British

1903
Daura-Baure became part of Zinder

1903
Damagaram became part of Zinder

1903
Misau became part of Northern Nigeria

1903
Hadejia submitted to the British

1903
Gumel became part of Northern Nigeria

1903
Most of Daura-Zango became part of Northern Nigeria

1903
The Uganda Railway venture completed

1903, Aug.
Seychelles broke away from Mauritius

1903, Oct.
Jemaari became part of Northern Nigeria

1903, Oct.
Katagum became part of Northern Nigeria

1903, Dec. 29
Moyen-Congo-Gabon split into two

1904, Jan. 4
Arthur Barclay became president of Liberia

1904, Feb. 13
Senegal Colony and Protectorate created

1904, Feb. 22
Starr Jameson became PM of Cape Colony

1904
Biu became permanent capital of Biu

1904
Morocco became a French sphere of influence

1904
The British ceded the Los Islands to French Guinea

1904
France occupied Figuig in Morocco

1904
Germans decimated the Hereros in Herero Rebellion

1904
Dakar became capital of French West Africa

1904, Oct. 18
Mauritania became a Civil Territory

1904, Oct. 18
Brakna became part of Mauritania

1904, Oct. 18
Senegambia & Niger renamed Upper Senegal & Niger

1905, Jan. 1
Togoland became a German colony

1905, March 16
Benadir Coast became Italian Somaliland

1905, April 1
Uganda transferred from Foreign to Colonial Office

1905
British Somaliland placed under the Colonial Office

1905
Tagant became part of Mauritania

1905
British refused Zionist home in British East Africa

1905
Entebbe became capital of Uganda

1905, May 12
Commandant Coppolani of Mauritania assassinated

1905
Nairobi became the capital of British East Africa

1905
The town of Lusaka founded

1905, Aug. 19
Letsie II designated king of Basutoland

1905, Sept. 19
Letsie II came to the throne in Basutoland

1906, Feb. 11
Ubangi-Shari and Chad united

1906, Feb. 16
Southern Nigeria Colony and Protectorate created

1906, April 7
Hadejia became part of Northern Nigeria

1906, April 8
France and Spain awarded control of Morocco

1906
Bangui became capital of Ubangi-Shari

1906
Mbabane became capital of Swaziland

1906
Tangier became an international town

1906
Germans finally pacified all of South West Africa

1906
Kazaure became part of Northern Nigeria

1906
Gold Coast Northern Territories military territory

1906
British garrison removed from Saint Helena

1906, Dec. 1
High Commission Territories created in South Africa
1906, Dec. 6
Orange River Colony achieved self-rule
1906, Dec. 6
Transvaal achieved self-rule
1907, Jan. 1
Gold Coast Northern Territories a civil territory
1907, Feb. 4
Louis Botha became first PM of Transvaal
1907
Yerwa became capital of Bornu
1907
Tagant occupied by the French
1907
France occupied Oujda in Morocco
1907
The Young Tunisian Party formed
1907, July 6
Nyasaland declared a British protectorate
1907, Aug. 4
French Morocco created
1907
Rabat became capital of French Morocco
1907, Sept. 30
Nyasaland protectorate went into effect
1908, Feb. 3
John Merriman became PM of Cape Colony
1908, April 9
Comoros became dependent territory of Madagascar
1908, May 16
Boundary fixed between Eritrea and Ethiopia
1908
Bamako became the capital of Upper Senegal & Niger
1908
Agaie became part of Northern Nigeria
1908
Coetivy transferred from Mauritius to Seychelles
1908
Lapai became part of Niger Province, in Nigeria
1908, Aug. 20
Belgian government took over the Congo
1908, Nov. 12

Butros Ghali became PM of Egypt
1908, Nov. 15
Congo became Belgian Congo
1909, Jan. 9
Adrar became part of Mauritania
1909, June 3
Wadai became a part of Chad
1909
Adrar occupied by the French
1909
Bakwanga founded as a town
1909
Potiskum became capital of Fika Province
1910, Jan. 15
French Congo became French Equatorial Africa
1910, Jan. 15
Brazzaville became capital of French West Africa
1910, Feb. 22
Muhammad Sa'id Bey became PM of Egypt
1910, May 31
Union of South Africa created
1910, May 31
Walvis Bay became part of South Africa
1910, June 22
Zinder renamed Niger
1910
The French took large part of Liberian hinterland
1910
The town of Elisabethville built
1910
Mutum Biyu became the capital of Muri
1910
Haile Selassie became governor of Harar
1910, July 1
South Africa became a dominion
1910, July
Italian Somaliland became a crown colony
1910, Sept. 15
Louis Botha became first PM of South Africa
1911, May 15
Lij Iyasu became emperor of Ethiopia
1911, June 24
Dahomey Colony and Dependencies created
1911
The French occupied Fez and Meknes

1911
Zinder became the capital of Niger
1911
The Agadir Incident
1911, July 16
Lord Kitchener became British consul in Egypt
1911, Aug. 17
Northern Rhodesia formed
1911, Aug. 17
Southern Rhodesia became a British protectorate
1911, Nov. 5
Tripolitania became an Italian protectorate
1911, Dec. 9
Sayid Khalifa became sultan of Zanzibar
1912, Jan. 1
Daniel Howard became president of Liberia
1912, March 30
The French declared a protectorate over Morocco
1912, May 24
Hubert Lyautey became resident-general of Morocco
1912
Canary Islands became a Spanish protectorate
1912
Tetuán replaced Ceuta as Spanish Morocco capital
1912, Oct. 15
Cyrenaica and Fezzan conquered by the Italians
1912, Nov. 27
Spanish Morocco created
1912, Nov. 27
Río de Oro became Spanish West Africa
1912, Nov. 27
Melilla became a comandáncia
1912, Nov. 27
Ifni became a Spanish protectorate
1912
Sidi Ifni became capital of Ifni
1913, Feb.
Griffith designated king of Basutoland
1913, April 11
Griffith came to the throne in Basutoland
1913
Negotiations began to make Tangier international
1913
Doma became the capital of Gombe

1913, July 1
Zanzibar became part of British East Africa

1914, Jan. 1
Nigeria came into being

1914, Jan. 1
Zungeru became capital of Nigeria Northern Region

1914, Feb. 23
Comoros became a French colony

1914, April 5
Hussein Rushdi Pasha became PM of Egypt

1914
The Italians occupied the Fezzan

1914
Sayid Khalifa of Zanzibar knighted

1914
Douala became capital of Kamerun

1914
Gondokoro and Nimule, in Uganda, given to the Sudan

1914, Aug. 15
Portuguese West Africa became the colony of Angola

1914, Aug. 31
Germans surrendered Togoland

1914, Sept. 16
Abeokuta became part of Nigeria

1914, Sept. 26
British and French captured Kamerun

1914, Nov. 14
German resistance to Allies in East Africa ended

1914, Dec. 18
Egypt became officially British

1914, Dec. 19
Hussein Khamil became sultan of Egypt

1915
Darfur revolted against Anglo-Egyptian rule

1915, July 15
SW Africa became a South African protectorate

1916, Feb. 18
Germans formally surrendered Kamerun

1916, March 4
Kamerun divided between French and British

1916, April 12
Ubangi-Shari–Chad split into two

1916, May 21

Ruanda and Burundi taken by Belgium

1916
Azare became the capital of Katagum

1916, Sept. 30
Haile Selassie became Emperor of Ethiopia

1916, Oct. 9
German East Africa occupied by Britain and Belgium

1916, Nov. 6
Darfur became a province of the Sudan again

1916, Dec. 27
Togo divided between French and British

1917, Jan. 1
Sir Lee Stack became governor-general of Sudan

1917, Jan. 1
Rex Wingate became high commissioner in Egypt

1917
The town of Enugu founded in Nigeria

1917
Jalingo became the capital of Muri

1917
Kaduna became capital of Nigeria Northern Region

1917, Oct. 9
Fuad became sultan of Egypt

1918, Nov. 16
Tripolitanian Republic created

1919, March 1
Colony of Upper Volta created

1919, April 21
Muhammad Sa'id Pasha became PM of Egypt

1919, May 17
Cirenaica became an Italian colony

1919, May 17
Tripolitania became an Italian colony

1919, May 30
Ruanda-Urundi awarded to Belgium

1919
The town of Doma became Gombe

1919, June 28
Treaty of Versailles

1919, Sept. 3
Jan Smuts became PM of South Africa

1919, Oct. 9
Gordon Guggisberg became governor of Gold Coast

1919, Oct. 17
Lord Allenby became high commissioner in Egypt

1919, Nov. 28
Yusef Wahba Pasha became PM of Egypt

1920, Jan. 5
Charles King became president of Liberia

1920, Jan. 10
German East Africa divided between Belgium and UK

1920, Jan. 10
Tanganyika came into being

1920, Jan. 10
Mozambique gained the Kionga Triangle from Germany

1920, March 17
Chad became a French colony

1920, May 19
Tewfiq Nesim Pasha became PM of Egypt

1920
Biu became an amirate

1920
The Destour Party created in Tunisia

1920
Ruanda-Urundi formed

1920, July 22
Cameroun mandates became effective

1920, July 23
Kenya Colony and Protectorate came into being

1920, Sept. 30
League of Nations mandates given for Togo

1920, Dec. 4
Upper Senegal & Niger became French Sudan

1920, Dec. 4
Civil Territory of Niger created

1921, Jan. 1
Mauritania became a French colony

1921, Jan. 1
South West Africa made a League of Nations mandate

1921, March 15
Adli Yègen Pasha became PM of Egypt

1921, March 23
Cameroun given limited autonomy by France

1921, Sept. 4
Chief Sobhuza II of Swaziland became king

1922, March 1

Abdul Khalik Pasha Sarwat became PM of Egypt

1922, March 15
Fuad became King of Egypt

1922
Amirantes transferred from Mauritius to Seychelles

1922
Providence Group transferred to the Seychelles

1922
Ascension made a dependency of Saint Helena

1922
Farquhar & Des Roches Islands went to Seychelles

1922
The bey of Tunisia threatened to abdicate

1922
Walvis Bay assigned to South West Africa

1922
Yaoundé became capital of Cameroun

1922
Egypt. Independence from Britain

1922, Nov. 30
Tewfiq Pasha became PM of Egypt

1923, Feb.
Rif Republic formed

1923
Léopoldville became capital of Belgian Congo

1923
Tangier became an international zone

1923
Tripolitanian Republic became part of Tripolitania

1923, Aug. 23
Ruanda-Urundi became a League of Nations mandate

1923, Sept. 21
Southern Rhodesia became a British colony

1923, Oct. 11
British Togoland ruled from Gold Coast

1922, Oct. 13
Niger became a French colony

1923, March 15
Yehia Ibrahim Pasha became PM of Egypt

1924, Jan. 28
Sa'd Zaghlul Pasha became PM of Egypt

1924, April 1

Northern Rhodesia became a British protectorate

1924
Potiskum became capital of Fika Amirate

1924
Bujumbura became the capital of Ruanda-Urundi

1924, June 30
J.B.M. Hertzog became PM of South Africa

1924, July 15
Jubaland ceded to Italy from Britain

1924, Oct. 20
Ruanda-Urundi mandate went into effect

1924, Nov. 19
Sir Lee Stack assassinated in Cairo

1924, Nov. 25
Ahmad Pasha Ziwar became PM of Egypt

1925, Jan. 5
Geoffrey Archer became governor-general of Sudan

1925
Comoros given their own local administration

1925, Aug. 21
Ruanda-Urundi split administratively

1926, May 27
Rif Republic came to an end

1926, June 6
Adli Yegen Pasha became PM of Egypt

1926
Spanish Guinea created as a colony

1926
Firestone granted a million acres in Liberia

1926, July 1
Jubaland became part of Italian Somaliland

1926
Rudolph Province of Uganda given to Kenya

1926
Jema'an Sarari became capital of Jemaari

1926
Niamey became the capital of Niger again

1926
Jemaari transferred from Kano to Bauchi Province

1927, April 18
Abdul Khalik Pasha Sarwat became PM of Egypt

1927
Canary Islands split into two provinces

1927, Nov. 27
Muhammad V became sultan of Morocco

1928, March 16
Nahhas Pasha became PM of Egypt

1928
Enugu became capital of Nigeria Southern Provinces

1928, June 25
Muhammad Mahmud Pasha became PM of Egypt

1929, Jan. 24
Cirenaica and Tripolitania united to form Libia

1929, Oct. 2
Adli Yegen Pasha became PM of Egypt

1929, Dec. 31
Nahhas Pasha became PM of Egypt

1930, June 21
Ismail Sidqi Pasha became PM of Egypt

1930, Dec. 3
Scandal brought down the Liberian government

1930, Dec. 3
Edwin Barclay became president of Liberia

1931
Katsina Province formed in Nigeria

1931, Dec. 11
South Africa became self-governing

1932, Sept. 5
Dismemberment of Upper Volta agreed upon

1933, Jan. 1
Upper Volta dismembered by the French

1933, March 24
Yehia Ibrahim Pasha became PM of Egypt

1933
Katanga was made part of the Belgian Congo

1933
Kafanchan became the capital of Jema'a

1933
Cyprian Bkekuzulu became king of the Zulus

1933, July 5
George Mitchell first PM of Southern Rhodesia

1933, Sept. 12
Godfrey Huggins became PM of Southern Rhodesia
1934, Jan. 1
Libia became an Italian colony
1934
The Neo-Destour founded in Tunisia
1934
Abidjan became the capital of the Ivory Coast
1934
Ifni occupied by Spanish troops
1934, June 30
French West Africa became a colony
1934, June 30
Ubangi-Shari became a region of the A.E.F.
1934, June 30
Chad became a region of the A.E.F.
1934, June 30
Moyen-Congo became a region of the A.E.F.
1934, Nov. 15
Muhammad Tewfiq Nesim became PM of Egypt
1935
Asmara became capital of Eritrea
1935
Lusaka became capital of Northern Rhodesia
1935
Jubaland became part of Italian East Africa
1935
Direct French military rule in Wadai ceased
1935, Oct. 3
Italy invaded Ethiopia
1936, Jan. 30
Nahhas Pasha became PM of Egypt
1936, April 28
Farouk became King of Egypt
1936, May 9
Italy conquered Ethiopia
1936, May 9
Eritrea became a province of Italian East Africa
1936, May 10
Nahhas Pasha became PM of Egypt
1936, May 22
Rodolfo Graziani governor of Italian East Africa
1936
Bahr al-Ghazal united with Equatoria

1936
Badeggi-Lapai became capital of Lapai
1936
Last British High Commissioner left Egypt
1937, Feb.
Ethiopian attempt to assassinate Graziani
1937, Dec. 30
Muhammad Mahmud Pasha became PM of Egypt
1937, Dec. 31
Ubangi-Shari became a French overseas territory
1937, Dec. 31
Chad became a French overseas territory
1937, Dec. 31
Moyen-Congo became a French overseas territory
1937, Dec. 31
Gabon became a French overseas territory
1938, Jan. 1
Upper Ivory Coast was created by the French
1938
Spanish Guinea became Gulf of Guinea Settlements
1938
Tristan da Cunha became a dependency of St. Helena
1938, Oct. 25
Libia declared part of Italy
1939, Jan. 9
Libia became, in effect, a part of Italy
1939
Nigeria's Southern Provinces split into two parts
1939
Abeokuta became part of Nigeria Western Region
1939, Aug.
Seeiso became new king of Basutoland
1939, Aug. 18
Ali Maher Pasha became PM of Egypt
1939, Sept. 5
Jan Smuts became PM of South Africa
1940
Douala became capital of Cameroun again
1940
Madagascar declared in favor of Vichy France
1940, June 14

Spain took control of Tangier
1940, June 28
Hassan Sabry became PM of Egypt
1940, Oct. 19
Hubert Huddleston became governor-general of Sudan
1940, Nov. 14
Hussein Sirry Pasha became PM of Egypt
1940, Nov.
Tangier became part of Spanish Morocco
1940, Dec.
MaNtsebo became Queen Regent of Basutoland
1941, Feb. 26
Dissolution of Italian East Africa
1941, May 5
Eritrea captured by the British
1941, May 5
Haile Selassie regained throne of Ethiopia
1941
Hargeysa became capital of British Somaliland
1941, Sept. 26
Italian Somaliland taken by the British
1942, Feb. 8
Nahhas Pasha became PM of Egypt
1942
al-Marj became capital of Cyrenaica
1942
Cyrenaica taken from the Italians by the Allies
1942, Sept. 25
Britain took over Madagascar
1942, Nov.
French West Africa joined the Free French
1942, Dec. 15
Tripolitania taken by the Allies
1943
Fezzan taken by the Allies
1943, Jan. 29
Libya split up by the Allies
1943
Sabha became capital of Fezzan
1943
Benghazi became capital of Cyrenaica
1944
Kenya included a black in legislative council
1944
Istiqlal, Moroccan independence movement, founded

1944, Jan. 1
William Tubman became president of Liberia
1944, Oct. 9
Ahmad Pasha became PM of Egypt
1945
Central African Council created
1945
Gold Coast Colony region created
1945, Feb. 24
Nokrashy Pasha became PM of Egypt
1945, Oct.
Tangier returned to being an international zone
1946
Yaoundé became capital of Cameroun again
1946, Feb. 8
Ismail Sidqi Pasha became PM of Egypt
1946, March 19
Réunion became an overseas department of France
1946, Oct. 13
Senegal became an overseas territory of France
1946, Oct. 13
Britain returned Madagascar to France
1946, Oct. 13
Dahomey became an overseas territory of France
1946, Oct. 13
Comoros became an overseas territory of France
1946, Oct. 13
French Guinea became an overseas territory
1946, Oct. 13
Ivory Coast became an overseas territory of France
1946, Oct. 13
French Sudan became an overseas territory of France
1946, Oct. 13
Niger became an overseas territory of France
1946, Dec. 3
Ruanda-Urundi became a UN Trusteeship of Belgium
1946, Dec. 9
Nokrashy Pasha became PM of Egypt
1946, Dec. 11
South Africa refused UN South West Africa mandate
1946, Dec. 13

British Togoland became a UN Trust Territory
1946, Dec. 13
French Togoland became a UN Trust Territory
1946, Dec. 11
Tanganyika became a UN Trust Territory
1946, Dec. 13
Cameroun became UN Trust Territory
1946, Dec. 13
British Cameroons became a UN Trust Territory
1947
Upper Ivory Coast became part of Upper Volta
1947
The town of Lilongwe established
1947, Feb.
Italy renounced all claims in Africa
1947, Sept. 4
Upper Volta became an overseas territory of France
1947, Sept. 4
Upper Ivory Coast dismantled
1948
Seretse Khama married Englishwoman Ruth Williams
1948
The Mau Mau formed in Kenya
1948
Italy re-admitted as part of Tangier government
1948, June 3
Daniel Malan became PM of South Africa
1948, Dec. 28
Abdul Hidi Pasha became PM of Egypt
1949, June 1
Kingdom of Libya proclaimed by Idris
1949, July 26
Hussein Sirry Pasha became PM of Egypt
1949, Aug. 7
Mauritania became an overseas territory of France
1950
France promised autonomy for Tunisia
1950, Jan. 12
Nahhas Pasha became PM of Egypt
1950, April 1
Italy received Italian Somaliland as a UN trust
1951

Gold Coast. Self-rule
1951, Feb. 8
Gold Coast granted internal autonomy
1951, March 29
Idris I formed a Libyan government
1951, June 11
Angola became an Overseas Province of Portugal
1951, June 11
Portuguese Guinea an Overseas Province of Portugal
1951, June 11
Cape Verde became an overseas province of Portugal
1951, June 11
São Tomé became an overseas province of Portugal
1951, June 11
Mozambique became an overseas province of Portugal
1951, Dec. 24
Libya. Independence from Britain and France
1952
Ifni became part of Spanish West Africa
1952
Violent nationalist riots in Tangier
1952, Jan. 2
Libyan independence came into effect
1952, Jan. 27
Ali Maher Pasha became PM of Egypt
1952, March 1
Naguib al-Hilaili Pasha became PM of Egypt
1952, March 5
Kwame Nkrumah became PM of Gold Coast
1952, May
Nnamdi Azikiwe became Chief Minister of Nigeria
1952, July 2
Hussein Sirry Pasha became PM of Egypt
1952, July 23
Egyptian Army seized power in Egypt
1952, July 24
Ali Maher Pasha became PM of Egypt
1952, July 26
Fuad II became king of Egypt
1952, Sept. 7
Muhammad Naguib became PM of Egypt

1952, Sept. 11
Eritrea became autonomous
1952, Oct. 20
State of emergency declared in Kenya
1952, Oct. 22
The Sudan achieved self-rule
1953
Gold Coast "regions" idea dropped
1953, Jan. 5
Press censorship re-introduced in Egypt
1953, Jan. 16
All political parties dissolved in Egypt
1953, June 18
Egypt became a republic
1953, June 18
Muhammad Naguib became president of Egypt
1953, Aug. 14
Muhammad V of Morocco deposed by the French
1953, Sept. 7
Garfield Todd became PM of Southern Rhodesia
1953, Oct. 23
Federation of Rhodesia and Nyasaland began
1953, Dec. 18
Godfrey Huggins PM of Fed. of Rhodesia & Nyasaland
1954
Milton Margai became chief minister of Sierra Leone
1954, Jan. 1
First elected Sudanese parliament opened
1954, Jan. 6
Ismail al-Azhari elected first PM of Sudan
1954, Jan. 13
Egypt dissolved the fanatical Muslim Brotherhood
1954, Jan. 15
UK troops captured General China, Mau Mau No. 2 man
1954, Feb. 22
Naguib resigned from all his posts in Egypt
1954, Feb. 25
Gamal Abdel Nasser became PM of Egypt
1954, Feb. 27
Naguib became president of Egypt again
1954, March 3
British–Mau Mau truce began in Kenya

1954, March 8
Naguib became PM of Egypt again
1954, April 11
British–Mau Mau talks broke down
1954, April 18
Gamal Abdel Nasser became PM of Egypt again
1954, April 24
3,679 Mau Mau members rounded up in Nairobi
1954, July 31
France agreed to independence for Tunisia
1954, Aug. 15
French troops seized the Arab quarter of Fez
1954, Sept. 2
Neo-Destour nationalist party legalized in Tunisia
1954, Oct. 1
British Cameroons joined partly-autonomous Nigeria
1954, Nov. 14
President Naguib was relieved of his post
1954, Nov. 17
Gamal Abdel Nasser became president of Egypt
1954, Dec. 2
Johannes Strijdom became PM of South Africa
1955, June
Habib Bourguiba returned to Tunisia from exile
1955, Nov. 1
Muhammad V of Morocco brought back to power
1955, Dec. 14
Libya became a UN member
1956
French Somaliland achieved internal autonomy
1956, Jan. 1
Sudan. Independence from Britain
1956, Jan. 1
Ismail al-Azhari became first PM of the Sudan
1956, Jan. 2
President Tubman of Liberia re-elected
1956, Jan. 11
Algeria's Kabylia region placed under military rule
1956, Jan. 19
Sudan became 9th member of the Arab League
1956, Feb. 1

South Africa expelled the Russians
1956, Feb. 6
French premier threatened by rioters in Algiers
1956, March 2
Morocco. Independence from France
1956, March 15
Sudan and USSR agreed to diplomatic ties
1956, March 20
Tunisia. Independence from France
1956, April 5
Heavy action in Gaza Strip between Egypt and Israel
1956, April 7
Spain gave up its portion of Morocco
1956, April 12
Egyptian jet fighter shot down by Israel over Negev
1956, April 7
Ceuta and Melilla became plazas of Spain
1956, April 10
Habib Bourguiba became PM of Tunisia
1956, May 10
Eastern Algeria placed under martial law
1956, May 19
Abdallah Issa became PM of British Somaliland
1956, May 22
French Army burned Algerian village of Ouled Djerra
1956, May 27
French troops sealed off the Algiers Casbah
1956, June 19
End of martial law and censorship in Egypt
1956, June 24
Military junta in Egypt was dissolved
1956, July 26
Egypt seized the Suez Canal
1956, Aug. 12
Massive British troop-lift to the Middle East
1956, Aug. 30
Togo became a partially autonomous republic
1956, Sept. 9
Suez talks ended in failure
1956, Sept. 12
Sylvanus Olimpio became Chief Minister of Togo

1956, Sept. 19
Second round of Suez talks began in London
1956, Oct. 29
Tangier given back to Morocco
1956, Oct. 29
Israeli forces invaded Egypt in the Sinai
1956, Oct. 30
Britain and France resolved to attack Egypt
1956, Oct. 31
British bombers attacked air fields in Egypt
1956, Nov. 1
Roy Welensky PM of Fed. of Rhodesia & Nyasaland
1956, Nov. 3
Israeli troops reached the Suez Canal
1956, Nov. 3
Britain and France reject UN demand for ceasefire
1956, Nov. 5
British and French forces seized Port Said
1956, Nov. 5
USSR threatened military action in Middle East
1956, Nov. 5
USA warned USSR not to intervene in Middle East
1956, Nov. 7
Ceasefire on the Suez Canal
1956, Nov. 7
UN demanded UK/France/Israel withdrawal from Egypt
1956, Nov. 10
UN Police Force arrived in Egypt
1956, Nov. 12
Morocco, Tunisia and Sudan became UN members
1956, Nov. 13
British action against Mau Mau in Kenya ended
1956, Dec. 3
Britain and France agreed to withdraw from Egypt
1956, Dec. 13
British Togoland became part of Gold Coast
1956, Dec. 22
British and French withdrew from Egypt
1956, Dec. 24
Egypt demanded reparations from Britain and France
1957
Djibo Bakari became first PM of Niger

1957, Jan. 6
Libya and Tunisia signed a treaty of friendship
1957, Feb. 7
Gold Coast independence received royal assent
1957, March 6
Gold Coast. Independence from Britain as Ghana
1957, March 8
Ghana admitted as 81st member of the UN
1957, March 30
Tunisia and Morocco signed a friendship treaty
1957, March 31
Suez Canal re-opened
1957, May 15
André-Maria Mbida became first PM of Cameroun
1957, July 25
Tunisia became a republic
1957, July 25
Habib Bourguiba became the first Tunisian president
1957, Aug. 11
The sultanate of Morocco became a kingdom
1957, Aug. 19
7 Moroccans killed by Spanish in fighting in Ifni
1957, Sept. 1
French troops crossed to Tunisia pursuing Algerians
1957, Sept. 2
Abubaka Tafawa Balewa became Premier of Nigeria
1957, Sept. 9
Tunisia declared a state of emergency on its border
1957, Dec. 26
African People's Conference began in Cairo
1958
Comoros voted to remain part of France
1958
Patrice Lumumba founded Congolese National Movement
1958
SWAPO founded in South West Africa
1958
French Somaliland became an overseas territory
1958
Kampala became the capital of Uganda
1958, Jan. 5

French Army in Cameroun to quell Communist uprising
1958, Jan. 10
Spanish Sahara created
1958, Jan. 10
El-Aaiún became the capital of Spanish Sahara
1958, Jan. 14
Ifni became a separate Spanish province
1958, Jan. 14
Ghana and USSR agreed to diplomatic ties
1958, Feb. 1
Egypt and Syria formed the UAR
1958, Feb. 1
Egypt and Syria formed the United Arab States
1958, Feb. 8
Edgar Whitehead became PM of Southern Rhodesia
1958, Feb. 8
French bombed Tunisian village near Algerian border
1958, Feb. 9
French bases in Tunisia blockaded by Tunisians
1958, Feb. 12
Tunisia demanded evacuation of all French troops
1958, Feb. 17
France and Tunisia accepted arbitration
1958, Feb. 18
Ahmadou Ahidjo became PM of Cameroun
1958, Feb. 20
Tunisian police forcibly closed 4 French consulates
1958, March 12
UAR abolished all Syrian political parties
1958, April 8
243 Algerian rebels killed in French action
1958, April 10
Spanish West Africa came to an end
1958, April 15
First Conference of Independent African States
1958, April 27
Nicolas Grunitzky became first PM of Togo
1958, May 13
French troops seized Algiers in defiance of Paris
1958, May 16
Sylvanus Olimpio became PM of Togo

1958, May 25
Tunisia mobilized Army against France

1958, June 16
Raoul Salan became delegate-general of Algeria

1958, June 17
France agreed to evacuate Tunisia (but not Bizerte)

1958, July 20
Jordan ended diplomatic ties with UAR

1958, July 26
Jacques Opangoult became first PM of Congo

1958, Aug. 14
Milton Margai became first PM of Sierra Leone

1958, Sept. 3
Hendrik Verwoerd became PM of South Africa

1958, Sept. 18
Algerian Government formed in exile in Cairo

1958, Oct. 2
French Guinea. Independence as Guinea

1958, Oct. 2
Ahmed Sékou Touré interim head of state of Guinea

1958, Oct. 14
Madagascar became semi-autonomous Malagasy Republic

1958, Oct. 15
Tunisia cut diplomatic ties with UAR

1958, Oct. 25
Britain announced Nigerian independence for 1960

1958, Nov. 1
Morocco and China established diplomatic ties

1958, Nov. 1
Tunisia replaced the franc with the dinar

1958, Nov. 12
Ahmed Sékou Touré became head of state of Guinea

1958, Nov. 17
Bloodless coup in the Sudan led by Ibrahim Abboud

1958, Nov. 18
Sudan declared a democratic republic

1958, Nov. 24
French Sudan now semi-autonomous Sudanese Republic

1958, Nov. 25
Senegal became an autonomous republic

1958, Nov. 28
French Equatorial Africa dissolved

1958, Nov. 28
Chad became an autonomous republic

1958, Nov. 28
Congo became an autonomous republic

1958, Nov. 28
Gabon became an autonomous republic

1958, Nov. 28
Léon M'Ba became chief minister of Gabon

1958, Nov. 28
Mauritania became a semi-autonomous republic

1958, Dec. 1
C.A.R. became an autonomous republic

1958, Dec. 4
Dahomey became an autonomous republic

1958, Dec. 4
Ivory Coast became an autonomous republic

1958, Dec. 8
Barthélémy Boganda became PM of the C.A.R.

1958, Dec. 8
Fulbert Youlou became PM of Congo

1958, Dec. 11
Upper Volta became an autonomous republic

1958, Dec. 14
Hamani Diori became PM of Niger

1958, Dec. 19
Niger became an autonomous republic

1958, Dec. 19
Paul Delouvrier became delegate-general for Algeria

1959
Sahel-Bénin Union created

1959
The Hutu revolted in Rwanda and overthrew monarchy

1959
Oil discovered in Libya in a big way

1959
Ruanda-Urundi divided into Rwanda and Burundi

1959, Jan. 1
Cameroun became an autonomous republic

1959, Jan. 1

UAR began rounding up Communists

1959, Jan. 5
Belgian Congo Army fired on independence protesters

1959, Jan. 15
France formally recognized Guinea diplomatically

1959, Jan. 17
Mali Federation became a fact on paper

1959, Jan. 21
Administration ended in French West Africa

1959, Jan. 25
Violent riots in Matadi, Belgian Congo

1959, Feb. 18
French troops move in to quell Brazzaville riots

1959, Feb. 24
Troops fired on nationalist mobs in Nyasaland

1959, Feb. 26
State of emergency declared in Southern Rhodesia

1959, Feb. 27
Léon M'Ba became first PM of Gabon

1959, March 3
State of emergency declared in Nyasaland

1959, March 3
Hastings Banda arrested and deported from Nyasaland

1959, March
Modibo Keita became president of Sudanese Republic

1959, March 4
Ibrahim Abboud assumed full control of the Sudan

1959, March 24
François Tombalbaye became PM of Chad

1959, March 29
Barthélémy Boganda, PM of C.A.R., died

1959, April 4
Mali Federation went into effect

1959, April 4
Modibo Keita became premier of Mali Federation

1959, April 6
French West Africa officially came to an end

1959, April 6
French troops flown in to Dahomey to stop riots

1959, April 16
Modibo Keita became PM of

Sudanese Republic
1959, April 27
Philibert Tsiranana became Malagasy president
1959, May 2
Félix Houphouët-Boigny became PM of Ivory Coast
1959, May 5
David Dacko became PM of C.A.R.
1959, May 6
President Tubman of Liberia re-elected
1959, May 22
Hubert Maga became PM of Dahomey
1959, May 26
Transkei created
1959, June 1
Tunisia adopted new constitution based on USA
1959, June 23
Mokhtar Ould Daddah became PM of Mauritania
1959, July 23
French troops move against Kabyle rebels in Algeria
1959, Aug. 16
UAR resumed diplomatic relations with Jordan
1959, Aug. 20
End of French-Tunisian customs union
1959, Oct. 16
France agreed on Algerian self-determination
1959, Oct. 30
Anti-white rioting in Stanley-ville, Belgian Congo
1959, Nov. 7
Northern Cameroons voted to stay British
1959, Nov. 8
President Bourguiba of Tunisia re-elected
1959, Nov. 12
State of emergency declared in Ruanda-Urundi
1959, Dec. 11
Maurice Yaméogo first president of Upper Volta
1959, Dec. 22
Krim Belkassim became PM of Algerians in exile
1959, Dec. 31
30 people killed at Douala, Cameroun
1959, Dec. 12
Nnamdi Azikiwe became president of Nigeria

1960
Sultanate abolished in Baguirmi
1960
Failed French attempt to topple Touré in Guinea
1960
Dr. Hastings Banda released from British prison
1960, Jan. 1
Cameroun. Independence from France
1960, Jan. 1
Spanish Guinea Overseas Provinces created
1960, Jan. 12
State of emergency ended in Kenya
1960, Jan. 19
Ferhat Abbas PM of Algerian Government in Exile
1960, Jan. 20
Tubman of Liberia inaugurated for fourth term
1960, Jan. 22
Gen. Jacques Massu, Algiers Army commander, fired
1960, Jan. 24
State of siege declared in Algiers
1960, Jan. 29
French Army ordered to restore order in Algiers
1960, Feb. 1
Colon uprising in Algeria collapsed
1960, Feb. 3
British PM criticized South Africa's racial policy
1960, Feb. 10
Algerian home guard dissolved
1960, Feb.
Parti National Africain founded in Chad
1960, March 5
Guinea first free country to recognize East Germany
1960, March 6
Ghana's plans for a republic published
1960, March 12
Moshoeshoe II became paramount chief in Basutoland
1960, March 21
Sharpeville incident in South Africa
1960, March 26
France agreed to Malagasy independence
1960, March 26
South Africa relaxed racial pass laws temporarily

1960, March 30
State of emergency in most of South Africa
1960, April 4
France agreed to Mali Federation's independence
1960, April 6
South Africa re-imposed racial pass laws
1960, April 7
1500 blacks rounded up and arrested near Cape Town
1960, April 8
Britain officially deplored S. Africa racial policy
1960, April 9
Attempted assassination of Verwoerd in South Africa
1960, April
Gen. Jean Crépin new commander in chief in Algeria
1960, April 18
Tangier's international zone status abolished
1960, April 27
Togo. Independence from France
1960, April 27
Sylvanus Olimpio became Togo head of state
1960, May 3
Tunisia established diplomatic relations with USSR
1960, May 5
Togo established diplomatic relations with USSR
1960, May 5
Ahmadou Ahidjo became first president of Cameroun
1960, May 10
Black riots in Northern Rhodesia copper country
1960, June 8
Guinea and USSR signed cultural exchange agreement
1960, June 17
Joseph Kasavubu became PM designate of Congo
1960, June 19
Kasavubu became first PM of Congo
1960, June 20
Mali Federation. Independence from France
1960, June 21
Patrice Lumumba became PM of Congo
1960, June 24
Kasavubu became first president of Congo

1960, June 24
Mobutu became Congolese State Secretary for Defense

1960, June 26
British Somaliland became Somalia

1960, June 26
Muhammad Ibrahim Egal became PM of Somalia

1960, June 26
Malagasy Republic. Independence from France

1960, June 29
Algerian peace talks ended in failure

1960, June 30
Belgian Congo independence as Congo (Léopoldville)

1960, July 1
Somalia and Italian Somaliland formed Somalia

1960, July 1
Aden Abdallah Osman Daar president of Somalia

1960, July 1
Muhammad Ibrahim Egal became PM of Somalia

1960, July 1
Ghana became a republic

1960, July 1
Kwame Nkrumah sworn in as first president of Ghana

1960, July 6
Congolese Army mutinies reported

1960, July 10
Belgian troops flew into the Congo

1960, July 10
Mobutu became Chief of Staff of the Congolese Army

1960, July 11
Katanga seceded from Congo (Léopoldville)

1960, July 11
France agreed to independence for Dahomey

1960, July 11
France agreed to independence for Niger

1960, July 11
France agreed to independence for Ivory Coast

1960, July 11
France agreed to independence for Upper Volta

1960, July 12
France agreed to independence for C.A.R.

1960, July 12

France agreed to independence for Chad

1960, July 12
France agreed to independence for (their) Congo

1960, July 12
Europeans fled the Congo en masse

1960, July 12
Abdi Rashid Shermarke became PM of Somalia

1960, July 14
UN voted to send troops to the Congo

1960, July 15
First UN troops (Tunisians) arrived in Congo

1960, July 15
Lumumba demanded Belgian withdrawal from Congo

1960, July 15
France agreed to independence for Gabon

1960, July 17
Congo gave deadline for withdrawal of Belgians

1960, July 22
UN asked Belgians to withdraw quickly from Congo

1960, July 25
Tshombe threatened any UN troops entering Katanga

1960, July 27
Iran severed diplomatic relations with the UAR

1960, July 28
Dag Hammarskjöld arrived in Léopoldville

1960, July 28
France agreed to independence for Mauritania

1960, July 29
Ghana boycotted South Africa

1960, July 30
Congo demanded immediate UN invasion of Katanga

1960, Aug. 1
Dahomey. Independence from France

1960, Aug. 1
Hubert Maga became head of state of Dahomey

1960, Aug. 3
Niger. Independence from France

1960, Aug. 3
Hamani Diori became interim president of Niger

1960, Aug. 5
Upper Volta. Independence from France

1960, Aug. 5
UN canceled invasion plans for Katanga

1960, Aug. 5
Maurice Yaméogo re-styled PM of Upper Volta

1960, Aug. 7
Ivory Coast. Independence from France

1960, Aug. 7
Houphouët-Boigny interim president of Ivory Coast

1960, Aug. 8
South Kasai seceded from Congo (Léopoldville)

1960, Aug. 9
UN demanded Belgian troop withdrawal from Katanga

1960, Aug. 11
Chad. Independence from France

1960, Aug. 12
François Tombalbaye became first president of Chad

1960, Aug. 12
Hammarskjöld led the UN into Katanga

1960, Aug. 13
C.A.R. Independence from France

1960, Aug. 13
David Dacko became interim president of C.A.R.

1960, Aug. 14
Belgian troops surrendered Elisabethville to UN

1960, Aug. 15
Congo. Independence from France

1960, Aug. 15
Fulbert Youlou became first president of Congo

1960, Aug. 16
Martial law declared in Congo by Lumumba

1960, Aug. 17
Gabon. Independence from France

1960, Aug. 17
Léon M'Ba first became president of Gabon

1960, Aug.
South Kasai and Katanga created a federation

1960, Aug. 20
Mali Federation came to an end

1960, Aug. 20
Léopold Senghor interim president of Senegal

1960, Aug. 20

Sudanese Republic. Independence from France

1960, Aug. 20
Mamadou Dia became PM of Senegal

1960, Aug. 24
Congolese troops entered Kasai

1960, Aug. 25
Delegates of 13 African states met at Léopoldville

1960, Aug. 27
South Kasai captured by Congolese forces

1960, Sept. 2
Julius Nyerere became PM of Tanganyika

1960, Sept. 5
President Kasavubu of Congo fired Lumumba as PM

1960, Sept. 5
Joseph Ileo became PM elect of Congo

1960, Sept. 5
Republic of Senegal formally proclaimed

1960, Sept. 6
UN closed all major Congolese airfields

1960, Sept. 6
Léopold Senghor became president of Senegal

1960, Sept. 7
Lumumba's dismissal invalidated by Congo chamber

1960, Sept. 10
Congo Army agreed to ceasefire in Katanga and Kasai

1960, Sept. 11
France recognized independence of Senegal

1960, Sept. 14
Congo (Léopoldville) coup led by Mobutu

1960, Sept. 16
Congo expelled Soviet and Czech ambassadors

1960, Sept. 20
Chad became a member of the UN

1960, Sept. 20
Cameroun became a member of the UN

1960, Sept. 20
C.A.R. became a member of the UN

1960, Sept. 20
Ivory Coast became a member of the UN

1960, Sept. 20
Upper Volta became a member

of the UN

1960, Sept. 20
Togo became a member of the UN

1960, Sept. 20
Somalia became a member of the UN

1960, Sept. 20
Congo (Brazzaville) became a member of the UN

1960, Sept. 20
Dahomey became a member of the UN

1960, Sept. 20
Niger became a member of the UN

1960, Sept. 20
Gabon became a member of the UN

1960, Sept. 20
Malagasy Republic became a member of the UN

1960, Sept. 22
Sudanese Republic renamed Mali

1960, Sept. 28
Mali and Senegal joined the UN

1960, Oct. 1
Nigeria. Independence from Britain

1960, Oct. 5
South Africa narrowly voted for a republic

1960, Oct. 7
Nigeria became the 99th member of the UN

1960, Oct. 7
USSR recognized Algerian government in exile

1960, Oct. 10
Rwanda formed its own government

1960, Oct. 30
Guinea and the US signed economic aid agreement

1960, Nov. 4
France agreed to Algerian self-determination

1960, Nov. 7
Britain agreed to Zanzibar independence

1960, Nov. 9
Hamani Diori became president of Niger

1960, Nov. 15
Morocco accepted Soviet military aid

1960, Nov.
The trial of leaders of Algiers January revolt

1960, Nov. 16
Nnamdi Azikiwe became governor-general of Nigeria

1960, Nov. 17
David Dacko became president of C.A.R.

1960, Nov. 18
Congo broke off diplomatic relations with Ghana

1960, Nov. 21
Fighting broke out between Congolese Army and UN

1960, Nov. 22
Congo (Léopoldville) became a member of the UN

1960, Nov. 27
Houphouët-Boigny first president of Ivory Coast

1960, Nov. 28
Mauritania. Independence from France

1960, Nov. 28
Patrice Lumumba fled Léopoldville arrest

1960, Dec. 1
Congo broke off diplomatic relations with UAR

1960, Dec. 1
Lumumba captured by Congolese Army in Kasai

1960, Dec. 2
Lumumba returned to Léopoldville for trial

1960, Dec. 8
UAR received big agricultural loans from Soviets

1960, Dec. 8
Maurice Yaméogo re-styled president of Upper Volta

1960, Dec. 9
De Gaulle in Algeria to win support for referendum

1960, Dec. 11
Large scale rioting in Algiers. May killed

1960, Dec. 11
Hubert Maga became president of Dahomey

1960, Dec. 12
Morocco and Guinea withdrew UN troops from Congo

1960, Dec. 13
De Gaulle's Algerian trip canceled amid rioting

1960, Dec. 13
French Army fired on European protesters in Bône

1960, Dec. 13
Stanleyville seceded from Congo (Léopoldville)

1960, Dec. 14
Revolt in Addis Ababa against Haile Selassie's rule

1960, Dec. 17
Haile Selassie regained control of Ethiopia

1960, Dec. 19
UN came out for Algerian independence

1961
Britain rejected Barotseland statehood

1961
Swaziland kingdom recognized by Britain

1961
United Arab States dissolved

1961
Syria withdrew from the U.A.R.

1961, Jan. 8
French voters supported De Gaulle's Algerian policy

1961, Jan. 15
Ahmed Sékou Touré became president of Guinea

1961, Jan. 18
Lumumba transferred to a prison in Katanga

1961, Jan. 26
Burundi formed local government

1961, Jan. 26
Joseph Cimpaye became first PM of Burundi

1961, Jan. 26
Britain and UAR resumed diplomatic relations

1961, Jan. 28
Rwanda proclaimed a republic and abolished monarchy

1961, Jan. 28
Dominique Mbonyumutwa first president of Rwanda

1961, Feb. 5
Rioting in Luanda. Angola

1961, Feb. 9
Congo returned to civil rule

1961, Feb. 12
Patrice Lumumba murdered

1961, Feb. 26
Hassan II became king of Morocco

1961, March 2
The last French troops left Morocco

1961, March 5
A UN force surrendered to the Congolese Army

1961, March 15
South Africa announced plans to leave Commonwealth

1961, March
Pierre N'Jie became chief minister of Gambia

1961, March 22
Britain again denounced South Africa's racial policy

1961, March 30
Albert Kalonji declared himself emperor of Kasai

1961, April 7
UN denounced South West Africa's racial policy

1961, April 12
Sylvanus Olimpio became president of Togo

1961, April 13
UN again denounced South Africa's racial policy

1961, April 22
Algiers taken over by insurrectionists under Challe

1961, April 26
Army mutiny in Algiers collapsed

1961, April 26
Moise Tshombe of Katanga seized by Congolese troops

1961, April 27
Sierra Leone. Independence from Britain

1961, May 1
Tanganyika achieved full internal self-government

1961, May 1
Julius Nyerere became PM of Tanganyika

1961, May 5
3,400 Portuguese troops sent to Angola

1961, May 18
Charles Swart became president of South Africa

1961, May 20
France began negotiations with Algerian rebels

1961, May 31
South Africa became republic and left Commonwealth

1961, June 1
Northern Cameroons became integral part of Nigeria

1961, June 2
Hassan of Morocco took over PM role as well

1961, June 12
Hammarskjöld said Congo troubles seemed to be over

1961, June 13
France broke off peace talks with Algerian rebels

1961, June 22
Tshombe freed from jail in Congo after peace deal

1961, June 28
Tshombe, back in Katanga, reneged on peace deal

1961, July 2
Benedicte Kiwanuka became chief minister of Uganda

1961, July 4
Sierra Leone boycotted South Africa

1961, July 5
General strike in Algeria. 80 Muslims killed

1961, July 19
Tunisian troops and civilians besieged Bizerte

1961, July 20
French Army ended siege of Bizerte naval base

1961, July 24
UN investigation of Bizerte crisis began

1961, Aug. 1
Cyrille Adoulla became PM of Congo

1961, Aug. 5
Stanleyville re-incorporated into Congo

1961, Aug.
Jomo Kenyatta released from prison

1961, Aug.
Salah ben Yusuf assassinated in Algeria

1961, Aug. 20
Mokhtar Ould Daddah became president of Mauritania

1961, Aug. 21
Jomo Kenyatta released from prison

1961, Aug. 25
UN asked France to withdraw from Bizerte base

1961, Aug. 31
Last Spanish troops left Morocco proper

1961, Sept. 13
UN troops attacked Katanga

1961, Sept. 18
France agreed to evacuate Bizerte and other bases

1961, Sept. 18
Dag Hammarskjöld died in plane crash

1961, Sept. 21
Tshombe of Katanga and UN ceased fire

1961, Sept. 26

Seewoosagur Ramgoolam chief minister of Mauritius

1961, Sept. 27
Sierra Leone became a UN member

1961, Sept. 29
Burundi given limited self-rule

1961, Sept. 30
Marrakesh, last French Morocco air base, given back

1961, Oct. 1
Southern Cameroons became part of Cameroun

1961, Oct. 3
French troops left Bizerte

1961, Oct. 9
Britain announced Uganda's future independence

1961, Oct. 9
Volcano on Tristan da Cunha erupted

1961, Oct. 26
Grégoire Kayibanda came to power in Rwanda

1961, Oct. 27
Mauritania became a UN member

1961, Oct. 30
Congolese Army invaded Katanga

1961, Nov. 5
Congolese Army routed by Katangans

1961, Dec. 5
UN and Katangan forces began fighting again

1961, Dec. 9
Tanganyika. Independence from Britain

1961, Dec. 14
Tanganyika became a member of the UN

1961, Dec. 22
Comoros became autonomous state

1961, Dec. 22
Sa'id Muhammad Sheikh became first PM of Comoros

1961, Dec. 26
Nasser ended union of UAR and Yemen

1961, Dec. 27
Congo and Belgium resumed diplomatic relations

1962, Jan. 2
A free zone established in Tangier

1962, Jan. 20
Antoine Gizenga placed under Léopoldville arrest

1962, Jan. 22
Rashidi Kawawa became new PM of Tanganyika

1962, Jan. 23
South Africa announced future Transkeian self-rule

1962, Jan. 30
UN demanded that Portugal cease Angola repression

1962, March 28
Abdur Rahman Farès president of Algeria in exile

1962, Feb. 19
French-Algerian peace talks ended successfully

1962, March 1
Uganda became self-governing

1962, March 18
French-Algerian ceasefire signed

1962, March 22
OAS attacked French security forces in Algiers

1962, March 22
Insurrection in Oran and Algiers

1962, March 25
French Army fought Europeans in Oran for five hours

1962, April 5
Angolan Revolutionary Government in Exile set up

1962, April 8
French voters approved Algerian peace settlement

1962, April
Jomo Kenyatta became PM of Kenya

1962, April 15
Edmond Jouhaud, OAS No. 2 man, sentenced to death

1960, April 20
Raoul Salan, chief of the OAS, arrested in Algiers

1962, April 23
François Tombalbaye became president of Chad

1962, April 25
Milton Obote became PM of Uganda

1962
Moroni became capital of the Comoros

1962
South Kasai Republic was declared dead

1962
First major South Sudan independence group formed

1962
FRELIMO began independence war in Mozambique

1962
Eritrean Liberation Front formed

1962, May
Dawda Jawara became first PM of Gambia

1962, May 14
17 Europeans killed by Muslims in Algiers

1962, May 23
Raoul Salan sentenced to life imprisonment

1962, May 29
State of emergency in Western Nigeria

1962, May 31
OAS began 6 day truce in Algeria

1962, June 12
Dawda Jawara sworn in as PM of Gambia

1962, June 17
OAS suspended terrorism in Algeria

1962, July 1
Rwanda and Burundi. Independence from Belgium

1962, July 3
Algeria. Independence from France

1962, July 5
Yusuf ben Khedda became provisional PM of Algeria

1962, July 6
OAS resumed terrorist activities in Algeria

1962, July
The province of North Katanga came into being

1962, July 21
UAR launched rockets in the desert

1962, Aug. 4
Ahmed ben Bella became provisional PM of Algeria

1962, Sept. 11
Northern Rhodesia achieved self-rule

1962, Sept. 22
State of emergency in Accra

1962, Sept. 24
Ali Sabry became PM of Egypt

1962, Sept. 25
Ahmed ben Bella became PM of Algeria

1962, Oct. 9
Uganda. Independence

1962, Oct. 20
Fighting broke out again in Katanga

1962, Oct. 25
Uganda became the 110th member of the UN
1962, Nov. 2
Julius Nyerere became president of Tanganyika
1962, Nov. 14
Eritrea became the 14th province of Ethiopia
1962, Nov. 29
Algeria banned the Communist Party
1962, Dec. 9
Tanganyika became a republic
1962, Dec. 9
Julius Nyerere sworn in as president of Tanzania
1962, Dec. 16
Winston Field became PM of Southern Rhodesia
1962, Dec. 29
UN forces captured Elisabethville
1963
SANU formed in Southern Sudan
1963
The Anya Nya formed in Southern Sudan
1963, Jan. 13
President Olimpio of Togo gunned down
1963, Jan. 15
Katanga re-united with Congo (Léopoldville)
1963, Jan. 16
Nicolas Grunitzky became acting president of Togo
1963, Jan. 21
Kolwezi, the last Katangan stronghold, taken by UN
1963, Feb. 1
Nyasaland awarded self-rule
1963, Feb. 1
Dr. Hastings Banda became PM of Nyasaland
1963, March 17
51 of the Tristan da Cunha evacuees returned home
1963, March 18
France exploded nuclear bomb in the Sahara
1963, April 11
Britain refused Southern Rhodesia independence
1963, April 27
Libya became a unitary state
1963, May 5
Nicolas Grunitzky became president of Togo

1963, May 8
President Tubman of Liberia elected for fifth term
1963, May 9
Self-rule went into effect for Nyasaland
1963, May
Transkei achieved self-rule
1963, May 25
Algeria and Tunisia resumed diplomatic relations
1963, May 28
Jomo Kenyatta named first PM of Kenya
1963, June
Lualaba & East Katanga Province came into being
1963, June
Kenya became partially self-governing
1963, June 24
Zanzibar achieved self-rule
1963, July 15
South Africa withdrew from UN Economic Commission
1963, July 17
Rebels controlled 15 percent of Portuguese Guinea
1963, July 26
Agreement to dissolve Fed. of Rhodesia & Nyasaland
1963, Aug. 11
End of 32-African nation conference in Dakar
1963, Aug. 15
Fulbert Youlou forced to resign in Congo
1963, Aug. 16
Alphonse Massemba-Débat acting president of Congo
1963, Sept. 15
Ahmed ben Bella elected president of Algeria
1963, Sept. 20
Ahmed ben Bella took office as president of Algeria
1963, Sept. 30
Moroccan troops poised to invade Algeria
1963, Oct. 1
Nigeria became a federal republic
1963, Oct. 1
Algeria nationalized all French-owned lands there
1963, Oct. 3
Gambia achieved self-rule
1963, Oct. 8
Battle between Morocco and Algeria at Hassi Beida
1963, Oct. 9

Uganda became a commonwealth
1963, Oct. 9
Sir Edward Mutesa II became president of Uganda
1963, Oct. 12
Algeria put down a Kabyle rebellion
1963, Oct. 14
Morocco invaded Algeria
1963, Oct. 16
Algerian Army mobilized
1963, Oct. 28
Dahomey. Coup
1963, Oct. 30
Algerian-Moroccan ceasefire
1963, Nov. 10
Last of Tristan da Cunha evacuees returned home
1963, Nov. 11
Kabyle rebellion in Algeria formally ended
1963, Nov. 21
Congo expelled all Soviet diplomats
1963, Dec. 4
UN urged arms embargo against South Africa
1963, Dec. 9
Pres. Senghor of Senegal sworn in for second term
1963, Dec. 10
Zanzibar. Independence from Britain
1963, Dec. 12
Kenya. Independence from Britain
1963, Dec. 15
Spanish Guinea became Equatorial Guinea
1963, Dec. 16
Last two US bases in Morocco handed back
1963, Dec. 19
Alphonse Massemba-Débat became president of Congo
1963, Dec. 24
Pascual Lissouba became PM of Congo
1963, Dec. 25
Kenya declared state of emergency in NE region
1963, Dec. 29
Kenya sealed off border with Somalia
1963, Dec. 31
Federation of Rhodesia and Nyasaland came to an end
1964
Fernando Po gained autonomy
1964

Lilongwe chosen as new capital of Malawi

1964
Nelson Mandela imprisoned for life in South Africa

1964, Jan. 2
Attempted assassination of Kwame Nkrumah

1964, Jan. 10
Tunisia and China established diplomatic ties

1964, Jan. 12
Zanzibar coup led to declaration of republic

1964, Jan. 19
Tanganyikan Army mutiny put down by Britain

1964, Jan. 21
State of emergency in Kwilu province, Congo

1964, Jan. 22
Northern Rhodesia's self-rule became effective

1964, Jan. 22
Kenneth Kaunda became first PM of Northern Rhodesia

1964, Jan. 25
Army mutinies in Kenya, Tanganyika and Uganda

1964, Feb. 4
Anti-US riots in Accra, Ghana

1964, Feb. 19
The last US diplomat expelled from Zanzibar

1964, Feb. 20
Morocco and Algeria agreed to end border conflict

1964, Feb. 21
Ghana became a one-party state

1964, Feb. 23
Libya refused to renew US & UK military base leases

1964, Feb. 23
US, UK & others recognized new Zanzibar government

1964, Feb. 27
Sudan deported 300 missionaries for subversion

1964, Feb. 28
Morocco and UAR resumed diplomatic ties

1964, March 3
UAR and Saudi Arabia resumed diplomatic ties

1964, March 8
Zanzibari government nationalized all farms

1964, March 11
South Africa left International Labor Organization

1964, March 12
Seewoosagur Ramgoolam became PM of Mauritius

1964, April 13
Ian Smith became PM of Southern Rhodesia

1964, April 26
Tanganyika and Zanzibar united

1964, June 19
Rebels captured Albertville, North Katanga

1964, June 26
Moise Tshombe returned to Congo from European exile

1964, June 30
UN forces left Congo

1964, July 6
Nyasaland. Independence from Britain as Malawi

1964, July 10
Moise Tshombe became PM of Congo

1964, July 30
UK agreed to Gambia independence for Feb. 18, 1965

1964, Aug. 1
High Commission Territories in Southern Africa end

1964, Aug. 1
Lesotho granted self-rule

1964, Aug. 1
Moshoeshoe II became king of Basutoland

1964, Aug. 1
Democratic Republic of the Congo (ex–Belgian Congo)

1964, Aug. 4
The leone currency introduced in Sierra Leone

1964, Aug. 5
Stanleyville captured by rebels in Congo

1964, Aug. 21
Congo troops recaptured Bukavu from rebels

1964, Aug. 30
Congo troops recaptured Albertville from rebels

1964, Sept. 7
Stanleyville People's Republic came into being

1964, Oct. 7
Congo troops and mercenaries captured Uvira

1964, Oct. 24
Northern Rhodesia. Independence as Zambia

1964, Oct. 24
Kenneth Kaunda became first president of Zambia

1964, Oct. 28
State of emergency declared in the Sudan

1964, Oct. 29
Tanganyika and Zanzibar became Tanzania

1964, Nov. 6
Congo troops and mercenaries captured Kindu

1964, Nov. 10
Kenya became a one-party state

1964, Nov. 15
President Abboud resigned in the Sudan

1964, Nov. 24
Belgian paratroopers occupied Stanleyville

1964, Nov. 26
Belgian paratroopers occupied Paulis, in the Congo

1964, Dec. 12
Kenya became a republic

1964, Dec. 12
Jomo Kenyatta became first president of Kenya

1964, Dec. 23
UAR admitted to helping Congolese rebels

1965
Gaborone became capital of Bechuanaland

1965
Seewoosagur Ramgoolam knighted

1965
Milton Margai knighted

1965
SANU split into two factions in Southern Sudan

1965
Azania Liberation Front formed in Southern Sudan

1965
Sudan African Liberation Front formed

1965, Jan. 7
Nigerian government crisis ended

1965, Jan. 10
Sudan admitted helping Congolese rebels

1965, Jan. 23
Borkou-Ennedi-Tibesti became part of Chad

1965, Jan. 23
Congolese rebels captured Nkolo

1965, Jan. 30
Burundi broke diplomatic ties with China

1965, Feb. 18

Gambia. Independence from Britain

1965, March 3
Seretse Khama became first PM of Bechuanaland

1965, March 29
Congo troops and Mercenaries captured Watsa

1965, April 18
Uganda formally denounced US action in Vietnam

1965, April 29
Kenya rejected USSR weapons gift

1965, April 30
Basutoland achieved internal self-government

1965, May 7
Ian Smith's party won overwhelmingly in Rhodesia

1965, June 2
The Gambia agreed to become a republic in 1966

1965, June 6
Sekhonyana Maseribane became first PM of Basutoland

1965, June 7
State of emergency declared in Morocco

1965, June 10
Ismail al-Azhari became president of the Sudan

1965, June 19
Boumedienne became Algerian president after a coup

1965, July 1
Former Belgian Congo became Congo (Kinshasa)

1965, July 1
Stanleyville People's Republic came to an end

1965, July 1
Léopoldville became Kinshasa

1965, July 7
Leabua Jonathan became PM of Basutoland

1965, July 19
Ghana adopted the new currency of the cedi

1965, July 20
Malawi agreed to become a republic on July 6, 1966

1965, Sept. 24
Britain agreed to Mauritius independence

1965, Sept. 29
Zahariah Mohieddin became PM of Egypt

1965, Oct. 13
Moise Tshombe dismissed as Congolese PM

1965, Oct. 13
Britain agreed to Bechuanaland independence

1965, Oct. 19
Léopold Biha, PM of Burundi, shot during revolt

1965, Nov. 5
State of emergency declared in Rhodesia

1965, Nov. 8
British Indian Ocean Territory created

1965, Nov. 11
Ian Smith's UDI in Rhodesia

1965, Nov. 12
UN condemned Rhodesia

1965, Nov. 16
Britain agreed to impose sanctions on Rhodesia

1965, Nov. 20
UN agreed to end economic relations with Rhodesia

1965, Nov. 22
Guinea and France broke off diplomatic relations

1965, Nov. 25
Mobutu came to power in Congo (Kinshasa) after coup

1965, Nov. 28
Leonard Mulamba became the PM of Congo

1965, Nov. 29
Bloodless coup in Dahomey

1965, Dec. 16
Ghana broke diplomatic ties with UK over Rhodesia

1965, Dec. 17
Britain imposed an embargo on Rhodesia

1965, Dec. 28
Rationing of gasoline and diesel oil in Rhodesia

1966
Dawda Jawara knighted

1966
Bakwanga (in Kasai) renamed Mbuji Mayi

1966
Stanleyville renamed Kisangani

1966
Elisabethville became Lubumbashi

1966, Jan. 1
Jean Bedel Bokassa came to power in C.A.R.

1966, Jan. 3
Lamizana came to power in Upper Volta after coup

1966, Jan. 3
Dahomey broke off diplomatic

relations with China

1966, Jan. 6
C.A.R. broke off diplomatic relations with China

1966, Jan. 15
Abubaka Tafawa Balewa toppled and killed in Nigeria

1966, Feb. 9
Emergency powers granted to Liberian president

1966, Feb. 22
Milton Obote seized power in Uganda

1966, Feb. 24
Kwame Nkrumah ousted in Ghana coup

1966, March 2
Milton Obote became acting president of Uganda

1966, March 2
Kwame Nkrumah arrived in Guinea as official guest

1966, April 15
Uganda declared a republic

1966, April 15
Milton Obote sworn in as president of Uganda

1966, April 15
Pascal Lissouba, PM of Congo, resigned

1966, April 15
Rhodesia closed its embassy in London

1966, May 6
Ambroise Noumazalay named PM of Congo

1966, May 9
Talks began between Britain and Rhodesia

1966, May 20
British-Rhodesian talks suspended

1966, May 24
Nigeria dissolved the federation of its states

1966, May 25
Uganda crushed two-day uprising

1966, May 25
Mutesa II, King of Buganda, fled Uganda

1966, May 28
Clashes between Ibo and Hausa tribesmen in Nigeria

1966, June 2
Former Congo PM Evariste Kimba executed

1966, June 10
Uganda dissolved the kingdom of Buganda

1966, June 17
Britain agreed on Basutoland's independence

1966, July 6
Malawi became a republic

1966, July 6
Hastings Banda became first president of Malawi

1966, July 8
Prince Charles Ndiziye seized power in Burundi

1966, July 13
Michel Micombero became PM of Burundi

1966, July 29
Yokubu Gowon came to power in Nigeria after coup

1966, Aug. 25
Independence riots in Djibouti

1966, Sept. 6
Hendrik Verwoerd, South Africa PM, stabbed to death

1966, Sept. 10
Sidqi Suleiman became PM of Egypt

1966, Sept. 13
John Vorster became PM of South Africa

1966, Sept. 24
Portuguese embassy sacked in Kinshasa

1966, Sept. 25
Kisangani recaptured by Congo troops from rebels

1966, Sept. 27
Ghana expelled Cuban diplomats

1966, Sept. 30
Bechuanaland became Botswana

1966, Sept. 30
Sir Seretse Khama became first Botswana president

1966, Oct. 1
Nigerian troops mutinied in Kano and attacked Ibos

1966, Oct. 3
Tunisia broke off diplomatic relations with UAR

1966, Oct. 4
Basutoland. Independence from Britain as Lesotho

1966, Oct. 17
Lesotho and Botswana admitted as UN members

1966, Oct. 27
UN removed South Africa's South West Africa mandate

1966, Nov. 8
Guinea expelled Peace Corps and other US agencies

1966, Nov. 21
Togo coup attempt crushed by Army

1966, Nov. 28
Kingdom of Burundi became a republic after coup

1966, Nov. 28
Michel Micombero became president of Burundi

1966, Dec. 4
Harold Wilson and Ian Smith met on the "Tiger"

1966, Dec. 5
Rhodesia rejected British peace proposals

1967
Ugandan monarchies abolished

1967
Southern Sudan Provisional Government formed

1967
Seychelles gained a certain autonomy

1967
Jomo Kenyatta allowed an opposition party in Kenya

1967, Jan. 4
Swahili replaced English as the Tanzanian language

1967, Jan. 13
Kléber Dadjo became president of Togo after coup

1967, Feb. 6
Failed coup in Sierra Leone

1967, March 13
Moise Tshombe sentenced to death in absentia

1967, March 17
Siaka Stevens elected PM of Sierra Leone

1967, March 19
French Somaliland voted to remain French

1967, March 21
Sierra Leone coup led by David Lansana

1967, March 23
David Lansana arrested in Sierra Leone

1967, March 23
Ambrose Genda headed Sierra Leone government

1967, March 27
Genda deposed by Andrew Juxon-Smith in Sierra Leone

1967, April 14
Étienne Éyadéma came to power in Togo

1967, April 18

Étienne Éyadéma became president of Togo

1967, April 25
Swaziland became self-governing

1967, April 25
Makhosini Dhlamini became first PM of Swaziland

1967, May 30
Biafra seceded from Nigeria and declared a republic

1967, June 5
Six-Day War began in Middle East

1967, June 6
Nasser closed the Suez Canal

1967, June 6
UAR broke off diplomatic relations with USA

1967, June 10
Abdi Rashid Shermarke became president of Somalia

1967, June 10
Six-Day War ended in Middle East

1967, June 10
Muhammad Ibrahim Egal became PM of Somalia again

1967, June 30
Moise Tshombe kidnapped

1967, July 1
UAR and Israeli forces clashed at Suez Canal

1967, July 5
Rebellion in Katanga

1967, July 6
French Somaliland became Afars and Issas

1967, July 6
Ali Aref Bourhan became PM of Afars & Issas

1967, July 6
Biafran War began

1967, Sept. 8
Uganda's republic status ratified

1967, Oct. 4
Nigerian forces captured Biafran capital of Enugu

1967, Oct.
Umuahia became capital of Biafra

1967, Oct. 19
UAR resumed diplomatic relations with Britain

1967, Nov. 4
Katanga rebellion ended

1967, Nov. 28
Omar Bongo became president of Gabon

1967, Dec. 15
Attempted coup in Algeria

1967, Dec. 17
Bloodless coup in Dahomey
1968
Gatsha Buthelezi became regent
of the Zulus
1968, Jan. 1
Guinea. President Touré re-
elected
1968, Jan. 30
Egypt and Israel exchanged fire
across Suez Canal
1968, Jan. 31
Kenya and Somalia resumed
diplomatic relations
1968, Feb. 19
South Africa. Jim Fouché elected
president
1968, Feb. 25
Senegal. Senghor re-elected
president
1968, March 12
Mauritius. Independence from
Britain
1968, April 10
Fouché sworn in as president of
South Africa
1968, April 10
Algeria and Mali resumed diplomatic ties with UK
1968, April 10
Mauritania & Congo resumed
diplomatic ties with UK
1968, April 13
Tanzania recognized Biafra as a
state
1968, April 18
Sierra Leone coup toppled the
Army from power
1968, April 24
Mauritius became UN mem-
ber
1968, May 6
Nigeria-Biafra peace talks began
in London
1968, May 7
Tunisia broke off diplomatic relations with Syria
1968, May 18
Nigerians captured Port Har-
court from Biafrans
1968, May 23
Nigeria-Biafra peace talks began
in Kampala
1968, May 31
Biafra withdrew from Kampala
peace talks
1968, June 12
South West Africa renamed Namibia
1968, June 23

UAR and Israeli forces clashed at
Ismailia
1968, July 17
Rhodesia agreed to become a republic in the future
1968, July 17
Dahomey returned to civilian
rule after 2 years
1968, July 19
Nigeria & Biafra agreed to Addis
Ababa peace talks
1968, Aug. 9
Biafra rejected Nigerian peace
proposals
1968, Aug. 10
Nigeria fired on relief planes to
Biafra
1968, Aug. 13
Nigeria rejected Biafran peace
counter-proposals
1968, Aug. 15
Nigeria refused Red Cross effort
to relief Biafrans
1968, Sept. 4
President Massemba-Débat of
Congo forced to resign
1968, Sept. 6
Swaziland. Independence. UK's
last African colony
1968, Sept. 16
Nigerians captured Biafran town
of Owerri
1968, Sept. 24
Swaziland became UN mem-
ber
1968, Sept. 29
Spanish Guinea. Macías
Nguema elected president
1968, Oct. 2
Ovamboland created as a bantustan
1968, Oct. 12
Equatorial Guinea. Independence from Spain
1968, Oct. 12
Biyogo became president of
Equatorial Guinea
1968, Oct. 13
Harold Wilson and Ian Smith
met on the "Fearless"
1968, Oct. 26
UAR and Israeli forces clashed
along Suez Canal
1968, Nov. 11
New flag replaced Union Jack in
Rhodesia
1968, Nov. 12
Equatorial Guinea became UN
member
1968, Nov. 13

Nigeria agreed on Biafran relief
from UN
1968, Nov. 16
British-Rhodesian talks failed
1968, Nov. 19
Army under Moussa Traoré took
over in Mali coup
1968, Nov. 24
UAR closed all its universities to
stop rioting
1968, Dec. 2
UN condemned South Africa
over apartheid
1968, Dec. 24
Nigeria rejected Christmas truce
with Biafra
1969, Jan. 1
Marien Ngouabi became president of Congo
1969, Jan. 1
Biafra called for a limited truce
1969, Jan. 4
Ifni given back to Morocco
1969, Jan. 29
Nigeria launched a final offensive against Biafra
1969, Feb. 1
Red Cross airlifts to starving Biafrans resumed
1969, Feb. 3
FRELIMO leader Mondlane assassinated in Tanzania
1969, Feb.
Samora Machel became new
head of FRELIMO
1969, March
Nile Provisional Government
formed in the Sudan
1969, March 3
State of emergency in Equatorial
Guinea
1969, March 3
Biafrans encircled Owerri in
counter-offensive
1969, March 13
Nigeria rejected Biafran truce
1969, April 23
Umuahia, Biafran HQ, taken by
Nigerian forces
1969, May 22
Biafran planes raided Port Har-
court
1969, May 25
Ja'far an-Numayri came to
power in the Sudan
1969, June 20
Rhodesia declared a republic
1969, June 24
Clifford Dupont became acting
president of Rhodesia

1969, June 30
Ifni formally handed back to Morocco

1969, July 5
Tom Mboya, Kenyan economic minister, assassinated

1969, July 7
Open warfare resumed on Suez Canal

1969, July 20
Israeli jets bombed UAR installations on Suez Canal

1969, July 24
Israeli and UAR forces clashed in major battle

1969, Aug. 1
The Pope hosted Nigeria-Biafra talks in Uganda

1969, Aug. 11
Zambia planned to nationalize the copper industry

1969, Aug. 25
State of emergency declared in Zambia

1969, Aug. 28
Nnamdi Azikiwe withdrew support of Biafra secession

1969, Sept. 1
Qadaffi came to power in Libyan coup

1969, Sept. 11
Israel shot down 11 UAR planes

1969, Sept. 19
Moussa Traoré became president of Mali

1969, Oct. 15
President Shermarke of Somalia assassinated

1969, Oct. 21
Somalia coup; country renamed Democratic Republic

1969, Oct. 21
Muhammad Siyad Barre came to power in Somalia

1969, Oct. 22
UAR planes attacked Israel in the Sinai

1969, Nov. 8
UAR Navy shelled Israeli posts in the Sinai

1969, Dec. 3
Major Nigerian offensive against Biafra

1969, Dec. 10
Dahomey coup

1969, Dec. 19
President Obote of Uganda shot in Kampala

1970

Sultanate re-established in Baguirmi

1970
Seychelles achieved more autonomy

1970
James Mancham became chief minister of Seychelles

1970, Jan. 1
Former French Congo now People's Republic of Congo

1970, Jan. 2
Nigeria cut Biafra into three sections

1970, Jan. 3
Zambian guerrillas raided Rhodesia

1970, Jan. 10
Owerri, new Biafran HQ, taken by Nigerian forces

1970, Jan. 12
Biafra surrendered

1970, Jan. 15
Biafran War formally over

1970, Jan. 18
Israeli jets bombed military targets near Cairo

1970, Jan. 30
UN condemned South African presence in SW Africa

1970, Jan. 30
State of emergency declared in Lesotho

1970, Feb. 28
Abdou Diouf became PM of Senegal

1970, March 2
Republic of Rhodesia became effective

1970, March 18
UN condemned Rhodesia

1970, March 31
King Moshoeshoe II of Lesotho ordered into exile

1970, April 14
Clifford Dupont became first president of Rhodesia

1970, April 16
Clifford Dupont sworn in as president of Rhodesia

1970, April 23
Gambia became a republic

1970, April 24
Dawda Jawara became first president of Gambia

1970, May 1
Uganda nationalized its banks

1970, May 7
Hubert Maga became president of Dahomey again

1970, May 15
South Africa expelled from the Olympic Games

1970, June 20
Mahmoud Fawzi became PM of Egypt

1970, July
Failed coup in Libya

1970, July 23
UAR agreed to cease fire in Middle East war

1970, July 24
Morocco ended 5-year state of emergency

1970, July 30
Israel shot down four UAR planes over Suez Canal

1970, July 31
Israel agreed to cease fire in Middle East war

1970, Aug. 7
90-day truce went into effect on Suez Canal

1970, Aug. 31
Edward Akufo-Addo became president of Ghana

1970, Sept. 15
UAR declared an end to the truce in the Middle East

1970, Sept. 28
President Nasser of Egypt died of a heart attack

1970, Sept. 29
Anwar as-Sadat became interim president of Egypt

1970, Oct. 1
President Diori of Niger re-elected

1970, Oct. 15
Anwar as-Sadat became president of Egypt

1970, Oct. 31
President Nyerere of Tanzania re-elected

1970, Nov.
Exiles and mercenaries invaded Guinea

1970, Nov. 29
Ivory Coast president Houphouët-Boigny re-elected

1970, Dec. 4
Moshoeshoe II of Lesotho ended exile in Netherlands

1970, Dec. 15
The two Congos resumed diplomatic ties

1970, Dec. 16
State of emergency declared in parts of Eritrea

1971, Jan. 5

UAR resumed peace talks with Israel

1971, Jan. 25
Idi Amin came to power in Uganda after a coup

1971, Jan. 27
South Africa agreed to plebiscite for SW Africa

1971, Feb. 20
Idi Amin became president of Uganda

1971, Feb. 24
Tunisia and Spain agreed to resume diplomatic ties

1971, March 5
UN urged Israel to withdraw from occupied territory

1971, March 22
Unsuccessful coup in Sierra Leone

1971, March 30
South Africa agreed to talks with black leaders

1971, April 19
Sierra Leone became a republic

1971, April 19
Christopher O. Cole acting Sierra Leone president

1971, April 21
Siaka Stevens became president of Sierra Leone

1971, May 13
Unsuccessful coup in Egypt

1971, July 6
Hastings Banda became President for Life in Malawi

1971, July 10
Unsuccessful coup in Morocco

1971, July 19
Coup in the Sudan

1971, July 22
Ja'far an-Numayri became president of the Sudan

1971, July 23
William Tolbert became president of Liberia

1971, Aug. 24
Border clashes between Uganda and Tanzania

1971, Aug. 27
Unsuccessful coup in Chad

1971, Aug. 27
Chad broke off diplomatic relations with Libya

1971, Sept. 2
U.A.R. became Arab Republic of Egypt

1971, Sept. 18
Egyptian and Israeli rocket fire over Suez Canal

1971, Oct. 21
Congo (Kinshasa) became Zaire

1971, Nov. 23
Rhodesian independence agreed by Britain

1972, Jan. 3
William Tolbert inaugurated as Liberian president

1972, Jan. 12
Mobutu changed his name to Mobutu Sese Seko

1972, Jan. 13
Ghana PM Kofi Busia deposed in coup

1972, Jan. 17
Aziz Sidqi became PM of Egypt

1972, Feb. 4
Kenneth Kaunda banned all rival parties in Zambia

1972, Feb. 22
Bokassa became president for life of C.A.R.

1972, March
East Caprivi created as a bantustan

1972, March 28
President Jawara of Gambia re-elected

1972, March 30
Idi Amin closed Israeli embassy in Kampala

1972, April 1
KwaZulu created

1972, April 1
Gatsha Buthelezi became chief minister of KwaZulu

1972, April 6
Egypt broke off diplomatic relations with Jordan

1972, April 7
Sheikh Abeid Amani Karume of Zanzibar assassinated

1972, April 12
Chad and Libya resumed diplomatic relations

1972, April 26
Louis Lansana Béavogui became PM in Guinea

1972, April 29
Burundi failed coup marked start of Hutu Rebellion

1972, May 18
Soviet-backed coup in Malagasy

1972, May 18
Gabriel Ramanantsoa came to power in Malagasy

1972, June 1
Bophuthatswana became self-governing

1972, June 2

Cameroun became United Republic of Cameroun

1972, June 13
Air battle between Israel and Egypt

1972, July 14
Biyogo president for life in Equatorial Guinea

1972, July 23
Qadaffi proposed merger of Egypt and Libya

1972, July 26
Israel made peace offer to Egypt

1972, July 27
Egypt rejected Israeli peace offer

1972, July 31
Bokassa supervised fatal beatings of jail inmates

1972, Aug. 1
Ciskei achieved self-rule

1972, Aug. 2
Libya and Egypt agreed to unite politically

1972, Aug. 5
Amin began expulsion of British-passported Asians

1972, Aug. 16
Hassan of Morocco narrowly avoided assassination

1972, Aug. 17
Moroccan Defense Minister Oufkir committed suicide

1972, Aug. 22
Rhodesia banned from the Olympic Games

1972, Sept. 17
War broke out between Tanzania and Uganda

1972, Sept. 18
First Asians actually expelled from Uganda

1972, Oct. 2
Lebowa achieved self-government

1972, Oct. 5
Peace treaty between Uganda and Tanzania

1972, Oct. 10
Kavangoland created as a bantustan

1972, Oct. 26
Dahomey coup ousted Ahomadegbé

1972, Oct. 27
Mathieu Kérékou became president of Dahomey

1972, Dec. 26
Ahmad Abdallah became PM of the Comoros

1973

End of Hutu Rebellion in Burundi
1973
Local government set up in São Tomé
1973
Huge phosphate deposit found in Spanish Sahara
1973
POLISARIO founded
1973
Severe drought in Northwest Africa
1973
Bathurst became Banjul
1973, Jan. 9
Rhodesia closed its border with Zambia
1973, Feb. 1
GazaNkulu achieved self-government
1973, Feb. 1
Venda achieved self-government
1973, Feb. 21
Israel shot down a Libyan commercial jet over Cairo
1973, Feb. 26
Rhodesia suspended postal service with Zambia
1973, March 1
Civil War broke out in Rwanda
1973, March 21
Libyan fighter planes attacked unarmed US plane
1973, March 26
Aziz Sidqi resigned as Egyptian PM under pressure
1973, May 1
Ovamboland achieved self-rule
1973, May 22
South Africa granted blacks limited right to strike
1973, May 28
Tanzania and Uganda signed new peace treaty
1973, July 5
Juvenal Habyarimana came to power in Rwanda coup
1973, July 6
Amin detained 112 Peace Corps workers in Entebbe
1973, July 9
Egypt-Libya merger talks failed
1973, Aug. 28
Mainza Chona became PM of Zambia
1973, Aug. 29
Egyptian-Libyan Union agreement signed
1973, Sept. 1

Egyptian-Libyan Union never went into effect
1973, Sept. 6
Fort Lamy became N'Djamena
1973, Sept. 12
Egypt and Jordan resumed diplomatic relations
1973, Sept. 16
50,000 dead announced in Ethiopian famine
1973, Sept. 24
Portuguese Guinea became Guinea-Bissau
1973, Sept. 26
Luis de Almeida Cabral president of Guinea-Bissau
1973, Oct. 6
The October War began between Egypt and Israel
1973, Oct. 8
Egypt claimed east bank of Suez Canal
1973, Oct. 15
Heavy fighting on west bank of Suez Canal
1973, Oct. 23
Full-scale war between Egypt and Israel
1973, Oct. 23
Ethiopia broke off diplomatic relations with Israel
1973, Oct. 28
Possible 100,000 reported dead in Ethiopian famine
1973, Nov. 7
Egypt and USA resumed diplomatic relations
1973, Nov. 8
USA closed its embassy in Uganda
1973, Nov. 11
Egypt and Israel signed cease fire agreement
1973, Dec. 1
Libya closed its embassy in Cairo
1973, Dec. 5
President Kaunda of Zambia reelected
1974
Dahomey became a Communist country
1974, Jan. 25
Israel pulled out from the Suez Canal zone
1974, Feb. 26
Army mutiny in Ethiopia
1974, April 15
Hamani Diori ousted in Niger coup
1974, April 17

Seyni Kountché came to power in Niger
1974, Aug. 26
Portugal agreed to Portuguese Guinea independence
1974, Sept. 10
Portuguese Guinea. Independence as Guinea-Bissau
1974, Sept. 12
Haile Selassie deposed in Ethiopia
1974, Sept. 20
FRELIMO began administration in Mozambique
1974, Sept. 20
Joaquim Chissanó became PM in Mozambique
1974, Sept. 25
Abdul Aziz Hegazy became PM of Egypt
1974, Sept. 30
Portugal agreed on Mozambique independence
1974, Nov. 1
QwaQwa achieved self-government
1974, Nov. 28
Teferi Benti came to power in Ethiopia
1974, Dec. 21
São Tomé and Príncipe achieved autonomy
1974, Dec. 22
Comoros voted on independence from France
1974, Dec. 22
Mayotte voted to remain French
1974, Dec. 30
Ruling council in power in Cape Verde
1974, Dec. 31
Cape Verde achieved self-rule
1975, Jan. 1
Lilongwe became the capital of Malawi
1975, Jan. 2
Élisabeth Domitienne first woman PM in Africa
1975, Jan. 31
Transitional government replaced Portugal in Angola
1975, Jan. 31
Eritrean rebels attacked military installations
1975, Feb. 5
Richard Ratsimandrava became Malagasy president
1975, Feb. 6
1200 Eritreans reported dead in Asmara in one week

1975, Feb. 11
Malagasy president Ratsimandrava assassinated

1975, Feb. 11
South African PM John Vorster
visited Liberia

1975, Feb. 15
State of emergency declared in
northern Eritrea

1975, Feb. 21
War broke out between Ethiopia
and Eritrean rebels

1975, March
Ethiopian monarchy abolished

1975, March 18
Habib Bourguiba became Tunisian president for life

1975, April 13
President Tombalbaye assassinated in Chad coup

1975, April 13
Mamdouh Salem became PM of
Egypt

1975, April 15
Félix Malloum came to power in
Chad

1975, April 16
Léon Mébiame became PM of
Gabon

1975, April 19
Nicolaas Diederichs new president of South Africa

1975, June 5
The Suez Canal re-opened after
8 years

1975, June 15
Didier Ratsiraka came to power
in Malagasy

1975, June 21
Angolan rival liberation groups
agreed to ceasefire

1975, June 25
Mozambique.   Independence
from Portugal

1975, June 25
Samora Machel became president of Mozambique

1975, June 30
Paul Biya became PM of Cameroun

1975, July 5
Cape Verde. Independence from
Portugal

1975, July 6
Comoros. Unilateral independence from France

1975, July 7
Ahmad Abdallah became first
president of Comoros

1975, July 8

Aristides Pereira became president of Cape Verde

1975, July 9
Angolan rival groups began civil
war again

1975, July 12
São Tomé. Independence from
Portugal

1975, July 12
Manuel Pinto da Costa became
São Tomé president

1975, July 12
Miguel Trovoada became PM of
São Tomé

1975, July 15
Pedro Pires became PM of Cape
Verde

1975, July 29
Gen. Gowon deposed in bloodless Nigeria coup

1975, Aug. 3
Ali Soilih took power in Comoros coup

1975, Aug. 14
Portugal resumed control in Angola

1975, Aug. 27
Haile Selassie died in Addis Ababa

1975, Sept. 4
Peace treaty signed between
Egypt and Israel

1975, Sept. 5
Failed coup in the Sudan

1975, Oct. 1
Seychelles became self-governing

1975, Oct. 1
James Mancham became first
PM of Seychelles

1975, Nov. 6
The Green March in Spanish Sahara

1975, Nov. 9
The Green March ended in failure

1975, Nov. 11
Angola. Independence from Portugal

1975, Nov. 11
Antonio Agostinho Neto became
president of Angola

1975, Nov. 14
Spanish Sahara now Spanish,
Moroccan & Mauritanian

1975, Nov. 30
Dahomey renamed Benin

1975, Dec. 4
Dahomey became Benin

1975, Dec. 13
Louis-Sylvain Ngoma became
PM of Congo

1975, Dec. 21
Malagasy now Democratic Republic of Madagascar

1975, Dec. 21
Didier Ratsiraka became president of Madagascar

1976
Saharan Arab Democratic Republic created

1976, Jan. 3
Ali Soilih became president of
the Comoros

1976, Jan. 5
Libya became Libyan Arab People's Republic

1976, Jan. 14
John Wrathall became president
of Rhodesia

1976, Feb. 3
Lourenço   Marques   renamed
Maputo

1976, Feb. 9
Mayotte vote made it overseas
department of France

1976, Feb. 13
Olusegun Obasanjo came to
power in Nigeria

1976, Feb. 26
Mauritania took southern Spanish Sahara

1976, Feb. 28
Spain finally evacuated Spanish
Sahara

1976, April 7
Bokassa   proclaimed   himself
marshal of the C.A.R.

1976, April 14
Morocco and Mauritania divided Spanish Sahara

1976, June 16
Soweto uprisings in South Africa

1976, June 25
Idi Amin became president for
life in Uganda

1976, June 29
Seychelles. Independence from
Britain

1976, June 29
James Mancham became first
president of Seychelles

1976, June 29
France-Albert René became PM
of Seychelles

1976, Oct. 26
Transkei achieved "independence"

1976, Nov. 9
Jean-Baptiste Bagaza took power
in Burundi

1976, Dec. 4

C.A.R. now Central African Empire (Emperor Bokassa)

1976, Dec. 8
Ange-Félix Patassé became PM of the C.A.R.

1977
KwaZulu became self-governing

1977, Jan. 17
Major riots in Cairo over price increases

1977, Jan. 17
Catholic schools in South Africa defied color bar

1977, Feb. 3
Teferi Benti shot and killed in Ethiopia

1977, Feb. 11
Mengistu Haile Mariam came to power in Ethiopia

1977, March 2
Libya became the Libyan Arab Jamahiriyya

1977, March 18
Congo president Ngouabi assassinated

1977, March 27
Canary islands air disaster worst in history

1977, April 1
Failed coup in Chad

1977, May 19
Kenya banned big-game hunting

1977, June 5
Seychelles coup brought F-A. René to power

1977, June 24
Hassan Gouled Aptidon president of Afars & Issas

1977, June 27
Afars & Issas. Independence from France as Djibouti

1977, July 21
Start of four-day Libyan war with Egypt

1977, Aug.
Walvis Bay incorporated into South Africa

1977, Sept. 12
Steve Biko, black leader, died in S. African jail

1977, Sept. 15
1200 blacks arrested in S. Africa over Biko death

1977, Sept. 25
Steve Biko's funeral in South Africa

1977, Sept. 20
Djibouti became a member of the UN

1977, Sept. 20
Idi Amin banned most Christian churches from Uganda

1977, Oct.
KwaNdebele achieved self-government

1977, Nov. 9
Major permanent Egypt-Israel peace initiatives

1977, Nov. 13
Somalia expelled Soviets and Cubans

1977, Nov. 20
Sadat of Egypt addressed the Knesset in Israel

1977, Nov. 24
Ian Smith offered black suffrage in Rhodesia

1977, Dec. 4
Bokassa was crowned emperor in the C.A.R.

1977, Dec. 6
Bophuthatswana. "Independence" from South Africa

1977, Dec. 6
Lucas Mangope became president of Bophuthatswana

1978
KaNgwane given a legislative assembly

1978
Sierra Leone introduced a one-party system

1978, Jan. 26
State of emergency declared in Tunisia

1978, Feb. 15
Ian Smith agreed to black rule in Rhodesia

1978, March 15
Somalia withdrew last of its troops from Ethiopia

1978, March 21
New transitional government formed in Rhodesia

1978, March 24
Ethiopia crushed the Eritrean rebels

1978, April 25
South Africa agreed to Namibian independence

1978, May 4
South African forces raided Angola

1978, May 11
Civil War began in Zaire

1978, May 13
Coup in Comoros led by French mercenaries

1978, July 10

Mokhtar Ould Daddah toppled in Mauritania coup

1978, Aug. 22
Jomo Kenyatta died in Kenya

1978, Aug. 22
Daniel arap Moi became president of Kenya

1978, Aug. 29
Hissène Habré became PM of Chad

1978, Sept. 10
Parts of Rhodesia placed under martial law

1978, Sept. 17
Camp David meeting on Middle East a success

1978, Sept. 20
Rhodesia raided guerrilla bases in Mozambique

1978, Sept. 20
John Vorster resigned as South African PM

1978, Sept. 21
12-year old state of emergency in Nigeria ended

1978, Sept. 28
Piet Botha became PM of South Africa

1978, Sept. 29
John Vorster became president of South Africa

1978, Sept. 30
Barket Gourad Hamadou became PM of Djibouti

1978, Oct. 2
Mustafa Khalil became PM of Egypt

1978, Oct. 10
Racial segregation ended in Rhodesia

1978, Oct. 12
Clash between Uganda and Tanzania

1978, Oct. 14
Daniel arap Moi sworn in as Kenyan president

1978, Oct. 22
Ahmad Abdallah became president of Comoros again

1978, Nov. 2
Jack Pithey became acting president of Rhodesia

1978, Dec. 27
President Boumédienne of Algeria died

1979, Feb. 8
Denis Sassou-Nguesso interim president of Congo

1979, Feb. 9
Chadli Bendjedid became presi-

dent of Algeria

1979, March
Egypt regained the Sinai

1979, March 15
Civil War ended in Chad

1979, March 23
Goukouni Oueddi came to power in Chad

1979, March 31
Denis Sassou-Nguesso became president of Congo

1979, April 11
Idi Amin forced from power in Uganda

1979, April 13
Yusufu Lule became president of Uganda

1979, April 14
Food price riots in Liberia

1979, April 18
Bokassa executed over 100 children

1979, April 21
Abel Muzorewa won first free election in Rhodesia

1979, April 21
Rhodesia became Zimbabwe-Rhodesia

1979, April 30
UN condemned election in Rhodesia

1979, May 23
Josiah Gumede became president of Zimbabwe-Rhodesia

1979, May 29
Abel Muzorewa became PM of Zimbabwe-Rhodesia

1979, May 31
First black government in Rhodesia began

1979, June 4
John Vorster resigned as South African president

1979, June 5
Jerry Rawlings came to power in Ghana

1979, June 16
Acheampong, former head of state, executed in Ghana

1979, June 19
Marais Viljoen became president of South Africa

1979, June 20
President Lule forced from office in Uganda

1979, June 20
Godfrey Binaisa became president of Uganda

1979, June 26
Two more former heads of state

executed in Ghana

1979, July 4
ben Bella released from 14-year custody in Algiers

1979, Aug. 3
Equatorial Guinea. Biyogo toppled in coup

1979, Aug. 5
Mauritania withdrew from Western Sahara

1979, Aug. 11
Morocco seized Western Sahara

1979, Sept. 13
Venda achieved "independence" from South Africa

1979, Sept. 13
Patrick Mphephu became first president of Venda

1979, Sept. 20
Coup in C.A.R.

1979, Sept. 21
Bokassa went into exile in the Ivory Coast

1979, Sept. 21
David Dacko became president of C.A.R. again

1979, Sept. 21
José Eduardo dos Santos became president of Angola

1979, Sept. 29
Former Equatorial Guinea president Biyogo executed

1979, Oct. 1
Alhajji Shehu Shagari became president of Nigeria

1979, Oct. 11
Equatorial Guinea. Teodoro Obiang new president

1979, Oct.
Miguel Trovoada toppled and arrested in São Tomé

1979, Oct. 10
Mbasogo became president of Equatorial Guinea

1979, Dec. 11
UDI terminated and Britain took power in Rhodesia

1979, Dec. 12
British governor-general arrived in Zimbabwe

1979, Dec. 12
Britain lifted trade sanctions against Rhodesia

1979, Dec. 21
Peace treaty signed by all concerned with Rhodesia

1980, Jan. 4
Muhammad Ould Haidalla became Mauritania president

1980, Jan. 13

Joshua Nkomo returned to Zimbabwe from exile

1980, Jan. 27
Robert Mugabe returned to Zimbabwe from exile

1980, Feb. 4
French embassy burned in Libya

1980, March 4
Canaan Banana became president of Zimbabwe

1980, March 4
Robert Mugabe became PM of Zimbabwe

1980, March 21
Civil War broke out in Chad

1980, April 12
William Tolbert toppled and killed in Liberia coup

1980, April 12
Samuel Doe came to power in Liberia

1980, April 18
Zimbabwe-Rhodesia became Zimbabwe

1980, April 18
Banana and Mugabe sworn in in Zimbabwe

1980, May 12
The Army took over Uganda

1980, June
Libyan troops entered Chad

1980, July
Ovamboland finished as a bantustan

1980, July 13
Seretse Khama of Botswana died

1980, July 18
Quett Masire sworn in as president of Botswana

1980, Aug. 25
Zimbabwe became the 153rd member of the UN

1980, Sept. 17
Milton Obote became president of Uganda again

1980, Oct. 10
Two massive earthquakes hit al-Asnam, Algeria

1980, Oct. 26
President Nyerere re-elected in Tanzania

1980, Oct. 28
Saudi Arabia severed diplomatic ties with Libya

1980, Nov. 14
João Vieira came to power after Guinea-Bissau coup

1980, Nov. 14
Cape Verde–Guinea-Bissau unification plans canceled

1980, Nov. 25
Saye Zerbo came to power after coup in Upper Volta
1980, Dec.
Bokassa sentenced to death in absentia in C.A.R.
1980, Dec. 12
Libyan troops became active in Chad Civil War
1981
Miguel Trovoada exiled to Lisbon from São Tomé
1981
Salisbury renamed Harare
1981, Jan. 1
Senegal PM Abdou Diouf became president
1981, March 15
President Dacko re-elected in C.A.R.
1981, March 15
Failed coup in Mauritania
1981, April
KaNgwane achieved self-rule
1981, Aug. 24
South Africa raided Angola
1981, Aug. 28
South Africa pulled out of Angola
1981, Sept. 1
Bloodless coup in the C.A.R. led by André Kolingba
1981, Oct. 6
Sadat assassinated in Cairo
1981, Oct. 7
Hosni Mubarrak became PM of Egypt
1981, Oct. 10
Sufi Abu Talib became acting president of Egypt
1981, Oct. 10
Sadat's funeral in Cairo
1981, Oct. 13
Hosni Mubarrak became president of Egypt
1981, Nov.
Libyan troops left Chad
1981, Nov. 25
Failed coup in the Seychelles
1981, Dec. 4
Ciskei. "Independence" from South Africa
1981, Dec. 4
Lennox Sebe became first president of Ciskei
1981, Dec. 17
Senegambia Confederation agreed upon
1981, Dec. 31
Coup in Ghana

1982, Jan. 2
Ahmad Fuad Mohieddin became PM of Egypt
1982, Feb. 1
Senegambia Confederation came into being
1982, Feb. 1
Abdou Diouf president of Senegambia Confederation
1982, Feb. 17
Joshua Nkomo relieved of Cabinet post in Zimbabwe
1982, Feb. 23
Uganda Freedom Movement attacked Kampala
1982, March 14
Ugandan government crackdown on rebels began
1982, April 7
Ugandan government arrested 10,000 rebel suspects
1982, April 10
Ugandans arrested 1,000 more rebel suspects
1982, April 15
The assassins of Sadat were executed
1982, April 25
Egypt ceremonially took control of eastern Sinai
1982, April 30
P.W. Botha and Kenneth Kaunda met for talks
1982, June
Rebel forces entered Chad
1982, June 7
Hissène Habré came to power in Chad coup
1982, June
Unsuccessful plan to merge KaNgwane with Swaziland
1982, June 11
Aneerood Jugnauth became PM of Mauritius
1982, June 19
Hissène Habré became head of state of Chad
1982, Aug.
Equatorial Guinea. New constitution
1982, Aug. 1
Failed coup in Kenya by members of the Air Force
1982, Aug. 15
Equatorial Guinea. New PM, Cristino Seriche Bioko
1982, Aug. 21
Kenyan government dismissed entire Air Force
1982, Oct. 21

Hissène Habré became president of Chad
1982, Nov. 6
Paul Biya became president of Cameroun
1982, Nov. 23
Ghana suppressed a rebellion
1983, Jan. 10
Thomas Sankara became PM of Upper Volta after coup
1983, Jan. 16
Libya and Saudi Arabia resumed diplomatic relations
1983, Jan. 17
Nigeria expelled 2 million illegal aliens
1983, Jan. 18
South Africa reasserted direct control over Namibia
1983, March 9
Joshua Nkomo fled Zimbabwe for his life
1983, March 17
Chad asked for UN help over Libya border dispute
1983, May 8
Canary Islands became autonomous province
1983, May 17
Thomas Sankara, PM of Niger, arrested in purge
1983, Aug. 4
Thomas Sankara came to power in Upper Volta coup
1983, Aug. 6
President Shagari of Nigeria re-elected
1983, Aug. 10
Chad rebels took town of Faya-Largeau
1983, Aug. 16
Joshua Nkomo returned to Zimbabwe from London exile
1983, Aug. 17
Joshua Nkomo resumed seat in Zimbabwe parliament
1983, Oct. 6
Failed coup in Niger
1983, Nov. 2
Coloreds & Asians given limited rights in S. Africa
1983, Dec. 31
President Shagari deposed in bloodless Nigeria coup
1984, Jan
Riots in Morocco over food price increases
1984, Jan. 3
State of emergency declared in Tunisia after riots

1984, Jan. 21
Cameroun now Republic of Cameroun
1984, Feb. 11
Gross corruption exposed in Nigeria
1984, March 2
Major inter-tribal warfare in Nigeria
1984, March 26
President Sékou Touré of Guinea died
1984, April
Cyclone Kamisey wreaked havoc in Madagascar
1984, April 3
Lansana Conté came to power in Guinea after coup
1984, April 5
Lansana Conté became president of Guinea
1984, April 6
Failed coup in Cameroun
1984, April 17
Nigerian government repressed the press
1984, April 29
State of emergency declared in the Sudan
1984, May 8
Failed coup in Libya
1984, June 5
Kamal Hassan Ali became acting PM of Egypt
1984, July 5
Britain expelled Nigerian diplomats
1984, July 7
Egypt and USSR resumed diplomatic relations
1984, July 17
Kamal Hassan Ali became PM of Egypt
1984, July 26
Liberia restored political freedoms
1984, Aug. 5
Upper Volta became Burkina Faso
1984, Aug. 11
Ange-Édouard Poungui became PM of Congo
1984, Sept. 5
Madagascar banned practice of martial arts
1984, Sept. 10
Ethiopia became Communist
1984, Sept. 14
Piet Botha became president of South Africa

1984, Nov. 5
1st mass anti-apartheid demonstration in S. Africa
1984, Dec. 12
Coup in Mauritania ousted President Haidalla
1985, Feb. 10
Nelson Mandela refused freedom from imprisonment
1985, March 8
Failed coup in the Comoros
1985, April 6
Coup in the Sudan ousted Numayri
1985, April 9
Transitional military council set up in the Sudan
1985, July 4
Failed coup in Guinea
1985, July 8
Egypt banned religious bumper stickers
1985, July 20
State of emergency declared in South Africa
1985, July 27
The Army took over Uganda again in coup
1985, Aug. 30
Ibrahim Babangida became president of Nigeria
1985, Sept.
Ivory Coast became Côte d'Ivoire
1985, Sept. 4
Ali Lutfi became PM of Egypt
1985, Sept. 26
Tunisia severed diplomatic ties with Libya
1985, Nov.
Unsuccessful coup in Liberia
1985, Nov. 5
Julius Nyerere resigned in Tanzania
1985, Nov. 5
Ali Hassan Mwinyi new president of Tanzania
1985, Nov. 28
Joseph Saidu Momoh became president of Sierra Leone
1985, Dec. 15
Sudan became the Republic of the Sudan
1985, Dec. 19
Failed coup in Nigeria
1985, Dec. 24
Zulu-Pondo clash near Durban
1986
Burkina Faso declared a Muslim republic
1986, Jan. 6

Samuel Doe became president of Liberia
1986, Jan. 20
Chief Leabua Jonathan deposed in Lesotho coup
1986, Jan. 23
Zulu-Pondos tribal conflict renewed near Durban
1986, Jan. 24
Justin Lekhanya came to power in Lesotho
1986, Jan
South Africa imposed a blockade on Lesotho
1986, Jan. 13
President Pereira of Cape Verde re-elected
1986, Jan. 29
Yoweri Museveni took power in Uganda
1986, Feb. 25
Military police rioted in Cairo
1986, March 7
State of emergency ended in South Africa
1986, March 24
Libyan and US forces clashed over Gulf of Sidra
1986, April 14
US planes bombed Libya
1986, April 25
Mswati III became king of Swaziland
1986, June 12
State of emergency declared in South Africa
1986, July
Equatorial Guinea. Unsuccessful coup attempt
1986, Aug. 26
Volcanic toxic gas disaster in Cameroun
1986, Sept. 23
Failed coup in Togo
1986, Sept. 30
Djibouti and Egypt resumed diplomatic relations
1986, Oct. 23
Bokassa returned to the C.A.R.
1986, Oct. 19
Joaquim Chissanó became president of Mozambique
1986, Nov. 9
President Bongo of Congo re-elected
1986, Nov. 12
Atif Sidqi became PM of Egypt
1987, March
Libyan forces finally forced out of Chad

1987, May 14
Egypt broke off diplomatic relations with Iran

1987, May 19
Australia expelled Libyan diplomats

1987, Aug. 30
Black African miners strike ended unsuccessfully

1987, Sept. 3
Pierre Buyoya took power in Burundi coup

1987, Sept. 10
Ethiopia became the People's Democratic Republic

1987, Sept. 10
Mengistu Haile Mariam became president of Ethiopia

1987, Sept. 18
5 Ethiopian regions (inc. Eritrea) gained autonomy

1987, Sept. 24
Gen. Bantu Holomisa came to power in Transkei

1987, Oct. 15
Blaise Campaoré came to power in Burkina Faso coup

1987, Nov. 7
Habib Bourguiba deposed in Tunisia

1987, Nov. 7
Zine ben Ali became president of Tunisia

1987, Nov. 10
President Kountché of Niger died

1987, Nov. 10
Ali Seibou became president of Niger

1987, Dec. 31
Robert Mugabe became executive president of Zimbabwe

1988, Feb.
Bokassa's death sentence commuted to life in prison

1988, Feb. 10
Lucas Mangope president of Bophuthatswana again

1988, Dec. 22
South Africa agreed on Namibian independence

1989
Civil War began in Liberia

1989, June 30
Umar al-Bashir came to power in the Sudan

1989, Aug. 15
F.W. deKlerk became president of South Africa

1989, Sept.

Senegambia Confederation came to an end

1989, Nov. 26
Sa'id Muhammad Djohar became president of Comoros

1990
Beginning of five-year Tuareg revolt in Niger

1990, Feb. 11
Nelson Mandela freed from prison after 27 years

1990, March 21
Namibia. Independence from South Africa

1990, March 21
Sam Nujoma became first president of Namibia

1990, Sept. 9
Samuel Doe ousted and killed in Liberia

1990, Nov. 12
Letsie III became king of Lesotho

1990, Nov. 22
Amos Sawyer became president of Liberia

1990, Nov. 30
Mozambique abandoned Communism

1990, Dec. 2
Chad coup

1991, Jan. 8
Louis-Sylvain Ngoma became PM of Congo again

1991, Jan. 28
Carlos Veiga became PM of Cape Verde

1991, Feb.
People's Republic of Congo became Republic of Congo

1991, March
First free elections in Benin in 30 years

1991, March 22
Antonio Mascarenhas Monteiro Cape Verde president

1991, March 26
Moussa Traoré ousted in Mali coup

1991, April 3
Miguel Trovoada became the president of São Tomé

1991, May 18
Somaliland Republic declared

1991, May 21
Mengistu Haile Mariam toppled in Ethiopia

1991, May 27
Meles Zenawi provisional president of Ethiopia

1991, May 29

Provisional government formed in Eritrea

1991, July 21
Meles Zenawi became president of Ethiopia

1991, Nov. 2
Kenneth Kaunda lost power in Zambia

1991, Nov. 2
Frederick Chiluba became new president of Zambia

1991, Dec. 12
Abuja replaced Lagos as capital of Nigeria

1991, Dec.
Unsuccessful invasion of Chad by rebels

1992
Tanzanian multi-party elections held for first time

1992, March 12
Mauritius became a republic

1992, April 29
Valentine Strasser came to power in Sierra Leone

1992, June 8
Alpha Oumar Konaré became president of Mali

1992, July
UN declared Somalia a country without a government

1992, Aug. 7
Truce signed between Mozambique and RENAMO

1992, Aug. 20
Pascaul Lissouba became president of Congo

1992, Dec. 4
Idriss Déby became president of Chad

1993
Ugandan native kingdoms restored

1993
First free elections held in Niger

1993, March 9
Albert Zafy became president of Madagascar

1993, April 16
Mahamane Ousmane became president of Niger

1993, April 25
Referendum in Eritrea for independence voted yes

1993, May 24
Eritrea. Independence from Ethiopia

1993, May 24
Isaias Afwerki first president of Eritrea

1993, Oct. 21
Burundi coup. President Ndadaye assassinated
1993, Oct. 22
Ange-Félix Patassé became president of C.A.R.
1993, Nov. 17
Gen. Sani Abacha came to power
in Nigeria
1993, Dec. 7
Houphouët-Boigny's ends rule
in Côte d'Ivoire
1994
South Africa held first free elections
1994
Free elections held in Malawi for
the first time
1994, March 1
Walvis Bay given to Namibia by
South Africa
1994, March 13
South Africa. White rule finished
1994, April 6
Presidents of Rwanda and Burundi killed
1994, May 9
South African bantustans came
to an end
1994, May 10
Nelson Mandela became president of South Africa
1994, May 17
Hastings Banda ended rule in
Malawi
1994, May 21
Bakili Muluzi became new president of Malawi
1994, July 19
Pasteur Bizimungu became president of Rwanda
1994, July 22
Dawda Jawara ousted in bloodless coup in Gambia
1994, July 23
Yahya Jammeh came to power in
Gambia
1994, Sept.
Ceuta and Melilla achieved a
certain autonomy
1994, Dec.
Peace treaty between Djibouti
and Afar rebels
1995
French Army deposed coup
leaders in Comoros
1995
Peace agreement between Niger
and Tuareg rebels

1995, Jan. 25
Moshoeshoe II restored to
throne of Lesotho
1995, Aug. 22
Negasso Gidada became president of Ethiopia
1995, Nov. 23
Benjamin William Mkapa became president of Tanzania
1995, Dec. 27
Navim Ramgoolam became PM
of Mauritius
1996
Niger coup
1996, Jan. 4
Kamal al-Ganzouri became PM
of Egypt
1996, Jan. 27
Ibrahim Baré Maïnassara became president of Niger
1996, Feb. 7
Letsie III became king of Lesotho
1996, March 29
Ahmad Tejan Kabbah becan.e
president of Sierra Leone
1996, April 4
Mathieu Kérékou became president of Benin
1996, July 25
Military coup in Burundi led by
Buyoya
1996, Sept. 3
Ruth Perry first African female
head of state
1997, Jan. 3
The Army took over in Somalia
1997, Feb. 9
Didier Ratsiraka became president of Madagascar
1997, May 16
Mobutu toppled from power in
Zaire
1997, May 17
Zaire became Democratic Republic of the Congo
1997, May 17
Laurent Kabila became president
of Congo (Zaire)
1997, May 25
Johnny Paul Koroma took power
in Sierra Leone
1997, Aug. 2
Charles Taylor became president
of Liberia
1997, Aug. 4
Nzwani declared independence
in the Comoros
1997, Sept. 7
Zaire. Former President Mobutu
died

1997, Oct. 12
Cameroun. President Biya won
re-election
1997, Oct. 15
Congo. Denis Sassou-Nguesso
captured Brazzaville
1997, Oct. 25
Congo. Denis Sassou-Nguesso
became president again
1997, Nov. 25
Malawi. Hastings Banda, former
president, died
1997, Dec. 12
Mauritania. President Taya won
re-election
1997, Dec. 29
Kenya. President Moi won re-
election
1998, Feb. 12
Sierra Leone. Capital taken by
Nigerian-led army
1998, Feb. 12
Ahmad Tejan Kabbah president
of Sierra Leone again
1998, March 22
Seychelles. René re-elected president
1998, May 8
Houngbédji, PM of Benin, resigned
1998, May 14
Post of Prime Minister abolished
in Benin
1998, May 28
Mosisili elected PM of Lesotho
1998, June 8
Sani Abacha, ruler of Nigeria,
died
1998, June 9
Abdulsalami Abubakar new ruler
of Nigeria
1998, June 11
Buyoya sworn in as president of
Burundi
1998, July 3
Loum new PM of Senegal
1998, July 23
Andrianarivo new PM of Madagascar
1998, Nov. 6
President Abdulkarim of the Comoros died
1998, Nov. 16
Chekia Ould Muhammad
Khouna appointed PM of Mauritania
1998, Nov. 22
Abbas Djoussouf appointed PM
of the Comoros
1998, Dec. 3

Francisco Fadul appointed PM of Guinea-Bissau

1998, Dec. 14
Algerian PM Ouyahia resigned

1998, Dec. 15
Liamine Zéroual appointed new PM of Algeria

1999, Jan. 5
Guilherme da Costa sworn in as PM of São Tomé and Príncipe

1999, Jan. 23
Emane appointed PM of Gabon

1999, Jan. 29
Post of PM abolished in Angola

1999, Feb. 1
Dologuélé appointed PM in Central African Republic

1999, March 8
PM Touré dismissed in Guinea. Sidimé replaced him

1999, April 9
Ismail Guelleh elected president of Djibouti

1999, April 9
President Maïnassara assassinated in Niger

1999, April 15
Bouteflika elected president of Algeria

1999, April 21
Daouda Wanké new head of state in Niger

1999, April 27
Bouteflika took office as new president of Algeria

1999, April 30
Coup in the Comoros

1999, May 6
Assoumani new head of state in the Comoros

1999, May 7
President Vieira overthrown in Guinea-Bissau

1999, May 8
Guelleh sworn in as president in Djibouti

1999, May 21
Abdoboli new PM of Togo

1999, May 29
Obasanjo took office as new president of Nigeria

1999, June 14
Thabo Mbeki elected new president of South Africa

1999, June 16
Thabo Mbeki sworn in as new president of South Africa

1999, July 22
Hassan II, King of Morocco, died

1999, Oct. 5
Ebeid new PM of Egypt

1999, Oct. 14
Julius Nyerere of Tanzania died

1999, Nov. 17
Ghannouchi new PM of Tunisia

1999, Nov. 25
Said Abeid named new Pm of Nzwani

1999, Dec. 2
Tarmidi new Pm of the Comoros

1999, Dec. 13
Yamassoum new PM of Chad

1999, Dec. 22
Tandja sworn in as president of Niger

1999, Dec. 23
Hamdouri, PM of Algeria, resigned. Ahmad ben Bitour replaced him

1999, Dec. 24
Bédié ousted in Côte d'Ivoire coup

1999, Dec. 25
Robert Guéi new head of state in Côte d'Ivoire

2000, Feb. 15
Mande Sidibe new PM of Mali

2000, Feb. 17
Ialá sworn in as president of Guinea-Bissau

2000, Feb. 19
Caetano N'Tchoma new PM of Guinea-Bissau

2000, March 1
ash-Shamikh new general secretary in Libya

2000, March 8
Makuza new PM of Rwanda

2000, March 19
Abdulaye Wade new president of Senegal

2000, March 23
Bizimungu resigned as president of Rwanda

2000, April 1
Abdulaye Wade took office as president of Senegal

2000, April 5
Niasse, new PM of Senegal, took office

2000, April 6
Habib Bourguiba of Tunisia died

2000, April 17
Paul Kagam elected president of Rwanda

2000, April 22
Kagame sworn in as new president of Rwanda

2000, May 8
Hubert Maga of Benin died

2000, May 18
Seydou Diarra new PM of Côte d'Ivoire

2000, Aug. 26
Ahmad ben Bitour, PM of Algeria, resigned

2000, Aug. 26
Abdiqasim Hassan elected new president of Somalia

2000, Aug. 27
Benflis, new PM of Algeria, took office

2000, Aug. 27
Abdiqasim Hassan took office as new president of Somalia

2000, Aug. 27
Adoboli, PM of Togo, resigned

2000, Aug. 29
Kodjo named new PM of Togo

2000, Aug. 31
Kodjo took office as new PM of Togo

2000, Sept. 29
Carlos Veiga resigned as PM of Cape Verde

2000, Oct. 5
Gualberto do Rosario new PM of Cape Verde

2000, Oct. 8
Ali Khalif Galaid new PM of Somalia

2000, Oct. 14
President Hassan and PM Galaid return to Somalia from exile

2000, Oct. 22
Robert Guéi elected president of Côte d'Ivoire

2000, Oct. 25
President Guéi fled Côte d'Ivoire

2000, Oct. 26
Laurent Gbagbo sworn in as new president of Côte d'Ivoire

2000, Nov. 7
Paramanga Yonli new PM of Burkina Faso

2000, Nov. 29
Hamada Madi new PM of the Comoros

2001, Jan. 7
John Kufuor took office as new president of Ghana

2001, Jan. 16
Laurent Kabila, president of Congo (Zaire) assassinated

2001, Jan. 17
Joseph Kabila named new interim president of Congo (Zaire)

2001, Jan. 26

Joseph Kabila sworn in as new president of Congo (Zaire)

2001, Feb. 1

Neves took office as new PM of Cape Verde

2001, Feb. 6

Hamedou resigned as PM of Djibouti

2001, March 3

Niasse resigned as PM of Togo. Boye replaced him

2001, March 4

Dileita named new PM of Djibouti

2001, March 4

Cándido Rivas new PM of Equatorial Guinea

2001, March 7

Dileita sworn in as new PM of Djibouti

2001, March 19

N'Tchoma fired as PM of Guinea-Bissau

2001, March 21

Imbali new PM of Guinea-Bissau

2001, March 22

President Pires of Cape Verde sworn in

2001, April 1

Dologuélé, PM of Central African Republic, fired. Zinguélé replaced him

2001, July 1

Yusuf Nur new acting president of Puntland

2001, Aug. 9

Military junta seized power in Nzwani

2001, Aug. 25

Muhammad Bacar new head of state in Nzwani

2001, Sept. 3

de Menezes took office as new president of São Tomé and Príncipe

2001, Sept. 18

Da Costa, PM of São Tomé and Príncipe, dismissed

2001, Sept. 25

Carvalho appointed new PM of Saõo Tomé and Príncipe

2001, Sept. 26

Carvalho sworn in as new PM of São Tomé and Príncipe

2001, Oct. 8

Girma Wolde-Giorgis Lucha elected president of Ethiopia

2001, Nov. 1

Buyoya sworn in as president of Burundi

2001, Nov. 12

Hassan Farah new PM of Somalia

2001, Nov. 14

Jama Ali Jama elected president of Somalia

2001, Nov. 21

Rebels captured Garowe in Puntland

2001, Dec. 7

Imbali, PM of Guinea-Bissau, fired

2001, Dec. 8

Alamara Nhassé new PM of Guinea-Bissau

2001, Dec. 9

Nhassé sworn in as new PM of Guinea-Bissau

2001, Dec. 20

Leopold Senghor of Senegal died

2002, Jan. 2

Mwanawasa took office as new president of Zambia

2002, Jan. 17

Assoumani resigned as president of the Comoros

2002, Feb. 15

Uteem resigned as president of Mauritius

2002, Feb. 18

Acting president Chettiar of Mauritius resigned

2002, Feb. 22

Marc Ravalomanana declared himself president of Madagascar

2002, Feb. 25

Karl Offmann elected president of Mauritius

2002, Feb. 26

Jacques Sylla named new PM of Madagascar

2002, March 3

Gabriel Costa named new PM of São Tomé and Príncipe

2002, March 18

Mande Sidibe, PM of Mali, resigned

2002, March 27

Dagomba ruler Yakuba II killed in tribal clash in Ghana

2002, March 31

Muhammad Bacar elected president of Anjouan (Nzwani)

2002, April 1

The new state of Southwestern Somalia proclaimed, with Shatigadud as president

2002, May 3

President Egal of Somaliland Republic died

2002, May 6

Marc Ravalomanana sworn in as new president of Madagascar

2002, May 8

Assoumani declared president of the Comoros

2002, May 12

Amadou Touré elected president of Mali

2002, May 19

President Fazul of the Comoros took office

2002, May 26

Assoumani sworn in as new president of the Comoros

2002, June 8

Amadou Touré took office as new president of Mali

2002, June 9

Ahmad Hamani new PM of Mali

2002, June 11

Yamassoum, PM of Chad, resigned

2002, June 12

Haroun Kabadi new PM of Chad

2002, June 27

Kodjo, PM of Togo, fired. Koffi Sama replaced him

2002, June 29

Koffi Sama sworn in as new PM of Togo

2002, July 5

Didier Ratsiraka fled Madagascar

2002, Aug. 28

Geingob, PM of Namibia, fired

2002, Sept. 19

Former president Guéi of Côte d'Ivoire killed in battle

2002, Oct. 3

María das Neves named Pm of São Tomé and Príncipe

2002, Oct. 9

Driss Jettou appointed new PM of Morocco

2002, Oct. 13

Sir Garfield Todd, former PM of Southern Rhodesia, died

2002, Oct. 15

Claude Wong Su appointed chief executive of Rodrigues

2002, Oct. 24

Claude Wong Su installed as chief executive of Rodrigues

2002, Nov. 4

Boye fired as PM in Senegal. Seck replaced him

2002, Nov. 15

Nhasse fired as PM in Guinea-Bissau

2002, Nov. 16
Pires new Pm in Guinea-Bissau

2002, Nov. 20
dos Santos proposed as new Pm of Angola

2002, Dec. 5
dos Santos named as new PM of Angola

2002, Dec. 6
dos Santos installed as new PM of Angola

2002, Dec. 15
President Mbasogo of Equatorial Guinea re-elected

2002, Dec. 27
Kibaki elected president of Kenya

2002, Dec. 30
Kibaki sworn in as new president of Kenya

2003, Jan. 25
Diarra named PM of Côte d'Ivoire

2003, Feb. 4
Serge Clair chief commissioner of Rodrigues

2003, Feb. 10
Diarra sworn in as PM of Côte d'Ivoire

2003, March 15
Coup in Central African Republic

2003, March 16
Bozizé declared himself president of Central African Republic

2003, March 23
Abel Goumba named new PM of Central African Republic

2003, April 14
President Khain of Somalia re-elected

2003, April 30
Ndayizeye sworn in as president of Burundi

2003, May 5
Benflis, PM of Algeria, fired. Ouyahia replaced him

2003, June 1
Éyadéma re-elected president of Togo

2003, June 8
Failed coup in Mauritania

2003, May 14
ash-Shamikh fired as general secretary of Libya. Replaced by Shukri Ghanem

2003, June 24
Faki new PM of Chad

2003, July 6

Sghair Ould M'Bareck new PM of Mauritania

2003, July 16
Coup in São Tomé and Príncipe

2003, Aug. 1
Maria das Neves, PM of São Tomé and Príncipe, resigned

2003, Aug. 7
Charles Taylor, president of Liberia, resigned

2003, Aug. 11
Moses Blah new president of Liberia

2003, Aug. 16
Idi Amin of Uganda died

2003, Sept. 14
President Ialá of Guinea-Bissau deposed in coup

2003, Sept. 29
Barnabas Dhlamini fired as PM of Lesotho

2003, Sept. 30
Jugnauth resigned as PM of Mauritius

2003, Oct. 1
Offmann resigned as president of Mauritius

2003, Oct. 7
Jugnauth elected president of Mauritius

2003, Oct. 14
Gyude Bryant new head of state in Liberia

2003, Oct. 15
Mokhtar Ould Daddah of Mauritania died

2003, Nov. 10
Canaan Banana of Zimbabwe died

2003, Nov. 14
Themba Dhlamini named new PM of Swaziland

2003, Nov. 20
David Dacko of Central African Republic died

2003, Dec. 11
Abel Goumba, PM of Central African Republic, fired

2003, Dec. 12
Celestin Gaombalet new PM of Central African Republic

2004, Feb. 17
Luisa Diogo named PM of Mozambique

2004, Feb. 23
Fall new PM of Guinea

2004, April 8
Bouteflika re-elected president of Algeria

2004, April 13

Albert René resigned as president of Seychelles

2004, April 23
Mbeki re-elected president of South Africa unopposed

2004, April 28
Ag Hamani resigned as PM of Mali

2004, April 29
Maïga appointed PM of Mali

2004, April 30
Maïga installed as PM of Mali

2004, April 30
Fall, PM of Guinea, resigned

2004, May 9
Carlos Gomes Júnior new Pm of Guinea-Bissau

2004, May 10
Carlos Gomes Júnior installed as Pm of Guinea-Bissau

2004, May 20
Mutharika elected president of Malawi

2004, May 24
Mutharika sworn in as new president of Malawi

2004, June 11
Rivas resigned as PM of Equatorial Guinea

2004, June 14
Boricó named new PM of Equatorial Guinea

2004, July 9
Ebeid, PM of Egypt, resigned. Nazif replaced him

2004, Sept. 15
María das Neves, PM of São Tomé and Príncipe, fired

2004, Sept. 17
d'Almeida new PM of São Tomé and Príncipe

2004, Sept. 18
d'Almeida sworn in as new PM of São Tomé and Príncipe

2004, Oct. 11
Biya re-elected president of Cameroun

2004, Oct. 24
Jean-Claude Pierre-Louis chief executive of Rodrigues

2004, Oct. 24
Zine ben Ali re-elected president of Tunisia

2004, Nov. 16
Pohamba elected president of Namibia

2004, Dec. 8
Inoni new PM of Cameroun

2004, Dec. 9
Diallo new PM of Guinea

2005, Feb. 2
Guebuza sworn in as president of Mozambique
2005, Feb. 3
Faki, PM of Chad, resigned. Replaced by Yoadimnaji
2005, Feb. 5
Éyadéma, president of Togo, died
2005, Feb. 7
Faure Gnassingbé sworn in as president of Togo
2005, Feb. 25
Faure Gnassingbé resigned as president of Togo
2005, March 21
Pohamba sworn in as president of Namibia
2005, March 21
Nahas Angula appointed PM of Namibia
2005, April 26
Former PM Élisabeth Domitienne of Central African Republic, died

2005, April 27
Defeated candidate Emmanuel Akitani Bob declared himself president of Togo
2005, May 4
Togolese president Gnassingbé sworn in
2005, May 8
Bozizé elected president of Central African Republic
2005, June 2
d'Almeida, PM of São Tomé and Príncipe, resigned
2005, June 8
New PM Silveira of São Tomé and Príncipe, installed
2005, June 9
Edem Kodjo, new PM of Togo, sworn in
2005, June 11
Gaombalet, PM of Central African Republic, resigned
2005, June 13
Bozizé sworn in as president of Central African Republic

2005, July 5
Navin Ramgoolam installed as PM of Mauritius
2005, July 9
John Garang sworn in as first vice-president of Sudan
2005, July 9
John Garang became president of the newly-created Southern Sudan
2005, July 24
João Bernardo "Nino" Vieira elected president of Guinea-Bissau
2005, July 30
John Garang killed in helicopter crash in Sudan
2005, Aug. 3
Coup in Mauritania
2005, Aug. 4
Salva Kiir replaced John Garang in Sudan
2005, Aug. 19
Pierre Nkurunziza elected president of Burundi

Appendix A
The Modern Countries with Their Historical Constituents

Following each bold heading is a list of all the entries in this book that fall within the geographical boundaries of the present-day country.

Algeria

Aghlabid Empire
Algeria
Algerian Republic (Provisional Government)
Algiers
Almohad Empire
Almoravid Empire
Arab North Africa
Barbary States
Byzantine North Africa
Constantine
Fatimid North Africa
Hafsid Kingdom
Hammadid Kingdom
Idrisid State
Mascara
Mauretania
Mauretania Caesariensis
Mauretania East
Mauretania Sitifensis
Numidia
Omayyad and Abbasid North Africa
Oran
Rustumid Amirate
Tlemcen
Vandal North Africa
Zirid Kingdom

Angola

Angola
Angola Democratic People's Republic

Angola Revolutionary Government in Exile
Dutch West Africa
Kongo
Ndongo

(Atlantic Ocean Area)

Ascension
Canary Islands
Cape Verde
Funchal
Gough Island
Gran Canaria
Machico
Madeira
Porto Santo
Príncipe
Saint Helena
São Tomé
São Tomé and Príncipe
Tenerife
Tristan da Cunha

Benin

Allada
Benin [ii]
Cotonou
Dahomey
Dahomey Portuguese Protectorate
French West Africa
Porto-Novo
Whydah

Botswana

Bakgatlaland
Bakwenaland
Bamaleteland
Bamangwatoland
Bangwaketseland
Barolongland
Batlokwaland
Batwanaland
Bechuanaland Protectorate
Botswana
Griqualand West
Rozwi

Burkina Faso

Burkina Faso
French West Africa
Gurma
Gwiriko
Kenedugu
Mossi States
Upper Ivory Coast
Wagadugu
Yatenga

Burundi

Burundi [i]
Burundi [ii]
German East Africa
Ruanda-Urundi

303

Cameroun

Adamawa
Ambas Bay
Bamoun
Cameroun
Fulani Empire
Kamerun
Kom
Mandara

Central African Republic

Central African Republic
French Equatorial Africa
Ubangi-Shari–Chad

Chad

Baguirmi
Chad
French Equatorial Africa
Kanem
Ubangi-Shari–Chad
Wadai
Zaghawa Kingdom

Congo

Congo
French Equatorial Africa
Kamerun
Kongo
Lower Congo–Gabon
Portuguese Congo

Congo (Zaïre)

Congo (Zaïre)
Katanga Republic
Kazembe
Kongo
Luba Empire
Lunda
South Kasai Republic
Stanleyville People's Republic
Stanleyville Republic

Côte d'Ivoire

Baule
Côte d'Ivoire
Denkyira
French West Africa
Gonja
Kong

Djibouti

Adal [ii]
Djibouti
Punt

Egypt

Egypt
Lower Egypt
Upper Egypt

Equatorial Guinea

Annobón
Bight of Biafra
Bights of Biafra and Benin
Equatorial Guinea
Fernando Po
Río Muni

Eritrea

Adal [ii]
Assab
Eritrea
Italian East Africa
Massawa
Punt

Ethiopia

Adal [ii]
Assab
Axum
Eritrea
Ethiopia
Gojjam
Harar
Ifat
Italian East Africa
Punt
Massawa
Shoa

Gabon

French Equatorial Africa
Gabon
Lower Congo–Gabon

Gambia

British West Africa
Fort James
French Gambia
Gambia
Senegambia Colony
Senegambia Confederation

Ghana

Akim
Akwamu
Ashanti
Bono
British Togoland
British West Africa

Dagomba
Danish Gold Coast
Denkyira
Dutch Gold Coast
Ghana
Gold Coast Colony Region
Gold Coast Northern Territories
Gonja
Hollandia
Mossi States
Portuguese Gold Coast
Swedish Gold Coast
Togoland

Guinea

French West Africa
Futa Jallon
Guinea
Samory's Empire

Guinea-Bissau

Bissau
Cacheu
Guinea-Bissau

(Indian Ocean Area)

Agalega Islands
Aldabra Islands
Amirante Islands
Andruna
Anjouan
Assumption Island
Astove
British Indian Ocean Territory
Coetivy
Comoros
Cosmoledo Islands
Diego Suarez
Europa Island
Farquhar and Des Roches Islands
Fort-Dauphin
Glorioso Islands
Gran Comoro
Juan de Nova Island
Libertalia
Louisbourg
Madagascar
Mauritius
Mayotte
Mayotte Department
Mohéli
Mwali
Nossi-Bé
Nzwani
Providence Group
Réunion
Rodrigues
Saint Brandon Islands

Sainte Marie de Madagascar
Seychelles

Kenya

Kenya
Mombasa
Zeng Empire
Lesotho
Lesotho

Liberia

Bassa Cove
Edina
Liberia
Maryland
Mississippi-in-Africa
New Georgia
Petit Dieppe

Libya

Africa [i]
Africa Proconsularis
Arab North Africa
Barbary States
Byzantine North Africa
Cyrenaica
Egypt
Fezzan
Hafsid Kingdom
Libia
Libya
Omayyad and Abbasid North
    Africa
Pentapolis
Phazania
Tripolitania
Tripolitanian Republic
Vandal North Africa
Zirid Kingdom

Malawi

Federation of Rhodesia and
    Nyasaland
Malawi

Mali

French West Africa
Ghana Empire
Kangaba
Kenedugu
Mali
Mali Empire
Mali Federation
Masina
Segu
Songhai

Timbuktu
Tukolor Empire

Mauritania

Adrar
Brakna
French West Africa
Ghana Empire
Kaarta
Mauritania
Tagant
Trarza
Western Sahara

Morocco

Almohad Empire
Almoravid Empire
Barbary States
Bou Regreg
Ceuta
French Morocco
Idrisid State
Ifni
Masmouda
Mauretania
Mauretania Tingitana
Mauretania West
Melilla
Morocco
Rif Republic
Santa Cruz de la Mar Pequeña
Spanish Morocco
Tangier
Western Sahara

Mozambique

Gazaland
Mozambique
Mwene Mutapa Empire
Zeng Empire

Namibia

Hereroland
Namibia
Oorlam Territory
Ovamboland
Rehoboth
Walvis Bay
Witbooi Territory

Niger

Biram
Bornu Empire
Damagaram
Daura
Daura-Baure
Daura-Zango

French West Africa
Fulani Empire
Gobir
Hausa States
Kororofa
Niger
Zamfara

Nigeria

Abeokuta
Abuja
Adamawa
Agaie
Argungu
Bauchi
Bedde
Benin [i]
Biafra
Bight of Benin
Bight of Biafra
Bights of Benin and Biafra
Biram
Biu
Bonny
Bornu
Bornu Empire
Brass
British West Africa
Cameroons
Daniski
Daura
Doma
East Nupe
Fika
Fulani Empire
Gobir
Gombe
Gumel
Gwandu
Hadejia
Hausa States
Ibadan
Ife
Igala
Ijebu
Ilorin
Jema'a
Jemaari
Kano
Katagum
Katsina
Kazaure
Keana
Keffi
Kontagora
Kororofa
Lafia
Lafiagi
Lagos

Lapai
Misau
Muri
New Calabar
Nigeria
Nigeria Eastern Region
Nigeria Northern Region
Nigeria Southern Provinces
Nigeria Western Region
Northern Nigeria
Nupe
Opobo
Oyo
Potiskum
Rabih's Empire
Southern Nigeria
Southern Nigeria Colony and
   Protectorate
Warri
Wase
West Nupe
Yauri
Zamfara
Zaria

Rwanda

German East Africa
Ruanda
Ruanda-Urundi
Rwanda

Senegal

Baol
Dyolof
French West Africa
Futa Toro
Gorée
Gorée and Dependencies
Kayor
Mali Empire
Mali Federation
Senegal
Senegambia Colony
Senegal Confederation
Songhai
Walo

Sierra Leone

Aku
Banana Island
British West Africa
Bumpe
Koya-Temne
Shenge
Sierra Leone

Somalia

Adal [i]
British Somaliland

Ifat
Italian East Africa
Italian Somaliland
Jubaland
Mogadishu
Punt
Puntland
Somalia
Somaliland Republic
Southwestern Somalia
Zeng Empire

South Africa

Adam Kok's Land
Bechuanaland Protectorate
Bophuthatswana
British Bechuanaland
British Kaffraria
British Pondoland
Cape Colony
Ciskei
Cornelis Kok's Land
Dutch African Republic
Fingoland
GazaNkulu
Goshen
Graaff-Reinet
Griqualand East
Griqualand West
Idutywa
KaNgwane
Klipdrift Republic
Kreli's Country
KwaNdebele
KwaZulu
Lebowa
Little Free State
Lydenburg
Lydenrust
Natal
New Republic
Ohrigstad
Orange Free State
Pondoland
Pondoland East
Pondoland West
Port Natal
QwaQwa
Sekonyela's Land
South Africa
Stellaland
Swellendam
Tembuland
Tongaland
Transkei
Transkeian Territories
Transorangia
Transvaal
United States of Stellaland

Utrecht
Venda
Winburg
Zoutpansberg
Zululand

Sudan

Alwah
Axum
Bahr al-Ghazal
Darfur
Dongola
Equatoria Province
Funj Sultanate
Kordofan
Kush
Mukurra
Nubia
Southern Sudan
Sudan
Zaghawa Kingdom

Swaziland

Swaziland

Tanzania

German East Africa
Karagwe
Mirambo
Tanganyika
Tanzania
Zanzibar
Zeng Empire

Togo

Little Popo
Togo
Togoland

Tunisia

Africa [i]
Africa [ii]
Africa Proconsularis
Aghlabid Empire
Almohad Empire
Arab North Africa
Barbary States
Byzacena
Byzantine North Africa
Carthage
Fatimid North Africa
Hafsid Kingdom
Omayyad and Abbasid North
   Africa
Tunis
Tunisia
Vandal North Africa
Zirid Kingdom

Uganda

Buganda
Bunyoro
Nkore
Uganda

Zambia

Barotseland
Federation of Rhodesia and
　Nyasaland

Kazembe
North Eastern Rhodesia
North Western Rhodesia
Rhodesia
Zambia

Zimbabwe

Federation of Rhodesia and
　Nyasaland
Gazaland

Matabeleland
Mwene Mutapa Empire
Rhodesia Protectorate
Rozwi
Zimbabwe

Appendix B
The Colonial Powers'
Holdings

The European powers involved in African colonization were (in order of number of possessions held there): Great Britain, France, Spain, Portugal, Italy, Germany, Denmark, Sweden, Netherlands, Brandenburg (or Prussia), Courland (now part of Latvia). There was also the interesting case of Liberia, settled from the United States.

There was also a great deal of colonization done in Africa by other African powers, most notably the Islamic powers, but also by such countries as South Africa. This type of colonization is distinct from that whereby one power simply conquers another, of which there have been countless examples over the centuries, most notably those of the Muslims and the Turks.

The following are the colonial entries to be found in this book, arranged by imperial country; numbers in parentheses refer to that country's total number of possessions.

Great Britain (95)

Adam Kok's Land
Agalega Islands
Aldabra Islands
Ambas Bay
Amirante Islands
Ascension
Ashanti
Assumption Island
Astove
Bechuanaland Protectorate
Bight of Benin
Bight of Biafra
Bights of Biafra and Benin
Botswana
British Bechuanaland
British Indian Ocean Territory
British Kaffraria
British Pondoland
British Somaliland
British Togoland
British West Africa
Buganda

Cameroons
Cape Colony
Ceuta
Coetivy
Cosmoledo Islands
Cyrenaica
Djibouti
Egypt
Eritrea
Farquhar and Des Roches Islands
Federation of Rhodesia and
   Nyasaland
Fernando Po
Fort James
Gambia
Ghana
Gold Coast Colony Region
Gold Coast Northern Territories
Gorée
Griqualand West
Idutywa
Italian Somaliland
Jubaland
Kamerun

Kenya
Lagos
Lesotho
Liberia
Madagascar
Malawi
Matabeleland
Mauritius
Mombasa
Natal
Nigeria
Nigeria Eastern Region
Nigeria Northern Region
Nigeria Southern Provinces
Nigeria Western Region
North Eastern Rhodesia
North Western Rhodesia
Northern Nigeria
Orange Free State
Port Natal
Providence Group
Réunion
Rhodesia
Rodrigues

Saint Brandon Islands
Saint Helena
Senegal
Senegambia Colony
Seychelles
Sierra Leone
South Africa
Southern Nigeria
Southern Nigeria Colony and
  Protectorate
Sudan
Swaziland
Tanganyika
Tangier
Togoland
Tongaland
Transkeian Territories
Transorangia
Transvaal
Tripolitania
Tristan da Cunha
Uganda
Walvis Bay
Zambia
Zanzibar
Zimbabwe
Zululand

France (66)

Agalega Islands
Aldabra Islands
Algeria
Allada
Amirante Islands
Assumption Island
Baguirmi
Benin [ii]
Burkina Faso
Cameroun
Central African Republic
Chad
Coetivy
Comoros
Congo
Cosmoledo Islands
Côte d'Ivoire
Cotonou
Dahomey
Diego Suarez
Djibouti
Egypt
Europa Island
Farquhar and Des Roches Islands
Fezzan
Fort-Dauphin
French Equatorial Africa
French Gambia
French Morocco
French West Africa

Gabon
Glorioso Islands
Gorée
Gorée and Dependencies
Guinea
Juan de Nova Island
Kamerun
Liberia
Little Popo
Louisbourg
Lower Congo–Gabon
Madagascar
Mali
Mali Federation
Mauritania
Mauritius
Mayotte Department
Muri
Niger
Nossi-Bé
Petit Dieppe
Porto-Novo
Providence Group
Réunion
Rodrigues
Sainte Marie de Madagascar
Senegal
Seychelles
Tangier
Togo
Togoland
Tunisia
Upper Ivory Coast
Wadai
Wagadugu
Whydah

Portugal (24)

Angola
Annobón
Bissau
Cacheu
Canary Islands
Cape Verde
Ceuta
Dahomey Portuguese Protec-
  torate
Fernando Po
Funchal
Guinea-Bissau
Machico
Madeira
Mombasa
Mozambique
Porto Santo
Portuguese Congo
Portuguese Gold Coast
Príncipe
São Tomé

São Tomé and Príncipe
Tangier
Tristan da Cunha
Zanzibar

Rome (18)

Africa [i]
Africa [ii]
Africa Proconsularis
Byzacena
Carthage
Ceuta
Cyrenaica
Egypt
Mauretania
Mauretania Caesariensis
Mauretania Sitifensis
Mauretania Tingitana
Numidia
Pentapolis
Phazania
Tangier
Tripolitania
Tunis

Spain (17)

Annobón
Canary Islands
Ceuta
Equatorial Guinea
Fernando Po
Gran Canaria
Ifni
Melilla
Oran
Río Muni
Santa Cruz de la Mar Pequeña
Spanish Morocco
Tangier
Tenerife
Tripolitania
Tunis
Western Sahara

Italy (12)

Assab
British Somaliland
Cyrenaica
Eritrea
Ethiopia
Fezzan
Italian East Africa
Italian Somaliland
Jubaland
Libya
Massawa
Tripolitania

Holland (11)

Cape Colony
Dutch Gold Coast
Dutch West Africa
Fort James
Gorée
Graaff-Reinet
Mauritius
Saint Helena
São Tomé
Swellendam
Tristan da Cunha

Turkey (9)

Algiers
Egypt
Fezzan
Harar
Massawa
Oran
Sudan
Tripolitania
Tunis

United States (7)

Bassa Cove
Edina
Liberia
Maryland
Mississippi-in-Africa
New Georgia

Germany (6)

German East Africa
Kamerun
Kenya
Lydenrust
Namibia
Togoland

Belgium (4)

Burundi
Congo (Zaire)
Ruanda-Urundi
Rwanda

Byzantium (2)

Byzantine North Africa
Egypt

Greece (2)

Egypt
Pentapolis

Prussia (1)

Hollandia

Brandenburg (1)

Hollandia

Knights of Malta (1)

Tripolitania

Normandy (1)

Tripolitania

Denmark (1)

Danish Gold Coast

Courland (1)

James Fort

Sweden (1)

Swedish Gold Coast

Appendix C
Dates of Admission into the United Nations

1945, Oct. 24. Egypt
1945, Nov. 2. Liberia
1945, Nov. 7. South Africa
1945, Nov. 13 Ethiopia
1955, Dec. 14. Libya
1956, Nov. 12. Morocco
1956, Nov. 12. Sudan
1956, Nov. 12. Tunisia
1957, March 8. Ghana
1958, Dec. 12. Guinea
1960, Sept. 20. Cameroun
1960, Sept. 20. Central African Republic
1960, Sept. 20. Chad
1960, Sept. 20. Congo (Brazzaville)
1960, Sept. 20. Dahomey
1960, Sept. 20. Gabon
1960, Sept. 20. Ivory Coast
1960, Sept. 20. Malagasy Republic

1960, Sept. 20. Niger
1960, Sept. 20. Somalia
1960, Sept. 20. Togo
1960, Sept. 20. Upper Volta
1960, Sept. 28. Mali
1960, Sept. 28. Senegal
1960, Oct. 7. Nigeria
1960, Nov. 22. Congo (Léopoldville)
1961, Sept. 27. Sierra Leone
1961, Oct. 27. Mauritania
1961, Dec. 14. Tanganyika
1962, Sept. 18. Burundi
1962, Sept. 18. Rwanda
1962, Oct. 8. Algeria
1962, Oct. 25. Uganda
1963, Dec. 16. Kenya
1963, Dec. 16. Zanzibar
1964, Dec. 1. Malawi
1964, Dec. 1. Zambia
1965, Sept. 21. Gambia

1966, Oct. 17. Botswana
1966, Oct. 17. Lesotho
1968, April 24. Mauritius
1968, Sept. 24. Swaziland
1968, Nov. 12. Equatorial Guinea
1974, Sept. 17. Guinea-Bissau
1975, Sept. 16. Cape Verde
1975, Sept. 16. Mozambique
1975, Sept. 16. São Tomé and Príncipe
1975, Nov. 12. Comoros
1976, Sept. 21. Seychelles
1976, Dec. 1. Angola
1977, Sept. 20. Djibouti
1980, Aug. 25. Zimbabwe
1990, April 23. Namibia
1993, May 28. Eritrea

Bibliography

Adams, Michael, ed. *The Middle East*. New York: Facts on File Publications, 1988.

Addison, John. *Ancient Africa*. New York: John Day, 1970

Africa Digest. London: African Publications, quarterly, 1949–.

Africa News. North Carolina: Africa News Science, biweekly, later weekly, 1973–.

Africa Report. New York: African-American Institute, bimonthly, 1957–.

Africa Research Bulletin. United Kingdom: Africa Research, previously monthly and bimonthly, 1964–.

The Africa Review. United Kingdom: World of Information, annual, 1976–.

Africa South of the Sahara. London: Europa, annual, 1970–.

Africa Today. Denver: Africa Today Assocs., quarterly, 1954–.

Africa Year Book and Who's Who. London: African Journal, annual, 1976–.

African Affairs. London: Royal African Society, quarterly, 1901–.

African Encyclopaedia. Oxford: Oxford Univ. Press, 1974.

The African Experience. Ed. John N. Paden, and Edward W. Soja. 4 vols. Evanston, Ill.: Northwestern Univ. Press, 1970.

African Recorder. Indian Publications, biweekly, 1960–83.

The Annual Register. London: Longman, annual, 1758–.

Appiah, L.H. Ofosu, ed. *Dictionary of African Biography*. 20 vols. Algonac, Mich.: Encyclopedia Africana, 1977.

Area Handbook/Country Studies Series. 102 vols. to date. Washington D.C.: Government Printing Office, 1956–.

Asante, Molefi Kete. *The Book of African Names*. Trenton, N.J.: Africa World Press, 1991.

Ayany, Samuel G. *A History of Zanzibar*. Nairobi: East Africa Literature Bureau, 1970.

Balandier, Georges, and Jacques Maquet. *Dictionary of Black African Civilization*. New York: Amiel, 1974.

Best, Alan C., and Harm J. de Blij. *African Survey*. New York: Wiley, 1977.

Bidwell, Robin. *Bidwell's Guide to Government Ministers*. London: Cass, 1973.

Brace, Richard M. *Morocco, Algeria, Tunisia*. Englewood Cliffs, N.J.: Prentice-Hall, 1964.

Brownlie, Ian. *African Boundaries*. London: Hurst, 1979.

Budge, Wallis. *A History of Egypt*. London: Kegan, Paul, 1902.

Bulpin, T.V. *Discovering Southern Africa*. 3rd edition. Cape Town: Books of Africa, 1983.

Burns, Sir Alan. *History of Nigeria*. London: Allen and Unwin, 1929.

Butler, Audrey. *Everyman's Dictionary of Dates*. London: Dent, 1964.

The Cambridge History of Africa. 8 vols. Cambridge: Cambridge Univ. Press, 1984.

Castagno, Margaret F. *Historical Dictionary of Somalia*. Metuchen, N.J.: Scarecrow, 1975.

Claridge, W. Walton. *A History of the Gold Coast and Ashanti*. 2 vols. London: Cass, 1964.

Clements' Encyclopedia of World Governments. Political Research, 1974.

Colonialism in Africa, 1870–1960. 5 vols. Cambridge: Cambridge Univ. Press, 1969.

The Columbia Lippincott Gazetteer of the World. New York: Columbia Univ. Press, 1962.

Colvin, Lucie G. *Historical Dictionary of Senegal*. Metuchen, N.J.: Scarecrow, 1981.

Cook, Chris, and David Killingray. *African Political Facts Since 1945*. 2nd edition. New York: Facts on File Publications, 1991.

Crosby, Cynthia A. *Historical Dictionary of Malawi*. Metuchen, N.J.: Scarecrow, 1980.

Crow, Ben, and Alan Thomas. *The Third World Atlas*. Philadelphia: Open Univ. Press, 1985.

Crowder, Michael, and Obaro Ikime, eds. *West African Chiefs*. New York: Africana, 1970.

Davidson, Basil. *The Growth of African Civilisation: West Africa, 1000–1800*. London: Longman, 1965.

Decalo, Samuel. *Historical Dictionary of Chad*. Metuchen, N.J.: Scarecrow, 1977.

_____. *Historical Dictionary of Dahomey*. Metuchen, N.J.: Scarecrow, 1975.

_____. *Historical Dictionary of Niger.* Metuchen, N.J.: Scarecrow, 1979.

_____. *Historical Dictionary of Togo.* Metuchen, N.J.: Scarecrow, 1976.

Dickie, John, and Alan Rake. *Who's Who in Africa.* African Development, 1973.

Diggs, Ellen Irene. *Black Chronology.* Boston: Hall, 1983.

Egan, E.W., et al., eds. *Kings, Rulers and Statesmen.* New York: Sterling, 1967.

Encyclopaedia Britannica. London, various editions.

The Encyclopaedia of Africa. London: MacDonald Educational, 1976.

Encyclopedia of the Third World. New York: Facts on File Publications, annual, 1972–.

Europa Year Book. London: Europa, annual, 1926–.

Facts on File. New York: Facts on File Publications, monthly, 1966–.

Fage, J.D. *An Atlas of African History.* New York: Africana, 1978.

Foray, Cyril Patrick. *Historical Dictionary of Sierra Leone.* Metuchen, N.J.: Scarecrow, 1977.

Freeman-Grenville, G.S.P. *Chronology of World History.* London: Collins, 1975.

Gailey, Harry A., Jr. *Historical Dictionary of the Gambia.* Metuchen, N.J.: Scarecrow, 1975.

_____. *The History of Africa in Maps.* Chicago: Denoyer-Geppert, 1967.

_____. *A History of the Gambia.* New York: Praeger, 1965.

Gardinier, David E. *Historical Dictionary of Gabon.* Metuchen, N.J.: Scarecrow, 1981.

Gazetteer of the Northern Provinces of Nigeria. London: Cass, 1972.

Gerteiny, Alfred G. *Historical Dictionary of Mauritania.* Metuchen, N.J.: Scarecrow, 1981.

_____. *Mauritania.* New York: Praeger, 1967.

Glastrow, Shelagh. *Who's Who in South African Politics.* 4th revised edition. New York: Zell, 1993.

Glickman, Harvey, ed. *Political Leaders of Contemporary Africa South of the Sahara: A Biographical Dictionary.* New York: Greenwood Press, 1992.

Green, Lawrence M. *Islands Time Forgot.* London: Putnam, 1962.

Griffiths, Ieuan L.L. *The Atlas of African Affairs.* 2nd edition. London: Routledge, 1993.

Grotpeter, John J. *Historical Dictionary of Swaziland.* Metuchen, N.J.: Scarecrow, 1975.

_____. *Historical Dictionary of Zambia.* Metuchen, N.J.: Scarecrow, 1979.

Gurney, Gene. *Kingdoms of Asia, the Middle East and Africa.* New York: Crown, 1986.

Hahn, Lorna. *Historical Dictionary of Libya.* Metuchen, N.J.: Scarecrow, 1981.

Haliburton, Gordon. *Historical Dictionary of Lesotho.* Metuchen, N.J.: Scarecrow, 1977.

Hallett, Robin. *Africa Since 1875.* Ann Arbor: Univ. of Michigan Press, 1974.

_____. *Africa to 1875.* Ann Arbor: Univ. of Michigan Press, 1970.

Harms, John. *Romance and Truth in the Canaries.* Acorn, 1965.

Harper Encyclopedia of the Modern World. New York: Harper and Row, 1970.

Harrabin, J.F. *An Atlas of Africa.* New York: Praeger, 1960.

Harrison, Christopher. *France and Islam in West Africa, 1860–1960.* New York: Cambridge Univ. Press, 1988.

Hastings, Adrian. *A History of African Christianity, 1950–1975.* Cambridge: Cambridge Univ. Press, 1979.

Heggoy, Alf Andrew. *Historical Dictionary of Algeria.* Metuchen, N.J.: Scarecrow, 1981.

Henderson, K.D.D. *Sudan Republic.* New York: Praeger, 1965.

Henige, David P. *Colonial Governors.* Madison: Univ. of Wisconsin Press, 1970.

Historical Atlas of Africa. Cambridge: Cambridge Univ. Press, 1985.

Holt, David K., and M.W. Daly. *The History of the Sudan.* London: Longman, 1988.

Hugon, Anne. *The Exploration of Africa: From Cairo to Cape.* London: Thames and Hudson, 1993.

Hull, Richard W. *African Cities and Towns Before the European Conquest.* New York: W.W. Norton & Co., 1976.

Imperato, Pascal James. *Historical Dictionary of Mali.* Metuchen, N.J.: Scarecrow, 1977.

Ingham, Kenneth. *A History of East Africa.* New York: Praeger, 1962.

The International Who's Who. London: Europa, various editions.

The International Year Book & Statesmen's Who's Who. West Sussex: Thomas Skinner Directories, annual, 1953–.

Journal of African Administration. British Government, 1949–61.

Journal of African History. Cambridge: Cambridge Univ. Press, quarterly, 1960–.

Journal of Modern African Studies. Cambridge: Cambridge Univ. Press, quarterly, 1963–.

Julien, Charles-André. *History of North Africa.* New York: Praeger, 1970.

Kalck, Pierre. *Historical Dictionary of the Central African Republic.* Metuchen, N.J.: Scarecrow, 1980.

Kane, Robert S. *Africa A-Z.* revised edition. New York: Doubleday, 1972.

Keller, Helen Rex. *Dictionary of Dates.* New York: Hafner, 1971.

Kirk-Greene, Anthony H.M. *Biographical Dictionary of the British Colonial Governors.* Brighton, England: Harvester Press, 1980.

Kurian, George Thomas. *The Encyclopedia of the Third World.* 2nd edition. New York: Facts on File Publications, 1987.

Kurtz, Laura S. *Historical Dictionary of Tanzania*. Metuchen, N.J.: Scarecrow, 1978.

Langer, William L. *An Encyclopedia of World History*. Boston: Houghton Mifflin, 1972.

Langville, Alan R. *Modern World Rulers*. Metuchen, N.J.: Scarecrow, 1979.

Laroui, Abdallah. *The History of the Maghrib*. Princeton, N.J.: Princeton Univ. Press, 1977.

Legum, Colin. *Africa: A Handbook to the Continent*. New York: Praeger, 1966.

_____, ed. *Africa Contemporary Record*. New York: Africana, annual, 1968–.

Lentz, Harris M., III. *Assassinations and Executions*. Jefferson, N.C.: McFarland, 1988.

_____. *Heads of States and Governments*. Jefferson, N.C.: McFarland, 1994.

Levine, Victor T. *The Cameroon Federal Republic*. Ithaca, N.Y.: Cornell Univ. Press, 1971.

_____. *The Cameroons: From Mandate to Independence*. Berkeley: Univ. of California Press, 1964.

Lewis, Paul H., and Roger P. Nye. *Historical Dictionary of Cameroon*. Metuchen, N.J.: Scarecrow, 1974.

Lineberry, William P. *East Africa*. New York: Wilson, 1968.

Liniger-Goumaz, Max. *Historical Dictionary of Equatorial Guinea*. Metuchen, N.J.: Scarecrow, 1979.

Lipschutz, Mark R., and R. Kent Rasmussen. *Dictionary of African Historical Biography*. Chicago: Aldine, 1978.

Lobban, Richard. *Historical Dictionary of Guinea-Bissau*. Metuchen, N.J.: Scarecrow, 1979.

McEvedy, Colin. *The Penguin Atlas of African History*. London: Penguin Books, 1980.

McFarland, Daniel Miles. *Historical Dictionary of Upper Volta*. Metuchen, N.J.: Scarecrow, 1978.

Malwal, B. *The Sudan: A Second Challenge to Nationhood*. New York: Thornton Books, 1985.

Manning, P. *Francophone Sub-Saharan Africa, 1880–1985*. Cambridge: Cambridge Univ. Press, 1985.

Mansor, Menahem, ed. *Political and Diplomatic History of the Arab World, 1900–1967*. 7 vols. Washington, D.C.: NCR/Microcard Editions, 1972.

Martin, Phyllis. *Historical Dictionary of Angola*. Metuchen, N.J.: Scarecrow, 1980.

The Middle East and North Africa. London: Europa, annual, 1953–.

Mostyn, Trevor, ed. *The Cambridge Encyclopaedia of the Middle East and North Africa*. Cambridge: Cambridge Univ. Press, 1988.

Murray, Jocelyn, ed. *Cultural Atlas of Africa*. New York: Facts on File Publications, 1981.

Ogot, Bethwell A. *Historical Dictionary of Kenya*. Metuchen, N.J.: Scarecrow, 1981.

Oliver, Roland. *The African Experience*. London: Weidenfeld and Nicholson, 1991.

_____, and Michael Crowder, eds. *The Cambridge Encyclopaedia of Africa*. Cambridge: Cambridge Univ. Press, 1981.

Olsen, James S, ed. *Historical Dictionary of the Spanish Empire, 1402–1975*. New York: Greenwood, 1992.

_____. *Peoples of Africa: An Ethnohistorical Dictionary*. Westport, Conn.: Greenwood Press, 1996.

O'Toole, Thomas. *Historical Dictionary of Guinea*. Metuchen, N.J.: Scarecrow, 1978.

Oxford History of South Africa. Oxford: Oxford Univ. Press, 1969.

Pachai, B. *Malawi: The History of the Nation*. London: Longman, 1973.

Palmer, Alan. *The Facts on File Dictionary of 20th Century History*. New York: Facts on File Publications, 1979.

Phillips, Claude S. *The African Political Dictionary*. Santa Barbara, Calif.: ABC-Clio, 1984.

Political Handbook of the World. Lakemont, Ga.: CSA, annual, 1975–.

Prouty, Chris, and Eugene Rosenfeld. *Historical Dictionary of Ethiopia*. Metuchen, N.J.: Scarecrow, 1981.

Rack, Alan. *Who's Who in Africa: Leaders for the 1990s*. Metuchen, N.J.; Scarecrow, 1992.

Rasmussen, R. Kent. *Historical Dictionary of Rhodesia/Zimbabwe*. Metuchen, N.J.: Scarecrow, 1979.

Reusch, Richard. *History of East Africa*. New York: Ungar, 1961.

Richmond, J.C.B. *Egypt, 1798–1952*. London: Methuen, 1972.

Riviere, Lindsay. *Historical Dictionary of Mauritius*. Metuchen, N.J.: Scarecrow, 1982.

Room, Adrian. *African Placenames*. Jefferson, N.C.: McFarland, 1994.

Rosenthal, Eric. *Encyclopaedia of Southern Africa*. London: Warne, 1961; and 7th edition, Cape Town: Juba, 1978.

Rulers and Governments of the World. vol. 1 by Martha Ross. vols. 2 & 3 by Bertold Spuler. London: Bowker, 1977–78.

Schwarz, Walter. *Nigeria*. New York: Praeger, 1968.

Shimoni, Yaacov, and Evyatar Levine, eds. *Political Dictionary of the Middle East in the 20th Century*. New York: Quadrangle, 1974.

South Africa: Official Yearbook of the Republic. South Africa: Chris Van Rensburg, annual, 1974–.

Spencer, William. *Historical Dictionary of Morocco*. Metuchen, N.J.: Scarecrow, 1980.

Standard Encyclopaedia of Southern Africa. 12 vols. Parow, South Africa: Nasou, 1970.

The Statesmen's Year Book. New York: St. Martin's, annual, 1864–.

Stevens, Richard P. *Historical Dictionary of Botswana*. Metuchen, N.J.: Scarecrow, 1975.

Stewart, John. *African States and Rulers*. Jefferson, N.C.: McFarland, 1989 (and 2nd ed., 1999).

Stratton, Arthur. *The Great Red Island*. Scribner's, 1964.

Tarikh. Essex, England: Longman, biennially, 1964–80.

Taylor, Sidney, ed. *The New Africans*. New York: Putnam, 1967.

Theal, George M. *History of South Africa*. 10 vols. in toto. London: Allen and Unwin.

Thompson, Virginia, and Richard Adloff. *Historical Dictionary of the Congo (Brazzaville)*. Metuchen, N.J.: Scarecrow, 1974.

Tindall, P.E.N. *A History of Central Africa*. New York: Praeger, 1968.

Truhart, Peter. *Regents of Nations*. 4 vols. Germany: Saur, 1984.

Ufahamu. Los Angeles African Activist Assoc., three times annually, 1970–.

UNESCO General History of Africa. 7 vols. 1981.

Vatikiotis, P.J. *The Modern History of Egypt*. New York: Praeger, 1969.

Vincent, Benjamin. *Haydn's Dictionary of Dates*. New York: Putnam, 1898.

Voll, John. *Historical Dictionary of Sudan*. Metuchen, N.J.: Scarecrow, 1978.

Weinstein, Warren. *Historical Dictionary of Burundi*. Metuchen, N.J.: Scarecrow, 1976.

Whitaker's Almanack. London: Whitaker, annual, 1868–.

Wiedner, Donald M. *A History of Africa South of the Sahara*. New York: Vintage, 1962.

Wilcocks, Julie. *Countries and Islands of the World*. 2nd edition. London: Clive Bingley, 1985.

Williams, Gwyneth, and Brian Hackland. *The Dictionary of Contemporary Politics of Southern Africa*. New York: Macmillan, 1989.

Who's Who in the Arab World. London: Bowker, annual, 1966–.

The World Almanack. New York: annual, 1885–.

World Rulers. Web page

Index of Places and Persons

This is a list of name elements in the main entries:
placenames and proper names not of rulers.

El-Aaiún: Western Sahara
Abaseni: Axum
Abdullahi, King of Bagdad: Gobir
Abéché: Wadai
Abidjan: Côte d'Ivoire
Abiras: Central African Republic
Abu Abdallah ash-Shi'i: Fatimid
  North Africa
Abu al-Futuh Buluggin: Algiers
Abu Hafs Umar: Hafsid Kingdom
Acatife: Canary Islands
Accada: Hollandia
Accra: Dutch Gold Coast; Ghana;
  Gold Coast Colony Region
Adama: Axum
Adama Lulu: Nupe
Addis Ababa: Ethiopia
Queen Adelaide: British Kaffraria
Aden: British Somaliland
Battle of Adowa: Ethiopia
Afonso V of Portugal: Cape Verde
Agadir: Morocco
Agadir: Tlemcen
Agama Kasha: Bedde
Agouz: Morocco
Aisa: Kanem
Ajdir: Rif Republic
Ajmat: Almoravid Empire
Alaric: Vandal North Africa
Alasora: Madagascar
Alcazarseguer: Morocco
Alexandria: Egypt
Algeciras Act: Spanish Morocco;
  Tangier
Alkalawa: Gobir
Amazons: Dahomey
Ambodifototra: Sainte Marie de
  Madagascar
Ambohidrabiby: Madagascar
Ambohidratimo: Madagascar
Ambohimanga: Madagascar
Ambuttai: Katsina
American Colonization Society:
  Liberia
Anamabo: Swedish Gold Coast

Anane: Lafia
Rev. Anderson: Griqualand West
Anfa: Morocco
Anka: Zamfara
Ankober: Shoa
Antananarivo: Madagascar
Anya Nya: Southern Sudan
Apollonia: Pentapolis
Apollonia: Swedish Gold Coast
Ardo Hassana: Adamawa
Guillaume d'Arse: Mauritius
Arsinoë: Pentapolis
Arzila: Morocco
Aseremankese: Akwamu
Ashir: Zirid Kingdom
Asila: Morocco
al-Askar: Egypt
Askari: Eritrea
Asmara: Eritrea
Assyria: Egypt
Asumenya Santemanso: Ashanti
Aswan: Kush
Lake Aswan: Upper Egypt
Atar: Adrar
Attah: Nupe
Augustus Caesar: Africa [i]; Tangier
Aussa: Assab
Avaris: Egypt
Axim: Dutch Gold Coast
Ayandawaase: Akwamu
Azammour: Morocco
Azania Liberation Front: Southern
  Sudan
Azare: Katagum
Aziziyah: Tripolitanian Republic

Badeggi-Lapai: Lapai
Bagamoyo: German East Africa
Bagauda: Kano
Bagida: Togoland
Baidoa: Southwestern Somalia
William Balfour Baikie: Northern
  Nigeria
Bakwanga: South Kasai Republic
Balearic Islands: Carthage

Bamako: Mali
Bandama River: Baule
Bandiagara: Tukolor Empire
Bangui: Central African Republic;
  Ubangi-Shari–Chad
Henry Barkly: Klipdrift Republic
Barkly West: Klipdrift Republic
Heinrich Barth: Adamawa
Bata: Equatorial Guinea
Bathoen: Botswana
Bawo: Gobir; Hausa States
Bayajidda: Hausa States; Kano;
  Zaria
Bbanda: Buganda
Bedeghi: Nupe
Behdet: Lower Egypt
Belisarius: Vandal North Africa
Benghazi: Cyrenaica
Berbera: British Somaliland
Sultan Berehan of Raheita: Assab
Berenice: Pentapolis
Juan de Béthencourt: Canary Islands
Reynaud de Béthencourt: Canary
  Islands
Biaghi: Nupe
Bida: Nupe
Bida-Nupiko: Nupe
Bin Yauri: Yauri
Louis Binger: Kong
Bingerville: Côte d'Ivoire
Birni Kimi: Bornu Empire
Birni Ngazargamu: Bornu Empire
Birnin-Bedr: Bedde
Birnin Kebbi: Argungu
Birnin Lalle: Gobir
Birnin Zamfara: Zamfara
Bisho: Ciskei
Bismarck: Lydenrust
Bissandugu: Samory's Empire
Bizerte: Tunisia
Jan Bloem: Klipdrift Republic
Bloemfontein: Orange Free State;
  South Africa; Transorangia
Bo: Kom
Bolama: Guinea-Bissau

Boma: Congo (Zaire); Ruanda-Urundi
Napoleon Bonaparte: Ascension; Egypt; Réunion; Saint Helena; Tristan da Cunha
Bono-Mansu: Bono
Bordj-Jedid: Carthage
Louis Botha: New Republic
Louis Bouët-Willaumez: Guinea
Bougie: Barbary States
Bougoula: Kenedugu
Comte de la Bourdonnais: Seychelles
Bremersdorf: Swaziland
British East Africa Company: Uganda; Kenya
British South Africa Company: Rhodesia; Zambia; Zimbabwe
Bubastis: Egypt
Buea: Cameroons; Kamerun
Buffalo River: Utrecht
Bujumbura: Burundi [i]; Burundi [ii]; Ruanda-Urundi
Bukharas: Nubia
Bukoba: Karagwe
Bulawayo: Matabeleland
Richard Burton: Benin [i]; Harar
Butha-Buthe: Lesotho
Buto: Lower Egypt
Butri: Swedish Gold Coast

Augustus Caesar: Africa [i]; Numidia; Tangier
Julius Caesar: Numidia
Caesarea Mauretaniae: Mauretania Caesariensis
Cairo: Egypt
Diogo Cam: Angola; Kongo
Cambe: Carthage
Diogo Cão: Angola; Kongo
Cape Coast Castle: Ghana; Swedish Gold Coast
Cape Esterias: Gabon
Cape Palmas: Maryland
Carlsborg: Swedish Gold Coast
Casablanca: Morocco
Castile: Canary Islands
Catherine de Braganza: Tangier
Catherine of Castile: Canary Islands
François Cauche: Réunion
Thomas Cavendish: Saint Helena
Antonio Cecchi: Italian Somaliland
Cekna: Baguirmi
Chai Chai: Gazaland
Chaka: Port Natal
Charles II of England: Fort James; Saint Helena; Tangier
Charles X of France: Algeria
Cherchel: Mauretania Caesariensis
Chingoni: Comoros; Mayotte; Sainte Marie de Madagascar
Chipata: North Eastern Rhodesia
Chisimaio: Jubaland
Christiansborg: Swedish Gold Coast
Cibinda Ilunga: Lunda
El Cid: Almoravid Empire
Cirta: Constantine; Numidia

George Clerk: Sekonyela's Land
Colbert's Compagnie des Indes Occidentales: Senegal
Colonia Iunonia: Carthage
Colonia Julia Carthago: Africa [i]; Africa [ii]; Carthage
Colonia Justiniana Carthago: Carthage
Como River: Gabon
Compagnie d'Afrique: Senegal
Compagnie des Indes Orientales: Senegal
Compagnie du Guinée: Senegal
Compagnie Normande: Senegal
Company of Adventurers of London: Fort James
Company of Devon and London Merchants: Fort James
Company of London Merchants: Ghana
Company of Merchants Trading to Africa: Fort James; Ghana
Company of Merchants Trading to Guinea: Ghana
Company of Royal Adventurers: Ghana
Conakry: Guinea
River Congo: Congo (Zaire)
Emperor Constantine; Saint Helena
Coptic Church: Ethiopia
Courland: Fort James
Elliott Cresson: Bassa Cove
Tristão da Cunha: Tristan da Cunha
Cyprus: Carthage

Tristão da Cunha: Tristan da Cunha
Vasco da Gama: Mozambique; Port Natal
João da Nova Castela: Ascension; Saint Helena
Dakar: French West Africa; Mali Federation; Senegal; Senegambia Confederation
Damberta: Kazaure
Dan Mairam: Daura
Danqaz: Ethiopia
Danshuhunni: Daura
Dar es-Salaam: German East Africa; Tanganyika; Tanzania
Guillaume d'Arse: Mauritius
Dazuli: Wagadugu
Juan de Béthencourt: Canary Islands
Reynaud de Béthencourt: Canary Islands
Charles de Gaulle: Algeria
Admiral de Hell: Nossi-Bé
Comte de la Bourdonnais: Seychelles
Comte de Modave: Fort-Dauphin
Marques de Ponbal: Bissau
Admiral De Ruyter: Ghana; Gorée
Ruy de Sequeira: Annobón
Pedro de Sintra: Liberia
Debra Markos: Gojjam
Delagoa Bay: Gazaland
Delphic Oracle: Pentapolis
Bob Denard: Comoros

William Deng: Southern Sudan
Dendi: Songhai
Destour party: Tunisia
Dhlo Dhlo: Rozwi
Bartolomeu Dias: Cape Colony
Diogo Dias: Diego Suarez; Madagascar
Diniz Diaz: Gorée
Dido: Carthage
Dikwa: Rabih's Empire
Dingaan: Port Natal
Diocletian: Africa [i]; Mauretania Sitifensis; Tripolitania
Djeriba: Mali Empire
Fernão do Po: Fernando Po
Dodoma: Tanzania
Dodu: Kangaba
Domoni: Anjouan
Doqait: Shoa
Douala: Cameroun; Kamerun
Francis Drake: Cape Verde
Drakensberg Mountains: Adam Kok's Land; Griqualand East
Dulo: Mandara
Durban: Port Natal
Benjamin D'Urban: British Kaffraria; Port Natal
Durbita Kusheyi: Katsina
Durombsi: Katsina
Dutsi: Zamfara
Dzaoudzi: Comoros

Edinburgh: Tristan da Cunha
El-Aaiún: Western Sahara
El Mina: Dutch Gold Coast; Portuguese Gold Coast
El Obeid: Kordofan
Elangeni: Swaziland
Elem Kalabari: New Calabar
Elisabethville: Congo (Zaire); Katanga Republic
Elissa: Carthage
Queen Elizabeth: Fort James
Elmina: Dutch Gold Coast; Portuguese Gold Coast
Entebbe: Uganda
Entoto: Ethiopia
Enugu: Biafra; Nigeria Eastern Region
Eshowe: Zululand

Louis Faidherbe: Mali; Walo
Falls Station: Stanleyville People's Republic
Fara: Zamfara
Faras: Nubia
al-Fasher: Darfur
Fatima: Egypt; Fatimid North Africa
al-Fayyum: Egypt
Prince Ferdinand of Portugal: Cape Verde
J. F. Ferreira: Little Free State
Fez: Almoravid Empire; French Morocco; Idrisid State; Morocco
Filonardi Company: Italian Somaliland
Firestone: Liberia

Fomboni: Mohéli
Fort Augustenborg: Danish Gold Coast
Fort Christiansborg: Danish Gold Coast
Fort d'Aumale: Gabon
Fort Dorothea: Hollandia
Fort Frederiksborg: Danish Gold Coast; Swedish Gold Coast
Fort Jameson: North Eastern Rhodesia
Fort Lamy: Chad
Fort Peddie: Transkeian Territories
Fort Salisbury: Rhodesia
Foumban: Bamoun
Bishop Frumentius: Ethiopia
al-Fustat: Egypt

Chief Gaberone Matlapin: Botswana
Gaberones: Bamaleteland; Batlokwaland; Botswana
Gabès: Tunisia
Gaborone: Botswana
Gafsa: Tunisia
Vasco da Gama: Mozambique; Port Natal
Gambia Adventurers: Fort James
Ganua: Wase
Garin Gabas: Biram
Garowe: Puntland
Garrison: Ascension
Gashua: Bedde
Gaul: Mauretania Tingitana; Tangier
Charles de Gaulle: Algeria
Gayin: Bedde
Gazai: Bedde
Gbara: East Nupe; Nupe
Geiserich: Vandal North Africa
George Town: Ascension
Gibeon: Namibia; Witbooi Territory
Gibraltar: Carthage; Tangier
Gidgid: Bedde
Giyani: GazaNkulu
William Glass: Tristan da Cunha
Golden Stool: Ashanti
George Goldie: Northern Nigeria
Juan Gonçalves Zarco: Funchal
Goncho: Ifat
Goran Rami: Gobir
Charles Gordon: Buganda
Gorgoram: Bedde
Capt. Goubert: Réunion
Capt. Gough: Gough Island
Gourcy: Yatenga
Gouveia: Gazaland
Grahamstown: British Kaffraria
Grão-Pará Company: Bissau
James Green: Mississippi-in-Africa
Grootfontein: Lydenrust
Gueza: Damagaram
Guilongou: Wagadugu
Gun War: Lesotho
Gurin: Adamawa
Ralph Randolph Gurley: Liberia

Hamdallahi: Masina
Harare: Zimbabwe

Hargeysa: British Somaliland; Somaliland Republic
Robert Goodloe Harper: Liberia; Maryland
Joe Harris: Bassa Cove
James Hastie: Madagascar
Admiral de Hell: Nossi-Bé
Hellville: Nossi-Bé
Prince Henry of Portugal: Canary Islands
Henry III of Castile: Canary Islands
Heracleopolis: Egypt
Hierakonpolis: Upper Egypt
Ho: British Togoland
Mike Hoare: Seychelles
Robert Holmes: Gorée
Hornacheros: Bou Regreg
Hornacho: Bou Regreg
Horus: Lower Egypt
Huambo: Angola; Angola Democratic People's Republic

Ibrahim: Kanem
Idj-Towy: Egypt
Ikopa Valley: Madagascar
Ilunga Mbili: Luba Empire
Imerinanjaka: Madagascar
Imhotep: Egypt
Ras Imru: Italian East Africa
Indonesia: Madagascar
Inhambane: Gazaland
Inkil: Bauchi
Inyati: Matabeleland
Iol: Mauretania; Mauretania East
Ireshe: Yauri
Ireshe Bino: Yauri
Mulay Ismail as-Samin: Ceuta; Tangier
Ismai'ili movement: Fatimid North Africa
Ismailia: Equatoria Province
Istiqlal: Morocco
Italy: Byzacena; Carthage; Mauretania Caesariensis

Jalingo: Muri
James II: Saint Helena
James, Duke of Courland: Fort James
Jamestown: Saint Helena
Jebba: Nupe
Jema'an Darroro: Jema'a
Jema'an Sarari: Jema'a
Jerusalem: Egypt
King Jimmy: Sierra Leone
Jimunli: Nupe
Joalaboholo: Sekonyela's Land
João II of Portugal: Cape Verde
Jobolio: Adamawa
Joe Harris: Bassa Cove
Juba: Southern Sudan
Julian: Ceuta
Julius Caesar: Numidia
Justinian: Byzantine North Africa; Ceuta

Kabodha: Buganda
Kaduna: Nigeria Northern Region

Kafanchan: Jema'a
Kampala: Uganda
Kanye: Bangwaketseland
Kasar Sa'id: Tunisia
Kawar: Kanem; Zaria
Kayès: Mali
Col. Keating: Mauritius
Kei River: British Kaffraria
Keiskamma River: British Kaffraria; Transkeian Territories
Kentani: Kreli's Country
Keta: Danish Gold Coast
Khama III: Botswana
Kharijite doctrine: Rustumid Amirate
Khartoum: Sudan
Kianza: Damagaram
Kiawa: Zamfara
Kigali: Ruanda; Rwanda
Kikandwa: Buganda
Kiki: Kangaba
Kilimiro: Burundi [i]
Kimberley: Griqualand West; Klipdrift Republic
Kinshasa: Congo (Zaire)
Kirtha: Numidia
Kisangani: Stanleyville People's Republic; Stanleyville Republic
Kismayu: Jubaland
Francis Kofi: Ghana
Kogu: Biu
Kokstad: Griqualand East; Transkeian Territories
Kongosteen: Danish Gold Coast
Kormantin: Dutch Gold Coast; Ghana
Rev. Kramer: Griqualand West
Kukawa: Bornu Empire
Kukya: Songhai
Kumasi: Ashanti
Kumbi: Ghana Empire
Kumbu River: Baule
Kuruman: Bechuanaland Protectorate
Kusseri: Rabih's Empire
Kwargdom: Daura

La: Wagadugu
Comte de la Bourdonnais: Seychelles
La Marsa: Tunisia
Labuji: Nupe
Lafian Beri-Beri: Lafia
Lafiya Moi: Fika
Laikom: Kom
Lambaye: Baol
Jonathan Lambert: Tristan da Cunha
François Lamy: Chad
Lau: Muri
Lealui: Barotseland; North Western Rhodesia
Lebowakgomo: Lebowa
Libreville: French Equatorial Africa; Gabon
Lilongwe: Malawi
Limbur: Biu
Limpopo River: Matabeleland; Mwene Mutapa Empire

Linger: Dyolof
Linguère: Dyolof
al-Lisht: Egypt
Livingstone: Zambia
David Livingstone: Bechuanaland
 Protectorate; Zambia
Lobatsi: Barolongland
Logone: Rabih's Empire
Lokko: Koya-Temne
Lomé: British Togoland; Togo; To-
 goland
London Convention: United States
 of Stellaland
London Missionary Society: Griqua-
 land West
Longwood: Saint Helena
Fernão López: Saint Helena
Louis XV: Louisbourg
Louisiana State Colonization Society:
 Mississippi-in-Africa
Lourenço Marques: Mozambique
Luapula Valley: Kazembe
Lubaga: Buganda
Lubumbashi: Katanga Republic
Lüderitz: Namibia
Frederick Lugard: Uganda; Katsina
Lady Lugard: Nigeria
Lugusi: Wagadugu
Lumbila: Wagadugu
Patrice Lumumba: Katanga Republic
Lusaakas: Zambia
Lusaka: Zambia

Robert Machim: Machico
Mad Mullah: British Somaliland
Mafeking: Botswana
Magdala: Ethiopia
al-Mahdiya: Fatimid North Africa;
 Tunis
Bertrand-François Mahé: Seychelles
Maiduguri: Bornu Empire
Maigali: Gobir
Henry Mainwaring: Masmouda
Makau: Abuja
Malabo: Equatorial Guinea
Malaya: Madagascar
Mamoutzou: Mayotte Department
Manda Bay: Kenya
Manuel of Portugal: Cape Verde
al-Mansuriyah: Egypt
al-Mansuriyya: Fatimid North Africa
Maputo: Mozambique
Maramba: Zambia
F. I. Maritz: Little Free State
Marrakesh: Almohad Empire;
 Almoravid Empire; Morocco
Pedro Mascarenhas: Réunion
Maseru: Lesotho
Massa: Morocco
Massenya: Baguirmi
Mau Mau: Kenya
Maun: Batwanaland
Honoratus Maynier: Graaff-Reinet
Mazagan: Morocco
Mbabane: Swaziland
Mbanza: Kongo

Mbanza Kabassa: Ndongo
Mbarara: Nkore
Tom Mboya: Kenya
Mbuji Mayi: South Kasai Republic
Mbul: Kayor
Duke of Medina Sidonia: Melilla
Mehdia: Morocco
Meknes: French Morocco; Morocco
Memphis: Egypt
Mendes: Egypt
Mengo: Buganda
Mfom Ben: Bamoun
Milanese Commercial Society: Italian
 Somaliland
Missionary Road: United States of
 Stellaland
Mmabatho: Bophuthatswana
Mochudi: Bakgatlaland
Comte de Modave: Fort-Dauphin
Robert Moffat: Bechuanaland Pro-
 tectorate
Mokotjo: Sekonyela's Land
Molepolole: Bakwenaland
Molopo River: Bechuanaland
 Protectorate
Eduardo Mondlane: Mozambique
James Monroe: Liberia
Mora: Mandara
Moree: Dutch Gold Coast
Maro Morgan: Southern Sudan
Moriscos: Bou Regreg
Col. Morland: Kano
Moshete: Goshen
Mount Fura: Mwene Mutapa Empire
Mparo: Bunyoro
Msamboro: Mayotte
Muhammad ibn Abdallah Hassan:
 British Somaliland
Muhammad ibn Tumart: Almohad
 Empire
Mulago: Buganda
Richard Munden: Saint Helena
Muniyo: Bornu Empire
Munza: Luba Empire
Murya: Daura
Murzuq: Fezzan; Phazania
Muscat: Zanzibar
Musumba: Lunda
Mutsamudu: Anjouan; Nzwani
Mutum Biyu: Muri
Mwibele: Luba Empire
Mzizima: German East Africa

Naba Zoungourana: Wagadugu
Nabulagala: Buganda
Nairobi: Kenya
Nakatema: Buganda
Napata: Kush
Charles Napier: Ethiopia
Napoleon Bonaparte: Ascension;
 Egypt; Réunion; Saint Helena;
 Tristan da Cunha
Napoleonic Wars: Ceuta; Gambia
Naqadah: Upper Egypt
Maurits von Nassau: Mauritius
Nazaret: Axum

N'Djamena: Chad
Nedega: Mossi States
Nekheb: Upper Egypt
Neni-Nesu: Egypt
Neo-Destour party: Tunisia
New York and Pennsylvania
 Colonization Societies: Bassa
 Cove; Edina
Ngoi: Segu
Nguru: Daura
Ngwese: Namibia
Niamey: Niger
Niani: Mali Empire
Nightingale: Tristan da Cunha
Njimi: Bornu Empire; Kanem;
 Zaghawa Kingdom
Nnakawa: Buganda
Nntamo: Congo
Nongoma: KwaZulu
Nooigedacht: Klipdrift Republic
Nouakchott: Mauritania
João da Nova Castela: Ascension;
 Saint Helena
Nova Lisboa: Angola
Nowe: Egypt
Nqamakwe: Fingoland
Nsauoen: Akim
Nuwe: Egypt
Nyamasane: KaNgwane
Nyandeni: Pondoland West

OAS: Algeria
El Obeid: Kordofan
Oduduwa: Ife; Ijebu
Joseph Oduho: Southern Sudan
Ohopoho: Namibia
John Okello: Zanzibar
Old Dunqulah: Mukurra
Omdurman: Sudan
Prince of Orange: Cape Colony
Orange River: Griqualand West;
 Orange Free State
Oshakati: Ovamboland
Osiris: Egypt
Osu: Ghana; Swedish Gold Coast
Otjimbigwe: Namibia
Oubritenga: Wagadugu
Ouidriaogo: Mossi States
Oujda: French Morocco
Ozi River: Kenya

Pachoras: Nubia
Panther Incident: French Morocco
Papendorp: Cape Colony
Cosmo Parkinson: Tanganyika
Pategi: Nupe
Payi: Lapai
Pedro VII: Kongo
Pembi: Gonja
Karl Peters: Buganda; Kenya
Ptolemy Philadelphus: British
 Somaliland
John Philip: Adam Kok's Land
Phoenicians: Algiers; Carthage
Phuthaditjhaba: QwaQwa
Lazare Picault: Seychelles

Pietermaritzburg: Natal
Pi-Ramesse: Egypt
Fernão do Po: Fernando Po
Podor: Futa Toro
Poeni: Carthage
Marques de Ponbal: Bissau
Pongolo River: Swaziland
Port Clarence: Fernando Po
Port Lokko: Koya-Temne
Port Louis: Mauritius
Port Mathurin: Rodrigues
Port St Johns: Pondoland
Hendrik Potgieter: Natal
Poughtoenga: Wagadugu
Praia: Cape Verde
Prester John: Ethiopia
Pretoria: Matabeleland; South
   Africa; Transvaal
Jacques Pronis: Réunion
Ptolemy Philadelphus: British
   Somaliland
Punic Wars: Carthage
Pygmalion: Carthage

al-Qahir: Egypt
Qakeni: Pondoland East
al-Qalat: Hammadid Kingdom
al-Qata'i: Egypt
al-Qayrawan: Aghlabid Empire; Arab
   North Africa; Fatimid North Africa;
   Omayyad and Abbasid North
   Africa; Zirid Kingdom; Tunisia
Qundi: Shoa

Ra: Egypt
Raba: Nupe; West Nupe
Rabat-Salé: Barbary States; Bou
   Regreg; French Morocco; Morocco
Raheita: Assab
Raqqada: Fatimid North Africa;
   Zirid Kingdom
Ras Imru: Italian East Africa
Ratsimilaho: Madagascar
Rauta: Bauchi
Rawa: Mossi States
Re: Egypt
Red Crown: Upper Egypt; Lower
   Egypt
Remboue River: Gabon
Piet Retief: Zululand
Cecil Rhodes: Katanga Republic;
   Rhodesia
Riala: Mossi States
Ribadu: Adamawa
Rikoci: Zaria
Arthur Rimbaud: Harar
Río Nuñez: Guinea
Robanna: Koya-Temne
Holden Roberto: Angola
Rokel River: Sierra Leone
Sylvain Roux: Madagascar
Royal Adventurers Trading in Africa:
   Fort James
Royal African Company: Fort James;
   Ghana; Senegal; Senegambia Col-
   ony

Royal African Corps: Gambia
Royal Company of Adventurers:
   Liberia
Royal Company of Senegal: Senegal
Rundu: Namibia
Rustenburg: Cape Colony
Ruwan Gora: Zamfara
Admiral De Ruyter: Ghana; Gorée

Sabaeans: Ethiopia
Sabha: Fezzan
Sabon Gari: Fulani Empire; Zamfara
Sabra al-Mansuriyah: Zirid Kingdom
Safi: Morocco
Sagmaga: Bedde
Saint Denis: Réunion; Sainte Marie
   de Madagascar
St. John River: Bassa Cove
Saint Louis: French Gambia; French
   West Africa; Gorée; Guinea;
   Mauritania; Senegal; Senegambia
   Colony; Trarza
Saint Paul: Réunion
Sainte Rita: Agalega Islands
Sais: Egypt
Saladin: Central African Republic
Salah ad-Din Ahmad: Central
   African Republic
Salah ben Yusuf: Tunisia
Raoul Salan: Algeria
Salé: Bou Regreg
Salisbury: Federation of Rhodesia and
   Nyasaland; Rhodesia; Zimbabwe
Lord Salisbury: Rhodesia
Sallee Rovers: Barbary States; Bou
   Regreg
San Antonio de Praia: Annobón
Santa Isabel: Equatorial Guinea;
   Fernando Po
Santo Antonio: Príncipe
Santorini: Pentapolis
São Jorge da Mina: Portuguese Gold
   Coast
São José de Bissau: Bissau
São Paulo de Loanda: Angola
São Salvador: Kongo
Giuseppe Sapeto: Assab
Saqqarah: Egypt
Sardinia: Carthage
Satako: Bedde
Lohure Saturnino: Southern Sudan
Savi: Whydah
Jonas Savimbi: Angola: Angola
   Democratic People's Republic
Schoemansdal: Zoutpansberg
Sebe: Togoland
Sebele I: Botswana
Sebennytus: Egypt
Sebu: Kanem
Segu-koro: Segu
Sena: Gazaland; Mozambique
Ruy de Sequeira: Annobón
Serowe: Bamangwatoland
Seth: Upper Egypt
Sétif: Mauretania Sitifensis
Sfax: Tunisia

Shaka: Port Natal
Shamama: Brakna
Shari River: Central African Republic
Granville Sharp: Sierra Leone
Flora Shaw: Nigeria
Queen of Sheba: Ethiopia
Sheme: Kano
Siberia: Louisbourg
Sicily: Aghlabid Empire; Carthage;
   Fatimid North Africa
Sidon: Carthage
Sifawa: Fulani Empire
Sijilmassa: Fatimid North Africa
Pedro de Sintra: Liberia
Sitifis: Mauretania Sitifensis
Siyabuswa: KwaNdebele
Sla al-Jadid: Bou Regreg
Sla al-Qadim: Bou Regreg
Henry Smeathman: Sierra Leone
Harry Smith: Orange Free State;
   Transorangia
Soba: Alwah
Società di Navigazione Rubattino:
   Assab
King Solomon of Israel: Egypt;
   Ethiopia
Sorbo Haoussa: Niger
Sous: Morocco
Spain: Almohad Empire; Almoravid
   Empire; Morocco; Tangier
John Hanning Speke: Buganda
Henry M. Stanley: Congo (Zaire);
   Stanleyville People's Republic
Subah: Alwah
Suez Crisis: Egypt
Suleiman Solong: Kordofan
Surame: Argungu
Hendrik Swellengrebel: Swellendam
Syria: Egypt

Tafilalt: Morocco
Tafna: Mascara
Tagdemt: Mascara
Tagrart: Tlemcen
Tahert: Mascara; Rustumid Amirate
Empress Taitu: Ethiopia
Takoradi: Dutch Gold Coast;
   Swedish Gold Coast
Tamale: Gold Coast Northern
   Territories
Tamatave: Madagascar
Tananarive: Madagascar
Tanis: Egypt
Tashena: Katagum
Taza: Morocco
Tegulat: Ethiopia
Tell al-Amarna: Egypt
Tete: Mozambique
Tetuán: Spanish Morocco
Abd ar-Rahman at-Thaalibi: Tunisia
Thaba Bosiu: Lesotho
Thebes: Egypt
Thera: Pentapolis
Thinis: Egypt
Thohoyandou: Venda
Thompson Town: Liberia

Tiaret: Mascara; Rustumid
   Amirate
Timbo: Futa Jallon
Tindouf: Western Sahara
Tingis: Mauretania Tingitana;
   Mauretania West; Tangier
Tinmallal: Almohad Empire
King Tom: Sierra Leone
Nuno Tristão: Cacheu
Tsibiri: Gobir
Tsirkau: Daura
Tsofon Birni: Daura
Tumbi: Gumel
Turunku: Zaria
Tuwon: Brass
Twon: Brass
Tyre: Carthage

al-Ubaid: Kordofan
Ubaydallah: Fatimid North Africa
Uccialli: Ethiopia
Ulad Abd Allah Dynasty: Brakna
Ulad Saiyyid Dynasty: Brakna
Ulad Yayha ibn Uthman: Adrar
Ulundi: KwaZulu
Umbandine: Little Free State
Umtata: Tembuland; Transkei
Umuahia: Biafra
Umzinkulu River: Transkeian
   Territories
UNITA: Angola; Angola Democratic
   People's Republic
Unyanyembe: Mirambo
USA: Louisbourg; Tangier;
   Tripolitania

Usama: Benin [i]
Usumbura: Burundi [i]; Ruanda-
   Urundi
Jacobus Uys: Natal
Utica: Carthage

Vaal River: Matabeleland; Orange
   Free State; Transvaal
Valencia: Almoravid Empire
Victoire: Libertalia
Victoria Nyanza: Kenya
Vila de Porto Santo: Porto Santo
Villa Cisneros: Western Sahara
Villa de Praia: Cape Verde
Visigoths: Ceuta
Vittorio Emanuele: Ethiopia
Maurits von Nassau: Mauritius
Vrijburg: British Bechuanaland
Vryburg: British Bechuanaland

Walwal: Italian East Africa
Wareba: Baule
Charles Warren: Bechuanaland
   Protectorate
Waw: Bahr al-Ghazal
Weltwitschia: Namibia
West India and Guinea Company:
   Danish Gold Coast
White Crown: Upper Egypt; Lower
   Egypt
White Wall: Egypt
Louis Bouët-Willaumez: Guinea
William IV of Britain: British
   Kaffraria
Ruth Williams: Botswana

Windhoek: Namibia; Oorlam
   Territory
Orde Wingate: Ethiopia; Italian East
   Africa
Hendrik Witbooi: Namibia
Garnet Wolseley: Zululand
Wuciciri: Zaria
Wudi: Bornu Empire

Xai Xai: Gazaland
Xois: Egypt

Yadega: Yatenga
Yamia: Bornu Empire
Yamoussoukro: Côte d'Ivoire
Yaoundé: Cameroun
Yelwa: Yauri
Yemen: Egypt; Gobir
Yendi: Dagomba
Yenenga: Mossi States
Yerwa: Bornu Empire
Yoruba Civil Wars: Abeokuta
Young Men's Colonization Society of
   Pennsylvania: Bassa Cove

Zambesi River: Zambia
Juan Gonçalves Zarco: Funchal;
   Porto Santo
Zionist homeland: Kenya
Ziri ibn Manad at-Talkali: Algiers;
   Zirid Kingdom
Zomba: Malawi
Zugurma: Nupe
Zungeru: Nigeria Northern Region

Index of Rulers

Because of the multiplicity of forms, stylings and naming traditions, and the attendant confusion as to what constitutes a Western style "last name," the names of rulers are not inverted. This index of rulers is arranged alphabetically. In many cases, where the entry is a long one in the bulk of the book, the ruler's basic dates are given, as a locating aid. Names are alphabetized under all reasonable permutations, eliminating the need for cross-referencing. Each name has a bold letter in it, representing the place where that ruler would be found in a more traditional inverted index. Names after "ibn" in multipart names are not listed alphabetically, as this means "son of."

The Arab forms ad-, al-, an-, ar-, as-, ash-, at-, and az- are treated as the English "the," and therefore not indexed at all in their place under "a." The name "al-Asi," for example, will be found under "Asi," but listed as "al-Asi," with the "A" of "Asi" in bold.

The honorifics Haj, al-Haj, Hajji, al-Hajj, and similar forms indicate a man who made the pilgrimage to Mecca, and are therefore titles, not names as such. Unless the name Haj or a variation thereof forms an integral part of a ruler's name, such as Alhaji, or al-Hajj (which, because that was the ruler's full name, will be found indexed under H), names are not alphabetized by these titles. The same practice is observed for Sa'id, Sa'd, Sayid, Seyid, and other forms; Sheikh, Shehu, and other forms; Sid, Sidi, and other forms; and Mallam. These titles are listed alphabetically where appropriate, but the bold letter will again show the correct name of the ruler.

For ease of reference, this index has been alphabetized by word, rather than by letter. So, for example, all the "Abd" entries appear before the "Abdallah" entries, even though on a letter by letter basis "Abdallah" would come before "Abd al-Malik."

Alphabetization follows the following pattern: all Abdallahs (for instance) are arranged alphabetically according to country, then chronologically when there are two or more from the same country. After the Abdallahs come the names in which Abdallah forms the last of two or more components, e.g. "Yahya Abdallah" or "Hassan Yakub Abdallah." In these cases it is the very first letter of the person's name that determines his/her position in the order. After this group come the Abdallahs who have a number after their names, e.g. "Abdallah I" or "Abdallah IV," arranged numerically, so that all rulers with the name "Abdallah II" are arranged together, and immediately after them come those with additional names after the number, such as "Abdallah II al-Hatim." Next comes "Abdallah III," then "Abdallah III Hazarmard," and so on. After this group come those with a name or names after the "Abdallah" component, e.g. Abdallah ibn Suleiman. These are arranged alphabetically, the key word being that after the name "Abdallah."

The following should be noted:

The Arabic-based "Abd al-" followed by another name can also be found under "Abdul," or "Abdel." For Abdul (the English version of Abd al-), and Abdel (the French version), see Abd al-.

The Arabic-based "Abd ar-" followed by another name, for example "Abd ar-Rahman," can also be found as "Abdarrahman," "Abderrahman" or "Abdurrahman."

Abu Bakr, Abu-Bakr, Abu Bakar, Abubakar, Abubakr, Abu Bekr and Abu-Bekr are all the same in essence.

Names containing the particle "De" or "de" are found in two places, under the letter "D" as well as under the next component of the name. Note: The Spanish, French and Portuguese tend to use "de," while the Dutch and Italians tend to use "De." There is no difference alphabetically. The

British are not constant in this regard, such names being from diverse origins anyway.

The Dutch particles "Van" and "Van Der" are indexed under "Van" as well as under the next component of the name. The German-based "von" is listed as such, and also under the next component of the name.

In the index (but not in the text) superfluous titles (such as Col., Sir, etc.) are omitted. However, peerage titles are included, because in most cases if there is no title given the person cannot be easily identified.

A

A'alaf Sagad: Ethiopia (1667–82)
Niels Aarestrup: Danish Gold Coast (1772–77)
Sani Abacha: Nigeria (1993–98)
Muhammad Abali: Fika
Abalokun: Oyo
Abarshi: Zamfara
Abdullahi Abarshi: Yauri
Dauda Abasama I: Kano (1565)
Dauda Abasama II: Kano (1776–80)
S.Y. Abashi: Yauri
Abayajidda: Daura
Abaza: Damagaram
Hassan Abaza: Tripolitania (1679–83)
Abba: Adamawa
Abbad al-Balkhi: Egypt (812–13)
Abbas: Egypt (1153–54)
al-Abbas: Timbuktu (1688)
Abu'l Abbas: Egypt (910)
Ahmad II al-Abbas: Morocco (1655–59)
Ferhat Abbas: Algerian Republic (Provisional Government)
Muhammadu Abbas: Kano (1903–19)
Muhammadu Inuwa Abbas: Kano (1963)
Abbas I: Egypt (1848–54)
Abbas II Hilmi: Egypt (1892–1914)
Abu al-Abbas Ahmad: Hafsid Kingdom
Abu al-Abbas Ahmad: Tlemcen (1430–62)
Abu al-Abbas Ahmad al-Fadl: Hafsid Kingdom
Abu'l Abbas Ahmad: Hafsid Kingdom; Morocco (1374–84)
al-Abbas ibn Musa: Egypt (814)
Abbas Bonfah: Togo (2005)
Abbas Djoussouf: Comoros (1998–99)
Obeydallah al-Abbasi: Egypt (805–806)
Abbiye: Shoa
Ibrahim Abboud: Sudan (1958–64)
Abd al-Ali al-Obeidi: Libya
Abd al-Aziz: Morocco (1894–1908)
Abd al-Aziz: Wadai
Abu Faris Abd al-Aziz: Hafsid Kingdom
Abu'l Faris Abd al-Aziz I: Morocco (1366–72, 1393–96)
Abd al-Hafiz: Morocco (1908–12)
Abd al-Halim: Morocco (1361)
Abd al-Hamid al-Bakkush: Libya

Abd al-Ja'far I: Timbuktu (1721–22)
Abd al-Ja'far II: Timbuktu (1748)
Abd al-Jalil: Fezzan
Abd al-Jalil: Kanem
Abd al-Kadim: Bornu Empire (1260–88)
Abd al-Kadir I: Funj Sultanate
Abd al-Kadir II: Funj Sultanate
Abd al-Kadiri: Ilorin
Sidi Abd al-Kadiri: Zaria (1853–54)
Abd al-Karim: Katsina (1631–34)
Abd al-Karim: Rif Republic
Abd al-Karim: Wadai
Abd al-Karim: Zaria (1834–46)
Abd al-Karim ar-Ragrag: Tunis (1195–1200)
Abd al-Karim ibn Muhammad: Harar
Abd al-Kedir: Baguirmi (1846–58)
Abd al-Kedir: Baguirmi (1918–35)
Abd al-Krim: Wadai
Abd al-Latif Pasha: Sudan (1850–51)
Abd al-Majid Kubar: Libya
Abd al-Malik: Arab North Africa
Abd al-Malik: Morocco (1728)
Abd al-Malik II: Morocco (1628–31)
Abd al-Malik III: Morocco (1624–26)
Abd al-Malik al-Ghazi: Morocco (1576–78)
Abd al-Malik ibn Marwar: Egypt (750)
Abd al-Malik ibn Rifa'a: Egypt (714–717, 727)
Abd al-Malik ibn Salih: Egypt (795–796)
Abd al-Mu'min: Hafsid Kingdom
Abd al-Mu'min al-Kumi: Almohad Empire
Abd al-Qadir: Mascara
Abd al-Qadir: Timbuktu (1711–12)
Abd al-Qadir Badri: Libya
Abd al-Qadir Pasha Hilmi: Sudan (1882–83)
Abd al-Qrim: Rif Republic
Abd al-Wahhab: Rustumid Amirate
Abd al-Wahid: Tripolitania (1397–1401)
Abu Malik Abd al-Wahid: Tlemcen (1412–24, 1429–30)
Abu Muhammad Abd al-Wahid: Tripolitania (1207–21); Tunis (1207–21)
Abd al-Wahid II: Almohad Empire
Abd al-Wahid al-Makhluwi: Almohad Empire

Abd al-Wahid ibn Yahya: Egypt (851–852)
Abd ar-Rahman: Egypt (1651–52)
Abd ar-Rahman: Egypt (1676–80)
Abd ar-Rahman: Morocco (1822–59)
Abd ar-Rahman: Omayyad and Abbasid North Africa
Abd ar-Rahman: Tagant
Abd ar-Rahman al-Youssoufi: Morocco (1998–2002)
Abu Sa'id Abd ar-Rahman: Tripolitania (1221); Tunis (1221, 1223–26)
Abu Sa'id Uthman II Abd ar-Rahman: Tlemcen (1348–52)
Abd ar-Rahman I: Timbuktu (1634–35)
Abd ar-Rahman II: Timbuktu (1666–67)
Abd ar-Rahman III: Timbuktu (1726)
Abd ar-Rahman Ahmad Ali Tur: Somaliland Republic
Abd ar-Rahman al-Youssoufi: Morocco (1998–)
Sayid Abd ar-Rahman ibn al-Mahdi: Sudan (1952–53)
Abd ar-Rahman ibn Ghadam: Egypt (684–685)
Abd ar-Rahman ibn Khalid: Egypt (735–737)
Abd ar-Rahman ibn Muhammad: Harar
Abd ar-Rahman ibn Musa: Tlemcen (1411)
Abd ar-Rahman ibn Rustum: Rustumid Amirate
Abd ar-Rahman Musa: Omayyad and Abbasid North Africa
Abd ar-Rahman Siwar ad-Dahab: Sudan (1985–86)
Abd ar-Rahman Yaqub: Tripolitania (1236–47)
Sheikh Abd as-Salaam al-Asman: Tripolitania (1480–82)
Abd as-Salami: Ilorin
Abd as-Salami: Zaria (1854–57)
Abd ash-Shakur ibn Yusuf: Harar
Abdaku: Zaria (1611–18)
Abdal-Salem Jallud: Libya
Abdallah: Baguirmi
Abdallah: Bornu Empire (1563–70)
Abdallah: Egypt (1729–33)
Abdallah: Harar
Abdallah: Morocco (1396–98)
Abdallah: Morocco (1729–34, 1736, 1740–57)

Abu Muhammad Abdallah: Tripolitania (1053)

Ahmad Abdallah: Comoros (1972–75, 1978–89)

Sayid ibn Abdallah: Zanzibar (1960–63)

Abdallah I: Aghlabid Empire

Abdallah I: Anjouan

Abdallah I: Kanem

Abdallah I: Timbuktu (1678)

Abu Muhammad Abdallah I: Tlemcen (1397–1400)

Abdallah II: Aghlabid Empire

Abdallah II: Anjouan

Abdallah II: Bornu Empire (1326–46)

Abdallah II: Morocco (1613–24)

Abdallah II: Timbuktu (1687)

Abu Muhammad Abdallah II: Tlemcen (1527–41)

Abdallah II Abu Muhammad al-Abdil: Almohad Empire

Abdallah III: Anjouan

Abdallah III: Timbuktu (1695–96)

Abdallah III Dakumuni: Bornu Empire (1435–42)

Abdallah IV: Timbuktu (1697–98, 1700, 1704–05, 1707, 1712)

Abdallah V: Timbuktu (1713–15, 1716, 1722–25, 1726–27, 1729–31)

Abdallah Derow Isaq: Somalia

Abu Muhammad Abdallah Abu: Tunis (1226–28)

Abdallah al-Ghalib: Morocco (1557–74)

Abu Abdallah as-Si'i al-Muhtasab: Tunis (909–10)

Abdallah ibn Abd al-Malik: Egypt (703–709)

Abdallah ibn Abderrahman: Egypt (769–772)

Abdallah ibn Ali al-Kasri: Bou Regreg

Abdallah ibn al-Mussayab: Egypt (793)

Abdallah ibn Amr: Egypt (664)

Abdallah ibn Gad: Zanzibar (1746)

Abdallah ibn Hamish: Mombasa (1837–60)

Abdallah ibn Hasan: Zeng Empire (1483–84)

Sayid Abdallah ibn Khalifa: Zanzibar (1963)

Abdallah ibn Muhammad: Harar

Abdallah ibn Muhammad: Mombasa (1773–82, 1811–25)

Abdallah ibn Muhammad at-Taashi: Sudan (1885–98)

Abdallah ibn Sa'd: Arab North Africa; Egypt (644–654, 655–656)

Abdallah ibn Tahir: Egypt (826–828)

Abdallah ibn Yalluf: Tripolitania (973)

Abdallah Ibrahim: Morocco (1958–60)

Abdallah Ibrahim: Nzwani

Abdallah Issa: British Somaliland

Hajji Abdallah Izmirli: Tripolitania (1684–87)

Abdallah Kamil: Djibouti (1978)

Abdallah Kassim Hanga: Zanzibar (1964)

Abdallah Khalil: Sudan (1956–58)

Abu Abdallah Muhammad: Tripolitania (1014–22)

Abu Abdallah Muhammad I: Tlemcen (1400–11)

Abu Abdallah Muhammad I al-Mustansir: Hafsid Kingdom

Abu Abdallah Muhammad II: Tlemcen (1424–27, 1430)

Abu Abdallah Muhammad II Abu Asida: Hafsid Kingdom

Abu Abdallah Muhammad III: Tlemcen (1462–68)

Abu Abdallah Muhammad IV: Tlemcen (1468–1504)

Abu Abdallah Muhammad IV al-Muntasir: Hafsid Kingdom

Abu Abdallah Muhammad V: Hafsid Kingdom; Tlemcen (1504–17)

Abu Abdallah Muhammad VI: Tlemcen (1543)

Abu Abdallah Muhammad ibn Ahmad az-Ziyani: Bou Regreg

Aden Abdallah Osman Daar: Somalia

Abdarrahman: Bornu Empire (1853–54)

Abdarrahman: Fulani Empire

Abdarrahman: Jema'a

Abdarrahman ar-Rashid: Darfur

Abdaweyh ibn Gaabela: Egypt (830–831)

Abdel Kadir Woli: Baguirmi

Abdel Krim: Rif Republic

Gamel Abdel Nasser: Egypt (1954–70)

Muhammad Abdelazizz: Western Sahara

Muhammad Abdelghani: Algeria (1979–84)

Abdelhamid Brahimi: Algeria (1984–88)

Abdelkader: Futa Jallon

Abdelkader Taleb Oumar: Western Sahara

Abdelkedir: Mascara

Abdellatif Filali: Morocco (1994–98)

Said Abeid Abderemane: Nzwani

Abderrahman Bey: Tripolitania (1904)

Abderrahman Guarang I: Baguirmi

Abderrahman Guarang II: Baguirmi

Ibrahim Abderrahman Halidi: Comoros (1993)

Abderrahman Woli: Baguirmi

Abderrahman Youssoufi: Morocco (1998–2002)

Belaid Abdesalam: Algeria (1992–93)

Abdi: Egypt (1714–17, 1727)

Kurd Abdi: Algiers (1724–31)

Muhammad Abdi Hashi: Puntland

Abdi Rashid Shermarke: Somalia

Abdi Rizak Hajji Hussein: Somalia

Muhammad Abdi Yusuf: Somalia

Abdinur Ahmad Darman: Somalia

Abdiqasim Salad Hassan: Somalia

Ahmad Abdou: Comoros (1996–97)

Abdou Diouf: Senegal (1970–80, 1981–2000)

Muhammad Abdou Mahdi: Comoros (1994)

Abdou Muhammad Hussein: Nzwani

Abdu: Biram

Abdu: Daura-Baure

Gwari Abdu: Daura

Bako Abdu Ashkuku: Zaria (1611–18)

Abdu Fari: Zamfara

Abdu Kakkadi: Zamfara

Abdu Kawo: Daura

Abdu na Makaki: Zamfara

Abdu na Tamane: Zamfara

Abdu Waliyi: Nupe

Abdu Zanga: Keffi

Abdul Aziz: Egypt (1405)

Abdul Aziz Hegazy: Egypt (1974–75)

Abdul Bu Bakar: Futa Toro

Abdul Hidi Pasha: Egypt (1948–49)

Abdul Khalik Pasha Sarwat: Egypt (1922, 1927–28)

Abdul Raman Osman: Mauritius (1970, 1971–79)

Idris Abdul Wakil: Zanzibar (1985–99)

Modi Abdulaye: Futa Jallon

Souley Abdulaye: Niger (1994–95)

Abdulaye Sékou Sow: Mali (1993–94)

Abdulaye Wade: Senegal (2000–)

Abdulkadir: Gwandu

Abdulkadiri: Hadejia (1847–48)

Abdulkadiri: Hadejia (1909–25)

Abdulkadiri: Katagum

Abdulkadiri: Lafiagi

Abdulkadiri: Lapai

Abdulkadiri II: Katagum

Abdulkadiri III: Katagum

Muhammad Taki Abdulkarim: Comoros (1992, 1995, 1996–98)

Abdulkeder: Futa Toro

Abdullahi: Agaie (1832–57)

Abdullahi: Agaie (1926–35)

Abdullahi: Gumel

Abdullahi: Jema'a (1833–37)

Abdullahi: Jema'a (1881–1911, 1915–26)

Abdullahi: Kano (1498–1508)

Abdullahi: Kano (1855–82)

Abdullahi: Keffi

Abdullahi: Lafia

Abdullahi: Nupe

Abdullahi: Yauri

Abdullahi: Zaria (1857–71, 1874–79)

Usuman Dan Abdullahi: Kano (1919–26)

Abdullahi I: Wase

Abdullahi II: Wase

Abdullahi Abarshi: Yauri

Abdullahi Ba Demba: Futa Jallon

Abdullahi Bayero: Gwandu

Abdullahi Burja: Kano (1437–52)

Abdullahi Chiroma Bayero: Kano (1926–53)

Abdullahi Dalla: Lafia

Abdullahi Dalla Bahagu: Lafia

Abdullahi Dan Fodio: Gwandu

Abdullahi Gade: Zamfara

Abdullahi Gallo: Yauri

Abdullahi Issa Muhammad: Italian Somaliland (1956–60)

Abdullahi Maikano III: Wase

Abdullahi Muhammad: Comoros (1976–78)
Abdullahi Toga: Argungu (1754–75)
Abdullahi Toga: Argungu (1860–83)
Yamta Abdullahi Ula: Biu
Abdullahi Yusuf Ahmad: Puntland; Somalia
Abdullai I: Dagomba
Abdullai II: Dagomba
Abdullai III: Dagomba
Muhammad Abdullai IV: Dagomba
Muhammad Abdullai IV: Dagomba
Abdur Rahman Farès: Algeria (1962); Algerian Republic (Provisional Government)
Abdurahman: Katagum
Abdurrahim: Lafiagi
Abdurrahman: Daura-Zango
Abdusalam Abubakar: Nigeria (1998–99)
Abe: New Calabar
Abiye Abebe: Eritrea
Said Abed: Mwali
Abede Aragai: Ethiopia (1958–60)
Said Abeid Abderemane: Nzwani
Abeid Amani Karume: Zanzibar (1964–72)
Amani Abeid Karume: Zanzibar (2000–)
Jean-Baptiste Abel: Algeria (1919–21)
Mustafa Aberchán: Melilla (1999–2000)
Ras Abeto Haylu: Gojjam
Sayid Muhammad al-Abid: Fezzan
Zayin al-Abidin: Morocco (1745)
Sheikh Abidin al-Bakha'i: Masina
Abiodun: Oyo
Abipa: Oyo
Abiye Abebe: Eritrea
Johan D'Ableing: Cape Colony (1707–08)
Matthew Abor: Southern Sudan
Abore: Biram
Aboshe: Doma
Aboshi: Doma
Abou Sekin Muhammad: Baguirmi
Aboud Jumbe: Zanzibar (1972–84)
Theodore Hoskins-Abrahall: Nigeria Western Region
Abraham: Dongola
Abraham Kok: Adam Kok's Land
Álvaro Abranches: Mozambique (1598–1601)
Abreha: Axum
Ella Abreha: Axum
Julio de Abreu: Cape Verde (1924–26)
Luis de Abreu: São Tomé (1611–13, 1614–16)
Pedro de Abreu: Mombasa (1609–10)
Vasco de Abreu: Mozambique (1507–08)
Paulo de Abreu e Lima: Cacheu (1707)
Rodrigo de Abreu e Lima: Mozambique (1843–47)
Marcos de Abreu e Meneses: Mozambique (1812–17)
Domingos de Abreu Picaluga: Bissau (1825)

Jean Abrial: Algeria (1940–41)
Hassan Abshir Farah: Somalia
Abu: Kano (1893–1903)
Monan Abu: Zaria (1505–30)
Abu Abdallah as-Si'i al-Muhtasab: Tunis (909–910)
Abu Abdallah Muhammad: Tripolitania (1014–22)
Abu Abdallah Muhammad I: Tlemcen (1400–11)
Abu Abdallah Muhammad I al-Mustansir: Hafsid Kingdom
Abu Abdallah Muhammad II: Tlemcen (1424–27, 1430)
Abu Abdallah Muhammad II Abu Asida: Hafsid Kingdom
Abu Abdallah Muhammad III: Tlemcen (1462–68)
Abu Abdallah Muhammad IV: Tlemcen (1468–1504)
Abu Abdallah Muhammad IV al-Muntasir: Hafsid Kingdom
Abu Abdallah Muhammad V: Hafsid Kingdom; Tlemcen (1504–17)
Abu Abdallah Muhammad VI: Tlemcen (1543)
Abu Abdallah Muhammad ibn Ahmad az-Ziyani: Bou Regreg
Abu al-Abbas Ahmad: Hafsid Kingdom
Abu al-Abbas Ahmad: Tlemcen (1430–62)
Abu al-Abbas Ahmad al-Fadl: Hafsid Kingdom
Abu al-Baqa Khalid I: Hafsid Kingdom
Abu al-Baqa Khalid II: Hafsid Kingdom
Abu al-Futuh Buluggin: Zirid Kingdom
Abu al-Misq Kafur: Egypt (946–965, 965–968)
Abu al-Yaqzan Muhammad: Rustumid Amirate
Abu Ali: Egypt (1130–31)
Abu Amr Uthman: Hafsid Kingdom
Abu Amran Musa: Tripolitania (1224–26)
Abu Abdallah Muhammad II Abu Asida: Hafsid Kingdom
Abu Awn: Egypt (751–753, 755–758)
Abu Bakar: Keffi
al-Hajj Abu Bakar: Biram
Abu Bakr: Adal [ii]
Sayid Abu Bakr: Anjouan
Abu Bakr: Egypt (1341)
Abu Bakr: Egypt (1727–29, 1734)
Abu Bakr: Harar
Abu Bakr: Mayotte
Abu-Bakr: Nupe
Abu Bakr: Rustumid Amirate
Abu Bakr: Tripolitania (1371–92)
Abu Bakr: Tripolitania (1482–89)
Badi II Abu Daqan: Funj Sultanate
Abu Yahya Abu Bakr: Hafsid Kingdom
Abu Yahya Abu-Bakr: Morocco (1244–58)

Abu Yahya Abu Bakr ash-Shahid: Hafsid Kingdom
al-Adil Abu Bakr I: Egypt (1200–18)
al-Adil Abu Bakr II: Egypt (1238–40)
Abu Bakr I: Mali Empire
Abu Bakr II: Mali Empire
Abu Bakr Awadullah: Sudan (1969)
Abu Bakr ibn Abd al-Mannan: Harar
Abu Bakr ibn Umar: Almoravid Empire
Abu Bakr Kolo: Nupe
Abu Bakr Liyatu: Bornu Empire (1392–94)
Abu Dabbus: Almohad Empire
Badi II Abu Daqan: Funj Sultanate
Abu Darba: Hafsid Kingdom
Abu Faris: Hafsid Kingdom
Abu Faris Abd al-Aziz: Hafsid Kingdom
Abu Ghazali: Wadai
Abu Hajjaj Yusuf: Tlemcen (1393)
Abu Halid Yazid: Omayyad and Abbasid North Africa
Abu Hafs Umar I: Hafsid Kingdom
Abu Hafs Umar II: Hafsid Kingdom
Abu Hammu I Musa; Tlemcen (1308–18)
Abu Hammu II ibn Abi Yaqub: Tlemcen (1359–70, 1372–89)
Abu Hammu III Musa: Tlemcen (1517–27)
Abu Hatim Rawh: Omayyad and Abbasid North Africa
Abu Hatim Yusuf: Rustumid Amirate
Abu Inan Faris: Morocco (1348–58)
Abu-Iqal al-Aghlab: Aghlabid Empire
Abu Ishaq Ibrahim: Hafsid Kingdom
Abu Ishaq Ibrahim: Tunis (1159)
Abu Ishaq Ibrahim: Tunis (1221)
Abu Ishaq Ibrahim I: Hafsid Kingdom
Abu Ja: Abuja; Zaria (1825–28)
Ismail Pasha Abu Jabal: Sudan (1852–53)
Abu Ja'far Hazarmard Umar: Omayyad and Abbasid North Africa
Abu Jemal Yusuf: Algiers (1640–42)
Abu Kwaka: Abuja
Abu Malik Abd al-Wahid: Tlemcen (1412–24, 1429–30)
Abu Muhammad Abd al-Haqq I: Morocco (1196–1218)
Abu Muhammad Abd al-Haqq II: Morocco (1428–65)
Abu Muhammad Abd al-Wahid: Tripolitania (1207–21); Tunis (1207–21)
Abu Muhammad Abdallah: Tripolitania (1053)
Abu Muhammad Abdallah I: Tlemcen (1397–1400)
Abu Muhammad Abdallah II: Tlemcen (1527–41)
Abu Muhammad Abdallah Abu: Tunis (1226–28)
Abu s-Sadat Uthman: Egypt (1453)
Abu Sa'id Abd ar-Rahman: Tripolitania (1221); Tunis (1221, 1223–26)
Abu Sa'id al-Aflah: Rustumid Amirate

Abu Sa'id ibn Musa: Tlemcen (1411–12)

Abu Sa'id Jaqmaq: Egypt (1438–53)

Abu Sa'id Uthman I: Tlemcen (1283–1304)

Abu Sa'id Uthman II: Morocco (1310–31)

Abu Sa'id Uthman II Abd ar-Rahman: Tlemcen (1348–52)

Abu Sa'id Uthman III: Morocco (1398–1420)

Abu Salih Yahya: Egypt (779–780)

Abu Salim Ali II: Morocco (1359–61)

Badi IV Abu Shulukh: Funj Sultanate

Amara II Abu Sukaykin: Funj Sultanate

Abu Suleiman: Rustumid Amirate

Abu Suleiman: Zeng Empire (1217–59)

Sufi Abu Talib: Egypt (1981)

Abu Tashufin I Abd ar-Rahman: Tlemcen (1318–36)

Abu Tashufin II Abd ar-Rahman: Tlemcen (1389–93)

Abu Tashufin III: Tlemcen (1468)

Abu Thabit: Tlemcen (1348–52)

Abu Thabit II Yusuf: Tlemcen (1393)

Abu Thabit Amir: Morocco (1307–08)

Abu Umar Tashufin: Morocco (1361)

Abu Umays Mahmud: Tripolitania (1711)

Ahmad Pasha Abu Wadan: Sudan (1838–43)

Sheikh Abu Yahya: Tripolitania (1146–48, 1160–72)

Abu Yahya Abu Bakr: Hafsid Kingdom

Abu Yahya Abu-Bakr: Morocco (1244–58)

Abu Yahya Abu Bakr ash-Shahid: Hafsid Kingdom

Abu Yahya al-Hassan: Tunis (1168)

Abu Yahya Amran: Tripolitania (1222–23)

Abu Yahya Yaghmurasan ibn Zayyan: Tlemcen (1236–83)

Abu Yahya Zakariyya I: Hafsid Kingdom

Yusuf II Abu Yakub: Almohad Empire

Abu Yakub al-Mustansir: Almohad Empire

Abu Yakub Yusuf: Morocco (1286–1307)

Abu Yusuf al-Mansur: Almohad Empire

Abu Yusuf Yakub: Morocco (1258–86)

Abu Zaiyid: Tripolitania (1224)

Abu Zakariyya Yahya: Tunis (1228–36)

Abu Zakariyya Yahya I: Hafsid Kingdom

Abu Zakariyya Yahya II: Hafsid Kingdom

Abu Zakariyya Yahya II al-Wathiq: Hafsid Kingdom

Abu Zayyan I Muhammad: Tlemcen (1304–08)

Abu Zayyan II Muhammad: Tlemcen (1393–97)

Abu Zayyan Ahmad: Tlemcen (1541–50)

Abu Zayyan Muhammad: Tlemcen (1360)

Abu Zayyan Muhammad III: Morocco (1361–66)

Abu Zayyan Muhammad IV: Morocco (1372–74)

Abuako Dako: Akwamu

Abubaka Tafawa Balewa: Nigeria (1957–66)

Abubakar: Damagaram

Abubakar: Muri

Abubakar: Zamfara

Abdusalam Abubakar: Nigeria (1998–99)

Abubakar I: Agaie

Abubakar II: Agaie

Abubakar Jatau: Yauri

Adamu Abubakar Maje: Hadejia (2002–)

Abubakar Modibbo: Kontagora

Abubakar Ukar: Argungu

Sidiq Abubakr: Fulani Empire

Abubakr: Gombe

Abubakr: Gumel

Abubakr: Hadejia

Abubakr: Katsina (1887–1904)

Abubakr: Mogadishu

Abubakr: Wase (1838–80)

Abubakr: Wase (1929–47)

Abubakr: Zaria (1871–74)

Abubakr Atiku I: Fulani Empire

Abubakr Atiku II: Fulani Empire

Abubakr Ceceko: Lafiagi

Abubakr Kado: Kano (1565–72)

Abubakr Kawu: Lafiagi

Abubakr Maje Haruna: Hadejia (1984–2002)

Abu'dh Dhahab: Egypt (1773–75)

Abu'l Abbas: Egypt (910)

Abu'l Abbas Ahmad: Hafsid Kingdom; Morocco (1374–84)

Abu'l Aish Ahmad: Idrisid State

Sa'id Abu'l Ala Idris: Tripolitania (1221–23); Tunis (1221–23)

Abu'l Faris Abd al-Aziz I: Morocco (1366–72, 1393–96)

Abu'l Hassan Ali: Algiers (1636–38)

Abu'l Hassan Ali: Tripolitania (1037–38)

Abu'l Hassan Ali I: Morocco (1331–48)

Abu'l Hassan Ali al-Mandari: Tangier (1437–71)

Abu'l Hassan Yanis: Tripolitania (1000–01)

Sheikh Muhammad Abu'l Kaylak: Kordofan

Hasan Abu'l Mawahib: Zeng Empire (1308–34)

Abu'l Muhagir Dinar: Arab North Africa

Abu'l Qasim: Darfur

Abu'l Rabi Suleiman: Morocco (1308–10)

Abut: Ifat

Abuta Eje: Igala

Zoilo Acafia: Fernando Po

Jerónimo de Saavedra Acevedo: Canary Islands (1983–87, 1991–93)

Achaimenes: Egypt (27th Dynasty)

Ignatius Acheampong: Ghana (1972–78)

Simon Achidi Achu: Cameroun (1992–96)

Achoris: Egypt (29th Dynasty)

Achthoes: Egypt (9th Dynasty)

Simon Achidi Achu: Cameroun (1992–96)

Decius Aciniancius Albinus: Africa Proconsularis (430–431)

Peter Acland: Cyrenaica

Aconius Catullinus: Africa Proconsularis (341–342)

Álvaro de Acosta: Gran Canaria

Rodrigo de Acuña: Gran Canaria

Acyl: Wadai

Ada Doki: Daura

Ada Gamu: Daura

Ada Guguwa: Daura

Ada Hamta: Daura

Ada Inda: Daura

Ada Jabu: Daura

Ada Kube: Daura

Ada Sabau: Daura

Ada Sunguma: Daura

Ada Yaki: Daura

Adago: Doma

Dakin al-Adal: Funj Sultanate

Adam: Biram

Adam: Fika

Adam: Wadai

Paul Adam: Central African Republic (1910–11); Gabon (1912–14)

Pierre Adam: Central African Republic (1913–16)

Adam Bakam: Daniski

Adam Kok II: Adam Kok's Land; Cornelis Kok's Land; Griqualand West

Adam Kok III: Adam Kok's Land; Griqualand East

Fara Penda Adam Sal: Walo (1823–37)

Adama: Adamawa

Kola Adama: Mandara

Theodore Adams: Nigeria Northern Region

Hamilton Goold-Adams: Botswana; Orange Free State (1901–02, 1907–10)

Adamu: Jema'a

Adamu Abubakar Maje: Hadejia (2002–)

al-Hajj Ibrahim Adamu: Kazaure

Adamu ibn Abdulmumini: Kazaure

Adamu Jumba: Bauchi

Suleiman Tiya Adamu Jumba: Bauchi

Adamu Karro: Gumel

Adanzan: Dahomey

Adasho: Keana

Adbar Sagad: Ethiopia (1716–21)

Muhammadu Adda: Jema'a

Muhammad Muse Hersi Adde: Puntland

Addi I: Trarza
Addi II: Trarza
William Addis: Seychelles (1953–58)
Dan Addo: Yauri
Suleimanu Dan Addo: Yauri
Edward Akufo-Addo: Ghana
  (1970–72)
Adebo: Oyo
Idoko Adegbe: Igala
Adegos: Axum
Adele I: Lagos (1811–21, 1833–34)
Alaiyeluwa Oba Adeniji Adele II:
  Lagos (1949–64)
Okunade Adele Sijuwade Olubuse:
  Ife
Adelu: Oyo
Ademola I: Abeokuta
Ademola II (Ladapo Ademola):
  Abeokuta
Aden Abdallah Osman Daar: Somalia
Alaiyeluwa Oba Adeniji Adele II:
  Lagos (1949–64)
Adeniran: Oyo
Adeqetali: Kush (137–146)
Daniel Adesanya Gbelegbura II: Ijebu
Adesoji: Ife
Aderemi Adesoji: Ife
Sikiru Adetona Ogbagba II: Ijebu
Adeyemi I: Oyo
Lamidi Adeyemi II: Oyo
Adeyinka Oyekan II: Lagos (1965–)
Adhana: Axum (374–379)
Adhana: Axum (418–424)
Adherbal: Numidia
Matsweu Adi: Kororofa
al-Adid: Egypt (1160–71)
Muhammad al-Adil: Zeng Empire
  (1416–25)
al-Adil Abu Bakr I: Egypt (1200–18)
al-Adil Abu Bakr II: Egypt (1238–40)
al-Adil ad-Din Ketbugha: Egypt
  (1294–96)
al-Adil al-Musta'in: Egypt (1412)
al-Adil Ruzzik: Egypt (1161–63)
al-Adil Salamish: Egypt (1279)
Adimu: Ife
Aholuho Adja: Allada
Adjakpa: Allada
De Adjara: Allada
Umar Adjara: Mandara
Boukari Adji: Niger (1996)
Adjossogbé: Whydah
Late Adjromitan: Little Popo
Adlan I: Funj Sultanate
Adlan II: Funj Sultanate
Adli Yegen Pasha: Egypt (1921–22,
  1926–27, 1929)
Admas Sagad: Ethiopia (1559–63)
Ado: Akwamu
Ado: Lagos (ca. 1740)
Ado Bayero: Kano (1963–)
Adolf Frederick, the Herzog of Meck-
  lenburg: Togoland
Adolo: Benin [i]
Cyrille Adoulla: Congo (Zaire)
  (1961–64)
Adra: Doma
Adreaz: Axum

Shehu Musa Yar Adua: Nigeria
  (1976–83)
Adyam Sagad: Ethiopia (1682–1706)
Adyam Sagad: Ethiopia (1755–69)
George Cosmas Adyebo: Uganda
  (1991–94)
Adyoma: Kanem
Aedemon: Mauretania
Aelius Gallus: Egypt (25–24 B.C.)
Lucius Aelius Lamia: Africa [i] (15–16)
Aelius Palladius: Egypt (374–375)
Aemilianus: Egypt (ca. 275)
Aemilius Rectus: Egypt (37, 42–47)
Aemilius Saturninus: Egypt (197–202)
Bukar Afade: Mandara
al-Afdal Shahanshah: Egypt
  (1094–1121)
Afena Diamono: Bono
Afena Yaw: Bono
Afera Kuma: Akwamu
Sheikh al-Afia Ould Muhammad
  Khouna: Mauritania (1996–2003)
Abu Sa'id al-Aflah: Rustumid Amirate
Afonja: Ilorin
García II Afonso: Kongo
Martím Afonso: Portuguese Gold
  Coast (1564)
Afonso I: Kongo
Afonso II: Kongo
Afonso III: Kongo
Stettius Africanus: Egypt (82–86)
Akwasi Afrifa: Ghana (1969–70)
Christiaan Afrikaner: Oorlam Terri-
  tory
Jager Afrikaner: Oorlam Territory
Jan Jonker Afrikaner: Oorlam Terri-
  tory
Junker Afrikaner: Oorlam Territory
Kade Afunu: Bornu Empire
  (1399–1400)
Isaias Afwerki: Eritrea
Ahmad Ag Hamani: Mali (2002–04)
Agabe: Axum
Agabi: Doma
Agabo: Doma
Agada: Igala
Agada Nagogo: Gobir
Agadi: Keana
Agagnon: Allada
Aganju: Oyo
Agba Fubra: Bonny
Agbaa: Bonny
Agbamy: Whydah
Agbande: Allada
Agbangba: Allada
Agbangia: Whydah
Té-Agbanlin I: Porto-Novo
Agbo Agoli: Dahomey
Agboluje: Oyo
Agbu Kendja: Kororofa
Agbu Manu I: Kororofa
Agbu Manu II: Kororofa
Agenapoje: Igala
Aggrey Jaden: Southern Sudan
Hassan Agha: Algiers (1535–43,
  1561–62)
Ramadan Agha: Tripolitania (1631)
Haydar Agha Zade: Egypt (1646–47)

al-Aghlab: Omayyad and Abbasid
  North Africa
Abu-Iqal al-Aghlab: Aghlabid Empire
Agigbi: Kororofa
Ago: Keana
Agbo Adoli: Dahomey
Agonglo: Dahomey
S.A. Agoro: Lagos (1964–65)
Agudu Manu: Kororofa
Agudum: Potiskum
Aguessi Dagba: Whydah
Diego de Águila y Toledo: Gran Ca-
  naria
Conde de Aguilar de Inestrillas: Oran
  (1608–16)
Manuel de Aguilar y Diosdado: Span-
  ish Morocco (1901–03)
Juan de Mur Aguirre y Argaiz: Canary
  Islands (1719–22)
Johnson Aguiyi-Ironsi: Nigeria (1966)
Aguja: Dahomey
Agulu: Doma
Isa Mustafa Agwa: Lafia
Agwabi: Kororofa
Agwaragi: Katsina (1784–1801)
Muhamman Agwe I: Lafia
Muhamman Agwe II: Lafia
Agyekum Owari I: Akim
Agyekum Owari II: Akim
Agyekum Owari III: Akim
Agyen Kokobo: Akwamu
Aha: Egypt (1st Dynasty)
Sayid Muhammad al-Ahabagi: Zanz-
  ibar (1823–32)
Ahaha: Denkyira
Vincent de Paul Ahanda: Cameroun
  (1965)
Ahenenre Apopi II: Egypt (15th Dy-
  nasty)
Ahenkpaye: Benin [i]
Ahenzae: Benin [i]
Ahmadou Ahidjo: Cameroun
  (1960–82)
Ahihi: Denkyira
Sidi Ahmad: Adrar
Ahmad: Aghlabid Empire
Ahmad: Algiers (1562)
Ahmad: Algiers (1653–55, 1656–58)
Sheikh Ahmad: Anjouan
Hajji Ahmad: Constantine
Ahmad: Egypt (968–969)
Ahmad: Egypt (1342–43)
Ahmad: Egypt (1461)
Ahmad: Egypt (1523–24)
Ahmad: Egypt (1615–18)
Ahmad: Egypt (1633–35)
Ahmad: Egypt (1649–51)
Ahmad: Egypt (1675–76)
Ahmad: Egypt (1689–91)
Ahmad: Egypt (1748–52)
Ahmad: Egypt (1762–65)
Sayid Ahmad: Gran Comoro
Ahmad: Hafsid Kingdom
Ahmad: Mayotte
Ahmad: Tripolitania (1609)
Abu al-Abbas Ahmad: Hafsid King-
  dom
Abu al-Abbas Ahmad: Tlemcen

Abu'l Abbas Ahmad: Hafsid Kingdom; Morocco (1374–84)
Abu'l Aish Ahmad: Idrisid State
Arab Ahmad: Algiers (1571–74)
Deli Ahmad: Algiers (1588–89)
Hafiz Ahmad: Egypt (1591–95)
Muhammad Ahmad: Comoros (1978)
Muhammad Ahmad (The Mahdi): Sudan (1881–85)
Muhammad Lamine Ould Ahmad: Western Sahara
al-Mukhtar Ahmad: Adrar
al-Muzaffar Ahmad: Egypt (1421)
Sa'd ad-Din Ahmad: Ifat
Soidri Ahmad: Mwali
Su'aidi Ahmad: Tagant
Ahmad I: Algiers (1695–98)
Ahmad I: Fezzan
Ahmad I: Timbuktu (1617–18)
Ahmad I: Tripolitania (1711–45)
Ahmad I: Tunis (1837–55)
Ahmad I al-Araj: Morocco (1517–25)
Ahmad II: Adrar
Ahmad II: Algiers (1805–08)
Ahmad II: Fezzan
Ahmad II: Timbuktu (1646–47)
Ahmad II: Tripolitania (1795)
Ahmad II: Tunisia (1929–42)
Ahmad II al-Abbas: Morocco (1655–59)
Ahmad II al-Mansur: Morocco (1578–1603)
Sidi Ahmad III: Adrar
Ahmad III: Timbuktu (1689–89)
Sidi Ahmad IV: Adrar
Ahmad IV: Timbuktu (1694)
Ahmad V: Timbuktu (1701–02)
Ahmad Abdallah: Comoros (1972–75, 1978–89)
Ahmad Abdou: Comoros (1996–97)
Ahmad adh-Dhahabi: Morocco (1727–29)
Ahmad Ag Hamani: Mali (2002–04)
Abu al-Abbas Ahmad al-Fadl: Hafsid Kingdom
Ahmad al-Hiba: Brakna
Ahmad al-Kollo: Constantine
Muhammad Ahmad al-Mangush: Libya
Ahmad al-Mirghani: Sudan (1986–89)
Ahmad al-Muraiyid: Tripolitanian Republic
Ahmad al-Wattasi: Morocco (1524–45, 1547–49)
Abd ar-Rahman Ahmad Ali Tur: Somaliland Republic
Ahmad Arabi: Egypt (1882)
Si Ahmad at-Tazi: Tangier (1954–56)
Sheikh Ahmad az-Zarraq: Tripolitania (1489–94)
Ahmad Bahmini: Morocco (1963–65)
Ahmad Bakr ibn Musa: Darfur
Ahmad Balafrej: Morocco (1958)
Ahmad ben Bitour: Algeria (1999–2000)
Ahmad ben Sheikh Attoumane: Comoros (1993–94)
Ahmad Dini: Djibouti (1977)

Ahmad Dunama IV: Bornu Empire (1451–55)
Ahmad Fuad I: Egypt (1917–36)
Ahmad Fuad Mohieddin: Egypt (1982–84)
Sid Ahmad Ghozali: Algeria (1991–92)
Ahmad Gran ibn Ibrahim: Harar
Ahmad ibn Abu Bakr: Harar (1756–83)
Ahmad ibn Abu Bakr: Harar (1852–56)
Ahmad ibn Ali: Bornu Empire (1793–1808)
Ahmad ibn Ali: Bou Regreg
Ahmad ibn Daman: Trarza
Ahmad ibn Ismail: Egypt (803–805)
Ahmad ibn Keyghalagh: Egypt (923–924, 933–934)
Ahmad ibn Muhammad: Harar
Ahmad ibn Muhammad: Mombasa (1782–1811)
Ahmad ibn Muzahim: Egypt (868)
Ahmad ibn Suleiman: Zeng Empire (1461–62)
Ahmad ibn Tulun: Egypt (868–884)
Ahmad Kérékou: Benin [ii] (1972–91, 1996–)
Ahmad Laraki: Morocco (1969–71)
Muhammad Mahmud Ould Ahmad Louly: Mauritania (1979–80)
Ahmad Muhammad Sani: Gumel
Sidi Ahmad Ould Bneijara: Mauritania (1980–81)
Ahmad Ould Bouceif: Mauritania (1979)
Ahmad Ouyahia: Algeria (1995–98, 2003–)
Ahmad Pasha: Egypt (1944–45)
Ahmad Pasha Abu Wadan: Sudan (1838–43)
Ahmad Pasha al-Manikli: Sudan (1844–45)
Ahmad Pasha Ziwar: Egypt (1924–26)
Ahmad Reda Guedira: Morocco (1961–63)
Ahmad Saif an-Nasir: Fezzan
Salim Ahmad Salim: Tanzania
Ahmad Salum: Trarza
Ould Sidi Ahmad Salum: Trarza
Sidi Ahmad Taya: Mauritania (1981–)
Ahmad Tejan Kebbah: Sierra Leone (1996–97, 1998–)
Ahmaddu I: Brakna
Ahmaddu II: Brakna
Ahmadou Ahidjo: Cameroun (1960–82)
Ahmadu: Adamawa
Ahmadu: Gumel
Ahmadu: Lafiagi
Ahmadu: Masina
Ahmadu: Tukolor Empire
Bobbo Ahmadu: Adamawa
Ahmadu I: Argungu
Ahmadu I: Damagaram
Ahmadu I: Keffi
Ahmadu II: Damagaram
Ahmadu III: Damagaram

Ahmadu Atiku: Fulani Empire
Ahmadu Barmo: Zamfara
Alhajji Ahmadu Bello: Nigeria Northern Region
Ahmadu Dan Amaru: Argungu
Ahmadu Dara Alfaya: Futa Jallon
Ahmadu Jerabana: Yauri
Ahmadu Maikwato: Keffi
Ahmadu Rufai: Fulani Empire; Katsina (1869–70)
Ahmadu Sego: Futa Toro
Ahmadu Waziri: Misau
Badi III al-Ahmar: Funj Sultanate
Ahmayada: Brakna
Ahmed ben Bella: Algeria (1962–65)
Ahmed Fawzi: Tripolitania (1908–09)
Hajji Ahmed Izzet: Tripolitania (1848–49)
Ahmed Izzet: Tripolitania (1858–60, 1879–80)
Ahmed Rasim: Tripolitania (1881–96)
Ahmed Sékou Touré: Guinea (1958–84)
Ahmose Khnemibre: Egypt (26th Dynasty)
Ahmose Nebpehtire: Egypt (17th Dynasty, 18th Dynasty)
Johan Ahnholm: Danish Gold Coast (1799–1802)
Aholin: Little Popo
Aholuho Adja: Allada
Justin Ahomadegbé: Benin [ii] (1964–65, 1972–72)
Ahratan: Kush (350–335 B.C.)
Helmut von Ahrenstorff: Danish Gold Coast (1831)
Martti Ahtissari: Namibia (1977–82)
Sidi Muhammad al-Hadi al-Ahwa: Tunisia (1932–42)
Aibak: Egypt (1250–57)
Aiezanes: Axum
Étienne Mengin Duval d'Ailly: Réunion (1830–32)
Ainal: Egypt (1453–61)
Aisa: Mayotte
Abu'l Aish Ahmad: Idrisid State
Aissa Kili: Bornu Empire (1570–80)
Aitogbuwa: Warri
as-Salih Aiyub: Egypt (1240–49)
Luis Aizpuru: Spanish Morocco (1923–24)
José Aizpuru y Lorriez Fontecha: Spanish Morocco (1879–81)
Ajagbo: Oyo
Ajaka: Oyo
Aji: Fika
Mai Bukar Aji: Mandara
Aji Daka: Daniski
Ajiboyede: Oyo
Ajika: Oyo
Ajohan: Porto-Novo
Ak Mehmed: Tripolitania (1678–79)
Akaba: Dahomey
Boadu Akafo Berempon: Denkyira
Akal: Gobir
Akal: Gobir
Akau: Doma
Akenbedo: Benin [i]

Akengboi: Benin [i]
Akengbuda: Benin [i]
Akengbuwa: Warri
Akenzua I: Benin [i]
Akenzua II: Benin [i]
Akhedakhetiwal: Kush (320–325)
Rameses VIII Usermare Akhenamun: Egypt (20th Dynasty)
Akhenaton: Egypt (18th Dynasty)
Siptah Akhenre Merneptah: Egypt (19th Dynasty)
Thutmose II Akheperenre: Egypt (18th Dynasty)
Thutmose I Akheperkare: Egypt (18th Dynasty)
Osorkhon IV Akheperre: Egypt (22nd Dynasty)
Psusennes I Akheperre: Egypt (21st Dynasty)
Sheshonk V Akheperre: Egypt (22nd Dynasty)
Amenhotep II Akheprure: Egypt (18th Dynasty)
Akhtoy: Egypt (9th Dynasty)
Akili Dan Chuba: Gobir
Akinidad: Kush (24–15 B.C.)
Akinshemoyin: Lagos (1805)
Samuel Akintola: Nigeria Western Region
Akitoye I: Lagos (1841–45, 1852–53)
Akli Khider: Mayotte Department
Tshafe Tezaz Aklilu Habte-Wold: Ethiopia (1961–74)
Do-Aklim: Dahomey
Akogu: Igala
Akoi: Songhai (873–885)
Akolu: Allada
Akolu I: Lagos (2003–)
Akonde: Allada
Akotia: Akwamu
Yau Akoto: Ashanti
Oguche Akpa: Igala
Aku Odiba: Igala
Akuete Zankli Lawson I: Little Popo
Frederick Akuffo: Ghana (1978–79)
Edward Akufo-Addo: Ghana (1970–72)
Tatila Akufuna: Barotseland
Akumfi I: Bono
Akumfi II: Bono
Dugum Akuya: Bedde
Akwa Bini: Baule
Takyi Akwamo: Bono
Akwano Panyini: Akwamu
Akwasi Afrifa: Ghana (1969–70)
Akwe I: Doma
Akwe II: Doma
Akwei: Doma
Owusu Akyem Ohenkoko: Akim
Owusu Akyempo: Bono
al-Mansur Al'a ad-Din: Egypt (1368–80)
Al'a ad-Din Kujuk: Egypt (1341–42)
Ala ad-Din Pasha Siddiq: Sudan (1883)
Sa'd Abu'l Ala Idris: Tripolitania (1221–23); Tunis (1221–23)
Aladoga: Keana

Alagbariye: Bonny
Alago: Keana
Alaiyeluwa Oba Adeniji Adele II: Lagos (1949–64)
Alam Sagad: Ethiopia (1632–67)
Alamami: Tukolor Empire
Alamara Nhassa: Guinea-Bissau (2001–02)
Fernando Alameda y Liancourt: Melilla (1898–99)
Eugène Alaniou: Comoros (1946–48)
Gabriel Alapetite: Tunisia (1907–18)
Alara: Kush (ca. 850 B.C.)
Francisco de Alarcão e Souto-Maior: Mozambique (1719–21)
Pedro Alardo: Ceuta (1509–12)
Alassane Ouattara: Côte d'Ivoire (1990–93)
Alawi: Anjouan
Sayid Alawi: Anjouan
Alawi II: Anjouan
Alawma: Bornu Empire (1580–1603)
Ibrahim Alayali: Tripolitania (1709–10)
Alayaman: Songhai (837–849)
Francisco de Alba: Melilla (1757–58)
Diogo Soares de Albergaria: Portuguese Gold Coast (1545, 1550–52)
Lopo Soares de Albergaria: Portuguese Gold Coast (1493)
Paul Alberge: Tangier (1926–29)
Albert I: South Kasai Republic
Decius Aciniancius Albinus: Africa Proconsularis (430–431)
Albishir: Yauri
Moi Albo: Daniski
François Albrand: Sainte Marie de Madagascar
Henning Albrecht: Danish Gold Coast (1662–69)
Afonso de Albuquerque: Portuguese Gold Coast (1522–24)
Antonio Albuquerque: Ceuta (1623–24)
João de Albuquerque: Mozambique (1817–18)
Joaquim de Albuquerque: Mozambique (1896–97)
Manuel de Albuquerque: Angola (1819–21)
Manuel de Albuquerque: Portuguese Gold Coast (1536–39)
Paulo de Albuquerque: Angola (1726–32)
Antonio de Albuquerque Cota Falcão: Bissau (1858)
Diogo de Alcáçova: São Tomé (1516–17)
Alonso, Conde de Alcandete: Oran (1558–64)
Francisco, Conde de Alcandete: Oran (1596–1604)
Martín, Conde de Alcandete: Oran (1534–58)
José Alcántara Pérez: Melilla (1895–98)
Gonçalo Alcoforado: Ceuta (1625)

Fernão, Conde de Alcoutim: Ceuta (1491–1509)
Pedro, Conde de Alcoutim: Ceuta (1512–17, 1524–25)
Pedro Alcubierre: Equatorial Guinea; Ifni; Western Sahara
José García Aldave: Melilla (1910–12); Spanish Morocco (1908–10)
Aldawa Nanda: Mandara
Aleit: Trarza
Joseph Alem: Côte d'Ivoire (1862–63)
Bernardo Alemañy y Perote: Melilla (1871–73)
Alenzae: Benin [i]
Alexander: Egypt (390–391)
Alexander: Egypt (468)
Alexander: Koya-Temne
Cyril Alexander: Nigeria Northern Region; Nigeria Southern Provinces
Henry Alexander: Natal (1880)
Julius Alexander: Egypt (68–71)
Ptolemy X Alexander I: Egypt (110–109 B.C., 107–88 B.C.)
Ptolemy XI Alexander II: Egypt (80 B.C.)
Alexander the Great: Egypt (332–323 B.C.); Pentapolis
Alexandre Boevi Lawson II: Little Popo
Alezzi Kalajuna: Gobir
Alfa Ibrahima Sori: Futa Jallon
Matteo Alfassa: Congo (1919–22); French Equatorial Africa (1921–22, 1924, 1925, 1929–30, 1931, 1932–33); Mali (1935–36)
Felipe Alfau y Mendoza: Spanish Morocco (1910–13)
Ahmadu Dara Alfaya: Futa Jallon
Alfenius Ceionius Camenius: Africa Proconsularis (380)
Robert Alford: Saint Helena (1958–62)
Hamid Algabid: Niger (1983–88)
Marqués de Algava: Oran (1678–81)
Algoje: Zamfara
Alhaji: Bedde
Moma Alhaji: Misau
Alhajji Ahmadu Bello: Nigeria Northern Region
Ali: Adal [ii]
Hajji Ali: Algiers (1665–71)
Ali: Anjouan
Ali: Biram
Ali: Brakna
Ali: Egypt (1623–24)
Ali: Egypt (1668–69)
Ali: Egypt (1691–95)
Ali: Egypt (1717–20)
Ali: Egypt (1734–41, 1755–56)
Ali: Gobir
Sayid Ali: Gran Comoro
Ali: Mali Empire
Ali: Omayyad and Abbasid North Africa
Ali: Segu
Ali: Tripolitania (1607–09)
Ali: Wadai
Sayid Ali: Zanzibar (1902–11)

Seyid Ali: Zanzibar (1890–93)
Ali: Zaria (1578–84)
Ali: Zirid Kingdom
Abu Ali: Egypt (1130–31)
Abu'l Hassan Ali: Algiers (1636–38)
Abu'l Hassan Ali: Tripolitania (1037–38)
Baba Ali: Timbuktu (1780)
Bako Ali: Zaria (1621–46)
Eulj Ali: Algiers (1568–77); Tripolitania (1565–68)
Kamal Hassan Ali: Egypt (1984)
Kilik Ali: Tripolitania (1576–87)
Muhammad Ali: Egypt (1805–48)
Osman Jama Ali: Somalia
Qat-Ali: Ifat
Salim ben Ali: Comoros (1978–82)
Sonni Ali: Songhai (1464–92)
Sunni Ali: Songhai (1464–92)
Yawuz Ali: Egypt (1601–03)
Zine ben Ali: Tunisia (1987–)
Ali I: Algiers (1710–18)
Sidi Ali I: Brakna
Ali I: Idrisid State
Ali I: Masina
Ali I: Mayotte
Ali I: Timbuktu (1612–17)
Ali I: Tripolitania (1754–93)
Ali I: Tunis (1735–56)
Abu'l Hassan Ali I: Morocco (1331–48)
Ali II: Algiers (1754–66)
Sidi Ali II: Brakna
Ras Ali II: Gojjam
Ali II: Masina
Ali II: Mayotte
Ali II: Timbuktu (1628–32)
Ali II: Tunis (1759–82)
Abu Salim Ali II: Morocco (1359–61)
Ali II Burghul: Tripolitania (1793–95)
Ali II ibn Umar: Idrisid State
Ali II Zainami: Bornu Empire (1545–46)
Ali III: Bornu Empire (1645–85)
Ali III: Masina
Ali III: Timbuktu (1632)
Ali III: Tripolitania (1832–35)
Ali III al-Miqdam: Idrisid State
Ali III ar-Rasul: Algiers (1808–09)
Ali IV: Algiers (1809–15)
Ali IV: Almohad Empire
Ali IV: Timbuktu (1661–62)
Ali IV ibn Haj Hamdun: Bornu Empire (1755–93)
Ali V: Timbuktu (1662)
Ali V Khoja: Algiers (1817–18)
Ali VI: Timbuktu (1672–75)
Ali VII: Timbuktu (1684)
Ali VIII: Timbuktu (1697)
Ali IX: Timbuktu (1702–03, 1712)
Ali X: Timbuktu (1707–08, 1713)
Ali XI: Timbuktu (1716)
Ali XII: Timbuktu (1750)
Ali al-Araj: Morocco (1734–36)
Abu'l Hassan Ali al-Mandari: Tangier (1437–71)
Ali al-Mukni: Fezzan
Abd al-Ali al-Obeidi: Libya

Ali Aref Bourhan: Djibouti (1967–77)
Ali Asker: Tripolitania (1838–42)
Ali Baba: Dongola
Mahfud Ali Beiba: Western Sahara
Ali Benflis: Algeria (2000–)
Ali Bey al-Kabir: Egypt (1768–73)
Ali Bijnin: Algiers (1645)
Ali Bilma: Futa Jallon
Ali Buri N'Dyaye: Dyolof
Ali Delatumi: Bornu Empire (1846)
Ali Dian: Gwiriko
Ali Dinar ibn Zakariyya: Darfur
Sidi Ali Diombot: Trarza
Ali Fai: Songhai (897–909)
Ali Ghajideni: Bornu Empire (1472–1504)
Ali Hassan Mwinyi: Zanzibar (1984–85)
Ali ibn Ammar: Tripolitania (1392–97)
Ali ibn Baskhat: Zeng Empire (1022–27)
Ali ibn Daud: Harar
Ali ibn Daud: Zeng Empire (1259–74)
Ali ibn Daud I: Zeng Empire (1064–90)
Ali ibn Daud II: Zeng Empire (1090–1100)
Ali ibn Hasan: Zeng Empire (980–1022)
Ali ibn Hasan: Zeng Empire (1484–86)
Ali ibn Suleiman: Egypt (786–787)
Ali ibn Suleiman the Lucky: Zeng Empire (1206–17)
Ali ibn Uthman al-Mazrui: Mombasa (1746–55)
Ali ibn Yahya: Egypt (841–843, 849–850)
Ali ibn Yusuf: Almoravid Empire
Ali Jezairli: Tripolitania (1683–84)
Ali Kafi: Algeria (1992–94)
Sa'id Ali Kamal: Comoros (1995)
Ali Khadim: Egypt (1559–60)
Ali Khalif Galaid: Somalia
Ali Kojja Bey: Constantine
Ali Konon: Songhai (1332–40)
Ali Koro: Songhai (1196–1215)
Ali Kuri: Trarza
Ali Lutfi: Egypt (1985–86)
Ali Mahdi Muhammad: Somalia
Ali Maher Pasha: Egypt (1936, 1939–40, 1952)
Ali Mroudjae: Comoros (1982–84)
Sa'id Ali Muhammad: Comoros (1993)
Ali Muhammad Ghedi: Somalia
Ali Murabus: Katsina (1543–68)
Ali Muraly: Egypt (1725–26)
Ali Musa Bey Sawqi: Bahr al-Ghazal
Hassan Ali Pasha Arnavut: Kordofan
Ali Pasha Jarkis: Sudan (1855–57)
Ali Pasha Jazairli: Egypt (1803–04)
Ali Pasha Sirri: Sudan (1854)
Ali Reza: Tripolitania (1867–70, 1872–73)
Ali Sabry: Egypt (1962–65)
Muhammad Ali Samatar: Somalia
Ali Sandura: Trarza

Ali Seibou: Niger (1987–93)
Ali Semiz: Egypt (1549–53)
Ali Shehu Shagari: Nigeria (1979–83)
Ali Silek: Wadai
Ali Soilih: Comoros (1975, 1976–78)
Ali Sufu: Egypt (1564–66)
Abd ar-Rahman Ahmad Ali Tur: Somaliland Republic
Abel Alier: Southern Sudan
Alii: Igala
Alikolo Tankari: Nupe
Alimah I: Anjouan
Alimah II: Anjouan
Alimah III: Anjouan
Alimani Lahai Bundu: Koya-Temne
Mallam Alimi ibn Zubeiru: Ilorin
Baba Alimu: Futa Jallon
Aliou Mahamidou: Niger (1990–91)
James Alison: Fort James
Aliyu: Agaie
Aliyu: Fulani Empire
Aliyu: Gwandu
Aliyu: Lafiagi (1833–34, 1845–53)
Aliyu: Lafiagi (1882–91)
Aliyu: Lapai
Aliyu: Nupe
Aliyu: Yauri
Aliyu: Zamfara
Aliyu: Zaria (1788–93)
Aliyu: Zaria (1903–20)
Bako Su Aliyu: Zaria (1597–1608)
Bako Aliyu: Zaria (1670–78)
Bako Aliyu: Zaria (1718–27)
Bayero Aliyu: Gwandu
Maidalla Mustafa Aliyu: Biu
Muhammadu Aliyu: Biu
Nufu Aliyu: Zaria (1902–03)
Shi'ta Aliyu: Ilorin
Aliyu Baba: Kano (1893–1903)
Aliyu Jan Hazo I: Katsina (1589–95)
Aliyu Jan Hazo II: Katsina (1612–14)
Aliyu Karami: Fulani Empire
Aliyu Karya Giwa: Katsina (1572–85)
Aliyu Lafiya: Yauri
Aliyu Mustafa: Adamawa
Allagoa: Brass
Bawan Allah: Daura
Fadl-Allah: Bornu Empire (1900–01); Rabih's Empire
Ubayd Allah: Omayyad and Abbasid North Africa
Ziyadat-Allah I: Aghlabid Empire
Ziyadat-Allah II: Aghlabid Empire
Ziyadat-Allah III: Aghlabid Empire
Allal: Timbuktu (1659–59)
Colin Allen: Seychelles (1973–76)
Edmund, Lord Allenby: Egypt (1919–25)
Alphonse Alley: Benin [ii] (1967–68)
Erifasi Otema Alliamdi: Uganda (1980–85)
Joseph Allison: Orange Free State (1863)
Fallonius Probus Allypsius: Africa Proconsularis (378–380)
Lourenço de Almada: Angola (1705–09); Madeira (1688–90)
Dedem Almaz: Axum

Damião Vaz d'Almeida: São Tomé and Príncipe (2004–05); Príncipe (ii)

Antonio de Almeida: Mozambique (1869)

Armindo Vaz de Almeida: São Tomé and Príncipe (1995–96)

Duarte de Almeida: Cape Verde (1781–82)

Francisco de Almeida: Angola (1592–93)

Francisco de Almeida; Ceuta (1637–41)

Januario de Almeida: Cape Verde (1860–61)

Jerónimo de Almeida: Angola (1593–94)

João de Almeida: Cape Verde (1926–27)

João de Almeida: Mozambique (1703–06, 1712–14)

João de Almeida: Mozambique (1857–64)

José d'Almeida: Mozambique (1889)

José da Costa Almeida: Mozambique (1964–69)

Lopo de Almeida: Mozambique (1525–28)

Lopo de Almeida: Mozambique (1623–24)

Luis de Almeida: Tangier (1661–62)

Manuel de Almeida: Cacheu (ca. 1670)

Miguel de Almeida: Mozambique (1686–89)

Nicolau de Almeida: Mozambique (1736–39)

Luis de Almeida Cabral: Guinea-Bissau (1973–80)

Caetano de Almeida e Albuquerque: Angola (1876–78); Cape Verde (1869–76)

Isidro de Almeida Sousa e Sá: Mozambique (1801–05)

Almu: Gobir

Almustafa: Gwandu

Mariano Alonso: Equatorial Guinea; Western Sahara

Idris Alooma: Bornu Empire (1580–1603)

José María Alós: Ceuta (1810–13)

Alpha Oumar Konaré: Mali (1992–2002)

Bernardo de Alpoim: Cape Verde (1562–65)

Joaquim Alpoim: Bissau (1845–47)

Mania Alsali: Fika

Jean d'Alteyrac: Gorée and Dependencies

Altine: Daura

Leonel d'Alva: São Tomé and Príncipe (1974–75)

Francisco de Alva Brandão: São Tomé (1744–45)

Norberto José d'Alva Costa Alegre: São Tomé and Príncipe (1992–94)

Pedro Álvares da Cunha: Madeira (1712–15)

Fernando Álvarez de Sotomayor y

Flórez: Spanish Morocco (1907–08)

Manuel Álvarez Maldonaldo: Melilla (1862–63); Spanish Morocco (1864–65)

Álvaro I: Kongo

Jaga Álvaro II: Kongo

Álvaro III: Kongo

Álvaro IV: Kongo

Álvaro V: Kongo

Álvaro VI: Kongo

Álvaro VII: Kongo

Álvaro VIII: Kongo

Álvaro IX: Kongo

Inacio Alves: Mozambique (1870)

Vasco Alves: Angola (1943–47)

Eugenio de Alvorado y Perales Hurtado y Colomo: Oran (1770–74)

Alonso de Alvorado y Ulloa: Gran Canaria

Muhamma Alwali: Kano (1780–1807)

François Pierre-Alype: Djibouti (1937–38)

As Ama ibn Amr: Egypt (785)

Nii Amaa Ollennu: Ghana (1970)

Amabilis: Byzantine North Africa

Amacho: Igala

Amada: Mandara

Amadi Dyor: Baol

Amadi Sire: Masina

Amadou Cissé: Niger (1995, 1996–97)

Amadou Hama: Niger (1995–96)

Amadou Seeku: Dyolof

Amadou Toumani Touré: Mali (1991–92, 2002–)

Amadu: Futa Jallon

Amadu: Hadejia

Amadu: Misau (1833–50)

Amadu: Misau (1900–03)

Amadu Faaduma: Walo (1251–71)

Amaga: Igala

Amah: Whydah

Amai: Dongola

Amain: Brass

Amakiri: Bonny

Amakiri: New Calabar

Amakiri II: New Calabar

Amakiri III: New Calabar

Amakiri IV: New Calabar

Amaku: Doma

Opu Amakubu: Bonny

Amakuru: New Calabar

Amale: Biram

Amamu: Allada

Aman Andom: Ethiopia (1974)

Kobia Amanfi: Ashanti

Abeid Amani Karume: Zanzibar (1964–72)

Amani Abeid Karume: Zanzibar (2000–)

Amanibakhi: Kush (310–295 B.C.)

Amanikhalika: Kush (103–108)

Amanikhatashan: Kush (62–85)

Amaninatakilebte: Kush (538–519 B.C.)

Amanislo: Kush (275–260 B.C.)

Amanitaraqide: Kush (35–45)

Amanitekha: Kush (250–235 B.C.)

Amanitenmemide: Kush (45–62)

Mukhtar Ould Amar: Trarza

Amar Faatim Borso: Walo (1812–21)

Amara II Abu Sakaykin: Funj Sultanate

Amara Dunkas: Funj Sultanate

Francisco Ferreira do Amaral: Angola (1882–86); São Tomé and Príncipe (1879)

José do Amaral: Angola (1854–60, 1869–70)

José do Amaral: Mozambique (1870–73)

Manuel Amaral: Cape Verde (1953–57); São Tomé and Príncipe (1957–63)

Francisco do Amaral Cardoso: Mozambique (1805–07)

Amari: Baol

Amari: Kayor (1549–93)

Amari: Kayor (1790–1809)

Amari: Kayor (1883)

Ahmadu Dan Amaru: Argungu

Yamta Amba: Biu

Ambrosio: Kongo

Amda Iyasus: Ethiopia (1433–34)

Amda Seyon: Ethiopia (1314–44)

Amda Seyon II: Ethiopia (1494)

Immanuel Amde Michael: Eritrea

Ame: Igala

Ameda: Axum (386–401)

Ameda: Axum (436–446)

Giovan-Battista Ameglio: Cyrenaica; Tripolitania (1915–18)

Amenemhet I Shetepibre: Egypt (12th Dynasty)

Amenemhet II Nubkaure: Egypt (12th Dynasty)

Amenemhet III Nemare: Egypt (12th Dynasty)

Amenemhet IV Makherure: Egypt (12th Dynasty)

Amenemhet V Sekhemkare: Egypt (13th Dynasty)

Amenemhet VI Sehetepibre: Egypt (13th Dynasty)

Amenemnisu Hekawise Neferkare: Egypt (21st Dynasty)

Amenemope Usermare: Egypt (21st Dynasty)

Amenhotep I Djeserkare: Egypt (18th Dynasty)

Amenhotep II Akheprure: Egypt (18th Dynasty)

Amenhotep III Nebmare: Egypt (18th Dynasty)

Amenhotep IV: Egypt (18th Dynasty)

Amenmesse Menmire: Egypt (19th Dynasty)

Ameyaw Kese: Bono

Ameyaw Kwaakye: Bono

Ella Amida: Axum

al-Amin: Songhai (1612–18)

Idi Amin: Uganda (1971–79)

Kiyari Muhammad al-Amin: Bornu Empire (1893)

Muhammad al-Amin: Baguirmi

Muhammad VIII al-Amin: Tunisia (1943–57)

Muhammad al-Amin al-Kanemi: Bornu Empire (1817–24)

Amina: Mayotte

Muhammad V Aminami: Bornu Empire (1526–45)

Muhammadu Aminu: Zaria (1959–)

al-Amir: Egypt (1101–30)

Abu Thabit Amir: Morocco (1307–08)

Yekuno Amlak: Ethiopia (1270–85)

Tahar ben Ammar: Tunisia (1954–56)

Ammar I: Timbuktu (1599–1600)

Ammar II: Timbuktu (1662–65)

Ammar III: Timbuktu (1714)

Ammehayes: Shoa

Amoaka Atta I: Akim

Amoaka Atta II: Akim

Amoaka Atta III: Akim

Amocheje: Igala

Amodo: Oyo

Amonirdisu: Egypt (28th Dynasty)

Pedro do Amorim: Angola (1916–17); Mozambique (1918–19)

Salmin Amour: Zanzibar (1999–2000)

Warempe Ampem: Denkyira

Twum Ampoforo Okasu: Akim

Boa Amponsem: Denkyira

Amr: Bornu Empire (1456–56)

Amr ibn al-As: Egypt (642–644, 658–664)

Abu Amr Uthman: Hafsid Kingdom

Amra: Upper Egypt

Abu Yahya Amran: Tripolitania (1222–23)

Abu Amran Musa: Tripolitania (1224–26)

Wajkare Amtalqa: Kush (568–555 B.C.)

Amuniwaiye: Oyo

Amyrtaeus: Egypt (28th Dynasty)

Anagiri: Daura

Yebowa Ananta: Bono

Anao: Doma

Anastasius: Egypt (629–641)

Anawo: Doma

Bernardino de Anaya: Gran Canaria

Anbanga: Daniski

Anbasa Bazar: Ethiopia (1494–1508)

Anbasa ibn Ishaq: Egypt (852–856)

José Anchorena: Fernando Po

Jean Anciaux: Réunion (1986–89)

Andani I: Dagomba

Andani II: Dagomba

Andani III: Dagomba

Andani Sigili: Dagomba

George Anderson: Mauritius (1849–50)

John Anderson: Liberia (1830)

Francisco de Andía Irarrazábal y Zárate: Canary Islands (1625–26)

Aman Andom: Ethiopia (1974)

Andoma: Doma

Alfredo de Andrade: Mozambique (1906–10)

Antonio de Andrade: Mombasa (1596–98)

Bernardim Freire de Andrade: São Tomé (1677–80)

Francisco de Andrade: Ceuta (1591–92)

Francisco Nunes de Andrade: Cacheu (1634)

Gaspar de Andrade: Cape Verde (1578–83)

José Baptista de Andrade: Angola (1862–65, 1873–76)

Manuel de Andrade: Cape Verde (1555–58, 1565–69)

Pedro de Andrade: São Tomé (1604)

Rafael de Andrade: Mozambique (1891–93)

Andramanelo: Madagascar (1540–75)

Edward Andrews: Ghana (1860–62)

Gilles Andriamahazo: Madagascar (1975)

Andriamanetaha: Mohéli

Andrianamasinavalma: Madagascar (1675–1710)

Andrianametaka: Mayotte

Andrianampoinimerina: Madagascar (1794–1810)

Tantely Andrianarivo: Madagascar (1998–)

Andrianerimerina: Madagascar (1300–20)

Andrianjaka: Madagascar (1610–30)

Andriantsimitoviaminanandrandehibe: Madagascar (1650–70)

Andriantsitakatrandriana: Madagascar (1630–50)

Andriantsuli: Mayotte

Andries Waterboer: Griqualand West

Anedjib: Egypt (1st Dynasty)

Aneerood Jugnauth: Mauritius (1982–95, 2000–03)

Sa'id Muhammad Jaffar al-Angadi: Comoros (1972)

Gabriel Angoulvant: Côte d'Ivoire (1908–16); Djibouti (1900); French Equatorial Africa (1917–20); French West Africa (1918–19)

Nahas Angula: Namibia (2005–)

Muhammadu Angulu: Lafia

Musa Angulu: Abuja

Anicetus: Africa Proconsularis (350–352)

Anim Kokobo Boadee: Denkyira

Bar Kaina Ankabi: Songhai (1362–70)

Smenkhare Ankheprure: Egypt (18th Dynasty)

Ankhikare Anlamani: Kush (623–593 B.C.)

Psamtik III Ankhkaenre: Egypt (26th Dynasty)

Ankhkare Nastasen: Kush (335–310 B.C.)

Muhammad Ankony: Zeng Empire (1504–05)

Joseph Ankrah: Ghana (1966–69)

Ankhikare Anlamani: Kush (623–593 B.C.)

Anna de Souza Nzina: Ndongo

Armand Annet: Benin [ii] (1938–40); Djibouti (1935–37); Madagascar (1941–42)

Annius Syriacus: Egypt (163–165)

Frederico Anrich: Fernando Po

Joaquín Gómez Ansa: Ceuta (1835–36)

Ansa Saseraku I: Akwamu

Ansa Saseraku II: Akwamu

Ansa Saseraku III: Akwamu

Ansa Saseraku IV: Akwamu

M. Anselme: Seychelles (1772–75)

Yerim Mbanyik Anta Dyop: Walo (1735)

Pedro de Antas e Meneses: Madeira (1807–13)

Anthemius: Egypt (477–478)

Pierre Anthonioz: Mauritania (1959–60)

Anthony Ockiya: Brass

Raphaël Antonetti: Benin [ii] (1909–10, 1911); Côte d'Ivoire (1918–24); Djibouti (1905); French Equatorial Africa (1924–34); Mali (1916–17); Senegal (1914–16)

Louis Antonin: Guinea (1929–31); Mauritania (1933–34)

Antoninus: Egypt (384)

Antonio I: Kongo

Antonio de Mingo: Warri

Antonius: Africa Proconsularis (377–378)

Antonius Marcellinus: Africa Proconsularis (340–341)

Flavius Antonius Theodorus: Egypt (338–354)

Antwi: Ashanti

Antyemsaf I Merenre: Egypt (6th Dynasty)

Antyemsaf II Merenre: Egypt (6th Dynasty)

Muhammad Anwar as-Sadat: Egypt (1970–81)

Enrico Anzilotti: Italian Somaliland (1955–58)

Aole: Oyo

Duca D'Aosta: Ethiopia (1941–41); Italian East Africa

Aparaku: Akim

Apeanin Kwaframoa Woyiawonyi: Akim

Aphilas Bisi-Dimele: Axum

Apia: Bonny

Sourou Apithy: Benin [ii] (1958–59, 1964–65)

Auserre Apopi I: Egypt (15th Dynasty)

Ahenenre Apopi II: Egypt (15th Dynasty)

Appinya: Bonny

Appius Sabinus: Egypt (250)

William Appleton: Sierra Leone (1815)

Apries Wahimbre: Egypt (26th Dynasty)

Caius Vipstanus Apronianus: Africa [i] (68)

Lucius Apronius: Africa [i] (18–21)

Hassan Gouled Aptidon: Djibouti (1977–99)

Aqrakamani: Kush (132–137)

Aquila: Egypt (17)
Subatianus Aquila: Egypt (202–215)
Arab Ahmad: Algiers (1571–74)
Ahmad Arabi: Egypt (1882)
Arabion: Numidia
Marquês de Aracaty: Mozambique (1837–38)
Lucius Aradius Valerius Proculus Felix: Africa Proconsularis (333–336)
Sidi Muhammad ben Mulay Arafa: Morocco (1953–55)
Abede Aragai: Ethiopia (1958–60)
Ahmad I al-Araj: Morocco (1517–25)
Ali al-Araj: Morocco (1734–36)
Arakil Bey al-Armani: Sudan (1857–59)
Birayamb Aram: Dyolof
Naatago Aram Bakar: Walo (1674–1708)
N'dyak Aram Bakar Teedyek: Walo (1708–33)
Yerim Mbanyik Aram Bakar: Walo (1640–74)
José de Aramburu: Oran (1738–42)
Juan Francisco de Araña: Ceuta (1705–09, 1720); Oran (1701–04)
Miguel Porcel y Manrique de Araña Menchaca y Zaldívar: Ceuta (1784–91)
Mar Arandan: Songhai (1449–56)
Eduardo Arantes e Oliveira: Mozambique (1969–71)
Daniel arap Moi: Kenya (1978–2002)
Antonio Vaz de Araújo: Cacheu (1775)
Jorge de Araújo: Cape Verde (1646–48)
Nicolau Pino de Araújo: Bissau (1753); Cacheu (1741)
Luis de Araújo e Silva: Cacheu (1786)
João de Araújo Gomes: Cacheu (1821)
Manuel Arcaya: Melilla (1847–48)
Diego de Arce: Melilla (1655–56, 1672–74)
Archelaus: Byzantine North Africa
Archelaus: Egypt (397)
Geoffrey Archer: British Somaliland; Sudan (1925–26); Uganda (1922–25)
José Archer: Tangier (1951–54)
Louis Archinard: Mali (1888–91, 1892–93)
Carlos de Arcos: Mozambique (1881–82)
Charles Arden-Clarke: Botswana; Ghana (1949–57); Lesotho (1942–46)
Albert Ardin d'Elteil: Cotonou
Muhammadu Ba Are: Argungu
Harbi Ar'ed: Ifat
Safya Ar'ed: Ethiopia (1344–72)
Senfa Ar'ed: Ethiopia (1294–95)
Wedem Ar'ed: Ethiopia (1299–1314)
Ali Aref Bourhan: Djibouti (1967–77)
Areobindus: Byzantine North Africa
Arfed: Axum
Francisco Bens Argandoña: Western Sahara

Martín de Argote: Oran (1512–17)
Arghuz Tarkhan: Egypt (868)
Argi: Kanem
Ari: Doma
Ari I: Biu
Ari II: Biu
Ari Paskur: Biu
Aritenyesbekhe: Kush (108–132)
Aritse: Kanem
Arju: Kanem
Khnemabre Arkaqamani: Kush (295–275 B.C.)
Mar Arkena: Songhai (1442–49)
Kobrina Arku Korsah: Ghana (1957)
Foli Arlonko: Little Popo
Armah: Axum
Rema Armah: Axum
Furcy Augustin Armanet: Nossi-Bé
Arakil Bey al-Armani: Sudan (1857–59)
Alexandre Armény de Paradis: Gorée
Cecil Armitage: Ashanti; Gambia (1921–27); Gold Coast Northern Territories
Robert Armitage: Malawi (1956–61)
Georges Arnaud: Comoros (1956–59)
Robert Arnaud: Burkina Faso (1927–28)
Hassan Ali Pasha Arnavut: Kordofan
Arnavut Halil: Tripolitania (1673–75)
Arnekhamani: Kush (235–218 B.C.)
Louis Arnoux: Nossi-Bé
Dan Aro: Daura-Zango
Juan Arolas y Esplugues: Melilla (1894)
Domingos Arouca: Cape Verde (1836–37)
Yakob Arous: Wadai
Arqamani: Kush (218–200 B.C.)
Satrius Arrianus: Egypt (307–323)
Antonio Arrobas: Cape Verde (1854–58)
Edwin Arrowsmith: Lesotho (1951–56)
Arsecilaus: Pentapolis
Arsecilaus II: Pentapolis
Arsecilaus III: Pentapolis
Arsecilaus IV: Pentapolis
Arsenius: Egypt (487)
Arsha: Egypt (31st Dynasty)
Arsinoe II: Egypt (277–270 B.C.)
Arsinoe III: Egypt (217–204 B.C.)
Artabanus: Byzantine North Africa
Artakhshayarsa I: Egypt (27th Dynasty)
Artakhshayarsa II: Egypt (27th Dynasty)
Artakhshayarsa III: Egypt (31st Dynasty)
Artaxerxes I: Egypt (27th Dynasty)
Artaxerxes II: Egypt (27th Dynasty)
Artaxerxes III: Egypt (31st Dynasty)
Umar Arteh Ghalib: Somalia
Artemi: Canary Islands (1402–05)
Artemius: Egypt (360–362)
Leonard Arthur: Ghana (1902)
Prince Arthur of Connaught: South Africa (1920–23)
Aruj: Algiers (1516–18)

Aryandes: Egypt (27th Dynasty)
Aryesbekhe: Kush (209–228 B.C.)
As Ama ibn Amr: Egypt (785)
Asabo: Doma
Asabysos: Dongola
Asae Pokou: Baule
Asagum: Axum
Asaman: Bono
Dan Asan: Biram
Kofi Asante Baninyiye: Akim
Otumfo Asare: Akwamu
Asawa: Biram
Asbeha: Axum
Asehere Khamudy: Egypt (15th Dynasty)
Aseil: Doma
Carlos Asensio: Spanish Morocco (1940–41)
Asfa Wossen: Shoa
Asfa Wossen II: Shoa
Betwoded Asfaha Wolde Mikael: Eritrea
Asfeh: Axum
Ella Asfeha: Axum
Muhammad V al-Asgher: Morocco (1636–55)
Ashafa: Katsina (1634–35)
Bako Mairari Ashaka Okao: Zaria (1758–60)
ibn Ashe: Gobir
Ashikpa: Lagos (ca. 1720)
Bako Abdu Ashkuku: Zaria (1611–18)
Jehudi Ashmun: Liberia (1822–28)
al-Ashraf Barsabay: Egypt (1422–38); Tripolitania (1412–21)
al-Ashraf Khalil: Egypt (1290–93)
al-Hajj Muhammad at-Tazi Bu Ashran: Tangier (1923–41, 1945–54)
Ashu Manu I: Kororofa
Ashu Manu II: Kororofa
Ashu Manu III: Kororofa
al-Asi: Egypt (642–644, 658–664)
Abu Abdallah Muhammad II Abu Asida: Hafsid Kingdom
Asiki: Keana
Asil: Wadai
Mustafa Asim: Tripolitania (1849–52, 1874–75)
Asim Warfaguma: Omayyad and Abbasid North Africa
Asimini: Bonny
Okpara Asimini: Bonny
Askalis: Mauretania West
Ali Asker: Tripolitania (1838–42)
Askia the Great: Songhai (1493–1528, 1537–38)
Askiu: Lower Egypt
Asma Giyorgis: Ethiopia (1721–30)
Sheikh Abd as-Salaam al-Asman: Tripolitania (1480–82)
Muhammad Asmani al-Mazrui: Mombasa (1826–35)
Asnaf Sagad: Ethiopia (1603–04)
Pobi Asomaning: Akim
Merkare Aspelta: Kush (593–568 B.C.)
Ptolemaios Aspion: Pentapolis
Lucius Nonius Asprenas: Africa [i] (12–15)

Bahr Asqad: Ethiopia (1294–95)
Hezba Asqad: Ethiopia (1295–96)
Kedma Asqad: Ethiopia (1296–97)
Saba Asqad: Ethiopia (1298–99)
Earl of Oxford and Asquith: Seychelles (1961–67)
Asrar Sagad: Ethiopia (1708–11)
Ras Asrata-Medhin Kassa: Eritrea
Assafa: Damagaram
Charles Assalé: Cameroun (1960–65)
Louis Van Assenburgh: Cape Colony (1708–11)
Charles Assier de Pompignan: Benin [ii] (1943–46); Gabon (1935–36, 1942–43)
Rafael Assin y Bazán: Melilla (1888–89)
Azali Assoumani: Comoros (1999–2002, 2002–)
Estanislau de Assunção e Almeida: São Tomé and Príncipe (1864–65, 1867–69)
Manuel de Assunção e Almeida: São Tomé and Príncipe (1876–79)
Riccardo Astuto: Eritrea
Atabor: Igala
Muhammad Atahiru I: Fulani Empire
Muhammad Atahiru II: Fulani Empire
Atahiru Ahmadu: Fulani Empire
Estévão de Ataíde: Mozambique (1607–09, 1611–12)
João de Ataíde e Azevedo: Madeira (1701–04)
Atapa: Aku
Athanasius: Byzantine North Africa
Earl of Athlone: South Africa (1924–30)
Ati Kwame: Bono
Atiba: Oyo
Atif Sidqi: Egypt (1986–96)
Atiku: Lapai
Ahmadu Atiku: Fulani Empire
Abubakr Atiku I: Fulani Empire
Abubakr Atiku II: Fulani Empire
Hukare Atlanersa: Kush (653–643 B.C.)
Atman: Daniski
Ato Tedla Bairu: Eritrea
Atona: Jema'a
Atta I: Doma
Amoaka Atta I: Akim
Nana Ofori Atta I: Akim
Atta II: Doma
Amoaka Atta II: Akim
Nana Ofori Atta II: Akim
Atta III: Doma
Amoaka Atta III: Akim
Atta IV: Doma
Atta Biwom: Akim
Atta Panyin: Akim
Atta Wusu Yiakosan: Akim
Atticus: Africa Proconsularis (384)
Ahmad ben Sheikh Attoumane: Comoros (1993–94)
Sa'id Attourmani: Comoros (1978)
Muhammar Atu: Gumel
Atuma: Kano (1452)
Atuwatse II: Warri

Jean-Hilaire Aubame (1964)
Laurent Aube: Gabon (1867–68)
Col. Aubert: Mauritania (1908–10)
Pierre Aubert: Cameroun (1937–38); Réunion (1939–42)
René Audéoud: Mali (1898–99)
Jean Augagneur: French Equatorial Africa (1920–23); Madagascar (1905–09)
Auhammadu: Gwandu
Louis Aujas: Benin [ii] (1932–33)
Ptolemy XII Auletes: Egypt (80–58 B.C., 55–51 B.C.)
Aulus Vibius Habitus: Africa [i] (16–17)
Aulus Vitellius: Africa [i] (60–61)
Duc d'Aumale: Algeria (1847–48)
Marcus Aurelius Papirius Dionysius: Egypt (193)
Quintus Aurelius Symmachus: Africa Proconsularis (373)
Auserre Apopi I: Egypt (15th Dynasty)
Ausu: Doma
Marqués de Miranda de Auta: Ceuta (1641–44)
Dan Auwa: Gumel
José de Avellaneda: Canary Islands (1789–91)
Visconde de Santa Clara de Avellido: Oran (1628–32)
Manuel Avello: Spanish Morocco (1934–36)
François Bertin d'Avesnes: Réunion (1763–67)
Avidius Heliodorus: Egypt (139–148)
João d'Ávila: Mozambique (1882)
José da Ávila: Bissau (1852–53)
Marcelino de Ávila: Cape Verde (1761)
Avillius Flaccus: Egypt (32–37)
Avissu: Dahomey
Lucius Hedius Rufus Lollianus Avitus: Africa [i] (157–158)
Abu Bakr Awadullah: Sudan (1969)
Awal Ibrahim: Abuja
Awani: Potiskum
Awibre Hor: Egypt (13th Dynasty)
Yao Awirri: Denkyira
Abu Awn: Egypt (751–53, 755–58)
Obafemi Awolowo: Nigeria Western Region
Awonbioju: Oyo
Awura Danse: Baule
Awura Pokou: Baule
Awusa: Bonny
Ay Kheperkheprure Itnute: Egypt (18th Dynasty)
Ayagba: Igala
Gonçalo de Gamboa Ayala: Cacheu (1644–49)
Ibrahim Ayalai: Abuja
Bernard Ayandho: Central African Republic (1979–80)
Luc Ayang: Cameroun (1983–84)
Ayaton: Porto-Novo
Hussein Aydid: Somalia
Muhammad Farah Aydid: Somalia
Ayekeraa: Denkyira
Dan Ayi: Yauri

Ayibi: Oyo
Ayikpe: Porto-Novo
Pantaleón Ayllón: Fernando Po
Joseph Aymerich: Cameroun (1916); Kamerun (1914–16); Niger (ca. 1905)
Sheikh Mahl Aynin: Brakna
Ayohuan: Whydah
Juan Bautista de Ayora: Tenerife
Eli Ayres: Liberia (1821–22)
Fara Aysa Naalem: Walo (1563–65)
Combo Ayuba: Comoros (1995)
Ayyub: Egypt (1644–46)
Ayyub ibn Shurahbil: Egypt (717–720)
Ayzur: Axum
Azagia I: Keana
Azagia II: Keana
Azali Assoumani: Comoros (1999–2002, 2002–)
Diogo de Azambuja: Portuguese Gold Coast (1482–84)
João de Azambuja: São Tomé and Príncipe (1778–82)
Diogo de Azambuja e Melo: Madeira (1595–1600)
Jean-Baptiste Azéma: Réunion (1745)
Antonio de Miranda de Azevedo: Portuguese Gold Coast (1504)
João de Azevedo: Mozambique (1612–14)
Rui Gomes de Azevedo: Portuguese Gold Coast (1562)
Simão de Azevedo: Mozambique (1512–15)
Victor Hugo de Azevedo Coutinho: Mozambique (1924–26)
José de Azevedo e Silva: Mozambique (1911–12)
Ismail al-Azhari: Sudan (1954–56, 1965–69)
Nnamdi Azikiwe: Nigeria (1952–54, 1959–66); Nigeria Eastern Region
al-Aziz: Egypt (975–996)
Abdul Aziz: Egypt (1405–05)
Abu Faris Abd al-Aziz: Hafsid Kingdom
Abu'l Faris Abd al-Aziz I: Morocco (1366–72, 1393–96)
Abdul Aziz Hegazy: Egypt (1974–75)
al-Aziz ibn al-Mansur: Hammadid Kingdom
Aziz Sidqi: Egypt (1972–73)
al-Aziz Uthman: Egypt (1193–98)
al-Aziz Yusuf: Egypt (1438)
Azoton: Allada
Azzedine Laraki: Morocco (1986–92)

B

Bodyan Mori Ba: Kaarta
Muhammadu Ba Are: Argungu
Deni Ba Bo: Kaarta
Abdullahi Ba Demba: Futa Jallon
Umaru Ba Demba: Futa Jallon
Ba-Haddu II: Timbuktu (1714, 1715, 1719–21, 1727–29)

Ba-Haddu III: Timbuktu (ca. 1760)
Ba-Haddu Salim: Timbuktu (1683)
Musa Ba Kikala: Futa Jallon
Nuhu Ba Kikala: Futa Jallon
Daoula Ba Traore: Kenedugu
Daoula Ba Traore II: Kenedugu
Ba'ala Segab: Ethiopia (1784–88)
Mallam Baba: Agaie
Baba: Zaria (1770–88)
Ali Baba: Dongola
Aliyu Baba: Kano (1893–1903)
Baba Ali: Timbuktu (1780)
Baba Alimu: Futa Jallon
Baba Osman: Tripolitania (1677–78)
Baba Saiyid I: Timbuktu (1693)
Baba Saiyid II: Timbuktu (1740–41, 1745–46)
Umar Baba Ya Mairami: Bornu Empire (1969–)
Baba Zaki: Kano (1768–76)
Babakar I: Timbuktu (1710–11)
Babakar II: Timbuktu (1748–49)
Babakr an-Nur: Sudan (1971)
Babami: Damagaram
Muhammad Babana: Trarza
Ibrahim Babangida: Nigeria (1985–93)
Babar: Egypt (1622)
Dan Gudi Dan Babari: Gobir
Nafata Dan Babari: Gobir
Yakuba Dan Babari: Gobir
Babari Dan ibn Ashe: Gobir
Babba: Gobir
Babba I: Zamfara
Babba II: Zamfara
Babemba Traore: Kenedugu
René Babin: Mauritania (1945–46)
Mallam Babu Saba: Damagaram
Lawan Babuje: Bedde
Muhammad Bacar: Mwali
Eduardo Baccari: Cyrenaica
Hedi Baccouche: Tunisia (1987–89)
Salah Eddine ben Muhammad Baccouche: Tunisia (1943–47, 1952–54)
Bachiri: Gobir
Bachiri: Gobir
Baciri VII: Gobir
Bada: Songhai (1325–32)
Badadella: Gobir
Badari: Upper Egypt
N.J. Badenhorst: KaNgwane
Badi I Sid al-Qum: Funj Sultanate
Badi II Abu Daqan: Funj Sultanate
Badi III al-Ahmar: Funj Sultanate
Badi IV Abu Shulukh: Funj Sultanate
Badi V: Funj Sultanate
Badi VI: Funj Sultanate
Badi Sidi: Masina
Badi Tali: Masina
Badimo: Bamaleteland
Badirile: Barolongland
Badis: Zirid Kingdom
Badis ibn al-Mansur: Hammadid Kingdom
Badlai: Adal [ii]
Pietro Badoglio: Eritrea; Italian East Africa; Libia

Badr al-Jamali: Egypt (1074–94)
Abd al-Qadir Badri: Libya
Ba'eda Maryam I: Ethiopia (1468–78)
Ba'eda Maryam II: Ethiopia (1795)
Ba'eda Maryam III: Ethiopia (1826)
Bagauda: Kano (998–1063)
Jean-Baptiste Bagaza: Burundi [ii]
Governor Baggs: Ghana (1697–1701)
Baghama: Gurma
Umaru Bago: Lapai
Abdullahi Dalla Bahagu: Lafia
Francisco Franco Bahamonde: Spanish Morocco (1936)
Thlama Bahara: Biu
Miguel Baharem: São Tomé (1616–20)
Umar Bahaushe: Nupe
Baher Ikela: Axum
Bahi Ladgham: Tunisia (1969–70)
Bahir Keuse: Egypt (1760–62)
Ahmad Bahmini: Morocco (1963–65)
Bahr Asqad: Ethiopia (1294–95)
Bahram: Egypt (1134–37)
Bai Foki: Koya-Temne
Bai Kanta: Koya-Temne
Bai Kompa: Koya-Temne
Fernão Baião: Mozambique (1646–48)
Inacio Baião: Bissau (1777)
Baibars I: Egypt (1260–77)
Baibars II: Egypt (1309–10)
Jean Georges le Baillif des Mesnager: Gorée
Victor Bailly: Côte d'Ivoire (1952–54); Mali (1952); Senegal (1950–52)
Bailutle: Bamaleteland
Bairam: Egypt (1626–28)
David Baird: Cape Colony (1806–07)
Ato Tedla Bairu: Eritrea
Pierre Chapon-Baissac: Benin [ii] (1921–22); Côte d'Ivoire (1922); Djibouti (1924–32)
Baji: Lapai
Baka Kodu: Dyolof
Bakaa-Tam Buri-Nyabu: Dyolof
Bakaffa: Ethiopia (1721–30)
Adam Bakam: Daniski
Bakan-Tam Khaari: Dyolof
Bakan-Tam Yaago: Dyolof
Bakar: Tagant
Abdul Bu Bakar: Futa Toro
al-Hajj Abu Bakar: Biram
Abu Bakar: Keffi
Naatago Aram Bakar: Walo (1674–1708)
Yerim Mbanyik Aram Bakar: Walo (1640–74)
Bu Bakar III: Futa Jallon
Bu Bakar IV: Futa Jallon
N'dyak Aram Bakar Teedyek: Walo (1708–33)
Bakare Tanuatamun: Kush (ca. 650 B.C.)
Bakari: Futa Jallon
Bakari: Segu
Djibo Bakari: Niger (1957–58)
Bakary Watara: Kong
Umaru Bakatara: Gwandu
Bakawa: Zamfara
Francis Baker: Saint Helena (1994–98)

Samuel Baker Pasha: Equatoria Province
Bakgatla: Bakgatlaland
Sheikh Abidin al-Bakha'i: Masina
Ramadani Baki: Zanzibar (1983–84)
Bakili Muluzi: Malawi (1994–)
Sidi al-Bakka: Masina
Abd al-Hamid al-Bakkush: Libya
Bako: Biram
Bako: Zaria (1710–18)
Dan Bako: Zamfara
Muhamman Bako: Biram
Bako Abdu Ashkuku: Zaria (1611–18)
Bako Ali: Zaria (1621–46)
Bako Aliyu: Zaria (1670–1678)
Bako Aliyu: Zaria (1718–27)
Bako Bawa: Zaria (1762–64)
Bako Brima: Zaria (1618–21, 1647–60)
Bako Brima Hasko: Zaria (1678–82)
Bako Dan Musa: Zaria (1727–36)
Bako Hamza: Zaria (1611)
Bako Ishihako: Zaria (1736–38)
Bako Mahama Gabi: Zaria (1608–11)
Bako Mahama Rubo: Zaria (1682–1710)
Bako Mairari Ashaka Okao: Zaria (1758–60)
Bako Majirua: Zaria (1584–97)
Bako Makam Danguma: Zaria (1738–50)
Bako Makam Gaba: Zaria (1757–58)
Bako Makam Rubu: Zaria (1646–47)
Bako Moru Watara: Gwiriko
Bako Musa: Zaria (1608)
Bako Ruhawa: Zaria (1750–57)
Bako Shukunu: Zaria (1660–70)
Bako Su Aliyu: Zaria (1597–1608)
Bakolopang: Barolongland
Bakon Dare: Gobir
Bakr: Egypt (1765–66)
Abu Bakr: Adal [ii]
Sayid Abu Bakr: Anjouan
Abu Bakr: Egypt (1341)
Abu Bakr: Egypt (1727–29, 1734)
Abu Bakr: Harar
Abu Bakr: Mayotte
Abu Bakr: Rustumid Amirate
Abu Bakr: Tripolitania (1371–92)
Abu Bakr: Tripolitania (1482–89)
Abu Yahya Abu Bakr: Hafsid Kingdom
Abu Yahya Abu-Bakr: Morocco (1244–58)
Muhammad al-Bakr: Tagant
Rashid Bakr: Sudan (1976–77)
Abu Bakr I: Mali Empire
al-Adil Abu Bakr I: Egypt (1200–18)
Abu Bakr II: Mali Empire
al-Adil Abu Bakr II: Egypt (1238–40)
Abu Yahya Abu Bakr ash-Shahid: Hafsid Kingdom
Abu Bakr Awadullah: Sudan (1969)
Abu Bakr ibn Abd al-Mannan: Harar
Ahmad Bakr ibn Musa: Darfur
Abu Bakr ibn Umar: Almoravid Empire
Abu Bakr Kolo: Nupe

Abu Bakr Liyatu: Bornu Empire (1392–94)
Bakurukuru: Zamfara
Bakwa Turunku: Zaria (1536–39)
Bakwante: Akim
Ahmad Balafrej: Morocco (1958)
Hassan al-Balazi: Fezzan
Claudius Balbillus: Egypt (56–60)
Italo Balbo: Libia
Antonio Baldissera: Eritrea; Massawa
Abubaka Tafawa Balewa: Nigeria (1957–66)
Bali Javush: Tripolitania (1672–73)
Abbad al-Balkhi: Egypt (812–13)
Gaspard de Ballade: Réunion (1745–47, 1748–49)
Noël Ballay: French West Africa (1900–02); Gabon (1886–89); Guinea (1890–1900)
Victor Ballot: Benin [ii] (1894–99); Porto-Novo
Younoussa Bamana: Mayotte Department
Bambilanga: Tembuland
Joseph Bamina: Burundi [ii]
Canaan Banana: Zimbabwe (1980–87)
Banaturumi: Gobir
Hastings Banda: Malawi (1963–94)
Ziblim Bandamda: Dagomba
Yamtara Bangwe: Biu
Muhammad Bani: Songhai (1586–88)
Kofi Asante Baninyiye: Akim
Banja Tejan-Sie: Sierra Leone (1968–71)
Kunia Banna: Koya-Temne
Banna Bubu: Ghana Empire
James Bannerman: Ghana (1850–51)
Bantu Holomisa: Transkei
Banydoba: Gurma
Baogho: Yatenga
Baogo: Wagadugu
Baogo II: Wagadugu
Baqa: Mauretania
Abu al-Baqa Khalid I: Hafsid Kingdom
Abu al-Baqa Khalid II: Hafsid Kingdom
Baqirdji: Egypt (1633–35)
Bar: Baguirmi
Bar Kaina Ankabi: Songhai (1362–70)
Barah: Dongola
Francisco Barahona: Canary Islands (1685–89)
Sa'id Barakh Khan: Egypt (1277–79)
Barama-Ngolo: Segu
Barandamasu: Kano (1306–42)
Barankimi: Gobir
Barankimi: Gobir
Baraonendana: Kangaba
Francisco Barata: São Tomé and Príncipe (1953–54)
Oreste Baratieri: Eritrea
Bashir Suleimanu Barau: Abuja
Suleimanu Barau: Abuja
João Barba: Mozambique (1763–65)
Pedro Barba de Campos: Canary Islands (1415–18)
Barbandoma: Gobir

Barbarossa: Algiers (1518–20, 1525–46); Tunis (1534–35)
Rubrius Barbarus: Egypt (13–7 B.C.)
Francisco Barbosa: Guinea-Bissau (1885–86)
Inacio Barbosa: Cape Verde (1683–87)
José Barbosa: Angola (1810–16); Bissau (1839–40)
José Barbosa: Cape Verde (1737–38)
Sebastião Barbosa: São Tomé and Príncipe (1928–29)
Francis Barbrius: Dutch Gold Coast (1740–41)
Barbushe: Kano (ca. 950)
Arthur Barclay: Liberia (1904–12)
Edwin Barclay: Liberia (1930–44)
Bardau: Zamfara
Bardiya-Gaumata: Egypt (27th Dynasty)
Ibrahim Baré Maïnassara: Niger (1996–99)
Quintus Marcius Barea Soranus: Africa [i] (41–43)
Barend Lucas: Adam Kok's Land
Barend Barends: Griqualand West
Victor Bareste: Cotonou
Sayid Barghash: Zanzibar (1870–88)
Isaac Bargues: Madagascar (1950–53)
Kanou-ba-Nyouma Bari: Segu
Barikurgu: Biram
Evelyn Baring: Egypt (1882, 1883–91, 1892–1907)
Evelyn Baring: Kenya (1952–59); South Africa (1944–51); Zimbabwe (1942–44)
Barka Mbody: Walo (1211–25)
Barket Gourad Hamadou: Djibouti (1978–2001)
Henry Barkley: Cape Colony (1870–77); Mauritius (1863–70)
Arthur Barkly: Seychelles (1882–88)
Barma Dan Moi Bunowo: Daniski
Barma Mustafa: Damagaram
Ahmadu Barmo: Zamfara
Barnabas Sibusiso Dhlamini: Swaziland (1996–2003)
John Barnes: Senegal (1763–65)
Jean-Baptiste Barnier: Nossi-Bé
Bisi Baro: Songhai (1295–1325)
Zenko Baro: Songhai (1275–95)
Barquq: Egypt (1382–89, 1390–99)
José de Barrasa: Fernando Po
Muhammad Siyad Barre: Somalia
Antonio de Barredo: São Tomé (1693–94)
Antonio de Barreido: Madeira (1591–95)
Fortunato Barreiros: Cape Verde (1851–54)
José Barrera: Fernando Po
Ángel Barrera y Luyando: Fernando Po
Francisco Barreto: Mozambique (1569–73)
Honorio Barreto: Bissau (1836–39, 1840–41, 1855–59); Cacheu (1846–47)
João Barreto: Cacheu (1785–86)

Jerónimo Barreto: Mozambique (1564–67)
Julião de Campos Barreto: São Tomé (1673–77)
Pedro Barreto: Cape Verde (1653–58)
Francisco Barreto de Meneses: São Tomé (1632)
Augusto de Castilho Barreto e Noronha: Mozambique (1885–89)
Pedro de Barrionuevo y Melgoza: Gran Canaria
Jerónimo de los Barrios: Melilla (1595–96)
João de Barros: Portuguese Gold Coast (1524–25)
José Correia de Barros: Cacheu (1820–21)
Pedro de Barros: Cacheu (1723)
Pedro de Barros: Mozambique (1958–61)
Roque de Barros do Rego: Cape Verde (1648)
al-Ashraf Barsabay: Egypt (1422–38); Tripolitania (1412–21)
Bartare: Kush (260–250 B.C.)
Col. Bartels: Congo (Zaire) (1900)
Cornelis Bartels: Dutch Gold Coast (1798–1804)
René Barthes: French West Africa (1946–48)
Francis Barton: Zanzibar (1908–13)
Muhammad II al-Bartuqali: Morocco (1505–24)
Baru: Songhai (1492–93)
Suleiman al-Baruni: Tripolitania (1915–17); Tripolitanian Republic
Barwa: Biram
al-Hajj Muhammadu Bashar: Daura-Zango
Bashe: Batlokwaland
Bashikarr: Zaria (ca. 1450)
Bashir Suleimanu Barau: Abuja
Umar al-Bashir: Sudan (1989–)
Muhammadu Bashiru: Gwandu
Basileios: Dongola
Basilianus: Egypt (218–219)
Baskakaren: Kush (405–404 B.C.)
Bassaeus Rufus: Egypt (167–175)
Denis Basset: Senegal (1682–84)
José de la Puente Basseve: Fernando Po
Bassi: Ghana Empire
Bassianus: Egypt (381–382)
Bassoh: Whydah
Bassus: Africa Proconsularis (426–427)
Flavius Bassus: Africa Proconsularis (435, 437–439)
Ettore Bastico: Libia
Joseph Bastide: Réunion (1696–98)
Damião de Bastos: Cacheu (1737)
Marcelino Bastos: Cape Verde (1796–1802)
Basuo: Brass
Changamire Baswi: Rozwi
Bata tare: Katsina (1180–1250)
ibn al-Batai'hi: Egypt (1121–25)
Batatume: Daura

Batchande: Gurma
Bathoen: Bangwaketseland
Kgosi Bathoen: Bangwaketseland
William Battershill: Tanganyika
Battus I: Pentapolis
Battus II: Pentapolis
Battus III: Pentapolis
Battus IV: Pentapolis
Baturi: Gobir
Batutua: Gobir
Léon Bauche: Togo (1923, 1925)
Baude: Hadejia
Auguste Baudin: Senegal (1847–50)
Charles Baur: Gabon (1863–66)
Bauya: Potiskum
Bawa: Gobir
Bawa: Ilorin
Bawa: Kano (1659–70)
Bawa: Lapai
Bawa: Zaria (1871–74)
Muhammadu Bawa: Gobir
Rabon Bawa: Zaria (1505–30)
Bako Bawa: Zaria (1762–64)
Bawa Dan Gima: Katsina (1802–04)
Bawa Dan Gwamki: Gobir
Bawa Jan Gwarzo: Gobir
Bawa Kayi: Daniski
Bawa Nesso: Gobir
Bawan Allah: Daura
Bawo: Daura
Jean Alingué Bawoyea: Chad (1991–92)
Charles Bayardelle: Djibouti (1942–43); French Equatorial Africa (1944–46)
Bayelekhaya: Tembuland
Abdullahi Bayero: Gwandu
Abdullahi Chiroma Bayero: Kano (1926–53)
Ado Bayero: Kano (1963–)
Bayero Aliyu: Gwandu
Pierre Bayle: Mayotte Department
Jean-Marie Bayol: Guinea (1882–90); Porto-Novo
Johann Bax: Cape Colony (1676–78)
Ambasa Bazar: Ethiopia (1494–1508)
Charles Bazoche: Réunion (1841–46)
Anthony Beale: Saint Helena (1672–73)
William Beaton: Ashanti
Alexander Beatson: Saint Helena (1808–13)
Laurent Beauchamp: Réunion (1896–1900)
Leicester Beaufort: North Eastern Rhodesia
Pedro Beaumont y Peralta: Melilla (1868–71)
Pierre de Beausse: Fort-Dauphin
Joseph Beauvollier de Courchant: Mauritius (1718–22); Réunion (1718–23)
Louis Lansana Béavogui: Guinea (1972–84)
M. Bech: Madagascar (1942–43)
Paul Béchard: French West Africa (1948–51)
Roland Béchoff: Réunion (1950–52)

Angelo Beda: Southern Sudan
Marie-Alphonse Bedeau: Algeria (1847)
Henri Konan Bédié: Côte d'Ivoire (1993–99)
Marqués de Bedmar: Canary Islands (1589–91); Gran Canaria
Paul de Beeckmann: Porto-Novo
John Beecroft: Bight of Biafra; Fernando Po
Edward Beetham: Botswana; Swaziland
Biyai Bei: Songhai (921–933)
Mahfud Ali Beiba: Western Sahara
Juan Beigbeder y Atienza: Spanish Morocco (1937–39)
Bekenrinef Wahkare: Egypt (24th Dynasty)
Bekir: Fezzan
Muhammad II Bektash: Algiers (1706–10)
Belaid Abdesalam: Algeria (1992–93)
Baron Belasyse: Tangier (1665–66)
Henry Belfield: Kenya (1912–19)
Belisarius: Byzantine North Africa
Krim Belkassim: Algerian Republic (Provisional Government)
Charles Bell: Ghana (1756–57, 1761–63)
Gawain Bell: Nigeria Northern Region
Hesketh Bell: Mauritius (1916–25); Uganda (1905–10)
John Bell: Cape Colony (1835–35)
Ahmed ben Bella: Algeria (1962–65)
Jean Lapeyre-Bellair: Nossi-Bé
William Bellairs: Natal (1880)
Bellama: Damagaram
Guillaume de Bellecombe: Réunion (1767–73)
Martin-Adrien Bellier: Réunion (1767)
Bello: Daura
Bello: Nupe
Alhajji Ahmadu Bello: Nigeria Northern Region
Muhammad Bello: Fulani Empire
Muhammad Bello: Kano (1882–92)
Muhammadu Bello: Adamawa
Muhammadu Bello: Agaie
Muhamman Bello: Katsina (1844–69)
Muhamman Bello: Lafiagi
Bello Bouba Maigari: Cameroun (1982–83)
Bemfa: Kaarta
Ben: Segu
Zine ben Ali: Tunisia (1987–)
Tahar ben Ammar: Tunisia (1954–56)
Ahmed ben Bella: Algeria (1962–65)
Ahmad ben Bitour: Algeria (1999–2000)
Yusuf ben Khedda: Algeria (1961–62); Algerian Republic (Provisional Government)
Sidi Muhammad ben Mulay Arafa: Morocco (1953–55)
Si Halil Bu Hajib ben Salim: Tunisia (1926–32)

Sidi Muhammad ben Yusuf: Morocco (1927–53, 1955–61)
Francisco de Benavides: Tenerife
Juan Alonso de Benavides: Gran Canaria
Juan Pacheco de Benavides: Gran Canaria
Martín de Benavides: Gran Canaria
Bartolomé Benavides y Campuzano: Melilla (1864–66)
Chadli Bendjedid: Algeria (1979–92)
Samuel Benedict: Liberia (1847)
Ali Benflis: Algeria (2000–03)
Muhammad Benhima: Morocco (1967–69)
Demetrio María de Benito y Hernández: Melilla (1839–47)
Benjamin: Egypt (616–628)
al-Fah Benkano: Timbuktu (1683)
Pierre-Benoît Dumas: Mauritius (1727–29)
John Benoy: Eritrea
Francisco Bens Argandoña: Western Sahara
Arthur Benson: Nigeria (1952); Zambia (1954–59)
Stephen Benson: Liberia (1856–64)
Teferi Benti: Ethiopia (1974–77)
Rudolf Bentinck: South Africa (1923–24)
Jean-Louis Bérard: Togo (1955–57)
Bereibibo: Bonny
Boadu Akafo Berempon: Denkyira
Berempon Katakyira: Bono
Paul Berenger: Mauritius (2003–)
Dámaso Berenguer y Fuste: Spanish Morocco (1919–22)
Berenice: Pentapolis
Berenice I: Egypt (290–282 B.C.)
Berenice II: Egypt (245–221 B.C.)
Berenice III: Egypt (101–80 B.C.)
Berenice IV: Egypt (58–55 B.C.)
George Beresford-Stooke: Sierra Leone (1947–52)
Alexandre Berg: Nossi-Bé
Ernest Berkeley: Kenya (1891–92); Uganda (1894–99)
George Berkeley: Lagos (1872–73); Sierra Leone (1874)
Léandre Berlin-Duchâteau: Senegal (1847, 1848)
Francisco Fernández Bernal: Spanish Morocco (1903–07)
François Bernard: Burkina Faso (1930–31)
Henri Bernard: Comoros (1963–66); Mauritania (1958–59)
Joseph Bernard: Gabon (1924–31); Madagascar (1933–34)
Bernardin Mungul Diaka: Congo (Zaire) (1991)
Bernardo I: Kongo
Bernardo II: Kongo
Pedro Berquó: São Tomé and Príncipe (1907–08)
M. Berthelot de la Coste: Seychelles (1781–83)
Max Berthet: Burkina Faso (1958–59)

Baron Berthezène: Algeria (1831)

Hugues Berthier: Madagascar (1926–27, 1929–30)

Eugène Bertin: Côte d'Ivoire (1896)

François Bertin d'Avesnes: Réunion (1763–67)

J.B. Bertrand: Senegal (1781–82)

Ras Beru Gugsa: Gojjam

Besekal: Zaria (ca. 1400)

Besele: Barolongland

Besele II: Barolongland

Hajji Beshir Pasha: Algiers (1543–44)

Birni Bessé: Baguirmi

Thomas Besson: Côte d'Ivoire (1843–44)

Beta Esrael: Axum

Maciot de Béthencourt: Canary Islands (1405–15)

Georges Betnui Lawson III: Little Popo

José de Bettencourt: Mozambique (1941–46)

Betwoded Asfaha Wolde Mikael: Eritrea

Beur Tyaaka Loggar: Walo (1576–1640)

Maurice Beurnier: Côte d'Ivoire (1919); Senegal (1929–30, 1931–36)

P.S. Beves: Namibia (1915)

Maritius Beynowski: Louisbourg

Jean-Louis Beyriès: Djibouti (1945); Mauritania (1936, 1938–44)

Antonio Bezerra: Cacheu (1676–82, 1687–88)

Antonio Bezerra: Cape Verde (1761–64)

Antonio Bezerra, Jr.: Cacheu (1715–18, 1721, 1731)

Bhekimpi Dhlamini: Swaziland (1983–85)

Cyprian Bhekuzulu: Zululand

Zwelithini Goodwill Ka Bhekuzulu: Zululand

Biamusu: Gobir

Isa Bige N'Gone: Kayor

Léopold Biha: Burundi [ii]

Ali Bijnin: Algiers (1645–45)

Kyebambe II Bikaju: Bunyoro

Joaquim Biker: Cape Verde (1911–15); Guinea-Bissau (1900–03)

Bikorom: Kanem

Muhammad Gharib Bilal: Zanzibar (1995–2000)

Di Jigi Bilali: Kangaba

Bilbay: Egypt (1467)

Silvestre Siale Bileka: Equatorial Guinea

Bill Pepple: Bonny

Jørgen Billsen: Danish Gold Coast (1744–45)

Ali Bilma: Futa Jallon

Nganda Bilonda: Kazembe

Godfrey Binaisa: Uganda (1979–80)

Merneptah Binere Meryamun Hotphimae: Egypt (19th Dynasty)

Louis-Gustave Binger: Côte d'Ivoire (1893–95)

Akwa Bini: Baule

Henry Binns: Natal (1897–99)

Julius Maada Bio: Sierra Leone (1996)

Cristino Seriche Bioko: Equatorial Guinea

Andreas Biørn: Danish Gold Coast (1789–92)

Ngarba Bira: Baguirmi

Birahim I: Masina

Birahim II: Masina

Biram: Biram

Biram Manga: Kayor

Birama: Ghana Empire

Birawa Keme: Dyolof

Birayamb: Dyolof

Birayamb Aram: Dyolof

Birayamb Kumba-Gey: Dyolof

Birayamb Ma-Dyigen: Dyolof

Birayma Dyeme-Kumba: Dyolof

Birayma Faatim-Penda: Kayor

Birayma-Fal: Kayor

Birayma Fatma: Baol

Birayma Fatma: Kayor

Birayma Kodu: Kayor

Birayma Kuran Kan: Dyolof

Birayma Mbenda-Tyilor: Kayor

Birayma N'Dyeme Eter: Dyolof

Birayma Penda: Dyolof (1605–49)

Birayma-Penda: Dyolof (1849)

Birayma Yaasin-Bubu: Kayor

Birayma Yamb: Kayor

Henry Bird: Ghana (1858–60)

Kashim Biri: Bornu Empire (1260–88)

Biri I: Kanem

Biri II Ibrahim: Bornu Empire (1288–1307)

Biri III: Bornu Empire (1400–32)

Faustin Birindwa: Congo (Zaire) (1993–94)

Dalo Birni: Baguirmi

Birni Bessé: Baguirmi

Casimir Biros: Benin [ii] (1955–58)

Birtakiskis: Gobir

Jakwa Birtitik: Biu

Duhaga II Bisereko: Bunyoro

Bishr ibn Safwan: Egypt (720–721)

Bisi Baro: Songhai (1295–1325)

Aphilas Bisi-Dimele: Axum

Bisr: Omayyad and Abbasid North Africa

John Bissett: Natal (1865–67)

Murray Bissett: Zimbabwe (1926, 1928)

Rabah Bitat: Algeria (1978–79)

Mamari Biton: Segu

Ahmad ben Bitour: Algeria (1999–2000)

Atta Biwom: Akim

Di Biya: Biu

Mari Biya: Biu

Paul Biya: Cameroun (1975–)

Biyai Bei: Songhai (921–933)

Biyai Kaina Kimba: Songhai (1101–20)

Biyai Koi Kimi: Songhai (1063–82)

Biyai Komai: Songhai (909–921)

Bukaar Biye-Sungule: Dyolof

Francisco Macías Nguema Biyogo: Equatorial Guinea

Pasteur Bizimungu: Rwanda

Louis-Placide Blacher: Benin [ii] (1932); Djibouti (1932–34); Guinea (1935, 1936–40); Niger (1930–31)

Samuel Blackall: Sierra Leone (1862–68)

Travers Blackley: Tripolitania (1943–51)

John Blackmore: Saint Helena (1678–90)

Quintus Junius Blaesus: Africa [i] (21–23)

Moses Blah: Liberia (2003)

Paul Celeron de Blainville: Comoros (1887–88)

François Blanchot de Verly: Senegal (1786–1801, 1802–07)

Louis Blandinières: Sainte Marie de Madagascar

Caius Rubellius Blandus: Africa [i] (35–36)

Michel Blangy: Réunion (1984–86)

Jacob Blanquet de la Haye: Fort-Dauphin

Ti-Kse Bldi: Mandara

Ernest Bleu: Cameroun (1924–25, 1926, 1929, 1931–32)

Hercule Blévec: Sainte Marie de Madagascar

Pieter Blignaut: Orange Free State (1888–89, 1895–96)

Philip Bloncq: Hollandia

Hilary Blood: Gambia (1942–47); Mauritius (1949–53)

John Bloome: Ghana (1691)

Francis Blunt: Seychelles (1880–82)

Grant Blunt: Saint Helena (1884–87)

Matthew Blyth: Lesotho (1883–84)

Sidi Ahmad Ould Bneijara: Mauritania (1980–81)

Deni Ba Bo: Kaarta

Moussa Koura Bo: Kaarta

Bo-Boliko Lokonga: Congo (Zaire) (1979–80)

Boa Amponsem: Denkyira

Boa Siante: Denkyira

Anim Kokobo Boadee: Denkyira

Boadu Akafo Berempon: Denkyira

Boakye I: Akim

Boakye II: Akim

Boakye III: Akim

Boakyi: Bono

Capitão Bobadilha: Portuguese Gold Coast (1508–09)

Bobbo Ahmadu: Adamawa

Luis de Bocanegra: Oran (1574–75)

Bocchoris Wahkare: Egypt (24th Dynasty)

Bocchus I: Mauretania East

Bocchus II: Mauretania West

Bocchus III: Mauretania; Mauretania East

Sheku Bochari Kawusu Conteh: Sierra Leone (1970)

Bodian Moriba: Kaarta

Émanuel Bodjolle: Togo (1963)

Bodyan Mori Ba: Kaarta

Georg Boers: Dutch Gold Coast (1867–69)

Boethius: Byzantine North Africa
Boethus: Egypt (476–477)
Alexandre Boevi Lawson II: Little Popo
Frederick Boevi Lawson V: Little Popo
Barthélémy Boganda: Central African Republic (1958–59)
Bogatsu: Bakgatlaland
Bogatswe: Batlokwaland
Bogora: Gurma
Bogud: Mauretania East
Bogud II: Mauretania West
Bohari: Hadejia
Félix Houphouët-Boigny: Côte d'Ivoire (1959–93)
Charles Boilève: Mali (1883–84)
Philippe Boisadam: Mayotte Department
Jacques-Alphonse Boissier: Benin [ii] (1949)
Pierre-François Boissons: Cameroun (1937, 1938); French Equatorial Africa (1939–40); French West Africa (1938–39, 1940–43)
Jules Boitard: Gabon (1876–78)
Bokassa I: Central African Republic (1976–79)
Jean-Bédel Bokassa: Central African Republic (1966–79)
Bokoye: New Calabar
Hamada Bolero: Comoros (2000–02, 2002)
Bo-Boliko Lokonga: Congo (Zaire) (1979–80)
Conde de Bolognino: Oran (1767–70)
Likulia Bolongo: Congo (Zaire) (1997)
Bomi: Biram
Maurice Bompard: Madagascar (1889–91)
José Pascual de Bonanza: Spanish Morocco (1883)
Napoléon Bonaparte: Egypt (1798–99)
Prince Napoléon Bonaparte: Algeria (1858–59)
Nguza Karl-I-Bond: Congo (Zaire) (1980–81, 1991–92)
François Bonelle: Mayotte Department
Robert Bones: Sierra Leone (1811)
Bonewamang: Bakwenaland
Abbas Bonfah: Togo (2005)
Charles-Henri Bonfils: Benin [ii] (1951–55); Guinea (1955–56)
Philibert Bonfils: Comoros (1851–53)
Bonga: Yatenga
Bongani Finca: Ciskei
Stéphane-Maurice Bongho-Nouarra: Congo (1992)
Luigi Bongiovanni: Cyrenaica
Albert-Bernard Bongo: Gabon (1967–)
Omar Bongo: Gabon (1967–)
Pierre Bonhomme: Côte d'Ivoire (1898)
Adrien Bonhoure: Djibouti (1900–04); Réunion (1906–07)

Charles Boniface: Gorée
Auguste Bonnecarrère: Cameroun (1920–21, 1932–34); Togo (1922–31)
Pierre Bonnefont: Central African Republic (1933–34, 1935); Chad (1935–36); Congo (1930–31)
Yves Bonnet: Mayotte Department
François Bonnier: Mali (1893)
Emilio De Bono: Eritrea; Italian East Africa; Tripolitania (1925–28)
Mansa Bonsu: Ashanti
Osei Bonsu: Ashanti
Kasongo Bonswe: Luba
Louis Bonvin: Gabon (1931–37); Madagascar (1931–32)
John Booker: Fort James
Dako Booman: Akwamu
Boon: Swaziland
Varela Borca: São Tomé and Príncipe (1797–98)
Pierre Bordes: Algeria (1927–30)
Francis De Bordes: Dutch Gold Coast (1736–40)
Henry Bordiaux: Senegal (1883–84)
Paul Bordier: Central African Republic (1958–60); Niger (1956–58)
Borea I: Koya-Temne
Borea II: Koya-Temne
Raffaele Borea Ricci D'Olmo: Tripolitania (1911)
Jacob Borghorst: Cape Colony (1668–70)
Gustave Borgnis-Desbordes: Mali (1880–83)
Custodio de Borja: Angola (1904); São Tomé and Príncipe (1879–80, 1884–86)
Felipe de Borja: Oran (1571–73)
Boroma Dangwarangwa: Mwene Mutapa Empire
Pedro Borrás: Melilla (1716–19)
Enewald Borris: Danish Gold Coast (1736–40)
Amar Faatim Borso: Walo (1812–21)
Hendrik Bosch: Dutch Gold Coast (1838–40)
Jacobus Boshof: Orange Free State (1855–59)
Jules Van Der Bossche: Dutch Gold Coast (1857)
Henry Lightfoot-Boston: Sierra Leone (1962–67)
Manuel da Silva Botelho: Cacheu (1640)
Pedro Botelho: Mombasa (1631–35)
Pedro Botelho: São Tomé (1558–58)
Sebastião Botelho: Madeira (1819–21)
Xavier Botelho: Mozambique (1825–29)
Louis Botha: South Africa (1910–18, 1919); Transvaal (1907–10)
Pieter W. Botha: South Africa (1978–89)
Botha Sigcau: Transkei
Botlolo: Bakgatlaland
Afonso Gonçalves Botofago: Portuguese Gold Coast (1557)

Maati Bouabid: Morocco (1979–83)
Bello Bouba Maigari: Cameroun (1982–83)
Sidi Muhammad Ould Boubakar: Mauritania (1992–96)
Ibrahim Boubakar Keita: Mali (1994–2000)
Ahmad Ould Bouceif: Mauritania (1979)
Adolphe Le Boucher: Senegal (1883)
Antoine Desforges-Boucher: Mauritius (1723–25); Réunion (1723–25)
Antoine Marc Desforges-Boucher: Mauritius (1759–67); Réunion (1749, 1757)
Benjamin Boucher: Saint Helena (1711–14)
Charles Boucher: Gorée; Senegal (1769–69, 1790–92)
Muhammad Boudiaf: Algeria (1992–92)
Robert Boudry: Madagascar (1946)
Louis Bouët-Willaumez: Gabon (1839–43); Senegal (1843)
Stanislas de Boufflers: Senegal (1786, 1787)
Thomas Bougeaud de la Piconnerie: Algeria (1841–45)
Boukari Adji: Niger (1996)
Boukhary Koutou: Wagadugu
M. de Boulay: Senegal (1661–64)
G.C. du Boulay: Ghana (1930, 1931)
Jean-Jules Boulay: Côte d'Ivoire (1848–50)
Boulli: Yatenga
Houari Boumedienne: Algeria (1965–78)
Bernard Bourdillon: Nigeria (1935–43); Sudan (1940); Uganda (1932–35)
Ernest Bourdon de Grammont: Senegal (1846–47)
Bernard François Mahé, Comte de la Bourdonnais: Mauritius (1735–46); Réunion (1735)
Frédéric Bourgarel: Gabon (1868–69)
Yvon Bourges: Burkina Faso (1956–58); French Equatorial Africa (1958)
Maurice Bourgine: Benin [ii] (1935–37); Côte d'Ivoire (1927–28); Niger (1933–34); Togo (1930, 1934)
Raoul Bourgine: Côte d'Ivoire (1931–32)
Hippolyte Bourgoin: Gabon (1869–71)
Habib Bourguiba: Tunisia (1956–87)
Jean Bourguignon: Senegal (1693–97)
Ali Aref Bourhan: Djibouti (1967–77)
Nourdine Bourhane: Comoros (1997–98)
Richard Bourke: Cape Colony (1826–28)
Bourkomanda I: Baguirmi
Bourkomanda II: Baguirmi
Bourkomanda III: Baguirmi
Bourkomanda Tad Lélé: Baguirmi
Comte Bourmont: Algeria (1830)
Abdul Aziz Bouteflika: Algeria (1999–)

Jean-Paul Boutonnet: Côte d'Ivoire (1930–31)

Alfred Claeys-Boúúaert: Ruanda-Urundi

Athanase Bouvet de Lozier: Réunion (1815–17)

Jean-Baptiste Bouvet de Lozier: Mauritius (1750–56); Réunion (1750–52, 1757–63)

Charles du Bouzet: Algeria (1870–71)

George Bowen: Mauritius (1879–80)

James Bowker: Lesotho (1868–70)

John Bowker: Transkeian Territories

Charles Bowring: Kenya (1912); Malawi (1924–29)

King Boy: Brass

Bfantz Boye: Danish Gold Coast (1711–17)

Madior Boye: Senegal (2001–02)

Comte Boyer de la Tour du Moulin: French Morocco; Tunisia (1954–55)

Alexander Boyle: Nigeria Southern Provinces

Cavendish Boyle: Mauritius (1904–11)

Boyoma: Kanem

Bukar Dalla Boyonbo: Songhai (1386–94)

Edmond Boys: Natal (1849–50, 1852–53)

Simon Bozanga: Central African Republic (1981)

François Bozizé: Central African Republic (2003–)

John S. Brabant: Malawi (1894)

Conde de Bracamonte: Oran (1687)

Henry Bradshaw: Fort James

Duque de Bragança: Ceuta (1447–50)

Raul Bragança: São Tomé and Príncipe (1996–99)

Muhammad Salum Ould Brahim: Trarza

Abdelhamid Brahimi: Algeria (1984–88)

Brajesh Chandra Mishra: Namibia (1982–87)

Fernand de Brancamont: Tripolitania (1538–42)

Marqués de Branciforte: Canary Islands (1784–89)

Eugenio Branco: São Tomé and Príncipe (1924–26)

João Branco: Madeira (1734–37)

Nicolau Branco: Angola (1823–29)

George Brand: Bight of Benin

Jan Brand: Orange Free State (1863–72, 1873–88)

Francisco de Alva Brandão: São Tomé (1744–45)

Gaspar Brandão: Madeira (1757–59)

Pedro Brandão: Madeira (1684–88)

Nathaniel Brander: Liberia (1835)

Joseph Le Brasseur: Gorée

Alexander Bravo: Gambia (1869–71); Ghana (1873); Sierra Leone (1873)

Pierre Savorgnan de Brazza: Congo (1883–86); French Equatorial Africa (1886–97); Gabon (1886)

Luis de la Breche: Melilla (1860–61)

Jacobus Van Der Breggen Paauw: Dutch Gold Coast (1826–28)

Coenrad Van Breitenbach: Cape Colony (1671–72)

Joseph Brénier: Réunion (1749–50, 1752–56)

Thomas Brereton: Senegal (1814–16)

Louis Bressalles: Côte d'Ivoire (1938–39)

Jean de la Bretesche: Fort-Dauphin

Albert Van Breughel: Cape Colony (1672)

Jules Brévié: Côte d'Ivoire (1930); French West Africa (1930–36); Niger (1921–29)

Gabriel Briand: Chad (1912–13, 1915–16)

Eloi Bricard: Côte d'Ivoire (1892)

Ottavio Briccolo: Cyrenaica

Tobias Bridges: Tangier (1664)

Louis Brière de l'Isle: Senegal (1876–80)

Antoine de la Brillane: Mauritius (1776–79)

Bako Brima: Zaria (1618–21, 1647–60)

Bako Brima Hasko: Zaria (1678–82)

Michel Gbzera-Brio: Central African Republic (1997–99)

André Brisset: Comoros (1853–55); Gabon (1844–46, 1847); Nossi-Bé; Sainte Marie de Madagascar

Fernão de Brito: Cape Verde (1603–06)

José de Brito: Guinea-Bissau (1886–87)

João de Brito: Madeira (1680–84)

João de Brito: São Tomé and Príncipe (1824–30)

Joaquim de Brito: São Tomé and Príncipe (1901–02)

Lourenço de Brito: Mozambique (1589–90)

Paulo de Brito: Mozambique (1829–32)

Cristóvão de Brito e Vasconcelos: Mozambique (1631–32)

Luis de Brito Freire: Mozambique (1706–07)

Antonio de Brito Pacheco: Mozambique (1640–41)

João Brito-Sanches: Mozambique (1819–21)

Íñigo de Brizuela y Urbina: Canary Islands (1634–38)

Niels Brøch: Danish Gold Coast (1825–27, 1831–33)

Victor Brochard: Réunion (1919–20)

Thomas Brock: Danish Gold Coast (1745)

Robert Brooke: Saint Helena (1788–1800)

Robert Brooke-Popham: Kenya (1937–40)

Frederick Broome: Mauritius (1880–82)

Charles Brossard de Corbigny: Côte d'Ivoire (1857)

Jean-Jacques Brot: Mayotte Department

Pierre Brou: Senegal (1829–31)

Denis de Brousse: Mauritius (1725–27)

Malcolm Brown: Lagos (1878)

George Browne: Nigeria Northern Region

Thomas Browne: Saint Helena (1851–56)

Charles Bruce: Mauritius (1897–1903)

Edmund Brückner: Togoland

André Bruë: Senegal (1697–1702, 1714–20)

Jean-Baptiste Estoupan de la Bruë: Senegal (1746–58)

Paul Bruë: Gabon (1861–63)

Nicolas de Regnac des Brulys: Réunion (1806–09)

Pierre Brun: Côte d'Ivoire (1909)

João Baptista Brunachy: São Tomé and Príncipe (1863–64, 1865–67)

Auguste Brunet: Mali (1918–19)

Charles Brunet: Benin [ii] (1908); French West Africa (1919); Madagascar (1923–24)

Joseph Brunet-Millet: Gabon (1866–67)

Giuseppe Bruni: Libia

Richard Brunot: Cameroun (1938–40); Central African Republic (1935–36); Chad (1933–34, 1935); Côte d'Ivoire (1924–25); Mauritania (1934–35)

Jean Brunteau de Sainte-Suzanne: Réunion (1809–10)

Mahmud Brusali: Algiers (1645–47)

Mehmed Brusali: Algiers (1642–45)

Charles Bruton: Swaziland

Noël Bruyas: Côte d'Ivoire (1856)

Herbert Bryan: Ghana (1903–04, 1905, 1906, 1907–08, 1909, 1910, 1911, 1912)

Gyude Bryant: Liberia (2003–)

Sheikh Sa'd Bu: Trarza

al-Hajj Muhammad at-Tazi Bu Ashran: Tangier (1923–41, 1945–54)

Bu Bakar: Futa Jallon

Abdul Bu Bakar: Futa Toro

Bu Bakar III: Futa Jallon

Bu Bakar IV: Futa Jallon

Si Halil Bu Hajib ben Salim: Tunisia (1926–32)

Buba: Biram

Buba Yero: Gombe

Banna Bubu: Ghana Empire

Birayma Yaasin-Bubu: Kayor

Yerim N'date Bubu: Walo (1733–34)

Bubu I: Masina

Bubu II: Masina

Bubu III: Masina

Thomas Buchanan: Liberia (1839–41)

Walter Buchanan-Smith: Nigeria Southern Provinces

Max Buchner: Kamerun (1884–85)

Buchraya Hamoudi: Western Sahara

Dan Buddi: Gobir

Sule-Budu: Futa Toro

Dugum Bugia: Bedde
Buhaya: Kano (1385–89)
Muhammad Buhari: Nigeria (1984–85)
Émile Buhot-Launay: Chad (1929, 1936, 1938); Congo (1932)
Fernando Gómez de Buitrón: Ceuta (1813–14, 1820–22)
Bukaar Biye-Sungule: Dyolof
Muhammad Bukalmarami: Bornu Empire (1603–17)
Bukar Afade: Mandara
Mai Bukar Aji: Mandara
Bukar Dalla Boyonbo: Songhai (1386–94)
Bukar D'Gjiama: Mandara
Bukar Garbai: Bornu Empire (1902–22)
Bukar Kura: Bornu Empire (1881–84)
Bukar Narbanha: Mandara
Bukar Zonko: Songhai (1378–86)
Redvers Buller: Natal (1881)
Willem Bullier: Dutch Gold Coast (1718–22)
Bulu: Kanem
Abu al-Futuh Buluggin: Zirid Kingdom
Buluggin ibn Muhammad: Hammadid Kingdom
Lunda Bululu: Congo (Zaire) (1990–91)
Henry Bulwer: Natal (1875–80, 1882–85)
Ziblim Bunbiogo: Dagomba
Raouf Bundhun: Mauritius (2003–)
Bundi: Potiskum
Alimani Lahai Bundu: Koya-Temne
Muhammad Bunkan: Songhai (1531–37)
Bunowo: Daniski
Barma Dan Moi Bunowo: Daniski
Bunu: Swaziland
Bupuor: Bonny
Buraima: Fika
Moi Buraima: Daniski
Buraima Wamu: Daniski
Burba: Muri
Geoffrey Burden: Gold Coast Northern Territories
Ali Bure N'Dyaye: Dyolof
Joaquín Bureau: Ceuta (1826)
Burema: Zaria (1618–21)
Lieven Van Burgen Van Der Grijp: Dutch Gold Coast (1787–90, 1794–95)
Schalk Burger: Transvaal (1900–02)
Thomas Burgers: Transvaal (1872–77)
Ali II Burghul: Tripolitania (1793–95)
Ricardo Burguete y Lana: Spanish Morocco (1922–23)
Buri: Biram
al-Buri Dyakher: Dyolof
Gireun Buri Dyelen: Dyolof
Ali Buri N'Dyaye: Dyolof
Bakaa-Tam Buri-Nyabu: Dyolof
Mba Buri-Nyabu: Dyolof
al-Buri Penda: Dyolof
al-Buri Peya: Dyolof

al-Buri Tam: Dyolof
Pedro de la Buría: Canary Islands (1811–20)
Abdullahi Burja: Kano (1437–52)
Lt.-Col. Burke: Sierra Leone (1821)
Alan Burns: Ghana (1942–47); Nigeria (1942)
Dayendranath Burrenchobay: Mauritius (1979–86)
Knapp Burrow: Lagos (1884–85)
Richard Francis Burton: Bight of Biafra
Sáenz de Buruaga: Spanish Morocco (1936)
Buruguyomda: Dagomba
Tasgarim Burum: Zanfara
Burum I: Zamfara
Burum II: Zamfara
Burwai: Biram
Kofi Busia: Ghana (1969–72)
Bussei: Kaarta
Gatsha Buthelezi: KwaZulu; Zululand
Butros Ghali: Egypt (1908–10)
Charles Butler: Ashanti
William Butler: Cape Colony (1898–99)
Buuna: Dyolof
Viscount Buxton: South Africa (1914–20)
Sidi Buya: Trarza
Buyanga: Yauri
Álvarez Buylla: Spanish Morocco (1936)
Pierre Buyoya: Burundi [ii]
Buzame: Kano (ca. 900)
Bwana Fuma ibn Ali: Mayotte
Bwana Kombo I: Mayotte
Bwana Kombo II: Mayotte
Bwarenga: Nkore
Ruganza Bwimba: Ruanda
Kalemera Bwirangenda: Karagwe
Horace Byatt: British Somaliland; Tanganyika
Edward Byfield: Saint Helena (1727–31)
Joseph Byrne: Kenya (1931–36); Seychelles (1921–27); Sierra Leone (1927–31)

C

Caabi al-Yachurtu: Comoros (1995–96)
Cabe: Pondoland
Amancio Cabral: Cape Verde (1904–07); São Tomé and Príncipe (1899–1901)
Augusto Cabral: São Tomé and Príncipe (1885–86)
Baltasar Cabral: Mozambique (1897–98)
Cristóvão de Cabral: Cape Verde (1632–36)
Filomeno Cabral: Angola (1918–19, 1929–30)
José Cabral: Mozambique (1926–38)

Luis de Almeida Cabral: Guinea-Bissau (1973–80)
M. Cadest: Senegal (1833)
Edmond Cadier: Congo (1919); Gabon (1922–23)
Joseph Cadier: Senegal (1926)
Caecillianus: Africa Proconsularis (409)
Caecina Tuscus: Egypt (67–68)
Ptolemy XV Caesar: Egypt (44–30 B.C.)
Caesarion: Egypt (44–30 B.C.)
Caesarius: Byzantine North Africa
M. Caille: Senegal (1847)
Henri Caillet: Diego Suarez
Caius Julius Juba II: Mauretania
Caius Rubellius Blandus: Africa [i] (35–36)
Caius Vipstanus Apronianus: Africa [i] (68)
Caius Vivius Marsus: Africa [i] (26–29)
Afonso Caldeira: Portuguese Gold Coast (1510–13)
Álvaro Caldeira: Bissau (1869–71)
Caleb: Axum
Alexander, Earl of Caledon: Cape Colony (1807–11)
Sebastião de Calheiros e Meneses: Angola (1861–62)
Thomas Callaghan: Gambia (1871–73)
Callistus: Egypt (422)
Lucius Calpurnius Piso: Africa [i] (38–39)
Caludius: Ethiopia (1540–59)
Auguste Calvel: Mali (1942–46); Niger (1936)
Calvisius Statianus: Egypt (175–177)
Manuel Camacho: Mozambique (1921–23)
João da Câmara: Angola (1779–82)
Jorge da Câmara: Madeira (1614–18)
José da Câmara: Bissau (1696–99); Cape Verde (1711–15); São Tomé (1722–27)
José da Câmara: Madeira (1800–03)
Luis da Câmara: Mozambique (1707–12)
Manuel da Câmara: Cape Verde (1692–96); São Tomé (1697–1702)
Jules Cambon: Algeria (1891–97)
Paul Cambon: Tunisia (1882–86)
Cambyses: Egypt (27th Dynasty)
Alfenius Ceionius Camenius: Africa Proconsularis (380–380)
Quintus Sulpicius Camerinus Peticus: Africa [i] (56–57)
Donald Cameron: Nigeria (1921, 1931–35); Tanganyika
Edward Cameron: Gambia (1914–20)
William Cameron: Cape Colony (1891–92, 1894)
Camillo De Camillis: Eritrea
Marcus Furius Camillus: Africa [i] (17–18)
Duque de Caminha: Ceuta (1592–94, 1597–1601, 1605–16, 1623, 1625–26)

Teodoro Camino y Alcobendas: Melilla (1886–87)

Blaise Campaoré: Burkina Faso (1987–)

Benjamin Campbell: Bight of Benin

Henry Campbell: Sierra Leone (1835–37)

John Campbell: Cornelis Kok's Land

Neil Campbell: Ghana (1826); Sierra Leone (1826–27)

Juan del Campo: Tenerife

Príncipe de Campo Flórido: Ceuta (1719–21)

Marqués de Campo Santo: Oran (1789–90)

Marqués de Campofuerte: Ceuta (1739–45)

Antonio Peláez Campomanes: Spanish Morocco (1866)

Adolfo Campos: Ifni

Alberto Campos: São Tomé and Príncipe (1963)

Artur de Campos: Cape Verde (1911)

Manuel de Campos: Mombasa (1663–67, 1673–76)

Julião de Campos Barreto: São Tomé (1673–77)

Marqués de la Cáñada Ibáñez: Canary Islands (1779–84)

Domingo Canal y Soldevila: Melilla (1697–1703)

Henri Canard: Senegal (1881–82)

Eric Vully de Candole: Cyrenaica; Italian Somaliland (1948)

Carlo Caneva: Tripolitania (1911–12)

Tomás de Cangas: Gran Canaria; Tenerife

Hernando de Cañizares: Tenerife

Antonio Cano: Fernando Po

Canreba: Bumpe

Duque de Cansano: Oran (1692–97)

Antonio de Canto e Castro: Mozambique (1864–67)

André Capagorry: Réunion (1942–47)

Jean Capagorry: Congo (1942)

Bernard Capdebosq: Mauritania (1905–07)

Guilherme Capelo: Angola (1886–92)

Pierre Capest: Côte d'Ivoire (1898); French West Africa (1902)

Jacinto Díaz Capilla: Melilla (1814–21)

Virgilius Capito: Egypt (48–54)

Luis Cappa y Rioseco: Melilla (1824–26, 1830–35)

Capt. Caraccioli: Libertalia

Carlos Carafa: Oran (1704–07)

Jean-Louis Carayon: Sainte Marie de Madagascar

Jules Carde: Algeria (1930–35); Cameroun (1919–23); Congo (1916–17); French West Africa (1923–30)

John Carden: North Western Rhodesia

Luis de Cárdenas: Oran (1523–25)

Frederic Cardew: Sierra Leone (1894–1900)

Antonio Cardoso: Angola (1975)

Bento Cardoso: Angola (1611–15)

Francisco Cardoso: Angola (1865–68)

Francisco do Amaral Cardoso: Mozambique (1805–07)

Leonel Cardoso: Angola (1975)

Pedro Cardoso: Cape Verde (1650–51)

Lott Carey: Liberia (1828)

Jean Carilès: Gabon (1846–47)

Joseph Carle: Nossi-Bé

Tommaso Carletti: Italian Somali land (1907–08)

Hendrik Carlof: Swedish Gold Coast

Bernt Carlsson: Namibia (1987–88)

María do Carmo Silveira: São Tomé and Príncipe (2005–)

Francisco Carneiro: Cape Verde (1790–95)

Manuel Carneiro: São Tomé (1640)

José Caroço: Guinea-Bissau (1921–26)

Francesco Saverio Caroselli: Italian Somaliland (1937–40)

Frederick Carr: Nigeria Eastern Region

J. Carr: Sierra Leone (1841)

Hubert Carras: Cameroun (1943–44)

Albert du Carré: Chad (1918–20)

Jean Joseph Carreau: Mali (1924)

Miguel Carreño: Ceuta (1755–60)

Frederick Carrington: Bechuanaland Protectorate; British Bechuanaland

José Carrión y Andrade: Melilla (1772–77)

Edvard Carstensen: Danish Gold Coast (1842–1850)

Beresford Carter: South Africa (1920)

Gilbert Carter: Gambia (1886–91); Lagos (1891–97)

Luis de Carvajal: Oran (1778–79)

Ramón Carvajal: Canary Islands (1810–11)

Ramón de Carvajal: Ceuta (1807–08)

Antero de Carvalho: Angola (1924–25)

Antonio de Carvalho: Angola (1722–25)

Antonio de Carvalho: São Tomé (1636)

Augusto de Carvalho: Cape Verde (1888–90)

Bernardim de Carvalho: Tangier (1553–62)

Domingos de Carvalho: Cacheu (1690–91)

Evaristo Carvalho: São Tomé and Príncipe (1994)

Feliciano Carvalho: São Tomé (1613–14)

Fernando de Carvalho: São Tomé and Príncipe (1910)

Filipe de Carvalho: Cape Verde (1921–22)

Inacio de Carvalho: Mozambique (1667–70)

João de Carvalho: Cacheu (1733–34)

João de Carvalho: São Tomé and Príncipe (1872–73)

José Carvalho: Angola (1947–55)

Manuel de Carvalho: São Tomé and Príncipe (1797)

Ruis de Carvalho: Tangier (1572–73)

Vasco de Carvalho: São Tomé (1597–98)

José de Carvalho e Meneses: Cape Verde (1864–69); Mozambique (1874–77)

Vasco de Carvalho e Meneses: Angola (1878–80); Cape Verde (1878–79)

Vasco de Carvalho e Meneses: Mozambique (1854–57)

Marqués de Casa Cagigal: Canary Islands (1803–09)

Marqués de Casa Tremañes: Ceuta (1776–83)

M. Casamata: Chad (1950–51)

Antonio Casarramona: Ceuta (1999–2001)

Luis de las Casas y Aragorri: Oran (1785–89)

Marqués de Casasola: Oran (1697–1701)

Fernand Casimir: Niger (1952–53)

Robert Casimir: Cameroun (1947, 1949–50)

Jean-Baptiste Castaing: Côte d'Ivoire (1896); Djibouti (1908–09, 1911)

Santos Castanho: Cacheu (1691–1707)

Eusebio Castella do Vale: Guinea-Bissau (1887)

Antonio de Castelo Branco: São Tomé (1741)

Baltasar de Castelo Branco: Cacheu (1615–16)

Jorge Castelo Branco: Cape Verde (1651–53)

Nuno Vaz de Castelo Branco: Portuguese Gold Coast (1502–04)

Marqués de Castelo Mendo: Ceuta (1662–65)

Jorge de Castilho: Cape Verde (1636–39)

Nicolau de Castilho: Cape Verde (1614–18)

Augusto de Castilho Barreto e Noronha: Mozambique (1885–89)

Pedro de Castilla: Gran Canaria

Álvaro de Castro: Mozambique (1915–18)

Gabriel do Castro: São Tomé and Príncipe (1802–05)

João do Castro: Portuguese Gold Coast (1613)

José Bautisto de Castro: Ceuta (1798–1801)

José do Castro: São Tomé (1702–09)

Luis Tomé de Castro: Portuguese Gold Coast (ca. 1627)

Mario Castro: São Tomé and Príncipe (1950–52)

Pedro de Castro: Mozambique (1577–82)

Antonio Castro e Ribafria: Angola (1709–13)

Jaime de Castro Morais: Angola (1917–18)

José de Castro y Méndez: Melilla (1850–54)

George Cathcart: Cape Colony (1852–54)
Honoré Catron: Comoros (1913–14)
Georges Catroux: Algeria (1943–44, 1956)
Aconius Catullinus: Africa Proconsularis (341–342)
Paul Caudière: Gabon (1878–79)
Lt.-Col. Caulfeild: Sierra Leone (1895, 1897, 1900)
Charles Caulker: Bumpe
George Stephen Caulker I: Shenge
George Stephen Caulker II: Shenge
James Canreba Caulker: Bumpe
James Cleveland Caulker: Banana Island
Richard Canreba Caulker: Bumpe
Stephen Caulker: Banana Island
Thomas Caulker: Banana Island; Bumpe
Thomas Neale Caulker: Shenge
Thomas Stephen Caulker: Shenge
Thomas Theophilus Caulker: Bumpe
William Caulker: Banana Island
Jean Caullier: Senegal (1641–48)
Eugène Cavaignac: Algeria (1848)
Jerónimo de Cavalcanti e Albuquerque: Cape Verde (1639–40)
Basil Cave: Zanzibar (1904–08)
Léon Cayla: French West Africa (1939–40); Madagascar (1930–39, 1940–41)
Laurent Cayrel: Réunion (2005–)
Abubakr Ceceko: Lafiagi
Jean Cédile: Togo (1948–51)
Alfenius Ceionius Camenius: Africa Proconsularis (380)
Celerinus: Egypt (ca. 275)
Paul Celeron de Blainville: Comoros (1887–88)
Cellou Diallo: Guinea (2004–)
Juan de Cepeda: Tenerife
Louis Cercus: Gabon (1923–24)
Rafael Cerero: Melilla (1894–95)
José de la Cerna: Fernando Po
Martín Cerón: Gran Canaria
Giovanni Cerrina-Ferroni: Eritrea; Italian Somaliland (1906–07, 1916–20)
Cetewayo: Zululand
Cetshwayo: Zululand
Servius Cornelius Cethegus: Africa [i] (36–37)
Álvaro Chacón: Ceuta (1822–23)
Ignácio Chacón: Melilla (1848–50)
Gonzalo Chacón y Arellano Sandoval y Rojas: Ceuta (1709–15)
Carlos Chacón y Michelena: Fernando Po
Antonio Chacón y Ponce de León: Ceuta (1677, 1678–79)
Chadli Bendjedid: Algeria (1979–92)
Chado: Nupe
Francisco das Chagas: São Tomé (1747–48)
Pierre Parat de Chaillenest: Réunion (1710–15)
Chaka: Zululand

William B. Chalmers: Idutywa
Jean Chalvet: Central African Republic (1946–48); Djibouti (1944–46)
André Chalvet de Souville: Réunion (1781–85)
Chamassi Sa'id Umar: Nzwani
Col. Chamberlayne: Sierra Leone (1865–66)
Jean-Georges Chambon: Benin [ii] (1948–49); Congo (1952–53)
Louis Moreau de Chambonneau: Senegal (1684–89, 1690–93)
Diego Chamorro: Fernando Po
Luc de Champmargou: Fort-Dauphin
Aimé Champy: Nossi-Bé
John Chancellor: Mauritius (1911–16); Zimbabwe (1923–28)
Brajesh Chandra Mishra: Namibia (1982–87)
Changamire: Mwene Mutapa Empire
Changamire I: Rozwi
Changamire II: Rozwi
Changamire Baswi: Rozwi
Changamire Chirisamaru: Rozwi
Changamire Dunbo: Rozwi
Changamire Negamo: Rozwi
Changamire Tohwechipi: Rozwi
Changara: Mwene Mutapa Empire
Nicolas Changarnier: Algeria (1848)
Chanomi: Warri
Antoine Chanzy: Algeria (1873–79)
Alan Chaplin: Lesotho (1956–61)
Drummond Chaplin: Zambia (1921–23); Zimbabwe (1914–23)
Pierre Chapon-Baissac: Benin [ii] (1921–22); Côte d'Ivoire (1922); Djibouti (1924–32)
João de Mata Chapuzet; Cape Verde (1822–26)
François Desbordes de Charanville: Réunion (1709–10)
M. de Charbonnes: Senegal (1801)
Guillaume Charmasson de Puy-Laval: Senegal (1839–41)
Charmosinus: Egypt (422)
Charmosynus: Egypt (395–396)
Comte de Charny: Ceuta (1725–31); Oran (1691–92)
Baron Charon: Algeria (1848–50)
David Charpentier de Cossigny: Mauritius (1790–92); Réunion (1788–90)
Samuel Charters: Port Natal
Comte de Chasseloup-Laubat: Algeria (1859–60)
Yves Chataigneau: Algeria (1944–48)
Yves Chatel: Algeria (1941–43)
Arthur Chater: British Somaliland
Milne Chatham: Egypt (1914–15)
Jean-Baptiste Barthélemy Chaudié: French West Africa (1895–1900); Senegal (1895)
Paul Chauvet: French Equatorial Africa (1951–58); French West Africa (1951–52)
Fortuné de Chavannes: Congo (1889–94); Gabon (1889–94)
Antonio Chaves: Cacheu (1842–44)

Francisco Chaves: Angola (1925–26)
José de Chavez y Osorio: Canary Islands (1718–19)
Pasques de Chavonne: Cape Colony (1714–24)
René Chazal: Mauritania (1928, 1929–31)
Jean-Baptiste Chazelas: Mauritania (1934, 1935); Niger (1938–39)
Joseph Cheeseman: Liberia (1892–96)
Achille de Penfentenio de Cheffontaines: Réunion (1826–30)
Amadou Cheiffou: Niger (1991–93)
Muhammad Chenik: Tunisia (1950–52)
Cheops: Egypt (4th Dynasty)
Chephren: Egypt (4th Dynasty)
Cheri: Gumel
Louis Chérier: Nossi-Bé
Dominique de Chermont: Réunion (1790–92)
Henri Chessé: Burkina Faso (1929–30, 1932–33)
Angidi Chettiar: Mauritius (2002)
Pierre de Chevigné: Madagascar (1948–50)
Aleixo Chicorro: Mozambique (1538–41)
Luis Chicorro: Angola (1654–58)
Chida: Gobir
John Chidley: Fort James
Chikkoku: Zaria (1793–95)
Chikombi Iyavu: Lunda
Muteba Chikombu: Linda
Chikuyo Chisamarengu: Mwene Mutapa Empire
Frederick Chiluba: Zambia (1991–2002)
Chimbindu Kasang: Lunda
Chioko: Mwene Mutapa Empire
François Chirat: Côte d'Ivoire (1853–54)
Chikuyo Chisamarengu: Mwene Mutapa Empire
Chirisamaru: Rozwi
Changamire Chirisamaru: Rozwi
Changamire Chirisamaru II: Rozwi
Chiroma: Gobir
Chiroma: Gobir
Muhammadu Dan Chiroma: Gobir
Abdullahi Chiroma Bayero: Kano (1926–53)
Negomo Chisamburu: Mwene Mutapa Empire
James Chisholm: Ghana (1822, 1824)
Humphrey Chishull: Fort James
Joaquim Chissanó: Mozambique (1974–75, 1986–2005)
Chivere Nyasoro: Mwene Mutapa Empire
Chiwayo: Mwene Mutapa Empire
Hugh Cholmondeley: Tangier (1670–72)
Mainza Chona: Zambia (1973–75, 1977–78)
Alphonse Choteau: Benin [ii] (1924); Mauritania (1928–29); Niger (1929–30); Réunion (1934–36)

Geminius Chrestus: Egypt (219–232)
Christiaan Afrikaner: Oorlam Territory
Akili Dan Chuba: Gobir
Chuba Dan Muhammadu: Gobir
Henry Churchill: Zanzibar (1865–70)
Cibinda Ilunga: Lunda
Francisco de Paula Cid: Cape Verde (1902–03); São Tomé and Príncipe (1903–07)
Conde de Cifuentes: Oran (1682–83)
Cilwayo: Pondoland
Joseph Cimpaye: Burundi [ii]
Cinkonkole: Kazembe
Cinyanta Munona: Kazembe
Amadou Cissé: Niger (1995, 1996–97)
Muhammadu Dan Ciwa: Argungu
Umaru Ciwa: Argungu
Alfred Claeys-Boúúaert: Ruanda-Urundi
Serge Clair: Rodrigues (ii)
Michael Clancy: Saint Helena (2004–)
George Villiers, Earl of Clarendon: South Africa (1931–37)
William Clark: South Africa (1935–40)
Alured Clarke: Cape Colony (1795)
Arden Clarke: Botswana; Ghana (1949–57); Lesotho (1942–46)
Charles Arden-Clarke: Botswana; Ghana (1949–57); Lesotho (1942–46)
Edward Clarke: Zanzibar (1909–13)
John Clarke: Senegambia Colony
Marshall Clarke: Lesotho (1884–94); Zululand
Percy Selwyn-Clarke: Seychelles (1947–51)
John Clarkson: Sierra Leone (1792)
Col. Claudel: Mauritania (1909)
Claudius Balbillus: Egypt (56–60)
Claudius Maximus: Africa [i] (158–160)
Claudius Septimus Eutropius: Egypt (392)
Comte Clausel: Algeria (1830–31, 1835–37)
Roger Seydoux Fornier de Clausonne: Tunisia (1955–56)
Alexander Cleeve: Fort James
Félix Clément: Gabon (1875–76)
Léon Clément-Thomas: Senegal (1888–90)
Cleopater: Egypt (435)
Cleopatra I: Egypt (193–176 B.C.)
Cleopatra II: Egypt (173–164 B.C., 163–115 B.C.)
Cleopatra III: Egypt (136–116 B.C., 115–101 B.C.)
Cleopatra IV: Egypt (116–115 B.C.)
Cleopatra V Selene: Egypt (115–110 B.C., 109–107 B.C.)
Cleopatra VI Traephaeana: Egypt (80–58 B.C.)
Cleopatra VII: Egypt (52–30 B.C.)
Henri Cleret de Langavant: Réunion (1922–23)
George Clerk: Orange Free State (1853–54)

Jules Hanet-Cléry: Gabon (1880–82)
Bede Clifford: Mauritius (1937–42)
Henry Clifford: Cape Colony (1880); Natal (1880)
Hugh Clifford: Ghana (1912–19); Nigeria (1919–25)
Abraham Cloete: Tristan da Cunha
Henry Cloete: Natal (1843–44)
Joseph Clozel: Côte d'Ivoire (1902–07); French West Africa (1915–17); Mali (1909–15)
Cnaeus Hosidius Geta: Africa [i] (57–58)
Jack Coby: Koya-Temne
Sextus Cocceius Severianus Honorinus: Africa [i] (163–164)
Arent Cocq: Dutch Gold Coast (1650–51)
Robert Codrington: North Eastern Rhodesia; North Western Rhodesia
Alfredo Coelho: Mozambique (1915)
Agostinho Coelho: Guinea-Bissau (1879–81); Mozambique (1882–85)
Bento Coelho: Cape Verde (1733–37)
José Coelho: Bissau (1843–44)
Manuel Coelho: Angola (1911–12)
Pedro Coelho: Angola (1623)
Andrew Cohen: Uganda (1952–57)
Pieter Col: Mauritius (1672–73)
Geoffrey Colby: Malawi (1948–51, 1954–56)
Christopher Okoro Cole: Sierra Leone (1971)
Lowry Cole: Cape Colony (1828–33); Mauritius (1820–23)
Thomas Cole: Sierra Leone (1834–35, 1837)
William Coleman: Liberia (1896–1900)
George Colley: Idutywa; Natal (1880–81)
William Collins: Orange Free State (1872–73)
Joseph Colomb: Comoros (1864–71)
Don-Jean Colombani: Niger (1958–60); Senegal (1955–57)
Ignace Colombani: Central African Republic (1950–51); Chad (1951–56); Niger (1949–50)
Bonaventure Colonna de Lecca: Porto-Novo
Archibald Colquhoun: Rhodesia (1890–91)
Antoine Columbani: Comoros (1966–69)
Edward Columbine: Sierra Leone (1810–11)
Charles Colville: Mauritius (1823–33)
Henry Colville: Uganda (1893–94)
Diego, Conde de Comares: Oran (1573–74, 1589–94)
Diego, Marqués de Comares: Oran (1517–22)
Luis, Marqués de Comares: Oran (1522–23, 1525–31)
Antoine Combes: Mali (1884–85)
Combo Ayuba: Comoros (1995)
Jacques Compain: Djibouti (1958–62)

Francisco de Conceição: São Tomé (1744–44)
Richard Coney: Saint Helena (1671–72)
Tairou Congacou: Benin [ii] (1965)
M. Conjard: Côte d'Ivoire (1845–47)
Prince Arthur of Connaught: South Africa (1920–23)
Henry Connor: Ghana (1854–57)
Joseph Conombo: Burkina Faso (1978–80)
David Conradie: Namibia (1933–43)
Edward Conran: Ghana (1865–67)
Daniel Constantin: Réunion (1989–91)
Constantine I: Ethiopia (1434–68)
Constantine Sereng Seeiso: Lesotho (1960–64, 1970–90)
Constantius: Egypt (592)
Constantius: Africa Proconsularis (373–374)
Lansana Conté: Guinea (1984–)
Patrick Conteh: Sierra Leone (1968)
Sheku Bochari Kawusu Conteh: Sierra Leone (1970)
Ramón Conti: Melilla (1800–14)
Manuel Contrim: Cacheu (1658–62)
Thomas de Conway: Mauritius (1789–90)
William Cooke: Fort James
Georges de Cools: Gorée and Dependencies
Henry Cooper: Natal (1855–56)
Miles Cooper: Lagos (1870)
Jules de Coppet: Benin [ii] (1933–34); Chad (1926–28, 1929–32); Djibouti (1934–35); French West Africa (1936–38); Madagascar (1939–40, 1946–47); Mauritania (1935–36)
Xavier Coppolani: Mauritania (1903–05); Trarza
Camille-Aimé Coquilhat: Congo (Zaire) (1891–92)
Charles Brossard de Corbigny: Côte d'Ivoire (1857)
Sebastián de Corcuera y Gaviría: Canary Islands (1659–61)
Harry Cordeaux: British Somali land; Saint Helena (1911–20); Uganda (1910–11)
Benedict de Cordemoy: Réunion (1895–96)
Philippe Jacob de Cordemoy: Réunion (1795–1803)
Cristóbal de Córdoba: Oran (1765–67)
Diego de Córdoba: Oran (1510–12)
Francisco de Córdoba: Melilla (1568–71)
Pedro de Córdoba: Melilla (1561–68)
Luis de Córdoba y Arce: Canary Islands (1638–44)
Henri Core: Madagascar (1910); Réunion (1908); Senegal (1911–14)
Thomas Corker: Fort James
Daniel Corneille: Saint Helena (1782–88)

Henri Cornelis: Congo (Zaire) (1958–60)

Cornelis Kok II: Cornelis Kok's Land

Servius Cornelius Cethegus: Africa [i] (36–37)

Publius Cornelius Dolabella: Africa [i] (23–24)

Cornelius Gallus: Egypt (30–26 B.C.)

Servius Cornelius Scipio Salvidienus Orfitus: Africa [i] (62–63)

Servius Cornelius Scipio Salvidienus Orfitus: Africa [i] (164)

Charles Cornewall: Fort James

Guido Corni: Italian Somaliland (1928–31)

Bernard Cornut-Gentille: French Equatorial Africa (1948–51); French West Africa (1952–56)

Jean Cornut-Gentille: Gabon (1883–85)

Joaquín Coronado: Ifni; Western Sahara

Alonso del Corral: Gran Canaria

Antonio Correia: Cape Verde (1957–58); Guinea-Bissau (1958–62)

Carlos Correia: Guinea-Bissau (1991–94, 1997–98)

Fernão Lopes Correia: Portuguese Gold Coast (1517–19)

Francisco Correia: São Tomé and Príncipe (1858)

Luis Correia: Tangier (1945–48)

Tomé Correia: Mozambique (1692–93)

José Correia de Barros: Cacheu (1820–21)

João Correia e Lança: Mozambique (1894, 1896)

Joaquim da Graça Correia e Lança: Guinea-Bissau (1888–90); São Tomé and Príncipe (1897–99)

Miguel Correia y García: Spanish Morocco (1891–94)

Rafael Correia y García: Spanish Morocco (1894–98)

Hassan Corso: Algiers (1556–57)

João Corte-Real: Cape Verde (1628–32)

Marqués de Cortes: Oran (1575–85)

Robert Coryndon: Kenya (1922–25); Lesotho (1915–17); North Western Rhodesia; Rhodesia (1897–1900); Swaziland (1907–16); Uganda (1918–22)

David Charpentier de Cossigny: Mauritius (1790–92); Réunion (1788–90)

Gabriel Costa: São Tomé and Príncipe (2002)

Abel da Costa: Cape Verde (1915–18)

Celestino Rocha da Costa: São Tomé and Príncipe (1988–91)

Eduardo da Costa: Angola (1903–04, 1906–07)

Estévão da Costa: Mozambique (1694–95)

Firmeno da Costa: São Tomé and Príncipe (1890–91)

Francisco da Costa: Mozambique (1695–96)

Francisco Meneses da Costa: Mozambique (1797–1801)

Gil da Costa: Ceuta (1586–91)

Guilhermo Posser da Costa: São Tomé and Príncipe (1999–2002)

José da Costa: Angola (1725–26)

José da Costa: Mombasa (1671–73)

José da Costa: São Tomé and Príncipe (1839–43)

Júlio da Costa: Mozambique (1900)

Leandro da Costa: São Tomé and Príncipe (1837–38, 1843, 1849–51)

Leonardo da Costa: Mombasa (1682–86)

Manuel Pinto da Costa: São Tomé and Príncipe (1973–74, 1975–91)

Manuel Saturnino da Costa: Guinea-Bissau (1994–97)

Rodrigo da Costa: Madeira (1690–94)

Veríssimo da Costa: Cape Verde (1687–88)

Vitoriano da Costa: Cape Verde (1688–90)

Norberto d'Alva Costa Alegre: São Tomé and Príncipe (1992–94)

José da Costa Almeida: Mozambique (1964–69)

José da Costa Moura: São Tomé and Príncipe (1862–63)

Manuel da Costa Pessoa: Cape Verde (1667–71, 1678–83)

M. Berthelot de la Coste: Seychelles (1781–83)

François La Coste: French Morocco

Jean-Paul Coste: Mayotte Department

Robert La Coste: Algeria (1956–58)

João Cota: Mombasa (1667–70)

Antonio de Albuquerque Cota Falcão: Bissau (1858)

Henrique Couceiro: Angola (1907–09)

Pierre Coudert: Comoros (1950–56)

Jacques de la Cour de la Saulais: Réunion (1699–1701)

Michel Jajolet de la Courbe: Senegal (1689–90, 1706–10)

Joseph Beauvollier de Courchant: Mauritius (1718–22); Réunion (1718–23)

Pierre Cournarie: Cameroun (1940–43); French West Africa (1943–46)

Joseph Court: Mali (1930–31); Niger (1935–38); Réunion (1938–39)

Hilaire Lafitte de Courteil: Réunion (1817–18)

Juan de Courten: Oran (1791–92)

Jean-Marie Cousirou: Mayotte Department

Paul Cousserau: Réunion (1969–72)

Paul Cousturier: Côte d'Ivoire (1895); Gabon (1905); Guinea (1892–93, 1895–96, 1898–1904)

Antonio Coutinho: Angola (1974–75)

Diogo Coutinho: Madeira (1781–98)

Diogo Coutinho: Mozambique (1793–97)

Fonseca Coutinho: Angola (1748–49)

Francisco de Sousa Coutinho: Angola (1764–72)

Inacio Coutinho: São Tomé and Príncipe (1797)

João Coutinho: Angola (1602–03)

João Coutinho: Madeira (1777–81)

João Róis Coutinho: Portuguese Gold Coast (1586–95)

Lopo de Sousa Coutinho: Portuguese Gold Coast (1541, 1548–50)

Lopo Coutinho: São Tomé (1734–36); São Tomé and Príncipe (1755)

Manuel Coutinho: Angola (1630–35); Mombasa (1643–46)

Manuel Coutinho: Madeira (1609–14)

Victor Hugo de Azevedo Coutinho: Mozambique (1924–26)

Walter Coutts: Uganda (1961–63)

Francis Cradock: Cape Colony (1811–14)

James Craig: Cape Colony (1795–97)

Joost Cramer: Danish Gold Coast (1659–62)

Col. Crane: Burkina Faso (1898–1904)

José do Crato: Bissau (1871); Cacheu (1844–46)

Frederick Crawford: Seychelles (1951–53); Uganda (1957–61)

Gerald Creasy: Ghana (1948–49)

Jan Cremer: Dutch Gold Coast (1833)

Victor Crespo: Mozambique (1974–75)

Col. Cristofari: Niger (1910)

Joaquín Cristón y Gasatín: Spanish Morocco (1868–70)

Horace Crocicchia: Côte d'Ivoire (1939–41); Guinea (1942–44)

Marqués de Croix: Ceuta (1751–55)

Lord Cromer: Egypt (1882, 1883–91, 1892–1907)

J.J. Crooks: Sierra Leone (1891–92)

Hendrik Crudop: Cape Colony (1678–79)

Brodie Cruickshank: Ghana (1853–54)

Conrad Crul: Danish Gold Coast (1674–80)

Andrés Cuadra y Bourman: Melilla (1873–79)

gBon Cuilbaly: Kong

Pierre Cuinier: Réunion (1879–86)

Culcianus: Egypt (303–307)

Lorenzo Cullén: Canary Islands (1988–91)

Conde de Cumbre Hermosa: Oran (1790–91)

Duncan Cumming: Cyrenaica; Eritrea

Álvaro da Cunha: Guinea-Bissau (1897–98, 1899–1900)

Antonio da Cunha: Angola (1753–58)

Bartolomeu da Cunha: Angola (1653–54)

Francisco da Cunha: Angola (1635–39); Cacheu (1655); Cape Verde (1624–28)

Francisco da Cunha: Mozambique (1877–80)

João da Cunha: Cape Verde (1640–45)

João da Cunha: São Tomé (1598–1601, 1609, 1611)

João da Cunha: São Tomé (1683–86)

Pedro da Cunha: Angola (1845–48)

Pedro da Cunha: Ceuta (1553–53, 1564–65)

Pedro da Cunha: São Tomé (1620–21)

Pedro Álvares da Cunha: Madeira (1712–15)

Pedro da Silva da Cunha: Madeira (1655–60)

Tristão da Cunha: Angola (1666–67)

Luis Antonio da Cunha d'Eça: Cape Verde (1752–57)

Nunho da Cunha e Ataíde: Mozambique (1595–98)

Manuel da Cunha e Teive: Portuguese Gold Coast (1616–24)

Sebastião da Cunha Souto-Maior: Bissau (1770–75)

Adolphe Cureau: Central African Republic (1900–04); Congo (1906–10); French Equatorial Africa (1910)

John Curlewis: South Africa (1937)

Walter Currie: Lesotho (1868)

Curtius: Africa Proconsularis (407–408)

Quintus Curtius Rufus: Africa [i] (58–59)

Antonio Curto: Angola (1897–1900, 1904–06)

Guillermo de la Peña Cusi: Western Sahara

Gaston Cusin: French West Africa (1956–58)

Jacques Cuvillier: Réunion (1832–38)

Cwa I Mali Rumoma Mahanga: Bunyoro

Cwa I Nabaka: Buganda

Daudi Cwa II: Buganda

Cwa II Kabarega: Bunyoro

Duhaga I Cwa Mujwiga: Bunyoro

Ndahiro II Cyaamatare: Ruanda

Cyilima II Rujugira: Ruanda

Cyilima Rugwe: Ruanda

Cyprian Bhekuzulu: Zululand

D

José da Ávila: Bissau (1852–53)

João da Câmara: Angola (1779–82)

Jorge da Câmara: Madeira (1614–18)

José da Câmara: Bissau (1696–99); Cacheu (1689–90); Cape Verde (1711–15)

José da Câmara: Madeira (1800–03)

José da Câmara: São Tomé (1722–27)

Luis da Câmara: Mozambique (1707–12)

Manuel da Câmara: Cape Verde (1692–96); São Tomé (1697–1702)

Abel da Costa: Cape Verde (1915–18)

Celestino Rocha da Costa: São Tomé and Príncipe (1988–91)

Eduardo da Costa: Angola (1903–04, 1906–07)

Estévão da Costa: Mozambique (1694–95)

Firmeno da Costa: São Tomé and Príncipe (1890–91)

Francisco da Costa: Mozambique (1695–96)

Francisco Meneses da Costa: Mozambique (1797–1801)

Gil da Costa: Ceuta (1586–91)

Guilhermo Posser da Costa: São Tomé and Príncipe (1999–2002)

José da Costa: Angola (1725–26)

José da Costa: Mombasa (1671–73)

José da Costa: São Tomé and Príncipe (1839–43)

Júlio da Costa: Mozambique (1900)

Leandro da Costa: São Tomé and Príncipe (1837–38, 1843, 1849–51)

Leonardo da Costa: Mombasa (1682–86)

Manuel Saturnino da Costa: Guinea-Bissau (1994–97)

Manuel Pinto da Costa: São Tomé and Príncipe (1973–74, 1975–91)

Rodrigo da Costa: Madeira (1690–94)

Veríssimo da Costa: Cape Verde (1687–88)

Vitoriano da Costa: Cape Verde (1688–90)

José da Costa Almeida: Mozambique (1964–69)

José da Costa Moura: São Tomé and Príncipe (1862–63)

Manuel da Costa Pessoa: Cape Verde (1667–71, 1678–83)

Álvaro da Cunha: Guinea-Bissau (1897–98, 1899–1900)

Antonio da Cunha: Angola (1753–58)

Bartolomeu da Cunha: Angola (1653–54)

Francisco da Cunha: Angola (1635–39); Cacheu (1655); Cape Verde (1624–28)

Francisco da Cunha: Mozambique (1877–80)

João da Cunha: Cape Verde (1640–45)

João da Cunha: São Tomé (1598–1601, 1609, 1611)

João da Cunha: São Tomé (1683–86)

Pedro da Cunha: Angola (1845–48)

Pedro da Cunha: Ceuta (1553, 1564–65)

Pedro da Cunha: São Tomé (1620–21)

Pedro Álvares da Cunha: Madeira (1712–15)

Pedro da Silva da Cunha: Madeira (1655–60)

Tristão da Cunha: Angola (1666–67)

Luis Antonio da Cunha d'Eça: Cape Verde (1752–57)

Nunho da Cunha e Ataíde: Mozambique (1595–98)

Manuel da Cunha e Teive: Portuguese Gold Coast (1616–24)

Sebastião da Cunha Souto-Maior: Bissau (1770–75)

André da Fonseca: Mozambique (1674)

Antonio da Fonseca: São Tomé and Príncipe (1867)

Joaquim da Fonseca: São Tomé and Príncipe (1830–34)

José da Fonseca: São Tomé and Príncipe (1909–10)

Manuel da Fonseca: Mozambique (1919–21, 1923–24)

Rodrigo da Fonseca: Bissau (1699–1707); Cacheu (1688–89); Cape Verde (1707–11)

Antonio da Gama: Angola (1807–10)

Cristóvão da Gama: Portuguese Gold Coast (1596–1608)

Duarte da Gama: Cape Verde (1587–91)

Duarte Lobo da Gama: Portuguese Gold Coast (1595–96)

Estévão da Gama: Portuguese Gold Coast (1529)

Francisco da Gama: Cape Verde (1596–1603)

João da Gama: Madeira (1715–18)

Pedro da Gama e Castro: Mozambique (1743–46)

Joaquim da Graça Correia e Lança: São Tomé and Príncipe (1897–99)

Da Kaba: Segu

Amaro da Luz: Cape Verde (1974–75)

Manuel da Maia Magalhães: Cape Verde (1919–21)

Manuel da Mota: São Tomé and Príncipe (1798–99)

Mendio da Mota: Portuguese Gold Coast (1574)

Luis da Mota e Melo: São Tomé and Príncipe (1758–61)

Luis da Mota Feo e Torres: Angola (1816–19)

Francisco da Pina Rolo: São Tomé and Príncipe (1853–55)

Paulo da Ponte: São Tomé (1641–42)

José da Ponte e Horta: Angola (1870–73)

Antonio da Rocha Magalhães: Portuguese Gold Coast (1634–42)

Sebastião da Rosa: Cacheu (1674)

João da Sera e Morais: Portuguese Gold Coast (1629)

Diogo da Silva: Mombasa (1646–48)

Duarte da Silva: São Tomé (1591–92)

Francisco da Silva: Cape Verde (1606–11)

Francisco da Silva: Guinea-Bissau (1887–88); Mozambique (1893–94); São Tomé and Príncipe (1882–84)

João da Silva: Mozambique (1824–25)

João Baptista da Silva: São Tomé and Príncipe (1799–1802)

José da Silva: Bissau (1853–54)

José da Silva: Mombasa (1658–63)

Júlio Moniz da Silva: Mozambique (1642–46)

Luis da Silva: Angola (1684–88)

Manuel da Silva: Madeira (1648–51, 1674–76)

Martim da Silva: Ceuta (1549–50, 1553–55)
Martinho da Silva: Portuguese Gold Coast (1505)
Paulo da Silva: Cacheu (1634)
Pedro da Silva: Madeira (1618–22); Portuguese Gold Coast (1613–15)
Pedro da Silva: São Tomé (1661)
Pedro da Silva: Tangier (1578)
Simão da Silva: Mozambique (1673–74)
Manuel da Silva Botelho: Cacheu (1640)
Pedro da Silva da Cunha: Madeira (1655–60)
Gomes da Silva de Vasconcelos: Ceuta (1519–21, 1525–29)
João da Silva e Sousa: Angola (1680–84)
Francisco da Silveira: Mozambique (1641–42)
Conde da Tôrre: Ceuta (1624–25)
Tristão da Veiga: Madeira (1585–91)
Tase Daagulen: Dyolof
Kherfi Khari Daano: Walo (1837–40)
Aden Abdallah Osman Daar: Somalia
Naatago Kbaari Daaro: Walo (1565–76)
Daba: New Calabar
Owerri Daba: New Calabar
Abu Dabbus: Almohad Empire
Dabila: Kong
Christian Dablanc: Djibouti (1974–76)
Johan D'Ableing: Cape Colony (1707–08)
Ibrahim Dabo: Kano (1819–45)
Dabulamanzi: Tembuland
Umaru Dacili: Gobir
David Dacko: Central African Republic (1959–65, 1979–81)
Antoine Dacosta: Congo (1992–93)
Mokhtar Ould Daddah: Mauritania (1957–78)
Dadi: Kano (1670–1702)
Maji Dadi: Zaria (ca. 1400)
Kléber Dadjo: Togo (1967)
Dadju: Kororofa
Herman Daendels: Dutch Gold Coast (1816–18)
al-Gizouli Dafalla: Sudan (1985)
Idris Wad Daftar: Bahr al-Ghazal
Charles Dagain: Chad (1938–39); Senegal (1943–45)
Dagajirau: Daura
Dagamu: Daura
Aguessi Dagba: Whydah
Abd ar-Rahman Siwar ad-Dahab: Sudan (1985–86)
Mwine Kombe Dai: Luba
Dai Mande: Luba
Étienne Mengin Duval d'Ailly: Réunion (1830–32)
Daniel Lima dos Santos Daio: São Tomé and Príncipe (1991–92)
Aji Daka: Daniski
Langawa Daka: Daniski
Dakauta: Kano (1452–52)

Dakin al-Adil: Funj Sultanate
Joseph Dakins: Fort James
Dakka I: Zamfara
Dakka II: Zamfara
Abuako Dako: Akwamu
Dako Booman: Akwamu
Dakodonu: Dahomey
Dakwai: Biu
Dala: Bornu Empire (1563–70)
Dala: Kanem
Dala: Kano (ca. 900)
Dalai: Baguirmi
Thomas Dalby: Ghana (1701–08)
16th Earl of Dalhousie: Federation of Rhodesia and Nyasaland
Dalindyebo: Tembuland
Daliza: Kreli's Country
Lucas Dall: Danish Gold Coast (1839–42)
Abdullahi Dalla: Lafia
Abdullahi Dalla Bahagu: Lafia
Bukar Dalla Boyonbo: Songhai (1386–94)
Dalla Dawaki: Gobir
Dalla Gungumi: Gobir
Umaru Dallaji: Katsina (1806–35)
Charles Dallas: Saint Helena (1828–36)
Dallatu: Zaria (1920–24)
Damião Vaz d'Almeida: São Tomé and Príncipe (2004–05); Príncipe (ii)
José d'Almeida: Mozambique (1889)
Dalo Birni: Baguirmi
John Dalrymple: Mauritius (1818–19)
Jean d'Alteyrac: Gorée and Dependencies
Leonel d'Alva: São Tomé and Príncipe (1974–75)
Norberto José d'Alva Costa Alegre: São Tomé and Príncipe (1992–94)
Henry Daly: Rhodesia (1897–98)
Archibald Dalzel: Ghana (1792–98, 1800–02)
Hen Kon Wanko Dam: Songhai (1044–63)
Damad: Egypt (1687–89, 1707–09)
Khaliji-Zade-Damad: Egypt (1656–57)
Suleiman Daman: Songhai (1456–64)
Dambo: Kazaure
Col. Dame: Namibia (1905–06)
Damgalke: Gumel
Damram: Akim
Usuman Dan Abdullahi: Kano (1919–26)
Dan Addo: Yauri
Suleimanu Dan Addo: Yauri
Ahmadu Dan Amaru: Argungu
Dan Aro: Daura-Zango
Dan Asan: Biram
Dan Auwa: Gumel
Dan Ayi: Yauri
Dan Gudi Dan Babari: Gobir
Nafata Dan Babari: Gobir
Yakuba Dan Babari: Gobir
Dan Bako: Zamfara
Dan Buddi: Gobir
Muhammadu Dan Chiroma: Gobir

Akili Dan Chuba: Gobir
Muhammadu Dan Ciwa: Argungu
Soba Dan Doro: Gobir
Abdullahi Dan Fodio: Gwandu
Modibbo Dan Fodio: Gobir
Usman Dan Fodio: Fulani Empire
Uthman Dan Fodio: Fulani Empire
Dan Gado: Zamfara
Dan Gajere: Yauri
Muhammadu Dan Gigala: Zamfara
Bawa Dan Gima: Katsina (1802–04)
Dan Gudi Dan Babari: Gobir
Bawa Dan Gwamki: Gobir
Babari Dan ibn Ashe: Gobir
Dan Ibrahimu: Yauri
Maliki Dan Ibrahimu: Argungu
Musa Dan Jaji: Lafia
Dan Juma I: Gumel
Dan Magaji: Gobir
Gidan Dan Masakanan: Zaria (1530–32)
Barma Dan Moi Bunowo: Daniski
Chuba Dan Muhammadu: Gobir
Bako Dan Musa: Zaria (1727–36)
Yunfa Dan Nafata: Gobir
Muhammadu Dan Tagande: Argungu
Dan Tanoma: Gumel
Dan Tunku: Kazaure
Muhammadu Dan Wari: Katsina (1704–06)
Danagaram Tumo: Kangaba
Henri Danel: Réunion (1893–95)
Dango: Biram
Dango: Daura
Dangoma: Gobir
Bako Makam Danguma: Zaria (1738–50)
Boroma Dangwaranga: Mwene Mutapa Empire
Daniel: Kongo
Rowland Daniel: Botswana
Daniel Adesanya Gbelegbura II: Ijebu
Danieri Mwanga: Buganda
Yama Danka Kibao: Songhai (969–981)
Dankawa: Katagum (1816–46)
Dankwafan: Biram
Danmaigatiny Uata: Gumel
Comte de Danrémont: Algeria (1837)
Awura Danse: Baule
Antonio Dantas: Angola (1880–82)
Danyawa: Gumel
Danyuma: Gumel
Danzaki: Zaria (ca. 1150)
Barão de Santa Comba Dão: Angola (1829–34)
Muhammad Dao: Songhai (1402–10)
Yama Dao: Songhai (1158–77)
Giuseppe Daodice: Eritrea
Duca D'Aosta: Ethiopia (1941)
Daouda Wanké: Niger (1999)
Daoula Ba Traore: Kenedugu
Daoula Ba Traore II: Kenedugu
Dappa: Bonny (?)
Dappa: Bonny (1835–53)
Dappo: Bonny
Badi II Abu Daqan: Funj Sultanate
Ahmadu Dara Alfaya: Futa Jallon

Darayavahush I: Egypt (27th Dynasty)

Darayavahush II: Egypt (27th Dynasty)

Darayavahush III: Egypt (335–332 B.C.)

Abu Darba: Hafsid Kingdom

George D'Arcy: Gambia (1859–66)

Bakon Dare: Gobir

Ibrahim Yanka Dari: Katsina (1410–52)

Darimani: Dagomba

Darius II: Egypt (27th Dynasty)

Darius III: Egypt (335–332 B.C.)

Darius the Great: Egypt (27th Dynasty)

Kosai Dariya: Songhai (1025–44)

Darizegu: Dagomba

Charles Darling: Cape Colony (1854)

Ralph Darling: Mauritius (1819–20)

Abdinur Ahmad Darman: Somalia

Tyaaka Daro Khot: Walo (1496–1503)

Rodolphe Darricau: Réunion (1858–64)

Baron Dartmouth: Tangier (1683–84)

Yves de Daruvar: Comoros (1962–63)

Francisco das Chagas: São Tomé (1747–48)

Maria das Neves: São Tomé and Príncipe (2002–04)

Dase: Kaarta

Dassa: Allada

Dassu: Allada

Dassu: Whydah

Ibrahim Dasuki: Fulani Empire

Datorli: Dagomba

Valerius Datus: Egypt (216–218)

Jean Daubigny: Réunion (1998–2001)

Daud: Egypt (1538–49)

Daud: Omayyad and Abbasid North Africa

Daud: Wadai

Daud ibn Ali: Zeng Empire (1027–32)

Daud ibn Suleiman: Zeng Empire (1117–58)

Daud ibn Suleiman: Zeng Empire (1177–80)

Daud ibn Suleiman: Zeng Empire (1334–57)

Daud Nigalemi: Bornu Empire (1377–86)

Dauda: Damagaram

Dauda: Kano (1421–37)

Dauda Abasama I: Kano (1565)

Dauda Abasama II: Kano (1776–80)

Dauda Demba: Kayor

Dauda Maza: Lapai

Daudi Cwa II: Buganda

Duc d'Aumale: Algeria (1847–48)

Marius Daumas: Porto-Novo

Domingos de Oliveira Daun: Angola (1836)

Daura: Daura

Dauti III: Ethiopia (1716–21)

Martín Dávalos y Padilla: Melilla (1596–1601)

François Bertin d'Avesnes: Réunion (1763–67)

David: Axum

David: Dongola

David I: Ethiopia (1382–1411)

David II: Dongola

David II: Ethiopia (1508–40)

David III: Ethiopia (1716–21)

Pierre David: Mauritius (1747–50); Senegal (1738–46)

Letsie David Seeiso: Lesotho (1990–94, 1996–)

Walter Davidson: Seychelles (1904–12)

Wilfred Davidson-Houston: Malawi (1929)

Alfonso Dávila: Tenerife

João d'Ávila: Mozambique (1882)

Marqués de Flores Dávila: Oran (1632–39, 1647–52)

Alfonso Dávila y Guzmán: Canary Islands (1650–59)

Steuart Davis: Saint Helena (1932–38)

Dalla Dawaki: Gobir

Dawda Jawara: Gambia (1962–94); Senegambia Confederation

Dawema: Wagadugu

William Dawes: Sierra Leone (1792–94, 1795–96, 1801–03)

Dawi: Kororofa

Dawi Moda: Biu

Dawit I: Ethiopia (1382–1411)

Lebna Dengel Dawit II: Ethiopia (1508–40)

Dawit III: Ethiopia (1716–21)

Muhammad I Dawra: Darfur

Dawra ibn Dakin: Funj Sultanate

Joseph Dawson: Ghana (1816–17)

Dawud: Songhai (1549–82)

Dawud II: Songhai (1618–35)

Dawud ibn Yezid: Egypt (790–791)

Dawuda: Argungu

William Day: Sierra Leone (1803, 1805)

Dayendranath Burrenchobay: Mauritius (1979–86)

Dayeni: Pondoland

Julio de Abreu: Cape Verde (1924–26)

Luis de Abreu: São Tomé (1611–13, 1614–16)

Pedro de Abreu: Mombasa (1609–10)

Paulo de Abreu e Lima: Cacheu (1707)

Vasco de Abreu: Mozambique (1507–08)

Rodrigo de Abreu e Lima: Mozambique (1843–47)

Marcos de Abreu e Meneses: Mozambique (1812–17)

Domingos de Abreu Picaluga: Bissau (1825)

Álvaro de Acosta: Gran Canaria

Rodrigo de Acuña: Gran Canaria

De Adjara: Allada

Diego de Águila y Toledo: Gran Canaria

Conde de Aguilar de Inestrillas: Oran (1608–16)

Manuel de Aguilar y Diosdado: Spanish Morocco (1901–03)

Francisco de Alarcão e Souto-Maior: Mozambique (1719–21)

Francisco de Alba: Melilla (1757–58)

Diogo Soares de Albergaria: Portuguese Gold Coast (1545, 1550–52)

Lopo Soares de Albergaria: Portuguese Gold Coast (1493)

Afonso de Albuquerque: Portuguese Gold Coast (1522–24)

João de Albuquerque: Mozambique (1817–18)

Joaquim de Albuquerque: Mozambique (1896–97)

Manuel de Albuquerque: Angola (1819–21)

Manuel de Albuquerque: Portuguese Gold Coast (1536–39)

Paulo de Albuquerque: Angola (1726–32)

Antonio de Albuquerque Cota Falcão: Bissau (1858)

Diogo de Alcáçova: São Tomé (1516–17)

Alonso, Conde de Alcandete: Oran (1558–64)

Francisco, Conde de Alcandete: Oran (1596–1604)

Martín, Conde de Alcandete: Oran (1534–58)

Fernão, Conde de Alcoutim: Ceuta (1491–1509)

Pedro, Conde de Alcoutim: Ceuta (1512–17, 1524–25)

Marqués de Algava: Oran (1678–81)

Lourenço de Almada: Angola (1705–09); Madeira (1688–90)

Antonio de Almeida: Mozambique (1869–69)

Armindo Vaz de Almeida: São Tomé and Príncipe (1995–96)

Duarte de Almeida: Cape Verde (1781–82)

Francisco de Almeida: Angola (1592–93)

Francisco de Almeida: Ceuta (1637–41)

Januário de Almeida: Cape Verde (1860–61)

Jerónimo de Almeida: Angola (1593–94)

João de Almeida: Cape Verde (1926–27)

João de Almeida: Mozambique (1703–06, 1712–14)

João de Almeida: Mozambique (1857–64)

Lopo de Almeida: Mozambique (1525–28)

Lopo de Almeida: Mozambique (1623–24)

Luis de Almeida: Tangier (1661–62)

Manuel de Almeida: Cacheu (ca. 1670)

Miguel de Almeida: Mozambique (1686–89)

Nicolau de Almeida: Mozambique (1736–39)

Luis de Almeida Cabral: Guinea-Bissau (1973–80)

Caetano de Almeida e Albuquerque: Angola (1876–78); Cape Verde (1869–76)

Isidro de Almeida Sousa e Sá: Mozambique (1801–05)

Bernardo de Alpoim: Cape Verde (1562–65)

Francisco de Alva Brandão: São Tomé (1744–45)

Eugenio de Alvorado y Perales Hurtado y Colomo: Oran (1770–74)

Alonso de Alvorado y Ulloa: Gran Canaria

Bernardino de Anaya: Gran Canaria

Francisco de Andía Irarrazábal y Zárate: Canary Islands (1625–26)

Alfredo de Andrade: Mozambique (1906–10)

Antonio de Andrade: Mombasa (1596–98)

Bernardim Freire de Andrade: São Tomé (1677–80)

Francisco de Andrade: Ceuta (1591–92)

Francisco Nunes de Andrade: Cacheu (1634)

Gaspar de Andrade: Cape Verde (1578–83)

José Baptista de Andrade: Angola (1862–65, 1873–76)

Manuel de Andrade: Cape Verde (1555–58, 1565–69)

Pedro de Andrade: São Tomé (1604)

Pedro de Antas e Meneses: Madeira (1807–13)

Rafael de Andrade: Mozambique (1891–93)

Marquês de Aracaty: Mozambique (1837–38)

José de Aramburu: Oran (1738–42)

Juan Francisco de Araña: Ceuta (1705–09, 1720); Oran (1701–04)

Miguel Porcel y Manrique de Araña Menchaca y Zaldívar: Ceuta (1784–91)

Antonio Vaz de Araújo: Cacheu (1775)

Jorge de Araújo: Cape Verde (1646–48)

Nicolau Pino de Araújo: Bissau (1753); Cacheu (1741)

Luis de Araújo e Silva: Cacheu (1786)

João de Araújo Gomes: Cacheu (1821)

Diego de Arce: Melilla (1655–56, 1672–74)

Carlos de Arcos: Mozambique (1881–82)

Martín de Argote: Oran (1512–17)

Estanislau de Assunção e Almeida: São Tomé and Príncipe (1864–65, 1867–69)

Manuel de Assunção e Almeida: São Tomé and Príncipe (1876–79)

Estêvão de Ataíde: Mozambique (1607–09, 1611–12)

João de Ataíde e Azevedo: Madeira (1701–04)

Marqués de Miranda de Auta: Ceuta (1641–44)

José de Avellaneda: Canary Islands (1789–91)

Visconde de Santa Clara de Avellido: Oran (1628–32)

Marcelino de Ávila: Cape Verde (1761)

Juan Bautista de Ayora: Tenerife

Diogo de Azambuja: Portuguese Gold Coast (1482–84)

João de Azambuja: São Tomé and Príncipe (1778–82)

Diogo de Azambuja e Melo: Madeira (1595–1600)

Antonio de Miranda de Azevedo: Portuguese Gold Coast (1504)

João de Azevedo: Mozambique (1612–14)

Rui Gomes de Azevedo: Portuguese Gold Coast (1562)

Simão de Azevedo: Mozambique (1512–15)

Victor Hugo de Azevedo Coutinho: Mozambique (1924–26)

José de Azevedo e Silva: Mozambique (1911–12)

Gaspard de Ballade: Réunion (1745–47, 1748–49)

José de Barrasa: Fernando Po

Antonio de Barredo: São Tomé (1693–94)

Antonio de Barreido: Madeira (1591–95)

Pedro de Barrionuevo y Melgoza: Gran Canaria

João de Barros: Portuguese Gold Coast (1524–25)

José Correia de Barros: Cacheu (1820–21)

Pedro de Barros: Cacheu (1723)

Pedro de Barros: Mozambique (1958–61)

Roque de Barros do Rego: Cape Verde (1648)

Damião de Bastos: Cacheu (1737)

Pierre de Beausse: Fort-Dauphin

Marqués de Bedmar: Canary Islands (1589–91); Gran Canaria

Paul de Beeckmann: Porto-Novo

Guillaume de Bellecombe: Réunion (1767–73)

Francisco de Benavides: Tenerife

Juan Alonso de Benavides: Gran Canaria

Juan Pacheco de Benavides: Gran Canaria

Martín de Benavides: Gran Canaria

Demetrio María de Benito y Hernández: Melilla (1839–47)

Maciot de Béthencourt: Canary Islands (1405–15)

José de Bettencourt: Mozambique (1941–46)

Paul Celeron de Blainville: Comoros (1887–88)

Luis de Bocanegra: Oran (1574–75)

Rodrigo de Bohorques: Tenerife

Conde de Bolognino: Oran (1767–70)

José Pascual de Bonanza: Spanish Morocco (1883)

Emilio De Bono: Eritrea; Italian East Africa; Tripolitania (1925–28)

Francis De Bordes: Dutch Gold Coast (1736–40)

Custódio de Borja: Angola (1904); São Tomé and Príncipe (1879–80, 1884–85, 1886)

Felipe de Borja: Oran (1571–73)

Stanislas de Boufflers: Senegal (1786–87)

M. de Boulay: Senegal (1661–64)

Conde de Bracamonte: Oran (1687–87)

Duque de Bragança: Ceuta (1447–50)

Fernand de Brancamont: Tripolitania (1538–42)

Pierre Savorgnan de Brazza: Congo (1883–86); French Equatorial Africa (1886–97); Gabon (1886)

Fernão de Brito: Cape Verde (1603–06)

João de Brito: Madeira (1680–84)

João de Brito: São Tomé and Príncipe (1824–30)

Joaquim de Brito: São Tomé and Príncipe (1901–02)

José de Brito: Guinea-Bissau (1886–87)

Lourenço de Brito: Mozambique (1589–90)

Paulo de Brito: Mozambique (1829–32)

Cristóvão de Brito e Vasconcelos: Mozambique (1631–32)

Luis de Brito Freire: Mozambique (1706–07)

Antonio de Brito Pacheco: Mozambique (1640–41)

Íñigo de Brizuela y Urbina: Canary Islands (1634–38)

Denis de Brousse: Mauritius (1725–27)

Fernando Gómez de Buitrón: Ceuta (1813–14, 1820–22)

Sáenz de Buruaga: Spanish Morocco (1936)

Cristóvão de Cabral: Cape Verde (1632–36)

Sebastião de Calheiros e Meneses: Angola (1861–62)

Camillo De Camillis: Eritrea

Duque de Caminha: Ceuta (1592–94, 1597–1601, 1605–16, 1623, 1625–26)

Príncipe de Campo Flórido: Ceuta (1719–20)

Marqués de Campo Santo: Oran (1789–90)

Marqués de Campofuerte: Ceuta (1739–45)

Artur de Campos: Cape Verde (1911)

Manuel de Campos: Mombasa (1663–67, 1673–76)

Pedro Barba de Campos: Canary Islands (1415–18)

Julião de Campos Barreto: São Tomé (1673–77)

Eric Vully de Candole: Cyrenaica; Italian Somaliland (1948)

Tomás de Cangas: Gran Canaria; Tenerife

Hernando de Cañizares: Tenerife

Duque de Cansano: Oran (1692–97)

Antonio de Canto e Castro: Mozambique (1864–67)

Luis de Cárdenas: Oran (1523–25)

Luis de Carvajal: Oran (1778–79)

Ramón de Carvajal: Ceuta (1807–08)

Antero de Carvalho: Angola (1924–25)

Antonio de Carvalho: Angola (1722–25)

Antonio de Carvalho: São Tomé (1636)

Augusto de Carvalho: Cape Verde (1889–90)

Bernardim de Carvalho: Tangier (1553–62)

Domingos de Carvalho: Cacheu (1690–91)

Fernando de Carvalho: São Tomé and Príncipe (1910)

Filipe de Carvalho: Cape Verde (1921–22)

Inacio de Carvalho: Mozambique (1667–70)

João de Carvalho: Cacheu (1733–34)

João de Carvalho: São Tomé and Príncipe (1872–73)

Manuel de Carvalho: São Tomé and Príncipe (1797)

Ruis de Carvalho: Tangier (1572–73)

Vasco de Carvalho: São Tomé (1597–98)

José de Carvalho e Meneses: Cape Verde (1864–69); Mozambique (1874–79)

Vasco de Carvalho e Meneses: Angola (1878–80); Cape Verde (1878–79)

Vasco de Carvalho e Meneses: Mozambique (1854–57)

Marqués de Casa Cagigal: Canary Islands (1803–09)

Marqués de Casa Tremañes: Ceuta (1776–83)

Marqués de Casasola: Oran (1697–1701)

Antonio de Castelo Branco: São Tomé (1741)

Baltasar de Castelo Branco: Cacheu (1615–16)

Nuno Vaz de Castelo Branco: Portuguese Gold Coast (1502–04)

Marqués de Castelo Mendo: Ceuta (1662–65)

Jorge de Castilho: Cape Verde (1636–39)

Nicolau de Castilho: Cape Verde (1614–18)

Augusto de Castilho Barreto e Noronha: Mozambique (1885–89)

Pedro de Castilla: Gran Canaria

Álvaro de Castro: Mozambique (1915–18)

José Bautisto de Castro: Ceuta (1798–1801)

Luis Tomé de Castro: Portuguese Gold Coast (ca. 1627)

Pedro de Castro: Mozambique (1577–82)

Jaime de Castro Morais: Angola (1917–18)

José de Castro y Méndez: Melilla (1850–54)

Jerónimo de Cavalcanti e Albuquerque: Cape Verde (1639–40)

Juan de Cepeda: Tenerife

Pierre Parat de Chaillenest: Réunion (1710–15)

Louis Moreau de Chambonneau: Senegal (1684–89, 1690–93)

Comte de Charny: Ceuta (1725–31); Oran (1691–92)

Luc de Champmargou: Fort-Dauphin

François Desbordes de Charanville: Réunion (1709–10)

M. de Charbonnes: Senegal (1801)

Comte de Chasseloup-Laubat: Algeria (1859–60)

Fortuné de Chavannes: Congo (1889–94); Gabon (1889–94)

José de Chavez y Osorio: Canary Islands (1718–19)

Pasques de Chavonne: Cape Colony (1714–24)

Achille de Penfentenio de Cheffontaines: Réunion (1826–30)

Dominique de Chermont: Réunion (1790–92)

Pierre de Chevigné: Madagascar (1948–50)

Conde de Cifuentes: Oran (1682–83)

Roger Seydoux Fornier de Clausonne: Tunisia (1955–56)

Diego, Conde de Comares: Oran (1573–74, 1589–94)

Diego, Marqués de Comares: Oran (1517–22)

Luis, Marqués de Comares: Oran (1522–23, 1525–31)

Francisco de Conceição: São Tomé (1744–44)

Thomas de Conway: Mauritius (1789–90)

Georges de Cools: Gorée and Dependencies

Jules de Coppet: Benin [ii] (1933–34); Chad (1926–28, 1929–32); Djibouti (1934–35); French West Africa (1936–38); Madagascar (1939–40, 1946–47); Mauritania (1935–36)

Charles Brossard de Corbigny: Côte d'Ivoire (1857)

Sebastián de Corcuera y Gaviría: Canary Islands (1659–61)

Benedict de Cordemoy: Réunion (1895–96)

Philippe Jacob de Cordemoy: Réunion (1795–1803)

Cristóbal de Córdoba: Oran (1765–67)

Diego de Córdoba: Oran (1510–12)

Francisco de Córdoba: Melilla (1568–71)

Pedro de Córdoba: Melilla (1561–68)

Luis de Córdoba y Arce: Canary Islands (1638–44)

Marqués de Cortes: Oran (1575–85)

David Charpentier de Cossigny: Mauritius (1790–92); Réunion (1788–90)

Joseph Beauvollier de Courchant: Mauritius (1718–22); Réunion (1718–23)

Hilaire Lafitte de Courteil: Réunion (1817–18)

Juan de Courten: Oran (1791–92)

Marqués de Croix: Ceuta (1751–55)

Conde de Cumbre Hermosa: Oran (1790–91)

Comte de Danrémont: Algeria (1837)

Yves de Daruvar: Comoros (1962–63)

Conde de Desallois: Melilla (1715–16)

Domingo de Dieguez: Melilla (1612–17)

Antonio Domínguez de Durán: Melilla (1687–88)

Antonio de Eça: Angola (1915–16)

Conde de Ericeira: Tangier (1656–61)

Tomás Mejía de Escobedo: Melilla (1633–35)

Adolfo de España y Gómez de Humarán: Fernando Po

Juan Antonio de Escoiquiz: Oran (1752–58)

Juan de Espinosa: Tenerife

Duque de Estrada: Tenerife

Luis de Evangelho: Cape Verde (1558–62)

Antonio de Faria: Cape Verde (1752–52)

Francisco de Faria: Mombasa (1676–79)

Antonio de Faria e Maia: Cape Verde (1785–90)

Príncipe de Faza: Mombasa (1697–98)

Vincenzo De Feo: Eritrea

Amadeu de Figueiredo: São Tomé and Príncipe (1941–45)

Antonio de Figueiredo: Cape Verde (1931–41)

Francisco de Figueiredo: São Tomé (1584–87)

João de Figueiredo: Cape Verde (1943–49)

Jacinto de Figueiredo e Abreu: São Tomé (1680–83)

Henrique de Figueiredo e Alarcão: Angola (1717–22)

Joaquim de Figueiredo e Góis: Cacheu (1811–14)

Diego de Figueroa: Tenerife

Francisco de Figueroa: Cape Verde (1658–63)

Étienne de Flacourt: Fort-Dauphin

Germain de Fleuricourt: Réunion (1678–80)

Chevalier de Fleury: Mauritius (1785)

Diego de Flores: Melilla (1707–11)

Marqués de Flores Dávila: Oran (1632–39, 1647–52)

Juan de Fonseca: Tenerife

Jean Terasson de Fougères: Mali (1920, 1921–24, 1925–30)

Diogo Lopes de França: Ceuta (1574–77)

Antonio de Freitas: Cape Verde (1903–04)

Felipe de Freitas: São Tomé and Príncipe (1817–24)

Charles de Fresne: Mauritius (1785)

Louis Desaulses de Freycinet: Réunion (1821–26)

Marqués de Fuensagrada: Canary Islands (1689–97)

Narciso de Fuentes y Sánchez: Spanish Morocco (1889–91)

Pedro de Gambôa: Mombasa (1629–31)

Gonçalo de Gamboa Ayala: Cacheu (1644–49); Cape Verde (1650)

Oreste De Gasperi: Cyrenaica

Paul de Gentilhomme: Madagascar (1943)

Nikolaas Van Der Nood De Gieterre: Dutch Gold Coast (1754–55)

Marqués de Gironella: Ceuta (1702–04)

Pedro de Godoy: Oran (1531–34)

Manuel de Gois: Portuguese Gold Coast (1509–10)

Francisco de Gouveia: São Tomé (1564–69)

Manuel de Gouveia: Bissau (1805–11); Cacheu (1800)

Pedro de Gouveia: Guinea-Bissau (1881–84, 1895–97)

Luis de Gouveia e Almeida: Madeira (1813–14)

Cornelis Van De Graaff: Cape Colony (1785–91)

Carlos de Graça: São Tomé and Príncipe (1994–95)

Ernest Bourdon de Grammont: Senegal (1846–47)

Conde de Guaro: Canary Islands (1681–85); Oran (1687–91)

Manuel de Guerra: Cape Verde (1622–24)

Juan de Guevara: Tenerife

Alonso de Guevara y Vasconcelos: Melilla (1719–30)

Comte de Gueydon: Algeria (1871–73)

Robert de Guise: French Equatorial Africa (1923–24); Guinea (1931–32); Togo (1931–33)

Enrique de Guzmán, Count of Niebla: Canary Islands (1418)

Fernán de Guzmán: Gran Canaria

Hernán de Guzmán: Oran (1565–67)

Pedro de Guzmán: Canary Islands (1644–50)

Jean de Hauteclocque: Tunisia (1952–53)

Philippe Leclerc de Hauteclocque: Cameroun (1940)

Charles Panon de Hazier: Gabon (1873–75)

Louis de Hell: Réunion (1838–41)

Diego de Herrera: Canary Islands (1444–76)

Miguel de Herredia: Canary Islands (1768–75)

Pedro de Herredia: Melilla (1603–11)

Pedro de Herrera: Gran Canaria

Diego de Herro: Gran Canaria

Francisco de Horta: Ceuta (1805–07)

Adolfo de España y Gómez de Humarán: Fernando Po

Conde de Aguilar de Inestrillas: Oran (1608–16)

Charles de Kerhallet: Côte d'Ivoire (1843)

De-Koro: Segu

Mattheus De Krane: Dutch Gold Coast (1723)

Bernard François Mahé, Comte de la Bourdonnais: Mauritius (1735–46); Réunion (1735)

Luis de la Breche: Melilla (1860–61)

Jean de la Breteche: Fort-Dauphin

Antoine de la Brillane: Mauritius (1776–79)

Jean-Baptiste Estoupan de la Bruë: Senegal (1746–58)

Pedro de la Buría: Canary Islands (1811–20)

Marqués de la Cáñada Ibáñez: Canary Islands (1779–84)

José de la Cerna: Fernando Po

M. Berthelot de la Coste: Seychelles (1781–83)

Jacques de la Cour de la Saulais: Réunion (1699–1701)

Michel Jajolet de la Courbe: Senegal (1689–90, 1706–10)

Jan de la Fontaine: Cape Colony (1724–27, 1729–37)

Juan de la Fuente: Tenerife

José de la Gándara: Fernando Po

Jean-Paul de la Grange: Sainte Marie de Madagascar

Claude Le Lardoux de la Gastière: Gorée

Jacob Blanquet de la Haye: Fort-Dauphin

Patrício Gómez de la Hoz: Melilla (1714–15)

José de la Ibarra: Fernando Po

Mariano de la Iglesia y Guillén: Melilla (1887–88)

Marqués de la Matilla: Ceuta (1751)

Conde de la Monclova: Oran (1681–82)

François de la Morlière: Mauritius (1800–03)

Alexandre de la Mothe: Oran (1742–48)

Henri de la Mothe: French Equatorial Africa (1897–1900); Senegal (1890–95)

Willem de la Palma: Dyolof

Diego de la Peña: Ceuta (1795)

Guillermo de la Peña Cusi: Western Sahara

Thomas Bougeaud de la Piconnerie: Algeria (1841–45)

José de la Puente Basseve: Fernando Po

Salvador de la Puente Pita: Spanish Morocco (1851–54)

Marqués de la Real Corona: Oran (1748–52)

Pierre Poncet de la Rivière: Gorée

Jean-Baptiste Montagniès de la Roque: Senegal (1841–42)

Jean Levens de la Roquette: Senegal (1726–33)

Francisco de la Rúa: Gran Canaria

Jacques de la Cour de la Saulais: Réunion (1699–1701)

Conde de la Torre: Tangier (1628–37)

Jules Ventre de la Touloubre: Comoros (1871–78); Nossi-Bé

Comte Boyer de la Tour du Moulin: French Morocco; Tunisia (1954–55)

Pedro de la Vega: Tenerife

René de la Villebague: Mauritius (1756–59)

Antonio de Lacerda: Mozambique (1867–68)

João de Lacerda: Cape Verde (1886–89, 1898–1900)

Jacques de Lahure: Réunion (1671–74)

Christophe de Lamoricière: Algeria (1845–47)

François Magallon de Lamorlière: Réunion (1803–05)

Ventura de Landaeta y Horna: Canary Islands (1713–18)

Henri Cleret de Langavant: Réunion (1922–23)

Frans de Lange: Hollandia

Louis de Lanneau: Senegal (1880–81)

Gabriel de Lara: Gran Canaria

René de Larminat: French Equatorial Africa (1940–41)

Luis de las Casas y Aragorri: Oran (1785–89)

M. de Launay: Seychelles (1770–72)

Duc de Lauzun: Senegal (1779–79)

Bonaventure Colonna de Lecca: Porto-Novo

Bernardino de Ledesma: Gran Canaria

Mendo de Ledesma: Ceuta (1594–97)

Juan de Legarte: Gran Canaria

Juan de Leiva: Tenerife

Eduardo de Lemos: São Tomé and Príncipe (1920–21)

Gonçalo de Lemos Mascarenhas: Cape Verde (1702–07)

Antonio de Lencastre: Angola (1772–79)

Antonio de Lencastre: Cape Verde (1803–18)

Dinís de Mascarenhas de Lencastre: Ceuta (1627)

João de Lencastre: Angola (1688–91)

José de Lencastre: Cape Verde (1831–33)

Rodrigo de Lencastre: Tangier (1653–56)

Andrés Ponce de León: Oran (1564–65)

Lázaro de León: Tenerife

Jacinto de León y Barreda: Seychelles (1898–1901)

Diego de Leyva: Melilla (1619–20)

Duarte de Lima: Portuguese Gold Coast (1608–13)

Francisco de Lima: Mozambique (1652–57)

Joaquim de Lima: Angola (1821–22)

José de Lima: Canary Islands (1744–45)

Conde de Linhares: Ceuta (1487–91)

Conde de Linhares: Tangier (1624–28)

Alfonso de Llarena: Tenerife

Louis de Lormel: Réunion (1869–75)

Jerónimo de los Barrios: Melilla (1595–96)

Marqués de los Tabalosos: Canary Islands (1775–79)

Marqués de los Vélez: Oran (1666–72)

Luis de Loureiro: Tangier (1552–53)

Marquês de Lovradio: Angola (1749–53)

Athanase Bouvet de Lozier: Réunion (1815–17)

Jean-Baptiste Bouvet de Lozier: Mauritius (1750–56); Réunion (1750–52, 1757–63)

Alonso de Lugo: Tenerife

Pedro de Lugo: Tenerife

Bernardo de Macedo: Cape Verde (1907–09)

Ernesto de Macedo: Angola (1975)

Lopes de Macedo: Cape Verde (1876–78)

Marçal de Macedo: Mombasa (1626–29)

Sebastião de Macedo: Mozambique (1604–07)

Diogo de Madeira: Mozambique (1612)

Antonio de Magalhães: Guinea-Bissau (1927–31)

Henrique de Magalhães: Angola (1694–97)

João de Magalhães: Angola (1738–48)

Joaquim de Magalhães: Mozambique (1851–54)

José de Magalhães: Mozambique (1912–13)

Luis de Magalhães: Cacheu (1640–41)

Fernão de Magalhães e Meneses: Cape Verde (1893–94); Mozambique (1894–95)

Duc de Magenta: Algeria (1864–70)

Vicente de Maia e Vasconcelos: Mozambique (1781–82)

Marqués de Malagón: Ceuta (1645–46)

Duc de Malakoff: Algeria (1860–64)

Joseph de Malartic: Mauritius (1792–1800)

Louis de Malavois: Seychelles (1789–92)

Francisco de Maldonaldo: Gran Canaria

Marqués de Malmusi: Spanish Morocco (1925–28, 1931)

Duque de Maqueda: Oran (1616–25)

Édouard de Martimprey: Algeria (1864)

Filipe de Mascarenhas: Mozambique (1633–34)

Francisco de Mascarenhas: Madeira (1665–68); Mozambique (1651–52)

Francisco de Mascarenhas: Mozambique (1714–15)

Manuel de Mascarenhas: Mozambique (1661–64)

Pedro de Mascarenhas: Portuguese Gold Coast (1632–34)

Simão de Mascarenhas: Angola (1623–24)

Vasco de Mascarenhas: Mozambique (1601–04)

Dinís de Mascarenhas de Lencastre: Ceuta

João de Mata Chapuzet: Cape Verde (1822–26)

Joaquim de Matos: Bissau (1822, 1825–27, 1830, 1834)

José Norton de Matos: Angola (1912–15, 1921–24)

Henri de Mauduit: Chad (1949–50); Côte d'Ivoire (1945–46); Mauritania (1948–49)

Charles de Maugras: Niger (1912–13)

Nicolas de Maupin: Mauritius (1729–35)

Diego de Melgarejo: Gran Canaria

Antonio de Melo: Madeira (1698–1701); Mombasa (1696–97)

Antonio de Melo: Mozambique (1730–33)

Antonio de Melo: Mozambique (1837)

Brás de Melo: Cape Verde (1591–95)

Duarte de Melo: Mombasa (1688–93)

Fernão de Melo: São Tomé (1499–1510)

Florencio de Melo: Madeira (1815–19)

Henriques de Melo: Mozambique (1973–74)

João de Melo: Cape Verde (1839–42, 1848–51)

João de Melo: Mozambique (1758)

João de Melo: São Tomé (1517–22)

José de Melo: Cape Verde (1890–93)

José de Melo: São Tomé e Príncipe (1860–62)

Manuel de Melo: Cape Verde (1671–76)

Miguel de Melo: Angola (1797–1802)

Rodrigo de Melo: Madeira (1821–22)

Rui de Melo: Portuguese Gold Coast (1552–55)

Rui Soares de Melo: Mombasa (1598–1606)

Ruis de Melo: Tangier (1471)

Miguel de Melo e Albuquerque: São Tomé (1640–41)

Vicente de Melo e Almada: São Tomé and Príncipe (1880–81)

Diogo de Melo e Alvim: Guinea-Bissau (1953–56)

Álvaro de Melo e Castro: Mombasa (1728–29); Mozambique (1721–23)

Antonio de Melo e Castro: Mozambique (1664–67)

Antonio de Melo e Castro: Mozambique (1786–93)

Caetano de Melo e Castro: Mozambique (1682–86)

Francisco de Melo e Castro: Mozambique (1750–58)

Antonio de Melo e Castro de Mendonça: Mozambique (1809–12)

Jerónimo de Melo Fernando: São Tomé (1623–27)

Fernando de Santiago y Díaz de Mendívil: Western Sahara

Manuel de Mendívil y Elío: Equatorial Guinea

Antonio de Melo e Castro de Mendonça: Mozambique (1809–12)

João de Mendonça: Angola (1594–1602)

Nunho de Mendonça: Tangier (1605–10)

Jorge de Mendonça Pessanha: Ceuta (1527–34)

Luis de Mendoza: Gran Canaria

Antonio de Meneses: Cacheu (1785)

Antonio de Meneses: Mombasa (1648–51)

Antonio de Meneses: Mozambique (1528–31)

Brás Teles de Meneses: Ceuta (1634–36)

Diogo de Meneses: Mozambique (1624–27, 1632–33)

Duarte de Meneses: Tangier (1522–31)

Duarte de Meneses: Tangier (1574–78)

Fernando de Meneses: São Tomé (1593–97)

Fernão de Meneses: Ceuta (1557–62, 1563–64)

Fernão Teles de Meneses: Ceuta (1637)

Francisco Barreto de Meneses: São Tomé (1632)

Francisco Teles de Meneses: São Tomé (1611)

Gonçalo de Meneses: Angola (1691–94)

João de Meneses: Madeira (1634–36)

João de Meneses: Tangier (1531–52)

Jorge de Meneses: Mozambique (1586–89)

Luis de Meneses: Angola (1697–1701)

Pedro de Meneses: Angola (1639–45)

Pedro de Meneses: Ceuta (1550–53)

Rodrigo de Meneses: Angola (1732–38)

João de Meneses Drumont: Cacheu (1819)

Fradique de Menezes: São Tomé and Príncipe (2001–)

Jacques de Menou: Egypt (1800–01)

Marqués de Santa Cruz de Mercenado: Oran (1732–33)

Benoît de Merkel: Tunisia (1900–01)

Diogo de Mesquita: Mozambique (1551–53)

Francisco de Mesquita: Mozambique (1693–94)

Manuel de Mesquita Perestrelo: Portuguese Gold Coast (1562)

Philippe de Mester: Mayotte Department

Pierre-Bernard de Milius: Réunion (1818–21)

Antonio de Mingo: Warri

Antonio de Miranda: Portuguese Gold Coast (1539–41)

Francisco de Miranda: São Tomé and Príncipe (1891–94)

José de Miranda: Ceuta (1818–20, 1824–26)

Juan de Miranda: Gran Canaria; Tenerife

Marqués de Miranda de Auta: Ceuta (1641–44)

Antonio de Miranda de Azevedo: Portuguese Gold Coast (1504)

Camilo de Miranda Rebocho Vaz: Angola (1966–72)

Jacob de Mist: Cape Colony (1803–04)

Barão de Moçâmedes: Angola (1784–90)

Guillem de Moncada: Tripolitania (1511–20)

Gaspar de Mondragón: Melilla (1617–18)

Conde de Monsanto: Tangier (1522)

Marquês de Montalvão: Tangier (1621–24)

Antoine Louis Desmarets de Montchaton: Gorée

Marquis de Montdevergue: Fort-Dauphin

Louis Lecoupé de Montereau: Senegal (1820–21)

João da Sera de Morais: Portuguese Gold Coast (1629)

Carlos de Morais e Almeida: São Tomé and Príncipe (1847)

Francisco de Moura: Cape Verde (1618–22)

Miguel de Moura: São Tomé (1587–91)

Alexandre de Moura e Albuquerque: Madeira (1676–80)

Juan de Mur Aguirre y Argaiz: Canary Islands (1719–22)

Guillaume de Mustellier: Senegal (1710–11)

M. Motais de Narbonne: Seychelles (1786–89)

Ernest de Nattes: Côte d'Ivoire (1957–60)

Pedro de Navarra: Tripolitania (1510)

Marqués de Navarrés: Oran (1567–71)

André de Negreiros: Angola (1661–66)

João de Neves Leão: Bissau (1799)

Pedro de Nhuya: Mozambique (1505–06)

Francisco de Nóbrega Vasconcelos: Cape Verde (1726–28)

Afonso de Noronha: Ceuta (1540–49)

Afonso de Noronha: Ceuta (1602–05); Tangier (1610–14)

Antão de Noronha: Ceuta (1549)

Antonio de Noronha: Angola (1839); Madeira (1822–23)

Fernando de Noronha: Angola (1802–06)

Fernando de Noronha: São Tomé (1609)

Fernando de Noronha: São Tomé and Príncipe (1836–37)

João de Noronha: Angola (1713–17)

João de Noronha: Ceuta (1481–87)

João de Noronha: Ceuta (1522–24)

José de Noronha: Cape Verde (1845–47)

Lourenço de Noronha: Mozambique (1739–43)

Nunho de Noronha: Ceuta (1529–39)

Paulo de Noronha: São Tomé (1669–71)

Paulo Dias de Novais: Angola (1575–89)

De Nufion: Allada

Denis de Nyon: Mauritius (1722–23)

José de Oca: Fernando Po

Domingo de Ochoa: Melilla (1618–19)

Conde de Odemira: Ceuta (1450–60)

Antonio Ros de Olano: Spanish Morocco (1847–51)

Conde de Oliveira: Tangier (1486)

Henrique de Oliveira: São Tomé and Príncipe (1910)

João de Oliveira: Cacheu (1685–86)

José de Oliveira: Mozambique (1938–40)

Domingos de Oliveira Daun: Angola (1836)

Conde de Oliveto: Oran (1509–09)

Antonio de Oro Pulido: Western Sahara

Marqués de Osera: Oran (1683–85)

Miguel de Otazo: Canary Islands (1701–05)

Antonio de Otero y Santallana: Canary Islands (1791–99)

Pedro de Padilla: Oran (1585–89)

Francisco de Paiva: São Tomé (1546–54)

João de Paiva: São Tomé (1485–90)

Juan de Palafox y Centurión: Ceuta (1745–46)

Marqués de Santa Cruz de Paniagua: Oran (1685–87)

Alexandre Armény de Paradis: Gorée

Francisco de Paula Cid: Cape Verde (1902–03); São Tomé and Príncipe (1903–07)

Armenteros de Paz: Tenerife

Visconde de Pedralva: Angola (1920–21)

Gabriel de Penalosa y Estrada: Melilla (1637–48)

Achille de Penfentenio de Cheffontaines: Réunion (1826–30)

Melchor de Pereda: Tenerife

Pedro Moreno y Pérez de Oteyro: Canary Islands (1764)

José de Perlasca: Canary Islands (1799–1803)

Marie-Auguste Deville de Perrière: Senegal (1881)

Baron Jacob De Petersen: Dutch Gold Coast (1741–47)

Visconde de Pinheiro: Angola (1853–54)

Charles Assier de Pompignan: Benin [ii] (1943–46); Gabon (1935–36, 1942–43)

Juan de Pontons y Mujica: Ceuta (1816–18)

Conde de Portalegre: Ceuta (1518–19)

Diego de Portugal: Ceuta (1677–78); Oran (1672–75)

Manuel de Portugal e Castro: Madeira (1823–27)

Alphonse de Pouzois: Côte d'Ivoire (1935)

Miguel de Prado: Equatorial Guinea

Conde de Puertolano: Canary Islands (1666–71)

De Barolet de Puligny: Réunion (1850–51)

Conde de Puñonrostro: Ceuta (1679–81)

Guillaume Charmasson de Puy-Laval: Senegal (1839–41)

Bernardin de Quimper: Réunion (1680–86)

Jean-Baptiste Quéau de Quincy: Seychelles (1794–1811)

Jerónimo de Quiñones: Canary Islands (1661–65)

Pierre de Rastel de Rocheblaye: Gorée

Arnaldo de Rebelo: Cape Verde (1900–02)

Nicolas de Regnac des Brulys: Réunion (1806–09)

Louis Le Gardeur de Repentigny: Senegal (1784–86)

Jayme de Requesens: Tripolitania (1510–11)

Carlos Tovar de Revilla: Fernando Po

Pierre de Richebourg: Senegal (1711–13)

M. de Richemont: Senegal (1668–73)

Pierre de Rivau: Fort-Dauphin

Juan de Rivera y Zambrana: Canary Islands (1629–34)

Miguel Primo de Rivera y Orbaneja: Spanish Morocco (1924–25)

Pierre de Rastel de Rocheblaye: Gorée

Izaak De Roever: Dutch Gold Coast (1804–05)

Rui Díaz de Rojas: Oran (1509–10)

M. Saint-Amant de Romainville: Senegal (1778–81)

Gualberto de Rosario: Cape Verde (2000–01)

Duc de Rovigo: Algeria (1831–33)

Angelo De Rubeis: Italian Somali land (1936)

Antonio de Sá: Portuguese Gold Coast (1570)

Caetano de Sá: Mozambique (1746–50)

Cristóvão de Sá; São Tomé and Príncipe (1782–88)

José de Sá: Madeira (1759–67)

Pantaleão de Sá: Mozambique (1560–64)

Sebastião de Sá: Mozambique (1557–60)

Serafim de Sá: Cape Verde (1716–20)

Salvador de Sá e Benavides: Angola (1648–51)

Pantaleão de Sá e Melo: Madeira (1694–98)

Jerónimo de Saavedra Acevedo: Canary Islands (1983–87, 1991–93)

Miguel Fernández de Saavedra: Melilla (1767–72)

Jean-François de Saint-Alary: Togo (1941–42)

Charles-Max Masson de Saint-Félix: Central African Republic (1936–39); Chad (1936–38); Congo (1931–32)

Thomas Renault de Saint-Germain: Senegal (1831–33)

Paul de Saint-Mart: Madagascar (1944–46)

Pierre de Saint-Mart: Central African Republic (1939–42); Madagascar (1943–44)

Didier de Saint Martin: Mauritius (1740, 1746–47); Réunion (1743–45, 1747–48)

Joseph Murinay de Saint-Maurice: Réunion (1779–81)

Nicolas Després de Saint-Robert: Senegal (1720–23, 1725–26)

Jean Brunteau de Sainte-Suzanne: Réunion (1809–10)

Eugenio de Salazar: Tenerife

Federico de Salazar y Nieto: Western Sahara

Domingo de Salcedo: Ceuta (1783–84)

Antonio de Saldanha: Mozambique (1509–12)

Fernão de Saldanha: Madeira (1625–26)

João de Saldanha e Albuquerque: Madeira (1672–76)

Manuel de Saldanha e Albuquerque: Madeira (1754–57)

Pedro de Saldanha e Albuquerque: Mozambique (1759–63, 1782)

Antonio de Sampaio: Cape Verde (1879–81)

Manuel de Sampaio: Mozambique (1657–61)

Duque de San Lúcar: Oran (1660–66)

Marqués de San Román: Oran (1652–60)

Francisco Rodríguez de Sanabria: Melilla (1620–22)

Gaspard de Sanguesse: Tripolitania (1530–33)

Conde de Santa Clara: Ceuta (1794–95)

Visconde de Santa Clara de Avellido: Oran (1628–32)

Barão de Santa Comba Dão: Angola (1829–34)

Marqués de Santa Cruz: Ceuta (1731–38)

Marqués de Santa Cruz de Mercenado: Oran (1732–33)

Marqués de Santa Cruz de Paniagua: Oran (1685–87)

João de Santa Maria: Cape Verde (1741–52)

Ramón de Santallana: Western Sahara

Jean de Santi: Benin [ii] (1934–36); Mali (1938–40)

Fernando de Santiago y Díaz de Mendívil: Western Sahara

Francisco de São Simão: Cape Verde (1782–83)

Conde de Sarzedas: Tangier (1637–43)

Francisco de Seixas e Cabreira: Mombasa (1635–39, 1651–53)

Marqués de Sentar: Ceuta (1665–72)

Diogo de Sepúlveda: Mozambique (1521–25)

João de Sepúlveda: Mozambique (1541–48)

Diogo Lopes de Sequeira: Portuguese Gold Coast (1504–05)

Francisco de Sequeira: Cape Verde (1611–14)

João de Sequeira: Mozambique (1905–06)

Simão de Silveira: Mozambique (1577)

Carlo De Simone: Italian Somali land (1940–41)

Christopher de Solefertan: Tripolitania (1542–51)

Lope de Sosa y Mesa: Gran Canaria

Gustavo de Sostoa y Sthamer: Equatorial Guinea

Jerónimo de Sotomayor: Tenerife

José de Sotomayor: Ceuta (1791–92)

Luis de Sotomayor: Melilla (1625–32, 1649)

Fernando Álvarez de Sotomayor y Flórez: Spanish Morocco (1907–08)

François de Souillac: Mauritius (1779–87); Réunion (1776–79); Seychelles (1783–86)

Afonso de Sousa: São Tomé and Príncipe (1948–50, 1953)

Antonio de Sousa: Angola (1851–53)

Carlos de Sousa: Bissau (1847–48)

Cristóvão de Sousa: Madeira (1600–03)

Cristóvão de Sousa: São Tomé (1560–64)

Diogo de Sousa: Mozambique (1553–57)

Fernão de Sousa: Angola (1624–30)

Francisco de Sousa: Madeira (1628–34)

João de Sousa: Angola (1621–23); Cacheu (1614–15)

Pedro de Sousa: Mozambique (1590–95)

Francisco de Sousa Coutinho: Angola (1764–72)

Lopo de Sousa Coutinho: Portuguese Gold Coast (1541, 1548–50)

José de Sousa e Faroo: São Tomé and Príncipe (1915)

Álvaro de Sousa e Macedo: Madeira (1830–34)

Antonio de Sousa e Meneses: Cape Verde (1777–81)

Jorge de Sousa e Meneses: Madeira (1718–24)

Manuel de Sousa e Meneses: Cape Verde (1757–61)

Pires de Sousa e Meneses: Angola (1676–80); Madeira (1669–72)

Luis de Sousa e Vasconcelos e Funchal: Mozambique (1947–48)

Bento de Sousa Lima: São Tomé (1686–89)

Bartolomeu de Sousa Tigre: Cape Verde (1764–66)

M. de Soussy: Senegal (1649–50)

Filipe de Souto-Maior: Bissau (1763)

Francisco de Souto-Maior: Angola (1645–46)

Francisco de Souto-Maior: Mozambique (1715–19)

Francisco de Souto-Maior: Portuguese Gold Coast (1624–25)

Lourenço de Souto-Maior: Mozambique (1634–39)

André Chalvet de Souville: Réunion (1781–85)

Anna de Souza Nzina: Ndongo

Antonio de Spínola: Guinea-Bissau (1968–73)

Conde de Tarouca: Tangier (1486–89, 1501–08)

Conde de Tarouca: Tangier (1614–17)

Álvaro de Távora: Madeira (1751–54)

Álvaro de Távora: Mozambique (1648–51)

Cristóvão de Távora: Mozambique (1515–18)

Fernão de Távora: Mozambique (1548–51)

Francisco de Távora: Angola (1669–76)

Francisco de Távora: Cacheu (1622)

João de Távora: Cacheu (1748–51)

Lourenço de Távora: São Tomé (1628–50)

Lourenço de Távora: Tangier (1564–66)

Conde de Teba: Oran (1604–07)

Antonio de Tejada: Melilla (1571–95)

Marqués de Tenorio: Ceuta (1653–61)

Charles de Ternay: Mauritius (1772–76)

Juan de Toledo; Canary Islands (1665–66)

Diego de Toledo y Guzmán: Oran (1607–08)

Íñigo de Toledo y Osorio: Oran (1675–78)

Marqués de Torcifal: Ceuta (1646–53)

Antonio de Torres: Gran Canaria

Conde de Torres Vedras: Ceuta (1672–77)

Sancho de Tovar: Mozambique (1501–05, 1515, 1518–21)

Louis de Trentinian: Mali (1895–99)

Blas de Trincheria: Melilla (1704–07)

José de Urbanski: São Tomé and Príncipe (1838–39)

Juan de Urbina: Canary Islands (1747–64)

Alonso de Urrea: Melilla (1556–59)

José de Urrutia y las Casas: Ceuta (1792–94)

Cesare De Val Cismon: Italian Somaliland (1923–28)

Marqués de Valdecañas: Ceuta (1695–98); Oran (1707–08)

Jerónimo de Valderrama y Tovar: Gran Canaria

Lope de Valenzuela: Gran Canaria

Marqués de Valhermoso: Canary Islands (1723–35)

Fray Gaspar de Valier: Tripolitania (1551)

Marqués de Valparaíso: Ceuta (1692–95)

Antonio de Vasconcelos: Angola (1758–64)

Bartolomeu de Vasconcelos: Madeira (1651–55)

Caetano de Vasconcelos: Cape Verde (1826–30)

Diogo de Vasconcelos: Mozambique (1639–40)

Gomes da Silva de Vasconcelos: Ceuta (1519–21, 1525–29)

João de Vasconcelos: Cape Verde (1881–86)

Luis de Vasconcelos: Angola (1617–21)

Mateus de Vasconcelos: Mombasa (1593–96)

José de Vasconcelos e Almeida: Mozambique (1780–81)

Luis de Vasconcelos e Sá: Guinea-Bissau (1891–95)

João Rodrigues de Vasconcelos Ribeiro: Ceuta (1464–79)

Rui Mendes de Vasconcelos Ribeiro: Ceuta (1479–81)

Henri Habet de Vauboulon: Réunion (1689–90)

Abraham De Veer: Dutch Gold Coast (1810–16)

Jacobus De Veer: Dutch Gold Coast (1790–94)

Marqués de Velada: Oran (1625–28)

Jerónimo de Velasco: Canary Islands (1677–81)

Juan Jerónimo Ungo de Velasco: Melilla (1711–14)

Francisco de Velasco y Tovar: Ceuta (1681–89)

Luis de Velázquez y Angulo: Melilla (1656–69)

Abraham Van De Velde: Mauritius (1703–10)

Pedro de Vera: Gran Canaria

François Blanchot de Verly: Senegal (1786–90, 1792–1801, 1802–07)

Duarte, Conde de Viana: Ceuta (1430–34, 1437–38)

Marqués de Viana: Oran (1643–47)

Pedro, Conde de Viana: Ceuta (1415–30, 1434–37)

Francisco de Vide: São Tomé and Príncipe (1799)

Luis de Vigil: Gran Canaria

Francisco de Vila Nova: São Tomé (1592–93)

Conde de Vila Real: Ceuta (1562–63)

Conde de Vila Real: Ceuta (1616–22)

Duque de Vila Real: Ceuta (1567–74, 1577–78)

Fernão, Conde de Vila Real: Ceuta (1438–45)

Pedro, Conde de Vila Real: Ceuta (1461–64)

Marqués de Villadarias: Ceuta (1698–1702); Oran (1733)

Jean-Baptiste de Villers: Réunion (1701–09)

Jacob de Villiers: South Africa (1930–31)

John, Baron de Villiers: South Africa (1912, 1914)

Charles Le Myre de Villiers: Madagascar (1886–88, 1894–95)

Jan de Visser: Hollandia

Marqués de Warmarch: Ceuta (1760–63)

Johannes Van De Wath: Namibia (1968–71)

Christiaan De Wet: Orange Free State (1902)

Jannie De Wet: Namibia (1970–90)

Nicolaas De Wet: South Africa (1943–45)

Francis de Winton: Congo (Zaire) (1884–87); Kenya (1890–91)

Gabriel de Zúñiga: Oran (1594–96)

Antonio de Zúñiga y la Cerda: Melilla (1692–97)

Agustín de Zurbarán: Gran Canaria

Jean-Jacques Debacq: Mayotte Department

Joseph Debat: Fort James; Senegambia Colony

Alphonse Massemba-Débat: Congo (1963–68)

Debbe Haile Maryan: Eritrea

Idriss Déby: Chad (1990–)

Almeida d'Eça: Cape Verde (1974–75)

João d'Eça: Madeira (1603–09)

Jose d'Eça: Cape Verde (1795–96)

Luis Antonio da Cunha d'Eça: Cape Verde (1752–57)

Charles Décaen: Mauritius (1803–10)

Eugène Décazes: Benin [ii] (1903–04); Central African Republic (1894)

Decius Aciniancius Albinus: Africa Proconsularis (430–431)

Dedele: Whydah

Dedem Almaz: Axum

Defter: Egypt (1585–87)

Defterdar: Egypt (1661–64)

Defterdar: Egypt (1675–76)

Degnajan: Axum

Dehwe Mapunzagutu: Mwene Mutapa Empire

Sidi Ould Deid: Trarza

Berthold von Deimling: Namibia (1906–07)

Adolphe Deitte: Central African Republic (1930–35); Chad (1928–29, 1934–35); Gabon (1926–27, 1928–29); Mauritania (1934)

Dejaz Ma'red Gwalo: Gojjam

Dejaz Saude: Gojjam

Dejaz Walad Rafael: Gojjam

Ras Dejazmatch Tafari: Ethiopia (1916–74)

Deka: Allada

Del Nead: Axum

Juan del Campo: Tenerife

Alonso del Corral: Gran Canaria

Felipe del Espinar: Melilla (1861–62)

Juan Pérez del Hacho y Oliván: Melilla (1823–24)

Bernardo del Nero: Gran Canaria

Conde del Palmar: Canary Islands (1697–1701)

Duque del Parque: Canary Islands (1810)

Fernando del Piño Villamil: Spanish Morocco (1876–77)

Antonio del Rey y Caballero: Spanish Morocco (1868)

Victor Díaz del Río: Equatorial Guinea

Juan Andrés del Thoso: Melilla (1730–32)

Manuel del Villar: Melilla (1854–56, 1858–60)

Marqués del Viso: Oran (1639–43)

Ali Delatumi: Bornu Empire (1846)

Robert Delavignette: Cameroun (1946–47)

Carlos Sáenz Delcourt: Spanish Morocco (1872–73)

José González Deleito: Western Sahara

Rafael Delgado y Moreno: Melilla (1835–38)

Deli: Egypt (1635–37)

Deli Ahmad: Algiers (1588–89)

Louis Hubert-Delisle: Réunion (1852–58)

Paul Delouvrier: Algeria (1958–60)

Léonce Delpech: Togo (1941)

Petrus Jacobus Delport: Swellendam

Albert Ardin d'Elteil: Cotonou

Pierre Delteil: Central African Republic (1949–50)

Delwa Kassire Koumakoye: Chad (1993–95)

Paul Demange: Réunion (1947–50)

Demawedem: Axum

Demba: Segu

Abdullahi Ba Demba: Futa Jallon
Dauda Demba: Kayor
Tié-Yaasin Demba: Baol
Umaru Ba Demba: Futa Jallon
Dembaane Yerim: Walo (1331–36)
Mamadou Dembelé: Mali (1986–88)
Tonmassa Dembele: Segu
Demetrios: Pentapolis
Demetros: Ethiopia (1799–1801)
Demophanes: Pentapolis
Den: Egypt (1st Dynasty)
Daniel Van Den Henghel: Cape Colony (1737–39)
Gatluak Deng: Southern Sudan
Sahla Dengel: Ethiopia (1832–40, 1841–50, 1851–55)
Sarsa Dengel: Ethiopia (1563–97)
Za Dengel: Ethiopia (1603–04)
Lebna Dengel Dawit II: Ethiopia (1508–40)
Dengella Koli I: Futa Jallon
Dengella Koli II: Futa Jallon
Dixon Denham: Sierra Leone (1828)
Edward Denham: Gambia (1928–30); Mauritius (1921)
Deni Ba Bo: Kaarta
Denibabo: Kaarta
Auguste Denis: Côte d'Ivoire (1958–59)
George Denton: Gambia (1900–11); Lagos (1889–90)
Joseph d'Entrecasteaux: Mauritius (1787–89)
Jules Van Der Bossche: Dutch Gold Coast (1857)
Jacobus Van Der Breggen Paauw: Dutch Gold Coast (1826–28)
Anthony Van Der Eb: Dutch Gold Coast (1837–38, 1840–46, 1847–52)
Lieven Van Burgen Van Der Grijp: Dutch Gold Coast (1787–90, 1794–95)
Anton Van Der Meden: Hollandia
Nikolaas Van Der Nood De Gieterre: Dutch Gold Coast (1754–55)
Jacobus Van Der Puye: Dutch Gold Coast (1780)
Symon Van Der Stel: Cape Colony (1679–99)
Willem Van Der Stel: Cape Colony (1699–1707)
Barend Van Der Walt: Namibia (1971–77)
Jacob Van Der Well: Dutch Gold Coast (1645–50)
Énoch Dérant Lakoué: Central African Republic (1993)
Salih Deret: Wadai
Charles Dériaud: Congo (1958–59)
Comte d'Erlon: Algeria (1834–35)
Abdallah Derow Isaq: Somalia
Vincent Derussat: Nossi-Bé
W.G.F. Derx: Dutch Gold Coast (1846–47, 1856–57)
Jean-Georges le Baillif des Mesnager: Gorée
Nicolas de Regnac des Brulys: Réunion (1806–09)

Charles Martin des Pallières: Côte d'Ivoire (1851–53)
Jean des Perriers: Fort-Dauphin
Jean Desailles: Côte d'Ivoire (1890–92)
Conde de Desallois: Melilla (1715–16)
Jean Desanti: Benin [ii] (1934–36); Mali (1938–40)
Louis Desaulses de Freycinet: Réunion (1821–26)
Gustave Borgnis-Desbordes: Mali (1880–83)
François Desbordes de Charanville: Réunion (1709–10)
Gabriel Descemet: Burkina Faso (1932); Mali (1926, 1928–29, 1931); Mauritania (1931–34)
Hubert Deschamps: Côte d'Ivoire (1941–42); Djibouti (1938–40); Senegal (1942–43)
Étienne Deschanel: Gabon (1848–49)
Antoine Desforges-Boucher: Mauritius (1723–25); Réunion (1723–25)
Antoine Marc Desforges-Boucher: Mauritius (1759–67); Réunion (1749, 1757)
René Desjardins: Mali (1933)
Venancio Deslandes: Angola (1961–62)
Antoine Louis Desmarets de Montchaton: Gorée
Jacques Desnouys: Côte d'Ivoire (1863–64)
Eugène Desperles: Gabon (1848)
Nicolas Després de Saint-Robert: Senegal (1720–23, 1725–26)
François Desroches: Mauritius (1769–72)
Desse Koro: Kaarta
Georges Destenave: Burkina Faso (1895–98); Chad (1900–01)
Dethialaw: Kayor
Detye Fu-N'Diogu: Kayor
Detye Maram N'Galgu: Kayor
Sebastien Devaulx: Senegal (1733–38)
Colville Deverell: Mauritius (1959–62)
Marie-Auguste Deville de Perrière: Senegal (1881)
Antoine Devoisins: Gabon (1843–44)
Jacques Dewatre: Réunion (1991–92)
Dexter: Africa Proconsularis (395)
Bukar D'Gjiama: Mandara
Abu'dh Dhahab: Egypt (1773–75)
Ahmad adh-Dhahabi: Morocco (1727–29)
Robert d'Hallebast: Tangier (1955–56)
Francis Dhanis: Congo (Zaire) (1896–1900)
Comte d'Hautpoul: Algeria (1850–51)
Pierre d'Héguerty: Réunion (1739–43)
Barnabas Sibusiso Dhlamini: Swaziland (1996–2003)
Bhekimpi Dhlamini: Swaziland (1983–85)
Prince Jameson Mbilini Dhlamini: Swaziland (1993–96)
Makhosini Dhlamini: Swaziland (1967–76)

Mandabala Fred Dhlamini: Swaziland (1979–83)
Maphevu Dhlamini: Swaziland (1976–79)
Obed Dhlamini: Swaziland (1989–93)
Sotsha Ernest Dhlamini: Swaziland (1985–89)
Themba Dhlamini: Swaziland (2003–)
Dhuka ar-Rumi: Egypt (915–919)
Di Biya: Biu
Di Forma: Biu
Di Jigi Bilali: Kangaba
Nobile Giacomo Di Martino: Cyrenaica; Eritrea; Italian Somaliland (1910–16)
Giuseppe Volpi Di Misurata: Tripolitania (1921–25)
Di Rawa: Biu
Alessandro Di San Marzano: Massawa
Mario Di Stefani: Italian Somaliland (1958–60)
Kokoroko Dia: Gwiriko
Mamadou Dia: Mali Federation (1959–60); Senegal (1958–62)
Diaba Lompo: Gurma
Bernardin Mungul Diaka: Congo (Zaire) (1991)
Yoro Diakité: Mali (1968–69)
Cellou Diallo: Guinea (2004–)
Afena Diamono: Bono
Ali Dian: Gwiriko
Diara Traoré: Guinea (1984)
Diare: Warri
Diare Kante: Ghana Empire
Kambine Diaresso: Ghana Empire
Seydou Diarra: Côte d'Ivoire (2000, 2003–)
Cristóvão Dias: Angola (1823)
Paulo Dias de Novais: Angola (1575–89)
Jacinto Díaz Capilla: Melilla (1814–21)
Rui Diaz de Rojas: Oran (1509–10)
Victor Díaz del Río: Equatorial Guinea
Dunama Dibbelemi: Bornu Empire (1256–59); Kane, (1221–56)
Dibolayang: Batwanaland
Thomas A. Dickson: Swaziland (1928–35)
Pierre Didelot: Senegal (1921–25)
Henri Didier: Algeria (1870)
Labi Diebo: Gurma
Nicolaas Diederichs: South Africa (1975–78)
Alfred Diefenbacher: Réunion (1963–66)
Domingo de Dieguez: Melilla (1612–17)
Herr Diehl: Kamerun (1900)
Tié-Yaasin Dieng: Baol
Roelof Dieodati: Mauritius (1692–1703)
Yves Digo: Gabon (1952–58); Togo (1951–52)
Digope: Bamaleteland
Dihirahi: Zaria (ca. 1475)
Muhammadu Dikko: Katsina (1906–44)

Mamman Diko: Agaie
Dileita Muhammad Dileita: Djibouti (2001–)
Nathaniel Dillinger: Hollandia
Dimani: Dagomba
Aphilas Bisi-Dimele: Axum
al-Mansur Al'a ad-Din: Egypt (1368–80)
Fahr ad-Din: Mogadishu
Fakhr ad-Din: Adal [ii]
Gamal ad-Din: Wadai
Haqq ad-Din I: Ifat
Haqq ad-Din II: Ifat
Jamal ad-Din I: Ifat
Jamal ad-Din II: Adal [ii]
Khair ad-Din: Algiers (1518–20, 1525–46); Tripolitania (1534–35)
Nur ad-Din: Egypt (1257–59)
Sa'id ad-Din: Egypt (1756–57)
Salah ad-Din: Egypt (1169–93)
Shahah ad-Din: Adal [ii]
Shams ad-Din: Adal [ii]
Sabr ad-Din I: Ifat
Sabr ad-Din II: Adal [ii]
Sa'd ad-Din Ahmad: Ifat
al-Adil ad-Din Ketbugha: Egypt (1294–96)
Al'a ad-Din Kujuk: Egypt (1341–42)
al-Mansur ad-Din Muhammad: Egypt (1361–63)
Nasir ad-Din Muhammad: Egypt (1198–1200)
Ala ad-Din Pasha Siddiq: Sudan (1883)
Abu'l Muhagir Dinar: Arab North Africa
Ali Dinar ibn Zakariyya: Darfur
Dingaan: Zululand
Dingana: Zululand
Si Mustafa Dingizli: Tunisia (1922–26)
Ahmad Dini: Djibouti (1977)
Tesfaye Dinka: Ethiopia (1991)
Dinuzulu: Zululand
Solomon Dinuzulu: Zululand
Dinzaki: Zaria (ca. 1150)
Diogo I: Kongo
Luisa Diogo: Mozambique (2004–)
Diogore: Yatenga
Marcus Aurelius Papirius Dionysius: Egypt (193)
Hélie Dioré: Réunion (1725–27)
Hélie Dioré: Réunion (1785–88)
Hamani Diori: Niger (1958–74)
Diori Watara: Gwiriko
Dioscorus: Egypt (535)
Abdou Diouf: Senegal (1970–80, 1981–2000)
Mallam Dipchairina: Nigeria (1966)
Dira: Bamaleteland
Dira Wala: Biu
Henri Dirat: Central African Republic (1920–21)
Dirgham: Egypt (1163–64)
Diringa Mori: Kaarta
Disa: Fika
Disa Siri: Fika
Duc d'Isly: Algeria (1841–45)

Charles Disnematin-Dorat: Porto-Novo
Nawej Ditend: Lunda
Ditend Yavu: Lunda
Dithapo I: Batwanaland
Diwitdar: Egypt (1768)
William Dixon: Saint Helena (1917–19)
Djedkare Izezi: Egypt (5th Dynasty)
Djedneferre Dudimose: Egypt (13th Dynasty)
Setpenanhur Irmaerne Djeho: Egypt (30th Dynasty)
Sekhemre Smentowe Djehuty: Egypt (15th Dynasty)
Djer: Egypt (1st Dynasty)
Amenhotep I Djeserkare: Egypt (18th Dynasty)
Horemheb Djeserkheprure: Egypt (18th Dynasty)
Djet: Egypt (1st Dynasty)
Djibo Bakari: Niger (1957–58)
Djidingar Done Ngardoum: Chad (1982)
Djidomingba: Allada
Djihento: Allada
Koibla Djimasta: Chad (1995–97)
Mar Fai Kolli-Djimbo: Songhai (1434–42)
Djin: Ethiopia (1297–98)
Sa'id Muhammad Djohar: Comoros (1989–96)
Djoser: Egypt (3rd Dynasty)
Abbas Djoussouf: Comoros (1998–99)
Do-Aklim: Dahomey
Francisco Ferreira do Amaral: Angola (1882–86); São Tomé and Príncipe (1879)
José do Amaral: Angola (1854–60, 1869–70); Mozambique (1870–73)
Francisco do Amaral Cardoso: Mozambique (1805–07)
Pedro do Amorim: Angola (1916–17); Mozambique (1918–19)
Maria do Carmo Silveira: São Tomé and Príncipe (2005–)
Gabriel do Castro: São Tomé and Príncipe (1802–05)
José do Castro: São Tomé (1702–09)
José do Crato: Bissau (1871); Cacheu (1844–46)
Baltasar do Lago: Mozambique (1765–79)
João do Nascimento: Madeira (1747–51)
Lopo do Nascimento: Angola (1975–78)
Cristóvão do Rego: São Tomé (1656–57)
Jaime do Rego: São Tomé and Príncipe (1910, 1911)
Domingos do Vale: Mozambique (1847–51)
Eusebio Castella do Vale: Guinea-Bissau (1887)
Docemo: Lagos (1853–85)
Ibrahim Dodo Musa: Abuja
Dodon Gwari: Abuja

Samuel Doe: Liberia (1980–90)
Hendrik Doedens: Dutch Gold Coast (1650)
Dogo: Biu
Dogon Sarki: Abuja
Dogon Sharki: Yauri
Doguma: Daura
Richard Doherty: Sierra Leone (1837–40)
Ada Doki: Daura
Dokua: Akim
Dola: Warri
Publius Cornelius Dolabella: Africa [i] (23–24)
Albert Dolisie: Congo (1894–99); Gabon (1894–99)
Raffaele Borea Ricci D'Olmo: Tripolitania (1911)
Anicet Georges Dologuélé: Central African Republic (1999–2001)
Enrique Serrano Dolz: Spanish Morocco (1870–72)
Yama Dombo: Songhai (957–969)
Dom Domingo: Warri
Antonio Domínguez de Durán: Melilla (1687–88)
Élisabeth Domitienne: Central African Republic (1975–76)
Domitius Honoratus: Egypt (165–166)
Gi-gla No-Don Gbé-non Mau: Allada
Kengo wa Dondo: Congo (Zaire) (1982–86, 1988–90)
Léon Kengo wa Dondo: Congo (Zaire) (1994–97)
Djidingar Done Ngardoum: Chad (1982)
Theophilus Dönges: South Africa (1966, 1967)
Rufane Donkin: Cape Colony (1820–21)
Charles Disnematin-Dorat: Porto-Novo
Louis Doret: Réunion (1851–52)
Henri Esse d'Orgeret: Réunion (1674–78)
Dori: Gojjam
Maurice Dorman: Sierra Leone (1956–62)
Camille d'Ornano: Djibouti (1976–77)
Soba Dan Doro: Gobir
Uban Doro: Gobir
Christian Dorph: Danish Gold Coast (1743–44)
Zeferino dos Prazeres: Príncipe (ii)
Antonio dos Santos: Cape Verde (1971–74)
Augusto dos Santos: Guinea-Bissau
Delfim dos Santos: Cacheu (1838)
Fernando dos Santos: Angola (2002–)
José Eduardo dos Santos: Angola (1979–)
Libanio dos Santos: Bissau (1852)
Daniel Lima dos Santos Daio: São Tomé and Príncipe (1991–92)
Dosumu: Lagos (1853–85)
Elie Doté: Central African Republic (2005–)

Dothapo II: Batwanaland
Muhammad Doud Mourrah: Wadai
Ángel Serafín Seriche Dougan: Equatorial Guinea
Robert Dougan: Sierra Leone (1854, 1855)
Doulougou: Wagadugu
Daniel Doustin: Chad (1957–59)
Dowi: Potiskum
Dragut: Tripolitania (1553–65)
Dramani: Gwiriko
Boston Drayton: Maryland
Pacatus Drepanius: Africa Proconsularis (390)
Francis Drew: Eritrea
Jean-Baptiste Drouillard: Réunion (1686–89)
Luigi Druetti: Tripolitania (1914–15)
Edward Drummond-Hay: Saint Helena (1856–63)
João de Meneses Drumont: Cacheu (1819)
Dsahai Sagad: Ethiopia (1711–16)
G.C. du Boulay: Ghana (1930, 1931)
Charles du Bouzet: Algeria (1870–71)
Albert du Carré: Chad (1918–20)
Jean-Baptiste Vigoureux du Plessis: Réunion (1792–94)
Wenzel du Plessis: Namibia (1963–68)
Gerhardus du Toit: Orange Free State (1872–73)
Kwaka Dua I: Ashanti
Kwaka Dua II: Ashanti
Kwaka Dua III: Ashanti
Teófilo Duarte: Cape Verde (1918–19)
Albert Dubarry: Djibouti (1903, 1904)
Julien Dubellay: Senegal (1723–25)
Henri Dubief: Algeria (1925)
André Dubois: French Morocco
Nicolas Dubois: Hollandia
Édouard Dubosc-Taret: Congo (1908, 1910–11)
Léandre Berlin-Duchâteau: Senegal (1847, 1848)
Djedneferre Dudimose: Egypt (13th Dynasty)
Francisco Dueñas: Fernando Po
Dugu: Kanem
Dugum Akuya: Bedde
Dugum Bugia: Bedde
Duhaga I Cwa Mujwiga: Bunyoro
Duhaga II Bisereko: Bunyoro
Otto Duim: Dutch Gold Coast (1795–96)
Dukagin: Egypt (1553–56)
Dulano Seezo: Batwanaland
Ernesto Dulio: Italian Somaliland (1897, 1898–1905)
Duma: Gobir
John Dumaresq: Lagos (1875–78)
Charles Dumas: Mauritania (1938)
Jean Dumas: Mauritius (1767–68)
Pierre-Benoît Dumas: Mauritius (1727–29); Réunion (1727–35)
Augustin Dumont: Gabon (1879–80)
Anne-Guilin Dumontêt: Senegal (1782–84)

Dun-Nun I: Timbuktu (1679, 1681, 1694)
Duna: Bedde
Dunama: Lafia
Dunama I ibn Hume: Kanem
Dunama III: Bornu Empire (1433–35)
Ahmad Dunama IV: Bornu Empire (1451–55)
Dunama V Ngumaramma: Bornu Empire (1546–63)
Dunama VI: Bornu Empire (1704–23)
Dunama VII Ghana: Bornu Empire (1752–55)
Dunama Dibbelemi: Bornu Empire (1256–59); Kanem (1221–56)
Dunama Lafiami: Bornu Empire (1808–10, 1814–17)
David Dunbar: Saint Helena (1743–47)
Changamire Dunbo: Rozwi
Andrew Duncan: Rhodesia (1893–94)
Daniel Kablan Duncan: Côte d'Ivoire (1993–99)
Patrick Duncan: South Africa (1937–43)
Charles Dundas: Uganda (1940–44)
Francis Dundas: Cape Colony (1798–99, 1801–03)
Fernando Van Dunem: Angola (1991–92, 1996–2002)
Dungari: Potiskum
Amara Dunkas: Funj Sultanate
Justin Dupérier: Nossi-Bé
Georges Dupoizat: Tunisia (1954)
Clifford Dupont: Zimbabwe (1965–76)
Christian Dupont: Djibouti (1942)
Alfred Lémery-Dupont: Réunion (1735–39)
Pierre Duprat: Réunion (1913–19)
Marc Dupré: Réunion (1865–69)
Guy Dupuis: Mayotte Department
Thomas Dupuis: Nossi-Bé
José Duque: Guinea-Bissau (1914–15, 1918–19)
Antonio Domínguez de Durán: Melilla (1687–88)
Jean-Pierre Durand: Sainte Marie de Madagascar
Oswald Durand: Côte d'Ivoire (1947–48); Mauritania (1936–38); Senegal (1946–47)
Benjamin D'Urban: Cape Colony (1834–38)
Abu Za'id Umar Durda: Libya
Durdur: Wadai
Baron Durieu: Algeria (1870)
Duro: Songhai (1255–75)
Sheger ad-Durr: Egypt (1249–50)
Dutsi: Yauri
John Dutton: Saint Helena (1659–61)
Étienne Mengin Duval d'Ailly: Réunion (1830–32)
Dwambera: Bono
Majan Dyabe Sisse: Ghana Empire
N'dyak Kumba Sam Dyakekh: Walo (1336–43)
al-Buri Dyakher: Dyolof

Dyakhere: Kayor
Sumayla Ndewura Dyakpa: Gonja
Dyakpa Lanta: Gonja
Majan Dyallo: Masina
Fara Penda Langan Dyam: Walo (1552–56)
Mari Dyara: Segu
Ngolo Dyara: Segu
Mali Kumba Dyaring: Baol
Gireun Buri Dyelen: Dyolof
Birayma Dyeme-Kumba: Dyolof
Fara Penda Dyeng: Walo (1519–31)
Birayamb Ma-Dyigen: Dyolof
Joseph Van Dyke: Lydenburg
Khuredya Kumba Dyodyo: Kayor
Ma-Dyodyo: Kayor
Fara Koy Dyon: Walo (1542–49)
Fara Koy Dyop: Walo (1549–52)
N'dyak Khuri Dyop: Walo (1736–80)
Yerim Mbanyik Anta Dyop: Walo (1735)
Dyor: Kayor
Amadi Dyor: Baol
Isa Tein-Dyor: Baol; Kayor
Lat-Dyor: Kayor
Dzeliwe Shongwe: Swaziland (1982–83)
Alois Dziezaski: Bissau (1851)
Dzuda: Mwene Mutapa Empire

E

Anthony Van Der Eb: Dutch Gold Coast (1837–38, 1840–46, 1847–52)
Atef Ebeid: Egypt (1999–2004)
Ebelejonu: Igala
Karl Ebermaier: Kamerun (1904, 1912–18)
Félix Éboué: Chad (1938, 1939–40); French Equatorial Africa (1941–44); Mali (1935)
Almeida d'Eça: Cape Verde (1974–75)
Antonio de Eça: Angola (1915–16)
João d'Eça: Madeira (1603–09)
José d'Eça: Cape Verde (1795–96)
Luis Antonio da Cunha d'Eça: Cape Verde (1752–57)
Ecdicius: Egypt (362–367)
Salah Eddine ben Muhammad Baccouche: Tunisia (1943–47, 1952–54)
Edegi: Nupe
Edem Kodjo: Togo (1991–94)
Ederisu: Nupe
Edhem Pasha: Sudan (1872–72)
Edimini: Bonny
Edoni: Benin [i]
Bonifacio Ondo Edu: Equatorial Guinea
Hussein Effendi: Tripolitania (1903–04, 1909–10)
Phillip Effiong: Biafra
Muhammad Ibrahim Egal: British Somaliland; Somalia; Somaliland Republic
Egbani: Bonny

Egbeka: Benin [i]
Egbeka II: Benin [i]
Walter Egerton: Lagos (1904–06); Southern Nigeria; Southern Nigeria Colony and Protectorate
Egrilius Plarianus: Africa [i] (160–161)
Egunoju: Oyo
Egwa: Keana
Egwala Seyon: Ethiopia (1801–18)
Ehengbuda: Benin [i]
Ehenmihen: Benin [i]
Abutu Eje: Igala
Ekalaga: Igala
Ekdelos: Pentapolis
Eklewudem: Axum
Kala-Ekule: Brass
El-Eshaba: Axum
Eshugbayi Eleko: Lagos (1900–20, 1931–32)
Henry Elias: Dutch Gold Coast (1862–65)
Filemon Elifas: Ovamboland
Elizabeth: Batwanaland
Ella Abreha: Axum
Ella Amida: Axum
Ella Asfeha: Axum
Jules Ellenberger: Botswana
Charles Elliot: Saint Helena (1863–70); Zanzibar (1900–04)
George Elphinstone: Cape Colony (1795)
Albert Ardin d'Elteil: Cotonou
Lt. Emery: Mombasa (1824–26)
Emidio Tafeng Lodongi: Southern Sudan
Mehmed Emin: Tripolitania (1870–71)
Mehmed Emin Pasha: Equatoria Province
Francisco Emparan: Canary Islands (1735–41)
Makonnen Endalkatchon: Ethiopia (1941–58, 1974)
Endreyas: Ethiopia (1429–30)
Antonio Enes: Mozambique (1895)
J.J. Engelbrecht: Ciskei
Carl Engmann: Danish Gold Coast (1752–57)
Ennius Proculus: Africa [i] (ca. 150)
Enriques I: Kongo
Joseph d'Entrecasteaux: Mauritius (1787–89)
Epagathus: Egypt (250)
Ptolemy V Epiphanes: Egypt (205–180 B.C.)
David Erasmi: Dutch Gold Coast (1760–63)
Daniel Erasmus: Transvaal (1871–72)
Erejuwa: Warri
Eresonyen: Benin [i]
Muhammad VII Erghamma: Bornu Empire (1737–52)
Eri: Warri
Conde de Ericeira: Tangier (1556–61)
Edvard Ericksen: Danish Gold Coast (1844)
Eriomulu: Warri
Comte d'Erlon: Algeria (1834–35)

Thomas Ernsthuis: Dutch Gold Coast (1683–85)
D. Erskine: Walvis Bay
Erythrius: Egypt (388–390)
Tomás Mejía de Escobedo: Melilla (1633–35)
Juan Antonio de Escoiquiz: Oran (1752–58)
Harry Escombe: Natal (1897)
Ernest Sweet-Escott: Seychelles (1899–1904)
El-Eshaba: Axum
Eshugbayi Eleko: Lagos (1900–20, 1931–32)
Esigie: Benin [i]
Eskender: Ethiopia (1478–94)
Charles Esnouf: Seychelles (1792–94)
Felipe del Espinar: Melilla (1861–62)
Carlos Espinosa: Ceuta (1835)
Juan de Espinosa: Tenerife
Diogo Esquivel: Cape Verde (1690–91)
Beta Esrael: Axum
Henri Esse d'Orgeret: Réunion (1674–78)
Frédéric Estèbe: Central African Republic (1911–13); Comoros (1911); French Equatorial Africa (1913–14, 1919); Réunion (1920–22)
Jean Walsin-Esterhazy: Algeria (1870)
Jean-Pierre Estéva: Tunisia (1940–43)
Vasco Estevens: São Tomé (1522)
Jean-Baptiste Estoupan de la Bruë: Senegal (1746–58)
Duque de Estrada: Tenerife
Alonso Esudero: Gran Canaria
Salvador-Jean Etcheber: Burkina Faso (1953–56); Mali (1952–53)
Birayma N'Dyeme Eter: Dyolof
Euagrius: Africa Proconsularis (339–340)
Euagrius: Egypt (391–392)
Charles Euan-Smith: Zanzibar (1888–91)
Valerius Eudaemon: Egypt (139)
Ptolemy III Euergetes I: Egypt (247–221 B.C.); Pentapolis
Ptolemy VIII Euergetes: Egypt (170–163 B.C., 145–116 B.C.); Pentapolis
Eulj Ali: Algiers (1568–77); Tripolitania (1565–68)
Eusebius: Africa Proconsularis (395–396)
Eusignias: Africa Proconsularis (386–387)
Eustathius: Egypt (501)
Euthalius: Egypt (404)
Eutrechius: Egypt (485)
Claudius Septimus Eutropius: Egypt (392)
Luis de Evangelho: Cape Verde (1558–62)
Augustine Evans: Sierra Leone (1829–30)
Edward Evans: South Africa (1933)
Fred Evans: Lagos (1883)
Auguste Éven: Central African Republic (1948–49, 1950); Chad (1945–46)

Henry Everard: Zimbabwe (1978)
Ewedo: Benin [i]
Eweka I: Benin [i]
Ewuakpe: Benin [i]
Ewuare: Benin [i]
Étienne Éyadéma: Togo (1967–)
Gnassingbé Éyadéma: Togo (1967–2005)
Jacques-Joseph Eyriès: Senegal (1779–81)
Ezana: Axum
Ezoti: Benin [i]
José Morcillo Ezquerra: Melilla (1856–58)

F

Fa Sine: Segu
Amadu Faaduma: Walo (1251–71)
Amar Faatim Borso: Walo (1812–21)
Birayma Faatim-Penda: Kayor
Carlos Fabião: Guinea-Bissau (1974)
Louis Fabre: Réunion (132–34)
Morgan Facey: Fort James
Fadana: Tembuland
Fadazu: Songhai (1177–96)
Muhammad III al-Fadhl: Darfur
al-Fadl: Omayyad and Abbasid North Africa
Abu al-Abbas Ahmad al-Fadl: Hafsid Kingdom
Sheikh Muhammad Fadl: Trarza
Fadl-Allah: Bornu Empire (1900–01); Rabih's Empire
al-Fadl ibn Salih: Egypt (785–786)
Uthman Ould Fadl Ould Sinan: Adrar
Francisco Fadul: Guinea-Bissau (1998–2000)
al-Fah Benkano: Timbuktu (1683)
al-Fah Ibrahim III: Timbuktu (1738)
al-Fah Ibrahim IV: Timbuktu (1738)
al-Fah Mahmud: Timbuktu (1746–48)
Fahr ad-Din: Mogadishu
Umar Bey Fahri: Sudan (1865)
Ali Fai: Songhai (897–909)
Mar Fai Kolli-Djimbo: Songhai (1434–42)
Louis Faidherbe: Senegal (1854–61, 1863–65)
Mustafa Faik: Fezzan
al-Fa'iz: Egypt (1154–60)
Alfonso Fajardo: Gran Canaria
Leele Fuli Fak: Dyolof
Fakhr ad-Din: Adal [ii]
Moussa Faki: Chad (2003–05)
Faku: Pondoland
Andreas Fakudze: Swaziland (1993)
Birayma-Fal: Kayor
Mr Falconbridge: Sierra Leone (1791)
Falkari: Zamfara
Ernst Falkenthal: Togoland
François Fall: Guinea (2004)
George Fall: Senegambia Colony
Fallonius Probus Allypsius: Africa Proconsularis (378–380)
Falolu: Lagos (1932–49)

Maurice Falvy: Niger (1940–42)

Faly: Kayor

Famagan denn Tieba: Gwiriko

Famagan Watara: Gwiriko

Famorhoba: Kenedugu

Monavo Fani: Mayotte

Fara Aysa Naalem: Walo (1563–65)

Fara Khet: Walo (1343–48)

Fara Ko Ndaama: Walo (1556–63)

Fara Koy Dyon: Walo (1542–49)

Fara Koy Dyop: Walo (1549–52)

Yerim Khode Fara Mbuno: Walo (1735–36)

Naatago Fara N'dyak: Walo (1503–08)

Tani Fara N'dyak: Walo (1531–42)

Fara Penda Adam Sal: Walo (1823–37)

Fara Penda Dyeng: Walo (1519–31)

Fara Penda Langan Dyam: Walo (1552–56)

Fara Penda Teg Rel: Walo (1488–96)

Fara Penda Teg Rel: Walo (1780–92)

Fara Toko: Walo (1485–88)

Fara Yerim: Walo (1304–16)

Hassan Abshir Farah: Somalia

Faraq: Egypt (1399–1405, 1405–12)

Abdur Rahman Farès: Algeria (1962); Algerian Republic (Provisional Government)

Francis Farewell: Port Natal

Fari: Zamfara

Abdu Fari: Zamfara

Muhammad Fari: Songhai (1418–26)

Muhammadu Fari: Zamfara

Antonio Faria: Bissau (1803)

Antonio de Faria: Cape Verde (1752)

Francisco de Faria: Mombasa (1676–79)

Luis Faria: São Tomé and Príncipe (1954–55)

Antonio de Faria e Maia: Cape Verde (1785–90)

Farima I: Koya-Temne

Farima II: Koya-Temne

Farima III: Koya-Temne

Farima IV: Koya-Temne

Muhammadu Farin Gani: Zamfara

Abu Faris: Hafsid Kingdom

Abu Inan Faris: Morocco (1348–58)

Abu Faris Abd al-Aziz: Hafsid Kingdom

Abu'l Faris Abd al-Aziz I: Morocco (1366–72, 1393–96)

José Sousa Faro: Angola (1930–31)

Pierre Faron: Réunion (1875–79)

Farouk: Egypt (1936–52)

Robert Farquhar: Mauritius (1810–17); Réunion (1810, 1811)

Umaru Faruku: Katagum

Fashane: Zamfara

Fasiladas: Ethiopia (1632–67)

Fathi al-Kikhya: Cyrenaica

Fati I: Zamfara

Fati II: Zamfara

Fatima: Koya-Temne

Jumbe Fatimah: Mohéli

Birayma Fatma: Baol

Birayma Fatma: Kayor

Manuel Faustino: Cape Verde (1974–75)

Faustinus: Africa Proconsularis (410)

Favorinus: Egypt (560)

Peter Fawcus: Botswana

Ahmed Fawzi: Tripolitania (1908–09)

Ibrahim Pasha Fawzi: Equatoria Province

Mahmoud Fawzi: Egypt (1970–72)

Jean-Baptiste Fayout: Niger (1929)

Príncipe de Faza: Mombasa (1697–98)

Muhammad Said Fazul: Mwali

Eric Featherstone: Swaziland (1942–46)

Mustafa Fehmy Pasha: Egypt (1891–93, 1895–1908)

Fehr Sagad: Ethiopia (1779–84, 1788–89, 1794–95, 1795–96, 1798–99, 1800)

Muhiaddin Fekini: Libya

Mavura Mhande Felipe: Mwene Mutapa Empire

Felipe II: Koya-Temne

Lucius Aradius Valerius Proculus Felix: Africa Proconsularis (333–336)

Munatius Felix: Egypt (150–154)

Petrus Marcellinus Felix Liberius: Egypt (539–542)

Angel Feltrer: Equatorial Guinea

Nikolaj Fensman: Danish Gold Coast (1687–91)

Vincenzo De Feo: Eritrea

Feresanay: Axum

Jan Fergusson: Dutch Gold Coast (1871)

William Fergusson: Sierra Leone (1841–42, 1844–45)

Ferhad Bey: Constantine

Luis Fernandes: São Tomé and Príncipe (1929–33)

Manuel Fernandes: Mozambique (1506)

Vasco Fernandes Pimentel: Portuguese Gold Coast (1579)

Manuel Fernández: Ceuta (1823)

Francisco Fernández Bernal: Spanish Morocco (1903–07)

Miguel Fernández de Saavedra: Melilla (1767–72)

Fernando Fernández Martín: Canary Islands (1987–88)

Francisco Fernández y Rivadeo: Ceuta (1715–19, 1720–25)

Jerónimo Fernando: Madeira (1626–28)

Jerónimo de Melo Fernando: São Tomé (1623–27)

Ivens Ferraz: Mozambique (1926)

Álvaro Ferreira: Angola (1893–96, 1909); Mozambique (1898–1900)

Antonio Ferreira: Angola (1926–28)

Carlos Ferreira: Guinea-Bissau (1917–18)

Inacio Ferreira: Cacheu (1718)

João Ferreira: São Tomé and Príncipe (1903, 1918–19)

José Ferreira: Cacheu (1835)

José Ferreira: Mozambique (1889–90)

Pedro Ferreira: Bissau (1854)

Vicente Ferreira: São Tomé and Príncipe (1770–78)

Francisco Ferreira do Amaral: São Tomé and Príncipe (1879)

Luciano Ferrer: Spanish Morocco (1931–33)

François Ferriez: Nossi-Bé

William Ferris: British Somaliland

Giovanni Cerrina-Ferroni: Eritrea; Italian Somaliland (1906–07, 1916–20)

Arthur-Paul Feutray: Nossi-Bé

João Fidalgo: Cacheu (1650–54)

Gregory Field: Saint Helena (1674–78)

John Field: Saint Helena (1962–68)

Winston Field: Zimbabwe (1962–64)

William Fielde: Ghana (1789–91)

Eustace Twistleton-Wykeham-Fiennes: Seychelles (1918–21)

Fifen: Bamoun

Amadeu de Figueiredo: São Tomé and Príncipe (1941–45)

Antonio Figueiredo: Bissau (1811)

Antonio de Figueiredo: Cape Verde (1931–41)

Francisco de Figueiredo: São Tomé (1584–87)

João de Figueiredo: Cape Verde (1943–49)

Jacinto de Figueiredo e Abreu: São Tomé (1680–83)

Henrique de Figueiredo e Alarcão: Angola (1717–22)

Joaquim de Figueiredo e Góis: Cacheu (1811–14)

Diego de Figueroa: Tenerife

Francisco de Figueroa: Cape Verde (1658–63)

Fijabi: Ibadan

Fikre Selassie Wogderess: Ethiopia (1987–89)

Abdellatif Filali: Morocco (1994–98)

Mele Filata: Daniski

Victor Fillon: Djibouti (1916–18)

Vincenzo Filonardi: Italian Somaliland (1893–97)

Bongani Finca: Ciskei

Alexander Findlay: Gambia (1826–30); Sierra Leone (1830–33)

Josiah Finley: Mississippi-in-Africa

Firari: Egypt (1697–99)

Michel Firélin: Réunion (1690–93)

Firmus: Egypt (ca. 275)

Abraham Fischer: Orange Free State (1906–10)

Gerald Fisher: British Somaliland

Charles Fitzgerald: Gambia (1844–47)

John Fitzgerald: Tangier (1664–65)

Alexander Fitzjames: Sierra Leone (1859–60)

James Fitzpatrick: Ghana (1849–50, 1853)

Avillius Flaccus: Egypt (32–37)

Étienne de Flacourt: Fort-Dauphin

Pierre Flandin: Tunisia (1918–20)

Flavianus: Africa Proconsularis (393–394)

Flavianus: Africa Proconsularis (431–432)

Lucius Tampius Flavianus: Africa [i] (51–52)

Maenius Flavianus: Egypt (180–181)

Nicomachus Flavianus: Africa Proconsularis (377–378)

Marcus Pompeius Silvanus Staberius Flavinus: Africa [i] (53–56)

Flavius Antonius Theodorus: Egypt (338–354)

Flavius Bassus: Africa Proconsularis (435, 437–439)

Flavius Philippus: Africa Proconsularis (353–354)

Flavius Priscus: Egypt (181)

Flavius Titianus: Egypt (126–134)

Flavius Titianus: Egypt (166–167)

Titus Flavius Vespasianus: Africa [i] (63–64)

Francis Fleming: Mauritius (1887–88); Sierra Leone (1892–94)

Capt. Fleuriau: Senegal (1817–19)

Germain de Fleuricourt: Réunion (1678–80)

Chevalier de Fleury: Mauritius (1785)

Jens Flindt: Danish Gold Coast (1827–28)

Florentius: Egypt (384–385, 386–388)

Diego de Flores: Melilla (1707–11)

Luis Antonio Flores: Ceuta (1815–16)

Marqués de Flores Dávila: Oran (1632–39, 1647–52)

Florus: Egypt (453)

Percy Flynn: Zimbabwe (1923)

Heinrich Fock: Fort James

Muhammadu Fodi: Argungu

Abdullahi Dan Fodio: Gwandu

Modibbo Dan Fodio: Gobir

Usman Dan Fodio: Fulani Empire

Uthman Dan Fodio: Fulani Empire

Opuke Fofie: Ashanti

João Fogaça: Portuguese Gold Coast

Bai Foki: Koya-Temne

Foli Arlonko: Little Popo

Tye-Folo: Segu

John Foncha: Cameroun (1961–68)

Jean-Baptiste Fonsagrives: Benin [ii] (1899)

André da Fonseca: Mozambique (1674)

Antonio da Fonseca: São Tomé and Príncipe (1867)

Joaquim da Fonseca: São Tomé and Príncipe (1830–34)

José da Fonseca: São Tomé and Príncipe (1909–10)

Juan de Fonseca: Tenerife

Manuel da Fonseca: Mozambique (1919–21, 1923–24)

Rodrigo da Fonseca: Bissau (1699–1707); Cacheu (1688–89); Cape Verde (1707–11)

Claude Fontaine: Comoros (1875); Nossi-Bé

Jan de la Fontaine: Cape Colony (1724–27, 1729–37)

Juan Fontán y Lobé: Equatorial Guinea

Henry Foote: Bight of Benin

Patrick Forbes: Rhodesia (1895–97)

King Forday: Brass

Thomas Forde: Fort James

Manuel Forjaz: Angola (1607–11)

Di Forma: Biu

Giovanni Fornari: Italian Somaliland (1949–53)

Roger Seydoux Fornier de Clausonne: Tunisia (1955–56)

Foro-Kolo: Kaarta

Aubrey Forsyth-Thompson: Botswana; Lesotho (1946–51)

Gabriel Fortune: Congo (1941–45)

Maj. Foster: Sierra Leone (1889)

Jim Fouché: South Africa (1968–75)

Christian Fouchet: Algeria (1962)

Jean Terasson de Fougères: Mali (1920, 1921–24, 1925–30)

Fernand Foureau: Comoros (1906–08)

Gaston Fourn: Benin [ii] (1917–28); Togo (1916–17); Togoland (1914–16)

Alfred Fourneau: Gabon (1905–06)

Jacques-Georges Fourneau: Congo (1947–50); Guinea (1944–46)

Lucien Fourneau: Cameroun (1916–19); Central African Republic (1909–10); Congo (1911–16)

Albéric Fournier: Burkina Faso (1928–32); Cameroun (1923); Mali (1924–25)

Hubert Fournier: Réunion (1992–95)

Louis Fousset: Burkina Faso (1929); Mali (1931–35)

Henry Fowley: Lagos (1872)

Diogo Lopes de França: Ceuta (1574–77)

David Francis: Fort James

Édouard Franck: Central African Republic (1991–92)

Carlos Franco: Angola (1860–61); Cape Verde (1861–64)

Manuel Franco: Mombasa (1679)

Francisco Franco Bahamonde: Spanish Morocco (1936)

Joseph François: Nossi-Bé

Kurt von François: Namibia (1891–95)

Pierre François: Central African Republic (1923–24)

William Franklyn: Seychelles (1868–74)

Alexander Fraser: Sierra Leone (1830)

Louis Fraser: Bight of Benin

Frederick Boevi Lawson V: Little Popo

Sanford Freeling: Ghana (1876–78)

Henry Freeman: Lagos (1862–63)

Ascenso Freire: Madeira (1803–07)

Francisco Freire: Madeira (1724–27)

João Freire: Mozambique (1670–73, 1676–82)

Luis de Brito Freire: Mozambique (1706–07)

Nunho Freire: Madeira (1642–45)

Bernardim Freire de Andrade: São Tomé (1677–80)

Antonio de Freitas: Cape Verde (1903–04)

Felipe de Freitas: São Tomé and Príncipe (1817–24)

George French: Sierra Leone (1874–75)

Bartle Frere: Cape Colony (1877–80)

Capt. Frerejean: Mauritania (1905)

Charles de Fresne: Mauritius (1785)

Henri Frey: Mali (1885–86)

Louis Desaulses de Freycinet: Réunion (1821–26)

Antoine Frezouls: Guinea (1904–06)

José Frias: Melilla (1675–80)

Gonthier Friederici: Réunion (2001–04)

Simon Frijkenius: Cape Colony (1792–93)

Ernest-Emmanuel Froger: Diego Suarez

Johan Frohlich: Danish Gold Coast (1770–72)

Antonio Fróis: Mozambique (1726–30)

Luigi Frusci: Eritrea

Detye Fu-N'Diogu: Kayor

Fuad: Egypt (1917–36)

Ahmad Fuad I: Egypt (1917–36)

Fuad II: Egypt (1952–53)

Ahmad Fuad Mohieddin: Egypt (1982–84)

Osman Fuad Pasha: Tripolitania (1918)

Fubra: Bonny

Agba Fubra: Bonny

Fubra II: Bonny

Félix Fuchs: Congo (Zaire) (1912–16)

al-Fudail: Zeng Empire (1496–1500)

Marqués de Fuensagrada: Canary Islands (1689–97)

Juan de la Fuente: Tenerife

Narciso de Fuentes y Sánchez: Spanish Morocco (1889–91)

Fula Mansa Gbanka: Koya-Temne

Fulakoro: Kaarta

Fulful: Tripolitania (1007–09)

Leele Fuli Fak: Dyolof

Herr Full: Kamerun (1913–14)

Francis Fuller: Ashanti

Bwana Fuma ibn Ali: Mayotte

Jacques Fuméchon: Senegal (1631–41)

Jacques Fuméchon: Senegal (1674–82)

Fundakira: Mirambo

Fune: Kanem

Joseph Le Fur: Tangier (1929–40)

Ibrahimu Na Mai Fura: Gobir

Marcus Furius Camillus: Africa [i] (17–18)

Diogo Furtado: Madeira (1660–65)

Mele Fusan: Daniski

Abu al-Futuh Buluggin: Zirid Kingdom

G

Bako Makam Gaba: Zaria (1757–58)
Sambo Gabaima: Jemaari
Gabaro: Lagos (ca. 1750)
Ottone Gabelli: Eritrea
Bako Mahama Gabi: Zaria (1608–11)
Gabir ibn al-Ashath: Egypt (811–812)
Gaborone I: Batlokwaland
Kgosi Gaborone II: Batlokwaland
Michael Gaborone: Batlokwaland
Moshibidu Gaborone: Batlokwaland
Gabra Krestos: Ethiopia (1832)
Gabra Maskal Lalibela: Ethiopia
  (1172–1212)
Gabra Masqal: Axum
Gabra Maskal: Ethiopia (1314–44)
Charles Gabrié: Comoros (1860–64)
Gabriel: Shoa
Muammar al-Gadaffi: Libya
Wanis al-Gadaffi: Libya
Gadar Gadar: Daura
Gadbo: Biram
Abdullahi Gade: Zamfara
Henri Gaden: Mauritania (1916–27)
Gadi: Zaria (1608–11)
Dan Gado: Zamfara
Winyi IV Gafabusa: Bunyoro
Gaga: Daura
Mammadi Gaganga: Fika
Gagoangwe: Bangwaketseland
Yuhi III Gahandiro: Ruanda
Yuhi I Gahima: Ruanda
Riek Gai: Southern Sudan
Gaika: British Kaffraria
Manuel Gaivão: Angola (1955–56)
Gajemasu: Kano (1095–1133)
Gajere: Yauri
Dan Gajere: Yauri
Gakuna: Daura
Ali Khalif Galaid: Somalia
Galawdewos: Ethiopia (1540–59)
Servius Sulpicius Galba: Africa [i]
  (44–46)
Galerius: Egypt (21–31)
Mustafa Galibuli: Tripolitania (1701–
  02)
Joaquín Gallardo: Fernando Po
Servaas Gallé: Dutch Gold Coast
  (1784–85, 1786–87)
Joseph Galliéni: Madagascar (1896–
  1905); Mali (1886–88)
Gallo: Masina
Abdullahi Gallo: Yauri
Tié-Yaasin Gallo: Baol
Ya Gallo: Masina
Aelius Gallus: Egypt (25–24 B.C.)
Cornelius Gallus: Egypt (30–26
  B.C.)
Antonio Galvão: Cape Verde
  (1663–67)
Henry Galway: Gambia (1911–14);
  Saint Helena (1903–11); Southern
  Nigeria
Henry Gallwey: Gambia (1911–14);
  Saint Helena (1903–11); Southern
  Nigeria
Antonio da Gama: Angola (1807–10)

Cristóvão da Gama: Portuguese Gold
  Coast (1596–1608)
Duarte da Gama: Cape Verde (1587–
  91)
Duarte Lobo da Gama: Portuguese
  Gold Coast (1595–96)
Estévão da Gama: Portuguese Gold
  Coast (1529)
Francisco da Gama: Cape Verde
  (1596–1603)
João da Gama: Madeira (1715–18)
Pedro da Gama e Castro: Mozambique
  (1743–46)
Gamajiya da yau: Biram
Gamal Abdel Nasser: Egypt (1954–70)
Gamal ad-Din: Wadai
Gamata: Daura
Sulu Gambari: Ilorin
Zulkarnayni Gambari: Ilorin
Geoffrey Gamble: Italian Somaliland
  (1948–49)
Pedro de Gambôa: Mombasa (1629–
  31)
Gonçalo de Gamboa Ayala: Cacheu
  (1644–49); Cape Verde (1650)
Ibrahim Gamda: Katsina (1635–44)
Gamdi: Yauri
Umaru Gamdi: Yauri
Ada Gamu: Daura
Musa Gana: Lafia
Sachi Gana Machi: Nupe
Ganamace: Nupe
Charles-David Ganao: Congo (1996–
  97)
Carlos Gand: Ceuta (1809–10)
José de la Gándara y Navarro: Fer-
  nando Po
Edvard von Gandil: Danish Gold
  Coast (1834)
Giacomo Gandolfi: Eritrea
Gandowo: Daniski
Gane: Ghana Empire
Gangia Sidje: Allada
Gangkpe: Dahomey
Ganhwa: Allada
Gani: Daura
Muhammadu Farin Gani: Zamfara
Muhamman Gani: Abuja
al-Qasim Gannum: Idrisid State
Ganye Hesu: Dahomey
Kamal al-Ganzouri: Egypt (1996–99)
Muhammad Gao: Songhai (1591)
Celestin Gaombalet: Central African
  Republic (2003–05)
Garageje: Kano (ca. 920)
Garan: Kaarta
John Garang: Southern Sudan
Bukar Garbai: Bornu Empire (1902–
  22)
Hubert Garbit: Madagascar (1909–10,
  1914–17, 1920–23); Réunion (1912–
  13)
García I: Kongo
Garcia II Afonso: Kongo
Estanislao García: Equatorial Guinea
Manuel García: Melilla (1826–29)
José García Aldave: Melilla (1910–12);
  Spanish Morocco (1908–10)

Juan García Torres: Spanish Morocco
  (1877)
Juan García y Margallo: Melilla (1891–
  93)
Evaristo García y Reyna: Melilla
  (1880–81)
Louis Le Gardeur de Repentigny:
  Senegal (1784–86)
Allan Gardiner: Port Natal
Anthony Gardner: Liberia (1878–83)
Garga Kopchi: Biu
Garga Moda: Biu
Garga Kwomting: Biu
Gariba: Dagomba
Italo Garibaldi: Libia
Vincenzo Garioni: Cyrenaica; Tripo-
  litania (1913–14, 1918–19)
Garko: Hadejia
Gabriel Garnier-Mouton: Comoros
  (1911–13)
Gustave Garrand: Gabon (1871–73)
Edward Garraway: Botswana; Lesotho
  (1917–26)
Henry Garrioch: Mauritius (1977–78)
Lourenço Garro: Cape Verde (1645–
  46)
Gaseitsiwa: Bangwaketseland
Gasiyonga I: Nkore
Gasiyonga II: Nkore
Jacopo Gasparini: Eritrea
Oreste De Gasperi: Cyrenaica
Manuel Gasset Mercader: Spanish
  Morocco (1858)
Claude Le Lardoux de la Gastière:
  Gorée
Gatamma: Zamfara
Gatluak Deng: Southern Sudan
Gatsha Buthelezi: KwaZulu; Zululand
Gatsi Rusere: Mwene Mutapa Empire
Gauda: Numidia
Antoine Gaudart: Benin [ii] (1908);
  Senegal (1909)
Henri-François Gaudillot: Togo
  (1945)
Bardiya-Gaumata: Egypt (27th Dy-
  nasty)
Fulgencio Gávila y Solá: Spanish Mo-
  rocco (1873–75)
Sebastián de Corcuera y Gaviría: Ca-
  nary Islands (1659–61)
Gawata: Kano (1133–35)
John Gawler: Idutywa
Ernest Gayon: Benin [ii] (1937–38)
Mustafa Gazari: Yauri
Gazaura: Daura
Pietro Gazzera: Ethiopia (1941)
gBagwe: Allada
Gbadebo I: Abeokuta
Gbadebo II: Abeokuta
Laurent Gbagbo: Côte d'Ivoire
  (2000–)
Fula Mansa Gbanka: Koya-Temne
Gbara: Nupe
Gi-gla No-Don Gbé-non Mau: Allada
Gbedissin: Porto-Novo
gBehanzin: Dahomey
Gbehinto: Porto-Novo
Gbelegbura I: Ijebu

Daniel Adesanya Gbelegbura II: Ijebu
Christophe Gbenye: Stanleyville People's Republic
Gbesso Toyi: Porto-Novo
Gbeyon: Porto-Novo
gBon Cuilbaly: Kong
Gboro: Brass
Michel Gbzera-Brio: Central African Republic (1997–99)
Gcaleka: Kreli's Country
Lucien Geay: Benin [ii] (1928–29); Burkina Faso (1950); Mali (1949–50, 1953–56); Mauritania (1947); Niger (1948–49); Senegal (1952–54)
Tesfaye Gebre Kidan: Ethiopia (1991)
Geda: Yatenga
Gedajan: Axum
Geigler Pasha: Sudan (1882)
Hage Geingob: Namibia (1990–2002)
Geiserich: Vandal North Africa
Léon Geismar: French West Africa (1938); Togo (1935–36)
Gelele: Dahomey
Gelimer: Vandal North Africa
Geminius Chrestus: Egypt (219–232)
Titus Prifernius Paetus Rosianus Geminus: Africa [i] (140–141, 161–162))
Ambrose Genda: Sierra Leone (1967)
Carlo Gene: Massawa
Gennadius: Byzantine North Africa
Gennadius: Egypt (396)
Jules Genouille: Senegal (1886–88)
Émile Gentil: Congo (1902–06); French Equatorial Africa (1903, 1904–08); Gabon (1899–1902, 1903)
Paul de Gentilhomme: Madagascar (1943)
Bernard Cornut-Gentille: French Equatorial Africa (1948–51); French West Africa (1952–56)
Jean Cornut-Gentille: Gabon (1883–85)
George: Bonny
Georges Betnui Lawson III: Little Popo
Georgios I: Dongola
Georgios II: Dongola
Georgios III: Dongola
Georgios IV: Dongola
Gui-Noël Georgy: Congo (1959–60)
M. Gerbidon: Senegal (1827–28)
Daniel Germa: Porto-Novo
Germa Safar: Axum
Gaëtan Germain: Djibouti (1940)
Germanus: Byzantine North Africa
Carl Gerotz: Graaff-Reinet
J. Gerrard: Lagos (1871–72)
Philotée Gerville-Réache: Comoros (1885–87)
Romolo Gessi Pasha: Bahr al-Ghazal
Cnaeus Hosidius Geta: Africa [i] (57–58)
Getachew Nadu: Eritrea
Birayamb Kumba-Gey: Dyolof
Tekin al-Khassa al-Gezeri: Egypt (910–915, 919–921, 924–933)

Gezo: Dahomey
Ghaji: Bornu Empire (1456–61)
Ali Ghajideni: Bornu Empire (1472–1504)
Butros Ghali: Egypt (1908–10)
Abdallah al-Ghalib: Morocco (1557–74)
Umar Arteh Ghalib: Somalia
Kure Ghana as-Saghir: Bornu Empire (1350–51)
Muhammad Ghannouchi: Tunisia (1999–)
Abu Ghazali: Wadai
Abd al-Malik al-Ghazi: Morocco (1576–78)
Shahsuwar-Zade-Ghazi: Egypt (1657–60)
Ali Muhammad Ghedi: Somali
Sid Ahmad Ghozali: Algeria (1991–92)
al-Ghuri: Egypt (1501–16)
Félix Giacobbi: Guinea (1940–42)
Edward Gibbons: Cameroons
George Gibbs: Gold Coast Northern Territories
Humphrey Gibbs: Zimbabwe (1959–69)
Garretson Gibson: Liberia (1900–04)
Negasso Gidada: Ethiopia (1995–2001)
Gidan Dan Masakanan: Zaria (1530–32)
Hans Giede: Danish Gold Coast (1839)
Nikolaas Van Der Nood De Gieterre: Dutch Gold Coast (1754–55)
Muhammadu Dan Gigala: Zamfara
Gigar: Ethiopia (1821–26, 1826–30)
Gi-gla Gunhu Hugnon: Allada
Gi-gla No-Don Gbé-non Mau: Allada
Gigma: Yatenga
Venancio Gil: Western Sahara
Alexander Giles: Lesotho (1961–66)
Giliga: Wagadugu
Gima: Gurma
Bawa Dan Gima: Katsina (1802–04)
Gimba: Yauri
Gimba II: Yauri
Gimba III: Yauri
Gimshikki: Zamfara
Mama Gimsi: Daniski
Gino: Daura
Ginsarana: Gobir
Ginuwa I: Warri
Ginuwa II: Warri
Henri Gipoulon: Mali (1956–58)
Capt. Giraud: Sainte Marie de Madagascar
Gireun Buri Dyelen: Dyolof
Girma Wolde-Giorgis Lucha: Ethiopia (2001–)
Marqués de Gironella: Ceuta (1702–04)
Percy Girouard: Kenya (1909–12)
Girza: Upper Egypt
Mibambwe II Gisanura: Ruanda
Joseph Gitera: Rwanda
Aliyu Karya Giwa: Katsina (1572–85)
Karya Giwa II: Katsina (1706–15)

Karya Giwa III: Katsina (1751–58)
Karya Giwa IV: Katsina (1767–84)
Asma Giyorgis: Ethiopia (1721–30)
Takla Giyorgis: Ethiopia (1779–84, 1788–89, 1794–95, 1795–96, 1798–99, 1800)
Takla Giyorgis II: Ethiopia (1878–82)
Gizirgizit: Daura
al-Gizouli Dafalla: Sudan (1985)
Mammadi Gizze: Daniski
Herbert John, 1st Viscount Gladstone: South Africa (1910–14)
Otto Gleim: Kamerun (1904–05, 1906–07, 1910–11)
Glele: Dahomey
Lord Glenbervie: Cape Colony (1801–03)
Vincent Glenday: British Somali land; Zanzibar (1946–51)
Glin Lawson VI: Little Popo
John Glover: Lagos (1864–70)
Henry Glynne: Fort James
gNansunu: Dahomey
Faure Gnassingbé: Togo (2005–)
Gnassingbé Éyadéma: Togo (1967–2005)
Louis-Sylvain Goba: Congo (1975–84, 1991)
Gobaz: Axum (402–404)
Gobaz: Axum (463–474)
Jaime Godins: Angola (1892–93); São Tomé and Príncipe (1894–95)
Pedro de Godoy: Oran (1531–34)
Godwin Mbikusita: Barotseland
Heinrich Goering: Namibia (1886–90)
Tanor Gogne: Baol
Gohar: Egypt (969–973)
Manuel de Gois: Portuguese Gold Coast (1509–10)
Goji: Gobir
Muhammadu Goji Yerima: Jemaari
Frederic Goldsmid: Congo (Zaire) (1884)
Herbert Goldsmith: Nigeria Northern Region
Ambrosio Gomes: Cacheu (ca. 1670)
João de Araújo Gomes: Cacheu (1821)
Rui Gomes de Azevedo: Portuguese Gold Coast (1562)
Carlos Gomes Júnior: Guinea-Bissau (2004–)
Domingo Gómez: Canary Islands (1764–68)
Joaquín Gómez Ansa: Ceuta (1835–36)
Fernando Gómez de Buitrón: Ceuta (1813–14, 1820–22)
Patrício Gómez de la Hoz: Melilla (1714–15)
Francisco Gómez Jordana y Sousa: Spanish Morocco (1928–31)
Ramón Gómez Pulido: Spanish Morocco (1858–64, 1865–66)
Francisco Gómez y Jordana: Spanish Morocco (1915–18)
William Gomm: Mauritius (1842–49)
Caetano Gonçalves: Angola (1910–11)

João Gonçalves: São Tomé and Príncipe (1973–74)
Octavio Gonçalves: São Tomé and Príncipe (1956–57)
Afonso Gonçalves Botofago: Portuguese Gold Coast (1557)
Henri-Ernest Gondry: Congo (Zaire) (1891)
Faustino González: Equatorial Guinea
José González Deleito: Western Sahara
Richard Goode: Zambia (1923–24, 1927)
William Goodenough: Cape Colony (1897)
João Goodolfim: Cacheu (1815, 1823–25)
Zwelithini Goodwill Ka Bhekuzulu: Zululand
John Goodwin: Saint Helena (1738–39)
Thomas Goodwin: Saint Helena (1707–08)
Hamilton Goold-Adams: Botswana; Orange Free State (1901–02, 1907–10)
Pieter Goosen: Ciskei
John Gootheridge: Fort James
John Gordon: Ghana (1791–92, 1799–1800)
Arthur Hamilton-Gordon: Mauritius (1871–74)
Charles Gordon Pasha: Equatoria Province; Sudan (1877–79, 1884–85)
J.C. Gore: Sierra Leone (1897)
William Ormsby-Gore: South Africa (1941–44)
Gorewang: Bamangwatoland
Howard Gorges: Namibia (1915–20)
Carlos Gorgulho: São Tomé and Príncipe (1945–48)
Gori: Gurma
Manuel Gorjão: Mozambique (1900–02)
Eldon Gorst: Egypt (1907–11)
Ras Gosho II: Gojjam
Isbrand Goske: Cape Colony (1672–76)
Ras Goskol: Gojjam
M. Gosse: Sainte Marie de Madagascar
Jacques Gosselin: Niger (1946)
Adolf von Götzen: German East Africa
François Gouhot: Nossi-Bé
Daniel Goujon: Senegal (1954)
Goukouni Oueddi: Chad (1979–82)
Valesius Gouldsbury: Gambia (1877–84)
Hassan Gouled Aptidon: Djibouti (1977–99)
Abel Goumba: Central African Republic (1959, 2003)
Barket Gourad Hamadou: Djibouti (1978–)
Henri Gouraud: Chad (1904–06); French Morocco; Mauritania (1907–09); Niger (1901–04)

Maurice Gourbeil: Senegal (1908–09)
Capt. Gourgas: Gabon (1887)
Francisco de Gouveia: São Tomé (1564–69)
Manuel de Gouveia: Bissau (1805–11); Cacheu (1800)
Pedro de Gouveia: Guinea-Bissau (1881–84, 1895–97)
Lt.-Col. San Gouveia: Guinea-Bissau (1974)
Luis de Gouveia e Almeida: Madeira (1813–14)
William Gowers: Nigeria Northern Region; Uganda (1925–32)
Yokubu Gowon: Nigeria (1966–75)
Joshua Oupa Gqozo: Ciskei
Cornelis Van De Graaff: Cape Colony (1785–91)
Carlos de Graça: São Tomé and Príncipe (1994–95)
Joaquim da Graça Correia e Lança: São Tomé and Príncipe (1897–99)
Marc Antoine Gradassi: Togo (1938–39)
Joseph Graëb: Réunion (1846–48)
Robert Graham: British Kaffraria
Ernest Bourdon de Grammont: Senegal (1846–47)
Nyaralen Gran: Kaarta
Ahmad Gran ibn Ibrahim: Harar
José Granados: Melilla (1782–86)
Gilbert Grandval: French Morocco
Jean Paul de la Grange: Sainte Marie de Madagascar
Francisco Grans: Cape Verde (1728–33)
Alexander Grant: Gambia (1816–26); Sierra Leone (1820–21)
John Gray: Sierra Leone (1799, 1800–01)
William Gray: Saint Helena (1941–47)
Rodolfo Graziani: Cyrenaica; Italian East Africa; Italian Somaliland (1935–36); Libia
Hugh Greatbatch: Seychelles (1969–73)
Félix Grébert: Sainte Marie de Madagascar
Henry Green: Orange Free State (1852–54)
William Greenhill: Ghana (1660)
Gregorius: Africa Proconsularis (336–337)
Gregorius: Byzantine North Africa
Thomas Gresham: Fort James
Albert Grévy: Algeria (1879–81)
Earl Grey: Rhodesia (1896–97)
George Grey: Cape Colony (1854–62)
Henry Grey: Cape Colony (1807, 1811)
William Grey-Wilson: Saint Helena (1887–97)
Griffith: Lesotho (1913–39)
Brandford Griffith: Lagos (1880, 1883–84)
Charles Griffith: Lesotho (1871–81)
Thomas Griffith: Seychelles (1888–95)
William Griffith: Ghana (1880–81, 1882, 1885–95)

Edward Grigg: Kenya (1925–31)
Lieven Van Burgen Van Der Grijp: Dutch Gold Coast (1787–90, 1794–95)
Louis Grimald: Central African Republic (1951–54)
Pedro Grimarest: Ceuta (1813, 1814–15)
Arthur Grimble: Seychelles (1936–42)
Adriaan Grobbe: Hollandia
Johannes Grobelaar: Transvaal (1860)
Louis Grodet: French Equatorial Africa (1900–04); Gabon (1902–03); Mali (1893–95)
Bartolomaus von Gronestein: Danish Gold Coast (1669–74)
John Grossle: Ghana (1769–70)
Nicolas Grunitzky: Togo (1956–58, 1963–67)
Guarafia: Canary Islands (1400–05)
Abderrahman Guarang I: Baguirmi
Abderrahman Guarang II: Baguirmi
Conde de Guaro: Canary Islands (1681–85); Oran (1687–91)
Gubarau: Zamfara
Gubbo: Potiskum
Dan Gudi Dan Babari: Gobir
Luis Gudiel y Ortiz: Tenerife
Muhammadu Mai-sa-Maza-Gudu: Katsina (1595–1612)
Gudumua Muska: Zaria (1530–32)
Armando Guebuza: Mozambique (2005–)
Antonio Guedes: São Tomé and Príncipe (1910–11)
Antonio Guedes Vaz: Cape Verde (1927–31)
Ahmad Reda Guedira: Morocco (1961–63)
Robert Guéi: Côte d'Ivoire (1999–2000)
Gueladio: Masina
Nassour Guelendoussia Ouaido: Chad (1997–99)
Pedro Guelfi: Oran (1779–85)
Ismael Guelleh: Djibouti (1999–)
Yves Guéna: Côte d'Ivoire (1960)
Mimosa Guera: Angola (1919–20)
Antonio Guerra: Fernando Po
Henrique Guerra: Guinea-Bissau (1919–20)
Manuel de Guerra: Cape Verde (1622–24)
Martin Gueston: Fort-Dauphin
Guetsalwe: Batwanaland
Juan de Guevara: Tenerife
Alonso de Guevara y Vasconcelos: Melilla (1719–30)
Comte de Gueydon: Algeria (1871–73)
Gordon Guggisberg: Ghana (1919–27)
Ras Beru Gugsa: Gojjam
Ada Guguwa: Daura
Gaston Guibet: Cameroun (1936–37)
Guidado: Masina
Augustin Guillaume: French Morocco
Louis Guillet: Senegal (1836–37)
Théophile Guillet: Gabon (1853–57)
Armand Guillon: Tunisia (1936–38)

Henri Guilman: Porto-Novo
João Guimarães: São Tomé and Príncipe (1902–03)
Robert de Guise: French Equatorial Africa (1923–24); Guinea (1931–32); Togo (1931–33)
Gujjua: Kano (1247–90)
Gulbi: Gobir
Gulussa: Numidia
Josiah Gumede: Zimbabwe (1979)
Gumidafe: Canary Islands (1350–1402)
Gumsara: Gobir
Gundamund: Vandal North Africa
Gungobili: Dagomba
Gunguma: Zaria (1010)
Dalla Gungumi: Gobir
Gungunyane: Gazaland
Gi-gla Gunhu Hugnon: Allada
Gurgur: Biu
Theo-Ben Gurirab: Namibia (2002–05)
Francisco Gurjão: Madeira (1737–47)
Gurji: Egypt (1604–05)
Gurji: Egypt (1660–61)
Gurori I: Masina
Gurori II: Masina
Camille Guy: Guinea (1910–12)
G.C. Guy: Saint Helena (1977–81)
Lucien Guy: Réunion (1908–10); Senegal (1902–07)
Casimir Guyon: Côte d'Ivoire (1911–12, 1913); Gabon (1914–17); Madagascar (1919–20)
Enrique de Guzmán, Count of Niebla: Canary Islands (1418)
Fernán de Guzmán: Gran Canaria
Hernán de Guzmán: Oran (1565–67)
Pedro de Guzmán: Canary Islands (1644–50)
Alfredo Guzzoni: Eritrea
Dejaz Ma'red Gwalo: Gojjam
Gwamki: Gobir
Bawa Dan Gwamki: Gobir
Dodon Gwari: Abuja
Gwari Abdu: Daura
Gwarma: Biram
Bawa Jan Gwarzo: Gobir
Gwebinkumbi: Kreli's Country
Tsagarana Gwozo: Katsina (1801–02)
Ntim Gyakari: Denkyira
Gyako I: Bono
Gyamfi: Bono

H

Kin-Ha: Allada
Haaibre Wahimbre: Egypt (26th Dynasty)
Uthman al-Habashi: Harar
Henri Habet de Vauboulon: Réunion (1689–90)
Habib: Omayyad and Abbasid North Africa
Muhammad IV al-Habib: Trarza
Muhammad VI al-Habib: Tunisia (1922–29)

Habib Bourguiba: Tunisia (1956–87)
Habib Thiam: Senegal (1981–83, 1991–98)
Aulus Vibius Habitus: Africa [i] (16–17)
Hissène Habré: Chad (1978–79, 1982–90)
Tshafe Tezaz Aklilu Habte-Wold: Ethiopia (1961–74)
Habu: Daura-Baure
Juvenal Habyarimana: Rwanda
Juan Pérez del Hacho y Oliván: Melilla (1823–24)
August Hackenborg: Danish Gold Coast (1745–46)
William Hackett: Ghana (1864)
Pieter Hackius: Cape Colony (1670–71)
Magnus Hacksen: Danish Gold Coast (1751–52)
Haddu: Timbuktu (1618–19)
Ba-Haddu Salim: Timbuktu (1683)
Seymour Haden: Natal (1893)
Sa'id al-Hadermi: Mombasa (1735–39)
Muhammad IV al-Hadi: Tunisia (1902–06)
Sidi Muhammad al-Hadi al-Ahwa: Tunisia (1932–42)
El Hadj Saeidou Nyimoluh Nyoju: Bamoun
Hadrianus: Egypt (377–380)
Rufus Synesius Hadrianus: Africa Proconsularis (400–405)
Synesius Hadrianus: Africa Proconsularis (413–414)
Hae Phoofolo: Lesotho (1994)
al-Hafiz: Egypt (1131–49)
Hafiz Ahmad: Egypt (1591–95)
Hafiz Mehmed: Tripolitania (1900–03)
Hafs ibn al-Walid: Egypt (727, 742–745)
Abu Hafs Umar I: Hafsid Kingdom
Abu Hafs Umar II: Hafsid Kingdom
Hage Geingob: Namibia (1990–2002)
Frantz von Hager: Danish Gold Coast (1793–95)
Haholo: Whydah
Muhammad Ould Haidalla: Mauritania (1979–84)
Mengistu Haile Mariam: Ethiopia (1977–91)
Debbe Haile Maryan: Eritrea
Haile Selassie: Ethiopia (1916–74)
Hailu Yemenu: Ethiopia (1989–91)
Moma Haji: Katagum
Si Halil Bu Hajib ben Salim: Tunisia (1926–32)
al-Hajj: Egypt (1748–52)
al-Hajj: Kano (1648–49)
al-Hajj: Songhai (1582–86)
Ibrahim al-Hajj: Egypt (1603–04)
Umar al-Hajj: Tukolor Empire
al-Hajj Abu Bakar: Biram
al-Hajj al-Mukhtar: Timbuktu (1659–60)
ben Hajj Hatmi: Rif Republic

al-Hajj Ibrahim Adamu: Kazaure
al-Hajj Muhammad at-Tazi Bu Ashran: Tangier (1923–41, 1945–54)
al-Hajj Muhammadu Bashar: Daura-Zango
Abu Hajjaj Yusuf: Tlemcen (1393)
Hassan al-Hajjam: Idrisid State
Mamman al-Hajji: Misau
as-Salih Hajji: Egypt (1380–82, 1389–90)
Hajji I: Egypt (1345–47)
Hajji Abdallah Izmirli: Tripolitania (1684–87)
Hajji Ahmad: Constantine
Hajji Ahmed Izzet: Tripolitania (1848–49)
Hajji Ali: Algiers (1665–71)
Hajji Beshir Pasha: Algiers (1543–44)
Hajji Hasan: Zeng Empire (1505–06)
Abdi Rizak Hajji Hussein: Somalia
al-Hajji Kabe: Kano (1743–52)
Hajji Mehmed Nazir: Bahr al-Ghazal
Hajji Rejeb: Tripolitania (1711)
al-Hajji Saidu Naemaska: Kontagora
Hajji Shaban: Algiers (1592–94)
al-Hakim: Egypt (996–1021)
Muhammad IV al-Hakim: Fezzan
Hakimzade: Egypt (734–741, 755–756)
Hakor Khnemmaere: Egypt (29th Dynasty)
Halbo: Daniski
Mehmed Halid: Tripolitania (1870–71)
Abu Halid Yazid: Omayyad and Abbasid North Africa
Ibrahim Abderrahman Halidi: Comoros (1993)
Magajin Halidu: Katsina (1805–06)
Halil: Algiers (1659–60)
Halil: Tripolitania (1706–09)
Arnavut Halil: Tripolitania (1673–75)
Si Halil Bu Hajib ben Salim: Tunisia (1926–32)
Halilu: Gwandu
Ibrahim Halilu: Lafiagi
Halim: Fezzan
Halim Bey: Kordofan
Halimah: Anjouan
Haliru I: Gwandu
Haliru II: Gwandu
Douglas Hall: British Somaliland
Gage Hall: Mauritius (1817–18)
James Hall: Maryland
John Hall: Uganda (1945–52); Zanzibar (1937–40)
Kenneth Hall: Malawi (1934)
Robert Hall: Sierra Leone (1952–56)
Hallaru: Daura-Baure
Robert d'Hallebast: Tangier (1955–56)
Amadou Hama: Niger (1995–96)
Hama Manga: Misau
Hama Wabi I: Jemaari
Hamad: Zanzibar (1832–33)
Seif Hamad: Zanzibar (1984–88)
Hamada: Zaria (1846)
Muhammad Shamte Hamadi: Zanzibar (1961–64)

Hamadi Madi: Comoros (2000–)
Barket Gourad Hamadou: Djibouti (1978–2001)
Hamadu: Muri
Hamadu I: Masina
Hamadu II: Masina
Hammadu III: Masina
Hamama: Daura
Hamama: Kangaba
Ahmad Ag Hamani: Mali (2002–04)
Hamani Diori: Niger (1958–74)
Hamata: Daura
Hamdan: Bornu Empire (1723–37)
Ismail Hamdani: Algeria (1998–99)
Musa Pasha Hamdi: Kordofan; Sudan (1862–65)
Hamdogu: Daura
Sayid Hamed: Zanzibar (1893–96)
Hamed Karoui: Tunisia (1989–99)
Gerhardus Van Hamel: Dutch Gold Coast (1796–98)
Atkins Hamerton: Zanzibar (1840–57)
Hamid: Harar
Hamid: Timbuktu (1647)
Hamid: Wadai
Abd al-Hamid al-Bakkush: Libya
Hamid al-Hiba: Brakna
Hamid Algabid: Niger (1983–88)
Hamid Bey: Fezzan
Hamida: Daura
Hamida: Hafsid Kingdom
Hamidu Karima: Zamfara
Hamidu Umar: Mandara
Hamilcar: Carthage (485–465 B.C.)
Hamilcar: Carthage (240 B.C.)
Daniel Hamilton: Sierra Leone (1824–25)
Arthur Hamilton-Gordon: Mauritius (1871–74)
Hammad ibn Buluggin: Hammadid Kingdom
Hammadi I: Masina
Hammadi I: Timbuktu (1651–54)
Hammadi II: Masina
Hammadi II: Timbuktu (1696, 1699–1700)
Hammadi III: Masina
Hammadi III: Timbuktu (1708–09)
Hammadi IV: Masina
Hammadi IV: Timbuktu (1735–36, 1737)
Hammadi V: Masina
Hammadi V: Timbuktu (1738)
Hamman: Muri
Hamman I: Wase
Hamman II: Wase
Hamman Lawal: Adamawa
Hamman Ruwa: Muri
Andreas Hammer: Danish Gold Coast (1792–93)
Hammu I: Timbuktu (1621–22)
Abu Hammu I Musa: Tlemcen (1308–18)
Hammu II: Timbuktu (1660–61)
Abu Hammu II ibn Abi Yaqub: Tlemcen (1359–70, 1372–89)
Abu Hammu III Musa: Tlemcen (1517–27)

Hammuda: Tunis (1782–1814)
Hammuda Pasha: Tunis (1631–59)
Buchraya Hamoudi: Western Sahara
Mouloud Hamroche: Algeria (1989–91)
Ada Hamta: Daura
Hamtiuri: Gurma
Sayid Hamud: Zanzibar (1896–1902)
Hamza: Egypt (1683–87)
Hamza: Egypt (1766–67)
Bako Hamza: Zaria (1611)
Sayid Hamza: Gran Comoro
Musa al-Hanafi: Egypt (834–839)
Hanatari: Daura
John Hanbury: Fort James
Henry Hand: Bight of Benin
Handhala ibn Safwan: Egypt (721–724, 737–742)
Jules Hanet-Cléry: Gabon (1880–82)
Abdallah Kassim Hanga: Zanzibar (1964)
Hangbe: Dahomey
Charles Hanin: Chad (1951); Gabon (1951–52)
Edward Hankinson: Bassa Cove
Hannibal: Carthage
Hanno: Carthage
Herr Hansen: Kamerun (1909, 1910, 1911–12)
Hanuf: Gwandu
Hanzala: Omayyad and Abbasid North Africa
Abu Muhammad Abd al-Haqq I: Morocco (1196–1218)
Abu Muhammad Abd al-Haqq II: Morocco (1428–65)
Haqq ad-Din I: Ifat
Haqq ad-Din II: Ifat
Harbi Ar'ed: Ifat
Arthur Hardinge: Egypt (1891–92); Zanzibar (1894–1900)
John Hare: British Kaffraria
William Hare: Ghana (1957–60)
James Harford: Saint Helena (1954–58)
Hieronimus Haring: Dutch Gold Coast (1711–16)
Baron Harlech: South Africa (1941–44)
Robert Harley: Ghana (1872–73); Sierra Leone (1873)
Charles King-Harman: Mauritius (1894); Sierra Leone (1900–04)
Haroun Kabedi: Chad (2002–03)
Charles Harper: Ashanti; Saint Helena (1925–32)
Suleiman Bey Harputli: Kordofan
Percy Wyn-Harris: Gambia (1949–58)
George Harrison: Seychelles (1822–37)
Jean-Paul Harroy: Burundi [ii]; Ruanda–Urundi
Hartama: Omayyad and Abbasid North Africa
Reginald Harte: South Africa (1912)
Harthama ibn an-Nadr: Egypt (848)
Harthama ibn Ayan: Egypt (794–795)

George Hartley: Bights of Biafra and Benin
Haru: Hadejia
Harun: Egypt (896–904)
Harun: Gwandu
Harun: Songhai (1599–1612)
Haruna: Daura-Zango
Haruna: Gombe
Haruna: Hadejia (1906–09)
Haruna: Hadejia (1950–84)
Abubakr Maje Haruna: Hadejia (1984–2002)
Mustafa Haruna Jokolo: Gwandu
al-Hasan: Zirid Kingdom
Hajji Hasan: Zeng Empire (1505–06)
Hasan I: Algiers (1682–83)
Hasan II: Algiers (1698–99)
Hasan III: Algiers (1791–98)
Hasan Abu'l Mawahib: Zeng Empire (1308–34)
Hasan Bey Salamah: Sudan (1859–61)
al-Hasan ibn Abdallah: Tlemcen
Hasan ibn Daud: Zeng Empire (1100–15)
Hasan ibn Ismail: Zeng Empire (1462–72)
Hasan ibn Suleiman: Zeng Empire (1035–64)
Hasan ibn Suleiman: Zeng Empire (1181–1200)
Hasan ibn Suleiman: Zeng Empire (1487–91)
Hasan ibn Talut: Zeng Empire (1274–93)
Suleiman al-Hasan the Great: Zeng Empire (1158–77)
Hasdrubal: Carthage (500–485 B.C.)
Hasdrubal: Carthage (220 B.C.)
Hasdrubal II: Carthage
Muhammad Abdi Hashi: Puntland
Hashim: Bornu Empire (1885–93)
Hashim: Harar
Hashim: Kordofan
Hashim Bey: Tripolitania (1899–1900)
Bako Brima Hasko: Zaria (1678–82)
Hassab Rabihi: Funj Sultanate
Ibrahim Hassabe Mayaki: Niger (1997–)
Hassan: Algiers (1598–99)
Hassan: Anjouan
Hassan: Arab North Africa
Hassan: Bauchi
Hassan: Constantine
al-Hassan: Dagomba
Hassan: Egypt (1347–51, 1354–61)
Hassan: Egypt (1580–83)
Hassan: Egypt (1687)
Hassan: Egypt (1687–89, 1707–09)
Hassan: Gombe
Mulay Hassan: Morocco (1961–)
Hassan: Muri
al-Hassan: Omayyad and Abbasid North Africa
al-Hassan: Timbuktu (1686)
Hassan: Tripolitania (1838)
Hassan: Tripolitania (1867)
Hassan: Wase
Hassan: Zamfara

Abdiqasim Salad Hassan: Somalia
Abu Yahya al-Hassan: Tunis (1168)
Kalyan Hassan: Constantine
Tsagarana Hassan: Katsina (1728–40)
Hassan I: Mayotte
Hassan I: Morocco (1873–94)
Hassan II: Idrisid State
Hassan II: Morocco (1961–99)
al-Hassan II: Timbuktu (1732–33)
al-Hassan III: Timbuktu (1741)
Hassan Abaza: Tripolitania (1679–83)
Hassan Abshir Farah: Somalia
Hassan Agha: Algiers (1535–43, 1561–62)
Hassan al-Balazi: Fezzan
Hassan al-Hajjam: Idrisid State
Abu'l Hassan Ali: Algiers (1637–38)
Abu'l Hassan Ali: Tripolitania (1037–38)
Kamal Hassan Ali: Egypt (1984)
Abu'l Hassan Ali I: Morocco (1331–48)
Abu'l Hassan Ali al-Mandari: Tangier (1437–71)
Hassan Ali Pasha Arnavut: Kordofan
Hassan ash-Sharawi: Egypt (1752–55)
Mulay Hassan ben al-Mahdi: Spanish Morocco (1925–56)
Hassan Bey: Oran (1831)
Hassan Bey Hilmi: Darfur
Hassan Corso: Algiers (1556–57)
Hassan Gouled Aptidon: Djibouti (1977–)
Hassan Husni: Tripolitania (1903–04, 1909–10)
al-Hassan ibn at-Takhtah: Egypt (808–810)
Hassan ibn Atahiya: Egypt (745)
Hassan ibn Hussein: Egypt (1605–07)
Hassan Muhammad Nur Shatigadud: Southwestern Somalia
Ali Hassan Mwinyi: Zanzibar (1984–85)
Hassan Pasha: Algiers (1544–52, 1557–68)
Hassan Sabry: Egypt (1940)
Hassan Shahu: Fulani Empire
Hassan Veneziano: Algiers (1557–88)
Abu'l Hassan Yanis: Tripolitania (1000–01)
Sheikh Hassana: Adrar
Haterius Nepos: Egypt (121–126)
Hatim ibn Harthama: Egypt (810–811, 849)
Abu Hatim Rawh: Omayyad and Abbasid North Africa
Abu Hatim Yusuf: Rustumid Amirate
ben Hajj Hatmi: Rif Republic
Hatshepsut Makare: Egypt (18th Dynasty)
James Haugh: Cyrenaica
Jean de Hauteclocque: Tunisia (1952–53)
Philippe Leclerc de Hauteclocq: Cameroun (1940)
Comte d'Hautpoul: Algeria (1850–51)
Arthur Havelock: Natal (1886–89);

Sierra Leone (1881–84); Seychelles (1879–80)
Nicolaas C. Havenga: South Africa (1954)
Hawadle Madar: Somalia
Edward Hawkesworth: Ashanti
al-Hawthara ibn Suheyl: Egypt (745–748)
Charles Hay: Cape Colony (1870)
James Hay: Gambia (1886); Sierra Leone (1886–87, 1888–91)
Edward Drummond-Hay: Saint Helena (1856–63)
Hayarum: Trarza
Sadou Hayatou: Cameroun (1991–92)
Haydar Agha Zade: Egypt (1646–47)
Jacob Blanquet de la Haye: Fort-Dauphin
Joseph Hayes: Comoros (1868–69); Nossi-Bé
Hayla Melekot: Shoa
Ras Abeto Haylu: Gojjam
Tedla Haylu: Gojjam
Takla Haymanot: Ethiopia (1706–08)
Takla Haymanot II: Ethiopia (1769–77)
Abu Ja'far Hazarmard Umar: Omayyad and Abbasid North Africa
Charles Panon de Hazier: Gabon (1873–75)
Hazo: Daura
Aliyu Jan Hazo I: Katsina (1589–95)
Aliyu Jan Hazo II: Katsina (1612–14)
Jan Hazo III: Katsina (1715–28)
William Heath: Fort James
Paul Heckman: Côte d'Ivoire (1892–93)
Hedi Baccouche: Tunisia (1987–89)
Hedi Nouira: Tunisia (1970–80)
Lucius Hedius Rufus Lollianus Avitus: Africa [i] (157–158)
Nesbanebded Hedjkheperre: Egypt (21st Dynasty)
Sheshonk I Hedjkheperre: Egypt (22nd Dynasty)
Takelot II Hedjkheperre: Egypt (22nd Dynasty)
Abdul Aziz Hegazy: Egypt (1974–75)
Pierre d'Héguerty: Réunion (1739–43)
Ludvig von Hein: Danish Gold Coast (1831)
Rameses IV Hekamare Setpenamun: Egypt (20th Dynasty)
Amenemnisu Hekawise Neferkare: Egypt (21st Dynasty)
Sheshonk II Hekenkheperre: Egypt (22nd Dynasty)
Willem Helot: Cape Colony (1711–14)
Avidius Heliodorus: Egypt (139–148)
Louis de Hell: Réunion (1838–41)
Knox Helm: Sudan (1955)
Walter Hely-Hutchinson: Cape Colony (1901–10); Natal (1893–1901)
Conrad von Hemsen: Danish Gold Coast (1777–80)
Hen Kon Wanko Dam: Songhai (1044–63)

Daniel Van Den Henghel: Cape Colony (1737–39)
John Pope-Hennessey: Ghana (1872); Mauritius (1883–87); Sierra Leone (1872–73)
Herbert Henniker: Gambia (1918–19, 1920–21)
Francisco Henriques: Madeira (1622–24)
João Henriques: Cape Verde (1766–67)
Lopo Henriques: Cacheu (1798)
Pedro Henriques: Mombasa (1682)
Rodrigo Henriques: Angola (1652–53)
Joseph Henry: Congo (Zaire) (1916–21)
Philippe Henry: Mali (1912–13, 1915)
Heperkare Maluiane: Kush (463–435 B.C.)
Hephaestus: Egypt (527)
Bernard Hepp: Benin [ii] (1958)
Septimius Heracleitus: Egypt (215–216)
Heraclius: Byzantine North Africa
Miguel de Heredia: Canary Islands (1768–75)
Sekhemre Herhimae Intef: Egypt (17th Dynasty)
Marius Herignon: Réunion (1906)
Herihor: Egypt (21st Dynasty)
Neferabre Herinutarekamen: Kush (431–405 B.C.)
Hermogenes: Africa Proconsularis (349–350)
Enrique Hernández: Melilla (1998–99)
Venancio Hernández y Fernández: Melilla (1899–1904)
David Hernn: Danish Gold Coast (1722–23)
Pedro de Herredia: Melilla (1603–11)
Diego de Herrera: Canary Islands (1444–76)
Pedro de Herrera: Gran Canaria
Diego de Herro: Gran Canaria
Muhammad Muse Hersi Adde: Puntland
Muhammad Siyad Hersi Morgan: Jubaland
James (J.B.M.) Hertzog: South Africa (1924–39)
Sameramne Herusaatef: Kush (404–369 B.C.)
Édouard Hesling: Burkina Faso (1919–21, 1922–27)
Hesperius: Africa Proconsularis (378–382)
Ganye Hesu: Dahomey
Hetepibre: Egypt (13th Dynasty)
Hetepsekhemwy: Egypt (2nd Dynasty)
J. Christian Heunis: South Africa (1989)
Heupruladze: Egypt (1729–33)
Edward Hyde Hewett: Bights of Biafra and Benin; Southern Nigeria
Hezba Asqad: Ethiopia (1295–96)
Hezba Nan: Ethiopia (1430–33)

Hezba Seyon: Axum
Hezekiyas: Ethiopia (1789–94)
Hiakpon: Porto-Novo
Hiassae: Mandara
Ahmad al-Hiba: Brakna
Hamid al-Hiba: Brakna
Muhammad al-Hiba: Brakna
Abdul Hidi Pasha: Egypt (1948–49)
Hiempsal I: Numidia
Hiempsal II: Numidia
Hifekepenye Pohamba: Namibia (2005–)
James Higginson: Mauritius (1851–57)
Naguib al-Hilaili Pasha: Egypt (1952)
Hilal ibn Bedr: Egypt (921–923)
Hilal Limann: Ghana (1979–81)
Maecilius Hilarianus: Africa Proconsularis (354–355)
Hilarius: Africa Proconsularis (396)
Hilderich: Vandal North Africa
Stephen Hill: Ghana (1851–54); Sierra Leone (1854–61)
William Hill: Sierra Leone (1861–62)
Worsley Hill: Ghana (1843–45)
Abbas II Hilmi: Egypt (1892–1914)
Abd al-Kadir Pasha Hilmi: Sudan (1882–83)
Hassan Bey Hilmi: Darfur
Albert Hime: Natal (1899–1903)
Himilco: Carthage
George Hingston: Ghana (1828)
Hintsa: Kreli's Country
John Hippisley: Ghana (1766)
James-Édouard Hirtzman: Chad (1912)
Hisham: Morocco (1792–93)
Talib Hiyar: Brakna
Hizr: Algiers (1589–92, 1594–96, 1603–05, 1621)
Col. Hocquart: Niger (1911–12)
Frederic Hodgson: Ghana (1889–90, 1891–91, 1893–94, 1896, 1897–1900)
Muhammadu Hodi: Argungu
Arnold Hodson: Ghana (1934–41); Sierra Leone (1931–34)
René Hoffherr: Cameroun (1947–49)
Josias Hoffman: Orange Free State (1854–55)
Gysbert Hofmeyer: Namibia (1920–26)
Friedrich Höhne: Orange Free State (1872)
Ismail Hoja: Tripolitania (1710–11)
King Holiday: Bonny
Hugh Hole: North Western Rhodesia
David Hollamby: Saint Helena (1999–2004)
Claud Hollis: Sierra Leone (1913); Zanzibar (1924–29)
Oliver Holmes Jr.: Maryland
Bantu Holomisa: Transkei
Vasco Homem: Mozambique (1573–77)
Evelyn Hone: Zambia (1959–64)
Montagu Honey: Seychelles (1928–34); Swaziland (1916–28)

Domitius Honoratus: Egypt (165–166)
Petronius Honoratus: Egypt (148–150)
Maevius Honorianus: Egypt (232)
Sextus Cocceius Severianus Honorinus: Africa [i] (163–164)
Johannes Hoogenboom: Dutch Gold Coast (1807–08)
Petrus Hoogenhout: Namibia (1943–51)
Gijsbrecht Van Hoogveldt: Hollandia
Alan Hoole: Saint Helena (1991–95)
John Hope Smith: Ghana (1817–22)
Hophra Wahimbre: Egypt (26th Dynasty)
David Hopkins: Bights of Biafra and Benin
Awibre Hor: Egypt (13th Dynasty)
Horemheb Djeserkheprure: Egypt (18th Dynasty)
Waldemar Horn: Togoland
Ventura de Landaeta y Horna: Canary Islands (1713–18)
Francisco de Horta: Ceuta (1805–07)
Cnaeus Hosidius Geta: Africa [i] (57–58)
Theodore Hoskins-Abrahall: Nigeria Western Region
Muhammad Hosni Mubarrak: Egypt (1981–)
Merneptah Binere Meryamun Hotphimae: Egypt (19th Dynasty)
M. Hoube: Senegal (1846)
Danie Hough: Namibia (1980–83)
Khalifa Houmadi: Comoros (1994–95)
Adrien Houngbédji: Benin [ii] (1996–98)
Félix Houphouët-Boigny: Côte d'Ivoire (1959–93)
Jasper Van Houssen: Dutch Gold Coast (1659–62)
Wilfred Davidson-Houston: Malawi (1929)
Abraham Houtman: Dutch Gold Coast (1722–23)
Daniel Howard: Liberia (1912–20)
Robert Howe: Sudan (1947–54)
Patrício Gómez de la Hoz: Melilla (1714–15)
Louis Hubert-Delisle: Réunion (1852–58)
Hubert Huddleston: Sudan (1940–47)
Hude: Porto-Novo
Hudji: Porto-Novo
Robert Hudson: Zimbabwe (1944–45, 1946–47)
Hueze: Allada
Hueze: Porto-Novo
Huffon: Porto-Novo
Huffon: Whydah
Jan Hugenholz: Dutch Gold Coast (1871)
Walter Huggard: South Africa (1940–41, 1944)
Godfrey Huggins: Federation of

Rhodesia and Nyasaland; Zimbabwe (1933–53)
Horatio Huggins: Sierra Leone (1877)
Gi-gla Gunhu Hugnon: Allada
Hubert Hugo: Mauritius (1673–77)
Hukare Atlanersa: Kush (653–643 B.C.)
Richard Hull: Fort James
Pierre Humbert: Mali (1891–92)
Humé ibn Abd al-Jalil: Kanem
Humeyd ibn Kahtaba: Egypt (760–762)
Hunefertemre: Kush (ca. 671 B.C.)
Hunerich: Vandal North Africa
Huni: Egypt (3rd Dynasty)
William Hunt: Nigeria Southern Provinces
Frederick Hunter: British Somaliland
Henry Huntley: Gambia (1840–41)
Hunungungu: Allada
al-Hurr ibn Yusuf: Egypt (724–727)
Husain I: Algiers (1683–86)
Husain I: Tunis (1705–35)
Husain II: Tunis (1824–35)
Husain II Khoja: Algiers (1705–06)
Husain III: Algiers (1818–30)
Najib Husaini: Kazaure
Hassan Husni: Tripolitania (1903–04, 1909–10)
Muhammad IV Hussain: Darfur
Sheikh Hussein: Algiers (1613–16, 1617–19, 1638–40)
Hussein: Algiers (1627–34)
Hussein: Anjouan
Hussein: Egypt (1573–75)
Hussein: Egypt (1620–22)
Hussein: Egypt (1635–37)
Hussein: Egypt (1673–75)
Hussein: Egypt (1697–99)
Hussein: Ifat
Hussein: Tripolitania (1588–95)
Abdi Rizak Hajji Hussein: Somalia
Abdou Muhammad Hussein: Nzwani
Mokhtar Muhammad Hussein: Somalia
Hussein Effendi: Tripolitania (1903–04, 1909–10)
Hussein ibn Suleiman: Zeng Empire (1358–64, 1392–1416)
al-Hussein ibn Gemil: Egypt (806–808)
Mehmed Hussein Javush Bey: Tripolitania (1711)
Hussein Khamil: Egypt (1914–17)
Hussein Maziq: Libya
Kuchuk Hussein Pasha: Egypt (1801–02)
Hussein Rushdi Pasha: Egypt (1914–19)
Hussein Sirry Pasha: Egypt (1940–42, 1949–50, 1952)
Louis Husson: French Equatorial Africa (1940)
Thomas Hutchinson: Bight of Biafra
Walter Hely-Hutchinson: Cape Colony (1901–10); Natal (1893–1901)
Charles Hutchison: Saint Helena (1747–64)

Jan Huydecooper: Dutch Gold Coast (1759–60, 1764–69)
Huyi: Porto-Novo
H.B. Hyde: Sierra Leone (1815)
Edward Hyde Hewett: Bights of Biafra and Benin; Southern Nigeria
Mari Vira Hyel: Biu
Hypatius: Africa Proconsularis (382–383); Egypt (383–384, 392–392)

I

Alphonse Iaeck: Central African Republic (1904–05)
Kumba Ialá: Guinea-Bissau (2000–03)
Wahibre Iayeb: Egypt (13th Dynasty)
Marqués de la Cáñada Ibáñez: Canary Islands (1779–84)
Francisco Ibáñez y Rubalcava: Melilla (1719)
José de la Ibarra: Fernando Po
Sayid ibn Abdallah: Zanzibar (1960–63)
Sayid Jamshid ibn Abdallah: Zanzibar (1963–64)
ibn al-Batai'hi: Egypt (1121–25)
ibn Kallis: Egypt (973–991)
Mallam ibn Maina: Damagaram
ibn as-Salar: Egypt (1152–53)
Ibrahim: Algiers (1655–56, 1658–59)
Ibrahim: Algiers (1686–88)
Ibrahim: Bauchi
Ibrahim: Bornu Empire (1817–46)
Ibrahim: Bornu Empire (1884–85)
Ibrahim: Darfur
Ibrahim: Egypt (1525)
Ibrahim: Egypt (1583–85)
Ibrahim: Egypt (1622–23)
Ibrahim: Egypt (1661–64)
Ibrahim: Egypt (1667–68)
Ibrahim: Egypt (1669–73)
Ibrahim: Egypt (1709–10)
Ibrahim: Egypt (1848)
Ibrahim: Gobir
Ibrahim: Katsina (1870–82)
Ibrahim: Keffi
Ibrahim: Lapai
Ibrahim: Masina
Ibrahim: Muri
Ibrahim: Tripolitania (1595–1600)
Ibrahim: Tripolitania (1910–11)
Ibrahim: Tunis (1704–05)
Ibrahim: Wadai
Ibrahim: Zaria (1924–37)
Abdallah Ibrahim: Morocco (1958–60)
Abdallah Ibrahim: Nzwani
Abu Ishaq Ibrahim: Hafsid Kingdom
Abu Ishaq Ibrahim: Tunis (1159)
Abu Ishaq Ibrahim: Tunis (1221)
Awal Ibrahim: Abuja
Biri II Ibrahim: Bornu Empire (1288–1307)
Maje Ibrahim: Katsina (1614–31)
Nyoja Ibrahim: Bamoun
Ibrahim I: Adal [ii]
Ibrahim I: Algiers (1710)
Ibrahim I: Bornu Empire (1307–26)

Ibrahim I: Damagaram
Ibrahim I: Timbuktu (1627–28)
Abu Ishaq Ibrahim I: Hafsid Kingdom
Ibrahim II: Adal [ii]
Ibrahim II: Aghlabid Empire
Ibrahim II: Algiers (1731–45)
Ibrahim II: Bornu Empire (1442–50)
Ibrahim II: Damagaram
Ibrahim II: Timbuktu (1691–94)
Kuchuk Ibrahim II: Algiers (1745–48)
Ibrahim III: Bornu Empire (1617–25)
al-Fah Ibrahim III: Timbuktu (1738)
al-Fah Ibrahim IV: Timbuktu (1738)
Ibrahim Abboud: Sudan (1958–64)
Ibrahim Abderrahman Halidi: Comoros (1993)
al-Hajj Ibrahim Adamu: Kazaure
Ibrahim al-Hajj: Egypt (1603–04)
Ibrahim Alayali: Tripolitania (1709–10)
Ibrahim ash-Sharif: Tunis (1702–04)
Ibrahim Ayalai: Abuja
Ibrahim Babangida: Nigeria (1985–93)
Ibrahim Baré Maïnassara: Niger (1996–99)
Ibrahim Bey: Egypt (1790–98)
Ibrahim Boubakar Keita: Mali (1994–2000)
Ibrahim Dabo: Kano (1819–45)
Ibrahim Dasuki: Fulani Empire
Ibrahim Dodo Musa: Abuja
Muhammad Ibrahim Egal: British Somaliland; Somalia; Somaliland Republic
Ibrahim Gamda: Katsina (1635–44)
Ibrahim Halilu: Lafiagi
Ibrahim Hassabe Mayaki: Niger (1997–)
Ibrahim ibn al-Aghlab: Aghlabid Empire
Sa'id Ibrahim ibn Ali: Comoros (1970–72)
Ibrahim ibn Ismail al-Hafs: Tripolitania (1221)
Ibrahim ibn Muhammad: Zeng Empire (1491–96)
Ibrahim ibn Muhammadu Urada: Wadai
Ibrahim ibn Salih: Egypt (781–784, 792–793)
Ibrahim ibn Suleiman: Zeng Empire (1500–04, 1507–08)
Ibrahim ibn Tashufin: Almoravid Empire
Ibrahim Jelebi: Tripolitania (1676)
Ibrahim Kabay: Songhai (1347–54)
Ibrahim Misirli-Oglu: Tripolitania (1675–76)
Ibrahim Muhammad Maccido: Fulani Empire
Ibrahim Musa: Futa Jallon
Ibrahim Nagamatse: Kontagora
Yehia Ibrahim Pasha: Egypt (1923–24, 1933–34)
Ibrahim Pasha Fawzi: Egypt (1970–72)
Ibrahim Ruzili: Tunis (1587–90)

Ibrahim Sura: Katsina (1541–43)
Ibrahim Terzi: Tripolitania (1687)
Ibrahim Yanka Dari: Katsina (1410–52)
Ibrahim Zakiyul Kalbi: Katagum
Ibrahima: Nupe
Alfa Ibrahima Sori: Futa Jallon
Ibrahima Sori I: Futa Jallon
Ibrahima Sori II: Futa Jallon
Ibrahima Sori III: Futa Jallon
Ibrahimu: Yauri
Dan Ibrahimu: Yauri
Maliki Dan Ibrahimu: Argungu
Ibrahimu I: Argungu
Ibrahimu II: Argungu
Ibrahimu Na Mai Fura: Gobir
Ibrihimu: Zaria (1539–66)
Sayid Idarus: Anjouan
Idewu Ogulari: Lagos (1832–33)
Idoko: Igala
Idoko Adegbe: Igala
Sa'id Abu'l Ala Idris: Tripolitania (1221–23); Tunis (1221–23)
Idris I: Libya
Idris I ibn Abdallah: Idrisid State
Idris I Nigalemi: Bornu Empire (1353–77)
Idris II: Idrisid State
Mulay Idris II: Idrisid State
Idris III al-Ma'mun: Almohad Empire
Idris IV: Bornu Empire (1685–1704)
Idris IV Abu l'Ula al-Wathiq: Almohad Empire
Idris Abdul Wakil: Zanzibar (1985–99)
Idris al-Mahdi as-Sanusi: Cyrenaica; Libya; Tripolitania (1922–51)
Idris Alooma: Bornu Empire (1580–1603)
Idris Katarkamabi: Bornu Empire (1504–26)
Idris Wad Daftar: Bahr al-Ghazal
Idriso: Daniski
Idriss Déby: Chad (1990–)
Idrissa: Fika
Idrissa Seck: Senegal (2002–04)
Idrisu I: Nupe
Idrisu II: Nupe
Willem Van Idzinga: Dutch Gold Coast (1866–67)
Igbani: Bonny
Igbessa: New Calabar
Mariano de la Iglesia y Guillén: Melilla (1887–88)
José Iglesias: Spanish Morocco (1945–51)
Igonibaw: New Calabar
Ikaneng: Bamaleteland
Ikata: Brass
Baher Ikela: Axum
Muhammad al-Ikhshid: Egypt (935–946)
Joseph Ileo: Congo (Zaire) (1960–61)
Iliyasu: Nupe
Ilo: Masina
Ilunga: Kazembe
Cibinda Ilunga: Lunda
Yavu Ilunga: Lunda

Ilunga Kaabala: Luba
Ilunga Kalala: Luba
Ilunga Sunga: Luba
Ilute: Barotseland
Mehmed Imam: Tripolitania (1702–06)
Mehmed Imam Kerdeki: Tripolitania (1687–1701)
Imam Sa'if ibn Sultan: Mombasa (1698)
Imasiku: Barotseland
Faustino Imbali: Guinea-Bissau (2001)
Immanuel Amde Michael: Eritrea
Mikael Imru: Ethiopia (1974)
Imwiko Lewanika: Barotseland
Abu Inan Faris: Morocco (1348–58)
Earl of Inchiquin: Tangier (1675–80)
Ada Inda: Daura
Conde de Aguilar de Inestrillas: Oran (1608–16)
Eduard Van Ingen: Dutch Gold Coast (1833–34)
Mustafa Inglis: Constantine
Thomas Ingram: Gambia (1837–38, 1839–40, 1841–43)
William Ingrams: Gold Coast Northern Territories
Merhetepre Ini: Egypt (13th Dynasty)
Innagari: Daura
James Rose-Innes: South Africa (1920, 1923–24)
James Rose-Innes, Jr.: Griqualand West
Innocentius: Byzantine North Africa
Ephraim Inoni: Cameroun (2004–)
Nubkheperre Intef: Egypt (17th Dynasty)
Sehertowy Intef: Egypt (10th Dynasty)
Sekhemre Herhimae Intef: Egypt (17th Dynasty)
Sekhemre Wepmae Intef: Egypt (17th Dynasty)
Intef II: Egypt (10th Dynasty)
Intef III: Egypt (10th Dynasty)
Muhammadu Inuwa Abbas: Kano (1963)
Inyambo: Barotseland
Ioannes: Egypt (582, 588, 606)
Ioannes Laxarion: Egypt (542)
Iphthas: Mauretania West
Ipuor: Bonny
Abu-Iqal al-Aghlab: Aghlabid Empire
Francisco de Andía Irarrazábal y Zárate: Canary Islands (1625–26)
Setpenanhur Irmaenre Djeho: Egypt (30th Dynasty)
Johnson Aguiyi-Ironsi: Nigeria (1966)
Isa: Egypt (905, 906–910)
Isa: Mayotte
Isa: Omayyad and Abbasid North Africa
Isa Bige N'Gone: Kayor
Isa Dan Muhammadu: Jema'a
Isa ibn Lukman: Egypt (778–779)
Isa ibn Mansur: Egypt (831–832, 843–847)
Isa ibn Yezid: Egypt (829–830)
Isa Muhammadu: Jema'a

Isa Mustafa Agwa: Lafia
Isa Tein-Dyor: Baol; Kayor
Isa-Tende: Kayor
Isaac I: Ethiopia (1414–29)
Isaac Benjamin Pratt: Aku
Isang: Bakgatlaland
Olimi III Isansa: Bunyoro
Abdallah Derow Isaq: Somalia
Isawi: Kordofan
Ishak Bey: Tripolitania (1918)
Mallam Ishaku: Daura
Ishaq: Zaria (1736–38)
Ishaq I: Songhai (1539–49)
Ishaq II: Songhai (1588–91)
Ishaq ibn Ali: Almoravid Empire
Ishaq ibn Suleiman: Egypt (793–794)
Abu Ishaq Ibrahim: Hafsid Kingdom
Abu Ishaq Ibrahim: Tunis (1159)
Abu Ishaq Ibrahim: Tunis (1221)
Abu Ishaq Ibrahim I: Hafsid Kingdom
Ishaq Jatau: Zaria (1796–1802)
Ishifi: Gobir
Bako Ishihako: Zaria (1736–38)
Ishihako Jatai: Zaria (1796–1802)
Isike: Mirambo
Isingoma Mpuga Rukidi: Bunyoro
Isitoso: Swaziland (1899)
Iskander: Egypt (1556–59)
Tsherkes Iskander: Egypt (1568–71)
Iskender: Tripolitania (1600–06)
Louis Brière de l'Isle: Senegal (1876–80)
Duc d'Isly: Algeria (1841–45)
Ismail: Algiers (1659–71)
Ismail: Egypt (1343–44)
Ismail: Egypt (1695–97)
Ismail: Egypt (1863–79)
Ismail: Songhai (1538–39)
Ismail: Songhai (1635–40)
Ismail al-Azhari: Sudan (1954–56, 1965–69)
Mulay Ismail as-Samin: Morocco (1672–1727)
Ismail Bey: Egypt (1777–78, 1786–90)
Ismail Hamdani: Algeria (1998–99)
Ismail Hoja: Tripolitania (1710–11)
Ismail ibn Badi: Funj Sultanate
Ismail ibn Hussein: Zeng Empire (1447–60)
Ismail ibn Isa: Egypt (798)
Ismail ibn Salih: Egypt (797–798)
Ismail Pasha: Sudan (1872–77)
Ismail Pasha Abu Jabal: Sudan (1852–53)
Ismail Sidqi Pasha: Egypt (1930–33, 1946–46)
Ismaila: Fika
Mbala Kmong Isot: Lunda
Israel: Dongola
Abdallah Issa: British Somaliland
Abdullahi Issa Muhammad: Italian Somaliland (1956–60)
Muhammadou Issoufou: Niger (1993–94)
Istabanos: Dongola
Miftah al-Istah: Libya
Minicius Italus: Egypt (105–109)

Ay Kheperkheprure Itnute: Egypt (18th Dynasty)
Itodo: Igala
Iuput I: Egypt (23rd Dynasty)
Iuput II: Egypt (23rd Dynasty)
Iustinus: Egypt (566)
Iustinus: Egypt (600–603)
Merneferre Iy: Egypt (13th Dynasty)
Muhammadu Yerima Iya: Adamawa
Lij Iyasu: Ethiopia (1911–16)
Iyasu I: Ethiopia (1682–1706)
Iyasu II: Ethiopia (1730–55)
Iyasu III: Ethiopia (1784–88)
Iyasu IV: Ethiopia (1830–32)
Amda Iyasus: Ethiopia (1433–34)
Sarwe Iyasus: Ethiopia (1433)
Tasfa Iyasus: Ethiopia (1270–85)
Chikombi Iyavu: Lunda
Mbal Iyavu: Lunda
Iyoas I: Ethiopia (1755–69)
Iyoas II: Ethiopia (1818–21)
Djedkare Izezi: Egypt (5th Dynasty)
Hajji Abdallah Izmirli: Tripolitania (1684–87)
Luis Ramos Izquierdo: Fernando Po
Hajji Ahmed Izzet: Tripolitania (1848–49)
Ahmed Izzet: Tripolitania (1858–60, 1879–80)

J

Abu Ja: Abuja; Zaria (1825–28)
Ja'afaru: Zaria (1937–59)
Jaaku: Daura
Adriaan Van Jaarsveld: Graaff-Reinet
Ismail Pasha Abu Jabal: Sudan (1852–53)
Jabu: Daura
Ada Jabu: Daura
Jack Coby: Koya-Temne
Francis Jackson: Ashanti; British Togoland; Gold Coast Northern Territories
Frederick Jackson: Uganda (1894, 1897, 1911–18)
John Jackson: Ghana (1828–30)
Wilfred Jackson: Mauritius (1930–37); Tanganyika
Jackson Kpavuvu Lawson IV: Little Popo
Jacob: Axum
Jacob II: Axum
Adriaan Jacobs: Dutch Gold Coast (1624–38)
Thomas Jacobsen: Danish Gold Coast (1694–96)
M. Jacquet: Senegal (1664–68)
Aggrey Jaden: Southern Sudan
Jadkaure Shebitku: Kush (ca. 650 B.C.)
Ja'far: Algiers (1580–82)
Ja'far: Egypt (1618–19)
Ja'far: Tripolitania (1569–80)
Ja'far an-Numayri: Sudan (1969–85)
Abu Ja'far Hazarmard Umar: Omayyad and Abbasid North Africa

Ja'far Pasha Mazhar: Sudan (1866–71)
Ja'far Pasha Sadiq: Sudan (1865–66)
Sai'd Muhammad Jaffar: Comoros (1975–76)
Sa'id Muhammad Jaffar al-Angadi: Comoros (1972)
Jaga Álvaro II: Kongo
Jagba: Whydah
Jager Afrikaner: Oorlam Territory
Jaja: Bonny
Jaja: Opobo
Jaji: Potiskum
Musa Dan Jaji: Lafia
Michel Jajolet de la Courbe: Senegal (1689–90, 1706–10)
Jaka: Daura
Jaketake: Daura
Jakwa Birtitik: Biu
Abdal-Salem Jallud: Libya
Jama: Zululand
Osman Jama Ali: Somalia
Jama Ali Jama: Puntland
Jamal ad-Din I: Ifat
Jamal ad-Din II: Adal [ii]
Badr al-Jamali: Egypt (1074–94)
Jamata: Daura
Jambalat-Zade: Egypt (1673–75)
Frederick James: Liberia (1822)
Leander (Starr) Jameson: Cape Colony (1904–08); Rhodesia (1891–95)
Prince Jameson Mbilini Dhlamini: Swaziland (1993–96)
Yahya Jammeh: Gambia (1994–)
Sayid Jamshid ibn Abdallah: Zanzibar (1963–64)
Bawa Jan Gwarzo: Gobir
Aliyu Jan Hazo I: Katsina (1589–95)
Aliyu Jan Hazo II: Katsina (1612–14)
Jan Hazo III: Katsina (1715–28)
Jan Jonker Afrikaner: Oorlam Territory
Jan Rina: Yauri
Janbalat: Egypt (1500–01)
Jangilizwe: Tembuland
Hudson Janisch: Saint Helena (1873–84)
Jankare: Kano (998)
Ernest Jansen: South Africa (1951–59)
Camille Janssen: Congo (Zaire) (1887–91)
Jan Janssens: Cape Colony (1803–06)
Jantabu: Lapai
Abu Sa'id Jaqmaq: Egypt (1438–53)
Cipriano Jardim: São Tomé and Príncipe (1897–99)
Douglas Jardine: Sierra Leone (1937–41); Tanganyika
Ali Pasha Jarkis: Sudan (1855–57)
Jarnanata: Katsina (1250–1300)
Mari Jata I: Kangaba; Mali Empire
Mari Jata II: Mali Empire
Ishihako Jatai: Zaria (1796–1802)
Jatau: Abuja
Jatau: Biram
Jatau: Zamfara
Abubakar Jatau: Yauri
Ishaq Jatau: Zaria (1796–1802)

Jean-Bernard Jauréguiberry: Senegal (1861–63)
Bali Javush: Tripolitania (1672–73)
Mehmed Hussein Javush Bey: Tripolitania (1711)
Dawda Jawara: Gambia (1962–94); Senegambia Confederation
Muhammad Jawda: Wadai
Jayin: Oyo
Jaysh: Egypt (896)
Ali Pasha Jazairli: Egypt (1803–04)
Jaziwi: Ifat
Mehmed Jelaleddin: Tripolitania (1876–78)
Ibrahim Jelebi: Tripolitania (1676)
Abu Jemal Yusuf: Algiers (1640–42)
Jemba: Buganda
Jenhako: Zaria (ca. 1480)
Robert Jenkins: Saint Helena (1739–41)
Ahmadu Jerabana: Yauri
Suleimanu Jerabana: Yauri
Jerabana I: Yauri
Jerabana II: Yauri
John Jeremie: Sierra Leone (1840–41)
Jordán Jerez: Melilla (1649–50)
Hubert Jerningham: Mauritius (1892–97)
Henry Jervis: Port Natal
Christian Jessen: Danish Gold Coast (1757–62)
Driss Jettou: Morocco (2002–)
Ali Jezairli: Tripolitania (1683–84)
Jia: Nupe
Jibo: Daura-Baure
Jibrilu: Keffi
Jibrilu: Nupe
Jibrilu: Yauri (1835–44, 1848–69)
Jibrilu: Yauri (1904–15)
Jibrin: Nupe
Jiga: Nupe
Jigba: Nupe
Di Jigi Bilali: Kangaba
Jil: Kanem
Jilabataji: Gobir
Jilim: Kanem
Jimada: East Nupe
Jimami: Biram
Jimir Dakka: Zamfara
Jimirra: Zamfara
Jimmy: Koya-Temne
Jina: Kom
Teslim Jinadu-Eko: Lagos (2003)
Jinga: Ndongo
Jinjiku: Zaria (ca. 1480)
Jirau: Zamfara
Jiro: Daura
João: Warri
João I: Kongo
João II: Kongo
Richard Jobson: Fort James
Joda: Wadai
Johannes: Africa Proconsularis (412–413, 422)
Johannes: Byzantine North Africa
Johannes: Byzantine North Africa
Johannes: Dongola

Johannes Rogathinos: Byzantine North Africa
Johannes Troglita: Byzantine North Africa
John I: Ethiopia (1667–82)
John II: Ethiopia (1769–69)
John III: Ethiopia (1840–41, 1850–51)
John IV: Ethiopia (1872–89)
Don John of Austria: Tunis (1573–74)
John Macaulay: Aku
Edward Johnson: Saint Helena (1719–23)
Elijah Johnson: Liberia (1822, 1823)
Hilary Johnson: Liberia (1884–92)
Joshua Johnson: Saint Helena (1690–93)
Harry Johnston: Malawi (1889–96); Uganda (1899–1901)
William Johnston: Ghana (1874)
Mustafa Haruna Jokolo: Gwandu
Jean Joliet: Comoros (1905–06)
Leabua Jonathan: Lesotho (1965–86)
Edward Jones: Gold Coast Northern Territories
Glyn Jones: Malawi (1961–66)
Rokeby Jones: Ghana (1865)
W.H.Q. Jones: Sierra Leone (1892–93, 1894)
William Jones: Gold Coast Northern Territories
Jongintaba: Tembuland
Celestin Jonnart: Algeria (1900–01, 1903–11, 1918–19)
Francisco Gómez Jordana y Sousa: Spanish Morocco (1928–31)
Léonce Jore: Madagascar (1936–37); Niger (1923–25); Senegal (1926–29)
Peter Jørgensen: Danish Gold Coast (1740–43)
Joshua: Barolongland
Piet Joubert: Transvaal (1875–76, 1880–84)
Willem Joubert: Lydenburg
Maxime Jourdan: Senegal (1954–55)
George Joy: Saint Helena (1947–54)
Joyi: Tembuland
Juba I: Numidia
Caius Julius Juba II: Mauretania
Jean Guillaume Jubelin: Senegal (1828–29)
Jubo Jubogha: Opobo
Judith: Axum
Aneerood Jugnauth: Mauritius (1982–95, 2000–03)
Jugurtha: Numidia
Alphonse Juin: French Morocco
Julianus: Egypt (ca. 240)
Julianus: Egypt (380)
Col. Julien: Chad (1901–02)
Gustave Julien: Côte d'Ivoire (1913–14)
Édouard Julien-Laferrière: Algeria (1898–1900)
Julius Alexander: Egypt (68–71)
Caius Julius Juba II: Mauretania
Julius Lupus: Egypt (71)

Sextus Julius Major: Africa [i] (141–142)

Julius Postumus: Egypt (47–48)

Julius Severus: Egypt (32)

Julius Vestinus: Egypt (60–67)

Philippe Jullien: Réunion (1910)

Dan Juma I: Gumel

Omar Ali Juma: Zanzibar (1988–95)

Adamu Jumba: Bauchi

Suleiman Tiya Adamu Jumba: Bauchi

Aboud Jumbe: Zanzibar (1972–84)

Jumbe Fatimah: Mohéli

Oko Jumbo: Bonny

Eugène Jungers: Congo (Zaire) (1947–51)

Pierre Jungers: Ruanda–Urundi

Carlos Gomes Júnior: Guinea-Bissau (2004–)

Quintus Junius Blaesus: Africa [i] (21–23)

Junius Quartus Palladius: Africa Proconsularis (416–421)

Marcus Junius Silanus: Africa [i] (29–35)

Junju: Buganda

Junker Afrikaner: Oorlam Territory

Henri Justamont: Réunion (1715–18)

Juwan Qapiji Sultanzade: Egypt (1637–40)

Andrew Juxon-Smith: Sierra Leone (1967–68)

K

Zwelithini Goodwill Ka Bhekuzulu: Zululand

Ilunga Kaabala: Luba

Mustafa Kaak: Tunisia (1947–50)

Da Kaba: Segu

Mukas Munying Kabalond: Lunda

Cwa II Kabarega: Bunyoro

Ibrahim Kabay: Songhai (1347–54)

al-Hajji Kabe: Kano (1743–52)

Haroun Kabedi: Chad (2002–03)

Kabelepile: Barolongland

Kabigumere: Bunyoro

Joseph Kabila: Congo (Zaire) (2001–)

Laurent Kabila: Congo (Zaire) (1997–2001)

Ali Bey al-Kabir: Egypt (1768–73)

Kabir Dan Uthman Nagogo: Katsina (1981–)

Kure Kura al-Kabir: Bornu Empire (1351–52)

Mehmed Bey al-Kabir: Oran (1792)

Muhammadu Kabir Umar: Katagum

Muhammadu Kabiya: Katsina (1740–50)

Daniel Kablan Duncan: Côte d'Ivoire (1993–99)

Marc-Christian Kaboré: Burkina Faso (1994–96)

Kasongo Kabundulu: Luba

Muhammad Kace: Damagaram

Kada: Yauri

Kadai: Bornu Empire (1450–51)

Kade: Bornu Empire (1259–60); Kanem (1259–60)

Kade Afunu: Bornu Empire (1399–1400)

Kadilo: Luba

Abdel Kadir Woli: Baguirmi

Sidi Abd al-Kadiri: Zaria (1853–54)

Abubakr Kado: Kano (1565–72)

Kadri: Katagum

Kafadyougou: Segu

Ali Kafi: Algeria (1992–94)

Kafow: Zaria (1576–78)

Abu al-Misq Kafur: Egypt (946–965, 965–968)

Paul Kagame: Rwanda

Kagulu: Buganda

Ntare II Kahaya I: Nkore

Kahaya I: Nkore

Kahaya II: Nkore

Dahir Riyale Kahir: Somaliland Republic

Bar Kaina Ankabi: Songhai (1362–70)

Biyai Kaina Kimba: Songhai (1101–20)

Kaina Shinyunbo: Songhai (1120–39)

Kaiser Matanzima: Transkei

Abdu Kakkari: Zamfara

Kala-Ekule: Brass

Kalabari: New Calabar

Kalagba: New Calabar

Alezzi Kalajuna: Gobir

Ilunga Kalala: Luba

Ibrahim Zakiyul Kalbi: Katagum

Kalema: Buganda

Kayenje Kalemera II: Karagwe

Kalemera Bwirangenda: Karagwe

Kalgo: Gumel

Kalifah: Daura

Olimi I Kalimbi: Bunyoro

Uthman III Kaliwama: Bornu Empire (1432–33)

ibn Kallis: Egypt (973–991)

Kasongo Kalombo: Luba

Mbala Kalong: Lunda

Shemakone Kalonga Wina: Barotseland

Albert Kalonji: South Kasai Republic

Kalyan Hassan: Constantine

Sa'id Ali Kamal: Comoros (1995)

Kamal al-Ganzouri: Egypt (1996–)

Kamal Hassan Ali: Egypt (1984)

Kamalo: New Calabar

Kamalu: Bonny

Kamanya: Buganda

Kamba: Bonny

Kamba: Lunda

Kambambori: Gurma

Jean Kambanda: Rwanda

Kambine Diaresso: Ghana Empire

Kambujiyah II: Egypt (27th Dynasty)

Kamharapasu Mukombwe: Mwene Mutapa Empire

Abdallah Kamil: Djibouti (1978)

Malik al-Kamil: Egypt (1218–38)

al-Kamin: Wadai

Wadjkheperre Kamose: Egypt (17th Dynasty)

Kampadi: Gurma

Kampadiboaghi: Gurma

Herr von Kamptz: Kamerun (1900)

Kamu: Daura

Kamurasi: Bunyoro

Kamutu: Daura

Kamuwa: Yauri

Birayma Kuran Kan: Dyolof

Kana: Yauri

Uthman Kanafa: Songhai (1354–62)

Kanajeji: Kano (1389–1409)

Kandeya: Mwene Mutapa Empire

Kandia Mamadi: Kaarta

Muhammad al-Amin al-Kanemi: Bornu Empire (1817–24)

Kangapu Nawej: Lunda

Kango: Yatenga

Kaniembo: Kazembe

Kaniembo Ntemena: Kazembe

Kankan Musa: Mali Empire

Kankarau: Biram

Moman Kankia: Hadejia

Kanou-ba-Nyouma Bari: Segu

Kanran: Oyo

Kanta: Masina

Bai Kanta: Koya-Temne

Diare Kante: Ghana Empire

Muhammadu Kantu: Argungu

Anatole Kanyenkiko: Burundi [ii]

Kanyorozi Ntare VI: Karagwe

Kao: Zaria (1760–62)

Kaogho: Yatenga

Nyambu Kapararidze: Mwene Mutapa Empire

Mustafa Kapudan: Tripolitania (1676–77)

Clemens Kapuuo: Namibia (1970–90)

Karafau: Zamfara

Karai: Songhai (933–945)

Karaiga: Nkore

Karama: Wadai

Karama: Zaria (1566–76)

Aliyu Karami: Fulani Empire

Karamoko: Gwiriko

Karamoko: Kong

Karanoko: Segu

Yama Karaonia: Songhai (945–947)

Karara I: Nkore

Karari: Argungu

Karbifo: Songhai (1426–34)

Kareshi: Keffi

Karfo: Wagadugu

Karibo: New Calabar

Karikari: Ashanti

Abd al-Karim ar-Ragrag: Tunis (1195–1200)

Muhammad Karim Lamrani: Morocco (1971–72, 1983–86, 1992–94)

Hamidu Karima: Zamfara

Karkamani: Kush (519–510 B.C.)

Nguza Karl-I-Bond: Congo (Zaire) (1980–81, 1991–92)

Hamed Karoui: Tunisia (1989–99)

Adamu Karro: Gumel

Karu: Wase

Kitahimbwa Karukare: Bunyoro

Abeid Amani Karume: Zanzibar (1964–72)

Amani Abeid Karume: Zanzibar (2000–)

Aliyu Karya Giwa: Katsina (1572–85)
Karya Giwa II: Katsina (1706–15)
Karya Giwa III: Katsina (1751–58)
Karya Giwa IV: Katsina (1767–84)
Lij Kasa: Ethiopia (1855–66)
Ras Kasa: Gojjam
Kasafogi: Yauri
Kasagurbi: Yauri
Chimbindu Kasang: Lunda
Kasasira: Nkore
Joseph Kasavubu: Congo (Zaire) (1960–65)
Kasdi Merbah: Algeria (1988–89)
Mpinga Kasenda: Congo (Zaire) (1977–79)
Kashim Biri: Bornu Empire (1260–88)
Kashta: Kush (860 B.C.)
Kashta II: Kush (ca. 800 B.C.)
Kasim: Tripolitania (1631)
Olimi IV Kasoma: Bunyoro
Kasongo Bonswe: Luba
Kasongo Kabundulu: Luba
Kasongo Kalombo: Luba
Kasongo Mwine Kibanza: Luba
Kasongo Nyembo: Luba
Ras Asrata-Medhin Kassa: Eritrea
Abdallah Kassim Hanga: Zanzibar (1964)
Delwa Kassire Koumakoye: Chad (1993–95)
John Kastell: Fort James
Kasu: Gobir
Mbumb Muteba Kat: Lunda
Suleiman Katanya: Algiers (1616–17)
Muteba Kat Kateng: Lunda
Berempon Katakyira: Bono
Katapka: Kororofa
Muhammadu Katar: Zamfara
Idris Katarkamabi: Bornu Empire (1504–26)
Kataruza: Mwene Mutapa Empire
Muteba Kat Kateng: Lunda
Katerrega: Buganda
Katuri: Kanem
Kauchi: Zaria (ca. 1250)
Kaumb: Lunda
Kaumbo: Luba
Kenneth Kaunda: Zambia (1964–91)
Kawanissa: Zaria (1535–36)
Rashidi Kawawa: Tanganyika; Tanzania
Kawel II: Lunda
Abdu Kawo: Daura
Kawu: Biram
Abubakr Kawu: Lafiagi
Sa'du Kawu Khaliru: Lafiagi
Sheku Bochari Kawusu Conteh: Sierra leone (1970)
Kaya Maja: Ghana Empire
Muhammadu Kaye: Argungu
Kayemba: Buganda
Kayenje Kalemera II: Karagwe
Bawa Kayi: Daniski
Mama Kayi: Daniski
Grégoire Kayibanda: Rwanda
Kayima: Buganda
Sheikh Muhammad Abu'l Kaylak: Kordofan

Kayunga: Nkore
Kazuru: Daura
Siti Kazurukamusapa: Mwene Mutapa Empire
Naatago Kbaari Daaro: Walo (1565–76)
Keaboha Khamane: Bamangwatoland
Keana: Keana
Robert Keate: Ghana (1873); Natal (1867–72); Sierra Leone (1873); Seychelles (1850–52)
Henry Keating: Réunion (1811–15)
Ahmad Tejan Kebbah: Sierra Leone (1996–97, 1998–)
Richard Kedgwin: Saint Helena (1673–74)
Kedma Asqad: Ethiopia (1296–97)
Kege Mari: Segu
Ibrahim Boubakar Keita: Mali (1994–2000)
Modibo Keita: Mali (1959–68); Mali Federation
Modibo Keita II: Mali (2000–02)
Sundiata Keita: Kangaba; Mali Empire
Keita Narifa Majan: Kangaba
Kekenya: Luba
Kekere: Lagos (1805–08)
Kibangu Keleka: Kazembe
Kelemogile: Bamaleteland
Richard Kelinge: Saint Helena (1693–97)
Manuel Keller y García: Spanish Morocco (1873)
Kema: Batlokwaland
Kemba: Wagadugu
Birawa Keme: Dyolof
John Kendall: Sierra Leone (1869–69, 1871, 1872)
Agbu Kendja: Kororofa
Kengo wa Dondo: Congo (Zaire) (1982–86, 1988–90)
Léon Kengo wa Dondo: Congo (Zaire) (1994–97)
Kenken: Songhai (993–1005)
Arthur Kennedy: Gambia (1852); Sierra Leone (1852–54, 1868–72)
John Kennedy: Zimbabwe (1947–53)
Donald Mackenzie-Kennedy: Malawi (1939–42); Mauritius (1942–49); Zambia (1931)
Jomo Kenyatta: Kenya (1962–78)
Francis Kerby: Fort James
Mai-Kere: Katsina (1740–50)
Kere Massa: Gwiriko
Ahmad Kérékou: Benin [ii] (1972–91, 1996–)
Mathieu Kérékou: Benin [ii] (1972–91, 1996–)
Keremeera Rwaaka: Ruanda
Charles de Kerhallet: Côte d'Ivoire (1843)
M. Le Roux de Kermeseven: Seychelles (1775–78)
Adriaan Van Kervel: Cape Colony (1737)
Ameyaw Kese: Bono
Kesitihoe: Bamangwatoland

Philip Kessler: Mayotte Department
al-Adil ad-Din Ketbugha: Egypt (1294–96)
Ketswerebothata: Bamaleteland
Ketumile Masire: Botswana
Bahir Keuse: Egypt (1760–62)
Kewo: Zaria (ca. 1300)
Keydar: Egypt (832–834)
Keys ibn Sa'd: Egypt (654–655)
Kgabo I: Bakwenaland
Kgabo II: Bakwenaland
Kgabosetso II Mosielele: Bangwaketseland
Kgafela: Bakgatlaland
Kgamanyane: Bakgatlaland
Kgari: Bamangwatoland
Kgari II: Bakwenaland
Kgosi Kgari Setshele III: Bakgatlaland
Kgomo: Bamaleteland
Kgosi: Batlokwaland
Kgosi Bathoen: Bangwaketseland
Kgosi Gaborone II: Batlokwaland
Kgosi Kgari Setshele III: Bakwenaland
Kgosi Molefi II: Bakgatlaland
Kgosikwena: Bakwenaland
Kgosimotse: Bangwaketseland
Kgotlamaswe: Bakgatlaland
Kgwefane: Bakgatlaland
Sebekhotep V Khaankre: Egypt (13th Dynasty)
Bakan-Tam Khaari: Dyolof
Kha'ba: Egypt (3rd Dynasty)
Khababasha: Egypt (338–335 B.C.)
Kharut al-Khabir: Wadai
Khadim: Egypt (1525–35)
Khadim: Egypt (1575–80)
Khadim: Egypt (1580–83)
Khadim: Egypt (1651–52)
Ali Khadim: Egypt (1559–60)
Khafre: Egypt (4th Dynasty)
Sebekhotep VI Khahotepre: Egypt (13th Dynasty)
Khair ad-Din: Algiers (1518–20, 1525–46); Tripolitania (1534–35)
Kha'ir Bey: Egypt (1517–22)
Senwosre III Khakaure: Egypt (12th Dynasty)
Sesostris III Khakaure: Egypt (12th Dynasty)
Senwosre II Khakheperre: Egypt (12th Dynasty)
Sesostris II Khakheperre: Egypt (12th Dynasty)
Khalaf: Harar
Muhammad al-Khalangi: Egypt (905–906)
Khalid: Zanzibar (1840–54)
Khalid: Zeng Empire (1200–06)
Abu al-Baqa Khalid I: Hafsid Kingdom
Abu al-Baqa Khalid II: Hafsid Kingdom
Sayid Khalid: Zanzibar (1896)
Khalid ibn Bekr: Zeng Empire (1032–35)
Khalid Pasha: Sudan (1846–49)
Ali Khalif Galaid: Somalia
Khalifa: Mali Empire

Khalifa: Tripolitania (1022–28)
Sayid Khalifa I: Zanzibar (1888–90)
Sayid Khalifa ibn Harub: Zanzibar (1911–60)
Sheikh al-Khalifa: Trarza
Khalifa Houmadi: Comoros (1994–95)
The Khalifah: Sudan (1885–98)
Sa'id Barakh Khan: Egypt (1277–79)
Sirr al-Khatim al-Khalifah: Sudan (1964–65)
Khaliji-Zade-Damad: Egypt (1656–57)
Abdul Khalik Pasha Sarwat: Egypt (1922, 1927–28)
Khalil: Egypt (1631–33)
Khalil: Egypt (1710–11)
Khalil: Gwandu
Abdallah Khalil: Sudan (1956–58)
al-Ashraf Khalil: Egypt (1290–93)
Mustafa Khalil: Egypt (1978–80)
Sa'du Kawu Khaliru: Lafiagi
Khama I: Bamangwatoland
Khama II: Bamangwatoland
Khama III: Bamangwatoland
Seretse Khama: Bamangwatoland; Botswana
Ian Seretse Khama: Bamangwatoland
Tshekedi Khama: Bamangwatoland
Keaboha Khamane: Bamangwatoland
Rasebolai Khamane: Bamangwatoland; Botswana
Hussein Khamil: Egypt (1914–17)
Khamis ibn Rashid: Mombasa (1837)
Asehere Khamudy: Egypt (15th Dynasty)
Khansoo: Egypt (1498–1500)
Kharif: Wadai
Yusuf Kharifain: Wadai
Kharut al-Khabir: Wadai
Kharut as-Sarhir: Wadai
Khasekhem: Egypt (2nd Dynasty)
Neferhotep I Khasekhemre: Egypt (13th Dynasty)
Khasekhemwy: Egypt (2nd Dynasty)
Tekin al-Khassa al-Gezeri: Egypt (910–915, 919–921, 924–933)
Khasseki: Egypt (1652–56)
Sirr al-Khatim al-Khalifah: Sudan (1964–65)
Khawuta: Kreli's Country
Sewesewenre Khayan: Egypt (15th Dynasty)
Khaznadar: Egypt (1691–95)
Khazrun: Tripolitania (1038)
Yusuf ben Khedda: Algeria (1961–62); Algerian Republic (Provisional Government)
Meu Mbody Kumba Khedy: Walo (1734–35)
Userkare Khendjer: Egypt (13th Dynasty)
Nekhtnebef Kheperkhare: Egypt (30th Dynasty)
Senwosre I Kheperkare: Egypt (12th Dynasty)
Sesostris I Kheperkare: Egypt (12th Dynasty)

Ay Kheperkheprure Itnute: Egypt (18th Dynasty)
Rameses X Khepermare Setpenre: Egypt (20th Dynasty)
Kherfi Khari Daano: Walo (1837–40)
Fara Khet: Walo (1343–48)
Akli Khider: Mayotte Department
Khidr: Egypt (1598–1601)
Khnemabre Arkaqamani: Kush (295–275 B.C.)
Ahmose Khnemibre: Egypt (26th Dynasty)
Achoris Khnemmaere: Egypt (29th Dynasty)
Hakor Khnemmaere: Egypt (29th Dynasty)
Yerim Khode Fara Mbuno: Walo (1735–36)
Ali V Khoja: Algiers (1817–18)
Husain II Khoja: Algiers (1705–06)
Khosej: Egypt (1710–11)
Khoshkhakham: Egypt (1461–67)
Tyaaka Daro Khot: Walo (1496–1503)
Sheikh al-Afia Ould Muhammad Khouna: Mauritania (1996–2003)
Khshayarsa I: Egypt (27th Dynasty)
Khshayarsa II: Egypt (27th Dynasty)
Khufu: Egypt (4th Dynasty)
Khumarawayh: Egypt (884–896)
Khuredya: Kayor
Khuredya Kumba Dyodyo: Kayor
N'dyak Khuri Dyop: Walo (1736–80)
N'dyak Kumba Khuri Yay: Walo (1792–1801)
Khurshid Pasha: Egypt (1803, 1804–05); Sudan (1826–38)
Khusrau Pasha: Egypt (1802–03)
Khusrev: Algiers (1622)
Khusru: Egypt (1525–36)
Khut: Egypt (850–851)
Khutowere: Egypt (13th Dynasty)
Khutwane: Bangwaketseland
Khutwe: Bangwaketseland
Kiaya: Egypt (1717–20)
Mufattish Kiaya: Egypt (1689–91)
Mwai Kibaki: Kenya (2002–)
Kibangu Keleka: Kazembe
Kasongo Mwine Kibanza: Luba
Yama Danka Kibao: Songhai (969–981)
Kida: Wagadugu
Tesfaye Gebre Kidan: Ethiopia (1991)
Kien: Brass
Kigaya: Zamfara
Kigeri I Mukobanya: Ruanda
Kigeri II Nyamuheshera: Ruanda
Kigeri III Ndabarasa: Ruanda
Kigeri IV Rwabugiri: Ruanda
Kigeri V Ndahundirwa: Ruanda
Kiggala: Buganda
Jean-Paul Kihl: Mayotte Department
Salva Kiir: Southern Sudan
Ntare V Kiitabanyoro: Karagwe
Musa Ba Kikala: Futa Jallon
Nuhu Ba Kikala: Futa Jallon
Fathi al-Kikhya: Cyrenaica
Umar Mansur al-Kikhya: Cyrenaica
Kikulwe: Buganda

Aissa Kili: Bornu Empire (1570–80)
Kilik Ali: Tripolitania (1576–87)
Biyai Kaina Kimba: Songhai (1101–20)
Kimbugwe: Buganda
Kimera: Buganda
Biyai Koi Kimi: Songhai (1063–82)
Kin-Ha: Allada
Moribu Kindo: Koya-Temne
Sylvio Kinigi: Burundi (ii)
Charles King: Liberia (1920–30)
Charles King-Harman: Mauritius (1894); Sierra Leone (1900–04)
Kintu: Buganda
Jens Kiøge: Danish Gold Coast (1780–88)
Johan Kipnasse: Danish Gold Coast (1788–89)
Mar Kirai: Songhai (1394–1402)
Kirari: Zaria (ca. 1477)
Mustafa Kiridli: Kordofan
John Kirk: Zanzibar (1870–86)
Piercy Kirke: Tangier (1681–83)
Mwezi II Kisabo: Burundi [i]
Kisagare: Yauri
Samson Kisekka: Uganda (1986–91)
Muhamman Kisoki: Kano (1508–64)
Kissun: Yatenga
Ntare IV Kitabanyoro: Nkore
Kitahimbwa Karukare: Bunyoro
Kitamba: Luba
Horatio, Lord Kitchener: Egypt (1911–14); Sudan (1898–99)
Kitera: Nkore
Harold Kittermaster: British Somaliland; Malawi (1934–39)
Ntare II Kivimira: Burundi [i[
Muhammad Kiwab: Zeng Empire (1496)
Benedicte Kiwanuka: Uganda (1961–62)
Muteba II Kiwena: Buganda
Kiyari Muhammad al-Amin: Bornu Empire (1893)
Umar Sanda Kiyarimi: Bornu Empire (1937–69)
Kiyimbo: Buganda
Kiyungi: Mirambo
Ruhinda Kizarabagabe: Karagwe
Jean-Baptiste Kléber: Egypt (1799–1800)
Kleomenes of Naucratis: Egypt (332–323 B.C.)
J.C. Klopper: Utrecht
Kwassi Klutse: Togo (1996–)
Mbala Kmong Isot: Lunda
Eduard von Knorr: Kamerun (1885)
Fara Ko Ndama: Walo (1556–63)
N'dyak Ko N'Dyay Mbanyik: Walo (1367–80)
Kobgha: Yatenga
Kobia Amanfi: Ashanti
Muhammadu Kobo: Lapai
Kobrina Arku Korsah: Ghana (1957)
Lat-Koddu: Dyolof
Yerim Kode: Walo (1415–85)
Edem Kodjo: Togo (1991–94)
Baka Kodu: Dyolof
Birayma Kodu: Kayor

Lat-Kodu: Dyolof
Ma-Kodu: Kayor
Kodu Kumba: Kayor
Ma-Kodu Kodu Kumba: Baol
Ma-Kodu Kumba: Baol
Kofano: Daura
Kofi Asante Baninyiye: Akim
Kofi Busia: Ghana (1969–72)
Kofu: Bono
August Köhler: Kamerun (1900);
  Togoland
Za Koi: Songhai (849–861)
Biyai Koi Kimi: Songhai (1063–82)
Koibla Djimasta: Chad (1995–97)
Koiranga: Gombe
Sherif Koja: Algiers (1619–21)
Ali Kojja Bey: Constantine
Osei Kojo: Ashanti
Abraham Kok: Adam Kok's Land
Adam Kok II: Adam Kok's Land; Cor-
  nelis Kok's Land; Griqualand West
Adam Kok III: Adam Kok's Land;
  Griqualand East
Cornelis Kok II: Cornelis Kok's Land
Kokai Kokai: Zamfara
Koko: Brass
Agyen Kokobo: Akwamu
Anim Kokobo Boadee: Denkyira
Kokoroko Dia: Gwiriko
Kola Adama: Mandara
Bernard Kolelas: Congo (1997)
Kolera: Wagadugu
Dengella Koli I: Futa Jallon
Dengella Koli II: Futa Jallon
André Kolingba: Central African Re-
  public (1981–93)
Mar Fai Kolli-Djimbo: Songhai
  (1434–42)
Ahmad al-Kollo: Constantine
Abu Bakr Kolo: Nupe
Foro-Kolo: Kaarta
Kom: Yatenga
Kom I: Wagadugu
Kom II: Wagadugu
Kom II: Yatenga
Kom III: Yatenga
Mwine Kombe Dai: Luba
Bwana Kombo I: Mayotte
Bwana Kombo II: Mayotte
Biyai Komai: Songhai (909–921)
Bai Kompa: Koya-Temne
Mba Kompaas: Dyolof
Kon Maran: Segu
Hen Kon Wanko Dam: Songhai
  (1044–63)
Alpha Oumar Konaré: Mali (1992–
  2002)
Kondwana: Pondoland
Jean-Marie Koné: Mali (1957–59)
Yerim Mbanyik Kobegil: Walo (1398–
  1415)
Kongolo: Luba
Jan Koning: Dutch Gold Coast
  (1808–10)
Muhammad Konkiya: Songhai (1410–
  18)
Ali Konon: Songhai (1332–40)
Garga Kopchi: Biu

Mari Kopchi: Biu
Kopon: Allada
Korau: Katsina (1350–1410)
Muhammadu Korau: Katsina (1492–
  1541)
Kori: Oyo
Ali Koro: Songhai (1196–1215)
De-Koro: Segu
Desse Koro: Kaarta
Nntin Koro: Kaarta
Touro-Koro Mari: Segu
Johnny Paul Koroma: Sierra Leone
  (1997–98)
Kobrina Arku Korsah: Ghana (1957)
Cornelius Kortright: Gambia (1873–
  75); Sierra Leone (1875, 1876–77)
Mama Korya: Daniski
Kosai Dariya: Songhai (1025–44)
Köse: Algiers (1605–07)
Köse Mustafa: Algiers (1610–13, 1616)
Za Kosoi: Songhai (1005–25)
Kosoko: Lagos (1845–52)
Koswika: Mirambo
Maurice Kouandété: Benin [ii]
  (1967–70)
Kouda: Wagadugu
Koudoumie: Wagadugu
Kougri: Wagadugu
Ahmand Koulamallah: Chad (1959)
Delwa Kassire Koumakoye: Chad
  (1993–95)
Seyni Kountché: Niger (1974–87)
Moussa Koura Bo: Kaarta
Koutou: Bamoun
Koutou: Wagadugu
Boukhary Koutou: Wagadugu
Fara Koy Dyon: Walo (1542–49)
Fara Koy Dyop: Walo (1549–52)
Gabriel Koyambounou: Central
  African Republic (1995–96)
Kpassé: Whydah
Jackson Kpavuvu Lawson IV: Little
  Popo
Kpengla: Dahomey
David Kpormakor: Liberia (1994–
  95)
Mattheus De Krane: Dutch Gold
  Coast (1723)
Kreli: Kreli's Country
Gabra Krestos: Ethiopia (1832)
Newaya Krestos: Ethiopia (1344–72)
Sarsa Krestos: Gojjam
Yemrehana Krestos: Ethiopia (1133–
  72)
Abdel Krim: Rif Republic
Krim Belkassim: Algerian republic
  (Provisional Government)
T. Krogh: Swaziland (1895–1902)
Gert Kruger: Dutch African Republic
Paul Kruger: Transvaal (1880–1900)
Kruli Mbaaba: Walo (1806–12)
J. Philippus von Krusenstierna:
  Swedish Gold Coast
Ti-Kse Bldi: Mandara
Ku: Songhai (885–897)
Abd al-Majid Kubar: Libya
Ada Kube: Daura
Kubri ibn Surun: Dongola

Kuchuk Hussein Pasha: Egypt (1801–
  02)
Kuchuk Ibrahim II: Algiers (1745–48)
Kudanbes: Dongola
Kudandam: Zamfara
John Kufuor: Ghana (2001–)
Kufuru: Daura
Kujera: Biram
Al'a ad-Din Kujuk: Egypt (1341–42)
Kukorai: Songhai (981–993)
Muhamman Kukuna: Kano (1650–59)
Kulo: Brass
Kultum: Omayyad and Abbasid North
  Africa
Ziblim Kulunku: Dagomba
Afera Kuma: Akwamu
Kumanbong: Kom
Kumari: Biram
Kumayo: Katsina (1015–1100)
Birayma Dyeme-Kumba: Dyolof
Kodu Kumba: Kayor
Ma-Kodu Kodu Kumba: Baol
Ma-Kodu Kumba: Baol
Umar Kumba II: Trarza
Mali Kumba Dyaring: Baol
Khuredya Kumba Dyodyo: Kayor
Birayamb Kumba-Gey: Dyolof
N'dyak Kumba-gi tyi Ngelogan: Walo
  (1348–55)
Kumba Ialá: Guinea-Bissau (2000–03)
Meu Mbody Kumba Khedy: Walo
  (1734–35)
N'dyak Kumba Khuri Yay: Walo
  (1792–1801)
N'dyak Kumba-Nan Sango: Walo
  (1355–67)
Mali Kumba N'Gone: Baol
N'dyak Kumba Sam Dyakekh: Walo
  (1336–43)
Kumbari: Kano (1730–43)
Abd al-Mu'min al-Kumi: Almohad
  Empire
Kumong: Kom
Kumongye: Nkore
Kumpaugum: Yatenga
Kumwimba: Luba
Kumwimba Ngombe: Luba
Kuna: Zaria (ca. 1300)
Kunde: Lunda
Kunia Banna: Koya-Temne
Kunto: Gobir
Kuntunkununku: Akim
Kuntunkununku II: Akim
Yamta Kupaya Wadi: Biu
Bukar Kura: Bornu Empire (1881–84)
M'Bissan Kura: Baol
Umar Sanda Kura: Bornu Empire
  (1922–37)
Kure Kura al-Kabir: Bornu Empire
  (1351–52)
Musa Kurabo: Kaarta
Kurada: Biram
Kurakara: Kong
Birayma Kuran Kan: Dyolof
Kurd: Egypt (1595–96)
Kurd Abdi: Algiers (1724–31)
Kure Ghana as-Saghir: Bornu Empire
  (1350–51)

Kure Kura al-Kabir: Bornu Empire (1351–52)
Ali Kuri: Trarza
Kurita: Yatenga
Kurra ibn Sharik: Egypt (709–714)
Herr Kurz: Kamerun (1890)
Kutagamoto: Mirambo
Hosea Kutako: Hereroland; Namibia (1966–70)
Olugun Kutere: Lagos (1808–11)
al-Mudhaffar Kuts: Egypt (1259–60)
Kutumbi: Kano (1622–48)
Kuwya: Kororofa
Ameyaw Kwaakye: Bono
Kwabchi: Biu (1740–50)
Kwabchi: Biu (1783–93)
Ofusu Kwabi: Akwamu
Kwadwo: Ashanti
Apeanin Kwaframoa Woyiawonyi: Akim
Abu Kwaka: Abuja
Kwaka Dua I: Ashanti
Kwaka Dua II: Ashanti
Kwaka Dua III: Ashanti
Ati Kwame: Bono
Osei Kwame: Ashanti
Kwame Nkrumah: Ghana (1952–66)
Kwasari: Zaria (ca. 1250)
Kwasi Obodun: Ashanti
Kwasso: Zaria (1897–1902)
Kwena: Bakwenaland
Kwo: Kom
Garga Kwomting: Biu
Kyabaggu: Buganda
Nyarma Omuzarra Kyaro: Bunyoro
Kyebambe I Omuzikiya: Bunyoro
Kyebambe II Bikaju: Bunyoro
Kyebambe III Nyamutukura: Bunyoro
Kyebambe IV: Bunyoro
Kyereme: Bono
Frantz Kyhberg: Danish Gold Coast (1768–69)
Kyriakos: Dongola

L

Bernard François Mahé, Comte de la Bourdonnais: Mauritius (1735–46); Réunion (1735)
Luis de la Breche: Melilla (1860–61)
Antoine de la Brillane: Mauritius (1776–79)
Jean-Baptiste Estoupan de la Bruë: Senegal (1746–58)
Pedro de la Buría: Canary Islands (1811–20)
Marqués de la Cáñada Ibáñez: Canary Islands (1779–84)
José de la Cerna: Fernando Po
M. Berthelot de la Coste: Seychelles (1781–83)
François La Coste: French Morocco
Robert La Coste: Algeria (1956–58)
Jacques de la Cour de la Soulais: Réunion (1699–1701)
Michel Jajolet de la Courbe: Senegal (1689–90, 1706–10)

Jan de la Fontaine: Cape Colony (1724–27, 1729–37)
Juan de la Fuente: Tenerife
José de la Gándara y Navarro: Fernando Po
Jean-Paul de la Grange: Sainte Marie de Madagascar
Claude Le Lardoux de la Gastière: Gorée
Jacob Blanquet de la Haye: Fort-Dauphin
Patrício Gómez de la Hoz: Melilla (1714–15)
José de la Ibarra: Fernando Po
Mariano de la Iglesia y Guillén: Melilla (1887–88)
Marqués de la Matilla: Ceuta (1751)
Conde de la Monclava: Oran (1681–82)
François de la Morlière: Mauritius (1800–03)
Alexandre de la Mothe: Oran (1742–48)
Henri de la Mothe: French Equatorial Africa (1897–1900); Senegal (1890–95)
Willem de la Palma: Dutch Gold Coast (1702–05)
Diego de la Peña: Ceuta (1795)
Guillermo de la Peña Cusi: Western Sahara
José de la Puente Basseve: Fernando Po
Salvador de la Puente Pita: Spanish Morocco (1851–54)
Marqués de la Real Corona: Oran (1748–52)
Pierre Poncet de la Rivière: Gorée
Jean-Baptiste Montagniès de la Roque: Senegal (1841–42)
Jean Levens de la Roquette: Senegal (1726–33)
Jacques de la Cour de la Soulais: Réunion (1699–1701)
Conde de la Torre: Tangier (1628–37)
Jules Ventre de la Touloubre: Comoros (1871–78); Nossi-Bé
Comte Boyer de la Tour du Moulin: French Morocco; Tunisia (1954–55)
Pedro de la Vega: Tenerife
René de la Villebague: Mauritius (1756–59)
Na'akueto La'ab: Ethiopia (1212–60)
Jan Van Laar: Hollandia; Mauritius (1667–68)
Labi Diebo: Gurma
Labo Salau: Gobir
Eirik Labonne: French Morocco; Tunisia (1938–40)
M. Laborel: Senegal (1843–44)
Laborinde: Ibadan
Étienne Lacascade: Comoros (1893–96)
Antonio de Lacerda: Mozambique (1867–68)
Antonio Lacerda: São Tomé (1689–93)

João de Lacerda: Cape Verde (1886–89, 1898–1900)
M. Lacoste: Madagascar (1891–92)
Henri LaCour: Central African Republic (1946)
William Lacy: Senegambia Colony
Ladapo Ademola II: Abeokuta
John Ladd: Fort James
Bahi Ladgham: Tunisia (1969–70)
Sule Ladi: Daniski
Ladigbolu I: Oyo
Ladigbolu II: Oyo
Ladime Sidimé: Guinea (1999–2004)
Maecius Laetus: Egypt (202)
Édouard Julien-Laferrière: Algeria (1898–1900)
Aliyu Lafia: Yauri
Dunama Lafiami: Bornu Empire (1808–10, 1814–17)
Hilaire Lafitte de Courteil: Réunion (1817–18)
Lafiya I: Yauri
Lafiya II: Yauri
Laganfiela Moru: Gwiriko
Léonce Lagarde: Djibouti (1884–99)
Godfrey Lagden: Lesotho (1894–1901)
al-Mansur Lagin: Egypt (1296–99)
Baltasar do Lago: Mozambique (1765–79)
Joseph Lagu: Southern Sudan
Alimani Lahai Bundu: Koya-Temne
Jacques de Lahure: Réunion (1671–74)
Christian Laigret: Congo (1946); Mauritania (1944–45)
Ma'at Laila: Ifat
Lakanle I: Ibadan
Lakanle II: Ibadan
Lakhideamani: Kush (300–308)
Énoch Dérant Lakoué: Central African Republic (1993)
Lala Shahin: Egypt (1560–64)
Gabra Maskal Lalibela: Ethiopia (1172–1212)
Lamadje Pokonu: Allada
Alexis Lambert: Algeria (1871)
Thomas Lambert: Saint Helena (1741)
Thomas Lambert: Senegal (1626–31)
Auguste Lamblin: Central African Republic (1917–20, 1921–29)
Lambwegha: Yatenga
Pierre Lami: Côte d'Ivoire (1956–57); Senegal (1957–60)
Lucius Aelius Lamia: Africa [i] (15–16)
Lamidi Adeyemi II: Oyo
Mamadou Lamine Loum: Senegal (1998–2000)
Muhammad Lamine Ould Ahmad: Western Sahara
Laminu: Bornu Empire (1817–24)
Laminu: Lafia
Sangoulé Lamizana: Burkina Faso (1966–80)
Col. Lamolle: Niger (ca. 1909)
Christophe de Lamoricière: Algeria (1845–47)
François Magallon de Lamorlière: Réunion (1803–05)
Isaäc Lamotius: Mauritius (1677–92)

Lampadius: Africa Proconsularis (409–410)

Miles Wedderburn Lampson: Egypt (1934–36)

Muhammad Karim Lamrani: Morocco (1971–72, 1983–86, 1992–94)

Heinrich Lamy: Hollandia

Julien Lamy: Côte d'Ivoire (1936)

Louis Lamy: Central African Republic (1906)

Martin Lamy: Nossi-Bé

Robert Lamy: Réunion (1975–77)

Ventura de Landaeta y Horna: Canary Islands (1713–18)

Bernard Landouzy: Réunion (1977–80)

Langa: Matabeleland

Fara Penda Langan Dyam: Walo (1552–56)

Henri Cleret de Langavant: Réunion (1922–23)

Langawa: Daniski

Langawa Daka: Daniski

Frans de Lange: Hollandia

Lanlassé: Yatenga

Louis de Lanneau: Senegal (1880–81)

Christiaan Lans: Dutch Gold Coast (1834–36)

David Lansana: Sierra Leone (1967)

Lansana Conteh: Guinea (1984–)

Dyakpa Lanta: Gonja

Owen Lanyon: Griqualand West; Transvaal (1879–80)

Maurice Lapalud: Côte d'Ivoire (1916–18, 1925–30); French Equatorial Africa (1920); Gabon (1918–19); Réunion (1923–24)

Jean Lapeyre-Bellair: Nossi-Bé

Pierre Lapie: Chad (1940–41)

Marcel Treich-Laplène: Côte d'Ivoire (1886–90)

Jean Pinet-Laprade: Senegal (1863, 1865–69)

Juan Lara: Ceuta (2001–)

Gabriel de Lara: Gran Canaria

Ahmad Laraki: Morocco (1969–71)

Azzedine Laraki: Morocco (1986–92)

Claude Le Lardoux de la Gastière: Gorée

Étienne Largeau: Chad (1902–04, 1906–08, 1911–12, 1913–15)

René de Larminat: French Equatorial Africa (1940–41)

Hippolyte Laroche: Madagascar (1895–96)

Ángel Larrando: Western Sahara

Marino Larrasquito: Ifni

Arthur Larrouy: Madagascar (1888–89, 1892–94)

Luis de las Casas y Aragorri: Oran (1785–89)

Bibye Lasage: Seychelles (1812–15)

Louis Laserre: Senegal (1801–02)

Frederick Last: Dutch Gold Coast (1821–23, 1825–26, 1828–33)

José María Lastres: Ceuta (1813)

Lat-Dyor: Kayor

Lat-Koddu: Dyolof

Lat-Kodu: Dyolof

Lat-Samba: Dyolof

Lat Sukaabe: Baol; Kayor

Lata: Gonja

Late Adjromitan: Little Popo

Latem: Axum

Lathyrus: Egypt (116–110 B.C., 109–107 B.C., 88–80 B.C.)

Latosisa: Ibadan

André Latrille: Central African Republic (1942); Chad (1941–43); Côte d'Ivoire (1943–45, 1946–47)

Comte de Chasseloup-Laubat: Algeria (1859–60)

M. de Launay: Seychelles (1770–72)

Émile Buhot-Launay: Chad (1929, 1936, 1938); Congo (1932)

Agustín Laurenzana: Canary Islands (1705–09)

Jules Lauret: Djibouti (1918–24)

Duc de Lauzun: Senegal (1779)

Guillaume Charmasson de Puy-Laval: Senegal (1839–41)

Fernand Lavit: Chad (1920–23); Guinea (1919–20)

Hamman Lawal: Adamawa

Lawan Babuje: Bedde

Lawani: Oyo

Arthur Lawley: Rhodesia (1896–1900); Transvaal (1902–05); Zimbabwe (1900–01)

Arthur Lawrance: British Somaliland

G.C. Lawrence: Zanzibar (1961)

Robert Lawrie: Fort James

Akuete Zankli Lawson I: Little Popo

Alexandre Boevi Lawson II: Little Popo

Frederick Boevi Lawson V: Little Popo

Georges Betnui Lawson III: Little Popo

Glin Lawson VI: Little Popo

Jackson Kpavuvu Lawson IV: Little Popo

Ioannes Laxarion: Egypt (542)

Paul Le Layec: Chad (1948–49); Congo (1950–52)

Tamirat Laynie: Ethiopia (1991–95)

Jean-Georges le Baillif des Mesnager: Gorée

Georges Le Beau: Algeria (1935–40)

Adolphe Le Boucher: Senegal (1883)

Joseph Le Brasseur: Gorée

Joseph Le Fur: Tangier (1929–40)

Louis Le Gardeur de Repentigny: Senegal (1784–86)

Claude Le Lardoux de la Gastière: Gorée

Paul Le Layec: Congo (1950–52)

Alexandre Le Maître: Nossi-Bé

Charles Le Myre de Villiers: Madagascar (1886–88, 1894–95)

Jules Le Prince: Congo (1917–19)

John Le Rougelet: South Africa (1951–55)

M. Le Roux de Kermeseven: Seychelles (1775–78)

Leabua Jonathan: Lesotho (1965–86)

Fernão Leal: Mozambique (1869–69)

José Leal: Mozambique (1733–36)

Leandros: Pentapolis

Augusto Leão: São Tomé and Príncipe (1881–82)

João de Neves Leão: Bissau (1799)

João Leão: Mombasa (1694–96)

Learchus: Pentapolis

Lebna Dengel Dawit II: Ethiopia (1508–40)

Jean-Pierre Lebouder; Central African Republic (1980–81)

Auguste Lebrun: Comoros (1844–46)

Bonaventure Colonna de Lecca: Porto-Novo

Honoré Léchelle: Nossi-Bé

Philippe Leclerc de Hauteclocq: Cameroun (1940)

Marie-Alexandre Leclos: Nossi-Bé

Louis Lecoupé de Montereau: Senegal (1820–21)

Hermann Ledeganck: Congo (Zaire) (1888–89)

Bernardino de Ledesma: Gran Canaria

Mendo de Ledesma: Ceuta (1594–97)

Leeapeetswe: Bamagwatoland

Leele Fuli Fak: Dyolof

Leema: Bangwaketseland

Charles Lees: Ghana (1876, 1878–79); Lagos (1873, 1874–75); Mauritius (1889–92)

N'dyelen Mbey Leeyti: Dyolof

Leeyti Tyukuli: Dyolof

Claude Lefebvre: Niger (1919–20)

Louis Lefebvre: Senegal (1936–38)

M. Leferre: Réunion (1858)

Mustafa Lefkeli: Egypt (1618)

Legabo: Bakgatlaland

Juan de Legarte: Gran Canaria

Robert Legendre: Benin [ii] (1946–48)

Alexis Leger: Cameroun (1946)

L.G. Leguay: Comoros (1869)

Legwale: Bakwenaland

Lehana: Sekonyela's Land

Arthur Walker-Leigh: Gold Coast Northern Territories

Herr Leist: Kamerun (1890–91, 1893–94)

João Leitão: Madeira (1581–85)

Avelino Leite: São Tomé and Príncipe (1919–20)

José Leite: Angola (1842–43)

Juan de Leiva: Tenerife

Henri Lejeune: Mali (1909–10)

M. Lejuge: Senegal (1733)

Justin Lekhanya: Lesotho (1986–91)

Lekoko: Barolongland

Bourkomanda Tad Lélé: Baguirmi

Umar Lele: Darfur

Lelingoanna: Sekonyela's Land

Jean-Baptiste Lemaire: Congo (1899–1902); French Equatorial Africa (1900)

Joseph Lemaire: Côte d'Ivoire (1895–96)

Joseph LeMaître: Senegal (1702–06)

M. Lemayeur: Réunion (1693)

Alfred Lémery-Dupont: Réunion (1735–39)

Antonio Lemos: São Tomé (1686)

Vitor Lemos e Melo: São Tomé and Príncipe (1907, 1908–09)

Eduardo de Lemos: São Tomé and Príncipe (1920–21)

Gonçalo de Lemos Mascarenhas: Cape Verde (1702–07)

Antonio de Lencastre: Angola (1772–79)

Antonio de Lencastre: Cape Verde (1803–18)

Dinís de Mascarenhas de Lencastre: Ceuta (1627)

João de Lencastre: Angola (1688–91)

José de Lencastre: Cape Verde (1831–33)

Julio Lencastre: Angola (1934–35)

Rodrigo de Lencastre: Tangier (1653–56)

Lentswe: Bakgatlaland

Lentswe II: Bakgatlaland

Andrés Ponce de León: Oran (1564–65)

Lázaro de León: Tenerife

Jacinto de León y Barreda: Spanish Morocco (1898–1901)

Roger Léonard: Algeria (1951–55)

Léopold, King of the Belgians: Congo (Zaire) (1884–1908)

João Leote: São Tomé and Príncipe (1788–97)

Louis Lépine: Algeria (1897–98)

Charles Louis Lepreux: Madagascar (1905)

Lerotholi: Lesotho (1891–1905)

Leshage: Batlokwaland

Leshomo: Barolongland

Lesokwana: Bamaleteland

Alphonse Seignac-Lesseps: Nossi-Bé; Senegal (1884–86)

Gordon Lethem: Seychelles (1934–36)

Letla Moreng: Barolongland

Letla Moreng II: Barolongland

Letsebe: Bakgatlaland

Letsholathebe: Batwanaland

Letsholathebe II: Batwanaland

Letsie I: Lesotho (1870–91)

Letsie II: Lesotho (1905–13)

Letsie III: Lesotho (1990–94, 1996–)

Letsie David Seeiso: Lesotho (1990–94, 1996–)

Theodor Leutwein: Namibia (1895–1905)

Michel Levallois: Réunion (1981–84)

Pierre Levasseur: Senegal (1807–09)

Fernand Lévecque: Senegal (1917–20)

Jean Levens de la Roquette: Senegal (1726–33)

Lewanika: Barotseland

Imwiko Lewanika: Barotseland

John, Baron Lewellin: Federation of Rhodesia and Nyasaland

Lewi: Axum

al-Leyth ibn al-Fadl: Egypt (798–803)

Diego de Leyva: Melilla (1619–20)

Joseph Lhuerre: Benin [ii] (1906)

Liamine Zéroual: Algeria (1994–)

Sempronius Liberalis: Egypt (154–159)

Liberius: Africa Proconsularis (409)

Petrus Marcellinus Felix Liberius: Egypt (539–542)

Licinius: Egypt (520)

Charles Liébault: Côte d'Ivoire (1860–62)

Eduard von Liebert: German East Africa

Percivale Liesching: South Africa (1955–58)

Henry Lightfoot-Boston: Sierra Leone (1962–67)

Ligidi: Yatenga

Lij Iyasu: Ethiopia (1911–16)

Lij Kasa: Ethiopia (1855–66)

Likulia Bolongo: Congo (Zaire) (1997)

James Lilley: Ghana (1845–46)

Bento de Sousa Lima: São Tomé (1686–89)

Duarte de Lima: Portuguese Gold Coast (1608–13)

Francisco de Lima: Mozambique (1652–57)

Joaquim de Lima: Angola (1821–22)

José de Lima: Canary Islands (1744–45)

Hilal Limann: Ghana (1979–81)

Ulpius Limenius: Africa Proconsularis (347–349)

Daniel Limodin: Mayotte Department

Heinrich Lind: Danish Gold Coast (1828–31, 1833–34)

Friedrich von Lindequist: Namibia (1905–07)

Conde de Linhares: Ceuta (1487–91)

Conde de Linhares: Tangier (1624–28)

Pieter Linthorst: Dutch Gold Coast (1805–07)

Victor Liotard: Benin [ii] (1900–06); Central African Republic (1894–99); Guinea (1908–10)

Oyebade Lipede: Abeokuta

Maurice Lippens: Congo (Zaire) (1921–23)

Luis Lisboa: São Tomé and Príncipe (1805–17)

Tobias Lisle: Fort James

Lissoangui: Gurma

Pascal Lissouba: Congo (1963–66, 1992–97)

Earl of Listowel: Ghana (1957–60)

Daniel Lisulo: Zambia (1978–81)

Litia: Barotseland

Stanislas Livet: Comoros (1849–51)

Charles Livingstone: Bight of Biafra; Bights of Biafra and Benin

Abu Bakr Liyatu: Bornu Empire (1392–94)

Alfonso de Llarena: Tenerife

Robert Llewellyn: Gambia (1891–1900)

George Lloyd: Egypt (1925–29)

Lobengula: Matabeleland

Joaquim Lobo: Cape Verde (1768–77)

Manuel Lobo: Cacheu (1726)

Duarte Lobo da Gama: Portuguese Gold Coast (1595–96)

Henry Loch: Cape Colony (1889–95)

Emidio Tafeng Lodongi: Southern Sudan

Loel: Baguirmi

William Logan: Seychelles (1942–47); Zambia (1941)

Beur Tyaaka Loggar: Walo (1576–1640)

Bo-Boliko Lokonga: Congo (Zaire) (1979–80)

Lokpon: Porto-Novo

Lol Muhammad Shawa: Chad (1979)

Lucius Hedius Rufus Lollianus Avitus: Africa [i] (157–158)

Lollianus Mavortius: Africa Proconsularis (356)

Diaba Lompo: Gurma

George London: Ghana (1941–42, 1947–48)

Longinianus: Africa Proconsularis (406–407)

Longinianus: Egypt (354–357)

Mahmud Longo III: Timbuktu (1604–12)

Stephen Longrigg: Eritrea

Lo'o: Kom

Henri Lopes: Congo (1973–75)

Pedro Lopes: São Tomé and Príncipe (1869–72)

Fernão Lopes Correia: Portuguese Gold Coast (1517–19)

Diogo Lopes de França: Ceuta (1574–77)

Diogo Lopes de Sequeira: Portuguese Gold Coast (1504–05)

Basilio López: Ceuta (1995–96)

José López: Western Sahara

Francisco López Moreno: Melilla (1687)

Victoriano López Pinto: Spanish Morocco (1877–78)

Juan López Pinto y Marín Reyna: Spanish Morocco (1883–89)

Percy Loraine: Egypt (1929–33)

Louis de Lormel: Réunion (1869–75)

James Loro: Southern Sudan

Marqués de los Tabalosos: Canary Islands (1775–79)

Marqués de los Vélez: Oran (1666–72)

Mamman na Lota: Gumel

Jean-Baptiste Lougnon: Réunion (1886)

Jean-Claude Pierre-Louis: Rodrigues (ii)

Muhammad Mahmud Ould Ahmad Louly: Mauritania (1979–80)

Mamadou Lamine Loum: Senegal (1998–2000)

Luis de Loureiro: Tangier (1552–53)

Edmond Louveau: Mali (1946–52); Upper Ivory Coast

Arthur Loveridge: Ashanti; Gold Coast Colony Region; Gold Coast Northern Territories

Marquês de Lovradio: Angola (1749–53)

William Low: Ghana (1898–99, 1900)

Hudson Lowe: Saint Helena (1816–23)
Auguste Loze: Algeria (1897)
Francis Loyd: Swaziland (1964–68)
Athanase Bouvet de Lozier: Réunion (1815–17)
Jean-Baptiste Bouvet de Lozier: Mauritius (1750–56): Réunion (1750–52, 1757–63)
Lubatko: Baguirmi
Lubosi: Barotseland
Barend Lucas: Adam Kok's Land
Pierre Lucas: Nossi-Bé
Lucciali: Algiers (1768–77); Tripolitania (1565–68)
Girma Wolde-Giorgis Lucha: Ethiopia (2001–)
Lucius Aelius Lamia: Africa [i] (15–16)
Lucius Apronius: Africa [i] (18–21)
Lucius Aradius Valerius Proculus Felix: Africa Proconsularis (333–336)
Lucius Calpurnius Piso: Africa [i] (38–39)
Lucius Hedius Rufus Lollianus Avitus: Africa [i] (157–158)
Lucius Mappius: Byzantine North Africa
Lucius Minicius Natalis: Africa [i] (121)
Lucius Minicius Natalis Quadronius Verus: Africa [i] (153–154)
Lucius Nonius Asprenas: Africa [i] (12–15)
Lucius Salvius Otho: Africa [i] (40–41)
Lucius Tampius Flavianus: Africa [i] (51–52)
Lucius Vitellius: Africa [i] (61–62)
Herr von Lücke: Kamerun (1895)
Thomas Ludlum: Sierra Leone (1799–1800, 1803–05, 1806–08)
Ludvonga: Swaziland (1868–74)
Luedji: Lunda
Frederick Lugard: Nigeria (1914–19); Southern Nigeria Colony and Protectorate; Uganda (1890–93)
Alonso de Lugo: Tenerife
Pedro de Lugo: Tenerife
Charles Luizet: French Equatorial Africa (1947)
Carlos Luján: Canary Islands (1809–10); Ceuta (1808–09)
Mulumba Lukeji: Congo (Zaire) (1991)
Mari Luku: Biu
Lukudi: Daura-Zango
Lukwesa: Kazembe
Yusufu Lule: Uganda (1979)
Hugh Lumley: Ghana (1827–28); Sierra Leone (1827–28)
Patrice Lumumba: Congo (Zaire) (1960)
Lunda Bululu: Congo (Zaire) (1990–91)
Frank Lupton: Bahr al-Ghazal
Julius Lupus: Egypt (71)
Rutilius Lupus: Egypt (116–117)
Luro: Dagomba

Maurice Lush: Tripolitania (1942–43)
Lusius: Egypt (54–55)
Charles Lutaud: Algeria (1911–18)
Ali Lutfi: Egypt (1985–86)
Georg Lutterodt: Danish Gold Coast (1844)
Magnus Lützow: Danish Gold Coast (1751)
Amaro da Luz: Cape Verde (1974–75)
Hubert Lyautey: French Morocco
Erik Lygaard: Danish Gold Coast (1696–98, 1705–11)
Hans Lykke: Danish Gold Coast (1684–87)
James Lynslager: Bight of Biafra; Fernando Po

M

Birayamb Ma-Dyigen: Dyolof
Ma-Dyodyo: Kayor
Ma-Kodu: Kayor
Ma-Kodu Kodu Kumba: Baol
Ma-Kodu Kumba: Baol
Yala Maaku: Lunda
Mbeu Mbody Maalik: Walo (1840–55)
Maaouya Ould Sidi Ahmad Taya: Mauritania (1981–)
Ma'at Laila: Ifat
Ma'azu: Nupe
J.T. Mabandla: Ciskei
Mabe: Barolongland
Jonas Mabena: KwaNdebele
Mabeo: Barolongland
Mabi Mulumba: Congo (Zaire) (1987–88)
Mabudi: Barolongland
Mabura Maobwe: Mwene Mutapa Empire
Enos Mabuza: KaNgwane
Charles Macarthy: Ghana (1822–24); Sierra Leone (1814, 1815–24); Senegal (1811–14)
George, Earl Macartney: Cape Colony (1797–98)
John Macaulay: Aku
Kenneth Macaulay: Sierra Leone (1826)
Zachary Macaulay: Sierra Leone (1794–95, 1796–99)
Sean MacBride: Namibia (1973–77)
Henry McCallum: Lagos (1897–99); Natal (1901–07)
C.D. McCarthy: Eritrea
Gino Macchioro: Italian Somaliland (1908–10)
Ibrahim Muhammad Maccido: Fulani Empire
William McCoskry: Bight of Benin; Lagos (1861–62)
Capt. MacDonald: Uganda (1893)
Claude MacDonald: Southern Nigeria; Zanzibar (1887–88)
George McDonald: Sierra Leone (1842–44)

Malcolm MacDonald: Kenya (1963–64)
Norman MacDonald: Sierra Leone (1845–52)
Sydney MacDonald-Smith: Gold Coast Northern Territories
Richard Macdonnell: Gambia (1847–52)
Bernardo de Macedo: Cape Verde (1907–09)
Duarte Macedo: Cape Verde (1830–31)
Ernesto de Macedo: Angola (1975)
Lopes de Macedo: Cape Verde (1876–78)
Marçal de Macedo: Mombasa (1626–29)
Sebastião de Macedo: Mozambique (1604–07)
George McGill: Liberia (1833–34)
Samuel F. McGill: Maryland
James MacGregor: Botswana; Lesotho (1913)
William MacGregor: Lagos (1899–1902)
Joaquim Machado: Mozambique (1890–91, 1900, 1914–15)
José Machado: Bissau (1841–42)
José Machado: São Tomé and Príncipe (1955–56)
Pedro Machado: São Tomé and Príncipe (1913–15)
Riek Machar: Southern Sudan
Samora Machel: Mozambique (1975–86)
Sachi Gana Machi: Nupe
Machikai: Zaria (ca. 1355)
Machu: Jema'a
Mario Machungo: Mozambique (1986–94)
Macianus: Africa Proconsularis (394)
Manuel Macías y Casado: Melilla (1879–80, 1881–86, 1893–94)
Francisco Macías Nguema Biyogo: Equatorial Guinea
Antonio Maciel: São Tomé (1575–82)
George Mackenzie: Kenya (1888–90, 1891–91)
John Mackenzie: Bechuanaland Protectorate
William Mackenzie: Botswana
Donald Mackenzie-Kennedy: Malawi (1939–42); Mauritius (1942–49); Zambia (1931)
William Mackie: Gambia (1838–39)
George Mackinnon: British Kaffraria
George Maclean: Ghana (1830–43)
John Maclean: British Kaffraria; Transkeian Territories
Arthur MacMahon: Egypt (1915–17)
Harold MacMichael: Tanganyika
Matthias MacNamara: Senegambia Colony
John MacPherson: Nigeria (1948–55)
Naevius Sertorius Macro: Egypt (38–39)
Macrobius: Africa Proconsularis (410)
Macwa: Nkore

Madafu: Keana
Muhammad Hawadle Madar: Somalia
Shu'aibu Madara: Yauri
Madaura: Gobir
Diogo de Madeira: Mozambique (1612)
Edward Madge: Seychelles (1815–22)
Hamadi Madi: Comoros (2000–)
Madior Boye: Senegal (2001–02)
Madirana: Bamangwatoland
Sayid Madjid: Zanzibar (1854–70)
Charles Madre: Réunion (1900–01)
Madu: Bonny
Maidalla Madu: Biu
Volusius Maecianus: Egypt (159–160)
Maecilius Hilarianus: Africa Proconsularis (354–355)
Maecius Laetus: Egypt (202)
Maenius Flavianus: Egypt (180–181)
Pierre Maestracci: Senegal (1945–46)
Maevius Honorianus: Egypt (232)
Peter Mafani Musonge: Cameroun (1996–2004)
John Maffey: Sudan (1926–34)
Muhammadu Mafindi: Muri
Hubert Maga: Benin [ii] (1959–63, 1970–72)
Dan Magaji: Gobir
Magajin Halidu: Katsina (1805–06)
Antonio de Magalhães: Guinea-Bissau (1927–31)
Antonio da Rocha Magalhães: Portuguese Gold Coast (1634–42)
Henrique de Magalhães: Angola (1694–97)
João de Magalhães: Angola (1738–48)
Joaquim de Magalhães: Mozambique (1851–54)
José de Magalhães: Mozambique (1912–13)
Luis de Magalhães: Cacheu (1640–41)
Manuel da Maia Magalhães: Cape Verde (1919–21)
Fernando de Magalhães e Meneses: Cape Verde (1893–94)
Fernão de Magalhães e Meneses: Mozambique (1894–95)
François Magallon de Lamorlière: Réunion (1803–05)
Magan Oule Watara: Gwiriko
Magas: Pentapolis
Mageba: Zululand
Duc de Magenta: Algeria (1864–70)
Mama Magha: Mali Empire
Magha I: Mali Empire
Magha II: Mali Empire
Magha III: Mali Empire
Suleiman al-Maghrebi: Libya
Magnilius: Africa Proconsularis (393–394)
A. Magnin: Dutch Gold Coast (1865–66)
Pactumeius Magnus: Egypt (177–180)
Mago: Carthage
Mago II: Carthage
Diogo Magro: Cape Verde (1583–87)
Mahama I: Dagomba
Mahama II: Dagomba

Mahama III: Dagomba
Bako Mahama Gabi: Zaria (1608–11)
Bako Mahama Rubo: Zaria (1682–1710)
Mahamane Ousmane: Niger (1993–96)
Aliou Mahamidou: Niger (1990–91)
Cwa I Mali Rumoma Mahanga: Bunyoro
Muhammad Ahmad (The Mahdi): Sudan (1881–85)
Muhammad II al-Mahdi: Morocco (1525–57)
Muhammad Abdou Mahdi: Comoros (1994)
Mulay al-Mahdi: Spanish Morocco (1913–23)
Mulay Hassan ben al-Mahdi: Spanish Morocco (1925–56)
Sadiq al-Mahdi: Sudan (1966–67, 1986–89)
Idris al-Mahdi as-Sanusi: Cyrenaica; Libya; Tripolitania (1922–51)
Ali Mahdi Muhammad: Somalia
al-Mahdi Ubaydallah: Fatimid North Africa
Bertrand-François Mahé, Comte de la Bourdonnais: Mauritius (1735–46); Réunion (1735)
Ali Maher Pasha: Egypt (1936, 1939–40, 1952)
Maherero: Hereroland
Samuel Maherero: Hereroland
Mahfud Ali Beiba: Western Sahara
Mahhu Bey: Sudan (1826)
Silahdar Mahir: Egypt (1766–77)
Muhammad Mahjub: Sudan (1965–66, 1967–69)
Sheikh Mahl Aynin: Brakna
George Mahlangu: KwaNdebele
Prince James Mahlangu: KwaNdebele
Mahmadi Makia: Mandara
Mare Mawa Mahmadu: Katsina (1804–05)
Mahmoud Fawzi: Egypt (1970–72)
Mahmud: Egypt (1566–67)
Mahmud: Tunis (1814–24)
Abu Umays Mahmud: Tripolitania (1711)
al-Fah Mahmud: Timbuktu (1746–48)
Yulk Mahmud: Tripolitania (1683)
Mahmud I: Timbuktu (1591–94)
Mahmud IV: Timbuktu (1725–26)
Mahmud Bey: Fezzan
Mahmud Bey Muntasir: Libya
Mahmud Brusali: Algiers (1645–47)
Mahmud Longo III: Timbuktu (1604–12)
Mahmud Nedim Bey: Tripolitania (1860–67)
Muhammad Mahumd Ould Ahmad Louly: Mauritania (1979–80)
Muhammad Mahmud Pasha: Egypt (1928–29, 1937–39)
Mahmud Sami: Egypt (1882)
Mahmud Taba II: Timbuktu (1597–99)

Mahmun ibn Hamal: Egypt (921)
Mahoma Sani: Zaria (1846–53)
Mai Bukar Aji: Mandara
Ibrahim Na Mai Fura: Gobir
Mai Haman Maigano: Zaria (1795–96)
Mai-Kere: Katsina (1740–50)
Muhammadu Mai-sa-Maza-Gudu: Katsina (1595–1612)
Vicente de Maia e Vasconcelos: Mozambique (1781–82)
Manuel da Maia Magalhães: Cape Verde (1919–21)
Maidalla Madu: Biu
Maidalla Mustafa Aliyu: Biu
Henri Maidou: Central African Republic (1978–79)
Umaru Maidubu: Kontagora
Ousman Maïga: Mali (2004–)
Mai Haman Maigano: Zaria (1795–96)
Maigardo: Daura
Maigari: Adamawa
Bello Bouba Maigari: Cameroun (1982–83)
Léopold Maignot: Porto-Novo
Abdullahi Maikano III: Wase
Maikota: Gumel
Ahmadu Maikwato: Keffi
Pierre Mailhetard: Côte d'Ivoire (1854–55, 1858–59); Gabon (1859–60)
J. Mailing: Sierra Leone (1814–15)
Joseph Maillard: Chad (1910–11)
Théodore Maillet: Mali (1920–21); Senegal (1925–26, 1930–31)
Mallam ibn Maina: Damagaram
Maina Mamman: Gumel
Ibrahim Baré Maïnassara: Niger (1996–99)
Yusufu Mainassara: Argungu
Mainassara Maji: Gobir
Maio: Bamaleteland
Bako Mairari Ashaka Okao: Zaria (1758–60)
Umar Baba Ya Mairami: Bornu Empire (1969–)
Peregrine Maitland: Cape Colony (1844–47)
Alexandre Le Maître: Nossi-Bé
Muhammad Maiturare: Fulani Empire
Maizabo: Keffi
M. Maizière: Gorée
Kaya Maja: Ghana Empire
Keita Nari fa Majan: Kangaba
Majan Dyabe Sisse: Ghana Empire
Majan Dyallo: Masina
Majan Wagadu: Ghana Empire
Majanjara: Gobir
Adamu Abubakar Maje: Hadejia (2002–)
Abubakr Maje Haruna: Hadejia (1984–2002)
Maje Ibrahim: Katsina (1614–31)
Majeogbe: Oyo
Maji: Biram
Maji: Gobir
Mainassara Maji: Gobir

Maji Dadi: Zaria (ca. 1400)
Abd al-Majid Kubar: Libya
Majidada: Zaria (ca. 1400)
Umar Majigi: Nupe
Majigu: Gobir
Bako Majirua: Zaria (1584–97)
Majiya: West Nupe
Majiya I: Nupe
Majiya II: Nupe; West Nupe
Sextus Julius Major: Africa [i] (141–142)
Majotu: Oyo
Makaba I: Bangwaketseland
Makaba II: Bangwaketseland
Makabe: Batlokwaland
Abdu na Makaki: Zamfara
Bako Makam Danguma: Zaria (1738–50)
Bako Makam Gaba: Zaria (1757–58)
Bako Makam Rubu: Zaria (1646–47)
Mutesa I Walugembe Makaobya: Buganda
Hatshepsut Makare: Egypt (18th Dynasty)
Muhamman Makau: Zaria (1802–05)
Makgasama: Bamangwatoland
Makgotso: Bakgatlaland
Amenemhet IV Makherure: Egypt (12th Dynasty)
Abd al-Wahid al-Makhluwi: Almohad Empire
Makhosini Dhlamini: Swaziland (1967–76)
Mahmadi Makia: Mandara
Mehmed Bey Makkalas: Oran (1804)
Makkam: Zaria (1802–04)
Makonnen Endalkatchon: Ethiopia (1941–58, 1974)
Maku: Oyo
Bernard Makuza: Rwanda
Makwangiji Na'ali: Lafia
Rocky Peter Israel Malabane-Metsing: Bophuthatswana
Marqués de Malagón: Ceuta (1645–46)
Malak Sagad: Ethiopia (1563–97)
Malak Sagad: Shoa
Duc de Malakoff: Algeria (1860–64)
Malam: Ilorin
Daniel Malan: South Africa (1948–54)
François Malan: South Africa (1918–19)
Henri Malan: Benin [ii] (1909–11)
Malandela: Zululand
Malangana: Transkeian Territories
Joseph de Malartic: Mauritius (1792–1800)
Louis Malavois: Senegal (1836)
Louis de Malavois: Seychelles (1789–92)
Malchus: Carthage
Antonio Manso Maldonaldo: Ceuta (1738–39)
Francisco de Maldonaldo: Gran Canaria
Manuel Álvarez Maldonaldo: Melilla

(1862–63); Spanish Morocco (1864–65)
John Malecela: Tanzania
Malehe: Bakwenaland
Malekeleke: Bakgatlaland
Timothée Malendoma: Central African Republic (1992–93)
Maleqerabar: Kush (308–320)
Edwin Malet: Egypt (1882–83)
Malete: Bamaleteland
Justin Malfeyt: Ruanda–Urundi
Manuel Malheiro: Angola (1839–42)
Mali Kumba Dyaring: Baol
Mali Kumba N'Gone: Baol
Cwa I Mali Rumoma Mahanga: Bunyoro
Malik: Gwandu
Malik: Nupe
Redha Malik: Algeria (1993–94)
Shah Malik: Tripolitania (1095)
Abd al-Malik al-Ghazi: Morocco (1576–78)
Abu Malik Abd al-Wahid: Tlemcen (1412–24, 1429–30)
Malik al-Kamil: Egypt (1218–38)
Malik ibn Delhem: Egypt (808)
Malik ibn Keydar: Egypt (839–841)
Abd al-Malik ibn Rifa'a: Egypt (714–717, 727)
Abd al-Malik ibn Salih: Egypt (795–796)
Malik Si: Futa Jallon
Maliki: Lafiagi
Malimba Masheke: Zambia (1989–91)
Mallam Maliki: Lafiagi
Maliki: Zamfara
Maliki Dan Ibrahimu: Argungu
Mallam Alimi ibn Zubeiru: Ilorin
Mallam Baba: Agaie
Mallam Babu Saba: Damagaram
Mallam Dipchairina: Nigeria (1966)
Mallam ibn Maina: Damagaram
Mallam Ishaku: Daura
Mallam Maliki: Lafiagi
Mallam Musa: Daura-Zango
Mallam Musa: Zaria (1804–21)
Mallam Uthman: Jema'a
Mallam Zaki: Katagum
Mallius Theodorus: Africa Proconsularis (397–399)
Félix Malloum: Chad (1975–79)
Marqués de Malmusi: Spanish Morocco (1925–28, 1931)
Malo: Baguirmi
Malope: Bakwenaland
Malope: Bangwaketseland
Maloto: Barolongland
J.M. Maltby: Sierra Leone (1888, 1889–90)
Malu: Zamfara
Heperkare Maluiane: Kush (463–435 B.C.)
1st Viscount Malvern: Federation of Rhodesia and Nyasaland
Mama: Fika
Mama Gimsi: Daniski
Mama Kayi: Daniski
Mama Korya: Daniski

Mama Magha: Mali Empire
Mama Mulu: Daniski
Kandia Mamadi: Kaarta
Tandja Mamadou: Niger (1999–)
Mamadou Dembelé: Mali (1986–88)
Mamadou Dia: Mali Federation (1959–60); Senegal (1958–62)
Mamadou Lamine Loum: Senegal (1998–2000)
Mamadu: Biram
Mamadu Mustafa: Damagaram
Mamalik Thioro: Baol
Oumarou Mamane: Niger (1983, 1988–89)
Mamaohato: Lesotho (1970–70, 1994–95, 1996)
Mamari Biton: Segu
Mamarikan-dyan: Kaarta
Mamdouh Salem: Egypt (1975–78)
Mamertinus: Africa Proconsularis (362–365)
Petronius Mamertinus: Egypt (134)
Mami I: Timbuktu (1703, 1705–06, 1713)
Mowa Mamili: Barotseland
Mamma: Nupe
Mammadi Gaganga: Fika
Mammadi Gizze: Daniski
Maina Mamman: Gumel
Mamman al-Hajji: Misau
Mamman Diko: Agaie
Mamman Manga: Misau
Mamman Manga III: Misau
Mamman na Lota: Gumel
Mamman Sali: Misau
Mamman Wari: Nupe
Mamosecane: Barotseland
al-Mamun: Egypt (832)
al-Mamun: Egypt (1121–25)
Muhammad IV al-Ma'mun: Morocco (1610–13)
Mamuru: Segu
Man-nsor: Segu
Seba-Mana: Kaarta
François Manceron: Tunisia (1929–33)
James Mancham: Seychelles (1970–77)
Francisco Pérez Mancheño: Ceuta (1719)
Jean-Luc Mandaba: Central African Republic (1993–95)
Mandabala Fred Dhlamini: Swaziland (1979–83)
Mandalela: Zululand
Abu'l Hassan Ali al-Mandari; Tangier (1437–71)
Dai Mande: Luba
Mande Sidibe: Mali (2000)
Nelson Mandela: South Africa (1994–99)
Louis Manès: Réunion (1888–93)
Manga: Baguirmi
Biram Manga: Kayor
Hama Manga: Misau
Mamman Manga: Misau
Mamman Manga III: Misau
Moma Manga: Misau
Mangete: Matabeleland
Mangi Suku: New Calabar

Thorleif Mangin: Ghana (1949); Gold Coast Colony Region
Mangisi Zitha: KaNgwane
Lucas Mangope: Bophuthatswana
Muhammad Ahmad al-Mangush: Libya
Mania Alsali: Fika
Ahmad Pasha al-Manikli: Sudan (1844–45)
Manikusa: Gazaland
Thutmose III Mankheperre: Egypt (18th Dynasty)
William Manning: British Somaliland; Malawi (1907–08, 1911–13)
Manuel Mano: Angola (1939–41)
Miguel Porcel y Manrique de Araña Menchaca y Zaldívar: Ceuta (1784–91)
Mansa Bonsu: Ashanti
Fula Mansa Gbanka: Koya-Temne
Nyani Mansa Muhammad: Mali Empire
Antonio Manso: Melilla (1780–82)
Mele Manso: Daniski
Antonio Manso Maldonaldo: Ceuta (1738–39)
al-Mansur: Fatimid North Africa
al-Mansur: Fezzan
al-Mansur: Zirid Kingdom
Abu Yusuf al-Mansur: Almohad Empire
Ahmad II al-Mansur: Morocco (1578–1603)
al-Mansur I: Ifat
al-Mansur I: Timbuktu (1594–97)
al-Mansur II: Adal [ii]
al-Mansur II: Timbuktu (1688, 1698–99, 1716–19)
al-Mansur III: Timbuktu (1712–13)
al-Mansur ad-Din Muhammad: Egypt (1361–63)
Umar Mansur al-Kikhya: Cyrenaica
al-Mansur Al'a ad-Din: Egypt (1368–80)
al-Mansur ibn al-Nasir: Hammadid Kingdom
Mansur ibn Muhammad: Harar
Mansur ibn Yezid: Egypt (779)
al-Mansur Lagin: Egypt (1296–99)
al-Mansur Qala'un: Egypt (1279–90)
Mantennius Sabinus: Egypt (193–195)
MaNtsebo: Lesotho (1940–60)
Agbu Manu I: Kororofa
Agbu Manu II: Kororofa
Agudu Manu: Kororofa
Ashu Manu I: Kororofa
Ashu Manu II: Kororofa
Ashu Manu III: Kororofa
Martim Manuel: Mombasa (1639–42)
Pedro Manuel: Tangier (1617–21)
Manuel Otobia: Warri
Manukure: Akwamu
Mustafa Bey al-Manzalah: Oran (1800)
Manzuma: Lafiagi
Mabura Maobwe: Mwene Mutapa Empire
Maoke: Bamaleteland

Maphalaola: Bamaleteland
Maphevu Dhlamini: Swaziland (1976–79)
Lucius Mappius: Byzantine North Africa
Dehwe Mapunzagutu: Mwene Mutapa Empire
Maqdum Musallam: Kordofan
Duque de Maqueda: Oran (1616–25)
Maqsud: Egypt (1642–44)
Mar Arandan: Songhai (1449–56)
Mar Arkena: Songhai (1442–49)
Mar Fai Kolli-Djimbo: Songhai (1434–42)
Mar Kirai: Songhai (1394–1402)
André Maracote: São Tomé (1627–28)
Detye Maram N'Galgu: Kayor
Kon Maran: Segu
Marari: Ethiopia (1117–33)
Antonius Marcellinus: Africa Proconsularis (340–341)
Petrus Marcellinus Felix Liberius: Egypt (539–542)
Marcellus: Africa [i] (154–155)
Jean-Ernest Marchaisse: Nossi-Bé
Charles Marchal: Benin [ii] (1902, 1906–08)
Jean Marchand: Congo (1919, 1923–25); Gabon (1919–22)
Théodore Marchand: Cameroun (1923–32)
Marcel Marchessou: Congo (1929–30); French Equatorial Africa (1935–36)
Marcianus: Byzantine North Africa
Quintus Marcius Barea Soranus: Africa [i] (41–43)
Marcius Turbo: Egypt (117–118)
Alfred Marcorati: Ruanda–Urundi
Marcus Antonius Zeno: Africa [i] (164–165)
Marcus Aurelius Papirius Dionysius: Egypt (193)
Marcus Furius Camillus: Africa [i] (17–18)
Marcus Junius Silanus: Africa [i] (29–35)
Marcus Pompeius Silvanus Staberius Flavinus: Africa [i] (53–56)
Marcus Servilius Nonianus: Africa [i] (46–47)
Mare: Bakgatlaland
Mare Mawa Mahmudu: Katsina (1804–05)
Dejaz Ma'red Gwalo: Gojjam
Ras Ma'red: Gojjam
Milton Margai: Sierra Leone (1954–67)
Kege Mari: Segu
Touro-Koro Mari: Segu
Mari Biya: Biu
Mari Dyara: Segu
Mari Jata I: Kangaba; Mali Empire
Mari Jata II: Mali Empire
Mari Kopchi: Biu
Mari Luku: Biu
Mari Vira Hyel: Biu
Mari Watila Tampta: Biu

Mari Watirwa: Biu
Victor Saúde María: Guinea-Bissau (1982–84)
Mengistu Haile Mariam: Ethiopia (1977–91)
Sahle Mariam: Ethiopia (1889–1911)
Maribbi Rabbu: Brakna
Édouard Marie: Comoros (1882–83)
José Marina y Vega: Melilla (1905–10); Spanish Morocco (1913–15)
Joaquim Marinho: Cape Verde (1835–36, 1837–39); Mozambique (1840–41)
José Marinho: Guinea-Bissau (1919)
Marinianus: Africa Proconsularis (422–423)
Gerrit Maritz: Natal (1836–37, 1838)
Marjani: Mohéli
Markos: Dongola
Maroki: Zamfara
Jaime Marquês: Angola (1962–66, 1974)
Joaquim Marquês: Bissau (1863)
José Marquês: São Tomé and Príncipe (1843–46, 1851–53)
Silvinio Marquês: Cape Verde (1958–63)
Francisco Marquez y Pedrosa: Gran Canaria
Hugh Marshall: North Eastern Rhodesia
Hugo Marshall: Nigeria Western Region
Caius Vivius Marsus: Africa [i] (26–29)
Clément Martelly: Chad (1916–18)
Rhammius Martialis: Egypt (118–121)
Édouard de Martimprey: Algeria (1864)
Fernando Fernández Martín: Canary Islands (1987–88)
Jean Martin: Côte d'Ivoire (1864–66); Gabon (1849–50)
Adán Martín Menis: Canary Islands (2003–)
Félix Martiné: Guinea (1939)
Albert Martineau: Comoros (1902–05)
Alfred Martineau: Djibouti (1899–1900); Gabon (1907)
Henri Martinet: Benin [ii] (1937, 1938)
Antonio Martínez: Fernando Po
Ferdinando Martini: Eritrea
Enrico Martino: Italian Somaliland (1953–55)
Nobile Giacomo Di Martino: Cyrenaica; Eritrea; Italian Somaliland (1910–16)
Alfredo Martins: Guinea-Bissau (1903–04)
José Martins: Cape Verde (1941–43)
Manuel Martins: Cape Verde (1833–35)
Mariano Martins: São Tomé and Príncipe (1911–13)
Marumo: Bamaleteland
Allan Marwick: Swaziland (1935–37)

Brian Marwick: Swaziland (1956–64)
Baʼeda Maryam I: Ethiopia (1468–78)
Baʼeda Maryam II: Ethiopia (1795)
Baʼeda Maryam III: Ethiopia (1826)
Newaya Maryam: Ethiopia (1372–82)
Takla Maryam: Ethiopia (1430–33)
Debbe Haile Maryan: Eritrea
Masaba: Nupe
Gidan Dan Masakanan: Zaria (1530–32)
Filipe Mascarenhas: Madeira (1727–34)
Filipe de Mascarenhas: Mozambique (1633–34)
Francisco de Mascarenhas: Madeira (1665–68); Mozambique (1651–52)
Francisco de Mascarenhas: Mozambique (1714–15)
Gonçalo de Lemos Mascarenhas: Cape Verde (1702–07)
Manuel Mascarenhas: Madeira (1645–48)
Manuel de Mascarenhas: Mozambique (1661–64)
Pedro de Mascarenhas: Portuguese Gold Coast (1632–34)
Simão de Mascarenhas: Angola (1623–24)
Vasco de Mascarenhas: Mozambique (1601–04)
Dinís de Mascarenhas de Lencastre: Ceuta (1627)
Antonio Mascarenhas Monteiro: Cape Verde (1991–)
Masellane: Bakgatlaland
Masepha: Barolongland
Sekkonyana Maseribane: Lesotho (1965)
Mashamba: Bunyoro
Malimba Masheke: Zambia (1989–91)
Mashobane: Matabeleland
Mashqadat: Dongola
Masih: Egypt (1575–80)
Masilo: Bakgatlaland
Masilo I: Bakwenaland
Masilo II: Bakwenaland
Salima Masimba: Mohéli
Masinissa: Numidia
Ketumile Masire: Botswana
Quett Masire: Botswana
Gabra Maskal: Ethiopia (1314–44)
Gabra Maskal Lalibela: Ethiopia (1172–1212)
Maslama ibn Mukhallad: Egypt (667–682)
Maslama ibn Yahya: Egypt (789)
Alexander Mason Bey: Equatoria Province
Gabra Masqal: Axum
Massa: Kaarta
Kere Massa: Gwiriko
Massatana: Segu
Alphonse Massemba-Débat: Congo (1963–68)
Justin Massicault: Tunisia (1886–92)
John Massingham: Saint Helena (1981–84)
Émile Masson: Gabon (1882–83)

Georges Masson: Gabon (1938–40)
Paul Masson: Burkina Faso (1959–60)
Charles-Max Masson de Saint-Félix: Central African Republic (1936–39); Chad (1936–38); Congo (1931–32)
Tajjidine ben Saʼid Massonde: Comoros (1996, 1998–99)
Charles Mast: Tunisia (1943–47)
Mastanabal: Numidia
Masud: Timbuktu (1637–42)
Masud ibn Nasir: Mombasa (1755–73)
Pie Masumboko: Burundi [ii]
Maswaza: Zaria (ca. 1150)
Mataa: Barotseland
Matani: Zaria (ca. 1050)
Matantu: Gojjam
George Matanzima: Transkei
Kaiser Matanzima: Transkei
Matazo: Zaria (ca. 1050)
Antonio Mateos y Malpartida: Melilla (1821–23)
Antonio Mateus: Angola (1935–39)
Mathiba: Bamangwatoland
Mathiba: Batwanaland
Edoardo Matienzo: Eritrea
Marqués de la Matilla: Ceuta (1751)
Nkonda Matit: Lunda
Matlala: Batlokwaland
Maurice Matlala: Lebowa
Matlapeng: Batlokwaland
Matope Nyanhehwe Nebedza: Mwene Mutapa Empire
João Matos: São Tomé (1696–97)
Joaquim de Matos: Bissau (1822, 1825–27, 1830, 1834)
José Norton de Matos: Angola (1912–15, 1921–24)
Matshego: Bakgatlaland
Matsheng: Bamangwatoland
Matsweu Adi: Kororofa
Lloyd Matthews: Zanzibar (1890–1901)
Gi-gla No-Don Gbé-non Mau: Allada
Jean Mauberna: Central African Republic (1948); Guinea (1958)
John Maud: South Africa (1959–61)
Muhammadu Maudo: Jemaari
Henri de Mauduit: Chad (1949–50); Côte d'Ivoire (1945–46); Mauritania (1948–49)
Charles de Maugras: Niger (1912–13)
Nicolas de Maupin: Mauritius (1729–35)
Maʼura: Gonja
Lollianus Mavortius: Africa Proconsularis (356)
Mavura Mhande Felipe: Mwene Mutapa Empire
Mawa: Baol
Mare Mawa Mahmadu: Katsina (1804–05)
Hasan Abuʼl Mawahib: Zeng Empire (1308–34)
Mawanda: Buganda
Mawewe: Gazaland
Maximus: Egypt (A.D. 1)

Claudius Maximus: Africa [i] (158–160)
Petronius Maximus: Africa Proconsularis (433–437, 439–442)
Vibius Maximus: Egypt (103–105)
Col. Maxwell: Ghana (1874)
Charles Maxwell: Senegal (1809–11); Sierra Leone (1811–14)
James Maxwell: Sierra Leone (1921); Zambia (1927–32)
John C. Maxwell: Ashanti; Ghana (1923, 1924, 1925, 1926, 1927)
William Maxwell: Ghana (1895–97)
Ti-Maya: Mandara
Mayaki: Gobir
Ibrahim Hassabe Mayaki: Niger (1997–)
Muhammadu Mayaki: Keffi
Muhamman Mayaki: Kazaure
John Maybin: Nigeria (1935); Zambia (1938–41)
Maye: Ibadan
Mayebre Sheshni: Egypt (15th Dynasty)
Gordon Mayen: Southern Sudan
Antonio Maymó: Fernando Po
Dauda Maza: Lapai
Muhammadu Mai-sa-Maza-Gudu: Katsina (1595–1612)
Mazakes: Egypt (333–332 B.C.)
Jaʼfar Pasha Mazhar: Sudan (1866–71)
Yuhi II Mazimpaka: Ruanda
Hussein Maziq: Libya
Muhammad Asmani al-Mazrui: Mombasa (1826–35)
Casimir Oyé-M'Ba: Gabon (1990–94)
Léon M'Ba: Gabon (1958–67)
Nyene-Mba I: Segu
Nyene-Mba II: Segu
Mba Buri-Nyabu: Dyolof
Mba Kompaas: Dyolof
Kruli Mbaaba: Walo (1806–12)
Sidi Mbairika: Trarza
Mbal Iyavu: Lunda
Mbala Kalong: Lunda
Mbala Kmong Isot: Lunda
Ngola Nzinga Mbandi: Ndongo
Mbandzeni: Swaziland (1874–89)
Mbang Waad: Walo (1202–11)
Mbany Naatago: Walo (1380–81)
Mbanyi Paate: Dyolof
N'dyak Ko N'Dyay Mbanyik: Walo (1367–80)
Yerim Mbanyik: Walo (1271–78)
Yerim Mbanyik Anta Dyop: Walo (1735)
Yerim Mbanyik Aram Bakar: Walo (1640–74)
Yerim Mbanyik Konegil: Walo (1398–1415)
Yerim Mbanyik Teg: Walo (1821–23)
M'Bar: Baol
Tyaaka Mbar: Walo (1225–42)
Sghair Ould M'Bareck: Mauritania (2003–)
Teodoro Obiang Nguema Mbasogo: Equatorial Guinea
M'Bathio Samb: Kayor

Mbay Yerim: Walo (1316–31)
Mbeikuo: Bamoun
Thabo Mbeki: South Africa (1999–)
Nkang Mbemba: Kongo
Nzinga Mbemba: Kongo
Birayma Mbenda-Tyilor: Kayor
N'Dyelen Mbey Leeyti: Dyolof
Mbeu Mbody Kumba Khedy: Walo (1734–35)
Mbeu Mbody Maalik: Walo (1840–55)
André-Marie Mbida: Cameroun (1957–58)
Godwin Mbikusita: Barotseland
Prince Jameson Mbilini Dhlamini: Swaziland (1993–96)
M'Bissan Kura: Baol
M'Bissan N'Della: Baol
Barka Mbody: Walo (1211–25)
Saayodo Yaasin Mbody: Walo (1801–06)
Mbeu Mbody Maalik: Walo (1840–55)
Dominique Mbonyumutwa: Rwanda
Mboo: Barotseland
Mbouombouo: Bamoun
Mbumb Muteba Kat: Lunda
Mbumba: Lunda
Yerim Khode Fara Mbuno: Walo (1735–36)
Robert Meade: Cape Colony (1813–14)
Budgett Meakin: Tangier (1674–75)
Léon Mébiame: Gabon (1975–90)
Félix Méchet: Niger (1918–19)
Joseph Mechlin, Jr.: Liberia (1829–33)
Adolf Frederick, the Herzog of Mecklenburg: Togoland
Anton Van Der Meden: Hollandia
Ras Asrata-Medhin Kassa: Eritrea
Francisco Medina y Salazar: Canary Islands (1709–13)
Abraham Meermans: Dutch Gold Coast (1676–80)
Mehiga: Karagwe
Mehmed: Algiers (1650–53)
Mehmed: Bahr al-Ghazal
Ak Mehmed: Tripolitania (1678–79)
Hafiz Mehmed: Tripolitania (1900–03)
Mehmed Brusali: Algiers (1642–45)
Mehmed Bey: Egypt (1773–75)
Mehmed Bey: Kordofan
Mehmed Bey al-Kabir: Oran (1792)
Mehmed Bey Makkalas: Oran (1804)
Mehmed Emin: Tripolitania (1842–47)
Mehmed Emin Pasha: Equatoria Province
Mehmed Halid: Tripolitania (1870–71)
Mehmed Hussein Javush Bey: Tripolitania (1711)
Mehmed Imam: Tripolitania (1702–06)
Mehmed Imam Kerdeki: Tripolitania (1687–1701)

Mehmed Jelaleddin: Tripolitania (1876–78)
Mehmed Nazif: Tripolitania (1880–81)
Hajji Mehmed Nazir: Bahr al-Ghazal
Mehmed Rashid: Tripolitania (1871–72)
Mehmed Reis: Tripolitania (1835–37)
Mehmed Reuf Pasha: Equatoria Province
Mehmed Sa'id Pasha Wahbi: Kordofan
Mehmed Saqizli: Tripolitania (1631–49)
Mehreka Nan: Ethiopia (1433)
Manuel Meira: Bissau (1868–69)
Tomás Mejía de Escobedo: Melilla (1633–35)
Maurice Meker: Djibouti (1957–58)
Melchior Ndadaye: Burundi [ii]
Mele Filata: Daniski
Mele Fusan: Daniski
Mele Manso: Daniski
Muhammad Melek: Egypt (1752, 1767)
Hayla Melekot: Shoa
Meles Zenawi: Ethiopia (1991–)
Diego de Melgarejo: Gran Canaria
Melitius: Africa Proconsularis (410–412)
Antonio de Melo: Madeira (1698–1701); Mombasa (1696–97)
Antonio de Melo: Mozambique (1730–33)
Antonio de Melo: Mozambique (1837)
Brás de Melo: Cape Verde (1591–95)
Duarte de Melo: Mombasa (1688–93)
Fernão de Melo: São Tomé (1499–1510)
Florencio de Melo: Madeira (1815–19)
Henriques de Melo: Mozambique (1973–74)
João de Melo: Cape Verde (1839–42, 1848–51)
João de Melo: Mozambique (1758)
José de Melo: Cape Verde (1890–93)
João de Melo: São Tomé (1517–22)
José de Melo: São Tomé and Príncipe (1860–62)
Manuel de Melo: Cape Verde (1671–76)
Miguel de Melo: Angola (1797–1802)
Rodrigo de Melo: Madeira (1821–22)
Rui de Melo: Portuguese Gold Coast (1552–55)
Rui Soares de Melo: Mombasa (1598–1606)
Ruis de Melo: Tangier (1471)
Miguel de Melo e Albuquerque: São Tomé (1640–41)
Vicente de Melo e Almada: São Tomé and Príncipe (1880–81)
Diogo de Melo e Alvim: Guinea-Bissau (1953–56)
Álvaro de Melo e Castro: Mombasa (1728–29); Mozambique (1721–23)
Antonio de Melo e Castro: Mozambique (1664–67)
Antonio de Melo e Castro: Mozambique (1786–93)

Caetano de Melo e Castro: Mozambique (1682–86)
Francisco de Melo e Castro: Mozambique (1750–58)
Antonio de Melo e Castro de Mendonça: Mozambique (1809–12)
Jerónimo de Melo Fernando: São Tomé (1623–27)
Thomas Melvill: Ghana (1751–56)
Michael Melville: Sierra Leone (1833)
Antonio Mena: Cape Verde (1696)
Fernando Mena: Angola (1947)
Menander: Africa Proconsularis (320–322)
Menas: Egypt (595)
Miguel Porcel y Manrique de Araña Menchaca y Zaldívar: Ceuta (1784–91)
Francisco Mendes: Guinea-Bissau (1973–78)
Rui Mendes de Vasconcelos Ribeiro: Ceuta (1479–81)
Fernando de Santiago y Díaz de Mendívil: Western Sahara
Manuel de Mendívil y Elío: Equatorial Guinea
Antonio Mendonça: São Tomé (1717–20)
João de Mendonça: Angola (1594–1602)
Nunho de Mendonça: Tangier (1605–10)
Jorge de Mendonça Pessanha: Ceuta (1627–34)
Luis de Mendoza: Gran Canaria
Menelik II: Ethiopia (1889–1911); Shoa
Menes: Egypt (1st Dynasty); Upper Egypt
Antonio de Meneses: Cacheu (1785)
Antonio de Meneses: Mombasa (1648–51)
Antonio de Meneses: Mozambique (1528–31)
Brás Teles de Meneses: Ceuta (1634–36)
Diogo de Meneses: Mozambique (1624–27, 1632–33)
Duarte de Meneses: Tangier (1522–31)
Duarte de Meneses: Tangier (1574–78)
Fernando de Meneses: São Tomé (1593–97)
Fernão de Meneses: Ceuta (1557–62, 1563–64)
Fernão Teles de Meneses: Ceuta (1637–37)
Francisco Teles de Meneses: São Tomé (1611)
Francisco Barreto de Meneses: São Tomé (1632)
Gonçalo de Meneses: Angola (1691–94)
João de Meneses: Madeira (1634–36)
João de Meneses: Tangier (1531–52)
Jorge de Meneses: Mozambique (1586–89)
Luis de Meneses: Angola (1697–1701)

Pedro de Meneses: Angola (1639–45)
Pedro de Meneses: Ceuta (1550–53)
Rodrigo de Meneses: Angola (1732–38)
Sebastião Meneses: Cape Verde (1858–60)
Francisco Meneses da Costa: Mozambique (1797–1801)
João de Meneses Drumont: Cacheu (1819)
Fradique de Menezes: São Tomé and Príncipe (2001–)
Menetewab: Ethiopia (1730–55)
Mengap: Bamoun
Étienne Mengin Duval d'Ailly: Réunion (1830–32)
Mengistu Haile Mariam: Ethiopia (1977–91)
Meni: Egypt (1st Dynasty); Upper Egypt
Tunka Menin: Ghana Empire
Adán Martín Menis: Canary Islands (2003–)
Menkare: Egypt (6th Dynasty)
Menkauhor: Egypt (5th Dynasty)
Menkaure: Egypt (4th Dynasty)
Menkheperre: Egypt (21st Dynasty)
Thutmose IV Menkheprure: Egypt (18th Dynasty)
Rameses XI Menmare Setneptah: Egypt (20th Dynasty)
Seti Menmare Merneptah: Egypt (19th Dynasty)
Amenmesse Menmire: Egypt (19th Dynasty)
Meno: Batwanaland
Jacques de Menou: Egypt (1800–01)
Rameses I Menpehtire: Egypt (19th Dynasty)
Mentuhotep I: Egypt (10th Dynasty)
Sankhenre Mentuhotep: Egypt (17th Dynasty)
Mentuhotep II Nebhepetre: Egypt (10th Dynasty, 11th Dynasty)
Mentuhotep III Sankhkare: Egypt (11th Dynasty)
Mentuhotep IV Nebtowere: Egypt (11th Dynasty)
Vittorio Menzinger: Tripolitania (1919–20)
Muhammadu Mera: Argungu
Kasdi Merbah: Algeria (1988–89)
Manuel Gasset Mercader: Spanish Morocco (1858)
Albert Mercadier: Togo (1943–44)
Luigi Mercatelli: Tripolitania (1920–21); Italian Somaliland (1905–06)
Marqués de Santa Cruz de Mercenado: Oran (1732–33)
Eulogio Merchán: Fernando Po
José Merello y Calvo: Spanish Morocco (1881–83)
Antyemsaf I Merenre: Egypt (6th Dynasty)
Antyemsaf II Merenre: Egypt (6th Dynasty)
Edward Merewether: Sierra Leone (1910–15)

Merhetepre Ini: Egypt (13th Dynasty)
Merikare: Egypt (10th Dynasty)
Merimde: Upper Egypt
Merkare Aspelta: Kush (593–568 B.C.)
Benoît de Merkel: Tunisia (1900–01)
Merkurios: Dongola
Amédée Merlaud-Ponty: French West Africa (1908–15); Mali (1899–1907)
Victor-Emmanuel Merlet: Central African Republic (1905–06, 1916–17)
Martial Merlin: French Equatorial Africa (1898–99, 1908–17); French West Africa (1907–08, 1919–23); Madagascar (1917–18)
Pierre-Balthasar Mermier: Sainte Marie de Madagascar
Merneferre Iy: Egypt (13th Dynasty)
Seti Menmare Merneptah: Egypt (19th Dynasty)
Seti II Usikheperure Merneptah: Egypt (19th Dynasty)
Siptah Akhenre Merneptah: Egypt (19th Dynasty)
Merneptah Binere Meryamun Hotphimae: Egypt (19th Dynasty)
John Merriman: Cape Colony (1908–10)
Neferhotep II Mersekhemre: Egypt (13th Dynasty)
Merso: Gojjam
Meruserre Yakhuber: Egypt (15th Dynasty)
Émile Merwaert: Benin [ii] (1911–12); Central African Republic (1905–09); Côte d'Ivoire (1904–05)
Rameses VI Nebmare Meryamun: Egypt (20th Dynasty)
Rameses VII Usermare Meryamun: Egypt (20th Dynasty)
Tausert Sitre Meryamun: Egypt (19th Dynasty)
Merneptah Binere Meryamun Hotphimae: Egypt (19th Dynasty)
Pepi I Meryre: Egypt (6th Dynasty)
M. Mésineau: Senegal (1651–58)
Jean-Georges le Baillif des Mesnager: Gorée
Diogo de Mesquita: Mozambique (1551–53)
Francisco de Mesquita: Mozambique (1693–94)
Manuel de Mesquita Perestrelo: Portuguese Gold Coast (1562)
Valerius Messala: Africa Proconsularis (399–400)
Messe: Porto-Novo
Messi: Porto-Novo
Pierre Messmer: Cameroun (1956–58); Côte d'Ivoire (1954–56); French Equatorial Africa (1958); French West Africa (1958–59); Mauritania (1952–54)
Philippe de Mester: Mayotte Department
Paul, 3rd Baron Methuen: Natal (1910)
Metius Modestus: Egypt (55–56)

Metius Rufus: Egypt (90–95)
Pomponius Metrodorus: Egypt (357–360)
Meu Mbody Kumba Khedy: Walo (1734–35)
Meumbody N'dyak: Walo (1381–98)
Hartvig Meyer: Danish Gold Coast (1703–04)
Jørgen Meyer: Danish Gold Coast (1691–92)
Lukas Meyer: New Republic
Meyi: Porto-Novo
Mwongo Mfwama: Kazembe
Nyamaende Mhande: Mwene Mutapa Empire
Mavura Mhande Felipe: Mwene Mutapa Empire
Abdou Mhindi: Nzwani
Rameses II the Great Usermare Miamun: Egypt (19th Dynasty)
Mibambwe I Mutabaazi: Ruanda
Mibambwe II Gisanura: Ruanda
Mibambwe III Seentaabyo: Ruanda
Mibambwe IV Rutulindwa: Ruanda
Michael: Dongola
Immanuel Amde Michael: Eritrea
Michael Gaborone: Batlokwaland
James Michel: Seychelles (2004–)
Micipsa: Numidia
Michel Micombero: Burundi [ii]
Louis Micon: Comoros (1897–99)
George Middlemore: Saint Helena (1836–42)
Earl of Middleton: Tangier (1669–74)
John Middleton: Gambia (1927–28); Mauritius (1914)
Miftah al-Istah: Libya
Mijo: Allada
Mikael: Axum
Betwoded Asfaha Wolde Mikael: Eritrea
Mikael Imru: Ethiopia (1974)
Muhammad Mikat: Zeng Empire (1506–07)
Miketo: Luba
Mikpon: Porto-Novo
Richard Miles: Ghana (1777–80, 1782–84)
Pierre-Bernard de Milius: Réunion (1818–21)
David Mill: Ghana (1770–77)
Thomas Milles: Natal (1873)
Joseph-Marie Millet: Gabon (1844)
René Millet: Tunisia (1894–1900)
Joseph Brunet-Millet: Gabon (1866–67)
Constant Millot: Chad (1908–09)
Alfred Milner: Cape Colony (1897–1905); Orange Free State (1902–05); Transvaal (1902)
André Milongo: Congo (1991–92)
William Milton: Rhodesia (1897–1900); Zimbabwe (1900–14)
Min: Egypt (1st Dynasty); Upper Egypt
Minas: Ethiopia (1559–63)
Mindji: Allada
Mingi I: Brass

Mingi II: Brass
Mingi III: Brass
Mingi IV: Brass
Mingi V: Brass
Mingi VI: Brass
Mingi VII: Brass
Mingi IX: Brass
Mingi X: Brass
Mingi XI: Brass
Antonio de Mingo: Warri
Minicius: Africa [i] (139–140)
Minicius Italus: Egypt (105–109)
Lucius Minicius Natalis: Africa [i] (121)
Lucius Minicius Natalis Quadronius Verus: Africa [i] (153–154)
Ali III al-Miqdam: Idrisid State
Antonio de Miranda: Portuguese Gold Coast (1539–41)
Francisco de Miranda: São Tomé and Príncipe (1891–94)
José de Miranda: Ceuta (1818–20, 1824–26)
Juan de Miranda: Gran Canaria; Tenerife
Marqués de Miranda de Auta: Ceuta (1641–44)
Antonio de Miranda de Azevedo: Portuguese Gold Coast (1504)
Camilo de Miranda Rebocho Vaz: Angola (1966–72)
José Mirelis y González: Melilla (1889–91)
Ahmad al-Mirghani: Sudan (1986–89)
Miri: Egypt (1620–22)
Mirindi: Nkore
Yahya al-Miruki: Tripolitania (1204–07)
Brajesh Chandra Mishra: Namibia (1982–87)
Ibrahim Misirli-Oglu: Tripolitania (1675–76)
Abu al-Misq Kafur: Egypt (946–965, 965–968)
Capt. Misson: Libertalia
Jacob de Mist: Cape Colony (1803–04)
Giuseppe Volpi Di Misurata: Tripolitania (1921–25)
Charles Mitchell: Natal (1881–82, 1889–93)
George Mitchell: Zimbabwe (1933)
Philip Mitchell: Kenya (1944–52); Uganda (1935–40)
Louis Mizon: Djibouti (1899); Muri (1892–93)
Benjamin William Mkapa: Tanzania
Edward Mkinga: GazaNkulu
Mmusi: Bakgatlaland
Mmusi: Bamaleteland
Mnguni: Transkeian Territories
Joseph Desiré Mobutu: Congo (Zaire) (1965–97)
Mobutu Sese Seko: Congo (Zaire) (1965–97)
Barão de Moçâmedes: Angola (1784–90)
W.E. Mockler: Ghana (1865)

Marcolino Moco: Angola (1992–96)
Pascoal Mocumbi: Mozambique (1994–2004)
Dawi Moda: Biu
Garga Moda; Biu
Metius Modestus: Egypt (55–56)
Modi Abdulaye: Futa Jallon
Abubakar Modibbo: Kontagora
Modibbo Dan Fodio: Gobir
Modibo Keita: Mali (1959–68); Mali Federation
Modibo Keita II: Mali (2000–02)
Modiboya: Barolongland
Modimokwana: Bakgatlaland
Festus Mogae: Botswana
Mogala: Bakgatlaland
Mogalakwe: Batwanaland
Mogoboya Ramodike: Lebowa
Juan Mogrobejo: Canary Islands (1671–76)
Mohama Wabi II: Jemaari
Ahmad Fuad Mohieddin: Egypt (1982–84)
Zahariah Mohieddin: Egypt (1965–66)
Daniel arap Moi: Kenya (1978–2002)
Moi Albo: Daniski
Barma Dan Moi Bunowo: Daniski
Moi Buraima: Daniski
Moise: Dongola
Moithali: Bakwenaland
Mokamba: Barotseland
Mokdad Sifi: Algeria (1994–95)
Mokgatsha Mokgadi: Bamangwatoland
Mokgadi: Bamangwatoland
Mokgatsha Mokgadi: Bamangwatoland
Mokgojwa: Bamaleteland
Mokgopha: Barolongland
Mokgosi I: Bamaleteland
Mokgosi II: Bamaleteland
Mokgosi III: Bamaleteland
Mokgwa: Bamaleteland
Mokgwa: Batlokwaland
Mokgware: Bamaleteland
Ntsu Mokhehle: Lesotho (1993–98)
Mokhtar Muhammad Hussein: Somalia
Mokhtar Ould Daddah: Mauritania (1957–78)
Molefe: Bakgatlaland
Molefi I: Bakgatlaland
Molefi II: Bakgatlaland
Kgosi Molefi II: Bakgatlaland
Juan Moles: Spanish Morocco (1933–34, 1936)
Molete: Bamangwatoland
Molete: Bangwaketseland
Alexandre Moll: Chad (1909–10)
Alfred Moloney: Gambia (1884–86); Ghana (1882); Lagos (1878–80, 1883, 1886–89, 1890–91)
John Molteno: Cape Colony (1872–78)
Molwa: Bamangwatoland
Moma: Ilorin
Moma Alhaji: Misau

Moma Haji: Katagum
Moma Manga: Misau
Moma Sali: Misau
Moman Kankia: Hadejia
Ernesto Mombelli: Cyrenaica
Joseph Saidu Momoh: Sierra Leone (1985–92)
Monaamabura: Batwanaland
Monan Abu: Zaria (1505–30)
Monavo Fani: Mayotte
Francisco Moncada: Angola (1900–03)
Guillem de Moncada: Tripolitania (1511–20)
Conde de la Monclova: Oran (1681–82)
Gaston Mondon: Côte d'Ivoire (1936–38)
Gaspar de Mondragón: Melilla (1617–18)
Mongala: Bangwaketseland
Mongatane: Bamaleteland
Júlio Moniz da Silva: Mozambique (1642–46)
Monjou: Bamoun
Jérôme Monléon: Gorée and Dependencies'
Fernando Monroi: Mozambique (1577)
Jean Mons: Tunisia (1947–50)
Conde de Monsanto: Tangier (1522)
Michel Montagné: Togo (1936–38, 1939–41)
Jean-Baptiste Montagniès de la Roque: Senegal (1841–42)
Ernest Montagu: Zimbabwe (1920, 1922–23)
Marquês de Montalvão: Tangier (1621–24)
Gilles Montaubam: Fort-Dauphin
Antoine Louis Desmarets de Montchaton: Gorée
Marquis de Montdevergue: Fort-Dauphin
Antonio Monteiro: São Tomé (1601–04)
Antonio Mascarenhas Monteiro: Cape Verde (1991–2001)
José Monteiro: Madeira (1828–30)
Leão Monteiro: Cape Verde (1963–70)
Ricardo Vaz Monteiro: Guinea-Bissau (1941–45); São Tomé and Príncipe (1933–41)
Martinho Montenegro: Cape Verde (1909–10)
Louis Lecoupé de Montereau: Senegal (1820–21)
Arend Montfort: Dutch Gold Coast (1639–41)
Montshiwa: Barolongland
Mookgami: Bangwaketseland
Enraght Mooney: Swaziland (1902–07)
Frederick Moor: Natal (1906–10)
Ralph Moor: Southern Nigeria
Henry Moore: Kenya (1930, 1940–44); Sierra Leone (1934–37)
Harry Moorhouse: Nigeria Southern Provinces

George Mooring: Zanzibar (1960–63)

Pieter Moorthamer: Dutch West Africa

Tsiame Kenneth Mopale: QwaQwa

Antonio Mora: Angola (1928–29)

Jaime de Castro Morais: Angola (1917–18)

João da Sera de Morais: Portuguese Gold Coast (1629)

Carlos de Morais e Almeida: São Tomé and Príncipe (1847)

Morare: Barolongland

Frederik Mørch: Danish Gold Coast (1834–39)

José Morcillo Ezquerra: Melilla (1856–58)

Louis Moreau de Chambonneau: Senegal (1684–89, 1690–93)

Bernardo Moreira: Bissau (1867–68)

Charles Morel: Comoros (1857–60); Nossi-Bé

Moremi I: Batwanaland

Moremi II: Batwanaland

Moremi III: Batwanaland

Letla Moreng: Barolongland

Letla Moreng II: Barolongland

Francisco López Moreno: Melilla (1687–87)

Pedro Moreno y Perez de Oteyro: Canary Islands (1764)

Pedro Moreo: Melilla (1632–33)

David Morgan: Swaziland (1950–56)

Muhammad Siyad Hersi Morgan: Jubaland (ii)

Diringa Mori: Kaarta

Bodyan Mori Ba: Kaarta

Moriba: Koya-Temne

Bodian Moriba: Kaarta

Moribu Kindo: Koya-Temne

Jean Morin: Algeria (1960–62)

François de la Morlière: Mauritius (1800–03)

Álvaro Morna: Angola (1942–43)

Morolong: Barolongland

Arthur Morris: Gold Coast Northern Territories

Laganfiela Moru: Gwiriko

Bako Moru Watara: Gwiriko

Morvakgomo: Bakwenaland

Mosadi: Bamaleteland

Moselekatze: Matabeleland

Moshibidu Gaborone: Batlokwaland

Moshoeshoe I: Lesotho (1822–70)

Moshoeshoe II: Lesotho (1960–90, 1995–96)

Kgabosetso II Mosielele: Bangwaketseland

Mosime: Batlokwaland

Pakalitha Mosisili: Lesotho (1998–)

Kintu Mosoke: Uganda (1994–99)

Manuel da Mota: São Tomé and Príncipe (1798–99)

Mendio da Mota: Portuguese Gold Coast (1574)

Wessels Mota: QwaQwa

Luis da Mota e Melo: São Tomé and Príncipe (1758–61)

Luis da Mota Feo e Torres: Angola (1816–19)

M. Motais de Narbonne: Seychelles (1786–89)

al-Motasim: Egypt (830)

Alexandre de la Mothe: Oran (1742–48)

Henri de la Mothe: French Equatorial Africa (1897–1900); Senegal (1890–95)

Mothubane: Batlokwaland

R. Motlhadledi: Barolongland

Motlotle: Bakgatlaland

Motsodhi: Bakwenaland

Motswasele I: Bakwenaland

Motswasele II: Bakwenaland

Moukhtar Sidi: Brakna

Jacob Mould: Ghana (1798–99, 1802–05)

Mouloud Hamroche: Algeria (1989–91)

Fidèle Moungar: Chad (1993)

Francisco de Moura: Cape Verde (1618–22)

José da Costa Moura: São Tomé and Príncipe (1862–63)

Miguel de Moura: São Tomé (1587–91)

Alexandre de Moura e Albuquerque: Madeira (1676–80)

Jacques Mouradian: Comoros (1969–75)

Albert Mouragues: Burkina Faso (1948–53); Mali (1953); Mauritania (1954–55, 1956–58)

Charles Mouret: Mauritania (1912–14)

James Mourgan: Ghana (1784–87)

Gaston Mourgues: Burkina Faso (1947–48)

Charles Mourin: Niger (1915–18)

Muhammad Doud Mourrah: Wadai

Pierre Moussa: Congo (1990–91)

Moussa Faki: Chad (2003–05)

Moussa Koura Bo: Kaarta

Moussa Toroma: Kenedugu

Moussa Traoré: Mali (1968–91)

Moustapha Niasse: Senegal (1983, 2000–01)

João Moutinho: Cacheu (1664)

Gabriel Garnier-Mouton: Comoros (1911–13)

Louis Mouttet: Côte d'Ivoire (1896–98); Senegal (1895)

Hendrik Mouwe: Dutch Gold Coast (1824)

Mowa Mamili: Barotseland

Mowashi: Zamfara

Fernando Moyano: Melilla (1798–1800)

Mpande: Zululand

Patrick Mphephu: Venda

Mpinga Kasenga: Congo (Zaire) (1977–79)

Isingoma Mpuga Rukidi: Bunyoro

Mqikela: Pondoland East

Ali Mroudjae: Comoros (1982–84)

Msavila: Mirambo

Arthur Mshiyeni: Zululand

Msindra: Anjouan

Cleopa David Msuya: Tanzania

Mswati: Swaziland (1836–68)

Mswati III: Swaziland (1986–)

Mswazi: Swaziland (1836–68)

Mthikrakra: Tembuland

Klaas Mtshiweni: KwaNdebele

Francisco Muacho: Bissau (1827)

Sheikh al-Mu'aiyad: Egypt (1412–21)

Muatiba: Wagadugu

Mu'awaiyah: Arab North Africa

Mu'azu: Fulani Empire

Mu'azu: Kontagora

Muhammad Hosni Mubarrak: Egypt (1981–)

al-Mubarrak I: Timbuktu (1685, 1693)

al-Mubarrak II: Timbuktu (1697)

al-Mubarrak III: Timbuktu (1706)

Mubarrak ash-Shamikh: Libya

Mubarrak ibn Rashid: Mombasa (1860–73)

Mubukwanu: Barotseland

Nawej Mufa Muchimbunj: Lunda

Baldwin Mudau: Venda

Elijah Mudenda: Zambia (1975–77)

Mudib: Lunda

al-Mudhaffar Kuts: Egypt (1259–60)

Nawej Mufa Muchimbunj: Lunda

Mufattish Kiaya: Egypt (1689–91)

Robert Mugabe: Zimbabwe (1980–)

Mugalula: Mirambo

Nyabongo II Mugenyi: Bunyoro

al-Mughira ibn Obeydallah: Egypt (748–750)

Abu'l Muhagir Dinar: Arab North Africa

Muhamma Alwali: Kano (1780–1807)

Muhamma Nazaki: Kano (1617–22)

Muhamma Sharefa: Kano (1702–30)

Muhammad: Adrar

Sayid Muhammad: Anjouan

Muhammad: Brakna

Sidi Muhammad: Brakna

Muhammad: Egypt (1496–98)

Muhammad: Egypt (1553–56)

Sayyid Muhammad: Egypt (1596–98)

Muhammad: Egypt (1604–05)

Muhammad: Egypt (1607–11)

Muhammad: Egypt (1611–15)

Muhammad: Egypt (1622)

Muhammad: Egypt (1628–30)

Muhammad: Egypt (1637–40)

Muhammad: Egypt (1646–47)

Muhammad: Egypt (1647–49)

Muhammad: Egypt (1652–56)

Muhammad: Egypt (1657–60)

Muhammad: Egypt (1699–1704)

Muhammad: Egypt (1704–06)

Muhammad: Egypt (1721–25)

Muhammad: Egypt (1726–27)

Muhammad: Egypt (1733–34)

Muhammad: Egypt (1744–48)

Muhammad: Egypt (1767–68)

Muhammad: Egypt (1768)

Muhammad: Fika

Muhammad: Gumel

Mulay Muhammad: Hafsid Kingdom; Tunis (1573–74)

Muhammad: Harar

Muhammad: Mali Empire

Muhammad: Mayotte

Sheikh Muhammad: Mogadishu

Muhammad: Mohéli

Muhammad: Nupe

Muhammad: Omayyad and Abbasid North Africa

Muhammad: Tripolitania (1053)

Muhammad: Tripolitania (1327–48)

Muhammad: Tripolitania (1645–54)

Muhammad: Tunis (1675–96)

Abdullahi Muhammad: Comoros (1976–78)

Abdullahi Issa Muhammad: Italian Somaliland (1956–60)

Abou Sekin Muhammad: Baguirmi

Abu Abdallah Muhammad: Tripolitania (1014–22)

Abu al-Yaqzan Muhammad: Rustumid Amirate

Abu Zayyan Muhammad: Tlemcen (1360)

Abu Zayyan I Muhammad: Tlemcen (1541–50)

Abu Zayyan II Muhammad: Tlemcen (1393–97)

Sa'id Ali Muhammad: Comoros (1993)

Ali Mahdi Muhammad: Somalia

al-Mansur ad-Din Muhammad: Egypt (1361–63)

Murtala Ramat Muhammad: Nigeria (1975–76)

Nasir ad-Din Muhammad: Egypt (1198–1200)

Nyani Mansa Muhammad: Mali Empire

as-Salih Muhammad: Egypt (1421–22)

Muhammad I: Adal [ii]

Muhammad I: Aghlabid Empire

Muhammad I: Algiers (1671–82)

Muhammad I: Anjouan

Muhammad I: Bornu Empire (1352–53)

Muhammad I: Fezzan

Muhammad I: Gwandu

Muhammad I: Kordofan

Muhammad I: Morocco (1240–44)

Muhammad I: Timbuktu (1619–21)

Muhammad I: Tunis (1756–59)

Abu Abdallah Muhammad I: Tlemcen (1400–11)

Abu Abdallah Muhammad I al-Mustansir: Hafsid Kingdom

Muhammad I ash-Sharif: Morocco (1631–35)

Muhammad I Dawra: Darfur

Muhammad II: Adal [ii]

Muhammad II: Aghlabid Empire

Muhammad II: Anjouan

Muhammad II: Bornu Empire (1455–56)

Muhammad II: Gwandu

Muhammad II: Kordofan

Muhammad II: Mali Empire

Muhammad II: Morocco (1635–64)

Muhammad II: Songhai (1582–86)

Muhammad II: Timbuktu (1642–46)

Muhammad II: Trarza

Muhammad II: Tunis (1855–59)

Abu Abdallah Muhammad II: Tlemcen (1424–27, 1430)

Abu Abdallah Muhammad II Abu Asida: Hafsid Kingdom

Muhammad II al-Bartuqali: Morocco (1505–24)

Muhammad II al-Mahdi: Morocco (1525–57)

Muhammad II as-Sa'id: Morocco (1358–59)

Muhammad II Bektash: Algiers (1706–10)

Muhammad II Nasir: Fezzan

Muhammad II Tairab: Darfur

Muhammad III: Algiers (1718–24)

Muhammad III: Bornu Empire (1456)

Muhammad III: Fezzan

Muhammad III: Mali Empire

Muhammad III: Morocco (1736–38, 1748, 1757–90)

Muhammad III: Timbuktu (1654)

Muhammad III: Trarza

Abu Abdallah Muhammad III: Tlemcen (1462–68)

Abu Zayyan Muhammad III: Morocco (1361–66)

Muhammad III al-Fadhl: Darfur

Muhammad III al-Mutawakkil: Morocco (1574–76)

Muhammad III al-Qasri: Morocco (1545–47)

Muhammad III an-Nasir: Almohad Empire

Muhammad III as-Sadiq: Tunis (1859–81); Tunisia (1881–82)

Muhammad IV: Algiers (1748–54)

Muhammad IV: Bornu Empire (1467–72)

Muhammad IV: Morocco (1859–73)

Muhammad IV: Timbuktu (1655–57)

Abu Abdallah Muhammad IV: Tlemcen (1468–1504)

Abu Zayyan Muhammad IV: Morocco (1372–74)

Muhammad IV al-Habib: Trarza

Muhammad IV al-Hadi: Tunisia (1902–06)

Muhammad IV al-Hakim: Fezzan

Muhammad IV al-Ma'mun: Morocco (1610–13)

Abu Abdallah Muhammad IV al-Muntasir: Hafsid Kingdom

Muhammad IV Hussain: Darfur

Muhammad V: Algiers (1766–91)

Muhammad V: Morocco (1927–53, 1955–61)

Muhammad V: Timbuktu (1657–59)

Abu Abdallah Muhammad V: Hafsid Kingdom; Tlemcen (1504–17)

Muhammad V al-Asgher: Morocco (1636–55)

Muhammad V al-Mustansir: Fezzan

Muhammad V Aminami: Bornu Empire (1526–45)

Muhammad V an-Nasir: Tunisia (1906–22)

Muhammad VI: Algiers (1815)

Muhammad VI: Morocco (1953–55)

Muhammad VI: Morocco (1999–)

Muhammad VI: Timbuktu (1665)

Abu Abdallah Muhammad VI: Tlemcen (1543)

Muhammad VI al-Habib: Tunisia (1922–29)

Muhammad VII: Timbuktu (1670)

Muhammad VII al-Muncif: Tunisia (1942–43)

Muhammad VII Erghamma: Bornu Empire (1737–52)

Muhammad VIII: Bornu Empire (1810–14)

Muhammad VIII: Timbuktu (1671, 1682)

Muhammad VIII al-Amin: Tunisia (1943–57)

Muhammad IX: Timbuktu (1680, 1684)

Muhammad X: Timbuktu (1697, 1704)

Muhammad XI: Timbuktu (1701, 1703)

Muhammad XII: Timbuktu (1708, 1715–16, 1733–34, 1737–38)

Muhammad XIII: Timbuktu (1731–32)

Abu Muhammad Abd al-Haqq I: Morocco (1196–1218)

Abu Muhammad Abd al-Haqq II: Morocco (1428–65)

Abu Muhammad Abd al-Wahid: Tripolitania (1207–21); Tunis (1207–21)

Abu Muhammad Abdallah: Tripolitania (1053)

Abu Muhammad Abdallah I: Tlemcen (1397–1400)

Abu Muhammad Abdallah II: Tlemcen (1527–41)

Abu Muhammad Abdallah Abu: Tunis (1226–28)

Muhammad Abali: Fika

Muhammad Abdelazziz: Western Sahara

Muhammad Abdelghani: Algeria (1979–84)

Muhammad Abdi Hashi: Puntland

Muhammad Abdi Yusuf: Somalia

Muhammad Abdou Mahdi: Comoros (1994)

Muhammad Abdullai IV: Dagomba

Sheikh Muhammad Abu'l Kaylak: Kordofan

Muhammad Ahmad: Comoros (1978)

Muhammad Ahmad (The Mahdi): Sudan (1881–85)

Muhammad Ahmad al-Mangush: Libya

Sayid Muhammad al-Abid: Fezzan

Muhammad al-Adil: Zeng Empire (1416–25)

Sayid Muhammad al-Ahabagi: Zanzibar (1823–32)

Kiyari Muhammad al-Amin: Bornu Empire (1893)
Muhammad al-Amin: Baguirmi
Muhammad al-Amin al-Kanemi: Bornu Empire (1817–24)
Muhammad al-Bakr: Tagant
Sidi Muhammad al-Hadi al-Ahwa: Tunisia (1932–42)
Muhammad al-Hiba: Brakna
Muhammad al-Ikhshid: Egypt (935–946)
Muhammad al-Khalangi: Egypt (905–906)
Muhammad al-Mukni: Fezzan
Muhammad al-Muqri: Morocco (1908–09, 1911–13, 1917–55)
Muhammad al-Mustansir: Idrisid State
Muhammad al-Qa'im: Morocco (1511–17)
Muhammad Ali: Egypt (1805–48)
Muhammad Ali Samatar: Somalia
Muhammad an-Nasir: Egypt (1293–94, 1299–1309)
Muhammad Ankony: Zeng Empire (1504–05)
Muhammad Anwar as-Sadat: Egypt (1970–81)
Muhammad ar-Rajal: Brakna
Muhammad as-Salih: Tunisia (1954)
Muhammad as-Saqizli: Cyrenaica; Libya
Muhammad ash-Sheikh: Morocco (1465–1505)
Muhammad Asmani al-Mazrui: Mombasa (1826–35)
al-Hajj Muhammad at-Tazi Bu Ashran: Tangier (1923–41, 1945–54)
Muhammad Atahiru I: Fulani Empire
Muhammad Atahiru II: Fulani Empire
Muhammad az-Zaruq Rajab: Libya
Muhammad Babana: Trarza
Salah Eddine ben Muhammad Baccouche: Tunisia (1943–47, 1952–54)
Muhammad Bani: Songhai (1586–88)
Muhammad Bello: Fulani Empire
Muhammad Bello: Kano (1882–92)
Sidi Muhammad ben Mulay Arafa: Morocco (1953–55)
Sidi Muhammad ben Yusuf: Morocco (1927–53, 1955–61)
Muhammad Benhima: Morocco (1967–69)
Muhammad Bey Rasileh: Sudan (1861–62)
Muhammad Boudiaf: Algeria (1992)
Muhammad Buhari: Nigeria (1984–85)
Muhammad Bukalmarami: Bornu Empire (1603–17)
Muhammad Bunkan: Songhai (1531–37)
Muhammad Chenik: Tunisia (1950–52)
Muhammad Dao: Songhai (1402–10)

Sa'id Muhammad Djohar: Comoros (1989–96)
Muhammad Doud Mourrah: Wadai
Sheikh Muhammad Fadl: Trarza
Muhammad Fari: Songhai (1418–26)
Muhammad Gao: Songhai (1591)
Muhammad Hosni Mubarrak: Egypt (1981–)
Abdou Muhammad Hussein: Nzwani
Muhammad ibn Abd al-Malik: Egypt (724)
Muhammad ibn Abdel Kadir: Bou Regreg
Muhammad ibn Abderrahman: Egypt (772)
Muhammad ibn Abu Bakr: Egypt (656–658)
Muhammad ibn Abu Bakr: Tripolitania (1318–27)
Abu Abdallah Muhammad ibn Ahmad az-Ziyani: Bou Regreg
Muhammad ibn al-Ashath: Egypt (759–760)
Muhammad ibn Ali: Harar
Muhammad ibn as-Sari: Egypt (820–822)
Muhammad ibn Aus al-Ansari: Omayyad and Abbasid North Africa
Muhammad ibn Hussein: Zeng Empire (1510–15)
Muhammad ibn Ibrahim: Harar
Muhammad ibn Isa: Tripolitania (1283)
Muhammad ibn Maslama: Egypt (682)
Muhammad ibn Muqatil: Omayyad and Abbasid North Africa
Muhammad ibn Nasir: Harar
Muhammad ibn Nasir: Zanzibar (1822–23)
Muhammad ibn Qurhub: Tripolitania (869)
Muhammad ibn Salah Raïs: Algiers (1567–68)
Muhammad ibn Suleiman: Egypt (905)
Muhammad ibn Tekin: Egypt (933, 934–935)
Muhammad ibn Tugh ("The Ikhshid"): Egypt (933)
Muhammad ibn Uthman al-Mazrui: Mombasa (1739–46)
Muhammad ibn Yazid: Omayyad and Abbasid North Africa
Muhammad ibn Zuheyr: Egypt (789–790)
Muhammad Ibrahim Egal: British Somaliland
Sa'id Muhammad Jaffar: Comoros (1975–76)
Sa'id Muhammad Jaffar al-Angadi: Comoros (1972)
Muhammad Jawda: Wadai
Muhammad Kace: Damagaram
Muhammad Karim Lamrani: Morocco (1971–72, 1983–86, 1992–94)
Sheikh al-Afia Ould Muhammad Khuna: Mauritania (1996–)

Muhammad Kiwab: Zeng Empire (1496)
Muhammad Konkiya: Songhai (1410–18)
Muhammad Lamine Ould Ahmad: Western Sahara
Ibrahim Muhammad Maccido: Fulani Empire
Muhammad Mahjub: Sudan (1965–66, 1967–69)
Muhammad Mahmud Ould Ahmad Louly: Mauritania (1979–80)
Muhammad Mahmud Pasha: Egypt (1928–29, 1937–39)
Muhammad Maiturare: Fulani Empire
Muhammad Melek: Egypt (1752, 1767)
Muhammad Mikat: Zeng Empire (1506–07)
Muhammad Muse Hersi Adde: Puntland
Muhammad Naguib: Egypt (1952–54)
Muhammad Ndayako: Nupe
Hassan Muhammad Nur Shatigadud: Southwestern Somalia
Muhammadu Nya: Muri
Muhammad Nzali: Tunisia (1980–86)
Sidi Muhammad Ould Boubakar: Mauritania (1992–96)
Muhammad Ould Haidalla: Mauritania (1979–84)
Muhammad Sa'id: Egypt (1743–44, 1757–60)
Muhammad Sa'id: Egypt (1854–63)
Muhammad Sa'id Bey: Egypt (1910–14)
Muhammad Sa'id Pasha: Egypt (1919)
Muhammad Sa'idi: Futa Jallon
Muhammad Salum Ould Brahim: Trarza
Ahmad Muhammad Sani: Gumel
Muhammad Sayid Madjid: Zanzibar (1854–70)
Muhammad Sayin: Tagant
Muhammad Shamte Hamadi: Zanzibar (1961–64)
Muhammad Sharif: Wadai
Lol Muhammad Shawa: Chad (1979)
Sheikh Muhammad Shayin: Tagant
Sa'id Muhammad Sheikh: Comoros (1961–70)
Muhammad Sidi: Brakna
Muhammad Siyad Barre: Somalia
Muhammad Siyad Hersi Morgan: Jubaland (ii)
Muhammad Taki Abdulkarim: Comoros (1992, 1995, 1996–98)
Muhammad Tambari: Fulani Empire
Muhammad Tewfiq Nesim: Egypt (1934–36)
Muhammad Touray: Songhai (1493–1528, 1537–38)
Muhammad Tukur: Yauri
Muhammad Tunjur: Wadai
Muhammad Urada: Wadai
Muhammad Yarik: Zeng Empire (1460–61)
Muhammad Yusuf: Baguirmi

Muhammadou Issoufou: Niger (1993–94)
Muhammadu: Agaie
Muhammadu: Argungu
Muhammadu: Bauchi
Muhammadu: Gobir
Muhammadu: Gumel
Muhammadu: Hadejia
Muhammadu: Jema'a
Muhammadu: Katagum
Muhammadu: Yauri
Chuba Dan Muhammadu: Gobir
Isa Muhammadu: Jema'a
Muhammadu I: Wase
Muhammadu II: Wase
Muhammadu III: Wase
Muhammadu IV: Wase
Muhammadu Abbas: Kano (1903–19)
Muhammadu Adda: Jema'a
Muhammadu Aliyu: Biu
Muhammadu Aminu: Zaria (1959–)
Muhammadu Angulu: Lafia
Muhammadu Ba Are: Argungu
al-Hajj Muhammadu Bashar: Daura-Zango
Muhammadu Bashiru: Gwandu
Muhammadu Baw: Gobir
Muhammadu Bello: Adamawa
Muhammadu Bello: Agaie
Muhammadu Dan Adamu: Kazaure
Muhammadu Dan Chiroma: Gobir
Muhammadu Dan Ciwa: Argungu
Muhammadu Dan Gigala: Zamfara
Muhammadu Dan Isa: Jema'a
Muhammadu Dan Tagande: Argungu
Muhammadu Dan Wari: Katsina (1704–06)
Muhammadu Dikko: Katsina (1906–44)
Muhammadu Fari: Zamfara
Muhammadu Farin Gani: Zamfara
Muhammadu Fodi: Argungu
Muhammadu Goji Yerima: Jemaari
Muhammadu Hodi: Argungu
Muhammadu ibn Idrissa: Fika
Muhammadu ibn Muhammadu: Jema'a
Muhammadu Inuwa Abbas: Kano (1963)
Muhammadu Kabir Umar: Katagum
Muhammadu Kabiya: Katsina (1740–50)
Muhammadu Kantu: Argungu
Muhammadu Katar: Zamfara
Muhammadu Kaye: Argungu
Muhammadu Kobo: Lapai
Muhammadu Korau: Katsina (1492–1541)
Muhammadu Mafindi: Muri
Muhammadu Mai-sa-Maza-Gudu: Katsina (1595–1612)
Muhammadu Maudo: Jemaari
Muhammadu Mayaki: Keffi
Muhammadu Mera: Argungu
Muhammadu na Sifawa: Argungu
Muhammadu Nya: Muri
Muhammadu Sama: Argungu
Muhammadu Sani: Argungu

Muhammadu Sanusi: Kano (1954–63)
Muhammadu Shefe: Argungu
Muhammadu Toya Rero: Katsina (1568–72)
Muhammadu Toya Rero II: Katsina (1684–1701)
Muhammadu Tukur: Muri
Muhammadu Tura: Kazaure
Muhammadu Wabi I: Jemaari
Muhammadu Wabi III: Jemaari
Muhammadu Wabi IV: Jemaari
Muhammadu Wari: Katsina (1644–55)
Muhammadu Wari II: Katsina (1701–04)
Muhammadu Wari III: Katsina (1758–67)
Muhammadu Yerima Iya: Adamawa
Muhammadu Zayanu: Yauri
Muhamman: Daura
Muhamman: Gobir
Muhamman: Keffi
Muhamman Agwe I: Lafia
Muhamman Agwe II: Lafia
Muhamman Bako: Biram
Muhamman Bello: Katsina (1844–69)
Muhamman Bello: Lafiagi
Muhamman Gani: Abuja
Muhamman Kisoki: Kano (1508–64)
Muhamman Kukuna: Kano (1650–59)
Muhamman Makau: Zaria (1802–25)
Muhamman Mayaki: Kazaure
Muhamman Rumfa: Kano (1462–98)
Muhamman Sha: Daura-Zango
Muhamman Shashere: Kano (1572–82)
Muhamman Zaki: Kano (1582–1617)
Muhamman Zangi: Kazaure
Muhammar: Gwandu
Muhammar Atu: Gumel
Muhiaddin Fekini: Libya
André Muhirwa: Burundi [ii]
Muhsin: Hammadid Kingdom
Abu Abdallah as-Si'i al-Muhtasab: Tunis (909–910)
al-Mu'izz: Egypt (973–975); Fatimid North Africa
al-Mu'izz: Zirid Kingdom
Juan de Pontons y Mujica: Ceuta (1816–18)
Ndai Mujinga: Luba
Duhaga I Cwa Mujwiga: Bunyoro
Mukas Munying Kabalond: Lunda
Mukas Waranankong: Lunda
Mutand Mukaz: Lunda
al-Hajj al-Mukhtar: Timbuktu (1659–60)
Mukhtar II: Trarza
Mukhtar III: Trarza
al-Mukhtar Ahmad: Adrar
Mukhtar Ould Amar: Trarza
Ali al-Mukni: Fezzan
Muhammad al-Mukni: Fezzan
Yusuf al-Mukni: Fezzan
Kigeri I Mukobanya: Ruanda
Nyahuma Mukombero: Mwene Mutapa Empire

Kamharapasu Mukombwe: Mwene Mutapa Empire
Mulaji Namwan: Lunda
Léonard Mulamba: Congo (Zaire) (1965)
Mulambwa: Barotseland
Mulay al-Hassan: Hafsid Kingdom
Mulay al-Mahdi: Spanish Morocco (1913–23)
Mulay Hassan: Morocco (1961–99)
Mulay Hassan ben al-Mahdi: Spanish Morocco (1925–56)
Mulay Idris II: Idrisid State
Mulay Ismail as-Samin: Morocco (1672–1727)
Mulay Muhammad: Hafsid Kingdom; Tunis (1573–74)
Mulay Rashid: Morocco (1664–72)
Mule: Mali Empire
Herr Oberst Müller: Kamerun (1906)
W.R. Mullinar: Lagos (1863–64)
Muloba: Luba
Mama Mulu: Daniski
Étienne Tshisekedi wa Mulumba: Congo (Zaire) (1991, 1992–93, 1997)
Mabi Mulumba: Congo (Zaire) (1987–88)
Mulumba Lukeji: Congo (Zaire) (1991)
Mulundo: Buganda
Bakili Muluzi: Malawi (1994–)
Abd al-Mu'min al-Kumi: Almohad Empire
Mumtaz Pasha: Sudan (1871–72)
Mumuromfi: Denkyira
Munatius Felix: Egypt (150–154)
Muhammad VII al-Muncif: Tunisia (1942–43)
Richard Munden: Saint Helena (1673)
Nalumino Mundia: Zambia (1981–85)
Neshangwe Munembire: Mwene Mutapa Empire
Bernardin Mungul Diaka: Congo (Zaire) (1991)
Cinyanta Munona: Kazembe
Juan María Muñoz: Ceuta (1823–24, 1826–30)
Muntaga: Tukolor Empire
al-Muntasir: Tripolitania (1068)
Abu Abdallah Muhammad IV al-Muntasir: Hafsid Kingdom
Mahmud Bey Muntasir: Libya
Umar Mustafa al-Muntasir: Libya
Mukas Munying Kabalond: Lunda
Johann Münz: Hollandia
Muqallab: Tripolitania (1078)
Muhammad al-Muqri: Morocco (1908–09, 1911–13, 1917–55)
Juan de Mur Aguirre y Argaiz: Canary Islands (1719–22)
Ali Murabus: Katsina (1543–68)
Murad: Algiers (1623–26)
Murad: Tripolitania (1551–53)
Murad: Tripolitania (1580–81)
Murad: Tunis (1612–31)
Murad II: Tunis (1659–75)
Murad III: Tunis (1699–1702)

Murad Bey: Egypt (1775–77, 1778–86, 1790–98)
Ahmad al-Muraiyid: Tripolitanian Republic
Ali Muraly: Egypt (1725–26)
Joseph Murinay de Saint-Maurice: Réunion (1779–81)
Murjim: Tripolitania (1279–82)
Murnai: Daura
Dermot Murphy: Saint Helena (1968–72)
James Murray: South Africa (1914)
Umar I al-Murtada: Almohad Empire
Mallam Musa: Daura-Zango
Musa: Egypt (1630–31)
Musa: Ghana Empire
Musa: Hadejia
Musa: Jema'a
Musa: Katsina (1882–87)
Musa: Lafia
Musa: Morocco (1384–86)
Musa: Songhai (1370–78)
Musa: Songhai (1528–31)
Mallam Musa: Zaria (1804–21)
Abd ar-Rahman Musa: Omayyad and Abbasid North Africa
Abu Amran Musa: Tripolitania (1224–26)
Abu Hammu I Musa: Tlemcen (1308–18)
Abu Hammu III Musa: Tlemcen (1517–27)
Bako Musa: Zaria (1608)
Bako Dan Musa: Zaria (1727–36)
Ibrahim Musa: Futa Jallon
Ibrahim Dodo Musa: Abuja
Kankan Musa: Mali Empire
Yan Musa: Zaria (1821–34)
Yusufu Musa: Lafia
Musa I: Biram
Musa I: Mali Empire
Musa II: Biram
Musa II: Mali Empire
Musa III: Mali Empire
Musa al-Hanafi: Egypt (834–839)
Musa Angulu: Abuja
Musa Ba Kikala: Futa Jallon
Ali Musa Bey Sawqi: Bahr al-Ghazal
Musa Dan Jaji: Lafia
Musa Gana: Lafia
Musa ibn Isa: Egypt (787, 791–792, 796–797)
Musa ibn Ka'ab: Egypt (758–759)
Musa ibn Musab: Egypt (784–785)
Musa ibn Olayy: Egypt (772–778)
Musa ibn Suleiman: Darfur
Musa Kurabo: Kaarta
Musa Pasha Hamdi: Kordofan; Sudan (1862–65)
Shehu Musa Yar Adua: Nigeria (1976–83)
Maqdum Musallam: Kordofan
Musananyanda: Barotseland
Musanawina: Barotseland
Muhammad Muse Hersi Adde: Puntland
Yoweri Museveni: Uganda (1986–)
Anthony Musgrave: Natal (1872–73)

Benjamin Musgrave: Walvis Bay
Mushidi: Lunda
Musidi: Lunda
Yuhi IV Musinga: Ruanda
Gudumua Muska: Zaria (1530–32)
Kebby Musokotwane: Zambia (1985–89)
Peter Mafani Musonge: Cameroun (1996–2004)
al-Mustadi ibn Ismail: Morocco (1738–40)
Mustafa: Adamawa
Mustafa: Algiers (1594, 1596–98)
Mustafa: Algiers (1621–22)
Mustafa: Egypt (1522–23)
Mustafa: Egypt (1619–20)
Mustafa: Egypt (1623, 1624–26)
Mustafa: Egypt (1640–42)
Mustafa: Egypt (1647)
Mustafa: Egypt (1656–57)
Mustafa: Egypt (1660–61)
Mustafa: Egypt (1760–62)
Mustafa: Futa Toro
Mustafa: Tripolitania (1584–88)
Mustafa: Tripolitania (1870, 1875–76)
Mustafa: Tukolor Empire
Mustafa: Tunis (1835–37)
Aliyu Mustafa: Adamawa
Barma Mustafa: Damagaram
Köse Mustafa: Algiers (1610–13, 1616)
Mamadu Mustafa: Damagaram
Mustafa I: Algiers (1699–1705)
Mustafa II: Algiers (1798–1805)
Isa Mustafa Agwa: Lafia
Umar Mustafa al-Muntasir: Libya
Maidalla Mustafa Aliyu: Biu
al-Wali Mustafa as-Sayyid: Western Sahara
Mustafa Asim: Tripolitania (1849–52, 1874–75)
Mustafa Bey al-Manzalah: Oran (1800)
Si Mustafa Dingizli: Tunisia (1922–26)
Mustafa Faik: Fezzan
Mustafa Fehmy Pasha: Egypt (1891–93, 1895–1908)
Mustafa Galibuli: Tripolitania (1701–02)
Mustafa Gazari: Yauri
Mustafa Haruna Jokolo: Gwandu
Mustafa Inglis: Constantine
Mustafa Kaak: Tunisia (1947–50)
Mustafa Kapudan: Tripolitania (1676–77)
Mustafa Khalil: Egypt (1978–80)
Mustafa Kiridli: Kordofan
Mustafa Lefkeli: Egypt (1618)
Mustafa Negib: Tripolitania (1835)
Mustafa Nuri: Tripolitania (1852–55)
Mustafa Ould Saleck: Mauritania (1978–89)
Mustafa Pehlevan: Tripolitania (1675)
Mustafa Sherif: Tripolitania (1620–31)
al-Adil al-Musta'in: Egypt (1412)
al-Musta'li: Egypt (1094–1101)
al-Mustansir: Egypt (1036–94)

Abu Abdallah Muhammad I al-Mustansir: Hafsid Kingdom
Abu Yakub al-Mustansir: Almohad Empire
Muhammad V al-Mustansir: Fezzan
Muhammad al-Mustansir: Idrisid State
al-Mustansir ibn Muhammad: Fezzan
Mustari: Egypt (1647)
Guillaume de Mustellier: Senegal (1710–11)
Domingo Mustrich: Fernando Po
Mibambwe I Mutabaazi: Ruanda
as-Sa'id al-Mu'tadid: Almohad Empire
Mutaga I Seenyamwiiza: Burundi [i]
Mutaga II: Burundi [i]
Mutambuka: Nkore
Mutand Mukaz: Lunda
Mutara I Seemugeshi: Ruanda
Mutara II Rwoogera: Ruanda
Mutara III Rudahigwa: Ruanda
Yahya V al-Mu'tasim: Almohad Empire
Muhammad III al-Mutawakkil: Morocco (1574–76)
Muteba III: Lunda
Muteba IV: Lunda
Muteba Chikombu: Lunda
Mbumb Muteba Kat: Lunda
Muteba Kat Kateng: Lunda
Mutebi: Buganda
Mutebi II Kiwena: Buganda
Edward Mutesa: Uganda (1963–66)
Mutesa I Walugembe Makaobya: Buganda
Mutesa II: Buganda; Uganda (1963–66)
Nyatsimba Mutota: Mwene Mutapa Empire
al-Muttalib: Egypt (813–815)
André Mutter: Algeria (1958)
William Mutter: Ghana (1763–66)
Paulo Muwanga: Uganda (1980, 1985)
Muyunda: Barotseland
al-Muzaffar Ahmad: Egypt (1421)
al-Muzaffar ibn Keydar: Egypt (834)
Muzahim ibn Khakan: Egypt (867–868)
Muzakha I: Gobir
Muzakha II: Gobir
João Muzanty: Guinea-Bissau (1906–09)
Muzgai: Potiskum
Abel Muzorewa: Zimbabwe (1979)
Isidore Mvouba: Congo (2005–)
Mwaaka: Lunda
Yakub al-Mwakir: Wadai
Mwambutsa I: Burundi [i]
Mwambutsa II: Burundi [i]
Mwana Silundu: Barotseland
Mwananyanda: Barotseland
Levy Mwanawasa: Zambia (2002–)
Mwanawina I: Barotseland
Mwanawina II: Barotseland
Mwanawina III: Barotseland
Danieri Mwanga: Buganda
Mwauluka: Barotseland
Mwezi I: Burundi [i]

Mwezi II: Burundi [i]
Mwezi II Kisabo: Burundi [i]
Kasongo Mwine Kibanza: Luba
Mwine Kombe Dai: Luba
Ali Hassan Mwinyi: Zanzibar (1984–85)
Mwonga Nsemba: Kazembe
Mwongo Mfwama: Kazembe
Mycerinus: Egypt (4th Dynasty)
Charles Mylius: Seychelles (1839–50)
Charles Le Myre de Villiers: Madagascar (1886–88, 1894–95)
William Myres: Senegambia Colony
Muhammad Mzali: Tunisia (1980–86)
Mzila: Gazaland
Mzilikazi: Matabeleland

N

Ibrahimu Na Mai Fura: Gobir
Ziblim Na Saa: Dagomba
Na'akueto La'ab: Ethiopia (1212–60)
Fara Aysa Naalem: Walo (1563–65)
Makwangiji Na'ali: Lafia
Mbany Naatago: Walo (1380–81)
Naatago Aram Bakar: Walo (1674–1708)
Naatago Fara N'dyak: Walo (1503–08)
Naatago Kbaari Daaro: Walo (1565–76)
Naatago Tany: Walo (1287–1304)
Naatago Yerim: Walo (1508–19)
Naba: Gonja
Cwa I Nabaka: Buganda
Yakubu Nabame: Argungu
Nabasere: Yatenga
Gustav Nachtigal: Kamerun (1884); Togoland
Getachew Nadu: Eritrea
Marcel Naegelen: Algeria (1948–51)
al-Hajji Saidu Naemaska: Kontagora
Naevius Sertorius Macro: Egypt (38–39)
Yunfa Dan Nafata: Gobir
Nafata Dan Babari: Gobir
Nagalogu: Dagomba
Nagama: Daura (16th cent.)
Nagama: Daura (17th cent.)
Ibrahim Nagamatse: Kontagora
Nagib: Fezzan
Agada Nagogo: Gobir
Kabir Dan Uthman Nagogo: Katsina (1981–)
Usman Nagogo: Katsina (1944–81)
Cornelis Nagtglas: Dutch Gold Coast (1857–62, 1869–71)
Muhammad Naguib: Egypt (1952–54)
Naguib al-Hilaili Pasha: Egypt (1952)
Naguji: Kano (1193–1247)
Umaru Nagwamatse: Kontagora
Nahas Angula: Namibia (2005–)
Nahhas Pasha: Egypt (1928, 1929–30, 1936–37, 1942–44, 1950–52)
Shamsi Nahodha: Zanzibar (2000–)
Naimbanna I: Koya-Temne
Naimbanna II: Koya-Temne

Naji: Daura
Najib Husaini: Kazaure
Nakibinge: Buganda
Naldawa Nazariza: Mandara
Namagula: Buganda
Namega: Wagadugu
Mulaji Namwan: Lunda
Hezba Nan: Ethiopia (1430–33)
Mehreka Nan: Ethiopia (1433)
N'dyak Kumba-Nan Sango: Walo (1355–67)
Nana Ofori Atta I: Akim
Nana Ofori Atta II: Akim
Nana Olomu: Warri
Aldawa Nanda: Mandara
Nani To: Kororofa
Nanka Traore: Kenedugu
Na'od: Ethiopia (1494–1508)
George Napier: Cape Colony (1838–44)
Napoléon Bonaparte: Egypt (1798–99)
Prince Napoléon Bonaparte: Algeria (1858–59)
Naqqash: Egypt (1640–42)
Naqrisan: Kush (145–120 B.C.)
José Naranjo: Melilla (1786–88)
Bukar Narbanha: Mandara
M. Motais de Narbonne: Seychelles (1786–89)
Salman Nari: Songhai (1340–47)
Keita Nari fa Majan: Kangaba
Narmer: Egypt (1st Dynasty); Upper Egypt
Nasabo: Zaria (ca. 1200)
Nasakhma: Kush (468–463 B.C.)
Nasbire: Wagadugu
João do Nascimento: Madeira (1747–51)
Lopo do Nascimento: Angola (1975–78)
Guglielmo Nasi: Cyrenaica; Ethiopia (1941)
Nasih Pasha: Egypt (1801)
an-Nasir: Fezzan
Nasir: Ifat
Ahmad Saif an-Nasir: Fezzan
Muhammad an-Nasir: Egypt (1293–94, 1299–1309)
Muhammad II Nasir: Fezzan
Muhammad III an-Nasir: Almohad Empire
Muhammad V an-Nasir: Tunisia (1906–22)
Zaydan an-Nasir: Morocco (1603–28)
Nasir I: Timbuktu (1666)
Nasir II: Timbuktu (1667–70, 1706–07)
Nasir ad-Din Muhammad: Egypt (1198–1200)
an-Nasir ibn Alannas: Hammadid Kingdom
Nasir ibn Badi: Funj Sultanate
Nasir ibn Uthman: Harar
Naskyemde: Wagadugu
Nasr: Omayyad and Abbasid North Africa
Nasr ibn Abdallah: Egypt (832–834)

Nasr ibn Abdallah al-Mazrui: Mombasa (1698–1728)
Nasr ibn Ahmad: Mombasa (1835–36)
Nassege: Yatenga
Gamal Abdel Nasser: Egypt (1954–70)
Nassodoba: Yatenga
Nassour Guelengdoussia Ouaido: Chad (1997–99)
Ankhkare Nastasen: Kush (335–310 B.C.)
Natakamani: Kush (15 B.C.–A.D. 12)
Lucius Minicius Natalis: Africa [i] (121)
Lucius Minicius Natalis Quadronius Verus: Africa [i] (153–154)
Mathew Nathan: Ghana (1900–04); Natal (1907–09); Sierra Leone (1899)
Ernest de Nattes: Côte d'Ivoire (1957–60)
Nattia: Wagadugu
Tom Naude: South Africa (1967–68)
Umaru Na'uka: Kazaure
Pedro de Navarra: Tripolitania (1510)
Marqués de Navarrés: Oran (1567–71)
Eduardo Navarro: Western Sahara
Luis Navarro: Fernando Po
Usman No Yi Nawa: Katsina (1667–84)
Nawainchi: Zaria (ca. 1310)
Nawata: Kano (1133–35)
Yavu a Nawej: Lunda
Kangapu Nawej: Lunda
Nawej Ditend: Lunda
Nawej Mufa Muchimbunj: Lunda
Nawidemak: Kush (65–33 B.C.)
Nawwar: Funj Sultanate
Nayil ibn Anara: Funj Sultanate
Nayoga: Zaria (ca. 1300)
Muhamma Nazaki: Kano (1617–22)
Naldawa Nazariza: Mandara
Osman Nazhar: Tripolitania (1855–58)
Ahmad Nazif: Egypt (2004–)
Mehmed Nazif: Tripolitania (1880–81)
Hajji Mehmed Nazir: Bahr al-Ghazal
Sambwa Pida Nbagui: Congo (Zaire) (1988)
Nchare Yen: Bamoun
Ncindise: Pondoland
Ncqungushe: Pondoland
Fara Ko Ndaama: Walo (1556–63)
Ndaba: Tembuland
Ndaba: Zululand
Kigeri III Ndabarasa: Ruanda
Melchior Ndadaye: Burundi [ii]
Ndagara I: Karagwe
Nyamukuba Ndagara II: Karagwe
Ndahiro II Cyaamatare: Ruanda
Ndahiro Ruyange: Ruanda
Kigeri V Ndahundirwa: Ruanda
Ndai Mujinga: Luba
Ndamase: Pondoland West
Nyangelizwe Ndamase: Transkei
Yerim N'date Bubu: Walo (1733–34)
Ndawula: Buganda
Domitien Ndayizeye: Burundi (ii)

José Ndele: Angola Democratic People's Republic
M'Bissan N'Della: Baol
Tié N'Della: Baol
Sumayla Ndewura Dyakpa: Gonja
Ndi: Kom
Tyukuli N'Diklam: Dyolof
N'Diklam Sare: Dyolof
Pascal Firmin Ndimira: Burundi [ii]
Detye Fu-N'Diogu: Kayor
Charles Ndiziye: Burundi [i]
Ntare III Ndiziye: Burundi [i]
Ndlambe: British Kaffraria
Ndoba: Ruanda
Okapara Ndole: Bonny
Ruganza II Ndoori: Ruanda
Antoine Nduwayo: Burundi [ii]
N'Dya-N'Dya: Walo (1186–1202)
N'Dyadya N'Dyaye: Dyolof (1350–70)
Meumbody N'dyak: Walo (1381–98)
Naatago Fara N'dyak: Walo (1503–08)
Tani Fara N'dyak: Walo (1531–42)
N'dyak Aram Bakar Teedyek: Walo (1708–33)
N'dyak Khuri Dyop: Walo (1736–80)
N'dyak Ko N'Dyay Mbanyik: Walo (1367–80)
N'dyak Kumba-gi tyi Ngelogan: Walo (1348–55)
N'dyak Kumba Khuri Yay: Walo (1792–1801)
N'dyak Kumba-Nan Sango: Walo (1355–67)
N'dyak Kumba Sam Dyakekh: Walo (1336–43)
N'dyak Ko N'Dyay Mbanyik: Walo (1367–80)
Umaru Sanda Ndayako: Nupe
Ali Bure N'Dyaye: Dyolof
Sare N'Dyaye: Dyolof
N'Dyelen Mbey Leeyti: Dyolof
Birayma N'Dyeme Eter: Dyolof
Del Nead: Axum
Neale: Bakwenaland
Matope Nyanhehwe Nebedza: Mwene Mutapa Empire
Nyanhehwe Nebedza: Mwene Mutapa Empire
Mentuhotep II Nebhepetre: Egypt (10th Dynasty, 11th Dynasty)
Neferkare Nebirierau: Egypt (17th Dynasty)
Swadjenre Nebirierau: Egypt (17th Dynasty)
Tutankhamen Nebkheprure: Egypt (18th Dynasty)
Amenhotep III Nebmare: Egypt (18th Dynasty)
Rameses VI Nebmare Meryamun: Egypt (20th Dynasty)
Albert Nébout: Côte d'Ivoire (1902, 1905–06, 1907–08); Mali (1917)
Ahmose Nebpehtire: Egypt (17th Dynasty, 18th Dynasty)
Mentuhotep IV Nebtowere: Egypt (11th Dynasty)

Necho II Wehembre: Egypt (26th Dynasty)
Nectanebo: Egypt (30th Dynasty)
Nectarebe: Egypt (30th Dynasty)
Sebastian Nederburgh: Cape Colony (1792–93)
Mahmud Nedim Bey: Tripolitania (1860–67)
Nefaurud: Egypt (29th Dynasty)
Nefaurud: Egypt (29th Dynasty)
Neferabre Herinutarekamen: Kush (431–405 B.C.)
Neferankh Asrumeri Amen: Kush (ca. 660 B.C.)
Neferefre: Egypt (5th Dynasty)
Neferhotep I Khasekhemre: Egypt (13th Dynasty)
Neferhotep II Mersekhemre: Egypt (13th Dynasty)
Neferhotep III Sekhemre Sankhtowy: Egypt (13th Dynasty)
Psamtik II Neferibre: Egypt (26th Dynasty)
Neferirkare: Egypt (5th Dynasty)
Amenemnisu Hekawise Neferkare: Egypt (21st Dynasty)
Pepi II Neferkare: Egypt (6th Dynasty)
Neferkare Analmaaye: Kush (542–538 B.C.)
Neferkare Nebirierau: Egypt (17th Dynasty)
Rameses IX Neferkare Setpenre: Egypt (20th Dynasty)
Neferkare Shabaha II: Kush (ca. 700 B.C.)
Amenhotep IV Neferkheprure Waenre: Egypt (18th Dynasty)
Changamire Negamo: Rozwi
Negasse I: Shoa
Negasse II: Shoa
Negasso Gidada: Ethiopia (1995–)
Mustafa Negib: Tripolitania (1835)
Nego: Potiskum
Negomo Chisamhuru: Mwene Mutapa Empire
André de Negreiros: Angola (1661–66)
Nekhtharehbe Snedjembre: Egypt (30th Dynasty)
Nekhtnebef Kheperkhare: Egypt (30th Dynasty)
Amenemhet III Nemare: Egypt (12th Dynasty)
Nembe: Brass
Nemik Bey: Tripolitania (1896–99)
Ptolemy VII Neos Philopator: Egypt (147–145 B.C.)
Neoterius: Africa Proconsularis (385)
Nepherites I: Egypt (29th Dynasty)
Nepherites II: Egypt (29th Dynasty)
Haterius Nepos: Egypt (121–126)
Bernardo del Nero: Gran Canaria
Nesbanebded: Egypt (21st Dynasty)
Nesbanebded Hedjkheperre: Egypt (21st Dynasty)
Neshangwe Munembire: Mwene Mutapa Empire

Muhammad Tewfiq Nesim: Egypt (1934–36)
Tewfiq Nesim Pasha: Egypt (1920–21)
Bawa Nesso: Gobir
Nestorius Timonianus: Africa Proconsularis (337)
Antonio Agostinho Neto: Angola (1975–79)
Ángel Nevascués: Madeira (1888)
Antonio Neves: São Tomé (1751)
José Maria Neves: Cape Verde (2001–)
Maria das Neves: São Tomé and Príncipe (2002–04)
João de Neves Leão: Bissau (1799)
Newaya Krestos: Ethiopia (1344–72)
Newaya Maryam: Ethiopia (1372–82)
Harry Newlands: Ashanti
Francis Newton: Botswana; Zimbabwe (1914)
Ngalama: Barotseland
Detye Maram N'Galgu: Kayor
Nganda Bilonda: Kazembe
Ngangomhlaba: Kreli's Country
Ngapna: Bamoun
Ngarba Bira: Baguirmi
Djidingar Done Ngardoum: Chad (1982)
N'garta Tombalbaye: Chad (1959–75)
Ngbesa: New Calabar
Ngbetnkom: Bamoun
Ngconde: Transkeian Territories
Ngcwangu: Transkeian Territories
N'dyak Kumba-gi tyi Ngelogan: Walo (1348–55)
Pierre Ngendamdumwe: Burundi [ii]
François Ngeze: Burundi (ii)
Nggam: Kom
Ngoi Sanza: Luba
Ngola-a-Nzinga: Ndongo
Ngola Nzinga Mbandi: Ndongo
Barama-Ngolo: Segu
Nya Ngolo: Kaarta
Ngolo Dyara: Segu
Louis-Sylvain Ngoma: Congo (1975–84, 1991)
Ngombala: Barotseland
Kumwimba Ngombe: Luba
Isa Bige N'Gone: Kayor
Tié-Yaasin NGone: Baol
Marien Ngouabi: Congo (1968, 1969–77)
Ngouh I: Bamoun
Ngouh II: Bamoun
Ngouhouo: Bamoun
Ngouloure: Bamoun
Jean-Paul Ngoupande: Central African Republic (1997)
Ngoupou: Bamoun
Ngqika: British Kaffraria
Ngubencuka: Tembuland
Paulin Obame-Nguema: Gabon (1994–00)
Francisco Macías Nguema Biyogo: Equatorial Guinea
Teodoro Obiang Nguema Mbasogo: Equatorial Guinea
Affi N'Guessan: Côte d'Ivoire (2000–03)

Denis Sassou-Nguesso: Congo (1979–92, 1997–)
Nguia: Masina
Dunama V Ngumaramma: Bornu Empire (1546–63)
Nguza Karl-I-Bond: Congo (Zaire) (1980–81, 1991–92)
Ngwaketse: Bangwaketseland
Ngwane: Swaziland (1889–99)
Ngwato: Bamangwatoland
Alamara Nhassa: Guinea-Bissau (2001–02)
Pedro de Nhuya: Mozambique (1505–06)
Niago: Yatenga
Tieba Niandane Watara: Gwiriko
Moustapha Niasse: Senegal (1983, 2000–01)
Nicetas: Byzantine North Africa
Nicolaas Waterboer: Griqualand West
Henri Nicolas: Cameroun (1944–46)
William Nicolay: Mauritius (1833–40)
Edward Nicolls: Fernando Po
Nicomachus Flavianus: Africa Proconsularis (377–378)
Enrique de Guzmán, Count of Niebla: Canary Islands (1418)
Willie Van Niekerk: Namibia (1983–85)
Gerrit Van Niekerk: Stellaland; United States of Stellaland
Gerrit Van Niekerk Viljoen: Namibia (1979–80)
Johann Niemann: Hollandia
Jacobus Nieuwland: Mauritius (1664)
Daud Nigalemi: Bornu Empire (1377–86)
Idris I Nigalemi: Bornu Empire (1353–77)
Nii Amaa Ollennu: Ghana (1970)
Niketas: Egypt (614)
Nikostratos: Pentapolis
Ninetjer: Egypt (2nd Dynasty)
Ninmitoni: Dagomba
Nintasanai: Songhai (1082–1101)
Niokhor: Baol
Nishanji: Egypt (1721–25, 1726–27)
Niuserre: Egypt (5th Dynasty)
Njekwa: Barotseland
Pierre N'Jie: Gambia (1961–62)
Cornelius Njoba: Ovamboland
Nkang Mbemba: Kongo
Nkonda Matit: Lunda
Nkosiyamntu: Transkeian Territories
Kwame Nkrumah: Ghana (1952–66)
Nkuba: Nkore
Pierre Nkurunziza: Burundi (ii)
Nkwain: Kom
Nnamdi Azikiwe: Nigeria (1952–54, 1959–66); Nigeria Eastern Region
Nntin Koro: Kaarta
Gi-gla No-Don Gbé-non Mau: Allada
Usman No Yi Nawa: Katsina (1667–84)
Noboga: Yatenga
Francisco de Nóbrega Vasconcelos: Cape Verde (1726–28)
Col. Noël: Niger (1904)

Léon Noël: Côte d'Ivoire (1866–67)
Augustin Noguès: French Morocco
Nohir: Zaria (1532–35)
Nokrashy Pasha: Egypt (1945–48)
Noluntu: Tembuland
Nombate: Matabeleland
Marcus Servilius Nonianus: Africa [i] (46–47)
Lucius Nonius Asprenas: Africa [i] (12–15)
Nikolaas Van Der Nood De Gieterre: Dutch Gold Coast (1754–55)
Pieter Noodt: Cape Colony (1727–29)
Edmund Norcott: Gambia (1843–44)
Hugh Norman-Walker: Botswana; Seychelles (1967–69)
Afonso de Noronha; Ceuta (1540–49)
Afonso de Noronha: Ceuta (1602–05); Tangier (1610–14)
Antão de Noronha: Ceuta (1549)
Antonio de Noronha: Angola (1839); Madeira (1822–23)
Fernando de Noronha: Angola (1802–06)
Fernando de Noronha: São Tomé (1609)
Fernando de Noronha: São Tomé and Príncipe (1836–37)
João de Noronha: Angola (1713–17)
João de Noronha: Ceuta (1481–87)
João de Noronha: Ceuta (1522–24)
José de Noronha: Cape Verde (1845–47)
Lourenço de Noronha: Mozambique (1739–43)
Nunho de Noronha: Ceuta (1529–39)
Paulo de Noronha: São Tomé (1669–71)
Robert Norri: Dutch Gold Coast (1727–30)
Thomas Norris: Ghana (1787–89)
Geoffrey Northcote: Ghana (1931, 1932, 1934)
Edward Northey: Kenya (1919–22)
José Norton de Matos: Angola (1912–15, 1921–24)
Henry Norwood: Tangier (1666–69)
Noto: Barolongland
James Pyke-Nott: Nigeria Eastern Region
Pierre Nouailhetas: Djibouti (1940–42)
Charles Noufflard: Benin [ii] (1912–17); Gabon (1906–07)
Hedi Nouira: Tunisia (1970–80)
Ambroise Noumazalay: Congo (1966–68)
Nourdine Bourhane: Comoros (1997–98)
Jean Noutary: Togo (1944–48)
Édouard Pageot des Noutières: Senegal (1842–43)
Paulo Dias de Novais: Angola (1575–89)
Jean Noyer: Côte d'Ivoire (1863)
Hastings Noyoo: Barotseland

Caetano Nozolini: Bissau (1829–30, 1834)
Nqiliso: Pondoland West
Nqoko: Kreli's Country
Nsangou: Bamoun
Sylvestre Nsanzimana: Rwanda
Mwonga Nsemba: Kazembe
Dismas Nsengiyaremye: Rwanda
Ben Nsibandze: Swaziland (1979)
Apolo Nsimbambi: Uganda (1999–)
N'Singa Udjuu: Congo (Zaire) (1981–82)
Nsom: Kom
Nsoro Samukondo: Ruanda
Ntare I: Karagwe
Nyabugaro Ntare I: Nkore
Ntare I Rushatse: Burundi [i]
Ntare II: Karagwe
Ntare II Kagwejegyerera: Nkore
Ntare II Kivimira: Burundi [i]
Ntare II Rugaamba: Burundi [i]
Ntare III: Karagwe
Ntare III Ndiziye: Burundi [i]
Ntare III Rugaamba: Nkore
Ntare IV: Karagwe
Ntare IV Kitabanyoro: Nkore
Ntare V: Nkore
Ntare V Kiitabanyoro: Karagwe
Kanyorozi Ntare VI: Karagwe
Cyprien Ntaryamina: Burundi [ii]
Caetano N'Tchoma: Guinea-Bissau (2000–01)
Ntebogang: Bangwaketseland
Kaniembo Ntemena: Kazembe
Sylvestre Ntibantunganya: Burundi [ii]
Ntim Gyakari: Denkyira
Ntombi Thwala: Swaziland (1983–86)
Jean-François Ntoutoumane: Gabon (1999–)
Hudson Ntsanwisi: GazaNkulu
Ntsu Mokhehle: Lesotho (1993–98)
Nubar Pasha: Egypt (1878–79, 1882–83, 1884–88, 1894–95)
Amenemhet II Nubkaure: Egypt (12th Dynasty)
Nubkheperre Intef: Egypt (17th Dynasty)
De Nufion: Allada
Nufu Aliyu: Zaria (1902–03)
Nugbododhone: Whydah
Nuh: Songhai (1591–99)
Nuhu: Agaie
Nuhu: Daura-Zango
Nuhu Ba Kikala: Futa Jallon
Sam Nujoma: Namibia (1990–2005)
Nul: Funj Sultanate
Numainda: Potiskum
Ja'far an-Numayri: Sudan (1969–85)
Dun-Nun I: Timbuktu (1679, 1681, 1694)
Francisco Nunes de Andrade: Cacheu (1634)
Babakr an-Nur: Sudan (1971)
Yusuf Haji Nur: Puntland
Nur ad-Din: Egypt (1257–59)
Nur ibn Mujahid: Harar

Hassan Muhammad Nur Shatigadud: Southwestern Somalia
Mustafa Nuri: Tripolitania (1852–55)
Nuri Bey: Tripolitania (1917–18)
Nurmash: Brakna
Henry Nurse: Ghana (1685)
Siamon Nutekheperre: Egypt (21st Dynasty)
Pieter Nuyts: Dutch Gold Coast (1705–08)
Nwaiko: Zaria (ca. 1310)
Samuel Nxumalo: GazaNkulu
Sishayi Nxumalo: Swaziland (1996)
Muhammadu Nya: Muri
Nya Ngolo: Kaarta
Nyabongo I Rulemu: Bunyoro
Nyabongo II Mugenyi: Bunyoro
Bakaa-Tam Buri-Nyabu: Dyolof
Mba Nuri-Nyabu: Dyolof
Nyabugaro Ntare I: Nkore
Nyadfo: Wagadugu
Nyagse: Dagomba
Nyahuma Mukombero: Mwene Mutapa Empire
Nyaika: Bunyoro
Nyaika: Nkore
Nyakambira: Mwene Mutapa Empire
Nyakashaija: Nkore
Nyakum: Gobir
Nyamaende Mhande: Mwene Mutapa Empire
Nyambu Kapararidze: Mwene Mutapa Empire
Samatambira Nyamhandu I: Mwene Mutapa Empire
Nyamhandu II: Mwene Mutapa Empire
Albin Nyamoya: Burundi [ii]
Kigeri II Nyamuheshera: Ruanda
Nyamukuba Ndagara II: Karagwe
Kyebambe III Nyamutukura: Bunyoro
Nyanamagha: Kenedugu
Nyangelizwe: Tembuland
Nyangelizwe Ndamase: Transkei
Nyanhehwe Nebedza: Mwene Mutapa Empire
Matope Nyanhehwe Nebedza: Mwene Mutapa Empire
Nyani Mansa Muhammad: Mali Empire
Nyaralen Gran: Kaarta
Nyarma Omuzarra Kyaro: Bunyoro
Nyasoro: Mwene Mutapa Empire
Chivere Nyasoro: Mwene Mutapa Empire
Nyatsimba Mutota: Mwene Mutapa Empire
Nyatsutsu: Mwene Mutapa Empire
Nyawuza: Pondoland
Kasongo Nyembo: Luba
Nyene-Mba I: Segu
Nyene-Mba II: Segu
Nyenyedzi: Mwene Mutapa Empire
Julius Nyerere: Tanganyika; Tanzania
Oyo Nyimba: Bunyoro
El Hadj Saeidou Nyimoluh Nyoju: Bamoun
Nyingnyemdo: Wagadugu

Nyoja Ibrahim: Bamoun
El Hadj Saeidou Nyimoluh Nyoju: Bamoun
Denis de Nyon: Mauritius (1722–23)
Kanou-ba-Nyouma Bari: Segu
Édouard Nzambimana: Burundi [ii]
Anna de Souza Nzina: Ndongo
Nzinga: Kongo
Ngola-a-Nzinga: Ndongo
Nzinga Mbemba: Kongo
Ngola Nzinga Mbandi: Ndongo

O

Thomas Oates: Saint Helena (1972–77)
Alaiyeluwa Oba Adeniji Adele II: Lagos (1949–64)
Obafemi Awolowo: Nigeria Western Region
Obaje Ocheje: Igala
Paulin Obame-Nguema: Gabon (1994–99)
Obanosa: Benin [i]
Olusegun Obasanjo: Nigeria (1976–79, 1999–)
Obed Dhlamini: Swaziland (1989–93)
Abd al-Ali al-Obeidi: Libya
Obeydallah al-Abbasi: Egypt (805–806)
Obeydallah ibn al-Mahdi: Egypt (796–797)
Obeydallah ibn as-Sari: Egypt (822–826)
Obia: Brass
Obiri Yeboa: Ashanti
Obirikorane: Akim
Louis Obissier: Mauritania (1914–16)
Kwasi Obodun: Ashanti
Oboni: Igala
Milton Obote: Uganda (1962–71, 1980–85)
Charles O'Brien: Seychelles (1912–18)
Obunumankona: Bono
José de Oca: Fernando Po
Ochaki Rwangira: Bunyoro
Obaje Ocheje: Igala
Ocheje Onokpa: Igala
Domingo de Ochoa: Melilla (1618–19)
Ocholi: Igala
Anthony Ockiya: Brass
Ockiya VII: Brass
Luke O'Connor: Gambia (1852–59)
Odarawu: Oyo
Umaru Oke-Ode: Lafiagi
Conde de Odemira; Ceuta (1450–60)
Aku Odiba: Igala
Noël Odingar: Chad (1975)
Odogbo: Benin [i]
Oduduwa: Oyo
Odumegwu Ojukwu: Biafra
Oduro: Akim
Oduro: Akwamu
Karl Offmann: Mauritius (2002–03)
Ofinran: Oyo
Nana Ofori Atta I: Akim

Nana Ofori Atta II: Akim
Ofori Panin: Akim
Ofusu Kwabi: Akwamu
Oga I: Doma
Oga II: Doma
Ogalla: Igala
Ogbagba I: Ijebu
Sikiru Adetona Ogbagba II: Ijebu
Ogbebo: Benin [i]
Ogbodo: Brass
Oghuz: Egypt (1607–11)
Ogio: Brass
Ibrahim Misirli-Oglu: Tripolitania (1675–76)
Ogu: Doma
Oguche Akpa: Igala
Idewu Ogulari: Lagos (1832–33)
Ogunmola: Ibadan
Oguola: Benin [i]
Charles O'Hara: Senegambia Colony
Ohen: Benin [i]
Owusu Akyem Ohenkoko: Akim
Ohuan: Benin [i]
Ohuyole: Ibadan
Said Omar Oili: Mayotte Department
Ojigi: Oyo
Odumegwu Ojukwu: Biafra
Oka: Doma
Okabu: Doma
Okaku: Doma
Bako Mairari Ashaka Okao: Zaria (1758–60)
Okapara Ndole: Bonny
Twum Ampoforo Okasu: Akim
Okbar ibn Amr: Egypt (665–667)
Umaru Oke-Ode: Lafiagi
Tito Okello: Uganda (1985–86)
Oko Jumbo: Bonny
Okoliko: Igala
Michael Okpara: Nigeria Eastern Region
Okpara Asimini: Bonny
Okukenun: Abeokuta
Okunade Adele Sijuwade Olubuse: Ife
Antonio Ros de Olano: Spanish Morocco (1847–51)
Frantz Christian Oldenborg: Dutch Gold Coast (1818–20)
Olimi I Kalimbi: Bunyoro
Olimi II Ruhundwangeye: Bunyoro
Olimi III Isansa: Bunyoro
Olimi IV Kasoma: Bunyoro
Olimi V Rwakabale: Bunyoro
Sylvanus Olimpio: Togo (1958–63)
Conde de Oliveira: Tangier (1486)
Eduardo Oliveira: Guinea-Bissau (1895–95)
Henrique de Oliveira: São Tomé and Príncipe (1910)
José de Oliveira: Mozambique (1938–40)
Rafael Oliveira: São Tomé and Príncipe (1915–18)
João de Oliveira: Cacheu (1685–86)
Domingos de Oliveira Daun: Angola (1836)
Conde de Oliveto: Oran (1509)
Marcel Olivier: French West Africa

(1922); Madagascar (1924–29); Mali (1919–21)
Nii Amaa Ollennu: Ghana (1970)
François Ollivier: Senegal (1845–46)
Raffaele Borea Ricci D'Olmo: Tripolitania (1911)
Olomu: Warri
Nana Olomu: Warri
Bendt Olrich: Danish Gold Coast (1793)
Olua: Benin [i]
Oluaso: Oyo
Okunade Adele Sijuwade Olubuse: Ife
Oluewu: Oyo
Olugboda: Ibadan
Olugun Kutere: Lagos (1808–11)
Oluodo: Oyo
Olusegun Obasanjo: Nigeria (1976–79, 1999–)
Samusi Olusi: Lagos (1920–31)
Oluwajin: Abeokuta
Oluwole: Lagos (1834–41)
Olyedun: Ibadan
Omar: Baguirmi
Said Omar Oili: Mayotte Department
Omeyr ibn al-Wahid: Egypt (829)
Omuye: New Calabar
Nyarma Omuzarra Kyaro: Bunyoro
Kyebambe I Omuzikiya: Bunyoro
Julio O'Neill: Ceuta (1826)
Huybert Van Ongerdonk: Dutch Gold Coast (1667–68)
Onigbogi: Oyo
Onisile: Oyo
Ocheje Onokpa: Igala
Onuche: Igala
Onyatiko: Keana
Johannes Oosthuit: Dutch Gold Coast (1820–21)
Jacques Yhombi-Opango: Congo (1993–96)
Joachim Yhombi-Opango: Congo (1977–79)
Jacques Opangoult: Congo (1958)
Opeagbe: Ibadan
Ophellas: Pentapolis
Opobo: Bonny
Osei Opoku Ware: Ashanti
Opoku Ware II: Ashanti
Opu Amakubu: Bonny
Opuke Fofie: Ashanti
Opukoroye: New Calabar
Oranmiyan: Benin [i]
Oranyan: Oyo
Antonio Ordóñez: Ceuta (1844–47)
Oreoghene: Benin [i]
Baldassare Orero: Eritrea; Massawa
Orestes: Egypt (415)
Charles Orfeur: Fort James
Servius Cornelius Scipio Salvidienus Orfitus: Africa [i] (62–63)
Servius Cornelius Scipio Salvidienus Orfitus: Africa [i] (164)
Luis Orgaz y Yoldi: Spanish Morocco (1936–37, 1941–45)
Henri Esse d'Orgeret: Réunion (1674–78)
Orhogbua: Benin [i]

José Oribe Sans: Spanish Morocco (1866–68)
Louis Ormières: Djibouti (1901–02, 1905–06); Gabon (1904–05)
William Ormsby-Gore: South Africa (1941–44)
Camille d'Ornano: Djibouti (1976–77)
Antonio Ornelas: Cacheu (1662–64)
Antonio de Oro Pulido: Western Sahara
Orobiru: Benin [i]
Orompotu: Oyo
Joseph Orpen: Griqualand East; Griqualand West; Lesotho (1881–83)
Georges Orselli: Côte d'Ivoire (1948)
Antonio Ortigão: Cape Verde (1910–11)
Juan Ortiz: Melilla (2000–)
Ruhinda VI Orushongo: Karagwe
Oruwusi: Ibadan
Tomás O'Ryan y Vázquez: Melilla (1863–64)
Melmoth Osborn: Zululand
Osei Bonsu: Ashanti
Osei Kojo: Ashanti
Osei Kwame: Ashanti
Osei Opoku Ware: Ashanti
Osei Tutu: Ashanti
Osei Tutu II: Ashanti
Osei Tutu Quamina: Ashanti
Osemwede: Benin [i]
Marqués de Osera: Oran (1683–85)
Oshinlokun: Lagos (1821–32)
Oshu: Keana
Osiyago: Oyo
Osman: Tripolitania (1701)
Abdul Raman Osman: Mauritius (1970, 1971–79)
Ahmad Osman: Morocco (1972–79)
Baba Osman: Tripolitania (1677–78)
Osman Bey: Oran (1800)
Aden Abdallah Osman Daar: Somalia
Osman Fuad Pasha: Tripolitania (1918)
Osman Jama Ali: Somalia
Osman Nazhar: Tripolitania (1855–58)
Osman Reis as-Suhali: Tripolitania (1672)
Osman Saqizli: Tripolitania (1649–72)
Diego Osorio: Ceuta (1763–76)
Fernando Osorio: Gran Canaria
Francisco Osorio y Astorga: Melilla (1669–72)
Osorkhon I Sekhemkheperre: Egypt (22nd Dynasty)
Osorkhon II Usermare: Egypt (22nd Dynasty)
Osorkhon III: Egypt (23rd Dynasty)
Osorkhon IV Akheperre: Egypt (22nd Dynasty)
Niels Østrup: Danish Gold Coast (1723)
Peter Østrup: Danish Gold Coast (1720–22)
Osumanu: Kano (1342–49)

Osumanu: Kano (1845–55)
Osumanu II: Kano (1919–26)
Otaki: Keana
Miguel de Otazo: Canary Islands (1701–05)
Otba ibn Abi Sufyan: Egypt (664–665)
Pedro Moreno y Perez de Oteyro: Canary Islands (1764)
Antonio de Otero y Santallana: Canary Islands (1791–99)
Lucius Salvius Otho: Africa [i] (40–41)
Oti Akenten: Ashanti
Manuel Otobia: Warri
Sebastian Otobia: Warri
Joachim Otto: Danish Gold Coast (1770)
Otumfo Asare: Akwamu
Nassour Guelengdoussia Ouaido: Chad (1997–99)
Abdelkader Taleb Oumar: Western Sahara
Alassane Ouattara: Côte d'Ivoire (1990–93)
Oubri: Wagadugu
Pietre Van Oudtshoorn: Cape Colony (1772–73)
Goukouni Oueddi: Chad (1979–82)
Jean-Baptiste Ouedraogo: Burkina Faso (1982–83)
Kedre Desiré Ouedraogo: Burkina Faso (1996–2000)
Youssouf Ouedraogo: Burkina Faso (1992–94)
Muhammad Lamine Ould Ahmad: Western Sahara
Muhammad Ahmad Ould Ahmad Louly: Mauritania (1979–80)
Mukhtar Ould Amar: Trarza
Sidi Ahmad Ould Bneijara: Mauritania (1980–81)
Sidi Ahmad Ould Boubakar: Mauritania (1992–96)
Ahmad Ould Bouceif: Mauritania (1979)
Muhammad Salum Ould Brahimi: Trarza
Mokhtar Ould Daddah: Mauritania (1957–78)
Sidi Ould Deid: Trarza
Uthman Ould Fadl Ould Sinan: Adrar
Muhammad Ould Haidalla: Mauritania (1979–84)
Sheikh al-Afia Ould Muhammad Khouna: Mauritania (1996–2003)
Sghair Ould M'Bareck: Mauritania (2003–)
Ould Rizg: Tagant
Mustafa Ould Saleck: Mauritania (1978–79)
Ould Sidi Ahmad Salum: Trarza
Maaouya Ould Sidi Ahmad Taya: Mauritania (1981–)
Uthman Ould Fadl Ould Sinan: Adrar
Magan Oule Watara: Gwiriko
Cornelis Ouman: Dutch West Africa

Alpha Oumar Konaré: Mali (1992–2002)

Oumarou Mamane: Niger (1983, 1988–89)

Joshua Oupa Gqozo: Ciskei

Ousman Maïga: Mali (2004–)

Mahamane Ousmane: Niger (1993–96)

Ahmad Ouyahia: Algeria (1995–98, 2003–)

Antonius Van Overbeek: Dutch Gold Coast (1734–36)

Ovonramven: Benin [i]

Owagi: Brass

Agyekum Owari I: Akim

Agyekum Owari II: Akim

Agyekum Owari III: Akim

William Owen: Mombasa (1823–24)

William Owens: Fernando Po

Owerri Daba: New Calabar

Owoma: New Calabar

Owusu Aduam: Bono

Owusu Akyem Ohenkoko: Akim

Owusu Akyempo: Bono

Earl of Oxford and Asquith: Seychelles (1961–67)

Casimir Oyé-M'Ba: Gabon (1990–94)

Oyebade Lipede: Abeokuta

Oyekan I: Lagos (1885–1900)

Adeyinka Oyekan II: Lagos (1965–2003)

Oyekon: Abeokuta

Oyo Nyimba: Bunyoro

Ozolua: Benin [i]

Ozuere: Benin [i]

P

Mbanyi Paate: Dyolof

Jacobus Van Der Breggen Paauw: Dutch Gold Coast (1826–28)

Pacatus Drepanius: Africa Proconsularis (390)

Antonio Pacheco: Ceuta (1445–47)

Antonio de Brito Pacheco: Mozambique (1640–41)

Bernardinho Ribeiro Pacheco: Portuguese Gold Coast (1584)

Gaspar Pacheco: Cacheu (1682–85)

Juan Pacheco de Benavides: Gran Canaria

Duarte Pacheco Pereira: Portuguese Gold Coast (1519–22)

Diego Pacheco y Arce: Melilla (1684–86)

Pactumeius Magnus: Egypt (177–180)

Pedro de Padilla: Oran (1585–89)

Titus Prifernius Paetus Rosianus Geminus: Africa [i] (140–141, 161–162)

Johan Pagenstecher: Dutch Gold Coast (1824–25)

Édouard Pageot des Noutières: Senegal (1842–43)

Fred Pahl: Danish Gold Coast (1727)

Francisco de Paiva: São Tomé (1546–54)

João de Paiva: São Tomé (1485–90)

Pakalitha Mosisili: Lesotho (1998–)

Pedro Palacio y Guevara: Melilla (1651–55)

Antoine Paladi: Guinea (1927–28, 1933)

Juan de Palafox y Centurión: Ceuta (1745–46)

Lourenço Palha: São Tomé and Príncipe (1767–68)

Palladius: Egypt (382–383)

Aelius Palladius: Egypt (374–375)

Junius Quartus Palladius: Africa Proconsularis (416–421)

Charles Martin des Pallières: Côte d'Ivoire (1851–53)

Willem de la Palma: Dutch Gold Coast (1702–05)

Conde del Palmar: Canary Islands (1697–1701)

Richmond Palmer: Gambia (1930–34); Nigeria Northern Region

William Palmer, 2nd Earl of Selborne: Cape Colony (1905–09); Orange Free State (1905–07); Transvaal (1906–10)

Antonio Pamachamoso: Gran Canaria

Pami: Egypt (22nd Dynasty)

Panda: Zululand

Marqués de Santa Cruz de Paniagua: Oran (1685–87)

Ofori Panin: Akim

Charles Panon de Hazier: Gabon (1873–75)

Pantaleon: Byzantine North Africa

Atta Panyin: Akim

Akwano Panyini: Akwamu

Francis Panzera: Botswana

Clovis Papinaud: Comoros (1888–93, 1899–1900)

Marcus Aurelius Papirius Dionysius: Egypt (193)

Alexandre Ar.mény de Paradis: Gorée

Paramanga Yonli: Burkina Faso (2000–)

Pierre Parat de Chaillenest: Réunion (1710–15)

Lt.-Col. Parent: Gabon (1940–41)

Parima: Yatenga

Georges Parisot: Gabon (1937–38); Senegal (1938–40)

Jean-Paul Parisot: Guinea (1953–55); Mauritania (1955–56)

Stafford Parker: Klipdrift Republic

Parnasius: Egypt (357)

Duque del Parque: Canary Islands (1810)

Pierre Pascal: Benin [ii] (1899–1900); Comoros (1900–02); Côte d'Ivoire (1896); Djibouti (1904–15)

Théophile Pascal: Senegal (1920–21)

Ari Paskur: Biu

Adrião Passálaqua: São Tomé and Príncipe (1855–57)

João Pássaro: Cape Verde (1676)

Pierre Passot: Comoros (1846–49); Nossi-Bé

Pastorius: Africa Proconsularis (385)

Rui Patalim: Mozambique (1508–09)

Ange-Félix Patassé: Central African Republic (1976–78, 1993–2003)

Lt.-Col. Patchett: Sierra Leone (1889)

Charles Patey: Gambia (1866–69); Lagos (1866); Sainte Helena (1871–73)

Henri Patey: Mauritania (1910–12)

M. Patte: Djibouti (1906)

John Patterson: Nigeria Northern Region

Robert Patton: Saint Helena (1801–08)

John Paul: Gambia (1962–66)

Francisco Paula: Cape Verde (1842–45)

Francisco de Paula Cid: Cape Verde (1902–03); São Tomé and Príncipe (1903–07)

Paulinus: Egypt (82)

Paulinus: Egypt (380–381, 385–386)

Paulus: Byzantine North Africa

Paulus: Egypt (585)

James Payne: Liberia (1868–70, 1876–78)

Armenteros de Paz: Tenerife

Octave Péan: Côte d'Ivoire (1890)

Francis Pearce: Malawi (1903, 1906–07, 1910); Zanzibar (1913–22)

João Rodrigues Peçanha: Portuguese Gold Coast (1584)

Laurent Péchoux: Côte d'Ivoire (1948–52); French Equatorial Africa (1947); Togo (1952–55)

Visconde de Pedralva: Angola (1920–21)

Pedro: Koya-Temne

Pedro I: Kongo

Pedro II: Kongo

Pedro III: Kongo

Pedro IV: Kongo

Pedro V: Kongo

Robert Peel: Saint Helena (1920–25)

José Pegado: Mozambique (1834–36)

Vicente Pegado: Mozambique (1531–38)

Mustafa Pehlevan: Tripolitania (1675–75)

Antonio Peláez Campomanes: Spanish Morocco (1866)

Pierre-François Pelieu: Côte d'Ivoire (1952); Gabon (1949–51)

Aimable Pelissier: Algeria (1860–64)

Joseph Pellegrin: Côte d'Ivoire (1844–45)

Christian Pellerin: Mayotte Department

Lewis Pelly: Zanzibar (1861–62)

Adrian Pelt: Cyrenaica

Diego de la Peña: Ceuta (1795)

Guillermo de la Peña Cusi: Western Sahara

Gabriel de Penalosa y Estrada: Melilla (1637–48)

Birayma Penda: Dyolof (1605–49)

Birayma-Penda: Dyolof (1849)

Birayma Faatim-Penda: Kayor

al-Buri Penda: Dyolof

Fara Penda Adam Sal: Walo (1823–37)
Fara Penda Dyeng: Walo (1519–31)
Fara Penda Langan Dyam: Walo (1552–56)
Fara Penda Teg Rel: Walo (1488–96)
Fara Penda Teg Rel: Walo (1780–92)
Jean Penel: Benin [ii] (1904–04); Côte d'Ivoire (1898)
Achille de Penfentenio de Cheffontaines: Réunion (1826–30)
Gen. Pennequin: Madagascar (1899–1900)
Pentadius: Egypt (403–404)
Francisco Penteado: São Tomé and Príncipe (1929)
Pepi I Meryre: Egypt (6th Dynasty)
Pepi II Neferkare: Egypt (6th Dynasty)
Daniel Pepper: Fort James
Bill Pepple: Bonny
Captain Pepple: Bonny
William Pepple: Bonny
Guillén Peraza I: Canary Islands (ca. 1430)
Guillén Peraza II: Canary Islands (1444)
Melchor de Pereda: Tenerife
André Pereira: Angola (1591–92)
Antonio Pereira: São Tomé and Príncipe (1921–24)
Aristides Pereira: Cape Verde (1979–91)
Carlos Pereira: Guinea-Bissau (1910–13)
David Marquês Pereira: Mozambique (1758–59)
Diogo Pereira: São Tomé (1541–45)
Dionisio Pereira: Ceuta (1578–80)
Duarte Pereira: Madeira (1704–12)
Duarte Pacheco Pereira: Portuguese Gold Coast (1519–22)
Félix Pereira: São Tomé (1621–23)
Francisco Pereira: Ceuta (1566–67)
Francisco Pereira: Mombasa (1620–25)
Francisco Sodré Pereira: Cacheu (1625)
Gaspar Pereira: Mombasa (1606–09)
Henrique Pereira: São Tomé (1531–35)
João Rodrigues Pereira: Ceuta (1553)
João Pereira: Madeira (1767–77)
João Pereira: São Tomé (1490–93)
Manuel Pereira: Angola (1603–06, 1615–17); Mombasa (1610–14)
Nunho Pereira: Mozambique (1582–86)
Nunho Pereira: Mozambique (1609–11, 1618–23, 1627–31)
Simão Pereira: Mombasa (1614–20)
Nunho Vaz Pereira: Mozambique (1506–07)
Luis Pereira e Horta: São Tomé and Príncipe (1859–60)
Perekule: Bonny
João Perestrelo: Cacheu (1729–31)
Manuel de Mesquita Perestrelo: Portuguese Gold Coast (1562)

Peresuo: Brass
Gentien Pereton: Comoros (1896–97); Porto-Novo
José Alcántara Pérez: Melilla (1895–98)
Pedro Moreno y Pérez de Oteyro: Canary Islands (1764)
Juan Pérez del Hacho y Oliván: Melilla (1823–24)
Francisco Pérez Mancheño: Ceuta (1719)
Pergamius: Egypt (482)
Peribsen: Egypt (2nd Dynasty)
Louis Périllier: Tunisia (1950–51)
Louis Periquet: Mali (1917–18)
José de Perlasca: Canary Islands (1799–1803)
Lt.-Col. Péroz: Niger (1900–01)
Jean-François Perreau-Pradier: Réunion (1956–63)
Marie-Auguste Deville de Perrière: Senegal (1881)
Jean des Perriers: Fort-Dauphin
François Perriez: Comoros (1875, 1880–82)
Ruth Perry: Liberia (1996–97)
Giovanni Pesenti: Italian Somaliland
Carlos Pessanha: Guinea-Bissau (1904–06)
Jorge Pessanha: Ceuta (1580–86)
Jorge de Mendonça Pessanha: Ceuta (1627–34)
José Pessôa: São Tomé and Príncipe (1848–49)
Manuel da Costa Pessoa: Cape Verde (1667–71, 1678–83)
Álvaro Vaz Pestano: Portuguese Gold Coast (1486)
Giulio Pestalozza: Ashanti
Earl of Peterborough: Tangier (1662–63)
Karl Peters: German East Africa
Harding Petersen: Danish Gold Coast (1692–94)
Baron Jacob De Petersen: Dutch Gold Coast (1741–47)
Peter Petersen: Danish Gold Coast (1705)
Quintus Sulpicius Camerinus Peticus: Africa [i] (56–57)
Léon Pétillon: Congo (Zaire) (1951–58); Ruanda–Urundi
Jean Petitbon: Djibouti (1954–57)
Léon Pêtre: Niger (1934–35); Togo (1928–29, 1933–34)
Gilbert Petrie: Ghana (1766–69)
Petronius: Egypt (26–25 B.C., 24–13 B.C.)
Petronius Honoratus: Egypt (148–150)
Petronius Mamertinus: Egypt (134)
Petronius Maximus: Africa Proconsularis (433–437, 439–442)
Sextus Petronius Probus: Africa Proconsularis (358, 367–375, 383–384, 387–388)
Petronius Secundus: Egypt (95–98)
Petrus: Byzantine North Africa
Petrus: Egypt (600–603)

Petrus Marcellinus Felix Liberius: Egypt (539–542)
Gey Van Pettius: Goshen
Jean Peuvergne: Benin [ii] (1908–09); Guinea (1913–15); Mali (1906–08); Senegal (1909–11)
al-Buri Peya: Dyolof
Marcel Peyrouton: Algeria (1943); French Morocco; Tunisia (1933–36, 1940)
Markus Graf Pfeil: Kamerun (1890)
Phalo: Transkeian Territories
Phatle: Bamaleteland
Cedric Phatudi: Lebowa
Arthur Phayre: Mauritius (1874–79)
Pherendates I: Egypt (27th Dynasty)
Pherendates II: Egypt (31st Dynasty)
Pheto I: Bakgatlaland
Pheto II: Bakgatlaland
Ptolemy II Philadelphus: Egypt (285–247 B.C.)
Arthur J. Philbrick: Ghana (1923); Gold Coast Northern Territories
Philemon: Pentapolis
Pierre Philip: Réunion (1952–56)
Flavius Philippus: Africa Proconsularis (353–354)
Mr Phillips: Southern Nigeria
Ptolemy VI Philometor: Egypt (180–164 B.C., 163–145 B.C.)
Ptolemy IV Philopator: Egypt (221–205 B.C.)
Ptolemy VII Neos Philopator: Egypt (147–145 B.C.)
Ptolemy XIII Theos Philopator: Egypt (52–47 B.C.)
Ptolemy XIV Theos Philopator II: Egypt (47–44 B.C.)
Phokotsea: Bakwenaland
Hae Phoofolo: Lesotho (1994)
Phunga: Zululand
Physcon: Egypt (170–163 B.C., 145–116 B.C.); Pentapolis
Piankh: Egypt (21st Dynasty)
Piankhi I: Kush (ca. 820 B.C.)
Piankhi II: Kush (ca. 665 B.C.)
Piankhi III: Kush (653 B.C.)
Domingos de Abreu Picaluga: Bissau (1825)
Eugène Pichon: Tunisia (1901–06)
Thomas Bougeaud de la Piconnerie: Algeria (1841–45)
Albert Picquié: Madagascar (1910–14)
Sambwa Pida Nbagui: Congo (Zaire) (1988)
Pie Masumboko: Burundi [ii]
Louis Pienaar: Namibia (1985–90)
François Pierre-Alype: Djibouti (1937–38)
Jean-Claude Pierre-Louis: Rodrigues (ii)
Piga I: Yatenga
Piga II: Yatenga
Adolphe Pigeon: Côte d'Ivoire (1847–48)
Andrés Pignately: Canary Islands (1741–44)
John Pigott: Kenya (1892–95)

C. Pike: Lagos (1885–86)
Theodore Pike: British Somaliland
Pilane: Bakgatlaland
Ariranga Pillay: Mauritius (2002)
Guy Pilling: Saint Helena (1938–41); Zanzibar (1941–46)
Pimay Usermare: Egypt (22nd Dynasty)
Francelino Pimentel: Guinea-Bissau (1909–10)
Jorge Pimentel: Cape Verde (1550–55)
Vasco Fernandes Pimentel: Portuguese Gold Coast (1579)
Carlos Pimentel e Melo: São Tomé and Príncipe (1910)
Francisco da Pina Rolo: São Tomé and Príncipe (1853–55)
Paul Pindar: Fort James
Benjamin Pine: Ghana (1857–58); Natal (1850–52, 1853–55, 1873–75)
Richard Pine: Ghana (1862–65)
Jean Pinet-Laprade: Senegal (1863, 1865–69)
Visconde de Pinheiro: Angola (1853–54)
Joaquim Pinheiro: Angola (1974)
Vicente Pinheiro: São Tomé (1709–10)
Franas Pinkett: Sierra Leone (1881, 1883, 1884–85)
John Pinney: Liberia (1834–35)
Johnny Pinnock: Angola Democratic People's Republic
Nicolau Pino de Araújo: Bissau (1753); Cacheu (1741)
Fernando del Piño Villamil: Spanish Morocco (1876–77)
Pintieba Watara: Gwiriko
Adrião Pinto: Angola (1848–51)
Alexandre Serpa Pinto: Cape Verde (1894–98)
Guilherme Pinto: São Tomé and Príncipe (1952–53)
João Pinto: Cacheu (1803)
José Antonio Pinto: Bissau (1793–96)
Luis Pinto: Madeira (1636–40)
Manuel Pinto: Mozambique (1689–92)
Victoriano López Pinto: Spanish Morocco (1877–78)
Juan López Pinto y Marín Reyna: Spanish Morocco (1883–89)
Luigi Pintor: Cyrenaica
Pinudjem I: Egypt (21st Dynasty)
Pinudjem II: Egypt (21st Dynasty)
Mário Pires: Guinea-Bissau (2002–03)
Manuel Pires: Bissau (1757–59)
Pedro Pires: Cape Verde (1975–91, 2001–)
Pisakar: Kush (17–35)
Lucius Calpurnius Piso: Africa [i] (38–39)
Jack Pithey: Zimbabwe (1978–79)
Placidus: Africa Proconsularis (344–346)
Pompeius Planta: Egypt (98–103)
Egrilius Plarianus: Africa [i] (160–161)

Joost Platfusz: Danish Gold Coast (1746–51)
William Platt: Eritrea
Robert Playfair: Zanzibar (1862–65)
Sr. Plaza: Tenerife
Clement Pleass: Nigeria Eastern Region
Herr Plehn: Kamerun (1902)
Jean-Baptiste Vigoureux du Plessis: Réunion (1792–94)
Wenzel du Plessis: Namibia (1963–68)
Joachim Van Plettenberg: Cape Colony (1771–85)
Arnaud Plumet: Senegal (1726)
Robert Plunkett: Fort James
Alphonse Poaty-Souchalaty; Congo (1989–90)
Pobi: Akim
Pobi Asomaning: Akim
Pogopi: Bakgatlaland
Hifekepenye Pohamba: Namibia (2005–)
Jean-Louis Poiret: Guinea (1912–13, 1914, 1915–29)
Georges Poirier: Mauritania (1946–47)
Stephen Poirier: Saint Helena (1697–1707)
Lamadje Pokonu: Allada
Asae Pokou: Baule
Awura Pokou: Baule
Polemius: Africa Proconsularis (390)
Ludovico Pollera: Eritrea
Vitrasius Pollio: Egypt (17–21, 31–32, 39–42)
Robert Pommies: Réunion (1995–98)
Pompeius: Egypt (302–303)
Pompeius Planta: Egypt (98–103)
Marcus Pompeius Silvanus Staberius Flavinus: Africa [i] (53–56)
Charles Assier de Pompignan: Benin [ii] (1943–46); Gabon (1935–36; 1942–43)
Pomponius Metrodorus: Egypt (357–360)
Andrés Ponce de León: Oran (1564–65)
Pierre Poncet de la Rivière: Gorée
Dominique Ponchardier: Djibouti (1969–71)
Henri Ponsot: French Morocco
Bartolomeu Ponte: São Tomé (1715–16)
Paulo da Ponte: São Tomé (1641–42)
José da Ponte e Horta: Angola (1870–73)
Juan de Pontons y Mujica: Ceuta (1816–18)
Amédée Merlaud-Ponty: French West Africa (1908–15); Mali (1899–1907)
Poo I: Bamaleteland
Poo II: Bamaleteland
Willem Poolman: Dutch Gold Coast (1823–24)
John Pope-Hennessey: Ghana (1872–72); Mauritius (1883–89); Sierra Leone (1872–73)

Robert Brooke-Popham: Kenya (1937–40)
Miguel Porcel y Manrique de Araña Menchaca y Zaldívar: Ceuta (1784–91)
Gerald Portal: Uganda (1893); Zanzibar (1891–92)
Conde de Portalegre: Ceuta (1518–19)
Portogenes: Africa Proconsularis (427–428)
João Portugal: Mombasa (1686–88)
Diego de Portugal: Ceuta (1677–78); Oran (1672–75)
Manuel de Portugal e Castro: Madeira (1823–27)
Guilhermo Posser da Costa: São Tomé and Príncipe (1999–2002)
Possinga: Yatenga
Lourenço Possolo: Angola (1844–45)
José Maria Velasco Postigo: Spanish Morocco (1878–79)
Julius Postumus: Egypt (47–48)
Potamius: Egypt (392–395)
D. Potgieter: Transkei
Hendrik Potgieter: Dutch African Republic; Ohrigstad; Winburg; Zoutpansberg
Pieter Potgieter: Zoutpansberg
Col. Pothous: Tangier (1942–45)
Henry Potter: Zanzibar (1954–59)
Henry Pottinger: Cape Colony (1847)
Georges Poulet: French Equatorial Africa (1913); Gabon (1911–12); Guinea (1907–08, 1910)
Ange-Édouard Poungui: Congo (1984–89)
Alphonse de Pouzois: Côte d'Ivoire (1935)
Alfred Pouzols: Côte d'Ivoire (1867–69)
George Powell: Saint Helena (1741–43)
Peveril William-Powlett: Zimbabwe (1954–59)
M. Prade: Réunion (1693)
César Pradier: Gabon (1860–61)
Georges Pradier: Gabon (1885–86)
Jean-François Perreau-Pradier: Réunion (1956–63)
Miguel de Prado: Equatorial Guinea
Praetextatus: Africa Proconsularis (384–385)
Magnus Prang: Danish Gold Coast (1681)
Jan Pranger: Dutch Gold Coast (1730–34)
Isaac Benjamin Pratt: Aku
Zeferino dos Prazeres: Príncipe (ii)
Roland Pré: Burkina Faso (1952–52); Cameroun (1954–56); Djibouti (1954); Gabon (1946–47); Guinea (1950–51)
Prempeh I: Ashanti
Prempeh II: Ashanti
W.R. Preston: Natal (1853)
Andries Pretorius: Dutch African Republic; Lydenburg; Natal (1838–42); Winburg

Marthinus Pretorius: Dutch African Republic; Orange Free State (1860–63); Transvaal (1856–60, 1864–71, 1880–83)

Thomas Price: Ghana (1787)

Harold Priestman: South Africa (1944)

Titus Prifernius Paetus Rosianus Geminus: Africa [i] (140–141, 161–162)

Ulpius Primianus: Egypt (195–197)

Miguel Primo de Rivera y Orbaneja: Spanish Morocco (1924–25)

Jules Le Prince: Congo (1917–19)

Principius: Africa Proconsularis (385–386)

G.D.P. Prinsloo: Lydenrust

Flavius Priscus: Egypt (181)

Sextus Petronius Probus: Africa Proconsularis (358, 367–375, 383–384, 387–388)

Fallonius Probus Allypsius: Africa Proconsularis (378–380)

Leslie Probyn: Sierra Leone (1904–10)

Proculus: Africa Proconsularis (423–426)

Ennius Proculus: Africa [i] (ca. 150)

Valerius Proculus: Egypt (160–163)

Lucius Aradius Valerius Proculus Felix: Africa Proconsularis (333–336)

Jacques Pronis: Fort-Dauphin

Auguste Prôtet: Gorée and Dependencies; Senegal (1850–54)

William A. Prout: Maryland

Henry Prout Bey: Equatoria Province

Georges-David Prouteaux: Central African Republic (1926–28, 1929–30); Chad (1932–33)

Psamtik I Wahibre: Egypt (26th Dynasty)

Psamtik II Neferibre: Egypt (26th Dynasty)

Psamtik III Ankhkaenre: Egypt (26th Dynasty)

Setneptah Usire Pshenmut: Egypt (29th Dynasty)

Psibkhaemne Akheperre: Egypt (21st Dynasty)

Psibkhaemne Titkheprure: Egypt (21st Dynasty)

Psusennes I Akheperre: Egypt (21st Dynasty)

Psusennes II Titkheprure: Egypt (21st Dynasty)

Ptolemaeus: Mauretania

Ptolemaios Aspion: Pentapolis

Ptolemy: Egypt (323–282 B.C.); Pentapolis

Ptolemy I Soter I: Egypt (323–282 B.C.); Pentapolis

Ptolemy II Philadelphus: Egypt (285–247 B.C.)

Ptolemy III Euergetes I: Egypt (247–221 B.C.); Pentapolis

Ptolemy IV Philopator: Egypt (221–205 B.C.); Pentapolis

Ptolemy V Epiphanes: Egypt (205–180 B.C.)

Ptolemy VI Philometor: Egypt (180–164 B.C., 163–145 B.C.)

Ptolemy VII Neos Philopator: Egypt (147–145 B.C.)

Ptolemy VIII Euergetes: Egypt (170–163 B.C., 145–116 B.C.); Pentapolis

Ptolemy IX Soter II: Egypt (116–110 B.C., 109–107 B.C., 88–80 B.C.)

Ptolemy X Alexander I: Egypt (110–88 B.C.)

Ptolemy XI Alexander II: Egypt (80–80 B.C.)

Ptolemy XII Auletes: Egypt (80–58 B.C., 55–51 B.C.)

Ptolemy XIII Theos Philopator: Egypt (52–37 B.C.)

Ptolemy XIV Theos Philopator II: Egypt (47–44 B.C.)

Ptolemy XV Caesar: Egypt (44–30 B.C.)

Ptolemy Soter: Egypt (323–282 B.C.)

Gabriel Puaux: French Morocco

Publius: Egypt (370–372)

Publius Cornelius Dolabella: Africa [i] (23–24)

Publius Sextilius: Carthage

Publius Sitius: Numidia

Publius Tullius Varro: Africa [i] (142–143)

Salvador de la Puente Pita: Spanish Morocco (1851–54)

Conde de Puertolano: Canary Islands (1666–71)

Louis Pujol: Senegal (1834–36)

Ramón Gómez Pulido: Spanish Morocco (1858–64, 1865–66)

De Barolet de Puligny: Réunion (1850–51)

Punga: Zululand

Conde de Puñonrostro: Ceuta (1679–81)

R. Purdie: Sierra Leone (1815)

Edward Purdon: Ghana (1824–25)

Antonio Pussich: Cape Verde (1818–22)

Jesko von Puttkamer: Kamerun (1887, 1890, 1895, 1896–1906); Togoland

Guillaume Charmasson de Puy-Laval: Senegal (1839–41)

Jacobus Van Der Puye: Dutch Gold Coast (1780–80)

Isaac Pyke: Saint Helena (1714–19, 1731–38)

James Pyke-Nott: Nigeria Eastern Region

Q

Qa'a: Egypt (1st Dynasty)

Muammar al-Qadaffi: Libya

Wanis al-Qadaffi: Libya

Abd al-Qadir Badri: Libya

al-Qa'id: Hammadid Kingdom

Qa'id Ramadan: Tripolitania (1581–84)

al-Qa'im: Fatimid North Africa

Muhammad al-Qa'im: Morocco (1511–17)

Qait Bey: Egypt (1468–96)

al-Mansur Qala'un: Egypt (1279–90)

Qanun: Dongola

Juwan Qapiji Sultanzade: Egypt (1637–40)

Qara: Egypt (1623, 1624–26)

Qara: Egypt (1699–1704)

Qaraqash: Egypt (1668–69)

Qaraqush: Tripolitania (1172–90, 1202)

Qasa: Mali Empire

Qasim: Egypt (1523, 1524–25)

Abu'l Qasim: Darfur

al-Qasim Gannum: Idrisid State

Muhammad III al-Qasri: Morocco (1545–47)

Qat-Ali: Ifat

Qu: Mali Empire

Badi I Sid al-Qum: Funj Sultanate

Lucius Minicius Natalis Quadronius Verus: Africa [i] (153–154)

Cornelis Van Quaelbergen: Cape Colony (1666–68)

Osei Tutu Quamina: Ashanti

Junius Quartus Palladius: Africa Proconsularis (416–421)

Quastantinos: Axum

Jean-Baptiste Quéau de Quincy: Seychelles (1794–1811)

Ernesto Queirolo: Tripolitania (1927)

Germain Quernel: Senegal (1833–34)

Jean-Baptiste Quéau de Quincy: Seychelles (1794–1811)

Quett Masire: Botswana

Bernardin de Quimper: Réunion (1680–86)

Jerónimo de Quiñones: Canary Islands (1661–65)

Quintus Aurelius Symmachus: Africa Proconsularis (373)

Quintus Curtius Rufus: Africa [i] (58–59)

Quintus Junius Blaesus: Africa [i] (21–23)

Quintus Marcius Barea Soranus: Africa [i] (41–43)

Quintus Sulpicius Camerinus Peticus: Africa [i] (56–57)

Quintus Voconius Saxa Fides: Africa [i] (162–163)

Enrique Quirce: Western Sahara

Mariano Quirce: Ifni

Antonio Quiroga: Ceuta (1823)

R

Rabah Bitat: Algeria (1978–79)

Maribbi Rabbu: Brakna

Abu'l Rabi Suleiman: Morocco (1308–10)

Rabih az-Zubayr ibn Fadl-Allah:

Bornu Empire (1893–1900); Rabih's Empire

Hassab Rabihi: Funj Sultanate

Rabon Bawa: Zaria (1505–30)

Rachid Sfar: Tunisia (1986–87)

Radama I: Madagascar (1820–28)

Radama II: Madagascar (1861–63)

Ra'djedef: Egypt (4th Dynasty)

Rafael: Dongola

Rafael: Kongo

Dejaz Walad Rafael: Gojjam

Jean-Baptiste Raffenel: Sainte Marie de Madagascar

Rafohy: Madagascar (1500–20)

Giuseppe Salvago-Raggi: Eritrea

Raghib: Egypt (1744–48)

Ragib: Tripolitania (1847–48)

Ragib Pasha: Egypt (1882)

Ottavio Ragni: Tripolitania (1912–13)

Ragongo: Yatenga

Abd al-Karim ar-Ragrag: Tunis (1195–1200)

M. Raguenet: Senegal (1658–61)

Rahman: Mogadishu

Abu Sa'id Uthman II Abd ar-Rahman: Tlemcen (1348–52)

Abu Sa'id Abd ar-Rahman: Tripolitania (1221); Tunis (1221, 1223–26)

Abu Tashufin I Abd ar-Rahman: Tlemcen (1318–36)

Abu Tashufin II Abd ar-Rahman: Tlemcen (1389–93)

Sayid Abd ar-Rahman ibn al-Mahdi: Sudan (1952–53)

Abd ar-Rahman Musa: Omayyad and Abbasid North Africa

Abd ar-Rahman Siwar ad-Dahab: Sudan (1985–86)

Abd ar-Rahman Yaqub: Tripolitania (1236–47)

Sekhemre Wahkha Rahotep: Egypt (17th Dynasty)

Arthur Raikes: Zanzibar (1906–08)

Rainilaiarivony: Madagascar (1864–96)

Salah Raïs: Algiers (1552–57)

Rajab: Egypt (1720–21)

Muhammad az-Zaruq Rajab: Libya

Muhammad ar-Rajal: Brakna

Desiré Rakotoarijaona: Madagascar (1977–87)

Joel Rakotomalala: Madagascar (1975–76)

Pascal Rakotomavo: Madagascar (1997–98)

Justin Rakotoniaina: Madagascar (1976–77)

Emmanuel Rakotovahiny; Madagascar (1995–97)

Ralambo: Madagascar (1575–1610)

T.G. Ramabulana: Venda

Ramadan: Algiers (1660–61)

Qa'id Ramadan: Tripolitania (1581–84)

Ramadan Agha: Tripolitania (1631)

Jean-Paul Ramadier: Cameroun (1958); Guinea (1956–58); Niger (1954–56)

Elias Tutsoane Ramaema: Lesotho (1991–93)

Victor Ramahatra: Madagascar (1987–91)

Albano Ramalho: Guinea-Bissau (1898–99)

Abdul Raman Osman: Mauritius (1970, 1971–79)

Gabriel Ramanantsoa: Madagascar (1972–75)

Murtala Ramat Muhammad: Nigeria (1975–76)

Ramba-Ramba: Katsina (1100–80)

Ramdan: Algiers (1574–77)

Ramdan: Tunis (1696–99)

Rameses I Menpehtire: Egypt (19th Dynasty)

Rameses II the Great Usermare Miamun: Egypt (19th Dynasty)

Rameses III Usermare Meryamun: Egypt (20th Dynasty)

Rameses IV Hekamare Setpenamun: Egypt (20th Dynasty)

Rameses V Usermare Sekhepereure: Egypt (20th Dynasty)

Rameses VI Nebmare Meryamun: Egypt (20th Dynasty)

Rameses VII Usermare Meryamun: Egypt (20th Dynasty)

Rameses VIII Usermare Akhenamun: Egypt (20th Dynasty)

Rameses XI Neferkare Setpenre: Egypt (20th Dynasty)

Rameses X Khepermare Setpenre: Egypt (20th Dynasty)

Rameses XI Menmare Setneptah: Egypt (20th Dynasty)

Navin Ramgoolam: Mauritius (1995–2000)

Seewoosagur Ramgoolam: Mauritius (1961–82)

Rami: Egypt (1704–06)

Mateo Ramírez: Ceuta (1833–35)

Mogoboya Ramodike: Lebowa

Jesús Ramos: Ceuta (1996–99)

Luis Ramos Izquierdo: Fernando Po

Bernabé Ramos y Miranda: Melilla (1688–91)

Simon Ramsay: Federation of Rhodesia and Nyasaland

Gabriel Ramushwana: Venda

Ranavalona I: Madagascar (1828–61)

Ranavalona II: Madagascar (1868–83)

Ranavalona III: Madagascar (1883–97)

Heinrich Randad: Togoland

Richard Randall: Liberia (1828–29)

Comte Randon: Algeria (1851–58)

Ranfi: Funj Sultanate

Paul Rang: Comoros (1843–44)

Rangita: Madagascar (1520–40)

John Rankine: Nigeria Western Region; Zanzibar (1952–54)

Richard Rankine: Malawi (1921, 1923–24); Zanzibar (1929–37)

Alfred Raoul: Congo (1968–69)

Jean Rapenne: Mali (1940–42); Niger (1939–40)

Amador Raposo: Cape Verde (1595–96)

Rarabe: British Kaffraria

Ras Abeto Haylu: Gojjam

Ras Ali II: Gojjam

Ras Asrata-Medhin Kassa: Eritrea

Ras Beru Gugsa: Gojjam

Ras Dejazmatch Tafari: Ethiopia (1916–74)

Ras Gosho II: Gojjam

Ras Goskol: Gojjam

Ras Kasa: Gojjam

Ras Ma'red: Gojjam

Ras Sahle Selassie: Shoa

Ras Wossen Seged: Shoa

Rasebolai Khamane: Bamangwatoland; Botswana

Mulay Rashid: Morocco (1664–72)

Abdarrahman ar-Rashid: Darfur

Mehmed Rashid: Tripolitania (1871–72)

Rashid I: Almohad Empire

Rashid Bakr: Sudan (1976–77)

Rashid ibn Hamish: Mombasa (1873–95)

Rashid ibn Salem: Mombasa (1836–37)

Abdi Rashid Shermarke: Somalia

Rashidi Kawawa: Tanganyika; Tanzania

Muhammad Bey Rasileh: Sudan (1861–62)

Ahmed Rasim: Tripolitania (1881–96)

Rasoaherina: Madagascar (1863–68)

Jean-Jacques Rasolondraibe: Madagascar (2002)

Gismalla Rassas: Southern Sudan

Pierre de Rastel de Rocheblaye: Gorée

Ali III ar-Rasul: Algiers (1808–09)

José Rato: São Tomé and Príncipe (1926–28)

Ratshidi: Barolongland

Richard Ratsimandrava: Madagascar (1975)

Norbert Ratsirahonana: Madagascar (1996–97)

Didier Ratsiraka: Madagascar (1975–93, 1997–2002)

Rauf Pasha: British Somaliland; Sudan (1879–82)

Maurizio Rava: Italian Somaliland (1931–35)

Marc Ravalomanana: Madagascar (2002–)

Frank N. Ravele: Venda

Francisque Ravony: Madagascar (1993–95)

Di Rawa: Biu

Abu Hatim Rawh: Omayyad and Abbasid North Africa

Jerry Rawlings: Ghana (1979, 1981–2001)

Charles Rayet: Comoros (1879)

Pierre Raynier: Central African Republic (1951)

Razakatsitakatrandriana: Madagascar (1670–75)

Guy Razanamasy: Madagascar (1991–93)

Philotée Gerville-Réache: Comoros (1885–87)

Herbert Read: Mauritius (1925–30)

Marqués de la Real Corona: Oran (1748–52)

Léon Réallon: Madagascar (1939)

Arnaldo de Rebelo: Cape Verde (1900–02)

Horacio Rebelo: Angola (1956–60)

Mariano Rebigliato: Spanish Morocco (1854–57)

Camilo de Miranda Rebocho Vaz: Angola (1966–72)

Benoît-Louis Rebonne: Senegal (1931)

Albrecht von Rechenburg: German East Africa

Aemilius Rectus: Egypt (37–37, 42–47)

Redebast Usermare: Egypt (23rd Dynasty)

The Red King: Akim

Ahmad Reda Guedira: Morocco (1961–63)

Redha Malik: Algeria (1993–94)

Gerald Reece: British Somaliland

Henry Reeve: Lagos (1902–04)

Nicolas de Regnac des Brulys: Réunion (1806–09)

Étienne Régnault: Réunion (1665–71)

Cristóvão do Rego: São Tomé (1656–57)

Jaime do Rego: São Tomé and Príncipe (1910, 1911)

Roque de Barros do Rego: Cape Verde (1648)

Jens Reiersen: Danish Gold Coast (1817–19)

Carlos Reis: Cape Verde (1974–75)

Mehmed Reis: Tripolitania (1835–37)

Osman Reis as-Suhali: Tripolitania (1672)

Francis Reitz: Orange Free State (1889–95)

J.J. Reitz: Mombasa (1824)

Hajji Rejeb: Tripolitania (1711)

Rejeb: Tripolitania (1904–08)

Fara Penda Teg Rel: Walo (1488–96)

Fara Penda Teg Rel: Walo (1480–92)

Rema Armah: Axum

Remigius: Egypt (396–397)

Roger Rémy: Comoros (1948–50)

Georges Renard: French Equatorial Africa (1934–35)

Maurice Renauld: Niger (1920)

Thomas Renault de Saint-Germain: Senegal (1831–33)

George Rendall: Gambia (1830–37)

France-Albert René: Seychelles (1977–2004)

Re'neb: Egypt (2nd Dynasty)

Patrick Renison: Kenya (1959–62)

Gilbert Rennie: Kenya (1942); Zambia (1948–54)

John Rennie: Mauritius (1962–68)

Willem Van Rensburg: Transvaal (1862–64)

Renseneb: Egypt (13th Dynasty)

Louis Le Gardeur de Repentigny: Senegal (1784–86)

Jules Repiquet: Cameroun (1934–36); Réunion (1925–32)

Jayme de Requesens: Tripolitania (1510–11)

Muhammadu Toya Rero: Katsina (1568–72)

Muhammadu Toya Rero II: Katsina (1684–1701)

Carl Resch: Danish Gold Coast (1762–66)

Dieudonné Reste: Benin [ii] (1929–31); Chad (1923–26); Côte d'Ivoire (1931–35); French Equatorial Africa (1936–39)

Rete'a: Axum

Piet Retief: Natal (1837–38)

Mehmed Reuf Pasha: Equatoria Province

Carlos Tovar de Revilla: Fernando Po

Paul Revoil: Algeria (1901–03)

Charles Rey: Botswana

Georges Rey: Côte d'Ivoire (1942–43); Senegal (1941–42)

Antonio del Rey y Caballero: Spanish Morocco (1868)

Ali Reza: Tripolitania (1867–70, 1872–73)

Rhammius Martialis: Egypt (118–121)

Johan Rhenius: Cape Colony (1791–92)

Albertus Van Rhijn: Namibia (1951–53)

Cecil Rhodes: Bechuanaland Protectorate; Cape Colony (1890–96)

Francis Rhodes: Rhodesia (1894–95)

Rhodon: Egypt (537)

Riaz Pasha: Egypt (1882, 1888–91, 1893–94)

Ferro Ribeiro: Mozambique (1974)

Gregorio Ribeiro: São Tomé and Príncipe (1873–76)

João Rodrigues de Vasconcelos Ribeiro: Ceuta (1464–79)

José Ribeiro: Mozambique (1910–11)

Rui Mendes de Vasconcelos Ribeiro: Ceuta (1479–81)

Bernardinho Ribeiro Pacheco: Portuguese Gold Coast (1584)

M. Ribes: Côte d'Ivoire (1898)

Carlo Ricci: Italian Somaliland (1920–23)

Raffaele Borea Ricci D'Olmo: Tripolitania (1911)

Jules Richard: Guinea (1906–07)

Arthur Richards: Gambia (1934–36); Nigeria (1943–47)

Edmund Richards: Lesotho (1939–42); Malawi (1942–47)

Étienne Richaud: Réunion (1886–87)

Léon Richaud: Gabon (1909–11)

Pierre de Richebourg: Senegal (1711–13)

Johan von Richelieu: Danish Gold Coast (1823–25)

M. de Richemont: Senegal (1668–73)

Johan Richter: Danish Gold Coast (1817)

Henry Ricketts: Ghana (1826–27, 1828); Sierra Leone (1828–29)

Manuel Rico: Fernando Po

Ridimba: Yatenga

Jan Van Riebeeck: Cape Colony (1652–62)

Rifau: Daura

Joseph Rigal: Togo (1957)

Christopher Rigby: Zanzibar (1857–60)

Rigo: Daura

Jean Rigotard: Mayotte Department

Jan Rina: Yauri

Veerasamy Ringadoo: Mauritius (1986–92)

Jean Risterucci: Gabon (1959–60)

Francisco Fernández y Rivadeo: Ceuta (1715–19, 1720–25)

Cándido Rivas: Equatorial Guinea

Pierre de Rivau: Fort-Dauphin

Ignacio Rivera: Melilla (1991–98)

José Rivera: Melilla (1788–98)

Miguel Primo de Rivera y Orbaneja: Spanish Morocco (1936)

Pierre Poncet de la Rivière: Gorée

Abdi Rizak Hajji Hussein: Somalia

Ould Rizg: Tagant

Rizvan: Algiers (1607–10)

Abraham Robberts: Dutch Gold Coast (1716–18)

Henri Roberdeau: Côte d'Ivoire (1898–1902); Réunion (1895)

King Robert: New Calabar

Holden Roberto: Angola Revolutionary Government in Exile

John Roberts: Ghana (1780–81)

John Roberts: Saint Helena (1708–11)

Joseph Roberts: Liberia (1841–56, 1872–76)

James Robertson: Nigeria (1955–60)

William Robertson: Ghana (1914)

A. Robin: Senegal (1858–59)

Hercules Robinson: Cape Colony (1881–97)

John Robinson: Natal (1893–97)

M.J. Roblin: Comoros (1878–79)

Francis Robson: Saint Helena (1800–01)

Carlos Roçadas: Cape Verde (1949–53)

José Roçadas: Angola (1909–10)

Celestino Rocha da Costa: São Tomé and Príncipe (1988–91)

Antonio da Rocha Magalhães: Portuguese Gold Coast (1634–42)

Pierre de Rastel de Rocheblaye: Gorée

Rennell Rodd: Zanzibar (1892–94)

John Rodger: Ghana (1904–10)

François Rodier: Réunion (1910–12)

Fernando Rodrigues: São Tomé and Príncipe (1953)

José Rodrigues: Guinea-Bissau (1973)

Manuel Rodrigues: Guinea-Bissau (1949–50); Mozambique (1961–64)

Vasco Rodrigues: Guinea-Bissau (1962–65)

João Rodrigues de Vasconcelos Ribeiro: Ceuta (1464–79)

João Rodrigues Peçanha: Portuguese Gold Coast (1584)

João Rodrigues Pereira: Ceuta (1553)

Francisco Rodríguez: Equatorial Guinea

José Rodríguez: Ifni

Román Rodríguez: Canary Islands (1999–2003)

Francisco Rodríguez de Sanabria: Melilla (1620–22)

José María Rodríguez Vera: Ceuta (1837–44)

Cecil Rodwell: Zimbabwe (1928–34)

Izaak De Roever: Dutch Gold Coast (1804–05)

Johannes Rogathinos: Byzantine North Africa

Jacques-François Roger: Senegal (1821–27)

Victor-Joseph Roger: Gabon (1847–48)

Roger II of Sicily: Tripolitania (1148–54)

A.S. Rogers: Zanzibar (1901–06)

Anthony Rogers: Fort James

Émmanuel Roget: Porto-Novo

Charles Rognon: French Equatorial Africa (1909–11); Gabon (1909)

Jacques Rogué: Chad (1943–48); Mauritania (1950–52)

Duarte Róis: Bissau (1759)

João Róis Coutinho: Portuguese Gold Coast (1586–95)

Manuel Rojas: Canary Islands (1993–99)

Rui Díaz de Rojas: Oran (1509–10)

Pedro Rolim: Mozambique (1567–69)

Emile Rolland: Lesotho (1877, 1878)

Louis Rollet: Niger (1958)

M. de Saint-Amant de Romainville: Seychelles (1778–81)

Johan Root: Dutch Gold Coast (1675–76)

Timoléon Ropert: Gorée and Dependencies

Jean-Baptiste Montagniès de la Roque: Senegal (1841–42)

Jean Levens de la Roquette: Senegal (1726–33)

Vincente Rorique: Ceuta (1820)

Antonio Ros de Olano: Spanish Morocco (1847–51)

Enrique Rosa: Guinea-Bissau (2003)

Sebastião da Rosa: Cacheu (1674)

Tomás Rosado: Mozambique (1902–05)

Francisco Rosalen y Burguet: Western Sahara

Gualberto de Rosario: Cape Verde (2000–01)

James Rose-Innes: South Africa (1920, 1923–24)

James Rose-Innes, Jr.: Griqualand West

Titus Prifernius Paetus Rosianus Geminus: Africa [i] (140–141, 161–162)

Baron Rosmead: Cape Colony (1881–97)

Patrick Ross: Saint Helena (1846–51)

William Ross: Ghana (1862)

Knud Røst: Danish Gold Coast (1717–20)

Pierre-Alexandre Roubaud: Réunion (1794–95)

John Le Rougelet: South Africa (1951–55)

Ferdinand Rougier: Mali (1936–38)

Francisco Roulim: Cape Verde (1622)

Ernest Roume: French West Africa (1902–07); Gabon (1903–04); Senegal (1902)

Théodore Rouston: Tunisia (1881–82)

Maurice Rouvier: Tunisia (1892–94)

Jean-Baptiste Roux: Sainte Marie de Madagascar

M. Le Roux de Kermeseven: Seychelles (1775–78)

Ernest-Eugène Rouys: Congo (1953–56)

Duc de Rovigo: Algeria (1831–33)

Samuel Rowe: Gambia (1875–77); Ghana (1881–84); Sierra Leone (1875–76, 1877–80, 1881, 1885–88)

William Rowe: Koya-Temne

Edward Roye: Liberia (1870–71)

Francisco de la Rúa: Gran Canaria

Winyi I Rubangiramasega: Bunyoro

Rubat I: Funj Sultanate

Angelo De Rubeis: Italian Somali land (1936)

Caius Rubellius Blandus: Africa [i] (35–36)

Winyi I Rubembeka: Bunyoro

Juan Rubío: Equatorial Guinea

Bako Muhama Rubo: Zaria (1682–1710)

Rubrius Barbarus: Egypt (13–7 B.C.)

Bako Makam Rubu: Zaria (1646–47)

Mutara III Rudahigwa: Ruanda

Rudamen: Egypt (23rd Dynasty)

Gerrit Rudolf: Natal (1842–43)

Rudwan: Egypt (1137–39)

Capt. Ruediger: German East Africa

Lucien Rueff: Niger (1920–21)

Ahmadu Rufai: Fulani Empire; Katsina (1869–70)

Vulcacius Rufinus: Africa Proconsularis (346–347, 352–353, 365–367)

Bassaeus Rufus: Egypt (167–175)

Metius Rufus: Egypt (90–95)

Quintus Curtius Rufus: Africa [i] (58–59)

Lucius Hedius Rufus Lollianus Avitus: Africa [i] (157–158)

Rufus Synesius Hadrianus: Africa Proconsularis (400–405)

Ntare II Rugaamba: Burundi [i]

Ntare III Rugaamba: Nkore

Ruganza II Ndoori: Ruanda

Ruganza Bwimba: Ruanda

Winyi III Ruguruka: Bunyoro

Cyilima Rugwe: Ruanda

Bako Ruhawa: Zaria (1750–57)

Ruhinda: Nkore

Ruhinda II: Karagwe

Ruhinda III: Karagwe

Ruhinda IV: Karagwe

Ruhinda V: Karagwe

Ruhinda VI Orushongo: Karagwe

Ruhinda VII: Karagwe

Ruhinda Kizarabagabe: Karagwe

Olimi II Ruhundwangeye: Bunyoro

Francisco Ruíz: Melilla (1622–24)

Cyilima II Rujugira: Ruanda

Isingoma Mpuga Rukidi: Bunyoro

Nyabongo I Rulemu: Bunyoro

Rumanyika: Karagwe

Rumanyika II: Karagwe

Muhamman Rumfa: Kano (1462–98)

Dhuka ar-Rumi: Egypt (915–919)

Cwa I Mali Rumoma Mahanga: Bunyoro

Murray Rumsey: Lagos (1884)

P.J. Runckel: Dutch Gold Coast (1856)

Ruqim: Egypt (1767–68)

Rusatira: Karagwe

Gatsi Rusere: Mwene Mutapa Empire

Rushango: Nkore

Ntare I Rushatse: Burundi [i]

Hussein Rushdi Pasha: Egypt (1914–19)

Alexander Russell: Zimbabwe (1934–35, 1942, 1946)

Alfred Russell: Liberia (1883–84)

Arthur Russell: Ashanti

John Russwurm: Maryland

Rustum Bey: Kordofan

Rustum Pasha: Sudan (1851–52)

Rutilius Lupus: Egypt (116–117)

Joseph Rutten: Congo (Zaire) (1923–27)

Mibambwe IV Rutulindwa: Ruanda

Hamman Ruwa: Muri

Upton Ruxton: Nigeria Southern Provinces

Ndahiro Ruyange: Ruanda

Jacob Ruyghaver: Dutch Gold Coast (1641–45, 1651–56)

Ibrahim Ruzili: Tunis (1587–90)

al-Adil Ruzzik: Egypt (1161–63)

Keremeera Rwaaka: Ruanda

Rwabirere: Nkore

Kigeri IV Rwabugiri: Ruanda

Louis Rwagasore: Burundi [ii]

Olimi V Rwakabale: Bunyoro

Ochaki Rwangira: Bunyoro

Rwebishengye: Nkore

Pierre-Celestin Rwigema: Rwanda

Mutara II Rwoogera: Ruanda

Pierre Ryckmans: Congo (Zaire) (1934–46); Ruanda–Urundi

S

Antonio de Sá: Portuguese Gold Coast (1570)

Caetano de Sá: Mozambique (1746–50)

Cristóvão de Sá: São Tomé and Príncipe (1782–88)

José de Sá: Madeira (1759–67)

Pantaleāo de Sá: Mozambique (1560–64)

Sebastião de Sá: Mozambique (1557–60)

Serafim de Sá: Cape Verde (1716–20)

Salvador de Sá e Benavides: Angola (1648–51)

Pantaleāo de Sá e Melo: Madeira (1694–98)

Sa'adu: Futa Jallon

Saanda: Adamawa

Jerónimo de Saavedra Acevedo: Canary Islands (1983–87, 1991–93)

Miguel Fernández de Saavedra: Melilla (1767–72)

Diego Saavedra y Magdalena: Fernando Po

Saayodo Yaasin Mbody: Walo (1801–06)

Mallam Babu Saba: Damagaram

Saba Asqad: Ethiopia (1298–99)

Sabah: Axum

Sabakes: Egypt (335–333 B.C.)

Saban Bey: Oran (1708–17)

Sabana: Gwiriko

Sabata: Tembuland

Ada Sabau: Daura

Sabhat ibn Muhammad: Zeng Empire (1486–87)

Sabinianus: Egypt (323–338)

Appius Sabinus: Egypt (250)

Mantennius Sabinus: Egypt (193–195)

Sabr ad-Din I: Ifat

Sabr ad-Din II: Adal [ii]

Sabri: Tripolitania (1878–79)

Ali Sabry: Egypt (1962–65)

Hassan Sabry: Egypt (1940)

Sabun: Wadai

Paul-Gustave Sachet: Nossi-Bé

Sachi Gana Machi: Nupe

Soumana Sacko: Mali (1991–92)

Edward Sackville: Tangier (1680–81)

Sa'd ad-Din Ahmad: Ifat

Sheikh Sa'd Bu: Trarza

Sa'd Zaghlul Pasha: Egypt (1924)

Muhammad Anwar as-Sadat: Egypt (1970–81)

Abu s-Sadat Uthman: Egypt (1453)

Ja'far Pasha Sadiq: Sudan (1865–66)

Muhammad III as-Sadiq: Tunis (1859–81); Tunisia (1881–82)

Sadiq al-Mahdi: Sudan (1966–67, 1986–89)

James Sadler: British Somaliland; Kenya (1905–09); Uganda (1901–05)

Sadou Hayatou: Cameroun (1991–92)

Numa-François Sadoul: Congo (1946–47); Djibouti (1950–54); Gabon (1944–46, 1947–49)

Sa'du Kawu Khaliru: Lafiagi

El Hadj Saeidou Nyimoluh Nyoju: Bamoun

Carlos Sáenz Delcourt: Spanish Morocco (1872–73)

Luis Saéz: Equatorial Guinea

Germa Safar: Axum

Saffah: Algiers (1551–52)

Safya Ar'ed: Ethiopia (1344–72)

A'alaf Sagad: Ethiopia (1667–82)

Adbar Sagad: Ethiopia (1716–21)

Admas Sagad: Ethiopia (1559–63)

Adyam Sagad: Ethiopia (1682–1706)

Adyam Sagad: Ethiopia (1755–69)

Alam Sagad: Ethiopia (1632–67)

Asnaf Sagad: Ethiopia (1603–04)

Asrar Sagad: Ethiopia (1708–11)

Dsahai Sagad: Ethiopia (1711–16)

Fehr Sagad: Ethiopia (1779–84, 1788–89, 1794–95, 1795–96, 1798–99, 1800)

Malak Sagad: Ethiopia (1563–97)

Malak Sagad: Shoa

Seltan Sagad: Ethiopia (1607–32)

Wasan Sagad: Axum

Louis Saget: Comoros (1960–62); Djibouti (1966–69)

Sagha: Yatenga

Sagha I: Wadai

Sagha II: Wadai

Kure Ghana as-Saghir: Bornu Empire (1350–51)

Sahan: Axum

Sahem: Axum

Sahla Dengel: Ethiopia (1832–40, 1841–50, 1851–55)

Sahle Mariam: Ethiopia (1889–1911)

Ras Sahle Selassie: Shoa

M. Sahoulba: Chad (1959)

Sahure: Egypt (5th Dynasty)

Sa'ib Pasha: Egypt (1848)

Sa'id: Bornu Empire (1398–99)

Sa'id: Nupe

Sa'id: Timbuktu (1675–78)

Sa'id: Tripolitania (1028–37)

Sa'id: Zanzibar (1710)

Muhammad II as-Sa'id: Morocco (1358–59)

Muhammad Sa'id: Egypt (1743–44, 1757–60)

Muhammad Sa'id: Egypt (1854–63)

Sa'id I: Timbuktu (1635–37)

Sa'id III: Timbuktu (1705)

Sa'id IV: Timbuktu (1734–35, 1736–37)

Sa'id V: Timbuktu (1738–39, 1741–42, 1743–45)

Sa'id VI: Timbuktu (1742–43, 1749–50)

Abu Sa'id Abd ar-Rahman: Tripolitania (1221); Tunis (1221, 1223–26)

Said Abed: Mwali

Said Abeid Abderemane: Nzwani

Sa'id Abu'l Ala Idris: Tripolitania (1221, 1222–23); Tunis (1221–23)

Sa'id ad-Din: Egypt (1756–57)

Abu Sa'id al-Aflah: Rustumid Amirate

Sa'id al-Hadermi: Mombasa (1735–39)

as-Sa'id al-Mu'tadid: Almohad Empire

Sa'id Ali Kamal: Comoros (1995)

Sa'id Ali Muhammad: Comoros (1993)

Sa'id Attourmani: Comoros (1978)

Sa'id Barakh Khan: Egypt (1277–79)

Muhammad Sa'id Bey: Egypt (1910–14)

Muhammad Said Fazul: Mwali

Sa'id ibn Hasan: Zeng Empire (1472–82)

Abu Sa'id ibn Musa: Tlemcen (1411–12)

Sa'id ibn Suleiman: Zeng Empire (1508–10)

Sa'id ibn Yezid: Egypt (682–684)

Sa'id Ibrahim ibn Ali: Comoros (1970–72)

Abu Sa'id Jaqmaq: Egypt (1438–53)

Tajjidine ben Sa'id Massonde: Comoros (1996, 1998–99)

Sa'id Muhammad Djohar: Comoros (1989–96)

Sa'id Muhammad Jaffar: Comoros (1975–76)

Sa'id Muhammad Jaffar al-Angadi: Comoros (1972)

Sa'id Muhammad Sheikh: Comoros (1961–70)

Muhammad Sa'id Pasha: Egypt (1919)

Said Muhammad Soefou: Mwali

Said Omar Oili: Mayotte Department

Mehmed Sa'id Pasha Wahbi: Kordofan

Chamassi Sa'id Umar: Nzwani

Abu Sa'id Uthman I: Tlemcen (1283–1304)

Abu Sa'id Uthman II: Morocco (1310–31)

Abu Sa'id Uthman II Abd ar-Rahman: Tlemcen (1348–52)

Abu Sa'id Uthman III: Morocco (1398–1420)

Muhammad Sa'idi: Futa Jallon

Joseph Saidu Momoh: Sierra Leone (1985–92)

al-Hajji Saidu Naemaska: Kontagora

Ahmad Saif an-Nasir: Fezzan

Imam Sa'if ibn Sultan: Mombasa (1698)

Lucien Saint: French Morocco; Tunisia (1921–29)

Jean-François de Saint-Alary: Togo (1941–42)

M. Saint-Amant de Romainville: Seychelles (1778–81)

Charles-Max Masson de Saint-Félix: Central African Republic (1936–39); Chad (1936–38); Congo (1931–32)

Thomas Renault de Saint-Germain: Senegal (1831–33)

William St. John: Ghana (1621–23)

Paul de Saint-Mart: Madagascar (1944–46)

Pierre de Saint-Mart: Madagascar (1943–44)

Didier de Saint Martin: Mauritius (1740, 1746–47); Réunion (1743–45, 1747–48)

Joseph Murinay de Saint-Maurice: Réunion (1779–81)

Nicolas Després de Saint-Robert: Senegal (1720–23, 1725–26)
Jean Brunteau de Sainte-Suzanne: Réunion (1809–10)
Saiwago: Zaria (ca. 1300)
Saiyid I: Timbuktu (1693)
Baba Saiyid I: Timbuktu (1693)
Baba Saiyid II: Timbuktu (1740–41, 1745–46)
Sakaina: Biram
Amara II Abu Sakaykin: Funj Sultanate
Sakazu: Yauri
Sakura: Mali Empire
Fara Penda Adam Sal: Walo (1823–37)
Sheikh Abd as-Salaam al-Asman: Tripolitania (1480–82)
Saladin: Egypt (1169–93)
Salah: Constantine
Salah ad-Din: Egypt (1169–93)
Salah Eddine ben Muhammad Baccouche: Tunisia (1943–47, 1952–54)
Salah Raïs: Algiers (1552–57)
Hasan Bey Salamah: Sudan (1859–61)
al-Adil Salamish: Egypt (1279)
Raoul Salan: Algeria (1958)
ibn as-Salar: Egypt (1152–53)
Salau: Gobir
Labo Salau: Gobir
Eugenio de Salazar: Tenerife
Luis Salazar: Canary Islands (1745–46)
Federico de Salazar y Nieto: Western Sahara
Domingo de Salcedo: Ceuta (1783–84)
José Salcedo y González: Melilla (1866–68)
Antonio de Saldanha: Mozambique (1509–12)
Fernão de Saldanha: Madeira (1625–26)
João de Saldanha e Albuquerque: Madeira (1672–76)
Manuel de Saldanha e Albuquerque: Madeira (1754–57)
Pedro de Saldanha e Albuquerque: Mozambique (1759–63, 1782)
Mustafa Ould Saleck: Mauritania (1978–79)
Saleh: Bedde
Mamdouh Salem: Egypt (1975–78)
Salem ibn Ahmad: Mombasa (1826–35)
Abdel-Salem Jallud: Libya
Diogo Salema: São Tomé (1571–75)
Tancredi Saletta: Massawa
Alejandro Salgado: Fernando Po
Antonio Salgado: Cape Verde (1698–1702)
Mamman Sali: Misau
Moma Sali: Misau
Pierre Saliceti: Benin [ii] (1940); Togo (1942–43)
Salih: Egypt (1351–54)
Salih: Mayotte
Muhammad as-Salih: Tunisia (1954)

as-Salih Aiyub: Egypt (1240–49)
Salih Deret: Wadai
as-Salih Hajji: Egypt (1380–82, 1389–90)
Salih ibn Ali: Egypt (750–751, 753–755)
Salih ibn Ruzzik: Egypt (1143–52, 1154–61)
Salih ibn Salih: Tangier (1421–37)
as-Salih Muhammad: Egypt (1421–22)
Abu Salih Yahya: Egypt (779–780)
Salihu: Futa Jallon
Salihu: Gobir
Salim: Anjouan
Sheikh Salim: Anjouan
Ba-Haddu Salim: Timbuktu (1683)
Salim Ahmad Salim: Tanzania
Si Halil Bu Hajib ben Salim: Tunisia (1926–32)
Salim I: Mayotte
Salim II: Anjouan
Salim II: Mayotte
Salim Ahmad Salim: Tanzania
Abu Salim Ali II: Morocco (1359–61)
Salim at-Teumi: Algiers (1516)
Salim ben Ali: Comoros (1978–82)
Salim ibn Sawada: Egypt (780–781)
Salim Pasha: Sudan (1853–54)
Salima Masimba: Mohéli
Salitis: Egypt (15th Dynasty)
Macky Sall: Senegal (2004–)
Michel Saller: Djibouti (1943–44)
Salman Nari: Songhai (1340–47)
Salmin Amour: Zanzibar (1999–2000)
Charles Salmon: Ghana (1871–72); Seychelles (1874–79)
Salomo: Dongola
Salomon: Byzantine North Africa
Salomon: Ethiopia (1777–79)
Walda Salomon: Ethiopia (1796–97, 1799)
Salomon I: Ethiopia (1285–94)
Ahmad Salum: Trarza
Ould Sidi Ahmad Salum: Trarza
Umar Salum: Trarza
Muhammad Salum Ould Brahim: Trarza
Giuseppe Salvago-Raggi: Eritrea
Servius Cornelius Scipio Salvidienus Orfitus: Africa [i] (62–63)
Servius Cornelius Scipio Salvidienus Orfitus: Africa [i] (164)
Lucius Salvius Otho: Africa [i] (40–41)
N'dyak Kumba Sam Dyakekh: Walo (1336–43)
Sama: Argungu
Muhammadu Sama: Argungu
Samaila: Argungu
Samaila II: Argungu
Samaila III: Argungu
Samaila IV: Argungu
Paul Samary: Réunion (1901–05)
Samatambira Nyamhandu I: Mwene Mutapa Empire
Muhammad Ali Samatar: Somalia
M'Bathio Samb: Kayor
Samba: Dyolof

Samba: Kayor (1593–1600)
Samba: Kayor (1883–86)
Lat-Samba: Dyolof
Sambigu: Futa Jallon
Sambo: Hadejia
Sambo: Zaria (1879–88)
Sambo Gabaima: Jemaari
Sambolei: Jemaari
Sambwa Pida Nbagui: Congo (Zaire) (1988)
Samembe: Ruanda
Sameramne Herusaatef: Kush (404–369 B.C.)
Mahmud Sami: Egypt (1882)
Samih: Tripolitania (1873–74)
Samih Bey: Fezzan
Mulay Ismail as-Samin: Morocco (1672–1727)
Samory Touré: Samory's Empire
Antonio de Sampaio: Cape Verde (1879–81)
Luis Sampaio: Mozambique (1696–99)
Manuel de Sampaio: Mozambique (1657–61)
Rui Sampaio: Mozambique (1614–18)
Sampu: Tembuland
Nsoro Samukondo: Ruanda
Samusi Olusi: Lagos (1920–31)
Lt.-Col. San Gouveia: Guinea-Bissau (1974)
Duque de San Lúcar: Oran (1660–66)
Alessandro Di San Marzano: Massawa
Marqués de San Román: Oran (1652–60)
Francisco Rodríguez de Sanabria: Melilla (1620–22)
Sanakafo: Gobir
Sanakht: Egypt (3rd Dynasty)
Sanau: Katsina (1300–50)
João Brito-Sanches: Mozambique (1819–21)
Umar Sanda Kiyarimi: Bornu Empire (1937–69)
Umar Sanda Kura: Bornu Empire (1927–37)
Umaru Sanda: Damagaram
Umaru Sanda Ndayako: Nupe
Sandaki: Mali Empire
Sandila: British Kaffraria
Gonzalo Chacón y Arellano Sandoval y Rojas: Ceuta (1709–15)
Ali Sandura: Trarza
Sanem: Wadai
Sanem: Yatenga
Sango: Oyo
N'dyak Kumba-Nan Sango: Walo (1355–67)
Sangrafare: Koya-Temne
Gaspard de Sanguesse: Tripolitania (1530–33)
Artur Sanhá: Guinea-Bissau (2003–04)
Malam Sanhá: Guinea-Bissau (1999–2000)
Ahmad Muhammad Sani: Gumel
Mahoma Sani: Zaria (1846–63)
Muhammadu Sani: Argungu

Sani Abacha: Nigeria (1993–98)
Sanibar I: Timbuktu (1691, 1694–95)
Francisco Sanjuanena: Ceuta (1836–37)
José Sanjurjo: Spanish Morocco (1925–28, 1931)
Thomas Sankara: Burkina Faso (1983–87)
Wilton Sankawulo: Liberia (1995–96)
Sankhenre Mentuhotep: Egypt (17th Dynasty)
Sankhibre: Egypt (13th Dynasty)
Mentuhotep III Sankhkare: Egypt (11th Dynasty)
Neferhotep III Sekhemre Sankhtowy: Egypt (13th Dynasty)
Sankré: Mandara
Louis Sanmarco: Central African Republic (1954–58); Gabon (1958–59)
José Oribe Sans: Spanish Morocco (1866–68)
Conde de Santa Clara: Ceuta (1794–95)
Visconde de Santa Clara de Avellido: Oran (1628–32)
Barão de Santa Comba Dão: Angola (1829–34)
Marqués de Santa Cruz: Ceuta (1731–38)
Marqués de Santa Cruz de Mercenado; Oran (1732–33)
Marqués de Santa Cruz de Paniagua: Oran (1685–87)
João de Santa Maria: Cape Verde (1741–52)
Santa'a: Timbuktu (1703)
Ramón de Santallana: Western Sahara
Enrique Santaló: Fernando Po
Jean de Santi: Benin [ii] (1934–36); Mali (1938–40)
Ruggero Santi: Italian Somaliland (1936–37)
Fernando de Santiago y Díaz de Mendívil: Western Sahara
Antonio Santos: Bissau (1842–42); Cacheu (1826)
Antonio dos Santos: Cape Verde (1971–74)
Augusto dos Santos: Guinea-Bissau (1890–91); Mozambique (1913–14)
Delfim dos Santos: Cacheu (1838)
Fernando dos Santos: Angola (2002–)
José Eduardo dos Santos: Angola (1979–)
Libanio dos Santos: Bissau (1852)
Manuel dos Santos: Mozambique (1971–73)
Fernando Santos e Castro: Angola (1972–74)
Idris al-Mahdi as-Sanusi: Cyrenaica; Libya; Tripolitania (1922–51)
Muhammadu Sanusi: Kano (1954–63)
Ngoi Sanza: Luba
Francisco de São Simão: Cape Verde (1782–83)
Alessandro Sapelli: Italian Somaliland (1906)
Saphadin: Egypt (1200–18)

Mehmed Saqizli: Tripolitania (1631–49)
Muhammad as-Saqizli: Cyrenaica; Libya
Osman Saqizli: Tripolitania (1649–72)
Sara-ba: Kaarta
Maurice Sarazac: Fezzan
N'Diklam Sare: Dyolof
Sare N'Dyaye: Dyolof
Kharut as-Sarhir: Wadai
as-Sari ibn al-Hakam: Egypt (815–816, 817–820)
Sarili: Kreli's Country
Dogon Sarki: Abuja
Uthman Sarki: Nupe
Augusto Sarmento: Mozambique (1880–81); São Tomé and Príncipe (1886–90)
Jácome Sarmento: Mozambique (1699–1703)
Pascual Sarmento: Mombasa (1693–94)
Serafim Sarmento: São Tomé (1727–34)
Joseph-Napoléon Sarda-Garriga: Réunion (1848–50)
Sarsa Dengel: Ethiopia (1563–97)
Sarsa Krestos: Gojjam
Pedro Sartorius y Tapia: Spanish Morocco (1875–76)
Abdul Khalik Pasha Sarwat: Egypt (1922, 1927–28)
Sarwe Iyasus: Ethiopia (1433)
Conde de Sarzedas: Tangier (1637–43)
Ansa Saseraku I: Akwamu
Ansa Saseraku II: Akwamu
Ansa Saseraku III: Akwamu
Ansa Saseraku IV: Akwamu
Numa Sasias: Comoros (1879–80)
Numa Sasias: Togo (1920)
Denis Sassou-Nguesso: Congo (1979–92, 1997–)
Satrius Arrianus: Egypt (307–323)
Manuel Saturnino da Costa: Guinea-Bissau (1994–97)
Aemilius Saturninus: Egypt (197–202)
Sa'ud I: Timbuktu (1632–34)
Sa'ud II: Timbuktu (1686, 1690)
Dejaz Saude: Gojjam
Victor Saúde María: Guinea-Bissau (1982–84)
Jacques de la Cour de la Saulais: Réunion (1699–1701)
Henri Sautot: Central African Republic (1942–46); French Equatorial Africa (1945)
Francesco Saverio Caroselli: Italian Somaliland (1937–40)
Savfet: Tripolitania (1878)
Gabriel Savignac: Comoros (1959–60)
Pierre Savorgnan de Brazza: Congo (1883–86); French Equatorial Africa (1886–97); Gabon (1886)
Sawadi: Masina
Sawadogho: Wadai
Ali Musa Bey Sawqi: Bahr al-Ghazal
Amos Sawyer: Liberia (1990–94)

Quintus Voconius Saxa Fides: Africa [i] (162–163)
Saye Zerbo: Burkina Faso (1980–82)
Sayid Abd ar-Rahman ibn al-Mahdi: Sudan (1952–53)
Sayid Abdallah ibn Khalifa: Zanzibar (1963)
Sayid Abu Bakr: Anjouan
Sayid Ahmad: Gran Comoro
Sayid Alawi: Anjouan
Sayid Ali: Gran Comoro
Sayid Ali: Zanzibar (1902–11)
Sayid Barghash: Zanzibar (1870–88)
Sayid Hamed: Zanzibar (1893–96)
Sayid Hamud: Zanzibar (1896–1902)
Sayid Hamza: Gran Comoro
Sayid ibn Abdallah: Zanzibar (1960–63)
Sayid Idarus: Anjouan
Sayid Jamshid ibn Abdallah: Zanzibar (1963–64)
Sayid Khalid: Zanzibar (1896)
Sayid Khalifa I: Zanzibar (1888–90)
Sayid Khalifa ibn Harub: Zanzibar (1911–60)
Sayid Madjid: Zanzibar (1854–70)
Muhammad Sayid Madjid: Zanzibar (1854–70)
Sayid Muhammad: Anjouan
Sayid Muhammad al-Abid: Fezzan
Sayid Muhammad al-Ahabagi: Zanzibar (1823–32)
Sayid Umar: Anjouan
Muhammad Sayin: Tagant
al-Wali Mustafa as-Sayyid: Western Sahara
Sayyid Muhammad: Egypt (1596–98)
Thomas Scanlen: Cape Colony (1881–84); Rhodesia (1898–99)
Friedrich von Schiele: German East Africa
Severin Schilderup: Danish Gold Coast (1735–36)
Georg Schilling: Tripolitania (1533–38)
Christian Schiønning: Danish Gold Coast (1807–17)
Julien Schmaltz: Senegal (1817, 1819–20)
Rasmus Schmidt: Danish Gold Coast (1847–50)
Heinrich Schnee: German East Africa
Friedrich Schnehage: Orange Free State (1872–73)
Karl von Schnitter: Hollandia
Eduard Schnitzer: Equatoria Province
Stephanus Schoeman: Transvaal (1860–63); Zoutpansberg
Hero Schomerus: Dutch Gold Coast (1852–56)
Adriaan Schoonheidt: Dutch Gold Coast (1709–11)
Abraham Schrameck: Madagascar (1918–19)
William Schreiner: Cape Colony (1898–1900)
Bruno von Schuckmann: Kamerun (1891–92); Namibia (1907–10)

Arnaldo Schultz: Guinea-Bissau (1965–68)

Carlos Alberto Schultz Xavier: Mozambique (1898)

Servius Cornelius Scipio Salvidienus Orfitus: Africa [i] (62–63)

Servius Cornelius Scipio Salvidienus Orfitus: Africa [i] (164)

Henry Scobell: Cape Colony (1909–10)

John Scott: Natal (1856–64)

John Scott: Tanganyika

Robert Scott: Ghana (1949–49); Mauritius (1954–59)

William E.H. Scupham: Italian Somaliland (1941–43)

Veríssimo Seabra: Guinea-Bissau (2003)

Henry Frowd Seagram: Gambia (1843)

Charles Sealy: British Somaliland

Seba-Mana: Kaarta

Sebastian Otobia: Warri

Antonio Sebastião: São Tomé and Príncipe (1963–72)

Sebekhnofru Sebbekhare: Egypt (12th Dynasty)

Sebe: Kaarta

Charles Sebe: Ciskei

Lennox Sebe: Ciskei

Sebego: Bangwaketseland

Sekhemre Shedtowe Sebekemsaf: Egypt (17th Dynasty)

Sebekemsaf I Sekhemre Wadjkhau: Egypt (13th Dynasty)

Sebekhnofru Sebbekhare: Egypt (12th Dynasty)

Sebekhotep I: Egypt (13th Dynasty)

Sebekhotep II: Egypt (13th Dynasty)

Sebekhotep III Sekhemre Sewadjtowy: Egypt (13th Dynasty)

Sebekhotep V Khaankre: Egypt (13th Dynasty)

Sebekhotep VI Khahotepre: Egypt (13th Dynasty)

Sebele I: Bakwenaland

Sebele II: Bakwenaland

Sebitwane: Barotseland

Seboko: Bamaleteland

Seboko II: Bamaleteland

Idrissa Seck: Senegal (2002–04)

Petronius Secundus: Egypt (95–98)

Sedimo: Bamangwatoland

Sedjefakare: Egypt (13th Dynasty)

Sedumedi: Batwanaland

Seeiso: Lesotho (1939–40)

Constantine Sereng Seeiso: Lesotho (1960–90, 1995–96)

Letsie David Seeiso: Lesotho (1990–94, 1996–)

Amadou Seeku: Dyolof

Mutara I Seemugeshi: Ruanda

Mibambwe III Seentaabyo: Ruanda

Mutaga I Seenyamwiiza: Burundi [i]

Seepapitso: Bangwaketseland

Seepapitso II: Bangwaketseland

Dulano Seezo: Batwanaland

Ba'ala Segab: Ethiopia (1784–88)

Ras Wossen Seged: Shoa

Ahmadu Sego: Futa Toro

Segotshane: Bangwaketseland

Enrique Segura y Campoy: Melilla (1905)

Sehertowy Intef: Egypt (10th Dynasty)

Amenemhet VI Sehetepibre: Egypt (13th Dynasty)

Ali Seibou: Niger (1987–93)

Alphonse Seignac-Lesseps: Nossi-Bé; Senegal (1884–86)

Seitlhamo: Bakwenaland

Theodor Seitz: Kamerun (1895–96, 1897, 1898, 1907–10); Namibia (1910–15)

Seius Strabo: Egypt (37–38)

Francisco de Seixas e Cabreira: Mombasa (1635–39, 1651–53)

Sejertawi: Kush (487–468 B.C.)

Sekamanya: Buganda

Sekeletu: Barotseland

Sekenenre Tao I: Egypt (17th Dynasty)

Sekenenre Tao II: Egypt (17th Dynasty)

Sekgathole: Batwanaland

Sekgoma: Batwanaland

Sekgoma I: Bamangwatoland

Sekgoma II: Bamangwatoland

Sekhekhet: Egypt (3rd Dynasty)

Amenemhet V Sekhemkare: Egypt (13th Dynasty)

Sekhemkare Malenaqen: Kush (555–542 B.C.)

Osorkhon I Sekhemkheperre: Egypt (22nd Dynasty)

Sekhemre Herhimae Intef: Egypt (17th Dynasty)

Neferhotep III Sekhemre Sankhtowy: Egypt (13th Dynasty)

Sebekhotep III Sekhemre Sewadjtowy: Egypt (13th Dynasty)

Sekhemre Shedtowe Sebekemsaf: Egypt (17th Dynasty)

Sekhemre Shedwast: Egypt (17th Dynasty)

Sekhemre Smentowe Djehuty: Egypt (17th Dynasty)

Sebekemsaf I Sekhemre Wadjkhau: Egypt (13th Dynasty)

Sekhemre Wahkha Rahotep: Egypt (17th Dynasty)

Sekhemre Wepmae Intef: Egypt (17th Dynasty)

Rameses V Usermare Sekhepereure: Egypt (20th Dynasty)

Sekherpereure Senkamanishen: Kush (643–623 B.C.)

Abou Sekin Muhammad: Baguirmi

Sekkonyana Maseribane: Lesotho (1965)

Seklocka: Whydah

Sekolo: Kaarta

Sekonyela: Sekonyela's Land

Abdulaye Sékou Sow: Mali (1993–94)

Ahmed Sékou Touré: Guinea (1958–84)

Sekplon: Whydah

Sekuba: Kaarta

Haile Selassie: Ethiopia (1916–74)

Ras Sahle Selassie: Shoa

Fikre Selassie Wogderess: Ethiopia (1987–89)

William Palmer, 2nd Earl of Selborne: Cape Colony (1905–09); Orange Free State (1905–07); Transvaal (1906–10)

Z.T. Seleki: Lebowa

Cleopatra V Selene: Egypt (115–110 B.C., 109–107 B.C.)

Seleucus: Africa Proconsularis (414–415)

Selim: Tripolitania (1606–07)

Selma: Bornu Empire (1346–50)

Seltan Sagad: Ethiopia (1607–32)

Percy Selwyn-Clarke: Seychelles (1947–51)

Semakookiru: Buganda

João Semedo: Bissau (1820–21)

João Semedo: Mombasa (1625–26)

Semenkhkare: Egypt (13th Dynasty)

Semenmedjatre: Egypt (17th Dynasty)

Semerkhet: Egypt (1st Dynasty)

Ali Semiz: Egypt (1549–53)

Sempronius Liberalis: Egypt (154–159)

Senakht Userkhaure: Egypt (20th Dynasty)

Senakhtenre: Egypt (17th Dynasty)

Sened: Egypt (2nd Dynasty)

Léopold Senghor: Mali Federation; Senegal (1960–80)

Nassau Senior: Ghana (1757–61)

Senwosre IV Seneferibre: Egypt (13th Dynasty)

Sesostris IV Seneferibre: Egypt (13th Dynasty)

Senfa Ar'ed: Ethiopia (1294–95)

Sekherpereure Senkamanishen: Kush (643–623 B.C.)

Marqués de Sentar: Ceuta (1665–72)

Jean Sentuary: Réunion (1763)

Senwelo: Bakgatlaland

Senwosre I Kheperkare: Egypt (12th Dynasty)

Senwosre II Kkakheperre: Egypt (12th Dynasty)

Senwosre III Khakaure: Egypt (12th Dynasty)

Senwosre IV Seneferibre: Egypt (13th Dynasty)

Senzangakhona: Zululand

Seogola: Bamangwatoland

Sepopa: Barotseland

Joseph Septans: Nossi-Bé

Septimius Heracleitus: Egypt (215–216)

Claudius Septimus Eutropius: Egypt (392)

Septimus Vegetus: Egypt (86–90)

Diogo de Sepúlveda: Mozambique (1521–25)

João de Sepúlveda: Mozambique (1541–48)

Diogo Lopes de Sequeira: Portuguese Gold Coast (1504–05)

Francisco de Sequeira: Cape Verde (1611–14)

João de Sequeira: Mozambique (1905–06)

José Sequeira: Guinea-Bissau (1913–14, 1915–17)

Antonio Sequeira e Faria: Mozambique (1723–26)

João da Sera de Morais: Portuguese Gold Coast (1629)

Constantine Sereng Seeiso: Lesotho (1960–90, 1995–96)

Seretse Khama: Bamangwatoland

Ian Seretse Khama: Bamangwatoland

Ángel Serafín Seriche Dougan: Equatorial Guinea

Cristino Seriche Bioko: Equatorial Guinea

Serkarer: Kush (12–17)

Alexandre Serpa Pinto: Cape Verde (1894–98)

Enrique Serrano Dolz: Spanish Morocco (1870–72)

Juan Serrano y Reyna: Melilla (1829–30)

Manuel Serrano y Ruíz: Melilla (1904–05)

Luis Serrão: Angola (1589–91)

Raimundo Serrão: Guinea-Bissau (1951–53)

Naevius Sertorius Macro: Egypt (38–39)

René Servatius: Senegal (1882–83)

André Servel: Gabon (1943)

Marcus Servilius Nonianus: Africa [i] (46–47)

Servius Cornelius Cethegus: Africa [i] (36–37)

Servius Cornelius Scipio Salvidienus Orfitus: Africa [i] (62–63)

Servius Cornelius Scipio Salvidienus Orfitus: Africa [i] (164)

Servius Sulpicius Galba: Africa [i] (44–46)

Sesostris I Kheperkare: Egypt (12th Dynasty)

Sesostris II Khakheperre: Egypt (12th Dynasty)

Sesostris III Khakaure: Egypt (12th Dynasty)

Sesostris IV Seneferibre: Egypt (13th Dynasty)

Setepkare Astabarqamen: Kush (510–487 B.C.)

Seti II Usikheperure Merneptah: Egypt (19th Dynasty)

Seti Menmare Merneptah: Egypt (19th Dynasty)

Setlhare: Barolongland

Rameses XI Menmare Setneptah: Egypt (20th Dynasty)

Setneptah Usire Pshenmut: Egypt (29th Dynasty)

Rameses IV Hekamare Setpenamun: Egypt (20th Dynasty)

Setpenanhur Irmaerne Djeho: Egypt (30th Dynasty)

Rameses IX Neferkare Setpenre: Egypt (20th Dynasty)

Rameses X Khepermare Setpenre: Egypt (20th Dynasty)

Setshele I: Bakwenaland

Setshele II: Bakwenaland

Seuserenre: Egypt (17th Dynasty)

Jean Seval: Réunion (1980–81)

Pierre Sevellac: Mayotte Department

Jan Van Sevenhuysen: Dutch Gold Coast (1696–1702)

Severus: Africa [i] (155–157)

Severus: Africa Proconsularis (382)

Julius Severus: Egypt (32)

Sebekhotep III Sekhemre Sewadjtowy: Egypt (13th Dynasty)

Sewesewenre Khayan: Egypt (15th Dynasty)

Publius Sextilius: Carthage

Sextus Cocceius Severianus Honorinus: Africa [i] (163–164)

Sextus Julius Major: Africa [i] (141–142)

Sextus Petronius Probus: Africa Proconsularis (358, 367–375, 383–384, 387–388)

Roger Seydoux Fornier de Clausonne: Tunisia (1955–56)

Seyid Ali: Zanzibar (1890–93)

Seyni Kountché: Niger (1974–87)

Amda Seyon: Ethiopia (1314–44)

Egwala Seyon: Ethiopia (1801–18)

Hezba Seyon: Axum

Yagbe'a Seyon: Ethiopia (1285–94)

Amda Seyon II: Ethiopia (1494)

Rachid Sfar: Tunisia (1986–87)

Sghair Ould M'Bareck: Mauritania (2003–)

Muhamman Sha: Daura-Zango

Shaabaan I: Egypt (1344–45)

Shaabaan II: Egypt (1363–68)

Shaba: Nupe

Neferkare Shabaha II: Kush (ca. 700 B.C.)

Shabaka: Egypt (25th Dynasty)

Hajji Shaban: Algiers (1592–94)

Shaban: Algiers (1661–65)

Shaban: Algiers (1688–95)

Shafau: Daura

Ali Shehu Shagari: Nigeria (1979–83)

Shah Malik: Tripolitania (1095)

Shahah ad-Din: Adal [ii]

al-Afdal Shahanshah: Egypt (1094–1121)

Shahel: Axum (401–402)

Shahel: Axum (446–448)

Abu Yahya Abu Bakr ash-Shahid: Hafsid Kingdom

Lala Shahin: Egypt (1560–64)

Shahsuwar-Zade-Ghazi: Egypt (1657–60)

Hassan Shahu: Fulani Empire

Shaka: Zululand

Shamamun: Dongola

Mubarrak ash-Shamikh: Libya

Shams ad-Din: Adal [ii]

Muhammad Shamte Hamadi: Zanzibar (1961–64)

Shanakdakhete: Kush (170–160 B.C.)

Sharaf: Egypt (1647–49)

Hassan ash-Sharawi: Egypt (1752–55)

Muhamma Sharefa: Kano (1702–30)

Sharif: Wadai

Ibrahim ash-Sharif: Tunis (1702–04)

Muhammad I ash-Sharif: Morocco (1631–35)

Muhammad Sharif: Wadai

Dogon Sharki: Yauri

Alfred Sharpe: Malawi (1894, 1896–1910)

Thomas Sharpless: Senegambia Colony

Sharuf: Wadai

Bryan Sharwood-Smith: Nigeria Northern Region

Muhamman Shashere: Kano (1572–82)

Shashimi: Daura

Shata: Daura

Hassan Muhammad Nur Shatigadud: Southwestern Somalia

John Shaw: Lagos (1874)

Lol Muhammad Shawa: Chad (1979)

Shawar: Egypt (1163, 1164–69)

Shawata: Daura

Shayban: Egypt (904–905)

Sheikh Muhammad Shayin: Tagant

Shebitku: Egypt (25th Dynasty)

Jadkaure Shebitku: Kush (ca. 650 B.C.)

Sekhemre Shedtowe Sebekemsaf: Egypt (17th Dynasty)

Sekhemre Shedwast: Egypt (17th Dynasty)

Muhammadu Shefe: Argungu

Sheger ad-Durr: Egypt (1249–50)

Shehu Musa Yar Adua: Nigeria (1976–83)

Ali Shehu Shagari: Nigeria (1979–83)

Shehu Umar Watara: Kong

Muhammad ash-Sheikh: Morocco (1465–1505)

Sa'id Muhammad Sheikh: Comoros (1961–70)

Sheikh Abd as-Salaam al-Asman: Tripolitania (1480–82)

Sheikh Abidin al-Bakha'i: Masina

Sheikh Abu Yahya: Tripolitania (1146–48, 1160–72)

Sheikh Abubakr: Mogadishu

Sheihk Ahmad: Anjouan

Sheikh Ahmad az-Zarraq: Tripolitania (1489–94)

Sheikh al-Afia Ould Muhammad Khouna: Mauritania (1996–2003)

Sheikh al-Khalifa: Trarza

Sheikh al-Mu'aiyad: Egypt (1412–21)

Ahmad ben Sheikh Attoumane: Comoros (1993–94)

Sheikh Hassana: Adrar

Sheikh Hussein: Algiers (1613–16, 1617–19, 1638–40)

Sheikh Mahl Aynin: Brakna

Sheikh Muhammad: Mogadishu

Sheikh Muhammad Abu'l Kaylak: Kordofan

Sheikh Muhammad Fadl: Trarza
Sheikh Muhammad Shayin: Tagant
Sheikh Sa'd Bu: Trarza
Sheikh Salim: Anjouan
Shekanda: Dongola
Shekkarau: Kano (1290–1306)
Shekkarau: Kano (1649–50)
Sheku Bochari Kawusu Conteh: Sierra
Leone (1970)
Shemakone Kalonga Wina: Barotse-
land
Capt. Sheppard: Sierra Leone (1871)
Shepsekaf: Egypt (4th Dynasty)
Shepseskare: Egypt (5th Dynasty)
Tefnakhte Shepsesre: Egypt (24th Dy-
nasty)
John W. Shepstone: Zululand
Theophilus Shepstone: Transkeian
Territories
W.G.B. Shepstone: Idutywa
Mustafa Sherif: Tripolitania (1620–31)
Sherif Koja: Algiers (1619–21)
Sherif Pasha: Egypt (1882, 1883–84)
Abdi Rashid Shermarke: Somalia
Mayebre Sheshni: Egypt (15th Dy-
nasty)
Sheshonk I Hedjkheperre: Egypt
(22nd Dynasty)
Sheshonk II Hekenkheperre: Egypt
(22nd Dynasty)
Sheshonk III Usermare: Egypt (22nd
Dynasty)
Sheshonk IV: Egypt (23rd Dynasty)
Sheshonk V Akheperre: Egypt (22nd
Dynasty)
Sheshonk VI: Egypt (23rd Dynasty)
Amenemhet I Shetepibre: Egypt (12th
Dynasty)
Shiazana: Axum
Uushona Shiimi: Ovamboland
Kaina Shinyunbo: Songhai (1120–39)
Sidney Shippard: Botswana; British
Bechuanaland
Shirkuh: Egypt (1169)
Shiruma: Gobir
Shishak: Egypt (22nd Dynasty)
Shi'ta: Ilorin
Shi'ta Aliyu: Ilorin
Shomoye: Abeokuta
Ernest Shonekan: Nigeria (1993)
Dzeliwe Shongwe: Swaziland (1982–
83)
Shu'aibu: Ilorin
Shu'aibu Madara: Yauri
John Shuckburgh: Nigeria (1940)
Bako Shukunu: Zaria (1660–70)
Badi IV Abu Shulukh: Funj Sultanate
George Shute: Nigeria Eastern Region
Shuwa: Kanem
Malik Si: Futa Jallon
Si Ahmad at-Tazi: Tangier (1954–56)
Si Halil Bu Hajib ben Salim: Tunisia
(1926–32)
Si Mustafa Dingizli: Tunisia (1922–
26)
Siamon Nutekheperre: Egypt (21st
Dynasty)
Boa Siante: Denkyira

Adrien Sibomana: Burundi [ii]
Barnabas Sibusiso Dhlamini: Swazi-
land (1996–2003)
Domenico Siciliani: Cyrenaica
Jean-Charles Sicurani: Mali (1958–
60)
Sid Ahmad Ghozali: Algeria (1991–
92)
Badi I Sid al-Qum: Funj Sultanate
Ala ad-Din Pasha Siddiq: Sudan
(1883)
Ahmad Salem Ould Sidi: Mauritania
(1979)
Badi Sidi: Masina
Moukhtar Sidi: Brakna
Muhammad Sidi: Brakna
Sidi Abd al-Kadiri: Zaria (1853–54)
Sidi Ahmad: Adrar
Sidi Ahmad III: Adrar
Sidi Ahmad IV: Adrar
Sidi Ahmad Ould Bneijara: Maurita-
nia (1980–81)
Ould Sidi Ahmad Salum: Trarza
Maaouya Ould Sidi Ahmad Taya:
Mauritania (1981–)
Sidi al-Bakka: Masina
Sidi Ali I: Brakna
Sidi Ali II: Brakna
Sidi Ali Diombot: Trarza
Sidi Buya: Trarza
Sidi Mbairika: Trarza
Sidi Muhammad: Brakna
Sidi Muhammad al-Hadi al-Ahwa:
Tunisia (1932–42)
Sidi Muhammad ben Mulay Arafa:
Morocco (1953–55)
Sidi Muhammad ben Yusuf: Morocco
(1927–53, 1955–61)
Sidi Muhammad Ould Boubakar:
Mauritania (1992–96)
Sidi Ould Deid: Trarza
Sidi Umaru: Keffi
Sidia Touré: Guinea (1996–99)
Mande Sidibe: Mali (2000)
Sidiku: Katsina (1835–44)
Lamine Sidimé: Guinea (1999–2004)
Sidiq Abubakr: Fulani Empire
Gangia Sidje: Allada
Atif Sidqi: Egypt (1986–96)
Aziz Sidqi: Egypt (1972–73)
Ismail Sidqi Pasha: Egypt (1930–33,
1946)
Sidqi Suleiman: Egypt (1966–67)
Banja Tejan-Sié: Sierra Leone (1968–
71)
Muhammadu na Sifawa: Argungu
Mokdad Sifi: Algeria (1994–95)
Sigcau: Pondoland East
Botha Sigcau: Transkei
Stella Sigcau: Transkei
Sigcawu: Kreli's Country
Andani Sigili: Dagomba
Sigiri: Wadai
Sigiri: Yauri
Abu Abdallah as-Si'i al-Muhtasab:
Tunis (909–910)
Okunade Adele Sijuwade Olubuse: Ife
Sikhomo: Transkeian Territories

Sikiru Adetona Ogbagba II: Ijebu
Sikomo: Transkeian Territories
Simon Sikosana: KwaNdebele
Silahdar: Egypt (1664–67)
Silahdar: Egypt (1733–34)
Silahdar Mahir: Egypt (1766–67)
Silamaran: Masina
Marcus Junius Silanus: Africa [i] (29–
35)
Ali Silek: Wadai
Silimela: Tembuland
Anthony Sillery: Botswana; Madagas-
car (1942–43)
Silumbu: Barotseland
Silumelume: Barotseland
Mwana Silundu: Barotseland
Diogo da Silva: Mombasa (1646–48)
Duarte da Silva: São Tomé (1591–92)
Francisco da Silva: Cape Verde (1606–
11)
Francisco da Silva: Guinea-Bissau
(1887–88); Mozambique (1893–
94); São Tomé and Príncipe (1882–
84)
João da Silva: Mozambique (1824–
25)
João Baptista da Silva: São Tomé and
Príncipe (1799–1802)
José da Silva: Bissau (1853–54)
José da Silva: Mombasa (1658–63)
Júlio Moniz da Silva: Mozambique
(1642–46)
Luis da Silva: Angola (1684–88)
Manuel da Silva: Madeira (1648–51)
Manuel da Silva: Mozambique
(1674–76)
Martim da Silva: Ceuta (1549–50,
1553–55)
Martinho da Silva: Portuguese Gold
Coast (1505)
Paulo da Silva: Cacheu (1634)
Pedro da Silva: Madeira (1618–22);
Portuguese Gold Coast (1613–15)
Pedro da Silva: São Tomé (1661)
Pedro da Silva: Tangier (1578)
Simão da Silva: Mozambique (1673–
74)
Manuel da Silva Botelho: Cacheu
(1640)
Pedro da Silva da Cunha: Madeira
(1655–60)
Gomes da Silva de Vasconcelos: Ceuta
(1519–21, 1525–29)
João da Silva e Sousa: Angola (1680–
84)
Marcus Pompeius Silvanus Staberius
Flavinus: Africa [i] (53–56)
Maria do Carmo Silveira: São Tomé
and Príncipe (2005–)
Francisco da Silveira: Mozambique
(1641–42)
Simão de Silveira: Mozambique (1577)
Luis Silvela y Casado: Spanish Mo-
rocco (1923)
Achille Silvestre: Djibouti (1935)
Simeon: Dongola
Sulpicius Simius: Egypt (109–116)
Simon: Dongola

Robert Simon: Guinea (1925–25)
Carlo De Simone: Italian Somaliland (1940–41)
Paul Simoni: Djibouti (1915–16)
F. Simpson: Lagos (1878)
W.H. Simpson: Ghana (1868–69); Lagos (1870–71)
Sinan: Egypt (1567–68, 1571–73, 1585–87); Tunis (1574–76)
Uthman Ould Fadl Ould Sinan: Adrar
John Sinclair: Zanzibar (1922–23)
Théodore Sindikubwayo: Rwanda
Sindozan: Dahomey
Fa Sine: Segu
al-Hajji Sir Farimang Singhateh: Gambia (1966–70)
Sini: Yatenga
Sipopa: Barotseland
Siptah Akhenre Merneptah: Egypt (19th Dynasty)
Sira Bo: Kaarta
Sirabo: Kaarta
Amadi Sire: Masina
Disa Siri: Fika
Paul Sirieix: Djibouti (1946–50); Guinea (1951–53)
Sirr al-Khatim al-Khalifah: Sudan (1964–65)
Ali Pasha Sirri: Sudan (1854)
Hussein Sirry Pasha: Egypt (1940–42, 1949–50, 1952)
Sirtengi: Gobir
Majan Dyabe Sisse: Ghana Empire
Siti Kazurukamusapa: Mwene Mutapa Empire
Publius Sitius: Numidia
Tausert Sitre Meryamun: Egypt (19th Dynasty)
Abd ar-Rahman Siwar ad-Dahab: Sudan (1985–86)
Muhammad Siyad Barre: Somalia
Ezekiel Skinner: Liberia (1835–36)
James Skinner: Fort James
John Skottowe: Saint Helena (1764–82)
Bernard Sladous: Togo (1927–28)
Ransford Slater: Ghana (1915, 1916–17, 1919, 1920, 1927–32); Sierra Leone (1922–27)
Rudolf Karl Slatin: Darfur
Herbert Sloley: Lesotho (1895, 1901–15)
Abraham Sluysken: Cape Colony (1793–95)
David Smallman: Saint Helena (1995–99)
Samuel Smart: Sierra Leone (1826, 1828)
Smendes: Egypt (21st Dynasty)
Smenkhare Ankheprure: Egypt (18th Dynasty)
Sekhemre Smentowe Djehuty: Egypt (17th Dynasty)
Smerdis: Egypt (27th Dynasty)
Samuel Smidt: Danish Gold Coast (1658–59)
Dirk Smient: Mauritius (1668–69)

Lt.-Col. Smith: Sierra Leone (1861–62)
Andrew Juxon-Smith: Sierra Leone (1967–68)
Bryan Sharwood-Smith: Nigeria Northern Region
Charles Euan-Smith: Zanzibar (1888–91)
George Smith: Malawi (1913–23); Mauritius (1911)
Harry Smith: British Kaffraria; Cape Colony (1847–52)
Ian Smith: Zimbabwe (1964–79)
James Smith: Liberia (1871–72)
John Smith: Saint Helena (1723–27)
John Hope Smith: Ghana (1817–22)
Lionel Smith: Mauritius (1840–42)
Reginald H. Smith: Italian Somaliland (1941)
Sydney MacDonald-Smith: Gold Coast Northern Territories
Victor Valentin-Smith: Gabon (1941–42)
Walter Buchanan-Smith: Nigeria Southern Provinces
Joel Smits: Dutch Gold Coast (1690–94)
Jan Smuts: South Africa (1919–24, 1939–48)
Henry Smyth: Cape Colony (1889)
Charles Smythe: Natal (1905–06)
Leicester Smythe: Cape Colony (1881, 1883–84)
Nekhtharehbe Snedjembre: Egypt (30th Dynasty)
Snefru: Egypt (4th Dynasty)
Snofru: Egypt (4th Dynasty)
John Snow: Fort James
Elias Snyman: Orange Free State (1859)
Lord Soames: Zimbabwe (1979–80)
Soarba: Wagadugu
João Soares: Angola (1924)
Diogo Soares de Albergaria: Portuguese Gold Coast (1545, 1550–52)
Lopo Soares de Albergaria: Portuguese Gold Coast (1493)
Rui Soares de Melo: Mombasa (1598–1606)
Soba Dan Doro: Gobir
Sobhuza I: Swaziland (1818–36)
Sobhuza II: Swaziland (1899–1982)
Sodeke: Abeokuta
Julius von Soden: German East Africa; Kamerun (1885–87, 1888–89)
Sodji: Porto-Novo
José Sodré: São Tomé (1695–96)
Francisco Sodré Pereira: Cacheu (1625)
Said Muhammad Soefou: Mwali
Sogdianos: Egypt (423)
Sogiji: Daura
Christophe Soglou: Benin [ii] (1963–64, 1965–67)
Nicéphore Soglou: Benin [ii] (1991–96)
Soidri Ahmad: Mwali

Ali Soilih: Comoros (1975, 1976–78)
Edward M. Sokoine: Tanzania
Christopher de Solefertan: Tripolitania (1542–51)
Léon Solomiac: French Equatorial Africa (1938–39); Mali (1933); Niger (1940); Senegal (1933)
Richard Solomon: Transvaal (1905–06)
Solomon Dinuzulu: Zululand
Suleiman Solong: Darfur
Soma: Segu
Lord Charles Somerset: Cape Colony (1814–26)
Somhlolo: Swaziland (1818–36)
Sonni Ali: Songhai (1464–92)
Quintus Marcius Barea Soranus: Africa [i] (41–43)
Alphonse Sordeaux: Gabon (1848)
Julien Soret: Senegal (1837–39)
Alfa Ibrahima Sori: Futa Jallon
Umaru Sori: Futa Jallon
Ibrahima Sori I: Futa Jallon
Ibrahima Sori II: Futa Jallon
Ibrahima Sori III: Futa Jallon
Giorgio Sorrentino: Italian Somaliland (1897–98)
Lope de Sosa y Mesa; Gran Canaria
Soshangane: Gazaland
Sosibius: Egypt (221–202 B.C.)
Gustavo de Sostoa y Sthamer: Equatorial Guinea
Sosus: Mauretania West
Ptolemy Soter: Egypt (323–282 B.C.); Pentapolis
Ptolemy I Soter I: Egypt (323–282 B.C.)
Ptolemy IX Soter II: Egypt (116–110 B.C., 109–107 B.C., 80 B.C.)
Jerónimo de Sotomayor: Tenerife
José de Sotomayor: Ceuta (1791–92)
Luis de Sotomayor: Melilla (1625–32, 1649)
Fernando Álvarez de Sotomayor y Flórez: Spanish Morocco (1907–08)
Sotsha Ernest Dhlamini: Swaziland (1985–89)
Jean-Louis Soucadaux: Cameroun (1950–54); French Equatorial Africa (1946–48); Madagascar (1953–60)
Alphonse Poaty-Souchalaty: Congo (1989–90)
François de Souillac: Mauritius (1779–87); Réunion (1776–79); Seychelles (1783–86)
Souley Abdulaye: Niger (1994–95)
Soumana Sacko: Mali (1991–92)
Sounsan: Kaarta
Jean-Michel Soupault: Congo (1956–58)
Sourou Apithy: Benin [ii] (1958–59, 1964–65)
Afonso de Sousa: São Tomé and Príncipe (1948–50, 1953)
Antonio de Sousa: Angola (1851–53)
Carlos de Sousa: Bissau (1847–48)
Cristóvão de Sousa: Madeira (1600–03)

Cristóvão de Sousa: São Tomé (1560–64)

Diogo de Sousa: Mozambique (1553–57)

Fernão de Sousa: Angola (1624–30)

Francisco de Sousa: Madeira (1628–34)

João de Sousa: Angola (1621–23); Cacheu (1614–15)

Pedro de Sousa: Mozambique (1590–95)

Francisco de Sousa Coutinho: Angola (1764–72)

Lopo de Sousa Coutinho: Portuguese Gold Coast (1541, 1548–50)

José de Sousa e Faroo: São Tomé and Príncipe (1915)

Álvaro de Sousa e Macedo: Madeira (1830–34)

Antonio de Sousa e Meneses: Cape Verde (1777–81)

Jorge de Sousa e Meneses: Madeira (1718–24)

Manuel de Sousa e Meneses: Cape Verde (1757–61)

Pires de Sousa e Meneses: Angola (1676–80); Madeira (1669–72)

Luis de Sousa e Vasconcelos e Funchal: Mozambique (1947–48)

Isidro de Almeida Sousa e Sá: Mozambique (1801–05)

Bento de Sousa Lima: São Tomé (1686–89)

José Sousa Faro: Angola (1930–31)

Bartolomeu de Sousa Tigre: Cape Verde (1764–66)

M. de Soussy: Senegal (1649–50)

Jacques Soustelle: Algeria (1955–56)

Richard Southey: Griqualand West

Thomas Southorn: Gambia (1936–42)

Abel Souto-Maior: Angola (1941–42)

Álvaro Souto-Maior: São Tomé (1493–99)

Filipe de Souto-Maior: Bissau (1763)

Francisco de Souto-Maior: Angola (1645–46); Portuguese Gold Coast (1624–25)

Francisco Souto-Maior: Cacheu (1751–55)

Francisco de Souto-Maior: Mozambique (1715–19)

José Souto-Maior: São Tomé (1736–41)

Leonardo Souto-Maior: Mombasa (1698)

Lourenço de Souto-Maior: Mozambique (1634–39)

Sebastião da Cunha Souto-Maior: Bissau (1770–75)

Sebastião Souto-Maior: Cacheu (1765–70)

André Chalvet de Souville: Réunion (1781–85)

Anna de Souza Nzina: Ndongo

Abdulaye Sékou Sow: Mali (1993–94)

Soyaki: Kano (1651)

Georges-Léon Spénale: Togo (1957–60)

Jean Spéville: Rodrigues (ii)

A.T. Spies: Utrecht

Antonio de Spínola: Guinea-Bissau (1968–73)

Gordon Sprigg: Cape Colony (1878–81, 1886–90, 1896–98, 1900–04)

Marcus Pompeius Silvanus Staberius Flavinus: Africa [i] (53–56)

Edward Stace: British Kaffraria

Lee Stack: Sudan (1917–24)

Herbert Stanley: South Africa (1931–36); Zambia (1924–27); Zimbabwe (1935–42)

Richard Stanley: Zambia (1947–48)

Jan Staphorst: Dutch Gold Coast (1694–96)

Robert Stapledon: Nigeria Eastern Region

Calvisius Statianus: Egypt (175–177)

Titus Statilius Taurus: Africa [i] (52–53)

Constantine Stavropoulos: Namibia (1967)

Théodore Steeg: Algeria (1921–25); French Morocco

Mario Di Stefani: Italian Somaliland (1958–60)

Peter Steffens: Danish Gold Coast (1821)

Jean Steinauer: Réunion (1773–76)

Herr Steinhausen: Kamerun (1910)

Pierre Steinmetz: Réunion (1995)

Symon Van Der Stel: Cape Colony (1679–99)

Willem Van Der Stel: Cape Colony (1699–1707)

Stella Sigcau: Transkei

Jean Stenauer: Mauritius (1768–69)

Léopold Stéphan: Senegal (1861)

Hugh Stephenson: Lesotho (1964–66)

Robert Sterndale: Saint Helena (1897–1903)

Wasey Sterry: Sudan (1924–25)

Stettius Africanus: Egypt (82–86)

Siaka P. Stevens: Sierra Leone (1967, 1968–85)

Hubert Stevenson: Ashanti; Sierra Leone (1941–47)

Malcolm Stevenson: Seychelles (1927–28)

William Stevenson: Mauritius (1857–63)

Donald Stewart: Ashanti; Kenya (1904–05)

Henry Stewart: Seychelles (1895–99)

Hermanus Steyn: Swellendam

J.C. Steyn: Utrecht

L.C. Steyn: South Africa (1961–61)

Marthius Steyn: Namibia (1977–79)

Marthinus Steyn: Orange Free State (1896–1902, 1906–10)

Otto Stiel: Fort James

Robert Frederick Stimson: Saint Helena (1988–91)

Andries Stockenstroom: British Kaffraria

George Beresford-Stooke: Sierra Leone (1947–52)

Ronald Storrs: Zambia (1932–34)

Seius Strabo: Egypt (37–38)

George Strahan: Cape Colony (1880–81); Ghana (1874–76); Lagos (1873–74)

Valentine Strasser: Sierra Leone (1992–96)

William Streeten: Sierra Leone (1880–81)

Johannes Strijdom: South Africa (1954–58)

Robert Stringer: Saint Helena (1661–71)

John Sturrock: Lesotho (1926–35); Uganda (1924)

John Styles: Saint Helena (2004)

Claude Wong Su: Rodrigues (ii)

Bako Su Aliyu: Zaria (1597–1608)

Su'aidi Ahmad: Tagant

Subatianus Aquila: Egypt (202–215)

Sufi: Egypt (1611–15)

Sufi: Egypt (1667–68)

Ali Sufu: Egypt (1564–66)

Sufi Abu Talib: Egypt (1981)

Sugunum: Yatenga

Suhal: Axum

Osman Reis as-Suhali: Tripolitania (1672)

Hendrik von Suhm: Danish Gold Coast (1724–27)

Lat Sukaabe: Baol; Kayor

Sukana: Zaria (1505)

Sukda: Mandara

Mangi Suku: New Calabar

Sule: Bedde

Sule: Fika

Sule-Budu: Futa Toro

Sule Ladi: Daniski

Suleiman: Algiers (1599–1603)

Suleiman: Egypt (1525–35, 1536–38)

Suleiman: Egypt (1704)

Suleiman: Fika

Suleiman: Ghana Empire

Suleiman: Gonja

Suleiman: Katsina (1655–67)

Suleiman: Mali Empire

Suleiman: Morocco (1793–1822)

Suleiman: Timbuktu (1600–04)

Suleiman: Tripolitania (1610–20)

Suleiman: Wase

Abu Suleiman: Rustumid Amirate

Abu Suleiman: Zeng Empire (1217–59)

Abu'l Rabi Suleiman: Morocco (1308–10)

Sidqi Suleiman: Egypt (1966–67)

Umar Suleiman: Bedde

Suleiman I: Damagaram

Suleiman II: Damagaram

Suleiman al-Baruni: Tripolitania (1915–17); Tripolitanian Republic

Suleiman al-Hasan the Great: Zeng Empire (1158–77)

Suleiman al-Maghrebi: Libya

Suleiman Bey Harputli: Kordofan

Suleiman Daman: Songhai (1456–64)

Suleiman ibn Ali: Mombasa (1825–26)

Suleiman ibn Daud: Zeng Empire (1357–58)
Suleiman ibn Ghalib: Egypt (816–817)
Suleiman ibn Hasan: Zeng Empire (1293–1308)
Suleiman ibn Hussein: Zeng Empire (1366–68)
Suleiman ibn Muhammad: Zeng Empire (1425–47)
Suleiman ibn Muhammad: Zeng Empire (1482–83)
Suleiman ibn Suleiman: Zeng Empire (1368–92)
Suleiman Katanya: Algiers (1616–17)
Suleiman Solong: Darfur
Suleiman the Tyrant: Zeng Empire (1115–17)
Suleiman Tiya Adamu Jumba: Bauchi
Suleimana: Argungu
Suleimana: Zamfara
Suleimanu: Daura-Zango
Suleimanu: Ilorin
Suleimanu: Katagum
Suleimanu I: Argungu
Suleimanu II: Argungu
Bashir Suleimanu Barau: Abuja
Suleimanu Barau: Abuja
Suleimanu Dan Addo: Yauri
Suleimanu Jerabana: Yauri
Suli: Gombe
Sulimano: Zaria (ca. 1180)
Sulimanu: Kano (1807–19)
Bartholomew Sullivan; Seychelles (1811–12)
Quintus Sulpicius Camerinus Peticus: Africa [i] (56–57)
Servius Sulpicius Galba: Africa [i] (44–46)
Sulpicius Simius: Egypt (109–116)
Juwan Qapiji Sultanzade: Egypt (1637–40)
Sulu Gambari: Ilorin
Sumanguru: Ghana Empire
Sumani Zoli: Dagomba
Frederick Sumaye: Tanzania
Sumayla Ndewura Dyakpa: Gonja
Gerald Summers: British Somaliland
Suna I: Buganda
Suna II: Buganda
Sundiata Keita: Kangaba; Mali Empire
Ilunga Sunga: Luba
Bukaar Biye-Sungule: Dyolof
Ada Sunguma: Daura
Sunni Ali: Songhai (1464–92)
Sunsa: Kaarta
Ibrahim Sura: Katsina (1541–43)
William Surmon: Lesotho (1870–71)
Susneyos: Ethiopia (1607–32)
George Sutton: Natal (1903–05)
Christian Svanekjaer: Danish Gold Coast (1819–21)
Peter Sverdrup: Danish Gold Coast (1704–05)
Swadjenre Nebirierau: Egypt (17th Dynasty)

Charles Swart: South Africa (1958, 1960–67)
Marthinus Swarte: Dutch Gold Coast (1834)
Eric Swayne: British Somaliland
Nikolaas Sweerts: Dutch Gold Coast (1685–90)
Ernest Sweet-Escott: Seychelles (1899–1904)
Hendrik Swellengrebel: Cape Colony (1739–51)
Syagrius: Africa Proconsularis (382)
Jacques Sylla: Madagascar (2002–)
Stewart Symes: Sudan (1934–40); Tanganyika
Symmachus: Byzantine North Africa
Quintus Aurelius Symmachus: Africa Proconsularis (373)
Christian Syndermann: Danish Gold Coast (1723–24)
Synesius Hadrianus: Africa Proconsularis (413–414)
Rufus Synesius Hadrianus: Africa Proconsularis (400–405)
Capt. Synge: Southern Nigeria
Annius Syriacus: Egypt (163–165)

T

Taanor: Dyolof
Mahmud Taba II: Timbuktu (1597–99)
Marqués de los Tabalosos: Canary Islands (1775–79)
Tabany-Yasy: Egypt (1628–30)
Tabarau: Zamfara
Tabirqa: Kush (200–185 B.C.)
Tabl: Funj Sultanate
Tabl II: Funj Sultanate
Bernardo Tacón: Ceuta (1837)
Bourkomanda Tad Lélé: Baguirmi
Ras Dejazmatch Tafari: Ethiopia (1916–74)
Tafarilu: Yauri
Abubaka Tafawa Balewa: Nigeria (1957–66)
Emidio Tafeng Lodongi: Southern Sudan
Tafida: Daura-Zango
Tafida: Muri
Muhammadu Dan Tagande: Argungu
Tagwai: Biram
Tahar ben Ammar: Tunisia (1954–56)
Taharqa: Egypt (25th Dynasty)
Taher Pasha: Egypt (1803–03)
Tahir: Tripolitania (1837–38)
Tahir I: Fezzan
Tahir II: Fezzan
Tahle: Pondoland
Muhammad II Tairab: Darfur
Campbell Tait: Zimbabwe (1945–46)
Tajjidine ben Sa'id Massonde: Comoros (1996, 1998–99)
Takelot I Usermare: Egypt (22nd Dynasty)
Takelot II Hedjkheperre: Egypt (22nd Dynasty)

Takelot III: Egypt (23rd Dynasty)
Takhos: Egypt (30th Dynasty)
Muhammad Taki Abdulkarim: Comoros (1992, 1995, 1996–98)
Takideamani: Kush (146–165)
Takla Giyorgis: Ethiopia (1779–84, 1788–89, 1794–95, 1795–96, 1798–99, 1800)
Takla Giyorgis II: Ethiopia (1868–72)
Takla Haymanot: Ethiopia (1706–08)
Takla Haymanot II: Ethiopia (1769–77)
Takla Maryam: Ethiopia (1430–33)
Takoi: Songhai (861–873)
Takyi Akwamo: Bono
Talakhamane: Kush (435–431 B.C.)
Abdelkader Taleb Oumar: Western Sahara
Talha: Harar
Talha ibn al-Abbas: Harar
Badi Tali: Masina
Sufi Abu Talib: Egypt (1981)
Talib Hiyar: Brakna
Talut ibn Hussein: Zeng Empire (1364–66)
Talut ibn Suleiman: Zeng Empire (1180–81)
al-Buri Tam: Dyolof
Bakaa-Tam Buri-Nyabu: Dyolof
Bakan-Tam Khaari: Dyolof
Bakan-Tam Yaago: Dyolof
Abdu na Tamane: Zamfara
Tamasiga: Bamangwatoland
Muhammad Tambari: Fulani Empire
Tamelerdeamani: Kush (266–283)
Tamim: Zirid Kingdom
Tamirat Laynie: Ethiopia (1991–95)
Tammam: Omayyad and Abbasid North Africa
Lucius Tampius Flavianus: Africa [i] (51–52)
Mari Watila Tampta: Biu
Tamsulat: Tripolitania (977–1000)
Tamusa: Zaria (ca. 1120)
Solomon Tandeng: Cameroun (1968–72)
Tandja Mamadou: Niger (1999–)
Tani Fara N'dyak: Walo (1531–42)
Tanimun: Damagaram
Tanimun II: Damagaram
Alikolo Tankari: Nupe
Tanoma: Gumel
Dan Tanoma: Gumel
Tanor Gogne: Baol
Tantiari: Gurma
Tanuatamon: Egypt (25th Dynasty)
Bakare Tanuatamun: Kush (ca. 650 B.C.)
Naatago Tany: Walo (1287–1304)
Tanyidamani: Kush (120–100 B.C.)
Sekenenre Tao I: Egypt (17th Dynasty)
Sekenenre Tao II: Egypt (17th Dynasty)
Pierre Tap: Guinea (1937–38)
Tapri Traore: Kenedugu
Taraore: Kangaba
Tarekeniwal: Kush (85–103)

Édouard Dubosc-Taret: Congo (1908, 1910–11)
Taritu: Zamfara
Arghuz Tarkhan: Egypt (868)
Tarkhunji: Egypt (1649–51)
Arthur Tarleton: Sierra Leone (1884)
Bianrifi Tarmidi: Comoros (1999–2000)
Conde de Tarouca: Tangier (1486–89, 1501–08)
Conde de Tarouca: Tangier (1614–17)
Tasau: Zamfara
Tase Daagulen: Dyolof
Tasfa Iyasus: Ethiopia (1270–85)
Tasgarin Burum: Zamfara
Abu Umar Tashufin: Morocco (1361)
Abu Tashufin I Abd ar-Rahman: Tlemcen (1318–36)
Abu Tashufin II Abd ar-Rahman: Tlemcen (1389–93)
Abu Tashufin III: Tlemcen (1460–68)
Tashufin ibn Ali: Almoravid Empire
Giulio Cesare Tassoni: Tripolitania (1915)
Tatianus: Egypt (367–370, 372–374, 375–377)
Tatila Akufuna: Barotseland
Tau: Barolongland
Taukobong: Batlokwaland
Taurus: Africa Proconsularis (355–361)
Titus Statilius Taurus: Africa [i] (52–53)
Tausert Sitre Meryamun: Egypt (19th Dynasty)
Louis Tautain: Porto-Novo
Álvaro Távares: Angola (1960–61); Guinea-Bissau (1956–58)
Bernardino Távares: Angola (1701–03)
Constantino Távares: São Tomé (1609–11)
Álvaro de Távora: Madeira (1751–54)
Álvaro de Távora: Mozambique (1648–51)
Cristóvão de Távora: Mozambique (1515–18)
Fernão de Távora: Mozambique (1548–51)
Francisco de Távora: Angola (1669–76)
Francisco de Távora: Cacheu (1622)
João de Távora: Cacheu (1748–51)
Lourenço de Távora: São Tomé (1628–50)
Lourenço de Távora: Tangier (1564–66)
Tawana: Barolongland
Tawana: Batwanaland
Tawana II: Batwanaland
Maaouya Ould Sidi Ahmad Taya: Mauritania (1981–)
Tayar Warinki: Biu
Charles Taylor: Liberia (1997–2003)
John Taylor: Sierra Leone (1788)
Si Ahmad at-Tazi: Tangier (1954–56)
al-Hajj Muhammad at-Tazi Bu Ashran: Tangier (1923–41, 1945–54)

Simon Tchoungi: Cameroun (1965–72)
Té-Agbanlin I: Porto-Novo
Conde de Teba: Oran (1604–07)
Tebandeke: Buganda
Tebele: Bakgatlaland
Tebele: Bakwenaland
Ato Tedla Bairu: Eritrea
Tedla Haylu: Gojjam
N'dyak Aram Bakar Teedyek: Walo (1708–33)
Teferi Benti: Ethiopia (1974–77)
Tefnakhte Shepsesre: Egypt (24th Dynasty)
Yerim Mbanyik Teg: Walo (1821–23)
Fara Penda Teg Rel: Walo (1488–96)
Fara Penda Teg Rel: Walo (1780–92)
Tegbesu: Dahomey
Tegenkoro: Kaarta
Isa Tein-Dyor: Baol; Kayor
Constantino Teixeira: Guinea-Bissau (1978)
Gabriel Teixeira: Mozambique (1948–58)
Antonio de Tejada: Melilla (1571–95)
Ahmad Tejan Kebbah: Sierra Leone (1996–97, 1998–)
Banja Tejan-Sie: Sierra Leone (1968–71)
José Tejero: Western Sahara
Tekelerli: Algiers (1557)
Tekin al-Khassa al-Gezeri: Egypt (910–915, 919–921, 924–933)
Francisco Teles: São Tomé (1569–71)
Brás Teles de Meneses: Ceuta (1634–36)
Fernão Teles de Meneses: Ceuta (1637)
Francisco Teles de Meneses: São Tomé (1611)
Édouard Telle: Gabon (1907–08)
Théophile Tellier: Benin [ii] (1931–32); Niger (1931–33)
Tembo: Buganda
Temerbeg: Egypt (1467–68)
Isa Tende: Kayor
Temmam: Fezzan
Charles Temple: Nigeria Northern Region
Octavius Temple: Sierra Leone (1833–34)
Jakob Tenhoof: Hollandia
Johann Tenhoof: Hollandia
Tenin: Gurma
Marqués de Tenorio: Ceuta (1653–61)
Teqerideamani: Kush (246–266)
Jean Terasson de Fougères: Mali (1920, 1921–30)
Teridnide: Kush (228–246)
Teritedakhetey: Kush (194–209)
Teriteqas: Kush (33–24 B.C.)
Charles de Ternay: Mauritius (1772–76)
Éduard Terrac: Guinea (1946–48); Mauritania (1949–50)
Antonio Terrero: Ceuta (1801–05)
Attilio Teruzzi: Cyrenaica
Ibrahim Terzi: Tripolitania (1687)

Tesfaye Dinka: Ethiopia (1991)
Tesfaye Gebre Kidan: Ethiopia (1991)
Teslim Jinadu-Eko: Lagos (2003)
Teti: Egypt (6th Dynasty)
Lambert Van Tets: Dutch Gold Coast (1758–59)
Salim at-Teumi: Algiers (1516)
Earl of Teviot: Tangier (1663–64)
Thomas Tew: Libertalia
Tewfik: Mogadishu
Tewfiq: Egypt (1879–92)
Tewfiq Nesim Pasha: Egypt (1920–21)
Tewfiq Pasha: Egypt (1922–23)
Tewodoros I: Ethiopia (1411–14)
Tewodoros II: Ethiopia (1855–66)
Tewoflos: Ethiopia (1708–11)
Tewosre: Egypt (19th Dynasty)
Tshafe Tezaz Aklilu Habte-Wold: Ethiopia (1961–74)
Tezifon: Allada
Thaara: Gonja
Abu Thabit: Tlemcen (1348–52)
Thabit I ibn Ammar: Tripolitania (1327)
Thabit II: Tripolitania (1348–55)
Abu Thabit II Yusuf: Tlemcen (1393)
Abu Thabit Amir: Morocco (1307–08)
Themba Dhlamini: Swaziland (2003–)
Theoctistus: Byzantine North Africa
Theoctistus: Egypt (478–479)
Theodore I: Ethiopia (1411–14)
Theodore II: Ethiopia (1855–66)
Theodorus: Africa Proconsularis (408–409)
Theodorus: Byzantine North Africa
Theodorus: Egypt (451)
Theodorus: Egypt (487)
Theodorus: Egypt (641–642)
Flavius Antonius Theodorus: Egypt (338–354)
Mallius Theodorus: Africa Proconsularis (397–399)
Theodosius: Africa Proconsularis (430)
Theodosius: Egypt (510)
Theognostus: Egypt (479)
Ptolemy XIII Theos Philopator: Egypt (52–47 B.C.)
Ptolemy XIV Theos Philopator II: Egypt (47–44 B.C.)
Fernand Theron: Réunion (1905–06)
Thes: Lower Egypt
Habib Thiam: Senegal (1981–83, 1991–98)
Thibela: Barolongland
Thibron of Sparta: Pentapolis
Louis Thiébaud: Mali (1915–16)
A. Thiebault: Comoros (1844)
Georges Thiercy: Djibouti (1971–74)
Adolph Thierens: Dutch Gold Coast (1785–86)
Mamalik Thioro: Baol
Thlama Bahara: Biu
Georges Thomann: Congo (1922–23); Gabon (1917–18, 1921)
Thomas: Byzantine North Africa
John Thomas: Natal (1864–65)
Pierre Thomas: Senegal (1844–45)

Shenton Thomas: Ghana (1932–34); Malawi (1929–32)

Walter Thomas: Zimbabwe (1950)

Léon Clément-Thomas: Nossi-Bé; Senegal (1888–90)

Thomas Will: Aku

B. Thompson: Sierra Leone (1787)

George Thompson: Fort James

Graeme Thompson: Nigeria (1925–30)

Thomas Thompson: Sierra Leone (1808–10)

Aubrey Forsyth-Thompson: Botswana; Lesotho (1946–51)

Eric Thompstone: Nigeria Northern Region

Matthias Thønning: Danish Gold Coast (1821–23)

James Thorburn: Ghana (1910–12); Southern Nigeria Colony and Protectorate

John Thorp: Seychelles (1958–61)

Juan Andrés del Thoso: Melilla (1730–32)

Thrasamund: Vandal North Africa

Thomas Thurloe: Fort James

Thutlwa: Barolongland

Thutmose I Akheperkare: Egypt (18th Dynasty)

Thutmose II Akheperenre: Egypt (18th Dynasty)

Thutmose III Mankheperre: Egypt (18th Dynasty)

Thutmose IV Menkheprure: Egypt (18th Dynasty)

Ntombi Thwala: Swaziland (1983–86)

Ti-Kse Bldi: Mandara

Ti-Maya: Mandara

Tiande: Baol

Tib: Songhai (1139–58)

Tibi: Gran Comoro

Tidarpo: Gurma

Tié N'Della: Baol

Tié Tieumbeul: Baol

Tié-Yaasin Demba: Baol

Tié-Yaasin Dieng: Baol

Tié-Yaasin Gallo: Baol

Tié-Yaasin Ngone: Baol

Famagan denn Tieba: Gwiriko

Tieba Niandane Watara: Gwiriko

Tieba Traore: Kenedugu

Tié Tieumbeul: Baol

Bartolomeu de Sousa Tigre: Cape Verde (1764–66)

Auguste Tilkens: Congo (Zaire) (1927–34)

Librecht Timmink: Dutch Gold Coast (1823)

Nestorius Timonianus: Africa Proconsularis (337)

Juan Antonio Tineo y Fuertes: Ceuta (1745)

Antonio Tinoco: Cape Verde (1569–78)

René Tirant: Benin [ii] (1958–60); Djibouti (1962–66)

Louis Tirman: Algeria (1881–91)

Jean-Claude Tissier: Guinea (1928–28)

Flavius Titianus: Egypt (126–134, 166–167)

Psusennes I Titkheprure: Egypt (21st Dynasty)

Titus Flavius Vespasianus: Africa [i] (63–64)

Titus Prifernius Paetus Rosianus Geminus: Africa [i] (140–141, 161–162)

Titus Statilius Taurus: Africa [i] (52–53)

Tiu: Lower Egypt

Suleiman Tiya Adamu Jumba: Bauchi

Tjamuaha: Hereroland

Nani To: Kororofa

Carlos Tobía: Spanish Morocco (1857–58)

Jean-François Toby: Côte d'Ivoire (1943); Niger (1942–54)

Garfield Todd: Zimbabwe (1953–58)

Tofa: Porto-Novo

Abdullahi Toga: Argungu (1754–75)

Abdullahi Toga: Argungu (1860–63)

Togu: Transkeian Territories

Changamire Tohwechipe: Rozwi

Gerhardus du Toit: Orange Free State (1872–73)

Fara Toko: Walo (1485–88)

Tokta: Wase

Tokurma: Gurma

William Tolbert: Liberia (1971–80)

Juan de Toledo: Canary Islands (1665–66)

Diego de Toledo y Guzmán: Oran (1607–08)

Íñigo de Toledo y Osorio: Oran (1675–78)

Toli: Porto-Novo

Tom I: Koya-Temne

Tom II: Koya-Temne

François Tombalbaye: Chad (1959–75)

N'garta Tombalbaye: Chad (1959–75)

Joseph Tombura: Southern Sudan

Tomman Bey I: Egypt (1516–1517)

Tomo: Argungu

Tonmansa: Segu

Tonmassa Dembele: Segu

Hendrikus Tonneboeijer: Dutch Gold Coast (1836–37)

Tonugum: Yatenga

Tooman Bey: Egypt (1501–01)

William Topp: Ghana (1836–38)

Marqués de Torcifal: Ceuta (1646–53)

Moussa Toroma: Kenedugu

Torquatus: Egypt (396)

George Torrane: Ghana (1805–07)

Conde da Tôrre: Ceuta (1624–25)

Conde de la Torre: Tangier (1628–37)

Xavier Torré: Cameroun (1958–60)

Henry Torrens: Cape Colony (1886)

Antonio Torres: Bissau (1842–43)

Antonio de Torres: Gran Canaria

Juan García Torres: Spanish Morocco (1877)

Conde de Torres Vedras: Ceuta (1672–77)

Bernardo Tortosa: Melilla (1777–79)

José Torvão: Cacheu (1802–03)

Diego Toscano y Brito: Melilla (1680–83)

Tossu: Dahomey

Totebalobo: Yatenga

Athanase Touchard: Réunion (1693–96)

Tougouri: Yatenga

Tougouri II: Yatenga

Jules Ventre de la Touloubre: Comoros (1871–78); Nossi-Bé

Amadou Toumani Touré: Mali (1991–92, 2002–)

Comte Boyer de la Tour du Moulin: French Morocco; Tunisia (1954–55)

Muhammad Touray: Songhai (1493–1528, 1537–38)

Ahmed Sékou Touré: Guinea (1958–84)

Amadou Toumani Touré: Mali (1991–92, 2002–)

Samory Touré: Samory's Empire

Sidia Touré: Guinea (1996–99)

Younoussi Touré: Mali (1992–93)

Touro-Koro Mari: Segu

Antoine Touzet: Chad (1925)

Sancho de Tovar: Mozambique (1501–05, 1515, 1518–21)

Carlos Tovar de Revilla: Fernando Po

Muhammadu Toya Rero: Katsina (1568–72)

Muhammadu Toya Rero II: Katsina (1684–1701)

Toyi: Porto-Novo

Gbesso Toyi: Porto-Novo

Toyon: Porto-Novo

John Tozer: Fort James

Cleopatra VI Traephaeana: Egypt (80–58 B.C.)

Babemba Traore: Kenedugu

Daoula Ba Traore: Kenedugu

Diara Traoré: Guinea (1984)

Moussa Traoré: Mali (1968–91)

Nanka Traore: Kenedugu

Tapri Traore: Kenedugu

Teba Traore: Kenedugu

Daoula Ba Traore II: Kenedugu

Johan Trawne: Danish Gold Coast (1698–1703)

Clarkson Tredgold: Zimbabwe (1919)

Robert Tredgold: Zimbabwe (1953–54)

Ferdinand Tredos: Senegal (1869)

Marcel Treich-Laplène: Côte d'Ivoire (1886–90)

Hamelin Trelawny: Saint Helena (1842–46)

Marqués de Casa Tremañes: Ceuta (1776–83)

Louis de Trentinian: Mali (1895–98, 1899)

Trifolius: Africa Proconsularis (388–389)

Blas de Trincheria: Melilla (1704–07)
Jean Troadec: Chad (1956–58)
Johannes Troglita: Byzantine North
  Africa
Lothar von Trotha: Namibia (1904–
  05)
Miguel Trovoada: São Tomé and
  Príncipe (1975–79, 1991–2001)
Léon Truitard: Benin [ii] (1940–43);
  Réunion (1936–38)
Tsado: Nupe (1721–42)
Tsado: Nupe (1834–35)
Usman Tsagarana: Katsina (1585–89)
Tsagarana Gwozo: Katsina (1801–02)
Tsagarana Hassan: Katsina (1728–40)
Tsagarana Yahya: Katsina (1750–51)
Tsamia: Kano (1306–42)
Tsaraki: Kano (1135–93)
Tshafe Tezaz Aklilu Habte-Wold:
  Ethiopia (1971–74)
Tshawe: Transkeian Territories
Tshekedi Khama: Bamangwatoland
Tsherkes Iskander: Egypt (1568–71)
Tshesebe: Barolongland
Tshetshedji: Egypt (1623–24)
Étienne Tshisekedi wa Mulumba:
  Congo (Zaire) (1991, 1992–94,
  1997)
Tshiwo: Transkeian Territories
Moise Tshombe: Congo (Zaire)
  (1964–65); Katanga Republic
Tshosa: Bakwenaland
Tshosa: Bangwaketseland
Tshwaana: Batlokwaland
Tsiame Kenneth Mopale: QwaQwa
Tsile: Barolongland
Tsimiharo: Andruna
Philibert Tsiranana: Madagascar
  (1959–72)
Tsoacha: Nupe
Tsoede: Nupe
Tsofo: Daura; Daura-Baure
William Tubman: Liberia (1944–71)
Ignacio Tudela: Fernando Po
Tufoyn: Kom
Tukuariki: Zaria (1532–35)
Tukudu: Zamfara
Tukur: Biram
Tukur: Gombe
Tukur: Kano (1892–93)
Muhammad Tukur: Yauri
Muhammadu Tukur: Muri
Tulatem: Axum
Ryk Tulbagh: Cape Colony (1751–71)
Publius Tullius Varro: Africa [i] (142–
  143)
Tumbulki: Gobir
Tumelo: Bamaleteland
Tumku: Biram
Danagaram Tumo: Kangaba
Tumsah: Zaria (ca. 1060)
Tumso: Zaria (ca. 1060)
Muhammad Tunjur: Wadai
Tunka Menin: Ghana Empire
Dan Tunku: Kazaure
Abd ar-Rahman Ahmad Ali Tur: So-
  maliland Republic
Muhammadu Tura: Kazaure

Turanshah: Egypt (1250)
Marcius Turbo: Egypt (117–118)
Richard Turnbull: Kenya (1957–58);
  Tanganyika
Charles Turner: Ghana (1825–26);
  Sierra Leone (1825–26)
Turranius: Egypt (7 B.C.–A.D. 1)
C.D. Turton: Lagos (1880–83)
Bakwa Turunku: Zaria (1536–39)
Caecina Tuscus: Egypt (67–68)
Tusuru: Yatenga
Tutankhamen Nebkheprure: Egypt
  (18th Dynasty)
Tutankhaton: Egypt (18th Dynasty)
Osei Tutu: Ashanti
Osei Tutu Quamina: Ashanti
Tutugri: Dagomba
Tuwayni: Zanzibar (1833–36)
Faustin Twagiramungu: Rwanda
Edward Twining: Tanganyika
Eustace Twistleton-Wykeham-
  Fiennes: Seychelles (1918–21)
Twum: Akim
Twum: Ashanti
Twum Ampoforo Okasu: Akim
Tyaaka Daro Khot: Walo (1496–1503)
Beur Tyaaka Loggar: Walo (1576–
  1640)
Tyaaka Mbar: Walo (1225–42)
Christian Tychsen: Danish Gold
  Coast (1766–68)
Tye-Folo: Segu
Tyemonkonko: Kenedugu
Birayma Mbenda-Tyilor: Kayor
William Tymewell: Ghana (1756)
Tyukli: Walo (1278–87)
Leeyti Tyukuli: Dyolof
Tyukuli N'Diklam: Dyolof

U

Danmaigatiny Uata: Gumel
Uban Doro: Gobir
Uban Yari: Katsina (1704–06)
Ubanu: Swaziland (1889–99)
Ubayd Allah: Omayyad and Abbasid
  North Africa
Ubayda: Omayyad and Abbasid North
  Africa
al-Mahdi Ubaydallah: Fatimid North
  Africa
Ubra: Wagadugu
Udagbedo: Benin [i]
N'Singa Udjuu: Congo (Zaire)
  (1981–82)
Abubakar Ukar: Argungu
Yamta Abdullahi Ula: Biu
Carlos Ullmann: Ceuta (1830–33)
Ulpius Limenius: Africa Proconsularis
  (347–349)
Ulpius Primianus: Egypt (195–197)
Roelof Ulsen: Dutch Gold Coast
  (1755–58)
Umar: Algiers (1815–17)
Sayid Umar: Anjouan
Umar: Bornu Empire (1824–81)
Umar: Egypt (1664–67)

Umar: Mayotte
Umar: Mayotte
Abu Ja'far Hazarmard Umar:
  Omayyad and Abbasid North Africa
Chamassi Sa'id Umar: Nzwani
Hamidu Umar: Mandara
Umar I: Lafia
Umar I: Trarza
Abu Hafs Umar I: Hafsid Kingdom
Muhammadu Kabir Umar: Katagum
Umar I al-Murtada: Almohad Empire
Umar II: Bornu Empire (1466–67)
Abu Hafs Umar II: Hafsid Kingdom
Umar II: Lafia
Umar III: Bornu Empire (1625–45)
Umar III: Trarza
Umar Adjara: Mandara
Umar al-Bashir: Sudan (1989–)
Umar al-Hajj: Tukolor Empire
Umar Arteh Ghalib: Somalia
Umar Baba Ya Mairami: Bornu Em-
  pire (1969–)
Umar Bahaushe: Nupe
Umar Bey Fahri: Sudan (1865)
Umar ibn Dunyahuz: Ifat
Umar ibn Idris: Bornu Empire (1394–
  98)
Umar Kumba II: Trarza
Umar Lele: Darfur
Umar Majigi: Nupe
Umar Mansur al-Kikhya: Cyrenaica
Umar Mustafa al-Muntasir: Libya
Umar Salum: Trarza
Umar Sanda Kiyarimi: Bornu Empire
  (1937–69)
Umar Sanda Kura: Bornu Empire
  (1922–37)
Umar Suleiman: Bedde
Abu Umar Tashufin: Morocco (1361–
  61)
Shehu Umar Watara: Kong
Umara: Bedde
Umaru: Bauchi
Umaru: Fulani Empire
Umaru: Gombe
Umaru: Hadejia (1805–08)
Umaru: Hadejia (1863–65)
Umaru: Kano (1409–21)
Sidi Umaru: Keffi
Umaru: Lapai
Umaru: Muri
Umaru Ba Demba: Futa Jallon
Umaru Bago: Lapai
Umaru Bakatara: Gwandu
Umaru Ciwa: Argungu
Umaru Dacili: Gobir
Umaru Dallaji: Katsina (1806–35)
Umaru Faruku: Katagum
Umaru Gamdi: Yauri
Umaru Maidubu: Kontagora
Umaru Nagwamatse: Kontagora
Umaru Na'uka: Kazaure
Umaru Oke-Ode: Lafiagi
Umaru Sanda: Damagaram
Umaru Sanda Ndayako: Nupe
Umaru Sori: Futa Jallon
Abu Umays Mahmud: Tripolitania
  (1711)

Umbandzeni: Swaziland (1874–89)
Umi: Gobir
Umthlangana: Zululand
Unas: Egypt (5th Dynasty)
Juan Jerónimo Ungo de Velasco: Melilla (1711–14)
Unis: Egypt (5th Dynasty)
Unsa I: Funj Sultanate
Unsa II: Funj Sultanate
Unsa III: Funj Sultanate
Untani: Gurma
Unujur: Egypt (946–960)
Thomas Upington: Cape Colony (1884–86)
Uqba: Arab North Africa
Muhammad Urada: Wadai
José de Urbanski: São Tomé and Príncipe (1838–39)
Juan de Urbina: Canary Islands (1747–64)
Urdamen: Kush (671 B.C.)
Col. Uriarte: Tangier (1941–42)
Alonso de Urrea: Melilla (1556–59)
Userkaf: Egypt (5th Dynasty)
Userkare: Egypt (6th Dynasty)
Userkare Khendjer: Egypt (13th Dynasty)
Senakht Userkhaure: Egypt (20th Dynasty)
Amenemope Usermare: Egypt (21st Dynasty)
Osorkhon II Usermare: Egypt (22nd Dynasty)
Pimay Usermare: Egypt (22nd Dynasty)
Rameses II the Great Usermare Miamun: Egypt (19th Dynasty)
Rameses III Usermare Meryamun: Egypt (20th Dynasty)
Rameses V Usermare Sekhepereure: Egypt (20th Dynasty)
Rameses VII Usermare Meryamun (20th Dynasty)
Rameses VIII Usermare Akhenamun (20th Dynasty)
Redebast Usermare: Egypt (23rd Dynasty)
Sheshonk III Usermare: Egypt (22nd Dynasty)
Takelot I Usermare: Egypt (22nd Dynasty)
Ushaq ibn Yahya: Egypt (850–851)
Seti II Usikheperure Merneptah: Egypt (19th Dynasty)
Setneptah Usire Pshenmut: Egypt (29th Dynasty)
Usman: Bauchi
Usman: Gwandu
Usman: Hadejia
Usman: Misau
Usman Dan Fodio: Fulani Empire
Usman Nagogo: Katsina (1944–81)
Usman No Yi Nawa: Katsina (1667–84)
Usman Tsagarana: Katsina (1585–89)
Usmanu: Wase
Herbert Ussher: Ghana (1867–72, 1879–80)

Stephen Ustick: Fort James
Usuman: Biram
Usuman: Gombe
Usuman Dan Abdullahi: Kano (1919–26)
Cassam Uteem: Mauritius (1992–2002)
Uthman: Egypt (1680–83)
Uthman: Egypt (1734)
Mallam Uthman: Jema'a
Uthman: Tagant
Uthman: Tunis (1590–1610)
Uthman: Tunis (1814)
Abu Amr Uthman: Hafsid Kingdom
Abu s-Sadat Uthman: Egypt (1453–53)
al-Aziz Uthman: Egypt (1193–98)
Uthman I: Bornu Empire (1386–91)
Uthman I: Kano (1845–55)
Uthman I: Morocco (1218–40)
Abu Sa'id Uthman I: Tlemcen (1283–1304)
Uthman II: Bornu Empire (1391–92)
Uthman II: Kano (1919–26)
Abu Sa'id Uthman II: Morocco (1310–31)
Abu Sa'id Uthman II Abd ar-Rahman: Tlemcen (1348–52)
Abu Sa'id Uthman III: Morocco (1398–1420)
Uthman III Kaliwama: Bornu Empire (1432–33)
Uthman IV: Bornu Empire (1461–66)
Uthman al-Habashi: Harar
Uthman Bey: Sudan (1825–26)
Uthman Dan Fodio: Fulani Empire
Uthman Kanafa: Songhai (1354–62)
Uthman Ould Fadl Ould Sinan: Adrar
Uthman Sarki: Nupe
Uthman Zaki: Nupe
Uushona Shiimi: Ovamboland
Uwaifiokun: Benin [i]
Uwakhuahen: Benin [i]
Uwan: Zaria (1535–36)
Uways: Egypt (1587–91)
Agathe Uwilingiyumana: Rwanda

V

Joseph Vadier: Guinea (1932–36)
Cesare De Val Cismon: Italian Somaliland (1923–28)
Peter Valck: Danish Gold Coast (1680–81)
Marqués de Valdecañas: Ceuta (1695–98); Oran (1707–08)
Jerónimo de Valderrama y Tovar: Gran Canaria
José Valdês: Madeira (1827–28)
Domingos do Vale: Mozambique (1847–51)
Eusebio Castella do Vale: Guinea-Bissau (1887)
Comte Valée: Algeria (1837–40)
João Valente: Guinea-Bissau (1904)
Victor Valentin-Smith: Gabon (1941–42)

Lope de Valenzuela: Gran Canaria
Valerius Datus: Egypt (216–218)
Valerius Eudaemon: Egypt (139)
Valerius Messala: Africa Proconsularis (399–400)
Valerius Proculus: Egypt (160–163)
Lucius Aradius Valerius Proculus Felix: Africa Proconsularis (333–336)
Marqués de Valhermoso: Canary Islands (1723–35)
Fray Gaspar de Valier: Tripolitania (1551)
François Victorien Valière: Senegal (1869–76)
Rafael Valiño y Marcen: Spanish Morocco (1951–56)
Jean Valkenburg: Dutch Gold Coast (1656–59, 1662–67)
Pieter Valkenier: Dutch Gold Coast (1723–27)
Ely Ould Muhammad Vall: Mauritania (2005–)
José Vallejo: Oran (1733–39)
Claude Valluy: Benin [ii] (1949–51)
Marqués de Valparaíso: Ceuta (1692–95)
Louis Van Assenburgh: Cape Colony (1708–11)
Coenrad Van Breitenbach: Cape Colony (1671–72)
Albert Van Breughel: Cape Colony (1672–72)
Lieven Van Burgen Van Der Grijp: Dutch Gold Coast (1787–90, 1794–95)
Cornelis Van De Graaff: Cape Colony (1785–91)
Abraham Van De Velde: Mauritius (1703–10)
Johannes Van De Wath: Namibia (1968–71)
Daniel Van Den Henghel: Cape Colony (1737–39)
Jules Van Der Bossche: Dutch Gold Coast (1857)
Jacobus Van Der Breggen Paauw: Dutch Gold Coast (1826–28)
Anthony Van Der Eb: Dutch Gold Coast (1837–38, 1840–46, 1847–52)
Lieven Van Burgen Van Der Grijp: Dutch Gold Coast (1787–90, 1794–95)
Anton Van Der Meden: Hollandia
Nikolaas Van Der Nood De Gieterre: Dutch Gold Coast (1754–55)
Jacobus Van Der Puye: Dutch Gold Coast (1780)
Symon Van Der Stel: Cape Colony (1679–99)
Willem Van Der Stel: Cape Colony (1699–1707)
Barend Van Der Walt: Namibia (1971–77)
Jacob Van Der Well: Dutch Gold Coast (1645–50)

Fernando Van Dunem: Angola (1991–92, 1996–2002)

Joseph Van Dyke: Lydenburg

Gerhardus Van Hamel: Dutch Gold Coast (1796–98)

Gijsbrecht Van Hoogveldt: Hollandia

Jasper Van Houssen: Dutch Gold Coast (1659–62)

Willem Van Idzinga: Dutch Gold Coast (1866–67)

Eduard Van Ingen: Dutch Gold Coast (1833–34)

Adriaan Van Jaarsveld: Graaff-Reinet

Adriaan Van Kervel: Cape Colony (1737)

Jan Van Laar: Hollandia; Mauritius (1667–68)

Gerrit Van Niekerk: Stellaland; United States of Stellaland

Willie Van Niekerk: Namibia (1983–85)

Gerrit Van Niekerk Viljoen: Namibia (1979–80)

Huybert Van Ongerdonk: Dutch Gold Coast (1667–68)

Pietre Van Oudtshoorn: Cape Colony (1772–73)

Antonius Van Overbeek: Dutch Gold Coast (1734–36)

Gey Van Pettius: Goshen

Joachim Van Plettenberg: Cape Colony (1771–85)

Cornelis Van Quaelbergen: Cape Colony (1666–68)

Willem Van Rensburg: Transvaal (1862–64)

Jan Van Riebeeck: Cape Colony (1652–62)

Albertus Van Rhijn: Namibia (1951–53)

Jan Van Sevenhuysen: Dutch Gold Coast (1696–1702)

Lambert Van Tets: Dutch Gold Coast (1758–59)

Joost Van Vollenhouven: French West Africa (1917–18); Guinea (1907); Senegal (1907)

Jan Van Voorst: Dutch Gold Coast (1747–54)

H.L.F.C. Van Vredenbusch: Tangier (1948–51)

Henrikus Van Wiessel: Dutch Gold Coast (1708–09)

Hermanus Van Wyk: Rehoboth

Nikolaas Van Ypren: Dutch Gold Coast (1638–39)

Brand Van Zyl: South Africa (1945–50)

Vante: Yatenga

Maurice Varnier: Algeria (1903)

Francisco Varona: Ceuta (1689–92)

Publius Tullius Varro: Africa [i] (142–143)

Antonio de Vasconcelos: Angola (1758–64)

Bartolomeu de Vasconcelos: Madeira (1651–55)

Caetano de Vasconcelos: Cape Verde (1826–30)

Diogo de Vasconcelos: Mozambique (1639–40)

Francisco de Nóbrega Vasconcelos: Cape Verde (1726–28)

Gomes da Silva de Vasconcelos: Ceuta (1519–21, 1525–29)

João de Vasconcelos: Cape Verde (1881–86)

Luis de Vasconcelos: Angola (1617–21)

Manuel Vasconcelos: Angola (1790–97)

Mateus de Vasconcelos: Mombasa (1593–96)

José de Vasconcelos e Almeida: Mozambique (1780–81)

Luis de Vasconcelos e Sá: Guinea-Bissau (1891–95)

João Rodrigues de Vasconcelos Ribeiro: Ceuta (1464–79)

Rui Mendes de Vasconcelos Ribeiro: Ceuta (1479–81)

Charles-Henri Vassal: Comoros (1879–79); Sainte Marie de Madagascar

José Vassallo: Ceuta (1795–98)

Henri Habet de Vauboulon: Réunion (1689–90)

Jean Vaudeville: Réunion (1966–69)

Camilo de Miranda Rebocho Vaz: Angola (1966–72)

Damião Vaz d'Almeida: São Tomé and Príncipe (2004–05); Príncipe (ii)

Armindo Vaz de Almeida: São Tomé and Príncipe (1995–96)

Antonio Vaz de Araújo: Cacheu (1775)

Nuno Vaz de Castelo Branco: Portuguese Gold Coast (1502–04)

Ricardo Vaz Monteiro: Guinea-Bissau (1941–45); São Tomé and Príncipe (1933–41)

Nunho Vaz Pereira: Mozambique (1506–07)

Álvaro Vaz Pestano: Portuguese Gold Coast (1486)

José Vázquez: Western Sahara

Narciso Vázquez y Nicuesa: Melilla (1758–67)

Abraham De Veer: Dutch Gold Coast (1810–16)

Jacobus De Veer: Dutch Gold Coast (1790–94)

José Marina Vega: Melilla (1905–10)

Pedro de la Vega; Tenerife

Septimus Vegetus: Egypt (86–90)

Carlos Veiga: Cape Verde (1991–2000)

Tristão da Veiga: Madeira (1585–91)

Georges Veillat: Guinea (1909–10)

Marqués de Velada: Oran (1625–28)

Jerónimo de Velasco: Canary Islands (1677–81)

Juan Jerónimo Ungo de Velasco: Melilla (1711–14)

José María Velasco Postigo: Spanish Morocco (1878–79)

Francisco de Velasco y Tovar: Ceuta (1681–89)

Luis de Velázquez y Angulo: Melilla (1656–69)

Marqués de los Vélez: Oran (1666–72)

José Vélez: São Tomé and Príncipe (1920)

Pires Veloso: São Tomé and Príncipe (1974–75)

Venantius: Africa Proconsularis (423)

Paul Venel: Niger (1910–11, 1913–15)

Hassan Veneziano: Algiers (1577–80, 1582–88)

Jacobus Venter: Orange Free State (1855, 1859–60, 1863)

Jules Ventre de la Touloubre: Comoros (1871–78); Nossi-Bé

José María Rodríguez Vera: Ceuta (1837–44)

José Vera: Fernando Po

Pedro de Vera: Gran Canaria

André-César Vérand: Comoros (1855–57); Senegal (1853–54)

Arthur Verdier: Côte d'Ivoire (1871–86)

Juan Verdugo: Tenerife

Raimond Vergès: Sainte Marie de Madagascar

Vergilius Capito: Egypt (48–54)

Charles Vergnes: Comoros (1908–11); French Equatorial Africa (1911, 1912–13)

Daniel Verhoutert: Dutch Gold Coast (1680–83)

François Blanchot de Verly: Senegal (1786–90, 1792–1801, 1802–07)

Jean-Louis Vernet: Côte d'Ivoire (1869–71)

Lucius Minicius Natalis Quadronius Verus: Africa [i] (153–154)

Hendrik Verwoerd: South Africa (1958–66)

Titus Flavius Vespasianus: Africa [i] (63–64)

Julius Vestinus: Egypt (60–67)

Dominique Vian: Réunion (2004–05)

Eduardo Viana: Angola (1931–34)

Marqués de Viana: Oran (1643–47)

Aulus Vibius Habitus: Africa [i] (16–17)

Vibius Maximus: Egypt (103–105)

Jules Vidal: Guinea (1922)

Manuel Vidal: Angola (1837–39)

Francisco de Vide: São Tomé and Príncipe (1799)

Antonio Viegas: Guinea-Bissau (1932–40)

Claude Vieillescazes: Réunion (1972–75)

Antonio Vieira: Bissau (1877–79)

Antonio Vieira: Cape Verde (1720–25)

Francisco Vieira: São Tomé and Príncipe (1901)

João Vieira: Angola (1658–61)

João Bernardo "Nino" Vieira: Guinea-Bissau (1978–99, 2005–)

Jorge Vieira: Ceuta (1555–57)

José Vieira: Bissau (1836)

Luis de Vigil: Gran Canaria
Alexis Vignon: Gabon (1850–53, 1857–59)
Jean-Baptiste Vigoureux du Plessis: Réunion (1792–94)
Francisco de Vila Nova: São Tomé (1592–93)
Conde de Vila Real: Ceuta (1562–63)
Conde de Vila Real: Ceuta (1616–22)
Duque de Vila Real: Ceuta (1567–74, 1577–78)
Fernão, Conde de Vila Real: Ceuta (1438–45)
Pedro, Conde de Vila Real: Ceuta (1461–64)
Daniel Viljoen: Namibia (1953–63)
Gerrit Van Niekerk Viljoen: Namibia (1979–80)
Marais Viljoen: South Africa (1979–84)
Marqués de Villadarias: Ceuta (1698–1702); Oran (1733)
Antonio Villalba y Angulo: Melilla (1732–57)
Juan Villalonga y Soler: Melilla (1888)
Fernando del Piño Villamil: Spanish Morocco (1876–77)
Miguel Villanueva: Spanish Morocco (1923–23)
Manuel del Villar: Melilla (1854–56, 1858–60)
René de la Villebague: Mauritius (1756–59)
Jean-Baptiste de Villers: Réunion (1701–09)
Charles Le Myre de Villiers: Madagascar (1886–88, 1894–95)
George Villiers; South Africa (1931–37)
Jacob de Villiers: South Africa (1930–31)
John, Baron de Villiers: South Africa (1912, 1914)
Aristide-Marie Villon: Senegal (1882)
Louis Vingarassamy: Gabon (1931)
Joseph Vintcent: Rhodesia (1895–96)
Maurice Viollette: Algeria (1925–27)
Théophile Viorol: Algeria (1833–34)
Caius Vipstanus Apronianus: Africa [i] (68)
Mari Vira Hyel: Biu
Marqués del Viso: Oran (1639–43)
Jan de Visser: Hollandia
Paul Visser: Witbooi Territory
Vitalius: Byzantine North Africa
Aulus Vitellius: Africa [i] (60–61)
Lucius Vitellius: Africa [i] (61–62)
Vitrasius Pollio: Egypt (17–21, 31–32, 39–42)
Vittorio Emanuele II: Italian East Africa
Caius Vivius Marsus: Africa [i] (26–29)
Quintus Voconius Saxa Fides: Africa [i] (162–163)
Gaspar Vogado: Cacheu (1649–50)
Charles Voisin: Ruanda–Urundi
Julien Voisin: Côte d'Ivoire (1892)

Pierre Voizard: Tunisia (1953–54)
Pieter Volkmar: Dutch Gold Coast (1780–84)
Joost Van Vollenhoven: French West Africa (1917–18); Guinea (1907); Senegal (1907)
Giuseppe Volpi Di Misurata: Tripolitania (1921–25)
Volusianus: Africa Proconsularis (428–429)
Volusius Maecianus: Egypt (159–160)
Volux: Mauretania East
Berthold von Deimling: Namibia (1906–07)
Kurt von François: Namibia (1891–95)
Adolf von Götzen: German East Africa
Herr von Kamptz: Kamerun (1900)
Eduard von Knorr: Kamerun (1885)
Eduard von Liebert: German East Africa
Friedrich von Lindequist: Namibia (1905–07)
Herr von Lücke: Kamerun (1895)
Jesko von Puttkamer: Kamerun (1887, 1890, 1895, 1896–1906); Togoland
Albrecht von Rechenburg: German East Africa
Johan von Richelieu: Danish Gold Coast (1823–25)
Friedrich von Schiele: German East Africa
Karl von Schnitter: Hollandia
Bruno von Schuckmann: Kamerun (1891–92); Namibia (1907–10)
Julius von Soden: German East Africa; Kamerun (1885–87, 1888–89)
Hendrik von Suhm: Danish Gold Coast (1724–27)
Lothar von Trotha: Namibia (1904–05)
Herrmann von Wissmann: German East Africa
Eugen von Zimmerer: Kamerun (1887–88, 1889–90, 1892–93, 1894); Togoland
John Vorster: South Africa (1966–79)
Tonnies Voss: Swedish Gold Coast
H.L.F.C. Van Vredenbusch: Tangier (1948–51)
Paul Vuillaume: Gabon (1943–44)
Vulcacius Rufinus: Africa Proconsularis (346–347, 352–353, 365–367)
Eric Vully de Candole: Cyrenaica; Italian Somaliland (1948)

W

Mbang Waad: Walo (1202–11)
Wabgho: Yatenga
Hama Wabi I: Jemaari
Muhammadu Wabi I: Jemaari
Mohama Wabi II: Jemaari
Muhammadu Wabi III: Jemaari
Muhammadu Wabi IV: Jemaari
Idris Wad Daftar: Bahr al-Ghazal

Ahmad Pasha Abu Wadan: Sudan (1838–43)
John Waddington: Zambia (1941–47)
Abdulaye Wade: Senegal (2000–)
George Wade: Seychelles (1852–62)
Thomas Wade: Cape Colony (1833–34)
Yamta Kupaya Wadi: Biu
Wadih: Egypt (779)
Wadih: Gonja
Sebekemsaf I Sekhemre Wadjkhau: Egypt (13th Dynasty)
Wadjkheperre Kamose: Egypt (17th Dynasty)
Amenhotep IV Neferkheprure Waenre: Egypt (18th Dynasty)
Anders Waerøe: Danish Gold Coast (1728–35)
Majan Wagadu: Ghana Empire
Zacharias Wagenaar: Cape Colony (1662–66)
Yusef Wahba Pasha: Egypt (1919–20)
Mehmed Sa'id Pasha Wahbi: Kordofan
Psamtik I Wahibre: Egypt (26th Dynasty)
Wahibre Iayeb: Egypt (13th Dynasty)
Abu Malik Abd al-Wahid: Tlemcen (1412–24, 1429–30)
Abu Muhammad Abd al-Wahid: Tripolitania (1207–21); Tunis (1207–21)
Abd al-Wahid al-Makhluwi: Almohad Empire
Abd al-Wahid ibn Yahya: Egypt (851–852)
Apries Wahimbre: Egypt (26th Dynasty)
Joseph Wahis: Congo (Zaire) (1892–96, 1900–12)
Sekhemre Wahkha Rahotep: Egypt (17th Dynasty)
Bekenrinef Wahkare: Egypt (24th Dynasty)
Bocchoris Wahkare: Egypt (24th Dynasty)
Waizam: Daura
Wajkare Amtalqa: Kush (568–555 B.C.)
Wake: Daura
Idris Abdul Wakil: Zanzibar (1985–99)
Dira Wala: Biu
Yamtara Wala: Biu
Dejaz Walad Rafael: Gojjam
Walda Salomon: Ethiopia (1796–97, 1799)
Wali: Egypt (1711–14)
al-Wali Mustafa as-Sayyid: Western Sahara
al-Walid: Morocco (1631–36)
al-Walid ibn Rifa'a: Egypt (727–735)
Abraham Waligo: Uganda (1985–86)
Abdu Waliyi: Nupe
Alexander Walker: Saint Helena (1823–28)
Hugh Norman-Walker: Botswana; Seychelles (1967–69)

Arthur Walker-Leigh: Gold Coast Northern Territories
Joseph Wall: Senegambia Colony
Lawrence Wallace: North Eastern Rhodesia; North Western Rhodesia; Zambia (1911–21)
Henry Wallis: Malawi (1910–11)
Hendrik Walmbeek: Dutch Gold Coast (1763–64)
Jean Walsin-Esterhazy: Algeria (1870)
Barend Van Der Walt: Namibia (1971–77)
Mutesa I Walugembe Makaobya: Buganda
Walzamu: Daura
Wambai Zozo: Zaria (1903)
Buraima Wamu: Daniski
Wanga: Baguirmi
Daouda Wanké: Niger (1999)
Hen Kon Wanko Dam: Songhai (1044–63)
Mukas Waranankong: Lunda
Swinburne Ward: Seychelles (1862–68)
Henry Warde: Mauritius (1811); Réunion (1811)
Henry Warden: Orange Free State (1848–52); Transorangia
Osei Opoku Ware: Ashanti
Opoku Ware II: Ashanti
Warempe Ampem: Denkyira
Asim Warfaguma: Omayyad and Abbasid North Africa
Warga: Wagadugu
Mamman Wari: Nupe
Muhammadu Wari: Katsina (1644–55)
Muhammadu Dan Wari: Katsina (1704–06)
Muhammadu Wari II: Katsina (1701–04)
Muhammadu Wari III: Katsina (1758–67)
Colston Waring: Liberia (1828)
Tayar Warinki: Biu
Joseph Warioba: Tanzania
Warisis: Kano (1063–95)
Marqués de Warmarch: Ceuta (1760–63)
Daniel Warner: Liberia (1864–68)
Charles Warren: Bechuanaland Protectorate
Warri: Bonny
Warru: Tripolitania (1009–14)
Wasan Sagad: Axum
Bakary Watara: Kong
Bako Moru Watara: Gwiriko
Diori Watara: Gwiriko
Famagan Watara: Gwiriko
Magan Oule Watara: Gwiriko
Pintieba Watara: Gwiriko
Tieba Niandane Watara: Gwiriko
Andries Waterboer: Griqualand West
Nicolaas Waterboer: Griqualand West
Johannes Van De Wath: Namibia (1968–71)
Alan Watherston: Gold Coast Northern Territories

Abu Zakariyya Yahya II al-Wathiq: Hafsid Kingdom
Wati: Mali Empire
Mari Watila Tampta: Biu
Mari Watirwa: Biu
Ahmad al-Wattasi: Morocco (1524–45, 1547–49)
Ahmadu Waziri: Misau
Waznar: Lower Egypt
Thomas Weaver: Fort James
Frédéric Weber: Gabon (1909)
Miles Wedderburn Lampson: Egypt (1934–36)
Wedem Ar'ed: Ethiopia (1299–1314)
Wedemdem: Axum
Wegbaja: Dahomey
Necho II Wehembre: Egypt (26th Dynasty)
Alain Weill: Mayotte Department
Roy Welensky: Federation of Rhodesia and Nyasaland
Jacob Van Der Well: Dutch Gold Coast (1645–50)
Weneg: Egypt (2nd Dynasty)
Sekhemre Wepmae Intef: Egypt (17th Dynasty)
Albertus Werth: Namibia (1926–33)
Martin West: Natal (1845–49)
Christiaan De Wet: Orange Free State (1902)
Jannie De Wet: Namibia (1970–90)
Nicolaas De Wet: South Africa (1943–45)
John Weuves: Ghana (1781–82)
Maxime Weygand: Algeria (1941)
William Wheelwright: Zululand
Edward White: Ghana (1807–16)
F.B.P. White: Ghana (1887)
Edgar Whitehead: Zimbabwe (1958–62)
Gerald Whiteley: Nigeria Western Region
Thomas Whitney: Fort James
Wibega: Dahomey
Dennis Wickham: Italian Somaliland (1943–48)
Henrikus Van Wiessel: Dutch Gold Coast (1708–09)
Johan Wilder: Danish Gold Coast (1745)
Bernhardt Wilkens: Danish Gold Coast (1842)
Richard W.H. Wilkinson: Ghana (1921); Sierra Leone (1916–22)
Mark Wilks: Saint Helena (1813–16)
Prince Will: New Calabar
Thomas Will: Aku
Louis Bouët-Willaumez: Gabon (1839–43); Senegal (1843)
Andreas Willennsen: Danish Gold Coast (1727–28)
Joseph Willey: Fort James
William: Bonny
William I of Sicily: Tripolitania (1154–60)
Peveril William-Powlett: Zimbabwe (1954–59)
William Rowe: Koya-Temne

Alexander Williams: Zambia (1954)
Anthony Williams: Liberia (1830, 1836–39)
Len Williams: Mauritius (1968–72)
Ralph Williams: Botswana
Dirk Wilré: Dutch Gold Coast (1662, 1668–75)
Arthur Wilson: Seychelles (1837–39)
William Grey-Wilson: Saint Helena (1887–97)
Laurent Wiltord: Senegal (1947–50)
Shemakone Kalonga Wina: Barotseland
Edward Windley: Gambia (1958–62)
Reginald Wingate: Egypt (1917–19); Sudan (1899–1916)
William Winniett: Ghana (1846–50)
Francis de Winton: Congo (Zaire) (1884–87); Kenya (1890–91)
Winyi I Rubembeka: Bunyoro
Winyi II Rubangiramasega: Bunyoro
Winyi III Ruguruka: Bunyoro
Winyi IV Gafabusa: Bunyoro
Herrmann von Wissmann: German East Africa
Hendrick Witbooi: Witbooi Territory
Kido Witbooi: Witbooi Territory
Moses Witbooi: Witbooi Territory
Peter With: Danish Gold Coast (1680)
Wobgho: Wagadugu
Philip Wodehouse: Cape Colony (1862–70)
Alfred-Louis Woelfel: Togo (1917–22)
Fikre Selassie Wogderess: Ethiopia (1987–89)
Tshafe Tezaz Aklilu Habte-Wold: Ethiopia
Girma Wolde-Giorgis Lucha: Ethiopia (2001–)
Betwoded Asfaha Wolde Mikael: Eritrea
Abdel Kadir Woli: Baguirmi
Abderrahman Woli: Baguirmi
Garnet Wolseley: Ghana (1873–74); Natal (1875); Sierra Leone (1873–74); Transvaal (1879–80)
Claude Wong Su: Rodrigues (ii)
Evelyn Wood: Natal (1881)
Pieter Woortman: Dutch Gold Coast (1769–80)
Richard Worge: Senegal (1758–63)
Asfa Wossen: Ethiopia (1974–75)
Asfa Wossen: Shoa
Asfa Wossen II: Shoa
Ras Wossen Seged: Shoa
Apeanin Kwaframoa Woyiawonyi: Akim
John Wrathall: Zimbabwe (1976–78)
Martin Wray: Botswana
Georg Wreede: Mauritius (1665–67, 1669–72)
Andrew Wright: Gambia (1947–49)
Rice Wright: Fort James
Gerhard Wrisberg: Danish Gold Coast (1769–70)
Johan Wrisberg: Danish Gold Coast (1795–1807)

Philip Wrisberg: Danish Gold Coast (1819)
Wubri: Wagadugu
Atta Wusu Yiakosan: Akim
Hermanus Van Wyk: Rehoboth
Eustace Twistleton-Wykeham-Fiennes: Seychelles (1918–21)
Percy Wyn-Harris: Gambia (1949–58)
Robert Wynyard: Cape Colony (1859–60, 1861–62)

X

Xhosa: Transkeian Territories

Y

Ya Gallo: Masina
Umar Baba Ya Mairami: Bornu Empire (1969–)
Bakan-Tam Yaago: Dyolof
Birayma Yaasin-Bubu: Kayor
Tié-Yaasin Demba: Baol
Tié-Yaasin Dieng: Baol
Tié-Yaasin Gallo: Baol
Tié-Yaasin Ngone: Baol
Saayodo Yaasin Mbody: Walo (1801–06)
Yabau: Daura
Caabi al-Yachurtu: Comoros (1995–96)
Yadega: Yatenga
Yagbe'a Seyon: Ethiopia (1285–94)
Abu Yahya Yaghmurasan ibn Zayyan: Tlemcen (1236–83)
Yahaya: Biram
Yahya: Algiers (1557)
Yahya: Dongola
Yahya: Egypt (1741–43)
Yahya: Futa Jallon
Yahya: Gwandu
Yahya: Tripolitania (1001–07)
Yahya: Tripolitania (1228–36)
Yahya: Tripolitania (1397–1401)
Yahya: Zirid Kingdom
Abu Salih Yahya: Egypt (779–780)
Sheikh Abu Yahya: Tripolitania (1146–48, 1160–72)
Abu Zakariyya Yahya: Tunis (1228–36)
Tsagarana Yahya: Katsina (1750–51)
Yahya I: Idrisid State
Yahya I: Timbuktu (1647–51)
Abu Zakariyya Yahya I: Hafsid Kingdom
Yahya II: Idrisid State
Yahya II: Timbuktu (1697)
Abu Zakariyya Yahya II: Hafsid Kingdom
Abu Zakariyya Yahya II al-Wathiq: Hafsid Kingdom
Yahya III: Timbuktu (1709)
Yahya IV: Idrisid State
Yahya IV: Timbuktu (1709–10)
Yahya V: Timbuktu (1739–40)

Yahya V al-Mu'tasim: Almohad Empire
Abu Yahya Abu Bakr: Hafsid Kingdom
Abu Yahya Abu-Bakr: Morocco (1244–58)
Abu Yahya Abu Bakr ash-Shaid: Hafsid Kingdom
Abu Yahya al-Hassan: Tunis (1168)
Yahya al-Miruki: Tripolitania (1204–07)
Abu Yahya Amran: Tripolitania (1222–23)
Yahya ibn al-Aziz: Hammadid Kingdom
Yahya ibn Ibrahim: Almoravid Empire
Yahya ibn Umar: Almoravid Empire
Yahya Jammeh: Gambia (1994–)
Abu Yahya Yaghmurasan ibn Zayyan: Tlemcen (1236–83)
Abu Yahya Zakariyya I: Hafsid Kingdom
Yaji I: Kano (1349–85)
Yaji II: Kano (1752–68)
Yakama: Daura
Yakaniya: Daura
Yakano: Kano (998–1063)
Meruserre Yakhuber: Egypt (15th Dynasty)
Yaki: Wase
Ada Yaki: Daura
Yidda Yaki: Katsina (1452–92)
Yako: Gobir
Yakob Arous: Wadai
Abu Yusuf Yakub: Morocco (1258–86)
Yusuf II Abu Yakub: Almohad Empire
Yakub I: Almohad Empire
Abu Yakub al-Mustansir: Almohad Empire
Yakub al-Mwakir: Wadai
Abu Yakub Yusuf: Morocco (1286–1307)
Yakuba: Yauri
Yakuba: Zaria (1770–88)
Yakuba Dan Babari: Gobir
Yakubu: Bauchi
Yakubu: Kano (1452–62)
Yakubu I: Dagomba
Yakubu I: Zamfara
Yakubu II: Bauchi
Yakubu II: Dagomba
Yakubu II: Zamfara
Yakubu III: Bauchi
Yakubu Nabame: Argungu
Yakufu: Kano (1564–65)
Yakumo: Daura
Yakunya: Daura
Yakwano: Daura
Yala Maaku: Lunda
Yama Danka Kibao: Songhai (969–981)
Yama Dao: Songhai (1158–77)
Yama Dombo: Songhai (957–969)
Yama Karaonia: Songhai (945–947)
Nagoum Yamassoum: Chad (1999–2002)
Birayma Yamb: Kayor

Maurice Yaméogo: Burkina Faso (1958–66)
Yamta Abdullahi Ula: Biu
Yamta Amba: Biu
Yamta Kupaya Wadi: Biu
Yamta ra Bangwe: Biu
Yamta ra Wala: Biu
Yamusa: Lapai
Yamusa: Wase
Yamusa II: Keffi
Yan Musa: Zaria (1821–34)
Yanazu: Yauri
Yanbamu: Daura
Yanghama: Gurma
Yanis: Egypt (1131–32)
Abu'l Hassan Yanis: Tripolitania (1000–01)
Ibrahim Yanka Dari: Katsina (1410–52)
Yanzo: Dagomba
Yao Awirri: Denkyira
Zara Yaqob: Ethiopia (1434–68)
Yaqob I: Ethiopia (1597–1603, 1604–07)
Abd ar-Rahman Yaqub: Tripolitania (1246–57)
Abu Hammu II ibn Abi Yaqub: Tlemcen (1359–70, 1372–89)
Yaqub ibn al-Aflah: Rustumid Amirate
Yaqut: Zanzibar (1804–22)
Abu al-Yaqzan Muhammad: Rustumid Amirate
Shehu Musa Yar Adua: Nigeria (1976–83)
Uban Yari: Katsina (1704–06)
Muhammad Yarik: Zeng Empire (1460–61)
Yarima: Biram
Tabany-Yasy: Egypt (1628–30)
Yau Akoto: Ashanti
Yaulumfao: Yatenga
Yauri: Yauri
Ditend Yavu: Lunda
Yavu a Nawej: Lunda
Yavu Ilunga: Lunda
Afena Yaw: Bono
Yawuz Ali: Egypt (1601–03)
N'dyak Kumba Khuri Yay: Walo (1792–1801)
Yazid: Morocco (1790–92)
Yazid: Omayyad and Abbasid North Africa
Abu Halid Yazid: Omayyad and Abbasid North Africa
al-Yazuri: Egypt (1050–58)
Obiri Yeboa: Ashanti
Yebowa Ananta: Bono
Adli Yegen Pasha: Egypt (1921–22, 1926–27, 1929)
Yehia Ibrahim Pasha: Egypt (1923–24, 1933–34)
Yekuno Amlak: Ethiopia (1270–85)
Yembirima: Gurma
Yemde: Yatenga
Hailu Yemenu: Ethiopia (1989–91)
Yempabu: Gurma
Yempadigu: Gurma

Yemrehana Krestos: Ethiopia (1133–72)
Nchare Yen: Bamoun
Yendabri: Gurma
Yenkirma: Gurma
Yenmianga: Gurma
Yentangu: Gurma
Yentiabri: Gurma
Yentuguri: Gurma
Dembaane Yerim: Walo (1331–36)
Fara Yerim: Walo (1304–16)
Mbay Yerim: Walo (1316–31)
Naatago Yerim: Walo (1508–19)
Yerim Khode Fara Mbuno: Walo (1735–36)
Yerim Kode: Walo (1415–85)
Yerim Mbanyik: Walo (1271–78)
Yerim Mbanyik Anta Dyop: Walo (1735)
Yerim Mbanyik Aram Bakar: Walo (1640–74)
Yerim Mbanyik Konegil: Walo (1398–1415)
Yerim Mbanyik Teg: Walo (1821–23)
Yerim N'date Bubu: Walo (1733–34)
Muhammadu Goji Yerima: Jemaari
Muhammadu Yerima Iya: Adamawa
Yero: Katsina (1905–06)
Yero: Zaria (1888–97)
Buba Yero: Gombe
Yesbekheamani: Kush (283–300)
Yeshaq I: Ethiopia (1414–29)
Yessu: Allada
Yeta I: Barotseland
Yeta II: Barotseland
Yeta III: Barotseland
Yetbarak: Ethiopia (1212–60)
Yezid ibn Abdallah: Egypt (856–867)
Yezid ibn Hatim: Egypt (762–769)
Jacques Yhombi-Opango: Congo (1993–96)
Joachim Yhombi-Opango: Congo (1977–79)
Usman No Yi Nawa: Katsina (1667–84)
Atta Wusu Yiakosan: Akim
Yidda Yaki: Katsina (1452–92)
Yo'ab: Axum
Pascal Yoadimnaji: Chad (2005–)
Joseph Yodoyman: Chad (1992–93)
Yohannes I: Ethiopia (1667–82)
Yohannes II: Ethiopia (1769)
Yohannes III: Ethiopia (1840–41, 1850–51)
Yohannes IV: Ethiopia (1872–89)
Yokubu Gowon: Nigeria (1966–75)
Yonas: Ethiopia (1797–98)
George Yonge: Cape Colony (1799–1801)
Gustavus Yonge: Sierra Leone (1867)
Paramanga Yonli: Burkina Faso (2000–)
Yonusa: Zaria (1764–70)
Yoro Diakité: Mali (1968–69)
Yosiboi: Songhai (1235–55)
Yostos: Ethiopia (1711–16)
Fulbert Youlou: Congo (1958–63)
Henry Young: British Kaffraria

Hubert Young: Malawi (1932–34); Zambia (1934–38)
Mark Young: Sierra Leone (1929–30); Tanganyika
William Young: Ghana (1884–85)
Younoussa Bamana: Mayotte Department
Younoussi Touré: Mali (1992–93)
Youssouf Ouedraogo: Burkina Faso (1992–94)
Abd ar-Rahman al-Youssoufi: Morocco (1998–2002)
Yoweri Museveni: Uganda (1986–)
Nikolaas Van Ypren: Dutch Gold Coast (1638–39)
Yu: Kom
Yubya: Barotseland
Yuhi I Gahima: Ruanda
Yuhi II Mazimpaka: Ruanda
Yuhi III Gahandiro: Ruanda
Yuhi IV Musinga: Ruanda
Yulk Mahmud: Tripolitania (1683)
Yunfa Dan Nafata: Gobir
Yunus: Algiers (1629)
Yusa: Kano (1135–93)
Yusef Wahba Pasha: Egypt (1919–20)
José Yuste: Tangier (1940–41)
Yusuf: Algiers (1557)
Yusuf: Algiers (1634–36, 1647–50)
Yusuf: Baguirmi
Yusuf: Harar
Yusuf: Mogadishu
Yusuf: Morocco (1912–27)
Yusuf: Tripolitania (1795–1832)
Yusuf: Tunis (1610–37)
Yusuf: Zirid Kingdom
Abdullahi Yusuf Ahmad: Puntland; Somalia
Abu Hajjaj Yusuf: Tlemcen (1393)
Abu Hatim Yusuf: Rustumid Amirate
Abu Jemal Yusuf: Algiers (1640–42)
Abu Thabit II Yusuf: Tlemcen (1393)
Abu Yakub Yusuf: Morocco (1286–1307)
Muhammad Abdi Yusuf: Somalia
Abu Yusuf al-Mansur: Almohad Empire
Abu Yusuf Yakub: Morocco (1258–86)
al-Aziz Yusuf: Egypt (1438)
Muhammad Yusuf: Baguirmi
Sidi Muhammad ben Yusuf: Morocco (1927–53, 1955–61)
Yusuf I: Timbuktu (1622–27)
Yusuf II: Timbuktu (1700–01, 1711, 1729)
Yusuf II: Wadai
Yusuf II Abu Yakub: Almohad Empire
Yusuf III: Almohad Empire
Yusuf al-Mukni: Fezzan
Yusuf ben Khedda: Algeria (1961–62); Algerian Government (Provisional Republic)
Yusuf Haji Nur: Puntland
Yusuf ibn Aiyub: Egypt (1171–93)
Yusuf ibn Tashufin: Almoravid Empire
Yusuf ibn Ziri: Fatimid North Africa
Yusuf Kharifain: Wadai
Yusufu: Daura

Yusufu: Daura-Zango
Yusufu Lule: Uganda (1979)
Yusufu Mainassara: Argungu
Yusufu Musa: Lafia

Z

Za Dengel: Ethiopia (1603–04)
Za Koi: Songhai (849–861)
Za Kosoi: Songhai (1005–25)
Zacharias I: Dongola
Zacharias III: Dongola
Zacharias IV: Dongola
Haydar Agha Zade: Egypt (1646–47)
Khaliji-Zade-Damad: Egypt (1656–57)
Shahsuwar-Zade-Ghazi: Egypt (1657–60)
az-Zafir: Egypt (1149–54)
Albert Zafy: Madagascar (1993–96)
Zagale: Dagomba
Antonio Zagalo: Bissau (1860–62)
Sa'd Zaghlul Pasha: Egypt (1924)
Zahariah Mohieddin: Egypt (1965–66)
az-Zahir: Egypt (1021–36)
Zailani: Gombe
Ali II Zainami: Bornu Empire (1545–46)
Abu Zaiyid: Tripolitania (1224)
Zakari: Daura-Baure
Abu Yahya Zakariyya I: Hafsid Kingdom
Abu Zakariyya Yahya: Tunis (1228–36)
Abu Zakariyya Yahya I: Hafsid Kingdom
Abu Zakariyya Yahya II: Hafsid Kingdom
Abu Zakariyya Yahya II al-Wathiq: Hafsid Kingdom
Mallam Zaki: Katagum
Baba Zaki: Kano (1768–76)
Muhamman Zaki: Kano (1582–1617)
Uthman Zaki: Nupe
Ibrahim Zakiyul Kalbi: Katagum
Zama: Daura
Zamnagawa: Kano (1342–49)
Zamnau: Daura
Zana: Wagadugu
Abdu Zanga: Keffi
Zangayella: Yatenga
Muhamman Zangi: Kazaure
Zangina: Dagomba
Akuete Zankli Lawson I: Little Popo
Zara Yaqob: Ethiopia (1434–68)
Sheikh Ahmad az-Zarraq: Tripolitania (1489–94)
Zartai: Zamfara
Muhammad az-Zaruq Rajab: Libya
Zaude: Zamfara
Zauditu: Ethiopia (1916–30)
Muhammadu-Zayanu: Yauri
Zaydan an-Nasir: Morocco (1603–28)
Zayin al-Abidin: Morocco (1745)
Abu Zayyan I Muhammad: Tlemcen (1304–08)

Abu Zayyan II Muhammad: Tlemcen (1393–97)
Abu Zayyan Ahmad: Tlemcen (1541–50)
Abu Zayyan Muhammad: Tlemcen (1360)
Abu Zayyan Muhammad III: Morocco (1361–66)
Abu Zayyan Muhammad IV: Morocco (1372–74)
Zazalita: Matabeleland
Julius Zech: Togoland
Meles Zenawi: Ethiopia (1991–)
Zenka: Timbuktu (1683)
Zenko Baro: Songhai (1275–95)
Marcus Antonius Zeno: Africa [i] (164–165)
Zerama: Gobir
Saye Zerbo: Burkina Faso (1980–82)
Zergaz: Axum
Juan Zermeño: Oran (1758–65)
Pedro Zermeño: Oran (1774–78)
Liamine Zéroual: Algeria (1994–99)
Ziblim Bandamda: Dagomba
Ziblim Bunbiogo: Dagomba
Ziblim Kulunku: Dagomba

Ziblim Na Saa: Dagomba
Martin Ziguélé: Central African Republic (2001–03)
Zike: Kororofa
Zikeenya: Kororofa
João Zilhão: Guinea-Bissau (1931–32)
Eugen von Zimmerer: Kamerun (1887–88, 1889–90, 1892–93, 1894–94); Togoland
Zine ben Ali: Tunisia (1987–)
Zinhummé: Whydah
Émile Zinsou: Benin [ii] (1968–69)
Zitana: Axum
Mangisi Zitha: KaNgwane
Ahmad Pasha Ziwar: Egypt (1924–26)
Ziyadat-Allah I: Aghlabid Empire
Ziyadat-Allah II: Aghlabid Empire
Ziyadat-Allah III: Aghlabid Empire
Zokuli: Dagomba
Corrado Zoli: Eritrea; Jubaland (i)
Sumani Zoli: Dagomba
Zoligu: Dagomba
Zombre: Wagadugu
Zondwa: Tembuland

Bukar Zonko: Songhai (1378–86)
Zonman: Dagomba
Zoser: Egypt (3rd Dynasty)
Wambai Zozo: Zaria (1903)
Zubair: Ifat
Rabih az-Zubayr ibn Fadl-Allah: Bornu Empire (1893–1900); Rabih's Empire
Zubeir Pasha: Bahr al-Ghazal
Zubeiru: Adamawa
Zubeiru: Daura
Zubeiru: Ilorin
Zubeiru: Nupe
Zulande: Dagomba
Zulkarnayni Gambari: Ilorin
Zulu: Zululand
Gabriel de Zúñiga: Oran (1594–96)
Antonio de Zúñiga y la Cerda: Melilla (1692–97)
Agustín de Zurbarán: Gran Canaria
Zwelidumile: Kreli's Country
Zwelithini Goodwill Ka Bhekuzulu: Zululand
Zwetembusma: Wagadugu
Brand Van Zyl: South Africa (1945–50)